Philadelphia

Philadelphia

A 300-YEAR HISTORY

A Barra Foundation Book

W · W · NORTON & COMPANY

NEW YORK · LONDON

The text of this book is composed in photocomposition Janson Alternate, with display type set in Roman Compressed No. 3 and Garamond Old Style. Composition by The Haddon Craftsmen, Inc. Printing and binding by The Murray Printing Company.

BOOK DESIGN BY MARJORIE J. FLOCK

Library of Congress Cataloging in Publication Data
Main entry under title:
Philadelphia: a 300-year history.
   Includes index.
    1. Philadelphia (Pa.)—History. I. Weigley,
Russell Frank. II. Wainwright, Nicholas B.
III. Wolf, Edwin, 1911–
F158.3.P5664 1982   974.8'11   82–8220

ISBN 0-393-01610-2

W. W. Norton & Company, Inc. 500 Fifth Avenue, New York, N. Y. 10110
W. W. Norton & Company Ltd. 37 Great Russell Street, London WC1B 3NU

3 4 5 6 7 8 9 0

To
Roy F. Nichols
and
Jeannette P. Nichols

ACKNOWLEDGMENTS

In 1967, aware of the approach of both the bicentennial of the United States—extending from the 200th anniversary of the Declaration of Independence in 1976 through that of the Constitution in 1987 —and the tercentenary of Philadelphia in 1982, a circle of Philadelphia historians gathered to discuss the feasibility of a new collaborative history of the city where the Declaration and the Constitution were written and William Penn essayed his Holy Experiment. Whitfield J. Bell, Jr., of the American Philosophical Society, initiated the gathering. In addition to the associate editors and many of the·chapter authors of this book, the organizing group included Hannah Benner Roach of the Genealogical Society of Pennsylvania and David H. Wallace of the National Park Service.

There had been no comprehensive history of Philadelphia since Ellis Paxson Oberholtzer's *Philadelphia: A History of the City and Its People* in 1912. The standard reference work was yet older, J. Thomas Scharf's and Thompson Westcott's *History of Philadelphia,* published in 1884.

Roy F. Nichols, vice-provost of the University of Pennsylvania and dean of its graduate school, took the lead in organizing the historians to write the new history with the support of the Barra Foundation. The president of the foundation, Robert L. McNeil, Jr., had become deeply involved in the project from the start, and the Barra Foundation has patiently borne its administrative and financial burdens through unforeseen vicissitudes.

Most important and most discouraging of those vicissitudes was the illness of Professor Nichols, the original editor of the project. Well before his death, Professor Nichols became unable to continue his accustomed firm yet kindly leadership, and in the early 1970s the history was in danger of foundering. Chapters remained uncompleted because authors doubted the history would ever be assembled. In 1972 the Barra Foundation accordingly invited Robert E. Spiller, professor emeritus of English at the University of Pennsylvania, to become editorial consultant to the foundation, with the mission of revitalizing the project. Professor Spiller's recommendations led to the appointment of the current editors and thus eventually to the completion of the work.

Everyone associated with the project owes special debts to Professors Nichols and Spiller. So many chapter authors received the help of so many

librarians, archivists, and colleagues that those debts cannot be fully enume-
rated. Yet the journey to completion was so long that several other persons'
special help to the editors has to receive specific recognition.

Lois Given Bobb was originally managing editor of the project and con-
ducted detailed administrative and editorial supervision for Professor Nichols.
When the new editors took over, she continued to provide indispensable help.
Two of the original chapter authors have died, Theodore Thayer and Wallace
E. Davies; Mrs. Bobb contributed much to the rounding out of Professor
Thayer's chapter and, presented with only a fragment of Professor Davies's
manuscript and almost illegible notes, she compiled a more than ample foundation of research for the eventual completion of the chapter by Nathaniel
Burt. Margaret B. Tinkcom, a member of Professor Nichols's original edito-
rial board, also continued to assist the present editors in many ways beyond
the writing of her own chapter. Gary B. Nash of the University of California
at Los Angeles shared his wealth of knowledge of colonial and revolutionary
Philadelphia to give advice and encouragement when the present editors were
just beginning to renew the project's momentum. The consulting editors,
Joseph E. Illick of San Francisco State University and Thomas Wendel of San
José State University, later contributed much to the final shaping of the
volume. Susan Gray Detweiler assembled the illustrations without which the
book would be much the poorer. Among others who were helpful in supply-
ing illustrations or information about illustrations are Edmund N. Bacon;
Kenneth Finkel and Philip Lapsansky of the Library Company of Philadel-
phia; George McDowell of the *Bulletin;* Fredric Miller and Kenneth Fones-
Wolf of the Temple University Urban Archives; Mr. and Mrs. Lennox Moak;
Peter J. Parker and Linda Stanley of the Historical Soceity of Pennsylvania;
Larry Shenk of the Phillies; and Warden Childs, Robert Mitchell, Jr., Richard
Levy, John Maass, and Al Strobl of the City of Philadelphia. Susan B. Danko,
Wendy H. Robbins, and A. Lucy Tinkcom contributed significant research
efforts. Gail H. Schmidt gave priceless administrative assistance as program
officer for the Barra Foundation. The help of Regina Ryan of Regina Ryan
Publishing Enterprises, publishing consultant to the Barra Foundation, was
notable, especially at the time when an excessively long series of manuscripts
had to be chopped down to reasonable size. The editor relied consistently on
the two associate editors' unexcelled knowledge of Philadelphia history. More
even than most collaborative histories, this book rests on the efforts of a host
of contributors, named or unnamed on the title page and in the table of
contents.

Russell F. Weigley

Philadelphia
March 18, 1982

Philadelphia

The Founding
1681-1701

by Mary Maples Dunn and Richard S. Dunn

> . . . a tract of land shall be survey'd; say fifty thousand acres to
> a hundred adventurers, in which some of the best shall be set out for towns
> or cities. . . .
>
> — WILLIAM PENN, in Some Account of the Province of Pennsylvania
>
> . . . of Citys and towns of concourse beware, . . . a country life and estate
> I like best for my Children.
>
> — PENN to his wife [1]

If ever one man created a city, William Penn founded Philadelphia. As soon as he received his charter for Pennsylvania, Penn advertised that he would establish "a large Towne or Citty" on the Delaware River. He named this capital city in advance, chose the site, devised the street plan, and distributed the house lots.

Penn's urban design was strikingly original, reflecting his tastes as an English landed gentleman and his ideals as a persecuted Quaker. Although he had been born in London and had spent much time in that city, in Amsterdam, Paris, the German Rhine cities, and such provincial British towns as Dublin and Bristol, he much preferred his country estate, Warminghurst Place, in Sussex. Most of Penn's income came from farm rents in England and Ireland, and he was inclined to view landed income as less corrupting than commercial wealth, so he wanted to build an urban center that would not contaminate his holy experiment in Pennsylvania. He remembered the bubonic plague in London in 1665 and the disastrous fire of 1666, so he wanted "a greene Country Towne, which will never be burnt, and allways be wholsome."[2] As a Quaker, Penn envisioned a place of refuge for the persecuted, where the spiritual union of all Christians might be more than a dream. He intended to live at peace with the Indians so he made no provision for city walls or fortifications or garrisons of soldiers. He hoped to liberate the townspeople from the factional politics in European cities so he made no provision for traditional municipal institutions. In short, Penn wanted his city of brotherly love to be radically different from any other town in the Western world.

But Philadelphia was also shaped by the hundreds of colonists who moved into the new settlement during the 1680s and 1690s. Three-quarters of Penn's chief backers, the so-called First Purchasers who bought tracts of Pennsylvania land, were merchants, shopkeepers, and artisans from London, Bristol, Dublin, and other British towns. Penn promised the First Purchasers city lots, and naturally they were attracted to the commercial possibilities of the port on the Delaware. Very quickly they developed Philadelphia into the third-largest port on the Atlantic seaboard, after Boston and New York. But they

William Penn (1644–1718), crayon drawing, c. 1695 by Francis Place (1677–1728).
HISTORICAL SOCIETY OF PENNSYLVANIA

also challenged Penn's conception of the city.[3] They complained about the proprietor's method of distributing house lots. They rejected his design for a green country town enveloped in gardens and orchards. A heterogeneous mix of Quakers, Anglicans, Presbyterians, and Baptists was drawn to the town by Penn's policy of religious toleration, but these people were not necessarily ready for spiritual union through brotherly love. Indeed the Philadelphia Quakers in the 1690s split into a fierce internal schism. And the political leaders of the town wanted to guarantee their control of local government through a municipal corporation as in English towns. Thus the story of the founding of Philadelphia is the interplay between Penn's radical vision and the tradition-bound expectations of the early settlers, who shared his hopes for peace and prosperity but wanted their new home on the Delaware to be essentially like the other towns they had come from in England and America.

I

Before Penn started his city in 1681 there was nothing resembling a commercial town in the Delaware Valley. Indians had lived along the great river since time immemorial, and Dutch, Swedish, and English colonists had explored, traded, and farmed along the Delaware since 1609, but very little had yet been done to exploit the valley's economic resources. In the early seventeenth century the Delaware (or Lenni Lenape) Indians occupied the site of Philadelphia, living in villages on Ridley Creek and Crum Creek below, and Neshaminy Creek above, the present-day city, as well as in the settlements of Wicoa, Passayunk, Shackamaxon, and Playwicky within or near the current city limits. By mid-century the Delawares had been pushed north and east, and they sold the whole western shore of their river to the Swedes and the Dutch.

The Europeans who displaced the native inhabitants made slow work of developing the Delaware Valley. The Dutch West India Company had planted settlers in Burlington Island and built two trading posts, Fort Nassau (now Gloucester, New Jersey) and Fort Beversrede (on the east bank of the Schuylkill, a quarter of a mile above the present George Platt Bridge). Swedes constructed Fort Christina (now Wilmington, Delaware), Fort Elfsborg (near present-day Salem, New Jersey), Fort Nya Korsholm (near Fort Beversrede), and with their then-compatriots the Finns, settled farms along the creeks and marshes running into the Schuylkill and built a grist mill on Cobbs Creek. In 1655 Dutch soldiers from New Netherland overran New Sweden and created New Amstel (now New Castle, Delaware), but less than a decade later the English supplanted the Dutch as masters of the Delaware. James, duke of York, the new proprietor of New York, had no interest in the region and gave the territory of New Jersey to his friends John Lord Berkeley and Sir George Carteret. In 1674 Berkeley sold his title for West New Jersey to two members of the Society of Friends, John Fenwick and Edward Byllynge, who soon fell to quarrelling, whereupon a third Friend, William Penn, was called in to mediate.[4]

A few years later, when Penn received his charter for Pennsylvania, the total European population along the Delaware River was less than 2000 (counting the newly arrived English settlers in New Jersey), and the total Indian population was not much larger. About fifty subsistence farmers were living within the limits of modern Philadelphia, mostly Swedes and Finns, with a few Dutch and English. Although some of them, such as the Dalbos, Rambos, Svenssons, and Cocks, had been there since the 1640s, most had moved to the site within the past decade. Their farms averaged about 200 acres in size, but the land was heavily wooded, and the clearings for fields relatively small. Snug log houses, built like Scandinavian peasant cottages, lay scattered along both banks of the Schuylkill, along the west bank of the Delaware, and inland up half a dozen tributary creeks. There was a small village at Kingsessing, the term borrowed from the Indians for the area between Cobbs Creek and the Schuylkill (Chingsessing, "a place where there is a meadow"). In a blockhouse at Wicaco the Swedish Lutherans had established a church. Rather than travel to the settlement at Upland (now Chester) every Sunday, they had offered their charge to the Rev. Jacobus Fabritius, a Dutch Lutheran who had come to America to minister to his countrymen on the Hudson, only to be banished because of his quarrelsome nature. He became in 1677 the first ordained clergyman in the future city of brotherly love.

It is evident from surviving records of court sessions held at Upland and Kingsessing between 1676 and 1681 that the settlers lived placid and simple lives.[5] The farmers here had little traffic with the outside world but were self-sufficient and comfortable enough, and on good terms with their Indian neighbors. (There were now few Delawares in the region.) Fines and fees were paid—if paid at all—in tobacco. The big issues were who killed a boar, who broke a calf's leg, or who owned four pigs running loose in the swamp. Such seemingly trivial questions were of vital importance to people who possessed very little livestock. A plantation of 200 acres, the only one inventoried in the court records, contained only four oxen, three cows, three sows, and two ewes. Such was the style of life on the site where William Penn would erect Philadelphia.

I I

In July 1681, shortly after obtaining his royal charter, Penn announced that he would lay out "a large Towne or Citty in the most Convenient place upon the River for health & Navigation."[6] In September 1681 he sent three commissioners to supervise the settlement of his province, and he instructed them to set aside 10,000 acres for the "great towne" on the Delaware. As soon as the commissioners arrived, however, they found that it was difficult to carry out this instruction. Practically all of the riverfront property along the western bank of the Delaware, as far as the falls at the present site of Trenton, was already patented to Swedish, Dutch, or English farmers. Penn had supposed that the new town could be constructed at Upland, but his commissioners ruled out this site because the Upland farmers were long established and it would have been awkward and expensive to buy them out. The commissioners explored the possibilities upstream, and finally in early 1682 they bought an undeveloped riverfront tract from three Swedes of Wicaco, the Svensson or Swanson brothers, Sven, Olave, and Andrew, sons of Sven Gunnasson.

Just north of Wicaco the land was high and firm in contrast to the swampy meadows to the south. There was a pine woods near the Delaware—the Lenni Lenape name for the place was Coaquannock, or "grove of pines"—but most of the tract was covered with a hardwood forest of oak, black walnut, chestnut, cypress, hickory, beech, and elm. During the summer Penn's surveyor-general, Capt. Thomas Holme, began to lay out the new town within this tract. The site extended about a mile along the river between the present South and Vine Streets. In September 1682 Holme and the commissioners supervised a street-by-street lottery to determine which town lots each of the First Purchasers would have.

In October the proprietor himself arrived on the scene. Dissatisfied both with the cramped site of his capital city and with the method of allocating town lots, Penn set aside the lottery and looked for ways to enlarge the town. Instead of expanding farther along the Delaware, he decided to expand west to the Schuylkill so that the city would face both rivers. He acquired a mile of river frontage on the Schuylkill parallel to his holdings on the Delaware. Philadelphia was now a rectangle of 1200 acres, stretching two miles in length from east to west between the two rivers, and one mile in width from north to south.

The site of the new city had serious disadvantages as a commercial entre-pôt. It lay about a hundred miles up a tortuous river, full of shoals and shallows. There was to be no lighthouse at the mouth of Delaware Bay until 1725 and no accurate chart of the river until the mid-eighteenth century. Buoys had to be maintained to warn ships off the more dangerous shoals. Once a ship reached the Philadelphia waterfront, it was difficult to load and unload cargo because of the thirty-foot-high riverbank between present South and Vine Streets. Philadelphia was not only 200 miles farther from England than New York, but its harbor froze more readily in winter, closing down the port and causing damage to quays and ships.[7]

Still, Philadelphia also had strong natural advantages. Shielded by the Appalachians from extremes of weather, Philadelphia offered a varied but not severe climate. The Delaware provided a deep and commodious harbor; dozens of big ships could anchor close to shore, and there was a cove—the Swamp, soon to be called the Dock or Dock Creek—and a sandy beach for small boats. The Schuylkill River, despite its rapids, offered the best highway to the interior of Pennsylvania. Most important, Philadelphia was surrounded by what would soon become the richest agricultural hinterland of any colonial city. It lay at the center of a circle of splendid farm country which reached fifty miles or more in every direction, drawing New Jersey as well as Pennsylvania and Delaware into its orbit. And the new settlers who poured into this region and cleared its forests in the late seventeenth and early eighteenth centuries not only produced commodities for Philadelphia merchants to export but also created a market for Philadelphia imports.[8]

The community that William Penn hoped to create at Philadelphia was, first of all, a truly peaceful one. The best remembered legend about Penn is that when he arrived on the Delaware in 1682 he made a Great Treaty of friendship with the Lenni Lenape under a spreading elm at the village of Shackamaxon, in what is now Kensington. The legend aptly enough captures the spirit of Penn's dealings with the Indians, for he did seek to win, and to deserve, their trust and friendship. He wrote to the Privy Council in 1683: "I have followed the Bishop of London's counsel, by buying, and not taking away, the natives' land."[9] During his visit to America from 1682 to 1684 he paid the Delawares generously by the standards of his time (£1000 in all) to extinguish their claims to land in Philadelphia, Chester, and Bucks Counties.

We should not claim too much for Penn's benevolent Indian policy. Like all the seventeenth-century settlers he had an essentially patronizing view of the Indians. He never supposed that they could become integral members of his Christian community. Furthermore he failed to understand that the Delawares had no conception of exclusive land ownership; they thought that they were merely affirming the right of the white men to share the use of the land. Fortunately for Penn, he arrived at a time when the Delawares were demoralized by seventy years of exposure to the Europeans; and the distant Five Nations of the Iroquois, who claimed control over the Indians of eastern Pennsylvania, were well satisfied with Penn's policy. At a time when all the other major towns in America had forts and walls, and when King Philip's War in New England and Bacon's war against the Virginia Indians were recent memories, Penn laid out his capital city as if to prove that it occupied the most peaceful corner of the world.

William Penn's Treaty with the Indians, *painted by Benjamin West (1738–1820) in London in 1771.*

PENNSYLVANIA ACADEMY OF THE FINE ARTS

If Philadelphia need not be a garrison, what else did the proprietor have in mind for it? Penn's initial thoughts for the creation of his city reflected his upper-class position. When he instructed his commissioners in 1681 to set aside 10,000 acres for a "great towne" on the Delaware, he was thinking in terms of a town inhabited chiefly by the largest landowners in the colony, the First Purchasers who had bought 5000-acre tracts of Pennsylvania land. Their houses, according to Penn's instructions, were to be set back a uniform distance from the riverbank, at least 600 feet, and at least 800 feet apart, surrounded by gardens, orchards, and fields. There was to be a modest commercial center, with quay, warehouses, market, and state house, but at this stage Penn was chiefly interested in setting up a congeries of gentlemen's estates stretching a dozen or more miles along the riverbank. This plan, conjured in England and reflecting Penn's style of life on his Warminghurst estate, did not fit the dimensions of his site in America. But the concept of uniform streets, symmetrically placed houses, and surrounding greenbelt was incorporated into Penn's later, modified scheme for Philadelphia.[10]

Penn's second plan, drawn in 1682, was a rectangular layout of 1200 acres providing far more generous city limits than in any other early American town, with enough expansion room to permit many years of orderly future growth. Penn offered the best building lots within the city to the First Purchasers and other early settlers, but he reserved more than half the city plots for future sale or rental. Beyond the urban limits he set aside about 8000 acres in what is now North and West Philadelphia as so-called liberty lands, where each purchaser of 5000 acres of Pennsylvania was entitled to a dividend of eighty acres. Keeping to his original idea of gentlemen farmers surrounding the commercial center, Penn expected the chief landowners in the colony to build their houses in a suburban belt from Kensington to Cobbs Creek. The proprietor himself proposed to build a house at Fairmount near the present Art Museum, overlooking the Schuylkill.

Thomas Holme advertised the layout of the new city in his famous plat or *Portraiture of the City of Philadelphia*, published in London in 1683. The *Portraiture* displays Penn's symmetrical gridiron pattern of wide streets intersecting large squares. High (now Market) and Broad Streets are each 100 feet wide, broader than the widest thoroughfares in seventeenth-century London. Most of the other streets are fifty feet wide. After they were first called by the names of prominent settlers who owned adjacent lots, the proprietor in 1684 renamed the east-west streets after local trees: Cedar (now South), Pine, Spruce, Walnut, Chestnut, Mulberry (now Arch), Sassafras (now Race), and Vine. And he numbered the cross streets, also in keeping with his taste for simplicity and order. Four squares (now Washington, Franklin, and Rittenhouse Squares, and Logan Circle) were set aside to be parks open to all.

At the intersection of High and Broad Streets, where City Hall now stands, Penn designated a central square or plaza of ten acres to be bordered by the principal public buildings, such as the Quaker meetinghouse, the state house, the market house, and the schoolhouse. Despite the two riverfronts, Penn's city had an inward-facing design, focusing on this central plaza. Penn

OVERLEAF: *Portraiture of Philadelphia, drawn by Thomas Holme (1624–1695) and published in London, 1683.*

HISTORICAL SOCIETY OF PENNSYLVANIA

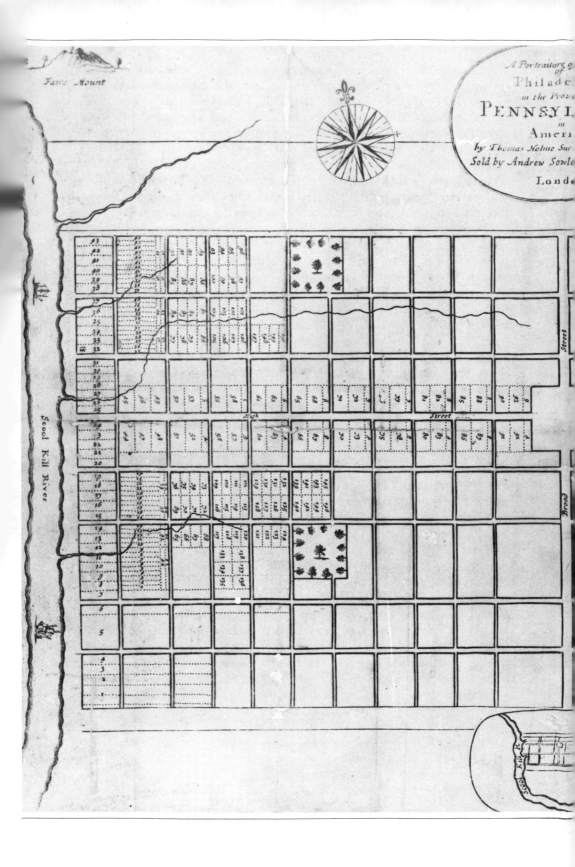

Fawe Mount

Scool Kill River

A Portraiture of
of
Philade...
in the Prove
PENNSYL...
in
Ameri...
by Thomas Holme Sur...
Sold by Andrew Sowle...
Londe...

Street

Broad

High Street

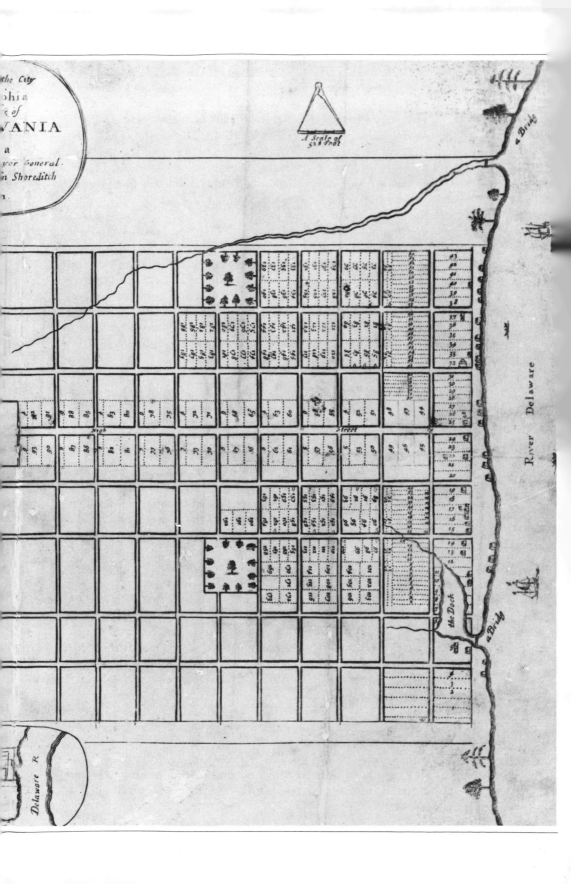

clearly hoped, as Holme's *Portraiture* shows, to distribute the first inhabitants across the city from river to river. He considered the best lots in the city to be those on Delaware Front Street, Schuylkill Front Street (now Twenty-second Street), and High Street, and he awarded these lots to the chief of the First Purchasers. On his plat Holme marked a total of 530 acre and half-acre city lots for the initial settlers. Even the smallest of the back lots, as Holme boasted, "hath room for House, Garden and small Orchard, to the great Content and Satisfaction of all here concerned."[11] The English country gentleman idea had not been abandoned.

There has been much speculation as to where Penn got his inspiration for the plan of Philadelphia. New ideas on city planning were in the air throughout Europe in the Baroque Age. Everywhere, designers were trying to find ways of opening up the overcrowded, walled medieval cities by introducing a more spacious arrangement of broad, straight avenues, regulated facades, monumental vistas, and dramatic open spaces. Both Penn and Holme had lived in Ireland and possibly they were influenced by the newly built Irish garrison towns such as Londonderry, with gridiron street patterns and central square,[12] though the fortress aspect of these places is of course absent from Philadelphia.

Undoubtedly the current building fashion in London had an impact on Penn. Holme observed that the public squares of Philadelphia were intended "for the Like [recreational] use as Moor Fields," which was developed after the London fire of 1666. The scheme for rebuilding that burned city drawn up by Richard Newcourt is a gridiron arrangement very similar in overall shape and inner detail to Penn's plan for Philadelphia, although there is no evidence that Penn had seen Newcourt's manuscript plan.[13] Probably Penn's design was chiefly conditioned by the long, narrow tract of land available to him and his basic aim of building a widely dispersed, low-density, countrified town. The five public squares of the city provide too little open space, yet Penn cannot be blamed for this since he assumed that each householder would have his own gardens and orchard. Being a Quaker community, Philadelphia was not designed like seventeenth-century Paris or Rome as a vehicle for Baroque display. Williamsburg, Virginia, laid out a few years later, is a far better example of Baroque planning in America, designed to place the chief public buildings, the College of William and Mary, the Capitol, and the Governor's Palace, as elegantly and effectively as possible. Penn's design for Philadelphia was prosaic by comparison. But while Williamsburg was—and has remained—a stylish village, Penn laid out a town that could and did grow into a twentieth-century metropolis far larger than seventeenth-century London.

I I I

During its first two decades Philadelphia grew rapidly, from a few hundred inhabitants in 1683 to over 2000 in 1700. Propagandists for the infant colony, writing home to England, boasted that the town was mushrooming with miraculous speed. They claimed 2500 inhabitants for Philadelphia in 1684 and 12,000 in 1697, and that there were 1400 houses in 1690 and over 2000 in 1698.[14] These totals were greatly exaggerated. Population advance through the first two decades can be traced with reasonable accuracy through tax lists and quitrent rolls for the city. In 1693 there were 356 taxpayers in Philadelphia; three years later there were 419. Demographers calculate that one out of four persons were taxables in colonial America, which suggests a total population of about 2000 for the city in 1700. This approximate figure is confirmed by two early quitrent rolls, which indicate how many building lots were patented within Philadelphia. In 1689, 377 lots were patented on the Delaware side of the town; by 1703 the number had risen to 516. The rent rolls show that a great many of these lots were unoccupied. Taking into account those persons who occupied unpatented lots, and those living on the Schuylkill side of town, it appears that Philadelphia had about 400 houses at the turn of the century. Reckoning six or seven persons to the average house, we arrive at a total population of between 2000 and 2500 in 1700.[15] Philadelphia was still a very small place, but it was already one of the three or four biggest towns in English America, almost as populous as New York, though well behind Boston.

During the 1680s and 1690s Philadelphia exhibited the characteristics of a raw frontier community. Some of its first inhabitants found shelter for several years in caves dug out of the riverbank. Penn was scandalized to hear that these rude dwellings were also the scenes of "clandestine loosness." Nor was he happy to discover one grotto full of hogs that rooted up his fence and ruined his grass plot. Pigs and goats ran freely through the avenues of early Philadelphia, no doubt enticed by the garbage. Front Street between Chestnut and Walnut, the very heart of the town, was an undrained sewer.

The first houses in town apparently were built of logs in the Swedish style, the earlier Scandinavian settlers teaching the English newcomers how to notch and fit the wood together without using nails. Soon, however, the English colonists returned to their native building habits of wood frame and brick construction. In November 1683 Penn warranted a site near Coaquan-nock Creek, just north of the city, for the manufacture of bricks from local clay. A year later Robert Turner, one of the largest investors in the province, built the first brick house, at the south corner of Front and Mulberry. By 1690 there was enough brick construction to occupy four brickmakers and ten bricklayers. In 1698 the Swedes themselves began the work of replacing their old wooden church at Wicaco with a new one of brick, now the oldest surviving building within the current limits of Philadelphia. Its dedication in 1700 was one of the major ceremonial events of the young city's history, a unique public musical event featuring a concert on viols, trumpets, and kettle-drums by the German monastic community of the "Hermits of the Wissahickon."

The Letitia Street House, circa 1710, removed to Fairmount Park in 1883, is probably a typical small Philadelphia house of the first generation, while

In 1685 Robert Turner wrote to William Penn: "The Town of Philadelphia it goeth on in Planting and Building to admiration . . . many brave Brick Houses are going up." These early houses in a photograph made in 1868 are thought to have been on Swanson Street in the Southwark district below Philadelphia proper.

FREE LIBRARY OF PHILADELPHIA

Gloria Dei Church, Old Swedes', off Delaware Avenue, represents early public architecture. Both structures are neat, solid, and homespun in appearance. Quaker plainness was much in evidence in early Philadelphia. Probably the largest building in town was the Great Meeting House, fifty feet square, which the Society of Friends constructed in 1696 at High and Second Streets, and this was hardly a pretentious structure. None of the other early meeting houses or churches was an impressive building. There were three brewhouses

Brick house of David Breintnall (d. 1731), north side of Chestnut Street between Third and Fourth, built c. 1700, demolished 1818. Elevation by William Strickland (1788–1854) for The Port Folio *(1818).*

LIBRARY COMPANY OF PHILADELPHIA

in town, and a half dozen or more taverns, including Griffith Jones's celebrated Blue Anchor on Dock Creek, opened in 1683. Market stalls, now represented only by the much later ones extending south on Second Street from the Head House at Pine to South, first appeared at High and Second in 1693. North of Vine Street were a ropewalk and several shipyards.[16] From the time when transplanted West India merchant Samuel Carpenter proposed to build the first wharf in 1684, Penn's Council had established rules for their construction, including provisions that no wharf should extend more than 250 feet into the river and that the builders must provide stairs from the water to the wharf and then from the wharf to the top of the bank.[17] The riverfront was soon covered over with wharves and the foot and top of the bank along the river with warehouses and shops.

The spirit of the place was observed by Andreas Rudman, the pastor of Gloria Dei in 1700, and just three years away from his native Sweden:

Gloria Dei (Old Swedes' Church), Swanson Street and Delaware Avenue, begun 1698 (photograph taken in 1854).

FREE LIBRARY OF PHILADELPHIA

If anyone were to see Philadelphia who had not been there [before], he would be astonished beyond measure [to learn] that it was founded less than twenty years ago. Even Uppsala, etc., would have to yield place to it. All the houses are built of brick, three or four hundred of them, and in every house a shop, so that whatever one wants at any time he can have, for money.[18]

And indeed with the focus of their energy on money-making, the first inhabitants of Philadelphia quickly altered Penn's design for the layout of the city. During the 1680s and 1690s they clustered as close to the Delaware as possible, refusing to spread out from river to river in accord with Penn's original scheme. By 1700 the Schuylkill side of the town was vacant, or virtually so, and on the Delaware side practically everyone lived within three or four blocks of the river—on much smaller, narrower, and more congested lots than Penn intended.

The Friends' Bank Meeting House, Front Street north of Arch, built in 1702 with materials from the dismantled meetinghouse in Centre Square. Conjectural nineteenth-century engraving.

QUAKER COLLECTION, HAVERFORD COLLEGE LIBRARY

This process started in 1683, as the first colonists began to stake out their city lots. Thomas Holme advertised in his *Portraiture* that 286 lots of an acre or a half acre were available for prospective settlers on the Delaware side of town, and 244 on the Schuylkill side. Holme and Penn expected the Delaware side to develop faster, and in fact assisted in the process by assigning most of the Schuylkill lots to First Purchasers who had not emigrated to the colony. By 1684, 187 of the Delaware lots had actually been warranted and surveyed, and only seventy-five of the Schuylkill lots.[19] During the next few years a large number of the more desirable Delaware lots, particularly along Front Street, were resold and subdivided, while hardly any of the Schuylkill lots changed hands.

By 1689 many of the original 43 lots along Front Street, each 102 feet wide, had been subdivided, so that there were now 70 smaller properties; and by 1703 they were further subdivided into 102 lots, many of which were less than twenty feet wide. East of Front Street, along the Delaware River bank, which Penn had originally intended as a public esplanade, there were 41 lots in 1689 and 110 lots in 1703, to accommodate the shops and warehouses of Philadelphia's burgeoning mercantile community. A few blocks inland a reverse process was taking place. West of Second Street on Walnut, Chestnut, High, and Mulberry Streets the lots were fewer but larger in 1703 than in 1689. The people who continued to live on these interior lots often had appropriated their neighbors' vacated land, and in several instances had increased their street frontage from 50 feet to 200 feet.[20]

But hardly anyone lived west of Fourth Street before 1703. Consequently Penn's design of a center square as the hub of his community had to be abandoned. The large Friends meeting house which was built in 1685 at the midpoint between the rivers was dismantled in 1702. Efforts to develop the Schuylkill waterfront likewise collapsed. Of the merchants, tradesmen, and craftsmen who can be identified as living in Philadelphia around 1690, 123 lived on the Delaware side of town and only 6 on the Schuylkill side. One of the latter, a tailor named William Boulding, complained that he had invested most of his capital in his Schuylkill lot, "so that he cannot, as others have done, Remove from the same."[21] Not until the mid-nineteenth century, long after the city had spilled northward and southward in an arc along the Delaware miles beyond its original limits, was the Schuylkill waterfront fully developed. Nor was Centre Square restored as the heart of Philadelphia until the construction of City Hall began in 1871.

Throughout the settled portion of the city near the Delaware, as the generously sized acre and half-acre lots that Holme surveyed in 1683 and 1684 were chopped up, a network of narrow alleys began to interlace Penn's large blocks and broad avenues. In part Holme was to blame for making the original lots so deep and narrow. The Front Street lots, approximately an acre in size, were 102 feet by 396 feet, and the Second Street lots, approximately half an acre in size, were 51 feet by 300 feet. It proved very easy to cut a twenty-foot alley lengthwise along the edge of a 102- by 396-foot property, and to face this alley with a row of narrow tenements. In this manner a lot designed for a single house could be converted into as many as twenty lots of row housing, each twenty by eighty-two feet. By 1698 nine lanes or alleys had already been cut through from Front to Second Street, and several had rows of narrow two-story workmen's houses on them. Soon dozens of other alleys appeared throughout the city, making Philadelphia one of the most congested communities in America, in utter violation of Penn's dream of a green country town.[22]

The early residents not only altered Penn's design for the new city; they protested vigorously against his method of allocating urban lots. As the First Purchasers understood their agreement of 1681 with Penn, they were entitled to ownership of the city land in its entirety, with real estate equally distributed by lot as dividends to 5000-acre purchasers. The big investors wanted their holdings allocated in the commercial center where population would grow most rapidly, where business would be conducted, and where real estate values would quickly appreciate. When Penn chose to give them their dividends largely in the outlying liberties, the First Purchasers grumbled. But they might have remained content had they received the full 1200 acres of city land. Penn, however, decided to reserve more than half the real estate within Philadelphia for renters and later purchasers. Furthermore he was determined to allocate the land himself rather than leave the pattern of settlement to chance. These decisions reflected his role as city planner and proprietor, but they ran contrary to his earlier enthusiastic promises to the First Purchasers.[23]

The advantages to be gained from controlled allocation of city land were certainly numerous. Population could be distributed rationally, with artisans, for example, located together in areas appropriate for trade; men likely to engage in overseas trade near the river; men of substance scattered along the river to encourage building and growth among them; and speculators who seemed likely to remain in England awarded more remote land so that their ownership of unimproved lots in the city would not retard growth. It is also possible that Penn hoped to reward his friends and weld together the most powerful men of the community into an alliance of interest that could govern in support of the proprietor.

Yet some of the most powerful persons immediately objected to the location of their holdings and had to be mollified. Robert Turner, an old friend and an early and heavy investor, thought his lot at the southeast corner of Front and Mulberry too far from Dock Creek and thus from the center of commerce. A valued citizen like Turner deserved special consideration. Penn pacified him by recalling that Turner had always said he wanted a quiet place, and that the Dock would hardly be serene, but at the same time he arranged that the local market and also the first yearly market or fair would be held on the bank in front of Turner's lot. When Turner applied to rent the bank plot opposite his own to build a wharf, he was granted a reduced rental and permission to dig vaults through the bank and under Front Street to his own lot. Similarly, Barnabas Willcox, a ropemaker of Bristol, was encouraged to emigrate with offers of choice land because Penn wanted industrial development. When surveyors' errors denied Willcox the lots he chose on Front Street and High Street, Penn intervened with a gift of Schuylkill lots in addition to his suburban ropewalk property.

The First Purchasers found especially galling Penn's retention of the Delaware River bank, which he leased with a shrewd requirement that rents would escalate with the rise of the economy. Injury was heaped on injury when landowners discovered that they were also to be charged quitrents—permanent rents due the proprietor—on city property, a quite unexpected imposition and one that raised the spectre of new conditions of tenure in the future. Purchasers, far from being welded together in the proprietor's interest, were growing alienated, feeling injured and defrauded of the city that they thought should be theirs.

In 1684 a formal petition, the "Humble Remonstrance & address of several, the Adventurers, Free holders & Inhabitants and others therein concerned," was presented to Penn, making it clear to him that the large investors disliked his policies and distrusted him. It was an unpleasant experience for Penn, especially since many of the remonstrants were Friends. Thomas Rudyard, author of the petition, was an old colleague who had joined with Penn to defend persecuted Quakers in England. Together they had charged that fines and similar punishments for unpopular religious beliefs were infringements on their property rights; now it was Penn's concept of property that was under attack.

In reply the proprietor defended quitrents on the ground that his purchase of land to enlarge the city to the Schuylkill should be recompensed. Indeed Penn always felt he gave his settlers more than he got. He claimed that his plan for allocation was to "preserve the Country from a Desolation" which the First Purchasers had agreed would be injurious; that he had never promised entire city ownership to the First Purchasers; that he wanted the riverbank available for common use; and that, despite quitrents, the remonstrants' hold on the land was secure.[24]

Penn included in his response a guarded promise that Philadelphia would become a borough, though in fact he did not issue a municipal charter until 1701. His gesture in 1684 may have temporarily muted complaints, but city real estate continued to be a matter dividing proprietor and colonists. Undoubtedly Penn and the colonists were all self-interested, but Penn had a larger sense of community in mind while his adversaries looked first to profit.

I V

Before the age of industry the economy of cities depended on trade. Cities grew because they were convenient places for the exchange of goods—the more convenient the location and the better the transportation network, the more likely the growth of the city. Other factors, such as proximity to fertile farmlands or attractiveness to skilled immigrants due to a policy of religious and ethnic tolerance, also created a kind of urban magnetism. To become a *major* urban center a city also had to develop financial services fundamental to the continuing conduct and growth of trade. The goodness of nature, the policies of the proprietor, and the canniness of the merchants provided Philadelphia with all of these features.

Pennsylvania had no "starving time" in its infancy, and Philadelphia got off to a strong start. In the earliest years trade nearly collapsed for a time when the first settlers had expended the specie they brought with them, leaving them with no satisfactory medium of exchange to purchase necessities from older settlements, but this proved to be only a temporary crisis. During the 1680s and 1690s Philadelphia rapidly established itself as the chief port of the Delaware River, serving as the commercial entrepôt for Pennsylvania, West New Jersey, and the three Lower Counties on the Delaware. The older Delaware River ports—New Castle, Chester, and Burlington—became commercial satellites of Philadelphia.[25]

True, in these early years Philadelphia business was small scale by the standards of Boston and New York; it took Penn's city fifty years to become a great commercial center. During the years 1697–1701, the first for which we have reasonably accurate trade statistics, Philadelphia exported £3400 in goods to England per annum and imported £12,300 in goods from England—a healthy trade for a new port, but only 1 percent of the total North American exports to England for 1697–1701, and only 3.5 percent of total North American imports from England. Not until about 1720 was Philadelphia to surpass Charleston's annual volume of trade.[26]

Philadelphia's economy did not develop along the lines anticipated by the proprietor and his chief English backers. They expected great things of the Free Society of Traders in Pennsylvania, a joint-stock company incorporated by Penn in 1682.[27] Over 200 subscribers, chiefly well-to-do Quaker merchants from London and the provincial towns, pledged £12,500 toward this enterprise, and actually paid about £6000 by September 1682. Penn granted the company a 20,000-acre tract (the Manor of Frank or Frankford) together with a 100-acre allotment in Philadelphia, extending from the Delaware to the Schuylkill between Spruce and Pine Streets. The prospectus that the Free Society of Traders issued in 1682 made it plain that the company expected to monopolize Pennsylvania's maritime commerce through its trading stations at Philadelphia and on Chesapeake Bay, as well as its London agents who would market the colony's exports and select its imports. Furthermore the society intended to handle Pennsylvania's fur trade with the Indians, build a glass factory, dig lead and iron mines, fish for whales, and produce linen cloth and wine for export.

Neither Penn nor the society anticipated the provincial suspicion of monopoly. The Pennsylvania Assembly refused to confirm the company's charter. Nevertheless the society set up a glassworks, tannery, sawmill, gristmill, and brick kiln at Frankford, and company fishermen actually caught several whales in Delaware Bay. But little profit was realized from these efforts. Colonists bought English goods from the society on credit but refused to cover with cash. Company employees began suing management for back wages. Investors in the society who emigrated to Pennsylvania, such as Thomas Holme and Robert Turner, showed more interest in their individual enterprises than in those that they shared with the society. By 1686 the Free Society, headed for bankruptcy, abandoned its trading operations, and in 1723 its last real estate holdings were dispersed. Today the only survival of this abortive commercial experiment is the name it has bequeathed to the Philadelphia neighborhood where its trading house once stood overlooking the Delaware—Society Hill.[28]

As the Free Society of Traders collapsed, economic leadership in Philadelphia was assumed by a group of Quaker merchants, many of whom had acquired experience in New World trading elsewhere before they came to Penn's city. Samuel Carpenter arrived from Barbados, Samuel Richardson, Isaac Norris, and Jonathan Dickinson from Jamaica, Humphrey Morrey and William Frampton from New York, Edward Shippen from Boston, and Anthony Morris from Burlington.[29] Such men brought knowledge of markets throughout America and ties with other Quaker entrepreneurs throughout the English-speaking world. Their connections with the English West Indian sugar islands proved to be especially valuable.

Philadelphia merchants faced the same basic problem as Boston and New York merchants: how to acquire the English goods they wanted when they had very little to sell on the English market. They copied the Boston and New York solution to this problem by looking to the West Indies for the currency or bills of exchange they could spend in England. They shipped out Pennsylvania's agricultural surplus—meat, grain, and especially flour—as well as forest products, chiefly barrel staves for the West Indian rum trade. For these cargoes they received bills of exchange or sugar, by which they purchased manufactured goods. By 1700 there were already four shipyards in Philadelphia building and repairing ocean-going vessels.

Even in these early years the merchants worked to build the commercial reputation of their prime export commodities by regulating the size and weight of packing casks and by appointing inspectors of exported meat and barrel staves, thus ensuring reliable quantity and quality. The first Pennsylvania law requiring the inspection of barrel staves was passed in 1683, and the first meat inspection law in 1693.[30] The colonists were much less careful to observe the strict commercial regulations laid down by the home government. In the 1690s a number of English officials charged that Philadelphia was the chief North American center of contraband trade with the Scots and the Dutch, and worse, a notorious haven for pirate ships. The reluctance of the Quaker colony to employ force for any purpose apparently helped lend substance to the latter charge; Robert Turner once wrote to Penn about the "Murtherings bloody Crew of Privateers whom we were become ye greatest harbourers of."[31] On the other hand the charges were inspired to some extent by jealousy of Philadelphia's economic growth.

There is no doubt that Philadelphia merchants flouted the English Navigation Acts, but so did merchants in all other colonies. As part of London's effort to strengthen the enforcement of the acts, the Crown appointed a Philadelphia customs collector in 1696, a vice-admiralty judge in 1697, and a customs surveyor in 1698. Henceforth Pennsylvania merchants were forced to operate with a double set of commercial rules, those devised by their local government to bolster the colony's trade, and those imposed by King and Parliament to keep the colonists dependent on the mother country.

Philadelphia became the trading center for the Delaware Valley not only because of its merchants but also because it attracted shopkeepers and craftsmen. Already by 1690 some twenty-two shopkeepers and 119 craftsmen were practicing thirty-five different trades and businesses in the town.[32] As a group these early Philadelphia artisans were persons of humble social origin—and far more representative of British Quakerism than Penn's major investors. Most of them had been manual workers in London, Bristol, Dublin, or the smaller British towns. Some came from the depressed northern and western counties of England, which was where the Quakers were most numerous.[33] Penn, though very anxious to attract the contributions of the well-to-do, also recognized that his colony could hardly function without carpenters, masons, smiths, and the like. He made a special point of inviting them to the city of brotherly love, and he succeeded in attracting a diversity of skills.

Of the 119 craftsmen who can be identified as living in Philadelphia around

1690, 34 were in the building industry—carpenters, sawyers, brickmakers, bricklayers, and plasterers. Another 26 were in the clothing industry—weavers, dyers, tailors, and shoemakers. Another 14 were food processors—bakers, butchers, brewers, and maltsters. Still another 22 manufactured a variety of household articles—pewterers, braziers, coopers, chandlers, potters, clockmakers, cabinetmakers, and the like. Four were in the shipbuilding industry, as carpenters and ropemakers. The remaining 19 were in service trades—barbers, physicians, tavernkeepers, and carters.[34] Obviously the country people for miles around Philadelphia depended on these craftsmen to supply many of their wants. Whatever consumer goods could not be made by Philadelphia craftsmen were imported and could be found on the shelves of Philadelphia's many shops.

One such craftsman was Nehemiah Allen, a cooper, whose account books illustrate the still primitive character of the Philadelphia economy around 1700. Allen made several hundred bread barrels and flour casks annually for both Samuel Carpenter and Isaac Norris, evidently for their export trade to the West Indies. Specie was scarce in Philadelphia throughout the early years and it was legal to pay in kind; Carpenter and Norris paid Allen in rum, flour, cheese, flannel, stockings, and other sundries. Allen's biggest customer was a brewer named Henry Badcock, who bought £100 worth of barrels annually and paid partly in cash and partly in beer. Another customer gave Allen the services of a slave named Moroka in exchange for his barrels. Allen unloaded some of the bartered goods he received from his customers onto his suppliers; he paid for his barrel staves in rum, salt, and molasses.[35]

Another craftsman, James West, a shipwright, practiced the same sort of barter. In 1701 he charged £39 for building a sloop, and in lieu of money he received raisins, flour, butter, sugar, and beer. These commodities were all useful to him, for he operated a tavern as well as a shipyard. Some of his workmen boarded at his tavern and most of them received a large part of their wages in drink. West repaired ships more often than he built them. Those he built must have been small vessels, for he finished them quickly. With seven or eight workmen he could build a brigantine in about a month. Labor was much more costly than materials. In building one ship West spent £3 for timber, £12 for carting, and £30 in wages for his workmen.[36]

But it was the merchants who were the mainspring of the economy in the preindustrial city. In the first Philadelphia generation, Samuel Carpenter, the former Barbadian who built Philadelphia's first wharf, was the most conspicuous trader, an industrious, creative, and ambitious Quaker entrepreneur. He joined Penn in the "Holy Experiment" out of the characteristic motives of his class, hoping to find in Pennsylvania profit, power, and the pleasures of freedom from the harassment that was so often the Quaker's lot elsewhere in England's empire.

Carpenter, born in 1649 in Horsham, Sussex, became a Quaker convert as a young man. By 1673 he was a merchant in Barbados and already prosperous. Quakers were unpopular in the West Indies as well as in England, however, and in 1673 and again in 1683 he had to pay fines for failure to provide armed men for the militia. These discomforts may have persuaded him to move on to Pennsylvania in 1684. He was well enough endowed to become one of the First Purchasers.[37]

Carpenter quickly displayed a talent for exploiting the possibilities of the new colony, both in land and in trade. His bargaining with Penn and the provincial Council to build his wharf occurred immediately, and he received permission to utilize double the width of a front lot, the one opposite his own and its adjoining plot. The wharf was constructed of tree trunks placed on top of each other; it was approximately 300 feet square, for Carpenter intended it to be "so far out that a ship of 100 tons or upward may come and unload or load on it."[38] Carpenter had to provide public access by a thirty-foot cartway along the front of the bank as well as the stairways from water to wharf and wharf to the top of the bank, but he was allowed to charge fees for the use of the quay. In a powerful position to enter the rapidly developing West Indian commerce, he became the leading figure in the Philadelphia flour and lumber trade.

Wealth and public responsibility were closely associated in the seventeenth century. The chief First Purchasers were men of substance, and they were immediately called on to assume public burdens of decision and settlement. Samuel Carpenter was no exception. Governor Penn was soon asking his advice on a wide range of problems: how to collect taxes, how to improve the postal service, and how to improve the colony's frame of government. He also served in a number of public offices: as deputy governor (1694–1698); councilor, both elected and appointed (1687–1695, 1697–1713); assemblyman (1693, 1694, 1696); and provincial treasurer (1704, 1710–1711, 1713).

In politics Carpenter could be counted upon as one of the proprietor's supporters, in part due to personal friendship, in part because Carpenter was a sincere Quaker who shared Penn's vision. Nevertheless he as much as anyone valued the political independence found in Pennsylvania. When Penn named John Blackwell, a Puritan and former military commander, to be deputy governor of the province in 1688, Carpenter supported the dissident Thomas Lloyd, keeper of the Great Seal of the province, who refused to recognize Blackwell's authority. When the Crown temporarily took over the province and appointed Benjamin Fletcher royal governor in 1692, Carpenter was a member of the Assembly and a party to that body's demands for powers they had not held under Penn. Earlier, Carpenter had refused to support the same demands because the colony was secure in the Quaker proprietor's hands. Indeed as a politician he never departed from the Quaker ethic, refusing to serve as a justice of the peace under Fletcher because he would not take the oaths and announcing his pacifism whenever war threatened.

Carpenter had an expansive enthusiasm for investment in the New World. In 1693 he was rated as the largest property holder in Philadelphia. In the course of little more than a decade he invested heavily in West Indies trade and erected not only Carpenter's Wharf, but at least ten warehouses, a lime kiln for mortar, and a crane. In addition to a large town house for himself, he built the famous Slate Roof House at Second Street and Hatton Lane (now Sansom Street), where William Penn stayed during most of his second visit to the colony. Carpenter also owned buildings in which a tavern and a coffeehouse were operated. He possessed extensive property in the liberties and the countryside as well; in both Bucks and Chester Counties he had an interest in grist and lumber mills. He and five other men proposed a "bank for money" in Philadelphia to ease the currency shortage in 1689, but nothing came of this idea. To the community he gave land for a meetinghouse and support for the incorporation of a Quaker school. But his greater contribution to Philadelphia was the energetic drive and enterprising force that fostered its unusually rapid economic development.

The "Slate Roof House," designed by James Porteus (d. 1737) for Samuel Carpenter and built c. 1687–1699. Watercolor by William L. Breton (1773–1855), 1830. The site at Second and Sansom Streets is now a small park.

HISTORICAL SOCIETY OF PENNSYLVANIA

In the end the city profited more than the man. Like many of the other first-generation Philadelphia merchants, Carpenter fell on hard times and failed to establish a lasting business enterprise. Philadelphia's overseas trade was hard hit by French privateers during King William's War in the 1690s, and again during Queen Anne's War, 1702–1713. In 1704, according to James Logan, Carpenter lost "the last stick . . . [he] was concerned in at sea" to a privateer, and in 1705 he was so depressed and indebted that he was selling land and city property. He retired from much of his business activity and moved to the country before he died in 1714.[39] A number of other first-generation merchants also went bankrupt or overextended themselves. It was not until the 1720s, at the beginning of a long era of international peace and prosperity, that Philadelphia's second generation of merchants began building more permanent dynastic fortunes.[40]

V

When Penn organized his new colony in 1682, he divided Pennsylvania into three counties, Philadelphia, Chester, and Bucks. A large part of Philadelphia County was agricultural hinterland, which included most of present-day Montgomery County. The 1693 tax list of Philadelphia City and County shows that about half of the inhabitants lived in the city, while the others resided in a dozen rural townships or districts, many of which were later annexed to the city. In Table 1 the last four districts—Cheltenham, Upper Precinct, Plymouth, and the Welsh Tract—are now in Montgomery County.

According to this tax list Philadelphians were paying nearly twice as much per capita as their rural neighbors. The villages in rural Philadelphia County were as yet neither populous nor wealthy. The rapid commercial development of the city discouraged the growth of secondary market towns within a radius of about thirty miles from Philadelphia. The one village in rural Philadelphia County that quickly developed its own independent economy was Germantown, a distinctive little community of Dutch Quakers and Mennonites, soon joined by German pietists. In 1683 the first settlers laid out their town. In 1686 they built a Quaker meetinghouse, constructed of logs. In 1691

Table 1 / Philadelphia County Tax List, 1693

Community	Number of taxables	Taxes paid
Philadelphia City	356	£200
Southwark	27	9
Beyond Schuylkill [West Philadelphia]	17	8
Northern Liberties	60	24
Germantown	51	13
Oxford	32	10
Bristol[a]	16	5
Dublin	27	9
Byberry	18	3
Cheltenham	24	8
Upper Precinct	5	2
Plymouth	2	1
Welsh Tract [Lower Merion]	70	23
Total	705	£315

[a] Not to be confused with Bristol, Bucks County, founded in 1697. The Bristol on this tax list was a Philadelphia County township in the area of the present Oak Lane.

they received a borough charter so that they could have their own mayor and council, court, and market. Germantown was laid out as a single-street village, stretching along what is now Germantown Avenue for about a mile in 1700, the houses surrounded by orchards. Francis Daniel Pastorius, a German agent of the Frankfurt Company who moved to Germantown in 1685, became the leading citizen of the community. He described his fellow townspeople as "mostly linen weavers and not any too skilled in agriculture."[41] But they proved to be very good at weaving. An English observer described Germantown in 1690, at a time when fewer than 200 people lived there: "five miles off is a town of Dutch and German people that have set up the linnen manufactory which weave and make many thousand yards of pure fine linnen cloth in a year."[42] Germantown cloth became known throughout the colonies. The village population, while ethnically heterogeneous from the beginning, was conspicuously more Germanic than Philadelphia's population in the colonial era.

Most of the other inhabitants of rural Philadelphia County in the 1690s were essentially subsistence farmers, as the Swedish peasants had been a generation earlier. In 1693 no taxpayer from the rural districts had an estate rated above £350. In the city, by contrast, twenty-eight Philadelphians owned estates valued from £350 to £1300. Analysis of the city taxables shows considerable stratification, with much of the property already concentrated in a few hands. The wealthiest 10 percent of the city population held 46 percent of the assessed property; the poorest 30 percent of the city population held only 2 percent of the assessed property.[43] The biggest Philadelphia taxpayers were merchants and brewers. Tavernkeepers, bakers, and coopers were rated fairly high. The average craftsman or shopkeeper had an estate valued at only £100, but low as this figure is, it was twice the rating of the average Philadelphia County farmer. The same picture emerges from a comparison of inventories of town and country estates probated in the 1680s and 1690s. The great majority of Chester and Bucks County farmers possessed large tracts of undeveloped land but very little livestock and very simple household furnishings. In Philadelphia inventories there is considerably more mention of silver spoons, linen cloths, walnut chairs, and black slaves.[44]

Given the economic dominance of Philadelphia in Pennsylvania, not to mention its special problems as a city, it is hardly surprising that urban inhabitants should have wanted greater control over their own affairs. Given Penn's concept of the city of brotherly love as a bucolic center for the chief landholders in the colony, it is not surprising that he made no provision for a distinct municipal government. The Assembly handled legislation for the city; the Council handled its administration. It was not, however, a one-sided matter since most of the colony's leaders lived in the city. Thanks to the agitation over city lots and liberty lands, already mentioned, Philadelphia became the center of antiproprietary sentiment in Pennsylvania. The antiproprietary Quakers who dominated the city wanted a corporate charter to enhance their municipal power. Penn knew his English history as well as his opponents did. Corporate charters granted by the Crown to towns had once served to protect the municipalities (and their economic interests) from local feudal lords. In the seventeenth century town corporations sent representatives to Parliament to engage in the struggle for power between King and Commons. In turn Charles II (and later James II) attacked municipal charters and attempted to pack corporations with royalists. Penn, though friendly with the Stuart monarchs, wanted no reenactment of this power struggle in Pennsylvania. He expressed his preference for the conduct of city affairs in the spirit of a Quaker meeting.

In 1691 the proprietor's political critics seized the initiative. At this time Penn was not only absent in England but in hiding because of his association with the recently deposed James II. Thomas Lloyd, acting governor of the province but part of the antiproprietary faction, issued a charter of incorporation for the City of Philadelphia, apparently based on the English model: a closed, self-perpetuating body whose major officers were mayor, recorder, sheriff, alderman, and councillors. These places were filled by firm supporters of Thomas Lloyd, and the membership of the corporation included only a few persons, such as Samuel Carpenter, who were sympathetic to the proprietor. Judging by the tax list of 1693 the membership consisted of prospering merchants, professionals, and artisans. Humphrey Morrey was mayor of the corporation, and he and a few minor corporation functionaries (for example, the overseer of the poor) appear fleetingly in the minutes of the provincial Council. The officials left behind no records of their own, however, and the charter of 1691 was not discovered by historians until late in the nineteenth century. Whether the corporation government was disallowed by Penn or disbanded by the royal governor who took office in 1692 is unknown. It never played a major role in city affairs, and by the end of the century there was certainly no corporation government in Philadelphia.

In 1699 William Penn returned to his colony after a fifteen-year absence. His political standing in England was insecure, as was the status of his colony. Both Crown and Parliament were taking an active interest in proprietary charters, and reports of Pennsylvania's pacifism, its evasion of the Navigation Acts, and its internal political and religious feuding further undermined his position. In Pennsylvania he was almost as vulnerable, as his opponents realized. He was presented with a petition of grievances in which complaints about Philadelphia land grants and quitrents were joined to a request for settlement of all land disputes in the courts, rather than by the proprietor and his agents. The antiproprietary Quakers in the Assembly were demanding a new constitution for the province and a charter of incorporation for the city. Penn soon regretted the extent to which he yielded to these demands, but at the time peace and stability in the colony seemed essential to maintain his proprietorship. Just before leaving Philadelphia for the last time, on October 25, 1701, he issued a charter for the city.

The Charter of 1701 conferred relatively limited authority upon the mayor, aldermen, and councilmen, who had full powers of justice within the city and the right to issue laws and ordinances, as well as to regulate markets and fairs, but no taxing power. And Penn held on to the vacant land in the western half of the city, from Broad Street to the Schuylkill, for future development.[45] Furthermore Penn appointed his friends to the three principal offices in the corporation: Edward Shippen became mayor; Thomas Story, recorder; and Thomas Farmer, sheriff. He had little choice but to give his opponents control of the self-perpetuating body of aldermen and councilmen. Of the twenty aldermen and councilmen in 1701, fourteen had signed the antiproprietary petition of grievances. The new qualifications for freemanship in the city contained franchise restrictions that favored the established antiproprietary men of means. A two years' residence requirement limited the political voice of new immigrants, and a new £50 means test eliminated the poorer men (30 percent of those of the tax list of 1696, for example). As in 1691 the corporation of 1701 was led by a well-to-do and primarily Quaker elite. David Lloyd, now the antiproprietary leader, was appointed recorder of Philadelphia when Story resigned a few months after the charter was granted. Within the city English tradition and an antiproprietary faction were in control.[46]

V I

What mattered most of all to William Penn was liberty of conscience. The persecution that he and other Friends suffered in England stimulated him to

William Penn's signature and his Provincial Seal attached to the 1701 City Charter, now in the mayor's reception room in City Hall.

PHILADELPHIA CITY ARCHIVES

campaign for toleration, but his ambitions were not narrow. He considered freedom of religion a fundamental right, and he believed that toleration would remove religious issues from the political arena. When he founded his colony he did not restrict the opportunities of the New World to Quakers, although Friends were to be the backbone of the new society and their meeting the model institution. He advertised far and wide the new liberty offered in the Pennsylvania wilderness, fully expecting to draw a religiously diverse group of immigrants while maintaining political unity.[47]

The proprietor's guarantees of freedom, combined with the rapid commercial growth of Philadelphia, did attract other religious groups, and by 1700 the Quakers probably accounted for only about 40 percent of the population of the town. Although they made up the largest single religious group and had four meetinghouses, other Protestant denominations worshipped unhindered in the city: the Swedish Lutherans built Gloria Dei, the Anglicans built a chapel in 1696, the Presbyterians worshipped in a warehouse at Second and Chestnut called Barbados Store, and the Baptists used Anthony Morris's brewhouse for services. But the Anglicans, who occupied a privileged position in England and in such neighboring colonies as New York and Virginia, found it difficult to accept Pennsylvania's religious pluralism. Although their presence was specifically protected by the charter, at the insistence of the bishop of London, and Crown officials were usually members of England's established church, the Anglicans complained of political repression by the powerful Quakers and repeatedly challenged the Quakers' hegemony in Philadelphia and Pennsylvania.

Diversity notwithstanding, the early leaders in the city as in the colony were Quakers who, not unnaturally, thought Pennsylvania would be theirs. It is likely that most of them never entirely shared the proprietor's radical vision of a new society. Instead they were principally concerned to duplicate to their own advantage an English economic and power structure in which they, as a religious faction, had never managed to acquire a major share and under which they had been severely repressed. This view is borne out by the rapidity with which a large group of Pennsylvania Quakers began to combat the proprietor in order to extend their political power and economic interest. The leader of this antiproprietary faction was Thomas Lloyd, a well-to-do merchant, president of the provincial Council, and multiple officeholder. In the years between 1684 when Penn returned to England and 1694 when Lloyd died, he was the most powerful political figure in the province, forceful enough to disregard Penn's instructions when they did not suit him and his fellow Quaker officeholders. Upon Thomas Lloyd's death another Welsh Quaker, David Lloyd, took over the political leadership of the antiproprietary forces.

As soon as the Quaker immigrants reached Pennsylvania they formed a religious structure replicating the one they knew in England. In 1683 they established Monthly and Quarterly Meetings in Philadelphia. In 1685 they combined with Friends in West Jersey to establish a Yearly Meeting, which met alternately in Philadelphia and in Burlington. Public Friends, who shaped Quaker policy and supervised the publication of Quaker books and pamphlets, had their own ministerial meetings in Philadelphia four times a year. Such institutional unity, supplemented by their preponderance in the province, allowed Quakers to enscribe the laws of a moral society on the statute books. The Ten Commandments provided the foundation, and in the statutes swearing, cursing, and profanity were prohibited; respect for the First or Lord's Day was commanded, as was respect for parents; a catalogue of sexual sins, including fornication, incest, sodomy, rape, and bigamy, established punishments ranging from a public whipping to life imprisonment, with second offenders all to be imprisoned for life. On the other hand in an era when a host of offenses warranted the death penalty in England, only premeditated murder and treason were capital crimes in Penn's colony.

Because a part of the Quaker's moral law was brotherly love, scolding, calumny or "defaming," scandalous reporting, and dueling were all punishable. People who indulged in such practices were "Enemies to the peace and Concord of the Province." Public order was considered conducive to brotherly love, and therefore stage plays, cards, dice, masques and revels, bull-baiting, and cock-fighting "which excite the people to rudeness, cruelty, looseness, and irreligion, shall be respectively discouraged, and severely punished." Even lying in conversation was legally offensive. Gov. Benjamin Fletcher, a royal appointee, complained in the 1690s that the Pennsylvanians made one bout of drunkenness as serious a crime as fornication, at least for officeholders.[48]

The importance of private property was everywhere recognized in this legal-moral code, which is hardly surprising in a seventeenth-century English colony. Felons and burglars had to make satisfaction to their victims; parents of raped daughters were to receive recompense in real property; boats, the rights to water use, trees, cattle—all articles of highest value in a new town in virgin land—were protected by law. Still, devotion to property must not subvert Christian virtue and brotherly love. The enforcement of standard weights, measures, and qualities and the outlawing of usury by setting upper limits for interest rates (8 percent) were ancient and familiar practices to Pennsylvanians, and were understood to be good for business as well. But in some instances Pennsylvania went further than her neighbors, with business principles dictated by the meetinghouse as well as by the countinghouse. The laws reminded government itself to exercise truth and uprightness in all its dealings and commerce.

The functions of the magistrates who administered these laws were determined by the desire to create a Christian community, but they were also limited by Quaker practice and the Quaker ideal of brotherly love. Quakers were suspicious of courts and lawyers, and they thought that men who stood in a loving and friendly relationship to each other should settle any differences among themselves without recourse to law. The court might render justice in a given dispute, but litigiousness could not help but create divisiveness.

Therefore Philadelphia and other Pennsylvania communities were to choose annually three "common peacemakers" who would arbitrate disputes in much the same way that Quakers settled disputes through the meeting; and in Penn's Holy Experiment punishments would be meted out to "Common Barrators," those who vexed their neighbors with "Unjust and Frequent Suits."

The law then demonstrated the belief that a better community than men had known since the fall of Adam could be created by appropriate punishment, by removing occasion of sin, and by the leadership of honest Christians. Particular attention was paid to the shaping of sound family life through the regulation of marriage. Quakers had for some time developed a slow and careful examination system for betrothed couples, partly to keep the religious ranks unbroken, partly as a means of moral restraint, partly to affirm conjugal affection.[49] This concept was transferred to Pennsylvania, where it was considered vital to the new community to encourage marriage, but also, in an immigrant society, to prevent "unseemly proceedings" and protect the sanctity of the family and its property. In fact the law regulating marriage was considered so important that it was made fundamental, equivalent to an article of a constitution.

The concept of a colonial Christian community that would prove to a wicked world the capability of man for better things was of course not original with William Penn and the Quakers. John Winthrop's "city on a hill" in Massachusetts comes immediately to mind. But Penn's Quaker vision was broader than Winthrop's Puritan one. The Quaker's emphasis on Christian love, mutual respect, and ability to live in harmonious understanding in some ways distinguishes Penn and Philadelphia from Winthrop and Boston. But a more important distinction is found in the Quakers' tolerance. Penn did not think religious uniformity and exclusiveness essential to the development of a Christian community, and further, although his concept of brotherly love was fundamentally a Christian one, he saw no need to exclude non-Christian Europeans from its benefits.

Africans, however, like native American Indians, did not qualify for membership. The black community in Philadelphia could trace its roots back to the earliest years of the city. The first blacks in the Delaware Valley, slaves brought by the Dutch, preceded William Penn by about half a century. In 1684 a slave ship from Bristol sold its cargo of 150 Negroes to eager Philadelphia buyers. Though there is no record of any other large shipment in the first years, Philadelphia merchants who traded with the sugar islands frequently imported small lots of blacks from Barbados or Jamaica. Samuel Carpenter, Jonathan Dickinson, Isaac Norris, and James Claypoole were among the Philadelphia Quakers who engaged in this traffic. By 1700 perhaps one Philadelphian in ten owned slaves; William Penn himself was a slave-owner.

Quakers as a group were troubled about the propriety of chattel slavery in the late seventeenth century, but not troubled enough to do much about it. Led by Pastorius, the Germantown Friends objected strenuously "against the traffick of men-Body" in 1688, as did the schismatic Friend George Keith in 1693; but the orthodox English Friends, in their Quarterly Meeting in Philadelphia, found the issue "a thing of too great a weight" to determine.[50] In 1693 the Philadelphia authorities tried to prevent the tumultuous gathering of blacks on Sundays by ordering that any slave caught "gadding abroad on the said first dayes of the week, without a tickett from their Master or Mistress" be publicly whipped with thirty-nine lashes—a tactic borrowed from the Barbados slave code rather than the spirit of brotherly love.[51]

The Quakers not only accepted racial slavery but they exhibited other repressive tendencies. Freedom of intellectual inquiry was discouraged in early Philadelphia. The Quakers supported free elementary education for the poor and a Latin school for the well-to-do, but they distrusted formal scholarship, which in their opinion bred arid disputation. Propagandists for Pennsylvania congratulated the colony on having few lawyers or physicians. William Penn, who during his career published well over a hundred tracts in England, did not really want a free press in Pennsylvania. The Quaker printer William Bradford worked in Philadelphia from 1685 to 1693, turning out a number of almanacs, broadsides, and tracts. But when he published tracts critical of the Quaker leadership he was forced to move his press to New York. Thereafter Philadelphia was without a printer until Reynier Jansen, a Dutch Mennonite, arrived in 1699.

Significantly, the first library in the city originated under Anglican auspices, when Thomas Bray, the bishop of London's commissary for Maryland and soon to be founder of the Society for the Propagation of the Gospel in Foreign Parts, made a gift of more than 200 volumes to the city's infant Anglican congregation in 1698. Andreas Rudman, the domine of Gloria Dei Church, who was evidently something of a snob, complained that he could find no one in Philadelphia to bind his books. "The reason," he observed sarcastically, "there are no bookbinders here, where all sorts of other craftsmen are found, is that there is no scholarship here, and nothing counts but chopping, digging, planting, plowing, reaping." The domine's charge would be echoed many times in the future.[52]

Although Francis Daniel Pastorius is associated chiefly with Germantown, he helped to shape the cultural life of Philadelphia, such as it was in the early days. Pastorius was one of the few intellectuals in the province and owned the biggest library, an impressive collection of 250 books, mostly theological, in English, Latin, German, Dutch, and French. He was also a prolific author and a compiler, who filled fifty manuscript volumes with chronicles, collections of moral sayings, poetry, and pedagogical exercises composed in several languages. Though he was not a Quaker, Pastorius taught in the Philadelphia Quaker school as well as in Germantown.[53]

The institutional and moral discipline instilled by Penn and his colleagues, and their isolation from intellectual developments outside their community, did not prevent the Philadelphia Quakers from quarreling very fiercely over religious issues. Between 1690 and 1694 the Keithian controversy took place, and split the Philadelphia Quakers into two bitterly opposed camps. George Keith, a Scottish Friend who came to the city in 1689 as a schoolmaster, wanted to introduce greater formality of creed among Quakers in this wilderness community, and he also argued that when Friends in government supported England's war against France in the 1690s, they were undermining Quaker principles of pacifism and nonresistance. The Quaker leadership accused Keith of heresy in the Monthly and Yearly Meetings, then carried the fight into the civil courts by arresting the printer William Bradford and trying him on the charge of publishing unlicensed books. Presently the magistrates forbade Keith to make speeches and issue pamphlets that disturbed the peace. The language of the dispute on both sides was entirely unrelieved by signs of brotherly love—"fools, idiots, silly souls . . . rotten ranters . . . Tyrants," cried Keith, and the orthodox answered with "Brat of Babylon" and "Pope Primate of Pennsylvania." The climax came in a scandalous pitched battle at the Bank Meeting House north of Mulberry Street.[54] Friends in both camps deserted principles and resorted to violence. The anti-Keithians adopted the persecuting tactics they had so long suffered under in England. The Keithians, infuriated at their treatment, remained in the city as a schismatic group even after their leader was rejected.[55] Neither spiritual nor political harmony could be restored.

In 1701, when Penn left his city for the last time, Philadelphia with its 2500 or so inhabitants was too small to be called a city, too crowded to be labeled a "green country town," too contentious to be seen as a model of brotherly love. It had seldom been the home of its creator who, even during his brief visits to America, preferred his country seat at Pennsbury in Bucks County. Indeed control of Philadelphia's affairs was passing from the hands of the proprietor into the clutches of the inhabitants. Yet William Penn's influence was everywhere clear, for it was he who recognized the initial need for planning and order in the wilderness, the commercial potential of the Delaware port, the importance of imposing Quaker ideals on human affairs. He had accomplished much and he deserves his place of eminence in the city today, standing atop City Hall, over thirty-six feet tall, making a solemn gesture of peace and friendship toward Penn Treaty Park and the Lenni Lenape Indians—and in a broader sense, a gesture of welcome to all people who believe in political and religious liberty.

Village into Town
1701-1746

by Edwin B. Bronner

Riches [are] the natural Effects of Sobriety, Industry and Frugality.
— James Logan

I too am taking the proper measures for obtaining leisure to enjoy life and my friends. . . .
— Benjamin Franklin [1]

The new charter that William Penn conferred upon Philadelphia in 1701 raised Penn's "greene Country Towne" to the status of a "city." The title, however, hardly described the raw frontier village of some 2500 inhabitants between the Schuylkill and the Delaware. A Swedish pastor, Andreas Sandell, described Philadelphia as "a very pretty town" of 500 brick houses in 1702, and by 1725 Christopher Saur estimated that there were "at least eight hundred important merchants and shopkeepers" in this "handsomely built" town. But Saur had become a Philadelphian, and even a pietist apparently might be a booster. As late as 1744 Dr. Alexander Hamilton, a Scottish physician of Annapolis, wrote on a visit, "I could not apprehend this city to be so very elegant or pritty as is commonly represented." Comparing it to a country market town of England, he mentioned dirty, unpaved streets, low buildings, and a lack of turrets or steeples to catch the eye from a distance. And as for her population, "They have that accomplishment peculiar to all our American colonys, viz, subtilty and craft in their dealings."[2]

The canny Scot was not much impressed with the Quaker town of 1744, but he did mention several of her buildings including the venerable Great Meeting House on the southwest corner of Second and High Streets. In 1701 the Great Meeting House (so-called to distinguish it from several other Quaker houses of worship) was the only structure in the newly designated "city" that could make any claim to consideration as a public building. It was of frame construction, fifty feet square, and had been built in 1696 at a cost of some £1000.[3] Among other buildings admired by Dr. Hamilton was Christ

Church, but in 1701 its location along Second Street between High and Mulberry was modestly occupied by the small Anglican chapel that had also been built in 1696. Farther north was another chapel where the supporters of the schismatic Quaker George Keith held services. To the south, in the once-separate village of Wicaco, stood the Swedes' little Gloria Dei.

If in 1744 Philadelphia did not seem particularly impressive, in 1701 it was even less so. The congregations of these several churches worked at the wharves or in the warehouses, some went for their evening tippling to one of the several taverns, and all returned home along unpaved streets down near the bank of the Delaware. There were several hundred dwellings, still mostly frame, many of them with an office, warehouse, or store on the first floor with living quarters above.

A few of these houses, it is true, were commodious for the time and place. Generally overlooking the river, these were large enough that, like the Slate Roof House and Mayor Edward Shippen's on Second Street near Dock Creek, they might even be called imposing. But even Philadelphia's few rich men felt a sense of isolation. Occasional letters arrived from the British Isles, but there were no local newspapers to circulate news or ideas. The world of real cities remained far away.

The South East Prospect of The City of Philadelphia By Peter Cooper Painter, *c. 1720. The earliest known view of the Philadelphia riverfront may have been commissioned by the Penns as the basis for a promotional engraving. Although several apocryphal steeples were included by the artist to enliven the skyline of the new city, the residences of leading citizens such as Samuel Carpenter and Edward Shippen as well as the Great Meeting House (1696) at Second and High Streets;*

I

Yet that world would soon grow nearer, with consequent stimulation of the attributes of city life in Philadelphia itself. When Penn granted the city charter just before departing his province forever in 1701, the only major trading area linked to Philadelphia remained the West Indies. Even trade with the British Isles was slight, largely due to the lack of an adequate medium of exchange with which to purchase manufactured goods. As long as these conditions prevailed, life necessarily continued to be simple and in large part self-sufficient. Within the next generation and a half, however, Philadelphia's exports were to grow enough to make the British Isles a major trading partner, and to add other outlets considerably enhancing the town's variety of imports and of exterior contacts.[4]

Philadelphia's rise to prosperity, nevertheless, would not be smooth. Her economy depended in large part on conditions beyond her control. The war that broke out in 1702—Queen Anne's War—ushered in over a decade of hard times for Philadelphia's citizens. For eleven years, in fact, Louis XIV's privateers wreaked havoc with the new city's all-important West Indian trade. Statistics vividly portray the story. While the 1693 tax list showed twenty-one

the Court House (1698/1709) in the middle of High Street near Second; the Bank Meeting House (1702) at Front Street, north of Arch; and the Penny Pot House (c. 1700), at Front and Vine, are accurately indicated. The arms of the Penn family are painted at the upper left, and the arms of the city, adopted in 1701, appear in the upper right.

Silver flagon made for the Anglican communion at the first Christ Church by Philip Syng, Sr. (1676–1739), in 1715. In July 1734 Syng advertised in Franklin's Pennsylvania Gazette *that his shop was "over against the Market House, next Door but one to the Crown."*

CHRIST CHURCH, PHILADELPHIA; PHOTOGRAPH COURTESY PHILADELPHIA MUSEUM OF ART

of the city's ratables with property worth more than £500, the 1709 list showed only Edward Shippen, William Trent, and Samuel Carpenter in this category —the latter maintaining his taxable wealth in spite of the severe losses he had incurred.[5]

The Treaty of Utrecht of 1713 brought an end to Queen Anne's War and humiliated the Bourbon powers. Nova Scotia, Gibraltar, and enlarged holdings in India increased British power and prestige, while the gaining of the *Asiento,* the monopoly contract for carrying slaves to the Spanish Empire, sparked the English carrying trade. Philadelphia's economy experienced the tidal wave of prosperity that now emanated from London to the farthest shores of the enlarged empire.

Yet once more Philadelphia's economy collapsed when in the early 1720s she felt the disastrous effects of the bursting of the so-called South Sea Bubble. Indeed, the failure of John Law's greatest speculative venture, one in which many if not most of England's great men had invested, appeared to threaten the Crown itself with bankruptcy. The consequent shrinkage of credit and trade was ameliorated only by the astringent medicine applied by the financial genius Robert Walpole. Meanwhile Philadelphians experienced another depression. In his *Autobiography* Benjamin Franklin remembered the look of the town upon his arrival there in early October 1723. "Most of the houses in

Walnut Street between Second and Front Streets," he recalled, had "Bills on their Doors, to be let; and many likewise in Chestnut Street, and other Streets; which made me then think the Inhabitants of the City were one after another deserting it."[6]

The young Franklin, of course, as well as the young town had a future. That future was bound up not only with the great prosperity of Walpole's England, but also with the tremendous population growth that characterized eighteenth-century America. Keen observer that he was, Franklin accurately forecast the doubling of America's population every twenty-five years. It was a formulation, incidentally, that later inspired Thomas Malthus to the framing of his famous population theory.

Philadelphia's recovery from the depression of the 1720s was in part a cause and in part a result of the growth of the population of Penn's colony. As the backcountry was transformed from forest to farm, Philadelphia's artisans and traders found new economic opportunities. These opportunities inspired larger families and also acted as a magnet to Europe's restless people.

Penn's tolerant, officially pacifist colony in fact had from the beginning been attractive to European pietist sectarians from the Germanies and elsewhere. German emigration to Pennsylvania had begun as early as the 1690s; the end of the 1720s saw the commencement of the human flood. Philadelphia's merchants and artisans thrived as they provided for the needs of an everincreasing tide of humanity. In the nineteenth century Philadelphia would give way to New York as the emigrants' chief port of entry. But in the eighteenth century Philadelphia was the funnel through which Europeans by the thousands passed on their way to creating new lives in America.

As if the magnet of New World opportunity were not enough to pull Europeans westward, conditions in the Old World worked toward the same result. Incessant wars, taxes, religious persecution, rack rents, crop failures, and famine brought thousands of people from central Europe, and after 1730 from impoverished Northern Ireland, where England's cruelly restrictive mercantilist policies added a further motive to emigrate.[7]

The consequent filling of the backcountry meant a great surge in Pennsylvania's agricultural production with obvious repercussions for Philadelphia's shipping and mercantile interests. Wheat, flour, and bread continued to be the staple Philadelphia exports. Fortunately, while weather in Europe had been bad, the immigrants enjoyed a succession of generally excellent crop years in Pennsylvania in the 1720s and 1730s. By the mid-1730s Philadelphia exports of breadstuffs approached an annual value of £50,000. Lumber products, especially barrel staves, remained another major export, and flaxseed also joined the list. And as a foretaste of her industrial future, mineral-rich Pennsylvania was soon viewed by the English iron masters as a dangerous rival.

In the economic revival and growth following the depression of the 1720s it was Philadelphia's direct trade with the British Isles that increased most in volume. With the waning of hard times and on through the 1730s clearances from Philadelphia for the British Isles quadrupled, while entries from British

home ports increased by two and a half times. The vessels arriving from
Britain, mainly from London and Bristol, of course brought the manufactured
goods whose acquisition was the main object of foreign trade. They also
brought the new immigrants, who generally arrived with at least some specie
in their pockets to help pay for imports. Though a 1728 estimate of £50 per
immigrant was surely an exaggeration, the chronic specie shortage was at least
moderated as long as immigrants were numerous.[8] Along with the trade with
England there grew a new trade with Ireland, which by the end of the 1730s
had attained a volume as great as that of the West Indies trade fifteen years
earlier. The same famine that sent immigrants from Ireland to the New
World created an Irish demand for Pennsylvania breadstuffs.

The Philadelphia shippers also found new markets in southern Europe. A
decline in Mediterranean and North African grain production and the effect
of the era's turbulent politics on grain supplies from northern Europe caused
the Iberian countries to seek new grain sources. Philadelphians sent Pennsylvania wheat, flour, and corn to help meet the demand. Any so-called
nonenumerated goods could be carried to southern Europe without running
afoul of the Navigation Acts, while with few exceptions European goods
exported to America had first to pass through England. One of these exceptions was wine from the Portuguese islands. Though temperance presumably
remained a Friendly virtue, madeira and port in astonishing quantities flowed
to Philadelphia cellars. But because even the most lavishly hospitable Philadelphia merchant and his guests eventually found limits to their capacity to
consume these new trade commodities, Portuguese wine and spirits threatened to glut the Philadelphia market. Pennsylvania felt obliged to spend more
than £200 to help win parliamentary acceptance of a bill allowing direct
importation of Portuguese and Spanish salt as well. Lisbon and Madeira were
the primary centers of Philadelphia's southern European trade, but gradually
Philadelphia ships began to navigate through the Straits of Gibraltar.

The southern European trade also produced bills of exchange to be negotiated for manufactured goods in England. Surplus wine and salt entered as
well into Philadelphia's rapidly growing coastal trade with the other North
American mainland colonies, there too to produce the means of purchasing
English manufactures. In this coastal commerce wheat was sent from the early
years to the tobacco and rice colonies to the south, and after bad harvests in
the north in 1737 Philadelphia grain and grain products also went in volume
to New England.

The rise of such other trading outlets coincided with a relative decline in
the value of the West Indian trade. The British West Indies were already
afflicted by declining soil fertility as well as by plant parasites, hurricanes, and
droughts. At the same time the Caribbean—that "cockpit of international
rivalries"—was an all but continuous theater of war during the unending
struggle between England and France and their allies. In order to discourage
trade with the still-productive French West Indies, Parliament passed the
famous Molasses Act of 1733 which contributed to that trade's decline. To be

sure, an indeterminate amount of smuggling occurred; illegal trade in rum and molasses probably accounts for some of the growing volume of the coastal trade, especially a rapid growth of trade with Rhode Island in the 1730s.

Trade with the West Indies was conducted by Philadelphia merchants mainly as a speculative venture, at the risk of the merchant. He bought up a cargo of flour, bread, lumber, and other Philadelphia products, shipped it to the islands without having assured buyers—several merchants together often investing in a ship's cargo—and sold the goods (and sometimes the ship too) either through a supercargo who accompanied the ship or more often through a resident factor in the islands. The factor acted as the Philadelphia merchant's agent, selling the cargo to West Indian planters, generally on several months' credit, and collecting produce and money from the planters to remit to Philadelphia. Only occasionally did the factor become more than an agent by buying a share of the venture.

More varied and distant trading partnerships prompted an increase in the size of the vessels that carried Philadelphia's commerce. In the early 1720s almost half of Philadelphia's tonnage was carried in sloops and schooners, but in the next decade the share of these smaller boats fell to about 15 percent, and the listing of brigs, snows, and ships in the port's trading registers increased sharply. More and larger vessels naturally meant a growing business for Philadelphia shipyards and employment for shipfitters. Twice as many ships were built in Philadelphia in 1726 as in any year before 1723. During the 1720s and 1730s, 235 Philadelphia-built ships cleared her port. A high proportion of this tonnage was evidently ocean-going.[9]

The immediate beneficiaries of the growth of Philadelphia's commerce included not only the great merchants but also the shipwrights and shipfitters, the men on the ropewalks, loftsmen, and chandlers. In fact the whole town experienced ever-widening ripples of prosperity. The absence of specie of course remained a problem, for without an adequate medium of exchange commerce would be severely restricted.

Scarcity of specie, it should be added, was not unique to Pennsylvania. England steadfastly refused such far-seeing suggestions as the establishment of a colonial mint. Fearful of colonial monetary independence, she also discouraged various land-bank schemes as well as the issuance of paper money by the various colonial legislatures. Her stand ultimately contributed to the coming of the Revolution.

Nevertheless, beginning with Massachusetts in 1691, the colonies had long since adopted various paper-money alternatives. Pennsylvania, arriving late on the scene, authorized the first of many issues of paper currency in the depression year of 1723, the year of Franklin's arrival in Philadelphia. In spite of proprietary fears of inflation, fears fueled by the runaway paper economy of South Carolina, Pennsylvania currency maintained its value and contributed to the colony's prosperity.

Lubricated by paper, Philadelphia's economy through the early decades of the eighteenth century slowly closed the gap with that of the older colonial seaports. By the end of the fourth decade of the century, of the American ports only Boston still surpassed Philadelphia in volume of shipping. At some time in the 1740s Philadelphia's population reached 10,000, leaving it second only to the Massachusetts capital. The outbreak of renewed warfare between England and the Bourbon powers in 1739 temporarily reversed the trend. But Philadelphia was destined to move to the forefront of colonial towns in the next major expansion of trade.[10]

I I

The year 1701 marks a turning point in Philadelphia's history not only because of its incorporation as a city and the final leave-taking of its founder, William Penn. This was also the year in which the twenty-seven-year-old James Logan took his place as the foremost representative of the proprietor's interests in Pennsylvania. Serious, intellectual, conservative, wise, acquisitive —in serving his employer he also generously served himself—Logan dominated the political and cultural life of the colony and city for almost half a century. At the same time he contributed to and benefited from the economic expansion within the Atlantic community of which Philadelphia would become the principal American outpost.

James Logan was born in 1674 in Ulster, the son of an impecunious if learned Scottish Quaker schoolmaster. The young man's intellectual bril-

James Logan *(1674–1751), painted by Gustavus Hesselius (1682–1755), c. 1716.*

liance headed him toward a similar career; he mastered Latin, Greek, Hebrew, French, and Italian, and taught himself mathematics, so that he became perhaps the only person in America in his time who could read and understand Newton's *Principia Mathematica*. Logan came to the attention of William Penn as a Bristol schoolteacher when Penn was living in that English city. Penn was impressed enough to ask the young man to become his secretary. Logan in fact proved the exception to the rule that the proprietor was a poor judge of men. The ex-schoolmaster proved both loyal and efficient. Left in charge of Penn's affairs in Pennsylvania, he both enriched himself and jealously guarded proprietary prerogatives.

Logan's positions of public trust facilitated his road to fortune. He was receiver-general of quitrents, a member of the governor's Council, and for one year, 1722–1723, mayor of Philadelphia. He held various judgeships including that of chief justice of the Pennsylvania Supreme Court. But it was through the offices of commissioner of property and proprietary Indian agent that Logan primarily saw to his own and the proprietor's welfare.

The basis of Logan's Pennsylvania fortune lay in his revitalizing and monopolizing the fur trade with the Indians, a trade that had been neglected in the Delaware Valley since the elimination of the Dutch and Swedes from the backcountry. Profits from fur enabled Logan to invest in lands whose value vastly increased with the increase in population. He also invested in Pennsylvania iron, one of his few failures though the industry soon prospered, and in British securities. By 1749 his estate came to some 18,000 prime acres in Pennsylvania and New Jersey as well as large holdings of securities and cash.[11]

Though Logan, as Penn's man in Pennsylvania, enjoyed peculiar advantages in the struggle for wealth, his rise was by no means unique. Nor was he unique, though he was among the first, to build for himself a comfortable country mansion where he could pursue his intellectual interests away from the increasing bustle of Philadelphia. Stenton, which Logan completed in 1730 near the Germantown Road and which he named after his father's birthplace, was the first Queen Anne-style building to be erected in the Delaware Valley. Approached through a graceful corridor of stately hemlocks, Stenton was of a simple symmetry except for decorative touches of bricks laid in Flemish bond (a feature anticipated by the Slate Roof House), a watertable of molded brick to mark the basement, a belt course to mark the second floor, and a denticulated cornice. Remarkably, Stenton stands to this day, though its spacious grounds have been reduced to a six-acre park engulfed by the city at Eighteenth and Courtland Streets.

James Logan preceded the transplanted Bostonian Benjamin Franklin as a Philadelphia contributor to the cultural life of the entire Atlantic world. Business and governmental activities never excluded Logan's real passion, the life of the mind. For the European scholar, thanks to Logan, Philadelphia soon conjured up no longer a frontier outpost of antiintellectual Quakers but a remarkable citadel of learning in the wilderness.

Mathematics fascinated Logan, and he not only kept up with all of the latest developments but made several contributions of his own, particularly in mathematical optics. Logan owned the first copy of Isaac Newton's *Principia Mathematica* known to have been brought to America. In botany he carried on experiments with Indian corn that demonstrated the manner in which pollen fertilized the seed. Through the agency of his English friend and correspondent the Quaker Peter Collinson, this work brought Logan to the attention of Carolus Linnaeus and won him the Swedish naturalist's praise as one of the heroes of science. The Dutch botanist Johann Friedrich Gronovius helped arrange the publication of Logan's plant experiments at Leyden in 1739 as *Experimenta et meletemata de plantarum generatione.*

Logan the linguist readily corresponded and published in the international scholarly language, Latin. In Pennsylvania he had continued his youthful language studies, adding Arabic, Persian, and Syriac as well as a smattering of others. In the margins of his editions of the classics he zestfully argued in Greek and Latin with the editors about their readings. He amused himself by translating into English couplets the medieval "Cato's Distichs," a collection of moralistic epigrams, a task in which for him the English versification was the only difficult part. When he was sixty-three Logan translated for his friend Isaac Norris Cicero's essay on growing old, the *Cato Major.* Franklin published both, the first published American translation of a classical author.

In all these fields James Logan had by the time of his death accumulated some 2500 volumes, a collection that not only made up one of the largest libraries in the colonies, but was also *the* largest in the sciences, linguistics, and classics. Because neither of his two sons shared his scholarly interests, Logan planned to bequeath his library as a public trust, a plan carried out by his heirs so that the Loganian Library remains today principally intact in the Library Company of Philadelphia.

Given the time and place and his forbidding personality, Logan's work was all but unnoticed by the provincial Philadelphians, but he nevertheless gathered about him a few disciples. It was Logan who taught Latin to the young botanical genius John Bartram, and who put Bartram in touch with the English naturalists and Linnaeus. When a young glazier, Thomas Godfrey, was working on his windows at Stenton, Logan discovered that Godfrey understood higher mathematics and made him another protégé with full access to his library. He reported Godfrey's improvement of the mariner's quadrant to Edmund Halley, the Astronomer Royal; and when John Hadley in England received the recognition of the Royal Society as the inventor of a suspiciously similar device, Logan stubbornly argued for Godfrey's priority. Logan also befriended and encouraged another young man whose personality precluded his being anybody's protégé, but who also possessed all the ingratiating characteristics and the ability to stimulate the cultural life of a whole community that Logan lacked. This was the bright young instigator of the Junto Club, Benjamin Franklin. In his encouragement of such men as Bartram, Godfrey, and Franklin lies James Logan's chief legacy to Philadelphia and to America.

I I I

James Logan died at age seventy-seven in 1751 still within the Quaker faith for which he and his parents had suffered in Ireland and England. But Quakerism, like Philadelphia itself, had changed from the days of George Fox. The late Quaker historian Frederick B. Tolles sums up that change in the title of his famous book *Meeting House and Counting House.* Though much more than a countinghouse merchant, Logan himself represented the secularization that followed increasing material wealth. Where the world made demands incompatible with faith Logan, unlike some of the more straight-backed Friends, was willing to bend.

As the "countinghouse" took precedence many Quakers not only lost zeal, but Quakerism in Philadelphia was losing its numerical preeminence as well. The growth of commerce and population brought about a cultural transformation from a Quaker community to a religiously and philosophically heterogeneous one. By the middle 1740s, helped by Scots-Irish immigration, Presbyterians were beginning to rival the Quakers in numbers. With the emergence of a diversity of competing religious denominations and sects, the cultural atmosphere, at least among the town's burgeoning upper class, moved away not only from Quakerism but also from traditional Christianity and toward the secularism of the Enlightenment. The work of men such as the Quaker Logan and later the Puritan-bred Franklin attests to this phenomenon.

But while Philadelphia and Boston were to shed at least some of their original religious zeal, so their separate religious origins had much in common. The persecuted English Quakers were to the latter part of the seventeenth century what the Puritans were to the 1620s and 1630s. In both cases the victims became the rulers, and in their new and unfamiliar role they perforce had to create new institutions of social cohesion.

For the Puritans the congregation and the town meeting fulfilled this need. For the Quakers the answer was a system of interlocking meetings of which the Philadelphia Monthly Meeting was the centerpiece. In the words of Frederick Tolles, "In addition to nourishing the religious life and guarding the the morals of its members, it functioned as a dispenser of poor relief, a loan office, a court of arbitration in economic matters, an employment agency, and a source of advice to new arrivals on the management of their affairs."[12] The Philadelphia Quaker meeting, in short, provided the nexus of the Quaker community.

With the growth of Philadelphia's population the monthly meeting became less involved in civil affairs—in the early years, for example, it had authorized the building of roads. But it always remained the prime agency for relief of human suffering. Widows were aided and their children given opportunity to learn a trade as apprentices. Quaker immigrants who arrived in Philadelphia without adequate funds were either lent money without interest or given grants. In 1713 Friends opened an Alms House on Walnut Street near Fourth, and it was enlarged in 1729. Here the poor lived in individual cottages instead of being thrown together, and they were encouraged to work part time at a trade. In this charitable instance Friendly concern was not merely exclusive; in the absence of a public almshouse until 1732 the Friends' Alms House was available to the indigent of all faiths.

While the local monthly meeting looked to such matters as Friendly charity, the Philadelphia Yearly Meeting attempted to make Philadelphia the center of American Quakerism, and assumed a special sense of responsibility for Friends throughout America.[13] The North American Friends in turn formed part of "The Atlantic Community of the Early Friends."[14] There was a constant exchange of "Public Friends" traveling in the ministry from one Quaker group to another. "Public Friends" continued to visit Philadelphia from England and Ireland each year, and more frequent visits were exchanged between Philadelphia and the other mainland colonies and the West Indies. Friends also exchanged letters of greeting and counsel, called epistles. In the first instance these went from one yearly meeting to another, but they were sent down to quarterly meetings and monthly meetings. Epistles to Philadelphia from the London Yearly Meeting were especially likely to set forth principles designed to help the American Quakers hew close to Truth.

Friends had their own schools and spent considerable time monitoring their operation. While most of them had little respect for higher education, the Quakers were concerned with basic instruction for their children. William Penn had provided in his First Frame of Government that the governor and Council should see to the erecting of schools, and the Friends' Public School, founded in 1689, and receiving a charter from the proprietor in 1701, was to evolve into the William Penn Charter School. The Friends' emphasis was on practical learning and the inculcation of Quaker virtues, but the early eighteenth-century growth of mercantile prosperity and concomitant social aspirations led to the founding and rapid growth of a Latin School—for the wealthy —within the Public School—which taught the three Rs to the less affluent. Girls were given a chance to learn as well as boys, which was a reflection of the Quaker view of the equality of the sexes.[15]

The international network of Quakers operated in matters of commerce as well as of conscience. When a Philadelphian such as Isaac Norris wished to deal with a merchant in a seaport in England, the West Indies, or one of the other mainland colonies, he naturally turned to a Quaker in those parts. If the man were not dependable, he could complain to the fellow Quaker's monthly meeting and have a reasonable expectation of finding satisfaction there. Within Philadelphia the Friends were likely to deal with one another, and the same guarantee of reliability was available.[16] In fact the leadership of the town's business, political, and religious life by an uncommonly exclusive and inward-looking sect set early Philadelphia apart from other cities of the

British Empire, at least until it ceased to be predominantly a Quaker city.

The most conspicuous way in which the Quaker character of early Philadelphia expressed itself within the town was in an increasingly detailed and rigid extension of Penn's effort to regulate daily life, both business and leisure, according to Quaker standards. In 1704 the Philadelphia Yearly Meeting prepared the first "Book of Discipline" compiled by Quakers anywhere, accompanied by "A Generall Testimony against all Looseness & vanity or what else may tend to ye Reproach of Truth and the hurt of ye Souls of the Youth or others. . . ." In the "Discipline" the meeting forbade drinking to excess, swearing, cursing, smoking in public, gambling, running races, engaging in competitive games, and in general such a catalogue of activities as suggested the beginnings of a considerable departure from the anticipated tranquility of an idealized "greene Country Towne." The Quaker-dominated General Assembly hardened similar restrictions into law, to apply to all inhabitants of Pennsylvania.[17]

The "Book of Discipline" tried also to regulate Quaker relationships with those puzzling new peoples encountered in the New World, the Indians and the blacks. It forbade selling spirits to Indians, and this regulation was among those written into statute law. When a revised "Discipline" appeared in 1719 it reiterated earlier Quaker misgivings about the trade in black slaves by expressing the hope "that none amongst us be Concerned in the fetching or importing Negro slaves from their own Country or elsewhere. . . ."[18] In 1711 the General Assembly prohibited further importation of slaves, but the Privy Council disallowed this statute. The provincial government then tried to achieve the same end with a prohibitory import duty of £20 on each slave brought to the colony, but the duty was also disallowed.[19] Yet the very necessity of seeking new weapons against the slave trade also suggests, and suggests accurately, that this was one of the areas where the professions of earnest Friends diverged from the practice of those less earnest.

Indeed, though the wealthy Friend Samuel Carpenter had subscribed to one of the earlier Quaker protests against the slave trade at the Philadelphia Monthly Meeting in 1698, in 1703 he himself was apparently importing and selling blacks.[20] As part of the expansion and diversification of Philadelphia commerce in the first decades of the eighteenth century the town's slave trade grew from an occasional importation of three or four black servants to frequent cargoes of perhaps thirty or forty slaves. Quaker merchants participated, Isaac Norris and Jonathan Dickinson being especially prominent among them. Although both these Quaker worthies expressed misgivings about this branch of their commerce, their misgivings sprang from the uncertainties of quality and sales and the prevalence of stomach disorders among the merchandise, not from moral revulsion.[21]

The protests against traffic in slaves published in Philadelphia by Ralph Sandiford in 1729 and by Benjamin Lay in 1737 are usually accounted landmarks in the rise of the Friends' protests against slavery. Sandiford's *Brief Examination of the Practice of the Times* spoke with outraged eloquence; Lay's

All Slave-Keepers Apostates rang with the fervor of the convert, Lay himself
having been recently a Barbadian slavekeeper. But Quakerism had changed
since the times of its fiery seventeenth-century martyrs, especially in the
increasingly comfortable Quaker town of Philadelphia; outrage and fervor no
longer seemed appropriate Quaker styles. Both Sandiford and Lay were
reprimanded in the meetings for excessive vehemence. In the first half of the
eighteenth century a Quaker front against slavery had not yet formed.

    The "Discipline" could deal more readily with war and preparation for
war, at least to the extent that the Quaker peace testimony coincided rather
than conflicted with the interests of an expanding mercantile community. But
even here there was tension, because while the Quakers rejected the use of
arms for themselves, Quakers of William Penn's generation and the early
eighteenth century acknowledged the right, indeed the duty, of government
to defend its citizenry—and in Pennsylvania the Quaker gentry of Philadelphia had achieved a considerable control of the government.

    It was a control, however, that the issue of defense would severely com-
promise, just as the same issue created a division within the Quaker community itself. In times of crisis some so-called defense Quakers were even induced to forgo the peace testimony altogether. As might be expected, the
learned, practical James Logan took the defense side over creedal purity. He
consistently aided efforts to provide Pennsylvania with ample defenses against
military threats either from the frontier or up the Delaware from the sea
toward Philadelphia. In 1741 he laid before the yearly meeting a long statement
on the peace testimony in which he observed of his fellow prosperous Quaker
merchants:

Although they allege they cannot for conscience-sake bear arms, as being contrary to
the peaceable doctrine of Jesus . . . yet, without regard to others of Christ's precepts,
full as express, against laying up treasure in this world, and not caring for tomorrow,
they are as intent as any others in amassing riches, the great bait and temptation to
our enemies to come and plunder the place.[22]

    Accurately foretelling future events, Logan reasoned that because all civil
government is founded on force, Friends who could not in good conscience
invoke force ought to eschew political participation. For himself he made no
pretense of literal adherence to either of the New Testament precepts to
which he had referred.

    It was a stance that succinctly summed up the Quaker dilemma. Philadel-
phia's conscience Quakers—"stiff-necked" as their opponents called them—
might later find a social role in the antislavery crusade and philanthropy, but
rigid adherence to their creed tended to isolate them as a people apart. For
the rest, they followed James Logan if not out of Quakerism then into such
compromises with the world that they were Quakers in name only. Few were
the Friends who successfully could bridge the gap between—in Professor
Tolles's terms—the meetinghouse and the countinghouse.

I V

Philadelphia's Quakers were not only torn between their duty to God and to the world as in the matter of defense. They also found themselves increasingly a minority in their own country. By mid-century, though they remained among the most influential groups, they made up only some one-sixth of the population. Immigration, of course, told the story. Between 1726 and 1755 some 40,000 Germans arrived in Philadelphia, and 30,000 Scots-Irish settled in Pennsylvania. The English and Welsh were now a minority counting some 25–30 percent of the population. The Scots-Irish equalled them in numbers while the 60,000 Germans were the largest ethnic group in the colony.[23]

As for Philadelphia's German population, immigrants of the Reformed faith were brought together into what proved a permanent congregation by George Michael Weiss, a clergyman who arrived in 1727. In 1747 they were to erect their first church structure, a picturesque octagonal building of stone, on the south side of Race Street just east of Fourth. Another Reformed clergyman, Samuel Guldin, preached in Germantown as early as 1718, and there a Reformed church was erected in 1733 where the Market Square Presbyterian Church now stands.

The German Lutherans also had a congregation in Germantown in 1726 and built a church there four years later; the present St. Michael's Lutheran Church is now on that northeast corner of Germantown Avenue and Phil-Ellena Street. In Philadelphia itself the Lutherans worshipped in a barn on Arch Street below Fifth from 1733 and acquired a lasting organization under the leadership of Henry Melchior Muhlenberg, who arrived in 1742. Muhlenberg, who had studied at the Universities of Göttingen and Halle, the latter the citadel of German pietism, heeded a call to America from the Hanoverian King George's German chaplain just in time to rescue the Philadelphia Lutheran flock from the seductions of Count Nicholas Zinzendorf into Moravianism.

Strengthened by Muhlenberg's pastorate, in March 1743 the Lutherans purchased a lot at the corner of Fifth Street and Appletree Alley, above Mulberry, where they erected St. Michael's Church. The first sermon was preached there in October, but in a building still without floor or windows. The church was eventually consecrated in 1748. St. Michael's was a relatively ambitious structure architecturally, later to be crowned with a tall steeple with bells.

As for the Moravians, having failed to appropriate the membership of the two major German faiths by pretending to be either Lutheran or Reformed as suited convenience, they settled down to a career as a third, though smaller, German denomination, with a church on the south side of Race Street between Second and Third.[24]

There were not yet many Presbyterians in Philadelphia when the adherents of this denomination in the Middle Colonies chose the town for their

St. Michael's Lutheran Church, Fifth Street and Appletree Alley (near Cherry), begun 1743, demolished 1872, engraving by William Birch (1800).
FREE LIBRARY OF PHILADELPHIA

assembly to organize the first American Presbytery in 1706. But they chose wisely, for the Scots-Irish immigration to Pennsylvania made their church the most rapidly growing one of the period. Philadelphia became the logical center of American Presbyterianism. From 1704 the Philadelphia Presbyterians had their own church building, the Buttonwood Church—so called from the trees around it—at the southeast corner of High and Bank Streets. Peter Kalm described the structure as "a half-hexagon" of "a middling size."[25] In 1717 or 1718 a synod of several presbyteries was created with a Philadelphia headquarters. As has so often been true in Christian history, the Presbyterians demonstrated their vitality through contentiousness. Jedediah Andrews, a Harvard graduate and pastor of the Buttonwood Church, emerged as the principal champion of leadership by a traditionally educated clergy against the Bucks County founder of the "Log College" at Neshaiminy, William Tennent. The emphasis of Tennent and his sons, William Jr. and Gilbert, on emotional religion prepared the way for the most dramatic demonstration of the continued importance of Christianity in Philadelphia's community life, the visits of George Whitefield in 1739–1740.

The eloquent apostle of the Great Awakening in the middle and southern colonies came to Philadelphia for the announced purpose of raising money for his Georgia orphanage. Even on that relatively mundane subject he could preach magnetically; the skeptical Franklin had calculated characteristically that it would be cheaper because of the lack of materials and workmen in Georgia to build the orphanage in Philadelphia, but he attended one of Whitefield's sermons on the subject, and as he tells it:

> . . . I silently resolved he should get nothing from me. I had in my Pocket a Handful of Copper Money, three or four silver Dollars, and five Pistoles in Gold. As he proceeded I began to soften, and concluded to give the Coppers. Another Stroke of his Oratory made me asham'd of that, and determin'd me to give the Silver, and he finish'd so admirably that I empty'd my Pocket wholly into the Collector's Dish, Gold and all.[26]

But Whitefield's impact far overshadowed the sums he collected for the orphanage. He brought a warm Christianity of individual communion with God that unsettled his fellow Anglicans, the conservative Presbyterians, and the Quakers, who in the Philadelphia area were decidedly no longer the "ranting" dissenters of the seventeenth-century English variety.

At first Whitefield preached daily at the Anglican Christ Church, a pulpit later denied him, and then to larger outdoor audiences from the Court House steps. The *Pennsylvania Gazette* reported a crowd of 6000 on a Sunday evening in mid-November 1739, and when Whitefield spoke again two weeks later the paper stated that 10,000 went to Society Hill to hear him preach. The following year he returned to Philadelphia in April, and this time the press estimated one of his audiences at 15,000. The skeptical Franklin utilized the scientific method to ascertain if it were true that the human voice could carry to such numbers. Both Market Street and Second Street, he remarked, were filled with Whitefield's "Hearers to a considerable Distance. Being among the hindmost in Market Street," Franklin continued,

I had the Curiosity to learn how far he could be heard, by retiring backwards down the Street towards the River, and I found his Voice distinct till I came near Front-Street, when some Noise in that Street, obscur'd it. Imagining then a Semi-Circle, of which my Distance should be the Radius, and that it were fill'd with Auditors, to each of whom I allow'd two square feet, I computed that he might well be heard by more than Thirty-Thousand. This reconcil'd me to the Newspaper Accounts of his having preach'd to 25000 People in the Fields, and to the antient Histories of Generals haranguing whole Armies, of which I had sometimes doubted.[27]

Whitefield stimulated the Tennents' attack on Presbyterian traditionalism, and his invasion precipitated a splitting of the Presbyterians into the "Old Lights" and the Tennents' "New Lights." The New Lights worshiped in a building erected by Whitefield's admirers to offer indoor comfort to as large as possible a portion of the crowds he attracted. Located on the east side of Fourth Street between High and Mulberry, the building was a "great and lofty hall" a hundred feet long and seventy feet wide. Significantly, neither the secular State House nor the latitudinarian Anglicans' Christ Church but Whitefield's hall was the largest building in Philadelphia.[28]

In Philadelphia, where divisions within sects as well as between sects created a broad religious heterogeneity, there existed a religious toleration that extended to Catholics as well as to Jews. In the spirit of the Holy Experiment, by which term William Penn had meant above all religious freedom, there were no laws in Pennsylvania against freedom of worship so long as the worshippers recognized the suzerainty of God.

The first Catholic chapel was built in 1733 in Willing's Alley on land conveyed by John Dixon, south of Walnut and just east of Fourth. Alongside it was constructed a residence for Fr. Joseph Greaton. Father Greaton, a onetime Jesuit missionary from Maryland, first held services in Philadelphia in 1720. Nine years later he chose to make the Quaker capital his home. There were not many Roman Catholics among the inhabitants, but enough to support St. Joseph's, as the parish was named.[29]

The first practicing Jew living in Philadelphia of whom there is a record was Nathan Levy, who was in the town by 1735; earlier there may have been former Jews, such as the convert Isaac Miranda. In 1740 David Franks moved to Philadelphia from New York, forming a mercantile partnership with Levy. Several other Jews came to the city, and the tradition is that by the 1740s services were held in a house on Sterling Alley, near Race Street, between Third and Fourth. The gathering was a simple minyan, with no name, no rules, and no official leader. Since the earliest Jews in the city were disproportionately male, some like David Franks married Christians and were absorbed into the Gentile community.[30]

V

Some of the churches, including the Lutherans' St. Michael's and most especially the Anglicans' Christ Church, contributed to the growing size and elaborateness of public architecture that was part of the gradual transformation of Philadelphia from a town toward a genuine city. Following the example of James Logan's Stenton, ambitious buildings in Philadelphia belatedly took up the London fashion of Georgian symmetry and balance.

From 1708 there was a Court House in the middle of High Street at Second. This early public structure remained in some ways a medieval building, with the disorder of market stalls on the ground floor, but nevertheless it was a handsome brick structure featuring a belfry and balcony.

In 1724 ten master builders formed the Carpenters' Company of the City and County of Philadelphia, to better instruct themselves in architecture, especially by gathering a library. As early as three years later one of the members, James Porteus, became the principal builder of the city's—indeed, America's—most ambitiously Palladian structure of the colonial era, the imposing Christ Church on Second Street north of Market. Dr. John Kearsley, a physician of the congregation, probably conceived the basic design. When the church was completed in 1744 the Palladian window of its east front was still exceptional in the architectural design of an American building. Also setting off the customary horizontal symmetries with especially opulent detail was a graceful balustrade decorated with wooden urns imported from London. A steeple was to be added in 1754.

The province itself built less ambitiously than the Anglicans. The legislators having previously met in private rooms and occasionally in the Court House, the Assembly appropriated funds for a government building in 1729 and named a building committee that included Andrew Hamilton, its speaker; Dr. Kearsley, who was also an assemblyman; and Thomas Lawrence of the Council. Hamilton selected a site on the western edge of the city over Kearsley's preference for a less remote location. Between 1730 and 1732 the province

A South East View of Christ's Church, *Second Street near Mulberry (Arch), probably designed by Dr. John Kearsley (1684–1772), engraved by Charles Willson Peale (1741–1827) for the* Columbian Magazine *(1787). One of the most impressive Georgian structures in the American colonies, Christ Church was begun in 1727 and finished in 1744. In 1750 the Penns (no longer Quakers) contributed funds for the steeple and bells.*

acquired the lots making up the present Independence Square, borrowing funds from Hamilton's wealthy son-in-law William Allen. When the whole Chestnut Street frontage between Fifth and Sixth, extending halfway to Walnut, was secured, construction began. Hamilton, another talented amateur architect, designed the Pennsylvania State House—later to become Independence Hall—in cooperation with another master builder, Edmund Woolley, who supervised construction.

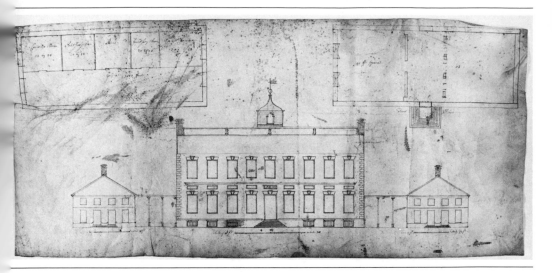

Plan of State House, *1732, unsigned ink drawing attributed to Edmund Woolley (c. 1695–1771), the carpenter-architect who was employed there from 1732 until at least 1754. The elevation shows the Assembly's building with its "torret" and two "offiscis" much as it appeared after the first phase of construction was completed in 1748.*

HISTORICAL SOCIETY OF PENNSYLVANIA

After nearly a decade of building, slowed in part by the young city's scarcity of skilled workmen, the Assembly became impatient and ordered its chamber readied for immediate occupancy in 1741. In the State House the setting off of the red brick with stone quoins, keystones, belt courses, and panels together with the balustrade and a steeple (at present not Woolley's original of about mid-century, but a William Strickland replacement of 1828) marks the designers' intentions that the structure should be monumentally worthy of the important institutions it housed.

The State House remained simply furnished, and so for the most part did the other Philadelphia buildings of the Queen Anne and early Georgian styles. Yet fine furniture craftsmanship began to appear in the city as the appropriate handmaiden of more ornate architecture. The earliest signed and dated piece of Philadelphia furniture is probably a walnut desk marked "Ed-

The State House in Philadelphia, *1778, from a detail in a painting by Charles Willson Peale (1741–1827), engraved by Illman Brothers (act. 1860). The tower and steeple were added by Edmund Woolley in 1750–1753 to support the famous bell which was prophetically inscribed "Proclaim Liberty Thro' all the Land to all the Inhabitants thereof." Low sheds beside the two office buildings are thought to have been built to house visiting Indian delegations. The sheds were replaced by Congress Hall on the west and Old City Hall (the Supreme Court) on the east in 1787–1791.*

AMERICAN PHILOSOPHICAL SOCIETY, PHILADELPHIA

ward Evans 1707," suitably architectural in its effect, with moldings and entablature that echo contemporary styles in room paneling.[31]

Architecture and furniture-making are the most practical of the arts, but the increasing worldliness of the Quaker town revealed itself in a growing Philadelphia interest in matters less utilitarian. Occasional plays were presented outside the city limits as early as 1723. Mayor James Logan—who was not exactly given to frivolity—tried to suppress them, but this was one of his losing fights. A marionette show appeared in 1742.

The Swedish immigrant Gustavus Hesselius provided Philadelphia with a trained portrait painter—"no bad hand," James Logan said, "who generally does justice to the men, especially to their blemishes."[32] The artist's portrait of Logan himself, for example, makes no effort to leaven the stern visage of the dour squire of Stenton. His paintings of the Lenni Lenapes Tishcohan and Lapowinsa, commissioned by John Penn and now, like the Logan portrait, at the Historical Society of Pennsylvania, further attest to the accuracy of

Logan's observation and also anticipate the reportorial Indian paintings of a George Catlin. By the 1720s Philadelphia was actually willing to accept from Hesselius classical mythological scenes—the earliest known painted in America—featuring nudity, a *Bacchus and Ariadne* and a *Bacchanale*. Philadelphia shared this gifted artist with neighboring Delaware and Maryland from the second to the sixth decade of the century.

Lapowinsa, *painted by Gustavus Hesselius (1682–1755) in 1735 at the request of John and Thomas Penn. Lapowinsa was one of the Lenni Lenape chiefs who were cheated in the infamous Walking Purchase Treaty arranged by James Logan in 1737.*

Nor was all the town's entertainment art. Billiards and bowling came to be allowed in Philadelphia, and dancing was fostered by a dancing school started in 1729.[33] Strange animals were exhibited at the taverns; a cameleopard, as the giraffe was then called, that was making the circuit of the colonial towns turned up at the Indian Queen at the southeast corner of Fourth and High. The citizens indulged in occasional horse races and even cock-fighting and bull-baiting. Quakers felt obliged to ask: "Are there any Friends that frequent Musick houses or go dancing and gaming?"[34]

On nearly every social level the convivial club became a feature of the Philadelphia scene, often encompassing purposes of mutual benevolence or self-improvement but always focusing on the potential of a growing population for enlarged sociability. The first Philadelphia club may have been an association of bachelors formed some time before 1728. In 1729 Welshmen of the town organized the "Society of Ancient Britons" to observe St. David's Day, promptly precipitating formation of a similar organization of Englishmen to give due honor to St. George's Day. Sportsmen formed themselves into fishing clubs, the first of which was the Colony in Schuylkill which had its birth in the same year that George Washington was born. The Colony was complete with governor, sheriff, and even a coroner, at its courthouse on the west bank of the Schuylkill near the present Girard Avenue Bridge, and was famous as the home of Fish House Punch. The prerevolutionary membership included such mayors of the city as Thomas Lawrence, William Plumstead, and Samuel Shoemaker. Having been founded on May 1, 1732, when what were to become the London clubs were still public coffeehouses, the State in Schuylkill holds claim to being the oldest organized men's club in the English-speaking world.[35]

Although it could not boast of so delectable an invention as Fish House Punch, Philadelphia's most famous eighteenth-century club did ultimately bring forth the American Philosophical Society. Benjamin Franklin organized his leather-apron cohorts in 1727 into a mutual and social benefit society whose members presented papers on scientific, moral, and social issues, known as the Junto. In connection with his Junto activities, Franklin in 1731 proposed what became the first subscription library in America, the Library Company of Philadelphia. Bibliophile James Logan consented to advise the original forty members on the purchase of books, which after 1741 were kept on the second floor of the new State House.

The Junto inspired several like clubs in Philadelphia, and Franklin in 1743 saw that similar clubs in other colonies might coalesce into an intercolonial organization paralleling London's Royal Society. The resulting American Philosophical Society failed at that time to attract much interest in other colonies. But with the maturation of colonial culture on the eve of the Revolution, it finally became an effective organization.[36]

V I

From one point of view the plethora of churches and faiths in Philadelphia would indicate the continuing vitality of religion during the eighteenth century. Surely the excitement created by a Whitefield would seem to attest to this phenomenon. On the other hand the growing proportion of the unchurched among the population would point to a lessening of religious zeal. The same might be said for the easygoing latitudinarianism of the Anglican church, the backsliding of the more worldly Quakers, and the appeal of

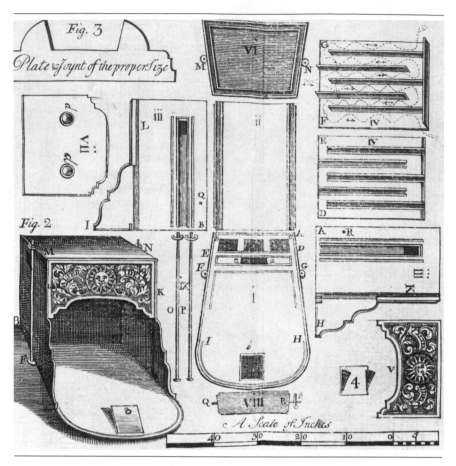

The last page of Benjamin Franklin's An Account of the New-Invented
Pennsylvanian Fire-Places, *drawn by Lewis Evans (c. 1700–1756), 1744. Franklin's treatise promoting the draft-free, iron fireplaces was published twenty-one
years after his arrival in Philadelphia as a runaway apprentice from Boston.*
HISTORICAL SOCIETY OF PENNSYLVANIA

"natural religion," i.e., Deism in any of its several manifestations, to Philadelphia's intellectuals. Once more James Logan and Benjamin Franklin come to
mind as representative figures of these latter groups.

But whatever its actual religious configuration, a visitor from our secular
times to the city at mid-century would be amazed at the continuing influence
of the churches over morals and education. Everyone, churched and unchurched, seemed to agree that religion was essential in upholding civilized
standards of living.

Such a visitor would be amazed in other ways as well. Religion might
teach that cleanliness was next to godliness. If so, Philadelphia had a way to

go in reaching that state of grace. Its streetscape presented a scene of dirt, mud, garbage, animal excrement, and general disorderliness all pervaded by the odor of decaying garbage and seething in accordance with the season with flies, mosquitos, and roaches. One would gladly accept an invitation from James Logan to stay with him at Stenton during one's visit to Philadelphia.

Temperance is another Christian virtue. But as with cleanliness, Philadelphia again fell somewhat short. By 1752 there were 120 licensed taverns in the city, to say nothing of numerous illicit "groggeries" to cater to sailors on the waterfront and other less than orderly elements of the population. Though America had no Hogarth to document the scene, for both England and her colonial offspring the eighteenth century was a drinking age.

There was a tavern—or more likely a multitude of taverns—for every pocketbook and every social class. Until 1729 it was thought suitable that the prison should have a tavern attached. To the more elegant surroundings of the Blue Anchor, the Indian Queen, the Three Tuns on Chestnut Street east of Letitia Street, or John Biddle's Indian King at High Street and Biddle Alley (east of Third)—which was said to serve the best meals in town and never dispensed liquor after eleven at night—to these, the mayor and corporation might retire for dinner.

If the tavern lubricated the political life of the city, so also business and social life depended on the relaxed atmosphere such a watering place offered. The London Coffee House at Front and High Streets, built about 1702 and opened under John Shubert's management in 1734, was a natural gathering place for merchants every noon, where they discussed news and business, arranged for cargoes and marine insurance, and set prices; later in the century the meetings here grew into a regularized merchants' exchange. A so-called coffeehouse, more genteel than the tavern, did serve coffee and tea, but likewise here headier, more spirited stuff remained the staple.[37]

Eighteenth-century Philadelphia's steaming streets with their ubiquitous taverns contradicted the traditional view of the city as a model of municipal planning. The neat pattern laid out by William Penn and his surveyor-general Thomas Holme encouraged a misleading impression of an orderly Philadelphia even from the beginning. But except for the small, and in the first half of the eighteenth century, increasingly crowded urban arc close to the Delaware, across most of the land between the Delaware and the Schuylkill the evidences of the Penn-Holme plan would have been hard to find. William Penn had completed his second visit and left his city forever long before all the tree stumps had been removed from the thoroughfares. As for paving the streets, the weakness of the medieval municipal corporation frustrated for decades all suggestions of a public effort, and until almost the end of the period at hand such street paving as occurred was the result of the private efforts of lot owners. The corporation lacked the financial means to support any considerable public works. Its revenues depended on the collection of various fees for doing business and fines for violating its ordinances, but it lacked adequate means for collecting even such limited sums; an effort to set up an inferior

The London Coffee House, southwest corner of Front and High (Market) Streets (photograph taken in 1854). In 1734 several prominent merchants in the city purchased an old (1702) building near the markets to use as a public house. The "old Coffee House" was superseded by the City Tavern during the Revolution and was eventually demolished in 1883.

FREE LIBRARY OF PHILADELPHIA

court in 1704 and thus facilitate receiving fees was disallowed by the governor on petition from the inhabitants.

Often the officers of the corporation themselves had to finance whatever municipal construction occurred, such as a new market house, hoping to be reimbursed "out of the first money raised."[38] On the other hand when the 1739 grand jury reported that many streets were not only unpaved but impassable, the corporation's jealousy for its prerogatives impelled it to secure a gubernatorial veto of a bill to turn over control of the streets to the Assembly. Only in this extremity did the corporation at last in the 1740s begin something of a program of municipal paving. The medieval custom of requiring each inhabitant to work on the roads several days each year persisted in Philadelphia law; but from 1712 the corporation allowed a money payment in lieu of actual labor, and whether in money or labor, this obligation was another that the corporation was evidently too weak to enforce regularly.

In 1727 the corporation at last ordered that inhabitants provide walks in front of their own properties; but this ordinance was also little enforced, and even a modicum of protection from dust and mud for pedestrians had to await the threat of provincial intervention in the 1740s. So it was also with bridges over the numerous creeks. Those that were built, such as a drawbridge erected in 1700 to carry Front Street across Dock Creek, were perennially being described as out of repair and dangerous, and the Front Street bridge was of little use until 1714 when a causeway was built over swampy ground to Society Hill, after which the resulting thoroughfare was forever being partially washed out and rendered impassable. Similarly, underground drainage systems of brick and stone had to depend mostly on private effort, though compared with other colonial towns Philadelphia made good progress with this problem toward the middle of the century.

It was not until 1727 that the corporation required that streets be so pitched that surface water might drain into watercourses in the middle of them. The streets, however, were still used by Philadelphia's citizens as convenient places on which to dump their garbage. Periodic legal warnings and threats of penalty did little to dissuade the householders from this traditional mode of garbage disposal.

Nor could much be done about the fact that the dust clouding the air on dry days and the mud sucking at shoes and wheels on wet days were composed not of earth alone but also of a generous admixture of animal droppings for which the horse was not the only source. Garbage removal, such as it was, was largely the work of scavenging animals. Hogs had the freedom of the streets in the early period. Later they yielded place to packs of dogs.

To complete the scene, in these same streets boisterous humans jostled the boisterous animals, and each other. Pickpockets early began to prey upon unwary travelers by day, and more menacing footpads upon wanderers after dark. The law interfered but little. It was supposed to be enforced by five constables. The constables received recompense for their activities out of fines and fees, yet they were anything but professional policemen. In a number of recorded instances disorderly persons with apparent impunity beat them up and drove them off. When youthful Gov. John Evans bruised the law-and-order men, having been interrupted in his nightly carousings, his high position might explain his exemption from prosecution. But in fact ordinary malefactors were equally successful in beating the law—and its keepers.

At night two of the constables were supposed to patrol the streets along with a watch of twelve citizens. The watch was unpaid; the well-to-do evaded their burdens, which fell disproportionately upon lesser tradesmen and mechanics who performed even less satisfactorily than the constables. While the City of Brotherly Love was still trailing behind Boston in population and volume of commerce, it seems already to have forged ahead of all the other colonial towns in assaults and robberies. Burglarizing appears to have become a favorite pastime.[39]

Philadelphians were also beginning to develop a reputation for riotousness that they would be at pains to cultivate in later years. Two early riots were touched off by angry parishioners of Christ Church in the affair of the rector, the Rev. Francis Philips, who boasted too much about his conquests of female parishioners, but who nevertheless found numerous male champions when he was arrested and prosecution was attempted. In 1726 riotous inhabitants of the lower classes attacked and destroyed the pillories and stocks next to the High Street market. In 1738 a provincial law against fish weirs and racks in the Schuylkill provoked a series of riots among the poor who feared deprivation of their fish.

Another series of riots in 1741 and 1742, their causes ranging from the price of bread to simple drunkenness among sailors, climaxed in the "Bloody Election" riots of October 1742. By that time another colonial war, the War of Jenkins' Ear, was again straining the Quaker peace testimony in politics; the Quaker party augmented its electoral strength by persuading pacifist Germans to eschew civic indifference and to vote; then a band of sailors armed with clubs and urged on by the advocates of military preparedness set upon Germans and Quakers, crying out to the "Quaker Sons of Bitches . . . Men with broad Hats and no pockets": "You are Damned Quakers, you are Enemies to King George, and we will knock you all in the head."[40]

If Philadelphia led the colonial towns in crime, it could take some small comfort in leading also in efforts to incarcerate the criminals rather than simply fining or branding them and letting them run loose. There had been a "Cage" as early as 1683. In 1687 a log prison was erected at Second and High Streets, which soon had to be supplemented by renting prison space from Patrick Robinson. A supposedly more escape-proof jail of stone surrounded by a high wall was completed at Third and High in 1722. But while it was the most solid prison in the colonies, and distinguished also by providing space for debtors separate from criminals, at least fifteen inmates escaped from it between 1729 and 1732.

Already in this early time, as on many occasions much later, the partisans of stricter law enforcement singled out the city's blacks as a special source of crime and disorder. Whites claimed that slaves had insatiable appetites for drink which, frequently indulged in, sent them reeling through the streets hurling threats, curses, and worse upon whites.[41]

But there was also plenty of potential for disorder among Philadelphia's white inhabitants. The troubles in Germany and Ireland that pushed immigration to Philadelphia also made it hard to pay passage to America and set down many immigrants on the Delaware docks destitute. To make passage possible at all, many came as indentured servants, bound to a term of labor up to seven years. With labor otherwise expensive in the New World, Benjamin Franklin estimated that physical work was performed chiefly by those bound by indentures.[42] In similar circumstances were the "redemptioners," immigrants, largely German, who could pay part of their transatlantic passage, but whose labor was sold by the ships' captains upon arrival to make up the rest of the passage fee.

In William Penn's day Philadelphia had welcomed all comers, but the influx of the poor stimulated a harsher attitude. As early as 1705 the municipal corporation required all newcomers to post a bond relieving the city of all charge for them for seven years. In 1717 the provincial Assembly decreed that all ships' captains must provide the Council with lists of their passengers, and that the city authorities must seek out vagabonds.

As usual, however, enforcement powers were insufficient and such laws had little effect. Increasingly the poor became a charge upon the city. In 1712 the Assembly authorized the corporation to employ the poor and to compel vagrants to labor. In 1717 the Assembly required that a workhouse open to the whole colony be erected in Philadelphia within three years. By this time relief of the poor was costing the city about £400 annually.

Fortunately the corporation had learned that it could rely heavily upon the Society of Friends. The Friends' Alms House was doing so much that the public authorities procrastinated over the construction of the mandated workhouse. When at last that facility was completed in 1732, it occupied the entire block between Third and Fourth, Spruce and Pine Streets. It ranked as a model public institution for its time. As the first de facto hospital in the city, it had an infirmary, rooms for the insane, and accommodations for the indigent. In 1735 the Assembly gave the mayor, recorder, and two aldermen power to set poor rates and the corporation authority to appoint overseers of the poor, one of the first major extensions of municipal authority.[43]

With its predominance of brick construction, Philadelphia largely escaped the extensive fires that plagued most other colonial towns. Well into the eighteenth century, however, the inhabitants had to find safety for themselves. The Assembly in 1696 required householders to provide themselves with leather buckets and ladders, but enforcement once more was left to the citizens' own initiative. In 1718 the corporation purchased a "ffire Engine," which was kept near the Friends Meeting House in Front Street, but for the next decade this manual pumping machine stood outdoors, weatherbeaten and neglected. In 1726 it was at last repaired and placed indoors, and two years later James Claypoole was hired as its caretaker. The town had its first large fire in 1730, when Fishbourn's Wharf and its warehouse burned together with nearby buildings. Thereupon the corporation roused itself to buy several hundred buckets and three London fire engines.

In the middle 1730s Benjamin Franklin opened a campaign of fire prevention education, which led in December 1736 to the founding of the Union Fire Company. The members provided themselves with leather buckets to carry water to fires, but initially as important a purpose was mutual protection against theft and looting. Other companies soon followed the Union's example. Andrew Bradford, Franklin's rival in printing and in almost everything

else, organized the Fellowship Fire Company in 1738, while another group
formed the Hand-in-Hand Fire Company in 1742. Franklin's company bought
its own engine in 1739, and through such nongovernmental initiative Philadelphia acquired a reputation for effective fire protection.[44]

VII

Philadelphia's development of those institutions that accompany city life
—welfare agencies, fire protection, prisons, and the like—paralleled her increasing importance as the marketing center for a vastly growing agricultural
hinterland. Market Days saw the crowded city ever more crowded as farmers
from within a radius of fifteen and more miles brought their sheep, cows, pigs,
vegetables, cider, and other products for direct sale to the townspeople. The
High Street Market was continuously enlarged throughout the period until
by 1736 it reached from Front Street to Third. By 1745 a New Market was
opened in Second Street between Pine and Cedar (South). The next year the
Callowhill Market in the Northern Liberties began operation.[45]

Along with Market Days, the institution of twice-yearly fairs persisted in
Philadelphia after similar trading days had been discontinued in other large
colonial towns. The fairs provided a means of bringing handmade goods from
outlying places to would-be buyers in the city. Linens and stockings from
Germantown, for example, were popular among Philadelphia's dames.[46]

Another popular form of occasional trade was the auction or "public
vendue." For obvious reasons retail merchants opposed these as well as the
fairs.[47] If efforts at achieving their eradication through governmental action
were less than successful, the ordinary course of economic development was
on the merchants' side. Increasing business specialization became the order
of the day. Export merchants became differentiated from their importing
counterparts. Though most stores still dealt in a variety of goods, specialty
shops began to appear.

Philadelphia's merchants generally prospered not only because Pennsylvania was undergoing tremendous economic and demographic growth. They
did their business, after all, in the capital city of the province. Not only did
they cater to the governor and his circle, but citizens from all over the colony
came to the capital for sessions of the Assembly and Council and the meetings
of the courts.

At the same time, as in the matters of law enforcement and other municipal services, the merchants along with other citizens had to suffer the ineffectual administration of the city corporation. This body was in such ill repute
that fines had to be prescribed for those persons who refused to accept office
in it when chosen. It was not uncommon, furthermore, for citizens to try to
avoid both office and fine by neglecting to qualify as freemen. The fines were
collected often enough to form a reasonably important part of the city's
constricted revenues. In 1745 Alderman Abraham Taylor refused to serve as
mayor and was fined £30; Joseph Turner, who was elected on the next ballot,
also refused and also was fined £30; on the third ballot James Hamilton was

elected and accepted the office. A classic episode occurred in 1747, when Anthony Morris fled to Bucks County to avoid notification of his election. When he could not be found within three days, a new election had to be arranged, at which the corporation reelected Mayor William Atwood for a second term.[48]

In spite of its difficulties the corporation could offer prestige in relation at least to the mayoralty. And a few offices, for example that of recorder, which oversaw the receipt of municipal fees, offered possibilities for monetary gain. As time passed officeholding in the corporation, as a matter of noblesse oblige, became more clearly identified with duty among the gentry. The first Edward Shippen, who could be described as having "the biggest person, the biggest house, and the biggest coach" in the city, set the precedent when he served as Philadelphia's first mayor. He was also an alderman and city treasurer.

Among others heeding the call—James Logan has already been mentioned as having graced the mayor's chair—was the Presbyterian grandee William Allen. Mayor of Philadelphia in 1735–1736, Allen was at mid-century probably the city's wealthiest individual. He was well known not only for support of the proprietary family, but also for the magnificence of his coach and of the four black horses that drew it, and for the opulence of his entertainment at that other favored means of conspicuous display, a fine country place, Mount Airy.

Allen in fact is a prime example of the admixture of politics and profit. He was recorder from 1741 to 1750, chief justice from 1751 to 1774, and at the same time served in both the provincial Assembly and the Philadelphia Council. Building upon a large fortune already accumulated by his father, Allen's business activities centered on trading but also included huge real estate investments, iron furnaces, a copper mine, a rum distillery, and stocks and loans at interest. He retired in 1753 when not quite fifty to devote the rest of his career to the province and the city. He was to be a lavish contributor to the Pennsylvania Hospital and the College of Philadelphia, and through gifts or loans he aided young John Morgan and Benjamin West to gain an education abroad. Both men were to make significant contributions, in the fields of medicine and art, respectively.[49]

The formidable careers of such worthies as Shippen and Allen should remind us that with eighteenth-century Philadelphia we are not dealing with an egalitarian society. If anything, with the development of the city came an increasingly emphatic social demarcation between an upper class of the wealthiest merchants and professional men and the lower orders of the population. The "Quaker grandees," and to the regret of those of them who had wanted a Quaker province, the grandees not Quaker, set themselves apart by means of a growing ostentation and display. Such men simply assumed their superior worth. Soon, as in England, social stratification became the norm.

It was all the more remarkable then that some men did acquire wealth and status primarily through their ability rather than their name. Generalizing

William Allen (*1704–1780*), *painting attributed to Robert Feke (c. 1707–1751/2), c. 1750.*

from his own exceptional career, Benjamin Franklin would warn would-be European emigrants that in America it is not who you are, but what you can do. And a few men, among whom printers would rank high on the list, did, as Franklin described his own achievement, emerge from poverty and obscurity "to a state of Affluence and some Degree of Reputation in the World."[50]

The press in Philadelphia, an institution Franklin would come to dominate, had begun as a Quaker institution, with its instrument—the printing press itself—the property of the meeting. William Bradford, printer for the Friends, underwent severe tribulations as he became involved in the Keithian controversy. Following his release from arrest by the authorities Bradford sought greener pastures as the king's printer in New York. While others undertook the Friends' printing, William in 1713 sent his son Andrew to Philadelphia as a partner to open an independent press.

Andrew Bradford arranged to rent the Quaker press for £10 annually, and it appears that he had brought with him from New York or shortly acquired some equipment of his own. In any case he printed many theological works, while at the same time he ventured into secular publication as well. Most notably Andrew Bradford established Philadelphia's first newspaper and the third in the colonies, the *American Weekly Mercury*. The first issue appeared on December 22, 1719.

Just as Bradford was branching out on his own, so the advent in Philadelphia of the brilliant if eccentric printer Samuel Keimer ended the concept of a single Quaker press in the town. Keimer was instrumental in helping cultivate in the city a wider taste for literature. He published the first translation of a Greek or Latin classic to appear in North America, Epictetus, *His Morals* (1729). In 1728 Keimer established in competition with Bradford's *American Mercury* a newspaper with the wonderful name of *The Universal Instructor in all Arts and Sciences: and Pennsylvania Gazette*. One purpose of the new paper was the serial reprinting in its enormous entirety of the whole of Chamber's *Cyclopaedia* from *A* to *Z*. Keimer did not even manage to get through *A*, however, before his erstwhile master pressman Benjamin Franklin brought about the paper's demise.[51]

Franklin only reluctantly and out of necessity had worked for Keimer, for whom the cocky younger man had only contempt. In partnership with a friend, Franklin managed to set up his own press when Keimer's curious encyclopedia project made its appearance. The older man had rendered himself peculiarly vulnerable to ridicule, a weapon most effective in the hands of an intelligent, self-confident youth.

Franklin immediately published several witty satires of Keimer's fatuous undertaking in the *American Weekly Mercury*. Keimer, still in the *A*s, had come to "abortion."

If [Keimer] proceed farther to expose the Secrets of our Sex, in that audacious manner, as he hath done in his Gazette, No. 5, under the Letters, A.B.O. To be read in all Taverns and *Coffee-Houses*, and by the Vulgar [wrote Martha Careful, i.e., Franklin]: I say if he Publish any more of that kind . . . my sister Molly and my Self, with some others, are Resolved to run the Hazard of taking him by the Beard, at the next Place we meet him, and make an Example of him for his Immodesty.

Martha Careful was joined in her condemnation of Keimer by Caelia Shortface, who presently was metamorphosed into a new character named "the Busy-Body." She too excoriated Keimer as well as disseminated her homely philosophy. One "Patience" in a letter to the Busy-Body complained of having to care for her thoughtless neighbor's children: "Thus, I have all the Trouble and Pesterment of Children, without the Pleasure of—calling them my own."[52]

Philadelphia's citizens were amused enough, as Franklin had hoped, to forgo Keimer's ponderous *Universal Instructor* for Bradford's *Mercury* with its waggish characters, Careful, Shortface, and the Busy-Body. The result was that with his creditors closing in on him, Keimer sold his newspaper to Franklin, who promptly reduced its cumbersome title to its last two words, *Pennsylvania Gazette*. In his first issue, dated October 2, 1729, Franklin, who shortly bought out his partner in the business, took wry notice of his former literary vehicle, the *American Weekly Mercury*. "There are many," wrote the young editor, "who have long desired to see a good News-Paper in Pennsylvania." Andrew Bradford must have fumed as the assured Franklin calmly promised to produce "as agreeable and useful Entertainment as the Nature of the Thing will allow."

And the *Pennsylvania Gazette*, "the Nature of the Thing allowing," was not only agreeable and entertaining, but it rapidly became the finest weekly published in the colonies. It was followed in 1733 by *Poor Richard's Almanac*, which soon outpaced all the competition in the field, including that of Andrew Bradford. Best remembered for his prudential maxims, Franklin made Richard Saunders a humorist as well as a moralist: "God heals, and the Doctor takes the fees"; "Fish and Visitors stink in 3 days"; "Neither a Fortress nor a Maiden head will hold out long after they begin to parley"; or "There's more old Drunkards than old Doctors." Sayings such as these as well as the *Almanac*'s useful information help explain its sales of over 10,000 copies a year throughout America.

As a publisher of books Franklin proved less venturesome than Keimer had been. He brought out Samuel Richardson's *Pamela*, the first novel published in America, and Logan's translations from the classics, another first. He made his fortune, however, by publishing standard religious works, official government printing, and forms and advertisements.

His enterprises nevertheless sometimes misfired. For the German immigrants, he issued in May 1732 the first German-American newspaper, the *Philadelphische Zeitung*, edited by Louis Timothée; but this paper died after two issues. After *The Gentleman's Magazine*, founded in 1731, proved a success in London, Franklin decided to emulate it in Philadelphia. Bradford heard of his plan and with his *American Magazine* probably anticipated by three days the first issue, in February 1741, of Franklin's *General Magazine and Historical Chronicle for All the British Plantations in America*. But the colonies were not yet ready to support such a publication, and both magazines failed within the year.

Franklin's famous propensity for forming organizations served as an additional means of advancing the number of his connections and his standing in the community. In 1736 he successfully petitioned to become clerk of the Pennsylvania Assembly, later writing candidly: "besides the Pay for the immediate Service as Clerk, the Place gave me a better Opportunity of keeping up an Interest among the Members, which secur'd to me the business of printing the Votes, Laws, Paper Money, and other occasional Jobs for the Public that, on the whole, were very profitable."[53] The following year he succeeded in replacing Bradford as postmaster, a similar valuable adjunct to his printing business (he had earlier had to bribe postmen to carry his *Gazette* in violation of Bradford's rule that they distribute only the *Mercury*).

Through the *Gazette, Poor Richard,* and the experiments in natural philosophy that he was already commencing—he invented the "Pennsylvania Fire-Place" or Franklin stove in 1741—Franklin made himself and his adopted city known throughout the colonies. He had assumed as his public persona that of the model Philadelphia craftsman, a skilled and solidly respectable artisan, and although he might be resented as an upstart by the city's old families, he could hardly be ignored. As his fame grew, the proprietors tried to gain his allegiance by appointing him a member of the city corporation and a justice of the peace. Shortly thereafter the people elected him to the provincial Assembly.

Franklin's emergence as a man of stature in the business, cultural, and political life of Philadelphia in part helped create, and in larger part was a reflection of, the coming of age of the city itself. Dr. Alexander Hamilton, it may be recalled, was not altogether charmed by what he saw on his visit to the city in 1744. But he nevertheless had the prescience to forecast that "in a few years hence, [Philadelphia] will be a great and flourishing place and the chief city in America."[54] The next few years would indeed fully justify the good doctor's prediction.

Town into City
1746-1765

by Theodore Thayer

Blessed be God, that it was our Lot to be sent to Pennsylvania, where our Wants have been relieved. . . .

— JOHN BAPTISTE GALERM,
speaking for French refugees from Nova Scotia

. . . why, I say, should that little island [England] enjoy in almost every neighbourhood more sensible, virtuous, and elegant minds than we can collect in ranging a hundred leagues of our vast forests? But 'tis said the arts delight to travel westward.

— BENJAMIN FRANKLIN [1]

The year 1751 was the fiftieth year of the Constitution of Pennsylvania: the famous Charter of Privileges. The bell ordered to commemorate this anniversary, an anniversary coinciding with that of Philadelphia's corporate charter, arrived the following year. Philadelphian Isaac Norris, Jr., speaker of the legislative Assembly, chose the prophetic inscription from Leviticus 25:10, an inscription prefaced in the Bible by the words "And ye shall hallow the fiftieth year": "Proclaim Liberty thro' all the Land to all the Inhabitants thereof." Though this famous Liberty Bell cracked on first ringing and twice had to be recast, its hanging in 1753 at the State House in a belfry especially built for it signaled the coming of age of Pennsylvania and its capital city.

I

The years 1750–1755 in fact proved crucial in the metamorphosis of town to city. A most obvious change was in the cityscape itself. A visitor approaching the city in 1750 would view the low unbroken skyline of any ordinary country market town, a skyline pierced only by the belfry at Second and High. Two years later the traveler toward the city would first see the grand new State House tower which would house the new bell. Before long the skyline would also present the upward thrust of the new spires of several churches, most notably the 196-foot steeple of Christ Church.

There were also less celestial changes in the city's physical aspect. Such matters as street paving may seem comparatively mundane, but they too serve to demarcate the city from the crossroads town. By mid-century most of the streets had brick or flagstone sidewalks, often bordered with posts that protected pedestrians from vehicular traffic. Some merchants now also took the initiative to have cobblestones or paving blocks laid in the streets in front of their places of business. Such private efforts continued until the city corporation itself in 1762 took on the responsibility, which it funded by a general tax and lotteries; at the same time the city took the giant step of hiring street cleaners.[2]

Philadelphia's merchants not only facilitated pedestrian and vehicular movement through the city's streets, but they also began to provide street lighting, another amenity not generally found in the ordinary town. In Philadelphia the evening's darkness was frequently penetrated by lamps hanging before the merchants' shops. In 1751, by means of a special tax, the principal streets were illuminated by whale-oil lamps suspended from lamp posts. The new globes, however, quickly became smudged with smoke, creating a maintenance problem. With his usual resourcefulness Franklin persuaded the corporation to adopt a square lamp fixture with four panes and with air holes to allow the smoke to escape. The frugal corporation recognized that a broken pane would be cheaper to replace than a globe.[3]

Since a supply of pure water was vital to a growing city, Philadelphia periodically took steps to see that the need was met. Most houses had wells situated in the rear, but some had them bordering the street. Both public and private wells lined High Street's marketplace teeming with people and horses during the busy hours. By mid-century the city was exercising some control over the privately owned street pumps, and in 1756 it took over most of them. Under new regulations the city made the city wardens responsible for inspecting the pumps, having new wells sunk when necessary, buying up private pumps, and assessing householders who used the city water. The wardens, like the overseers of the poor, formed a committee elected by the freeholders as provided by an act of the provincial Assembly. This was a means of circumventing the inactivity of the sluggish corporation on civic concerns.[4]

Another marked improvement followed the appointment of Benjamin Franklin as one of the two deputy postmasters-general for the colonies. Responsible for the postal service in the northern colonies, Franklin instituted three regular mail deliveries a week between Philadelphia and New York. In 1755 he provided one weekly delivery to Boston, a run that previously had no set schedule. Mail service to the west and south continued to be more sporadic, but Franklin eventually established regular service to Virginia, and by 1767 three stage lines were running south to Baltimore and beyond.[5] Under the aegis of two Franklins—Benjamin had appointed his son William comptroller —the post office on the corner of Church Alley and Third Street became a kind of symbol of the growing network of communications of which Philadelphia was the center.

The Battery

An East Prospect of the City of Philadelphia; taken by George Heap
[c. 1715–1752] from the Jersey Shore, under the Direction of Nicholas Scull
[1687–1761] Surveyor General of the Province of Pennsylvania (1754), engraved
by Gerard Vandergucht. The view of the city, printed in London from four copper
plates, measures nearly seven feet in length when the prints are assembled and
portrays the riverfront from below South Street to Callowhill Street on the north.
An inset at the left, near Windmill Island, depicts the fortification called the
Battery which was below the Swedish church in the vicinity of the present Federal

Street. The steeples in the center are those of the State House on Chestnut Street; Christ Church near Market Street; the Academy (a slender, lower steeple) on Arch Street at Fourth; the Presbyterian Church, also on Arch Street at Third; and the German Reformed Church on Race Street near Fourth. The Court House and Great Meeting House are visible in the center of Market Street.

HISTORICAL SOCIETY OF PENNSYLVANIA

(Panorama continues on the next two pages.)

   Improvements in transportation facilitated Franklin's expansion of the
postal service. Until Joseph Borden, Jr., and his partners started their stage
line in 1755 between Philadelphia and New York, there was no regular service
between the cities. The first lap of the journey was by a stageboat which left
the wharf at the Crooked Billet on Chestnut Street and sailed to Bordentown,
New Jersey. An overland stage continued the journey to Perth Amboy,
whence passengers were transported by water to New York. When the
weather cooperated the trip took three days; the cost was three pence per mile.
A rival line was soon started by John Butler. His stage left from the Sign of

the Death of the Fox on Strawberry Alley and traveled by way of Trenton
to New York. In 1766 another stage called the Flying Machine made the trip
to New York in two days. This remarkable feat was accomplished in a "stage
wagon" with seats suspended on springs. It ran twice a week and cost only
two pence a mile, putting all rivals at a definite disadvantage.[6]

An improved network of transportation and communication during the
century's middle years also meant a concomitant growth in trade. By mid-
century the most frequently used highway in America was the great Philadelphia Wagon Road that led out from the city to Lancaster. Over it moved

settlers seeking lands to the west, and, coming and going, wagons and cara-
vans of supplies and trade goods. To Lancaster from the west came the furs
and skins sent in by George Croghan and his partner William Trent, who
traded directly with the Indians on the Ohio. This trade alone had an annual
value of £40,000. The leading merchant in Lancaster was Joseph Simon, the
frontier representative of Levy and Franks. Franks, also associated in Philadelphia with William Plumstead, had a brother in London who looked after his
affairs abroad. Later the firm of Baynton, Wharton and Morgan with their
English correspondents would vastly increase the economic as well as the
political aspects of the western trade.

While overland transportation vastly improved during these years, the
Atlantic remained Philadelphia's principal avenue of trade. So rapid was the
growth of commerce in this period that more waterfront construction took
place in Philadelphia than in any other American port. According to an
Assembly report, the number of vessels clearing the port increased from 85
in 1723 to an average of 403 between 1749 and 1752. Most of these ships were
Philadelphia-owned, often collectively by a dozen or more merchants, and
they kept the city's shops well stocked with goods from all over the world.
There were linens from Ireland, wines from Portugal and Madeira, India
goods, expensive woolens and high-grade cutlery from England, rum and
molasses from the West Indies, and Rhode Island oysters that Edward Shippen thought were superior to any others.[7]

The great proportion of ships leaving Philadelphia's docks, however,
never ventured beyond American waters. These vessels were bound for ports
in sister colonies in a trade that surpassed overseas commerce in both value
and tonnage. Ships either in the coastal or overseas trade were often tied up
at Philadelphia's wharves for several weeks while their owners advertised for
and collected freight. The staple exports had not changed—mainly grain and
flour but also meat, lumber, barrel staves, flaxseed, pig and bar iron, deerskins,
and furs.

One lucrative aspect of foreign commerce continued to be the transportation of immigrants to America. The vast majority of them at mid-century
came from Germany. Twenty-two ships, the greatest number in any one year,
carrying about 7000 persons, arrived in Philadelphia in the autumn of 1749.
A year later fourteen ships brought 4000 to the swelling German population
in Pennsylvania. By comparison only about 1000 immigrants arrived that year
from Northern Ireland and Great Britain.[8] Many Germans stayed in nearby
Germantown or in Philadelphia, which had a sector that was almost completely German. The rapidly growing number of shops of all kinds in the city
welcomed them many of whom were skilled artisans. But so great was the
influx that some Philadelphians feared they would eventually take over and
make Philadelphia a German city.

Voyages to Philadelphia from Europe lasted about seven weeks. Carrying
an average of 300 passengers, the ships were dreadfully crowded. Hunger
added to this misery, and disease frequently took a frightful toll. In 1750 the

Assembly made an effort to improve the immigrants' lot by limiting the number of passengers a ship could carry. This proved to be little more than a well-meaning gesture. Despite untoward conditions most ships made the voyage without severe misfortunes and landed the bulk of their human cargo safely at Philadelphia. Many ships, like the *Edinburgh* and the *Two Brothers*, sailed year after year in the indentured servant trade; others made sporadic trips depending on market conditions.[9]

Immigrants of another kind also came into the city as Philadelphians expanded their importation of slaves, usually from the West Indies. Although the trade was not nearly so extensive as that of other colonial cities north and south, nevertheless throughout the 1750s "parcels" of slaves frequently arrived in Philadelphia along with cargoes of sugar and molasses. Prominent among those merchants handling slaves were William Allen, Joseph Turner, Thomas Willing, and Robert Morris. By this time most Quaker merchants, faced with growing opposition to slavery within the Society of Friends, would not allow their ships to carry slaves.[10]

Philadelphia's commerce of all kinds—raw materials, manufactured goods, and human beings—grew greatly during the French and Indian War. Imports, for example, skyrocketed from a value of £168,000 in 1757 to over £700,000 in 1760. According to the firm of Willing and Morris, the supply of cotton goods in 1758 was sufficient to last three years, a symptom of a general condition that at the end of the French and Indian War created a severe recession.

The export trade was richly if illicitly supplemented by supplying the French through neutral ports in the West Indies. The collector of the port, Abraham Taylor, and Chief Justice William Allen were accused of this offense, while Gov. William Denny himself appears to have made a business of selling flags of truce. Of course smuggling was nothing new; it was estimated in 1757 that out of 400 chests of tea received in the previous two years, only about sixteen were legally imported.[11]

All this trade depended on an ample number of ships for its cargoes. Boston had been the great shipbuilding center of the American colonies, but by 1750 this primacy was passing to Philadelphia, in large part because of the greater supply of ash and cedar in Pennsylvania and New Jersey. Moreover, because of lower costs of materials, ships constructed in the Philadelphia yards were about 10–15 percent cheaper than those built in England. These ships were not, however, so well built as those constructed in the mother country or in New England. "Our Ship Carpenters never season a stick," Lewis Evans complained. For all this, shipbuilding flourished. Scull and Heap's 1754 view of the city shows twelve shipyards in the mile between Old Swedes' Church and Poole's Bridge, over Coaquannock Creek (or Pegg's Run) at the northern edge of the city.[12]

Near the waterfront and often in the neighborhood of the shipyards, other industries, large and small, were operated. Many of them, such as the blacksmith shops, foundries, and ropewalks, were essential for the shipbuilding industry. There were tanneries, distilleries, breweries, carriage shops, fulling mills, and cooperages. Philadelphia rum was reputed to be as good as any in America. And the shoe industry prospered despite the fact that the best boots and shoes had to be made from imported leather because of the poor quality of the local product. To satisfy the needs of dressmakers and tailors, quantities of buckles, buttons, and hooks and eyes were manufactured in the city. Philadelphia shops even produced such specialties as mustard and chocolate.[13] All these industries created such a demand for labor that William Meyer opened an employment office in 1756 which supplied the services of journeyman artisans, apprentices, Negroes, and common laborers.[14]

One inevitable component of urbanization was the ever-increasing number of taverns in the city. At High and Water Streets, near the popular Indian King, Obadiah Bourne set up in 1748 a new tavern whose name held more than a bit of irony. Bourne, a sea captain, called it "Le Trembleur"—The Quaker—for his privateer which had brought terror to the French and Spanish during King George's War.[15] In Water Street was the Tun Tavern, commonly known as Peggy Mullen's Beefsteak House. It was a favorite meeting place for Freemasons. The Masons also often gathered at the Widow Pratt's Royal Standard on High Street, where the directors of the Library Company regularly met and the contributors to the Pennsylvania Hospital convened for a time.[16] The busiest tavern in the city remained the London Coffee House, acquired in 1754 by William Bradford, who promoted the house's reputation as a merchants' exchange.[17]

If the tavern was an inevitable ingredient of city life, so was the rising incidence of crime. There were such serious crimes as murder and grand larceny, with the last having a surprising number of women offenders. Most breaches of the law, however, were of a less serious nature—stealing, disorderly conduct, drunkenness, and gambling. Those convicted were overwhelmingly from the middle and lower classes; the rather few erring wealthy usually escaped punishment through their influential connections. The fathering of bastards, however, brought to account nearly all, regardless of class, who did not provide a settlement for the mother and child.[18]

Sentences were imposed by the city magistrates. For major crimes the punishment could be hanging, jailing, or forced departure from the colony. In 1718 the Assembly had forsaken Penn's humane limitations on capital punishment in favor of the rules practiced in England. This change arose from a bargain permitting Quakers to continue holding office in the province without taking oaths. Petty offenders faced being fined, whipped, jailed, and put in the public stocks at the discretion of the magistrate. Culprits, however, could appeal to the mayor, aldermen, and councilmen, who were usually lenient, partly out of compassion or out of consideration for the city budget if the sentence prescribed jailing. Because of Daniel Ford's poverty and bad health, for example, the board of appeals remitted his £20 fine for keeping an unlicensed tavern. Leonore Martin's fine of £10 for having a bastard child was remitted because she needed the money to support the child. Such examples

Trade card of Benjamin Harbeson (1728–1809), engraved c. 1764 by Henry Dawkins (act. 1753–1786). At his shop on Market Street, corner of Strawberry Alley (west of Second), Harbeson made tin and pewter articles in addition to the copper wares offered on his elegant card. A respected political leader among the craftsmen of Philadelphia, Harbeson signed the Nonimportation Agreement of 1765 and became a captain of the Second Battalion of Philadelphia Associators in 1776.

could be multiplied many times in the course of the years. One sentence, however, was seldom if ever set aside. When ordered, a public whipping at the whipping post in the Court House yard was dutifully carried out by Daniel Pellito, the city executioner.[19]

The ostracism of criminals and other undesirables was common practice in the eighteenth century. In 1749 a dozen or more lawbreakers in Philadelphia had their fines remitted when they agreed to leave the city. Even Samuel Jackson's capital sentence for the serious crime of counterfeiting was commuted in 1752, but only after he had been whipped. Two years later George Lee and Richard Davis, guilty of assaulting a nightwatchman, escaped punishment by enlisting on a British warship. In times of war most anyone could go free by joining the armed forces.[20]

Court sessions evidently offered an entertaining diversion for Philadelphia's citizenry. "On court days," writes Gottlieb Mittelberger, "young and old may enter the chamber and may listen to the cross-examinations and to the judgments, which often cause the listeners to burst into uproarious laughter." One such cross-examination involved a pregnant woman who wanted for a husband the man she accused of rape. The man during the trial pretended deafness, claiming that when he had "raped" the woman, "she had cried out so horribly that he had lost his hearing." When he said this, the woman angrily retorted, 'O, you godless villain, how can you say this? You remember I didn't say a word then." But of course if she had thought she would become pregnant, she "would certainly have cried for help. At this," Mittelberger concludes, "young and old broke into great laughter; and the man was at once acquitted and set free."[21]

On the evidence of Mittleberger's tale of the "deaf" man, sometimes crime in Philadelphia did pay. Philadelphians, nevertheless, were as desirous of preventing crime as of punishing the criminal. Street lighting helped. So did a paid nightwatch, which at last became a reality in 1751 when the Assembly authorized the city corporation to levy a property tax for this purpose.[22]

As it happened, however, the nightwatch proved as efficacious in the detection of fire as in the prevention of crime. By mid-century there were six fire companies ready to respond to an alarm sounded by the nightwatchman. Two more, the Britannia and the Hibernia, were formed in the early 1750s. The fire companies had many of the features of social clubs. They met regularly for inspection and relaxation, and drew their membership from particular groups in the city; for instance, the Hibernia was overwhelmingly Irish.

Philadelphia's fire companies provided some training for their men, but more important, by now they owned an impressive amount of firefighting equipment. Most of their manually operated pumping engines were purchased from Richard Newsam of London, who advertised throughout the colonies. In 1752 the Union Fire Company and the Hand-in-Hand jointly purchased a large fire bell that could be heard throughout the city from its belfry atop the academy in Fourth Street. More wells that could be used in firefighting were dug and public pumps installed. In 1755 the Philadelphia Contributionship for the Insurance of Houses ordered from harnessmaker Obadiah Elbridge twenty-four leather buckets to be hung at convenient places for the watch. In 1764 four of the fire companies elected a joint president and board of managers, to begin the process of amalgamating the companies into a cooperating union.[23]

A natural outgrowth of fire consciousness and protection was fire insurance. Following Charleston's abortive effort in this field in 1735, no other attempt was made until 1750 when the Union Fire Company under Franklin's aegis offered its members a mutual fire insurance scheme. Nothing immediately came of this plan, but two years later, again sponsored by Franklin, the Philadelphia Contributionship for the Insurance of Houses from Loss by Fire was established. Commonly known as the Hand-in-Hand from its firemark, the Contributionship was the first successful fire insurance company in America and has continued to serve the needs of Philadelphia's citizens down to the present day.[24]

The institutionalization of fire protection was one of the many results of the growth of Philadelphia as a great commercial center. So was her astonishing increase in population. In 1746 there were some 1500 dwellings in the town, housing an estimated population of about 10,000. In 1765 there were nearly 5000 habitations with a population of over 25,000. Boston on the other hand had remained virtually stable throughout this period, with a population of about 15,000. New York, with a population about equal to Philadelphia's in 1755, had fallen behind by 1765 and remained so until long after the American Revolution. To one English visitor in 1765, Philadelphia was a "great and noble City": a not inappropriate appelation, for Penn's "greene Country Towne" was now probably the fourth in size among the cities of the British world, behind only London, Edinburgh, and Dublin.[25]

II

"I never was before engaged in any study that so totally engrossed my attention and my time as this has lately done. . . ."[26] So exclaimed Benjamin Franklin as he launched his series of epoch-making "Philadelphia experiments" which gave rise to the modern science of electricity. His resulting *Experiments and Observations in Electricity* of 1751, to which he constantly added in subsequent editions, has been called the single most important book to come out of colonial America. The single-fluid theory of electricity and the proof of the identity of an electric spark and lightning—along with the invention of the lightning rod—placed Franklin in the forefront of the world's scientists. They also served to denominate Philadelphia as the American center in the world of an emerging Atlantic civilization.[27]

But Franklin was only the most outstanding of an ever-enlarging circle of science-minded men who since Logan's time had brought Philadelphia world renown. Ebenezer Kinnersley, for example, worked closely with Franklin in his electrical experiments. In the early 1750s while Franklin's work was gaining European favor, Kinnersley was becoming known and respected in colonial scientific circles through his extensive traveling and lecturing. He proved that electricity produces heat, and he invented an electrical air thermometer. The English scientist Joseph Priestley wrote of him: "Some of his observations . . . are very curious; and some later accounts . . . seem to promise that, if he continues his electrical inquiries, his name, after that of his friend, will be second to few in the history of electricity." After 1755 Kinnersley taught English and oratory at the College of Philadelphia while continuing his scientific researches.[28]

Benjamin Franklin (1706–1790), painted by Mason Chamberlin (d. 1787) in London in late July 1762 for Franklin's friend, Col. Philip Ludwell III. Franklin himself considered the portrait an accurate likeness, and he ordered more than a hundred copies of an engraving taken from Chamberlin's painting.

PHILADELPHIA MUSEUM OF ART MR. AND MRS. WHARTON SINKLER COLLECTION

Philip Syng, silversmith and another associate in the electrical experiments, was the inventor of a convenient friction machine for producing electricity. Robert Grace, like Syng, had been an original Junto member. A metallurgist, he cast the plates for Franklin's first invention, the Pennsylvania fireplace, and he now also assisted in the experiments with electricity.

The very much younger David Rittenhouse—he was only nineteen when Franklin published his electrical experiments—opened on his father's farm an instrument shop mainly devoted to clockmaking. Within the next years, however, he would invent a pocket metallic thermometer, experiment with the compressibility of water, and design his celebrated orrery, a mathematically precise model of the solar system in motion.

John Bartram, the protégé of James Logan, continued his botanical studies during this period. In the same year that Franklin published his electrical book Bartram's *Observations on the Inhabitants, Climate, Soil, etc. . . . made by John Bartram in his travels from Pennsylvania to Lake Ontario* appeared. Bartram's book was based on his journey of 1743, a journey that has been called the first scientific exploration by an American. Later, William Bartram would carry on his father's work.[29]

Exploration of the North American continent was not confined to the colonial mainland. Arctic expeditions whetted the scientific imagination of Philadelphia, in large part because of the unsuccessful English attempts to find a northwest passage to the Orient. Speculation about such a passage became active in Philadelphia in 1748 when Peter Collinson sent over a book on the subject. Five years later the first Philadelphia—or American—expedition to the frozen north was launched when the schooner *Argo*, sponsored by William Allen and other wealthy citizens, set sail under Capt. Charles Swaine. Stopped by an impasse of ice, Swaine returned with discouraging reports. A second expedition sent out the next spring took the *Argo* as far north as the sixty-third parallel, but it proved as fruitless as the first in finding a passage through the Arctic wastes. The expedition did, however, chart the Labrador coast and discovered good fishing banks hitherto unknown to Philadelphians.[30]

Of more immediate utility—it would be almost another century before Americans again attempted the Arctic regions—was the field of medicine, in which Philadelphians made significant contributions. The ubiquitous Franklin invented the first flexible catheter in America in 1752, and he had probably already begun his ruminations on lead poisoning. More young Philadelphians bent on a career in medicine were going abroad to study in the great medical schools of Europe. Following his training at Edinburgh—he was among the first Americans to study there—Dr. John Redman pursued his interest in obstetrics at the University of Leyden, where he wrote his dissertation, *De Abortu*. Obtaining practical experience in the hospitals of London and Paris, Redman returned to Philadelphia where he had a long and distinguished medical career both as a practitioner and as an instructor in the College of Physicians.[31]

Dr. Thomas Bond began his career at Annapolis, where he studied with the peripatetic Scotsman Dr. Alexander Hamilton—he who in the 1740s had pungently commented in his diary about Philadelphia and its citizens. Bond then attended medical schools in both Paris and London before settling in Philadelphia as a skilled surgeon with particular interests in hygiene and epidemiology. Bond also published in an English journal a paper on liver worms and discussed with physician to the Crown Dr. John Fothergill the use of Peruvian bark in the treatment of scrofula.[32]

Bond, furthermore, first conceived of a charity hospital for Philadelphia along the lines of those of London and Paris. Franklin publicized the project in the *Pennsylvania Gazette,* and the leading Quakers offered their support— perhaps, as some people suspected, in order to offset attacks on their pacifism. To raise funds for the project Franklin introduced what may have been the first dollar-matching scheme in American history. He prevailed upon the Assembly to grant £2000 to the hospital only when a like amount was privately raised. The plan was immediately successful, and in 1752 the Pennsylvania Hospital opened temporary quarters in the house of the late Justice John Kinsey on the southeast corner of Fifth and High Streets.

Two years passed before a permanent site for the hospital was acquired beyond the built-up area of the city, between Eighth and Ninth Streets on the north side of Pine. Subsequently the proprietors gave the hospital the

The Pennsylvania Hospital, *Pine Street at Eighth, begun 1755, engraving by William Birch (1755–1834), 1799. The hospital's east wing, designed in 1751 by Samuel Rhoads (1711–1784), was completed in 1756, the west wing in 1796, and the central building in 1794–1805.*

remaining land in the block, extending to the south side of Spruce Street. Samuel Carpenter, a master carpenter and one of the managers of the hospital, drew up the design for its buildings, a plan that was not to achieve completion until after the Revolution; the east wing, however, was built in 1755.

The need for the hospital was apparent from the beginning. The Quaker Alms House had become inadequate, and the St. Andrew's Society, founded by Dr. Thomas Graeme, James Burd, and John Inglis in 1749 for the relief of poor Scots, was helpful but limited. From the time the new hospital opened its doors, therefore, the list of patients awaiting its facilities was a long one. Most of the city's physicians, including Dr. Bond, offered their services without pay.[33]

Franklin, who served as a manager for several years and was the first secretary of the hospital's board of trustees as well as its second president, composed the inscription for the cornerstone of the building:

> IN THE YEAR OF CHRIST
> 1755
> GEORGE THE SECOND HAPPILY REIGNING
> (FOR HE SOUGHT THE HAPPINESS OF HIS PEOPLE)
> PHILADELPHIA FLOURISHING
> (FOR ITS INHABITANTS WERE PUBLIC SPIRITED)
> THIS BUILDING,
> BY THE BOUNTY OF THE GOVERNMENT,
> AND OF MANY PRIVATE PERSONS,
> WAS PIOUSLY FOUNDED,
> FOR THE RELIEF OF THE SICK AND MISERABLE.
> MAY THE GOD OF MERCIES
> BLESS THE UNDERTAKING![34]

God perhaps was listening, for the record of the Pennsylvania Hospital far surpassed those of London and Paris. In its first twenty-five years over half of almost 9000 persons admitted were completely cured.

In the same year that the cornerstone for the hospital was laid, the College of Philadelphia received its charter of incorporation. Franklin—of whom when he died it has been said that "no other town, burying its great man, ever buried more of itself than Philadelphia with Franklin"[35]—was again the catalyst. Eight years previously the successful printer had opined that though Philadelphia was a good place to live, it lacked two essentials: there was "no Provision for Defence, nor for a compleat Education of Youth."[36] The solution to the former was the military association he shortly organized. In pursuit of the latter he published his famous proposals *Relating to the Education of Youth in Pennsylvania,* in which he suggested the establishment of a nonsectarian academy. His idea won the support of such influential Anglicans as Tench Francis and Richard Peters and of such Presbyterians as William Allen and the Shippens. Of the first twenty-four trustees, eighteen were Anglicans.

The College of Philadelphia, *Fourth and Mulberry (Arch) Streets, sketch by Pierre Eugène Du Simitière (d. 1784), c. 1780. The Academy of Philadelphia held classes in a large hall which had been built in 1740 as a charity school and meeting-house by the followers of George Whitefield, the English evangelist. In 1755 the Academy was empowered to grant degrees to the graduates among its 300 students and to change its name to "The College, Academy, and Charitable School of Philadelphia." A dormitory, to the north of the main hall, was added in 1762.*

Although a few Quakers, such as Abel James, donated substantially to the project, and James Logan and Dr. Lloyd Zachary served on the original board of trustees, most Friends opposed it. Critical of higher education, they also feared a further loss of power, especially to the Anglicans. Despite this opposition £15,000 was raised within a year, and in 1751 the first classes of the academy were held in a warehouse owned by William Allen on Second Street. Shortly thereafter the academy moved to the large building on Fourth Street below Arch that had been erected for George Whitefield's religious meetings.

At its beginning the academy was headed by the Rev. David Martin, the Latin teacher, but upon his death within the year the position was taken by the noted Presbyterian minister and classical scholar Francis Alison. Franklin was not enthusiastic about the classical aspects of the curriculum, but in order to secure the backing of the wealthy William Allen and others he had agreed to dividing the academy into an English and a Latin school. In addition to Alison the first faculty included Theophilus Grew, who taught mathematics and geography, and David James Dove, who taught English. In 1754 the young Rev. William Smith joined the group as a teacher of humanities. His pamphlet *A General Idea of the College of Mirania,* which stressed practical subjects, had caught the interest of Franklin, who soon afterward secured Smith's appointment.[37]

When in 1755 the academy received college status with power to grant degrees, it became the College, Academy, and Charitable School of Philadelphia, commonly known as the College of Philadelphia. William Smith, who introduced the term in America, became the first provost, and Francis Alison, vice-provost. Among the first seven graduates in May 1757 were Jacob Duché, Hugh Williamson, John Morgan, and Francis Hopkinson, all of whom became distinguished in their fields. Since so many Philadelphians frowned on higher education, the college never had a large enrollment in its colonial days. Only 141 men were graduated before the Revolution. Nevertheless, except for Harvard, it offered the best education available in British America.

Harvard, like the College of Philadelphia, was a private institution. Harvard represented, however, the capstone to the longstanding Puritan commitment to education, privately as well as publicly supported. Philadelphia, on the other hand, had no publicly supported schools. Rather, previous to the academy Philadelphia's youth was educated solely in sectarian institutions or with private schoolmasters. The church-related schools usually provided free instruction to a few promising poor pupils, but others paid a tuition fee to cover operating costs. As Philadelphia grew more urbane, controversy had developed over the relative merits of classical as opposed to practical learning. By 1750 the Quakers themselves were allowing their schools to emphasize Latin along with the subjects taught in the English departments. Even the "ignorant" Baptists established a Latin grammar school five years later. There were those, naturally, who opposed this drift toward classical education. John Bartram, for example, wanted his son to receive an education that would enable him to make a "temperate, reasonable living." To meet the demand for practical studies several private schoolmasters taught such subjects as accounting, mathematics, navigation, and surveying. Anthony Lamb for twenty-six years taught "Italian," i.e., double-entry bookkeeping, writing, and arithmetic among other subjects, and prepared many of Philadelphia's youths for the world of business.[38]

Young women too had their opportunities for schooling beyond the expected social accomplishments of a well-bred lady. The Quakers for years had included girls in their schools, but in 1751 David James Dove conducted a private school for girls that offered a curriculum more advanced than the accepted elementary level. After his dismissal in 1753 from the College of Philadelphia where he also taught, Dove merged his tutorial interests and opened a boarding school in Vidal's Alley for both boys and girls. In the same year William Dawson inaugurated night classes for working girls which included psalmody in addition to the more useful writing and arithmetic. Inspired perhaps by the success of these private schools, Anthony Benezet in 1754 started a school for girls which became highly successful and in time included in its curriculum Latin and Greek, alongside needlework.[39]

Even before Benezet's interest in female education, the concern over slavery for which he is famous had led him to support education for Negroes. In 1750, in his own home, he began to conduct evening classes for black children, an undertaking he engaged in for twenty years. Later in the decade, in 1758, the Bray Associates, a group of Englishmen administering a fund left by the philanthropic Rev. Dr. Thomas Bray, were persuaded by Benjamin Franklin to open a school for blacks under the direction of the Rev. William Sturgeon of Christ Church. At its opening thirty black pupils were taught by a woman instructor to "Sew, Knit, read and write."[40]

Formal institutions of education were supplemented in Philadelphia by a proliferation of libraries. "You would be astonished," the Rev. Jacob Duché declared in 1774, "at the general taste for books, which prevails among all orders and ranks of people in this city." Because membership in the Library Company had become expensive, a group of professional men, tradesmen, and artisans in 1747 organized the Union Library Company, also a subscription library. By 1759 the Union Library owned more than 300 volumes and its membership had reached its limit of 100. A third company, the Association Library, was founded in 1757 by a group of artisans, mostly Quaker, which included such notables as printers William Bradford and David Hall, apothecary Christopher Marshall, and clockmaker Owen Biddle. Before long this library too had accumulated a sizable collection. At the same time that the artisans were forming the Association Library, a group of workingmen organized the Amicable Company, a smaller and less successful undertaking than the others. During the years that followed the feasibility of supporting so many similar libraries was increasingly questioned, and in 1769, after a series of mergers, the Library Company of Philadelphia absorbed them all, thus becoming once again the sole "public" library in the city, well endowed with money, members, and books.[41]

Just as libraries flourished, so did booksellers. One of the better known was William Bradford, nephew of Franklin's old competitor Andrew Bradford and publisher of the *Pennsylvania Journal*. William Bradford combined retailing with printing at the Sign of the Bible, next door to his London Coffee House. With the absence of copyright laws, Philadelphia printers increasingly published their own editions of English and European works. By the late 1760s, after the Nonimportation Agreement, Robert Bell industriously brought out popular titles of the day, the works of such authors as the historian William Robertson and the jurist William Blackstone and a whole series of English plays. In 1774 James Humphreys issued the first American edition of Lawrence Sterne's collected works.[42]

There were a half dozen or so printing shops by mid-century, with three printers—Franklin, William Bradford, and in Germantown, Christopher Saur—publishing newspapers. Bradford, later denominated "the patriot printer" for his activities during the Revolution, undertook in 1757 the ambitious plan of publishing a literary magazine modeled on similar English journals of the day. For his editor Bradford chose College Provost William Smith, under whose auspices *The American Magazine, or Monthly Chronicle for the British Colonies* managed a brief life of twelve issues before financial exigencies caused its demise. *The American Magazine*, which has been called the "most brilliant" publication to come out of colonial America, offered a forum for such Philadelphians as the versatile Francis Hopkinson, composer and inventor as well as versifier, and Thomas Godfrey, Jr. Godfrey, son of the improver of the mariner's quadrant, would soon author a play entitled *The Prince of Parthia*. Its production in 1767 made it the first drama by an American author to be professionally staged. Godfrey was probably the most talented of the literati surrounding Provost Smith, but death cut off his career in 1763 at the untimely age of twenty-seven.[43]

Five years before Godfrey's death Benjamin Franklin, who wrote in a less derivative, less pretentious style—the Smith group doted on English taste and manners—composed what would shortly become the most widely read American work of the century. *The Way to Wealth*, as it came to be called, was the preface to the 1758 *Poor Richard's Almanac*, the last to be edited by Franklin. Before the century was out Franklin's homely essay in the prudential virtues—a relevant lesson at a time when the mobility was replacing the nobility—had enjoyed 144 reprintings, including twenty-eight in French, eleven in Italian, three in German, and one each in Dutch, Gaelic, and Swedish.

Franklin, who in 1748 had other things on his mind such as politics and electricity, that year turned his printing business over to his partner David Hall. But his interest in journalism and printing remained keen, and early in the 1750s he again tried unsuccessfully to establish a German-language newspaper. He was not able, however, to compete with Christopher Saur (Sower), Sr., of Germantown, a man of much influence among the Germans who by 1753 claimed a circulation of 4000 for his *Pensylvanische Berichte*, a newspaper founded in 1739 as *Der Hoch Deutsch Pensylvanische Geschichte Schreiber* and destined for a number of metamorphoses. Until his death in 1758 Saur, and thereafter his son and grandsons, published a variety of books and tracts in both English and German. The elder Saur, who started out in Germantown as a clockmaker, is best known for his prayerbooks and Bibles. His German Bible published in 1748 was the first in a European language to be printed in America. Heinrich Miller's *Der Wochentliche Philadelphische Staatsbote* was able soon after its founding in 1762 to surpass Saur's publication as the most widely circulated German newspaper, not only in Philadelphia but throughout the German settlements in America.[44]

The German press was but one facet of the growth of educational opportunity for Philadelphia's citizens. From foreign-language periodicals to Franklin's homiletics, to schools for blacks, to libraries, to short-lived if ambitious literary projects such as Bradford's *American Magazine*—in short, in the general dissemination of the printed word, education, either formal or informal, became increasingly available. When at the same time the economic system afforded leisure to a significant portion of her citizens, the scene was set for the city to enjoy a modest flowering in the arts that depend on both education and leisure.

The so-called higher arts, painting, music, and the like, were patronized

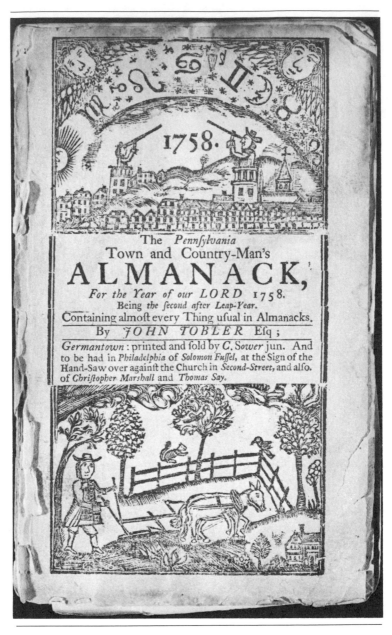

The Pennsylvania Town and Country-Man's Almanack, *by John Tobler, printed in 1758 by Christopher Sower (Saur), Jr. (1721–1784). Beginning in 1739 Christopher Saur and his sons printed German and English almanacs, as well as religious books, on their presses in Germantown, the early textile and paper manufacturing center.*

—though in Philadelphia with one exception—by those who could afford them. That exception included most of the wealthy Quakers, whose pietistic faith disdained worldly amusements as a waste of God-given time. Upper-class Anglicans and Presbyterians, however, increasingly supported the fine arts, most particularly the art of portrait painting. Their interest brought to Philadelphia a number of artists from abroad and from other American colonies. The Swedish painter and organ builder Gustavus Hesselius continued to live in the city much of the time. Some artists stayed only briefly, such as John Wollaston, who worked in the city around 1755 when he painted the portraits of Mayor William Plumstead and Judge William Peters. Likenesses of Mrs. Peters and of Attorney-General Tench Francis along with others had been painted some years earlier by Robert Feke, noted Rhode Island portrait-ist who made several visits to Philadelphia in the late 1740s.[45]

A clientele for portraits made Philadelphia attractive to artists. It is significant too that the Philadelphia Academy taught painting to local boys with talent. For their art supplies one of the best shops was the "oil and colour shop" run by Christopher Marshall under the Sign of the Golden Ball near the Three Tuns Tavern in Chestnut Street. Matthew Pratt, who became a popular Philadelphia portrait painter, learned his craft as an apprentice to his uncle James Claypoole.[46] Another artist who taught painting was William Williams, the versatile Welshman who came to the city about 1750 and achieved renown as the scene painter for David Douglass's 1759 theater on Society Hill in Southwark. More important, Williams introduced oil painting to the talented Benjamin West, a young student on the threshold of his career.[47] Encouraged also by Provost William Smith, West painted a few Philadelphia portraits in the manner of Williams, including one of Thomas Mifflin, before departing for European study in 1760, never to return.

As patrons of the dramatic arts, the non-Quaker gentry gave the theater a breath of life in a city still prejudiced against this form of entertainment. In August 1749 Walter Murray and Thomas Kean brought a troupe to Philadelphia to perform several plays including Joseph Addison's tragedy *Cato.* The large brick warehouse owned by William Plumstead on the banks of the Delaware at the foot of Pine Street served as a makeshift theater. Prodded by Quakers and other conservatives, the city Council ordered magistrates to bind the actors against the showing of any improper performances.[48]

Five years passed before another theatrical visit. This time the company was the better known group directed by Lewis Hallam, fresh from successful engagements in New York and Charleston. Using Plumstead's warehouse, now equipped with stage, pit, and gallery, Hallam opened the season in April 1754 with a tragedy, Nicholas Rowe's *The Fair Penitent,* and a farce, David Garrick's *Miss in Her Teens.* In the course of its thirty performances Hallam's company may well have performed some of the Shakespearean plays in their repertory.

Following Hallam's death in 1756 his widow married David Douglass, a theater manager and architect, and in 1759 they came to Philadelphia with a

1763. Der Wöchentliche 61 Stück.

Philadelphische Staatsbote,

Mit den neuesten Fremden und Einheimisch-Politischen Nachrichten;

Samt den

von Zeit zu Zeit in der Kirche und Gelehrten Welt sich ereignenden Merkwürdigkeiten.

Montags, den 14 Merz.

Diese Zeitung wird alle Montage ausgegeben, für Sechs Schillinge des Jahrs, bey Henrich Miller, Buchdrucker, zwischen der Wein- und Rees-strasse, in der Zweyten-strasse.

NB. Die Advertisements oder Benachrichtigungen, welche man in diese Zeitung will gesetzt haben, werden, samt der Zahlung, abgelegt, in Philadelphia bey eben benamtem Verleger, und dem Herrn Georg Honig, Gastgeb zum König von Preussen, in der Markt-strasse; und an andern Orten bey den folgenden Herren: In Germanton bey Augustin Neisser; in Lancaster bey Adam Müller; in Yorktaun bey Jacob Billmeyer; in Friederichstaun bey Conrad Grosch; in Reading bey Martin Kast; und in Neuyork bey Jacob Huth, auf dem Breiten Wege.

☞ Um Recommendation guter Kundleute wird freundlichst gebeten; und daß einer es dem andern sagen wolle.

☞ In dem vorhergehenden Stück dieser Zeitung, auf der 2ten Blattseite, in der 1ten Spalte, und 2ten Zeile von oben, lies: denn es ist kein; anstatt, denn es kein. Auf eben derselben Blattseite, in der 2ten Spalte, zu anfang der 2ten Zeile von unten, muß es heissen: Im 26ten grad 56 min. Norder breite; anstatt, Im 26 und 56ten grad.

[Folgendes ist aus Hrn. Franklins und Halls Zeitung.]

Ein Mittel wider den Rheumatismum, oder die Gliederkrankheit so von scharfen Feuchtigkeiten und Flüssen herrührt.

Nimm Eine Unze Polychrest-Balsam*, und mische solchen wohl mit einem Weinglas oder Theeschälchen voll des besten Wein-Brannteweins oder Rums: Wenn es solchergestalt gemischt ist, gieß es in eine zum theil mit starkem Spanischen Wein gefüllete Quart-Butellie, dann fülle die Butellie ganz auf mit derselbigen Art Weins, und laß es zusammen vier und zwanzig Stunden stehen, nach Verfliessung dieser Zeit ist es gut zum Gebrauch; und selbiger bestehet darin, daß der Kranke ein Weinglas voll, oder beynahe ein viertel Peint, von diesem Trank zu sich nimmt, wenn er zu Bette gehet.

* Der Polychrest-Balsam ist ein Zusammensatz vom Gum oder Harz des Franzosen- oder heiligen Holzes, vom Peruvianischen Balsam, und Weingeist oder Spiritus Vini.

Es ist zu merken: Daß in einigen Vorfällen ein Quart genug gewesen von dieser Krankheit zu genesen. Der Kranke solte sich warm gekleidet halten, um sich nicht zu verkälten. Ein Herr, der dieses Arzneymittel für einige seiner Bekannten angemacht hat, beobachtet, daß Wein-Brannteweín bequemer dazu ist als Rum; weil der erstere, als von Wein distillirt, sich besser mit Spanischem Wein vermischt, und weil der Geschmack und Geruch des Rums vielen Leuten zuwider ist.

Eine Acte, oder Landes-Gesetz, gewissen schädlichen Dingen in und bey der Stadt Philadelphia vorzubeugen und abzuhelfen.

Demnach von verschiedenen Einwohnern der Stadt und Vorstädte von Philadelphia grosse Klage geführt wird, daß die Distillirer, Seifensieder, und andere, öfters grosse Quantitäten unflätig und stinkenden Gewässers, das Gespühl aus ihren Distillir-Kesseln und Koch-Gefässen, auf den beyliegenden Grund, oder in die Rinnen der öffentlichen Strassen, Gassen oder Gänge ausleeren, zu grosser Beschwerde der Einwohner; oder durch Ausleerung desselben in die zu dem Ende gegrabene Pfühle, Gruben oder Anzüchte, ihrer Nachbarn Wasser beschädigt, wo nicht gänzlich verdorben haben; und daß noch allerhand andere Dinge in und nahe bey besagter Stadt sind, so den Einwohnern zum Ungemach und Schaden gereichen. Um nun solchen unschicklich- und schädlichen Dingen vorzubeugen: So wird hiemit gesetzmässig verordnet von dem Grosachtbaren James Hamilton, Esq. Guvernör-Lieutenant, unter den Grosachtbaren Thomas Penn, und Richard Penn, Esquires, wahren und vollkommenen Eigenthums-herren der Provinz Pennsylvanien, und Caunties New-Castle, Kent und Sussex an der Delaware, auf und mit dem Rath und Einwilligung der Representanten der freyen Einwohner besagter Provinz, in Allgemeiner Landsversammlung vereinigt, und vermög dererselben Gewalt, Daß wofern einige Distillirer, Seifensieder, oder Kerzenmacher, innerhalb besagter Stadt, dem Bezirk von Southwark, oder den bebauten Gegenden der Norder Freyheiten, nach öffentlicher Kundmachung dieses, für sich selbst, durch ihre Unterhändler, Arbeitsgesellen, oder Dienstboten, sich unterstehen werden, aus oder von einigem Distillirhause, oder Werkstatt, unflätiges und eckelhaftes Gewässer, von was Art es auch sey, in oder auf einigen beyliegenden Grund, oder in einigen Pfuhl, Grube oder Anzucht, innerhalb besagter Stadt, Bezirk oder Taunschip, auszuleeren, ein jeder so solchergestalt sich vergehen, und davon gesetzmässig wird überführt worden seyn in dem Gericht der Vierteljährigen Seßionen (Court of Quarter Seßions), so für den Frieden besagter Stadt und Caunty respective gehalten wird, für ein jedes dergleichen Verbrechen die Summe von Zwanzig Pfund verwirken und bezahlen soll.

Und, um das Wasser in besagter Stadt, dem Bezirk von Southwark, und den Norder Freyheiten, desto wirklicher gesund und zum Gebrauch tüchtig zu bewahren: So wird durch vorbesagte Gewalt gesetzmässig verordnet, Daß die nach den Gesetzen bestimmte Commissarien um die Strassen besagter Stadt zu pflastern, und die Aufseher des Bezirks Southwark, und Taunschips der Norder Freyheiten respective, mit Bewilligung des Bürgermeisters und Registrators, und einiger zween Rathsherren besagter Stadt, und einiger zwey oberkeitlichen Personen in vorbesagter Caunty von Philadelphia, die Tiefe aller Gruben, Pfühle und Anzüchte, vestsetzen, anordnen und bestimmen sollen, welche nach diesem für Secreter oder Abtritte sollen gegraben werden, in den bebauten Gegenden besagter Stadt, Bezirks, oder Taunschips, welche Einrichtung, nachdem sie vorbesagter massen gemacht ist, in der Pennsylvanischen Gazette kund gethan, und sodann in die Hände des Schreibers des Vierteljährigen Seßions-Gerichts für die Stadt und Caunty Philadelphia beygelegt werden soll, um von einigem Einwohner vorbesagter Stadt, Bezirks oder Taunschips, der sich darum meldet, nachgesehen zu werden. Und wenn einige Person oder Personen werden graben oder graben lassen eine dergleichen Grube, Pfuhl, oder Anzucht zu Secretern oder Abtritten, von grösserer Tiefe als vorbesagter massen vestgesetzt und bestimmet worden, so soll jede solche Person oder Personen, die dergestalt sich vergehen, und davon nach den rechten, wie vorgemeldet, werden überführt werden, die Summe von Zwanzig Pfund verwirken und bezahlen.

Und es wird durch vorbesagte Gewalt ferner gesetzmässig verordnet, Daß wofern einiger Distillirer, Seifensieder, oder Kerzenmacher, innerhalb besagter Stadt, Bezirks, oder Taunschips, einiges unflätiges oder eckelhaftes Gewässer auf vorgemeldete weise ausleeren wird von einigem Distillirhause, oder Werkstatt, so daß solches Gewässer in oder durch einige der Strassen, Gassen oder Gänge besagter Stadt, Bezirks oder Taunschips, hinfliessen wird; oder wofern einiger Seifensieder, oder Kerzenmacher, aufbehalten, sammlen, oder gebrauchen, oder aufbehalten, sammlen oder gebrauchen lassen wird, in einiger der bebaueten Gegend vorbesagter Stadt, Bezirks oder Taunschips, einiges altes, verfaultes, stinkendes Fett, Schmier, oder andere Materie; oder wofern einiger Metzger wird aufbehalten an oder bey seinem Schlachthause einiges Eingeweide, Abgänglinge oder Unreinlichkeit, was es auch sey, so einigem Nachbar, oder sonst jemanden, er sey wer er wolle, schädlich oder widerlich seyn kan, so soll er, sie, oder diejenigen, so sich also vergangen, und dessen vor einigem Friedensrichter besagter Stadt oder Caunty respective sind überführt worden, für jedes solches Vergehen die Summe von Fünf und Dreyßig Schillingen verwirken und bezahlen.

Und es wird durch vorbesagte Gewalt ferner gesetzmässig verordnet, Daß wofern einige Person oder Personen, nach öffentlicher Bekanntmachung dieses (Gesetzes sich unterstehen werden, einig todt Pferd, oder ander Aas von einem Vieh, Schaaf, Schwein oder Hunde, oder einigen Auswurf, oder Unflath, aus Anzüchten, Secreten oder Abtritten hinaus zu führen, zu tragen, zu schleppen, oder zu legen, auf einige Gegend des allgemeinen Weideganges besagter Stadt, oder auf oder nahe bey einige der Strassen, Gassen, Gänge, oder Landstrassen, innerhalb besagter Stadt oder Bezirks, oder an selbige stossenden Taunschips, und solche todte Thiere, Aas oder Unflath da liegen lassen werden, ohne dasselbige völlig und hinlänglich tief genug in die Erde zu begraben, so soll jede Person oder Personen, so sich solchergestalt vergangen, und dessen vor einigem Friedensrichter der Stadt oder Caunty von Philadelphia respective überwiesen werden, für jedes solches Verbrechen die Summe von Dreyßig Schillingen verwirken und bezahlen.

Und es wird durch vorbesagte Gewalt ferner gesetzmässig verordnet, Daß wofern jemand, nach öffentlicher Kundmachung dieses, wird werfen, schmeissen, oder legen, einiges Aas, todten Cörper, oder Unflath was es auch sey, oder einigen Koth, oder Schutt, oder sonst etwas schädliches oder verstopfendes, es sey was es wolle, in den allgemeinen Wassergang besagter Stadt, insgemein die Dock genannt, und wird dessen vor einigem Friedensrichter besagter Stadt wie vorgemeldet überwiesen werden, so soll ein jeder solcher Verbrecher für jegliches dergleichen Vergehen eine Summe Geldes verwirken, so sich nicht über Vierzig Schillinge beläufft, so wie besagter Friedensrichter, vor welchem der Verbrecher wird überwiesen werden, es billig erkennen wird.

Und demnach durch ausserordentliche Eingriffe der seith kurzer Zeit in den Strassen besagter Stadt gemachten Keller-Thüren, Hausthür-Staffeln, und Vorhöfe, der Abstandfenster, Vorbuden, und anderer hinderlichen Dinge, besagte Strassen gar sehr sind verlegt worden; und da von einer Anzahl Wasser-Röhren oder Dach-Rinnen, welche auf die Schoppen oder andere Oerter gelegt werden, eine grosse Menge Wassers zur Zeit des Regenwetters sich auf diejenigen ergeußt, welche nahe bey selbigen vorbey gehen: So wird daher durch vorbesagte Gewalt gesetzmässig verordnet, Daß wofern einige Person oder Personen, nach diesem machen, aufrichten werden, oder werden lassen machen oder aufrichten, in einiger Strasse von Fünfzig Fuß breit oder drüber, innerhalb besagter Stadt, einigen Vorhof, Keller-Thür, oder Staffel, so sich über Vier Fuß Drey Zoll in solche Strasse hinaus erstrecken wird, oder auf eine proportionirte Weite in einige engere Strasse hinaus, wo dergleichen gemacht oder aufgerichtet werden; und wenn einige Person oder Personen nach diesem werden machen und aufrichten, oder lassen machen und aufrichten, einige Vorbude, Abstandfenster, oder einige hinderliche Dinge, was es auch sey, wodurch der Weg in einiger Strasse verlegt wird; oder wird also legen, oder also legen lassen, einige Wasser-Röhre, oder Dach-Rinne, wodurch der Weg in einiger Strasse beschwerlich gemacht wird, so soll ein jeder, der sich also vergehet, und dessen vor einem Friedensrichter besagter Stadt den Gesetzen gemäß wird überwiesen werden, für ein jegliches solches Verbrechen, die Summe von Dreyßig Schillingen verwirken und bezahlen; und soll sofort besagtes schädliche Wesen wegschaffen, oder schaffen lassen.

Und es wird durch vorbesagte Gewalt ferner gesetzmässig verordnet, Daß ein Eigner, oder die Eigner eines jeden Hauses, innerhalb besagter Stadt, so da haben, zu der Zeit der öffentlichen Kundmachung dieses, einige Vorhöfe, Keller-Thüren, oder Staffeln, welche in einige Strasse hinaus sich erstrecken über das vorbesagte Ziel; oder haben angeheftet oder bevestigt an solch Haus einige Vorbude, Abstandfenster, oder ander hinderlich Ding was es auch sey, sollen jährlich, und jedes Jahr, bezahlen, an solche Person oder Personen, welche werden bestimmet werden selbiges zu empfangen und einzusammlen, solche Summe oder Summen Geldes als besagte Commissarien, und die Taxirer (oder Assessors) besagter Stadt, taxiren oder setzen

talented troupe of actors. Hoping to escape the inevitable opposition in the city proper, the company gave its performances in a new frame building on the southwest corner of Cedar and Vernon Streets (South and Hancock), just west of Front and, more important, across the street from the city boundary line. No sooner had the building been started than the provincial Assembly, prodded by church groups in Philadelphia, framed a bill banning theaters in Pennsylvania and sent it to Governor Denny. The liberal-minded governor, hoping to give the actors a reprieve, amended the bill and sent it back to the Assembly. This maneuver allowed the company to perform during the entire season from June until December. In 1761 the Privy Council in England disallowed the antitheater act, thus ending legislative attempts to ban the theater for the remainder of the colonial period.

The "Theatre on Society Hill" had only one season, but it was notable. It was for this theater that William Williams painted his scenery, and it was here that Philadelphia saw John Gay's *Beggar's Opera,* the first opera to be performed in Penn's colony. The season also included *Hamlet,* as well as a tragedy with music by Henry Purcell and some lighter interludes, both vocal and instrumental.

In 1766 Douglass's troupe became the American Company and permanently based itself in the northern colonies. On November 12 of that year the company opened a new Southwark Theater closer to the residences of most of the potential patrons, on the south side of Cedar Street at Apollo, west of Fourth. The inaugural performance was of *The Provoked Husband.* From the 1767 season onward until the Revolution Douglass and the Southwark Theater made drama an established feature of Philadelphia life.[49]

Music also was slowly entering Philadelphia's social life. The Quakers would have no part of it, but by 1750 there were organs in at least four of the city's churches—Christ Church, the Moravian church, St. Michael's Lutheran, and St. Joseph's—and interest was being shown in other instruments as well. John Beals, music master from London, in 1748 taught the violin, oboe, flute, recorder, and dulcimer. He was also willing to supply music for various occasions, and may perhaps have played for the Dancing Assemblies.[50]

German-language publications were printed by Benjamin Franklin and others to accommodate the estimated 58,000 German immigrants who had arrived through the port of Philadelphia by the early 1750s. In 1763 Der Wochentliche Philadelphische Staatsbote was issued every Monday by Heinrich Miller from his press on Second Street between Vine and Race. The distribution of Miller's readership is revealed by his list of advertising agents in Philadelphia, Germantown, Lancaster, York, Reading, Fredericktown (Maryland), and New York.

LIBRARY COMPANY OF PHILADELPHIA

Brig Nancy, N. Cooper to Madeira.
Sloop Lovely Peggy, A. Clarkson to Maryland.
Brig Philadelphia Packet, J. Harrison to South-Carolina.
Ship Ann, G. Forten to Ditto.
Sloop Speedwell, J. Sooy, Jun. to Ditto.
Brig Nancy, H. Dougherty to Barcelona.
Schooner Charming Nancy, J. Mullowny to Halifax.

By Authority.

NEVER PERFORMED BEFORE.

By the AMERICAN COMPANY,
At the NEW THEATRE, in Southwark,
On FRIDAY, the Twenty-Fourth of April, will be
presented, A TRAGEDY written by the late ingenious
Mr. Thomas Godfrey, of this city, called the

PRINCE of PARTHIA.

The PRINCIPAL CHARACTERS by Mr. HALLAM,
Mr. DOUGLASS, Mr. WALL, Mr. MORRIS,
Mr. ALLYN, Mr. TOMLINSON, Mr. BROAD-
BELT, Mr. GREVILLE, Mrs. DOUGLASS,
Mrs. MORRIS, Miss WAINWRIGHT, and
Miss CHEER.

To which will be added, A Ballad Opera called

The CONTRIVANCES.

To begin exactly at Seven o'Clock.--Vivant Rex & Regina.

April 23.

TO BE LETT,

TWO pasture LOTTS. situated near the Lower Ferry road,
on the first lane to the southward as you enter said road
from the commons land of Andrew Elliott's late in the

Advertisement in the Pennsylvania Journal and Weekly Advertiser,
April 23, 1767. The Southwark Theater, on Cedar (South) Street west of Fourth,
was built in 1766 for David Douglass and his American Company. Midway in the
first season, the group advertised performances of The Prince of Parthia, a tragedy
in blank verse recounting the love of a king's son for a captive maiden. The play
had been written by Thomas Godfrey, Jr. (1736–1763), in Philadelphia in 1759.

HISTORICAL SOCIETY OF PENNSYLVANIA

III

When a gentleman came to Philadelphia in 1747 to offer lessons not only in dancing but in "the noble art and science of defence, and pursuit of the small sword," Samuel Foulke, a leading Quaker, avowed that such evils would open the gates to a whole train of sins, including the wasting of time and all the afflictions of worldliness.[51] But Quaker attitudes themselves continued to undergo a gradual change. While some affluent Friends departed the meetings for the greater freedom of the Church of England, others such as Joseph Fox, who was censured by the Friends in 1759 for supporting the war with France, remained within the Society but adopted a mode of life that became more and more inconsistent with old Quaker precepts. In spite of their dogmatic utterances wealthy Quakers generally owned elegant houses, drank the best wines, and set luxurious tables. Their dress, though somber in hue, was stylishly cut from the finest materials. A good example of the new worldliness was Israel Pemberton, Jr. While consistently opposing all the arts, he had in 1747 purchased Clarke Hall on the southwest corner of Third and Chestnut Streets. Built in 1694, this attractive residence was surrounded by formal gardens. In reality, wealthy Quakers were increasingly hard to distinguish from their non-Quaker neighbors.[52]

Charles Norris is another example. His large three-story Georgian mansion on Chestnut Street between Fourth and Fifth contained a handsome wild-cherry staircase in its spacious hall and was gracefully furnished throughout. Back of the house were a greenhouse and a hothouse with pineapples, both buildings heated against the cold. Next to such mansions as these or in nearby courts and alleys stood the less pretentious residences and even the dwellings of the poor.

One of the most elegant of all the prerevolutionary town houses in Philadelphia was the mansion built by Charles Stedman and later purchased by Samuel Powel. Excepting two other dwellings, this imposing house and its gardens occupied the entire block on Third Street between Spruce and Willing's Alley. It was built in the usual manner of Philadelphia houses with red brick walls and white trimming. Inside, Powel made it a place of striking beauty with mahogany wainscoting, paneled pine walls painted in soft colors, and bas-relief plastered ceilings. Powel, grandson of the "rich carpenter" of the same name, occupied the house after returning from Europe in 1766. He used the wealth accumulated by his father and grandfather to grace his dwelling with Chippendale furniture, paintings by artists of renown, and costly carpets and rugs.[53]

Besides richly decorating their houses, Philadelphia's wealthy men of every faith also took great pride in their fine collections of books. Outstanding was the library of the Quaker Isaac Norris, Jr., a scholarly man, competent in Latin, Greek, Hebrew, and French. His collection was passed on to his daughter, the wife of lawyer and revolutionary "Pennsylvania Farmer" John Dickinson. The latter in 1785 presented a portion of the books to Dickinson

The second-floor front room taken from Samuel Powel's house, now in-stalled at the Philadelphia Museum of Art. Another room from the Powel house is in the Metropolitan Museum of Art in New York. The actual house on Third Street between Spruce and Willing's Alley has been restored by the Philadelphia Society for the Preservation of Landmarks and is open to the public.

College in Carlisle, Pennsylvania. The Rev. Richard Peters also owned a superb library, and Attorney-General Tench Francis could boast of a law library of more than 300 volumes. Christopher Marshall owned even more books of a miscellaneous character, and Lloyd Zachary had probably the best medical collection in town, most of which he left to the Pennsylvania Hospital.[54]

But for all one's fine town house with its rich furnishings and large library, the true mark of having arrived was the ownership of a country estate. Patterned after the great country seats of Old England, such mansions as have been preserved are today within the metropolitan area. In the eighteenth century they were within an hour's ride of the city, for example, on the banks of the Schuylkill or near Germantown. Most of the estates were farms as well as country homes, well stocked with horses, cows, and sheep, attended by indentured servants. In the mansions some of the landlords had collections of art bought in Europe. Outside the houses there were invariably large flower gardens, greenhouses, and fishponds. The country seats not only were places where the wealthy could go for the joys of country life, but also served as refuges when epidemics struck the city.[55]

Like persons of their station everywhere the Philadelphia gentry were lavish entertainers. Occasions like the sumptuous party given by Gov. James Hamilton in 1752 in honor of the king's birthday were not uncommon. Following the dinner at his country estate at Bush Hill, where in the early twentieth century the United States Mint would stand along Spring Garden Street west of Sixteenth, a grand ball and supper were held in the Long Gallery of the State House. Great banquets were given for incoming and outgoing governors and other dignitaries, and special events were similarly observed. In 1746, for instance, Gov. George Thomas celebrated the victory of Culloden Moor with a banquet for a hundred guests. Similarly, the Corporation of Philadelphia in 1757 "genteely entertained" Major-General Lord Loudoun, four colonial governors, and a number of high-ranking officers of the British army.[56]

Samuel Powel *(1738–1793), copy of the portrait painted in Rome (1764) by Angelica Kauffmann (1741–1807). Grandson of a Quaker carpenter, Powel was the last colonial mayor of Philadelphia and the first to hold the office under the new government in 1789.*

PHILADELPHIA SOCIETY FOR THE PRESERVATION OF LANDMARKS

Such entertainments were admittedly exclusive, but there were pastimes that could be enjoyed by all levels of society. Skating in winter and swimming in summer were both popular sports. Alexander Graydon recalled that Philadelphia had "the best and most elegant skaters in the world," and perhaps because of so many opportunities, excellent swimmers as well. Franklin took great pride in his skill as a skater and a swimmer. Although not allowed to frequent the places where males went swimming, girls were permitted to bathe in the ocean when the family vacationed on the Jersey shore.[57] For the spectator there was occasional bull-baiting, bear-baiting, and cock-fighting. But above all there was horse racing; along what is now Race Street and later at Centre Square, sportsmen would gather to bet on their favorite pacers.[58]

Some gentlemen kept race horses as well as coach and riding horses in their stables, and this ownership of horses reflects, in part, the class lines in Philadelphia. If they had them at all, the lower classes were able to own only an occasional work horse. Those who could afford horses added sleighriding to their winter pleasures, and throughout the year moved about town and to the country in sulkies and carriages whose swiftness was annoyingly impeded by the rutted condition of the roads. By the 1750s the very wealthy began to acquire luxurious coaches which naturally excited the envy of the less affluent. There were only eight four-wheeled vehicles in Philadelphia in 1736; twenty-five years later almost forty private carriages were in use. The rising demand for vehicles of all types gave impetus to the carriage-making trade in Philadelphia, despite the fact that many continued to be imported from England.[59]

The rage for carriages reflected the desire as well as the ability of Philadelphia's emergent upper class to emulate the social forms of the mother country. So did the Philadelphia Dancing Assemblies, first held in 1748. An institution whose social exclusiveness continues to the present day, the first Assembly had fifty-nine subscribers, none of whom was a Quaker. The list included such nabobs as Dr. Phineas Bond (brother of Thomas), Joseph Shippen, William Plumstead, James Hamilton, Archibald McCall, William Allen, Richard Peters, Lynford Lardner, and David Franks. Although tradition maintains that the first dance was held at the home of John Swift, treasurer of the Assemblies, most of the early affairs took place at Andrew Hamilton's warehouse. Light refreshments were served and music was provided for by a levy on the members. At one of the first Assemblies Anne Shippen Willing, wife of Mayor Charles Willing, had the honor of leading off the dance with Gov. James Hamilton. Also in attendance was the noted beauty Mrs. Jekyll, granddaughter of Edward Shippen, the city's first mayor.[60] Her marriage to a brother of Sir Joseph Jekyll, one-time secretary to Queen Anne, had given her the English association so greatly esteemed by America's upper class.

Writing of the Philadelphia of the 1720s, the prominent historian Carl Bridenbaugh states that in the city "there was little gaiety and less elegance; a dreary commercialism, clothed in the austere garb of Quaker principles, permeated the very air."[61] The same could no longer be said of Philadelphia twenty-five years later. Education, science, the arts, the pretentious emulation of the social mores of old England by a self-conscious minority of name and wealth, all of these contributed by the 1750s to the making of an unmistakably vibrant city.

I V

Philadelphia society by 1750, though no longer a tight circle of Quakers, was nonetheless closely knit. By then although many of their fathers were of humble origin, most members of the upper class were born to wealth and position. The importance of family or lineage separated the middle-class man who had attained wealth by his own means from the man who simply inherited it from his parents or grandparents. As with the Quakers, marriage ties among the non-Quakers tightened the circle of their society. The subscribers to the first Assembly offer a case in point. John Inglis, a director of the Assembly, was married to Catherine McCall, sister of Archibald McCall and daughter of George McCall, head of one of the city's leading merchant families. William Plumstead, another merchant, married Catherine's sister Mary in 1753, and the next year another sister, Eleanor, became the wife of Andrew Eliot, son of a Scottish nobleman. Col. Joseph Shippen, who married Jane Galloway, was the brother of Mrs. Charles Willing. Chief Justice William Allen married Anne Hamilton, daughter of the noted lawyer Andrew Hamilton. Anne's brother was James Hamilton, governor of the province from 1748 to 1754 and 1759 to 1763. In 1766 Allen's daughter married John Penn, grandson of the founder. These were but a few of the family connections that formed the web of Philadelphia's society.[62]

Not all of society, of course, enjoyed the manifold delights of life—the Dancing Assemblies, for example—that the city at mid-century could provide for those who could afford them. Philadelphia's upper class provided the glitter. The less wealthy—smaller merchants, traders, shopkeepers, some artisans, professional men and clergymen not of the front rank, lesser officials, teachers—provided much of the substance.

The more prestigious upper middle class included the talented craftsmen, the silversmiths and goldsmiths, the watch and clockmakers, the printers, instrument makers, and makers of coaches and fine furniture. Some of the more illustrious among them are frequently classed with the gentry, who were merchants and the owners of land and property. Amassing considerable wealth, they participated in civic and philanthropic undertakings and were patrons and members of various organizations. Silversmiths Philip Syng and John Leacock and clockmaker Thomas Stretch, for example, became members of the fashionable Colony in Schuylkill.

By the middle of the eighteenth century Philadelphia craftsmen were known throughout the colonies. Philadelphia cabinetmakers, many of them Quakers, had a reputation for fashioning durable furniture of fine workmanship and excellent design.[63] Especially distinguished were the city's silversmiths. Catering to a Quaker clientele, Joseph Richardson was noted for the beauty and simplicity of his designs. Philip Syng in 1752 made the silver inkstand for the provincial Assembly that would later be used in signing the Declaration of Independence. John Leacock, whose shop was the Sign of the Golden Cup in Front Street, the center of the city's silversmiths and goldsmiths, is remembered not only for his silver pieces, but as the author of *The Fall of British Tyranny: or, American Liberty Triumphant*, a popular play of 1776.[64] Another outstanding artisan, a craftsman in pewter, was Cornelius Bradford, who worked at his Sign of the Dish in Second Street opposite the George Tavern.[65]

Among Philadelphia's excellent clockmakers was Thomas Stretch, already mentioned, who in 1753 made the State House clock, with its dials at the east and west ends of the main building connected by rods to the clock movement in the middle of the building. Edward Duffield, like so many craftsmen of his day, not only produced his specialty, clocks, but was active in other affairs. He was a member of the American Philosophical Society and created perhaps the first commemorative medal in America, representing Col. John Armstrong's defeat of the Indians at Kittanning in 1756. Just beginning his career as a maker of clocks, watches, and other fine instruments was Owen Biddle, who some years later, as a mathematician, would be associated with David Rittenhouse in observing the 1769 transit of Venus.[66]

Less prestigious but more typical of Philadelphia's middle class were the small merchants, shopkeepers, taverners, and others of moderate income, who like the craftsmen lived with their families and apprentices at their places of business. Hanging out over the sidewalks, decorative, descriptive signs advertised many a tradesman's specialty. Wives and daughters frequently helped in the shops, and millinery and dressmaking were almost exclusively in the hands of widows and maiden ladies. Mary Cahell from Dublin, for example, worked for Mr. Burk, a peruke maker on Front Street, and made hats and bonnets, cloaks, bags for gentlemen's hair and wigs, and turbans for Negroes. Occasionally taverns were run by women, usually widows who took over the management after a husband's death. For the most part, however, women kept house and managed the family.

The skilled workmen, called mechanics or artisans, formed the largest part of the middle class. Prominent among these were the men who performed the skilled tasks in shipbuilding. In 1747 Elias Bland, a prominent London businessman, placed an order for a ship with the Quaker merchant John Reynell. James West was hired to construct the seventy-five-foot vessel at his shipyard at the foot of Vine Street, and contracts were let for outfitting the ship. Among those hired to outfit the vessel were Samuel Chandler, joiner; Joseph Oldman, blacksmith; Samuel Austin, blockmaker; and Henry Wells, carver. John Ridge and William Sims provided the rigging and Abraham Mason the sails; the chandlers were Henry Elves and William Spofford.[67]

Among the most numerous craftsmen were the coopers who supplied the barrels and tubs in which were shipped sugar, molasses, rum, and most every kind of produce. The demand was enormous, and cooperages dotted the waterfront. Their lumber was amply supplied by the white oak trees of the forests of Pennsylvania and New Jersey. Besides supplying the American market, coopers made barrels for overseas purchasers chiefly in the West Indies but in Europe as well.

Nearly everyone who worked in eighteenth-century Philadelphia worked as an individual or in a family group. The one-man workshop or store was the standard unit of labor. Even the great merchants had but a partner or two and a clerk. It was mainly in the shipyards, ropewalks, and distilleries that labor groups as large as five or ten were found. Within this individualistic scheme, the kind of work a man did largely determined his status in society.

Of slaves and most free blacks it might be said that they remained off the class ladder entirely. They were not a class in fact, but rather a caste separated from the rest of society by the ineradicable badges of race and color. That within their ranks their status varied according to occupation—from stable-hand to artisan—made no impress upon the white society they served. Next on the ladder were those indentured servants of whom some—again, according to occupation—might join in status the ranks of free unskilled labor: sailors, carters, hostlers, and others. The few indentured servants who had been artisans or mechanics in the Old World might, upon completion of their terms, open shops of their own.

Although there was social mobility beyond anything known in England, Philadelphia remained an eighteenth-century class-conscious social organism. Evidence of social distinction is clear, for example, in the city's election laws. The limitation of the franchise to a few helped fix status by delineating sharply who could share in political power. For the city, the ownership of personal property to the value of £50 was required to vote or hold office. Only about one in fifty of the inhabitants, it is estimated, met the property qualifications in Philadelphia. Furthermore, by the eve of the Revolution 10 percent of the people paying the highest taxes owned 89 percent of the taxable property. Fewer than 20 percent of Philadelphians owned their own homes, the rentals of which were a major source of income for the well-to-do.[68]

Whether they rented or owned their homes, many artisans of the "middling sort," and not a few wealthy families, used part of their houses as places of business. On Water Street, for example, Abel James, one of the foremost Quaker merchants of his day, lived on the second floor above his counting-house. By the 1760s about a fourth of the houses in Philadelphia were to be found in Mulberry Ward, which extended from Front to Seventh Streets between Mulberry (Arch) and Vine, the most populous of the city's ten wards. In the three wards lying between Mulberry and Walnut, Second and Seventh Streets, were a somewhat greater number of buildings in total. Dock Ward, between Walnut and Cedar (South), had half as many houses as Mulberry Ward and was steadily growing. The small wards bordering the waterfront—Walnut, Chestnut, High, and Lower Delaware—had developed early and remained fairly static in population during the rest of the colonial period.[69]

Within the wards containing most of the city's population, unlike the pretentious mansions of some of the wealthy, the typical Philadelphia house was of modest size, a plain, red-brick building of two or three stories with a garret. Representative of this style, Provost Smith's house had cedar shingles and was equipped with gutters and downspouts that protected pedestrians from the runoff in rainstorms. The woodwork, inside and out, was generally painted white; the rooms were plastered and whitewashed. Wallpaper was not yet in use, and though many houses had rag rugs, carpets were rare. Despite the monotony of the city's gridiron blocks and row houses, Peter Kalm in 1749 found that Philadelphia's aspect was agreeable and equal to any town in Europe. In 1755 the city's brick houses and pent roofs and shops reminded Thomas Pownall of Cheapside, London.[70]

Housing, of course, was one measure of class. So in Philadelphia was church membership, particularly at the top of the ladder. Most of the moneyed people, other than the Quakers, were Anglicans. In London, Thomas Penn himself, son of the founder and now chief proprietor, became an apostate from Quakerism and in 1751 joined the Church of England. In a few years Christ Church in Philadelphia found its membership increasing to such an extent that the building of St. Peter's, initially a chapel to the east of Christ Church, was begun on the southwest corner of Third and Pine Streets in 1758. The smaller St. Paul's, on the east side of Third below Walnut, was added in the 1760s.

St. Peter's, where services were first held in 1761, lacks Christ Church's imposing effects, but it is a most dignified and pleasing structure. Its designer, Robert Smith, a Quaker emigrant from Glasgow, had but recently built Nassau Hall at Princeton and would be responsible for other buildings from Providence to Williamsburg. A member of the Carpenters' Company, Smith probably had the best claim of any builder in the city to priority in achieving the transition from master carpenter to architect. St. Peter's is noted particularly for its Palladian window on the east front and its exceptional beauty within.[71]

As for Quakerism, in spite of the formidable social stature of several of the old families, membership in the meetings was in relative decline. The Hill Meeting House on Pine Street in the Society Hill area was erected in 1753 to serve the only new Quaker congregation to be added in Philadelphia before the Revolution. Two years later the Quakers tore down the Great Meeting House at Second and High Streets and replaced it with the Greater Meeting House. Nevertheless, by mid-century they comprised only a quarter of the city's population.[72]

Presbyterianism on the other hand continued its growth. Counting among its members some of Philadelphia's wealthiest citizens—most notably William Allen—this largest religious group in Philadelphia more nearly reflected the class structure of the city as a whole. For a time Presbyterians divided over the issue of evangelism. Drawing heavily from the middle and lower classes, the New Lights erected a church at Third and Arch Streets in 1750, adding a steeple two years later.[73] The more wealthy Presbyterians remained with the conservative Old Side, headed by the scholarly Rev. Francis Alison. But as enthusiasm generated by George Whitefield ran its course, such disputes faded. By 1758 the two groups of Presbyterians in the city achieved a rapprochement. In 1763 Whitefield himself, visiting Philadelphia for the seventh time, was welcomed even by the Anglican clergy who had been a target of his attacks on previous occasions.[74]

If religious enthusiasm subsided after the Great Awakening, religious prejudice remained. Catholicism, in the minds of many, still invoked memories of James II and Jacobitism. Particularly when England was at war with the Catholic Bourbon powers—a condition practically endemic in the eighteenth century—anti-Catholicism emerged with renewed vigor. Word of Maj.-Gen. Edward Braddock's defeat in the summer of 1755 aroused such fears that an anti-Catholic mob attempted to destroy St. Joseph's and was turned back only through the persuasion of some brave Quakers. Two years later known Catholics were not allowed to serve in the militia, though they were obliged to pay the militia tax.[75]

Despite such occasional evidences of tension and suspicion, it was generally acknowledged that all religions were entitled to religious freedom as guaranteed by Penn's Charter of Liberties, and the English, Irish, and German Catholics continued worshipping at their chapel. In 1757 Fr. Robert Harding, who had succeeded the Rev. Joseph Greaton in 1750, tore down the original St. Joseph's and built a larger one in its place. Father Harding's support of the Pennsylvania Hospital and other civic enterprises did much to soften dislike of Catholics, and under his guidance the parishioners gave their neighbors no cause to question their loyalty.[76]

Like the Catholics, both the German Reformed and the Lutherans built new houses of worship during these years, and in 1750 the latter installed at St. Michael's an organ brought from Germany. Meanwhile the proportion of unchurched Philadelphians seemed to grow. Gottlieb Mittelberger, who had accompanied the St. Michael's organ to America and who had found Philadelphia's court sessions amusing, was astonished at the numbers of Philadelphians who had no belief in "a true God," in heaven or hell, and who did not even know the Bible. Deism, of course, had its attractions for Philadelphia's cosmopolitan elite, while at the bottom of the social ladder the churches frequently failed to reach the city's burgeoning population. In any case it is a significant fact that Philadelphia by the time of the Revolution had no more than eighteen churches, large and small—one for every 1700 inhabitants.

With the exception of sporadic anti-Catholic outbursts, Philadelphians at mid-century, true to the founder's purpose and in the spirit of the Enlightenment, were moderate and tolerant in their religious attitudes. Mittelberger was struck by the absence of bigotry. "To speak the truth," he wrote, "one seldom hears or sees a quarrel among them [which is] the result of the liberty which they enjoy and which makes them all equal."[77]

Other visitors made similar comments. Lord Adam Gordon, who in 1765 had denominated Philadelphia "a great and noble City," went on to acclaim her "one of the wonders of the World." He particularly noted "the Magnificence and diversity of places of Worship (for here all Religions who profess the name of Christ are tolerated equally) . . .":

It is not an hundred years since the first tree was cut where the City now Stands, and at this time it consists of more than three thousand Six hundred Houses.—It is daily encreasing, and I doubt not in time, will reach all the way, from River to River,—the great and foreseeing Founder of it, Mr. Penn having wisely laid out the Space so far, which is daily taking and filling.[78]

Lord Adam's words serve as a reminder that although Philadelphia was indeed a true city, there was still plenty of "Space" to be filled in. The point needs making, for no true picture of mid-century Philadelphia can be drawn if it neglects the lingering "country" aspects that reflected its recent founding at the edge of a wilderness. Though visitors naturally emphasized its rapid growth, they also recognized that it had not yet lost the charm of its country origin.

Behind the houses of the more well-to-do, for example, could be found gardens and orchards, as well as outbuildings, such as a barn or stable, where chickens, geese, a cow, and perhaps a horse were kept. A few private gardens, like the "pretty pleasure garden" on the proprietor's estate at Springettsbury, along the Schuylkill north of the city proper, were open to the public; while some of the public gardens, like Cherry Garden which extended from Front Street to the Delaware, became retreats where one could capture a bit of rural serenity.[79] At Walnut and Sixth nearly six acres of ground, today's Washington Square, served as a potter's field. Jacob Shoemaker pastured his cows here until complaints forced the city corporation to charge him rent for its use. Two small plots between Chestnut and Walnut near the outskirts of the city were set aside by the proprietors in 1755 as a camping ground for visiting Indians. Beyond the built-up area to the west was a forest known as the Governor's Woods.[80]

Philadelphia then, for all its citified ways, was still close in time and setting to its pastoral origin. The land retained its ancient appeal. The artisan dreamed of a farm of his own, just as the wealthy merchant saw riches in western land schemes. Philadelphians would look askance at impediments to western settlement, be they in the guise of French power, Indian land claims, or official British policy.

But Philadelphia also fronted a seaway to the Atlantic. As an outpost of empire, the diverse city would respond in diverse ways as the outside world pressed on her from both east and west. In the successive crises to come her buoyant citizenry would simply bypass their outmoded and ineffectual government. In an effort to capture the essence of this baffling new phenomenon, Mittelberger quotes a saying he had heard in the province: "Pennsylvania is heaven for farmers, paradise for artisans, and hell for officials and preachers."[81] The coming years would generously attest that Mittelberger's saying was not far off the mark.

V

In the year 1701 when Penn bestowed his new charter of incorporation upon his town, England and France were getting set to undertake the second in a series of world wars that would not end until 1815 and the Battle of Waterloo. Four of these wars occurred during America's colonial period, while a by-product of the fifth was America's independence. But all of them one way or the other intimately affected the life of the American people.

Philadelphia of all the major cities of English America had the least capabilities of military defense. Boston had its Castle William, New York and Charleston had their various shore batteries, but Philadelphia long had nothing. The city's exposed condition was the product of three factors: first, her geographical location away from the sea gave her a false sense of security; second, Quaker principles impeded military preparedness; and third, money bills for defense were blocked in the legislature by a chronic deadlock between the Assembly and the proprietors over the power of the purse.

Therefore when in 1747 French and Spanish privateers cruised off the Delaware Capes and even raided plantations up the river in New Castle County, the citizens themselves acted. In November Franklin came forth with his famous pamphlet *Plain Truth*, in which he proposed a volunteer association for defense. Popular reaction was immediate and enthusiastic. James Logan approved Franklin's proposal, and it was hoped that other so-called defense Quakers would give their support. Within a week after *Plain Truth* appeared, Franklin, William Allen, provincial Secretary Richard Peters, and other non-Quaker leaders worked out a plan for an association for defense and submitted it to various groups in the city—tradesmen, mechanics, merchants, and gentlemen—for their endorsement. On November 24, 500 inhabitants signed the association, and in a matter of days more than 1000 men had joined.[82]

The associators were divided into companies in accordance with Philadelphia's wards and townships. Company officers were chosen by the rank and file. Among these were a number of members of the city corporation, such as Capt. Charles Willing and Thomas Bond. The company officers in turn gathered and elected their regimental officers: thus Abraham Taylor became colonel; Thomas Lawrence, lieutenant-colonel; and Samuel McCall, major. Each company had its own colors with some distinctive emblem, such as a lion, eagle, or elephant. Early in December the associators presented themselves in military formation to the provincial Council and received its approval and encouragement.[83]

The foremost problems facing the association and the city were fortifications and supplies. Two batteries were begun immediately. The smaller one, under Society Hill at today's Lombard Street, was completed in three days. The larger "Association Battery" was erected just south of the city below Gloria Dei Church; it eventually mounted twenty-seven cannons.[84] But procuring the cannons was more difficult than erecting fortifications. Franklin answered the need by arranging Philadelphia's first lottery, managed by William Allen, Charles Willing, Edward Shippen, and others. The city corporation, holder of the largest bloc of tickets, was one of the lottery winners, and to evidence its civic concern it turned its prize back to the association. James Logan bought the largest number of tickets by an individual. When the Union Fire Company subscribed, only one of the Quaker members showed up to register an objection.[85]

With the lottery proceeds the association ordered cannons from London, twelve of which were received in the summer of 1748. The provincial Council and city corporation already had sent appeals for guns to the proprietors, but their petitions were denied.[86] Thirty-nine new Spanish cannons ordered from Boston eventually arrived in Philadelphia, and a large thirty-two-pounder was contributed by the Colony in Schuylkill. To serve as a stopgap until the guns from London and Boston came, a committee consisting of Franklin, Thomas Lawrence, William Allen, and Abraham Taylor visited Gov. George Clinton of New York to ask his assistance. That worthy first refused, "but at a Dinner with his Council where there was great Drinking of Madeira Wine," Franklin later recalled, "he soften'd by degrees, and said he would lend us Six. After a few more Bumpers he advanc'd to Ten. And at length he very good-naturedly conceded Eighteen."[87]

Continued harassment of shipping by French and Spanish privateers during the spring and summer of 1748 in the waters near New Castle dramatized the need for strong defenses. A poem in the *Pennsylvania Gazette* expressed the fear that had seized the city:

> —While scarce a day but fresh Alarms
> Of Blood and Slaughter shock our Ears;
> Our Foes around us shine in Arms,
> And every Bosom beats with Fears.
> Some dread the butch'ring *Indians* most,
> And some the *Spaniards* on the Coast. . . .[88]

News of the Peace of Aix-la-Chapelle finally arrived in August 1748, and Philadelphians once again returned to their peacetime pursuits.

Peace, however, was of but a short duration. With the outbreak of the French and Indian War in 1754 Philadelphia was again confronted with the problem of living in an empire at war. This time the main danger to Pennsylvania came from the western frontier, where the French were moving to secure the Ohio Valley. Defense once more became the prime issue. Franklin, now an assemblyman, in 1755 managed through the legislature the first militia bill in Pennsylvania's history. Believing the measure to be too democratic— the men, New England style, elected their own officers—Gov. Robert Hunter Morris instituted "independent companies" under proprietary, not Assembly control. Philadelphia was now treated to the portentous scene of the Assembly militia's and the proprietary companies' staging competitive military exercises.

The Philadelphia City Regiment elected Franklin its colonel, and in an excess of military ardor fired several rounds before Franklin's door. This affectionate display did not altogether please the new colonel, for as he rue-fully explained, the resulting concussion "shook down and broke several Glasses of my Electrical Apparatus."[89]

While the first years of the French and Indian War proved a disaster for the English cause, Philadelphia became a city of refugees. There were the surviving soldiers from General Braddock's calamitous defeat along the Monongahela. There were civilian refugees from the West, driven from their homes by the aroused Indians, and there were some 450 of the 1000 Acadians whom the English, fearing them loyal to France, expelled from their Nova Scotia homes. Housed in a row of one-story wooden buildings on Pine Street and distrusted by British officialdom, the unfortunate Acadians found in Philadelphia's Quaker citizens their main protection and sympathy. Longfel-low's heroine Evangeline, it may be recalled, discovered her dying Gabriel in the Friends' Alms House in Philadelphia.

Wartime Philadelphia was not only burdened by refugees. Late in 1756 the city was ordered to house the new Royal American Regiment, British regu-lars recruited in the colonies. In compliance, the Assembly designated that they be quartered at inns, but the innkeepers refused to house the soldiers at the legislated fee. With the men freezing in makeshift quarters and sick with smallpox, Lt.-Col. Henry Bouquet appealed unsuccessfully to Mayor Plum-stead and the city corporation, and then turned to Governor Denny, who had succeeded Governor Morris. Denny's authorization to use private homes if public accommodations could not be found raised a predictable chorus of protest throughout the city. From New York, Lord Loudoun thundered that he was prepared to march troops to Philadelphia to seize the necessary quar-ters. Finally, when a committee appointed by the Assembly and headed by Franklin persuaded the tavern keepers to accept the prescribed rates, the affair blew over about as quickly as it had arisen.

The following year, in response to directives from London, army bar-racks, known popularly as the "British Barracks," were built in the Northern Liberties, around the present Third and Green Streets. The quartering of troops in Pennsylvania never again became a major issue with British authori-ties as it did in some other American colonies.[90]

The year 1758 proved a turning point for the British cause in America. Philadelphia, where each successive British victory was celebrated by fire-works, was the gala scene of preparation for Brig.-Gen. John Forbes's success-ful reduction of Fort Duquesne, renamed Fort Pitt. Philadelphians gave the ailing Forbes a hero's welcome on his return to the city. But the euphoric mood was shortly dissipated when Forbes died on March 11, 1759. Amid general mourning, he was interred with fitting ceremony at Christ Church.

The British victory ratified at Paris in 1763 did not spare Philadelphia from further alarms. The frontier was again in flames as Chief Pontiac led his followers in a desperate effort to contain the whites' incessant penetration into the interior. The city once more filled with refugees from the West. Among them was a small group of "Moravian Indians," who sought succor in the city both from Indians angry at their pacifism and from the white frontiersmen.

The Paxton Expedition, *engraved by Henry Dawkins (act. 1753–1786),
1764. This satirical cartoon, which depicts Franklin proclaiming his delegation's
success to the nervous citizens of Philadelphia, is one of the earliest street scenes of
the city. The Court House is shown in the middle of Market Street with the market*

stalls extending westward. The Greater Meeting House (1754)—which replaced the Great Meeting House (1696)—is at the southwest corner of Second and Market, and the house of John Speakman, apothecary, is shown at the northwest corner. The public pillory appears in the center foreground near the New Jersey stalls.

LIBRARY COMPANY OF PHILADELPHIA

Their need for such protection was vividly illustrated when angry frontiers-men massacred the defenseless and peaceful remnants of the Conestoga tribe at Lancaster. The so-called Paxton Boys—"Christian White Savages," Frank-lin called them—marched toward Philadelphia with the avowed purpose of destroying the Moravian Indians.

Philadelphia was thrown into a panic. The citizenry called upon Franklin to organize a defense. Within a few days he revived the association with eight companies of volunteers. Even some of the Quakers were seen shouldering muskets and marching with the militia.

When the Paxton Boys approached the city early in February 1764, they found the ford over the Schuylkill into Philadelphia so well guarded that they moved upriver and came by way of Germantown. Here Franklin met them at the head of a committee, and, as he said, "The fighting face we put on and the reasonings we used with the insurgents . . . turned them back and restored quiet to the city."[91] Soon afterward the Indians were defeated by Colonel Bouquet at Bushy Run and peace was restored on the frontier. As for the defenseless Moravian Indians, they were sent back to the frontier and were later destroyed during the turmoil of the American Revolution.

Philadelphia's experiences during the long and arduous French wars, experiences for which her governmental institutions proved inadequate, pro-vided a schooling for the trials yet to come during the years of the American Revolution. Philadelphians and all Pennsylvanians learned invaluable lessons in war and defense, lessons that included levying taxes, recruiting volunteers, organizing a militia, and erecting fortifications. As a time of testing the wars reinforced the process of maturation leading to Philadelphia's leadership in the nation soon to be born.

The crises solved by citizen initiative ultimately led to a more responsive governmental structure. The electoral base of the city broadened as the war-time economy enabled more men to acquire the means to qualify for the franchise. In consequence the mechanic element that would figure promi-nently in the American Revolution became a force in public affairs. The influence of the Quakers on the other hand, now but a fraction of the popula-tion, diminished.

The middle years of the eighteenth century had seen the flowering of colonial Philadelphia. Under an ever-growing cosmopolitanism, the city at-tained preeminence among the cities of colonial America. Not only was its material growth phenomenal, but its advancement in cultural attainments was as striking. The advent of the College of Philadelphia and the veritable explo-sion in the number of books owned by Philadelphians epitomized its intellec-tual growth. Already the cultural center of colonial America, Philadelphia would soon as well become the political center of the colonies from whence, in deeds as well as words, Liberty would be proclaimed "thro' all the Land to all the Inhabitants thereof."

The Revolutionary City
1765-1783

by Harry M. Tinkcom

> . . . they are determined to fall upon every measure to raise a
> revenue in America. We are to be their grand Milch Cow but if they are
> not prudent in their modes we shall turn dry upon their hands.
>
> — WILLIAM ALLEN

> It is happy for us that we have Boston in the front & Virginia in the rear
> to defend us. We are placed where Cowards ought to be placed, in the
> middle.
>
> — WILLIAM BRADFORD, JR. [1]

For many reasons Philadelphia was destined to play a stellar role
in the American Revolution. Its strategic location, wealth, industrial and commercial importance, large and cosmopolitan population, and professional and business classes combined to make it after 1774 the
hub of America's revolutionary activity.

The forces and circumstances that led to the attainment of Philadelphia's
critical position were as much a part of the city's prewar history as they were
of the Revolution itself. At the beginning of hostilities the city was successful
in so many areas of achievement that its potential for leadership within the
colonies was clearly evident. Ironically, though, many of the people who were
most responsible for this success, the erstwhile commercial and political leaders of the city, withdrew or were shoved aside by the revolutionary stream
of change grown so violent that it could not be navigated by the old methods.
From backwaters and eddies they watched new men, along with a few of their
own group, assume control of a movement that had started years before as a
result of parliamentary measures.

I

In 1763 the British Ministry, at the urging of George Grenville, chancellor
of the exchequer, had projected a defense plan for North America which
required the recruitment and maintenance of an army of 10,000 men. To the
British, a people already heavily taxed, it seemed reasonable to shift part of

the cost to the direct beneficiaries of the protective force, the colonists. Parliament responded with measures that seriously and directly affected all colonial entrepreneurs. The three pieces of legislation that produced the most violent reactions were the Stamp Act of March 1765, the Townshend Revenue Acts of June 1767, and modifications of the Tea Act in 1773.

Philadelphia's response to these and to various other irritants showed an intensity of feeling, expressed by people of all classes, that could only emanate from a community conscious of having suffered deep and serious injury. Proof of this was found in the ease with which chiming bells and pounding drums could summon capacity crowds of approximately 8000 people to the State House Yard to act on the latest developments. It found expression in the newspapers, then becoming more aware of the influence they wielded in helping to form public opinion. It burst forth passionately in the taverns and howled through the streets with the mobs. It put in ferment a city whose government was complacent and content, and generated mass meetings as vehicles of expression and committees as agents of force in a community that came to accept them almost as a way of life.

News of the Stamp Act was received in Philadelphia with resentment and anger. The first direct parliamentary levy on America, it taxed almost everything written or printed on paper or vellum—newspapers, diplomas, legal documents, licenses, almanacs, and even playing cards. Everyone was affected. Moreover the Stamp Act struck a city in distress after five years of economic dislocation. The close of the British army's active campaigning against the French in North America in 1760 had proven a mixed blessing. Economically it meant the abrupt withdrawal from colonial commerce of unprecedented quantities of specie, with which the army by purchasing subsistence and equipment stimulated economic activity everywhere in British North America. That resource removed, the colonies' perennial unfavorable balance of trade with Britain promptly pulled hard money back across the Atlantic. The colonial demand for bills of exchange then drove up the exchange rate unfavorably for colonial currencies. Merchants' debts to Britain became harder to pay; merchants' inventories proved to be overstocked. In turn the sudden end of wartime prosperity left the colonial customers in city and countryside deeply in debt to the merchants. The prices of imported manufactured goods fell and virtually eliminated profit margins. Despite this British exporters, accustomed to large colonial sales, continued to ship goods to America at practically the wartime rate. Philadelphia linen importers, for example, who had enjoyed an average markup of 33 percent in the booming war years 1758–1759 saw their markup fall to 16 percent in 1760–1762 and 13 percent in 1763–1765. Meanwhile the Currency Act of 1764 affirmed a British determination, already evident enough during the war, to curb the unsatisfactory colonial paper money.[2]

Meanwhile also, Philadelphia's West Indies trade, from the beginning a pivot of the city's commerce, was undergoing long-term changes that were discouraging. The decline of the productivity and prosperity of the British

Seventh-day Evenings for that purpose.

The FLYING MACHINE.

This is to give NOTICE to the PUBLIC,

THAT the FLYING MACHINE, kept by JOHN BARNHILL, in Elm ſtreet, near Vine-ſtreet, Philadelphia ; and JOHN MASHEREW, at the Blazing ſtar, performs the Journey from Philadelphia to New-York in two days, and from thence to Philadelphia in two days alſo; a circumſtance greatly to the advantage of the traveller, as there is no water carriage, and conſequently nothing to impede the Journey. It has already been performed to the general ſatisfaction of many genteel people. They ſet off from Philadelphia and New-York on Mondays and Thurſdays, punctually at Sunriſe, and change their paſſengers at Prince Town, and return to Philadelphia and New York the following days: paſſengers paying ten ſhillings to Princeton, and ten ſhillings to Powles's Hook oppoſite to New-York, ferriage free, and three-pence each mile any diſtance between. Gentlemen and Ladies who are pleaſed to favour us with their cuſtom may depend on due attendance and civil uſage, by their humble ſervants,

$　　JOHN BARNHILL and JOHN MASHEREW.

Pennsylvania Journal, *April 16, 1767.*

sugar islands was persisting, and with it the decline of the market for Philadelphia exports. The development of new sugar-growing areas, such as northern Jamaica, and the acquisition of Dominica, Grenada, St. Vincent, and Tobago from France in 1763 could only partially offset the deterioration of the older markets. At best the traditional Philadelphia method of trading with the islands, the speculative venture in which the merchant shipped cargoes at his own risk to undetermined customers, had paid handsomely only with careful calculation of prevailing conditions in the West Indies. If rains favored the Caribbean in a given season, the islands could grow enough provisions for themselves to curtail sharply the market for mainland grainstuffs. Altogether, a speculative voyage to the Indies was as likely to result in a loss as in a profit. The glory days of the West Indies trade were over.[3]

I I

The forms of protest against the Stamp Act varied, with the first serious action taken being to prevent the use of the stamped paper. John Hughes, appointed stampman for Pennsylvania as a mistaken act of friendship on the part of Benjamin Franklin, received pointed suggestions early in September 1765 that he should resign his commission. In spite of mounting pressure and threats to his person and property, he refused. His refusal may have been buttressed by the support he received from the White Oaks, a carpenters' association. On the night of September 16 the White Oaks gathered 800 men to defend the houses of Hughes and Franklin against a mob attack. The White Oaks were not friends of the Stamp Act, but they had supported Franklin and the Quakers in efforts to rid Pennsylvania of the proprietary regime, and they would not now abandon either Franklin or a principled opposition to violence as a means of achieving political ends.[4]

On October 5 when the *Royal Charlotte* appeared off Gloucester Point with the stamped paper on board, thousands of Philadelphians rushed to a meeting in the State House Yard. There a committee was appointed to demand Hughes's resignation. He refused again, but he did agree not to carry out his duties unless the Stamp Act was being executed in the neighboring colonies. When the hated paper was later put aboard the warship *Sardine* for safekeeping, a victory had been won by the community. Of equal importance was the fact that the force of law, as represented by the mayor of Philadelphia and the governor of Pennsylvania, had not supported the agent of the Crown.

The intimidation of local officialdom was only one phase of the struggle, which ended before November 1, the date set for the enforcement of the act. After that time any business transacted without the use of stamped paper would be illegal. Consequently shipowners worked feverishly to get their vessels away, and when the deadline arrived almost all ships had been "cleared out."[5] Thereafter for a time business almost ceased.[6]

To gain support for their protest in Britain, several merchants met in November and agreed to boycott British goods until the Stamp Act was repealed. They were then joined by more than 300 merchants and shopkeepers large and small who determined to buy no British goods, with the exception of certain items necessary for continued local industrial growth, such as utensils used in manufacturing and dyestuffs.[7]

The boycott was almost of necessity coupled with a tentative movement to increase home manufactures, with emphasis on textiles. A cloth market for locally made goods was established, and the resolutions of the Sun, Fellowship, Union, Crown, and Beaver Fire Companies to discourage the purchase of lamb in order to increase the amount of wool available for manufacture were printed by newspapers almost everywhere in the colonies.[8]

Resistance and confusion prevailed in Philadelphia until it was learned early in the spring of 1766 that the Stamp Act had been repealed. The news was received with jubilation, and was celebrated with a banquet at the State

---

N. B. It is supposed the said Woman is gone off with a Man and may pass for his wife.

March 12.

ALL Persons indebted to GEORGE FULLERTON, whose accounts are above twelve months unpaid, as well as those indebted to him by bond, bill or note, are requested to discharge the same before the first of May next, otherwise they may expect to be sued without respect of persons. §8w.

March 12,

Imported in the last vessels from London, Liverpool and Bristol, and to be sold wholesale or retail on the very lowest terms for cash only, by

ALEXANDER BARTRAM,

At his shop in Market street, next door to the sign of the Indian King.

A Neat assortment of DRY GOODS, suitable for the season, Likewise a large assortment of enameled and blue and white CHINA consisting of plates and dishes choco late cups with handles and saucers; halfpint bowls and saucers; coffee cups and saucers; tea-cups and saucers; teapots; sauce-boats; sugar dishes and cream Juggs.

Also, short pipes by the box; great choice of chimney tiles; a very large assortment of glass, delph blue and white, stone, and enameled stone ware, by the crate or smaller quantity; tea; coffee and chocolate

And on the 23d of this month will begin the sales of his Pennsylvania pencil'd tea potts, bowls and sugar dishes, which for beauty of colours, and elegance of figures, &c are allowed by the nicest Judges to exceed any imported from England

N. B. Those who are indebted to Bartram and Dundas are once more earnestly intreated immediately to pay their respective debts to Alexander Bartram, otherwise, he will be laid under the disagreeable necessity, of sueing them for the same, without further notice ; he hopes this will not be thought ungenerous or severe as he intends leaving the province soon.   the6w.

The 14th of the 3d month, called March

WHEREAS JOSIAH WOOD, who left this city some years past and has not been heard of since; if the said

---

Pennsylvania Journal, March 12, 1767.

House. On that occasion many Philadelphians who had bought homespun clothing to encourage local manufactures promised to give it to the poor. This generosity was laudable but premature, for Parliament had by no means given up its intention to tax the colonies.

It tried again in 1767 with the passage of the Townshend Revenue Acts, which levied duties on glass, lead, painters' colors, paper, and tea. Philadelphia's response to these taxes lacked the explosiveness and spontaneity that had characterized the reaction to the Stamp Act. For some months after the Townshend duties went into effect in November 1767 the attitude of the

---

MADE at the Subfcriber's Glafs-Works, and now on Hand, to be fold at his Houfe in Market-Street, oppofite the Meal-Market, either wholefale or retail, between Three and Four Hundred B O X E S of W I N D O W   G L A S S, confifting of the common Sizes, 10 by 12, 9 by 11, 8 by 10, 7 by 9, 6 by 8, &c. Lamp Glafs, or any uncommon Sizes, under 16 by 18, are cut upon a fhort Notice.   Where alfo may be had, moft Sorts of Bottles, Gallon, Half Gallon, and Quart, full Meafure Half Gallon Cafe Bottles, Snuff and Muftard, Receivers and Retorts of various Sizes; alfo electrifing Globes and Tubes, &c,   As the abovementioned Glafs is of American Manufactory, it is confequently clear of the Duties the Americans fo juftly complain of, and at prefent it feems peculiarly the Intereft of America to encourage her own Manufactories, more efpecially thofe upon which Duties have been impofed, for the fole Purpofe of raifing a Revenue,

   N. B.   He alfo continues to make the Philadelphia Brafs Buttons, well noted for their Strength, fuch as were made by his deceafed Father, and are warranted for feven Years.

   Philadelphia, Auguft 10.   R I C H A R D   W I S T A R.

WE hear fome Copies are to be had in Town of the famous North-Brittons, No. 50 and 51, for publifhing which Mr. Bingley is now under Confinement in the King's Bench Prifon in London.——Inquire at the Printing-Office.

Juft imported from the Maker, and original Inventer, now in London, the rightly prepared and improved
LIQUID   TRUE   BLUE.

New York Journal and General Advertiser, *August 17, 1769.*

generality of merchants seemed to mirror that of the Philadelphia Council, which, except for one negative action, officially ignored the rising storm. Appealed to by a Boston town meeting in October, the Council replied two months later that the interests of the colonies could best be served "by diffusing a spirit of Industry and Frugality." It declined to initiate any action.[9]

Similarly, the merchants' resistance to the Townshend duties was weak until they were goaded into action by boycotts and threats of mob violence. The opposition to the duties was by no means totally lacking in leadership by prominent citizens—such as the merchants Charles Thomson and Thomas Mifflin, the printer William Bradford, Jr., and the lawyer John Dickinson. Nevertheless dissatisfaction with British revenue measures was already being turned into a vehicle for the airing of class differences at home. When merchants' protests were lukewarm, mechanics and artisans and members of the lower orders more generally could vent their dislike of the merchants' economic and political domination of the city by charging the merchants with indifference to Philadelphia's and America's self-government and security. In March 1769, pushed thus from below and from the colonies to the north, more than 300 Philadelphia merchants signed nonimportation agreements.[10] This resolve once taken, thereafter Philadelphians cooperated with effect. Comparative import-export figures for 1768–1770 show that Philadelphia stuck to nonimportation more faithfully than the other colonial ports. Philadelphians were furious when New York reneged in 1770.

One of the major forces that impelled the merchants to join in nonimportation was the influence of the Philadelphia press. Departing from their former preoccupation with the wranglings of political factions, Bradford's *Pennsylvania Journal*, David Hall's and William Sellers's *Pennsylvania Gazette*, and William Goddard's *Pennsylvania Chronicle and Universal Advertiser*, founded in 1767, emphasized imperial matters. Radical in their opposition to the Townshend Acts, they not only reported but stimulated events.[11] It was the new *Pennsylvania Chronicle* that, beginning in the early winter of 1767, published a series of letters that in their influence and circulation exceeded any publication of the revolutionary era except Thomas Paine's *Common Sense*. These, the famous "Farmer's Letters" of John Dickinson, were copied in colonial newspapers everywhere and later published in pamphlet form as *Letters from a Farmer in Pennsylvania to the Inhabitants of the British Colonies.*[12]

The "farmer" was actually an outstanding Philadelphia lawyer, but it is likely that Dickinson was too well aware of the suspicion in which lawyers were held in some quarters to write as a member of that profession. In trenchant and logical prose he constructed a brief for constitutional government that was used not only in the trial of strength with Britain over the Townshend Acts, but in other trials that sorely tested the fortitude of Americans for years to come. Dickinson advocated caution and nonviolent action, but he made it clear that the Townshend duties were unconstitutional and a dangerous innovation; that there was no difference between external and internal taxes; and that the colonies needed to unite their efforts, for the cause of one was "the cause of all." A Boston public meeting was held in Dickinson's honor. Next to Franklin, he was possibly the best known Philadelphian of the prerevolutionary era. Writing at a time when there was probably more

The Patriotic Farmer, *John Dickinson (1732–1808), engraved by James Smither (d. 1797).*

ideological agreement in America than there would be again until England had been defeated, Dickinson may well be regarded as the first "Continental" spokesman, the first prenational patriotic hero.

After the lapse of the nonimportation agreement in 1770, resistance in Philadelphia to Parliament's taxing policy waned in the face of a creeping lethargy and conservatism that was not overcome by the newspapers, the mechanics, or the active Whigs—the political opponents of British impositions. The Pennsylvania Assembly did rouse itself sufficiently to send a petition to George III in March 1771 deploring the continuing tea levy as taxation without consent.[13] But the public had a means of persuasion that was more forceful than petitions, one that required less cooperation from merchants than nonimportation agreements. This was the determination to buy smuggled Dutch tea in preference to the product offered by the British East India Company that was subject to duty. The consequent loss in sales, along with other financial difficulties, brought the company to the verge of bankruptcy. To relieve its distress Parliament allowed it, by passage of the Tea Act in 1773, to bypass the duty collected in England and to send its tea directly to selected consignees in America. This procedure eliminated the profit of the English middleman and made it possible for Americans to buy tea at lower prices than the Dutch charged.

Philadelphia, July 12, 1770.

THE Inhabitants of the City of *New-York*, having broke their Non-Importation Agreement, and thereby endangered the Liberties of all *America*, the Inhabitants of this City and County, are therefore earneftly requefted to meet in the *State-Houfe*, on SATURDAY next, at *Three* o'Clock in the Afternoon, to confider what Steps may be neceffary on the prefent alarming Occafion.

From an unidentified press, July 12, 1770.
LIBRARY COMPANY OF PHILADELPHIA

The first protests against the Tea Act came from Philadelphia and New York, where smugglers were the most active. In addition to resentment over the tax levied under the Townshend Acts, which would still be collected at American ports, there was the fear that the use of designated American wholesale consignees was the first step toward the future monopolization of all American business by the British.[14] From the time in October 1773 when Philadelphians were warned that tea ships in England were loaded for transit to America[15] until one arrived in the Delaware River in December, the opposition to the Tea Act was carried on by the press, mass meetings, and committees. Once again, as in 1765, there was an opportunity to act directly upon individuals, in this case the tea consignees, and at a meeting in the State House Yard on October 16 a committee was appointed to persuade them to refuse the cargo. Some, notably Thomas Wharton, perhaps the most prominent merchant among them, did so within a few days, but others required "farther explanation."[16] The firm of Henry Drinker and Abel James, another prominent merchant house, did not surrender its agency until December. James was finally convinced by the appearance of a hostile crowd in front of his place.[17] If the tea were stored in warehouses, "A Countryman" warned in the *Pennsylvania Packet* for October 18, they should be built of stone or "asbestos" to prevent "trifling accidents." A "Committee for Tarring and Feathering" threatened violence to any pilot who brought the tea ship up the river, and they also planned to attack the ship with burning rafts.[18] To stop a price escalation when the tea supply decreased sharply, a committee visited dealers and persuaded them to charge not more than six shillings a pound.[19]

On December 24, as excitement mounted, the *Pennsylvania Packet* printed news of the Boston Tea Party. Amid rejoicing over that wet affair it was learned on the following day that Philadelphia's shipment of tea had arrived at Chester in the ship *Polly*. Another test had come, and the measures then taken, although lacking the flamboyance of Boston's, were more effective. To prevent the *Polly* from even reaching port, a delegation was sent to intercept her at Gloucester Point. There she was hailed and her commanding officer, a Captain Ayres, agreed to leave his ship and go to Philadelphia with the deputation. At a large meeting in the State House Yard on December 27— called at an hour's notice "to consider what is best to be done on this alarming crisis"[20]—Ayres was ordered to sail away without landing the tea or reporting his vessel at the custom house. Ayres agreed, and with a special committee dogging his shadow, fully complied with his instructions.[21]

As the *Polly* sailed down the Delaware the first phase of Philadelphia's resistance to Britain's new imperial program ended. The experience had taught the Whigs a few lessons, ones that would be put to use in the more

Monday Morning, December 27, 1773.

THE TEA-SHIP being arrived, every Inhabitant, who wishes to preserve the Liberty of America, is defired to meet at the STATE-HOUSE, This Morning, precifely at TEN o'Clock, to advife what is beft to be done on this alarming Crifis.

Notice circulated December 27, 1773.

LIBRARY COMPANY OF PHILADELPHIA

violent years ahead: if colonial protests could be expressed with sufficient vigor and unity, there was a good likelihood that objectionable legislation would be modified; if the Assembly became too conservative and timorous to take forceful action, then reliance would have to be placed on an aroused citizenry operating through the media of committees, meetings, and the press; if voluntary merchant associations failed to hold nonimportation lines, they would have to be forced to do so; and finally, if all the major commercial colonies did not act in unison, they would all suffer together.

I I I

Philadelphia was prepared, then, with a *modus operandi* when the second act of the revolutionary drama began. It opened when Paul Revere, silversmith, engraver, and horseman extraordinary, rode into town on May 19, 1774, with a plea for aid from the people of Boston. The port of that town was to be closed on June 1 by an act of Parliament as punishment for the destruction of the East India Company's tea. Would Philadelphia come to the aid of its fellow Americans?

To ardent Philadelphia Whigs a positive answer to that question was an absolute necessity for the welfare not only of Pennsylvania but of the colonies in general, and during the next two years they devoted their energies to that end. Led by Thomas Mifflin, merchant, Charles Thomson, merchant and former schoolteacher, and Joseph Reed, a brilliant young lawyer who had moved from New Jersey to Philadelphia a few years before, they realized the necessity of involving all of Pennsylvania as soon as possible.[22]

In the spring of 1774 the sentiment for unification of American efforts against British policies induced the Whigs in all the colonies to discuss the desirability of calling a general congress. Philadelphians, who embraced this idea with enthusiasm, petitioned Gov. John Penn in June to call the Pennsylvania Assembly into session. After Penn's refusal, which was not unexpected, thousands of people gathered for a meeting in the State House Yard on June 18. Presided over by John Dickinson and the merchant Thomas Willing, the meeting endorsed the idea of a colonial congress and the appointment of a special Committee of Correspondence for Philadelphia City and County to devise the best means of choosing Pennsylvania's delegates.[23]

The Committee of Correspondence, with Thomas Willing as chairman, persuaded Penn to convene the Assembly after all and then asked "proper Persons" in every county to arrange for the appointment of committees to attend a Provincial Conference of Committees in Philadelphia on July 15 to prepare instructions for the Assembly.[24] The Provincial Conference met on the designated day, approved the calling of a congress, and asked the Assembly to appoint delegates.[25] Obligingly, the Assembly did so on July 22. But before reaching that decision it had discussed resolutions and letters received from Massachusetts, Rhode Island, and Virginia, all in favor of a congress. A resolution of the Massachusetts Assembly of June 17, 1774, suggested Philadelphia as a possible location for the meeting.[26]

When the First Continental Congress met in Philadelphia in September, it began its sessions in the new and still incomplete Carpenters' Hall, constructed for the Carpenters' Company by one of the most distinguished of their number, Robert Smith. The Congress could count on a warmer reception from the Carpenters than it would have found in the chambers of the Assembly. As John Adams noted, an excellent library—the Library Company —was on the second floor.

The absence of general enthusiasm for it notwithstanding, the relationship between the city and the Congress was to continue for the next nine years, primarily because of the contributions Philadelphia could make during the Revolution.[27]

Many of the delegates to the First Congress were stunned by the magnificence they found there, in the manifestations of luxury. By 1774 its brilliant Chippendale style had reached the apogee of colonial achievement in its interpretation of the rococo and was to be seen in all its glory ornamenting the city's principal mansions. Builders such as Samuel Rhoads, David Evans, Thomas Nevell, and Robert Smith erected houses whose interiors displayed splendid paneling, carving, and gilding, impressive chimney pieces, elaborate stucco ceilings, portraits by Charles Willson Peale, furniture from the shops of Benjamin Randolph, Thomas Affleck, James Reynolds, and William Savery. Their silver illustrated the artistry of Philip Syng and the Richardsons. Most of these grand city and country houses had been created in the 1760s and early 1770s, and were in their prime. Such indeed were those of John Cadwalader on Second Street below Pine and Samuel Powel on Third Street, the only one of these great urban mansions still standing in restored condition. Silas Deane, a Connecticut delegate, dined with Cadwalader and observed that the Philadelphian's "furniture and house exceed anything I have seen in this city or elsewhere." John Adams also noted Cadwalader's "grand and elegant House and Furniture." Both delegates liked Philadelphia. Deane found that "hospitality itself resides" there, while Adams feared he would be killed with kindness. Many of the entertainments enjoyed by the delegates took place at the new City Tavern on the west side of Second Street between Walnut and Chestnut. Adams pronounced it the most genteel tavern in the colonies.[28]

Exposed to the visitors' admiring view were the sophisticated ways of life of the local aristocracy, their many diversions. Most prominent men belonged to the exclusive fishing clubs located several miles up the Schuylkill. The oldest of these, instituted in 1732, was the Schuylkill Fishing Company of the Colony in Schuylkill (it exists to this day with a change in its title, immediately after the Revolution, of the word "State" for "Colony"). Another similar club was the Fort St. David's Fishing Company. Its clubhouse was home to what may have been Pennsylvania's first museum, an accumulation of Indian materials and objects of natural history. Adams thought the collection admirable. In addition to the fishing clubs, local men of wealth maintained a Jockey Club founded in 1766 "to encourage the breeding of good horses and to

House at 224 Pine Street, probably built by John Stamper in 1765, demolished c. 1930 (photograph made c. 1860). Stamper, a wealthy merchant, was mayor of Philadelphia in 1759–1760.

FREE LIBRARY OF PHILADELPHIA

promote the pleasures of the turf" (visited by Washington in 1773) and a fox hunt established in 1767.

Philadelphia's public buildings and institutions—the commodious State House, which would house Congress after all following 1774, the Library Company of Philadelphia, the Barracks in the Northern Liberties, the Pennsylvania Hospital, and the Walnut Street Prison, a model jail built on Walnut Street east of Sixth in 1773 by Samuel Rhoads—all were of vital importance for the convenience of a Continental government. Living quarters for congressmen and the many visitors drawn to the capital were readily found in private homes, rented houses, and the many taverns. The excellent printing shops and the city's newspapers, by now seven in number, supplied with paper from the Wissahickon mills, met Congress's publishing needs.

The delegates to the First Continental Congress perceived the divisions that existed in Philadelphia over the proper measures to take in the attempt to obtain a redress of grievances from Britain. Would Congress take sides in the local disputes? It would, and the decisions promptly indicated its political bias. Congress originally chose to meet in Carpenters' Hall although Joseph Galloway, speaker of the Assembly, an adamant conservative and later a Tory, offered the State House as quarters.[29] The intercolonial delegates went on to select as secretary Charles Thomson, a zealous radical who was anathema to Philadelphia conservatives. Able, dedicated, and punctilious, Thomson would serve patiently and faithfully, at considerable expense to himself, until the establishment of the government under the federal Constitution.

And so the Congress set to work. Once again it is John Adams who gives a general idea of a delegate's life at that time: "We go to Congress at nine, and there we stay until three in the afternoon; then we adjourn, and go to dine with some of the nobles of Pennsylvania at four o'clock and feast upon a thousand delicacies, and sit drinking madeira, claret and Burgundy till six or seven and then go home fatigued to death with business, company and care."[30]

IV

To force the British into a change of policy the Congress adopted a resolution called the Association. It bound the colonies to a nonimportation, nonexportation, nonconsumption agreement that was to be enforced not by the merchants themselves but by local committees. Now, with sufficient backing to force reluctant merchants to honor such agreements, the Philadelphia Whigs reorganized the committee system. The Committee of Correspondence for the City and County of Philadelphia, elected on June 18, was dissolved[31] and a new one, for the city only, was chosen in a general election on November 12.

One of the first and most important actions of the new committee was the creation, on December 5, 1774, of the Philadelphia Committee of Inspection and Observation. This committee served zealously in enforcing the Association until its dissolution in September 1776. In an early move to strengthen its hand the Philadelphia Committee of Correspondence, which began to assume a tentative leadership for the entire province, issued a call for a provincial convention to meet in Philadelphia on January 23, 1775.

When the convention met in a three-day session, it passed resolutions to buttress the Association, promote domestic manufactures, and prohibit the importation of slaves. Then in an action of major importance to the city's revolutionary leadership, it made the Philadelphia committee a standing committee of correspondence for the eight counties represented at the convention.[32] As spokesman for the provincial convention, it became in effect an extralegal body in competition with the Assembly.

V

In 1775 the course of the revolutionary drama accelerated with the Second Continental Congress due to meet that May. Prior to that event came news of the bloody encounters at Lexington and Concord. The country was now in effect at war; an enraged irregular army beseiged the British army at Boston. The military movement in Philadelphia, which saw the Light Horse of the City (the First Troop Philadelphia City Cavalry, which is still in existence) organized on November 17, 1774, went into high gear with the recruiting of large bodies of men. Cols. John Dickinson and his first cousin John Cadwalader commanded two of the major units.

Charles Thomson *(1729–1824), appointed secretary of the Continental Congress in 1774, woodcarving by William Rush (1756–1833).*

It was onto this scene of excitement that the southern delegates to Congress came on May 9, 1775, George Washington among them, in his own carriage. They were escorted into town by a large, enthusiastic cavalcade of the militia and private citizens. The following day Congress, meeting in the State House, considered raising an army, but it was not until June 15 that Washington was unanimously elected to command the Continental forces. A week later, after a farewell dinner at the City Tavern, he set out for Boston, escorted as far as New York by the city's Light Horse. With Washington as aides went two Philadelphians, Thomas Mifflin and Joseph Reed.[33]

Although later in the year the Assembly expressly prohibited the Pennsylvania delegation to Congress from agreeing to any proposition that would lead to a separation from England or a change in the Pennsylvania government,[34] the move toward independence could not be stopped. The Second Continental Congress again inserted congressional influence into local politics with its resolution of May 10, 1776, calling for the establishment of governments freed of British authority in all the colonies.[35] Responding to this resolution, the Philadelphia committees led an attack on the Pennsylvania colonial government that would bring about its destruction. At a mass meeting in the State House Yard on May 20, chaired by merchant Daniel Roberdeau, a decision was made to inform the Assembly that the Committee of Inspection and Observation would call a provincial conference of county committees to meet in Philadelphia and plan for the election of a convention to set up a new government.[36]

Before the provincial convention could forgather, the United Colonies became the United States of America, despite the efforts of most of the members of the Pennsylvania delegation to Congress. On July 1, when Congress voted in committee of the whole on the question of independence, a majority of the delegation was opposed. On July 2, however, when a formal poll was taken, the affirmative votes of John Morton, James Wilson, and Benjamin Franklin aligned Pennsylvania with her sister states. Thomas Willing and Charles Humphreys opposed to the end, while John Dickinson and Robert Morris abstained from voting.[37] On July 4 Congress adopted "The unanimous Declaration of the Thirteen United States of America," a document that explained the reasons for the action of July 2. The Declaration was written during June by Thomas Jefferson, who had rented living quarters on the western edge of the city, in Jacob Graff's house on the southwest corner of Seventh and Market Streets.[38] When John Hancock, president of Congress, urged unanimity in the signing of the Declaration—"There must be no pulling different ways: we must all hang together"—Franklin is reputed to have agreed: "We must indeed all hang together, or most assuredly we shall all hang separately."[39]

To some Philadelphians the Declaration seemed a disaster, but those who felt otherwise proclaimed it on July 8 with military parades, gunfire, and the ringing of bells day and night. The sheriff, Lt.-Col. John Nixon, militia officer, merchant, and Whig leader, read the Declaration to a large crowd in the State House Yard, and in the evening the king's arms were taken from the courtroom in the State House and burned.[40]

The story of the ringing of the State House bell on July 4 to proclaim liberty throughout the land apparently originated with the nineteenth-century Philadelphia popular writer George Lippard, and the veneration of the bell as the "Liberty Bell" is also a development of the nineteenth century.[41] Almost as appealing to tourists as the Liberty Bell is that other shrine of nineteenth-century legend, the house presently numbered 239 Arch Street and associated with Elizabeth Griscom "Betsy" Ross. In this instance the patriotic tale—of Betsy's following up independence by fashioning the first Stars and Stripes—originated with the protagonist's grandson in 1870. Betsy's husband of the time, John Ross, the first of three husbands, did have an

Congress Voting Independence *in the Assembly Room of the State House on July 4, 1776, painting begun by Robert Edge Pine c. 1788.*

HISTORICAL SOCIETY OF PENNSYLVANIA

upholsterer's shop in Arch Street, and Betsy was a seamstress who is known to have made ships' colors during the Revolution.

VI

While partisans were quarreling over political control of the city and state, no one was unaware of the possibility that the British armed forces would sooner or later invade Pennsylvania. To repel attack upon the city, preparations had to be made on both land and water, but unfortunately the patriots had little or no local foundation upon which to build. At the outset of hostilities in Massachusetts in 1775 Pennsylvania was without a formal militia establishment or manned fortifications.[42] Until the Assembly passed a comprehensive militia law in March 1777 the city was forced to rely mainly on voluntary groups such as the Light Horse of the City of Philadelphia[43] and the Military Association. The latter had apparently diminished to two companies by early 1775, the Philadelphia Greens under Capt. (later Brig.-Gen.) John Cadwalader, and the Quaker Blues under Capt. (and Sheriff) Joseph Cow-

*House of Jacob Graff, southwest corner of Market and Seventh Streets,
where Thomas Jefferson wrote the Declaration of Independence in June 1776. The
house was demolished in 1883, but it has been reconstructed as part of Independence
National Historical Park.*

perthwait. The news of Lexington and Concord stimulated military activity,
however, and by August 1775 the Philadelphia Committee built up the Associators of Philadelphia to four infantry battalions, a rifle battalion, an artillery battalion, and the City Guards, a kind of patriot police force. In response
to a petition from the Committee, the Assembly on June 30, 1775, approved
of the Military Association and promised to pay wages to its members, but
only when they were engaged in repelling actual attacks.[44] At the same time

a provincial Committee of Safety was appointed to determine the time when it was necessary to call out the Associators and to supply them with equipment and ammunition. To the demands of the Philadelphia Committee in October 1775 that a regular militia be created, the Assembly responded by attempting to improve the Association, but without much effect.

Housing an unprecedented number of men under arms in Philadelphia presented serious problems. The Barracks were soon filled to capacity, and the overflow was distributed in the latter part of 1776 and early 1777 among private houses, the college, Quaker meetinghouses, churches, and any other available quarters. Although the number of soldiers in the armed service of Pennsylvania was small, 1365 in August 1776,[45] the facilities were overtaxed by other troops who were in transit, in training, or awaiting assignment.

Before the war the river defenses of Philadelphia never occasioned enough concern to warrant heavy or sustained expenditures for elaborate fortifications. In 1773 the Assembly appropriated money to purchase Mud Island (later called Fort Island), several miles below the city, and to build a stone fort to ward off raiding ships. The works were commenced in 1774 but remained uncompleted because of insufficient funds.[46]

Acutely aware of the possibility of British attack on Philadelphia from the Delaware, both Pennsylvania and Continental officials concerned themselves with planning and building defensive fleets and fortifications from the summer of 1775 to the autumn of 1777. Despite delays occasioned by conflicting authorities over methods of constructing and financing the defenses, they eventually reached a stage of development that made them serious obstacles to British control of the river. Topographically, the approaches to Philadelphia from Billingsport on the New Jersey shore north to the mouth of the Schuylkill lent themselves reasonably well to defense. The main channel ran along the eastern shore of Mud Island, just below the mouth of the Schuylkill, and thence south past Hog Island and Billings Island, opposite Billingsport. The basic plan of defense called for the erection of *chevaux-de-frise*—wooden obstacles with protruding stakes, literally looking like "frizzy horses"—to block the channels at Billings Island and Mud Island. To protect these underwater obstacles, forts were built at Billingsport; at Red Bank, New Jersey, just opposite the tip of Mud Island (Fort Mercer); and on the southwest extremity of Mud Island (Mud Fort, later Fort Mifflin), on a design first laid out in 1771 by the British military engineer Capt. John Montresor. To permit friendly shipping to use the river, secret openings were made in the *chevaux-de-frise* that were known to only a handful of pilots.[47]

In addition to stationary defenses Pennsylvania built a small navy of galleys and gondolas for operation in the Delaware. They were supported by floating batteries and fire rafts. By November 1776 it was estimated that there were 150 fire floats, two fire boats, two floating batteries, and seven cannon at Mud Island. In addition, forty *chevaux-de-frise* had been planted and a large chain stretched across the channel at that point.[48] The Pennsylvania navy in August 1776 numbered 768 men.[49]

Until the spring of 1776 Philadelphia experienced the milder and more pleasant sights and sounds of war—the parades, cheers on the training grounds, and the thrilling roll of drums. Then in March the British frigates *Roebuck* and *Liverpool* appeared at the mouth of Delaware Bay and instituted a blockade. The sealing of the harbor was virtually complete, and the shipping that had been the life blood of Philadelphia stood idle; but the demand for the manufacture of munitions, clothing, and equipment for the soldiers was so great, and consequently such was the demand for capital and labor, that the blockade had remarkably little impact on the city's prosperity. In May the first local armed clash occurred, when the *Roebuck* and the *Liverpool* ventured up river and engaged thirteen Pennsylvania galleys and the Continental sloop *Reprisal* near the mouth of the Christiana River. Spectators gathered on both banks of the Delaware. All turned out well when the intruders retired down the river under fire.[50]

The news of the fighting that took place between the American and British forces in and around New York during August and September alternated between bad and terrible. General Washington and the Continental Army were defeated in a series of engagements by the British army under Gen. Sir William Howe, and in November the remnants of Washington's badly mauled forces retreated across New Jersey toward the Delaware. Previously the Pennsylvania Council of Safety, apprehensive that Howe would invade the state, had asked Congress to consider the possibility of stationing troops near Philadelphia, and to name a general officer to command them.[51] Congress had no troops to spare, but on November 11, 1776, it did ask the Continental Board of War, its military administrative agency, to confer with the Council of Safety on Philadelphia's defense.[52] To consolidate defense Congress asked Washington to take direct command of all the troops in the Northern Department that had been raised in Pennsylvania and New Jersey.[53] In an effort to supplement Washington's forces the Council of Safety was requested to call out all the Associators in Philadelphia City and County and the counties of Chester, Bucks, and Northampton to serve for six weeks in the Continental forces.[54]

In the deepening crisis David Rittenhouse, vice-president of the Council of Safety, warned the city that only vigorous action could save it from invasion. To inspire courage and enthusiasm, on November 28 he and Thomas Mifflin, now quartermaster general of the Continental Army, addressed a mass meeting in the State House Yard. About 2000 men in the city responded to their appeals by taking up arms. The Philadelphia Associators, who about this time were reorganized as the Philadelphia Brigade, went into active service and eventually fought creditably. But while the city responded reasonably well to the military emergency, the countryside appeared lethargic, indifferent, and sometimes hostile to the cause.[55] The countrymen's failure to rally, and the apparent hopelessness of stopping the numerically and qualitatively superior British army, deepened the fear and frustration in the city, and thousands began leaving for the country as reports of British progress filtered in. When it was learned that the enemy had reached New Brunswick, the

Council of Safety requested that the schools be closed and that all inhabitants immediately spring to the city's defense. By December 7 the council thought that the British "may be hourly expected" in Pennsylvania, but curiously enough it asked that the "Schools in the City be opened on Monday next, and the Education of Youth be carried on as usual."[56]

The situation had not improved in the slightest, however, and while the children were thinking of resuming their studies, Congress was contemplating departure from a city that apparently could not be defended. But before it decamped on December 12 and headed for Baltimore, it made some last desperate efforts to save its place of residence. On December 9 it reinforced Washington's repeated requests for troops by asking the Council of Safety to scour the backcountry, and among other actions it directed the commanding officer in the city, Maj.-Gen. Israel Putnam, to defend it "to the utmost extremity."[57] Putnam imposed martial law, announced a ten o'clock curfew, and in the face of a general flight, ordered the inhabitants out to dig entrenchments.

Before the disorderly exodus from the city ended about half of the people had fled, and the roads to the west were covered with escapees in carts and wagons of all descriptions. "This city was, for days," wrote Robert Morris on December 21, "the greatest scene of distress that you can conceive; everybody but Quakers were removing their families and effects, and now it looks dismal and melancholy."[58] To add to the misery and disorder, smallpox and camp fever spread among the soldiers in epidemic proportions. The dead were buried by the hundreds in long shallow trenches in the area of the Walnut Street Prison.

Then, amid the pervasive gloom that marked the nadir of the revolutionary cause, came news of Washington's victory at Trenton on December 26. Four days later hundreds of Hessians captured in the fighting were marched through Philadelphia's streets.[59] Returning to New Jersey to fight again at Princeton on January 3, Washington cleared the enemy from that state, except in the easternmost part, and went into winter quarters near Morristown. From the hills there he could overlook the invasion route across New Jersey toward the Delaware and discourage another British overland advance by threatening its line of communications. The Philadelphia Light Horse, attached to the Continental Army for the emergency, won distinction in reconnaissance and in outpost actions during the course of the Trenton-Princeton campaign.

When the threat of invasion had receded, Philadelphia once again became its former bustling self as thousands of refugees returned. Congress too came back in March 1777, openly unrepentant, but nevertheless somewhat chagrined over its hasty departure.

Many suspected, however, that the city enjoyed a reprieve that was merely temporary, for every month that followed brought its alarms. In April the Pennsylvania Executive Council, warned by General Putnam that Howe would probably appear soon, encouraged Pennsylvanians to join the militia by assuring them that the city had once been saved by a few Associators, just as a "Divine Providence" had remarkably saved "the lives of the militia in every Battle during this just War."[60] Despite such reassurance many potential soldiers preferred to stay at home and give Providence an even better chance. Home also had its attractions for the Executive Council and the Assembly. Both responded to the April alarm by promptly adjourning. Congress immediately asked them to come back to Philadelphia, and in the meantime it decided "to watch over all matters" in Pennsylvania because the state's executive authority was "incapable of any exertion adequate to the present crisis."[61]

Again the patriots, as they had in the past and would in the future, turned to the committee system to get things done. On April 17 Owen Biddle, chairman of the Pennsylvania Board of War, announced that a Committee of Fifty had been named by the board to remove from Philadelphia all equipment and provisions that might fall into British hands.[62] It had the power to keep goods from coming into the city, to search for suspected hidden supplies, and to determine the amount of provisions any family might retain.

In the summer rumors of invasion increased, for on July 23 General Howe sailed out of New York harbor on his way by sea to wage a campaign in Pennsylvania and capture Philadelphia.[63] In a leisurely voyage he eventually reached the Virginia Capes, and coming up the Chesapeake, his troops debarked at Head of Elk on August 25.

VII

As the danger from the enemy outside Philadelphia increased, both the state and congressional authorities came to concern themselves more and more with the enemies, real and imagined, from within. Unfortunately the problem of detection and punishment was as complicated as it was vexatious. The political spectrum of Philadelphians ranged from patriot blue to bright British red, and while some held true to their colors, others had the habit of changing with perplexing frequency as the revolutionary tides rose and fell. But however annoying the chameleons were, the real danger would come from the men who might be waiting for the moment of greatest urgency to commit overt treason. Of course some saw Tories behind every teapot, but which ones were most likely to have hidden guns in the stable or the attic? They had to be identified as soon as possible.

Before the Declaration of Independence Tories were more outspoken than they were after that event. In 1775 the Pennsylvania Committee of Safety had required self-acknowledged Loyalists to recant. Isaac Hunt, a lawyer, was carted through the streets by a mob for refusing to apologize for having acted as an attorney for a Loyalist. Dr. John Kearsley, a Tory physician who sharply protested against this action, was then himself manhandled. Hunt later left for England, and Kearsley was sent as a prisoner to York.[64] For aiding South Carolinian Moses Kirkland to escape from Philadelphia in May 1776, Arthur Thomas and his sons were attacked in their home by a mob. After a term of imprisonment Thomas went in September to New York, the haven for several local Tories. Quite a few Loyalists left Philadelphia in the summer of 1776, including several sons of former Chief Justice William Allen. John Penn and Benjamin Chew, chief justice of Pennsylvania from 1774 to 1776, were exiled to New Jersey in 1777. The number of Loyalists, of whatever hue, who remained in Philadelphia could only be conjectured. The patriots suspected that they were numerous, but what they would do during a British invasion was the important question.

The Quakers presented a special problem. Throughout the colonies the Society of Friends was trying to keep its members true to their religious professions, urging them to avoid any participation in revolutionary activity. The Quaker community in Philadelphia, the strongest and most influential on the continent, served as a clearinghouse for information that was widely circulated, along with advice and earnest exhortations, to Friends everywhere in America.[65] At the same time their attitude was in accord with that of the Yearly Meeting in London, which in 1775 entreated American Friends to remain clear of any political commotions or rebellious activities against the king. They continued to insist on this policy throughout the war, and urged the colonials to have nothing to do with the new order and to refrain from sympathizing with it in any manner.[66]

The Pennsylvania Quakers needed no urging. While embracing the peace testimony as the foundation of their opposition to the Revolution, they enlarged it with political and economic pronouncements that angered most Whigs. Although many had joined in resistance to British policies in the 1760s, they began a definite withdrawal when the opposition took on more violent forms. To the English king, according to the Philadelphia Yearly Meeting of 1774, could be attributed the liberties enjoyed in America, and therefore all opposition to him, even the evasion of customs duties, should be discouraged. Yet more specific was the 1775 declaration by the Philadelphia Meeting for Sufferings that Quakers should oppose all violations of law as manifested in usurpation of power and the convening of "illegal assemblies."[67] The stand taken by the Meeting for Sufferings, as Anne T. Gary puts it, "was especially sympathetic to the political opinions and economic interests of prominent Quaker merchants, such as Israel Pemberton, who were instrumental in obtaining the official adherence of their meetings to British [Quaker] counsels. Thus the political pronouncements of colonial Quakerism were more loyalistic than a strictly logical interpretation of their dogmas demanded."[68]

It was on the recommendation of the Meeting for Sufferings that the Philadelphia Yearly Meeting in September 1776 discussed the Quaker position vis-à-vis the Declaration of Independence and its consequences. With all American yearly meetings represented but New York, the meeting adopted one of the most important and comprehensive statements yet made. Friends were strictly forbidden to participate in civil government under the Declaration, even in elections, to pay fines in lieu of military service, or to engage in business that was likely to help the war effort.[69]

In 1775 the Pennsylvania Quakers had begun to enforce a rigid code of conduct. By the end of that year 163 Friends had been investigated, of whom 65 were disowned. Some 353 more were disowned from 1776 through 1778.[70] No revolutionary government ever came close to compelling such obedience.

But behind the adamant stand of the Society of Friends in Philadelphia fundamental changes were taking place. The Revolution undoubtedly presented the severest test the Quakers had yet faced in Pennsylvania. Many of them met it by hearkening to the voices of reform which had become more insistent in recent years and by returning to the original simplicities of the faith, by living more plainly and withdrawing as much as possible from "worldly" influences.[71]

The various pronouncements and injunctions issued by the Quaker meetings had of course come to the attention of the government. They were taken so seriously that Congress, on August 28, 1777, as invasion became imminent, recommended that the Pennsylvania Executive Council arrest and confine three members of the Fisher family, three Pembertons, including Israel, and five other leading Quakers, because they were certainly and notoriously "disaffected to the American cause" and would be inclined "to communicate intelligence to the enemy."[72] The Executive Council was not only willing to comply with the recommendation but added the names of thirty more men whom it deemed dangerous to the public safety.[73] Accordingly, in the first week of September a number of persons, mostly Quakers, were rounded up and confined in the Freemasons' Lodge in Norris (Lodge) Alley just off Second Street.[74] Subsequently, just as the British and American armies were about to clash at the Brandywine, twenty of them were exiled to Virginia.

VIII

The problem of Loyalism was only one of many that faced Congress and the Executive Council as they sought means to save Philadelphia from British occupation or, failing that, to prevent valuable supplies from falling into enemy hands. In August the Committee of Fifty continued to remove superfluous stores to places of safety. People who refused to promise allegiance to the state were disarmed, lead spouts were torn from the houses, and frantic efforts were made to fill the militia ranks in the city and the nearby counties.[75]

General Howe stayed only a short time at Head of Elk before marching into Pennsylvania. Howe had come to force Washington into a general engagement which he was sure the Americans would have to accept to protect Philadelphia. Had he forced a fight in New England he would have had to contend with the local militia who he thought were "the most persevering of any in all North America," but he did not expect that Washington would be able to obtain any considerable increase in his forces in Pennsylvania.[76]

On August 24 Washington took his troops through Philadelphia, making "pathetically minute" preparations to ensure a show of strength that might impress the city's Tories and Quakers. The Continental Army came down Front Street and moved west out Chestnut, impressive in that they marched twelve deep and yet took over two hours to pass by, but even to John Adams's sympathetic eye not having "quite the air of soldiers," and trying to make up for their utter lack of uniforms by wearing sprigs of green leaves in their hats.[77] Then on September 11 around Chadd's Ford on the Brandywine Creek, outnumbered as well as overmatched in training and discipline, the Continentals met the British in battle.

In the city, where the firing could be heard, prayers were sent up for both sides.[78] There was little activity until the end of the day when reports began arriving from the battlefield. At first no two accounts agreed, but as night came on a horseman sped down to the Indian Queen with more definite news. At six o'clock the next morning Congress heard the worst when dispatches from Washington were read.[79] The Continental Army had been outgeneraled as well as otherwise overmatched and nearly trapped; it had extricated itself from the field, but Howe had badly beaten Washington.

In the days that followed, while the city was being scoured to remove any supplies that had been missed before, another exodus began. The city's bells, including the State House bell, were taken down and carted off to safety in Allentown. Thousands fled into the backcountry and across the Delaware into New Jersey. The Assembly and the Executive Council hurried to Lancaster, and Congress, after a brief stay there, went on to York. On the night of September 19, when rumor had it that the British were approaching, Mrs. Sarah Logan Fisher, whose happiness over the news was somewhat dampened by the exile of her Quaker husband to Virginia, saw "horses galloping, women running, children crying, delegates flying, and altogether the greatest consternation, fright and terror that can be imagined. Some of our neighbors took their flight before day, and I believe all the Congress moved off before 5 o'clock, but behold when morning came, it proved a false alarm."[80]

Mrs. Fisher, who described the American troops as "lawless banditti" and "dirty creatures," and Washington, Congress, and the Executive Council as "infernals," had to wait another week for the full triumph. It came on September 26, when huge crowds, composed for the most part of women, children, and Quakers, lined the streets and shouted with joy as Maj.-Gen. Charles Lord Cornwallis marched part of the victorious British army into the city.[81] Smoothness and good order marked the entrance. Since the soldiers were unacquainted with the locality, two Tories, Enoch Story and Phineas Bond, Jr., guided the light horse in. They were followed by a band; then, led by Cornwallis, came the main body of troops, the artillery, the Hessians, and another band. That was not all, though. Apparently the invaders had come to stay, for "Baggage wagons, Hessian women, and horses, cows, goats and asses brought up the rear." All of this was fitting and proper, thought Mrs. Fisher. Even the Philadelphia weather cooperated. As the British neared the city the clouds dispersed, "the sun shone out with a sweet serenity," and the air was cool enough to prevent the troops from being "incommoded with the heat."[82]

Philadelphia's capture was a serious blow to the Revolution; Washington at one time thought it would be fatal to the American cause. The reasons for his concern are clear when one considers the important role the city had played as a war center and arsenal. From 1775 the demands for armament, ships, cloth, and tents had greatly expanded Philadelphia's productive capacity. As a case in point, about 4000 women were engaged in their homes in the manufacture of textiles by the summer of 1776. In the latter part of the same year Robert Morris presented a graphic view of Philadelphia's importance. "You will consider Philadelphia," he wrote, "from its centrical situation, the extent of its commerce, the number of its artificers, manufactures and other circumstances, to be to the United States what the heart is to the human body in circulating the blood."[83] The loss of America's leading city, the disruption of government on all levels, and the population dislocation, including the flight of many in the industrial and commercial groups, undoubtedly hampered the war effort. Certainly one of the immediate effects of the loss was to force Washington's army to draw its supplies other than subsistence from distant areas.[84] With the revolutionary cause in such sad disarray, subsistence became hard to extract from southeastern Pennsylvania farmers who preferred to sell for British currency. The miseries of Valley Forge would come soon enough.

But there were some mitigating circumstances in the loss of Philadelphia. So long a period of warning had preceded the British approach in the late summer and early autumn that ample opportunity was afforded to remove war and industrial matériel. So much had been taken and so many people had left that for the moment the city was almost a hollow shell.

To prevent the British from using local printing facilities, Congress on September 18 had directed Brig.-Gen. John Armstrong to transport into the country the printing presses and type of the city and Germantown. During the first three weeks of September all the major English-language newspapers in Philadelphia suspended publication. All, incidentally, would resume operations in the city after it was reoccupied by the Americans. In the meantime David Hall and William Sellers issued their *Pennsylvania Gazette* from York, and the *Pennsylvania Packet* was published at Lancaster. Apparently General Armstrong did not make a clean sweep of the printing presses for Benjamin Towne's *Pennsylvania Evening Post*, which had suspended publication from September 23 to October 11, resumed under British control, and James Humphreys's *Pennsylvania Ledger*, a Tory paper which had been suspended during the previous year, resumed operation on October 10. In the same month Christopher Sower [Saur] brought his press in from Germantown and resumed publication of his *Pennsylvanische Staats-Courier*, the current version of the series of German papers initiated by his father the first Christopher Saur.[85]

The people who remained in the city, Southwark, and the Northern Liberties numbered 21,767, of whom 17,285 were women, children, and adolescents. Thus there remained only 4482 males over eighteen years of age.[86] Of the 5470 houses in these areas, 587 were untenanted, and many of the 287 stores were left vacant.[87] Within a short time, however, the population figures increased dramatically. Now open to avowed Tories, deserters, refugees, and opportunists of all descriptions, the city was overrun with strangers who sought to exploit the Whigs' misfortune.

To guard the city against Washington's army, Howe established his headquarters at Stenton, the Logan house near Germantown, and positioned much of his army about a mile to the northwest in the general region of Germantown's Market Square. Cornwallis's division occupied Philadelphia and began building works for its defense, and Howe planned to reduce the fortifications on the Delaware, which were still in American hands. Until he did so the British situation at Philadelphia was vulnerable, because supplies could not reach Howe's army by the Delaware River route. To cover the operations against the Delaware forts, however, Howe had to stretch his Germantown lines thin.

Washington took advantage of this deployment by attacking at Germantown on October 4 with 11,000 Continentals and militia. The American commander's complicated battle plan called for the converging of four columns against the British lines; such a difficult operation rarely works even with veteran troops led by professional officers. Inevitably, during their night march the timing of the American columns went awry and they did not attack simultaneously. Maj.-Gen. John Sullivan's column, which marched down the Germantown Road across Chestnut Hill and through Mount Airy, lost much of its momentum when Washington diverted troops from it to deal with six

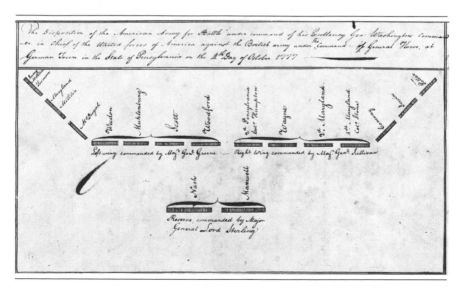

The Disposition of the American Army for Battle under the command of his Excellency Geo. Washington . . . against the British army under the Command of General Howe at German Town, *October 4, 1777. Page from an orderly book.*

small companies of Lt.-Col. Thomas Musgrave's 40th Regiment that retired into Cliveden, Benjamin Chew's house, and defended it sturdily. Nevertheless the British were much handicapped because the American attackers were coming at them out of a heavy fog. Sullivan's column and Maj.-Gen. Nathanael Greene's, which was approaching Market Square down the streets from the Limekiln Road farther north, actually drove the enemy before them —until the fog confused them too, and they commenced fighting each other. When the British counterattacked, the Americans began a retreat that degenerated into panic. The battle of Germantown, the second major engagement fought for Philadelphia, ended as another British victory. But the determination with which the Americans attacked, and their conviction that they had

Medal commemorating the British victory at Germantown and Lt.-Col. Thomas Musgrave's defense of Cliveden, the house of Benjamin Chew, October 4, 1777. The Chew mansion is now owned by the National Trust for Historic Preservation.

been on the verge of winning, did much for their morale and impressed the French government, which was contemplating an American alliance.

The determination of the American attack also impressed Howe to the extent that he withdrew his army into Philadelphia. Thus constricted, he more than ever needed access to the sea by way of the Delaware, but the American river defenses were proving stubborn. The British occupied an abandoned Billingsport on October 9, but on October 22 some 400 Rhode Island troops in Fort Mercer at Red Bank beat off an attack of 2000 Hessians. The next day the guns of Fort Mifflin and the Pennsylvania navy repulsed a British naval attack; six enemy warships were heavily damaged, and the sixty-four-gun ship *Augusta* and the sixteen-gun sloop *Merlin* ran aground. After the *Augusta* caught fire and blew up, the British destroyed the *Merlin*.

Washington hoped Howe would have to divert enough strength downriver and into New Jersey against the forts so that he could stage a second assault. This hope foundered, however, on the isolation of Fort Mifflin from effective American help and on the strength of Howe's artillery train and the Royal Navy. Though Province Island was a mud bank largely under water at high tide and thus hardly a good artillery platform, the British contrived to mount five heavy batteries on it within range of Fort Mifflin. They also brought a floating battery of twenty-two twenty-four-pounders within forty yards of the fort. On November 10 they opened a bombardment with these guns. Five days later their fleet also came into action. Fort Mifflin's guns were knocked out one by one until only two could fire, and by nightfall of November 15 its garrison had to move to Fort Mercer. But that post was now too isolated to be held, and it was abandoned on the night of November 20–21. The Pennsylvania navy also had to be given up, scuttled by its crews.[88]

Even then the rebels were not yet ready to cede undisputed control of the Delaware. David Bushnell, earlier the inventor of a primitive submarine called "Bushnell's Turtle," had suspended his experiments in trying to sink British ships with that underwater craft, but he conceived the idea of floating kegs laden with explosives from above Philadelphia down the Delaware on the ebb tide, to blow up among the British ships in the harbor. The kegs were readied, but a heavy frost on the night in January 1778 when they were put into the river happened to cause the ships to be moved to the city's wharves, out of danger. The kegs were discovered when a bargeman hauled one out of the water and it exploded in his arms, killing him and several companions. This incident touched off wild rumors that the fiendish rebels were coming down the Delaware in kegs that they were using as Trojan horses. British troops were drawn up on the riverbanks to fire at the kegs. One story has it that just as the alarm was subsiding, a marketwoman dropped a keg of cheese into the Delaware and touched off a frenzy all over again. Francis Hopkinson, the sole member of William Smith's old Anglophile literary circle to become a rebel, immortalized this "Battle of the Kegs" in verse.[89]

The whole tedious business of gaining control of the Delaware left the

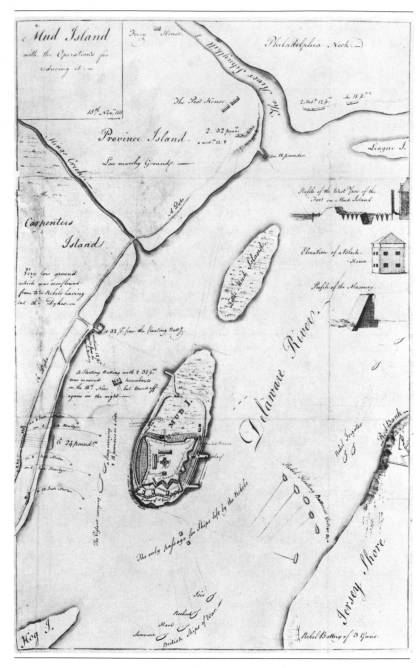

Mud Island with the Operations for reducing it, 15th Novr. 1777, *drawn by Maj. John André. Badly damaged during the Revolution, Fort Mifflin was rebuilt in 1798.*

Representation of the Action off Mud Fort in the River
Delaware . . . 15th Novr 1777. *Drawn and engraved by Lt. W. Elliot, 1787.*

British army feeling far less at ease in Philadelphia than they had anticipated. To ward off another attack by Washington, Howe erected a chain of ten redoubts, with connecting abatis, between the two rivers in a line running north of and parallel to Callowhill Street.[90] The construction of these works, begun while Howe was still in Germantown, was hampered by a labor shortage. Although Joseph Galloway was sure it would be a simple matter to get 500 civilians to do the digging, the most the British could obtain was about eighty. Few were interested in working all day for eight pence and a ration of salt provisions.[91] Many summer mansions that might have sheltered snipers along the defense line were burned to the ground, including John Dickinson's Fair Hill, formerly a residence of his father-in-law Isaac Norris II.

Washington continued scrutinizing the Philadelphia defenses, warding off Howe's lunge against him at Whitemarsh in early December, until he decided there were no longer any inviting openings and retired into winter quarters at Valley Forge on December 19. There, about twenty-two miles northwest of the city, the Continental Army took up a hilly defensive position that could command any enemy foray toward Congress at York or toward the remaining American supply depot in the area at Reading. There was an abundance of water and of wood for fuel and building. Food that the farmers would part with was less available, and for a time in midwinter the army was close to starvation. The soldiers were also so destitute of clothing that in mid-January many could not leave their huts. But famous though the suffering at Valley Forge has become, and real though it was, the winter fortunately was in fact rather mild. Beginning in March there was opportunity for the training program inaugurated by the new inspector-general of the army, Baron Friedrich Wilhelm Augustus von Steuben, to begin honing into soldierly discipline the raw warrior skills displayed in the vigor of the attack at Germantown.

I X

Less self-assured than when the Philadelphia campaign had begun, by the latter part of December the British settled down in relative comfort for the winter. The troops were quartered in the Barracks, available public buildings, and encampments, while officers lived in private houses. Lt.-Gen. Wilhelm Baron von Knyphausen, the Hessian commander, occupied John Cadwalader's residence. The Samuel Powels, who had elected to stay in the city, were relegated to the back of their house while high-ranking officers took over its front rooms. General Howe established his quarters in former Gov. Richard Penn's large house on Market Street, and all lived rather luxuriously. When news at last reached Franklin in France that Howe had taken Philadelphia, the philosopher remarked that, on the contrary, Philadelphia had taken Howe. This seemed to be the case, for Howe showed little interest in leaving his mistress and the comforts of the city.[92]

American prisoners, about 500 of them, were put into the two jails, the Walnut Street Prison and its predecessor at Third and Market; the officers were confined in the State House.[93] The deprivations suffered by the men in the jails were extreme. Fed barbarously restricted rations, they supplemented their diet with wood, leather, and rats. The provision baskets they hopefully suspended to the street level yielded very little.[94]

To govern Philadelphia, Howe enlisted the aid of Joseph Galloway, who made himself useful in the early days of the occupation by identifying rebels, directing an agency of about eighty spies, and administering oaths of allegiance to the inhabitants. In December he was appointed superintendant-general of the police and director of exports and imports.[95] He was in effect the civil governor of the city. Other Philadelphians also served Howe faithfully: Samuel Shoemaker and John Potts as police magistrates; George Roberts, James Reynolds, and several others as commissioners of the nightwatch. George Harding ferreted out spies, while Abraham Carlisle granted passports only to those above suspicion, and carefully watched the city's entrances for dangerous intruders. To secure the streets at night a curfew was imposed in January which required all pedestrians to carry lanterns.[96]

During his stay in the city Howe made strenuous efforts to recruit Loyalists, but without much success. The lack of enthusiasm was a repetition of what he had experienced on his march from Head of Elk. At that time, despite the assurances of Galloway that there were many Loyalists in southeastern Pennsylvania, Howe remained doubtful. He was suspicious of everyone but the Quakers, and he felt later that with very few exceptions they were the only people in Philadelphia who were really glad to see him occupy the city.[97] Because of their religion, however, the Quakers would not fight in the king's behalf; nor, for quite different reasons, would most of the other Loyalists in Philadelphia. After eight months of recruiting, according to Howe, only 974 men were raised, and quite a few of those had come in from Maryland and New Jersey.[98]

Joseph Galloway thought that the people who stayed in Philadelphia, with few exceptions, were Loyalists.[99] Some of the exceptions could very well have been such prominent Whigs as Dr. John Morgan and Thomas Willing. But Morgan's Whig patriotism was lukewarm at the time because he had been dismissed as director-general of hospitals in the Contintental Army. Moreover he was disgusted with what he regarded as the arbitrary conduct of the city committees.[100] Willing, whose business partner Robert Morris was of course not in the city, continued to work there, but he refused to take an oath of allegiance to the king.[101] Other exceptions were, according to Howe, Whigs who filtered back into town to carry out supplies and information to the rebel army, and to do all the damage they could to Howe's forces. In the opinion of James Allen, many of "the fiercest Whigs" stayed on unmolested.[102] There were also many neutralists who carried on business as usual and were cordially accepted by the British officers but whose conduct did not injure them in the eyes of the Whigs when the British departed.

During the early days of the occupation commodities of all kinds, provisions especially, were scarce, and prices were exorbitant. Tea sold for $60 a pound, silk commanded $100 a yard, wood was at times unobtainable, and the markets were often unable to provide flour, butter, and eggs.[103] The rebel blockade of the Delaware until Forts Mifflin and Mercer were taken, a refugee inundation, and plundering by the British troops contributed to the scarcity. Howe imposed price controls and restrictions on the sale of certain items, but enforcement, largely in the hands of the merchants, was not strict and prices consequently remained high throughout the winter.[104] The shortage of goods was considerably relieved after the Delaware was cleared for shipping and the cessation of major campaigning allowed a greater freedom of trade between the city and the local farmers. The steady flow of provisions into Philadelphia angered Washington, but he could not stop it. The Pennsylvania militia, to which this task was mainly entrusted, was so weak in numbers—at one time there were only sixty men in the field—that their scattered patrols were evaded with relative ease by farmers who preferred British specie to depreciated currency.[105] With the exception then of the very poor, among whom many in the swarms of Loyalist refugees could be included, the inhabitants of Philadelphia lived in moderate comfort while Washington's troops were starving at Valley Forge. During January and February, the worst months at the American camp, the city was said to be full of goods and provisions.[106] Toward the end of the occupation, however, food was again less plentiful. When Robert Morris entered Philadelphia in June shortly after the British left, he was struck by the underfed appearance of the inhabitants. "You cou'd know," he wrote, "a Country Refugee from a Citizen [of Philadelphia] the whole length of a square by the difference of their looks, but as the market begins to fill with wholesome provisions before I left them, I suppose they will fatten fast."[107]

The social season during the occupation was lively and exciting, with an understandable military orientation. It reached its height on May 18 with an extravaganza called, because "it was made up of a variety of entertainments," the Meshianza (as the ticket spelled it).[108] This affair honored the departure of General Howe, who had resigned in the face of adverse political pressure and discouragement and had been replaced by Gen. Sir Henry Clinton as commander in chief of the British forces. The fête included a trip on the Delaware to Walnut Grove, the estate of the absent Thomas Wharton south of the city, a mock medieval chivalric tournament, varied gustatory delights, fireworks, and dancing that lasted until four o'clock in the morning. The British officers came costumed as knights of old—but because it would have been awkward to dance in armor, in court costumes of the period of Henry IV. Since it would not do to have the American girls who attended, however Loyalist their sentiments, dressed as aristocratic ladies, they were costumed as Turkish maidens instead. In the later recollections of old women, the girls were not criticized by the Whigs for consorting with the enemy. When the American army returned and a dance was given for the French officers, many of the Meshianza girls were invited. With happy impartiality they accepted. The uniforms were different, but a dance was a dance.[109] In accepting the British invitations the girls may have been a bit daring, for rumors were circulating to the effect that their hosts' stay in Philadelphia would be short.

The British were in fact planning to return to New York. The French alliance with the rebels and the consequent threat of French naval activity off the American coast impelled them to consolidate their forces. To many of the merchants and refugees the news was appalling. In May tradesmen with large stocks of goods on their hands lowered prices sharply and tried to remove the remainder from the city.[110] Equally urgent was the necessity of collecting from the British troops to whom they had extended credit. In that effort they were only partially successful, for it was estimated that the uncollected debts on their books when the army left exceeded £10,000 sterling.[111]

The intended departure of the British left many Loyalists in a quandary over whether they should go along or stay and take a chance on Whig mercy. Certainly those who held commissions under the king or aided the enemies of the new governments of Pennsylvania and the United States, actions declared treasonable by a Pennsylvania law of February 11, 1777, were courting serious danger by remaining.[112] Under the curious delusion that they really had a choice, Galloway and other city magistrates asked General Howe for an opinion as to the best thing to do. Howe later recalled that he told them that if they chose to go with the army they would be safe, but he would not object if they stayed behind to ask protection from Washington and Congress.[113] Galloway's recollection of the matter was different. He was advised by Howe, he said, to make his peace with Washington.[114] But most of the men who held office during the occupation did not risk capture by the Whigs. The fate in store for them was further clarified by an act of the Assembly of March 6, 1778, which declared that all Pennsylvanians who voluntarily served the king during the war were attainted of high treason. This act also required Galloway, Samuel Shoemaker, and certain other Philadelphians to appear for examination by April 20 or suffer seizure of their property.[115] When the British army withdrew in June, 3000 civilians left with it, most of them on British ships. It is impossible to estimate with any accuracy the number of Philadelphians who were of this group, for it included runaway slaves and servants and the refugees who had flocked into the city during the previous months. The actual number of Philadelphians who were attainted of treason from 1778 to 1781 for serving under the British was 109.[116]

X

Fifteen minutes after the last enemy soldier left the city, on June 18, 1778, an American cavalry troop entered.[117] The reoccupation was accomplished quietly as the soldiers moved about on their missions. Two weeks before, on June 4, Congress had forbidden any molestation or pillaging of the inhabitants, and apparently those orders were observed. Gouverneur Morris of New York thought the citizens should be confined to their houses and forced to contribute £100,000 to the American cause, individual amounts to be determined by wealth and degree of disaffection. But Congress took milder action. It was primarily concerned with the supplies that might have been left by the British and with any goods belonging to people who could be regarded as British subjects. Their ownership would be decided by a committee appointed by Congress and the Pennsylvania Executive Council.[118]

To carry out congressional orders, Maj.-Gen. Benedict Arnold, who had been appointed military commander of the city, issued a proclamation on June 19. Prepared with the help of Joseph Reed, former adjutant-general of the army and now a delegate to Congress, and other influential Philadelphians, it placed the whole urban area under martial law until civil authority could be resumed. Lists of goods in the categories that concerned Congress were to be submitted to Arnold's officers by noon on June 20, and nothing could be sold or transferred without Arnold's permission.[119] With the suspension of all business in areas vital to the Continental Army, the supply officers were enabled to enter into contract arrangements with the merchants without competition.[120]

One week after Arnold's proclamation the Executive Council returned from Lancaster and restored civil government. Martial law ended, but Arnold would continue as military commander of Philadelphia until March 1779.[121] In the interval this former fighting general, once the best tactical commander in the Continental Army but now crippled by the leg wound he had received at Saratoga, developed a luxurious lifestyle. Quartered in the Market Street mansion that had recently sheltered General Howe, he fell under suspicion of excessive friendship with Tories, and the state government pursued him with charges that he financed his luxuries by using his office for illegal business partnerships and profiteering. Enough evidence to prove the charges never surfaced during Arnold's tenure, but they were true, and he left the Philadelphia command after an acrimonious court-martial, convicted of only minor charges—issuing an improper pass for a vessel to leave the city and using public wagons for private purposes—but distinctly under a cloud. Worse, of course, followed. While in Philadelphia Arnold courted and married the pretty and vivacious young Peggy Shippen, daughter of the jurist Edward Shippen (who was a great-grandson of the city's first mayor). Through Peggy, Arnold soon made contact with Capt. John André of General Clinton's staff, who had been one of the principal organizers of the Meshianza. With André, Arnold plotted still more illicit profits for himself by selling not contraband merchandise but the revolutionary cause.[122]

Congress, happy to leave its cramped quarters in the little town of York, adjourned its sessions there on June 27 and started back to Philadelphia. The State House, however, had been used by the British as a hospital, and had been left in a disgraceful condition. The air in the immediate vicinity was especially foul because the enemy had opened a large pit and used it for the disposal of garbage, dead horses, and dead men. Consequently Congress, which mustered a quorum on July 7, had to convene in a nearby meetinghouse and in College Hall until the State House was again fit for occupancy.[123] The congressmen were by no means the only ones disturbed by the condition of the city. Property destruction, much of it wanton, was everywhere to be seen. In 1782 it would be estimated that the losses due to vandalism and theft amounted to £187,280.[124] Even Fort St. David's and its museum were not spared; the Hessians sacked the place. Captain André, who had occupied Franklin's house, had seen nothing wrong in helping himself to books from its library, as well as the doctor's portrait.[125]

After their return to Philadelphia many Whigs were determined to take action against Loyalism in all of its degrees and manifestations. Its detection, although not easy, was less difficult than it had been before the occupation. The uncertainties and kaleidoscopic changes that had characterized the Revolution from the beginning, along with the political and military confusion that existed for months before the arrival of the British, had blurred lines of allegiance and permitted considerable dissimulation. But the invasion of Pennsylvania had brought more Loyalists unabashedly to light and aroused serious suspicions of others. The former were to be dealt with out of hand, and the others were to be discovered and punished. Inspired by the ratification of the French alliance in May 1778 and the departure of the British army, the Whigs went about their task.

Under Pennsylvania laws of 1777 legal procedures had been devised to ascertain the names of all who had sought protection under the British, joined their forces, or held office under their jurisdiction. In May 1778 a long list of Pennsylvanians charged with having entered the British army were required to report to justices of the peace by July 6 and stand trial or be attainted of high treason.[126] Those so attainted were subject to estate forfeiture. The actual seizure of the estates was entrusted to agents appointed by the Executive Council. Accordingly, in July 1778 it named William Will, Jacob Shriner, Charles Willson Peale, Robert Smith, hatter, and Samuel Massey to perform that function in Philadelphia. At the same time Chief Justice Thomas McKean, sitting at the city Court House, heard charges that were preferred against people accused of joining or aiding the British army.[127]

Fearful that many Tories would escape from the official net, 186 men in the area joined in a loose, extralegal association to expose all who were "notoriously disaffected to the American cause." Accusing the Tories of intimidating witnesses who might appear against them, the members guaranteed protection for all who were willing to testify. Among the 186 men who signed the association's statement on July 17, 1778, were Joseph Reed, Thomas Paine, Cadwalader Dickinson, Thomas and William Bradford, John Nicholson, and John Dunlap. Significantly absent were such conservative leaders as Robert Morris, James Wilson, Thomas Fitzsimons, and Thomas Mifflin.[128]

To assist Attorney-General Jonathan Sergeant in prosecuting Tories, the Assembly obtained the services of Joseph Reed in September 1778. During the following autumn the grand jury drew up forty-five bills charging treason, of which twenty-three cases came to trial. Only two persons received the death penalty: John Roberts, of Merion, and Abraham Carlisle, of Philadelphia, both Quakers.[129] Convicted of openly aiding the British, they were executed on November 4. Dozens of petitions signed by hundreds of Quakers could not save them. Individual Quakers protested vigorously, but the Meeting for Sufferings, which investigated the whole matter, did not officially intercede because the two men had not behaved in strict accordance with the principles of the Society of Friends. Cadwalader Dickinson, on the other hand, was disowned for serving as a judge during the trial, and for generally aiding the rebel cause.[130] To Reed the extensiveness of the subversive activity that came to light was a revelation. His conviction that it had to be suppressed in the future partly accounted for his willingness to take a leading part in government.

As a problem, Toryism was especially difficult to handle because of the varying degrees of seriousness in which it existed, or was suspected of existing, in individuals and groups. Although the Whigs thought that many people in Philadelphia hoped for the destruction of Congress, the American army, and the Pennsylvania government, they found relatively few who had joined the British forces or engaged in overt acts of treason to bring those things about. They were sure, though, that many Tories were trying to effect those same ends by encouraging inflation, diverting army supplies to civilian use, profiteering, and trading and corresponding with the enemy. To expose such activities, state agencies and extralegal bodies remained active, with varying degrees of thoroughness, during the war.

Inherent in the preoccupation of the radicals with Loyalism was a desire to bring institutions as well as individuals into conformity with the democratic spirit unleashed by the Revolution. An illustration of this outlook was the treatment accorded the College of Philadelphia. Despite Franklin's intentions at the founding, those most responsible for the college's administration and growth had thus far shown strong aristocratic and Anglican predilections, an attitude at variance with rising egalitarian and Presbyterian influences. With the coming of the Revolution much Whig antipathy was aroused by the negative position of Provost William Smith and the open Toryism of some of the trustees.[131] In January 1778, after some trustees had joined the British and others remained in the city under "the power" of General Howe, the Assembly suspended their authority for as long as the British occupied Philadelphia and three months thereafter.[132]

After its period of suspension the college tried to resume. Although the provost, all the professors, and some of the trustees took an oath of loyalty to Pennsylvania, that was not enough.[133] Strongly voiced suspicions of the college's loyalty continued, and the Assembly, after a long investigation, passed a law on November 27, 1779, that provided for a new board of trustees, under rules destroying the old Anglican dominance; changed the name of the college to the University of the State of Pennsylvania; and granted the institution an income of not more than £1500 a year.[134] New trustees and faculty members were then appointed. John Ewing, a Presbyterian minister of scientific attainments, became provost, and David Rittenhouse was named vice-provost. With its charter basically amended but not abrogated by the Assembly's action, the institution was thus made to align itself with the new revolutionary forces.[135]

Coincidental with the bitterness over Loyalism in 1779 was the outrage induced by a sudden and almost disastrous spurt in prices. Inflation had been worrisome for years of course, and the efforts made to thwart it by both Congress and the Pennsylvania Assembly had been hesitant and ineffectual. Whatever caused the upsurge in 1779—many in the ranks of officialdom attributed it to currency depreciation, scarcity of goods, and lack of information on market conditions—the distressed consumer, who saw prices jump 45 percent in one month and rise seven times above the level of the preceding year, was inclined to look about for conspirators.[136] These, he naturally assumed, were the merchants who asked ever higher prices for their goods. By early May runaway inflation had caused so much distress and anger in Philadelphia that leaderless gangs were roaming the streets looking for scapegoats.

Although most Philadelphians were victims of inflation in one way or another, it was the underprivileged workingman, often living on the verge of dire want, who suffered most. Beyond his comprehension were the fine points of economic theory, but when he compared his position to that of the wealthy, especially those who were living ostentatiously, he was inclined to attribute most of his ills to that class. Furthermore, among the wealthy, he thought, were most likely to be found Loyalists and their protectors, militia evaders, and price gougers. All these complaints were indicative of a general unrest that expressed itself in violence and disorder in 1779. It began in January when sailors, striking for higher wages, dismantled ships, disrupted work on the wharves, and precipitated a riot. Order was restored when the Executive Council called upon General Arnold to use his troops.[137]

The most violent episode, the Fort Wilson Riot, occurred on October 4, 1779, after the circulation of a handbill that urged the militia to expel from the city all disaffected persons and those who supported them. After gathering in the morning at Paddy Byrne's Tavern on Tenth Street between Race and Vine, a band of militiamen and street loiterers decided to capture James Wilson, signer of the Declaration of Independence but a conservative and a suspected profiteer, as a Loyalist sympathizer. Dr. James Hutchinson and Charles Willson Peale tried vainly to stop them. Wilson, warned that he was high on the list of the suspect because he had defended Philadelphians accused of treason, appealed to the Assembly and the Executive Council for protection. Not sure that the authorities could preserve order, he and about twenty of his friends met on Second Street and began practicing military maneuvers under Thomas Mifflin's command. When the mob arrived Mifflin withdrew his force into Wilson's house at Third and Walnut, and the battle was on. Unable to take the sturdily built house by assault, the militiamen ordered up a field piece. Before it appeared, Joseph Reed, president of the Executive Council, and the Light Horse with drawn sabers arrived on the scene and broke up the riot. The casualties numbered five dead and seventeen wounded.[138]

With inflation worsening and the Continental currency depreciated to the point where it was no longer accepted, Congress in February 1781 took a step to revive credit that had significance not only in Philadelphia but in the country at large. It created the office of superintendent of finance and unanimously elected Robert Morris to fill the position.[139]

His election came as no surprise. As a businessman of outstanding energy, intelligence, and experience, Morris was the leading figure in the most important financial community in the country. And it was from this community that he expected to receive primary assistance in laying what he considered to be the keystone of a national financial structure, the Bank of North America. Congress chartered the bank on December 31, 1781, and one week later it began operations. Thus was established the first modern bank in the United States.[140] From the time it started business until the end of the war it contributed important services to the government. Also conspicuous in mobilizing Philadelphia's financial resources to carry the Continental forces through the final campaigns, as broker for the Office of Finance and agent for the French in America, was Haym Salomon, a Polish Jew not only exiled from his homeland but an escapee from British-occupied New York, where he was twice imprisoned for his support of the Revolution before he came to Philadelphia.

The incorporation and establishment of the Bank of North America was a distinct victory for the Philadelphia conservatives, one that was in keeping with a return to political and social conservatism that came as a reaction to excesses of Tory hunting and out of dissatisfaction with the political groups most closely identified with the war and therefore with the troubles attendant upon war. Even before the victory at Yorktown in October 1781 many Philadelphians believed, or liked to believe, that the war was practically won, and that the danger of invasion which had stimulated leveling tendencies so disruptive of the old social serenity was a thing of the past. The fighting at least had moved elsewhere.

The financier Robert Morris (1734–1806), painted in 1782 by Charles Willson Peale (1741–1827).
INDEPENDENCE NATIONAL HISTORICAL PARK COLLECTION

For those in the dominant social and political levels in prewar Philadelphia the Revolution had been a traumatic experience indeed. Power formerly held by them—by the proprietary leaders and their placemen, and by the Quakers—had between 1775 and 1777 fallen into the hands of new men. The punitive action taken by the radical Whigs against Tories and "sunshine patriot[s]" in 1778 and 1779, however, and the radicals' failure to bring the considerable resources of Pennsylvania to bear on army supply problems encouraged the basic conservatism of Philadelphia to reassert itself. Of course there were elements in the unrest of 1779 that reflected the inherent class antagonism between the "better sort" and the "meaner sort," but the economic fluidity that had characterized Philadelphia in the eighteenth century worked as a safety valve to prevent a violent overturn in basic social structures. This fluidity, along with increased opportunities for economic self-aggrandizement, tended to encourage the growth of the middle class. It is true, of course, that Philadelphia had its very rich and its very poor, but the economic forces operating in the city tended to deemphasize the extremes at the top and the bottom and to magnify the middle. The contrasts evident in 1779 were more indicative of the frustrations and excesses of a long war than of any basic instability in the social structure.

When the conservatives began to reemerge politically after 1779 there was no great social or economic convulsion. From 1780 through 1783 the Republicans showed increasing strength in the elections for assemblymen. Their candidates won in Philadelphia year after year, and when John Dickinson was elected president of the Executive Council in November 1782 political opinion had come almost full circle.[141] But regardless of the politics of the men in the ascendancy at any time during Philadelphia's Revolution, their motivations were fundamentally constructive rather than destructive. Political turnovers were accomplished without assassination; no man on horseback appeared; no guillotine was introduced; and for obvious reasons, no "Bastilles" were attacked or "châteaux" burned. People went on with the task of making a living with a continuing respect for property, and the old habit of deferring to one's betters did not disappear.

X I

The same could be said for the principal cultural institutions—the College of Philadelphia, the Library Company, and the American Philosophical Society. The Library Company of Philadelphia, in existence forty-four years before the Revolution, had not been dismayed by the surrounding turmoil. It had books to lend and it lent them with generous impartiality to congressmen and British officers alike, as long as they obeyed the rules. Not unexpectedly, though, it did suffer some inconveniences. In the early summer of 1776 it had trouble obtaining a quorum of directors to make policy decisions. One year later the Library quarters in Carpenters' Hall were used to house sick American soldiers. During the war years it was extremely difficult to acquire new books. An attempt to bring some volumes from New York City in 1780 was thwarted when the Executive Council cited a state law that forbade the importation of anything manufactured in England. Finally, in the spring of 1783 the library sent its first money to England since 1774, an order for £200 worth of books.[142]

The sessions of the American Philosophical Society from 1774 to 1776 were sporadic, and from 1776 to 1779 they were suspended altogether. Enthusiasm for the organization still continued, however, and at a meeting at the University of Pennsylvania in December 1779 plans for its incorporation were prepared. They were approved by the Assembly in 1780 in an act that carefully detailed the purposes for which the society was created.[143]

Although the war in its early stages had damaging effects on the local humane and charitable organizations, interest in these matters by no means disappeared. When the American army took over the Bettering House, a larger successor to the City Alms House opened in 1767 on Spruce Street between Tenth and Eleventh, the Quakers offered their Fourth Street Meeting House as a refuge for the poor.[144] Poor relief was generally undertaken by private individuals and groups. For example, they contributed food and old clothing to the inmates of the prisons. From 1776 until the British occupation members of the Society for the Relief of Distressed Prisoners collected food for them in wheelbarrows which they pushed about in solicitation from house to house.[145] Food was also purchased through contributions of money dropped into charity boxes. Those imprisoned for debt were in the worst condition because they, unlike the criminals, received no subsistence from the county. In 1783 John Reynolds, a jailer, made a public appeal in behalf of confined debtors. Forty of the fifty-seven men and women under his control, he reported, were in great distress.[146]

In July 1781 there arose a special problem in poor relief that was too large and complicated to be solved by the casual methods usually employed. The city's lodging facilities were overtaxed with the arrival of refugees from the fighting in Georgia and South Carolina. Since many of them were destitute, Congress made arrangements for their support by setting up a committee to borrow money, the return of which was guaranteed by the government.[147]

In a time when frequent sickness was accepted as one of the inevitable trials of the human condition, Philadelphians became alarmed only when disease reached epidemic proportions. Two such outbreaks occurred during the war, the first in the winter of 1776–1777 when hundreds of soldiers died of camp fever and smallpox, and the second in 1780 when a great many people, including the wife of Joseph Reed, died of the flux.[148] But whether the amount of sickness was routine or abnormal, Philadelphia had the benefit of what was for the time a high quality of medical care administered by the Pennsylvania Hospital, a boon to both American and British soldiers, and by a group of excellent physicians, outstanding among whom were Benjamin Rush, James Hutchinson, William Shippen, Jr. (a cousin of Peggy Shippen's father), and John Morgan. Despite the growing political turmoil of the 1760s the city had also during that decade inaugurated systematic medical education in America. In November 1762 William Shippen, Jr., fresh from the completion of his doctoral thesis at the University of Edinburgh, instituted a series of medical lectures at the State House aimed at both medical students and seriously interested laymen. In May 1765 John Morgan, returned from his own Edinburgh studies, proposed the founding of a medical school to the trustees of the college. Morgan was promptly elected "Professor of the Theory and Practice of Physick." Unfortunately, jealousy between Shippen and Morgan impeded the subsequent growth of Philadelphia's medical education and efforts to apply the city's medical learning to the health of the Continental Army.[149]

Measures to protect the health of Philadelphians were undertaken both by citizens' groups and by governmental agencies. To provide emergency treatment for persons whose "animation may be suspended" by drowning, chokedamp, hanging, and sunstroke, the Humane Society was organized in 1780.[150] In the same year the city's "Inspector of Salt Provisions," decrying the fact that spoiled and contaminated meat had been fraudulently sold in the past, warned all provisioners and merchants that their goods could not be offered to the public until they had been inspected and approved.[151]

After the city was returned to American control in 1778 more attention was paid to the maintenance of safeguards against the constant peril of fire. The numerous fire companies had allowed their organizations to languish during the early years of the war, and after a "great fire" in the latter part of December 1778 the Pennsylvania Executive Council urged their revival.[152] Chimney blazes were the main hazard, and although fines were to be imposed on all who suffered these mishaps, many chimneys remained unswept because of householders' forgetfulness or indifference. Since many "owners" of chimney sweeps were unwilling to allow their boys to go out unless they had specific job orders in advance, householders often went unreminded of the condition of their chimneys until it was too late.[153]

The Philadelphia Contributionship, convinced that the numerous trees in the city constituted a fire hazard, reaffirmed in 1781 a decision it had made in 1774 to refuse to insure or reinsure houses located near trees.[154] When opposition to the decision developed considerable strength, the Assembly buttressed the company's policy with an act of April 15, 1782, that ordered the removal of all trees in streets, lanes, and alleys because they obstructed passage, destroyed watercourses, and spread fires. This ill-considered legislation aroused the immediate resentment of a number of petitioners who protested that trees "conduce much to the health of the inhabitants, and are in other respects of great public utility."[155] In response to the petition the Assembly repealed the offending section just five months after the original act was passed, and Philadelphia's trees were saved. The Contributionship stubbornly continued to adhere to its policy, however, a persistence that encouraged the establishment in 1784 of a competitor, the Mutual Assurance Company. The new company was willing to insure houses near trees, at an extra premium, provided the trees were not allowed to grow higher than the eaves of the adjacent houses. It took as its fire mark, and of course became popularly known as, the Green Tree.[156]

The effect of the war on organized entertainments and diversions in Philadelphia was at times dampening, but not always suppressive. Congress tried to set the tone for all of the colonies in 1774 when its Continental Association prohibited gaming, cock-fighting, plays, and all sorts of amusements. At that time the New England delegates were especially worried about the spirit of levity they believed prevailed in Philadelphia—for some of them,

Philadelphia was the first relaxed city they had ever seen, and was accordingly disturbing—and mainly at their behest a rule was passed to forbid congressmen themselves from participating in public entertainments. Samuel Adams was much upset at the behavior of southern congressmen who, he thought, should have done more praying and less dancing.[157] But southerners for the most part always enjoyed Philadelphia. Where Samuel Adams beheld sin in all its garish forms, Richard Henry Lee saw an "attractive scene of debauch and amusement."[158]

It was too much to expect that a city that had been transformed into a war capital, inundated with thousands of visitors, invaded, and then liberated, would behave with constant dignity and sobriety. When they had an opportunity Philadelphians liked to dance and revel at gargantuan feasts, and the war brought no cessation of those activities. "We have a great many balls and entertainments," wrote Mrs. Robert Morris in November 1778.[159] In the same month Col. Walter S. Stewart commented on the great changes that had occurred in manners and customs since his last visit:

Tis all gaiety, and from what I can observe, Every Lady and Gentleman Endeavours to outdo the other in Splendor and show. The manners of the Ladys is likewise much chang'd, they have really in a great measure lost that Native Innocence in their manners which formerly was their Characteristick, and supplied its place with what they call an easy behaviour, they have really got the art of throwing themselves into the most wanton and amorous Postures; which their free manner of speech adds not a little to. By Heaven tis almost too much for a Healthy, Vigorous, young Soldier to bear; to be plac'd on an Elegant Sofa along side one of them, when they are displaying both the artillery of their Tongues and Eyes. The Manner of Entertaining in this place has likewise undergone its change; you cannot conceive anything more Elegant than the Present Taste; you will hardly dine at a table but they present you with three Courses, and each of them in the Most Elegant manner.[160]

Yet Stewart's three-course dinner was frugal compared to one attended by Maj.-Gen. Nathanael Greene. He counted 160 dishes on the table.[161]

The "easy behaviour" noted by Stewart in women at the upper levels of society was evident to a much greater degree in other social areas. There are no statistics on the relative increase of immorality and crime in the city, but according to one observer in 1780, vice was so prevalent that the Devil himself "wou'd blush to be here."[162] In the same year another observer, disturbed by the increase in crime, suggested that the citizens, "without respect to persons," organize themselves into nightwatches to stop the spread of robberies.[163]

Whatever the increase in immorality or law-breaking might have been, it had to be assessed in light of the puritanical strictures imposed by legislative action during the war. Almost everything that was enjoyable was widely considered to be immoral or unpatriotic, and that covered a wide range within the blurred lines of the moral spectrum. One outstanding illustration was the banning of theatrical presentations. After the sudden flowering of the Philadelphia theater just before the war, Philadelphians must have been greatly disappointed when stage performances were listed among the forbidden diversions by Congress in 1774. Instead of relenting, Congress later reaffirmed its stand by prohibiting army officers from attending the theater. The Pennsylvania Assembly went even further in 1779 when it provided severe penalties for anyone guilty of building stages or acting on them anywhere in the state. That the law would be enforced was made clear by Plunkett Fleeson, president of the Philadelphia magistrates, in January 1782. He had seen an advertisement in the *Pennsylvania Packet* announcing that *Eugénie*, a farce, would be presented by Alexandre-Marie Quesnay and students of the French language for the benefit of the poor in the Pennsylvania Hospital and the soldiers in the Barracks. Fleeson did not stress the moral questions posed by the theater, but he implied that it would be wrong to present a public entertainment while the Indians and the British were still at war with America.[164]

Dancing and public celebrations nevertheless provided occasional diversions. The Dancing Assemblies continued and celebrations were held on every suitable occasion.[165] But with the exception of the Fourth of July and the French alliance there was not much to celebrate until 1781. Then came the ratification of the Articles of Confederation, the surrender of Cornwallis at Yorktown, and the arrival of the victorious Washington, all of which were publicly celebrated. Perhaps the most lavish demonstration occurred when 12,000 spectators watched 750 people help the French minister to the United States honor the birth of the dauphin in 1782.[166]

XII

After the great Franco-American victory at Yorktown, Philadelphians eagerly awaited peace. In the early spring of 1783 its signs were unmistakable when American prisoners of war arrived from New York and British prisoners passed through from Lancaster on their way to New York.[167] Finally, in April it was learned that King George had declared a cessation of arms two months earlier. Congress then issued a similar proclamation on April 11, and shortly thereafter the port of Philadelphia was opened to ships of all nations.[168]

With the strains and abrasions of warfare now in the past, Philadelphia and Congress would have to readjust to each other in times of peace, but before that could happen the two suddenly parted company under unfortunate and embarrassing circumstances. On Saturday, June 21, 1783, about 300 troops of the Pennsylvania Line, numbering some from the Barracks and about eighty from the Third Pennsylvania Regiment at Lancaster who had come to Philadelphia against the orders of their officers, surrounded the State House. Almost all were recent recruits. They feared that in the still parlous financial condition of Congress they would be sent home without a settlement of their pay, and they had come to seek redress of their grievances from the Executive Council, then in session at the State House. Congress, which had been vainly appealed to by some of the soldiers on June 13, was in adjournment for the weekend, but its president Elias Boudinot hastily summoned it to the State House just in time to be encircled.[169] When called upon by Congress to use the state militia, the Executive Council, headed by its president John Dickinson, refused. The disaffected troops eventually set a twenty-minute time limit for the surrounded Congress to assure redress of their grievances; but the time limit passed without violence, and when the congressmen mustered courage simply to walk out through the milling troops, they met nothing worse than insults, though by then the soldiers had been drinking freely. The troops returned to the Barracks, still mutinously inclined.

On June 22 and 23 Congress continued to insist that the state use force to compel the mutinous soldiers to accept the command of their officers, and although it coupled this demand with a threat to leave the city, the Executive Council still refused. The council was negotiating with the troops, who by now appeared to be peaceably disposed, and it feared that the use of militia would create even worse disorder. The soldiers finally subsided, finding discharge and going home even more important than firm assurances of pay, though their disorders, following close on the threat of an officers' coup at Newburgh, New York, reinforced traditional American and English suspicions of military power and helped assure Congress's virtually complete dissolution of the Continental Army in 1784.[170]

But Congress, meanwhile, would not wait to see the results of the state's negotiations with the soldiers. On June 24 Boudinot signed a proclamation summoning the delegates to meet at Princeton, New Jersey, two days later. Although the stated reason for the move was the refusal of the Executive Council to suppress troops still in "open revolt,"[171] many congressmen were eager to leave Philadelphia for reasons that did not appear in the proclamation. Weeks before the mutiny Oliver Ellsworth, delegate from Connecticut, reported that it was "generally agreed that Congress should remove to a place of less expense, less avocation and less influence than are to be expected in a commercial and opulent city."[172]

Philadelphia and Congress had endured the hard realities of war together, and each had contributed much to the other. Their abrupt and angry parting was unfortunate for all concerned, but the war was over and the city had served its purpose.

The Federal City
1783-1800

by Richard G. Miller

*... the mechanic labors under the double difficulty of the impracti-
cability of obtaining money to carry on his business and the profusion of
foreign goods which prevent the sale of such articles as he could finish.*
— A Philadelphia artisan

*... the men [of Philadelphia] are almost always immersed in their
business affairs and in political intrigue.*
— Francisco de Miranda

*The room became full before I left it, and the circle very brilliant. How
could it be otherwise, when the dazzling Mrs. Bingham and her beautiful
sisters were there; the Misses Allen, and Misses Chew; in short a constellation of beauties?*
— Abigail Adams [1]

Philadelphia ushered in its first postwar Christmas season with
festivities honoring a secular messiah. On the afternoon of December 8, 1783, Gen. George Washington approached the city on his
way from New York, just liberated from British occupation, heading toward
Annapolis, where he would resign his commission to the Confederation
Congress and go home to Mount Vernon.

John Dickinson, president of the Supreme Executive Council of Pennsylvania, Robert Morris, Maj.-Gen. Arthur St. Clair, Maj.-Gen. Edward Hand,
many other Philadelphia dignitaries, and the Light Horse Troop of the city
rode out to meet Washington at Frankford and escort him into town. When
he arrived at Philadelphia, the church bells rang out, cannon fired a thirteen-
gun salute, and even a Dutch ship at anchor in the harbor joined in the
celebratory firing of guns. Cheering citizens crowded the streets. [2]

It was Washington's first experience of so adulatory a welcome; many
more were to come, of course, including many in Philadelphia. The signing
of the peace treaty in Paris in September and the British evacuation of New
York had assured both American independence and the general's own place

as the first of the charismatic founder-figures of the modern new nations, the hero whom all subsequent nation-builders would strive to emulate. Even after Lord Cornwallis's surrender to him at Yorktown, Washington had passed through Philadelphia in the autumn of 1781 without arousing the sort of emotions that now burst forth, because then the war had not yet been certainly won and Washington's role in history was not yet quite certain either. From the welcome to Philadelphia in December 1783 onward, however, Washington would become accustomed to receiving adulation almost as a living god. His savoring of that role, furthermore, would continue to take place largely in Philadelphia; the years of the general's greatest glory through the remainder of the century were to be bound together with one of Philadelphia's eras of greatest civic glory, as national capital and presidential residence of the immortal Washington. Together for almost the next twenty years the city and the general were to share each other's pride and also each other's troubles and vexations.

I

Not yet quite accustomed to the part of a demigod, Washington was uncharacteristically effusive when he spoke to the General Assembly of Pennsylvania in the State House on December 9 to thank the legislators and the city for their approbation. Usually the most careful of accountants in presenting his lists of expenses to Congress for payment, he was flustered enough on this visit to the Confederation financial offices still located in Philadelphia to omit his customary stipulation requiring "lawful money" when he drew a warrant for £217 owed him; as a result he was paid in depreciated Pennsylvania currency and had to claim redress later.[3]

Perhaps he was also too distracted to look around carefully enough to see that troubles and vexations aplenty disturbed Philadelphia in the immediate wake of the war. Other visitors in 1783 found the city looking as if it had survived a fearful storm. Peeling paint and broken windows on houses and shops bespoke years of wartime neglect. The slightest rainfall turned broken pavements to mud. Public buildings that had housed soldiers and horses still reeked of human and animal waste.

The Philadelphia economy, so recently forced to redirect itself from maritime commerce to the manufacture of war materials, now had to reverse itself. The demand for military supplies naturally collapsed; instead the city's military depots held a large surplus of army equipage to be disposed of at reduced prices if at all. Wars always leave surpluses, no matter how desperate the shortages while the fighting is going on.

The British blockade, to be sure, no longer restricted passage of the Delaware, and the British Navigation Acts also no longer directly bound Philadelphia commerce. On the other hand in colonial times the Navigation Acts had probably been as much a help as a hindrance, permitting Philadelphia ships and merchants to share with other British vessels and subjects in a monopoly of the internal commerce of the British Empire. Now the familiar ports of the British West Indies were closed to Philadelphia ships. New trading partners would have to be found, while in the meantime the coming of peace also brought cheap British goods flooding into the Philadelphia market, often dispensed by agents of British exporters who bypassed Philadelphia merchants, and competing ruinously with local manufactures. In the postwar economic dislocation wages fell, artisans and laborers were thrown out of work, and industry stagnated. Shipbuilding was especially hard hit; as late as 1786 only thirteen ships were built in Philadelphia.[4]

Plan of Mr. Fitch's Steam Boat, *engraved for the* Columbian Magazine *(1786). John Fitch founded a company in Philadelphia to build the first steamboat in 1786.*

Departed along with the economic stimuli of the war were the Confederation Congress and the business its members and hangers-on had brought to keepers of taverns and boardinghouses, to printers, and to a host of other tradesmen. It may be that the welcome shown Washington was all the more fervent in the hope it would demonstrate that the mutiny against Congress the previous June, precipitating the national legislature's exodus, had in no way reflected the sentiments of the city. But the Confederation Congress stayed away. For the present all efforts to coax it back were unavailing. The efforts were compromised, moreover, by a quality of halfheartedness, reflecting in part the political malaise with which Pennsylvania state factionalism of the 1780s infected the city.

II

In the midst of the Revolution, Pennsylvania had adopted a state constitution in 1776 that granted the franchise to almost every male over twenty-one who paid taxes. It abolished Philadelphia's city charter—the state Assembly assumed control of city affairs—and it established a single-house legislature subject to annual elections.[5] The adoption of the 1776 constitution had ejected the colonial merchant upper class from political leadership and replaced them with radical Whigs, or Constitutionalists.

Dr. James Hutchinson, Jonathan Dickinson Sergeant (a lawyer), Blair McClenaghan (a merchant), and George Bryan (another lawyer) led the supporters of the constitution of 1776 in Philadelphia. These leaders of the Constitutionalists were themselves generally well-to-do merchants and professional men, but for the most part they were a rising business and professional group, standing apart from the old upper class and perceiving greater opportunity in a new political and social order than in stability and retention of the old order. The Constitutionalists had won approval of the new constitution from many of the city's skilled workingmen, its artisans. The artisans had assumed that with independence would come freedom from British competition.

After 1780, however, the Constitutionalists never achieved as much political success in Philadelphia as in the western areas of the state. In the city Constitutionalists lost the Assembly elections from 1780 to 1783, won in 1784, and lost all but one of the remaining elections until the parties of the 1780s broke apart with the adoption of another new state constitution in 1790. The Constitutionalist victory in 1784 occurred because that year the Anti-Constitutionalists or Republicans happened to conduct a poorly organized campaign. After 1784 the Constitutionalists failed more and more surely, because as the Revolution receded into the past they could no longer rely on cries of "Tory" or "traitor" and the anti-British emotions that these labels invoked. Eventually they also hastened their own decline by opposing the federal Constitution in 1787.[6]

Opposition to the constitution of 1776 came from many nouveau riche as well as from the colonial upper class. Exploitation of wartime economic opportunities had propelled into social as well as business prominence men such as Robert Morris, financier to Congress; Thomas Fitzsimons, Irish immigrant merchant and with Morris a co-founder of the Bank of North America; Thomas McKean, lawyer and former radical leader of Delaware politics who now had a house in Philadelphia, played the political game in both Pennsylvania and Delaware, and opposed the Pennsylvania constitution even though he was chief justice under it; Israel Israel, wealthy merchant and by avocation keeper of the popular Cross Keys Inn at Fourth and Chestnut; John Swanwick, another rising merchant, notable for his political ambition; and Dr. Benjamin Rush, who had played a major role in the local revolution of 1776 and the writing of the constitution but had grown disgruntled with the Constitutionalists' extremism. Ambitious men such as these worked with the old upper class to bring about the defeat of the Constitutionalists. Their new coalition engaged in a bitter political struggle with the supporters of the democratic constitution. Their goals were to recapture and solidify the political power lost by the upper class in 1776 and to win a new, far less radical state constitution. To develop a political organization, this faction had to adopt some of the democratic ideals unleashed by the Revolution in order to win the broad-based support necessary to defeat the Constitutionalists.[7]

Republicans feared the democratic constitution of Pennsylvania, believing that its single-house legislature unchecked by any other authority was susceptible to corruption by demagogues. The urban upper class had little confidence in the ability of common citizens to govern themselves unless guided by the natural leaders of society. More specifically, the Republicans saw the Constitutionalists as opposed to government aid to business. Issues such as banking reforms, protective tariff duties for American manufactures, encouragement of trade, and protection of private property were basic to the economic lifeblood of the merchant, lawyer, and artisan of Philadelphia, and the Republican members of those groups did not believe the Constitutionalists showed adequate regard for these issues.[8]

In particular, the Republicans sought to reincorporate the city of Philadelphia as a means of encouraging a return to political activity of the leaders of the old municipal corporation. Publicly, the Republican campaign was waged on the ground that efficiency demanded that the city govern itself. The Constitutionalists countered that corporations were irresponsible and that reincorporation would serve the "aristocrats." For the time being the Constitutionalists turned back the Republican effort.[9]

The chartering and operation of the Bank of North America also invoked a bitter political struggle throughout the 1780s. Because there was doubt of the power of the Confederation Congress to charter such an institution, the bank was incorporated under both United States and Pennsylvania charters; in fact New York and Massachusetts had also chartered it to assure the legality of its activities within their boundaries. Its chartering had been one of the first triumphs of the Republicans. The Constitutionalists would have preferred an institution such as the Bank of Pennsylvania of 1780, which was an impermanent organization created to raise funds for the Continental Army. The Bank of North America, in contrast, was a corporate bank in the modern sense, the first on the continent. Its corporate quality especially distressed the Constitutionalists because it seemed likely to them to become an immortal instrument forever using its power over credit to favor its stockholders, their friends, and other special interests. The Constitutionalists feared that "the accumulation of enormous wealth in the hands of a society who claim perpetual duration will necessarily produce a degree of influence and power which can not be entrusted in the hands of any set of men whatsoever without endangering the public safety."[10]

The Constitutionalists also disapproved the election as first president of the bank of Thomas Willing, who by remaining in Philadelphia to represent Willing, Morris and Company during the British occupation had in their eyes sold out to the enemy. The bank was governed by Willing, Morris, Fitzsimons, and a few other wealthy merchants who were Republicans in politics. Constitutionalists claimed also that its interest rates were too high, that it placed excessively narrow limits on currency issues and short-term mortgages, and that it had too much influence over state government.[11]

The radical Constitutionalists retained enough power in the western counties that on September 13, 1786, they succeeded in repealing the Pennsylvania charter of the Bank of North America. This was yet another blow to the Philadelphia economy as the city attempted to recover from the dislocations of the war. The bank continued to operate under its remaining charters, and Delaware granted it a new charter, opening the possibility that it might move its headquarters downriver. It did not do so, but meanwhile its uncertain status reduced confidence in its credit.

By this time, however, the drift of state as well as city politics was away from the Constitutionalists and the disruptive effect of their policies. The elections of 1785 gave neither party firm control of the legislature, but the Republicans were able to win recharter in March 1786. In Philadelphia, the combination of an economic slowdown that had worsened even before the revocation of the bank's charter with renewed Republican efforts to rally the artisan vote had brought about the defeat of all the Constitutionalist assemblymen from the city.[12]

Less critical to the city's well-being but dismally symptomatic of the chronic discontents that had come to be associated with the Constitutionalist regime was the ongoing battle between the University of the State of Pennsylvania and the College of Philadelphia. The trustees of the college, and most especially its provost, the Rev. William Smith, regarded the act of 1779 that created the university as an "abrogation of the charters" of 1753 and 1755 that had founded the college. The "abrogation," they held, was contrary to clauses in the Pennsylvania constitution of 1776 protecting existing corporations in their property rights and privileges.

The officials of the college nevertheless had surrendered the charters, minute books, and use of the buildings at Fourth and Arch to the officials of the new university, albeit Provost Smith delivered up only slowly and reluctantly the seal, the keys, and the accounts. Almost a year was required to pry Smith out of the provost's house.

Thereafter Smith, the college trustees, and increasingly the Republicans, grasping another partisan issue, went on denying the legitimacy of the university and inveighing against it as an invasion of property rights. In their invective, the university became a nest of "robbers" who had gotten control of the institution by "robbing the Original Owners." While this accusation confused trusteeship over property with ownership of it, such blurring of the facts did nothing to reduce the obstinacy of the college's stand or the growing enthusiasm with which Republicans endorsed it. Higher education in Philadelphia, long hindered by the Friends' distrust, was now foundering on political shoals.[13]

No doubt the university would have suffered troubles enough without having to wage a battle for its very right to legal existence. In establishing a state university the Pennsylvania Assembly had not only guaranteed to it the property of the earlier college, but had promised that sufficient charges would be made against confiscated Loyalist estates to assure an income from them not beyond £1500 a year. The returns from this source proved slow to come in, however, and meanwhile many persons who had pledged financial aid to the old college disavowed any obligation under the new circumstances. Continuing currency inflation as another attribute of political and economic instability kept expenses higher than anticipated. Within its first month the university had to appeal to the state for a £15,000 loan, which was not forthcoming. The institution simply could not make ends meet. During the 1780s its faculty had to teach with their salaries constantly in arrears. Properties along the waterfront and elsewhere in the city had to be sold off for ready cash, though the eventual increments in their value might one day have guaranteed the university's financial stability. By 1788 the university was regularly receiving an annual income of only about £2200 against normal annual expenses of £2800.[14]

These troubles were too numerous for the university to withstand the rise of Anti-Constitutionalist political fortunes. On March 6, 1789, a Republican-dominated Assembly voted to restore to the trustees and faculty of the college the property they had possessed in 1779 and their privileges under the charters of 1753 and 1755. William Smith, who had lately conducted his assaults on the university from Chestertown, Maryland, where he had founded Washington College, returned in triumph to the provost's house, and the college resumed instruction at Fourth and Arch Streets. The revitalized college board of trustees filled ten vacancies that had accumulated because of deaths and the departure of Loyalists. Yet the act of 1789 had not revoked the charter of the university. Though forced out of the old college buildings, the university continued to hold classes, first in the Masonic hall in Lodge Alley, then in a new building just being completed for the American Philosophical Society on the west side of Fifth Street within the State House Yard. Only dubiously capable of supporting a single college, Philadelphia now had two rival colleges within a few blocks of each other.[15]

I I I

For the second time Philadelphia staged a grand civic welcome for General Washington, when he arrived on May 13, 1787, to take his seat in the convention of the states to revise the Articles of Confederation. This convention had been authorized by Congress specifically in response to a call from a convention on interstate commerce meeting at Annapolis in 1786, but more generally in answer to many pleas like those of Philadelphia for national assistance to the economy.

Washington traveled this time from Mount Vernon, so a delegation of senior officers of his old army rode south from Philadelphia to meet him at Chester and dined with him there. The party crossed the Schuylkill at Gray's Ferry, where during the occupation the British had established a floating bridge since maintained by the Americans. The Light Horse Troop and other mounted citizens formed an enlarged escort from Gray's Ferry into the city, where once more the bells pealed forth the inhabitants' greetings. Washington was to have stayed at a boarding establishment run by a Mrs. House, probably at Fifth and Market Streets; but Robert Morris and Mrs. Morris so strongly repeated an earlier invitation that the general lodge with them that he now accepted. He moved his baggage into their commodious house at 190 High Street, the second house east of Sixth Street on the south side. Before the day ended Washington called on Benjamin Franklin, then eighty-one years old and feeble; Franklin had returned from his diplomatic missions in 1785 and was president of the Supreme Executive Council of Pennsylvania as well as a delegate to the forthcoming convention.[16]

Enough delegates had arrived by May 25 to open the convention on that day. The Constitutional Convention, as the meeting became, initially provided little information to fuel gossip in the taverns and on streetcorners. The members decided their work was so momentous—they quickly chose to exceed their instructions and to write a new federal Constitution—that they had to enfold their sessions in complete secrecy. The rule of silence was evidently well observed.

Their deliberations persisted through a hot summer and into September. Washington, who was immediately elected president of the convention, continued to ornament the city's most important social gatherings and to be seen on his way to or from occasional excursions into the countryside; during an intermission in the debates on July 31, he rode over the length and breadth of his army's encampment at Valley Forge. The comings and goings of other prominent men—Gov. Edmund Randolph of Virginia and George Mason, the author of the Virginia Bill of Rights; Alexander Hamilton of New York, very young but already famous as a hero of Yorktown and one of the stoutest advocates of stronger central government; John Rutledge, wartime governor of South Carolina, and many more—revived much of the atmosphere of the Continental capital. But the citizenry learned little of what was transpiring until the convention adopted an agreed-upon document and an enacting motion offered by Benjamin Franklin: "Done in Convention, by the unanimous consent of the States present the 17th of September, &c, in witness whereof we have hereunto subscribed our names." During the signing ceremony, Franklin made his remark that he was now satisfied that the sun depicted on the back of the president's chair was rising, not setting. The rule of secrecy was repealed, and the delegates proceeded to the City Tavern at Second and Walnut Streets for a dinner together and farewells.[17]

In Philadelphia and throughout Pennsylvania the news that the convention had drawn up a charter for a strong central government caused little alteration of existing party divisions. The Constitutionalists, who drew their name from the democratic state constitution of 1776, generally saw in the new federal Constitution a threat to Pennsylvania's democracy and a federal government that might reinforce the unwholesome financial operations of Robert Morris and his friends; thus, confusingly, most Constitutionalists became opponents of the new Constitution. The old Anti-Constitutionalists or Republicans became in general the friends of the new Constitution, or Federalists. They did so largely because they hoped the new government would do the very things their opponents feared, particularly that the clause of the new Constitution guaranteeing the obligation of contract would shield the Bank of North America from future assaults on its charter. In the background, however, was the sense among the friends of the new frame of government that by creating a larger political arena it might rescue Pennsylvania from much of the destructive factional squabbling that had plagued it since independence. This consideration beyond the motives of economic gain of one or another group of businessmen was important because the contest for Pennsylvania's ratification would be, within Philadelphia, mainly a contest for the votes of artisans, small tradesmen, and mechanics, the voting workingmen of the city; as always, the merchants and professional men were already divided between the two parties.

The contest for Pennsylvania's ratification also involved the efficiency of the Republican—now Federalist—party's recently constructed political machine. That machine was never to perform to better advantage. The Pennsylvania Assembly had been approaching the end of a session when the Constitutional Convention adjourned. The Republicans had determined to keep the session alive long enough to call a ratifying convention, rather than risk putting the arrangements into the hands of a new and possibly Constitutionalist Assembly to be elected in October. It was not until September 27, however, that the Confederation Congress formally submitted the new Constitution to the states. The Assembly was scheduled to adjourn on September 29 because its members could no longer delay returning home to prepare for the coming elections. A special courier brought the congressional resolution of submission to Philadelphia on the morning of September 28. Thereupon some of the Constitutionalist members absented themselves from the Assembly to prevent a quorum. The sergeant-at-arms and a clerk were sent into the streets to find at least two members to produce a quorum. Two being found refused to come, but Federalist bystanders dragged them forcibly to the State House. The Assembly then appointed the first Tuesday in November for the election of a ratifying convention.[18]

The Philadelphia Anti-Federalists worked up a strong ticket, attempting to confuse the voters by including Benjamin Franklin at the head of it, and publishing the objections to the Constitution drawn up by that champion of natural rights George Mason, who had refused to sign it. James Wilson, Philadelphia lawyer, frequent congressman, one of the Pennsylvania delegates to the Continental Congress who had voted for independence in July 1776,

member of the Constitutional Convention, and next to James Madison probably the single most important architect of the new Constitution, led the
oratorical battle in behalf of ratification. Wilson received more votes than any
Anti-Federalist for the ratifying convention, and the Federalists won all five
Philadelphia city and all five Philadelphia County delegates.

They also won two-thirds of the sixty-nine delegates who assembled at the
State House on November 21. This Federalist margin did not prevent vigorous debate, nor was it sufficient to forestall the Anti-Federalists from parliamentary maneuvers to prolong the convention for almost a month. Wilson
once more carried much of the burden of debate for the Federalists, enthusiastically seconded by Benjamin Rush. After a forty-six to twenty-three vote in
favor of ratification was at last recorded and announced to the public on
December 12, that afternoon a group of sailors and ship carpenters mounted
a boat on a wagon drawn by five horses and escorted it through the Philadelphia streets, pretending to take soundings as they went: "Three and twenty
fathoms, foul bottom"—in reference to the opposition vote—and "Six and
forty fathoms, safe anchorage."[19]

This small ratification-day procession may have helped inspire the holding
of parades in many other cities and towns to celebrate the progress of the
Constitution toward the nine ratifications necessary for the new government
to go into operation. When the ninth state, New Hampshire, happened to
ratify just before the Fourth of July, on June 21, 1788, the Federalists of
Philadelphia decided to celebrate again with the grandest procession of all, to
be held on the coming Fourth. Francis Hopkinson, poet, wit, signer of the
Declaration of Independence, and currently a judge of admiralty, became
director of the Federal Procession, one of the most spectacular civic observances in all of Philadelphia's history.

Eighty-eight numbered units comprised the procession. The ship *Rising
Sun*, anchored in the Delaware and decorated with the flags of many nations,
opened the festivities with a cannon salute at sunrise, echoed by the bells of
Christ Church. Ten other vessels anchored near the *Rising Sun* flew flags
bearing the names of the states that had ratified—Virginia had just followed
New Hampshire to make ten. At eight o'clock ten marshals, headed by
Maj.-Gen. Thomas Mifflin, wartime quartermaster-general and now a power-
ful Pennsylvania political leader, led off the parade from Third and South
Streets. It marched north on Third to Callowhill, west to Fourth, south to
Market, and thence to Union Green, a park in front of the Hamilton family
estate of Bush Hill, north of Market beyond Twelfth.

The Light Horse Troop marched near the head of the procession. The
features included Thomas Fitzsimons representing the French Alliance by
riding a horse that had belonged to the French hero of Yorktown, Général
le comte de Rochambeau, and carrying a flag that combined three fleurs-de-
lys with thirteen stars; Richard Bache, Franklin's son-in-law, as herald of a
new era, proclaimed in verse on a banner on the herald's staff; and a carriage
drawn by ten white horses and displaying the "New Roof, or grand Federal

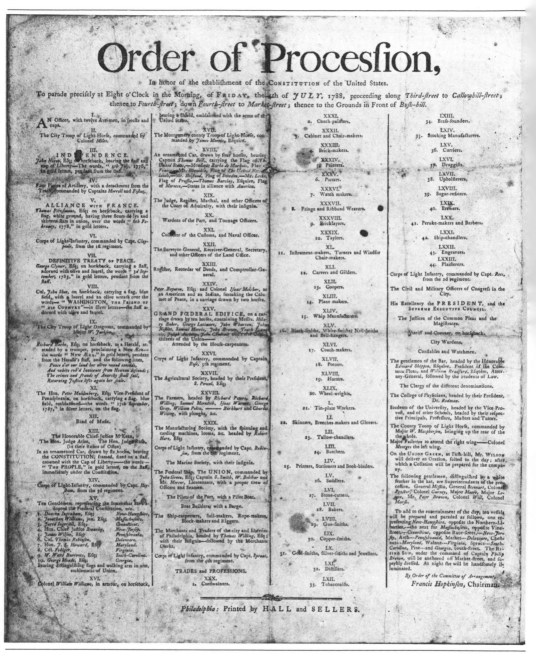

Order of Procession, In honor of the establishment of the Constitution of the United States, *printed by Hall and Sellers (1788).*

AMERICAN PHILOSOPHICAL SOCIETY

Edifice," a symbol based on an allegorical poem composed by Francis Hopkinson the previous December in which he ridiculed the Anti-Federalists for
preferring an old roof to a new one.

Mainly, however, the numbered units represented the trades of the city
—units thirty-three through seventy-seven in an order determined by lot.
Most of the trades were represented by impressive delegations, many in some
sort of uniform, most with various emblems of their trades and patriotic
slogans. The last, the stay-makers, were content to be "Represented by Mr.
Francis Serre, with his first journeyman carrying an elegant pair of ladies'
stays." The turn-out of tradesmen, like the results of the elections for the
ratifying convention, suggests the strength with which Philadelphia workingmen had accepted the Federalist arguments.[20]

I V

The Federal Procession aptly symbolized a clearing of Philadelphia's and
Pennsylvania's political air, permitting the resolution of many of the quarrels
that had bitterly divided local factions since 1776.

One such was the question of Philadelphia self-government. Through the
1780s Constitutionalists had feared that Anti-Constitutionalist political
strength in the city would yield immediate control of any new municipal
government to Robert Morris and his political and business associates. By the
end of the decade, however, the Anti-Constitutionalists in their new guise as
Federalists usually controlled the state as well as the city anyway. Furthermore they were willing to allow the city government to consist mainly of
elected officials, rather than coopted men as in the past. No compelling reason
to deny Philadelphia authority over its own affairs any longer existed. Declaring that "the administration of government within the city of Philadelphia is,
in its present form, inadequate to the suppression of vice and immorality, to
the advancement of the public health and order, and to the promotion of trade,
industry, and happiness," the Pennsylvania Assembly on March 11, 1789, at last
adopted "An Act to incorporate the city of Philadelphia."

The inhabitants of the city became a corporation and body politic styled
"The Mayor, Aldermen, and Citizens of Philadelphia." The freeholders were
to elect fifteen aldermen to serve seven-year terms and thirty common councilmen to serve three-year terms. A mayor was to be elected by the aldermen
from among their number and to serve a one-year term. A recorder was to
be chosen by the mayor and aldermen from among the city's freemen to serve
a seven-year term. The mayor, recorder, aldermen, and common councilmen
constituted the legislative power when assembled in Common Council. All
the property and rights of the colonial corporation were transferred to the
new corporation. When the taxing power of the new government proved
inadequate because it was too much bound by the limits of the old corporation, the Assembly supplemented the charter on April 2, 1790, to give the
Common Council power to raise and levy taxes "upon the persons of single
men, and upon the estates, real and personal, of the inhabitants, for the

purposes of lighting, watching, watering, pitching, paving, and cleansing the streets, lanes, and alleys of the city."

Samuel Powel, the last mayor under the colonial charter, was elected alderman and then chosen first mayor under the new charter. Powel had been counted a patriot during the Revolution, and among his fellow aldermen were such other old patriots as Francis Hopkinson and John Nixon. But the mood of reconciliation nourished by the federal Constitution and making possible the municipal charter also produced the election as common councilmen of such former Loyalists or suspected Loyalists as Benjamin Chew, Henry Drinker, Miers Fisher, Jared Ingersoll, and James Pemberton. On the other hand not one Anti-Federalist was elected to municipal office; the Federalists swept the races for alderman and carried twenty-two of the Common Council seats, the rest going to gentlemen or well-to-do artisans of similar sympathies.[21]

The mood of reconciliation also permitted replacing the Pennsylvania constitution of 1776 with the constitution of 1790, modeled closely on the federal Constitution, particularly in separating and balancing the legislative, executive, and judicial powers.

The general clearing away of old contentions extended to the contest between the college and the university. The 1789 live-and-let-live solution of permitting both institutions to function as neighbors fitted the conciliatory spirit of the times, but for the practical and particularly the financial requirements of higher education in Philadelphia it was an absurdity. The two boards of trustees consequently brought themselves to negotiate a compromise, merging boards and faculties. The new, unified trustees were to number twenty-four, the same number as each of the old boards; each of the contending boards was to select twelve. The Pennsylvania legislature approved this and other details of the merger on September 30, 1790.

The name of the merged institutions was to be the University of Pennsylvania, dropping "of the State of" from the designation given the university in 1779; common discourse had long since abandoned those cumbersome words. John Ewing, provost of the university and a Presbyterian minister, was to continue as provost. Despite the composition of the merged board, the name, and the final displacement of the Anglican clergyman William Smith by his Presbyterian rival, the merger proved essentially a triumph of the old college. While the governor of the state was always to be president of the board of trustees, and the university was bound to lay a financial statement before the legislature annually, the institution became again a private one of self-perpetuating trustees. The democratizing possibilities of state sponsorship —of initiating the American state university movement—were lost. Out of a complex of reasons, the faculty tended to become that of the college rather than of the university. Though the college itself had been intended, especially by Franklin, as a secular institution in a constellation of American church-related colleges, it had promptly developed an Anglican atmosphere, with William Smith's encouragement; the Anglican overtones soon prevailed again, notwithstanding the retention of John Ewing. The University of Pennsylvania was set on its course, for over a century, as a conservative institution, and one whose name would always be misleading. Along with conciliation, that outcome also was consistent with the temper of the Federalist times.[22]

V

On April 20, 1789, still in a festive mood—so strong and so widespread was the conviction that the federal Constitution could rescue both Philadelphia and the nation from postwar troubles—the city prepared yet again to welcome General Washington. It would be the most splendid of all the municipal welcomes to the revolutionary hero, for he would be traveling through Philadelphia to take up tasks fully comparable to those that had won him his laurels in war. He was on his way from Mount Vernon to New York, the temporary federal capital, to become the first president of the United States under the Constitution.

An honor guard comprised largely of Pennsylvania veterans of the Revolution relieved a similar Delaware guard of honor at the boundary between the two states. Among them was General Mifflin, president of the Supreme Executive Council of Pennsylvania. With the guard were also several of the city troops of horse. The escort apparently led a white horse out from Philadelphia to meet the president-elect, so that mounted on it when he entered the city he could be better seen by the populace than if he remained inside his coach. At Gray's Ferry Bridge, Washington beheld yet another welcoming delegation, headed by General St. Clair, along with remarkable decorative embellishments of the bridge arranged by the proprietors, the brothers C. and R. Gray, with the help of the Philadelphia artist Charles Willson Peale. Laurel arched each end of the floating bridge, and laurel and cedar lined its sides. Large banners flew above the approaches, announcing again the themes of the rising sun and the new era, along with the motto particularly appropriate to Philadelphia LET COMMERCE FLOURISH. The flags of all the states lined the north side of the bridge; alone from the center of the south side flew the flag of the Union. One report had it that Angelica Peale, daughter of the artist, lowered a laurel wreath to Washington's head; in other reports it was simply an unidentified girl or boy who performed this ritual.

From Gray's Ferry into the city "every fence, field and avenue" was thronged with people. As usual on these occasions cannon roared and bells pealed; the Philadelphia diarist Jacob Hiltzheimer happened to be in Bristol, Pennsylvania, on his way home from Trenton and recorded that he heard the guns that far away. Leading the procession now astride the white horse, Washington made his way through ever more tightly packed crowds down High Street to Second and to the City Tavern, where about 250 men joined him in a grand dinner and fourteen toasts. Washington again stayed overnight at Robert Morris's house. Inclement weather caused him for once to decline the escort of the City Light Horse when he resumed his journey the next day.[23]

An East View of Gray's Ferry, near Philadelphia with the Triumphal Arches, &c. erected for the Reception of General Washington, *engraved by James Trenchard (b. 1747) after Charles Willson Peale (1741–1827), for the* Columbian Magazine *(1789).*

THE LIBRARY COMPANY OF PHILADELPHIA.

Among the reasons for Philadelphia's hearty support of the federal Constitution was the hope that a new start in government would provide the occasion to bring the national capital back where it belonged, to the largest, wealthiest, and most centrally located city in the Union. If Philadelphia seemed too wickedly urban to puritanical and backwoods congressmen from New England and the South, then Pennsylvania, Philadelphia, and Bucks County were willing to unite in offering a nearby tract on which to locate a new federal district, while the public buildings of Philadelphia housed the government in the meantime. To Philadelphians, the city itself of course would be better yet. Tench Coxe, a rising power among the Federalists especially as a lobbyist, had sought through James Madison to persuade the First Congress under the Constitution to hold its sessions in Philadelphia. Benjamin Rush, who supported John Adams for the vice-presidency in the belief that his old revolutionary friend would support the transfer of the capital to Philadelphia, wanted to see it returned at once to prevent "the seat of government [moving] to a more southern . . . and less republican state" in the future.[24]

Suspicion of Philadelphia as the combined center of self-interested financiers and unruly urban mobs, concern about the city's high prices, and bad memories of the hasty 1783 departure of Congress under the spur of mutineers all remained strong. A bill setting the permanent site of the capital on the Potomac River but naming Philadelphia as the temporary capital failed during the first session of the new Congress. Opponents of Philadelphia feared that if the capital returned at all, then Philadelphia would muster the strength to assure that it should never leave. Fisher Ames of Massachusetts grumbled about the rival lobbying for Philadelphia and New York as a "despicable grog-shop contest, whether the taverns of New York or Philadelphia shall get the custom of Congress."

Secretary of the Treasury Alexander Hamilton—who was close to Tench Coxe, now the assistant secretary—meanwhile was suffering difficulties in his effort to secure from Congress federal assumption of the states' debts. The Treasury leaders decided to try harnessing together the issues of assumption and the federal capital, to combine enough votes to win satisfactory resolutions of both questions. In June 1790 Coxe and William Jackson, one of President Washington's secretaries who was to spend the latter part of his life as a Philadelphia businessman, proposed to Pennsylvania Reps. Thomas Fitzsimons and George Clymer, whom their opponents considered a Philadelphia congressional junto, that Philadelphia become the permanent capital in return for enough Pennsylvania votes to pass assumption. Robert Morris, now a United States senator, on hearing about this overture invited Hamilton to join him on his morning constitutional along the Battery for further discussion. Hamilton offered the votes for Germantown or the Falls of the Delaware to become the capital in return for one vote in the Senate and five in the House for assumption. But he was not ready to assure Philadelphia's becoming the temporary capital, and negotiations with the Pennsylvania delegation dragged on inconclusively for a time.[25]

Meanwhile Philadelphians were flooding Congress with petitions in favor of moving the capital to the Delaware. Philadelphia newspapers published the petitions in an attempt to arouse a public outcry. The *Federal Gazette* warned that the people might lose confidence in Congress if it stayed in an "improper place." Philadelphia, the paper claimed, was filled with "Americans who exhibited the ancient simple Republican manners of our country."[26]

Municipal officials also lobbied for the city. The city Council wrote to Congressman Fitzsimons, telling him that the city government would provide public buildings and funds to remodel houses for the use of federal officials. A new courthouse built on the same square as the State House could provide a meeting place for Congress. The city Council conducted a lottery to raise the necessary funds for remodeling old structures and for the building of a new city hall that could also help accommodate the federal government. In addition the Council voted funds to have Robert Morris's mansion on High Street remodeled for the use of the president. City officials hoped that once these buildings were turned over to the federal government, Philadelphia would in fact become the permanent capital.[27]

This flurry of activity notwithstanding, it is hard to escape the feeling that Philadelphia or at least a nearby site might have won the capital if only Philadelphians had altogether wanted it. But for whatever reason—disdain for a grog-shop contest, or Philadelphian self-doubt—their hearts were not quite in the effort. In the face of Hamilton's proposed bargain the Philadelphia and Pennsylvania congressmen dallied and bargained but failed to come to the point. While the Pennsylvanians dithered, Hamilton sealed instead his famous bargain with Secretary of State Thomas Jefferson of Virginia to locate the permanent capital not on the Delaware, but on the Potomac. Robert Morris and Tench Coxe had to settle for bringing the temporary capital to Philadelphia, for ten years, as Pennsylvania's part in the deal that finally achieved assumption.[28]

V I

At least Philadelphia had the temporary capital, and there remained those who, like Pennsylvania's other senator William Maclay, thought that once the seat of government was in the city inertia would cause it to remain.[29] Thus there would be yet another civic welcome for George Washington, and this time Philadelphia could expect to play host to him for the remainder of his presidential service. Traveling south from New York on September 2, 1790, Washington was met as usual some ten miles out of town by the City Light Horse, other militia, and distinguished citizens. Again the cannon fired and the bells rang when he approached Market Street. Again sumptuous dinners were offered to him, but for the time being he had to decline many of the invitations because he had decided to visit Mount Vernon before returning to Philadelphia to stay.

He did, however, pause to examine the Robert Morris house with an eye to its becoming the presidential mansion. The Morrises had graciously acceded to the city's wish that they make their place available by agreeing to move next door, to the house on the southeast corner of Sixth and Market, which had been Joseph Galloway's and from which the commissioners for confiscated estates had evicted Mrs. Galloway after her husband had fled with the British.

The Morris house had been built in 1761 by Mary Lawrence Masters, who in 1772 deeded it to her daughter, also named Mary, at the time of the daughter's marriage to Richard Penn, grandson of the founder. The Penns had gone to England in 1775 when the Continental Congress commissioned Richard to deliver its Olive Branch Petition, and they chose to remain across the Atlantic. During the war both Gen. Sir William Howe and Gen. Benedict Arnold had lived in the house during their respective military commands in the city. Robert Morris purchased it from the Penns in 1785 and immediately rebuilt it, among other purposes to raise the ceilings of the second floor to accommodate the current London fashion of entertaining chiefly in rooms above the ground floor. Despite Morris's changes Washington was not completely satisfied with the house as the prospective residence of the president: "It is, I believe, the best *single house* in the City; yet, without additions it is inadequate to the *commodious* accommodation of my family." So he wrote to his secretary Tobias Lear, who was given the task of supervising major additions and alterations while Washington tarried at Mount Vernon until late November. During his absence the president bombarded Lear with copious detailed instructions for the work. He returned to move in on November 22, thereby forcing the workmen to hasten the finishing touches.[30]

The Philadelphia where Washington took up residence stretched about nine blocks north and south along the Delaware and not far beyond the State House to the west. A large wooded area that had long remained between the settled portion and the Schuylkill had mostly been cleared during the British occupation.[31] In 1781 and 1782 a rural greenbelt area in the Northern Liberties had been sold by the state to speculators; land developers purchased over 1400 lots, which soon became housing sites.[32] The population of the city and the adjacent districts, estimated at 38,798 in 1782 despite the effects of war, had grown to 42,520 by the first federal census of 1790. This 9.6 percent growth rate was not spectacular by the standards of most of the earlier decades of the eighteenth century, but it nevertheless signified considerable economic recovery.[33]

View of Several Public Buildings in Philadelphia, *taken from the "Compting House Window of Wm Nancarrow, about 54 feet to the Northward of Walnut Street on the West side of eighth Street by Wm Thomas Bedwell of the Northern Liberties . . ." for the* Columbian Magazine *(1790). From the left, the*

Refurbishing since the war had made much of the city attractive again, with its red-brick houses facing red-brick foot pavements, rows of buttonwood, willow, and Lombardy poplar trees, main streets paved with pebbles and with brick or wooden gutters, and posts between carriage ways and footpaths to protect pedestrians. Architectural styles had changed little from the Georgian of the colonial era. In 1785 the Pennsylvania Assembly had somewhat surprisingly voted to grant to the American Philosophical Society a plot of ground within the State House Yard, along the west side of Fifth Street. There in 1787 the society began erecting the building it has occupied ever since, a relatively unadorned rectangular, symmetrical structure in harmony with the State House. The Library Company of Philadelphia had considered building a similar structure in the State House Yard, but it was unwilling to go so far west as the Sixth Street side as the Assembly wished. Meanwhile a Philadelphia County courthouse was erected along Chestnut Street just west of the State House in 1787–1789, and to balance it a city hall rose east of the State House in 1790–1791; these buildings also followed traditional Philadelphia red-brick Georgian lines, though cupolas gave them a slight air of pretension. With the arrival of the federal government, the first

buildings are: the Protestant Episcopal Academy; the County Court House, later Congress Hall; the State House; the American Philosophical Society; the Library Company of Philadelphia; and Carpenters' Hall. In 1790 a City Hall which soon housed the U.S. Supreme Court was built just east of the State House.

of these latter two structures became Congress Hall, accommodating the House of Representatives on its first floor, the Senate on the second; the City Hall took in the United States Supreme Court.[34]

Denied what it considered the most appropriate site within the State House Yard, the Library Company chose to build in 1789–1790 across the street, on the east side of Fifth Street just across from the hall of the Philosophical Society. The style of the new library building signaled the beginning of architectural change in the city. Library Hall was the first building by Dr. William Thornton, a young physician recently arrived from the West Indies, who won a competition for its design. Although Thornton had no architectural training, he was in touch with British architectural fashion, an awareness that stood him in good stead again when he later won the competition to design a Capitol for the new federal city on the Potomac. He gave to Library Hall an elegance and delicacy of detail hitherto rarely seen in Philadelphia— particularly in four pilasters and an ornamental balustrade—the whole representing a fuller and more literal Palladianism than had prevailed in Philadel-

Library and Surgeons Hall, in Fifth Street Philadelphia, *drawn and engraved by William Birch and Son (1799). The Library Company of Philadelphia's original building was demolished in 1888, but it was rebuilt to house the American Philosophical Society in 1959. Surgeons Hall, also called the Philadelphia Dispensary, was a clinic and outpatient service established in 1786.*

phia before, a style approaching the Robert Adam mode of current English building. When the wealthy merchant William Bingham offered to donate a white marble statue of Franklin for a niche on the front of the building, the impression of elegant classicism became complete; indeed at Franklin's own suggestion the statue was clothed in a toga. The original Library Hall was razed in the 1880s, but the present American Philosophical Society Library, built on the site in 1959, reproduces Thornton's facade.[35]

The elegance of the Adam style as transplanted to America to become the "Federal" style was perhaps best expressed in Philadelphia in David Evans, Jr.'s Central Pavilion of the Pennsylvania Hospital, facing south toward Pine Street between Eighth and Ninth, begun in 1794 and completed in 1805. The use of marble for the first story, the six marble Corinthian pilasters extending through the red-brick second and third stories to a finely detailed entablature with an equally finely worked pediment featuring a delicate oval window, and perhaps most important the circular balustrade which surrounds the skylight of the clinical amphitheater—all these details carried into a new architectural era a structure whose basic form nevertheless remained the familiar Georgian colonial rectangle with balanced windows and doors arranged along horizontal lines.[36]

The colonial and the Federal styles both echoed Greek and Roman architecture as filtered through Renaissance Italy and then through England. In part to carry the United States toward a larger cultural independence from England to accord with political independence—though at the same time, paradoxically, relying on trends in England itself—the era of the return of the capital to Philadelphia witnessed also a more literal borrowing of Greek and Roman design. After all, the leaders of the new American Republic liked to think of themselves as emulating the ancient Roman Republic.

In 1788 William Hamilton, grandson of Andrew Hamilton, brought the new, literal classicism to his estate outside Philadelphia, the Woodlands. In the process of transforming a fairly simple farmhouse into a pretentious mansion, he added a large Greek portico with two Doric columns. The first Philadelphia public building to adopt this classic temple facade with free-standing columns was a new First Presbyterian Church, built in 1793 on the site of the same congregation's earlier church on the south side of Market Street between Second and Third, at the east corner of Bank Alley. The church had four Corinthian columns.[37]

A centerpiece of Secretary of the Treasury Alexander Hamilton's program to use the federal Constitution not only to place the Union's finances on a sound footing but to encourage commerce with the help of federal power was a federally chartered bank. The United States government appointed only one-fifth of the directors of the resulting Bank of the United States, but the bank was to have a special relationship with the government, particularly as the depository of federal funds, against which it could issue notes that would circulate as currency, and extend loans. Receiving with the federal deposits the notes of state-chartered banks—several of which had appeared in

South East Corner of Third and Market Streets, *drawn and engraved by William Birch and Son (1799). A goldsmith and two French merchants occupied the corner building which was erected by Joseph Cooke in 1793. The Indian King Tavern appears at the far left on Market Street.*

HISTORICAL SOCIETY OF PENNSYLVANIA

addition to the Bank of North America—the bank could regulate the credit operations of those other banks by means of the promptness with which it demanded that notes be redeemed in specie. Chartered on February 25, 1791, the Bank of the United States opened for business in December 1791 in Carpenters' Hall. The experienced Thomas Willing became its first president. In 1794 the stockholders acquired a lot on the west side of Third Street between Chestnut and Walnut, across from the head of Dock Street, which had been built over the course of Dock Creek in 1784. Construction appears to have begun in 1795 on a design by Samuel Blodget, Jr., a New Hampshire–born businessman, militia captain, and amateur architect.

Blodget chose the newly popular classical "grand order," helping fix the Greco-Roman temple as a favored design for American banks for generations afterward. His temple facade was constructed of blue Pennsylvania marble, except for a wooden entablature and pediment featuring an American eagle. Six free-standing Corinthian columns support the entablature. Inside, eight

Corinthian columns support a balcony, and forty small Corinthian columns support a low dome with a skylight. The bank received an imposing head-quarters worthy of Hamilton's ambitions for the institution—except for one conspicuous cost-cutting change in Blodget's plan; as the architect complained, "the brick sides are an injurious deviation."[38]

No such economies of cost marred the most pretentious private residence built in Philadelphia during the 1790s. William Bingham, Federalist merchant and land speculator, associate of Robert Morris, son-in-law of Thomas Willing, and from 1795 to 1801 United States senator, modeled his house on the London showplace of the duke of Manchester. Built near Third and Spruce Streets, the house along with its formal gardens occupied most of the ground west to Fourth Street and north to Willing's Alley. Its marble stairs among similar features gave the house the "Roman air" now in fashion. "The chairs in the drawing-room were from Seddon's in London of the newest taste, the back in the form of a lyre, with festoons, of yellow and crimson silk. The curtains of the room a festoon of the same. The carpet, one of Moore's most expensive patterns. The room papered in the French taste, after the style of the Vatican in Rome." The mirrors lining the parlors reflected social gatherings rivaling in prestige those of the president's mansion itself.[39]

The lady of the house, Anne Willing Bingham, had married in 1780, when she was sixteen and her husband twenty-eight. From 1783 to 1786 the Binghams had traveled in England and on the continent, where Anne captivated and was captivated by the courts of St. James's, Versailles, and the Hague. Rich, attractive, intelligent, shrewd, witty, and elegantly dressed, Mrs. Bingham was welcomed to the fashionable salons of the European capitals and began to form the notion of presiding over a salon of her own in Philadelphia. She was especially struck by the "young and handsome" marquise de Cogny, who "takes a lead in all the fashionable Dissipations of life, and at more serious moments collects at her House an assembly of the Literati, whom she charms with her knowledge and her bel Esprit. The women of France interfere in the politics of the Country, and often give a decided Turn to the Fate of Empires."[40]

The empires to which Mrs. Bingham gave a turn with her Philadelphia dances, dinners, and receptions of the 1790s were those conjured up by the imaginations of the ambitious and the successful in the reigning Federalist party. As the politics of the new federal government increasingly divided between Hamilton's Federalists and the more democratically inclined Republicans led by Secretary of State Jefferson and Congressman Madison, few of the Republicans appeared at the glittering Bingham salon. Jefferson himself had long been a friend of the hostess and was always welcome, but he was uncomfortable amid imitations of the social life of a monarchical court, and many of his followers no more met Mrs. Bingham's standards of elegance than they themselves approved of aristocratic display. In 1795, indeed, a mob attacked the Bingham house to protest John Jay's Treaty with England, whose commercial concessions to the British the men of the streets thought an

Anne Willing Bingham *(1764–1801), painted by Gilbert Stuart (1755–1828) in 1797.*

PRIVATE COLLECTION

all-too-logical product of anglophilia like the Binghams'. But "the dazzling Mrs. Bingham," as Abigail Adams called her, would not allow such a passing incident among the lower orders to disturb seriously her round of entertainments of the Federalist notables, the aristocratic French emigrés such as the duc d'Orléans (later King Louis-Philippe) and the duc de la Rochefoucald-Liancourt, and such visiting English worthies as Alexander and Henry Baring, of the great financial house, who married two of her daughters.[41]

Even President Washington's frigid dignity warmed to the slightly risqué conversation of Mrs. Bingham. It was she who commissioned from Gilbert Stuart the full-length painting of the chief executive that, presented by her to Lord Lansdowne, became known in its original and the many copies as the "Lansdowne portrait."[42]

The portrait conveys the rather different tone of entertainment at the president's mansion, 190 High Street. It depicts Washington in the sort of black suit he wore at his formal levees for gentlemen on Tuesday afternoons from three to four o'clock. The awe in which Washington had come to be held even by most others in high places combined with the president's utter lack of small talk to render these affairs strictly ritualistic. A secretary or some similar associate of the president presented each caller, to whom Washington bowed, holding back his hands to discourage handshakes. After the presentations the visitors formed a circle and Washington went round it beginning on his right, exchanging a few words with every guest. Finally the president returned to his original position, whereupon the guests approached him, bowed, and departed.

The president's state dinners, held on Thursdays at four o'clock, were not much more jovial, though Mrs. Washington and other ladies sometimes attended. So humorless were the proceedings, so limited the conversation, that even a confirmed democrat might wish himself at the Binghams' instead. Attending such a dinner, the democratically inclined Senator Maclay thought the "dead silence almost" might at last give way to conversation once Mrs. Washington and the ladies had withdrawn. But it was not to be; the president occasionally spoke a sentence or two, he soon went upstairs for coffee, the company followed, and soon everyone went home. Yet Maclay acknowledged that viewing the affair simply as a dinner, the quality of the food was the best he had ever found at any comparable banquet.[43]

More sprightly, much more in keeping with the social life that well-placed Philadelphians had expected with the "federal court" in their midst, were the Friday evening "drawing rooms" hosted by Mrs. Washington—or "Lady Washington," for she too possessed her full share of regal dignity. These occasions began in the early evening, around seven, and might last as late as nine-thirty or ten o'clock, beyond the Washingtons' customary bedtime. The president's lady received her guests while seated with one or two friends; Mrs. Robert Morris was almost always at her right. The guests bowed to the hostess and chatted briefly, then mingled with informal groupings. Martha Washington usually seemed relaxed and kindly. Refreshments were served in an adjoining room—tea, coffee, cakes, sweetmeats, in warm weather orangeade or some other cold drink. "The room became full before I left it," Abigail Adams reported of an early "drawing room," "and the circle very brilliant. How could it be otherwise, when the dazzling Mrs. Bingham and her beautiful sisters were there; the Misses Allen, and Misses Chew; in short a constellation of beauties?" At least as dazzling as the beauties were the displays of jewelry adorning some of the foreign ministers' ladies, especially the wife of the Austrian minister, "who frequently appeared blazing with diamonds." (Mrs. Washington set herself off by wearing little jewelry.)[44]

The president himself unbent to a degree and mingled with the guests at Martha's "drawing rooms." Not only was the occasion informal, but he did not consider himself the host, and was therefore more at his ease.

Washington rode out from the Morris house in a coach and six, the handsome horses carefully matched, the coach freshly and elaborately repainted and reupholstered by the brothers David and Francis Clark of Chestnut Street when the capital moved to Philadelphia. In fact Washington's "coach of state" was too heavy and ornate for use on bad roads or at moderately rapid speeds; it served only for short trips within the city. Upon the shift of the capital from New York, Washington also purchased from the Clarks a lighter coach newly imported from England. This second vehicle was to cause historical confusion; Mrs. Samuel Powel, the mayor's wife, bought an identical coach from the Clark brothers at the same time, and it was hers that survived for many years, to be exhibited at the Centennial Exposition of 1876 as Washington's.[45]

The lighter coach took the president on jaunts into the countryside around Philadelphia. Had he enjoyed more free time, and had his personal finances been less tied up in Virginia lands, Washington would have liked to buy a southeastern Pennsylvania farm to experiment with the rich soil and to live the gentleman farmer's life he loved closer to the capital than Mount Vernon. Aloof though he was, his imposing coach and six traveling the streets was a welcome and reassuring sight to most Philadelphians, tangible evidence that the troubles of the Revolution had been left far behind and that the prosperity of the city and the independence of the nation seemed secure. And after all, Washington knew how to draw the line between an imposing display of authority and the mere fripperies of kingship. When a tradesman, Joseph Cook, proposed to affect British custom and to affix to his shop the Washington coat-of-arms and the inscription "silver Smith to the President," Washington promptly forbade it.[46]

VII

On August 19, 1793, a cloudy, not excessively warm, but rainless day following upon weeks of similar dry weather, Philadelphia's best known physician, Dr. Benjamin Rush, conferred with two other members of his profession about an illness whose appearance in the city had caused him growing alarm through the preceding two weeks. A signer of the Declaration of Independence, a principal shaper of the Pennsylvania constitution of 1776, more recently a champion of the new federal and state constitutions—thus a leading political light as well as professor of the institutes of medicine and clinical practice at the University of Pennsylvania, Rush somehow found time for a large private medical practice. Since early August he had treated several patients for a severe fever accompanied by nausea, eruptions of the skin, a black vomit, and eventually deep lethargy, rapid feeble pulse, incontinence, and a morbid yellow coloring of the skin. The little daughter of a colleague who had summoned Rush for help, Dr. Hugh Hodge, had died. Only the day before, Rush had lost another patient to the fever. Now he met with Dr. Hodge and Dr. John Foulke at a house on crowded, narrow Water Street, north of Arch. Hodge and Foulke wished to consult with Rush about yet another case of the new fever; Catherine LeMaigre, wife of a French importer, was dying horribly, gasping for breath and vomiting black bile.

The three physicians agreed that they had seen an uncommon number of such cases recently, all in the same area near the waterfront. Dr. Foulke called their attention to a pungent odor in the air. He reminded them of its source; the sloop *Amelia* out of Santo Domingo had dumped a cargo of damaged coffee on Bell's Arch Street wharf on July 24, and the coffee had putrified there. Rush, who remembered a yellow fever epidemic in Philadelphia in 1762 and had studied such plagues, immediately reached a terrifying conclusion. He believed that the fever was spread by noxious effluvia in the air, such as that of the rotting coffee. He pronounced the disease that had killed Hodge's daughter and was killing Mrs. LeMaigre to be bilious remitting yellow fever.[47]

Dr. Benjamin Rush *(1746–1813), painted by Thomas Sully (1783–1872) at unknown date.*

AMERICAN PHILOSOPHICAL SOCIETY

News of this conclusion by the city's most eminent physician soon spread through Philadelphia, and so did panic and terror. On August 22 Mayor Matthew Clarkson notified city officials of the presence of a contagious fever and ordered immediate removal of all filth from the streets. On August 25 the fellows of the Philadelphia College of Physicians, almost all the most prestigious doctors in the city, conferred in the hall of the American Philosophical Society "upon the treatment of the existing malignant fever." The first explicit newspaper notice of "the malignant and contagious fever which now prevails" appeared on August 28. By that date the epidemic needed no announcement in print, for it was reporting itself on the streets and in the graveyards.

On an average August day in Philadelphia there would have been three to five burials. On August 24 there were seventeen, on August 28 twenty-two, on August 29 twenty-four, and thereafter slight declines in burials were quickly followed by alarming increases. Though business at first went on as usual, the lassitude, glazed eyes, depression, even the yellow complexion and seizures of vomiting and delirium symptomatic of the disease could be found everywhere on the streets. By the end of the month Rush was advising "all the families that I attend, that can move, to quit the city." Jefferson, living beyond the town at Gray's Ferry, wrote to Madison that "Everybody who can, is flying from the city, and the panic of the country people is likely to add famine to the disease"—that is, fresh produce was coming in only in a trickle.[48]

There was good reason to fly. Medical science understood little about yellow fever, and the physicians' treatments could well hasten the course of the disease—though a fever that had killed at least one victim within twelve hours of its onset required little hastening. Philadelphia physicians promptly revived an old debate over the origins and means of contagion of the fever. Rush insisted that the source was putrescent refuse like the rotting coffee shipment and that the contagion involved the circulation of noxious matter from the refuse through the air. Other physicians, representing both a different tradition of medical belief and the local patriot's desire to find a foreign origin for the disease, noted that the plague was already widespread throughout the city from early August, far beyond the Arch Street wharf, and that hundreds of refugees from the recent and still tumultuous black uprising on Santo Domingo had come up the Delaware during the summer. Physicians who emphasized these observations tended to believe that the contagion proceeded from direct contact with infected persons, and that it had been brought to Philadelphia by the refugees.

An unusually rainy spring had preceded the prolonged drought of the 1793 summer, first creating flooded streams and numerous swamps, then leaving many stagnant pools. Almost everyone commented on the uncommonly large numbers of mosquitos infesting the city, and some Philadelphians felt intuitively that the swarms of mosquitos had something to do with the plague. But no one knew that the female *Aëdes aegypti* mosquito, biting a victim of the plague—almost certainly beginning with the Santo Domingo refugees—after twelve days transmitted the infection to the next person she bit, and could then inject the disease into a different person every three days, that is, as often as she fed.

More dismaying in retrospect than the physicians' debate over the source of the infection—there was little chance that the science of the time could have perceived enough to eradicate the source anyway—was the controversy over treatment. In the first days of the epidemic Rush was appalled not only by his conclusion that the dread yellow fever had returned, but also by his

MORTALITY.

—EACH MOMENT has its sickle, emulous
Of TIME's enormous scythe, whose ample sweep,
Strikes empires from the root; each MOMENT plays

His little weapon in the narrower sphere
Of sweet DOMESTIC comfort, and cuts down
The fairest bloom of sublunary bliss.

An Account of the BAPTISMS AND BURIALS in the United Churches of Christ Church and St. Peter's, by Matthew Whitehead and John Ormrod, Clerks; and Joseph Dolby, Sexton.
Also---An abstract of the Baptisms and Burials of the various Congregations of the City and Suburbs of Philadelphia. From December 25, 1792, to December 25, 1793.

BAPTISMS, Males, - - 74   BURIALS, Males, - - 228
Females, - 65   Females, - 170
139   398

Difference of Baptisms and Burials in Christ Church and St. Peter's between this year and last,

Baptisms decreased - - 41   Burials increased, - - 373

Buried under one year, - 23   From forty to fifty - 37
From one to three - - 31   to sixty - 31
to five - - 19   to seventy - 19
to ten - 26   to eighty - 18
to twenty - 42   to ninety - 7
to thirty - 81   to a hundred - 2
to forty - 63   to a hundred and five - 1

The Diseases and Casualties in Christ Church and St. Peter's, this year.

Apoplexy,	1	Gravel	2
Asthma,	1	Hooping Cough	5
Bilious Fever	3	Hives	5
Cholic	2	Mortification	3
Cancer,	2	Nervous Fever	3
Child-bed,	3	Old Age	5
Consumption	12	Purging and Vomiting	9
Dry Gripes		Palsey	7
Dropsy	9	Small-pox	16
Decay	44	Suddenly	4
Fits	17	Teeth and Worms	10
Fever	7	Worms	6
Flux	6	Yellow Fever	214
Gout	2		

St. PAUL's CHURCH.

Baptisms 143 Decreased 2   Burials 94 Increased 54

ROMAN CATHOLIC CHURCHES.

St. MARY's, Baptisms - 335 Decreased - - 13
Burials - 370 Increased - - 228

Holy Trinity, Baptisms - 53 Increased - - 6
Burials - 53 Increased - - 40

BAPTISMS INCREASED or DECREASED.

Swedes	42	Decreased	10
German Lutherans	506	Increased	66
Ditto Reformed	200	Decreased	1
First Presbyterians	45	Ditto	9
Second Do.	50	Ditto	26
Third Do.	60	Ditto	5
Scotch Do.			
The Associate Church	6	Decreased	2
Moravians	1	Ditto	6
Methodists	50	Ditto	30
Jews, or Hebrew Church	4		

Printed by William W. Woodward at Franklin's Head, No. 41, Chesnut-street.

BURIALS INCREASED or DECREASED.

Swedes	96	Increased	6
German Lutherans	802	Ditto	617
Ditto Reformed	224	Ditto	151
The Friends	482	Ditto	343
First Presbyterians	95	Ditto	58
Second Do.	147	Ditto	86
Third Do.	152	Ditto	100
Scotch Do.	31	Ditto	23
The Associate Church	15	Ditto	9
Moravians	18	Ditto	10
Society of Free Quakers	43	Ditto	28
Methodists	60	Ditto	20
Baptists	87	Ditto	55
Jews, or Hebrew Church	4	Ditto	2

BURIALS in the STRANGER's GROUND.

Whites - - 1639 Increased - - 524
Blacks - - 305 Ditto - - 276

BAPTISMS this Year, - 1634 Decreased - - 131
BURIALS Ditto, - 5304 Increased - - 3939

BURIALS in the GRAVE-YARDS, since the FIRST of AUGUST.

Christ Church and St. Peter's	229	Roman Catholics—St. Mary's	278
St. Paul's	77	Ditto — Holy Trinity	30
Swedes	79	The Associate Church	18
German Lutherans	658	Moravians	15
Ditto Reformed	265	Society of Free Quakers	50
The Friends	385	Methodists	35
First Presbyterians	76	Baptists	72
Second Do.	129	Kensington	178
Third Do.	112	Jews or Hebrew Church	4
Scotch Do.	18	Stranger's Ground	1426
		TOTAL since August	5019

How many precious souls are fled
To the vast regions of the dead!
Since to this day the changing sun
Through his last yearly period run.

We yet survive; but who can say?
That through this year, or month, or day,
"I shall retain this vital breath,
"Thus far, at least, in league with death."

That breath is thine, eternal God;
Tis thine to fix my soul's abode;
It holds its life from thee alone
On earth, or in the world unknown.

To thee our spirits we resign,
Make them and own them still as thine;
So shall they live secure from fear,
Though death should blast the rising year.

Thy children, panting to be gone,
May bid the tide of time roll on,
To land them on that happy shore,
Where years and death are known no more

No more fatigue, no more distress,
Nor sin, nor hell shall reach that place;
No groans to mingle with the songs,
Resounding from immortal tongues:

No more alarms from ghostly foes;
No cares to break the long repose;
No midnight shade, no clouded sun,
But sacred high eternal noon.

O, long expected year! begin;
Dawn on this world of woe and sin;
Fain would we leave this weary road,
To sleep in death, and rest with God.

Broadside bill of Mortality (1793).
LIBRARY COMPANY OF PHILADELPHIA

inability to treat it effectively. At the end of August Rush discovered Dr. John Mitchell's account of a yellow fever epidemic in Virginia in 1741, in which Mitchell related that the abdominal viscera of the victim were filled with blood, and that a thorough purging of the body's humors was essential for a cure. "An *ill-timed scrupulousness about the weakness of the body*" was fatal, Mitchell said.

Conscientious physician that he was, Rush resolved not to be overscrupulous about the weakness of the body. Having included mild bleeding and purging among his treatments heretofore, he now determined upon heroic bleeding and purging. For purging, he decided to use Dr. Thomas Young's

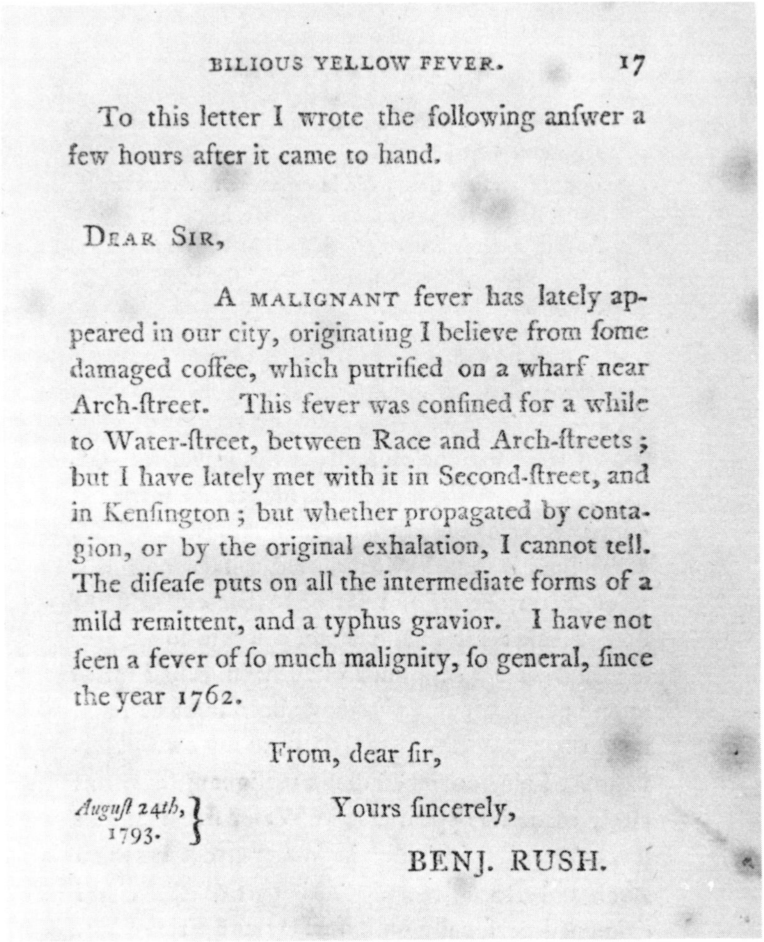

BILIOUS YELLOW FEVER.   17

To this letter I wrote the following anfwer a few hours after it came to hand.

DEAR SIR,

A MALIGNANT fever has lately appeared in our city, originating I believe from fome damaged coffee, which putrified on a wharf near Arch-ftreet. This fever was confined for a while to Water-ftreet, between Race and Arch-ftreets; but I have lately met with it in Second-ftreet, and in Kenfington; but whether propagated by contagion, or by the original exhalation, I cannot tell. The difeafe puts on all the intermediate forms of a mild remittent, and a typhus gravior. I have not feen a fever of fo much malignity, fo general, fince the year 1762.

From, dear fir,

Auguft 24*th*,⎫   Yours fincerely,
　1793.　⎭

BENJ. RUSH.

Letter from Dr. Benjamin Rush to Dr. James Hutchinson, in Rush's An Account of the Bilious Yellow Fever Philadelphia: T. Dobson, 1799).

PRIVATE COLLECTION

drastic formula, employed by Young among the vigorous, youthful soldiers of the Continental Army, of ten grains of calomel and ten of jalap. This dose was far stronger than most physicians believed safe; but when Rush's first experiments with it seemed to bring positive results, he increased the dosage of jalap to fifteen grains, prescribing three doses of "ten and fifteen," one every six hours, or until the patient had four or five large evacuations. For bleeding, Rush resolved on a still more heroic program; he thought the human body contained about twice as much blood as it really does, and he urged that four-fifths of the total volume, or twenty pounds, be drawn away. Once Rush had decided upon the cure, no amount of evidence of its disastrous impact could dissuade him from it.[49]

All too many Philadelphia physicians followed Rush into heroic purging and bleeding, but a few did not. Dr. William Currie restricted himself to mild dosages of medicinal barks and restorative liquids. Dr. Edward Stevens, a native of the West Indies, applied a mild "West Indies treatment" to, among other patients, his boyhood friend in the islands Alexander Hamilton, and to Mrs. Hamilton, both of whom recovered from the plague. A number of French doctors in the city, refugees from Santo Domingo or the French Revolution itself, represented a different tradition of medical education from Rush's Edinburgh, a tradition more fully acquainted with tropical fevers. One of the French physicians, Dr. David Nassy of Second Street, was to compile a remarkable record. Between August 28 and October 10 he treated 117 yellow fever victims and lost only nineteen. Of the latter, eleven were patients he saw only on the second to fifth day of the disease, after other physicians had treated them according to Rush's methods. Another of the French, Dr. Jean Devèze, was to be a hero of the quarantine center eventually established by the city, and eventually became recognized as perhaps the world's leading authority on yellow fever.

But Rush was the most prominent physician in the city—certainly after Dr. William Shippen early joined the exodus—and in the narrow, working-class streets where the plague struck hardest, Rush's methods of treatment tended to prevail. The ravages of the plague came to seem inexorable. From the last week of August to the middle of September at least 600 died. By then perhaps half the population had fled. Philadelphia, the federal capital, was a ghost city. Business withered away; not only were there too few merchants, clerks, or workers of any kind, but the external commerce on which almost everything else depended could not continue because other ports refused to receive ships and goods out of Philadelphia, lest they receive the infection as well. Almost all government was suspended, federal, state, and municipal. Persons obliged to walk the streets stayed in the middle to avoid infected houses. Old friends refused to pause to speak to one another. Tales circulated of husbands abandoning wives, parents abandoning children, victims dying forsaken and uncomforted; in confirmation of some of the rumors, many collapsed alone in the streets.

President Washington departed on September 10. He usually went to

Mount Vernon at this time of year, but the absence of his imposing, reassuring presence worsened the demoralization. When Hamilton and Mrs. Hamilton left only after contracting the disease, their prominence did not prevent their being shunned like lepers on their way to Albany. Soon almost all travelers from Philadelphia, sick or well, found themselves similarly ostracized, at least until they endured a quarantine period along the road. Secretary of War Henry Knox thus had to tarry in Elizabethtown, New Jersey, before he could pass through New York on his way home to Boston.

The governor of Pennsylvania, General Mifflin, had fled early, but Mayor Clarkson believed duty bound him to remain. Sixty years old, a transplanted New York aristocrat descended in the paternal line from a provincial governor and in the maternal line from the patroon families, successful in Philadelphia business through his own skills, and a notable amateur mathematician, astronomer, and engineer, Clarkson could count on almost none of the customary apparatus of government to sustain the city through the plague. He governed finally through an extralegal committee reminiscent of the Committee of Safety. This time, however, the group consisted of leaders altogether self-selected: the few assertive men of competence and bravery who remained in the city besides physicians and a handful of clergy.

Very early, to protect their other inmates from the disease, the Pennsylvania Hospital and the Almshouse refused to receive plague victims. The overseers and guardians of the poor—another civic group with a small core of courageous leaders, until they themselves fell to the fever—thereupon took possession of John Bill Ricketts's circus, on the outskirts of town at Twelfth and High Streets where the Philadelphia Saving Fund Society tower now stands. Ricketts, a famous Scots equestrian, had often attracted President Washington to his circus, but before the plague appeared he had gone to New York for the summer. With his building otherwise empty, it became the first depository of the victims of the plague who had nowhere else to go and nobody to care for them, and whom everyone wanted removed as sources of infection. But Ricketts's circus was not distant enough from the populated areas of Philadelphia, and encouraged by the mayor, the guardians found a more remote retreat by taking over, with dubious legal authority, Andrew Hamilton's old country seat, Bush Hill. By mid-September, however, Bush Hill had become a hell-hole of neglected, stinking, filthy victims of the fever wallowing in their own vomit and excrement, occasionally visited by physicians mainly of the Rush persuasion. Then Stephen Girard and Peter Helm, members of Clarkson's committee, took over.

At forty-three, Girard was not yet well known. He was only beginning his rise to the summit of Philadelphia and American finance, and James Hardie's *Philadelphia Directory and Register* listed him simply as "Girard Stephen, grocer, [number] 43, No. Front St." Peter Helm was a Race Street cooper of German extraction and Moravian religion; Washington had employed him occasionally to make barrels for the presidential household. At Bush Hill, Girard took charge of administration, maintenance of the rooms, and general care of the sick. Helm was superintendent of grounds and out-buildings, with charge over carting and receiving patients, burying the dead, staff accommodations, and sanitary facilities. Both men combined efficiency with tender care of the sick. They transformed Bush Hill from a place of hopelessness to a clean, airy hospital nourishing as much hope as the circumstances and the medicine of the day might permit. Bush Hill benefited especially from the executive talents that were to propel Girard to his fortune. At least as much, however, it benefited because Girard as a transplanted Frenchman knew the French physicians and brought Dr. Devèze to be medical supervisor of Bush Hill. Moving a French doctor into this post past the Rushites required a combination of forcefulness and guile such as perhaps no one in the city other than Girard possessed (Franklin had died three years previously). Most patients were desperately sick before they reached Bush Hill, but Devèze's cleanliness, cool liquids, cool baths, and mild medicines saved many nevertheless.

It remained mostly black carters who carried the sick to Bush Hill. In the early days of panic when Mayor Clarkson had first asked for volunteers to help fight the plague, only two men had stepped forth, the black clergymen Richard Allen and Absalom Jones. Both were pious men who despite their color had once attained a measure of leadership at St. George's Methodist Episcopal Church. Both had been driven away from there because black leadership was not wanted. Allen then established Mother Bethel, the founding church of black Methodism, and was to become the first bishop of the African Methodist Church of North America. Jones established the first Episcopal church for blacks in America, St. Thomas's, became a deacon, and was in time ordained the first black Episcopal priest in America. After they had volunteered, Mayor Clarkson used the Free African Society, which Allen and Jones had founded in 1787, as a major agency of relief work. The society ended 1793 in debt £177/9/8 largely because of its expenses for bedding and means of moving the fever victims. Besides working as carters, blacks recruited by the African Society served as nurses throughout the infected areas. Allen and Jones themselves were ubiquitous among the victims. Until sometime in September no blacks were reported as victims, and the whites at least thought blacks immune. When blacks began to fall by the score, few of them ceased to mingle with the sick as long as they retained the strength to help. In return they received white accusations of thievery and other misconduct.

Some physicians thought that rain would alleviate the plague, but drought persisted with only minor interruptions through most of October. So did the fever, despite cooler weather. Some believed the disease grew worse in October—that at least the torments preceding death became more prolonged and painful. How many died altogether is not certain. Mathew Carey, who achieved his first fame as a journalist by quickly publishing and then enlarging over the years his eyewitness account of the epidemic, listed in his book 4044 dead whom he named. His list omits, however, a number of the known dead, and it must surely have missed many of the anonymous poor, black, and youthful victims. Probably more than 5000 died—about a tenth of the population of Philadelphia.[50]

President Washington worried in October about the session of Congress scheduled to meet in December. Reports reaching him suggested that the plague might not abate even by then. He doubted whether congressmen would go to Philadelphia. Nevertheless, he informed his cabinet members that he would travel to Germantown to meet them there about November 1.

Comptroller of the Treasury Oliver Wolcott had moved his house and office to "Smith's Folly," an eyrie above the Falls of Schuylkill built by Provost William Smith, where Wolcott was one of the few federal officials to continue doing business in the vicinity of the capital. In late October Wolcott still warned Washington that it was dangerous to return, but on October 28 the president set out for Germantown, leaving Martha at Mount Vernon. On November 1 Washington arrived at the comfortable house in Germantown where Attorney-General Edmund Randolph, having preceded him, found quarters for him. The president opened his office for business the next morning.

He had learned that the fever was abating at last. Deaths declined precipitously in mid-October, only to rise to an appalling eighty-two on October 22, but then fell off again until on October 28, the mayor's committee learned, there were only twelve admissions to Bush Hill, only two deaths there, and no burials at all. October 28 began with a light frost. Fugitives began to return to the city.

Against the advice of most of his close associates, President Washington decided to ride into Philadelphia on November 10. It was a Sunday. He came all alone, and this time there was no welcome in the streets. He rode through the city, bowing with typical formality to the few people he met. The air was fresh and cool. He decided that Congress could meet in Philadelphia as planned, and from Germantown he sent out word accordingly. Washington himself would come back to stay by the opening of Congress at the beginning of December.[51]

VIII

Only one newspaper, Andrew Brown's *Federal Gazette*, went on publishing all through the epidemic. Shortages of workers and paper notwithstanding—neither vessels nor carts would bring paper up from the Wilmington mills that usually supplied Brown—the *Federal Gazette* kept up communication among citizens who, afraid even to converse in the streets, were otherwise isolated.

With Brown's columns of local news given over to the plague and the debates among the doctors about its source and treatment, it was possible, however, to regard the suspension of ordinary Philadelphia journalism as a small blessing for which to give thanks in the midst of the city's great tragedy. At least for the duration of the plague, Philadelphians were spared the vitriolic partisan excesses customary among many of the newspapers of the day.

In part such excesses were an unpleasant by-product of the presence of the federal capital. Somewhat surprisingly in light of the rise of the local Federalist party, before Congress and the president arrived in 1790 Philadelphia had four newspapers of Anti-Federalist proclivities and none supporting Washington's Federalist administration. To be sure, the journals were all relatively moderate in their opposition, but they were opposition papers for all that. Eleazar Oswald's *Independent Gazetteer* was the most outspoken of them. The others were Brown's *Federal Gazette* (in spite of its name); John Dunlap's *Pennsylvania Packet;* and a newcomer, the *General Advertiser*, whose proprietor was Benjamin Franklin Bache, Franklin's thirty-one-year-old grandson. Along with the capital there came from New York, however, John Fenno's *Gazette of the United States.* Fenno was a Bostonian who had been a secretary to Maj.-Gen. Artemas Ward during the Revolution and then mastered the newspaper business as an assistant editor of the *Massachusetts Centinel.* He had established his *Gazette* in New York soon after the inauguration of the new government, with apparent support from Alexander Hamilton and other Federalist leaders. The support was tangible enough in the form of public printing jobs that Fenno was able to dispense with the usual clutter of advertisements on the first page. His reciprocal endorsement of administration policies was fulsome to the point of obsequiousness. In New York, this editorial stance embroiled Fenno in a nasty feud with Thomas Greenleaf's *New-York Journal.* [52]

After moving to High Street in Philadelphia, Fenno was at first more circumspect, going so far as to give columns to letters from Anti-Federalists. Nevertheless when Jefferson and Madison moved toward open opposition over Hamilton's financial programs, and notwithstanding Jefferson's position as secretary of state, the two Virginians felt a need for a more emphatic rival to Fenno's *Gazette* than any of the existing Philadelphia papers. Madison therefore persuaded a Princeton classmate, Philip Freneau, to accept an appointment as "clerk for foreign languages" in Jefferson's State Department, with the understanding that Freneau's real mission would be to create a Jeffersonian newspaper.

Freneau was already well known as a poet, and he had newspaper experience as assistant to the editor of New York's *Daily Advertiser.* In fact the proprietor of the *Daily Advertiser*, Francis Childs, agreed to underwrite Freneau's Philadelphia paper, and it was to be printed by John Swaine, Childs's Philadelphia partner. The resulting *National Gazette* moved with surprising gradualness toward an open attack on Fenno's *Gazette of the United States*, but by early 1792 Freneau was hurling anathemas against both the secretary of the treasury and the paper that championed him. Freneau depicted Hamilton's policies as designed to drive the industrious middle class into peasantry while further enriching the already rich; he called Fenno and other Hamiltonians "Mad dogs! Such is the hue and cry raised [by Fenno] . . . against every man who writes on the measures of government without dipping his pen in molasses to sweeten every line with panegyrick." [53]

Fenno responded in kind and eventually raised the obvious questions about the legitimacy of Freneau's public employment, which forced the *National Gazette* briefly onto the defensive. The feud naturally took on extra heat as the presidential election of 1792 approached. Freneau began to aim cautiously at Washington himself when the president decided to seek reelection, enough to cause the thin-skinned hero to complain to Jefferson that Freneau's paper was a national menace. Mainly, however, Freneau concentrated on Washington's more vulnerable running mate, John Adams, hoping to transfer the vice-presidency to the Jeffersonian governor of New York, George Clinton.

Undaunted by the failure of that effort, Freneau seized eagerly the opportunity to open a new front when the French Revolution caused Hamiltonians and Jeffersonians to fall out over foreign as well as domestic policies. To embrace revolutionary France and all its works almost uncritically, however, as Freneau did, was to consign oneself as a hostage to erratic and arrogant leaders. In early 1793 this meant particularly to put oneself in the hands of France's brash young minister to the United States, Citizen Edmond Genêt. Puffed up by a rousing popular welcome when he landed in Charleston and proceeded overland to Philadelphia, Genêt tried to push American sympathies for fellow republicans farther then they would go, by not only recruiting Americans to do France's fighting as seamen on French privateers and as soldiers raiding British Canada and Spanish Louisiana, but also by setting up French maritime prize courts within the United States. His patent contempt for American sovereignty drew a rebuke from the president, whereupon Genêt used friendly newspapers such as Freneau's to appeal over Washington's head to the people, practically inciting revolution. A foreigner attacking Washington was going much too far. France felt obliged to recall Genêt, while Freneau by endorsing his actions suffered guilt by association.

Freneau's *National Gazette* was already in dangerous waters when the yellow fever arrived to add its perils. Whistling in the dark, Freneau wrote and published attempts at light and humorous verse about the plague:

> Priests retreating from their pulpits!—
> Some in hot, and some in cold fits
>   In bad temper
>   Off they scamper
> Leaving us—unhappy culprits!
>
> Doctors raving and disputing,
> Death's pale army still recruiting—
>   What a pother
>   One with t'other!
> Some a-writing, some a-shooting.[54]

The plague was too grim for humor even of the blackest sort. Freneau's approach failed. On October 11, 1793, he resigned his State Department clerkship, and on October 27 he announced the end of his paper.

Fenno's *Gazette of the United States* reappeared after the decline of the plague, and B. F. Bache was soon to reveal a disposition to take Freneau's place in the journalistic jousting. For an interval after the plague, however, those Philadelphians and federal officeholders who found envenomed personal journalism distasteful would continue to enjoy a respite, while those others who found it amusing had to seek diversion elsewhere.

The taverns came back to life, Ricketts's circus returned, and Charles Willson Peale's Museum was an attraction that had never departed—Peale nursed his wife through the fever and survived a brief attack himself. Peale had been well known before the Revolution as a fashionable portrait painter. He became enmeshed in the Revolution for a time as a soldier and a partisan of the Pennsylvania constitution of 1776, but he lacked the combative disposition suitable to active politics, and in the 1780s he returned to his painting and to scholarly interests. Many visitors came to his studio, and as a dedicated patriot he decided to make the studio a gallery of portraits of the heroes of the new nation. To this end he added a skylighted building to his house at Third and Lombard Streets. Here in 1784 a collection of mastodon bones assembled by Dr. John Morgan was also on display, while Peale made drawings of them. Some visitors found the bones more interesting than the paintings and urged Peale to develop a museum of similar scientific curiosities. "Cabinets" of such collections had long existed in Europe, and out of them modern museums were beginning to grow. Peale was receptive, and in 1786 he announced through the newspapers the opening of his "Repository for Natural Curiosities."[55]

Peale devoted the remaining forty-one years of his life chiefly to the development of his museum. He arranged specimens of living creatures according to the Linnaean classification and inanimate materials in a similar orderly fashion based on their places of origin. To mount the natural history specimens, Peale taught himself taxidermy—there was no other practitioner of the craft in Philadelphia. He employed his artistic skills to paint backgrounds which along with rocks and foliage created habitat arrangements, an idea he originated. His hope was to teach the public as well as to enlarge the knowledge of scholars. He succeeded well enough that the museum became his main source of income. In 1794 he moved the museum to Philosophical Hall in the State House Yard, where the American Philosophical Society leased to him all but two of its rooms. As part of the arrangement, he became the society's librarian and the curator of its scientific collection. The portrait gallery moved with the rest of Peale's collection but became a depiction of the types of mankind, of various ages, races, and conditions, as well as of patriotic leaders.

The theater was less able to escape politics than Peale had been, in several senses. First, government suppression returned during the Revolution, when the earnest and humorless radical regime of the constitution of 1776 saw to the local enforcement of a congressional resolution of 1774 calling on the provinces to encourage frugality and discourage such extravagances as the theater. In 1784 Lewis Hallam petitioned to have the act repealed, but all he could

The Long Room of Peale's Museum, painting begun by Charles Willson Peale (1741–1827) in 1822. In 1802 Peale was granted the use of the upper floors of the State House for his collections which had been in Philosophical Hall since 1794.

DETROIT INSTITUTE OF ARTS, FOUNDERS SOCIETY PURCHASE, DIRECTOR'S FUND

achieve was permission to present in the Southwark Theatre a *Monody to the Memory of the Chiefs Who Had Fallen in the Cause of American Liberty*. The rise of the Federalists did not bring about repeal of the prohibition until 1789. Then Hallam included Philadelphia on a circuit of port cities through which his American Company toured. When President Washington attended the Southwark for performances of the company, a box was specially fitted out for him, with cushioned seats, red draperies, and the coat-of-arms of the United States. The comedian Thomas Wignell, proprietor of the theater, would welcome the president with ritualistic ceremony, and a military guard would attend the box and the theater doors.[56]

Restored to life, the Philadelphia theater soon became entangled in the same political rivalries that agitated the newspapers. Wignell, hoping for a new and more elegant stage, found backing to begin construction of the Chestnut Street Theatre, on the north side of Chestnut west of Sixth, in 1791. The yellow fever epidemic delayed completion, and the theater opened for a regular season only on February 17, 1794. Wignell gathered for it a talented company, including Susanna Haswell Rowson, author of the most successful American imitation of Samuel Richardson's moralistic novels, *Charlotte, A Tale of Truth*, actually a tale of seduction and usually known as *Charlotte Temple*. "Old Drury," as the Chestnut Street came to be known, was the most impressive theater built to this time in North America, with three galleries holding 765 persons and a parquet that brought the total capacity to 1165. It boasted French-style lighting, with oil lamps that could be raised or dimmed depending on the scene and mood. But as the 1790s went on Old Drury also became enflamed in noisy demonstrations and counterdemonstrations between Federalists and Jeffersonian Republicans, a discouragement to further presidential theater-going or to serious interest in the drama by anyone else.[57]

It was Jay's Treaty of 1794 that rekindled political fires in the streets and the taverns as well as in the theater and the press, enraging Republicans not only because of commercial concessions to Great Britain, but also, and worse, by seeming to make the United States almost a partner of the British against revolutionary France. Bache's paper, now the *Aurora*, leaped into the forefront of partisan journalism with its attacks on the supposed terms of the treaty, whose text the president believed should be kept secret until the completion of Senate consideration. Fenno's *Gazette of the United States* of course promptly sprang to the defense. Eleazar Oswald's *Independent Gazetteer* weighed in with a long and vitriolic series of attacks signed "Franklin." When the Senate at length ratified the treaty on June 24, 1795, Washington decided to release its text, but Bache anticipated him by publishing an abstract in the *Aurora* on June 29 and then offering a pamphlet edition of the whole text two days later. Sen. Stevens T. Mason of Virginia, a Republican, said he had given Bache the text to correct false impressions left by the abstract.

Oswald's paper declared that the Fourth of July should henceforth be a day of mourning, because George III at last had administered a dose of poison to "Mrs. Liberty." On the night of the Fourth a mob carried an effigy of John Jay, depicted as saying to a group of senators, "Come up to my price and I will sell you my country." The mob paraded through the downtown streets and to Kensington, where they burned the effigy and stoned militia who were sent to disperse them.[58]

The street and press wars heightened further with the approach of another presidential election in 1796. Bache emulated Philip Freneau by opening his columns to the French minister for a letter assailing administration policy; the minister, Pierre Adet, a worthy successor to Citizen Genêt, thereby delivered to the public before he transmitted to the secretary of state a threat that "The flag of the [French] Republic will treat the flag of neutrals in the same manner as they shall suffer to be treated by the British."[59] Bache also republished the forged "Lund Washington Letters," which had been circulating from time to time since 1777 and attempted to discredit Washington by portraying him as a belated convert to American independence. Thus the president himself became increasingly a target of the journalists. He was not seeking reelection, but his imminent retirement made him appear all the more vulnerable, and the Republicans hoped to strike at his chosen successor, John Adams, through him. So Bache also accused Washington of overdrawing his salary, charged that the "perfidious" president declined to run again not from "a want of ambition or lust of power" but because he knew he could not win, and when John Adams won anyway, printed as a valedictory to Washington a letter from Tom Paine to the president whose climax summarized its message: "As to you, sir, treacherous in private friendship . . . and a hypocrite in public life, the world will be puzzled to decide, whether you are an apostate or an imposter; whether you have abandoned good principles, or whether you ever had any."[60]

From the month of Adams's inauguration, March 1797, the Federalists were represented in the Philadelphia press with equal scurrilousness, thanks to the emergence of William Cobbett's *Porcupine's Gazette*. Cobbett was a British subject and patriot whose prejudices accorded well with those of the most extreme anglophile Federalists. In Philadelphia he had also proven himself the peer of any abusive journalist through a series of pamphlets written under the pen name "Peter Porcupine" and directed against a fellow expatriate whom he loathed, the scientist and political and religious reformer Joseph Priestley. Hamilton and other Federalists had now arranged for Cobbett to enter regularly into the journalistic feuds, with subsidies similar to those earlier provided for John Fenno. The first issue of *Porcupine's Gazette* pounced upon Bache's *Aurora* as a "vehicle of lies and sedition." Bache, Cobbett soon further opined, was a "white-livered, black-hearted thing . . . that public pest and bane of decency."[61]

Cobbett benefited from a decided shift in public feeling in favor of the Federalists, when the fears of the francophiles and the threats of Adet about the consequences of Jay's Treaty were both realized in French assaults on American maritime commerce, leading to an undeclared naval war with France in 1798. Patriotic emotions hostile to France and auspicious for the Federalists peaked after President Adams informed Congress on March 5, 1798, of the XYZ Affair, in which the French foreign minister, Charles Maurice de Talleyrand-Périgord, had through intermediaries known as X, Y, and Z informed would-be peacemakers sent by Adams that they could not so much as consult with him without prior payment of a bribe. Charles Cotesworth Pinckney's angry retort "No, no, not a sixpence!" became translated into the Federalists' patriotic slogan "Millions for defense, but not one cent for tribute."

France and Republicanism nevertheless retained some local champions, and the rival theater demonstrations of the two parties along with his own convictions inspired a young actor, Gilbert Fox, to ask Francis Hopkinson's twenty-eight-year-old son Joseph, a Federalist lawyer of some poetic talent, to write a patriotic air appropriate to the times. To accompany the music of "The President's March," Hopkinson wrote "Hail, Columbia." On April 25 Fox introduced the song at the Chestnut Street Theatre. The place was filled

General Washington's Resignation, *drawn by John James Barralet (1747–1815) and engraved by Alexander Lawson (1773–1846) for* Philadelphia Magazine and Review *(January 1799). The engraving was based on an allegorical transparency prepared for the "splendid public dinner" given in 1797 by the merchants of Philadelphia for the retiring president.*

to capacity; thousands tried unsuccessfully to get in for the occasion. Fox had to encore the song again and again. The audience beat time with its feet, shouted approval at the call "Immortal patriots, rise once more," joined in the choruses, and finally, with the whole house standing for the final chorus, took the anthem out into the streets.[62]

To face the French, the frigate *United States*, designed like all her sister frigates of the infant American navy by Joshua Humphreys of Philadelphia and built in Philadelphia by Humphreys himself, went to sea under Commodore John Barry. Philadelphia citizens subscribed the funds to build another, somewhat smaller frigate, the *Philadelphia*, which was destined to be captured by Tripolitan pirates and then burned in the harbor of Tripoli by another Philadelphia naval hero, Stephen Decatur, to prevent the pirates' using her.[63]

Preparation for War to defend Commerce. The Swedish Church Southwark with the building of the Frigate Philadelphia, *drawn and engraved by William Birch and Son (1800).*

President Adams designated May 8, 1798, as a day of fasting and prayer. The street crowds intoxicated by "Hail, Columbia" preferred riotous disorder. On the eve of the fast day a mob of mostly drunken young men marched on Bache's house. The Republican editor was not at home, and with only women and children inside, the mob began bravely smashing away at doors and windows. Neighbors soon restrained their enthusiasm, but the next evening witnessed a return visit featuring additional shattered windows and a general skirmishing of Federalist and Anti-Federalist mobs. Later in the month a physical attack on Bache in his office produced for the assailant one of the briefest of incarcerations, because Federalist politicians apparently made prompt payment of his fifty-dollar fine.

Once more as in 1793 the crescendo of newspaper excesses was interrupted by the yellow fever. The fever had returned in 1794, 1796, and 1797, though never so virulently as in 1793. On August 17, 1798, it appeared in the city again, and this visit was to prove by far its worst since the great plague of five years before. Once more government and business alike dispersed along with many citizens who could afford it, and Philadelphia again became a ghost city. By October the remaining population was estimated at only 7000. Tent cities sprang up along the Schuylkill, sheltering those who could not afford to flee to more distant refuges. Downtown, again there were few sounds except the creaking of the carts that carried the dying and the dead away. Once more Benjamin Rush took to his heroic rounds, allowing no *"ill-timed scrupulousness about the weakness of the body"* to deter him from his regimen of purging and bleeding the victims. By the time the plague relented in early November, the number of deaths was estimated at 1292.

This time, however, the journalists' cacophony was not so nearly stilled as in 1793. Hatred of Rush as a Republican helped keep Peter Porcupine's quill scribbling, insisting day after day that the revered doctor was in truth a murderer, whose blood-letting killed nearly all the unfortunates who became his patients. William Cobbett's example may have helped hold John Fenno to the task of spewing forth similar invective, until in early September Fenno announced the suspension of his *Gazette* because Mrs. Fenno had died; then Fenno promptly followed his wife into the grave. Before the month was out their rival Bache was dead as well.[64]

John Ward Fenno resumed his father's paper, and soon he and Cobbett were in full cry after Bache's widow, who took up the *Aurora*. But during the epidemic the political winds shifted. When the city came back to life in November the Federalist mobs and their choruses of "Hail, Columbia" no longer dominated streets, taverns, and theaters. The new mood was represented by a letter in the *Aurora* excoriating John Adams for his flight from the fever—though in fact it was his usual custom to flee the Philadelphia summer, fever or not, to his home in Braintree, Massachusetts. But "An Old Soldier" described the president as "reveling and feasting at Boston and New York while our unhappy city was the prey of disease and death," and those who survived the plague could hardly restrain themselves from at least a small nod of agreement. There was no hearty welcome when the *Aurora* reported "the triumphal entry of his Serene Highness of Braintree into the city."[65]

The underlying reason for the shift in political sentiment was the war's becoming a fizzle, at least too much so to sustain patriotic frenzies. There were a few sea fights, but for the most part the American navy engaged only in long and uneventful patrols. The French, troubled enough by their European wars, had not bargained for another war with America, and they had soon sent out peace feelers and gradually ceased their raids on American commerce. Such American ship losses as still occurred were mainly at the hands of Caribbean privateers responsible to no government. Meanwhile the Alien and Sedition Acts that the Federalist Congress had passed in June and July to repress Republicanism as akin to treason had boomeranged against their authors; arresting opposition political leaders seemed no way to preserve the traditions of the American Revolution. The Federalist effort to recruit a large army—with only staunch Federalists as officers—backfired similarly, because whatever war there was took place at sea, with no need for a large land force. The Republicans suspected and effectively charged that the real purpose of the army, like the Alien and Sedition Acts, was to put down domestic dissent. The political signposts were pointing toward Thomas Jefferson's victory over John Adams in the "Revolution of 1800."

Another such signpost was the outcome of Benjamin Rush's libel suit against William Cobbett for the accusations of murder during the latest plague. After Cobbett's delaying maneuvers held off a decision until the end of 1799, a jury of the Supreme Court of Pennsylvania brought in a verdict assessing $5000 damages against Cobbett, an unprecedented sum in Pennsylvania. Cobbett's property was promptly seized and sold for $400. Cobbett fled to New York, where he briefly resumed denunciations of Rush, all other Jeffersonians, and now the people of Pennsylvania in a new paper called the *Rushlight*. In 1800, however, Cobbett returned to England.[66]

I X

The lifeblood of eighteenth-century Philadelphia was always its maritime commerce. When yellow fever was not ravaging the city, the 1790s were a propitious decade for this commerce. In fact a considerable commercial revival from the dislocations of the Revolution had already begun by the time of the Constitutional Convention to lay a foundation for the greater growth of the 1790s.

The glut of British exports to the United States that troubled American manufacturers immediately after the Revolution had fallen off following 1784; some British mercantile houses had overextended credit to America and gone bankrupt. Beginning in 1787 imports from Britain rose again, but this time evidently on a firmer basis of American ability to pay through the acquisition of foreign exchange. American merchants, including those of Philadelphia, learned to profit from their new ability to trade freely and legally beyond the British Empire.

In direct trade with France, for example, the United States showed a large and consistent favorable balance from 1783 onward. A major ingredient in this balance consisted of tobacco exports, for which Philadelphia's Robert Morris had negotiated a monopoly with the French Farmers-General whereby all American tobacco sold to France had to go through Morris. Goods from Holland, Germany, and even Russia also competed with British products in the Philadelphia market. So did goods from the Baltic countries; Christian Febiger, founder of a notable Philadelphia family, had arrived from Denmark before the war, risen to a brigadier-generalship during the conflict, and afterward represented Scandinavian mercantile houses.

More exotic ports of call soon beckoned to Philadelphia shippers. The ubiquitous Robert Morris was a part owner and prime mover in the 1784 voyage of the *Empress of China* from New York to Java and Canton, the first American ship to trade with the Far East. The *United States,* of Philadelphia, also set out for China in 1784, but she was troubled by scurvy and a drunken first mate and so she changed her destination to Coromandel, the east coast of India, to open American trade with the subcontinent. A transplanted Long Islander who had sailed privateers out of Philadelphia during the war, Capt. Thomas Truxtun, after bringing Franklin home on his ship *London Packet*, had the vessel overhauled in Joshua Humphreys's Philadelphia yard and renamed it *Canton* to enter the new Oriental trade. Sailing in 1786, Truxtun inaugurated Philadelphia's commerce with China.

Old skills in smuggling, cultivated when Britain had tried to bar American colonial trade from the foreign West Indies, were revived by the middle 1780s to help overcome whatever handicaps lay in no longer being part of the British navigation system. The new trade with the Orient soon brought back more Far Eastern products than the American market could consume, and the British Navigation Acts forbade reexport to the British Empire; but the British consul in Philadelphia, Phineas Bond, Jr., reported that Oriental tea was being shipped to the British West Indies hidden by a covering of Indian corn, and that the tea would soon no doubt go from Philadelphia to Britain and Ireland as well.[67]

By 1787 Philadelphia exports appear to have reached their highest level to that time. The volume of the city's trade may have been about half again as large as in the best years before the war. An average of some 45,000 tons of shipping a year had cleared Philadelphia in 1770–1772; by 1789 James Madison estimated Pennsylvania's—mainly Philadelphia's—comparable figure at 72,000 tons.[68]

The 1790s brought yet more accelerated commercial growth. Alexander Hamilton's reorganization of the nation's finances with a strong central bank, a stabilized economy encouraged by the new federal Union, and the funding of national and state debts aided Philadelphia merchants and artisans in their

efforts to increase both domestic and foreign trade. Close on the heels of
Hamilton's financial program, furthermore, the wars of the French Revolution brought an increased European demand for American farm produce and
a rise in prices for it. At the same time Philadelphia ships, like other American
vessels, were neutral carriers and protected from seizure by the belligerents
—the periods of British seizures before Jay's Treaty and French seizures late
in the decade were brief exceptions—so that they were able to take over much
of the world's transoceanic carrying trade.[69]

X

Yet all was not smooth sailing. At first Philadelphia's businessmen almost
unanimously favored Hamilton's plans for the Bank of the United States and
expecially for funding of the national and state debts incurred during the
Revolution. Philadelphia had been a center of speculation in government
securities, and for speculators who had bought the securities cheaply during
the uncertainties of the 1780s, Hamilton's funding program meant that their
investments would pay off. But the success of the funding program in turn
touched off a new speculative boom in all types of securities and negotiable
paper, with prices spiraling upward to inordinate heights until the summer
of 1791, when the boom collapsed into a financial panic. According to Jefferson, with the onset of the panic "ships are lying idle at the wharves, buildings
are stopped, capital withdrawn from commerce, manufacturing, art, and agriculture." The crisis proved short-lived, but it was followed by another, somewhat more severe panic ten months later.[70]

These two financial crises began to shake the Federalist preponderance in
Philadelphia politics. Men whose economic interests suffered began to blame
Federalist policies for their miseries. At the same time Philadelphians learned
of Hamilton's proposed federal excise tax on distilled liquor, designed to raise
money for the payment of the national debt. A tax increasing the price of
whiskey touched the pocketbooks and habits of a great many Philadelphians;
the whiskey excise provoked the strongest protests against any tax measure
since the various hated British duties before the Revolution.

The chief prospect of success for those opposing the Federalists in Philadelphia lay in organizing those citizens who at least since the days of revolutionary fervor had taken little interest in politicians. An emerging Anti-
Federalist political organization believed they had to convince large numbers
of artisans and unskilled laborers that their interests were involved in the
choice of candidates for office. Such an appeal would work only if Philadelphians were convinced that the new party wanted to ensure for every citizen
an equal opportunity regardless of his economic status. This idea challenged
the assumption of the city's upper class that only the wealthy should govern
society. Thus opponents of the Federalists hoped to use a revival of the ideals
and goals of the Revolution to form a heterogeneous urban political party that
drew support from as many diverse groups as possible. In so doing the
emerging Republican party—not to be confused with the very different Re-

publican party of the 1780s—represented itself as a direct antithesis to the exclusive practices of the Federalists.

The Philadelphia elections of 1791 and 1792 revolved around Hamilton's financial policies and their implications for opportunity and equality within the city. The Anti-Federalists organized under the leadership of Dr. James Hutchinson, fellow of the College of Physicians and during the Revolution the surgeon-general of Pennsylvania; John Swanwick, a politically ambitious merchant; and Alexander J. Dallas, who had emigrated from Jamaica in 1783 and quickly risen to prominence in the law. Party labels were not rigid but rather loosely applied during these early campaigns. Federalists still won the elections by wide margins, primarily because Anti-Federalists still lacked the organization of their opponents. The only exception was John Swanwick's victory for an Assembly seat over Federalist William Lewis. Yet the 1792 election was fought intensely enough to produce a turnout of about 30 percent of the eligible voters, an increase of almost 6 percent since 1789.[71]

Beginning the next year the issues of the French Revolution accelerated the development of a new two-party system. Republicans saw the French Revolution as an affirmation of the same values as the American Revolution, and they believed Americans should support a sister republic, all the more because France had aided America against the British. Federalists, on the other hand, viewed events in France with disdain. They believed the radicalism into which the French Revolution hastened was a threat to the social structure of the United States. They also feared the effect of European war on America's reviving trade with Great Britain. They strongly opposed any preferential treatment of France under the 1778 Treaty of Alliance.[72]

To crystallize their support of the French Revolution, the Republicans created pro-French, anti-Federalist "democratic societies," political clubs intended for active campaigning in support of both French and American varieties of republicanism. Dr. Hutchinson and Alexander J. Dallas organized the first Democratic Society in Philadelphia. About 25 percent of this society's members were artisans, 15.9 percent had some relation to manufacturing and maritime interests, and the remainder held a variety of occupations ranging from doctors to innkeepers. As usual, many of the leading opponents of the established upper class were themselves well to do, but ambitious to move closer to the inner circle. The Democratic Society lost a widely respected and even beloved leader when Dr. Hutchinson died early in the yellow fever epidemic of 1793.[73]

The similar German Republican Society was formed to organize German voters in the city and Philadelphia County. Its leaders included Maj.-Gen. Peter Muhlenberg, a Revolutionary War military hero, and Dr. Michael Leib, who was to discover that political organizing rather than medical practice was his true forte. The German population, until now usually politically inert, had the potential to become a major political force if only its leaders could mobilize it against the Federalists.[74]

During the spring of 1794 the Federalist Congress dealt its own partisan interests in Philadelphia another blow by approving excise duties on loaf sugar, snuff, carriages, sales of spiritous liquors, and auction sales. The taxes on loaf sugar and snuff were especially galling to Philadelphia manufacturers and artisans. By 1794 twenty-seven snuff and tobacco factories in Philadelphia employed over 400 workers. The city refined about 35,000 pounds of sugar that year. By exploiting Federalist sponsorship of the new duties, Republicans worked to broaden their political base still further.[75]

Nevertheless the Federalists generally hung on to win the series of elections from 1793 to 1799. Yet each election tended to become more hotly contested than the last, and the Republicans achieved some major individual triumphs along the way. In the 1794 congressional election the incumbent Federalist, the prominent conservative merchant Thomas Fitzsimons, was pitted against the Republican merchant John Swanwick. Swanwick won with 51.2 percent of the votes. He carried the day by capitalizing on sentiment against the excise taxes with the help of improved Republican organization, which increased voter participation by another 4 percent over the 1792 congressional election, to 34 percent. In 1796 Swanwick gained reelection despite Federalist successes in municipal and state races. Republicans tended to draw most of their strength from the peripheral wards. This strength spilled over into the 1796 presidential election, when Jefferson carried Philadelphia with 61.1 percent of the votes cast for electors. Yet in legislative elections the Federalists continued to average above 60 percent of the vote.[76]

The Federalists also recaptured the city's congressional seat after the death of Swanwick in 1798. With the aid of the pro-Federalist emotions accompanying the naval war with France, Robert Waln, a wealthy Quaker merchant, won overwhelmingly. The yellow fever epidemic may well have benefited the Federalists by reducing voter participation to 18 percent of the eligibles.[77]

But the Federalists had long been slipping, and the elections of 1800 and 1801 brought the end of their dominance of Philadelphia politics. The close of the war with France in 1800 practically destroyed their opportunity to charge their opponents with lack of patriotism. In the election of 1800 city voters sent Republican William Jones, a wealthy Anglican merchant, to Congress. His margin of victory was only fourteen votes, but Republicans won the seat by achieving a large voter turnout, 50 percent of the eligibles. Most of the increase in participation came in wards that were heavily populated by artisans and unskilled workers. In addition the Republicans captured one of the city's Assembly seats and one place on the city Council.[78]

With Jefferson's election to the presidency, Philadelphia's Federalists could no longer rely on federal patronage or the prestige of having the nation's capital in Philadelphia. The federal government departed as scheduled in 1800. Republicans, on the other hand, looked forward to the election of 1801 as their opportunity to grasp complete control of Philadelphia's elected offices. The results fulfilled Republican optimism. The party elected its entire ticket for the state Senate, the Assembly, and the recently divided Select and

Common Councils. (In 1796 the State Legislature had amended the incorporation act to vest municipal legislative power in a Select Council of twelve persons, chosen for staggered three-year terms, and a Common Council of twenty, elected annually, with the mayor now to be chosen by both Select and Common Councils from among the aldermen.)

With the 1801 results the Republicans controlled the Common Council for the first time in the city's history. They won 53 percent, 52.1 percent, 51.8 percent, and 51.5 percent of the votes for Assembly, Select Council, Common Council, and Senate, respectively. Most of their voting strength still came from the peripheral wards. In fact the election marked the first time that the Republicans carried a majority of the city's wards, winning in nine wards in the Assembly and eight in the other major races. The party also succeeded in turning out 50.4 percent of the eligible voters in an off-year election. The Federalist interest that had dominated Philadelphia since 1785 had passed into a minority position.[79]

X I

Before the Federalists' downfall the undeclared war with France had provided Philadelphia with one last opportunity to cheer the national hero whose fortunes were so closely bound to the city's own eminence as the federal capital. The Federalist efforts to strengthen the army for the war brought the master of Mount Vernon once more from his beloved country seat to the city, to accept a commission as lieutenant-general commanding the army and to establish headquarters in Philadelphia. Returning again just as the yellow fever subsided, on November 10, 1798, General Washington was welcomed by the usual tolling of bells and military guard of honor, the latter uncommonly large this time because of the war spirit. With John Adams occupying the presidential mansion at 190 High Street, the honor guard accompanied Washington to lodgings at the Widow Rosannah White's, 9 North Eighth Street. After he had seen to basic matters of military organization, Washington took advantage of the absence of any immediate military threat to consign active leadership of the army to the inspector-general, Maj.-Gen. Alexander Hamilton. On December 14, 1798, the old commander departed Philadelphia for Mount Vernon.[80]

Exactly one year later, on December 14, 1799, Washington died. The news reached Philadelphia during the night of December 17. The federal government still being in the city, Congress assembled at Sixth and High Streets as scheduled the next morning, but when confirmation of the death arrived during the morning the legislature adjourned. Mayor Robert Wharton requested that the bells of Christ Church be muffled for three days "as a mark of the deep regret with which the citizens of this place view the melancholy news." Congressional chambers, churches, and particularly the pew that Washington had occupied at Christ Church were shrouded in black. A joint committee of Congress drafted memorial resolutions and set December 26 as a day of formal mourning in the city. Sixteen cannon fired to open the day, and thereafter one of the cannon fired every half hour until an hour before noon, when a procession of military companies and federal and civic leaders formed in Chestnut Street at Sixth to escort a bier representing Washington's. Down Chestnut to Fifth, south on Fifth to Walnut, east on Walnut to

High Street, From the Country Market-place Philadelphia: with the procession in commemoration of the Death of General George Washington, December 26th 1799, *drawn and engraved by William Birch and Son (1800)*.

Fourth, and north to the Lutheran Church of Zion on the southeast corner of Fourth and Cherry, the largest church auditorium in the city, the procession marched. Bishop William White, long rector of Christ Church and one of the first American bishops who had founded the Protestant Episcopal church, conducted the service. Rep. Henry Lee of Virginia—"Light Horse Harry"—had been chosen by Congress to deliver the oration, because he had known Washington long and well. "First in war, first in peace and first in the hearts of his countrymen . . . ," Lee said of Washington. "Such was the man for whom our nation mourns."[81]

With Washington gone and the capital about to go, the federal era was passing, in its greatness—and in its frivolousness as well. The next winter Anne Willing Bingham contracted a cold during exposure to harsh weather, and like Washington's of December 1799 her cold worsened into a "lung fever" that the medicine of the day could not control. In hopes of halting her rapid decline William Bingham sailed with her for Maderia. But she died on the way, at St. George's in Bermuda. She was thirty-seven years old. Her husband died less than three years later.[82]

In the federal era Philadelphia had reached the peak of its eminence. In the new century its position as the leading American city would soon be lost. The nineteenth century would greatly alter its economy and society. Philadelphia would give way to New York as the largest and richest American city. After the federal capital moved to Washington, Philadelphia also lost its political preeminence. Even the state capital was gone; in 1799 rural suspicion of the city combined with the desire for a more central location to shift the state government to Lancaster, whence it moved again to Harrisburg in 1812. The end of the eighteenth century in a real sense closed out Philadelphia's colonial epoch. Manufacturing developed, trade became less dependent on Great Britain, and the city's political institutions became more democratic. A new nation had taken root, and Philadelphia had played a leading role in its planting.

OVERLEAF: Philadelphia [a] New Plan of the City and its Environs, *engraved by Joseph T. Scott (act. 1795–1800) after Peter Charles Varlé (act. 1794– c. 1835), first edition 1796, second edition 1802. The extension of the city west of the Schuylkill was proposed by Varlé. His plan of ovals, diagonals, and squares resembles L'Enfant's plan for Washington, D.C.*

HISTORICAL SOCIETY OF PENNSYLVANIA

The Athens of America
1800–1825

by Edgar P. Richardson

When I resided in the Athens of America. . . .

— Gilbert Stuart

> *. . . they had some [anthracite] brought down by teams. . . . They expended some three hundred dollars in experiments, but could not succeed in making it burn. . . . they became exasperated, threw a large quantity of the "black stones," as they called them, into the furnace, shut the doors and left the mill; it so happened that one of them had left his jacket in the mill, and in going there for it some time after, he discovered a tremendous fire in the furnace—the doors red with heat."*

— Charles V. Hagner [1]

In the year 1800 Philadelphia was the most successful example in North America of the seaport city, a kind of city that the eighteenth century had brought to perfection. It was a community of merchants, mariners, and mechanics. It was urban but preindustrial, a tree-lined checkerboard of red-brick houses trimmed in white.[2] Within the next twenty-five years it began to be transformed into something new—the first major American industrial city.

I

Philadelphia's ships and seamen were famous. The emblems of the city's coat of arms officially adopted in 1789—a plow and sheaves of wheat and a ship under full sail—were true emblems. The prosperity of the city rested, as it had in colonial times, upon the exchange of the products of the fertile soil of its hinterland for the commerce of the seas. The city directories of 1800–1805 give ample evidence of the dominance of merchants, shipowners, shipbuilders, and seamen in the economy of the city. A writer in *The Port Folio* underlined the importance of this trade: "The staple commodity of Philadelphia is flour, of which 400,000 barrels have been exported in a year."[3]

The first serious threat to the preeminence of Philadelphia came from the meteoric rise of Baltimore after 1783. From the newly opened farmlands of the

Susquehanna Valley grain and other produce were floated downriver by ark and raft from as far upstream as the southern counties of New York. Difficult and imperfect though navigation of the shallow Susquehanna was, it threatened to divert the trade of the interior of Pennsylvania to the mills and wharves of Baltimore. In the years 1798–1800 the value of Baltimore's exports exceeded that of Philadelphia's.[4] To meet this competition Philadelphia built the first paved turnpike in America, west to Lancaster. It was the city's first move in a long contest with Baltimore and later with New York as those rival cities tapped wider hinterlands than they had been able to reach in the colonial period. This economic battle was fought with turnpikes, canals, and finally railroads, to capture the trade of the interior.

In 1800 no one could have imagined the changes that were to shift the city's energies inland, away from the sea; by 1825 Philadelphia would find more attractive opportunities in the coal and iron of northeastern Pennsylvania, the factories of Kensington and Manayunk, the roads and canals spreading north and west. Looking westward as had the Philadelphia fur traders of an earlier century, a stage line to Pittsburgh was advertised in the newspapers of 1804. The stage was to leave weekly from John Tomlinson's hotel on Market Street; the fare was $20 and the journey was promised not to exceed seven days. The adventurous could go farther, floating in a keelboat or ark down the winding reaches of the wild Ohio to reach in twelve days the falls where the frontier settlement of Louisville had sprung up, projected two decades earlier by the Philadelphia Gratzes and their land-speculating associates. To go from Pittsburgh to New Orleans, which had just become American territory, was a journey of twenty to twenty-five days.[5] Farsighted Americans, notably Philadelphia- and Lancaster-based mercantile consortia and intrepid individuals such as the Pennsylvanian Daniel Boone, had long had their eyes fixed on the interior of the continent. But the rapid development of the West in the nineteenth century was made possible by two inventions of the industrial revolution, the steamboat and the railroad.

On the high seas the Napoleonic Wars from 1798 to 1815 absorbed so much of the shipping and manpower of Europe that the United States became the chief neutral carrier. The new opportunities afforded American merchants also exposed their ships to considerable risks. When Great Britain established a naval blockade to close all ports to French ships and to prevent supplies from reaching France, France and her allies retaliated. A long struggle ensued during which neutral ships were seized and the rights of noncombatants disregarded. From the earliest days the chief market for Pennsylvania's products shipped from the port of Philadelphia had been the sugar islands of the Caribbean. Since these were French, Spanish, Dutch, and English colonies, a naval war of blockade and seizure by British men-of-war and French privateers now raged about them.

The complications of the black uprisings against the French, notably in Saint Domingue where Negroes established their own government, and of the harassment of American vessels, made West Indian trade less and less

Arms of the City of Philadelphia, *painted by Thomas Sully (1783–1872)*
for the Mayor's Court in the former Supreme Court Chamber (c. 1821). The configu-
ration of Peace and Plenty with the scale of Justice as a crest was adopted in 1789
and is the basis for the city seal used today.

INDEPENDENCE NATIONAL HISTORICAL PARK COLLECTION

attractive to the Philadelphia merchants. Despite diplomatic peace in 1802,
naval warfare in the Caribbean continued. American mercantile losses were
heavy. By 1812 even Stephen Girard, the crabbed, one-eyed genius at making
money, had withdrawn from the West Indian trade. Girard, Richard Waln,
and other merchants once active there shifted their importing and exporting
commerce to China, India, Europe, and South America.[6]

Philadelphia played a major role in the China trade. This commerce, in
spite of the facts, has usually been associated with Boston and Salem. It was
Robert Morris of Philadelphia and Daniel Parker of New York who sent the
first American ship, the *Empress of China,* to Canton in 1784. The merchant
vessel *United States,* sailing from Philadelphia that same year, opened the trade
with India. When these voyages showed that the monopoly of the British East
India Company could be broken, other Philadelphia merchants—Tench
Coxe, Mordecai Lewis, James Large Mifflin, Joseph Sims, and the Walns,
Drinkers, Hazelhursts, Dales, Fishers, Willings, and Emlens—followed. In
1800 there were forty ships owned in Philadelphia and using it as their home
port that were devoted exclusively to the China trade.[7]

China was a difficult market to enter, yet the rewards were great. The Chinese wanted few products that American merchants could exchange for the tea, porcelains, and silk and cotton goods the Western world sought. The young American Republic could ship out only specie (of which it had but little), ginseng, furs, and some metals. But American seamen had become skilled in triangular trading. Their ships collected cargoes for Canton in Amsterdam, Antwerp, and Gibraltar; they stopped at Valparaiso for hides, at Smyrna for opium, in Batavia or Malacca for tin, and on the Malabar coast for sandalwood and pepper. As soon as the accounts of Capt. James Cook's voyages spread word of the rich, deep-piled sea otter skins of the Northwest coast of America—luxuriant furs were especially desired by the Chinese— American ships made the long voyage around Cape Horn and up the Pacific coast to barter knives and blankets with the Indians for those splendid pelts. The sealers in the South Atlantic and the Pacific harvested islands almost to the point of the extinction of the easily killed sea-going mammals. These were the outbound cargoes.

In return they brought home from Canton chiefly tea, and also silks, nankeens, porcelains, and camphor. During the War of 1812 the British bottled up the American ships in Canton and drove American vessels from the Northwest fur trade and from Hawaii, but as soon as the war ended they were back again. Of the American ships at Canton between June 6, 1816, and May

Philadelphia from the Jersey Shore, *painting by Thomas Birch (1779–1851), c. 1812. A China trade ship is greeted by its merchant owner and his family in the longboat.*

FRANK T. HOWARD

25, 1817, Boston was the home port of eleven, Philadelphia nine, New York seven, Salem five, Baltimore four, and Providence three. Contrary to the overemphasis on New England's China trade, the merchants of that region seem to have shared equally with those from the Middle Atlantic states. In 1825 business in the Celestial Empire was chiefly in the hands of four American firms of which two, Samuel Archer and Jones, Oakford and Company, were Philadelphian; the others were Perkins & Company of Boston and T. H. Smith of New York.[8]

The stimulating effect of the China trade was not limited to the value of the goods brought to the American home markets or reexported to Europe, or to the increasing number of fortunes made in the trade. Tea, porcelains, and textiles had found their way to America before the Revolution through the hands of the East India Company, but to most Americans Asia was little more than an Oriental fable. Now they had direct contact with the accumulated wealth and ancient culture of China.

A Dutch merchant, Andreas Everardus van Braam Houckgeest, who had spent years in China in the service of the Dutch East India Company, settled in Philadelphia in 1796, bought a farm on the Delaware near Bristol, and built a fifteen-room house called "China's Retreat," where he lived surrounded by the curiosities he had brought back with him and waited upon by Chinese servants and a Malay housekeeper. A description of his visit to the court of the Ch'ien Lung emperor was published in Philadelphia by Moreau de Saint-Méry in two handsome volumes in 1797–1798. His collection of Chinese art was soon sent across the Atlantic and sold at Christie's in London in February 1799. Other objects of Oriental workmanship arrived in Philadelphia. Exhibition pieces from the East Indies and China appeared in the accession book of the Peale Museum, and mementos of Asia accumulated in homes up and down the Delaware.

The son of one of the pioneer China merchants, Robert Waln, Jr., visited the Far Eastern mainland as a supercargo on his father's ships. In 1823 he published the first major work of its kind by an American, *China, Comprehending a View of the Origin, Antiquity, History, Religion, Morals, Government, Laws, Population, Literature, Drama, Festivals, Games, Women, Beggars, Manners, Customs, etc., of that Empire.* Some years later the architect John Haviland built the first great marble mansion on Chestnut Street for Charles Blight, an East India merchant; and Nathan Dunn, another merchant, opened a Chinese Museum on the northeast corner of Ninth and Sansom Streets to show his collections. The China trade was the beginning of a great enlargement of the nation's horizon. Mercantile contacts with South America, which began as early as 1799, were also to be of importance.[9]

In 1805 when Philadelphia's maritime trade was near its peak, 547 ships arrived at its Delaware wharfs from foreign ports, while 617 cleared; 1169 coasters arrived and 1231 cleared. A total of 3564 ships came up the river, anchored, unloaded, loaded, or sailed away, an average of better than ten a day, since the port was closed by ice for several weeks in the winter.[10] The maritime activity was brought to a sudden end in 1808 when President Jefferson placed an embargo on foreign commerce in answer to the British Orders in Council of December 1807, the final tightening of the screw of the naval blockade, and to Napoleon's retaliatory Milan Decree of the same month. Ships were tied up in port; shipbuilding stopped.

Mayor Robert Wharton wrote to his brother: "Our city as to traffic is almost a desert, wharves crowded with empty vessels, the noise and buz of commerce not heard, whilst hundreds of labourers are ranging the streets without employ or the means of getting bread for their distressed Families." In January 1808 hungry and discontented sailors marched behind the Stars and Stripes to City Hall at Fifth and Chestnut Streets to appeal to the mayor. Wharton first sternly told them to lower the flag, which they did; he then expressed his pity for their distress, asked them to disperse peaceably, and told them that the Chamber of Commerce would do what it could for them. Money was raised to aid the sufferers; it was only a palliative. By April the distress was so general that sailors drifted away to other places, many going to Halifax, Nova Scotia, to enter the British service.[11]

The lifting of the embargo in 1810 brought a brief revival of ocean trade; that was ended in 1812 by the declaration of war against Great Britain. In the first months of open hostilities the small American navy gave a gallant account of itself, but it was soon driven into port by overwhelming numbers of British ships. The United States had seven frigates and fifteen sloops-of-war and other smaller vessels to fight a British navy of 1060 sail, 800 of which were in commission.[12] The American frigates had been designed in Philadelphia. Nine of the sixteen gold medals of honor voted by Congress for naval gallantry went to officers from the bay and river Delaware: Jacob Jones for the capture of the *Frolic*, Stephen Decatur for taking the *Macedonian*, William Bainbridge for overcoming the *Java*, William Burrows for the capture of the *Boxer*, James Lawrence for taking the *Peacock*, Thomas Macdonough and Stephen Cassin for their victory on Lake Champlain, Charles Stewart for bringing in the *Cyane* and the *Levant*, and James Biddle for his success against the *Penguin*.[13] But from March 1813 until the end of the war a British blockading squadron, cruising off the capes of the Delaware from Egg Harbor to Chincoteague, effectively bottled up Philadelphia's shipping.

Although Col. Winfield Scott raised the Second Artillery Regiment in Philadelphia for service on the Canadian frontier,[14] only a direct threat to the city stimulated the mobilization of local land forces. In March 1813 the British squadron appeared at the mouth of the Delaware. It bombarded Lewes in April and the following month sailed upstream as far as Reedy Island. Excitement and alarm stirred the city. Volunteer companies were raised. The Philadelphia Blues, the Independent Volunteers, and the Washingotn Guards under the command of Col. Lewis Rush marched down the river to protect Wilmington and the du Pont powder mills.

The next year a strong British force sailed into the Chesapeake, burned Washington, and attacked Baltimore. It appeared that General Howe's 1777

advance from Elkton to Philadelphia might be repeated. Commanded by
Brig.-Gen. Thomas Cadwalader, the Philadelphia militia marched south, once
again to guard the line of the Brandywine. Citizens turned out with enthusiasm to fortify the approaches to the city, digging redoubts at Gray's Ferry,
at the Woodlands, on the west bank of the Schuylkill, along the Darby and
Lancaster Roads, and on the south side of Fairmount. With the death of
British Maj.-Gen. Robert Ross, at the head of a landing party near Baltimore,
the invasion came to an end. Philadelphia's troops were home by December.[15]

Independence Day Celebration in Centre Square, Philadelphia,
painted by John Lewis Krimmel (1786–1821), 1819.

HISTORICAL SOCIETY OF PENNSYLVANIA

After the war the port of Philadelphia never regained its former position.
Trade and shipbuilding returned for a time, only to be stifled by a depression
as European ships and men, released from half a generation of wartime
demands, resumed international commerce and supplanted American shipping. For a number of reasons New York now forged rapidly ahead of
Philadelphia. Its great ice-free harbor was more easily accessible. Its wharves
were not a hundred difficult miles from the ocean as were those of Philadelphia. Moreover British manufacturers who had accumulated large surpluses
of cottons and woolens chose New York as the port at which to dump their
textiles for "whatever they would bring." Buyers flocked in from all over the

country. To hold this trade New York in 1817 passed auction legislation that made the port so attractive that the flood of British manufactures continued to pour through it. More important still, in 1817 New York established the first line of regular packets, later called the Black Ball Line, to replace the old spring and fall sailings, thus initiating a new pattern of ocean commerce.[16]

During the constant naval wars of the eighteenth century the seas had been so dangerous and communication so uncertain that the captain and supercargo of a merchant ship were given great freedom to find a safe port and bring back a profitable cargo. When the *United States,* for example, sailed from Philadelphia for China in March 1784, her officers decided in mid-voyage, while taking on a cargo of madeira wine at Funchal, to go instead to the Coromandel coast, thus becoming the first American ship to venture to India.[17] Stephen Girard gave his officers this authority and rewarded them handsomely with a percentage of the profits. William Wagner, one of Girard's men, was able to retire quite young to devote himself to science and to found the Wagner Free Institute of Science.[18]

Stephen Girard *(1750–1831), painted by Bass Otis (1784–1861), c. 1831. Girard, a merchant and banker who purchased the Bank of the United States building on Third Street in 1812, was the wealthiest man in the United States at the time of his death.*

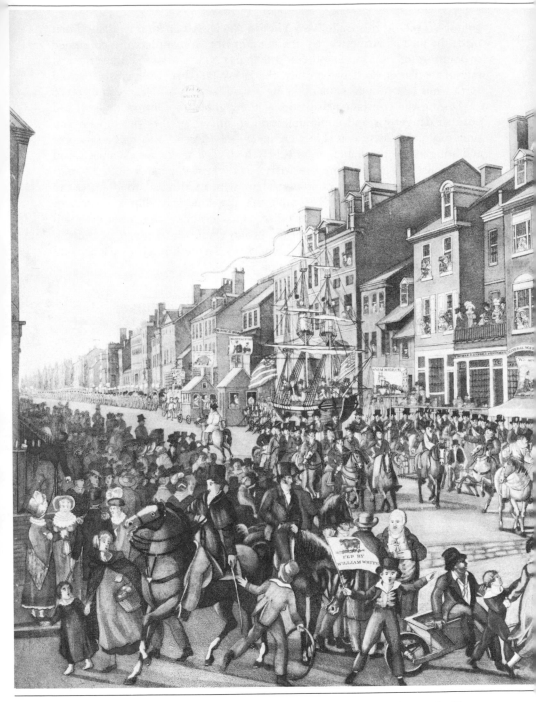

Procession of Victuallers, *aquatint and etching by Joseph Yeager*
(c. 1792–1859) after John Lewis Krimmel (1786–1821), 1821. An extraordinary parade

and livestock show which attracted 300,000 spectators is shown turning at the northwest corner of Fourth and Chestnut.

As the new era dawned, frequent and regular schedules replaced more adventurous voyaging. Successive packet lines to Liverpool, Le Havre, and London enabled New York, even before the opening of the Erie Canal, to forge ahead of Boston, Philadelphia, and Baltimore in ocean commerce.[19] Philadelphia nonetheless continued to be a center of shipbuilding and a major port for the South Atlantic and Gulf trade. But by 1824 its foreign commerce had declined to a poor third or fourth place in the nation. In the opinion of one maritime historian, this decline showed not so much lack of energy as extraordinary foresight.[20] Businessmen in Philadelphia had found other, more secure, more profitable uses for their talents and capital; they moved into the technological revolution.

I I

In 1800 Philadelphia was the biggest city in the United States; 67,787 people lived within the municipality and its contiguous suburbs of Southwark and the Northern Liberties.[21] The shape of the populated area had changed little over the past fifty years, but the half-moon of houses was expanding. To the south, beyond Old Swedes' Church, were farmlands and marshes. To the north, above Pegg's Run near Vine Street, were the houses and dockyards of the Northern Liberties. There were scattered structures west of Seventh Street, but Centre Square was at the fringe of open country. The fields, trees, and lawns of farms and country estates lined the banks of the Schuylkill. Here and there along its shores were famous private gardens, like Lemon Hill and the Woodlands, and public pleasure grounds such as Gray's Garden at the Lower Ferry and the Wigwam Baths at the end of Race Street, to which citizens walked, rode, or drove according to their means. Until 1818 a grove of walnut trees, a last remnant of the original forest, stood on Chestnut Street facing the State House.[22]

The semicircumference of the half-moon was being pushed farther and farther out into the fields. The city was growing rapidly, four to five hundred houses a year since the formation of the federal government in 1789.[23] In the new century its population increased by 40–50 percent in each decade, except during the troubled years 1810–1820 when growth was about halved. Fast as Philadelphia grew, New York grew faster. In the census of 1810 the latter became first in the nation. Numbers were not indicative, however, of the nature of the city. In some respects Philadelphia retained characteristics of a medieval town. Many merchants and craftsmen still lived over their shops; and people of every sort, gentleman and ironmonger, bishop and soap-boiler, resided pell-mell together. There was no "good neighborhood," although there were areas where certain groups tended to congregate. The Germans were in the northwest. The Negroes lived on the southeast edge of town where the Mother Bethel African Methodist Episcopal Church stands on Sixth Street below Pine, the oldest piece of property in continuous black ownership in the United States. Arch Street was a Quaker street. Third and Fourth Streets below Market, and Chestnut and Walnut Streets were especially handsome, with many of the houses of the wealthy.

Negroes in Front of the Bank of Pennsylvania, *painting by Pavel Petrovitch Svinin (1787/88–1839), 1811–1813. The bank, on the west side of Second Street above Walnut, was designed in 1789 by Benjamin H. Latrobe (1764–1820) and demolished c. 1871.*

Market Street too, not yet wholly devoted to business, still had great houses, mostly to the west, for the market at Second Street dominated the river end. When ships came into port, their cargoes from India, China, or the Mediterranean were bought by merchants up and down Front or Second Street and advertised in the papers. Many goods were disposed of by auction, as they had been in the eighteenth century, but gradually wholesale dealers with warehouses to store specialized goods and retail shops established a pattern of commerce more like that of today.

Philadelphia was a pretty city, as the views published in 1798–1800 by William Birch most pleasantly show. The citizens were proud of it, and most foreign travelers shared the opinion of the French botanist André Michaux that it was "the most extensive, the handsomest and most populous city in the United States."[24] Some, accustomed to the winding, crooked streets of European cities, thought its rectangularity monotonous. Sir Augustus Foster, who had been a young chargé d'affaires in Philadelphia before the War of 1812, considered it "built too much in the shape of a chess board to be beautiful," adding, "There is nothing surely so unfavorable to Architectural ornament as long lines of broad streets cutting each other at right angles." But the Swedish traveler Baron Axel Klinckowström described it as "one of the loveliest cities in the world."[25]

The highest form of flattery, however, came from fellow Americans. As new cities were laid out in the Old Northwest, along the Great Lakes and down the Ohio and Mississippi, the rectilinear pattern of Penn's first plat of his city-to-be was repeated over and over again. Philadelphia was the "model metropolis"; visitors to the West were struck by the similarity between the frontier cities and Philadelphia. And not only in urban regularity, but also in language and social and cultural trends, Middle America assumed the ways of the Quaker City rather than those of New England or the Old South.

In 1805 a writer describing the city in *The Port Folio* said of it:

The streets of Philadelphia are paved with pebblestones, and bordered with ample footways, raised one foot above the carriageway, for the ease and safety of passengers. They are kept cleaner than those of any city in Europe, excepting the towns of Holland. . . . London is the only capital in the world that is better lighted at night. Many of the New Streets have been latterly planted with Poplars. . . . Their introduction has already given to some sections the air of Public Walks, for ornament of which nothing is wanting but Fountains and Statuary.[26]

Statues and fountains were added in the first decade of the century. The Board of Managers of the Pennsylvania Hospital, proud of their striking new building, solicited works of art to adorn it. John Penn presented a leaden statue of his grandfather, which arrived in September 1804 on the ship *Pigou* and was set up on the lawn facing Pine Street.[27] The expatriate Benjamin West promised a large painting of *Christ Healing the Sick*, which arrived a decade later. It was housed in a special building on the Spruce Street side of the hospital's block, known as the West Picture House, the cost of which was more than paid for by public admissions.[28] In 1809 the city's first fountain,

The Nymph of the Schuylkill, carved in wood by William Rush, was erected in Centre Square. Two years later Rush was commissioned to supply life-size figures of Faith, Hope, and Charity for the new Masonic Hall designed by William Strickland on the north side of Chestnut Street between Seventh and Eighth.[29]

In Washington, diplomats and congressmen, irritated by the mud, emptiness, and inconveniences of the unfinished new capital, recalled longingly the city they had left. In February 1808 a congressman from New Jersey introduced a resolution that "it is expedient, and the public good requires, that the Seat of Government be removed to the city of Philadelphia." It passed on the first reading. But the members from Maryland, Virginia, and the Carolinas rallied; the debate went on for several days, and the proposal was talked to death.[30]

The congressmen had much to regret. Washington was a raw settlement of muddy roads and crowded boardinghouses, a hall for Congress in which no one could hear the speaker, a few scattered unfinished rows of houses— "like the ruins of Palmyra," one congressman said—empty distances and a malodorous swamp where the Mall now is. Philadelphia was an amusing and cosmopolitan city with good hotels, theaters, restaurants, circuses, bookshops, a fine library, a natural history museum, an art museum, the greatest scientific institution in America, and a galaxy of interesting and talented people. The poet Tom Moore—riding the peak of his Anglo-American popularity— remembered as a bright spot of his visit to America the evenings spent at the house of the talented lawyer Joseph Hopkinson, the picnics by the Schuylkill, and the young literati who gathered in the mornings at Asbury Dickins's bookstore opposite Christ Church.[31]

No longer did state legislators and federal officials vie for lodgings during the meetings of their respective bodies. No longer seen about the corner of Sixth and Chestnut Streets were Washington, now at the top of the pantheon of dead heroes; Hamilton, slain in a duel by Aaron Burr; Adams, now in Quincy, Massachusetts; and President Jefferson. Robert Morris, once a genial entertainer of guests, was in debtor's prison. Gone too were the speculators and the men who had collected on the raffish fringes of government. Philadelphia was settling down to its own particular kind of society, sometimes rich and extravagant, more often genteely cultured.

Pres. Jared Sparks of Harvard College found that John Vaughan, the treasurer, librarian, and most active member of the American Philosophical Society, was the cicerone and friend of all distinguished visitors to the city. Under Vaughan's guidance he was "at a society, or at a dinner, or at a tea every day and almost every hour . . . almost wholly among scientific men and artists."[32] "At the beginning of this century," an editor of Franklin's writings, Albert H. Smyth, wrote retrospectively as the nineteenth century came to a close, "Philadelphia was the most attractive city in America to a young man of brains and ambition."[33]

The city certainly was politically exciting. Although Congress no longer met there, it was the cockpit where the conflicting views and policies of the two emergent political parties were pitted against each other in the press and in pamphlets. The revolt against the Federalists which carried Jefferson to the presidency of the United States in 1801 first came to a head in Pennsylvania. It was led by three dominating figures, Gov. Thomas McKean, Dr. Michael Leib, and William Duane. McKean, whose election as governor of Pennsylvania in 1799 helped pave the way for Jefferson's electoral victory in 1800, was a tall, choleric, volatile Scots-Irish lawyer. During the Revolution he had been a fiery Whig; he was a Federalist when the Constitution was adopted; he went over to the radical side in the 1790s and had the distinction, while living in Philadelphia, of holding offices in two states, as chief justice of the Supreme Court of Pennsylvania and as a member of Congress from Delaware. A lawyer, he was a leader of the postrevolutionary democracy that feared and distrusted lawyers. Better educated and more experienced than his rural followers, he served at times as a brake on their "crude theories, fanciful alterations, new projects and pleasing visions," as he put it, vetoing a measure passed by his own party.

Dr. Leib, fond of power and office, seems to have enjoyed playing the sport of politics for its own sake. He was Philadelphia's first political boss. He successfully organized the voters—as well as those not entitled to vote—into a political machine, a coalition of dedicated Jeffersonians, anti-English Irish expatriates, and a mass of citizens who feared the rise of an aristocracy of wealth and position.

His ally in Philadelphia—and Jefferson's in the nation—was William Duane, who made his newspaper, the *Aurora*, the national voice of the new democracy. Jefferson is said to have attributed his election to its effective support. In an age of bitter and abusive partisanship, Duane was one of the most abusively partisan. His attacks on his opponents were so vitriolic that at one time he was defendant in more than sixty libel suits.

While the alliance of these three hot-tempered, domineering men held, they were unbeatable. Their party—then called "Republican"—captured the governorship and control of the lower house of the Assembly in 1799 and of the Senate in 1802. That latter year the Federalists, polling 17,125 votes for James Ross against 47,567 for McKean, were not so much defeated as annihilated; in 1803 they could not find candidates for all the offices slated.[34]

The "Revolution of 1800" was in Pennsylvania as much a social as a political turnabout. It was the revolt of the small farmer, the frontiersman, and the city's poor against the old ruling class of Philadelphia merchants and large landowners. Partisan feelings, on a national and international level rather than on a local one, particularly the sympathies aroused by the world war between France and England, were intense. Each party had its own armed militia units, and occasionally demonstrated its muscle. Yet these excited feelings expressed themselves only through ballots; the transfer of power in 1800 took place peacefully.

With the moving of the state and national governments to other cities, the buildings they had occupied reverted to local uses. Congress Hall, the westernmost of the State House complex, again became the courthouse; the east building, where the Supreme Court of the United States had sat, became the City Hall.[35] The municipal government, little more powerful than in the eighteenth century, consisted of a mayor, the Select and Common Councils, the Board of City Commissioners, and a registrar. Some of their functions were judicial as well as administrative. The mayor, elected for a term of one year, was, as he had been since the time of Penn's charter, a leading citizen —a merchant perhaps, like John Inskeep (1800–1801, 1804–1806) or Robert Wharton (1798–1800, 1806–1808, 1810–1811, 1814–1819, 1820–1824), or a lawyer like Michael Keppele (1811–1812). His duties were little more than those of a chief of not very effective police. In return for the honor of the post he was required to handle riots and tumults, which were not uncommon. Mayor Wharton was described by one who knew him:

This Mr. Wharton was Mayor of the City in 1798, and for many years after. He was bold, intrepid, and very active, ready at a moment's notice to quell a riot. His appearance at such gatherings with staff in hand, and hat tipped a little on one side of his head, with firm step, and independent authority, would scatter the ire and quell the fire of the most ferocious mob. Philadelphia never had a more efficient and popular municipal officer.[36]

Other functionaries and commissions of the city remained virtually unchanged from an earlier period. Constables and watchmen kept order by day and night. Authority lay with twelve "viewers" to lay out new streets, and another similar jury assessed damages for such appropriation. The Watering Committee of the Councils assumed greater importance as the pumping system of the city expanded, and the municipal guardians of the poor continued their traditional concern.[37] The administration of the port, a state responsibility, was reorganized in 1803 to consist of a master warden and six (later raised to twelve) assistants, the majority from Philadelphia and originally one from Southwark and one from the Northern Liberties.[38]

I V

The tradition of voluntary association was strong in Philadelphia. Protection from fire had been and would continue to be for many years the work of volunteer fire companies. The primitive engine, hauled to the scene of a fire, filled by a bucket brigade and expelling water from a metal nozzle at the top of the tank, was a hand-pumper operated by a horizontal bar on the side. Although the flexible fire hose had been invented in Holland in the seventeenth century, it did not reach Philadelphia until 1803. In that year, after a series of fires costly in damage and lives, a group of men met at the house of Reuben Haines on Bank Street to form the Philadelphia Hose Company. Money was raised by subscription to purchase a hose carriage and to build a house for it at 17 North Fourth Street. The new machine proved so valuable in quenching a stable fire in Whalebone Alley on March 3, 1804, that two more hose companies were organized. In 1811 the city Councils appropriated $1000 to support the fire and hose companies, the first use of public funds for such a purpose.[39]

The same pattern of self-help by private association prevailed in education, although the state at this time took the first tentative steps toward assuming responsibility. The churches remained active in sponsoring schools, orphanages, and free academies for the poor. The Quakers, Episcopalians, Presbyterians, Moravians, Baptists, Roman Catholics, and Lutherans all had schools, many of which in original form or by succession still exist. There were also numerous private academies, taught by men who conceived "that their business was to make their scholars good writers, good readers, good arithmeticians, and intelligent grammarians."[40] Further intellectual graces were left to self-education or to the host of teachers who advertised their ability to produce pupils competent in French, singing, dancing, drawing, and other such arts.

Alexander Wilson, who later became famous as an ornithologist, taught such a school in Darby Township. The Rev. Samuel Magaw, rector of St. Paul's Episcopal Church, was president of Poor's Academy for Young Ladies, a notable establishment for girls on Cherry Street. The Negro Episcopal and Methodist churches had started schools for their own people, and in 1804 a group of the black community, desiring education separated from religious instruction, formed the Society of Free People of Color to promote an independent institution.

The University of Pennsylvania in 1800 purchased for its college building the large house on Ninth Street built by the state as a mansion for the president of the United States. Yet the college, so influential and so productive of leaders before the Revolution, made slow recovery from its more recent, bitter divisions. Provost William Smith had been energetic but prickly; his successors were less prickly and less energetic. The first twenty years of the nineteenth century have been called "the lowest point in the history of the college."[41] One factor damping its revival was the sectarian emphasis of American education in the nineteenth century. The University of Pennsylvania was nonsectarian, part of its legacy from Franklin. As a result, Presbyterian boys went to Princeton or Dickinson, Germans to Franklin and Marshall; Quakers, though cultured and great readers, continued to consider advanced education superfluous. A further impediment to the institution was its organization as college, academy, and charity school, confusing its tone and its purpose. The one exception to this ineffectiveness was the university's medical school which, housed in Anatomy Hall on Fourth Street, was the outstanding center of medical training in the United States, basking in the reputation of the nation's most famous physician, Dr. Benjamin Rush.

At other levels the educational experiments going forward in Europe were making themselves felt in Philadelphia. William Maclure, who had observed

The University of Pennsylvania, *engraving published by Cephas Grier Childs after George Strickland (1797–1851), 1828.*

the schools for poor children started by Pestalozzi in Switzerland, brought a disciple of his, Joseph Neef, a German, to Philadelphia. In 1808 he established the first kindergarten in America in Provost William Smith's mansion near the Falls of Schuylkill.[42] Contemporaneously the Abbé Espée was developing in Paris a method of teaching children born deaf and dumb, who had hitherto been hopelessly cut off from a normal life. When his successor, the Abbé Sicard, toured America in 1816 to demonstrate this method, David G. Seixas, a Philadelphia tin and crockery merchant, became interested. Something of an inventor himself, Seixas introduced his own system of manual communication, and in 1820 founded the Philadelphia Institute for the Deaf and Dumb. After a bitter quarrel between the founder and some members of his board, he was ousted and the institution renamed the Philadelphia Asylum for the Deaf and Dumb. Its building, erected in 1825, still stands at Broad and Pine Streets as part of the Philadelphia College of Art.[43]

Meanwhile the feasibility of schools for the children of the poor, to be paid for by public taxes, was under discussion. Bills had been introduced in the state legislature for this purpose but had been defeated. The opposition consisted principally of Quakers and Lutherans, who supported their own schools without state aid and felt a general tax would be unfair to them; of the German sectarians, who wanted to educate their children in their own tongue as they had been doing; and of conservatives generally, who were against any new tax.[44] In 1802 an act was passed, applying only to the city and county of Philadelphia, which provided that children whose parents could not afford schooling might attend the most convenient private school at the county's expense.[45]

Far away, in Madras, India, the Rev. Dr. James Andrew devised a system by which children taught one another under the supervision of a master. The method was introduced into England by Joseph Lancaster and became known as the Lancastrian method. It was brought to Philadelphia in 1817. Although it eventually proved a failure, its promise of educating large numbers of children without the expense of paid teachers helped persuade the Assembly, during the depression year of 1818, to pass an act that set up the city and county of Philadelphia as the "First School District" of Pennsylvania and provided for education on the Lancastrian plan at public expense. In a real sense this marked the beginning of the public school system in the state.[46]

V

The great civic improvement of the period was the waterworks on the Schuylkill. Philadelphia, like all cities for centuries past, had drawn its water supply from wells and cisterns. These were in the lowland of the city proper, shallow, and easily contaminated by surface drainage from the streets and by the underground flow from the cesspools and outhouses. The death toll from the yellow fever epidemics of the 1790s had been appalling. Nothing was known about their cause, but it was believed that adequate good water would mitigate, if not prevent, the terrible scourge. It was also argued that existing water supplies were inadequate for fighting fires. In 1799 a petition signed by several hundred citizens asked the city Councils to seek a new source of water.

One proposal recommended that it be drawn from an unfinished canal, begun nearly ten years earlier, to connect the Delaware and Schuylkill Rivers near the line of Vine Street. Because of the low level of the land between the rivers, purer water was to be brought to the Vine Street area by a feeder canal from a point near Norristown, where the Schuylkill was nearly forty feet above its level in Philadelphia. Authority for the provision and sale of water to the city had been written into the charter of the Delaware and Schuylkill Canal Company which in 1792 had begun, but never completed, the construction of the feeder canal. The company now proposed that the state complete this canal and bring water to the city from Spring Mill Creek below Norristown.

The engineer-architect Benjamin Henry Latrobe was engaged by the city to survey the route. He reported that water could be brought by an aqueduct from Spring Mill, but that a better method would be to build a basin on the Schuylkill above Chestnut Street, the bottom of which would be three feet below low water. From this basin, water, lifted and forced by steam pumps, would be brought by canal and tunnel along the line of Chestnut Street to Broad and up Broad to a pump house in Centre Square. There another steam engine would raise it to a reservoir thirty feet above ground holding 16,000 gallons. Thence it would flow by gravity in wooden pipes throughout the

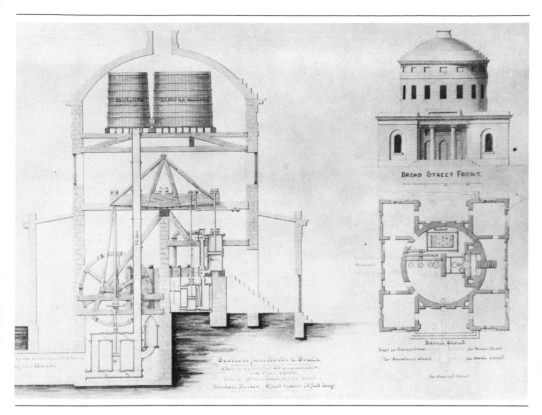

Centre Square Water Works, *colored drawing by Frederick C. Graff* (*1774–1847*), *c. 1828. Designed by Benjamin Henry Latrobe* (*1764–1820*) *in 1798–1800, the pumphouse at the intersection of Broad and Market Streets was built to be "ornamental as well as useful" and to "supply the City of Philadelphia with Wholesome Water," according to Latrobe's report of 1798.*

HISTORICAL SOCIETY OF PENNSYLVANIA

city. Latrobe's plan was adopted over the determined opposition of the canal company and the doubts of those who had no faith in steam engines.[47]

Latrobe himself designed the pump house in a new classical style in Centre Square, for years one of the sights of Philadelphia. A contract was made with Nicholas I. Roosevelt of New York to build the steam engines, which were to be capable of supplying a million gallons of water a day. Roosevelt was an inventor and machine builder of talent; among other improvements he designed the vertical paddlewheel that made Robert Fulton's steamboat successful. On January 27, 1801, with public rejoicing, the Latrobe-Roosevelt waterworks were put into operation. In the year that followed, sixty-three houses, four breweries, and a sugar refinery were supplied with Schuylkill water, and thirty-seven hydrants were installed in various parts of the city. But Roosevelt's low-pressure engines were unequal to their task; by 1804 he claimed he had lost $45,000 on his contract. After much dispute, the Watering Committee settled with him for $15,000, and put Frederick Graff in charge of the works.[48]

Frederick Graff, whose battered and neglected monument stands between the Water Works and the rocky slope of Fairmount, was one of Philadelphia's great civil servants before that term was invented. His grandfather, who came from Germany in 1741, and his father before him had been skilled master builders and contractors. The son, trained as a carpenter, had gained some skill also as a draftsman and was employed by Latrobe in erecting the pump house. On April 1, 1805, Graff was made superintendent and engineer in charge of the works. He was to serve the city for forty-two years and to become the leading American expert on hydraulic engineering. Graff created for the Water Works a new technology for control of the movement and delivery of water: iron pipes replaced the old piping of wooden logs; fire hydrants to which the fire engine could be directly con-

View of Centre Square, *water color, c. 1812, by Pavel Petrovich Svinin (1787/88–1839). The* Nymph of the Schuylkill *sculpture by William Rush (1756–1833) was added c. 1809.*

METROPOLITAN MUSEUM OF ART, ROGERS FUND, 1942

nected (Latrobe's hydrants delivered the water into a ground-level pool, from which the water was moved by hand pump into the tank of a fire engine); stopcocks to stop the flow of water in case of a leaking or broken pipe. His advice and innovations were followed by about thirty-five American cities and drawings of them sent to England. He changed the habits of the people of Philadelphia.[49]

After spending five years trying to make the original system work, Graff recommended that the intake be moved upstream. In December 1811 the city Councils approved his plan for a reservoir on top of Morris Hill (later Fairmount) with a pumping station at its base. In 1814 the Watering Committee bought from Oliver Evans a high-pressure steam engine to lift the water to the reservoir, but before the works were completed Graff decided to switch to a hydraulic system by which waterwheels supplied the power. In 1818 he began to replace the wooden mains with cast-iron pipes, an innovation that involved new problems. Graff himself designed the stopcocks and hydrants for the new distribution system, which was completed in 1822. Within two years the use of Schuylkill water and the handsome buildings by the river that

View of the Waterworks on Schuylkill—Seen from the Top of Fair Mount, *engraving published by Cephas Grier Childs after Thomas Doughty (1793–1856), 1829.*

housed the Water Works were the pride of the city. To visit Philadelphia without seeing Fairmount and its Water Works was, people said, like viewing London without seeing Westminster Abbey. Of all the views of the city, the Schuylkill at Fairmount was that which attracted most artists and resulted in most paintings and prints. Graff, as the result of his local success, was called for advice by New York when it installed the Croton water system in 1842 and by Boston in 1848.[50]

Despite the improvement in Philadelphia's water supply, yellow fever continued to recur periodically. Because of it, in 1810 the Board of Health opened a hospital for contagious diseases, with a capacity of about 500, out in the open country near the present intersection of Nineteenth Street and Fairmount Avenue.[51]

The city's authority, including its police and its water supply, were then, and would long continue to be, confined to the area from river to river between South and Vine Streets. As population increased and as houses were built outside these bounds, the environs were incorporated as separate boroughs, as Southwark had been in the 1760s. Frankford became a borough in 1800 and the southeast corner of Northern Liberties Township three years later. Penn Township was carved out of the western part of the Northern Liberties in 1807, and its western portion became Spring Garden Township in 1813. Moyamensing was incorporated in 1812, and Kensington in 1820. Although county courts and certain county offices were maintained, each borough had its own government and borough hall, its own lower courts and police. A quarter of a century after Schuylkill water was first introduced into the city proper, the boroughs of Spring Garden, the Northern Liberties, and Southwark contracted to have the system extended into their jurisdictions.

VI

Among the developments that made the modern city possible were the new forms of transportation created in the nineteenth century: bridges, turnpikes, canals, steamboats, and finally, railroads. The example of the macadamized Lancaster and Germantown pikes encouraged the organization of other turnpike companies. Following the chartering of the pike from Front Street through Germantown to Reading in 1798, a company was created to build a road from Third and Vine Streets to Germantown and Perkiomen (the Ridge Pike) in 1801. Two years later the Cheltenham and Willow Grove Turnpike Company was incorporated to run a pike from the Rising Sun Tavern to the Red Lion Inn on Old York Road, and another the same year was to go from Front Street through Frankford to Bustleton and Morrisville, where it connected with a ferry to New Jersey. These pikes broke through the checkerboard pattern of Philadelphia's streets and have remained thoroughfares. By 1821 eighty-five turnpikes had been chartered in the state, mostly financed by Philadelphia capital. A network of paved toll highways had been pushed out from the city to New York, Reading, Harrisburg, Lancaster, and Baltimore, and into New Jersey.[52]

But Philadelphia lay at the end of a narrow peninsula between two deep and navigable rivers; their tributaries were hardly less formidable barriers to travel by land. From the city's infancy there had been ferries; from the time of the Revolution two floating bridges crossed the Schuylkill. These expedient bridges were repeatedly swept away by freshets, and various designs for a bridge that could withstand storms and floods had been proposed. Although a model for an iron bridge had been produced by the pamphleteer Tom Paine and a design for a wooden truss bridge patented by the artist-inventor Charles Willson Peale,[53] it was not until 1798 that a company organized by Judge Richard Peters as president adopted a plan by Timothy Palmer for a wooden structure to cross the Schuylkill at Market Street. Its cornerstone was laid on

Judd's Hotel and the United States Mail Coach, *painted by an unknown artist (1817–1825). Judd's Hotel was at 27 South Third Street, and the U.S. Mail coach office was across the street at no. 30. Advertisements for the mail and passenger service promised arrival in New York "the same day" following a 5 A.M. departure.*

October 13, 1800, and the single-arch bridge, 552 feet long and 31 feet above the river at its greatest elevation, was opened on January 1, 1805.

At Judge Peters's insistence a protective wood cover was added that same year, and the covered highway across the river was embellished with two carved wood statues by William Rush, *Commerce* at one end and *Agriculture* at the other. A marble obelisk at the western approach bore a long inscription describing the bridge and praising those "who by enterprising, arduous, and persevering exertions achieved this extensively beneficial improvement." The city was immensely proud of the Permanent Bridge, as it was called. When a tavern near the western end caught fire one January night in 1806, the *United States Gazette* reported: "It is due to the respective Hose and Fire Companies, to state, that notwithstanding the distant situation of the fire, and the badness of the walking the citizens turned out with alacrity and ardor highly honorable—we understand that not less than 5,000 persons crossed the bridge on this occasion."[54]

The Permanent Bridge inaugurated a period of great activity in bridge building. On February 1, 1806, a bridge over the Delaware at Trenton, built by Theodore Burr, was formally opened: for the first time stagecoaches could travel all the way by land between Philadelphia and the Hudson opposite New York.[55] The Gray's Ferry Bridge Company was chartered in 1806; but only a floating bridge, first built by the British during their occupation of the city, actually crossed the river there until the Philadelphia, Wilmington and Baltimore Railroad built a bridge in 1838. In 1809 a bridge of novel design was erected at the Falls of Schuylkill. Its stone abutments and two stone piers supported two spans 253 feet long held up by chains. The bridge collapsed in 1811 under the weight of a drove of cattle; in 1816 its replacement fell down too. An inventive manufacturer, Josiah White, who had a wire factory at the Falls, then constructed a footbridge across the river, which is said to have been the first known suspension bridge of wire. Another bridge company was chartered in 1809 to build a bridge still farther up the Schuylkill at Flat Rock (Manayunk); it completed a bridge to Lower Merion in 1810.

The great bridge builder of Philadelphia, and of the age, was Lewis Wernwag. Coming to the city from Württemberg at the age of fifteen, he worked in his youth as a machinist. In 1810 he threw a wooden bridge across Neshaminy Creek on the road to New York, and the following year a wooden cantilever drawbridge across Frankford Creek at Bridesburg. His reputation made, Wernwag was asked to design a bridge across the Schuylkill just below Fairmount to replace a floating one that had been carried away by a freshet in 1810. The Upper Ferry Bridge, as it was called, was a single wooden arch whose chord (length) was 340 feet, 98 feet greater than the longest up to then built in North America. The crest of the arch rose thirty feet above the water. From a broad base at either end the roadway tapered to twenty feet in the center. The wooden casing protecting it from the weather was designed by the architect Robert Mills. Although Lewis Wernwag built over two dozen other bridges, worked on steel-mill machinery, and interested himself in

The Chain Bridge at the Falls of Schuylkill, *built 1809, collapsed 1811, painted by Thomas Birch (1779–1851), c. 1810.*

Permanent Bridge *(Market Street Bridge over the Schuylkill River), painting by John J. Barralet (1747–1815), c. 1810. The bridge was completed in 1804 and demolished in 1875.*

anthracite coal and canals and dams, his fame has all but vanished for his greatest achievements were in wood. The great Upper Ferry Bridge stood only twenty-six years; fire destroyed it in 1838.[56]

VII

Philadelphia had one advantage over any other seaport city except Baltimore: it was on the fall line and hence internally channeled by streams that could supply water power. The Delaware River, in its southwesterly course from Bristol to Wilmington, flows along the border between the granite hills of the Piedmont plateau and the sandy coastal plain. Waterpower sites on Philadelphia's streams ranged from Kensington in the northeast—where there had been mills since the city began—in an arc across the watershed through Germantown to the Schuylkill, into which flowed many useful tributaries. To the west and southwest, Cobbs, Darby, Ridley, and Chester Creeks offered abundant waterpower.[57] Streams that have long ago dried up or disappeared beneath the city streets once kept mill wheels turning. One example will suffice: James Traquair had a mill on Falls Creek, somewhere in the valley up which automobile traffic now climbs from the East River Drive to join Roosevelt Boulevard. There a waterwheel thirty-six feet in diameter worked a number of saws which cut the marble front steps and door frames of Philadelphia's brick houses.[58]

Such a basic source of power, easily accessible, gave the city an incalculable advantage at the beginning of the industrial revolution. In 1803 the Pennsylvania Society for the Encouragement of Useful Arts and Manufactures, founded in 1787, was reorganized with Dr. Benjamin Rush as its president and Tench Coxe as one of its vice-presidents.[59] Coxe was the first of a number of economists in Philadelphia who strongly advocated the establishment of manufactures in the United States. He had assisted in the composition of Alexander Hamilton's famous Report on Manufactures, encouraged planters in the South to grow cotton, and worked to nurture a cotton-spinning industry in Philadelphia. In 1805 Seth Craige acquired a site on Cohocksink Creek in Kensington, where the Penns had owned a flour mill, and there established the first large cotton mill in the state. By 1816 it was the largest manufactory of its kind in the country.[60]

The embargo of 1808, a disaster for the merchants, was an impetus to the establishment of factories to make the goods that could no longer be imported from Europe or Asia. When the foreign shipping trade was in desperate straits, the little mills around the city were prospering. The *Aurora*, a firm supporter of Jefferson and the embargo, on November 15, 1808, published a list of the principal manufacturers of the city:

Floor cloth & carpets	John Dorsey, Chestnut above 12
Oilcloth carpeting	John McNulty
Printed calicoes	John Thoburn & Co., north 3

Cottons & linens	Domestic Society's Warehouse, south 3
Calicoes	John Hewson, Jr. 3
Windsor & fancy soaps & sealing wax	W. Lehman, W. Smith & Son, south 2
Cotton bagging	Macclure & Robertson, south wharves
Earthenware (tea & coffee pots, sugar boxes)	Binny & Ronaldson, South St.
Window glass	Agent, Elisha Kane, south Front James Lee, agent John Wetherill North Front
Shot	Paul Beck, north Weber [whose shot tower was for many years one of the city's landmarks] Bishop & Co., South wharves
Red lead	R. Hovenden & Co., South Front
Catheters & bougies	Dr. Vincent King
Refining of camphor	Joseph Lehman, Market St.
Twine & cotton bagging	Capt. Towers
Woolen stocking cloth	Wm. Davy, Germantown[61]

The *Aurora* reported as among the toasts at the festival held in Pottstown to celebrate the election of Simon Snyder as governor: "American manufacturers—may they receive encouragement worthy of a free people," and "The American fair—may they soon substitute for the fineries of Europe, our own manufactures, and spurn from their sides the enemies of freedom."[62]

The *Aurora* failed to mention some of the industries most important for the future. Paper and paper-making machinery and printing presses, as well as Binny and Ronaldson's type foundry, were basic to Philadelphia's foremost position in the printing and publishing industry. Leather too was important. The city had become a center of boot and shoe manufacturing, with a lucrative export trade to the South. The cordwainers, as the makers of boots and shoes were called, had organized as masters and journeymen into traditional guilds. In the fall of 1805 the journeymen struck for a long time, but unsuccessfully, for higher wages. The next year eight of them were brought to trial before Judge Moses Levy for illegal combination and conspiracy, and were convicted. The journeymen's loss was a blow to what might have been the beginning of the trade union movement; on the other hand it speeded the transition from the handicraft to the factory system. The cotton industry, which sprang up at mill sites outside the city proper, being wholly new, was mechanized from the first. In contrast the extensive woolen, satinet, and rug businesses were long carried on by hand-weavers as home industries in South Philadelphia.[63] The first Jacquard loom in Philadelphia was put into operation by William H. Horstmann in 1824.

The most significant developments, however, were in the machine and foundry industries. Two men were representative of the new era. Josiah White was a successful merchant who abandoned that field when he was still

Northwest view of Mr. Paul Beck's Shot Tower near the Schuylkill, after a painting by Thomas Birch (1779–1851), in The Port Folio, December 1812. *The tower, near the present Twenty-First and Cherry Streets, was abandoned in 1828.*

LIBRARY COMPANY OF PHILADELPHIA

young to start a factory. He prospered from the time of the embargo until peace in 1815 brought in a flood of cheaper European goods and put him out of business. White's factory was at the Falls of Schuylkill, where in 1807 a tavern keeper, Robert Kennedy, had bought the right to build a bridge and to use the waterpower on condition that he build locks around the falls for freight boats coming down from Reading. Kennedy, in partnership with Conrad Carpenter, built a chain bridge but did nothing about the locks. Around 1809 they sold their water rights to Josiah White and Erskine Hazard, who built a rolling mill and wire factory there. At first they used bituminous coal from Virginia in their furnaces, but White became interested in the possibilities of Pennsylvania anthracite which, although it was abundant on the upper Schuylkill, no one then knew how to use. In 1815 luck solved the problem for White:

> . . . they had some [anthracite] brought down by teams at an expense of one dollar per bushel (twenty-eight dollars per ton). They expended some three hundred dollars in experiments, but could not succeed in making it burn. The hands in the mill got heartily sick and tired of it, and it was about being abandoned: but, on a certain

occasion, after they had been trying for a long time to make it burn without success, they became exasperated, threw a large quantity of the "black stones," as they called them, into the furnace, shut the doors and left the mill; it so happened that one of them had left his jacket in the mill, and in going there for it some time after, he discovered a tremendous fire in the furnace—the doors red with heat. He immediately called all hands and they ran through the rolls three separate heats of iron with that one fire.[64]

This accidental discovery of how to burn anthracite in mill furnaces is said to have been the first successful industrial use. White immediately threw his restless energies into experimenting with various kinds of cast-iron grates in which the hard coal could be burned in homes, and into the organization of a canal company to bring it down the Schuylkill to Philadelphia.[65]

Essential to the rise of an industrial age was a new kind of man. The inventor Oliver Evans is an early representative. He grew up in Delaware, a millwright by trade and the owner of a flour mill at Newport on the Christiana River. He turned his inventive genius first to the production of flour and, using waterpower as the source of energy, developed a method of continuous mechanical handling of the operation from unloading grain to sacking flour, a mechanization that revolutionized the milling industry.

All his life, however, Evans had been haunted by a dream of a steam-propelled carriage to move freight overland. In 1792 he moved to Philadelphia and established the Mars Works, which became the first important foundry and ironworks in the city. He filed the first specifications for a steam engine to be registered in the United States Patent Office, and in 1800–1801 began to build steam engines commercially. The *Aurora* in 1803 carried the first notice of the high-pressure engine, patented the following year, which was his greatest contribution to the new technology.

When Evans received an order in 1804 from the Board of Health for a steam-powered dredge to clear the wharf area of the Delaware, he saw an opportunity to prove his idea of a steam carriage. He built the dredge in his shop at Ninth and Market Streets, mounted it on a heavy wooden carriage, and connected the dredge's engine with the wheels of the carriage. For several days in June 1805 he demonstrated this remarkable self-propelled vehicle—to which he gave the equally remarkable name of "Orukter Amphibolis"—driving it around Centre Square and out Market Street to the Schuylkill. There he transferred its power to water propulsion wheels, to take it down the Schuylkill and up the Delaware as far as Dunk's Ferry, sixteen miles above Philadelphia, before finally returning to the city. Unfortunately as a dredge the machine does not seem to have been a success. But Evans had a successful career building high-pressure steam engines to power both mills and boats. To reach markets on the western waters, Evans opened a factory in Pittsburgh.[66] Evans was the first of a great line of designers of machines in Philadelphia in the nineteenth century.

The horse-powered railroad—wooden carts with cast-iron wheels pulled over wooden rails—built by Thomas Leiper in 1809 to move stone from his quarry on Crum Creek three-quarters of a mile to a dock on Ridley Creek was an isolated practical novelty.[67] Transportation by water ruled the thoughts of engineers. In 1807 on the Hudson River Robert Fulton launched the first successful steamboat, using a British engine and Nicholas Roosevelt's paddle-wheel. It was the culmination of earlier efforts made by Roosevelt, Chancellor Robert R. Livingston, and Livingston's brother-in-law John Stevens, the inventor. Stevens, who held a United States patent, was preparing to build a steamboat of his own design. In competition, Chancellor Livingston and Fulton secured a monopoly from the state of New York for their boat. Not to be completely defeated, Stevens brought his boat, the *Phoenix*, around by sea to Philadelphia in 1810 and initiated steamboat navigation on the Delaware. After demonstration trips to Chester and Bordentown, the *Phoenix* was advertised to leave Philadelphia at 2:30 P.M. each Monday, Wednesday, Thursday, and Friday for Bordentown, arriving in the evening and connecting with the stage lines for the Raritan River and New York.[68]

Industry could expand only within a narrow geographical area as long as the transport of goods was confined to horse and wagon. Water, chief source of power, was also the easiest highroad. Transportation by water was essential for heavy freight, and was far more pleasant for passengers than the stage-coach. Philadelphia had a great river leading to the sea, but her water routes to the interior—the upper Delaware and its tributaries, the Schuylkill and the Lehigh, leading westward—were hampered by swift currents, falls, and sudden changes in depth when droughts or floods occurred. Between the city and the next great river valley to the westward lay broken hills of Piedmont upland and, beyond the Susquehanna, range after range of the Appalachian Mountains. The industrial revolution required a revolution also in water transport. The geography of Pennsylvania interposed formidable obstacles.

A dream of canals had haunted the minds of Americans almost since the first settlement. "The parent of all canal projects in this country," said *A Connected View of the Whole Internal Navigation of the United States, Natural and Artificial, Present and Prospective*, published by the Philadelphia firm of Carey and Lea in 1826, was the Chesapeake and Delaware Canal, first seriously proposed in 1767 or 1768 but not built until sixty years later. During the 1790s several canal projects were started in Pennsylvania, but only the Conowingo Canal, a short-cut around the Conowingo rapids on the Susquehanna, was completed. The construction of Robert Morris's canal to connect the Delaware and Schuylkill Rivers was halted by lack of funds. A still more ambitious proposal to join the Delaware with the Susquehanna was twice surveyed by David Rittenhouse by authorization of the Assembly. By 1796 that project too was out of funds. In 1811 when the reopening of ocean commerce produced a spirit of optimism in Philadelphia, these two defunct plans were combined into one called the Union Canal, to be built from Reading along the line of the Tulpehocken and Swatara Creeks to the Susquehanna.[69]

After the war Josiah White's interest in anthracite coal led him to organize the Schuylkill Navigation Company to connect Philadelphia with the hard-coal country above Reading. Becoming dissatisfied with the management, he and his partner Erskine Hazard withdrew and in 1818 inaugurated a still more adventurous undertaking, the Lehigh Coal and Navigation Company, to canalize the Lehigh River.

Philadelphia thus had three canal projects underway in the years following the war, two to tap the anthracite coal beds north of the city and one to reach westward to the Susquehanna. The long postwar depression made their financing difficult, and it was not until after the revival of business in the 1820s that construction really got underway. By that time the Erie Canal, the mammoth state-financed project in New York to link the Hudson River with the Great Lakes, begun in 1817 and opened in October 1825, had given a tremendous impetus to canal building.

The importance of the Erie Canal as an engineering feat and as an element in the rise of New York City as a transfer point of inland products and ocean commerce has been well documented, while the significance of the Pennsylvania canals has been overshadowed. The Erie Canal extended from Albany to Buffalo through generally level country; it required only eighty-one locks in its 362-mile length. The Schuylkill Canal, when completed in 1825, measured 108 miles from Fairmount in Philadelphia to Port Carbon above Reading. It had fifty-eight miles of canals, fifty miles of pools, 129 locks, thirty-four dams, one tunnel 385 feet long, and a rise of 610 feet. The Union Canal began at a pool in the Schuylkill three miles above Reading, followed the Tulpehocken Creek forty-one miles to a high-point 498 feet above tidewater, ran along a summit level for seven miles, and then went down westward for thirty-four miles. The ascent and descent required ninety-three lifts and two guard locks, forty-nine culverts, 135 bridges, fourteen aqueducts, and one tunnel 729 feet long at the summit. The Lehigh Coal and Navigation Company canal, begun in 1827, was of a different type, being in essence the canalization of a mountain torrent. As designed by White and Hazard, it consisted of downward navigation only. Coal from the mines at its head came by gravity down a nine-mile railroad to Mauch Chunk; from that point the coal vehicles, called arks, floated down forty-seven miles of canals and pools, entering the Lehigh River above Easton. The route descended 364 feet, requiring nine dams and fifty-four locks, some of which were of great height.

Coal began to reach Philadelphia from the Lehigh in 1820, well before a canal facilitated its passage, and from the Schuylkill in 1823, although the whole latter canal from Port Carbon opened only in October 1825. In that year it was stated: "The coal trade is increasing with great rapidity; the demand for coal being, just now, much beyond the means of transporting it from the mines." Single-horse boats made the journey from the anthracite beds above Reading to the city in four days and returned in the same time; packet boats with passengers took half the time. Passengers for Reading left the White Swan Hotel on Race Street above Second by coach to Fairmount and there boarded a canal boat; the fare was two dollars. These canals, together with turnpikes, bridges, and steamboat lines, began to transform Philadelphia from a seaport to a manufacturing city looking inland and living by mine and mill.[70]

The industrial revolution could not have taken place without men competent to develop a new technology, able to invent, build, and use precision tools and precision machines. Philadelphia had such men; it was such assets, still in process of maturation, that persuaded the federal government, upon removal to Washington, to leave behind our institutions that required technically skilled management and workers—the United States Mint, two arsenals, and the Navy Yard.

One of the great sources of such skills was the long-established craft of the clock and watchmaker. Men trained in that trade turned their experience into other channels, as David Rittenhouse had become astronomer, builder of scientific instruments, and first director of the mint. Oliver Evans had been trained as a millwright; but Matthias W. Baldwin, a watchmaker, turned to the manufacture of locomotives for the infant railroad industry; and Joseph Saxton, who made the clock in the State House tower, became constructor and curator of the standard weighing apparatus at the mint, and called to Washington when Alexander Dallas Bache took over the direction of the Coastal Survey and the Office of Weights and Measures, furnished most of the states with their sets of linear, volumetric, and weight standards. (His standard balance scale may be seen in the collection of the American Philosophical Society.)[71]

The problems of metallurgy, precision tools, and precision balance scales for assay work encountered by the United States Mint and successfully solved in the first forty years of its existence were equally basic for the dawning industrial age. The importance of the mint's technical skills was illustrated by the contents of the *Mechanics Magazine,* a journal later absorbed into the *Journal of the Franklin Institute,* which in its first volume in 1825 printed six articles on the process of coining at the Royal Mint in London, seven on railways, and eighteen on steam engines.

November 1, 1800, marked the end of the use of the British monetary system by American merchants.[72] Brokers announced that they intended thereafter to buy and sell public bonds for dollars and cents. Conversion books were published for the use of those accustomed to the old method of computation.

The supply of coins was an old and a complicated problem. The most numerous hard coins in the early Republic were Spanish milled dollars, but there were also French louis and Portuguese, Spanish, and English gold coins. Each of the states also had its own coinage, and the various pieces were valued at varying rates.[73] To create order, the United States Mint was established in Philadelphia in 1792 to produce a decimal coinage in gold, silver, and copper for the new Republic. David Rittenhouse, recognized as the nation's foremost scientist and instrument-maker, was appointed its first superintendent. When the mint began operation it lacked not only the necessary machinery but even tools to build the machines. The only sources of power in the first mint buildings at Seventh and Filbert Streets were the muscles of men and of horses: a team of horses drove the rolling mill; men swinging a weighted screw press stamped the coins.[74] In 1816, after a fire destroyed the old wooden mill house, a steam engine was purchased from Oliver Evans to drive the rolling and drawing machines. It was only after the mint's director, Samuel Moore, sent Franklin Peale abroad in 1833 to study European mints and refineries that the mint technology became mechanized. By that time the great age of the Philadelphia machine designers had dawned.[75]

The federal government also maintained in Philadelphia a navy yard on the Delaware River at Southwark and two arsenals. The Navy Yard, for which the land was purchased in 1800–1801, was and remained important to the city's economy and to the development of American naval technology, although vessels were built also at other yards in Southwark and Kensington. The yard's two shiphouses, erected in 1821 and 1822 to protect the ways against the weather, were for half a century the largest, most conspicuous objects in and around the city. The Schuylkill Arsenal, constructed between 1802 and 1806, was primarily a storage depot. The Frankford Arsenal, established in 1816, was used both for storage and for the development and repair of military equipment. Mint, Navy Yard, and arsenals remained part of the fabric of Philadelphia. As the tempo and character of the times changed, so indeed did the activity and development of those federal institutions.[76]

The industrial revolution, whose freight of human good and human ills no one could foresee, was underway. The change amounted to the invention of a new kind of city, for the industrial city, based on unprecedented forms and uses of energy and techniques of work, and successor to the maritime city of the eighteenth century, was a new kind of social organism. While some other of the older seaport cities faded away before the thrust of machines, Philadelphia exploited its natural advantages to survive. It had the necessary ingredients for success. Its geographical situation provided abundant water-power and easy access to coal and iron. Because Philadelphia was the financial center of the country, there was ample investment capital available at hand. There were also human resources; the city was the home of inventors and engineers like Latrobe, Wernwag, Evans, and White. It had escaped the curse of slavery; its labor was skilled, hard-working, and free. Mechanical aptitude and commercial experience combined to unlock the door for the expansion of industry and trade.

VIII

Philadelphia had a tradition of science and technology inherited from Franklin and Rittenhouse and embodied in the American Philosophical Society, in the early nineteenth century the leading scientific institution of North America. Thomas Jefferson, third president of the United States, was the third president of the society as the century opened. It met twice a month to hear reports and papers, the more important of which appeared in its internationally distributed *Proceedings*. The contents of the volume that appeared in 1817 evidenced the broad interests of the society: geology, geography, the archeological remains and customs of the American Indians, metallurgy, mathematics, phonology, astronomy, anatomy, ichthyology, entomology, the vital statistics of the city of Philadelphia, and mechanical inventions. The society was living up to its full title, "for Promoting Useful Knowledge."

The role of the society in the life of the city was too general to be felt directly. Its influence arose rather from the fact that its members were not academic scholars and scientists; they were lawyers, merchants, physicians, farmers, clergymen, and publishers who combined their intellectual interests with busy and active careers. Meeting frequently and knowing each other well, they created a scientific community. Yet they were also diffused throughout the life of the city.[77]

As the nineteenth century progressed the sciences developed by an ever-increasing degree of specialization. Other institutions were founded to pursue more concentrated fields of study and research, and the American Philosophical Society's role gradually changed. It became a national institution for honoring men of scholarly and scientific distinction and for promoting and disseminating the results of their work. But the age of the specialist had not yet altogether arrived; men were still catholic in their interests. The same men who were active in the American Philosophical Society were among the founders of the institutions that sprang up around it, and in some instances evolved from it: the Pennsylvania Academy of the Fine Arts (1805),[78] the Academy of Natural Sciences (1812),[79] the Athenaeum of Philadelphia (1814),[80] the Franklin Institute (1824),[81] and the Historical Society of Pennsylvania (1824), as well as the innumerable societies for the improvement of personal and civic moral and economic good so characteristic of this period.

A brief mention of some of the American Philosophical Society's members and their activities suggests the influence and dynamism of the place and the time. William Maclure, properly called the founder of American geology, constructed the first geological map of the eastern United States.[82] Benjamin Henry Latrobe, as an engineer, advanced the society's concern in internal improvements and trained the young men who built America's first railroads, and as an architect, left his impress throughout the nation.[83] Benjamin Smith Barton, with his *Elements of Botany* in 1813, Thomas Nuttall, who published his *Genera of North American Plants* in 1818, and John Torrey, whose *Flora of the Northern and Middle Sections of the United States* appeared in 1824, were among the botanists who made Philadelphia the American center of the study of that science.[84] The Lewis and Clark expedition and other subsequent government-sponsored exploratory and surveying ventures were supplied in and received their scientific briefings from the city's resources of men and equipment.

The fact that so many of these men working in Philadelphia have been honored as the "father" of one or another American science gives testimony to the intellectual creativity their milieu engendered. Thomas Say has been called the father of American entomology, but that title rightfully belongs to Frederick Valentin Melsheimer, whose *Catalogue of Insects of Pennsylvania* appeared in 1806.[85] There is no doubt that Alexander Wilson, a Scottish poet and schoolmaster, made the first major contribution to American ornithology with his handsomely illustrated, nine-volume work issued in 1808–1813.[86] Scientific agriculture, economics, electricity, and other special fields all had their mentors and inventors.[87] There was even the beginning of the study of Indian linguistics with the important contributions of the lawyer Peter S. Du Ponceau, the Moravian missionary John Heckewelder, and the financial expert Albert Gallatin.[88]

The leaders, however, of Philadelphia's intellectual—and to a great extent civic and social—life were and remained for years her physicians and her lawyers. It was a brilliant period for medicine. The distinction of the city's doctors lay more in their role as teachers and in their skillful and sympathetic practice than in medical discovery or research. The surgeon Philip Syng Physick, the anatomist Caspar Wistar, and the obstetrician William P. Dewees set high standards for their profession. John Redman Coxe compiled the earliest American pharmacopeia, and Franklin Bache, the great-grandson of Benjamin Franklin, building on his knowledge of chemistry, laid the foundations for both the official *United States Pharmacopeia* and the *United States Dispensatory*. The brilliant physician Nathaniel Chapman, later to become the first president of the American Medical Association, in 1820 founded

Caspar Wistar *(1761–1818), painted by Thomas Sully (1783–1872) in 1830 after a portrait by Bass Otis (1784–1861), painted in 1817.*

AMERICAN PHILOSOPHICAL SOCIETY

the *Philadelphia*—or, as it was later called, the *American*—*Journal of the Medical Sciences*, which was the most important American medical periodical of the period, and the forerunner of the association's own journal.[89]

The most celebrated physician in America was the passionate reformer and stubborn medical theorist Benjamin Rush. His innovative treatment of the insane at the Pennsylvania Hospital and his book on the diseases of the mind, published in 1812, have obtained for him the accolade of being the founder of American psychiatry. Rush's greatest impact was as a teacher; dozens of the doctors who practiced medicine from New York to Georgia in the first half of the nineteenth century had received their training under him at the University of Pennsylvania's medical school. As a medical thinker, however, Rush was a builder of holistic systems in the manner of the medical past. The road to the future lay rather in the slow and patient study of pathologic anatomy, which was to be the achievement of other men.[90]

The University of Pennsylvania did not long maintain its monopoly in the field of medical education. In a storm of professional hostility, the popular teacher Dr. George McClellan in 1825 founded another medical school, Jefferson Medical College. The preparation of medicines used by physicians had become at this time a separate professional skill. To train qualified druggists the Philadelphia College of Pharmacy was founded in 1821; four years later it published its own journal, which in 1835 became the *American Journal of Pharmacy*.[91]

Lawyers were even more ubiquitous in Philadelphia's life than the doctors. They seem to have been in everything but medicine. At this period the Philadelphia lawyer was often a man of erudition, frequently of a philosophic mind. He took the lead in founding institutions and working for civic betterment. Whether one reads the writings of lawyers in *The Port Folio*, in the *Proceedings of the American Philosophical Society*, in the scores of addresses given on anniversaries and other celebrative occasions, or in the reports and decisions of the Supreme Court of Pennsylvania, one is struck by the amount of vigorous thinking that went on—and the voluminous flow of words.

The role of the judge and the lawyer in a new nation that had passed through revolution and was in the process of establishing a new form of government was one of great responsibility. Edward Shippen, Thomas McKean, and William Tilghman (successive chief justices of Pennsylvania), Richard Peters (who served on the District Court of Eastern Pennsylvania for thirty-six years), and Bushrod Washington (who, since the United States Supreme Court then rode circuit, spent much of his judicial career in Philadelphia, where he died), were among the jurists who gave dignity and strength to state and federal high courts at a critical period of American history. The federal bar before the Supreme Court was then almost a monopoly of Philadelphia, Maryland, and Virginia lawyers.

The leaders of the local bar, Jared Ingersoll and his two sons Charles J. and Joseph R., Joseph Hopkinson, William Rawle, John Sergeant, and Horace Binney set a tone of dignity, learning, and urbanity. Most of the city's lawyers, representative of the conservative mercantile class, were Federalists, but the leading Democrats, Alexander James Dallas, Charles J. Ingersoll, Richard Rush, and Peter S. Du Ponceau, were also in the upper stratum of society, well born and well educated. The dignity of the law is always vital, but its competence and stature at this time made an important contribution to the new Republic's stability and order.[92]

IX

In the arts, imagination sometimes turns toward nature and the normal experience all men share; at other times it coils inward to a private world of fantasy and dream. In the neoclassic period of the early nineteenth century the arts were outward-looking, based—as were medicine and law—on disciplined knowledge. Arts and sciences were related in their interests. Charles Willson Peale, a gifted portrait painter, provides an example of this interrelation; his museum has been called the first significant natural history museum in North America. When the offices of the government moved out of the State House, Peale got permission to move his museum into its second floor. In the long room where once banquets were held and official receptions given, above the cases containing habitat groups of animals, birds, fishes, and insects, he hung a double row of portraits from his own brush. They represented man in the great order of nature. They were also his own record of the men, his contemporaries and friends, who had led the country in the struggle for independence and the creation of the Republic. The museum's collections were dispersed in mid-century, but many of the portraits were acquired by the City of Philadelphia and long remained in Independence Hall. Now part of the National Historical Park collection, they are a unique historical record of the age.[93]

In 1805 the city acquired another museum. Joseph Allen Smith of South Carolina, the first American to form a collection of art in Italy, offered Philadelphia an assemblage of engravings, paintings, gems, and cameos, as well as a number of carefully made casts of classical sculpture. He considered the city the best location in America for the encouragement of artistic taste.[94] To accept the gift, a group of citizens organized the Pennsylvania Academy of the Fine Arts, with the elderly banker George Clymer, a signer of the Declaration of Independence, as its president. To house the gift, an elegant little classical building was erected on the north side of Chestnut Street above Tenth. Nicholas Biddle, in Paris as secretary to the American minister, purchased additional casts of classical statues with the advice of the famous sculptor Jean Antoine Houdon. There was some difficulty with the artists of Philadelphia, who considered that an academy was for artists rather than laymen, but under the leadership of Joseph Hopkinson, the second president of the academy, a *modus vivendi* was found. An annual exhibition for artists on the model of the Royal Academy in London began in 1811, and an art school was established. The Academy of the Fine Arts, still in existence both as a museum and a school, is the oldest museum and school in America and among the oldest in the world.[95]

The largest and most vital group of American artists was then in Philadel-

The Pennsylvania Academy of the Fine Arts, designed by John Dorsey (c. 1759–1821), built 1805, burned 1845. Engraving from The Port Folio *(June 1809).*

phia: painters, sculptors, and a large number of engravers, whose role was then more significant than it is today. Their interests were in man and his world and in nature; there was little of the historical retrospection that absorbed so many European artists. It was a great age of portrait painting. Gilbert Stuart, who had been in Philadelphia since 1794, left in 1802; Charles Willson Peale was absorbed in his museum and left portraiture to other members of his family. This opened that popular field to a new generation of which Thomas Sully, Bass Otis, Rembrandt Peale, and Jacob Eichholtz of Lancaster were the leaders. In two exhibitions sponsored by the Society of Artists of the United States, held in the academy in 1811 and 1812, artists from other cities joined local painters. The major themes of American art were enunciated in these exhibitions. There were portraits in oil and miniatures by many artists. There were landscapes and city views by William Russell Birch, William Strickland, and John J. Barralet; genre scenes by John Lewis Krimmel; monumental and portrait sculpture by William Rush; and still-life paintings by the American pioneers of that charming form, James and Raphaelle Peale. The earliest painter of the wild landscape of America, one of the dominant romantic themes of nineteenth-century painting, was Thomas Doughty, a Philadelphian, who first exhibited in 1816. This was a vigorous and distinguished period.[96]

Engraving was then a highly skilled form closely related to the art of painting, of which it was a delightful and relevant extension. The century began with one of its most attractive landmarks: William Russell Birch's volume of engraved plates, usually hand-colored, celebrating the beauty of Philadelphia, its buildings, streets, and port. Birch followed this in 1808–1809 with a smaller second volume, *The Country Seats of the United States.* The two form a most appealing record of the eighteenth-century city and its environs.[97] Engraving on copper was the technique most in use before the War of 1812. Birch used it, as did other engravers such as Alexander Lawson, who did the plates for Alexander Wilson's ornithology, and David Edwin, whose portrait engravings played a significant role in elevating the standard of book illustration. Relying on the freer and somewhat less demanding method of etching, William Charles, an immigrant from England, issued a number of wartime cartoons and a host of charming illustrations for children's books. Aquatinting was introduced in America after the war by W. J. Bennett and John Hill, also transplanted Englishmen. With a compatriot, Joshua Shaw, Hill produced a portfolio of aquatints, *Picturesque Views of American Scenery,* issued in Philadelphia in 1820–1821, which was a landmark in the dawning appreciation of the natural beauty of the American continent. To round out the printmaking techniques that took root and flourished in the city, Bass Otis in 1818 made the first American lithograph as an illustration in the *Analectic Magazine.*[98]

The census of 1820, taken during a major depression, listed by city only ten industries in the entire country whose annual sales exceeded $100,000. One of these was book publishing in Philadelphia, among the city's oldest industries. All the elements for the making of books were locally available: the Gilpin mill on the Brandywine produced high-quality woven paper; Binny and Ronaldson's foundry cast a full selection of the modish boldface type, with appropriate ornaments; Adam Ramage had his improved cast-iron press manufactured at Evans's Mars Iron Works. Joseph Hopkinson, in an 1810 address reviewing the state of the arts in Philadelphia, found the best augury for their future in the astonishing advances made by the city's printers and booksellers.[99] Looking back twenty-five years to the close of the War of Independence, he pointed out that in 1786 the whole book production of the city had been no more than 500 octavo volumes. By 1810 it had increased to at least 500,000 volumes, and possibly twice that number. In 1786, he said, four leading booksellers had hesitated a long time before combining to issue a small school edition of the New Testament in 3000 copies. Its success was such that four years later Dobson boldly undertook the first American edition of the *Encyclopaedia Britannica,* issued in 1790–1802 in twenty-two quarto volumes, with 542 copper plates.[100]

There were many notable publishing projects in these years. In 1804–1805 Caleb P. Wayne issued John Marshall's *Life of Washington* in five volumes. When C. and A. Conrad, with the financial backing of Robert Fulton, put out Joel Barlow's patriotic epic poem *The Columbiad* in 1807, they were ambitious to show that an American publisher could produce a sumptuously beautiful book. This they did, although they were obliged to use plates engraved in London. In publishing Wilson's *American Ornithology*, Samuel Bradford in the preface to the second volume noted: "Hitherto the whole materials and mechanical parts of this publication have been the production of the United States, except the colors." Advances in chemistry were overcoming this exception, and Bradford congratulated himself particularly upon a yellow "from the laboratory of Messrs. Peale and Son, of the Museum of this city."[101] National pride thus extended to every ingredient of the handsome set: paper, ink, colors, type, and presswork. Bradford also brought out an American edition of Rees's *Cyclopaedia; or Universal Dictionary of Arts, Sciences and Literature*, with American additions and emendations, in forty-one volumes of text and six of plates, which appeared in parts from 1810 to 1822.[102] Such projects attracted to the city numbers of printers and engravers. They seem to one glancing through the directories of the period only a little less numerous than merchants and sailors.

The most influential publisher in Philadelphia was the Irishman Mathew Carey, who developed a well-organized network of booksellers, particularly in the South and West, to distribute his books. Bibles were among his stock in trade, and the type of the "standing Bible" of 1801—30,000 pounds of metal —was kept standing for successive editions. Carey was a man of great energy and enterprise, of an inquiring mind and generous impulse. He was also a prolific and effective propagandist for political and economic causes. The *Olive Branch*, his appeal in 1814 to the good sense of both Federalists and Democrats to lay aside their differences during the war with Great Britain, went through ten editions.

Such an active mind was naturally drawn to the economic problems of his city. In 1810 he was one of the Democrats who supported the renewal of the charter of the first Bank of the United States. After the war Carey, originally a free trader, saw the city's industries overwhelmed by a flood of imported goods. He changed his point of view. In the *New Olive Branch* in 1820, *Essays on Political Economy* two years later, and numerous pamphlets, he made himself the spokesman for a combination of ideas new in American thought. He advocated tariff protection for American industries, internal improvements publicly financed, and a strong banking system to maintain a supply of credit. Carried into national politics as "the American System" by Henry Clay, Carey's ideas became the program of the new Whig party. Public spirited, charitable, and concerned, he left his mark on the life of the city in many ways.[103]

Carey's *American Museum* had been a successful, if short-lived, periodical before 1800. The new century saw Philadelphia become the center of magazine publishing in the United States. The first major continuing literary and critical journal on the continent, *The Port Folio*, began publication on January 3, 1801. It owed its initial success to the editorial skill and strong personality of its first editor, Joseph Dennie, a transplanted New Englander who, according to the inscription by Nicholas Biddle on his tombstone in St. Peter's

Churchyard, "devoted his life to the literature of his country." The professional literary man was a rarity in the first decades of the 1800s, but Dennie was one. A dandy and a bon vivant, a stout conservative in domestic politics and supporter of Great Britain in foreign affairs, the editor gathered about him a coterie of bright young men known as the Tuesday Club, which met initially at the bookshop of the Methodist publisher Asbury Dickins. Most of the members of the club were lawyers or doctors. One of them, Charles Brockden Brown, was a pioneer American novelist.[104]

In 1812 another influential periodical appeared, the *Analectic Magazine,* which Washington Irving edited in 1813–1814. The magazine was well illustrated, with many excellent portrait engravings, and in July 1818, as has been mentioned, carried the first lithograph made in America. Its contributors, like those of *The Port Folio,* were chiefly young lawyers and doctors for whom literature was an avocation.[105]

Another aspect of Philadelphia's publishing industry had been, was, and remained its excellent and important newspapers. In addition to the two Democratic papers, the *Aurora* and *Democratic Press,* there were others that supported the political conservatives, of which the chief were the *United States Gazette* edited by Enos Bronson, and *Poulson's Advertiser.* The latter was published by Zachariah Poulson, Jr., who had purchased Claypoole's *American Daily Advertiser* in 1800. Poulson, longtime librarian of the Library Company and active in many civic and humanitarian causes, reflected the quiet, benevolent commonsense conservatism of the Quaker community.[106]

The Quakers had long looked upon the stage as an abomination. Nonetheless the theater flourished in the city. It was closely linked to England; most of the plays produced were by English authors, and there was a constant coming and going of London stage companies in Philadelphia and New York. Actors like George Frederick Cooke, Thomas Abthorpe Cooper, Edmund Kean, and others made American tours, or, like Junius Brutus Booth, settled in America and founded a theatrical dynasty on this side of the ocean.

The principal playhouse in Philadelphia at this time was the Chestnut Street Theatre, on the north side of Chestnut Street above Sixth, a Palladian building modeled on the theater in Bath. From 1810 the theater was under the management of William Warren and William B. Wood, the most enterprising entrepreneurs of the American theatrical world. The old Southwark Theatre of the 1760s was in occasional use, and Ricketts's Circus on Fifth Street below Market still offered equestrian performances. In 1809 a new company of equestrians headed by Victor Pepin and John Breschard built another circus at Ninth and Walnut Streets. Enlarged in 1811, with a stage added, the building was rechristened the Olympic Theatre; now known as the Walnut Street Theatre, it is said to be the oldest in the English-speaking world that has remained in use for stage performances. In addition to the playhouses there were popular places of amusement like Vauxhall Garden, opened in 1814 at the northeast corner of Broad and Walnut Streets, and Columbian Garden, on Market Street between Thirteenth and Centre Square, where refreshments were served, with music and singing on a stage as complimentary attractions. Smaller theaters were opened in converted buildings from time to time, but had only a brief life. The Chestnut Street Theatre remained the best house, offering the best plays with the most competent actors and drawing the most distinguished audiences. When it burned in 1820, it was rebuilt on the same site in 1822 after a design by William Strickland, with the new splendor of gas lighting.[107]

Philadelphia also had an active musical life. Music can be said to have emerged from an amateur to a professional level in the period 1795–1825. The most influential of a group of well-trained and versatile musicians who emigrated to the city was Benjamin Carr. He was a performer, composer of orchestral pieces, music publisher, and proprietor of a music store. With its large publishing industry, it is not surprising that Philadelphia led in the publication of sheet music. Carr, George Willig, and Michael Hillegas were prominent in the business, but publishers like James Aitken, Robert Shaw, and Mathew Carey also issued music. In such a musically aware milieu it was inevitable that the manufacture of pianos—America's main musical industry in the nineteenth century—should have become centered in the city, with Charles Albrecht, Charles Taws, John T. Hawkins, and Thomas Loud the leading makers. To Taws and Hawkins together in 1800 is credited the inven-

The New Theatre in Chestnut Street Philadelphia, *engraving by William Birch (1755–1834), 1823. Designed by William Strickland (1788–1854), this, the second Chestnut Street Theatre, was demolished in 1856.*

PHILADELPHIA MUSEUM OF ART

tion of the upright piano, which did much to make the instrument popular in private homes.

A series of small string ensembles meeting in homes during the years 1816–1820 led to the founding in 1820 of the Musical Fund Society, which remained the center of musical life until the Civil War. It was created to meet two needs: to offer concerts, and to raise funds "for relief and support of decayed musicians and their families." For a few years its concerts were given in Washington Hall, the Chestnut Street Theatre, and St. Stephen's Church. In 1824 the society bought a church in the 800 block of Locust Street and engaged William Strickland to remodel it. Musical Fund Hall proved to be so acoustically perfect that it was the favorite auditorium of the city until the erection of the present Academy of Music.[108]

X

While the life of Philadelphia was changing, growing, and becoming richer in content, the city itself was being remade architecturally. Two modes of building were simultaneously at work. The first was that of the master builder, trained by apprenticeship in the traditional eighteenth-century Philadelphia style of construction—brick exterior walls with wooden interior frame and roof. In the new century the master builders continued to serve the city well, providing the quiet dignity of the brick residential town, much of which still survives between Front and Tenth Streets. An early outstanding example of this manner is the central building of the Pennsylvania Hospital, completed in 1805 from the design of David Evans, Jr. The exterior design may be a little flat, but within, the slender, airy elegance of the double staircase shows what grace this traditional mode could achieve.[109]

About the same time William Sansom, a Quaker philanthropist and builder of artistic taste, bought the block from Seventh to Eighth Streets on Walnut where Robert Morris's "folly" had been left unfinished. There, on the north side of Walnut Street he erected Sansom's Union Row, and on the south side of the newly cut Sansom Street Thomas Carstairs built his row. They introduced into the city block-long rows of houses, planned as a unit, such as had earlier been erected in the crescents and squares of London, Bath, and Dublin. These rows were a novelty in America, and when built elsewhere in the country such units were known as "Philadelphia rows."[110] Alterations have since almost obliterated Sansom's buildings, although one or two of them, now devoted to business, retain nearly their original exteriors. The dignity and elegance given the city by these long architectural units can still be seen in Stephen Girard's later row construction on Spruce Street between Third and Fourth, and elsewhere to the west on Spruce and Pine Streets.

While the master builder was creating a red city of brick, a new kind of construction appeared. The local blue-toned Schuylkill marble varied the pattern. In interiors, marble fireplaces and mantels, appropriate in scale to larger rooms and higher ceilings, took the place of carved wooden ones in the homes of the new city.[111] In public view, Benjamin Henry Latrobe inaugurated the new style. A well-trained professional architect, he had come to Philadelphia from London in the late 1790s, and through his own work and that of his pupils effected a fundamental change in building design. His Bank of Pennsylvania, on the west side of Second Street above Walnut, built in 1799–1801 and demolished in 1865, initiated what is called, somewhat misleadingly, the Greek Revival in American architecture. The bank building was of white marble, with a Greek Ionic temple portico facing Second Street and a similar portico in the rear. The banking room inside was a large rotunda, covered by a low marble dome crowned by a graceful lantern. Although some refined classical ornament was used in columns and moldings, the building was unlike any Greek structure. The large simplicity of the design, its spacious interior, and its unity foreshadowed a new national style. The men who created it—on occasion using Gothic ornament as well as Greek detail—were at the same time engineers who built canals, breakwaters, and bridges. The use of masonry arches and vaults was as characteristic of their work as was the classical portico.[112]

Shortly after the beginning of the new century President Jefferson appointed Latrobe the architect of the Capitol in Washington, and thereafter his career lay outside Philadelphia. His pupils, Robert Mills and William Strickland, and the London-trained John Haviland, continued what he had begun. James Traquair, who emigrated from Greenock, Scotland, in 1784, bringing with him the disciplined skill of the Scottish stonemason, was the first of the master stonecutters capable of carrying out the new designs.[113] He was succeeded by John Struthers, who executed most of Strickland's buildings.

Robert Mills was the most important architect working in the city from the time Latrobe left in 1802 until his own departure for Washington twelve years later. His construction was notable for its large scale and solidity. He created an auditorium-type structure for the Sansom Street Baptist Church in 1808, and the Octagon Unitarian Church on the northeast corner of Tenth and Locust in 1813. Washington Hall, on the west side of Third Street above Spruce, completed from his designs in 1816, gave the city an auditorium capable of holding 6000 people. But all these buildings have disappeared, and Mills's achievements can be seen today best in Washington and Charleston.[114]

John Haviland was trained in London as Latrobe had been. He came to Philadelphia in 1816, apparently planning to establish a school of architectural drawing with the artist Hugh Bridport. Together in 1818–1821 they published the three-volume *Builder's Assistant*, a work that made the Greek orders available for the first time in an American design book. Haviland, however, became immediately involved in practice rather than theory, and he showed himself a designer of originality and power. His major surviving works were executed after 1825.[115]

The fourth man to make Philadelphia the center of the new American architecture was William Strickland. He studied under Latrobe, but then earned his living for some years as an illustrator, drawing street views and scenes to be engraved. He began his long and fruitful career as an architect

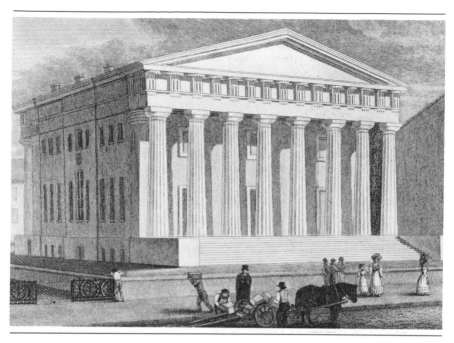

The Second Bank of the United States, *designed by William Strickland (1788–1854), engraving published by Cephas Grier Childs (1829). The building, part of Independence National Historical Park, now houses a portrait and special exhibitions gallery.*

FREE LIBRARY OF PHILADELPHIA

by winning, as his first major commission, the most important building project of the decade, the second Bank of the United States. It has been said that Nicholas Biddle, who had fallen in love with Greek temple architecture on a visit to Greece in 1806, used his influence as a director of the bank in favor of the Greek temple design submitted by the relatively untried young man. Unlike most of the buildings that have been mentioned, the second Bank of the United States still stands, on Chestnut Street between Fourth and Fifth. An English critic of the 1830s wrote that it "excells in elegance and equals in utility, the edifice, not only of the Bank of England, but of any banking house in the world." Even today this Greek temple, with its two fronts facing north and south, stands out strikingly from its surroundings. When it was built in 1819–1824 its eight massive white marble columns on each front and its monumental unity of design must have been astonishingly novel. The dignity given by the weight of heavy masonry was one source of its effect; another was the changing patterns of sunlight and shadow upon deeply carved white marble. In the main banking room with its barrel vault overhead and a rank of marble pillars—between which were the tellers' desks—along either side, Strickland achieved unity and grandeur.[116]

There was one bold project in these years that was never realized. In 1820 Paul Beck, merchant and philanthropist, proposed that the city acquire all the land along the Delaware River from South Street to Vine and clear away the congestion of waterfront buildings and narrow alleys which were believed to be the breeding place of yellow fever. He engaged Strickland to draw a plan for rebuilding from Front Street east to a new avenue along the river. The planner's estimate of the cost was $3,651,000. It was the first ambitious essay in city planning for Philadelphia since Penn's original design. The plan was blocked, partly, it was said, by the opposition of Stephen Girard; but when Girard wrote his will twelve years later, he left a legacy of half a million dollars to the city for the purpose of cutting a wide street along the Delaware.[117]

The impulse to improve and beautify the city, to transform it from brick to marble, would have made greater progress in the first quarter of the nineteenth century had not business conditions been so troubled. Architecture is closely related to economic life. The successive trade catastrophes of the embargo, the war, and the postwar depression postponed the greater part of the rebuilding of the city until the years after 1825.

X I

European visitors in the preceding century had been astonished to see so many religions living peacefully together in Pennsylvania. In the new century most denominations grew in numbers, and many new churches were built as the city expanded from one river toward the other. The great issues which had arisen in the past and would arise again were not, in these years, disruptive factors. To be sure, the German churches were troubled by the language controversy. The Roman Catholics were divided by a dispute over the control of church properties—the Hogan schism, or the trusteeship controversy, during which the bishop was for twenty years locked out of his own cathedral, St. Mary's, and withdrew to St. Joseph's. But the memorable religious achievement of the period was the creation of the black churches. It was in the churches that the black population of Philadelphia first had opportunity to develop its own leaders and create its own institutions.

In the census of 1790 fewer than 300 slaves remained in Pennsylvania; in the census of 1820 there were only three in the city and four in the northern suburbs, but there were 7579 free Negroes. Absalom Jones and Richard Allen, who had helped Girard as volunteers during the yellow fever epidemic of 1793,[118] had established the first two black churches in the city. Jones became the first Negro rector of an Episcopal church. By 1809 there were five black churches whose ministers, it is said, constituted the first Negro clergy in America: St. Thomas (Episcopal), founded by Jones; Bethel (Methodist), established by Allen and the parent church of the African Methodists who separated from the white Methodists in 1816; Zoar (Methodist), a mission of Methodist St. George's; Central (Presbyterian); and the African Baptist. The erection of these churches, destined to exert a mighty influence not only religious but social and educational upon the black people of America, was one of the original and significant achievements of the time.

There was the small beginning of a black middle class, even of wealth. James Forten made a fortune as owner of a sail loft and spent the greater part of it in buying the freedom of other Negroes and on charities for his people. Other men acquired ample means and reputation in the catering business, which became a black specialty. Robert Bogle had a celebrated catering establishment on Eighth Street near Sansom, and Peter Augustin in 1818 started a second firm which made Philadelphia catering famous throughout the country. The best and most elegant service of food at balls and parties was provided by black business.

There had been little racial friction in eighteenth-century Philadelphia and great hopes were held for the future of the black population. Following the War of 1812, as the city became a magnet for poor and untrained Negroes from the South and at the same time for poor and untrained white immigrants from Europe, competition for jobs between the two produced increasing racial bitterness and tension. The relations between the races were worse in 1825 than in 1800; they would continue to deteriorate.[119]

X I I

Growing pains were inevitable. In the first quarter of the nineteenth century Philadelphia was the metropolis of what was swiftly becoming the great industrial state of the nation. One source of its strength, as has been noted, was an abundant supply of capital. Yet as the city grew it passed through a series of severe financial and business crises—the embargo, the War of 1812 and the naval blockade of the Delaware, the panic of 1814 when every bank south of New England suspended specie payments, and postwar hard times culminating in a severe depression in 1819–1820. These troubles affected every aspect of the city's life and underlay the fluctuations of all its activities.

Although in 1800 Philadelphia was the financial center of the country, it had in the early years only three banks: the first Bank of the United States, which had a federal charter and a national purpose; and two state-chartered institutions, the Bank of North America and the Bank of Pennsylvania, which latter in a large degree was a state agency.[120] Thomas Willing, the head of one of the city's most prosperous mercantile firms, was president of the Bank of the United States, and his son-in-law, the former United States senator William Bingham, was its most influential director. By 1824 there were eight chartered banks in addition to the second Bank of the United States, of which Nicholas Biddle was the president. In 1800, however, financial institutions did not play the same role that they do today. Investments, loans, and the sale or mortgage of real estate were largely direct transactions between individuals. Lotteries were a common method of raising funds for every purpose from building a church to paving a road. Commercial banking and, still more so, investment banking were unorganized.[121]

The needs of homeowners had created fire insurance companies, and the needs of merchants and shipowners had created marine insurance companies, long before the chartered bank appeared. In 1816 the first bank for savings in the country, the Philadelphia Saving Fund Society, was organized. There were also private banking houses that assisted merchants in their foreign trading: Thomas Biddle, Alexander Brown and Sons, and Stephen Girard.[122]

But banks were neither understood nor trusted. The Bank of the United States had been founded when Alexander Hamilton was secretary of the treasury to help finance the operation of the federal government and stabilize its new currency. It had served its purpose well; yet when the renewal of its charter came before Congress in 1810, and was strongly recommended by Albert Gallatin, secretary of the treasury, Congress refused to renew it. During the War of 1812 the state banks financed the government, but the panic of 1814 brought a general suspension of specie payments. To find a way out of the financial confusion, Alexander James Dallas of Philadelphia, then secretary of the treasury, proposed to charter a second Bank of the United States to deal with the problem on a national basis. It was chartered in 1816 and went into operation the following year, but this bank too was strongly opposed both in Congress and out by those who believed in hard money and states' rights.[123]

With the coming of peace, American exports sank and European imports poured into the country. The nation's balance of trade was upset and the reserves of state banks ran down. When the banks after 1817 tried to call in their paper and return to specie payment, the great depression of 1819 resulted. Banknote circulation dropped from $110 million to $45 million. "The whole country was involved in one universal scene of distress and ruin," wrote a Philadelphia merchant.[124] *Niles' Weekly Register* reported in August 1819, "It is estimated that there are 20,000 persons *daily seeking* work in Philadelphia."[125] A year later, a director of the Bank of the United States wrote to a London colleague:

Houses which rented for 1,200 dollars, now rent for 450 dollars. Fuel which cost 12 dollars, now costs 5-½ dollars—flour which was 10 and 11 dollars, is now 4-½; beef 25 cents, now 8 cents—other things in proportion. . . . The farmer is become as poor as a rat—the labor of the farm costs him more than the produce is worth. He cannot pay the storekeeper, and the storekeeper cannot pay the merchant.[126]

When Nicholas Biddle became president of the second Bank of the United States in 1823, he reversed the tight-credit policy of his predecessor and recovery followed slowly.

In the quarter century 1800–1824, beset with difficulties and distresses, the people of Philadelphia accomplished remarkable things. They created the institutions and laid the foundations for the great scientific and industrial city that was to come. While doing so, they reached a higher level of intellectual and artistic life than any other city of the United States. Gilbert Stuart, after he removed to Boston, liked to remember this, and used to begin his anecdotes with "When I resided in the Athens of America."[127]

Exiles from the great convulsions of the Napoleonic Wars gravitated to the city—the vicomte de Noailles, the duc d'Orléans, Général Moreau, Joseph Bonaparte and Charles Lucien Bonaparte, Achille and Napoléon Murat, and the former Empress Itúrbide of Mexico. Life was agreeable and interesting; the location, halfway between New York and Washington, was convenient. Joseph Bonaparte's house and park, Point Breeze, near Bordentown, was filled with great works of art; it housed the country's first major art collection, dispersed in the 1840s. The count de Survilliers, as the one-time king of Spain called himself in exile, spent his winters in Philadelphia. One catches a pleasant glimpse of him walking on a Sunday morning to St. Joseph's Roman Catholic Church in Willing's Alley where he occupied a high-walled, old-fashioned pew, accompanied by his two children and a huge Newfoundland dog.[128] Both he and Charles Lucien Bonaparte, prince of Canino and Musignano, were members of the American Philosophical Society. Joseph presented a Greek kylix or drinking cup to its collections.[129] Charles Lucien, a naturalist, devoted himself to the preparation of a supplement to Wilson's ornithology, which appeared in 1825–1833. A new species which he described, the smallest and prettiest of the gulls, called after him Bonaparte's gull, is still commonly seen in spring and fall along the reedy shores of the Delaware.

The Age of Nicholas Biddle
1825-1841

by Nicholas B. Wainwright

Philadelphia is a city to be happy in. . . . Everything is well conditioned and cared for. If any fault could be found it would be that of too much regularity and too nice precision.
— NATHANIEL P. WILLIS

Mr. Biddle represented the money power of the country. . . . These causes, combined with his personal qualities, his manners, talents, varied accomplishments and the triumphant success which appeared for a long time to attend all his measures, gave him a degree of influence & popularity among the monied and educated classes equalled only by that of Genl. Jackson with the populace.
— SIDNEY GEORGE FISHER [1]

To the extent that any period of time in the history of a great city may be linked with the name of a single one of its citizens, there is justification in characterizing the Philadelphia years 1825–1841 as "The Age of Nicholas Biddle." These were the years of his prominence—a nationwide prominence unequalled by that of any other Philadelphian of the day, and approached by few in any other day. They were also years of impressive growth and prosperity for the city. If there is a parallel in the careers of the man and the place where he lived, however, it is nowhere closer than in the dismal year 1841, which brought catastrophe to both.

Nicholas Biddle was, to be sure, merely one in a sizable group that constituted Philadelphia's leadership, but in this group he was the "delight & ornament."[2] It was a compact, cohesive group, the last full flowering of colonial origins. At the head of many organizations—civic, cultural, and commercial—were men who in general shared the same attributes: descendants of well-established families, they composed the local aristocracy; of superior education, they were endowed with a deep sense of civic responsibility and were blessed with talents that brought them to the fore; through their wide range of interests they were perhaps the last representatives of the Enlightenment, as reflected by the memory of Franklin. Narrow specialization, concentration on a single goal, did not characterize them. When Nicholas Biddle left the scene, their predominance had also reached its end, and the old control, handed down generation to generation from early times, fell into the hands of a new order. As an entity Biddle's circle failed to leave successors able and willing to perpetuate the traditions of service suggested by their family names. Their descendants preferred to become "mere men of business," as Sidney George Fisher expressed it, or mild philanthropists, worthy gentlemen content to live in quiet ease on inherited wealth.

Biddle, on the contrary, devoted his life to "always seeking and achieving results."[3] Born in Philadelphia in 1786, he was named for his uncle, a captain in the Continental Navy who was killed in action during the Revolution, trying to overcome the odds favoring the sixty-four-gun *Yarmouth* over his thirty-two-gun frigate *Randolph*. Charles Biddle, father of the second Nicholas, came of a hardy breed, as his career and those of his formidable brothers proved. He was evidently the underlying influence in his son's life. From Charles, a former sea captain, Nicholas inherited an intense patriotism and also a sense of obligation to his community. His father's record was worth emulating. Among Charles Biddle's many public services was his office as vice-president of the Supreme Executive Council of Pennsylvania during the ailing Franklin's presidency. Charles left to Nicholas a book-length autobiography, which Nicholas must have read with considerable pride in his father's indomitable courage.[4]

Although he was never to compose so enthralling a narrative, Nicholas Biddle was the literary man his father never aspired to be. As a scholar, writer, and orator, he had few equals in the city. From his youth Biddle's progress had attracted attention. He was undeniably precocious. To begin with, he graduated in 1801 with highest honors from Princeton at the age of fifteen. Back in Philadelphia he read law, without much enthusiasm, and then in 1804 went off to Paris as secretary to the American minister. There he attended Napoleon's coronation, traveled extensively in Italy, and was the first American to visit Greece in the pure and simple role of a tourist. Contemplating the remains of ancient temples, he was seized with the lasting conviction that there were only two perfect truths in the world—the Bible and Greek architecture.[5] His European wanderings ended in London, where he served as secretary to James Monroe before returning to Philadelphia in 1807.

The practice of law interested him less than his association with Joseph Dennie, literary leader and editor of *The Port Folio;* when Dennie died, Biddle assumed its editorship. Before that event he edited the journals of Lewis and Clark at the request of Col. William Clark, who had been steered to him by Thomas Jefferson. While this work represents Biddle's chief literary contribution, an effort of greater personal value to his career was his digest of the laws of foreign nations affecting the commerce of the United States, a study suggested to him by Secretary of State John Quincy Adams.[6]

Biddle married an heiress, Jane Craig, and settled down to farming at Andalusia, his country seat on the Delaware. Always the student, he became an authority on farming, horticulture, and animal husbandry, subjects he pursued with intense interest throughout his life. His successful culture of grapes in Andalusia's extensive forcing houses, his importation of the first Alderney cattle to the United States, and his speeches before agricultural groups made him an authority in areas that were typically Jeffersonian. For many years Biddle served as president of the Philadelphia Society for the Promotion of Agriculture.

From time to time his literary and agricultural pursuits had been interrupted by legislative duties. In 1810 he was elected to the Pennsylvania House of Representatives, and there he gained some applause for his defense of the first Bank of the United States. On his twenty-fifth birthday Biddle made a reputation for himself as an expert on banking in a three-hour speech before the legislature, urging the recharter of the bank.

In 1819 President Monroe called him back to a measure of public life by appointing him one of the five governmental directors of the recreated Bank of the United States, the other twenty being elected by the stockholders. At this time the affairs of the bank were in bad shape. Its president, William Jones, was not qualified for his task, and under his administration the institu-

Nicholas Biddle (*1786–1844*), *engraved by John Sartain (1808–1897) after a portrait painted by Thomas Sully (1783–1872) in 1831. The portrait by Sully was destroyed in a fire in the 1850s.*

NICHOLAS B. WAINWRIGHT

tion had become much embarrassed. To rectify matters, curtailment of loans, attended by serious losses, became the order of the day. Jones resigned during the resultant financial crisis and Langdon Cheves of South Carolina took his place. Through strenuous deflationary policies and years when the bank paid no dividends, Cheves resolutely restored its capital—"the Bank was saved but the people were ruined."[7] Cheves's banking ability seems to have been limited to keeping the bank solvent; he refused to make it useful. Money remained scarce, credit difficult to obtain, and a nation verging on a period of unusual economic growth was kept on a leash. However, Cheves had no desire to preside long over the institution he had in large measure saved. On his retirement, Nicholas Biddle was elected president in January 1823. Hitherto, in Biddle's opinion, the bank had made more enemies than money. He reversed Cheves's tight-money measures and opened the bank's facilities to the legitimate requirements of the nation's growing credit needs.

Biddle's first major accounting of his stewardship was laid before the stockholders in September 1825 at their triennial meeting. His address on that occasion was summarized by newspaper publisher Zachariah Poulson: "The luminous and masterly statement of the present flourishing condition of the affairs of the Bank, presented by the President, was received with feelings of the strongest and most universal satisfaction."[8] On occasions such as this senior citizens were always present to extend their mark of approbation. This time it was Mathew Carey's turn. On behalf of the stockholders he arose to move their thanks to the president and directors "for their able, faithful, and successful administration."[9] Thus the condition of the national bank was sound, its future bright; but the future of Philadelphia had grown less promising.

On the surface all seemed well with the city, were one content with limited aspirations. At a testimonial dinner in 1825 Commodore John Barron held forth his glass and declaimed: "Philadelphia—justly acknowledged to be the first in the arts, and second to none in whatever can contribute to the grandeur, respectability, and comfort of a city!"[10] Yet in the arts Philadelphia was fast losing her place, and she had already lost her rank as the country's largest city and most important trading center.

I

To be sure, numerous vessels continued to ascend the Delaware—about 500 a year from foreign ports, two to three times that many plying the coastal trade.[11] Unloaded on the wharves that lined the city's front were cargoes of rice, cotton, and tobacco from the South; spermaceti oil from New Bedford; horse hides from Montevideo; coffee from Brazil and Java; toys from Germany; linen from Ireland; rum from St. Croix and Jamaica; sherry, madeira, claret, muscatel, and teneriffe from their points of origin; armagnac, bordeaux, and brandy from France; whisky from Scotland; mahogany from Nicaragua and Santo Domingo; indigo from Bengal; pepper from Sumatra; and opium

from Turkey. The most princely imports of all came from Canton, consigned
to merchants specializing in that trade. Every year about a dozen richly laden
ships hove into port from the Pearl River. Shortly after the ice had melted
in the early spring of 1825, the *Caledonia* sailed majestically upstream to
discharge her store of silks, curry powder, window blinds, umbrellas, porcelains, camphor trunks, bamboo baskets, fans, kites, fireworks, and vast quantities of tea—Hyson, Gunpowder, Imperial, Pouchong, Souchong.[12] These
Chinese luxuries found a ready market, but Philadelphia had little to export
to China in exchange. Her ships went out lightly freighted with gold and
silver to balance her trade with the Orient.[13] As a consequence her merchants
sought substitute markets. By 1820 English and French porcelain had largely
supplanted Chinese articles in that line,[14] and by 1825 the city had its own
porcelain factory, where the famous Tucker china was made. Tucker's masterpieces were said to surpass European imports "in soundness of body,
smoothness of glazing, and beauty of lustre."[15]

Part of the bullion exported to China was gained in Philadelphia's favorable trade with Latin America. In 1825 about a third of her foreign exports—
flour, lumber, furniture—went to Mexico and South America, bringing back
much hard money in exchange. Henry Pratt, Matthew Bevan, and Manuel
Eyre were prominent in this trade, which was the largest with Latin America
of any North American port.[16] Trading ties brought social ties. Many young
South Americans and Cubans were sent to school in Philadelphia, among
them Simon Bolívar's nephew Fernando, who attended Germantown Academy in the mid-1820s.[17]

In the order of their value, the city's largest foreign exports in 1825 went
to Mexico, Cuba, and England. In the same order, the largest foreign imports
came from England, China, and Cuba.[18] Most of this trade, which was so vital
to the city's economy, was carried in American ships, many of them Philadelphia-owned and built in the extensive Kensington and Southwark yards.
Six to ten thousand tons of new shipping slid annually down their ways into
the Delaware. In 1825 the 6292 tons launched were represented by seven ships,
eleven brigs, two schooners, one sloop, and one steamboat.[19]

Most of these vessels were built for the coastwise lines which furnished
regular service between Philadelphia and New York, Boston, Baltimore,
Charleston, New Orleans, and other ports. The city also had two Liverpool
lines, one owned by Thomas P. Cope and the other by John Welsh. The
Liverpool packets, with their ample cabin space—the trip to England cost $133
—and large holds for cargo, were among Philadelphia's most highly prized
vessels. Cope's *Tuscarora, Montezuma, Algonquin,* and *Alexander* and the
"New Line's" *Colossus, Delaware, Julius Caesar,* and *Bolivar* were proud sights
as they cleared the river under clouds of canvas.[20]

II

But commercially the city might have done better had she not been so
relaxed and comfortable. Philadelphia's easy-going southern overtones were

Vase made at the Tucker porcelain factory (1826–1838), c. 1832–1835. The building painted on the vase was the Tucker factory on the Schuylkill riverfront near Market Street.

PHILADELPHIA MUSEUM OF ART, GIVEN BY ELIZA AMANDA TUCKER IN MEMORY OF THOMAS TUCKER

in marked contrast to the hurly-burly, the raucous bustle of New York. Her ties with the South were close. During the sickly season families from South Carolina and Virginia summered in her vicinity, and there was much inter-marriage. From Charleston came Draytons, Hugers, Middletons, and Izards, some of them to remain as Philadelphians. The Virginia contingent, Carters, Tuckers, Pages, Riveses, was most distinguished.[21] In addition much of Phila-delphia's business was with the South. Seasonal visits filled her hotels with southern and western merchants, come to replenish their stocks of merchan-dise by large purchases from the local commission dealers.

Out-of-towners looked forward to their Philadelphia visits. The city was so neat and clean, its market the best in the country. The better stopping places, such as the United States Hotel, facing the Bank of the United States across Chestnut Street, were noted for their cuisines. Joseph Head's Mansion House at Third and Spruce Streets boasted French cooking, a style evidently considered unrivaled,[22] while Parkinson's celebrated restaurant at 161 Chest-nut Street advertised "Coffee à la mode de Paris."[23] Of all the exponents of the French mode, M. Latouche was unquestionably the leader. For eight years

Latouche had cooked for the prince D'Ecmuhl, then for three years he had presided over the kitchens of the duc de Rovigo. Coming to America, he had been employed in Washington by the Russian minister before settling in Philadelphia as a restaurateur and caterer. In addition to the oyster cellar he conducted under his Market Street restaurant, well stocked with the choicest wines, Latouche offered take-out dishes such as oyster pies (100 oysters), $1.25; fourteen mutton chops, $1.00; eight quail, roasted and larded, $1.00; sixteen pounds of beef à la mode, $3.00; and hogs' heads, trimmed with jelly, $2.50.[24] The prices seem low, but when it is realized that the pay of Philadelphia weavers averaged only five dollars a week, there could not have been too many calls for hogs' heads from the workingman.[25]

Latouche and his fellow caterers were kept well employed at public and private entertainments, which were numerous and to which visitors of distinction were ever welcome. Hardly anyone was more cosmopolitan in this regard than Nicholas Biddle. While some social leaders were rigorous in excluding all but the well-born elect, Biddle invited anyone whom he found of interest, and his tastes were catholic. Many hosts had not yet reached the point of inviting actors to their houses. By and large society frowned on wealthy Pierce Butler's marriage to Fanny Kemble,[26] and even Thomas A. Cooper, an English actor of tremendous popularity in Philadelphia, had experienced the local censure with which so many of the citizens regarded his profession. One day Cooper found himself closely scrutinized by a pair of filthy chimney sweeps. "I say, Bill," said one of them. "Look! there goes Cooper the player man." "Hold your tongue, John," returned the other, "who knows what you may come to yourself."[27]

In accordance with the custom of others in their position the Biddles gave at least one ball a year in their large town house, now 715 Spruce Street. Dances such as these were largely under the professional care of black men. One Shepherd, as an instance, was a waiter seen everywhere. Another, Robert Bogle, was even better known, for he united the vocations of public waiter and undertaker, frequently officiating at a funeral of an afternoon and at a party that evening, presenting on both occasions the same unchanging gravity of demeanor, although, so it was whispered, when the evening grew late he did rather well with the punch and performed a few *pas seuls* in private. In July 1829 Biddle wrote an eight-verse "Ode to Bogle," of which the following verse is an example:

> On Johnson's smooth and placid mien
> A quaint and fitful smile is seen;
> O'er Shepherd's pale, romantic face,
> A radiant simper we may trace;
> But on the Bogle's steadfast cheek,
> Lugubrious thoughts their presence speak;
> His very smile, severely stern,
> Like lighted lachrymary urn.
> In Church and State, in bower and hall,
> He gives, with equal face, to all

The wedding-cake—the funeral crape—
The mourning glove—the festive grape;
In the same tone, when crowds disperse,
Calls Powell's hack or Carter's hearse,
As gently grave, as sadly grim
At the quick waltz as funeral hymn.[28]

Even more famous than Bogle was Frank Johnson (he of the "smooth and placid mien" alluded to in the first line of the verse above), whose Negro band played at Biddle's parties. In addition to conducting his orchestra, the best in the city, Johnson gave music lessons, adapted tunes from new operas for use in quadrilles and cotillions, played these novel airs at social gatherings, and published them as sheet music. Ultimately, so great was his success that he took his band to London for a concert series. There, curiously enough, his musicians were mistaken for Indians.[29]

III

Although parties were frequent and life pleasant, the city lived to an excessive extent on the diminishing returns of a direction given to its economic life by men long since dead. A bold, aggressive new leadership was necessary lest Philadelphia's drowsiness lapse into a deep slumber. Profoundly agitated at the portents of the times, the city's men of business fully recognized the seriousness of the crisis. Comparing the past with the present, they were faced with figures that proved how badly their city had fallen behind her rivals.

Historically Philadelphia had prospered as the "bread basket" of the colonies and the young Republic; but the westward shift of population had cost her primacy in the export of flour. This was not because Pennsylvania was producing relatively less—59 of the 100 members of her House of Representatives were farmers in 1825[30]—but because her flour was slipping away to other ports. The produce of the western part of the state now went down the Susquehanna to Port Deposit, at the head of tidewater navigation. There, thousands of barrels of Pennsylvania flour and whiskey and vast quantities of wheat, corn, pork, and bacon were loaded on schooners for shipment to Baltimore.[31] Fleets of lumber rafts, which had floated downstream, were towed off to the same place. In 1820 Baltimore had exported 577,000 barrels of flour, already exceeding Philadelphia, which had only 400,000 barrels to ship out, but was still far ahead of New York's 267,000. The measure of Philadelphia's decline in this trade is seen in the comparable figures for 1825: Baltimore, 510,000; New York, 446,000; Philadelphia, 351,000. The completion of the Erie Canal, as Philadelphians were aware, would not improve the situation. In 1828, for example, New York was to ship out 722,000 barrels; Baltimore, 546,000; Philadelphia, 333,000.[32]

Brought up in the belief that their prosperity depended on foreign commerce, Philadelphians were dismayed at how, year by year, the shipping tonnage registered at their port was falling behind their competitors. Tonnage figures for 1825 showed New York in the lead with 304,484; Boston next with 152,868; Baltimore totaling a surprising 92,050; and Philadelphia trailing with 73,807.[33] As far as the rivalry between New York and Philadelphia was concerned, the figures were in balance with the values of their foreign imports and exports. In 1824 New York's imports were valued at $36,113,000—Philadelphia's at $11,865,000; New York's exports came to $22,897,000—Philadelphia's to $9,634,000.[34] The state of New York, having surpassed Pennsylvania in population before 1820, had a growth rate in the 1820s twice that of Pennsylvania, and that rate approximated the growing difference in size between her metropolis and Philadelphia.[35]

I V

Philadelphians realized that the economic health of their city depended on internal improvements, access to the interior wherein lay the future wealth of America. The turnpike spree was still in progress—by 1832 Pennsylvania chartered 220 turnpike companies which had built some 3000 miles of roads[36] —but for the shipment of heavy freight turnpikes were outmoded; canals were now the cry, and New York was in the lead. Her great state-built canal, 362 miles long and eight years in the building, was completed in 1825. Philadelphians had financed two lesser improvements: the Schuylkill Navigation Company, which was opened to Reading in 1825, and the Union Canal, which would soon permit canal navigation between Reading and the Susquehanna. Philadelphians were also heavily interested in the Chesapeake and Delaware Canal, but these three improvements did not reach the heartland of the country, the great western reaches that New York had tapped through her Erie Canal.

Determined that their city should not lose what was left of her commercial prestige, a group of Philadelphians, headed by John Sergeant, eminent lawyer, congressman, and champion of Henry Clay's American System, had founded the Pennsylvania Society for the Promotion of Internal Improvements late in 1824. The activities of this society resulted in a public meeting in January 1825, presided over by Chief Justice William Tilghman. Sergeant, the principal speaker, pointed out that canal navigation between the Delaware and the Susquehanna would soon become a reality, and that this development called for the next step—water communication between the Susquehanna and the Allegheny. Furthermore, from the Allegheny a canal to Lake Erie should be undertaken, and built at the expense of the state. The meeting enthusiastically endorsed Sergeant's resolutions. A suitable memorial to the legislature was prepared, and William Strickland was sent abroad by the internal improvements society to procure information on canals and railroads. "A large proportion of the western trade has been withdrawn from this city," reported the improvements society, "and the present exertions are calculated not merely to regain what is lost. The struggle assumes a more serious aspect. It is to retain what is left."[37]

Philadelphians next convened a canal convention at Harrisburg, attended by 113 delegates from thirty-six counties.[38] After a year of ceaseless effort by Sergeant and his friends the legislature passed an act that opened the way for the building of the canal at state expense. Ultimately the state improvement program embraced a railroad from Philadelphia to Columbia, the point on the Susquehanna where much of the western produce reached the river, and various lesser projects. A 394-mile "main line" of State Works was projected and completed in the mid-1830s: the Columbia Railroad, 82 miles; the Eastern Division Canal from Columbia to Hollidaysburg, 171 miles; the Allegheny Portage Railroad over the mountains to Johnstown, 37 miles; and the Western Division Canal from Johnstown to Pittsburgh, 104 miles.[39]

Long before all this was accomplished Strickland had returned from his foreign travels and published his influential *Reports on Canals, Railways, Roads, and Other Subjects,* which so much favored railroads over canals that his sponsors required him to tone down the emphasis.

V

After all, Pennsylvania was by this time committed to canals, and it was especially through the Schuylkill Navigation Company, a gilt-edged Phila-

Advertisement for portable iron boats used in the 394-mile system of rail and canal transportation between Philadelphia and Pittsburgh. Lithograph by P. S. Duval after George Lehman (d. 1870), c. 1840.

HISTORICAL SOCIETY OF PENNSYLVANIA

The Columbia Rail Road, part of the State Works, from Daniel Bowen,
A History of Philadelphia (*Philadelphia, 1839*).

delphia-owned investment, that the city was experiencing the promise of better days. Back in 1817 the company's managers had suggested the possibility that coal might eventually be carried on the canal; they had had no concept that, shortly after it went into operation, coal would constitute two-thirds of its traffic. Flour, lumber, whiskey, and all the multitude of country products were to take a back seat to anthracite. In 1826 coal accounted for half the canal's total freight of 32,000 tons; in 1840, of the 658,000 tons brought down the river, 452,000 came from Schuylkill County mines.[40]

The first coal of consequence to reach Philadelphia had been 365 tons brought down the Delaware from the Lehigh area in 1820. Under the guidance of its manager, Josiah White, the Lehigh Coal and Navigation Company struggled to make the mines at Mauch Chunk profitable. When the state agreed to build the Delaware Division of the Pennsylvania canal system, work began in 1827 on the Lehigh canal planned by White and Erskine Hazard, and within a few years both projects were completed.[41] At Easton, the Delaware Division of the state-owned works united with Josiah Wright's heroic enterprise, and provided slack-water navigation down the Delaware to tidewater.[42]

Coal worked miracles in Philadelphia. The city had always been a wood-burning community, its houses heated by hickory, oak, and maple. Wood was used for cooking and to fire the boilers of the recently invented steam engines —indeed, the appearance of steamboats on the rivers had caused the forests to recede, so great was their hunger for fuel. At first there was much suspicion and dislike of coal, but as stoves, grates, and furnaces were perfected for its use it won a grudging acceptance based on its cheapness. In the late 1820s central heating was introduced into some Philadelphia homes, but the change from wood to coal in domestic uses came slowly; in 1833, $741,000 worth of wood was burned in the city, only $404,000 of coal.[43]

The most notable physical change imposed on Philadelphia by the coming of coal was to be seen along her Schuylkill River front, where a solid mass of wharves was built. These were usually crowded with canal boats from the mines and bristling with the masts of the coastal shipping which distributed anthracite to ports along the Atlantic seaboard. Philadelphia's first exports of coal went out in four vessels in 1822. In 1837 some 350,000 tons in 3225 carriers cleared the port for coastal destinations. Gone forever was the old colonial concept that the city's economic life depended on foreign trade.[44]

An innovation in these years, made possible by the abundance of coal, was the application of steam power to industry. Philadelphia led early in the manufacture of steam engines for this purpose—stationary engines as opposed to those designed for steamboats and locomotives. By the late 1830s the role of the stationary engine was fully appreciated and steam was being used in every conceivable type of manufacture.

To keep up with New York, Philadelphians had done all they could to encourage manufacturing, but waterpower for mills was limited, as neither the Delaware nor the Schuylkill had sufficient fall to generate a great amount of power. Steam supplied the alternative. By 1838 there were more steam engines in Pennsylvania than any other state, with nearly all of those in Philadelphia of local manufacture. Made by forty-four different individuals or firms, they serviced twenty-five types of mills, supplying the power for such enterprises as carpet weaving, breweries, flour mills, and the iron industry. Rush & Muhlenberg and Levi Morris were among Philadelphia's leading enginemakers, and so famous were the city's workers in this trade that Joseph Harrison, Jr., later recalled: "Philadelphia skill has been sought for to fill responsible places in all parts of the United States, in the West Indies, in South America and in Europe, and even in British India."[45]

Now that factories were no longer dependent on the geographical necessities of waterpower, manufacturers were free to concentrate their mills wherever they wished, in Frankford and Kensington, where waterpower had first attracted industry and which had become textile centers, but also throughout the city. The stationary steam engine helped make possible another long step in changing Philadelphia from a commercial to a manufacturing town with all the implications that would have for the city's future.

V I

Philadelphia's prosperity continued, however, to depend in large measure on her port, and various steps were taken to make it more available to the outside world. A canal connecting Delaware and Chesapeake Bays, it was believed, would greatly enhance Philadelphia's southern commerce, and into such a project Philadelphians poured a great deal of money. In the fall of 1829 the thirteen-and-a-half-mile length of the Chesapeake and Delaware Canal was completed. To celebrate its opening, a large party of Philadelphians embarked on the steamer *William Penn*, chartered by the canal's directors. On board were two companies of militia in full dress, Frank Johnson's band, and

the best caterer available. The paddlewheel vessel churned her way down to
Delaware City at the eastern end of the canal, where her guests left for their
tour of inspection.[46]

The year that saw the completion of the Chesapeake and Delaware Canal
was notable also for the commencement of work on the great breakwater,
designed by William Strickland, at the entrance to Delaware Bay. Storms and
ice had brought disaster to 193 vessels in that vicinity during the past twenty
years, losses that would not have occurred had there been a place of shelter.[47]
Now that Pennsylvania was at the threshold of a new era to be created by its
system of internal improvements, safe navigation of the Delaware was more
than ever necessary to protect the increased commerce that was expected on
her waters. Philadelphians believed that the canals converging on their city
would provide the flourishing interior of the nation with its shortest route to
the Atlantic; Philadelphia, they hoped, would be the place to which the
western trade could be carried at the cheapest rate.[48]

There was, unfortunately, a fly in the ointment; Philadelphia was not an
ice-free port. The winter of 1831–1832 was unusually severe, and the port iced
in. On January 26, 1832, there were no fewer than 126 vessels listed as ready
to sail as soon as the ice broke up. The eventual departure of this large number
of ships, all sailing together, brought thousands of spectators to the wharves.
It was a beautiful sight.[49] In 1835–1836 the solid sheet of ice that spanned the
river again kept the shipping from coming up for more than two months. Not
until the middle of March was a passage between Chester and Philadelphia
possible, and then it was hammered out by the new steamer *Pennsylvania*,
built at Kensington by John Vaughan & Son and not designed primarily to
clear ice but to tow up ocean-going ships from the breakwater, thereby
creating "a new era in our foreign trade." "It was a cheering sight to see the
white canvas again on the river," wrote an observer. "Fully fifty square rigged
vessels arrived at the wharves, swelling the whole number of arrivals to near
one hundred." Many of the boats were loaded with firewood, which had been
in short supply. The day they unloaded, the price per cord dropped from
fifteen dollars to seven.[50]

While steam tow boats were a valuable navigational aid (in 1836 the *Pennsylvania* towed up 247 sail), the need for a real ice boat remained. In 1837 the
Delaware was again ice-fast and the public's patience was exhausted. As usual
the stoppage of trade threw hundreds of laborers out of work and drove
merchants to New York to buy their goods.[51] Urged on by resolutions
adopted at a town meeting, the city Councils appropriated $70,000 to build
an ice boat, which was launched the following August at Van Dusen and
Byerly's Kensington yard. The next year this boat, commanded by Capt. Levi
Lingo, was battling Delaware ice piled in ridges five feet thick.[52]

Launchings at Van Dusen and Byerly's and Philadelphia's other shipyards
were popular, well-attended affairs, but there never was such a launching as
that of the U.S.S. *Pennsylvania* in July 1837. It attracted the largest crowd,
estimated at 100,000, that had ever assembled in the county. Fifteen years

a-building and a-setting on the stocks in the giant shiphouse at the Navy Yard, the 120-gun ship-of-the-line *Pennsylvania* was the largest ship in the world and the most heavily armed man of war ever built. Designed by Philadelphia's naval architect Samuel Humphreys, her main gun deck was 212 feet long, and her beam 58.[53] To the delight of the multitudes clustered on rooftops and crowding the more than 200 vessels assembled for the event, the *Pennsylvania* glided smoothly down the ways. On board were several hundred guests and a German band playing patriotic American airs. Just as the vessel touched the water, Nicholas Biddle's brother, Commodore James Biddle, a veteran of thirty-seven years in the navy, christened her by smashing on her figurehead a bottle of Pennsylvania whiskey made in Union County in 1829, and a bottle of madeira, hoary with age, its label bearing a single word, the name "Cadwalader."[54] The career of the *Pennsylvania* was not fated to be as glorious as her launching. She was to spend many years tied up at the Norfolk Navy Yard, and there she was scuttled in 1861 to prevent her falling into the hands of the Confederates.

With navigation improved by the breakwater, tow boats, and the ice boat, its life stimulated by coal and other cargoes carried on the canals, the port of Philadelphia had never been more active. About five-sixths of the shad taken by Gloucester County's forty shad fisheries was marketed in Philadelphia. Every year about 1000 lumber rafts containing fifty million board feet in all descended the river from New York's Delaware and Sullivan Counties and Pennsylvania's Wayne County.[55]

Launch of the U.S. Ship Pennsylvania, *wood engraving by R. S. Gilbert (July 1837), from* A History of Philadelphia *(1839).*

But the enormous increase in the city's coastal trade was accompanied by a decline in her foreign commerce. Of her two packet lines to Liverpool, only Cope's remained. At New York, on the other hand, many lines provided regular sailings to a number of European ports, and it was to New York that the English steamers *Sirius* and *Great Western* made their way in 1838. With the practicability of transatlantic steam navigation established, Philadelphians yearned for steam packet service of their own, through whose "potent aid" they could "restore our city to the first rank among our commercial sisters . . . and bring back to the shores of the Delaware the forests of masts which in former times cheered the hearts of our fathers and laid the broad foundations of our wealth and power." But the $550,000 required to set up a steam line could not be raised. The effort was evidently unrealistic, based on nostalgia for the city's lost position and a desire to regain her former prestige in commerce. Philadelphia's destiny lay in other directions, in other kinds of wealth and economic might.[56]

VII

For Philadelphia was to have as much steam power as any other city, steam applied not to ocean-going lines but to railroads and factories, with the first locally financed road stimulated by a Germantown gathering in October 1830. Among those who thought that a railroad to Philadelphia would be profitable were Benjamin Chew, Jr., of Cliveden, P. R. Freas, editor of the *Germantown Telegraph,* and John F. Watson, the antiquarian whose *Annals of Philadelphia,* the city's first history, had just been published. The line these men wanted was to have a branch, crossing the Wissahickon near its mouth, to Norristown, where mills produced 40,000 barrels of flour a year. The possibilities of heavy freight and passenger service were so favorable, and the understanding that the line would eventually be connected with the coal regions so well understood, that the stock of the Philadelphia, Germantown & Norristown Railroad, when offered for sale, proved insufficient to meet the demands of frantic speculators who scrambled for it in riotous fashion.[57]

The railroad celebrated the successive opening of its divisions with much pomp. In June 1832 the Germantown run was inaugurated with thousands of curiosity seekers in attendance and the usual band of music. The cars, which resembled large stagecoaches, each seated about twenty passengers inside and fifteen outside, and were drawn by horses. The road's first locomotive, *Old Ironsides,* made by Matthias W. Baldwin, was placed on the rails the following November, but at first was used only in fair weather because its weight of a mere five tons did not give it enough traction to hold the rails in rain. Under the supervision of William Strickland, the Norristown branch reached Manayunk late in 1834, and in August 1835 service was initiated to Norristown. From there, arrangements were made with the Philadelphia and Reading to continue a railroad along the margin of the Schuylkill.[58]

Chartered in 1833, the Reading was to be the masterpiece of Virginia engineer Moncure Robinson. Financed in part with money Robinson had raised in England, the railroad was completed to Reading in 1838, thereby providing competition for the canal of the Schuylkill Navigation Company. A feature of the Reading was mine-to-ship transportation, from the coal regions to the port, for its line extended across Philadelphia County to Port Richmond at Kensington on the Delaware, where the railroad had its own wharves.[59]

Rail Road Depot at Philadelphia, *Ninth and Green Streets, lithograph by David Kennedy and William Lucas after William L. Breton (c. 1773–1855), 1832. On November 24, 1832, the* United States Gazette *reported, "The beautiful locomotive engine and tender, built by Mr. Baldwin, of this city . . . were for the first time placed on the road. The engine traveled about six miles, working with perfect accuracy and ease and with great velocity."*

LIBRARY COMPANY OF PHILADELPHIA

Not content with a railroad to Reading, Philadelphians had their eyes on the trade of a vast area of productive land along the branches of the Susquehanna. As early as 1830 they were calling for a railroad from Danbury and Sunbury to Pottsville, where it would connect with the Schuylkill Navigation Company's canal. Assisted by Mathew Carey and Thomas P. Cope, Nicholas Biddle had been the leading figure in this move to establish the Danville and Pottsville, or the Central Railroad as it was generally called. Moncure Robinson located the line, but funds for its complete construction could not be had. Still, by 1836 it had been run twelve miles beyond Pottsville to Girardville, the site designated for a town by the great Philadelphia merchant. In 1830 Girard had purchased at auction from the trustees of the old first Bank of the United States 30,000 acres in the rich Mahanoy coal region of Schuylkill County. Its cost to him, including the improvements he had made, was $170,000 at the time of his death, when he bequeathed it to the City of Philadelphia, probably the best investment ever made by one of her citizens.[60]

Philadelphians had not forgotten the importance they had placed back in 1825 on an access to Erie. The state-owned canal system had been opened to Pittsburgh in 1834, but a canal to Erie had not been undertaken from that point. Moreover entrepreneurs now favored railroads, because unlike the canals they did not have to shut down for the winter months. In 1836 a convention stimulated by Philadelphians was held at Williamsport to formalize plans for a railroad from Pittsburgh to Erie. Nicholas Biddle was elected president of the convention, and through his efforts a charter was obtained for the Sunbury and Erie Railroad with Biddle as president.[61] Surveys were run and some preliminary work on the road undertaken, but the Philadelphia and Erie, as it was later known, was not completed until long after its first president's death.

Meanwhile the Columbia Railroad's double-track line to the Susquehanna was completed in 1834, with horse-drawn, flanged-wheel coach connections from various points in the city across the new Columbia Avenue Bridge to an inclined plane up Belmont Hill, at the top of which the coaches were hooked together for the trip westward. Later this railroad's tracks were extended from Broad Street down Market to the Delaware (causing the demolition of the old Court House which had stood on Market at Second Street since 1708). It was also in 1834 that the Philadelphia and Trenton's thirty-mile line went into operation. Earlier the same year the Camden and Amboy Railroad across the river replaced the forty to fifty stagecoaches that had carried passengers, freight, and the mail overland from opposite Philadelphia to New York.[62] One remaining line of importance to Philadelphia continued in progress, the railroad to Baltimore. This road was built by three companies, with Latrobe laying out the Baltimore–Havre de Grace section, his former student Strickland in charge from Wilmington to the Susquehanna, and Strickland's former student Samuel H. Kneass handling the engineering of the Philadelphia-Wilmington division. The completion of the first two sections in July 1837 called for a celebration at their juncture on the Susquehanna, where a steamboat provided the unifying link. The next year the double-track line from Wilmington to Gray's Ferry was completed, a railroad bridge built over the Schuylkill, replacing the old Gray's Ferry floating bridge, and the rails laid to a depot on Broad Street at Prime (now Washington Avenue). The city now had its rail access to the South—the Philadelphia, Wilmington and Baltimore Railroad.[63]

VIII

With coal and iron in nearby abundance it was inevitable that Philadelphia in her transition from a mercantile center should become a manufacturing center. She had the raw materials and she had the men. John Bristed, in his *The Resources of the United States,* published in 1818, noted the city's trend in that direction: "There is no part of the world where, in proportion to its population, a greater number of ingenious mechanics may be found than in the City of Philadelphia and its immediate neighbourhood; or where, in proportion to the capital employed, manufactures thrive better."[64] *Niles' Register* in 1829 noted the improvement and wealth of Philadelphia, and the extension of her manufactures: "more than half the business of selling goods in our commercial cities, for the direct supply of the interior, is in domestic production. The *back shops* of Philadelphia are more valuable to her than the ranges of stores on the Delaware."[65] So great and swift was the rise of factories in Philadelphia that Peter S. Du Ponceau, in toasting the city in 1829, predicted: "Our good city of Philadelphia—In twenty years the Manchester and Lyons of America."[66]

The degree to which Philadelphia had pulled herself out of the doldrums of the 1820s can be appreciated by the surprised comments of a New Yorker on visiting this "great, beautiful, rich, and self-complacent city" in 1830:

The foreign commerce of Philadelphia suffers much in comparison and by the all commanding advantages of New York. But such is the countless wealth of the former city—such her internal resources and her indissoluable connections with a vast and rich interior—such the acknowledged superiority of her artists [engineers and mechanics]—of almost every description—there are so many established and productive manufactures—she has so much literature, science, and professional talents in her own bosom—that Philadelphia makes a world in itself, altogether independent of the accidental superiorities of her rival sister. And her growth within a few years last past has been more substantial and more rapid than at any former period. I had expected to see this city decline. But it is no longer a question. She is destined to rise and grow with the country.[67]

As these comments indicate, Philadelphia had continued to surge vigorously into the industrial revolution. Manufacturing and fine craftsmanship were encouraged by the Franklin Institute's annual exhibits, where all vied for the "premiums," or medals, awarded. In 1825 the institute offered prizes for the best specimens in eighty-two branches of manufactures.[68] Mathew Carey, president of the Pennsylvania Society for the Promotion of Manufactures and the Mechanic Arts, led the way in making Philadelphia the citadel of high-tariff theory.[69]

Large mills for spinning cotton and weaving wool were built with astonishing rapidity. They were particularly numerous at Manayunk (the old Indian name for the River Schuylkill), near "Flat Rock," five or six miles above Philadelphia. In 1820 there was only a toll house there, but by 1825 it was a thriving factory town, soon boasted of as the "Lowell of Pennsylvania."[70] The source of waterpower for mills had always been there, but it was the transportation facility of the Schuylkill Navigation Company and its dam and millrace that created Manayunk and helped push Philadelphia into the first rank in the textile field. By 1828 the city's 104 warping mills employed 4500 weavers and more than 5000 spoolers, bobbin winders, and dyers.[71]

Philadelphia also excelled in heavy industry. By 1830 nearly one-fourth of the nation's steel production centered there, and the city was preeminent in

Manayunk, *lithograph published by John T. Bowen (1801–1856), after John Caspar Wild (c. 1804–1846), 1838.*

the building of locomotives. Matthias W. Baldwin led off in this field with his first engine for the Germantown line in 1832, his Baldwin Locomotive Works soon becoming the largest producer in the country. By 1838, 45 percent of the domestically manufactured engines in use on American railroads bore his name.[72]

In some respects William Norris was even more famous than Baldwin. Starting in the locomotive business in 1832 as a partner in the American Steam Carriage Company, he moved its shop from Kensington to Bush Hill in 1835, and there built the *George Washington* for the Columbia Railroad. This engine's tremendous power brought him an order for seventeen like it for an English railroad, the Birmingham and Gloucester. From then on Norris's foreign business grew rapidly. Many of his machines went to Austria and elsewhere on the Continent; they were to be found in Cuba and South America.

Still another locomotive builder of spectacular attainments was Joseph Harrison, Jr., who became foreman in 1835 for Garrett and Eastwick, one of Philadelphia's pioneer locomotive concerns. Before long the firm had become Eastwick and Harrison. It is best remembered as the company that moved to Russia to build the engines and cars needed by the czar.[73]

Samuel V. Merrick was another industrialist comparable in achievements to the locomotive builders. In the 1820s he and his partner John Agnew won fame for their construction of an improved type of fire engine. Next, with John H. Towne, Merrick established the Southwark Foundry for the manufacture of heavy machinery and boilers. A founder of the Franklin Institute and destined to be the first president of the Pennsylvania Railroad, Merrick was one of the most forward-looking men in the city. Many naval vessels were powered by engines made by his firm, in particular the steam frigate U.S.S. *Princeton*, built at the Philadelphia Navy Yard in 1843, the first propeller-driven man-of-war ordered by the navy.[74]

The reputation of Philadelphia manufacturers spread far and wide. The city's famous coachmaker, William Ogle, exported many of his vehicles; his *volantes* went to South America and Mexico, and a record exists of his making a carriage for a gentleman in Scotland. In partnership with George W. Watson, Ogle constructed a factory near the Falls of Schuylkill, run by waterpower and a marvel of ingenuity and efficiency.[75]

The making of fire engines was a separate line of business, one in which Philadelphia became well known as the supplier of southern and western communities. George Jeffries was one of the principal builders in this trade, but John Agnew, late of Merrick & Agnew, was outstanding. In 1839 he made an engine for a company in Mobile that was the largest Philadelphians had ever seen—a "hydraulian" capable of throwing a stream of water 192 feet. The sides of its gallery were carved in bold, bronze scrollwork by Samuel Hemphill. All of its metal ornaments were silver plated, even to the axle boxes, and much of this was beautifully engraved with appropriate inscriptions and devices by Gaskill & Copper. The front locker was covered with an inscribed plate of German silver, the back by a magnificent ornamental painting by John A. Woodside. The moldings and paneling were blue and black, relieved with gold.[76]

Foundries and factories of all sorts proliferated in the Philadelphia of this era. Cornelius and Company's chandeliers were unsurpassed in beauty, hung in places as exalted as the United States Senate, and won fame at the Crystal Palace Exhibition. In a more mundane line, this company provided the countless gas fixtures required by Philadelphians in the late 1830s. McCalla's carpet factory at Bush Hill had achieved such a position in the trade that it was known as the Kidderminster of America. Indicative of the city's ties with Cuba were twelve sugar refineries, which made Philadelphia perhaps the largest sugar-refining center in the country, one destined to be later accused of monopolizing the business. One of the most curious industrial plants of all was the extensive Dyottsville Glass Works, on the Delaware just above Kensington. Of its 300 employees, 225 were boys, some not eight years of age.[77]

This kaleidoscopic view presents only a few of the fields in which Philadelphia's industry developed at such breakneck speed that by 1828 the city was recognized as the foremost manufacturer in the country.[78] Unfortunately the accomplishment achieved in transferring the making of products from the

Parke & Tiers Brass Bell & Iron Founders, Point Pleasant, Kensington, Philada., *engraving in* Picture of Philadelphia ... (*Philadelphia: E. L. Carey and A. Hart, 1831). The foundry, built by C. B. Parke in 1819, also made sugar mills, soap boiler pans, anvils, and hammers.*

T. W. Dyott, Wholesale and Retail Druggist and Warehouse, *northeast corner of Second and Race Streets, wood engraving from the* Philadelphia Directory and Register for 1820.

View of the Glass Works of T. W. Dyott at Kensington on the Delaware nr Philada., *lithograph probably by David Kennedy and William Lucas after W. L. Breton (c. 1773–1855), from* Picture of Philadelphia from 1811 to 1831 *(Philadelphia, 1831).*

LIBRARY COMPANY OF PHILADELPHIA

home or small shop to the factory almost totally neglected the human factor involved. The result was a labor problem of novel aspect to employers, who saw no reason to respect the "rights" of laborers. They had no rights: if they were dissatisfied, let them go elsewhere; there were plenty of men available to take their places. The justness of this attitude was endorsed by the clergy, public opinion, and the law.

But the voice of labor began to be heard in Philadelphia. In 1827 the journeymen house carpenters struck, complaining of the "grievous and slave-like system of labor." The reaction of the master carpenters was to advertise for journeymen in other cities.[79] There was no security for the workingman. Living in fear of losing his job, he was crowded into unsanitary dwellings and tenements, working from sunrise to sunset for pitifully low wages which were subject to drastic reductions. Mill owners at Blockley and Manayunk expected a fourteen-hour working day, six days a week, for a weekly salary of $4.33. Vacations were unknown, and July 4 was the only official holiday.[80]

Given these circumstances it was no accident that the American labor movement had its beginnings in Philadelphia. In 1827 a young cordwainer, William Heighton, published *An Address to the Members of Trade Societies and to Working Classes Generally*. Later in that strike-torn year he formed the Mechanics Union of Trade Associations, which served as a coordinating body for constituent trade unions. It founded six new trade societies and once embraced as many as fifteen. Heighton was also editor of the *Mechanics Free Press*, established in 1828, the first labor paper in America. From 1828 to 1831 the Working Men's party nominated candidates for public office who were proponents of such reforms as a universal free school system, abolition of imprisonment for debt, mechanics' lien laws, and other measures to protect the status and dignity of skilled craftsmen and artisans. As a class they fought against reduction to a proletariat; but as a party they could not compete successfully against the experienced politicians and the traditions of the major parties. Labor's antimonopoly and pro-hard-money views made it susceptible to absorption by the Democrats when Andrew Jackson undertook his war against the Bank of the United States.[81]

Long hours were the overt issue of the general strike of 1835, its basic goal the ten-hour day. Down at the grimy Schuylkill wharves the unskilled Irish coal-heavers walked off, and prevented others from working. The house painters went out next, denouncing the "present system of labor as oppressive and unjust and destructive of social happiness." Bricklayers, carpenters, masons, and many other trades also struck, parading with fife, drum, and banners which displayed their demands. When the city Councils accepted the ten-hour day for city employees, enough other employers reluctantly fell into line that the strike was considered won.[82]

Labor next concentrated on winning better wages, but with small success. When the coal-heavers struck on this issue in 1836, the dealers would not budge from the old one-dollar-a-day standard, with twelve and a half cents an hour overtime. "This with constant employment," the workers were told, "is great encouragement to those who wish to 'make hay while the sun shines,'" an allusion to wintertime when, with the canal closed, most of them would be out of work.[83]

Soon came the Panic of 1837, and the ensuing business depression and unemployment so weakened the bargaining position of labor that the Ten-Hour Movement of 1835 became the fond memory of a moment not to be approached again for generations. At that, the brief success of the movement was illusory. Though the ten-hour day was the tangible issue at hand, and though the unskilled participated in the Ten-Hour Movement, most of the impetus for the general strike of 1835 came from skilled artisans, whose basic concern was not the length of the working day but the loss of their historic status and independence. The independent artisan of the eighteenth century, who ran his own business from his dwelling place, was now losing control of his destiny to capitalists who bought up his products for distribution in a larger, big-city-wide or regional or national market, and who in the process reorganized the trades.

I X

The enormous increase in the city's industrial output brought about startling changes in her population. In 1820 the number of people living in Philadelphia County already exceeded those in the city proper by 72,922 to 63,713. Over the years both sections gained in population density, but the county with its new factory areas grew faster than the city, and in 1840 had outstripped her by 164,474 to 93,652. The old sections of the city began to run down. Few new buildings went up on the Delaware front; the houses once owned by wealthy colonial merchants were taken over as tenements or factories as blight set in. Back from the river more recent residential streets were transformed into rows of stores as the former residents moved westward. This drift was recognized as early as 1825 when the Middle Ward boundaries were extended from Fourth Street to Seventh. By 1830 the center of the city was around Sixth Street, since 37,500 people lived west of Seventh and 43,000 east of the new dividing line. The 1840 census shows a quickening of the westward trend—56,000 inhabitants west of Seventh Street, 37,500 east. Of course the areas to the north and south were also increasing in population. Southwark, the Northern Liberties, and Kensington doubled their numbers in this twenty-year period, while Spring Garden's jumped from 3500 to 28,000.[84]

Surprised by such changes, an Old Philadelphian recorded in 1828 that "Below South Street, east of Broad, has recently sprung up a new town. Where last summer the boys played, there are now solid blocks of brick buildings, grocery stores and taverns [and the] clitter clatter of the weavers' shuttle."[85] The quantity of buildings being erected was astonishing. In 1827 more houses were built in Philadelphia than in any two years previous, and in 1829 and 1830 it was estimated that 5000 residences and stores were erected in the city and county, yet rents were higher than ever.[86]

Building rows of handsome brick houses, three and four stories high, complete with baths and water closets, was one of Stephen Girard's favorite forms of investment carried on by him until his death: "He projects and executes schemes with the courage and ardour of a young man."[87] Examples can still be seen in the south side of Spruce Street between Third and Fourth. All were high in praise of Girard's superior and extensive building improvements. "He has been the means of beautifying this, his adopted city, and of employing large numbers of respectable artisans, who might otherwise have been thrown out of bread," observed a Chestnut Street merchant.[88]

"Philadelphia," wrote Nathaniel P. Willis, "is a city to be happy in. . . . Delightful cleanliness everywhere meets the eye. The sidewalks are washed constantly; the marble steps are spotlessly clean. . . . Everything is well conditioned and cared for. If any fault could be found it would be that of too much regularity and too nice precision."[89] As Latrobe had observed earlier of Philadelphia architecture, "so it was in the beginning, is now, and ever shall be."[90] But change was on its way; granite fronts were coming into vogue,[91] and among Girard's building efforts was the row of houses on Chestnut between Eleventh and Twelfth, which were distinguished by marble fronts and pillars. Rich men like Matthew Newkirk, railroad president, bank director, philanthropist, and, to his guest Henry Clay's dismay, teetotaller, built marble mansions.[92]

Of the three great architects of the period—Strickland, Haviland, and Thomas U. Walter—Strickland was probably the most outstanding. "He found us," said newspaper publisher Joseph R. Chandler, "living in a city of brick, and he will leave us in a city of marble."[93] The marble came from

North Side of Chestnut St: Extending from Sixth to Seventh St.,
*watercolor by Benjamin Ridgway Evans (fl. 1840–1885), 1851. The Philadelphia
Arcade, designed by John Haviland (1792–1852) stood between the Columbia House
and Bolivar House hotels. The second Chestnut Street Theatre is just east of the
Bolivar House. The Arcade was demolished in 1863.*

LIBRARY COMPANY OF PHILADELPHIA

quarries in Montgomery County and owed its perfection in appearance to the
Scotsman John Struthers, unquestionably the best marble mason in Philadelphia, if not in the country. Strickland's beautiful buildings did much to
enhance the appearance of the city and to provide her with many of her
"lions." His contributions were impressive: in addition to the second Bank
of the United States (1819–1824) at 420 Chestnut Street, there were the Naval
Asylum, near Gray's Ferry (1826–1829); a new building for the Unitarian
church on the Tenth and Locust site (1828); the Arch Street Theatre, on the
north side of Arch Street above Sixth (1828); the University of Pennsylvania's
Medical Hall (1829) and College Hall (1829–1830); the United States Mint at
the northwest corner of Chestnut and Juniper (1829–1833); the Almshouse at
Blockley west of the Schuylkill (1830–1834); the Merchants' Exchange on the
north side of Walnut between Third and Dock Streets (1832–1834); and the
Philadelphia Bank on the southwest corner of Fourth and Chestnut (1836–
1837), to mention some of the most notable. Of these, along with the Bank of
the United States, only the United States Naval Asylum and the Merchants'
Exchange still stand.

Merchants' Exchange, *lithograph by Deroy after Augustus Kollner (1813–1906), 1848. The Exchange, designed by William Strickland (1788–1854) in 1832, is now part of Independence National Historical Park.*

John Haviland's first important building was the Philadelphia Arcade, which, patterned on London's Burlington Arcade, owed its inception as the city's first office building to the restless energy of Peter A. Browne. Chief Justice William Tilghman having recently died, his ancient home, formerly the residence of Gov. Sir William Keith, was torn down and on its site on the north side of Chestnut Street between Sixth and Seventh Haviland's handsome marble building was erected in 1827. The tenancy of the ninety stores it housed was sold at auction, an odd way of establishing their rental value. Peale's Museum vacated Independence Hall to occupy the third floor. Interesting as the novel building was, it turned out a financial failure.[94]

The year after he completed the Arcade, Haviland, again in conjunction with Browne, built an even more curious structure, a Chinese pagoda. This lofty pile stood in a pleasure garden near the Schuylkill at Fairmount, and represented a tower on the banks of the Ta-ho, between Canton and Hoang-pou.[95] Alas, it too was unsuccessful.

Haviland achieved his greatest fame in prison design: cell blocks radiating like the spokes of a wheel from a central administration building. In 1829 he completed Philadelphia's Eastern State Penitentiary at Cherry Hill—now Fairmount Avenue at Twenty-first Street—according to this plan and surrounded it with a stone wall twelve feet thick at the base and thirty feet high, with castellated towers at its corners and a massive fortress-like entrance.[96] Having demonstrated his virtuosity in Greek Revival buildings, such as his Asylum for the Deaf and Dumb on the northwest corner of Broad and Pine (1824–1825) and St. George's Episcopal Church on Eighth Street south of Locust (1822), as well as his familiarity with medieval fortresses and Chinese temples, Haviland was next entranced by the "pure Egyptian." His plan for the Museum Building in 1835 was a transplant from the Nile.[97] In 1839 he designed a building for an insurance company on Walnut Street opposite Independence Square. This marble Egyptian edifice so took the fancy of a prominent New Yorker that the architect was commissioned to do one like it for that gentleman's residence. Haviland's work was well known in New York. After the great fire in 1835 he received several major commissions, including the building of the New York Exchange. This recognition of his worth caused a New York editor to write: "The best architectural taste in the country is found at Philadelphia, as her public buildings make manifest. It is not to be wondered at, therefore, that we are indebted to the American Athens, instead of our own."[98] The Eastern State Penitentiary; the original Franklin Institute (1826), on Seventh Street south of Market, now the Atwater Kent Museum; the Philadelphia College of Art and what is now St. George's Greek Catholic Church; and the much altered Walnut Street Theatre are the principal Haviland buildings surviving in Philadelphia today.

Philadelphia's third prominent architect, Thomas U. Walter, is noted for his Girard College, erected 1833–1847, but he also built the Philadelphia County Prison in Moyamensing in 1835 (demolished in 1967). This formidable Gothic stronghold, to which were transferred the prisoners from the antiquated Walnut Street Prison, was of granite from the Quincy quarries in Massachusetts. Next to it, Walter built an Egyptian-style debtors' prison of red Connecticut sandstone.[99] Many churches and other public structures owed their design to him, such as the Spruce Street Baptist Church at 426 Spruce. In domestic architecture, his outstanding work was the enlargement of Biddle's "Andalusia," and "Portico Row," west of Broad Street on Chestnut (not to be confused with "Portico Square," of similar construction on Spruce Street). Between 1825 and 1840 Walter and his friends Strickland and Haviland created more architecturally important buildings in Philadelphia than had ever been built there before.

X

Although her appetite for building improvements seemed insatiable, Philadelphia was often slow in accepting technological advances. For years voices had been heard vainly urging the establishment of a gasworks. Baltimore, New York, and Boston had gas plants, but the city Councils were timid. In 1831 they averred that gas lighting had not yet been brought to the necessary degree of perfection. They feared health hazards, danger of explosion, nauseous odors, and other perils and inconveniences.[100] Irritated by this nonsense, Samuel V. Merrick, advocating gas lighting, was elected a councilman and went abroad to study gas manufacture. His report resulted in an ordinance establishing a gasworks which he designed and superintended for several years. This plant was erected on Market Street next to the Schuylkill and went into general operation in 1836. The following year the city's principal streets were lighted by gas. Philadelphians were thrilled with the new light. "This evening," wrote Joseph Sill in 1836, "was rendered remarkable by the introduction of gas into my store and private entry of my dwelling . . . the most clear, dazzling, and bright light I ever saw."[101]

Among other improvements which came to the city in the 1830s were several in transportation. Until 1833 Philadelphians went about town either on foot, in private carriages, or in hired hacks. June 1, 1833, brought a new method, for on that day omnibus service was inaugurated. The *William Penn,* lineal ancestor of the horse car, trolley, and bus, started its hourly runs between the Merchants' Coffee House on Second Street and the Schuylkill. Immediately afterward line after line went into operation, their gay equipages fancifully painted and individually named—*Stephen Girard, Independence, Lady Washington, Union*—until there was scarcely a major avenue in Philadelphia without its ponderous-looking omnibus service.[102] Six years after the appearance of the *William Penn* another mode of conveyance, the cab, attracted favorable comment. Abbreviated from the French *cabriolet,* the cab carried two passengers inside and a driver outside on a box to the rear. Philadelphia's "Cab No. 1" was made by Robert E. Nuttle for Joseph M. Sanderson, the genial proprietor of the Merchants' Hotel on Fourth Street north of Market.[103]

XI

Another change of the times, brought on by population growth and the inadequacy of church burial yards, was the commercial cemetery. In 1827

Representation of the Gas Works, *Philadelphia, Market Street at Twenty-Second, drawn by Nicholson B. Devereux for* Gleason's Pictorial Drawing-Room Companion *(1853)*.

HISTORICAL SOCIETY OF PENNSYLVANIA

James Ronaldson, type founder and the enterprising president of the Franklin Institute, opened the Philadelphia Cemetery (usually called Ronaldson's) on Shippen (now Bainbridge) Street between Ninth and Tenth, a city landmark until 1950 when it was removed. Next, the concept of cemeteries set in peaceful, rural settings, modeled on Mount Auburn, near Boston, and Père la Chaise, Paris, became popular. In 1836 Laurel Hill, Joseph Sims's former countryseat on the Schuylkill, was purchased by a stock company and converted into a beautiful cemetery in the new style. Before long other similar burial grounds were in operation—Woodlands Cemetery on the Hamilton estate in West Philadelphia, and Monument Cemetery at North Broad Street and Turner's Lane, removed in recent years and the grounds transformed into a Temple University parking lot.[104]

The elaborate efforts to beautify cemeteries, particularly Laurel Hill where John Notman was employed as architect, were in the mood of the city's exceedingly appreciative interest in artistic endeavors. Traditional art activity in Philadelphia was sustained by the annual exhibitions of the Artists' Fund Society and of the Pennsylvania Academy of the Fine Arts, as well as by numerous special exhibitions at Masonic Hall and Earle's Gallery. This was the Philadelphia of Thomas Sully, her most popular portrait painter. He idealized his subjects, but he obtained likenesses and painted more Philadelphians than any other artists. His greatest triumph came in 1838 when he went to England to paint Queen Victoria. "The Queen, he told me," wrote Samuel Breck, "was exceedingly affable and granted him six sittings."[105]

John Neagle did not obtain as good likenesses as Sully, but his composition was far more interesting. His portrait of Thomas P. Cope, for example, shows one of Cope's packet ships in the background, while in the foreground, on a table, rests the charter of the Mercantile Library Company, of which Cope was founder and president. Neagle's best known work, *Pat Lyon at the Forge*, was completed in 1827. Behind Pat's brawny figure is the cupola of the Walnut Street Jail, where he was imprisoned in 1798 for a crime he did not commit. In his wealthy old age Lyon insisted on being painted not as the gentleman he had become but in the role of his early days, a blacksmith.[106]

Rembrandt Peale, Jacob Eichholtz, and Henry Inman were all prominent portrait painters in Philadelphia in this period, many of their works being made into prints by John Sartain, the best engraver of the day. In prolific Thomas Birch, the city rejoiced in one of the best marine painters of the time, his canvases selling usually for thirty dollars. Russell Smith had come into public notice when, failing to gain adequate support for his landscapes, he turned scene painter and did extraordinary work at the Walnut Street Theatre.[107] In John A. Woodside the city had one of the best ornamental painters in the country, famed for his stirring allegories which decorated fire engines. His signs, such as the one that hung in front of Lukens' Tavern in Kensington—*The Landing of Columbus*—were unexcelled.[108]

Visiting artists were invariably entranced by the Fairmount Water Works. In 1834 J. C. Wild's watercolors of Fairmount were exhibited at the Merchants' Exchange, and the next year Nicolino Calyo exhibited his large, highly colored city views at Masonic Hall. Scarce had Calyo been in town a month before he too had his view of Fairmount, and the ruins of the great fire that burned out fifty-five acres of New York City had hardly cooled before he was exhibiting pictures of the disaster.[109]

William Rush continued in his great tradition. His favorite carvings were ship figureheads of Indian chiefs. Sometimes they were shown in the act of shooting an arrow, or in solemn thought, arms folded within a tightly drawn blanket, or else fiercely threatening with raised tomahawk. But Rush was versatile. When the ship *John Sergeant* slid into the Delaware from John Vaughan's yard in 1831, her figurehead was an excellent likeness by Rush of Philadelphia's prominent citizen. On Rush's death in 1833, it was acknowledged that as a carver he had been unequalled. However, John Rush, his son, carried on capably, carving the figurehead for the mighty U.S.S. *Pennsylvania* —Hercules dressed in a lion's skin, armed with a club.[110]

Whether the banker's head ornamented the brig *Nicholas Biddle* at her launching at Southwark in 1838 is not recorded. She was a first-rate ship intended for the Brazil trade, and not the first to be named for him. Fortunately a description survives of the *Joseph Cowperthwait*, a brig launched two months later, named for Biddle's cashier. Cowperthwait's bust adorned the vessel, but not in the usual place under the bowsprit; it was placed at the stern. To starboard of this effigy in bold carving was the front of the Bank of the United States, while on the other side were carved representations of the cashier's books, desk, and the charter of the bank.[111]

Among the city's many excellent sculptors in marble was Nicholas Gevelot, whose statue of Apollo, god of music and poetry, was placed in the pediment of the Arch Street Theatre in 1830. It was Gevelot who carved the angels for St. John's Roman Catholic Church on Thirteenth Street, and who was commissioned to do the life-size marble statue of Girard at Girard College. His bronze busts of Edward Burd and William Strickland delighted Philadelphians who found them on exhibit at the Louvre in 1836.[112]

To provide Gevelot with some competition, E. Luigi Persico came to Philadelphia in 1831. Over a period of years Persico immortalized a number of Philadelphians in marble.[113] Much excellent sculpturing was done by artists whose names are lost. However, it is known that the brothers Peter and Philip Bardi did the elaborate capitals for the columns at the Merchants' Exchange, and that the pair of lions that guard its front were carved by Signor Fiorelli of 31 Dock Street.[114] At Struthers's marble yard highly skilled workers provided the city with its most elaborate mantelpieces, ornamented with delicately worked friezes of grapevines and Egyptian caryatids. Some of these men, such as Hugh Cannon, later set up their own studios. John Hill was presumably Struthers's best man, for it was he who lavishly executed Struthers's masterpiece according to designs provided by Strickland, the Washington sarcophagus.[115] True proportions were the ideal of the day. A sculptor exhibiting his statue of Cleopatra in Philadelphia displayed a certificate testifying to its anatomical exactness, signed by several of New York's most eminent physicians.[116]

Nicolo Monachesi, who made Philadelphia his home from 1831 until his death twenty years later, was a master of painting in fresco. In this medium he decorated the ceilings of the great room at the Exchange, St. John's sanctuary, and other Catholic churches. Some of the city's most costly residences bore testimony to his skill: "This tasteful manner of decorating the walls of noble mansions is becoming fashionable and seems to offer some encouragement to the fine arts." For Matthew Newkirk's house he provided a brilliant ceiling of Cornelia, the mother of the Gracchi, showing her jewels to Capuano. Sidney George Fisher thought that George Cadwalader's parlors were the handsomest in town; their walls and ceilings were "beautifully painted in fresco by Monachesi."[117]

One of the city's most active art patrons was the engraver Col. Cephas G. Childs. It was he who procured for the Pennsylvania Academy of the Fine Arts Benjamin West's masterpiece *Death on a Pale Horse*. Between 1827 and 1830 Childs published in parts his *Views in Philadelphia and Its Environs*, and in 1829 he became interested in lithography, the city's first lithographic firm having been established the year before. His major contribution to this art of inexpensive reproduction was bringing to Philadelphia an expert French lithographer, Peter S. Duval. Duval, and his competitor J. T. Bowen, turned out some of the most important lithographic artwork of the times, notably Thomas L. McKenny's and James Hall's three-volume *History of the Indian Tribes of North America*, John James Audubon's octavo *Birds of America*, and also the naturalist's *Quadrupeds of North America*.[118]

A pictorial process cheaper yet than lithography was at hand. On the afternoon of October 16, 1839, Joseph Saxton leaned out of a window at the mint, where he was employed, pointed a contraption housed in a cigar box at nearby Central High School, and took perhaps the first American daguerreotype. Other inventive Philadelphians immediately turned their hands to this fascinating innovation. Ralph Cornelius, a lamp manufacturer, obtained the first picture of a human face ever taken by Louis Daguerre's process. Dr. Paul Beck Goddard of the University of Pennsylvania improved on the technique, and in January 1840 made the first successful attempt at interior photography.[119] While many rejoiced at the prospect of cheap pictures, others had cause to mourn. Peter F. Rothermel, a promising young portrait painter, gave up portraiture, blaming loss of business on the daguerreotype.[120] The years that lay ahead were to bring a sharp decline in the quality of oil painting in Philadelphia, and with mass production and garish color processes, a falling off in the charm that had characterized lithographic work of the 1830s.

XII

However, Philadelphia in the 1830s survives visually in the hundreds of scenes drawn by its artists on stone. The elegance, color, ostentatious pride, and activity of the day vibrate in these exuberant prints. Never before had Philadelphians lived in so vivacious a style. The sober veil of Quaker origins had been rent to shreds; there was a sense of elation and gaiety in these times of accomplishment, of intense individualism held in check by pleasant formality, an ordered discipline.

Rowing clubs began to hold regattas on the Schuylkill in 1834, their members suitably dressed for the sport and their boats colored to suit their fancy. The *Metamora* barge was painted vermilion with a gold stripe; her rowers wore Canton hats, white jackets trimmed with blue, and white pantaloons. She competed against the *Sylph*, orange with red gunwales, her members clad in dark trousers, pink striped shirts, and red and white caps.[121]

There had never been so many stirring parades as in this day of fresh and ardent patriotism. The magnificence of the militia's uniforms was recorded by William H. Huddy and Peter S. Duval in their *U. S. Military Magazine.* The triennial processions of the fire companies were gorgeous, circus-like. Each company had its distinctive dress (one was garbed as Turks). Their engines and hose carriages, nearly all of them superbly decorated by Woodside, were drawn on these occasions by horses ridden by boys in fancy costumes. The officers, carrying silver speaking trumpets, were preceded by buglers and by standard bearers holding aloft imaginatively painted banners. Bands of music interspersed the column. Flowers and flags festooned the equipment. In the 1833 parade the William Penn Hose Company was led by members dressed as Penn, Indians, and Quakers, accompanied by seamen who bore gifts offered at the famous treaty.[122]

The most stupendous parade in these years took place in 1832 on the centennial of Washington's birth. At 10:30 that morning 15,000 marchers fell into line, headed by eighteen pioneers, large, athletic men in white frocks and leather caps, carrying axes. Next came a trumpeter and then the chief marshal, Col. Clement C. Biddle, whose father had been a marshal in the Grand Federal Procession of 1788. Included in the parade were the city's officials, the military, the fire companies, and the various trades, many of them in their individual full-dress attire. On elaborate floats, printers were busy with their press and handed out broadsides; the bakers served bread hot from their oven; tobacconists distributed "segars." The master mariners sailed up Chestnut Street in an amply manned full-rigged ship. From time to time a hand in the mizzen chains heaved the lead and announced the depth to the pilot. Every time the vessel came to a temporary halt her anchor was cast. The celebration, "the most imposing spectacle that has ever been exhibited at Philadelphia," concluded at Independence Hall, where William Rawle read Washington's Farewell Address and Bishop William White delivered a prayer.[123]

Parades of another sort marked the passing of famous men. On Girard's death in 1831, Bishop White's in 1836, Dr. Philip Syng Physick's in 1837, and Mathew Carey's in 1839, those who did not follow the coffin to the grave lined the streets through which it passed. Girard's funeral was the largest the city had yet seen; there were 3000 in the procession and 20,000 watchers. The head of Dr. Physick's funeral column had nearly reached Christ Church burial ground before its rear had left his house on Fourth Street. Carey was followed to the grave by unprecedented thousands of mourners.[124] The interest thus expressed, the ceremonial attention, reflected the close, personal feelings of involvement that characterized the Philadelphian of that day.

The town meeting furnished another outlet for demonstrations of public interest. When Chief Justice John Marshall died at Mrs. Crim's Walnut Street boardinghouse in 1835, the public met to record its respect. Bishop White presided and Joseph R. Ingersoll delivered the eulogy.[125] Silver presentations were another form of tribute and appreciation. On July 4, 1834, Mathew Carey was honored with a silver service in testimony to his public conduct. The old printer's friends deemed Carey's "whole career in life an encouraging example, by the imitation of which, without the aid of official station or political power, every private citizen may become a public benefactor." Most presentation pieces were made by Thomas Fletcher, although Carey's came from another silversmith, R. & W. Wilson.[126] Yet another form of tribute was the testimonial dinner. The English dramatist James Sheridan Knowles was thus honored in 1834, and in 1837, 200 of the city's cultural elite dined with Edwin Forrest at the Merchants' Hotel.[127]

In these prosperous years, fortunate Philadelphians lived very well, summering at inland watering resorts or at Long Branch and Cape May. Those who did not go out of town patronized Swaim's baths at Seventh and Sansom, an elegant establishment with forty-four baths and showers as well as a swimming pool for children. For ice cream there was no equal to Parkinson's, where one sat on sofas and dined off small marble tables. With its marble mosaic floor, its ceiling a glorious picture of the marriage of Jupiter and Juno by Monachesi, Parkinson's represented refinement *par excellence.*[128]

For bucolic pleasures, the drive to the Falls of Schuylkill was most pictur-esque, and the catfish and coffee to be had at the taverns there formed a favorite meal. Closer at hand, nature could be enjoyed at various botanical gardens and nurseries, such as Bartram's (run by Robert Carr), Daniel Maupay's, and the Landreths', which sold seeds and plants all over the coun-try and also to Europe and South America.[129] In the city proper were the public squares. In 1825 the city Councils gave them names—Penn, Logan, Washington, Franklin, Rittenhouse, and Independence.[130] By 1837 when the cemetery on Franklin Square was obliterated, they had nearly all been exten-sively improved with walks and plantings. On Washington Square fifty varie-ties of trees flourished.[131] Philadelphia's interest in flowers and shrubs was stimulated by the founding of the Pennsylvania Horticultural Society in 1828 with Horace Binney as president.

The city offered a wide range of entertainment, the most rewarding of which was a visit to the new marble Museum Building, opened at Ninth and Sansom on July 4, 1838. After ten years at the Arcade, the Peale family collection was moved to this location, where could be seen some of the best exhibits in the country. Its "grand saloon," 233 feet long, 64 feet wide, and a towering 32 feet in height, was said to be the largest room in America. In its center stood the prodigious skeleton of Peale's mastodon. In one of its lower rooms was Nathan Dunn's Chinese Collection, which he had assembled during a long residence in Canton. Some seventy to eighty life-size figures in costumes from that of mandarin to coolie, Chinese rooms and shops, landscapes and portraits, ship models and numerous other objects illustrated the arts, manners, pleasures, and characteristics of the celestial race.[132] A block from the museum, the Assembly Building offered the best facilities for balls and receptions. Its great hall, with its immense mirrors, rich pilasters, Corin-thian capitals, and gilded moldings, was likened to Aladdin's palace.[133] Here Signor Antonio Blitz, one of the most popular entertainers of the time, performed with his trained birds, his sleight-of-hand and magical tricks, and his feats of ventriloquism.[134] And as for the theater, staid Philadelphians were surprised to note that in 1840 there were seven of them in nightly operation.[135]

The glamor of the stage had its attractions for the city's men of letters. Dr. Robert Montgomery Bird, without doubt Philadelphia's ablest literary figure, created the role of Spartacus in *The Gladiator* for Forrest. In this part the famous thespian won ovations in New York, Philadelphia, and London. By 1853 this play had been performed a thousand times.[136] Another distinguished actor, Junius Brutus Booth, acted the principal role in *Sartorius*, a drama by David Paul Brown, one of the city's leading orators and criminal lawyers. Showing unusual modesty, Brown thought that it was not so remarkable that he "should have written two bad plays, but that he had been able to write any."[137] James Nelson Barker, collector of the Port of Philadelphia and for-mer mayor, was yet another dramatist. In 1836 one of his plays was performed at the Arch Street Theatre.[138]

For those not interested in the theater there was the field of sports to cultivate. Each year the United Bowmen celebrated their anniversary with a shoot attended by immense crowds. In white pantaloons, green caps, and frock coats trimmed with gold, the archers marched in ordered array from target to target, delivering their shafts with grace and precision to the music of Frank Johnson's band.[139] At Nicetown's Hunting Park, one of the leading tracks in the country in the 1830s, trotting races were all the rage. These races were under saddle, not sulky-drawn events. At Carlton, his Germantown estate, John C. Craig had his own racetrack and a large stud of race horses, whose portraits by Edward Troye hung on his walls.[140] Gen. Callender Irvine, a Philadelphian who seems to have preferred to race his horses at Saratoga, owned thirty-eight thoroughbreds at the time of his death in 1841.[141] Probably the city's outstanding horseman was George Cadwalader, grandson of Gen. John Cadwalader who had presided over the Jockey Club during George Washington's visit to attend the races in 1773. In October 1840 a diarist who crossed the Delaware to see the races at the Camden track recorded that "A great crowd was there. Three horses ran 4 mile heats. . . . George Cadwalader was there in the most complete and stylish equipage I ever saw. A barouche and four superb dark brown horses. The celebrated Ned Forrest, the fastest trotter in the world, and a steed of matchless beauty, was one of the leaders. . . . I suppose no man in this country or elsewhere can turn out such a splendid team. He had two servants in livery with him."[142]

A yachtsman and devotee of duck shooting, Cadwalader had a zest for all the good things in life and enjoyed the company of those similarly inclined. In 1834 he was a founder of Philadelphia's first city club in the modern sense, an organization appropriately named the Philadelphia Club. Sixteen years later the club moved into the Thomas Butler mansion at Walnut and Thirteenth Streets, where it remains to this day.[143]

In the pursuit of business and pleasure Philadelphians did not overlook the promotion of worthy causes. While most leading citizens participated in such work, four men were outstanding: Bishop White, an Episcopalian, was remarkable, nothing ever keeping him from the ballot box or attendance at public meetings of a religious or philanthropic nature; Roberts Vaux, a Quaker, a leading promoter of public schools and abolitionism, was active in many charities;[144] Alexander Henry, a Presbyterian, was president of the American Sunday School Union, and an officer of most other benevolent organizations of note; and Mathew Carey, a Catholic, had closest at heart the welfare of the poor. The promotion of temperance attracted them all, while the more controversial Sabbatarian movement was led by Robert Ralston and Henry, whose followers pledged "to refrain from all secular employment on that day, from travelling in steam boats, stages, canal boats, or otherwise, except in cases of necessity or mercy." Attempts were made to persuade the packet lines operating between Philadelphia, New York, and Baltimore not to run on Sundays.[145]

A more successful effort at moral improvement was that of Philadelphia reformers interested in penitentiaries. They championed the "Pennsylvania

System"—solitary confinement with labor—which was enacted into law in 1829 and was subsequently copied all over Europe. Cherry Hill, the Eastern State Penitentiary designed by Haviland, had large cells suitable for one-man workshops, and the cells were provided with high-walled exercise pens where individual prisoners could secure fresh air while remaining completely secluded. The theory was that solitary confinement prevented the prisoner from being contaminated by others and afforded the assurance that when he left prison he would at least be no worse than when he entered it. Solitude, forcing reflection, was considered a powerful moral medicine. Labor was necessary because it calmed the mind, made solitary confinement possible, and restored self-respect.[146]

Another reform, akin to the above, dealt with the growing concern over the treatment of juvenile delinquents, who were miserably lodged in the jails and almshouses. New York had opened its House of Refuge for juvenile offenders in 1825, and Boston had followed in 1826. Under John Sergeant's leadership the Philadelphia House of Refuge was built at Fairmount Avenue and Fifteenth Street, and received its first inmates in 1828.[147]

Yet another reform was the abolition of imprisonment for debt, just in time to render purposeless Walter's new Egyptian debtor's prison at Moyamensing. Of the 817 persons imprisoned for debt in Philadelphia between June 1829 and February 1830, it is of interest to note that 30 owed debts of less than one dollar; 233 owed between one and five dollars; only 98 owed more than $100.[148]

The benefactions of the period, which included Dr. Jonas Preston's bequest of the Preston Retreat, a lying-in charity for married women in indigent circumstances, and James Wills's bequest of the Wills Hospital "for the Indigent Blind and Lame," were overshadowed by Stephen Girard's action in leaving virtually all his estate to the city. The richest man in the country, Girard's property had a book value of more than $6 million; its true value was beyond anyone's wildest imagination. The chief feature of his will was the creation of Girard College for "poor white male orphans."[149]

It is doubtful that the city's black population—about one Philadelphian out of twelve in 1830[150]—was irritated by Girard's restriction of his college to whites. Segregation was the practice of the day. By coincidence the year of Girard's death, 1831, was the year that the first major effort was made by people of color in America for the improvement of their general condition. A "national convention" consisting of sixteen delegates from five states met in Philadelphia that June. Although not much was accomplished, the call for the meeting points up the fact that there was a growing black middle class in the city. It supported a Philadelphia Library Company of Colored Persons, various debating societies, lyceums and literary clubs, sixteen churches, and sixty-four benevolent organizations. James Cornish, Robert Purvis, and the Rev. William Douglass were among the leaders of the black community. Philadelphia black Protestantism grew rapidly, for blacks found religion the most congenial sphere in which to develop their talents.[151]

The feelings of the white laboring class were easily incensed against the blacks. Negro competition in the labor market was resented, and the activities of abolitionists frequently infuriated the mob and led to race riots.[152] It was an indication of the mood of the times that the Pennsylvania constitution of 1838, otherwise a Jacksonian document widening popular participation in state politics, deprived black men of the franchise which they had exercised under the constitution of 1790.

Although the mayor claimed with some reason that 99 percent of Philadelphia's citizens were opposed to abolition,[153] the city nevertheless maintained its Quaker-led priority in the antislavery movement. It was in Philadelphia that the American Anti-Slavery Society was founded in 1833, and the Pennsylvania Anti-Slavery Society in 1837,[154] and it was there that John Greenleaf Whittier took over the editorship of the *Pennsylvania Freeman* the following year.

Although the crescendo of antislavery activity was directed solely toward

A Sunday Morning View of the African Episcopal Church of St. Thomas in Philadelphia—Taken in June 1829, *lithograph by David Kennedy and William Lucas (act. 1829–1835) after W. L. Breton (c. 1773–1855). The church, on the west side of Fifth Street below Walnut, opened for services in 1794.*

the good of the African race, it brought disastrous consequences to Philadelphia's Negro community in the 1830s and sadly worsened that community's position. Antislavery came to be regarded as subversive; any action taken against it seemed legal. Mobs saw themselves in the role of patriots defending the established order against enemy encroachments. The abolitionist movement was deemed by many a conspiracy against the nation fomented by British agents. The alternative to slavery was regarded as either race war or miscegenation, and the charge that abolitionists desired a mixture of races could always stir up the brutality of the mob. The reaction to the antislavery crusade was thus an upsurge of violence in America in the mid-1830s. It affected all parts of the country and became a feature of American life.[155]

Those who bore the brunt of this disorder were the Negroes rather than the abolitionists. Turning public opinion against the blacks also was the rancor of the newly arrived Irish who found themselves competing with them for jobs. Attacks on Negroes by the Irish and others during the 1830s were distressingly frequent for a City of Brotherly Love.[156] Houses were burned, people were injured, several were killed in a series of race riots. In August 1835 rioters indulged themselves somewhat more picturesquely by emulating the Boston Tea Party. They seized a mass of antislavery pamphlets, took them to the middle of the Delaware River, and consigned them in small pieces to the water.[157]

The most spectacular violence of the period occurred in May 1838, when the unpopular abolitionists, unable to secure meeting rooms, dedicated a large,

Frontispiece from Pennsylvania Hall Association, History of Pennsylvania Hall, which was Destroyed by a Mob, on the 17th of May, 1838 *(Philadelphia: Merrihew and Gunn, 1838).*

handsome building of their own, Pennsylvania Hall, as a place where freedom of speech could be enjoyed. The Anti-Slavery Convention of American Women met there shortly after the hall was opened, and blacks and whites promenaded arm in arm. This was too much for the temper of the times. Inflamed beyond control, a mob burned the building to the ground. "Such is the force of public opinion when provoked!!!" approved the usually liberal Samuel Breck. "The abolitionist must be put down, or the Union of these states will be dissolved."[158] But the burning of Pennsylvania Hall only strengthened the antislavery cause. A reaction set in and the far more serious violence that was to mark Philadelphia's ensuing decade was to be directed at Irish Roman Catholics rather than at Negroes, a stroke, it might seem, of poetic justice.

Much of the city's laboring class, its factory and dock workers, was composed of recent Irish immigrants, a factor that presented a massive challenge to the Roman Catholic bishop. He found himself faced with an urgent need for more priests and churches. The Diocese of Philadelphia in 1828 had only thirty-two priests, twenty-five of them of Irish birth. To train new ones, Bishop Francis Patrick Kenrick established the seminary of St. Charles Borromeo in 1832. The 1830s were a great church-building period for the Catholics. Wherever manufacturing interests had attracted many Irish a church was built—among them St. John's in Manayunk in 1831; St. Michael's in Kensington in 1834; for the coal-heavers, St. Patrick's on the east bank of the Schuylkill in 1839; and St. Philip de Neri in Southwark in 1840. Also to serve the constantly increasing Irish-Catholic population, Bishop Kenrick established St. Mary's Moyamensing Cemetery.[159]

Probably the denomination most severely affected by the egalitarian impulse that characterized the Age of Jackson was the Society of Friends, which experienced in 1827 the Hicksite-Orthodox Separation, dividing it into two parts which have been reunited only in recent years. The causes for the separation were complex. In part it was a reaction against the wealthy, urban-dwelling businessmen who dominated the Philadelphia meetings, a struggle between aristocracy and democracy. The Hicksites, who took their name from Elias Hicks, were mainly traditionalists driven by a desire to preserve old ways of worship and to function under a weak central organization.[160] Whether Hicksite or Orthodox, the Quakers zealously adhered to the basic elements of their discipline. When Mrs. Roberts Vaux, for example, learned in 1838 that her son, a future mayor of Philadelphia but at the time a young attaché of the American legation in London, had danced with Queen Victoria at her coronation ball, the old lady remarked: "I hope my son Richard will not marry out of Meeting."[161]

Another influence in the Age of Jackson that disquieted religious circles was the rising controversy over slavery. The Unitarians were particularly affected by it. In 1825 William Henry Furness started his fifty-year career as the first full-time ordained minister of the city's small Unitarian congregation. His success was extraordinary. Three years after his installation the Unitarians found it necessary to build a new church seating nearly three times the number accommodated by the former building. The serenity of Furness's congregation was severely jolted in 1839, however, when he became an ardent, tireless, and outspoken abolitionist. Many influential parishioners abandoned his church in protest.[162]

Throughout these years agitation of a less alarming and more acceptable kind was directed toward the necessity of establishing a system of free public education. This was one of the goals promoted by William Heighton in the interest of labor. Another persistent advocate was Joseph R. Chandler, himself a former schoolteacher. Editorials in his *United States Gazette* consistently backed proposals that the necessary laws be passed. The man who spearheaded the drive for legislative action from 1818 to 1834 was the ubiquitous Roberts Vaux, head of the Philadelphia school system and president of the Pennsylvania Society for the Promotion of Public Schools. Thanks largely to Samuel Breck, a Philadelphia legislator, and to much favorable propaganda, the Pennsylvania Assembly passed the Free School Law of 1834, which, as amended in 1836, became the basis of a statewide system of tax-supported schools. Grade schools now replaced the primitive, monitorial Lancastrian system. The act of 1836 also authorized the establishment of Philadelphia's Central High School. The first in the country, Central High opened in 1838 on Juniper Street east of Penn Square, where its building was photographed a year later by Joseph Saxton. Alexander Dallas Bache served as its first principal.[163]

Central High School, Juniper Street (photograph made c. 1854). Originally on the present site of John Wanamaker's Department Store, Central High School is now at Ogontz and Olney Avenues.

Professional life in Philadelphia went more even-tempered, or complacent, ways. In the second quarter of the century the city's bar, continuing its leadership in almost every facet of civic and cultural life, was brilliantly headed by William Rawle, Horace Binney, John Sergeant, Charles Chauncey, Joseph R. and Charles J. Ingersoll, and John M. Scott. When the bar assembled of a morning, the courtroom, thronged with elegantly dressed gentlemen of refined manners, more nearly resembled a drawing room.[164] Distinguished for learning, ability, and eloquence, these were men of high professional honor and moral worth. Many of them served a term or two in Congress.

Their versatility was well expressed in their historical interests. William Rawle, first president of the Historical Society of Pennsylvania, contributed articles to its *Memoirs.* Charles J. Ingersoll found time to write a four-volume history of the War of 1812; his brother Joseph R. Ingersoll was the Historical Society's fifth president. From Binney's pen came *The Leaders of the Old Bar of Philadelphia* and countless pamphlets. "C. C." and "J. S.," the authors of a history of the French Revolution published in Philadelphia in 1830, are believed to be Charles Chauncey and John Sergeant. Sergeant's eminence in law and government is attested by his selection as the Whig vice-presidential candidate in 1832, and by the offers he received of a seat on the United States Supreme Court, a cabinet position, and the mission to England, all of which he declined.

The city's medical profession was no less eminent than its lawyers, for Philadelphia was still the most advanced medical center in America, with the oldest and largest medical schools, hospitals, and libraries.[165] Even after the death of the famous Dr. Physick, when his son-in-law Dr. Jacob Randolph became the leading surgeon, Philadelphia more than held its own. In fact with the establishment of Jefferson Medical College by Dr. George McClellan in 1825 the city strengthened its position. By 1841 Jefferson had an outstanding faculty, including such notable names as Robley Dunglison, Thomas D. Mütter, Charles D. Meigs, John K. Mitchell, and Franklin Bache.[166]

In addition to the activities of its many distinguished practitioners, specialists, and professors in the medical schools, notable advances were made in hitherto neglected areas of medical science and rehabilitation. In 1833 Julius R. Friedlander, backed by John Vaughan and Roberts Vaux, founded Philadelphia's famous school for the blind, with Bishop White as its first president.[167] About the same time Dr. Thomas Kirkbride undertook his pioneer work in the treatment of mental diseases, which led to his becoming superintendent of the Pennsylvania Hospital's department for the insane, better known as "Kirkbride's." In another area of medicine Dr. Isaac Hays, a specialist in diseases of the eye and an outstanding surgeon, was from 1826 to 1869 the editor of the *American Journal of the Medical Sciences,* which had been founded under another name in 1820 by Dr. Nathaniel Chapman.[168] In publishing medical material, the city had early won an unequalled reputation, one that it has retained.

Unquestionably the most dramatic and terrible challenge faced by the physicians of this time was the cholera epidemic of 1832. The disease had appeared in India on the banks of the Ganges in 1817 and started on its course around the world. In 1832 it reached Canada and then spread over the eastern part of the United States, arriving in Philadelphia in July. Carey and Lea, the country's leading publisher of medical books, promptly issued the *Cholera Gazette*, edited by Dr. Isaac Hays. This weekly publication informed the public of the progress of the disease and its treatment. With sixty to seventy people dying daily of the plague, Henry Carey wrote to James Fenimore Cooper: "The People now read only the Cholera Gazette."[169] Some 2314 cases of cholera and 985 deaths were reported by October when the pestilence disappeared. As a testimonial to the heroic role of the medical profession in battling the infection, the city Councils presented thirteen silver pitchers to the physicians who had been in charge of the hospitals, among whom were Nathaniel Chapman, John K. Mitchell, W. E. Horner, Charles D. Meigs, and Hugh L. Hodge.

Many literary journals made their appearance at this time, covering subjects of more cheerful note than that of the *Cholera Gazette*. In 1826 Samuel C. Atkinson started *The Casket*, a monthly magazine. Robert Walsh's serious *The American Quarterly Review* began its appearances the following year. *Godey's Lady's Book*, specializing in fashions, was brought out by Louis A. Godey in 1830. Among its contributors was Eliza Leslie, a prolific writer on subjects of interest to women. In 1836 she started her annual, *The Gift*, printing in its first issue Edgar Allan Poe's "MS Found in a Bottle." Subsequently she was editor of *Miss Leslie's Magazine*.

Poe came to Philadelphia, then the hub of the American publishing world, in 1837, and there he wrote many of his most famous stories and poems. In 1839 he became William E. Burton's assistant editor on *The Gentleman's Magazine*. This association was not entirely happy, and Poe hoped to edit a journal of his own, *The Penn Magazine*, but was unable to arouse sufficient interest.[170] Meanwhile George R. Graham had come on the scene, purchasing *The Casket* in 1839, and shortly after, *The Gentleman's Magazine*, merging the two in 1841 into the very successful *Graham's Magazine*.

Although Philadelphia failed to produce literary figures of lasting renown, she had in Henry Carey, Mathew's son, the leading political economist of the day. His three-volume *Principles of Political Economy* came out between 1837 and 1840. The want of literary genius did not discourage publishers, however. Under Henry Carey's leadership the publishing house of Carey and Lea dominated Philadelphia's and the nation's book trade. It was the publisher of James Fenimore Cooper and Washington Irving, active in the reprint trade of English authors, notably Sir Walter Scott and Charles Dickens, and dominant in the field of medical texts. When Henry Carey retired in 1838 the firm's great rival, Harper and Brothers, captured for New York preeminence in yet another field.[171]

Henry Carey had witnessed a revolution in the technique of printing. To begin with better presses were invented, and after 1825 the cylinder press replaced the old flat-bed press. Within a few years steam power was adapted to its use. Other technological advances in typesetting and printing methods —most important, stereotype plates—and in papermaking made possible cheap, mass production of books and at the same time unleashed a flood of newsprint upon the community in the 1830s.[172]

For news, Philadelphia continued to be served by more than a dozen papers, a fluid field with new papers being offered and mergers and sales removing old ones. In 1829 the *Philadelphia Inquirer* (first known as the *Pennsylvania Inquirer*) was launched as an organ dedicated to the principles of Andrew Jackson. It did not prosper and was soon acquired by Jesper Harding, a Bible publisher. Under Harding the *Inquirer* became a leading journal, broke with the Democrats, and assuming a tone of gentility, was deferential to commercial interests.[173]

In 1839 the *North American* was established, a paper that was destined to become most influential. It promptly swallowed up Zachariah Poulson's *American Daily Advertiser*, the oldest daily in the country. Since 1800 Poulson's had been a favorite with Philadelphia conservatives, a safe-and-sound family paper. The famous old *United States Gazette*, a Philadelphia fixture since 1790, was also to be sold to the *North American* a few years later. Under the guidance of Joseph R. Chandler, the *Gazette* was considered an infallible authority by many readers throughout the 1830s, and evidenced a mild Whig character while paying studious attention to the interests of trade and commerce.

The sale of newspapers had been limited by their high prices, six cents for the better ones. But in the 1830s the new printing processes and cheaper paper made possible the penny paper. In 1833 Benjamin Day brought out the *New York Sun*, that city's first popular penny gazette. Two years later James Gordon Bennett, after an unsuccessful newspaper career in Philadelphia, created an even more successful penny paper in his *New York Herald*. Philadelphia's first penny journal was the *Public Ledger*, founded in 1836. It had a lurid appeal in its handling of police reports and other sensational matters, and it gained notoriety through libel suits. So well did it flourish that its proprietors established a similar paper in Maryland, the *Baltimore Sun*. William M. Swain, editor of the *Ledger*, shocked Philadelphia's staid newspaper world with his innovations. Rather than waiting for news to be delivered to his office, he sent reporters about town, a most undignified procedure. The few reporters employed by the city's papers used to meet once a day to pool information. The *Public Ledger* was the first to hire enough reporters to free itself of this exchange method and to insist on exclusive news coverage. It was the policy of this enterprising sheet, moreover, to route newsboys through the streets, soliciting sales; other papers either mailed their issues or decorously delivered them to subscribers' doorsteps. Before long the *Ledger* had the largest circulation in Pennsylvania.

In the stories carried by Philadelphia's newspapers it is possible to trace the public's growing awareness of the city's history, for in the early part of the nineteenth century America began to identify its historical image. Historical societies were founded, sites were honored, documents preserved, historical writings published, and the historical theme found expression in orations, art, the theater, and literature.[174] The impulse that set this trend in action in Philadelphia had been Lafayette's visit in August 1824. Civic-minded citizens were pleased to recall the founding of the city. On October 24 they met in the Letitia House, a building then associated with William Penn, to commemorate the 142nd anniversary of his landing in 1682. Out of this dinner was born the Historical Society of Pennsylvania. "Our Penn Dinner has made a great stir, and is very popular," wrote the philanthropist Roberts Vaux to the antiquarian John Fanning Watson; "The Historical Soc'y will go on, and in short a new current of feeling seems to have set in."[175] The society was founded the next month with William Rawle, a leading member of the bar, as its first president. Rawle was succeeded in 1837 by the even more celebrated Peter S. Du Ponceau, another lawyer of note, a contributor to historical and linguistic literature, and president of the American Philosophical Society. Thus a good and enduring start was made and a worthy stream of publications soon attested to the society's program.

The attractions and importance of history in these years led Deborah Logan of Stenton to arrange and transcribe James Logan's correspondence. In 1827 a monument was erected near the site of the great elm at Kensington to commemorate Penn's treaty of 1682 with the Indians. Two years later, Thomas F. Gordon, a Philadelphia lawyer, published his history of Pennsylvania, and as already noted, in 1830 John Fanning Watson gave to the public the first history of Philadelphia.

Lafayette's visit also awakened interest in the State House (Independence Hall), which had hitherto been accorded little reverence. In 1828 the city Councils retained Strickland to restore its wooden steeple, taken down in 1781, and three years later John Haviland was commissioned to convert its Assembly room, where the Declaration had been signed, "to its ancient form."[176]

The collector was early on the scene. In John McAllister, Jr., an antiquarian who retired from business in 1835 to devote the rest of his long life to gathering materials on the history of Philadelphia, the city rejoiced in the most perceptive of scavengers who preserved significant records which would otherwise have been lost. And in David J. Kennedy, a skilled amateur artist who came to Philadelphia in 1836, the city gained a historically interested person who would record the appearance of its old buildings in hundreds of sketches.[177]

The contributions of these talented, historically interested people were overshadowed, however, by the city's most dynamic and dramatic issue, the future of the Bank of the United States.

XIII

When Nicholas Biddle became president of the bank it was his ambition to give the country better "notes" than it had ever seen before. Aside from the bank's own paper money, that in use was issued by state-chartered banks. There was always the tendency for them to overissue, and from this and other causes their notes had circulated at a discount. In return for a bonus paid for its charter and the services it rendered to the government without charge— the transfer of public money from place to place, the payment of the public debt, of pensions, of salaries for the civil list, the army, and the navy—the bank was made the depository of the public funds. These funds arose principally from taxes paid by importers to customs collectors and were largely in the form of state-bank notes. With these notes in hand the Bank of the United States was a creditor of the state banks, and by presenting their notes for payment could regulate their activities and keep them from lending too much, thereby preventing the depreciation of their paper money.[178]

Not only did the bank, the largest corporation in the nation, enforce a uniform standard of currency; it had eased financial crises and prevented others by the expansion or contraction of its credit facilities. By 1828 there was virtually no criticism heard of its operations. Relations with the bank's largest stockholder, the federal government, were excellent at the close of John Quincy Adams's administration. Secretary of the Treasury Richard Rush termed the institution "an indispensable and permanent adjunct to our political and fiscal system." That the new president, Andrew Jackson, did not harbor such friendly notions was no secret, but Biddle was sure that experience would convince him otherwise.[179] As far as party ideologies were concerned there was not as yet any question over the bank. Biddle himself had voted for Jackson in 1824 and again in 1828; many of his closest advisers, notably Gen. Thomas Cadwalader, were strong Jackson men.

Dissuaded from coming out against the bank in his inaugural address, Jackson raised the question of the bank's recharter in his first annual message to Congress. "Both the constitutionality and the expedience of the law creating the bank are well questioned," he averred, "by a large portion of our fellow-citizens, and it must be admitted that it has failed in the great end of establishing a sound and uniform currency." The currency Jackson wanted was one of hard money. Biddle, on the contrary, believed that a paper currency was the only practical medium of exchange; the country had never had such a currency as Jackson wanted, and it never would have. The parts of Jackson's message relating to the bank were referred to the appropriate committees of the Senate and the House, both of which reported in favor of the bank and its usefulness to the community. The statement from the House controverted the president's reasoning at every point, declaring, as had the Supreme Court, that the bank was constitutional. Moreover, it was highly expedient, and had "actually furnished a circulating medium more uniform than specie."[180]

Jackson's views were not yet party policy. Like many other Democratic leaders, Charles J. Ingersoll disapproved the president's financial theories. In 1831 Ingersoll urged the recharter of the bank in the Democratically controlled Pennsylvania legislature. Resolutions to this effect passed its Senate by a unanimous vote and its lower house by seventy-five to eleven. Despite the overwhelming proportions of these votes the *Globe*, spokesman for the administration in Washington, announced that the bank had purchased the passage of the resolutions by bribery. Ingersoll and his associates branded the accusation "an unfounded and attrocious libel."[181]

In December 1831 Secretary of the Treasury Louis McLane reported in favor of rechartering the bank. That same month the National Republican party, running Henry Clay for president and John Sergeant for vice-president, adopted the recharter of the bank as one of its goals. Cadwalader, after consultation with leaders of both parties, urged Biddle to apply immediately for recharter; there seemed little to be gained by postponing this increasingly agitated question. Accordingly, in January 1832 George Mifflin Dallas, Democratic senator from Pennsylvania, son of the man who had proposed the bank, long a counsel for it, and recently a director, presented Biddle's memorial for a renewal of the charter. Neither Biddle nor Cadwalader thought the application would have the slightest effect on the president's reelection, which they regarded as certain. Thus Biddle professed not to consider the application in an election year as politically motivated. To Ingersoll he wrote: "You know I care nothing about the election. I care only for the interests confided to my care."[182]

The recharter bill passed Congress. But Jackson, having urged the people to take into consideration the recharter of the bank, now that they had done so through their constituted representatives vetoed their decision. His veto message's strength rested in its appeal to the poor against the rich, the West against the East, democracy against privilege.[183] Questioning the very solvency of the bank, Jackson directed the secretary of the treasury to find out whether the public deposits could be considered safe. The Treasury's investigation was undertaken by a Democratic politician who found that there was no question as to the security of the deposits or the solvency of the bank. A congressional investigating committee endorsed this opinion: "there can be no doubt of the entire soundness of the whole Bank capital."[184]

The result of Jackson's veto was the worst possible for the bank, for it made the bank the central issue of the presidential election of 1832, a contest of extraordinary bitterness. Biddle was soon in the thick of it, getting up speeches and arguments for the bank and having them printed and distributed to defend the bank against the heavy attacks being made on it. The administration considered his activities as electioneering against Jackson. Perhaps it is impossible to separate the two, and there has been much criticism of Biddle's throwing the bank into politics. However, few leading men in Philadelphia opposed his activities, and while the defection of such Democrats as George Mifflin Dallas, Charles J. Ingersoll, and Richard Rush brought them political favor, it resulted in their social ostracism at home where an overwhelmingly anti-Jackson vote was registered.[185]

Obsessed by the idea that the bank was a hydra-headed engine of corruption, Jackson viewed his reelection as a mandate to destroy the "monster," which, in his message to Congress in December 1832, he announced was insolvent.[186] Disappointed by the results of all the investigations of the bank, he convoked a meeting of New York bankers to obtain their opinion on the removal of the deposits. Again he was disappointed. They urged him not to do it and repeated advice that he had heard before—removal of the deposits would bring on a financial crisis.[187] Opposed by his secretary of the treasury, he promoted McLane to be secretary of state, replacing him with William J. Duane, a known opponent of recharter from Philadelphia. When Duane refused to obey Jackson's request that he remove the deposits, Jackson dismissed him. Believing that unless the bank was broken it would break his administration, and that the removal of the deposits was "necessary to preserve the morals of the people, the freedom of the press, and the purity of the elective franchise," Jackson appointed Roger B. Taney secretary of the treasury, and the removal of the deposits was ordered, effective October 1, 1833.[188]

The government pledged that funds deposited in the bank would be withdrawn gradually as needed and that no funds would be transferred to state-bank depositories. Partially through the clumsiness of Taney, this pledge was immediately violated, and unannounced drafts totaling more than $2 million began to be presented for instant payment.[189] Faced with the necessity of reducing loans because of the forthcoming loss of the deposits and the closing of the bank itself in 1836, Biddle now feared that Jackson was actually trying to make good his threat to break the bank. There were runs on branches of the bank, as at Savannah, where at the height of a run a government paymaster from Charleston appeared with a Treasury draft to be paid for in specie, refusing to explain why he did not cash it in his own city. Such incidents convinced Biddle that the runs were politically inspired, and indeed such actions had been openly discussed by leaders of the administration.[190] Accordingly, for the safety of the bank Biddle ordered more drastic reductions in credit than would normally have been necessary.

Jackson at first refused to recognize the financial crisis that ensued, and of which he had been warned. But the distress was real, and the petitions that poured in on him from all over to restore the deposits to the bank and thus right the country's economy did nothing to soothe his temper. At length, when it became undeniable that he had placed the safety of the bank beyond Jackson's ability to destroy it, Biddle ordered an easing of credit restrictions and the crisis passed. His action liberalizing loan policy aroused the stern displeasure of many of his friends, including Horace Binney, who declared that Biddle's action was "a complete reversal of the Bank's policy and an abandonment of its only practical weapon of defense against the administration."[191]

The excitement in Philadelphia over the War on the Bank, or as Jackson would put it, the Bank's War on the People, was intense, and throughout the remainder of Jackson's administration the great majority of the city's voters was solidly against Old Hickory. The withdrawal of the deposits was protested as "executive usurpation," and numerous rallies were held during the financial crisis by every sort of trade and organization demanding the return of the deposits. In March 1834 the largest of these gatherings, 50,000 people, assembled at Independence Square. One of the memorials praying for the return of the deposits bore 10,259 signatures.[192]

Biddle proceeded to wind up the bank's affairs and close its branches. At this time, he and the bank stood high in the esteem of the commercial world. "In all the proceedings of this institution," wrote a business commentator, "a calm dignity, a moderation of temper, and a regard to the interests of the country are observable, which contrasts admirably with the perturbed and ferocious spirit that seems to animate its persecutors."[193] At their final meeting the stockholders expressed their entire approbation for the way the bank was run during its last seven years, during which period "the institution has been exposed to both persecution and obloquy, which the public investigation of its transactions, and their undeniable benefit to the nation have enabled them to know were unmerited and unjust."[194]

The failure of the bank five years later lent credence to Jackson's sagacity in having attacked the "monster," and made history's verdict appear that he was right and Biddle wrong. But it should be borne in mind that throughout the period of Jackson's presidency the bank was unquestionably solvent. Its subsequent troubles did not stem from its operations as the national bank.

When Jackson removed the deposits he made it impossible for Biddle to regulate the extension of credit by private banks, and this did much to make the Jacksonian inflation one of the worst in American history. During Jackson's presidency the number of banks in the country increased by 140 percent. Unfettered by control, they fostered a whirlwind of speculation that ended in panic, bankruptcy, and a long depression.[195]

The most notable victim of these disasters was the Bank of the United States, operating after the loss of its federal charter under a charter granted by Pennsylvania. According to the most recent study of this bank, it was "strong, solvent, and liquid" when forced to suspend specie payments in 1837 because of the general paralysis of bank credit occasioned by Jackson's Specie Circular of 1836.[196] Seeking to encourage the hard-money economy so dear to his heart, Jackson had ordered payment for government land to be made only in gold or silver. As a result specie was drained from the great commercial centers of the East, where it was most needed, to the frontier, where it was least needed. Two months after Jackson left office, every bank in the nation suspended specie payments.

In 1838 the Philadelphia banks, following the example set by New York, resumed, and with affairs looking reasonably prosperous, Biddle felt free to resign from the Bank of the United States the following March. Six months later the bank suspended again, as did all the other banks in Pennsylvania, the South, and most of the West. Forced by the legislature to resume in January 1841, it encountered staggering runs on its specie and was soon obliged to close its doors for a final time. In the ensuing panic the city's next two largest banks failed, as did four lesser ones.

The reason for the bank's failure lay in policies that caused its assets to become illiquid and the safety of the bank itself to be tied to the debtor sections of the nation, the South and West. Ever anxious to promote improvement programs, Biddle had subscribed heavily to state bond issues. Anxious to help the southern banks resume in 1838, he had come to their aid. The bank's portfolio, the largest in the country, filled up with state obligations and stocks of all sorts. When the boom ran out, the states, including Pennsylvania, stopped paying interest on their bonds, prices fell, and the bank could not convert its rapidly depreciating assets into liquid funds.

Philadelphia was profoundly shocked by the failure of the Bank of the United States and the disclosures of corruption in other banks. The Schuylkill Bank was ruined by its cashier and the Western Bank was compromised by one of its officers; the president of a local railroad sold its stock by the simple process of filling in blank shares and pocketing the money. In an atmosphere of bitter recrimination, criminal charges were lodged by stockholders against Biddle, but they were later dismissed as without foundation. "It is due to truth to say that his private and personal character has never, to my knowledge, been successfully impeached," observed Martin Van Buren.[197]

Industrial Development
and Social Crisis
1841-1854

by Elizabeth M. Geffen

Day after day in their personal visits did they breathe the pestiferous atmosphere of some degraded or illy-ventilated purlieus, where extremes of filth and misery and loathsome disease met the eye. . . .
— *Report of the Sanitary Committee of the Board of Health,* 1848

This is the fatal evil of Philadelphia—that the riotous and disorderly are convinced of the lukewarmness and timidity of the respectable part of society, and so they take full swing upon every occasion that arises.
— WILLIAM H. FURNESS

How . . . am I able to communicate a just notion of the intelligence, the refinement, the enterprise of Philadelphians—their agreeable and hospitable society, their pleasant evening-parties, their love of literature, their happy blending of the industrial habits of the north with the social usages of the south?
— WILLIAM CHAMBERS [1]

Between 1841 and 1854 Philadelphia came to terms with the industrial revolution. The cost was high and the rewards unevenly distributed. No one enjoyed the increasing noise and congestion of the city's streets, the degeneration of neighborhoods into slums. Workers —men, women, and children—newly regimented to the harsh discipline of factories, smarting under the demeaning impersonality of the emerging corporate order, experienced new anxieties. A new moneyed class, sometimes ill-mannered, challenged the old aristocracy for positions of power and won them with increasing frequency.

Contradictory and paradoxical readings of the significance of events destroyed consensus. Some Philadelphians deplored an apparent decline in public taste, while others rejoiced in the upward surge of the "common man." Some profited from novel opportunities for making great fortunes; others found themselves for the first time ground down into a poverty from which there was no escape. The period was marked by unprecedented civic violence, arising from many causes: an explosive increase in population; a complex and unreconciled ethnic, racial, and religious mixture; inadequate housing; a growing and ever more obvious maldistribution of wealth; a volatile social class structure—all exacerbated by political ineptitude or chicanery or a combination of both. With the political consolidation of city and county in 1854, Philadelphia at length worked out a formula for the reasonably peaceful coexistence of its conflicting constituencies. In the process it completed shedding its old identity as a seaport city on the eighteenth-century model and became definitively a nineteenth-century industrial city.

The civic transformation of the 1840s and 1850s sprang from old roots. The technological earthquake of the industrial revolution had long been gathering force beneath the foundation of the old way of life. From nearly the beginning of the century to 1841 the city had created the technological pattern for its future development. A massive reordering of the economy was achieved in the 1840s and early 1850s, and by 1854 the city had consolidated its position as the dynamic center of the most highly industrialized area in the United States. Of logical necessity its social and ideological adjustment to the new order lagged behind its technological achievements, and herein lay the basis for social misery and public alarm.

I

The year 1841 began in ice. The old year had gone out in hail, rain, and snow, and on January 1 the city was frozen stiff. "It will, perhaps, long be remembered by the present generation," wrote a contemporary historian, "that in the year 1841, there was, comparatively, no spring. Winter commenced on the 15th of November, and continued until the 15th of May."[2] Nature offered compensatory joys, however: the sleighing was excellent. "A large number of sleighs [went] dashing up and down the streets, the bells ringing out clear and sweet, the ladies looking rosy and animated, and full of glee, the gentlemen carefully wrapped up, and criticizing the comparative merits of their own and their neighbor's 'turn-out.' "[3] Suddenly, in typical Philadelphia fashion, the weather changed. A great thaw broke up masses of ice in the Delaware and sent floods roaring down the Schuylkill, inundating the western part of the city two blocks from the river. Extracting God's Providence from every calamity, one citizen noted that happily the poor were able to pick up enough driftwood to keep their home fires burning for the rest of the winter.[4] Prophetically, these days captured much of the essence of the entire period 1841–1854.

The city plunged into profound depression, psychic as well as economic, in February, when the Bank of the United States closed its doors for the last time. "If a volcano had opened its fiery jaws in our midst," Job Tyson wrote some years later, "or an earthquake had shaken the firmest edifices to their foundations, the popular terror could not have been more complete, the distress and dismay could not have been more painful and pervading." In April, James Fenimore Cooper, in town to confer with his publisher, wrote to his wife: "Philadelphia is struck by a paralysis."[5]

Nonetheless all vital signs indicated that Philadelphia was not only alive but growing at an unprecedented rate. The population of the city and its surrounding area increased 58 percent in the decade of the 1840s and another 38.3 percent in the 1850s, posing a staggering logistical problem in itself; but the difficulties were further intensified by the pattern of population distribution. Within the limits of the city proper the increase in the 1840s was 29.5 percent, from 93,665 in 1840 to 121,376 in 1850, while in the adjacent districts there was a 74.8 percent increase, from 164,372 in 1840 to 287,386 in 1850. A significant part of the increase was foreign-born. Debarkations at the port of Philadelphia quintupled from 3016 in 1849 to 15,511 in 1849, then rose again to 19,211 in 1853; yet thousands of others must have come overland from other ports as well, especially from New York, where 294,818 landed in 1853 alone. By 1850, in a total population of 408,672 in city and county, 121,699 (29.7 percent) were foreign-born. Of these, 72,312 had been born in Ireland, 22,750 in Germany, 17,500 in England. By 1860 Philadelphia's foreign-born population numbered 169,430 out of a total of 565,529. Unprecedentedly large numbers of the newcomers were Catholics, in a city that had always been a center of Protestantism and that in the 1840s had become the general propaganda center of militant anti-Catholicism. The Jewish community was small, numbering perhaps only 1800 in the mid-1840s, but growing at an accelerating rate as a result of increasing immigration from the Rhineland, southern Germany, Alsace, and Poland.[6]

There were 19,833 blacks in city and county in 1840, but this number decreased slightly to 19,761 in 1850, a significant fact in relation to the tremendous increase in the white population and attributable to the hostility and violence that whites directed against blacks in the 1830s and 1840s. In 1848 about one-third of the Negro population of Philadelphia County lived in Moyamensing, with the densest concentration in an area bounded by South and Fitzwater Streets from Fifth to Eighth, where 302 families lived. By 1860 the black population had increased to 22,185, of whom 65.1 percent still remained within the boundaries of the original municipality. The foreign-born, however, showed almost exactly the reverse pattern, with only 37.9 percent within the original city limits and 62.1 percent in the outer wards.[7]

To house the growing multitude the total number of dwellings in Philadelphia County increased from 53,078 in 1840 to 61,278 in 1850, about 23,600 more than in New York in the latter year. One Philadelphian, hoping to demonstrate the superiority of his native city to New York, calculated that Philadelphia in 1850 had only six and two-thirds persons per house, while New York had thirteen and five-eights. (Most of the new Philadelphia houses, to be sure, were two- or three-stories high, while New York's were taller and for multifamily use.) The number of houses increased to 89,979 by 1860 but still fell increasingly short of needs.[8]

More and more of the prosperous moved westward. Luxurious single homes and handsome new rows of dwellings with white marble steps and large-pane windows began to appear on tree-shaded sidewalks well beyond

Broad Street. By 1854, "The fashionable quarter, 'par excellence,' [was] south of Market street and west of Seventh street; but Walnut Street [was] the 'ton' street of the quarter. This region [was] thronged with spacious and elegant residences, built of sandstone, granite, marble, and fine-pressed or stuccoed brick, giving abundant evidence of affluence, taste, and luxurious ease, and comfort."[9] Many had garden yards, fragrant in the summertime with grape-vines, roses, honeysuckle, and clematis, which with the thick foliage of the trees produced an effect a contemporary found "indescribable and inconceiva-ble" in the midst of a populous city.[10] Many costly and ornate churches were built in the newly populous western section of the old city limits. Two of the most beautiful, in the Gothic Revival style, were on Locust Street: Calvary Presbyterian, above Fifteenth, and John Notman's St. Mark's Protestant Epis-

Interior of the Cathedral of Saints Peter and Paul, Logan Square, under construction 1846–1864. The cathedral was designed by John Notman (1810–1865) and Napoleon Le Brun (1821–1901) in association with church officials.

copal, a block farther west.[11] The largest and most spectacular of all would be the sandstone Roman-style Roman Catholic Cathedral of Sts. Peter and Paul by Napoleon Le Brun and later by Notman as well, being built on Logan Square.

Satellite communities expanded: Mantua, "a beautiful little village" on the high and airy ground across the Schuylkill opposite Fairmount, containing several country seats as well as the homes of many who worked in the city; Hamilton, "probably the prettiest village in the neighborhood of Philadelphia," about a mile west of the Market Street Bridge on the road to West Chester; Powelton, a new village between Philadelphia and Mantua; to the northeast, Nicetown, Germantown, Mount Airy, and Chestnut Hill.[12] By 1854 all of these bustled with new life, "thronged with cottages and villas."[13] Property values soared. One astute businessman in October 1849 bought thirty-one acres in Germantown from a private owner at $150 per acre and nineteen acres at public sale for $240 per acre. Two years later the adjoining land cost him $500 per acre.[14]

Three miles to the northeast on the Delaware River stood the new town of Port Richmond, which became the District of Richmond in 1847, the

Italian Villa, *lithograph by P. S. Duval after Samuel Sloan (1815–1884), from Sloan's* The Model Architect *(2 vols.; Philadelphia: John Leslie, 1852). Suburban villas designed by Sloan and other architects began to proliferate in the northern and western sections of Philadelphia with the extension of railroad lines and the consolidation of the city and county. A house of this design, built in 1854, stands in Chestnut Hill on Bethlehem Pike opposite the terminus of the Chestnut Hill Rail Road, also completed in 1854.*

eastern terminus of the Philadelphia and Reading Railroad, opened to there in 1842. By 1847 property in the district worth only $10,000 ten years previously was priced at $90,000. Two miles beyond Port Richmond lay Bridesburg, a new village of about thirty or forty homes and several business establishments in 1841 which became a borough in 1848.[15] Frankford, about five miles to the northeast, and Manayunk, eight miles west of the city, developed into "aggregations of manufactories" surrounded by the homes of workers. Holmesburg, on the Pennypack Creek about ten miles from the city, was another growing community of mills and other businesses.[16] By the early 1850s "almost every species" of manufacturing "abound[ed] in the suburbs," and almost everywhere was heard "the sound of the loom."[17]

Many old buildings in the heart of the city were replaced in the 1840s and 1850s by new and imposing business structures of red sandstone, granite, and iron. Though they embodied a wide range and mixture of architectural styles, including Greek Revival, Gothic, and Italianate, a British visitor in 1846 found them "much more regular and pleasing in [their] effect than [those] of either Boston or New York."[18] The city's first "skyscraper" was built in 1849–1850 on Chestnut Street below Third for Dr. David Jayne, a patent medicine manufacturer. The design of William L. Johnston, a young architect who died during its construction, its Venetian Gothic façade of Quincy granite soared eight stories, to which Johnston's successor, Thomas U. Walter, added an observation tower and large sculptured druggist's mortars and pestles. The first entirely cast-iron building in Philadelphia was constructed in 1850 of prefabricated units in "modern or florid Italian" style, designed by G. P. Cummings for the Penn Mutual Life Insurance Company on the northeast corner of Third and Dock Streets.[19]

On July 11, 1844, the *Public Ledger* reported that the only house on the south side of Chestnut Street between Eighth and Ninth that was still used exclusively as a dwelling was having its first story converted into a store. By 1854 Chestnut Street from Third westward to Broad had become a fashionable promenade of fine shops and hotels, "the Broadway of Philadelphia."[20] Beginning with the Girard stores, their Third Street facade in ornamented Byzantine and their Chestnut Street side in Italian, a succession of large-pane windows followed in unbroken line. The array of shops brought a notable change in city life, the coming of women to the downtown area in large numbers for the first time.

Market Street also had its impressive business establishments, mostly wholesale importing firms, occupying buildings from three to eight stories high. The market houses that had given the popular name to High Street were ordered demolished by city ordinance in 1853. Ironically, in the same year the city formally changed the name of High Street to Market Street. At the same time the popular names of three other streets were legalized: Mulberry, Sassafras, and Cedar became, respectively, Arch, Race, and South. West of Broad Street, the streets named Schuylkill Eighth to Front were renamed Fifteenth

The Jayne Building, designed by William L. Johnston (1811–1849) and Thomas Ustick Walter (1804–1887), built 1849–1850, demolished 1957, engraving by John M. Butler (act. 1841–1860).

to Twenty-second Streets, respectively, and Ashton Street became Twenty-third.[21]

New hotels were built—the increasingly larger "palaces of the people" that were a new American urban vogue. The American House, which opened in 1844 opposite the State House, contained 105 rooms but only two baths. The Washington House, however, opening on Chestnut Street above Seventh in 1845, boasted of its private baths. The Girard House, on the north side of Chestnut at Ninth, opened in 1852, was designed in the Italianate style of John McArthur, Jr., who used the same style for the La Pierre Hotel on the west side of Broad Street between Chestnut and Sansom, opened in 1853, a herald of the coming movement of hotels from east Chestnut Street to south Broad.[22]

Visitors who stayed at elegant hotels, strolled in the fashionable quarter, visited the famous public institutions, or enjoyed the hospitality of prosperous families were charmed by Philadelphia in these years. Countess Pulszky, who with her husband accompanied the Hungarian exile Louis Kossuth to America in 1850, found "the stamp of wealth and commerce wherever we cast our glance on the buildings and the inhabitants, and we cannot help feeling that the pulsation of life must be strong and genial in these precincts. . . ." William Chambers, an Englishman who visited the United States in the fall of 1853, decided: "There is something more than usually wonderful in the growth of

The Athenaeum of Philadelphia, *built 1845–1847, designed by John Notman (1810–1865), watercolor (c. 1847) by John Notman. Established in 1814 to provide a "set of Reading Rooms," the Athenaeum held a design competition in 1845 for a new building on the east side of Washington Square to house its collections. Notman's winning design was the inspiration for many Italianate buildings erected in Philadelphia in the 1850s.*

ATHENAEUM OF PHILADELPHIA

Philadelphia." Though it was now second in size to New York, it was "second, however, to none in beauty, regularity, and all the blessings attending on good order and intelligence." He found that "So far from being a dull or dismal town, Philadelphia is . . . a remarkably animated city," its streets crowded with fashionable people, its shops filled with luxury goods selected from the finest offerings of Paris and London, and no city in the Union was making more progress in the "unusually elegant style" of its public buildings.[23]

There was another side of Philadelphia's life that such visitors did not see. Many houses abandoned by the affluent deteriorated into cheap boardinghouses or tenements. Bandbox row houses, three stories high, with one room, about ten by twelve feet, on each floor—"Father, Son, and Holy Ghost houses," they were called—filled many courts and alleys running off secondary streets, or lined dead-end walls in the rear of larger houses facing on the street, with access by means of narrow passageways between the front houses. This pattern, well over a century old, proliferated to the saturation point in the 1840s and 1850s and expanded into the working-class districts north and south of the city. A typical, not special, block described by Dr. Isaac Parrish in his 1849 report for the American Medical Association's Committee on Public Hygiene contained six alleys and five closed courts filled with houses, all fronted by pleasant dwellings on the main street.[24]

In the building of their factories Philadelphia's new industrialists, wrote a contemporary admirer, had "not generally been governed by any other than reasons of convenience and economy . . . ; hence the factories are scattered throughout the city and its vicinity . . ." built along railroad lines or by creek, stream, or river.[25] As the city expanded, however, an effort was made to retain open green spaces. Kensington developed Shackamaxon Square, Norris Square, and Fairhill Square. Germantown Square was established in 1854. Logan, Rittenhouse, and Penn Squares—originally Northwest, Southwest, and Centre Squares—in the western part of the city were placed under stringent regulations in 1842 to guard them from abuse, and all were protected by the installation of iron railings in 1852.[26]

The most elaborate park system in the city and ultimately one of its greatest ornaments was initiated in 1844, when the city purchased from the Bank of the United States for $75,000 the Lemon Hill estate that had once been owned by Henry Pratt and later by Isaac S. Loyd. The purpose was to preserve the purity of Schuylkill water from possible pollution which might result if buildings were constructed adjacent to the Fairmount Water Works. For many years the property was leased to a tenant who made it a popular beer garden, and it was not dedicated as a public park, named Lemon Hill Park, until 1855.[27]

Laurel Hill Cemetery held quite as many attractions as any of the parks, however, for not only did its landscaping offer physical escape from the noise, dirt, and general confusion of the city and "a suitable place for the exercise of a pure and enlightened taste for ornament," but its special function provided the stimulus for moral reflection upon the precariousness of life.[28] By 1844, eight years after its founding, about 900 families owned lots there and had buried in them over 1000 persons. Laurel Hill became one of the city's "lions" to be shown to visitors, over 30,000 of whom enjoyed its beauty in 1846.[29]

The expansion of the city required better public transportation, but Philadelphia lagged behind other large cities in introducing streetcars. By the 1850s transportation in the city and districts was provided by some 400 hacks and cabs and over 300 horse-drawn omnibuses in regular service on several streets. Large, open sleighs, drawn by four horses, were substituted when the deep snows came. In April 1854 a franchise was granted to the Philadelphia and Delaware River Railroad Company to lay passenger lines for horse-drawn streetcars, but opposition from both the omnibus lines and the public, which feared increased congestion, noise, and accident hazards, prevented any further action for several years.[30]

The city streets were filled with railroad cars, however, from the four major lines and four lines serving the suburban area. Many objected to the added congestion of the streets and the ugliness, noise, dangers from collisions with other vehicles, and injury to pedestrians and children playing in the streets. A unique community endeavor in Kensington, combining the efforts of workingmen and their families, middle-class property-owners and employers, and politicians, and carried on from early 1840 until mid-1842, finally prevented the extension of the tracks of the Philadelphia and Trenton Railroad from its Tacony terminus down Front Street.[31]

Because most locomotives burned wood until the late 1850s and were recognized as fire hazards, an ordinance forbade their entry into the city. Depots were at the city's edge—Green Street, Callowhill Street, Washington Avenue. The trip from the west bank of the Schuylkill, where locomotives were replaced by horses, prompted various reactions from travelers, from one who found "The sudden transition from flying to creeping at the end of a railroad journey . . . an absolute misery," to the British visitor who was delighted by the "exciting trot" of the horses and the way in which the carriages whipped around rectangular street corners without losing speed.[32]

All public services were expanding to meet the city's growing needs. In the 1840s three private companies began to provide mail service in addition to that of the government: the American Mail Company, Hale's Independent Mail, and Blood's Despatch, popularly known as "Blood's Penny Post." Blood's was the only one to survive until 1861, when all private mail service was ended by Congress. Mail from Great Britain came to Philadelphia by way of New York or Boston in accordance with an agreement made by the two governments in 1848. The Philadelphia Board of Trade in its February 1854 report asked that the federal government take appropriate steps to eliminate this handicap suffered by the city.[33]

The city bought out the rights of the Philadelphia Gas Company in July 1841. Gas consumption, provided through 113 miles of pipe in the city and southern districts, by 1852 had reached a maximum of 1,123,000 cubic feet in one twenty-four-hour period. The city maintained 1718 lamps in its streets, squares, and market houses in that year. The works on the Schuylkill River at Market Street, with an aggregate capacity of about 1.5 million cubic feet, were no longer deemed adequate, so new gasworks were begun below Gray's Ferry, to contain 1.9 million cubic feet. Three new gas companies were incorporated outside the city, in the Northern Liberties and Spring Garden in 1844, and in Manayunk in 1853. Southwark and Moyamensing organized a company in 1846–1847, but it supplied no gas for several years.[34]

Philadelphia's water system had long been considered a universal marvel. It charged its customers in the adjoining districts, however, an average of a half-rate more than that paid by city dwellers. Resenting this discriminatory practice, Spring Garden and the Northern Liberties in December 1844 began the operation of their own waterworks, with a pumping station on the east bank of the Schuylkill about a mile above Fairmount and a reservoir with a capacity of 9.8 million gallons adjoining the northwest angle of the grounds of Girard College. Kensington also took its water from this project until 1850, when it built its own works on the Delaware. Southwark and Moyamensing continued to use Fairmount water under a ten-year renewal of their contract effective January 1, 1845.[35]

The substitution of iron water pipes for the original wooden ones, begun in 1820, was completed in 1848. At the end of 1848 there were almost seventy-eight miles of pipes in the city, over fourteen miles in Southwark, and almost nine miles in Moyamensing. Indoor plumbing became a normal part of the better housing, and in 1849 almost 17,000 tenants paid for water in the city. Unfortunately, about 3500 families still received their supply from public hydrant pumps.[36] "The practice of bathing was confined to a comparatively small number."[37] The city supplied Fairmount water to 4107 private baths in the city, 226 in Southwark, and 135 in Moyamensing. There were only five public baths within the city limits and one in the district of Spring Garden, from which the cost of admission, in any case, excluded the poor. By the end of 1853 the tenants paying for water in the city had increased to 20,409, and only about 3000 families depended on public hydrants.[38]

Industrial pollution of the upper reaches of the Schuylkill was brought to the attention of the city in 1846 by Frederick Erdmann, engineer of the waterworks, who recommended the installation of filters. After an investigation by a committee, however, and upon the advice of two conservative superintendents, Frederick Graff and his son, Frederick Jr., who succeeded him, the city rejected Erdmann's proposal. It noted with pleasure that Schuylkill water contained only 6.1 grams of solid matter per gallon while the water of the Croton Reservoir that supplied New York contained 10.94 grams.[39]

II

The Sanitary Committee of the Board of Health, assigned to clean up the city during the cholera epidemic in 1849, offered unimpeachable testimony to the wide gap between the fragrant "greene" city of the well-to-do and the fetid slums of the poor:

Day after day in their personal visits, did they breathe the pestiferous atmosphere of some degraded or illy-ventilated purlieus, where extremes of filth and misery and loathsome disease met the eye; where horrid heaps of manure from hog and cow pens; putrifying garbage and refuse of every kind; carcases in disgusting decomposition; filthy rooms and damp, dirty and mouldy cellars, full and foul privies in close and illy-ventilated locations gave off their noxious gases. Many of these localities were in close proximity to contracted and badly contrived houses, crowded by occupants, filthy and poor, without ventilation or drainage, or receptacles for refuse, or supply of water, or the common comforts of life.[40]

Public and professional concern for the city's health had always been marked in Philadelphia, and many civic leaders had been convinced of the connection between sanitation and disease. In 1849 the city responded promptly and with great thoroughness to the report of the investigating committee. Indeed one diarist noted on June 5, 1849: "Such a cleaning of streets and cleaning of houses never was known before for a long while."[41]

Philadelphia was unusual among large American cities in that its death rate had declined slightly after 1825, while that of other large cities had tended to rise from 1800 to 1850. The Philadelphia mortality rate, however, began to rise also after 1850 and remained relatively high, though it was still lower than that of New York, in 1853 being 1 to 43.61 of population compared to New York's 1 to 30.85. The only epidemics recorded as such in the city in the period 1841–1854 were those of Asiatic cholera in 1849, causing 1012 deaths; smallpox in 1852 with 427 deaths; and yellow fever in 1853 with 128 deaths. These statistics, however, took no account of more or less endemic fevers such as typhus, which broke out several times in Moyamensing in the 1840s and caused 205 deaths in 1848. Dysentery, endemic every summer, reached epidemic proportions in the poor districts from about 1845 on, with 315 deaths in 1848, 578 in 1849 (the cholera year), 432 in 1850, and 386 in 1851. In 1852, when smallpox killed 427 persons, 433 died of scarlet fever, 558 of dysentery, and 1204 of tuberculosis. Malarial fevers were prevalent in the area between Broad Street and the Schuylkill and in the low, flat lands to the south of the city between the rivers. It is estimated that more than ten times as many people died of malaria and tuberculosis as died of cholera, but they died gradually and quietly, "romantically" in the case of tuberculosis, whereas cholera killed with terrifying speed and ugliness. Cholera persisted, with a few cases every year from 1849 to 1854, when it disappeared, not to recur until 1866.[42]

The connection between poverty and disease became dramatically evident in the statistics of the cholera epidemic of 1849 which, though it appeared in all parts of the Philadelphia area, was especially prevalent in the poorer districts where more persons lived in closer proximity in a single dwelling. The highest rate of incidence was in Southwark, with 1 case per 132.09 of population, the next highest rate in Moyamensing with 1 to 134.58, compared with a total ratio of 1 to 246.82 for the city and surrounding districts.[43] Though the godly still tended to regard poverty as the wages of sin, the city in 1849, in a notable change from its reaction in previous epidemic years, relied on sanitary measures more than on prayer to fight the epidemic.

The medical profession was unfortunately ill-prepared to meet the health challenges of the 1840s. For over fifty years doctors had been slowly evolving a new approach to healing, but their work up to the mid-nineteenth century had been theoretical, neither intelligible nor of practical value to laymen. The public grew impatient. The enormous growth of population, the increased influx of impoverished immigrants, urban growth and deterioration, and industrialization—all contributed to the rising mortality rate. The political, economic, and social promises of "Jacksonian democracy," the improvements in public education, and the growth of the mass media all fed the demand for better health care. The regular medical profession could not supply the needs.

Philadelphia had long been the center of medical education in the United States and it retained this supremacy in the 1840s and 1850s, with approximately 1000 medical students in the city every year. Numerous among them were young southerners, particularly Virginians, and many of them became particularly conspicuous in these years through their violent antiabolitionist activities.[44]

The Medical Department of the University of Pennsylvania maintained its prestigious aura, but in 1850 its younger rival, Jefferson Medical College, surpassed it in the number of its annual graduates, 211 in that year compared with the university's 176. After many difficult years Jefferson had achieved the basis for stable growth with the appointment in 1841 of a new faculty, which worked together as "a solid phalanx."[45]

The number of medical schools in the United States more than doubled between 1830 and 1845 and continued to increase. Philadelphia shared this development. The best of the new institutions organized in the city at the beginning of the 1840s was the Medical Department of Pennsylvania College, a Lutheran institution in Gettysburg under whose auspices the Philadelphia school was chartered in 1840. It merged in 1859 with the Philadelphia College of Medicine, which had been chartered in 1847. The latter institution, offering a unique course of two terms which made it possible for its students to practice a year earlier than those of other schools, had produced 400 graduates between 1847 and 1854. In 1857 this course was given up, however, and the institution thereafter, until its demise in 1861, conformed to the standards adopted by the American Medical Association. The Franklin Medical College, chartered in January 1846, lasted only a few years.[46]

In 1846 the Medico-Chirurgical College, a professional society, not a school, was established to disseminate medical knowledge and to defend the rights and preserve the repute and dignity of the medical profession. The proliferation of medical schools, many with lowered standards to attract customers in a highly competitive situation, and the rise of "irregular" practice, prompted many attempts to establish regulatory agencies. Many also believed that even the best teaching program did not reflect the growing body of knowledge in the field. The American Medical Association, organized in Philadelphia in May 1847, attempted to meet all these needs.[47] It adopted uniform, standard, and expanded requirements for the granting of an M.D. degree, including the extension of the course of lectures to six months (the average was then four months); the extension of the total period of study to three years, including two full courses of lectures; and the rejection of any preceptor "who is avowedly and notoriously an irregular practitioner, whether he shall possess the degree of M.D. or not."[48] Three Philadelphia physicians were elected to major posts in the new association: Nathaniel Chapman, president; Alfred Stillé, one of the secretaries; Isaac Hays, treasurer (Hays was largely responsible for the code of medical ethics of the AMA). The Philadelphia County Medical Society was organized in 1848. In spite of all regulatory attempts, however, a committee of the County Medical Society in 1851 reported that in Philadelphia County, in addition to 397 physicians in "legitimate" practice, there were 42 homeopathists, 30 Thomsonians, 2 hydropathists, 32 advertising doctors, 37 druggist-physicians, and 42 "nondescripts."[49]

Although earlier attempts had been made to establish the teaching of homeopathic medicine elsewhere, the first such institution to succeed anywhere in the world, the Homeopathic Medical College of Pennsylvania, was organized in Philadelphia in 1848.[50] A system of healing developed by a German physician, Samuel Hahnemann, homeopathy treated disease with small doses of drugs that were "capable of producing in healthy persons symptoms like those of the disease to be treated."[51] The Homeopathic Hospital of Pennsylvania was opened in 1852. As a result of an internal dispute, a rival teaching institution, Hahnemann Medical College, was established in 1867, but two years later the two merged and under the name of the Hahnemann Medical College became a major center for the training of physicians in Philadelphia.[52]

Another divergence from "regular" practice was the short-lived Eclectic Medical College of Pennsylvania, chartered in 1850. Protesting against the harsh methods of "regular" physicians—such as cupping, leeching, and purging—it intended to employ all useful medical systems and reject all harmful ones. After ten successful years, however, it fell victim to a faculty quarrel which drew off many students and faculty to a rival institution established by the dissidents, and poor financial management completed its destruction.[53]

Hydropathy was introduced to Philadelphia by Charles Christian Schieferdecker, who had come to the United States from Germany in 1839 and had claimed at least one major cure in Philadelphia by 1843. In October 1846 he opened a "Hydriatic Institution" on the banks of the Schuylkill at Chestnut Street, in a forty-room house built for a "splendid hotel."[54] He claimed that adherence to his regimen would guarantee a life span of 150 to 200 years. So seriously was he taken, moreover, that such a man as John F. Watson, the Philadelphia annalist, and his wife and daughter spent about three months at a second "Hydropathic Institute" which Schieferdecker opened at Willow

Grove in 1848. Many other water-cure establishments were opened in Philadelphia during the late 1840s and the 1850s, but they were "mostly fleeting affairs."[55]

The oldest permanently organized medical school for women in the United States, after 1867 called the Woman's Medical College of Pennsylvania and in 1970 renamed the Medical College of Pennsylvania, was established as the Female Medical College by a group of Philadelphia physicians in 1850. Several of the city's doctors had been teaching women students in their homes since the early 1840s, but women had been barred from all of the medical schools. Even after the opening of the Female Medical College women medical students were denied clinical practice at the University of Pennsylvania, Jefferson Medical College, and the various hospitals, although their services were accepted as nurses. Not until 1868 were women physicians admitted to the municipal Blockley Almshouse. In 1869 the Pennsylvania Hospital permitted them to attend its Saturday clinics. They were barred from the Philadelphia County Medical Society until late in the nineteenth century.[56]

In 1852 the Philadelphia School of Anatomy, founded in 1838, was revived by Dr. D. Hayes Agnew and enjoyed great success under his direction for ten years. The Penn Medical College (named for William Penn), chartered in 1853, its name changed to the Penn Medical University in 1854, differed from other institutions in its graded curriculum and in its admission of women students on an equal basis with men and, in 1857, in the same classes with men, the only medical school in the United States so organized during this period. It went out of existence in 1881.[57]

Dr. George B. Wood in his "Introductory Lecture to the Course of Materia Medica" at the University of Pennsylvania in 1842 noted that the only really new remedies that had come into general use since he had begun practicing were iodine and its compounds. This fact did not discourage the purveyors of patent medicines. Several men had made great fortunes in Philadelphia by the mid-1840s by the manufacture and sale of such remedies, outstanding being William Swaim, who had amassed $400,000 with his "Panacea," advertised to cure even cancer, and Benjamin Brandreth, whose fortune of $150,000 had come largely from "Brandreth's Pills." A new giant developing in the field was Dr. David Jayne, who advertised his "Expectorant" in 1844 as "the only remedy that can arrest with certainty the various pulmonary affections under which thousands sink into the grave," while his "Carminative" would cure cholera morbus for fifty cents.[58]

The earliest efforts to develop pharmacy as a profession separate from medicine had been made in Philadelphia in the mid-eighteenth century, and the city had continued to be the center of pioneering developments in this field. The first national organization to govern the preparation and sale of drugs and to elevate the standards of pharmacy as a profession, the American Pharmaceutical Association, was formed in Philadelphia in 1852.[59]

The Pennsylvania Association of Dental Surgeons was organized in Philadelphia in 1845. Five years later the Philadelphia College of Dental Surgery was chartered, but it had completed only four sessions when it ceased operations because of a faculty dispute. The faculty got a new charter in 1856 for a new institution, the Pennsylvania College of Dental Surgery, which did survive. Supporting the profession was Samuel S. White, who began in 1844 the manufacture of the most life-like false teeth yet made anywhere. Well past the middle of the twentieth century the S. S. White Dental Manufacturing Company remained a leading maker of dental supplies.[60]

"Even strangers can see that medicine is a subject of general interest in Philadelphia," attested a visiting physician in late 1841, but then he added, "What other distinction has this city achieved except in medical science?"[61] He shared the "all or nothing" attitude of many native sons.

I I I

The Schuylkill Navigation Company's canal had long been bringing to Philadelphia the products of the Schuylkill Valley—lumber, grain, flour, whiskey, iron ore, the lime and limestone used for iron manufacture, and above all, coal. On January 1, 1842, the pattern changed, when the first train of the Philadelphia and Reading Railroad from Pottsville to Philadelphia, carrying the company's officers, completed the journey in four hours and forty-eight minutes running time, exclusive of stoppages. On January 10 a single engine drew seventy-five passenger cars containing 2150 passengers and three bands of music from Pottsville to a gala celebration in Philadelphia. Passengers and musicians paraded down Chestnut Street to the Merchants' Exchange and back to the Washington Hotel, where a small parcel of coal dug from the mines that morning was symbolically burned. A conservative Philadelphia diarist commented: "I am told the company had a carousing time of it all the way down."[62]

Running behind the passenger train had been another composed of fifty-two cars loaded with 180 tons of coal. On May 17 the railroad's branch line, built expressly to carry coal to the Delaware River, made its first run to the company's wharves at Port Richmond, and the Schuylkill Navigation Company's monopoly of the Schuylkill Valley traffic was broken. A "ruinous competition" ensued, during which the Schuylkill cut its rates from Port Carbon to Philadelphia from one dollar per ton in 1840 to fifty-four cents late in 1842, and to thirty-six cents in 1845. The railroad's cost in 1842 was an estimated fifteen cents per ton per 100-mile run. In that year it carried 49,390 tons of coal, the following year 218,711 tons, and 421,958 tons the year after that.[63]

By 1844 the Reading Railroad had won its war with the canal, its total tonnage in that year exceeding that of the canal at Fairmount locks by about 450,000 tons. The fight was bitterly fought, with mutual defamation in pamphlets and newspaper articles, but peace came with an agreement in 1846. The canal company shifted its market routes, with only 155,750 tons of its total tonnage of 888,695 going to Philadelphia in 1853, while 474,105 tons went to New York by the Raritan Canal.[64]

The Reading nearly doubled its tonnage in 1845 after opening up several short lateral roads. By 1847 it was considered the greatest freight road in the United States, carrying in that year more tonnage than the Erie Canal at almost half the cost per ton. The company bought additional land at Port Richmond, purchased the old State Works Columbia Bridge over the Schuylkill in 1850, and in the same year began leasing mines in order to control its coal supply. In 1852 more than 1,230,000 tons of coal were shipped from its wharves, where 100 ships could be loaded at one time.[65] Ultimately in the 1860s it procured its own fleet of ships and had taken Philadelphia into "the one branch of maritime activity [the coastwise coal trade] in which it surpassed New York and in which it also enjoyed national primacy."[66]

Although over $10 million had been spent on the State Works, by the 1840s it became obvious that they did not meet the growing needs of the West. Pittsburgh's insistence on an unbroken rail connection with the East developed into what one group of Philadelphia gentlemen described as "an obligation imposed on us by a kind Providence," and they decided that a new railroad must be built.[67] Public meetings in Philadelphia under the chairmanship of Thomas P. Cope, together with ferocious lobbying in Harrisburg, finally on April 13, 1846, produced an act incorporating the Pennsylvania Railroad. Many had opposed it, including Baltimore interests who wanted that city as the eastern terminus, canal supporters who saw a new central railroad as a threat to their investments, and those westerners who disliked Philadelphia on general principles well rooted in history and geography.[68]

The new railroad also encountered opposition in Philadelphia, but in November 1846 the city Councils authorized the mayor to subscribe in the name of the city for 50,000 shares, one-quarter of the railroad's total stock, at a cost of $2.5 million, which investment was later increased to $4 million. The new company organized in the Board of Trade room of the Philadelphia Exchange on March 30, 1847, elected thirteen directors, and the next day named Samuel V. Merrick the first president.[69]

The Pennsylvania began its passenger service on September 1, 1849, operating one trip daily between Harrisburg and Lewistown, a distance of sixty-one miles, with a total rolling stock of two passenger cars, one baggage car, and two locomotives. Its coaches—long boxes seating thirty-two passengers—had no steps, and more important, no brakes. It ordered seventy-five freight cars for its freight service opened in the same year. In February 1854 the main line from Philadelphia to Pittsburgh was completed, the first through line without inclined planes, with a running time of thirteen hours. It carried 250,095 tons of freight in its first year of operation.[70]

Only the Cope Line of sailing packets between Liverpool and Philadelphia provided regular transatlantic service from Philadelphia during the early 1840s, but by 1849 two additional lines, George McHenry and Company and Robert Taylor and Company, had entered the Liverpool trade.[71] One English traveler in 1846 found these ships fully as good as those serving New York, and the passage money was generally £5 cheaper; but he still did not recommend the Philadelphia lines, for the voyage to Philadelphia was "much longer and tedious." The passage up the Delaware, after rounding Cape May, although only about 100 miles, frequently took ten days or a fortnight "of the most disagreeable kind; the scenery is exceedingly flat, of one continued sameness, and by no means interesting."[72] New York attracted most of the transatlantic customers, with fifty-two packets sailing at the rate of three per week by 1845.[73]

Latin American trade was carried on by the Philadelphia firms of John F. Ohl & Sons, sailing to Havana, and the Dallett Brothers' "Red D Line" to La Guaira and Puerto Cabello in Venezuela.[74] Three of the Dalletts' three-masted barques in the 1840s came from the Kensington yard of John K. Hammitt, one of them, the *Thomas Dallett*, described in the *North American* on August 23, 1848, as "the handsomest vessel ever built at the port of Philadelphia."[75] The "Red D Line," originally trading Philadelphia soap and flour in return for coffee and hides, became exporters of American technology as well, carrying to Caracas machinery for its factories, and to La Guaira parts of its first railroad and all of the materials used for the building of its breakwater from 1843 to 1846 by the Philadelphia architect Thomas U. Walter. The Dalletts' trade made La Guaira one of the few ports in which Philadelphia enjoyed ascendancy over New York.

Philadelphia's transatlantic sailing lines built their ships for endurance and storage capacity rather than for speed and beauty, with the single exception of Isaac Jeanes & Co., for whom William Cramp in 1854 built a clipper ship for the Mediterranean trade. The Pacific and California trade, however, engaged many Philadelphia clippers, notably those owned by Bishop, Simons & Co. of the Pioneer Line to Fort Philip, Australia, and William Platt & Sons, operators by 1852 of the *White Squall, Messenger,* and *Canton* to California.[76]

Steamships entered into serious competition with sailing vessels in the 1840s. Thomas Clyde began a freight business between Philadelphia and New York with a single steamer in 1842. Others were added and lines began to other cities, including Charleston, Richmond, Norfolk, and Portsmouth. The Baltimore and Philadelphia Steamboat Company, later the Ericsson Line, chartered in 1844, used Ericsson screw-propeller vessels in the trade between Philadelphia and Baltimore by way of the Chesapeake and Delaware Canal. Four steamships of the Philadelphia, Albany, and Troy Line, a freight line established in 1844, at first carried coal by way of the Delaware and Raritan Canal. The Philadelphia and Atlantic Steam Navigation Company, chartered in 1848 for the Philadelphia-Charleston trade, failed after three or four years. The Philadelphia and New York Transportation Company was chartered in 1850 to carry passengers and freight between the two cities and intermediate points. Many small steam vessels operated on the Delaware and Schuylkill Rivers, one survey in 1847 enumerating seventy-seven, including tow boats and ferries on the Delaware.[77]

Transatlantic steam service became a European operation because of the Americans' continued preference for wooden ships. The Cunard Line, established in 1840 between Liverpool and Boston, began regular service to New York in 1848. Philadelphia did not have such service until 1850, when William Inman, a Liverpool merchant, began his line from Liverpool to Philadelphia. The *City of Glasgow* entered the Delaware on January 2, 1850, to the cheers of the populace. The *City of Manchester* followed in August, the *City of Pittsburgh* in January 1852. The *City of Philadelphia*, built some months later, never arrived in Philadelphia, going down off Cape Race on September 17, 1854, fortunately without losing any passengers. The *City of Glasgow*, sailing from Liverpool in March 1854 with more than 500 passengers, had disappeared without a trace. Still earlier, in October 1852 the *City of Pittsburgh* had been destroyed by fire at Valparaiso. Only the *City of Manchester* remained in 1854, running between Philadelphia and Liverpool until the beginning of the Crimean War, when it was taken by the British government as a troop transport. After the war the name of the line was changed to the Philadelphia, New York, and Liverpool Steamship Company, its offices were transferred to New York, and its vessels operated exclusively out of New York.[78]

As railroad and steamship speeded up the tempo of Philadelphia's life, another technological development of the 1840s added still another dimension to that quickening. In June 1846 Philadelphia was connected to New York and Washington by telegraph. When Amos Kendall had organized the Magnetic Telegraph Company in May 1845 to build a line from New York to Philadelphia, prominent on the first board of directors had been William M. Swain of the *Public Ledger*, who had editorialized a year earlier on behalf of Samuel F. B. Morse's plea that the federal government control the telegraph. Swain and his partners, Arunah S. Abell and Azariah H. Simmons, contributed $3500 of the $10,000 raised to carry the line from Philadelphia to Baltimore and Washington. In April 1848 the rival New Jersey Magnetic Telegraph Company began service between New York and Philadelphia, and by June 1849 still another, the North American Telegraph Company, was nearing Philadelphia from Washington.

The telegraph transformed the business of news reporting. Kendall's company encouraged the press's use of the new facility by reducing to one-third of the regular price any dispatch over 100 words, and the press quickly became the company's best customer. By the fall of 1846 some telegraphers began to specialize in news reporting, and the following spring the Philadelphia press, led by the *Ledger*, kept a telegraphic reporter at Fredericksburg to collect news from the South for them. In April 1847 Alexander Cummings issued the first number of *Cummings' Evening Telegraphic Bulletin*, later to become Philadelphia's leading evening newspaper, the *Evening Bulletin*.[79]

The telegraph was efficient but unsightly. As early as 1846 people were complaining that the telegraph poles were crooked, rough, and unpainted, to which the Magnetic Telegraph Company responded by painting the poles, but did nothing about straightening them. The poles, originally T-shaped, became uglier as cross-arms were added to carry additional wires for their expanding business.[80]

Philadelphia had $33,737,911 invested in manufacturing in the city and county in 1850, with 59,106 hands employed and a total production valued at $64,114,112. By 1857 Philadelphia had a greater number of textile factories than any other city in the world, with 260 manufacturing cotton and woolen goods. Cheap coal, making steam readily available, helped Philadelphia, alone among the older and larger cities, to remain a textile center. Machine shops capable of building textile mill equipment further contributed to the city's leadership in this field. Probably the most important of these firms outside of New England was Alfred Jenks and Son in Bridesburg.[81]

At the same time Philadelphia remained "the great seat of Hand-Loom Manufacturing and Weaving in America," with over 4700 looms operating as late as 1857. Over 2000 of these produced carpets, 2000 other textiles, and 700 hosiery. Half of the 15,000 textile workers in that year were hand-loom operators, producing about one-quarter of the total output. The men usually owned their own looms and worked at home. Immigrant Englishmen, Scots, and northern Irishmen made Kensington the great carpet center. Many knitters of fancy woolen hosiery, displaced by machinery in England by 1840, came to Philadelphia, especially from Nottingham and Leicester, and settling

Steam Sugar Refinery, Joseph S. Lovering & Co., No. 225 Church St., Philadelphia, *engraving by Van Ingen Snyder (c. 1860). In 1846 the annual value of production by Philadelphia's twelve sugar refineries was more than $1 million. One of the buildings in the Lovering complex, parts of which date to 1792, has recently been rehabilitated and adapted for apartments.*

HISTORICAL SOCIETY OF PENNSYLVANIA

in Kensington and Germantown, produced Philadelphia's "Germantown woolen goods," which became as famous as England's.[82]

Philadelphia excelled in iron manufactures. Levi, Morris and Co., makers of heavy machinery, founded in 1828, moved to Port Richmond in 1846, just south of the Reading wharves. Here they specialized in the production of outsize tools, one of which, a boring mill, could bore out a cylinder sixteen feet in diameter and eighteen feet long, and was claimed to be the largest in the world. This firm also built the largest engine ever constructed for smelting iron with anthracite. Another outstanding builder of heavy machinery was the Southwark Foundry of Merrick and Sons. They also operated large iron boatyards on the Delaware. Matthias W. Baldwin, leading American manufacturer of locomotives, in 1842 introduced the six- and eight-wheel connected engine, providing for adaptation to curves and uneven roadbeds, which saved 30 percent in railroad operating costs; his trade soon became international. Robert Wood's firm became famous all over the United States for its ornamental cast iron, at the height of its popularity in the 1850s used for "the adornment of the dwelling-places, breathing-places, and last resting-places" of Americans; much of Wood's ironwork still ornaments New Orleans, Savannah, and Mobile. The manufacture of chandeliers, lamps, and fixtures for gas lighting developed into an important industry in the 1840s, and Philadelphia became the leading American manufacturer of these items, by 1860 producing two-thirds of the American total. One firm alone, Cornelius & Baker, in 1851 employed 1000 persons in numerous buildings on Cherry Street.[83]

Shipbuilding continued to flourish on the Delaware, turning to a concentration on steamships in the mid-1840s. Within ten years Theodore Birely & Son in Kensington built 107 steamers. C. & N. Cramp's *Caroline*, launched in 1849, was claimed by its builders to be the fastest propeller ship then afloat. In 1857 it was estimated that Philadelphia shipbuilding for the previous five years had averaged $1,760,000 annually.[84]

I V

Many Philadelphians had amassed large fortunes by the mid-1840s. Although Philadelphia had no rich men to compare with New York's John Jacob Astor and his son William, who in 1846 shared $33 million between them, it did, according to an anonymous study in 1845, have ten fortunes of $1 million or more, compared with New York's five, and a total of 234 fortunes of $100,000 or more, compared with New York's 212. It had eleven between $500,000 and $1 million, nine between $250,000 and $500,000, 205 between $100,000 and $250,000, and 477 between $50,000 and $100,000. According to Charles Godfrey Leland, a contemporary Philadelphian, $50,000 "constituted the millionaireism or money aristocracy" of the mid-1840s, for this sum permitted a man to keep a carriage.[85]

Real estate speculation, mercantile pursuits, marriage to heiresses, or combinations of all three, predominated among the ways to wealth. By 1857

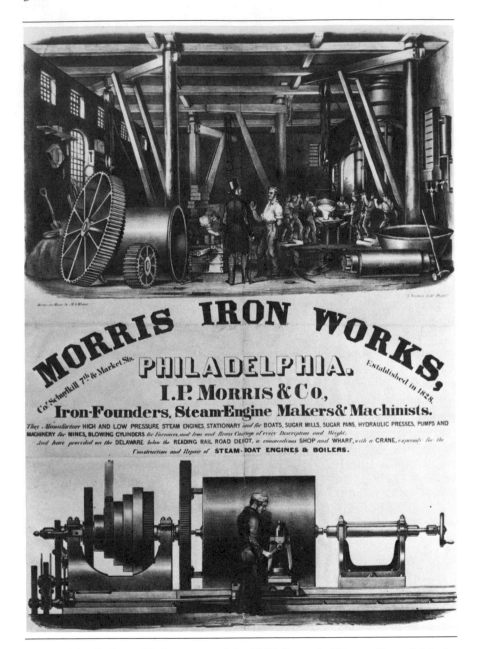

Morris Iron Works, corner Schuylkill Seventh (Sixteenth) and Market Streets, lithograph by T. Sinclair after M. S. Weaver (1840). The firm, now Morris Wheeler and Co., still exists in the Midvale and Frankford neighborhoods of Philadelphia.

HISTORICAL SOCIETY OF PENNSYLVANIA

Robert Wood & Co. Iron & Bronze Foundries, Philadelphia, 12th Street View, *engraving (c. 1860). The firm, located at Ridge Avenue and Twelfth Street, was founded in 1839. The omnibus, pictured at the left, ran between Chestnut and Fairmount on Twelfth Street. Other notable details in the picture include a fire truck and a telegraph pole and wires.*

HISTORICAL SOCIETY OF PENNSYLVANIA

Philadelphia's list of millionaires had increased to at least twenty-five by one estimate. Four on the 1845 list—John A. Brown, John J. Ridgway, Evans Rogers, and Jacob Steinmetz—were still in that class. Seven who had been said to be worth between $100,000 and $500,000 in 1845 had moved up into the millionaire group: Richard Ashhurst, merchant; George W. Carpenter, druggist; John B. Myers, auctioneer; the physicians J. Rhea Barton and James Rush, both married to daughters of Jacob Ridgway and through them sharing the Ridgway estate; James Dundas, retired president of the Commercial Bank; and Jacob L. Florance, "gentleman." Among others listed as millionaires were: Alexander Benson, broker; J. P. Crozer, manufacturer; Francis M. Drexel, broker; John Grigg, retired publisher; David Jayne, patent medicine manufacturer; J. S. Lovering, sugar refiner; and Joseph Harrison, Jr., mechanical engineer, famous for the construction of the St. Petersburg–Moscow Railroad.[86]

The mere acquisition of great wealth did not guarantee admission to the ranks of Philadelphia's upper class. "The exclusive feature of American society is no where brought so broadly out as it is in the city of Philadelphia," observed the British traveler Alexander Mackay in 1846. "It is, of course, readily discernible in Boston, New York, and Baltimore; but the line drawn in these places is not so distinctive or so difficult to transcend as it is in Philadelphia."[87] Family had always been valued above wealth, yet the upper class had also accepted some members of the "natural aristocracy" who had proved their right of entry by demonstration of talent and what was considered to be virtue. Many of the new industrial and financial leaders and successful speculators in real estate were admitted to the upper social stratum in the 1840s and 1850s.[88] Indeed one Philadelphia gentleman of old family in 1843 found few houses "from which vulgar people are excluded. . . ."[89] But many of the "new" men were not accepted. Charles Godfrey Leland, born in Philadelphia in 1824, testified:

The lines of demarcation in [Philadelphia] "society" were as strongly drawn as in Europe, or more so, with the enormous difference, however, that there was not the slightest perceptible shade of difference in the intellects, culture, or character of the people on either side of the line. . . . Very trifling points of difference, not perceptible to an outsider, made the whole difference between the exclusive and the excluded. . . .[90]

Most travelers agreed with the native aristocracy that upper-class Philadelphians were an attractive lot. Mackay found their society

intellectual without being pedantic, and sprightly without being boisterous. It seems to be a happy blending of the chief characteristics of Boston and New York society. . . . In their habitual intercourse with each other Philadelphians have an ease of manner which is perfectly charming. They are familiar without being coarse. . . . In many respects, Philadelphia life is the best counterpart which America affords of the social refinements of Europe.[91]

William Chambers, another British traveler, writing in 1853, found Philadelphia's social charms almost indescribable:

How . . . am I able to communicate a just notion of the intelligence, the refinement, the enterprise of Philadelphians—their agreeable and hospitable society, their pleasant evening-parties, their love of literature, their happy blending of the industrial habits of the north with the social usages of the south? All this must be left to conjecture, as well as the Oriental luxury of their dwellings, and the delicate beauty of their ladies.

He could find no fault. "Nothing is left to pine for on the banks of the lovely Schuylkill or the noble Delaware."[92]

The Philadelphia Assemblies continued to be held, though probably not every year, during the 1840s and 1850s.[93] However, the chronically disgruntled Sidney George Fisher found the April 1849 Assembly "very dull, not many there, & no one I cared to see or speak to," while the January 1850 ball was

"Crowded, dull & stupid. No beauty, grace, style or fashion. Very different from what they used to be when I was *young*. Our society is broken up & degenerated under the influence of democracy, which is destructive at least to all the refinements & embellishments of life."[94]

A series of three "private assemblies" was given on successive Thursdays in 1851, the first to celebrate the Philadelphia Club's occupation of its new home at Thirteenth and Walnut Streets, the old Butler house. The second was given by Mrs. George Willing at her house in Girard Row, the north side of Chestnut Street between Eleventh and Twelfth, distinguished for its aristocratic occupants. The third private assembly also took place in Girard Row, given by the Thomas Cadwaladers.[95]

Wistar Parties, restricted to gentlemen, were "sadly neglected [after] the demise of our lamented associate, Mr. John Vaughan," secretary of the American Philosophical Society who had been their leading spirit until his death in 1841; but they were soon reorganized with a new constitution and continued to serve as a focus of elite hospitality for "literary and scientific gentlemen" of Philadelphia and for distinguished visitors to the city.[96]

Gentlemen continued to participate in volunteer military organizations. Most outstanding in the early 1840s was the leadership given the Philadelphia Grays by George Cadwalader, then a captain. Providing at his own expense costly horses and equipment, Cadwalader made the Grays famous for their flying artillery drills, which usually took place on a large field on the west side of the Schuylkill beyond Mantua, drawing thousands of spectators. The captain's continuing military activity eventually brought him into action as a brigadier-general of militia to subdue the anti-Catholic riots in 1844 and later to win glory as a major-general of volunteers in the Mexican War.[97]

A unique recreational development among Philadelphia gentlemen was the playing of cricket, because it brought them into intimate association with men of the working class. Though the game had been introduced into the city late in the eighteenth century, at first it had not made much progress. An early cricketer said that even in the early 1840s "all field sports were looked down upon by our elders, and they neither aided nor abetted us in our cricketing endeavors, nor did the ladies smile upon our efforts."[98] Nevertheless English immigrant hosiery workers from the Wakefield Mills organized a cricket club early in the decade, and the Union Cricket Club was formed in 1842, chiefly by English importing merchants together with a few Americans. The first club formed by Americans was probably the Junior Cricket Club at the University of Pennsylvania, organized in 1843 or 1844 by about forty members, "all to the manor born." The Germantown Cricket Club of the same period included both young gentlemen and sons of English weavers. Cricket suffered from lack of money, enmity between northern and southern Englishmen, and civic indifference. The early clubs died out about 1852, but small groups continued to play informally. The Philadelphia Cricket Club, organized in February 1854, and the second Germantown Cricket Club, established six months later, were to survive.[99]

The upper classes continued to enjoy the old rural pastimes of walking, skating, riding, driving, fishing, and boating, but lack of leisure time or money or facilities for getting out of the city prevented most other Philadelphians from spending much time in such pursuits.[100] Those of the middle classes who could afford to take summer vacations happily "ruralized" in the country area lying within a radius of from five to ten miles outside the city, which abounded in summer boarding houses.

More and more wealthy Philadelphians were permanently withdrawing from city residence, building large country mansions costing from $10,000 to $40,000. Many of them were seeking the advice of the newly fashionable landscape architect Andrew Jackson Downing. At a fee of $20 per diem Downing in 1847 conferred with Harry Ingersoll, who was building "Medary" on Green Lane near Fern Rock Station in Germantown; with Joshua Francis Fisher about "Alverthorpe" on Meeting House Road near Jenkintown; and with Henry Fisher, planning "Brookwood" at Green Lane and County Line.[101]

The Fourth of July in the 1840s and 1850s marked the exodus of fashionable Philadelphians to various summer resorts, where they generally stayed until the middle of August. Many went to Newport, Saratoga, or, closer to home, Yellow Springs in Chester County. Most popular of all, however, was Cape May, which achieved national prominence by 1840 and was for fifty years second only to Saratoga in the elegance of its hotels and the numbers of famous visitors it attracted.[102] Nine large new hotels were built there between 1840 and 1854, the largest of which, the Mount Vernon, accommodated 2100 guests. Cape May had no railroad until 1863, but people flocked there by stage or private carriage or by steamers down the Delaware. One custom attested to in July 1854 by a visiting Philadelphian was the bathing in the ocean of about a hundred men, "at 5 A M, without clothing."[103]

A future rival to Cape May, but one that was not a serious threat until the 1880s, was Atlantic City. The dream of Dr. Jonathan R. Pitney, who visited the area in 1845 and envisioned "a second Cape May," it was almost entirely a Philadelphia project, financed by Philadelphia investors, who bought 200 acres at $17 per acre and built the Camden and Atlantic Railroad to the coast. The resort was officially opened on July 1, 1854, when the new railroad made its inaugural excursion, bearing 600 persons to a joyous celebration at the partly finished United States Hotel.[104]

For the middle class on the way up and for those who hoped to join them, an invaluable guide to what was believed to be fashionable behavior was provided by popular magazines. Here could be learned what the best dressed people were wearing, what kinds of houses they were building, how they were furnishing their houses, all presented in illustrations that were themselves works of art—copper and steel engravings, the best of them by John Sartain, American master of mezzotint engraving; lithographs by P. S. Duval, Christian Schuessele (most distinguished of chromolithographers), E. J. Pinkerton (who specialized in fashion plates), and many others.

Mrs. Sarah J. Hale, who had been editing *Godey's Lady's Book* from Boston since 1837, came to Philadelphia in 1841, and by the end of the decade under her expert guidance *Godey's* outdistanced all rivals. Taking stock for the year 1849, Mrs. Hale announced that *Godey's* had offered 916 pages, 116 pages more than its leading competitor, while its 281 engravings—20 colored and 93 full page—represented 136 more than its nearest rival. Each number had included a piece of music, separately printed; the "Ladies' Work Table," with patterns for all types of needlework; reading matter, "always moral and instructive," for the entire family; and the "Editor's Table," from which Mrs. Hale issued advice and crusaded for a better world for women and children.[105]

Sarah Josepha Hale *(1788–1879), engraving (c. 1860).*
HISTORICAL SOCIETY OF PENNSYLVANIA

Louis A. Godey himself had written in 1840: "We were the first to introduce the system of calling forth the slumbering talent of our country by offering an equivalent for the efforts of genius."[106] In other words he paid well, as did George R. Graham, who established the standard page rate for monthly magazines, paying $4 to $12 for a 1000-word page and $10 to $50 for a poem.[107] The magazines encouraged not only such outstanding writers as Edgar Allan Poe, Nathaniel Hawthorne, William Gilmore Simms, and Oliver Wendell Holmes, but also those whom Hawthorne described as "a d----d mob of scribbling women."[108]

Graham's, not primarily a woman's magazine, had to offer colored fashion illustrations to compete with *Godey's* in the $3 annual subscription field. In 1842 Graham and Charles J. Peterson, his partner in the ownership and management of the *Saturday Evening Post* and *Graham's*, began publishing *Peterson's Lady's National Magazine* at a $2 rate, with three engravings a month. Peterson eventually left the *Post* and *Graham's* and devoted full time to the new magazine, which surpassed *Godey's* circulation in the early 1860s. It carried on in the Godey tradition by appointing a woman editor, (Mrs.) Ann S. Stephens, herself an established writer of serialized fiction.

Eliza Leslie and Timothy Shay Arthur, both contributors to *Godey's*, began the joint editorship of *Miss Leslie's Magazine* in January 1843. A year later Arthur took over the monthly and changed it to *Arthur's Ladies Magazine of Elegant Literature and the Fine Arts*, which appeared until April 1846, merging in May with *Godey's*.[109] In 1850 Arthur began the *Home Gazette*, a weekly, which boasted of "Freedom from Vulgarity, Low Slang, Profanity, *or anything that can corrupt or deprave the mind.*" Out of selected articles from the journal, in 1852 Arthur began publishing the monthly *Arthur's Home Magazine*, which flourished for many years.[110]

All of these magazines contributed to the creation of the "genteel" ideal, which one suspects bore as much relationship to real life in the mid-nineteenth century as Hollywood movies and television soap operas bear to reality in the twentieth century. They also assisted in the feminization of American literature, which so enraged Hawthorne. On the other hand they did perform several useful functions, helping to support American writers, men as well as women, working for the equalization of human rights without regard to sex, and above all, expressing and helping to mold the aspirations of the multitude. By 1850 *Godey's* alone had a subscription list of over 60,000, which in the next decade increased to 150,000. In 1860 Godey claimed a readership of a million.[111]

Though sentimentality, banality, and too much "Home and Mother" characterized much of Philadelphians' reading fare in the 1840s and 1850s, the runaway bestseller among novels was George Lippard's *The Quaker City*, an extraordinary tale of lust and violence, published in 1844. It sold 60,000 copies in less than a year; ran through twenty-seven editions in five years, none of them of less than 1000 copies and some of 4000; was reprinted in London; and was translated into German. It was dramatized and scheduled to appear at the Chestnut Street Theatre in November 1844, but so great was the crowd that gathered in front of the theater before the doors were opened, and so violent had been the conservative objections to the whole production from the start, that Mayor Peter McCall, fearing a riot, persuaded Lippard to let the performance be cancelled.

The Quaker City was the first widely read American muckraking novel. Using a plot of seduction and murder based on real events in Philadelphia in February 1843, Lippard loosed his powerful imagination upon all the evils of the city's life as he had learned about them in his reporting for the *Spirit of the Times*, a Democratic newspaper.[112] He found his native place a "Whited

Sepulchre, without all purity, within, all rottenness and dead men's bones."
The city "which William Penn had built in hope and honor,—whose root was
planted deep in the soil of truth and peace," had produced "poison and
rottenness, Riot, Arson, Murder and Wrong."[113] He despised the upper
classes.

V

Poverty had become a fixed and terrible feature of Philadelphia's life in
the 1840s. Unskilled factory operatives received an average of 63¢ a day in 1841,
78¢ in 1854. In March 1844, at the height of the price rises of 1843–1844, one
group of Port Richmond coal-heavers was getting 80¢ a day, while another
got $1.00. In June 1844 the *Ledger* ran an advertisement for girls to work in
a match factory for $2.50 to $3.00 a week. In 1851 Philadelphia carpenters struck
for an advance of 25¢ a day to make a weekly wage of $10.50 for sixty hours.
Servant girls were paid $1.00 to $1.50 a week plus board to do general
housework in 1844.[114]

The grand jury investigating "the most degraded classes in the city" in
1853 reported thousands starving and homeless in the area bounded by Fifth
and Eighth Streets, Lombard to Fitzwater. This revelation so shocked Casper
Souder, Jr., a reporter for the *Evening Bulletin*, that he explored "the infected
district" himself with a guide and guard and found conditions so terrible that
he felt incapable of reporting their full horror to his readers. He estimated that
between 4000 and 5000 lived in this area chiefly by begging and stealing. A
common custom was for one person to rent a room for 12½¢ a day and then
sublet sleeping spaces on the floor for 2¢ each. Some shops charged a penny
for a meal made up of scraps begged at the back doors of the wealthy. Taverns
provided rum at a penny a glass.

Souder reflected the belief of many of his contemporaries that "rum is at
the root of the trouble." In 1841 the assessors reported 902 taverns in the city
and county, 388 of which were in the city wards, with the highest concentration in Chestnut Ward, where there were 59.[115] To combat this situation
Philadelphia in the 1840s and 1850s developed a strong temperance movement.
In 1841 the city and county supported nineteen temperance societies with a
total membership of 7000, while seven total abstinence societies claimed 10,000
members. In April 1843 the Philadelphia Division #1 of the nationally organized Sons of Temperance was instituted, the first of its kind in Pennsylvania,
and by 1847 the city had seventy divisions with 9180 members. The city's
greatest gift to the temperance movement, however, was the novel *Ten Nights
in a Bar-Room*, published in 1854 by Timothy Shay Arthur, who lived in
Philadelphia from 1841 until his death in 1885.[116]

Other social reformers attacked other evils. The movement of young girls
to the city, where they met unfamiliar temptations both as domestic servants
and as factory workers, the limited economic opportunities, and the legal and
social restrictions faced by all women drove many of them into prostitution
and associated vice. "To rescue from vice and degradation a class of women

who have forfeited their claim to the respect of the virtuous," the Rosine Association was formed in 1847, enlisting several hundred prominent church-women among its members.[117] The association opened a fourteen-room house on Eighth Street above Wood, where it cared for thirty women at a time. By April 1854 it had admitted 325, only 85 of whom were natives of Philadelphia, 80 coming from other counties in Pennsylvania, and 95 from England, Ireland, and Germany. In contradiction of the stereotype of the "sheltered" Victorian lady, the "genteel females" of the Rosine Association also conducted a visitation program to all of the brothels in their neighborhood, of which there were thirteen in one block alone. By April 1848 they had made upward of 160 of such visits. With great clarity their first annual report noted that "those who are the visitors and supporters of these houses and their inmates, are many of them the husbands, the fathers, the brothers, and the sons of virtuous women in our community. . . ."[118]

The tailoresses of the city and county went to the heart of their problem with equal directness. In an appeal for aid which they published in the *New York Tribune* on February 23, 1850, they called attention to the starvation wages being paid them. "The winter is upon us, and distress and want stare us in the face." They sought help in starting their own productive associations, "and then Rosines, and Magdalens, and children's prisons may want inmates!"[119]

In the mid-1840s the *Ledger* carried on an editorial campaign for women's rights, claiming in 1845 that women were actually morally and ethically superior to men in most respects. Women's most powerful journalistic champion, however, was Mrs. Hale of *Godey's*. "We are true to the creed that the civilization of the world is to be the work of woman," she wrote in 1847, "and so we keep the chronicle of her progress as the index of the world's advancement."[120] She was especially active in the cause of women's education, of which a high point was the establishment of the Women's Medical College in 1850.

Factories absorbed thousands of unskilled men, women, and children, binding them to the service of steam-driven machinery which required undivided attention from dawn to dark in a new pattern of servitude. The old hierarchical order of apprentice-journeyman-master, in which a man could work his way up to the enjoyment of guaranteed rights and privileges, was shattered. The factory degraded the worker, made him anonymous. He no longer bargained for his product; he delivered his life into the hands of a system that neither knew nor cared what became of him. The new system widened the gulf between the poor and the well-to-do, as a capable and fortunate few rose to become organizers and entrepreneurs, while most workingmen lost all prospect of the independence and status they might once have hoped to achieve when they became masters of a craft. Instead downward mobility—geographical, into the poorer districts of the city, and by implication social and economic—accelerated through the whole pre–Civil War era.

Philadelphia's workingmen watched the transformation of their lives and

delphia. Terms $18 per month. Board can be had in respectable families, at from $1 25 to $1 50 per week. Apply to the Subscriber, at the High School, at any time between the hours of 9 and 3, during the present week.　　j12-3t*　　JOHN S. HART.

WANTED—25 GIRLS, to work in a MATCH FACTORY. Such as will work steady can make from $2 50 to $3 per week. All wages are paid *every Saturday in cash.* Apply either at the FACTORY, No. 412 COATES Street, above Tenth, or at FATMAN BROTHERS & CO., No. 28 BANK Street.

　　Also, Wanted, a SERVANT GIRL, for doing Housework in a small family. Good recommendations required. Apply as above.　　je12-2t*

BAKER'S INTELLIGENCE OFFICE, established in May, 1811, (33 *years ago*,) at the Southeast corner of CHESNUT and (entrance in) THIRD Sts., *UP STAIRS*. Procures Clerks, Journeymen, *Apprentices,* Farmers, Gardeners, Coachmen, Waiters, Barkeep-

Advertisement, Public Ledger, *June 12, 1844.*

HISTORICAL SOCIETY OF PENNSYLVANIA

did not like what they saw. Many remained quiescent, still clinging to the promise of the Protestant Ethic, still dreaming the American Dream. Several thousand workingmen at a meeting in the State House Yard on August 1, 1842, discussed "the propriety of a procession" of unemployed, but adjourned without making any plans to march.[121] Two hundred fifty hand-loom weavers paraded a few weeks later in center city to protest their many grievances.[122] At other times and places the protest was not so peaceful. In the course of the competition between the Reading Railroad and the Schuylkill Navigation Company, the railroad company reduced the wages of its workmen. When the railroad's wooden bridge over the Schuylkill River burned down on August 25, 1842, everyone was convinced that the workmen—"lower classes, Irish probably"—had committed arson.[123] Sporadic rioting by the weavers became a familiar news item throughout the 1840s.[124]

　　The condition of the hand-loom weavers was desperate. Working in their homes on materials advanced to them on credit by the mill owners, skilled men, working fourteen hours a day, each with another person constantly assisting him, could earn as little as sixty cents. Many manufacturers paid even this pittance in store orders, which took another 8 to 10 percent of the worker's payment. Having exhausted all peaceful means of protest, "turning out" and refusing to work, the weavers exploded in violence, directed, ironically, against fellow weavers who refused to join them; they entered such workers' homes, destroyed their looms and materials, and beat men, women, and children. By 1843 wages were forced up to $4.25 to $4.75 per week, but they fell again to $2.50 in 1846.[125]

One clergyman called on the impoverished to be of good cheer, quoting John Bunyan to the effect that "He that is down needs fear no fall."[126] Quite different counsel was offered by a new, militant labor organization established in 1847 by the crusading journalist and novelist George Lippard. Calling themselves the "Brotherhood of the Union" and following a complicated secret ritual involving robes, countersigns, and the like, these workers began an organizational drive in 1849 in step with Lippard's publication of a newspaper called *The Quaker City*. The paper demanded action: "We would advise Labor to go to War, in any and all forms—War with the Rifle, Sword, and Knife! The War of Labor—waged with pen or sword—is a Holy War." No holocaust developed, but the brotherhood established branches in twenty-three states and survived into the twentieth century though with modified aims. One historian considers it the unsung parent of the Noble and Holy Order of the Knights of Labor, founded in Philadelphia in December 1869, for the first grand master workman of that organization was Uriah S. Stephens, who had begun working as a tailor in Philadelphia in 1845 and knew Lippard and the Brotherhood well.[127]

The major cities all had city industrial congresses of their workingmen by 1850, including Philadelphia. The nationally organized Industrial Congress, established in 1845–1846, held its fourth meeting in Philadelphia in 1848. In their discussion of the European revolutions of that year the members considered the possible applicability of revolutionary measures to their own problems, but the Philadelphia workmen felt they had gained a major victory in the passage of Pennsylvania's first statewide ten-hour law in March. Their joy was premature, as had been that over the ten-hour law for city workers in 1835, for the law was widely ignored. On July 4 many workers went on strike to force compliance by factory owners in the Philadelphia area. All the Fairmount mills went on a ten-hour schedule on July 6, but Manayunk and Delaware County mills either shut down, opened on a ten-hour schedule with reduced wages, or negotiated new contracts on the old basis.[128]

The 1850s began the era of modern trade unionism, in which skilled trades gave up their idealistic drive for the betterment of all workers and reverted to their earlier concentration on higher wages and better working conditions for themselves. Their new organizations specifically barred unskilled labor in general, and a few began to bar women. In 1854 there were forty-one organized trades in Philadelphia, three of which—the printers, hat finishers, and stone cutters—were affiliated with national organizations. Recurring seasonal crises finally brought stable organization by the mid-1850s to the building trades, which became the strongest group in Philadelphia and the first to band together in a "Central Union." One old carpenter, however, who had been a union member since 1852, said at a union meeting in 1869 that never more than a tenth of the city carpenters belonged to the union, most of them not even aware that it existed and caring even less about finding out. The weavers remained generally unorganized throughout the 1850s, with small groups flaring into protests from time to time, usually against individual manufacturers.[129]

Philadelphia's working class lacked articulate leadership of high quality, and their response to the changing conditions of labor was consequently fragmented. John Campbell, an immigrant Irishman who came to Philadelphia in 1843, a bookseller, publisher, prolific writer, and reporter of the Philadelphia labor movement for the *New York Tribune*, rose to prominence in the mid-1840s and for many years spoke at every important mass meeting.[130] In 1844 he was the first secretary of the Philadelphia Social Reform Society, and subsequently he founded other such organizations, such as the Social Improvement Society. However, he was not a member of any skilled trade, and his ideas were deeply tinged with the more radical theories of European socialism. By the end of 1851 his influence began to wane. He wrote in a letter to the *Tribune* in December 1850 that the main trouble with Philadelphia's workingmen was that they showed *"too much caution"*[131] (the italics were his). But his own radicalism did not extend to the inclusion of blacks in his reform efforts.

The strongest labor leader to develop in Philadelphia was William H. Sylvis, a molder by trade, who settled in the city in 1852. But Sylvis became more interested in the national and international aspects of the labor movement than in the purely local. He was to head the National Labor Union, the first great national labor movement in the United States, from 1863 until his death in 1869.

In general localism, strongly rooted in the skilled trades, became the characteristic feature of Philadelphia's labor movement, providing a future basis for the American Federation of Labor. Most of Philadelphia's workers were at best only very loosely knit together in any respect in the 1850s, barely conscious of their common interests but sharing middle-class aspirations. In this they were typical of American labor in general in this decade. Labor's chief problem in the 1850s, as it had been for half a century, was the industrial revolution. Labor did not know what to do about it any more than anyone else did.[132]

VI

Philadelphia's educational system yielded slowly to the demands of the times. The University of Pennsylvania, its oldest institution of higher learning, until mid-century displayed "a certain rigidity, a devotion to old, established practice, a complacency of Trustees and Faculty in the routine that had been long followed, a lack of imagination and of boldness of conception and action that had made it indifferent to new proposals and alien to the community that surrounded it."[133] Its strongest division, the Medical Department, enrolled from 400 to 500 students annually. In its Collegiate Department a faculty of four or five professors taught the classical curriculum to a group of from 80 to 120 young gentlemen, who tried to relieve the tedium of their lives by the organization of Greek letter societies, the first in 1849, two in 1850, and another in 1854. A minor renaissance was in the making, however. By 1854 the arts curriculum had been reorganized; the Law School, first established abortively in 1790–1791 with James Wilson as professor, was reestablished; two new degrees were instituted—Bachelor of Science and Bachelor of Laws; and a School of Mines, Arts and Manufactures was authorized. An attempt failed to transform the university into a postgraduate school, to be superimposed upon the college as the college had been imposed upon the original academy.[134]

The Central High School, opened by the controllers of the public schools in 1838, posed a challenge to the university's undergraduate program. Its arts curriculum compared favorably with that of the university for many years, and it was increasingly referred to as the "Poor Man's College." This raising of the specter of a free city college may have had something to do with the efforts made in 1842 to reduce the school's appropriations, but Central had able defenders. In 1849 the legislature gave the controllers the right to confer the bachelor of arts degree upon qualified graduates of the institution and also *in honoris causa*. In June 1854 the school occupied a new building erected at Broad and Green Streets at a total cost of $75,000.[135]

Girard College opened on January 1, 1848, with 100 students. In October an additional 100 were admitted, and another 100 in April 1849. The Jesuits founded St. Joseph's College in May 1851 at 317 Willing's Alley next to St. Joseph's Church. The Christian Brothers came to Philadelphia in 1853, opening St. Peter's School in that year. Ten years later they established a college, La Salle, initially at 1419 North Second Street.[136]

Public education made substantial gains with the state aid available under the act of April 1, 1834, that was the foundation of Pennsylvania's tax-supported public school system. With a combined population of 258,037 in the city and county in 1840, state and local funds of $125,740 were available for 23,192 students. By 1850, with the population increased to 408,762, the appropriations totaled $366,361 for 48,056 students. Although public distrust of the system was general until mid-century, conservative fears of the rising masses were even more general, and one of the most persuasive arguments for developing the public schools was their potential for directing the energies of the common man in ways thought proper by "the better sort." The *Ledger* expressed satisfaction in January 1845 that the young men trained in the public schools "will form no materials for social disorganization."[137]

Other efforts were made to keep young men in line. The Episcopal bishop Alonzo Potter, "painfully impressed with the rowdyism and apparent profligacy of multitudes" of youths, worked with laity and clergy in 1849 and 1850 to bring the members of Moyamensing gangs and others into night schools. Their efforts led to the organization of the Young Man's Institute and the Spring Garden Institute, among many similar institutions, in 1850.[138]

Ambivalence characterized the city's attitude toward the education of women. Alexander Dallas Bache had submitted to the controllers of the public schools in 1840 a plan for a four-year high school for girls and a seminary for training female teachers, but nothing came of his proposal until February 1848 when a normal school was opened offering a two-year course for girls. That it was not considered a high school can be deduced from the comment of a visiting educator in the early 1850s who, after seeing the normal school, remarked: "Yes, the High School for Girls!—that is what Philadelphia lacks. . . ."[139] Yet in 1851 Philadelphia had 699 women teachers and only eighty-two men teaching in the public schools. The School of Design, opened in 1850, provided training for young girls in "the useful arts."[140] The opening of the Female Medical College in the same year climaxed many years of effort.

VII

The diversions that were increasingly a feature of urban life helped reduce social tensions. Taverns still abounded, but they were no longer the only leisure-time alternative to the streets.

The theaters suffered, as did everything else, from the cyclical vagaries of economics and were in "miserable condition" financially from 1840 to 1846.[141] Nonetheless they continued to provide entertainment for every level of taste. In terms of the number of performances given, the most popular play in the period 1841–1854 was the national favorite, Edward Bulwer-Lytton's romantic drama *The Lady of Lyons,* which played 213 times. Shakespeare was the dramatist most frequently presented, *Hamlet, Richard III,* and *Macbeth* being the favorites, given, respectively, 124, 110, and 106 performances.[142] One ardent playgoer, however, in 1841 felt that the Bard had lost favor with the multitude, who could appreciate "nothing of higher excellence."[143] Vaudeville acts— dancers, popular singers, jugglers, acrobats, trained animals—were often presented between the acts of serious plays, and farces appeared as after-pieces.[144]

Audiences began to lionize American actors, foremost among them the Philadelphia-born Edwin Forrest, whose style, "striding, screeching, howling, tearing passions to tatters, disregarding the sacred bounds of propriety," according to hostile critics, in others satisfied a craving for excitement.[145] So devoted was Forrest's Philadelphia following in fact that when the rival English actor William C. Macready appeared at the Arch Street Theatre on November 20, 1848, he was greeted by hissing and a shower of rotten eggs; on the other hand this outburst was hardly to be compared with the fatal riot that greeted Macready's appearance in New York the following May.[146]

Women seldom went to the theater in Philadelphia in the 1840s and 1850s, generally avoiding the physical discomforts of hard seats, poor ventilation, and lack of heat in winter, the roisterous crowds, and the danger of fire. When they did attend, however, ladies went properly escorted by gentlemen and sat in the first or second tier of boxes, while "the other sort" sat with the lower classes in the third tier. The pit was exclusively male territory. Blacks were restricted to designated gallery areas, where they had to pay twice as much as other gallery occupants. Few of them attended.[147]

William E. Burton, "the keystone of the Philadelphia theatre" in the 1840s, reopened the Arch Street Theatre in June 1844 and made a bid for the family trade by announcing that "the Third Tier Nuisance" would be abolished, "improper characters will be prevented from obtaining admission to any part of the house; and the sale of alcohol, in any shops, will be discontinued. . . ."[148] The latter part of the announcement represented a daring innovation, since many theaters remained solvent because of rental fees collected from bars and stands selling fruit and oysters. Another innovation was the employment of women managers in 1842, Charlotte Cushman at the Walnut and Mary Elizabeth Maywood at the Chestnut.[149]

The middle and lower classes forming an ever-larger part of the audience loved melodramas, burlesques, comedies, and musical shows.[150] Minstrel shows became an established feature of the city's entertainment when Samuel Sanford collected a company that performed at Commissioners' Hall, Southwark, in the fall of 1844, appearing periodically thereafter at various places. In August 1853 Sanford opened his own establishment, "the first Ethiopan permanent opera-house," on the second floor of a building on Twelfth Street below Chestnut. This place burned down in December, but in April 1855 he reopened the Sanford Opera-House on Eleventh Street above Chestnut and remained there for several years.[151]

Philadelphians loved ephemeral pieces based on contemporary life. At least thirty-seven plays produced between 1841 and 1854 had the name of Philadelphia locales in their titles and reflected local conditions, such as *A Row at the Chesnut* [sic], *or Old Drury in an Uproar, Is the Philadelphian Dead, or Is He Alive and Merry?* and *Life in Philadelphia, or the Unfortunate Author*. The texts of these plays have disappeared, but something about their quality may be surmised from the comment of a theatergoer who stopped in at the Arch Street in May 1848 to see a new play called *Philadelphia in 1848*, but "found it so low that I was glad to get home again."[152]

Philadelphians did not turn out in large numbers to support lecture programs, although many were given by American and foreign celebrities, including Emerson, Thackeray, and the English geologist Charles Lyell. The number of lectures and the average attendance, however, were not high in terms of Philadelphia's population and claims to cultural leadership. "The rage for lectures . . . has passed away," the *Ledger* reported in 1845, citing as a major cause the fact that newspapers now gave free lectures in their editorial columns. The *Ledger* in that year was said to have achieved the largest circulation in the state. In 1846 it bought one of the new "type-revolving" presses invented in New York the year before, and in its first edition with the new equipment printed 4000 copies of the four-page paper per hour.[153]

A strident new voice had appeared in Philadelphia journalism in 1842 when *The Spirit of the Times* hired George Lippard, then a struggling law student, as an assistant editor. Lippard made local news his specialty, delving deeply into the city's more sensational happenings and unearthing scandals that he later used in his novel *The Quaker City*. He also increased the circulation of the paper until in January 1845 it claimed to have the largest circulation of any Democratic journal in the United States. It stopped publication in 1849 when its publisher, John S. DuSolle, went to New York to be confidential secretary to P. T. Barnum. Lippard began his own paper, *The Quaker City*, which lasted only a short time.[154]

For the new mass audiences there were many other types of diversions. The New National Theater at Ninth and Chestnut Streets was converted to a circus amphitheater in October 1846, and was well patronized until it burned down, together with the Chinese Museum, on July 5, 1854. The American Circus was opened in January 1849 on Fourth Street between Brown and Poplar. Ballard and Stickney opened a menagerie and circus on Walnut Street west of Eighth in December 1853.

The Chinese collection of Dunn's Philadelphia Museum was sent to London around 1842–1843, but the first floor of the building continued to be called the Chinese Museum. It was widely used for balls, concerts, public meetings, exhibitions, and similar purposes, the whole building being converted to such use when Peale's natural history collection on the second floor was sold around 1844. There were several other similar combinations of theater, museum, and meeting hall.[155]

Painting suffered from lack of support in Philadelphia. Many young painters came to the city to study under Sully, Neagle, and others, but found they could not make a living. The upper classes preferred European artworks to those produced in America, while successful manufacturers and merchants in general, unlike their peers in New York, showed little interest in the patronage of painting. One of the most notable exceptions, the merchant Joseph Sill, waged a lonely struggle in behalf of Philadelphia artists, with the publisher and bookseller Edward L. Carey one of his few allies. While serving as chairman of the Board of Managers of the Artists and Amateurs Association in 1841, Sill "made some severe strictures upon the wealthy part of our population for their total neglect of the Fine Arts."[156] In February 1843 he had the sad duty of supervising the winding up of the association's affairs. The following month he began organizing a new society to encourage and support local artists, an effort filled with frustrations, but his persistence finally produced the Art Union of Philadelphia and sustained it by main force through several years.[157] "How much of the labour and anxiety of the Art Union has fallen upon me!" he wrote in October 1848, "and how few of the Board of Managers take any trouble about it."[158] By 1848 only about 500 of the 800 members were Philadelphians. Sill finally withdrew in 1849. A gallery established by the Art Union in 1844 to sell the work of local artists sold only forty-three canvases in its best year, 1851. The organization finally dissolved in 1855.

The Artists' Fund Society, founded in 1835, continued to function, giving its first exhibition in the spring of 1841 in a gallery it had built over two shops on Chestnut Street with the permission of the Academy of the Fine Arts, which owned the property and occupied the back part of it. Sully refused to participate in this organization, because, according to John Sartain, he valued peace and tranquillity.[160]

A collection of portraits by Charles Willson Peale and others, long exhibited in conjunction with Peale's natural history collection, was sold at auction in 1854 for $11,672.06, the best part of it purchased by the city for Independence Hall.[161]

Sill had come to the conclusion in 1844 that "Philadelphia is not the place for an Artist's success. Indeed the taste for the Arts seems to be waning away in this City; and with our Commerce we shall lose our refinement also." Even Sully decided in 1848 that Philadelphia was "a sad place for artists," although he continued to live in the city until his death in 1872.[162] Younger painters more and more frequently went to New York, which became the center of the arts as well as commerce.[163]

The Pennsylvania Academy of the Fine Arts nevertheless continued in importance and influence. After a disastrous fire in 1845 the Academy re-opened in 1847, with antique and life classes under a group of local artists: James Reid Lambdin, Peter F. Rothermel, Samuel Waugh, William E. Winner, and Abraham Woodside. Gradually during this period the apprentice system of working under a single great master gave way to the academy form of instruction. An 1853 exhibit of 100 artists by the Academy, however, included only thirty Philadelphians. Engravers and lithographers fared better, with a great demand for illustrations from the city's busy publishers of books and magazines. Lithographers also pioneered in business advertising in their extensive production of trade cards, which incidentally became an invaluable addition to the city's iconography.[164]

Philadelphia's musical life reflected the social class structure. Gentlemen continued to enjoy amateur musicianship individually in their homes and in select clubs such as the Anacreontic Society and the Philharmonic Society. About thirty ladies and gentlemen formed a musical club, the Junto, in 1848–1849, with Dr. R. M. Patterson as president and Mrs. Hartman Kuhn as lady patroness. Opera choruses were their specialty, and they sang over sixty of them in that year. The following year a society of about seventy ladies and gentlemen, amateur vocalists, organized "Amateur Musical Soirees," presenting programs accompanied by a full orchestra of the best professional musicians in Philadelphia at the Musical Fund Hall.[165]

The Musical Fund Society on February 8, 1841, produced its first opera, Mozart's *Magic Flute*, with an orchestra of sixty-four performers, the first production of that work in the United States. The whole enterprise was said to have been underwritten by Matthias W. Baldwin, manufacturer of locomotives. It was a great success. Visitors came from as far away as Boston and New York to hear it. Of a long list of famous artists appearing at the hall in 1843, Ole Bull, the Norwegian violinist, created the most excitement, by his musicianship with the initiates, and by his distinctive headgear, a round fur creation, with the faddists, who made a popular craze of the "Ole Bull hat."[166]

The membership of the Musical Fund Society increased to about sixty in 1843–1844 and continued to rise. After four highly successful seasons the Musical Fund Hall was enlarged and altered in the summer of 1847, after plans drawn by Napoleon Le Brun.[167] Its orchestral concerts, employing from 80 to 120 musicians, continued to draw enthusiastic response. A peculiarity of Philadelphia audiences, however, was demonstrated in the 1844–1845 season, when the orchestra performed the Beethoven Symphony No. 1 in C major, but the names of the singers also on the program appeared in larger type, "perhaps . . . sugar for the pill," according to one knowledgeable critic.[168] The audiences usually had to have symphonies divided into "digestible slices," and "it would have been presumptuous to play continuously for forty-five minutes."[169]

All previous musical events were outshone by the Swedish singer Jenny Lind's concerts in 1850. *Godey's* rhapsodized: "The age of music has come for America. The national enthusiasm which has greeted and welcomed the sweet nightingale of Europe to our shores proves that our people have souls to appreciate the highest kind of this heavenly art, namely vocal music."[170] Tickets for Jenny Lind's first appearance on October 17 at the Chestnut Street Theatre were sold at auction, as was her management's custom, and the highest bidder, the well-known daguerreotypist Marcus Aurelius Root, paid $625 for his seat. He admitted, however, having hopes of thereby advertising his business as well as satisfying his love of music.[171] A contemporary critic felt that Jenny's success in Philadelphia "settled for ever the question of her reputation in America. She had sung before one of the most difficult audiences that could be collected on this continent."[172]

Adelina Patti, not eight years of age, also gave a celebrated concert in September 1852. Mme. Henriette Sontag became the leading vocal soloist in the 1852–1853 season. Among her other accomplishments was the smoking of cigars, which she and several of her fellow artists thought improved the voice.[173]

In the early 1850s increasing traffic in the vicinity of Eighth and Locust Streets made the location of the Musical Fund Hall more and more undesirable, and a lot was bought in June 1854 for a new concert hall in the fashionable new residential neighborhood at Broad and Locust Streets. The opening of the Academy of Music on January 26, 1857, marked the end of the public concerts of the Musical Fund Society, and the beginning of a new era in Philadelphia's musical life.[174]

"The year of the opera" was 1843, when two complete foreign opera companies, one French and one Italian, played long engagements at the Chestnut Street Theatre.[175] The company of Arthur and Anne Seguin, a bass-soprano couple, became the most popular troupe about 1841, supplanting Mr. and Mrs. Wood, who had "reigned" over the 1830s. A notable "first" of the Seguins was their world-première performance in June 1845 of *Leonora*, the work of William H. Fry, who had been the editor of the *Ledger* in 1844.

This "first American work worthy to be called an opera" was performed with an orchestra of fifty instruments and a chorus of seventy voices.[176]

Italian opera enjoyed considerable popularity in Philadelphia. Verdi was introduced in July 1847 by a new Italian company from Havana, which gradually surpassed the Seguin Company in both the number and quality of its productions and became the outstanding favorite until the early 1850s. The socially prominent Pierce Butler persuaded the company's leading tenor, Natale Perelli, to stay in Philadelphia and give singing lessons.[177]

While cultivated Philadelphians patronized French and Italian opera, older and socially less exalted forms of music continued to grow. Successful new German singing clubs were organized, such as the Junger Männerchor in 1850 and the Arion Singing Society in 1854, each having a membership of about sixty men. The sentimental songs of such writers as "Alice Hawthorne," who was the Philadelphian Septimus Winner, became national favorites. Winner's three most popular compositions typified a vital part of the *Zeitgeist:* "Listen to the Mocking Bird," "Whispering Hope," and "Home Without Mother."[178]

VIII

The volunteer firemen were an unfailing source of excitement. Although Philadelphia already had an excess of volunteer companies, between 1841 and 1854 twenty-nine new ones were organized in the city and surrounding districts. The whole volunteer system had for some time been identified in the public mind with violent street fighting, but in the 1840s this general lawlessness exploded more frequently and began to include arson, shooting, and murder. The city took action on May 21, 1840, in an ordinance requiring each company to submit to inspection by a committee of the city Councils, and a Board of Control was appointed to protect property and quell riots at fires. There was no immediate improvement. The geologist Charles Lyell, lecturing in Philadelphia in September 1841, noted: "We were five days here, and every night there was an alarm of fire, usually a false one; but the noise of the firemen was tremendous. . . ."[179]

The increasing number and violence of firemen's riots again led to the appointment of a joint special committee of the city Councils, which produced another ordinance on January 4, 1844, dividing the city and districts into three fire districts, and regulating the movement of fire companies out of their own districts, the use of fireplugs, and the number and age of active members of each company. All companies were to make annual reports of their activities, the number of fires attended, and the nature of their membership. Penalties were attached to noncompliance: the first offense called for withdrawal of the city appropriation, the second brought prohibition of the use of fireplugs, the third a $100 fine.

Many reasons have been suggested for the violence of the firemen—simple love of a good fight by active young males, the increasing number of lower-class artisans in the ranks (with the accompanying assumption that violence

The Philadelphia Firemen's Anniversary Parade March, *sheet-music cover, designed by James Queen, lithograph by P. S. Duval (c. 1842). The music was composed by Francis (Frank) Johnson, a popular band leader.*

is an ingredient of lower-class behavior), the desire to control their own communities and keep them "pure." Many members of organized gangs in the poorer districts also belonged to fire companies. A gang called the Killers actually took over the Moyamensing Hose Company under the leadership of William McMullin, who headed both organizations. The political ramifications of the situation are exemplified in the career of McMullin, who became a lieutenant of the marshal's police in 1852 and ultimately the Democratic boss of the Fourth Ward.[180]

On March 7, 1848, the state legislature gave the Court of Quarter Sessions special jurisdiction over riotous fire companies in the city and districts, with authority to put them out of service or disband them. By March 1853 twenty-five companies had been taken out of service under this law, yet the clerk of quarter sessions stated at that time that sixty-nine riots involving firemen had occurred during the previous year.[181]

Many fires of incendiary origin were openly attributed to the fire companies, who thus provided their own opportunities for the exercise of their professional talents. Yet the firemen also responded faithfully to the innumerable legitimate calls for their services. One of the city's worst fires began in a store on North Water Street below Vine on July 9, 1850, and eventually razed about eighteen acres, destroyed 367 buildings, and killed 28 and injured 100 persons, with a total property loss of $1.5 million. On December 27, 1851, the firemen fought against cold and a driving rain that froze almost all of the fireplugs, to bring under control a fire that destroyed publisher and bookseller Abraham Hart's building on the northeast corner of Sixth and Chestnut Streets and the Shakespeare Building opposite it on the northwest side of Sixth. These ruins were still smoldering three days later when Barnum's Museum on the southeast corner of Seventh and Chestnut Streets went up in flames. On July 5, 1854, Chestnut Street suffered still another major fire, which destroyed the whole south side of the street from Eighth to Ninth and back to Sansom Street, including the National Theater and the Chinese Museum.[182]

The maintenance of public order in the midst of unprecedented social change required political skill of the highest order. Unfortunately the political organization of Philadelphia during this period produced mixed results. The Pennsylvania constitution of 1838 had given the right to vote to all white male citizens over twenty-one years of age. The enlarged white electorate at the same time provided new possibilities for political exploitation and patronage. In keeping with the Jacksonian rhetoric of "power to the people," an increasing number of political offices became elective in the 1840s. In 1841 John Morin Scott, Princeton graduate and lawyer, became the first mayor of Philadelphia to achieve that office by popular election instead of appointment by the city Councils.[183] In many cases, however, while the administration of the city became ever more complicated and more demanding of talent, public officials were elected for reasons that had little to do with their qualifications for their jobs.

The Jacksonian premise that any (white) man could do anything he put his heart to ran counter to the facts of technological development, which demanded increasing specialization and professionalization of training as the price of success. Those who wanted to rise in the economic system had to devote their entire lives to business, and they had little or no time for municipal housekeeping chores. Keeping the city a fit place for the transaction of business was turned over to new specialists, professional politicians. One such was Joel Barlow Sutherland, who took control of the southern districts in the 1820s.[184] The colorful saloonkeeper William McMullin, erstwhile "Killer" and volunteer fireman, represented the "grass roots" of the new politics in the 1850s. By distribution of patronage and the placement of many friends on the police force, he brought order to his ward and delivered its voters to the party of his choice at each election.

The tradition of noblesse oblige weakened as "a new bourgeois ethic entered the genteel drawing-rooms around Washington and Independence Squares."[185] As early as September 1841 the Whigs were having trouble trying to get a "gentleman" to run for Congress to fill the vacancy left by the resignation of John Sergeant. One of them explained: "It has ceased to be an honor to be sent to Congress; the body itself has become so low and coarse, that a man of education & refinement finds himself out of place in it and is disgusted with its violence and blackguardism, and no one is found willing to make a sacrifice of comfort or interest to represent a city like this. . . ."[186] Yet they did find a gentleman Whig, Joseph Reed Ingersoll, to fill the post and to remain in Congress until 1849. His older brother, Charles Jared, the Democratic Ingersoll, was already there, having been elected in 1840, and he also served until 1849.[187]

Many other gentlemen entered public service as Democrats, among them Richard Rush, John Cadwalader, Richard Vaux, and most outstanding of all in this period, George Mifflin Dallas.[188] Vice-president of the United States from 1845 to 1849, Dallas felt, however, that "My personal life during the administration of Col. Polk has but poorly compensated me for the suspended enjoyments and pursuits of private and professional spheres."[189] He lacked the gusto of Vaux who, defeated for mayor in 1854, roared from the State House steps that he would run again. He won too, in 1856.[190]

It was generally believed that the Whigs were the party of the rich, the well-born, and the conservative of all classes, while the Democrats represented the masses and the occasional gentlemen who "betrayed" their own class by joining "the common sort." In the period 1841–1854 the Whigs usually dominated the city's elections, while the Democrats took the surrounding districts. The 1840 census had reported 93,665 persons living in the city while the rest of the county numbered 164,372. By 1850 these figures were respectively 121,376 and 287,386. Simple arithmetic provided one good reason why so many Whigs opposed consolidation of city and county. Yet oversimplified labels did not correspond to the realities. The Whigs as well as the Democrats drew followers from all social and economic levels. Many gentlemen-Demo-

George Mifflin Dallas (1792–1864), photograph, 1848. Dallas was mayor of Philadelphia in 1828, a U.S. senator, ambassador to Great Britain, and vice-president under James K. Polk. The city of Dallas, Texas, was named in his honor.

HISTORICAL SOCIETY OF PENNSYLVANIA

crats did not identify with the "common man" and offered conservative resistance to social change. Old hatreds forged new coalitions—anti-Negro, anti-Catholic, anti-Protestant, antiforeigner. The two major parties split within themselves for various reasons at various times, and while they quarrelled with each other, the new Native American Republican party offered a third choice. Capitalizing on the economic distress of the early 1840s, the ethnic animosities among English, Scots-Irish, and southern Irish, and the hostility felt toward all immigrants by the native-born, the Native Americans attracted dissidents from both major parties. Their power waned in the early 1850s, but the same sources of discontent fed a new coalition, the Know-Nothing party, which appeared in the mid-1850s.

The major political issue on which most Philadelphians were in agreement was the tariff. All recognized the central importance of iron in the city's economy, and the demand for protection crossed party lines. Mrs. Hale of *Godey's* expressed popular emotion in a poem of nine stanzas published in January 1847, ending:

> Thus, by Iron's aid, pursuing
> Through the earth their plans of love,
> Men our Father's will are doing,
> Here as angels do above![192]

The tariff reductions in 1841 and 1842 had coincided with the lowest depths of the depression. The lower tariff of 1846 was blamed when Philadelphia factories began to close down less than two weeks after its passage, and much of the abuse centered on Dallas, who as vice-president had cast the deciding vote in the Senate. Dallas was burned in effigy and received many threatening letters; barrels placed over chimneys of closed factories were called "Dallas Night Caps."[193]

The retired publisher Henry C. Carey and Stephen Colwell, leading iron manufacturer, supplied most of the ideological basis for Philadelphia protectionism. Having called himself a free trader for many years, Carey had begun to reexamine his position after the passage of the Act of 1842. The Tariff of 1846 had an even stronger effect on him, for suddenly one morning in 1847, he related: "I jumped out of bed, and dressing myself, was a protectionist from that hour."[194] Within ninety days he had written a 474-page treatise, *The Past, the Present, and the Future,* and thereafter he became a fount of books, pamphlets, newspaper articles, and conversation in defense of the protective principle. He never sought public office, but he did attract a fervent disciple, the lawyer and jurist William D. Kelley, who ceased to be a Democrat in protest over the Kansas question, helped to organize the Republican party in 1854, and went to Congress as a Republican in 1860, where he remained through fifteen consecutive reelections until his death in 1890.[195] Kelley earned the nickname of "Pig-Iron" for his devotion to Carey's cause.

Carey said of Stephen Colwell in 1871, "Between us there has never been any essential difference."[196] Colwell did, however, deviate in one extraordinary respect from the behavior expected of a Philadelphia gentleman. In 1851 he anonymously published *New Themes for the Protestant Clergy,* which attacked American Protestantism for its lack of charity, its materialism, and its general departure from Christian principles.[197] Many horrified Philadelphia clergymen were certain the author must be a Unitarian, while others thought he was a Jesuit in disguise; he was, in fact, a devout Presbyterian.[198] Carey defended his friend's theological approach to economics. "To my mind," he said, "it is clearly obvious that the religious writings of Mr. Colwell exhibit a healthy tone and a useful drift reflected from his economic studies."[199] Colwell attacked unbridled individualism; Carey praised free enterprise. Both ultimately arrived at protectionism.[200]

The Mexican War called forth a full spectrum of reactions. The Whigs tended to be opposed and the Democrats favorable, if only because a Democratic president was giving the orders. Polk's proclamation of war reached Philadelphia's newspapers on May 15, 1846, but two days earlier the journeymen printers had stated their intention, "as long as we have life and breath, [to be] found battling in the cause of freedom. . . ."[201] On May 16 several hundred young men of Spring Garden resolved to form a military corps, and ultimately Philadelphia offered thirty companies of volunteers. Maj.-Gen. Zachary Taylor's victories were enthusiastically celebrated on April 19, 1847, with a general illumination of the city and joyous crowds in the streets until after midnight. The First and Second Pennsylvania Regiments, both with Philadelphia companies, fought in all the principal battles of Maj.-Gen. Winfield Scott's campaign from Veracruz to the City of México. Some claimed, however, that "there is a widely spread conviction . . . that it is a wicked & disgraceful war."[202]

The churches, caught between the pacifist claims of Christianity and the desire for loyalty to the government, remained officially silent, but individual clergymen expressed divergent views, to the extent that denominational polity and their congregations permitted.[203] The minister of the First Unitarian Church, William H. Furness, preached that the war constituted "flat rebellion against Heaven" and deplored "the curse of . . . victories which provoke the appetite for conquest."[204] Many, on the other hand, welcomed the war as part of a Protestant crusade to save the world from Catholicism. The Catholics objected to the latter interpretation but nonetheless tended to support the war effort.

Philadelphia's blacks occupied a separate world, segregated by the color line. Unknown to most whites, a well-defined black upper class maintained a genteel standard of living. In 1847 black Philadelphians owned real estate worth $531,804. They supported nineteen churches and 106 beneficial societies. They maintained their own insurance societies, cemetery associations, building and loan associations, labor unions, and branches of fraternal organizations such as the Odd Fellows and Masons. They operated their own libraries and offered lectures, debates, and general adult education programs in such organizations as the Philadelphia Library Company of Colored Persons, the Rush Library and Debating Society, the Demosthean Institute, and the women's Edgeworth Literary Association and Minerva Literary Association. The truly remarkable proportions of these achievements, however, can be appreciated only when they are viewed in the context of the steady deterioration of the general living conditions of black Philadelphians in the 1840s.[205]

In the decade following Negro disfranchisement in 1838, although 30 percent more households were added to the black community, the number of real property holders decreased from 294 to 280, while per capita value of personal property decreased 10 percent. Three out of five households owned $60 or less of real and personal property. Of 302 black families living in Moyamensing in 1848, 176 together owned personal property worth only $603.50, or $4.43 per family.[206]

As a pioneer center of abolitionism and the first large city north of the Mason-Dixon Line, Philadelphia had long been a mecca for escaping slaves and free blacks who hoped to better themselves. By 1847, 47.7 percent of the black people living in the city proper had come there from somewhere else, the next highest percentages living in Moyamensing (46.3) and Southwark

(35.9). In that decade they were overwhelmed by competition from thousands of European immigrants, particularly the Irish, as impoverished and illiterate as themselves, equally unused to urban industrialism, far more numerous, and implacably hostile to them. Blacks were forced out of hod-carrying and stevedoring jobs which had traditionally been theirs. Less than half of 1 percent of adult black males found jobs in factories. Blacks found it increasingly difficult to obtain training in skilled trades, and by 1854 less than two-thirds of those who had trades could find employment in them. The one field in which they remained supreme was that of catering, with Henry Jones, Thomas Dorsey, and Henry Minton "ruling" the fashionable world from the mid-1840s until the mid-1870s.[207]

At the same time white hostility to black residential expansion, reinforced by daily incidents of overt violence, turned the Negroes back upon themselves in a pattern resembling the medieval ghetto. By 1847, of almost 20,000 blacks living in the city and county, only 1300 lived north of Vine and east of Sixth Street. Overcrowding, deteriorating housing, chronic unemployment, and increasing poverty were reflected in prison statistics. At the Eastern Penitentiary from 1840 to 1844, 29.8 percent of the inmates were blacks, most of them Philadelphians, although blacks constituted only 7.39 percent of the city's population. During the period 1836–1845 blacks comprised 48.29 percent of the inmates of Moyamensing Prison for less serious crimes and misdemeanors.[208]

White hatred of blacks burst into a spectacular riot on August 1, 1842, when a mob attacked a parade of the Negro Young Men's Vigilant Association, a Moyamensing temperance society, which was marching to commemorate the abolition of slavery in the West Indies. In rioting that recurred throughout the night and all of the next day, black men, women, and children were beaten, homes were looted, and the Smith Beneficial Hall, said to be an abolitionist meetingplace, and the Second Colored Presbyterian Church were burned to the ground. Only the use of the militia on August 2 ended the riot. On October 9, 1849, white hooligans expressed their fury against a mulatto married to a white woman by attacking a hotel he operated for Negroes at the corner of Sixth and St. Mary (Rodman) Streets. This action swelled into a two-day riot against all blacks in the area, with the blacks fighting back, until three whites and one Negro were killed and twenty-five of the injured were taken to hospitals.[209]

The violence directed against black people was deeply rooted in white racism. A visiting English Quaker, Joseph Sturge, in 1841 concluded that "Philadelphia appears to be the metropolis of this odious prejudice and that there is probably no city in the known world where dislike, amounting to hatred of the coloured population, prevails more than in the city of brotherly love!"[210] In the same year a southern Negro wrote of Philadelphia: "The exceedingly illiberal, unjust and oppressive prejudice of the great mass of the white community, overshadowing every moment of [the Negroes'] existence, is enough to crush—effectually crush and keep down—any people. It meets them at almost every step without their domiciles, and not infrequently follows even *there*."[211] Robert Purvis, outstanding Philadelphia black leader, shortly after the 1842 riot wrote to the white abolitionist Henry C. Wright: "Press, church, magistrates, clergymen and devils are against us. . . . I am convinced of our utter and complete nothingness in public estimation."[212]

Philadelphia's schools were segregated. The first law prohibiting exclusion of blacks from white public schools was not passed until 1881 and even then was widely evaded. Robert Purvis spoke for all of his people in 1853 when, in a bitter denunciation of the school system most of whose schools rejected his children, he refused to pay the school tax. The black community persevered in the construction of its own schools, which by 1854 numbered eight public schools (four opened since 1841), seven charity schools (four opened since 1841), thirteen private schools (ten opened since 1841), two schools in connection with benevolent and reform societies, and nineteen Sunday schools. About 2000 children were probably enrolled in 1854, although attendance was irregular, with approximately 1600 black children between the ages of eight and eighteen not accounted for in school statistics. There was no high school for Negroes, and black people were barred from all professional schools, even from attendance at lectures without credit, with the exception of the Eclectic Medical School, which had admitted blacks by 1852. The census of 1850 showed that of approximately 9000 Negroes over twenty years of age, 4123 were totally illiterate while 1686 could only read and could not write.[213]

Blacks provided the main strength of Philadelphia abolitionism, though their activities remained for the most part known only within the movement. A major "depot" of the Underground Railroad, Philadelphia maintained its service to fugitives through the constant devotion of such Negroes as William Still and Robert Purvis. Purvis served as president of the Philadelphia Vigilant Committee formed in 1839; chairman of its successor, the General Vigilance Committee, from 1852 to 1863; and president of the Pennsylvania Anti-Slavery Society from 1845 to 1850. Most of Philadelphia's blacks supported William Lloyd Garrison in his split with the American Anti-Slavery Society in 1840 and did not attempt to form their own black national organization, though many wished to do so.[214]

The first case under the Fugitive Slave Act of 1850 was tried in Philadelphia on October 21, 1850. Many Philadelphians opposed the law, but Edward D. Ingraham, a Philadelphia lawyer, who was one of the commissioners appointed under it, was a strong proslavery man, and the first to be appealed to by slaveholders or their agents.[215] The Pennsylvania Anti-Slavery Society accused Ingraham of "indecent readiness" to perform the "odious functions" of his office.[216] "You can have no idea of the suffering which the Fugitive Slave Law is producing among the colored people in this neighborhood," Dr. Furness wrote to a Massachusetts correspondent in April 1851. "Case after case has occurred of black persons kidnapped and dragged away in the night without even a form of law."[217] Antislavery men crowded into the courtrooms to give both legal advice and moral support to blacks brought to trial.

On the other hand a "Great Union Meeting" was held in the Chinese

Museum in November 1850 "under a call signed by upwards of 5,000 citizens," at which John Sergeant presided and, among many prominent speakers, George Mifflin Dallas denounced the "imported fanaticism" of the abolitionists, while Josiah Randall pleaded for "our Southern friends."[218] In the same year *Godey's* dropped "Grace Greenwood" from its list of contributors because of her antislavery sympathies, and it was rumored that a Philadelphia publisher had rejected the manuscript of *Uncle Tom's Cabin* because of its attacks upon the South.[219] *Graham's Magazine,* in a vitriolic review of *Uncle Tom's Cabin* in February 1853, entitled "Black Letters; or Uncle Tom-Foolery in Literature," exploded: "We have a regular incursion of the blacks. The shelves of booksellers groan under the weight of Sambo's woes done up in covers! . . . A plague of all black faces! We hate this niggerism and hope it may be done away with. . . . let us have done with this woolly-headed literature. . . ."[220] Nonetheless G. L. Aitken's dramatized version of the novel opened to a packed house at the Chestnut Street Theatre on September 26, 1853, and ran to sold-out houses for twenty-five consecutive nights.[221]

Philadelphia's interracial difficulties were complicated by the fact that it was both a "Garrisonian stronghold" and the most southern of northern cities. The conflict between its twin traditions of brotherly love and white racism was intensified by its desire for the goodwill of its southern neighbors, relatives, and customers. By the 1840s the moral dimensions of the problem had grown to major proportions.

No church could completely avoid the subject, but most of them tried. The Hicksite Quakers, led by such outstanding reformers as Lucretia Mott, Mary Grew, the Burleigh brothers, and James Miller McKim, conspicuously worked in the abolitionist cause and were often the targets of mob violence. The Quakers in general, however, were charged by one of their English brethren with having grown lukewarm in the cause, while the few black Quakers testified that they were forced to sit in segregated pews at the rear of the Arch Street Meeting House. The Unitarian pastor, William H. Furness, lost many of his wealthiest parishioners because of his antislavery activities, but persisted nonetheless, a familiar figure at abolitionist meetings and fugitive slave trials. The majority of churchgoers, however, praised the Presbyterian minister Albert Barnes, who advised that every Christian denomination should simply "detach itself from all connection with slavery, without saying a word against others. . . . Not a blow need be struck. Not an unkind word need be uttered. No man's motives need be impugned, no man's property rights invaded."[222] The Philadelphia Conference of Methodists from 1837 to 1847 asked every candidate for admission as a preacher, "Are you an Abolitionist?" and if he was, he was not received.[223]

Many Philadelphians looked to their clergy as they always had for moral guidance through the upheavals of their time, but the clergy had troubles of their own. In the nineteenth-century version of old quarrels, the Presbyterian New School did battle ideologically with the Old. The Episcopalians were divided by the High Church–Low Church controversy. The conservative defenders of "old measures" in the German Reformed Church struggled with the "new measures" of revivalism. The Jews wrestled with evolutionary trends toward Americanization of ritual and governance, as Philadelphia became a center in the development of Reform Judaism. Protestants grew frantic over the growth of Catholicism, as Irish and German immigrants of that faith poured into the city. The Irish-born bishop of Philadelphia's Roman Catholics from 1830 to 1851, the Right Rev. Francis P. Kenrick, became the target of complaints from the Germans in his flock, who felt themselves discriminated against in favor of the more numerous Irish. The increasing immigration of German Jews brought German congregations new power in that faith.[224]

To counter the public's preoccupation with business, revivalism was cultivated in the 1840s with some success, especially among the Presbyterians and the German Reformed churches of the Philadelphia area, although the enthusiasm of the latter began to die down in the mid-1840s and expired around 1853. Apparently Philadelphia needed such a program, for the Rev. Albert Barnes estimated that in 1841 there were more than 100,000 unchurched in the city. However, "the quest for personal holiness," the avowed object of revivalism, obviously did not appeal to as many Philadelphia Protestants in the 1840s as did the crusade against Catholicism. The necessity for vigilance against a papist conspiracy, the defense of Protestantism against its oldest enemy, constituted a recurrent theme in the revivalist preaching of this period.[225]

Philadelphia became a major operating base for what has been called "the Protestant Crusade" in the 1840s. Many local groups of anti-Catholic agitators had sprung up early in the decade, had combined in a Union of Protestant Associations, and by 1842 had established a Protestant Institute to distribute anti-Catholic literature. A newspaper, *The Protestant Banner*, began publication early in 1842 under the editorship of the German Reformed pastor Joseph F. Berg, a noted anti-Catholic, and continued for many years. Meanwhile the new political coalition to be called the Native American party had been organizing in various parts of the United States, demanding restriction of the suffrage to native-born Americans and only those immigrants who had been in the country for twenty-one years. It held its first meeting in the Philadelphia area in 1837 in Germantown.[226]

On November 2, 1842, twenty-six Philadelphia clergymen, representing a cross-section of Protestant denominations, invited to an organizational meeting all persons alarmed by the growing presence of Catholicism in their midst. Six days later the American Protestant Association was formed, with the names of ninety-eight clergy and laymen appended to its constitution. Many of the city's most influential congregations were represented by such clergymen as Stephen H. Tyng of St. Paul's Protestant Episcopal Church, George B. Ide of the First Baptist Church, Cornelius C. Cuyler of the Second Presbyterian and Henry A. Boardman of the Tenth Presbyterian Church, and Joseph F. Berg of the First German Reformed Church. Another signer, the Rev. Samuel B. Wylie, was a professor and vice-provost of the University of

Pennsylvania as well as pastor of the Reformed Presbyterian Church.[227] In ecumenical unity all pledged themselves to an unremitting ideological war on popery, through their own congregations and by appeals to others in books, tracts, and pamphlets. They had potent allies in the publishers of secular textbooks, for "No theme in these schoolbooks . . . [was] more universal than anti-Catholicism."[228]

Many forces coalesced in Philadelphia in the summer of 1844—Protestant clergy and laity, unchurched masses, the popular press, politicians—to produce the worst mob violence that had ever ravaged the city. The spark that set off the explosions was a letter written by Bishop Kenrick on November 14, 1842, to the board of controllers of the public schools, asking that Catholic children be allowed to use their own Bible and be excused from other religious instruction while attending the public schools.[229] During the following months of correspondence between the bishop and the controllers, this request was transformed by the anti-Catholic forces into an attack on Sacred Writ, with the result that the controversy turned into a holy war. According to a contemporary Protestant, the anti-Catholic crusade "arose in probably the least religious section of the city," and most of the rioters "would not have known the difference between the Protestant and Catholic Bible if it had been placed in their hands."[230]

The violence began in Kensington, where concentrations of skilled weavers from Northern Ireland had organized the anti-Catholic Orange Society of Philadelphia in the 1830s. In the 1840s they revived an old quarrel with the newly arrived southern Irish, who in addition to being Catholic were also unskilled laborers and so poor they were willing to work for less even than blacks. Meanwhile in December 1843 the political nativists formed the American Republican Association, which within five months had set up branches throughout the city. On May 3, 1844, one of their meetings in Kensington was broken up by southern Irishmen. Reprisals followed, with thirty Irish homes destroyed by fire on May 7. On May 8 mobs burned down St. Michael's Catholic Church and rectory at Second and Jefferson Streets, the Female Seminary of the Sisters of Charity at Second and Phoenix Streets, St. Augustine's Church on Fourth Street below Vine, with an adjoining school, and several private homes of Irishmen. An estimated fifty persons were injured, 200 had to leave their homes, and property damage totaled $150,000. The grand jury blamed the Irish Catholics for the riot.[231]

The Native Americans celebrated the Fourth of July, 1844, with a parade of fifty ward and township associations, but without the expected violence. Fighting broke out the next day at St. Philip de Neri's Catholic Church on Queen Street between Second and Third in Southwark. Militia units were called out, the violence ebbed and flowed, and fifteen were killed and fifty wounded before peace was finally restored on July 8.[232] An estimated total of 5000 militia had been used to quell the disturbance, which had, unlike the May riot, pitted citizens against the military, not simply Protestant against Catholic. In a sober mood, on July 11 the city passed an ordinance providing

Riot in Philadelphia, July 7th, 1844, *lithograph by James Baillie, New York. The Catholic Church of St. Philip de Neri, in the right background, still stands on Queen Street near Second.*

for its own armed force of one battalion of artillery, one regiment of infantry, and one or more full troops of horse, subject to call when necessary, "to provide for the preservation of the peace of the city." By September 26 the full complement was enlisted, totaling 1350 men.[233]

The Native American politicians had larger stakes in mind than a few Catholic churches. They sent eight men to the House and one to the Senate from Philadelphia County in the state elections in October, and in the presidential election in November helped the Whigs take control of the county away from the Democrats. In October 1848 five Native Americans were elected to the House from Philadelphia County with Whig aid, and they held the balance of power when the Assembly organized in 1849. The Native American leader in Philadelphia, Lewis C. Levin, was elected to Congress three times between 1844 and 1848, and in 1846 another Native American, Henry Lelar, was elected sheriff. Native American newspapers were established: Levin's *Daily Sun*, a penny paper, which lasted from 1843 to 1857; the daily *Native American*, begun in the 1844 campaign and lasting only a few months; the daily *American Advocate*, founded in 1844, which in 1845 became the *Native Eagle and Advocate* and survived until 1849; and the short-lived *American Citizen*, begun in 1845. The first national convention of the party was held in Philadelphia on July 4, 1845. The special brand of patriotism that the Native Americans sponsored, however, began to dissipate after the mid-1840s with the gradual decline of the party.[234]

I X

The political administration of Philadelphia became increasingly difficult during the 1841–1854 period. Officially the city's jurisdiction extended only from the Delaware River to the Schuylkill, north as far as Vine Street, south as far as South Street; but its burgeoning population had continued to spill over into the surrounding area until by 1854 there were thirteen townships, six boroughs, and nine districts surrounding the city. The city and county together included forty corporate or quasi-corporate bodies.[235] The result was an administrative nightmare in many respects, but especially for law enforcement officers, since criminals could break the law in the city and by a short flight over the city's narrow boundaries could pass quickly beyond the possibility of punishment. Furthermore as the prominent lawyer Eli Kirk Price pointed out in 1853: "The parent city [had] often evinced an illiberal policy toward her surrounding children, which they [had] more than requited by a spirit of retaliation."[236] Though the neighboring districts could not control their disorderly citizens, they refused to let the city intervene. One observer blamed the newspaper reporters, "hard put for subjects," whose daily news stories about violence gave the rioters "exactly the kind of fame they coveted."[237] Others blamed the general public. According to one clergyman: "This is the fatal evil in Philadelphia—that the riotous and disorderly are convinced of the lukewarmness and timidity of the respectable part of society, and so they take full swing upon every occasion that arises."[238]

The crux of the matter was the total inadequacy of the law enforcement agencies in the city and county. When the May 1844 riots had begun in Kensington, the only police officer available had been the sheriff, and he had neither an assistant nor the funds to pay or arm a *posse comitatus*. The militia had hesitated to respond to his call because they had not been reimbursed for expenditures they had made on previous occasions. By the time they did decide to help, matters were completely out of hand. Spurred by the events of that summer and acting on the recommendation of the city Councils, the state Assembly passed an act on April 12, 1845, requiring Philadelphia and the unincorporated districts of Spring Garden, Northern Liberties, and Penn and the township of Moyamensing to establish and maintain police forces of not less than one able-bodied man for every 150 taxable inhabitants. Yet in August 1849, in order to quell a serious riot in Moyamensing, a gang from a rival district was employed as a police force. A new attempt to improve the situation was made on May 3, 1850, when an act was passed by the legislature establishing a Philadelphia police district with a police force that had authority not only in the city but in seven surrounding districts as well.[239] This force was independent of watchmen and police already serving the city and county. A police board was created, composed of a marshal and four lieutenants, and new station houses were built in various parts of the city.

Consolidation of the city with the outlying districts had been proposed unsuccessfully several times. Many reasons other than the obvious need for better police and fire protection argued for the move. The city needed an extended tax base in order to provide the services—water, sewerage, street paving, street cleaning, street lighting, among others, in addition to police and fire departments—that a growing urban industrial center required for survival. Eli Kirk Price, who led the fight for consolidation in the early 1850s, pointed out that the existing city charter was a "procrustean bed" in which Philadelphia was "cramped, fettered, and paralyzed by a pernicious and complicated system of government."[240] Philadelphia was sinking to the status of a colony, for the center of the area's population was no longer in the city but north of Vine Street, where 206,885 persons lived between the two rivers, as compared with 188,802 who lived south of Vine. The rate of increase in the decade 1844–1854 indicated further disparity to come, for while the city's population grew by 29.5 percent, Spring Garden's increased 111.5 percent and Kensington's 109.5 percent, with only slightly lesser percentages in other districts. All of these considerations, together with many others, finally helped to overcome the objections of Whig leaders who feared Democratic domination in a city-county consolidation.

With all the city's leading newspapers supporting the movement, three men were elected to carry the cause to the state legislature: Eli Kirk Price for the Senate, and Matthias W. Baldwin and William C. Patterson for the House. A bill for a new charter was produced on December 20, 1853. In Price's memorial to the legislature on January 3, 1854, he presented an overwhelming mass of statistics to support the proposal, not the least of which was the fact that in the Philadelphia area there were nineteen sets of taxes, nineteen sets of tax collectors, and at least twelve distinct debts in connection with the nineteen distinct corporations of the city and county. He estimated that the proposed new charter would eliminate 168 tax collectors at least, with a saving of $100,000 a year. By January 31 the bill had passed both houses, and it was rushed to Gov. William Bigler, then in Erie, for signature. Roused out of bed before midnight on February 2, the governor signed the bill, this unseemly haste having been deemed necessary because certain districts were considering assuming new debts for railroad loans and similar projects, in the expectation that the consolidated city would have to pay them.[241]

Great was the rejoicing in Philadelphia on March 11, 1854, as the consolidation forces celebrated their victory. An excursion on the Delaware sponsored by the Board of Trade, a ball at the Chinese Museum, a banquet at the Sansom Street Hall, and visits by the governor, members of the legislature and city Councils to the public institutions of the city, with the whole city brilliantly illuminated at night, all attested to the general feeling of accomplishment. Saluting the new Philadelphia at the civic banquet, Governor Bigler asked rhetorically, "Who can doubt her future triumph?"[242]

The period from 1841 to 1854 constituted a watershed in Philadelphia's history. During these years the major problems of the industrial revolution had been confronted and solutions sought. A technological advance of unprecedented character had created productive capacity and great wealth, but it had also caused enormous social dislocation and misery. The physical and

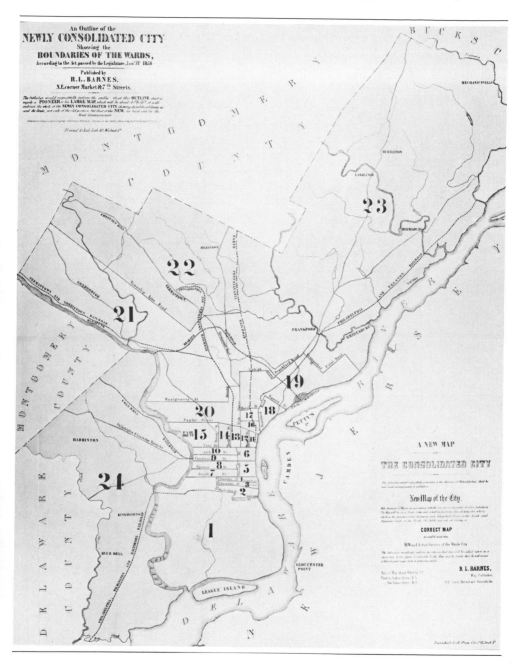

An Outline of the Newly Consolidated City, Showing the Boundaries of the Wards, According to the Act Passed by the Legislature, Jan. 31, 1854, *published by R. L. Barnes. The map also includes six railroad rights of way. The Main Line of the Pennsylvania Railroad was completed in February 1854.*

demographic expansion of the city, the influx of a new wave of immigrants, the maldistribution of wealth, the rising expectations of the masses—all presented problems of staggering magnitude. New social arrangements were urgently required, but how were men to be persuaded to do that which had to be done? Vested interests, human inertia, human ignorance, all constituted formidable obstacles.

The Border City in Civil War
1854-1865

by Russell F. Weigley

Colorphobia is more rampant here than in the pro-slavery, negro-hating city of New York.

— WILLIAM WELLS BROWN

Later in the day, I saw several hundred colored men in procession march up Sixth to Chestnut, and up Chestnut St. They were not uniformed nor armed, but were a good looking body of men. They had a drum and fife, and carrying inspirited banners. At Chelten Hills they have a camp, and are raising a regiment.

— GEORGE W. FAHNESTOCK [1]

Anthony Trollope remarked with characteristic condescension that if all cities were to stretch their boundaries as Philadelphia had done, "there would soon be no rural population left at all." The census takers would count everybody as urban. Like much of what he said about America, Trollope's remark was half true. There were still some 1500 farms and about 10,000 cattle in the 129 square miles between Cobbs and Poquessing Creeks declared by the Consolidation Act to be the city of Philadelphia. The city indeed, as Trollope observed, "takes in other towns connected with it by railway, but separated by large spaces of open country." Nevertheless the crowded precincts from Moyamensing and Southwark northward through the old city to Spring Garden, and along the Delaware as far as Kensington and Richmond, ranked the consolidated city among the great urban centers of the new industrial age. By 1860 its 565,529 inhabitants may well have made it the fourth-largest city in the Western world, as well as second in the United States. London and Paris were much larger, with about two million and a million and a half souls respectively. New York with its more than 800,000 (hard by Brooklyn's 266,000) was well ahead. But Baltimore, the next American city, was well behind; and Philadelphia's population compared with but surpassed such European capitals as Vienna and St. Petersburg and the somewhat similar industrial and commercial cities of Liverpool and Manchester.[2]

Panoramic View of Philadelphia, *lithograph by Asselineau after a water-color by John Bachman (act. 1850–1877), published by John Caspar Wild (c. 1855). Looking over the Schuylkill eastward to the Delaware River and Camden, the view shows the growth of the city at mid-century. The white columns of Girard College (finished 1847) are seen at the left edge of the picture, and the domes of the Cathedral of Sts. Peter and Paul (1846–1864) and the West Arch Street Presbyterian Church*

(1850–1855) are north of Market Street, which bisects the now empty Centre Square.
A reservoir tops a small hill above the waterworks near the Fairmount Bridge at
the lower left, and the old gasworks are near the Market Street Bridge. Development
has nearly surrounded Rittenhouse Square at Eighteenth and Walnut Streets,
southwest of Centre Square. The two shipbuilding houses of the Navy Yard are
visible on the Delaware riverfront at the upper right.

Philadelphia in the age of the American Revolution had been too big and too urban for the tastes of many members of the Continental Congress, but the city of 1776 had been a very small place compared with the Philadelphia of the mid-nineteenth century: industrial Philadelphia was one of the first of the world's truly big cities, something new under the sun, an agglomeration of people that made inherited notions of "a community" obsolete, for it was too populous and widespread to be truly a community. Its pace of growth from 161,410 inhabitants in the urbanized portion of Philadelphia County in 1830 had been staggering, not only to the imagination but to community cohesion and services. While violent riots threatened all vestiges of civic well-being, there were more mundane troubles as well. Early in the century, for example, the designers of the justly famous Schuylkill Water Works had built in an excess capacity they thought would last for generations—only three of eight waterwheels at Fairmount Dam had had to be used initially; but the waterworks became overtaxed, and three years before consolidation Philadelphia had to reject the request of West Philadelphia to share in the water.

With the hope that consolidation would overcome at least the worst of the big city's tensions and problems of rapid growth, confidence nevertheless overshadowed concern.

On some future day perhaps, the eighteenth-century past would transfix the city's imagination, the here-and-now would seem drab in contrast to the time of Benjamin Franklin and President Washington, and the conviction that a golden age was lost and gone would itself help breed drabness and stagnation. None of that was true on the morrow of consolidation. From consolidation to the Civil War, Philadelphia continued to enjoy exuberant growth. Living men who had themselves witnessed the creation of a city that was big on an unprecedented scale knew well that, for all the political and cultural eminence of the eighteenth century, they now inhabited a metropolis in comparison with which Franklin's Philadelphia had been a provincial town. If the city counted for less in the realm of books and the arts, it hardly mattered to the businesslike masters of Chestnut Street. If political capitals were gone, the first city of the Keystone State could still command votes and money enough to assure respectful attention to its interests in Harrisburg and Washington.

For the life of the city lay in finance, commerce, and industry—industry above all, an activity in which Philadelphia was a far closer rival to New York than in population. Population itself was still climbing rapidly, from 408,762 in the county in 1850 to the 565,529 of 1860. Philadelphia was disorderly and often ugly, yet thoroughly vital. If the city had experienced eras of greatness in the past, it was enjoying another now.

The gathering stormclouds of civil war did not imperil Philadelphia's economy as once they might have done. The businesses, banks, and first families of the city retained strong ties to the South, and partly for this reason sectional controversy divided opinion within the city as much as in New York and more than in any other northern center. But during the consolidation

Advertisement in Abner D. Jones's The Illustrated American Biography . . . (*New York: J. M. Emerson, 1853–1855*). *The sheds in Market Street were demolished to make way for the tracks of the Pennsylvania Railroad. Steam locomotives were used between Pittsburgh and the Schuylkill, but as a precaution against fire, horses were substituted to pull the cars through Philadelphia.*

year the Pennsylvania Railroad opened its mountain division to weld the last link in the rail connection between Philadelphia and Pittsburgh. By that time the rails also reached outward from Pittsburgh to the Mississippi River. In 1858 a direct railroad linked Pittsburgh and thus Philadelphia with Chicago. The Pennsylvania Railroad system cancelled much of the westward advantage New York had held since the opening of the Erie Canal and accelerated the turning of Philadelphia away from the South and toward the West. If intersectional war should come, moreover, Philadelphia's position as the northern city nearest to Washington and Virginia promised a grim but potentially profitable role as a center of northern mobilization.[3]

I

A principal motive of the Consolidation Act was to try to make the booming city governable. As a welter of tiny jurisdictions it clearly had not been so, especially in the elementary matter of law and order. Consolidation was intended to unsnarl legal complexities that impeded police activity; to make an adequate police force financially possible; to end the reign of hoodlums like the Moyamensing Killers and fifty-one other recorded street gangs of teenagers and young men who battled each other for territorial rights on street corners, mauled and terrorized passersby, and covered walls and fences with graffiti; to send the fire companies back to fighting fires instead of—in shifting alliances with the gangs—each other; and above all to forestall any recurrence of the great riots of 1844. The cry for public safety and police protection had been at the heart of the consolidation movement.[4]

The Consolidation Act vested executive power in a mayor, who was to be elected every two years. Appropriately, the clearest and strongest of the mayor's powers under the new charter pertained to the police. Unfortunately only the mayor's police powers were really clear and strong. Under the municipal charter of 1789 the Councils had continued to place administration of new city services as they developed, such as the waterworks and the supply of gas for lighting, under autonomous committees on the direct model of the colonial congeries of committees. Another of the explicit purposes of the Consolidation Act was to improve the municipal executive branch by putting in the mayor's charge the municipal administration and the executive departments, subject only to the Councils' general oversight and control of the purse. As events turned out, however, the Councils exploited their fiscal power to shift the locus of executive authority back into the Councils and committees created by the Councils. Here lay seeds of eventual trouble.

The Councils were cumbersome even as a legislative assembly. In accordance with the conventional wisdom of the day, the Select Council and Common Council were modeled on the state Senate and House of Representatives respectively, with analogous functions, privileges, and relationships. They were analogously large, with one member for each ward in the Select Council (for a total of twenty-four in 1854), and one member for every 1,200 taxable inhabitants (plus one for any fraction over 600) in the Common Council (for a total of seventy-four in 1854). Their size and organization unsuited them for executive and administrative activity. The first mayor under consolidation quickly complained that the Councils were usurping executive functions, and in spite of their unwieldiness they persisted in the habit.[5]

Only law and order posed problems of conspicuous enough intractability, and only here was the Consolidation Act explicit enough that the Councils observed restraint and the mayor approximated a strong executive. The charter gave him power to appoint police officers (with the advice and consent of the Select Council), dismiss them, prescribe their duties and rules and regulations, and command them. The memory of 1844 gave the mayor "the like powers and authority [to suppress riots and disturbances] as the sheriff of the county of Philadelphia," which is to say powers broad to the bounds of constitutional dubiety. From the commonwealth's antiriot statute of May 3, 1850, the mayor inherited authority to disperse groups as small as twelve persons, if he found them "riotously or unlawfully" assembled. He might call upon any citizen of appropriate age and abilities to assist the police in the process, and he might also call upon the commanding officer of the Philadelphia militia district.[6]

An early councilman thought the mayor's police powers formidable enough to deserve outward symbolism in the shape of a great tricorn hat which, like the lord mayor of London, the chief executive might don whenever he assumed the role of chief policeman.[7] Nothing came of the idea, but it is by their performances in the police role that the first mayors after consolidation are best known to history.

The first of them, Robert T. Conrad, was a Whig journalist and businessman carried narrowly into office by a combination of the traditional Whig strength in the old city and the American or Know-Nothing movement, which cut into Democratic voting north of Vine and below South Streets. Although the revulsion that followed 1844 had chastened and quieted Philadelphia nativism and anti-Catholicism, such resentments had continued to simmer, and they were brought to a boil again in the early 1850s by the visit of Monsignor Gaetano Bedini as a Vatican emissary charged with final settlement of the old trusteeship controversy, and by the rise of the Know-Nothings in other parts of the country. Fewer of the foreign-born lived in Philadelphia than in any other large northern city; but by 1860 there were to be 169,430, or better than one in four, and more than half of them—over 95,000—were the Irish whose presence had provoked the great riots. These circumstances offered enough fuel for the Know-Nothing party to give Conrad the mayoralty as the "American" candidate.[8] Mayor Conrad announced his intention to recruit a police force of 900 men—all of American birth.

The Councils reorganized the police department by an ordinance passed on July 28, 1854. Each ward was made a separate police district with its own police station, and a central police station was set up in City Hall at Fifth and Chestnut Streets. Conrad used the growing force most conspicuously to harass violators of the Sunday blue laws, thus invoking the sanctions of the

Quaker and Puritan past against the festive continental Sabbath of the immigrants. He enforced a new state law against Sunday liquor sales in taverns, tippling rooms, oyster houses, and amusement parks. He obstructed the distribution of Sunday newspapers. In the process he touched off a number of boisterous scuffles between citizens and police—the more boisterous because the police themselves were recruited from the kind of toughs who came out of the street gangs and were accustomed to beating up Irishmen and blacks. The early police specialized in legalized violence as their weapon against the unlegalized kinds.[9]

If, however, Mayor Conrad vented nativist prejudices in the most respectable fashion possible, by guarding the sanctity of the Christian Sabbath, he also provoked annoyance, not necessarily confined to immigrants, at police highhandedness and busybodyism. In 1856 he failed of renomination, and his party failed to win the city election. The Democrats elected Richard Vaux, son of the philanthropist Roberts Vaux. While Richard Vaux was an old-family Quaker, his political connections, significantly, were with Lewis C. Cassidy, leader of the Irish Catholic faction of the Democratic party.

No doubt forces other than nativism affected the outcome. Not only did the Whigs have to overcome a mainly Democratic tradition in the former suburbs, but by 1856 national politics was in flux; the Whig party was moribund and the American party unlikely to take its place as the principal opposition. Many former Whigs of conservative temperament were moving toward the Democrats because the new Republican party struck them as dangerously radical on the slavery question. To what extent national politics carried over into municipal elections is questionable, especially since the balloting for mayor took place in May; yet the confusion of national politics cannot have been entirely irrelevant to Philadelphia elections. In addition the Democrats employed an ever-popular theme when they chose as their cry against Whig control of the mayor's office: "No increase of taxes! No excursions of Councils! No Free Rum at expense of Councils! No Free Cigars! No Free Hack Hire! But a frugal and economical administration of municipal affairs!"[10]

Apart from the fame of his father, the new Democratic mayor may have been best known for the frivolous fact of his coronation-ball dance with Queen Victoria. But he had rejected an opportunity to enjoy similar frolics at the court of the czars by joining the American mission there, choosing instead to return to Philadelphia for a career of service and leadership to the city more in keeping with his father's example. A lawyer by profession, he maintained the family's humanitarian tradition through almost half a century as secretary and president of the Board of Inspectors of the State Penitentiary for the Eastern District. A relatively young man of forty when he was elected mayor, he was destined still to be serving his city and party in Congress as late as 1891. If there was a measure of incongruity in his political partnership with Lewis Cassidy and the Irish faction, here too Richard Vaux was following his father. Roberts Vaux had long been a powerful voice in the Philadelphia Democracy, albeit moving mostly behind the scenes. He had helped lend some social distinction to the party when, in the age of Nicholas Biddle, its leaders included a Charles Jared Ingersoll and a Richard Rush but overall it could not match the social qualifications of the Whigs. Richard Vaux was an early local specimen of an American phenomenon, the gentleman in politics who, by connecting himself with working-class interests and organizations—Vaux belonged to the Columbia Hose Company, for example—establishes himself as a champion of the common man.[11]

Richard Vaux (1816–1895), salt print by Richards and Betts (c. 1856).

By the time of Vaux's mayoralty the contrast with Know-Nothings and Black Republicans was affording the Democrats a respectability among the city's first families that they had not enjoyed at least since before Andrew Jackson assaulted the Bank of the United States. Vaux assisted his party's rise in respectability not only through his family credentials but by doing efficiently the mayor's main job, improving the police force and guarding law and order. Like Theodore Roosevelt in New York at a later date, Vaux liked to prowl the nighttime streets in person along with the police, joining them in their battles with the street gangs. While adopting a more tolerant view of the Sabbath laws than Conrad's, and while distributing patronage with due regard to the Cassidy alliance—that is, he appointed Irish police—Vaux secured enlargement of the police force to as many as 1000 men. As far as the rudimentary crime reporting of the day permits judgment, he apparently accomplished something toward pacification of the Moyamensing Killers, the Bleeders, the Blood Tubs, the Deathfetchers, the Gumballs, the Hyenas, the Smashers, the Tormenters, and the rest of their ilk. At all events the number of physical assaults committed on the streets declined during the 1850s. More important, and in direct fulfillment of the hopes of the champions of consolidation, there were no great riots.[12]

Vaux had the advantage of a police-and-fire-alarm telegraph system installed late in the Conrad administration, connecting 163 outlying stations with the central police office at City Hall. Modern writers on municipal problems of the nineteenth century have suggested that inadequate communications accounted for much of the trouble, indeed rendering the government of large cities almost impossible; the municipal telegraph at least moderated the difficulty. To exploit improved communications Vaux created a police reserve, normally stationed for the most part along Chestnut Street, but available for rapid deployment wherever it might be needed. He also initiated a fire detective bureau under a fire marshal; the consequent investigations into the crime of arson, often perpetrated by the volunteer fire companies themselves, reputedly cut the incidence of the crime by half.[13]

The greater test of law enforcement under consolidation awaited the next mayor, Alexander Henry, who had to face the climactic sectional crises and the tensions of civil war in a city of divided sentiment. On several occasions his city was to appear on the verge of a miniature civil war of its own, but always the mayor and the new police force met the test.

II

Its tempering of the city's violence was the consolidated government's most notable early success. Other than the police, the bureaus and departments of the municipal administration remained closely linked with the unwieldy Councils, and any improvement in them did not match the hopes that the Consolidation Act might have aroused. The early mayors, especially Vaux and Henry, were men of considerable ability; the personnel of Councils, in contrast, probably warranted the grumbling with which fastidious Philadelphians discussed them. The complexities of the new big city, along with those of managing the new industrial establishments, were prominent among the factors that in the nineteenth century made a political career and business leadership more and more specialized and therefore separate occupations. Councilmen were therefore less and less the prominent business, social, and civic figures they had been.

On the other hand the new municipal government did not yet afford enough patronage to make possible a well-disciplined and cohesive political organization with the virtues that discipline and cohesion imply, at least not beyond the boundaries of a single ward. Philadelphia's professional politicians did not yet wield strength much above the ward level. In Southwark and Moyamensing, for example, Joel Barlow Sutherland, who had exerted considerable power in the 1820s and 1830s but had come to grief in the Democracy by supporting the Bank of the United States, had been succeeded eventually as Democratic boss of what was now the Fourth Ward of the consolidated city by William McMullin. An alumnus of the street gangs, McMullin kept order in his ward by methods he had learned in that hard school.[14]

The extremes of violence had abated, but most of Philadelphia's problems of the preconsolidation years remained problems still. An abatement of the growing division between the well-to-do and the poor, the factory operator and the workingman who in the industrial age could no longer hope to be a master craftsman, obviously would have been beyond the reach of any mere municipal political reorganization. But there were too few improvements even within the purview of city government. Too many of the public thoroughfares continued to be abominations, quagmires in wet weather and at other times tangles of ruts and potholes where broken wheels and axles were a matter of course. Railroads penetrated the city amid constant complaint about the perils of unregulated grade crossings; but little was done about the crossings, and their gruesome accidents were a staple of the newspapers. The waterworks were becoming outdated rather than regarded as a model of technology; water was often filthy and in parts of the city sometimes too scarce to bathe in. The city retained, and despite professions of reluctance often had to use, the Kensington Water Works, opened in 1850; Kensington drew from a stretch of the Delaware that by the mid-1860s received over thirteen million gallons of sewage daily. Pigs still scavenged for garbage in some of the streets and carved out their wallows; hog raisers, driven from the central districts, still colonized foul precincts in the Neck—the peninsula between the Delaware and the Schuylkill south of the old city—and West Philadelphia. In the alleys of the old city and in clusters of jerry-built dwellings scattered around the urban periphery, blacks, immigrants, and the poor in general huddled amid cockroaches, rats, and assorted filth, inviting new epidemics—and in fact the consolidated city's response to the cholera epidemic of 1866 was to be in some ways less effective than that of the old municipalities to the epidemic of 1848.[15]

The growth rate of Philadelphia's population in the 1850s was 38 percent. As a city that was still young, and expanding at such a pace, Philadelphia had insoluble housing problems. The city was not old enough to have acquired any large reservoir of deteriorating older houses into which the poor might move as the better-off departed; some such housing existed in Southwark, Moyamensing, and the Northern Liberties, but not enough. The well-to-do still inhabited the general area where they had always lived, the central precincts of Chestnut, Walnut, Spruce, and Pine Streets. Unable to find much abandoned older housing, the poor had to build dwellings for themselves, taking up previously vacant ground—sometimes as squatters—in the Neck or Kingsessing or Richmond. The growth of the heavily populated districts at mid-century was mainly in the upper areas of Moyamensing—the worst of the city's slums—and Passyunk, and along the northern reaches of the old suburbs of Spring Garden, Penn, and Kensington. These circumstances brought poverty into convergence with building costs; the results were insufficiency and hazards to health and safety among the "hangers-on about the outskirts of the cities," the poor of the urban periphery who reversed the urban core-and-ring pattern that was to become familiar in the twentieth century.

There were already some foreshadowings of that later pattern. The main business section of the city had moved west from the immediate vicinity of the Delaware since the early years of the century, and the area between Third and Eighth Streets, Walnut and Market, was changing from residential to the prototype of the modern downtown shopping district. It differed, however, from a modern downtown in the profusion of manufacturing activities that persisted amid the shops. Philadelphia was an industrial city, but big factories dominated only a few industries—notably the manufacture of locomotives, certain kinds of textiles, gas fixtures, umbrellas, bricks, and iron machinery —while other manufacturers still operated in small shops—milliners, tailors, shoemakers, bookbinders, printers—that clustered in the downtown district. The factories tended to be on the outskirts of the city, such as the mills of Manayunk, Nicetown, and Germantown. But in a further presaging of later developments, also in the suburbs more and more not only of the wealthy but of the middle class were availing themselves of the railroads to transform summer homes into year-round retreats from the turmoil of downtown. Thus the circle of Ingersolls and Fishers with their friends and connections chronicled by Sidney George Fisher's diary was limning the future of Washington Lane and other environs of Germantown.[16]

Meanwhile, bad streets and the absence or expense of transportation also obliged workingmen to live as close as they could to the scenes of their labors. The houses of operatives tended to cluster around mills and factories, creating mill towns as enclaves within the larger city. Meanwhile too in the old city, especially between Chestnut Street and the former boundary at South Street, domestics and menial workers gathered in the alleys and side streets close behind the town houses of their employers. Altogether, in much of the nineteenth-century city wealth and poverty rubbed elbows in indiscriminate jumble and clutter. On Kent Street, now part of Panama Street and just behind Pine east of the Schuylkill, tiny bandbox houses sheltered linen weavers of the mills along the Schuylkill practically in the backyards of the somewhat more spacious Pine Street dwellings of foremen and clerks. The latter structures nudged and were dwarfed in turn by the town houses of notables just slightly farther east on Pine, such as Maj.-Gen. George Gordon Meade's at the time of his Gettysburg victory, at 2037.[17]

Yet it is Philadelphia that we are describing, and an impression of clutter and confusion must not be overdone. Charles Godfrey Leland remembered the Philadelphia of mid-century as

a very well-shaded, peaceful city, not "a great village," as it was called by New Yorkers, but like a pleasant English town of earlier times, in which a certain picturesque rural beauty still lingered. The grand old double houses with high flights of steps, built by the Colonial aristocracy—such as the Bird [Burd] mansion in Chestnut Street by Ninth Street—had a marked and pleasing character, as had many of the quaint black and red-brick houses, whose fronts reminded one of the chequer-board map of our city.[18]

William Russell of the *Times* of London saw a "vast extent of the streets of small, low, yet snug-looking houses. . . . Philadelphia must contain in comfort the largest number of small householders of any city in the world."[19]

Along with the snug-looking red-brick row houses, Philadelphia's neat gridiron street pattern marched outward from the old center to cover more and more of Philadelphia County. This phenomenon was a dubious inheritance from the "pleasant English town of earlier times," because however well the gridiron pattern fitted the small and comparatively level old city, it was much less satisfactory to extend the pattern mechanically over a far larger area. In the outlying districts hills were higher and more numerous, and the absence of diagonal avenues, except for a few old roads that were retained, lengthened travel distances unduly. Characteristically, as the gridiron expanded, the city Councils in 1858 extended to the whole city a plan begun for the old city in 1853, changing the names of some 900–1000 streets, courts, and alleys to make them consistent throughout the city, eliminating changes of a street's identity from district to district. In a related measure, in 1856 the Councils also regularized the numbering system for houses and other buildings, to run by hundreds within each full block, each new block beginning a new hundred. On east-west streets the numbering began at Front Street and ran westward, even numbers on the south side of the street, odd numbers on the north. Anyone confronted with the address 400 Walnut Street would henceforth know that he would find it on the southwest corner of Fourth and Walnut. On north-south streets the numbers ran northward or southward from Market, even numbers on the west side, odd numbers on the east. All householders were required to display their house numbers. This simple but enlightened arrangement still exists. Even the carping Anthony Trollope praised it while deploring the confusion of north-south addresses in New York, a contrast he might still draw.[20]

I I I

The Councils of the 1850s could also boast certain larger accomplishments. Their financial support was essential, of course, to the improvement of the police. They made a beginning toward control of the notoriously unruly fire companies. An ordinance of January 30, 1855, gave the companies their first central direction, in the form of a fire department headed by a chief engineer, with seven assistants, and a board of directors representing the companies. Henceforth companies had to come into the fire department to be recognized and assisted by the city. In joining they had to limit their membership, but they would be assured annual appropriations. For several months many companies haggled over the powers of the fire department and refused to come in, and their political power was such that the Councils felt obliged at last to promise a weak central direction and the preservation of much of each company's autonomy. Thus the accomplishment had to be restricted to be effected at all, but nevertheless a corner had been turned. About the same time the city was able to force the newly developed steam pumping engines upon the resistant companies. The members of the volunteer companies rightly foresaw that here was a much more decisive threat to their old ways. The steam engines were delicate machines that would require maintenance by skilled mechanics, not haphazard abuse by rowdies. The new engines were also so heavy that they had to be pulled by horses. That requirement cut down on the numbers of men who needed to run with the engines and thus justified the city in curtailing the membership rolls.[21]

Consolidation brought the Schuylkill River within the city limits for several miles above the Fairmount Water Works, and another of the early actions of the new Councils was to avail themselves of this development to protect and improve the purity of the Schuylkill water supply. Such was the official motive for the ordinance of September 15, 1855, which set aside the Lemon Hill area just north of the Fairmount Water Works as a common to be held in trust for the citizens of Philadelphia. But another motive was also present; the Councils were responding to the romantic vogue of naturally landscaped public parks, a popular movement that was concurrently inspiring Andrew Jackson Downing's campaign for an extensive park in mid-Manhattan and Pres. Millard Fillmore's overtures to Downing to beautify the public grounds of Washington in the area that later became the Mall. The ordinance of 1855 was the foundation of Fairmount Park.

The city had owned the old Robert Morris estate at Lemon Hill since 1844 but had leased it as a beer hall and garden. Transferred now to direct city management, the tract was enlarged in two years by the acquisition of an additional thirty-three acres, partially purchased by interested citizens on condition that the city complete the transaction. This acquisition carried the new park north past Benjamin Latrobe's Sedgely mansion. It also linked the park with the Spring Garden Water Works, which had served Spring Garden and the Northern Liberties since 1844 and had come into the city's hands through the Consolidation Act. Presently the city acquired also, by court action, a tract along Fairmount Avenue that separated Lemon Hill from the Fairmount Water Works. Altogether the city now held a park of some 110 acres, extending from the old waterworks to the present area of the rock garden near the Girard Avenue Bridge.

In 1859 the Pennsylvania legislature incorporated the Zoological Society of Philadelphia, which had plans to attach a zoological garden to Fairmount Park north of the Spring Garden Water Works. Meanwhile the Councils had agreed to accept a donation of forty-five acres including the Hunting Park Race Course, northeast of Fairmount Park. The municipal legislators were soon considering proposals for a street to connect the Hunting Park tract with Fairmount Park. In 1858 the Councils drew all these accessions together by

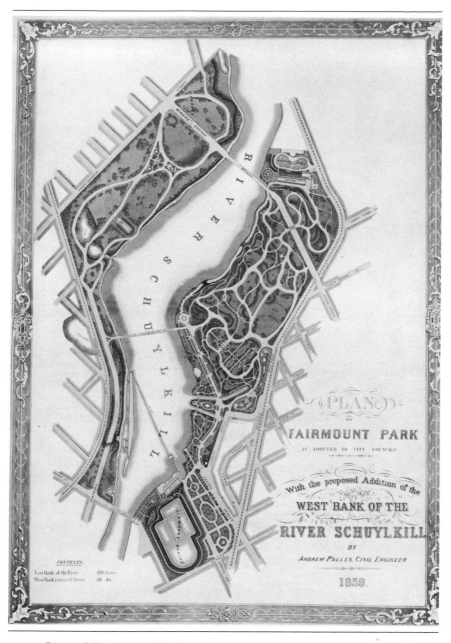

Plan of Fairmount Park, *lithograph by Louis Napoleon Rosenthal (act. 1850–1875) after Andrew Palles (n.d.), 1859. This plan by Palles, a civil engineer, won a design competition held by the city in 1858. Although the park was not laid out according to this specific design, the plan illustrates the intent of the city for expanding its public gardens and lands at the Waterworks and Lemon Hill.*

Home Run Quick Step, *sheet-music cover, lithograph by Thomas Sinclair (1860). The playing field of the Mercantile Base Ball Club was at Eighteenth and Master Streets, near Girard College. Other early baseball teams active in Philadelphia before the Civil War included the Minerva, the Keystones, the Athletics, the Equity, and the Swiftfoot.*

HISTORICAL SOCIETY OF PENNSYLVANIA

adopting a comprehensive plan for the development of Fairmount Park. The city's yearning for tranquility and order, which had accomplished consolidation and now felt the stimulus of the accomplishment, seemed to be reviving Penn's dream of the "greene Country Towne."[22]

But tranquility and urban progress were only rarely compatible. Because the large and growing consolidated city required improved intraurban transportation, the postconsolidation renaissance which created Fairmount Park also introduced new noise, clatter, and danger to the streets by inaugurating the first street railway lines, the horse cars. About the time of consolidation the North Penn Railroad was preparing to operate from a station at Front and Willow Streets into Bucks County. The railroad then proposed to connect its terminal with other sections of the city by means of horse-drawn cars. The city allowed it to lay rails for that purpose, and the first horse cars to travel on tracks moved in 1855. Other steam railways followed with similar horse-car spurs.

In New York and Boston, meanwhile, the same idea was being turned to expressly intraurban movement. Philadelphia was not long in following. The Philadelphia and Delaware River Railroad Company held a charter to build a steam railroad from Philadelphia to Easton. Its managers decided, however, that competition made that plan unpromising, and on July 7, 1857, the city Councils agreed to let them enter the intraurban railway business instead. They would operate horse cars south on Sixth Street and north on Fifth between Cherry Street in Kensington and Morris Street in Southwark, thus serving the most densely populated districts, which still followed the arc of the Delaware. They began service in January 1858, and they met immediate success. Riding over iron rails gave horse cars conspicuous advantages both in speed and in comfort over the older omnibuses which plied the rutted and cobblestoned streets. Councils promptly received a flurry of requests for additional charters. In March 1858 they chartered another horse-car line; in April, nine more.

By 1860 eighteen street railways held charters, and their tracks lined nearly all the major streets of the heavily populated areas. By the end of their first year of operation the intraurban horse cars were already carrying an estimated 46,000 riders daily. Their relative speed and convenience so improved travel that on the suburban line to Darby five cars could not keep up with a traffic for which one omnibus had been enough. In 1857 there were 322 omnibuses in the city; by 1864 there remained only one. In the early 1860s, again following Boston's lead, the Fifth and Sixth Streets and Broad Street lines experimented with steam-powered streetcars, but complaints about noise and fire hazards obliged them to remain with horse power.

The city paid a price even for the horse cars. By ordinance the streetcar lines were to maintain both their own tracks and the street surfaces immediately adjacent. But the railways neglected the streets, nobody did much to reprove them, and street surfaces became more abominable than before. The city's indifference to neglect, furthermore, pointed to the beginning of a larger issue. The street railways would contribute much to the unhappy political atmosphere of the later nineteenth century, when they would be conspicuous members of a coterie of private interests apparently capable of manipulating the representatives of the public interest at will.[23]

Fortunately not all of the streetcars' disruptions of municipal tranquility seem in retrospect to have been quite so serious. Before private tampering with the public interest assumed frightening dimensions, the first political furor occasioned by the streetcars involved the question of operating them on Sundays. Lines that attempted to do so were enjoined against it by the courts.

Third and Dock Streets (photograph 1859). Tracks of one of the eighteen street railways chartered in the city by 1860 as well as an omnibus are visible in this photograph of the banking and publishing center of Philadelphia. The first Bank of the United States had been taken over by Stephen Girard in 1812, and the small building to the left of the bank was the home of the Saturday Evening Post *from 1858 to 1860. In 1861 Jay Cooke & Co. rented office space in the brownstone building to the right of the bank.*

There thus developed a lively controversy between practical-minded citizens and the devout, the latter charging that streetcars on Sundays disturbed the worship of God, created a demand for intoxicating liquors, tempted the lower classes to squander their money, and exposed the suburbs to plunderers. Sunday operations generally ceased for the period of this chapter.

There were other early controversies: Was the five-cent fare exorbitant? Could something be done to keep the horses from collapsing and even dying with appalling frequency in the heat of the Philadelphia summer? Portentously, should blacks be allowed to ride the cars? Withal, the street railways soon grew indispensable to the unity of the expanding city; the big city desperately needed improved transportation.[24]

In 1857 the confident progress of the consolidated city wavered briefly during the financial panic of that year. Textbooks often date the panic from August 24, when the New York branch of the Ohio Life Insurance and Trust Company suspended specie payments. But the American phase of the world-wide panic entered its worst period with the failure of the Bank of Pennsylvania in Philadelphia on September 25. This event was especially unsettling because the bank had a relationship with the commonwealth similar to the old connection between the Bank of the United States and the federal government, and because the failure unveiled gross mismanagement in this key institution. Thereafter the suspension of specie payment became general throughout the nation. In the city, business distress grew severe enough to produce a rally of 10,000 unemployed in Independence Square. Over the economy-minded objections of the Councils, Mayor Vaux, the workingman's friend, initiated a limited municipal program of public works.

The banks gradually resumed specie payment toward the end of the year. No prolonged depression developed to follow the crisis. The Panic of 1857 proved to be one of the milder spasms of the business cycle, and although the Bank of Pennsylvania dealt Philadelphia a harder blow than many cities felt, confidence soon returned to Chestnut Street. The rapidity of recovery made the whole affair seem almost a confirmation rather than a denial of Philadelphia's essential economic solidity.[25]

The decade of consolidation resumed its course as a decade of progress. By the end of the 1850s the authorities in Washington endorsed Philadelphia as the most appropriate place for a display of American prosperity; specifically, they chose the city for a visit of the first official Japanese envoys to the Western world, where the Japanese might observe the wonders of an American metropolis at work. Philadelphia responded with zest. In what turned out to be the final display of municipal self-confidence and exuberance before the Civil War clouded everything, Philadelphians turned out en masse to welcome the Oriental visitors and open shops, factories, and theaters to them.

There were some seventy Japanese dignitaries and attendants. They came to the United States to exchange ratifications of the first commercial treaty between Japan and America, which according to the treaty had to take place in Washington. But from Washington the Japanese were eager to travel on to view an industrial city, and they especially hoped to visit the United States Mint in Philadelphia. The city eagerly arranged for them to see not only the mint but almost everything else of note. They toured a variety of industrial plants, they shopped, they witnessed a surgical operation performed under a general anesthetic, they attended a matinee that combined opera—including the voice of Adelina Patti—with farce and pantomine, and they marveled at a balloon ascension. They brought with them artists to record these spectacles; Western exotica such as bathtubs and kitchen forks attracted the artists as much as factories and machinery. To Philadelphia, however, it was the Japanese themselves who were the great attraction of the day, people of strange faces and stranger costumes and customs, but of a vivaciousness and verve not expected in natives of the supposedly long-slumbering East.

As many as half a million Americans, from far and wide across the country as well as from all over the city, were estimated to have crowded the downtown streets to catch a glimpse of the Orientals when they arrived by railroad from Washington on June 9, 1860, and made their way to the largest hotel, the Continental, just opened the previous February 16 on the southeast corner of Ninth and Chestnut Streets. For days thereafter the streets around the hotel remained packed with curious humanity. Five days after the arrival the city Councils could not muster a quorum because too many members were waiting upon the Japanese. "Japanese fever" was the rage of the city. "Japanese Tommy," an individual of ready wit, flirtatious disposition toward the ladies of Philadelphia, and competent English—he was one of the delegation's interpreters—was the special favorite of those who met the visitors.

Between presents bestowed on them by Philadelphians and their purchases in the stores, the Japanese envoys supposedly took some $100,000 worth of goods away from the city, which Philadelphians might regard as an auspicious beginning of a new avenue of commerce. The envoys also left $3000 to be divided among the police because they had been well protected.[26] If not a harbinger of any immediately important commercial developments for the city, hopes notwithstanding, the "Japanese fever" amusingly foreshadowed a second Japanese visit to Philadelphia. At the Centennial Exposition of 1876 Philadelphia's and America's enthusiasm for things Japanese was to rise again from the Japanese exhibits there, so much that it is from the Philadelphia Centennial Exposition that the American vogue of Oriental art and design is often dated.

For the present more traditional Western kinds of design prevailed in Philadelphia, but the consolidated city's prosperity seemed so complete that even a new golden age for culture and the arts seemed not beyond possibility with the coming of the 1860s. On February 25, 1857, the magnificent acoustics of Napoleon Le Brun's Academy of Music had resounded to their first opera, Verdi's *Il Trovatore*; it was here that the Japanese listened to Patti. The domed cathedral, designed by Le Brun and John Notman, was rising above Logan Square. On Twentieth Street north of Market, Notman built St. Clement's; following upon St. Mark's on Locust Street west of Sixteenth, St. Clement's

Academy of Music, Broad and Locust Streets, built 1855–1856 (photograph c. 1865), designed by Napoleon Le Brun (1821–1901) and Gustav Runge (1822–1900). A corner of Horticultural Hall (finished 1866, burned 1881) appears at the left, and Calvary Presbyterian Church (built c. 1853) is seen at Fifteenth and Locust Streets.

FREE LIBRARY OF PHILADELPHIA

was the second of his temples of High Church Anglicanism and another result of the westward movement of society and fashion as the residential district of the old city became more and more commercial. Where John Notman's hand touched, Philadelphia assumed a medieval aspect; still another of his churches was Holy Trinity on Rittenhouse Square, where the young Phillips Brooks ascended the pulpit in 1862. (In keeping with the mood of the new churches, brownstone advanced along the residential facades of Walnut, Locust, Spruce, and Pine west of Broad Street.)[27]

I V

But though at least faintly smug, the consolidated city could not concentrate on its own progress alone. More and more the sectional controversy diverted attention from municipal events.

At first Philadelphians were among those who could scarcely conceive that the slavery controversy might embroil the country in civil war. Except for a handful, they themselves had no intention of agitating the question to the annoyance of the South. On the contrary, Charles Godfrey Leland remarked that in Philadelphia "everything Southern was exalted and worshipped."[28]

To be sure, the antislavery Republican party chose the hall of the Musical

1724 Walnut Street, northeast corner Rittenhouse Square (photograph c. 1865). The brownstone palazzo in the newly fashionable Rittenhouse Square neighborhood was built c. 1850 for George W. Edwards, a wealthy hotel owner.

FREE LIBRARY OF PHILADELPHIA

Fund Society off Washington Square for its first national nominating convention in 1856. That same year, however, William B. Thomas won less than 1 percent of the city's vote as the first Republican candidate for mayor. The persistent Kansas troubles and the Charles Sumner–"Bully" Brooks affair stirred up somewhat more Republican sentiment by the time the city went to the state and national elections in the fall. But the nativist American party remained the principal successor to the Whigs as major opponent of the Philadelphia Democracy. Prominent former Whigs such as William B. Reed, Joseph Reed's grandson, were tending to become Democrats rather than associate with either nativism or antislavery. And the Republican showing remained so feeble in the October state elections that the American state chairman refused a coalition with the Republicans for the November presidential contest. In October the Democrats captured the whole Philadelphia congressional delegation and elected Lewis Cassidy district attorney. In November Pennsylvania's Democratic favorite son, James Buchanan, won 53 percent of the Philadelphia vote. The American party's Millard Fillmore took 36 percent and the Republican John C. Frémont, though he had been nominated in Philadelphia, only 11 percent.[29]

These results did not indicate merely that Philadelphia felt indifferent to antislaveryism. More than that, the Democratic campaign of 1856 candidly argued that a vote for Buchanan's party was a vote of unequivocal rejection of the antislavery party and the Negro. This argument evidently appealed to most Philadelphians. They would not agitate against the peculiar institution of the South, and they could hardly imagine the North's agitating the question to the extremity of civil war; they themselves did not like the Negro and wished to confine him to a restricted and menial role. The whole remaining history of the sectional crisis was to confirm that this was the principal attitude of Philadelphia, and to leave the attitude little changed.

With such an outlook Philadelphians did not expect civil war, but neither did they find the sectional controversy, so closely linked to questions of race, altogether remote and abstract. It would be a mistake to make the sectional controversy seem central to the lives of Philadelphians in the 1850s; it would be equally a mistake to pretend that the controversy was not a constant presence somewhere in the city's consciousness. The blacks themselves, after all, were present. They constituted about 4 percent of the population of the city, a small proportion by later standards but the largest of any northern city at the time. The 22,000 blacks of Philadelphia were in fact the largest black community in any city of the United States except Baltimore.

The black inhabitants of Philadelphia congregated, furthermore, in the very heart of the city, in and immediately adjacent to the wards of the old city where they were most visible and closest to the principal institutions of the city's life. In the Fourth Ward, that is, old Southwark from South Street to Fitzwater and from the Delaware to Broad Street, nearly 10 percent of the inhabitants were blacks. In the Seventh and Eighth Wards, from Chestnut Street to South and Seventh Street to the Schuylkill, over 11 percent were blacks. In the Fifth Ward, the very center of the old city between Washington Square and the Delaware and from Chestnut to South, 21 percent were blacks.

These proportions were easily large enough to cause disquiet. The blacks lived there, of course, because their occupations as domestic and menial workers for the best families of the city brought them here. (Their work as domestics is attested also by a striking disproportion of women among them.) Despite a few who were well-to-do, such as, at various times in the century, the sail manufacturer James Forten and the coal merchants William Still and Stephen Smith, the economic position of the blacks was steadily deteriorating from a very low base. Employment in the new factories remained generally closed to them. Semiskilled and unskilled occupations in which blacks had once predom-

inated, such as hod carrier and stevedore, had fallen to the Irish. The proportion of black craftsmen who possessed skills but were not practicing their trades
rose from 23 percent in 1838 to about 38 percent in 1856.[30] Socially as well as economically Philadelphia's impact on the the blacks was destructive. Blacks born
and living free in Philadelphia were less likely to have stable family lives than
those coming to the city out of slavery.[31] Prospects for improvement were
being cut off, like the power of the ballot in 1838; in 1854, for example, the state
legislature acted against equality in education by requiring separate schools
for blacks in districts where there were twenty or more colored pupils.[32]

Living at the core of the city, the blacks were perceived by white Philadelphians as a seemingly necessary but disturbing presence. They troubled the
very families in whose homes the overwhelming majority of their working
women served as domestics.[33] They infuriated the working-class whites who
competed with them on the lowest rung of the economic ladder, and who had
attacked them in a series of bloody riots from 1834 onward. New York had
a well-deserved reputation for antiblack racism, which was to erupt there in
the murderous riots of July 1863; but the black abolitionist William Wells
Brown said of Philadelphia in 1854, "Colorphobia is more rampant here than
in the pro-slavery, negro-hating city of New York." Frederick Douglass said:

There is not perhaps anywhere to be found a city in which prejudice against color
is more rampant than in Philadelphia. . . . It has its white schools and its colored
schools, its white churches and its colored churches, its white Christianity and its
colored Christianity, its white concerts and its colored concerts, its white literary
institutions and its colored literary institutions . . . and the line is everywhere tightly
drawn between them. Colored persons, no matter how well dressed or how well
behaved, ladies or gentlemen, rich or poor, are not even permitted to ride on any of
the many railways through that Christian city. Halls are rented with the express
understanding that no person of color shall be allowed to enter, either to attend a
concert or listen to a lecture. The whole aspect of city usage at this point is mean,
contemptible and barbarous. . . .[34]

The riots had halted the growth of Philadelphia's black population in the
1840s, but in the 1850s fugitives from the South helped restore the growth rate
to 12.26 percent, still much lower than that of the white population but another
disquieting tendency.[35]

Almost equally disquieting was the presence of the blacks' friends and
advocates, the abolitionists, a small and unpopular minority but a persistent
one, whose cries against slavery in the South carried overtones of racial
egalitarianism that seemed to threaten Philadelphia itself. The Pennsylvania
Society for the Promotion of the Abolition of Slavery, the Relief of Free
Negroes Unlawfully Held in Bondage, and for Improving the Condition of
the African Race, founded in 1775, had long since fallen into a very moderate
and very respectable type of reformism. The same was true generally of the
antislavery attitudes of the Society of Friends, who had initiated eighteenth-
century Pennsylvania abolitionism. Philadelphia Quakerism in the middle
nineteenth century was so distracted by the schism between Hicksites and

Orthodox, and so subdued by quietist principles and social conservatism, that its quest for worldly reform had largely withered away. Fears that antislavery agitation might lead to war confirmed Quaker silence. But as the older antislavery movement faded, new and more militant advocates rose in its place.

The Pennsylvania Anti-Slavery Society, founded in 1837, never attracted more than 300 persons to its state meetings, but it managed to remind Philadelphia of its existence in a variety of ways. The burning of its headquarters at Pennsylvania Hall by an anti-Negro mob in 1838 had done nothing to temper its inclinations toward militancy. When the national antislavery movement had divided at the beginning of the 1840s, the Pennsylvania Society joined with the radical Garrisonian faction. It followed William Lloyd Garrison in denouncing the United States Constitution as a proslavery document and proclaiming "No Union with Slaveholders." Its leading figure was J. Miller McKim, variously publishing agent and corresponding secretary, and a notable of the national movement as well. James Mott was president for a time, and his wife Lucretia a vice-president. More disturbingly, the leadership also included two Negroes, Robert Purvis, at various times president and vice-president, and William Still, the clerk at the society's post-1838 headquarters, 31 North Fifth Street. Under these auspices Philadelphia witnessed an annual antislavery fair, and a stream of antislavery lecturers came to address those who would listen. Propaganda flowed from North Fifth Street, and thence also agents of the society coordinated the Underground Railroad in the Philadelphia area.[36]

In the story of the Underground Railroad it is difficult to separate reality from myth, and the traditional version may contain more of the latter than the former. But thanks to the Anti-Slavery Society, Philadelphia was one place in the North where there did exist a fairly effective organization to succor escaping black men. A "Vigilance Committee" of the Anti-Slavery Society supervised the work. Both Philadelphia and neighboring Phoenixville were important junction points on the routes that slaves followed northward, where the fugitives knew they could find shelter and directions for further travel. The most spectacular exploit of the Philadelphia Underground station was the completion of the escape of Henry "Box" Brown, who in 1849 had himself shipped in a wooden box, via the Adams Express Company, from Richmond to the abolitionists in Philadelphia. During the 1850s the Philadelphia Vigilance Committee aided about a hundred fugitives a year, although the number fell off toward the end of the decade. Most fugitives proceeded to places farther north; but some stayed, and by augmenting the Negro population of the North the Philadelphia abolitionists did not augment their own popularity among their neighbors.[37]

Thus although a handful of Philadelphians worked as conductors on the Underground Railroad, most of the city by contrast appeared more conservative than the North in general on the question of the Fugitive Slave Act of 1850. That law provoked no remarkable outcry among white Philadelphians. Six cases developing from it were heard in the city during the 1850s. One of them, in 1851, was the famous trial of the Christiana rioters, in which Thaddeus Stevens and the prominent Philadelphia Democrat John M. Read defended twenty-seven Negroes and three white men against charges growing out of the Lancaster County killing of a Maryland slaveowner, Edward Gorsuch, while he was trying to capture an alleged runaway. In this instance antislaveryism seemed to triumph since the defendants were acquitted. But the triumph was not unequivocal. Victory in court followed from the prosecution's attempting too much; the charge was treason, and it was untenable. Outside the courtroom the antislavery movement had to bear a revulsion of popular feeling against the killing of Gorsuch. And in the more typical cases of the decade, while two Negroes were set free by a judge or commissioner unconvinced that they were fugitives, three were seized and sent south without obstruction or much excitement. The only people who in one case threatened to stand in the way of the law were a group of the city's Negroes, but as events turned out they did nothing more than form a crowd outside the State House, the scene of the hearing.[38]

In 1855 one of the members of the Vigilance Committee, a Quaker named Passmore Williamson, attracted notoriety when he approached three slaves of a North Carolina owner traveling through the city and told them they could claim their freedom. He based his appeal on a Pennsylvania law of 1847 that had withdrawn the right to bring slaves into the state in transit. Naturally the slaveowner and his attendants objected despite the law, but Williamson was accompanied by six local blacks, and a scuffle developed during which the slaves escaped. The participating Philadelphia Negroes were arrested, and two of them were eventually convicted of riot. Judge John K. Kane of the United States District Court ordered Williamson to produce the fugitives, but he did not do so and was thereupon jailed for contempt of court. The aftermath was characteristic of the city and state. The Republican party nominated Williamson for canal commissioner, the party's first candidate for state office in Pennsylvania, but he won less than 3 percent of the vote. Philadelphia Democrats persuaded a mass meeting to resolve that the state should restore permission for slaves to pass in transit.[39]

The city's congressional delegation showed little sympathy for antislaveryism. When William Millward, elected to the Thirty-fourth Congress in 1854 on the American ticket, deviated by shifting from a prosouthern record to support of the Republicans, he failed to win reelection. In the late 1850s none of the major newspapers was friendly to antislaveryism. Republicans bought the *Times* to give their party a journalistic voice in the campaign of 1856, but significantly the paper collapsed in 1857. Morton McMichael's *North American* also endorsed John Charles Frémont in 1856, but very cautiously and conservatively and without a clear embrace of the antislavery cause. The *Bulletin, Inquirer, News,* and *Sun* backed Fillmore in 1856. The *Public Ledger,* which had the largest circulation in the city, was officially independent but supported Buchanan. The *Argus* and the *Pennsylvanian* were Democratic papers, the latter rabidly antiabolitionist and prosouthern, since it was the Buchanan administration organ.[40]

The *Press*, founded in 1857, occupied a peculiar position because it was John W. Forney's paper. Forney was an upstate Pennsylvanian who had edited the Democratic party's Washington paper during the early 1850s and concurrently served as clerk of the national House of Representatives. With the elevation of a Pennsylvanian to the presidency Forney had aimed for higher things, principally a seat in the United States Senate. But he was not well liked among Philadelphia Democrats, and they had joined with other party dissidents to block his election. From that point Forney's luck continued bad. Buchanan thought of arranging the purchase of the *Pennsylvanian* for him as a consolation prize, but the owner's price proved too high. Forney then opened the *Press,* expecting that the lucrative contract for printing post office blanks would be transferred from the *Pennsylvanian* to him. It was not. Disgruntled, and not liking slavery anyway, Forney broke with Buchanan in 1857 over the administration's effort to admit Kansas to the Union under the proslavery Lecompton constitution.[41]

Forney was by no means representative of Philadelphia Democratic opinion. Much of the local Democracy was so sympathetic to the South and so hostile to blacks and abolitionists that it swallowed even the Lecompton constitution, though that document patently mocked the principle of popular sovereignty. United States District Attorney James Van Dyke was able to organize a successful mass meeting in support of Lecompton. Still, Mayor Vaux and his right-hand man Lewis Cassidy felt squeamish enough about Lecompton to abstain from becoming sponsors of the meeting, and their misgivings proved well placed. The Lecompton constitution, which denied Kansas white men control of their own institutions, shifted the terms of political debate enough to open the first chink in the prosouthern armor of Philadelphia politics. Doubts about official Democratic policy seem to have developed first among some of the former Whigs who had drifted into the party. Their defections from the Democracy largely explain why the party's share of Philadelphia ballots fell to 45 percent in the state elections of 1858.[42]

By that time, moreover, Lecompton had provided the means for building an American-Republican coalition. In the face of Lecompton, many Republicans were willing to emphasize popular sovereignty rather than explicit antislaveryism, and old Whigs and Americans were willing to take that ground too. With so much mutuality established, the Americans were amenable to softening their nativism into protection of American labor, whose implications could be as nativist as one chose to make them, but which more explicitly meant the protective tariff. A coalition manufactured of these materials won its first victory by unseating Mayor Vaux in favor of Alexander Henry in 1858. It chose for itself the label "People's party." In October it went on to defeat four of the city's five Democratic congressmen.[43]

But it must be emphasized that the coalition and its victories were possible only because the Republicans agreed to play down their antislaveryism; the city's opinions had changed in no essentials. John Brown's raid in 1859 horrified most articulate Philadelphians. When the Anti-Slavery Society scheduled a public meeting at National Hall on Market Street above Sixth to observe the hour of Brown's execution, Mayor Henry felt obliged to send 120 policemen to prevent the affair from turning into a riot, especially since many of the mourners were blacks, and many of the hecklers who predictably appeared were medical students from the South, who made up nearly half the enrollment in the medical schools of the city. Other Philadelphians, thinking of themselves as responsible citizens, and including some who would one day join in founding the Union League, felt called upon to organize a much larger meeting—over 6000 appeared—to deplore John Brown and to express solicitude for the constitutional rights of the South.[44]

Miller McKim accompanied Mrs. John Brown to Charlestown, Virginia, to claim her husband's body and take it to New York State for burial. Since no formal preparation of the body was permitted in Virginia, McKim planned to pause in Philadelphia and use the services of a local undertaker. As the body approached the city, however, a crowd gathered at the Philadelphia, Wilmington and Baltimore station at Broad and Prime Streets, once more mixing Negroes and abolitionists with southern medical students and southern sympathizers. Thereupon the mayor not only assembled another large police detachment but ordered that the body be moved through Philadelphia without pause. As a further precaution, the crowd was lured away from the railroad station with the ostentatious removal of a decoy coffin, after which the real coffin was quietly hurried to the Walnut Street wharf. Preparation for burial had to take place in New York City, where no one objected to turning over the body to an undertaker for two days.[45]

Two weeks later George William Curtis of Brook Farm and Horace Greeley's *New York Tribune* appeared at National Hall to share his New England antislavery propaganda with Philadelphia. The occasion provided Mayor Henry with the stoutest test yet of his ability to preserve the consolidated city's good record against rioting. A counterrally outside the building was advertised in the *Pennsylvanian* and the *Public Ledger*, and rumors spread that Curtis would be muzzled by force. A crowd estimated at 5000 gathered outside the hall to hear leading Democrats such as Charles Ingersoll, son of Charles Jared Ingersoll, offer speeches not notable for their restraint; the abolitionists were warned to call off their meeting under pain of various dire penalties. Stones began to fly at the windows, and fist fights broke out. The mayor urged Curtis to cancel his speech in the interest of public safety, but on the advice of Philadelphia abolitionists Curtis proceeded to talk. Mayor Henry also proceeded with his own duties. He stationed fifty policemen in front of the speaker's platform, scattered fifty more through the audience, and had another 400 in the rear and outside. The mayor himself, genteel scholar of the Greek and Hebrew languages turned symbol of law enforcement, took a seat at Curtis's side on the stage. The police made a number of arrests, including two of the ubiquitous southern medical students armed with loaded revolvers, and some former members of the police under the Vaux regime; but Mayor Henry kept the peace.[46]

V

"Slavery occupies all conversation now," Sidney George Fisher recorded. Though utterly unwilling to count himself an abolitionist, and with all his customary snobbishness a firm believer in the inferiority of the Negro race, Fisher thought that John Brown "has done more to reveal the true nature of the slavery question than all others who have acted on it; he has stirred the nation from its depths and it may turn out that he will be the proximate cause of the dissolution of the Union."

Slavery is a wrong, an injustice. It must either destroy the moral sentiment of the country or be destroyed by it. In this age of thought and free discussion, there is some hope that the destruction of slavery may be brought about by peaceful means. If John Brown had succeeded in his purpose of running off the Negroes in the neighborhood of Harper's Ferry, his success would have been a real failure. His death was necessary to his triumph. . . .[47]

So slavery occupied all conversation, but all hoped for settlement of the question by peaceful means, and few were willing yet to take as advanced a position as Fisher's. Mayor Henry had refused to be a sponsor or to speak at the meeting to deplore John Brown, but when parties formed for the 1860 presidential election, he rejected the Republicans and Abraham Lincoln for the Constitutional Unionists and John Bell. The Democrats characterized even Henry's moderate position as virtual abolitionism, however, and they focused their 1860 mayoralty campaign on Henry's support of the Curtis meeting. Their tactic almost worked, or perhaps did work; Henry was officially declared reelected, but tampering with the returns may have been necessary to accomplish that result. Henry helped prevent Curtis from making a return appearance in the fall of 1860.[48]

Philadelphia entered the critical presidential campaign of 1860 then with sentiments confused but still tending to shun even moderate Republicanism. The Pennsylvania Democratic party remained so prosouthern that its state chairman in 1859 was Robert Tyler, son of Pres. John Tyler, a Virginian in origin and a friend of slavery. The People's party determined to continue playing down the slavery issue, and while allying themselves with the national Republicans, to make tariff protection their main theme in Pennsylvania. William Thomas, who had been the first Republican mayoralty candidate, preferred a more candid antislavery position and became chairman of a separate Republican committee. More People's party leaders, however, were inclined to move in the opposite direction and to support John Bell for the presidency. Straddling the issue, they managed to elect Andrew Gregg Curtin governor of Pennsylvania in the October balloting, but the Democrats still polled 51 percent of the Philadelphia vote.[49]

If the People's party could not carry Philadelphia in the October elections despite playing down its antislavery associations, the divided Democrats had severe problems too in the national balloting in November. The Pennsylvania state committee remained tied to the Buchanan administration and thus favored the southern presidential candidate, John C. Breckinridge. In the city the Democrats of old family such as Charles Ingersoll and William B. Reed, recently President Buchanan's minister to China, supplied the Breckinridge leadership. Other party chieftains, including the Richard Vaux–Lewis Cassidy axis and generally the labor and immigrant factions in the city, believed the party could not retain its strength in a northern city and state if it persisted indefinitely in prosouthern policies. They favored Stephen A. Douglas. In Pennsylvania these two factions managed to agree on a slate of electors who would vote for either Breckinridge or Douglas, depending on which of them could defeat Lincoln or throw the election into the House of Representatives. But John Forney emerged to lead a separatist Douglas movement that sabotaged the agreement. Forney's motives are suspect, since behind the scenes he was already engaged in the consultations with People's party leaders that eventually returned him to the clerkship of the House. The political experts soon concluded that the fusion Democratic ticket and Forney's Douglas ticket would kill each other off, which they did. In the city many discouraged Democrats may well have stayed home. Lincoln took 52 percent of the Philadelphia vote and 57 percent of the state's.[50]

That encroachment of Republicanism notwithstanding, Philadelphia opinion had followed a consistent course all through the 1850s. Explicitly antislavery Republicanism made no headway in the city. The ticket that carried the city in November 1860 against a divided opposition called itself not Republican but the People's party, and its rallying cry was tariff protection, the force of whose appeal was to be apparent through the rest of the nineteenth century. The sectional crises of the late 1850s, especially the Sumner-Brooks incident and Lecompton, had somewhat dampened Philadelphia's longstanding southern sympathies. But the abolitionists remained a despised minority, and as late as May 1860 another fugitive slave was apprehended in Philadelphia and returned to the South without much excitement. If all the North had shared the attitudes of Philadelphia, the South would have had nothing to fear, and not even the most extreme of southern fire eaters could have conjured up a justification for secession. On the contrary, the attitude of Philadelphia encouraged southerners to believe that if they did secede in the face of Abraham Lincoln's election, much of the North would acquiesce in their departure.[51]

Up to a point the behavior of Philadelphia during the subsequent secession crisis bore out such a belief. On the day in December 1860 when George W. Curtis was to have made the return appearance that Mayor Henry scotched, the Councils sponsored instead a municipal expression of regard for both the Union and the South. Half the People's party councilmen joined in a call for all businesses to suspend for two hours for a conciliatory rally in Independence Square, to which delegations of factory workers were urged to parade. At the rally most of the speakers stressed the North's offenses against the South, which they said were driving the southern states to secession, and called upon the North to reassure the South by means of such measures as repeal of the state personal liberty laws.[52]

At the beginning of the new year business leaders of the city sponsored a meeting of the Board of Trade that petitioned the General Assembly of Pennsylvania to repeal any legislation that might be deemed unfriendly to the South. The next day over a hundred political leaders met at the same place for a somewhat less acquiescent purpose, namely, to plan a new rally that would call for the South's return to the Union. With People's party leaders present there was much disagreement, but after a two-day adjournment the meeting resolved that only peaceful measures should be used to accomplish the return. Meetings at Barr's Hotel on January 7 and 10 climaxed in resolutions admitting the right of secession and calling on Pennsylvania to choose between "fanatical New England" and "the South, whose sympathies are ours."[53]

On January 16 a mass meeting of anticoercionists heard encouraging remarks from George M. Wharton, Charles Ingersoll, Benjamin H. Brewster, and William B. Reed, all men of substance and social prestige. The meeting adopted Reed's resolution declaring that if the South seceded, Pennsylvania might be released from its own bonds to the Union and ought to hold a convention "to determine with whom her lot should be cast."[54] Abolitionists, blamed for the crisis, were more detested than ever. When the city's only vocal antislavery clergyman, William Henry Furness, preached at his First Unitarian Church, some of the congregation came armed to protect him against threats to his life. The Republican state legislature thought it wise to postpone the city's municipal elections until the fall. Peace rallies persisted through January, February, and March.[55]

But both the *Pennsylvanian* in the extreme prosouthern wing of the Democracy and pessimistic William Lewis in the People's party were wrong when they predicted civil war inside the North if the new federal administration should attempt to override secession with force. Not only did People's party leaders such as District Attorney William Mann, the party's most astute Philadelphia politician, move gradually to the conclusion that the Union must coerce the South if everything else failed; so did a growing number of Democrats, including Lewis Cassidy.[56]

With only one dissenting vote the Councils threw a significant straw into the wind by inviting the president-elect to include Philadelphia among the cities he would visit on his journey from Springfield, Illinois, to Washington. Lincoln agreed to join in the observance of Washington's Birthday at the State House, raising a new flag bearing a thirty-fourth star for the state of Kansas. Reporting on the event, the *Pennsylvanian* sarcastically observed that "negroes were delighted and turned out in unusual numbers." The president-elect also spoke from the balcony of the city's monumental new caravansary, the Continental Hotel at Ninth and Chestnut, where he drew prolonged applause by declaring "there is no need of bloodshed and war. . . . The Government will not use force unless force is used against it." But he also drew cheers and applause when he said at the State House:

I have often inquired of myself, what great principle or idea it was that kept this Confederacy so long together. . . . It was not the mere matter of the separation of the colonies from the mother land; but something in that Declaration giving liberty, not alone to the people of this country, but hope to the world for all future time. It was that which gave promise that in due time the weights should be lifted from the shoulders of all men, and that *all* should have an equal chance.[57]

Doubtless many who cheered those words would have shuddered instead had they not been caught up in the emotions of the place, the occasion commemorated, and the hour in their country's history. But the crowd that cheered Lincoln's words about equality on Washington's Birthday signaled a turn in the city's mood. It proved to be the first of many Philadelphia crowds that would cheer Lincoln and the Union before 1861 was over; for if Philadelphians disliked blacks and sympathized with the South, they also felt great pride in their city as the birthplace of the noble Declaration, the flag, and the Constitution. To abandon the Union without a struggle would be to abandon all that inheritance. As the birthplace of the American nation, the city could do no other than defend the nation. To do that, however, to defend the legacy of Jefferson's Declaration, meant, as Lincoln recognized, that the city must uphold the equality of all men in spite of itself.

At the State House, Lincoln said that rather than preserve the Union by surrendering the principles of the Declaration, he would prefer to be assassinated on the spot. The thought may have suggested itself because rumor of an assassination plot had reached him, and he departed Philadelphia by stealth to foil the assassins said to be awaiting him in Baltimore. In Washington he reaffirmed his dedication both to the Union and to the principles of Jefferson's Declaration, thereby convincing the leaders of the seceded states that they must take the initiative to remove all federal authority from their soil. Confederate artillery therefore fired on Fort Sumter in Charleston harbor on April 12, 1861, and the Civil War began. In Philadelphia the antislavery minister Furness exclaimed, "The long agony is over!" He too foresaw that if the North fought for the Union, it must fight for equality as well, in spite of itself.[58]

VI

In Philadelphia as everywhere throughout the North, homes, stores, and streetcars were bedecked with banners in the wake of Fort Sumter and the president's call for 75,000 militia. The city mobs which so recently had threatened abolitionists now turned on southern sympathizers instead. They visited the office of a small secessionist paper called the *Palmetto Flag* at 337 Chestnut Street, and it required action by the police and another personal appearance by Mayor Henry to keep them from destroying the place. The paper suspended publication. The mayor had to appear again at William B. Reed's house to prevent mayhem there. Joseph Baker, an old friend of Buchanan as well as holdover collector of the customs from the Buchanan administration, was forced to display the Stars and Stripes, as were others of suspected loyalties. Meanwhile the more important newspaper voices of the prosouthern Democracy began to die from lack of federal patronage as well as the change in popular opinion.[59]

The president's call for troops set men to drilling everywhere, preparing themselves to take the field should the state government and the federal War Department accept them. Philadelphia's quota was six regiments. In theory the city mustered a whole division of the state militia, the First, comprising three brigades, plus an additional reserve brigade. How much organized military strength actually existed was questionable. The word "militia" had always been used indiscriminately in the United States to designate two different things: the whole able-bodied military manpower of a district, all of whom owed military service under ancient English tradition sanctioned by the Constitution and written into federal and state law; and the volunteer companies composed of men of military inclinations who actually organized and equipped themselves and more or less frequently underwent military drill. Much of Philadelphia's share of the Pennsylvania militia existed only on muster rolls, in the legal obligation of all capable men to do military service. Parts of the First Division, but hardly a whole division, did exist as uniformed companies, such as the Gray Reserves; other volunteer companies in the city were separate from the First Division, such as the First City Troop.[60]

New volunteer formations had been springing up since the beginning of the secession crisis, and Governor Curtin accepted one of them to be Philadelphia's first contribution to the defense of Washington. At midnight on April 18, half of Brig.-Gen. William F. Small's "Washington Brigade" entrained at the Broad and Prime Streets station. Unfortunately the men of the Washington Brigade were not yet uniformed or armed. More unfortunately they followed the Sixth Massachusetts Regiment into Baltimore. The uniforms of the Bay Staters drew the fury of a secessionist Baltimore mob, which then fell on the Philadelphia men too and sent them bruised and bleeding in retreat to their homes. One of them, a German-born private named George Leisenring, died of stab wounds four days later at the Pennsylvania Hospital, Philadelphia's first casualty of the war.[61]

Eventually, after more cautious and thorough preparation, Philadelphia sent eight infantry regiments, the Seventeenth through Twenty-fourth Pennsylvania, into federal service under the president's first call. A regiment nominally counted about a thousand men, and the earliest regiments entered the service not much below that figure. An artillery company, the Commonwealth Artillery; an independent infantry company, the McMullin Rangers, raised from the Moyamensing Hose Company; and the First City Troop also joined the federal forces. None of them was at Bull Run; some served out their three-month terms on garrison duty, while most went into the Maryland and Shenandoah Valley command of their fellow Philadelphian Maj.-Gen. Robert Patterson, an elderly veteran of militia service as colonel in the War of 1812 and major-general in the Mexican War. The Twenty-third Infantry and the First City Troop fought in an action at Falling Waters on the Potomac on July 2, becoming the first Philadelphians to meet Confederate forces.[62]

The initial enthusiasm for the defense of the Union produced more volunteers than the War Department could equip and care for. Luckily much of that enthusiasm survived the defeat at Bull Run—or was renewed by the defeat—to provide new formations when the first units came home at the end of the three-month hitch to which the militia laws had restricted the president's first call. By then Congress was meeting and had authorized an army of a million men enlisted for three years or the war, and the president had become bold enough to begin enlisting them even before Congress completed the authorization. The Twenty-third Infantry, which saw the most action of Philadelphia's three-month regiments, also had the honor of being the only one of them to reenlist for three years. The Washington Brigade, which had turned back from Baltimore in April, entered the new army as the Twenty-sixth and Twenty-seventh Regiments, completing their organization early enough for the latter to be ready to screen the retreat from Bull Run, the only Philadelphia unit to participate in that campaign. The Twenty-eighth, Twenty-ninth, Thirty-first, Thirty-second, Thirty-third, Thirty-sixth, and Forty-first Pennsylvania Regiments were recurited in whole or in part in Philadelphia by the end of July, the latter five destined for special fame as part of the "Pennsylvania Reserves."[63]

Some forty-seven additional three-year regiments of infantry and cavalry were recruited wholly or partly in Philadelphia, in addition to various batteries of artillery, as well as some infantry regiments mustered in for only nine months or at the beginning of the 1864 campaign. After the Emancipation Proclamation opened the way for the War Department to accept black soldiers, eleven regiments of United States Colored Troops were organized in Philadelphia, with many of their recruits coming from the city's own black population. It is impossible to estimate just how many. With reenlistments having been common, it is also impossible to state accurately the number of white Philadelphians who served in the Union Army; but exclusive of three-month troops, between 89,000 and 90,000 men appeared on the muster rolls of Philadelphia units in federal service.[64]

V I I

The red, white, and blue bunting of the spring of 1861 faded and came down, but Philadelphia, the first large city above the Mason-Dixon line, became a city of war. Soldiers and sailors thronged the streets—marching through on the way to Washington, waiting for ships repairing or building at the Navy Yard, wistfully enjoying their leaves, or convalescing in the city's hospitals. Confederate prisoners came through also, en route to various northern stockades and to Fort Delaware on Pea Patch Island below the city. A garrison occupied Fort Mifflin to guard against an enemy foray up the Delaware, and there too deserters were imprisoned and sometimes executed.[65]

The Schuylkill Arsenal on Gray's Ferry Road was the principal depot of the Quartermaster's Department and the principal source of uniforms for the army. It gave work to hundreds of seamstresses scattered through the city, since the government still manufactured clothing by the "domestic system," farming out the various operations to workers in private homes and only

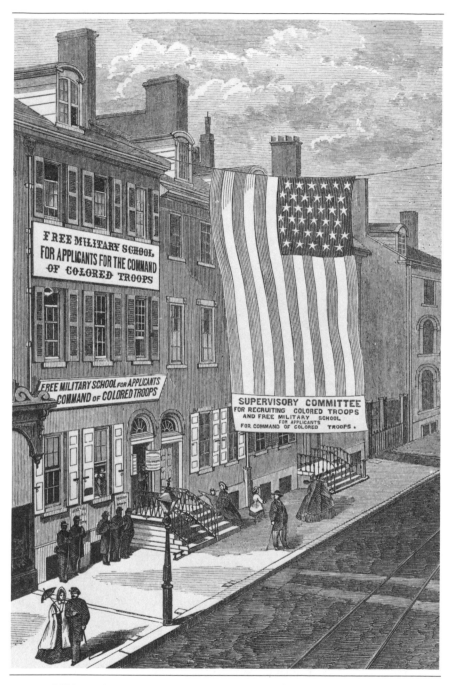

Military School for Officers of Negro Troops, 1210 Chestnut Street, engraving based on a photograph (c. 1863).

completing the assembling of the uniforms in its own shops. To the north, munitions manufacture at the Frankford Arsenal employed enough workers to extend Frankford and Bridesburg until the open country between them and the city was blotted out. To the south, Sharp and Rankin's factory on the west bank of the Schuylkill manufactured breech-loading rifles.[66]

At the Navy Yard at the foot of Federal Street, still occupying the site of Joshua Humphreys's shipyard of the Federalist era, as many as 3000 men labored during the war, and eleven warships were launched while many other vessels were fitted out for combat. Private shipyards built many additional warships, including the ironclad steam frigate *New Ironsides*, the greatest ship of the Civil War navy, whose machinery was constructed by Merrick & Son while William Cramp & Sons built her hull. The old Navy Yard at last proving too small, the United States in 1862 accepted from the city League Island at the mouth of the Schuylkill, although the transfer to the new site was delayed until after the war.[67]

Souvenir of the Coldest Winter on Record. Scene on the Delaware River at Philada. during the severe winter of 1856, *lithograph by P. S. Duval after James Queen (1856). Eleven warships were built in the Navy Yard's ship houses (erected 1820–1821) during the Civil War.*

FREE LIBRARY OF PHILADELPHIA

Troops from New England, New York, and New Jersey traveled to the battlefields by way of the Camden and Amboy Railroad across New Jersey and by ferry across the Delaware River, to be deposited at the foot of Washington Avenue. Thence they marched to the trains of the Philadelphia, Wilmington and Baltimore Railroad. Philadelphians greeted them with refreshments, writing papers, envelopes, free stamps, and as elaborate a welcome and as much companionship and conversation as time allowed. Two organizations directed this activity, the Union Volunteer Refreshment Saloon with head-quarters on Swanson Street below Washington Avenue, and the Cooper Shop Refreshment Saloon in an abandoned cooperage on Otsego Street, near Washington Avenue. Both organizations were established as early as May 1861.

When a troop train left Jersey City, the news was telegraphed to Philadelphia, whereupon a cannon at the foot of Washington Avenue fired a charge to notify the Union and Cooper volunteers to come to their posts.[68]

As soon as we reached the city [a soldier wrote home] we marched to the dining saloon, about ten or fifteen rods from the ferry. As soon as we got there we entered the wash-room, a room large enough to accommodate sixty or seventy men to wash at a time. Then we were marched into a splendid hall, with room enough to feed five hundred men at a time. There were gentlemen to wait on us, and they would come around and ask if we had plenty and urge us to eat more. We had nice white bread, beautiful butter, cold boiled ham, cheese, coffee, with plenty of milk and sugar. After we had eaten our fill, which was considerable, for we had eaten nothing since morning, we returned to the streets. Our knapsacks on the sidewalk were left without a guard, but they were almost covered with little children who were watching to see that no one disturbed them.[69]

Philadelphia also received the returning wounded. The Union Refreshment Saloon set up the first military hospital in the city, fifteen beds for the sick of the regiments passing through. Eventually the military hospitals of Philadelphia had almost 10,000 beds, in addition to the beds of the twenty-two civilian hospitals that sometimes served the soldiers. Twenty-four military hospitals functioned at one time or another, some of them temporarily occupying existing buildings, such as the 200-bed Haddington Hospital in the old Bull's Head Tavern at Sixty-fifth and Vine Streets, while the larger ones consisted of temporary frame buildings in the suburbs.

In September 1862, after George B. McClellan's and John Pope's campaigns brought the first flood of casualties from Virginia, a citizens' committee established the Citizens' Volunteer Hospital on Broad Street opposite the railroad station from the South. With a listed capacity of 400 beds, the hospital sometimes admitted as many as 700 men at a time. By its first anniversary it reportedly had served 30,000 soldiers. It took the most serious cases and then gradually distributed those it could to outlying hospitals. Eventually the smaller of these were closed down, and the army Medical Department concentrated most of its Philadelphia work in the largest military hospitals in the United States. These were the West Philadelphia or Satterlee General Hospital of 3124 beds, on the Baltimore Road and extending westward up the Mill Creek ravine from the present vicinity of Baltimore Avenue and Forty-third Street, and the Mower General Hospital designed for 4000 beds, covering twenty-seven acres along the Chestnut Hill Railroad, opposite the later Wyndmoor Station of the Reading Railroad. Large numbers of the wounded in the Philadelphia hospitals were Pennsylvanians, since the War Department

Union Volunteer Refreshment Saloon of Philadelphia, *Swanson Street below Washington Avenue, lithograph by Thomas Sinclair after James Queen (1861).*

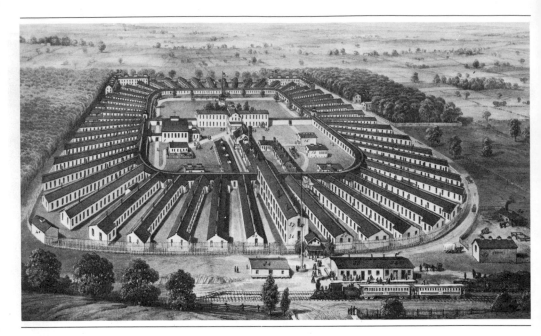

The Mower U.S. Army General Hospital, *Willow Grove Avenue, lithograph by P. S. Duval and Son after James Queen (c. 1863). The railroad right of way is now used by the Chestnut Hill East commuter line.*

HISTORICAL SOCIETY OF PENNSYLVANIA

cooperated with a state agency in returning casualties to hospitals near their homes. Altogether, some 157,000 soldiers and sailors received care in Philadelphia hospitals.[70]

VIII

As the pitiful tide of the wounded rolled up the railroad from Washington, enthusiasm for the war ebbed. Enthusiasm faded everywhere of course, but in Philadelphia it gave way to especially bitter dissension, as the city's traditional sympathy for the South and antipathy toward the black man once again clouded its dedication to the Union.

A few indications of returning disquiet appeared as early as the summer of 1861. Pierce Butler, the transplanted South Carolina patrician whose marriage to Fanny Kemble made him seem a more romantic personage than he really was, had given loud expression to secession sympathies. He said he would go south to fight, and at the end of 1860 in keeping with the threat he resigned from the Non-Active Roll of the First City Troop. When the war came his activities proved anticlimactically mild. He visited his Georgia plantation early in 1861, but financial troubles probably would have compelled him to do so anyway. While there he may have taken an oath of allegiance to the

Confederacy. But after the fighting commenced he returned to Philadelphia, neglecting his previous threats. Back in the city, however, he did resume his belligerently prosouthern conversation. By August 19 the federal authorities were jittery enough over rumors of disloyalty in the city to take advantage of Lincoln's suspension of habeas corpus and pack Butler off to a cell in Fort Hamilton in New York harbor, without a hearing or trial. About a month later Henry Fisher, the wealthy businessman brother of Sidney George Fisher, obtained his release on a promise of good behavior. There was something to be said for Sidney's view that it might have been just as well for Butler that he remain in confinement, "as it will keep him quiet and out of harm's way." But Butler returned relatively subdued, and he remained in Philadelphia until almost the end of the war, when his business problems took him back to the South where he thenceforth spent most of his time.[71]

About the time of Butler's arrest the federal authorities also suppressed a small weekly, the *Christian Observer*, which had expressed southern sympathies. They also arrested seven more men, releasing most of them promptly but holding William Winder, son of the War of 1812 general of that name, more than a year without trial. This sort of action provoked a newspaper debate over the legality of the suspension of habeas corpus, enabling the Democrats to get in some of their first licks against the Lincoln administration in the patriotic pose of defenders of the Constitution.[72]

They tried to retain that role as their attacks grew sharper and all-out partisanship resumed, but increasingly the supporters of the war came to see many of them as men who would try to save every crossed "t" and dotted "i" of the Constitution at the sacrifice of the federal Union itself. To their own way of thinking, Philadelphia's leading Democrats throughout the war were merely trying to preserve the Constitution and the Union as the founding fathers had conceived them. But it was too late for that. The Union and the Constitution were bound to be changed by a great civil war, no matter how the war ended. Preservation of the Union eventually became inseparable from constitutional and social revolution. To resist revolution was to resist winning the war, so that men who to themselves were simply constitutional Democrats became traitorous Copperheads in the eyes of their political opponents.

The first families of Philadelphia did not accept revolution gladly in 1776, and again they did not now. So Sidney George Fisher found himself almost alone as a defender of Lincoln in the social circles in which he moved, and men such as Charles J. and George W. Biddle, Charles and Edward Ingersoll, and William B. Reed moved to the forefront of the Democratic opposition to Lincoln's conduct of the war.[73]

Charles John Biddle, lawyer, Princeton graduate, and son of Nicholas Biddle, had served in the Mexican War as a captain of voltigeurs in Gen. George Cadwalader's brigade and won the brevet rank of major for gallantry at Chapultepec. Although he was a Democrat who hoped for sectional conciliation to the last, after Fort Sumter he felt he must take arms again, and on June 21, 1861, he received his commission as colonel of the Forty-second

Pennsylvania Regiment, called sometimes the First Bucktails or the Thirteenth Reserves. About the same time his party nominated him for Congress, to fill the vacancy in the Second District created by Lincoln's appointment of Edward Joy Morris as minister to the Sublime Porte. The Republicans nominated a party wheelhorse, a state legislator named Charles O'Neill, and Biddle won by about 200 votes in a listless campaign. Sidney George Fisher thought that any reasonably distinguished opponent could have beaten Biddle, who "is suspected of a leaning towards the South and justly suspected."[74]

If these words were excessively strong to describe a colonel of the Union Army, they were not altogether wide of the mark. Biddle might have liked to avoid the hard choices that a seat in Congress would force on him; he was offered a brigadiership and considered staying in the army, but he finally decided that his health was no longer good enough for campaigning and took his seat when Congress resumed in December 1861. Significantly, his resumption of vocal opposition, and that of most Philadelphia Democrats, began the next spring when the administration's war measures touched the slavery issue. Biddle opposed the act of March 13, 1862, with which Congress overturned the Fugitive Slave Act as far as it had obliged the military to return fugitives; the effort to abolish slavery in the District of Columbia; and the Second Confiscation Act of July 17, 1862, which freed the slaves of rebel owners.

He asserted that the South probably would have returned to the Union if her people had been offered "a spectacle of entire contentment and security upon this negro question"; thus he implied that blame for continuing the war rested on the North. He declared that slavery had been rooted in America by the Providence of God, and that only gradual action, not by the federal government but by the states, could safely uproot it. He discerned that the federal government was moving toward both constitutional and social revolution, and he opposed both: "I would leave to my children the Union that our fathers left to us." "Sir, the repugnance to Negro equality is as strong in the middle states as it is in the South." Emancipation in the South, he feared, would inundate his own Pennsylvania with black men.[75]

So the conjoined issues of slavery and race, with their implications for Philadelphia as well as for the South, came to cloud over much of Philadelphia's first resolution to support the war. Men of conservative inclinations for whom the preservation of the Union took precedence over other issues, such as Morton McMichael of the *North American* and the editors of the *Inquirer*, began the painful process of adjusting to revolution and accepting it. The *Inquirer* initially opposed the Second Confiscation Act, but within a month McClellan's setbacks before Richmond led its editors to advocate a more ruthless war and a new tack on slavery. On the other hand those for whom "the Union that our fathers left to us" was the only Union worth preserving began a movement into increasingly virulent and uncompromising opposition to Lincoln, the Republicans, and all they stood for. In July 1862 the Democratic state convention resolved that "Abolitionism is the parent of secessionism," and "That this is a government of white men, and was established exclusively for the white race; that the Negro race are not entitled to and ought not to be admitted to political or social equality with the white race."[76]

When Sidney George Fisher argued with his Democratic brother-in-law Charles Ingersoll about the legal tender act, Ingersoll began with the constitutional question but finally replied to Fisher's contention that paper money was necessary for carrying on the war by saying: "But we don't want the government to carry on this war." This, as Fisher noted, was "a speech that means a great deal." Within a month Charles Ingersoll said the same sort of thing in public, slightly toned down but plainly enough, and the federal provost marshal arrested him for discouraging enlistments. Judge John Cadwalader of the federal district court, a Democrat, issued a writ of habeas corpus and declared that the federal officials would be in contempt if they did not produce Ingersoll. On orders from Washington they freed him. The arrest of so distinguished a figure, grandson of a signer of the Constitution, caused local Republicans some embarrassment. But in the meantime Ingersoll had given a disturbing indication of whither the Democratic opposition was tending.[77]

Many Philadelphians shared Congressman Biddle's views on race, and those views were a persistent magnet pulling toward Ingersoll's position. But the *Inquirer* must have spoken for many Philadelphians also when it overcame its own misgivings about Republican policy on slavery and race by approving the argument that "in this war there can be but two parties, patriots and traitors." ". . . the man who is not thoroughly with us . . . is a traitor of as deep and black a dye as ever was Cataline or Arnold." In wartime this argument is hard to resist.[78]

Also working to overcome misgivings on the race issue was the prosperity that war stimulated in Philadelphia by 1862. Jay Cooke's use of public advertising to float the Treasury's war loans gave not only Cooke's own house but all of Philadelphia banking a renewed prominence in national finance.[79] The appeals of loyalty and prosperity overshadowed the race question enough to keep the Democrats submerged at the polls in 1862. A straight-out Republican could not yet capture the mayoralty, but Alexander Henry won a third term on the National Union ticket. Charles J. Biddle lost his seat in Congress to Charles O'Neill after all, and the Philadelphia congressional delegation would consist of four Republican–People's party men and one Democrat, Samuel Jackson Randall, who had taken the field with the First City Troop in 1861 and who, unlike Biddle, could be clearly counted a War Democrat. In November also a circle of substantial citizens prompted by Judge J. I. C. Hare, and including George H. Boker, Morton McMichael, and Horace Binney, Jr., having felt disturbed over prosouthern pronouncements at the Wistar Club, acted to demonstrate that not all the city's aristocracy opposed the war. They organized the Union Club as a "refuge for loyalty," asserting their counterclaim against the peace Democrats for the allegiance of the city's first families by choosing the traditional Saturday night of the best social clubs as their meeting time.[80]

Jay Cooke (1821–1905), photograph, 1892. Jay Cooke and Co. had branches in New York, Washington, and later (1870) London. The firm's financial failure precipitated the Panic of 1873.

HISTORICAL SOCIETY OF PENNSYLVANIA

On the other hand the Emancipation Proclamation could not help but aggravate unease over the race issue. It shattered the last hopes that Lincoln might yet lead a return to the Union of the fathers, and it drove the Democrats to redoubled efforts. "I found," wrote one observer of Philadelphia:

> I found, most gladly, no secession;
> But hatred strong of abolition,
> A willingness to fight with vigor
> For loyal rights, but not the nigger.

On January 8, 1863, a week after the final Emancipation Proclamation and on the anniversary of Andrew Jackson's victory at New Orleans, the peace Democrats replied to the founding of the Union Club by opening the Central Democratic Club, with Charles Ingersoll as president and George W. Biddle, John C. Bullitt, and George M. Wharton among the vice-presidents. It also would meet on Saturday nights. Late in March, William B. Reed proclaimed in a speech before the club: "I deplore and condemn the war and believe coercion to have been a mistake from the beginning, and pray, and hope and urge the necessity of Peace, and, if possible, 'Reconciliation'; but Peace, even if the bond of sympathy be, as I fear it is, irreparably broken."[81]

Two months later the same group moved to reestablish Philadelphia Democratic journalism by setting up a former private secretary to President Buchanan, Adam J. Glossbrenner of York, as proprietor of the *Age*, to propagate their views. As expressed by Glossbrenner, these views included the usual calls for a return to the Constitution and condemnation of the Emancipation Proclamation as a blunder that left the South "no other choice but war to the knife." The paper also rang the changes on the racial inferiority and brutishness of blacks and the dangers of miscegenation and racial amalgamation as offshoots of emancipation. The Democratic General Assembly at Harrisburg called for a constitutional convention to restore the Union.[82]

The founders of the Union Club responded in turn by abolishing their limitation of fifty members and transforming their intimate club into a much larger and, they hoped, more potent organization, the Union League. This change revolutionized the social character of the organization, for with several thousand members by the end of the war the Union League obviously ceased to be an adjunct of the Philadelphia aristocracy. Instead it tended to become an organization of the new business elite, the often self-made men who were rising with the economic opportunities of the war, or rather with the larger northern industrial boom that was too big even to be dependent on the war, but of which the war, the Union cause, and the Republican party were becoming the symbols. This change in turn doubtless troubled the Democrats of old-family background still more, for it signified that the revolutionary aspects of the time were touching them and their status yet more directly than the race question could.[83]

The Union League developed some of the political potency for which its founders hoped. Its efforts included the sponsorship of new regiments for the army and a vigorous pamphlet campaign for the Union and the Lincoln government, with Henry Charles Lea as an especially noteworthy and forceful pamphleteer. More than any other period of the war, however, the early months of 1863, with emancipation's renewal of the race question, suggested that the star of the peace party was rising. Charles J. Biddle was now chairman of the Democratic State Central Committee. Richard Vaux and the Cassidy faction had tended hitherto to remain aloof from the organizers of the Central Democratic Club, but they did not like the Emancipation Proclamation. They shifted their ground enough to join in a mass meeting to protest the arrest of the Ohio Peace Democrat Clement L. Vallandigham. The draft act of March 3, 1863, was not popular and played into the Peace Democrats' hands. "The 'Peace' Democracy are holding meetings to encourage their brethren in the South," diarist George W. Fahnestock wrote as the summer began. "These traitors are growing bolder every day; denouncing our government in the most unmeasured terms. A civil war in the North may not be far off."[84]

IX

Then the war itself took what some Peace Democrats hoped would be a decisive turn in their favor. Successive disasters for the Union arms and triumphs for the Confederacy emboldened Gen. R. E. Lee to march a Confederate army of invasion toward Pennsylvania.

Unhappily, so strong has grown the feeling of opposition to the present Administration [Fahnestock wrote the day Philadelphia received its first news of possible invasion], that many men are pleased with the prospect of invasion, carnage, blood, and smoking ruins! They walk our streets today, radiant with joy, led on by W. B. Reed, Charlie Ingersoll, Wharton, and a horde of old worn out Peace Democrats. Nothing would rejoice them more than to see our whole government laid in ashes![85]

Much in the aspect of the city might have contributed to the Peace Democrats' joy. As Lee's army entered Pennsylvania and accumulating reports confirmed its approach toward Harrisburg during the humid days of late June, no determined rally to the colors but a strange apathy marked the city's response. While Fahnestock addressed his diary in the confinement of a sickroom, he listened, impressed, to the rumble of the recruiting drums and the bells and whistles of trains he believed to be carrying thousands of troops to Harrisburg; but when he was well enough to venture out again to observe for himself he found "the people as quiet and apathetic as if it was all a false report. Thousands of able bodied young fellows are ever parading the streets, but no enlistments go on with spirit." As for preparations to defend the city, "there has been some little vaporing and quibbling in Councils, and that is the end of it. Not a spadeful of earth has been raised in the defence of Philadelphia."[86]

Sidney George Fisher recorded similar impressions:

The streets presented a strange aspect, most of them deserted, but Chesnut Street thronged with crowds of men, chiefly of the working classes, many of them vicious & ill-looking, wandering about apparently without a purpose. Recruiting parties were marching about with drum & flag, followed only by a few ragged boys—recruiting offices empty, taverns & grog shops full. The people looked careless & indifferent. There was no excitement. The same street presented a very different scene in April 1861 when the war broke out. Then it was fluttering with flags & filled by a crowd of agitated, earnest men. War was a novelty then; it is an old story now, and the demagogues have spread abroad the opinion that the administration is corrupt & imbecile, that it is impossible to conquer the South & that we ought to have peace now on any terms.[87]

At the beginning of his march Lee evaded the Union Army of the Potomac, and through most of June that army was trying to catch up while the Confederates advanced with no major forces in front of them. The War Department advised the Pennsylvania authorities that the state might have to defend itself, and on June 12 Governor Curtin appealed for enlistments to protect "homes, firesides, and property."[88]

The city's political rivalries divided even Philadelphia's home defense forces. Under emergency legislation of the General Assembly in 1861 the municipality itself had organized the Philadelphia Home Guard Brigade, hopefully listed as ten regiments. The city Councils which sponsored the brigade were Democratic, however, and the commanding officer, Brig.-Gen. Augustus J. Pleasonton, was so Democratic that some suspected him of southern leanings; therefore Republicans distrusted the Home Guard. They felt more confidence in the Philadelphia units of the state militia, especially the Reserve Brigade Infantry, including the Gray Reserves and the First and Second Blue Reserves. Suspicious of each other, neither reserve force was anywhere near its theoretical strength. The previous fall when Lee had invaded Maryland, the Home Guard Brigade had managed to send nineteen companies toward the seat of war, the Philadelphia militia three weak regiments. Neither organization had much equipment.[89]

One of the first responses of the War Department to Lee's movement northward was to erect two new military departments in Pennsylvania, with federal army officers and staffs to take charge of the defense of the state. Philadelphia fell within the Department of the Susquehanna, with headquarters at Harrisburg and under the command of Maj.-Gen. Darius N. Couch, a competent soldier who recently had commanded the II Corps of the Army of the Potomac. Under Couch, on June 26 Maj.-Gen. Napoleon Jackson Tecumseh Dana took command of the Military District of Philadelphia. Dana's assignment was to inject vigor into preparations for the defense of the city. Unfortunately he was a New Englander who proved to be not especially compatible with Philadelphians; and he was by no means so good a soldier as his parents when naming him evidently hoped he might become. Still, he began doing things to fortify the city where previously there had been only "vaporing and quibbling."[90]

On June 29 he asked Mayor Henry to find him 2000 men to dig entrenchments. The mayor produced a remarkable first contingent of 200 laborers and 100 volunteer clergymen, and by July 1 some 700 laborers had been found. Dana selected three sites for his principal fortifications: the Falls of Schuylkill, commanding the approach from the northwest; a hill at the west end of Gray's Ferry Bridge, commanding the approach from the west; and the east side of the Schuylkill near Gray's Ferry Road, looking toward the southwest. The designs were ambitious, with the Falls of Schuylkill works planned to accommodate 200 guns; in fact the earthworks cost the city the interesting sum of $51,537.37. But the rudiments of earthworks did not change the gloomy essentials of the defensive situation that Dana had found on his arrival; only 400 trained soldiers were on guard in the city, about 600 convalescents in the hospitals might be available, and there were ten pieces of artillery and 500 stand of arms at the disposal of the mayor. Neither the Home Guard nor the militia could add much very quickly.[91]

Perhaps it is true that, as some accounts say, thousands of Philadelphians were drilling in the public parks and the environs by the beginning of July. At the time, however, Governor Curtin was still disturbed about lack of energy in the city, and he arrived at the Continental Hotel to stimulate the authorities and to rally the populace with oratory. Two infantry regiments, five companies of another, and seven independent companies and batteries from Philadelphia eventually did join the emergency forces mustered into state service. In the Philadelphia troops' most notable action, the Twentieth Pennsylvania Emergency Regiment, under the zealous Republican William B. Thomas, skirmished with the enemy to protect the crossing of the Susquehanna at Wrightsville. The First City Troop, under Capt. and Cong. Sam Randall, was involved in the same action. They had to withdraw to the eastern shore of the river and set fire to the Columbia-Wrightsville bridge to prevent the Confederates from crossing.[92]

Such is the uninspiring story of a politically divided and doubtful city's response to the threat of invasion. Luckily, the Army of the Potomac arrived in Pennsylvania in time to cut the threat short. Commanded from June 28 by Philadelphia's Maj.-Gen. George G. Meade, that army won the Battle of Gettysburg on July 1–3. On those three days Meade rose to the occasion by outgeneraling the redoubtable Lee, and in defense of their own homes the Union soldiers at last outfought the Confederates. Meade became the city's great military hero of the Civil War, and deservedly so.

Maj.-Gen. George Gordon Meade (1815–1872), commander of the Army of the Potomac (photograph c. 1864). After the war General Meade served the city as a commissioner of Fairmount Park.

HISTORICAL SOCIETY OF PENNSYLVANIA

X

This outcome of Lee's invasion disappointed the Philadelphia Peace Democrats in more ways than one. Despite the city's passivity there are suggestions in the record of the invasion that the threat to Philadelphia cleared the air. If it did not restore the city's enthusiasm for the war, it provoked enough resentment against the South to make the Peace Democrats' notions of turning back the clock seem futile and to cause most Philadelphians to buckle down determined to see the war through. After the invasion, the hopes of the Peace Democrats, so recently bright, ingloriously fizzled.

The apathy of the invasion period itself was not merely a sign of division and confusion; it sprang partly too from confidence—confidence that the Union cause was too strong to permit the enemy's entrance into a great city such as Philadelphia. Such confidence proved in the end well placed. Apathy, furthermore, may have begun to dissolve by the time of Governor Curtin's visit; apparently there did develop a growing surge of patriotic feeling by the beginning of July, at last stimulating enlistments while uncertainty remained, and then erupting into fervent celebration of the victories at Gettysburg and Vicksburg.[93]

During the invasion, while white men were slow to mobilize for home defense, Pennsylvania for the first time authorized the enlistment of blacks within the state. They would not be permitted in the short-term emergency forces but must enlist for three years or the war, and with lower pay than white men received at that. On June 30 Fahnestock saw several hundred of them marching up Sixth Street to Chestnut, and thence up Chestnut, without uniforms but with fife and drum and "inspiriting banners," bound for a camp in the Chelten Hills, at the present La Mott, where they would organize. With Lee prowling the state, the city voiced little protest—although Mayor Henry was sufficiently fearful of a reaction that the black soldiers who paraded were not only without uniforms but also without weapons lest they provoke an attack on themselves. A few days later Republican Cong. William D. Kelley became the first elected politician in Philadelphia to address a black mass meeting in company with black leaders; doing so did not harm a highly successful political career.[94]

The draft began to be enforced in part of Philadelphia, the Fourth Congressional District, in July. But in this city fresh from its apprehensions over Lee's invasion there erupted no riots comparable to New York's. While the city's history indicated that it held plenty of riot potential, and while some Democratic leaders might not have been loath to see violence occur, Mayor Henry kept the lid on. He quietly suppressed minor disturbances before they got out of hand, aided by the Democratic militia general and Mexican War veteran George Cadwalader, who replaced the unpopular Dana in command of the military district.[95]

In the gubernatorial election in October, Philadelphia went Unionist by some 7000 votes, helping to reelect Curtin over the Peace Democrat Judge George W. Woodward. The next month the Supreme Court of the state, reacting to a test case encouraged by the Democrats, declared the draft law unconstitutional; but the decision was a partisan one by a margin of three to two. Since one of the Democratic judges had just failed of reelection, the court promptly reversed itself after he left the bench.[96]

The great public event of 1864 was a testimonial of loyalty and support for the army. The Philadelphia division of the United States Sanitary Commission, the soldiers' relief organization, held a huge "Central Fair" in Logan Square for several days in June for the benefit of the commission. Abraham Lincoln distinguished the festivities with a visit.[97]

Great Central Fair Buildings, *Logan Square, designed by H. E. Wrigley* *(engraving 1864). The rotundas contained the restaurant, horticultural exhibit, and* *"smoking divan," as well as commercial exhibits and sales booths. One visitor stated* *that the walls of the 500-foot-long picture gallery were covered with "admirable* *works of art, much the best I have ever seen."*

HISTORICAL SOCIETY OF PENNSYLVANIA

That summer the Central Democratic Club quietly subsided into insignificance. In its place an older group, the Keystone Club, was restored to life as the principal social club of the Democrats; but although some of the Central Club leaders were active in the Keystone Club, the latter appears to have been dominated by the Lewis Cassidy faction of the Democratic party. By now Cassidy had planted himself firmly in the war camp. The president of the Keystone Club was Col. William McCandless, twice wounded in the Union Army before he and his Thirty-first Pennsylvania Regiment (Second Reserves) were mustered out. Under such leadership the local Democratic organization turned cool to the peace plank of the Democratic platform in the 1864 elections.[98]

In these elections the city again went for the National Union party. For the first time that party won clear majorities in both Councils, and the city endorsed Lincoln and returned its loyal delegation of four Unionists and one Democrat to Congress. By that time Unionist political triumphs were assisted by the certainty that the Union would win the war. By that time too the result of Democratic opposition to the war was beginning to take shape as a party disaster. By opposing the war the Peace Democrats not only raised questions about their party's patriotism; by insisting on the futility of a war that was proving victorious they made themselves look foolish as well.[99]

Thus assisted by Democratic obtuseness, the National Unionists used the war to secure a foothold on Philadelphia politics firm enough to be made the foundation of nearly a century of Republican dominance. During the 1850s the city's congressional delegation had exhibited a rapid turnover of personnel; rarely did an individual serve two successive terms. The war began to transform political uncertainty into stability. Of the five congressmen who won their seats in the election of 1862 and were returned in 1864, all but one, who chose instead to become a judge, would still be in Congress at least until the 1870s. Kelley, O'Neill, and Randall would remain until the 1890s. All of them but Randall were Republicans, and to many of his party Randall often seemed a Republican in Democrat's clothing.

The rise of the wartime Republicans hastened a change in the social composition of the city's political leadership. Names such as Cadwalader and Biddle had still appeared on the city's congressional rosters during the political uncertainties of the 1850s and early 1860s. But when the upper class of the city identified themselves disproportionately with the peace wing of the Democracy, they helped ensure their disappearance from such rosters. Amid the war George W. Fahnestock found all the business streets filled with "Shoddy aristocracy . . . crazy to make a display. They buy up all the horses, carriages, drivers, stables, and everything else, in their haste to make a display." In the circumstances the Republican party was bound to be the party of these nouveaux riches. The situation did not encourage the old families' heading Republican electoral tickets, and with the party's growing ascendancy the Republicans could get along without their names anyway.[100]

During the war Princeton-educated Alexander Henry was already something of an anomaly as a municipal political leader, enough a gentleman that meeting him left Sidney George Fisher agreeably surprised. After the war a Wistar would reflect "that every observant person must admit that the educated and well-born, though hardly to be regarded as unfit or criminal on account of these advantages, are habitually distrusted by the democracy and, as a rule, excluded from popular favor and public affairs."[101]

In some areas the impact of the war on the permanent career of the city is harder to discern. The war interrupted the surge of civic pride and development touched off by consolidation. Wartime visitors to Fairmount Park, for example, found the ambitious plans for the park languishing and the place neglected; the zoo project was sidetracked so completely that when it reappeared after the war there was a fresh beginning at an entirely new site. But the postwar renewal that carried into the Centennial Exhibition suggests a mere temporary interruption, not the onset of the deeper municipal lassitude of the final years of the century.[102]

In economic development the war probably made no great change. Much wartime activity was too transient to contribute much to the city's long-term growth. The construction and staffing of the army hospitals was an example of such activity; their temporary presence may have helped confirm the city's place as a medical center, but of that little confirmation was needed. Some of the economic readjustments of the war may have harmed Philadelphia. Wartime efforts to achieve a direct and regular maritime connection with Europe failed; partly in consequence, Philadelphia shared little in the rise of the grain trade between the American West and Europe, and New York's commercial predominance was relatively greater at the end than at the beginning of the war. The financial prominence that Jay Cooke restored to the city proved largely ephemeral, even though the firm of A. J. Drexel enjoyed a more substantial growth in the shadow of the spectacular Cooke. The iron industry and its branches and associated activities profited from the war, and *New Ironsides* made the Cramp shipyards famous. It seems unlikely, however, that Philadelphia industry would not have found equal or greater returns and stimulus in the peaceful activity of a young industrial economy.[103]

In the long history of the city the greatest significance of the Civil War era was surely its raising the specter of the race question. The slavery question was at bottom the race question, and the race question belonged to Philadelphia as well as to the South. Congressman Biddle foresaw that by freeing the Negro to leave the South, the abolition of slavery would one day make Philadelphia's race question still more acute. With a large black population —by northern standards of the day and in some wards by twentieth-century standards—already within its gates, Philadelphia refused to join in the crusade against slavery, refused before and during the war to grant political power to the Republican party as such, and wavered even in its dedication to the Union once emancipation and Unionism were conjoined, until Confederate invasion of the North at last pushed the slavery issue into the background and made the safety of the Union appear clearly paramount.

But the race question would not remain in the background. For the safety of their city and the Union in the invasion crisis of 1863, Philadelphians acquiesced in blacks' donning uniforms and taking up arms. For black men who became soldiers the experience of recognition as being men would not permit them to lapse altogether into their former passivity. Black soldiers on leave or convalescing from wounds, and their wives and children attempting to visit them in the city's military hospitals, tried to ride the city's streetcars. In doing so they inspired a demand for access to the cars from the whole black community.[104]

Of nineteen streetcar and suburban railroad companies operating in Philadelphia during the early years of the Civil War, eleven did not permit black riders. The other eight grudgingly accepted black passengers, if they would ride on the platform with the driver, exposed to all kinds of weather. William Still had opened a campaign for the desegregation of the streetcars with a letter to the *North American* as early as August 31, 1859. In the manner of moderate-minded reformers, he piled up future troubles for himself by stressing the respectability of the blacks who would ride the cars, thus allowing militants to charge later that he wanted only well-to-do blacks like himself to be permitted to ride. Still's letter and his other early efforts created something of a stir in the abolitionist press but initially much less local agitation than the question of operating the horse cars on Sundays. Late in 1861 Still persuaded the Social, Civil and Statistical Association of the Colored People of Philadelphia, organized in 1860 to combat racial prejudice, of which he was corresponding secretary, to circulate among white business leaders a petition for open streetcars. By June 1862, 369 prominent white Philadelphians had signed, including Episcopal Bishop Alonzo Potter, the Rev. Phillips Brooks, Horace Binney, and Morton McMichael; but the defenders of the status quo pointed out that these substantial citizens enjoyed more private means of transportation and did not habitually ride streetcars themselves, so their protest might be ignored.

It was the outrageous exclusion of black men who were serving in the armed forces of the Union, and of their families, that late in the war finally began to crack the resistance of the streetcar companies and the indifference of white Philadelphia. Black soldiers were late in returning from the city to their duties at Camp William Penn in the Chelten Hills because they could not travel in the streetcars. Black women who had the temerity to enter a car when traveling to visit their wounded husbands were imprisoned in the car while the conductor informed them they would be taken to the depot and whitewashed. Robert Smalls, a hero of the Union siege of Charleston and a skilled seaman, but an escaped slave, could not travel by streetcar to visit his ship *Planter* when it was undergoing repairs at the Navy Yard. The streetcar committee of the Statistical Association joined with more militant younger Philadelphia blacks, including the schoolteacher Octavius V. Catto, to organize a mass meeting of blacks for open streetcars on March 3, 1864. On December 7, 1864, the streetcar committee met with the presidents of the street railway companies to plead with them and point out that New York had ended streetcar segregation. The West Philadelphia and Darby Road and the Fifth and Sixth Streets line then capitulated, announcing their cars would be open to all well-behaved persons, while the Girard College and Ridge Avenue Road and the newly established Union line agreed to run separate cars for colored people.

But no further concessions could be squeezed from the companies or the government and people of Philadelphia. On January 31, 1865, the day Congress adopted the Thirteenth Amendment abolishing slavery, the Philadelphia streetcar companies announced the result of a referendum among their passengers on the question "Shall colored persons be allowed to ride in all the cars?" The vote was predictably negative. The Frankford and Southwark Company announced it would admit Negroes nevertheless, but it reverted to special "colored" cars after one month because of a decline in white riders.

To desegregate the streetcars of Philadelphia required outside intervention, an act of the Pennsylvania legislature in 1867 requiring railroads and street railways to carry all passengers without distinction of color. The principal legislative sponsor and champion of the act was Republican state Sen. Morrow B. Lowry, representing Erie and Crawford Counties far upstate. The significance for Philadelphia's capacity to deal with its own racial divisions was hardly encouraging.

The Centennial City
1865-1876

by Dorothy Gondos Beers

Art in all its forms is after all with most people but a means of recreation after the serious business of life is attended to. . . . Good music is good, and good pictures are good, and good statuary is good, and good books are good, but we can do without them all and yet get along very comfortably and very happily. . . . An artist who is also a good business man will always do good work, the best he is capable of doing, but, like every other business man, he will manufacture the kind of goods his customers want to buy.
— Philadelphia *Evening Telegraph*, 1876

. . . of the events of the second half of the nineteenth century none had more profound effects on American art and taste than the preparations made in Philadelphia to celebrate the completion of one hundred years of American independence.
— GEORGE B. TATUM, 1961 [1]

On Saturday afternoon, April 22, 1865, a crowd of some 30,000 gathered around the Baltimore Depot at Broad and Prime Streets. They had come to honor the body of Abraham Lincoln, the martyred president.[2] Like the rest of the nation the city of Philadelphia was stunned by the events of the Good Friday just past. Sidney George Fisher said: "I felt as tho I had lost a personal friend. . . . Bet said she was as much agitated as if she had lost a relation."[3]

As the funeral train pulled in late in the afternoon the city's bells tolled. Philadelphia was draped in black. Spectators jammed the sidewalks and perched on the roofs of buildings on South Broad Street and along the route to Independence Hall to see the catafalque as it passed in solemn procession. Many soldiers guarded the way. The body was escorted to the Declaration chamber, where those with tickets were admitted from 10 P.M. to midnight. On the next day, Sunday, the public was allowed to view the body. Though the doors would not open until six, a crowd began to gather as early as four-thirty in the morning. In lines stretching for many blocks, most of the mourners waited patiently for hours. Some 85,000 persons filed through Independence Hall before evening. At one time soldiers had to be called to clear the surrounding streets except for the waiting queue. Early the next morning another parade carried the body to the Kensington Depot north of Harrison Street between Front Street and Frankford Road for a journey to New York and thence, ultimately, to Springfield, Illinois, for burial.[4]

Both the pent-up emotion of four years of civil strife and the regard for Lincoln that had gradually developed among most of the population caused trouble for those of unwary tongue or action who still sympathized with the fallen South. A mob threatening the offices of the Democratic *Age* was turned back by the police. On April 13, the day before Lincoln's assassination, Charles Ingersoll's brother Edward with unlucky timing had made a speech in New York still defending secession, and declaring the Union war debt unconstitutional. On April 27 a crowd met Edward Ingersoll at the Kensington Depot and hooted at him as he left the train. He was insulted by a Captain Withington and in self-protection drew a pistol, but was arrested for carrying a concealed weapon. His brother Charles, coming to the district police station to visit him, was pulled from his carriage by another mob and rescued by the police only after the crowd had had leisure to beat him savagely; it was obvious that the police sympathized with the attackers.

Pierce Butler provided another case in point. After Lincoln's death Butler failed to bow his shutters and hang them with black in accordance with the Philadelphia custom of observing a death in the family. By chance an abolitionist, Morris Davis, heard of the plans of some workingmen to attack Butler's home, and thanks to his own credentials Davis was able to persuade them against it.[5]

But soon, more cheerfully, the Philadelphia regiments were returning home. On June 10 the city held its grand review. Philadelphia's most successful soldier, Maj.-Gen. George Gordon Meade, hero of Gettysburg, and from that battle through Appomattox commander of the Army of the Potomac, led the veterans from Camp Cadwalader far out on Ridge Avenue, past reviewing stands of dignitaries and wounded soldiers near Penn Square, and on to the volunteer refreshment saloons in Southwark for a dinner. There the general disconcerted everybody by nearly fainting in the heat and humidity of an overcrowded building whose windows were closed against a heavy rain.

Over a year later, on July 4, 1866, as a climactic observance of the ending of the war, there came an extraordinary Independence Day celebration, the first of a succession of spectacular observances of the Fourth of July in the decade to come. This day the Pennsylvania regiments were to return their colors to the custody of the state. Citizens responded to a call to decorate and illuminate homes and business establishments. Throughout the day gun salutes were fired from Penn Square and from the wartime fortification in Fairmount Park on the hill above the east end of the present Girard Avenue Bridge; residents near Penn Square were warned to raise their windows about a foot to prevent the glass from breaking. Another grand parade with veteran units and commanders, this time headed by another local hero of Gettysburg,

Catafalque bearing the body of Abraham Lincoln on Broad Street, between Washington Avenue and Carpenter Street, at about five o'clock, April 22, 1865.
LIBRARY COMPANY OF PHILADELPHIA

Maj.-Gen. Winfield Scott Hancock, marched from Broad and Arch to Independence Square. There General Meade presented the colors to Governor Curtin.[6] The city had reverted from the gloom of the president's assassination to a confident good humor—a mood it generally managed to sustain through ten years of preparation, to its greatest celebration of all, the centennial of independence.

I

There was a feeling abroad that war's end meant a new beginning, a fresh approach to all aspects of living. Growth—in population, populated areas, new buildings, industry, commerce, cultural activities, educational opportunities, and finally in capacity to undertake and carry through the project of the Centennial Exposition—was certainly to be a central theme of the new period for Philadelphia. By 1870 the city's population was 674,022; on April 1, 1876,

a police estimate prepared for the Centennial set the population total at
817,000.[7] By the 1870s the densely populated portion of the city's area extended
about seven miles up and down the Delaware and some three to four miles
westward, having crossed the Schuylkill into West Philadelphia. This westward expansion was recognized and further stimulated by the completion of
new bridges across the Schuylkill, at Chestnut Street in 1866, at Callowhill
Street in 1874, at South Street in 1875 for pedestrians and in 1876 for vehicular
traffic, and most spectacularly, at Girard Avenue on the Fourth of July, 1874,
the bridge that was to carry visitors directly to the Centennial Exposition,
erected at a cost of over a million dollars and reputed to be the widest bridge
in the world.[8]

*Broad and Chestnut Streets, southwest corner (c. 1876). One of the city's
busiest corners, now the site of the Land Title Building, was occupied by the Adams
Express Company and a grocer when this photograph was made. The narrow
building at the left was the Academy of Natural Sciences until 1876 when the
Academy moved its collections and library to Nineteenth and Race Streets. The La
Pierre House with its prominent eagle was one of the city's luxury-class hotels.*

FREE LIBRARY OF PHILADELPHIA

The territorial expansion of the city goes far to explain its ability to
generate and maintain a mood of confidence. New York and Boston in
contrast were geographically constricted cities, and they paid penalties that
Philadelphia did not have to suffer. Apparently it was not until fairly late in
the century that Philadelphia was first called "The City of Homes," but if the
phrase was not yet in vogue, the city already enjoyed a reputation as outstanding among the great urban centers in the proportion of its housing that

consisted of single-family and owner-occupied homes. New York could absorb its growing population in the second half of the nineteenth century only by building vertically and pressing its inhabitants more and more into multi-story tenements that became notorious for filth, bad ventilation, and oppressive crowding. Boston also had to pack its newcomers tightly together, in deteriorating older houses in the South End. Philadelphia too had its slums, in long-decayed precincts of Southwark and Moyamensing and in alleys and courts hidden behind the principal streets of the old city. But in large part the ready availability and consequent cheapness of land for expansion permitted the continued outward march of the city's gridiron blocks and of the characteristic Philadelphia row houses, also cheap, but comfortable for one-family occupancy. By 1867 an average of 4500 such buildings a year were being added to Philadelphia's supply of housing.[9]

Along with cheap land, the rapid extension of the street railways was of course also indispensable to the Philadelphia pattern of dispersed housing. One hundred twenty-nine miles of track had been laid by 1864; by 1893 there were 212 miles, and over sixty-six million passengers were carried. The fare was seven cents, or four tickets for twenty-five cents; transfers were available for use at intersections of various lines. Early in the period more than a dozen companies, their cars distinguished by special colors, still operated the lines. But Peter A. B. Widener, a butcher who had founded his fortune with a contract to provide mutton for federal troops within ten miles of Philadelphia during the Civil War, was beginning to extend his interests by buying up streetcar lines. In 1875, in partnership with William Lukens Elkins, an oil magnate from western Pennsylvania, Widener commenced the systematic buying that was to create the Philadelphia Transportation Company monopoly of the lines by 1883.

Black people could now ride the cars. Gov. John W. Geary signed the Pennsylvania antidiscrimination bill on March 3, 1867. On March 25 Miss Carrie Lacount, a schoolteacher, was refused admission to a car at Ninth and Lombard. She immediately sought the aid of a magistrate, who arrested and fined the conductor. Philadelphia's black community soon held a victory meeting.[10]

To bring the growing ranks of row houses served by the expanding streetcar lines within the means of large numbers of Philadelphia's mechanics, factory workers, and clerks, the middle years of the nineteenth century had witnessed a burgeoning of building and loan associations. The first of these in the United States was founded in Philadelphia in 1831. They spread across the country, but they remained especially a Philadelphia institution. By 1876 over $50 million in housing investment had flowed through them since 1849; at least 450 of them, perhaps 600, were active in the city. The would-be owner invested his savings in shares at a moderate interest rate. In New York land values were too high to permit individuals of modest means to acquire the price of a home in this way; but in Philadelphia thousands of workingmen could thus buy the sixteen by thirty-one-feet, two-story brick row houses that sold, according to location, for from $1000 to $2500. An additional aid to cheap housing was the Philadelphia custom of ground rent, inherited from the proprietary period, whereby the purchaser of a house might not have to buy the lot it occupied, but instead might pay a nominal rent. And the simple extension of the gridiron street pattern, even outward across hills where it was no longer so appropriate as in the level center city, saved contractors and the city from planning costs that would have been entailed by refitting the streets to the terrain, and thus helped keep prices low.[11]

For all that, owner occupancy of homes in Philadelphia never exceeded 25 percent. Yet Philadelphia was well ahead of other large American cities in this respect. In 1880 Philadelphia homes had 5.7 occupants per dwelling, as compared with 16.36 in New York, 8.25 in Boston, and 8.24 in the new and geographically expansive city of Chicago.[12]

Among the social tensions eased by the availability of land and houses were those of assimilating immigrants. Philadelphia never became a center of immigrant settlement comparable to New York; but in the census of 1870 the proportion of foreign-born in the city's population reached a peak it was not to match again, 27 percent of the total, 183,624 of 674,022. At this time the great tide of immigration from southern and eastern Europe had of course scarcely begun; Philadelphia's immigrants when her foreign-born population reached this summit were still predominantly Germans and Irish, a majority Irish. Even before the potato famine had pushed Irish immigration to its crest, the riots of 1844 had dramatized the potential for trouble when Irish Catholic newcomers settled in the old Protestant city of Philadelphia. But by the 1870s the Irish inhabitants had dispersed themselves throughout the city, and with geographic mobility came an upward social mobility. The kinds of suspicions and hostilities that Irish ghettos in New York and Boston generated both within and without the ghetto boundaries were much less intense in Philadelphia. Not constricted as the Boston Irish were into narrow geographical limits, the Philadelphia Irish also enjoyed more rapid escape into the ranks of skilled workingmen and into independent businesses as grocers, dry goods dealers, commission merchants, real estate brokers, and especially construction contractors. They were the builders of many of the homes of the city of homes.[13]

If until very recently Philadelphia has looked like a late-nineteenth-century city, the reason is clear, for many of the structures that the Philadelphian regards as the landmarks of his city were erected in the 1860s and 1870s. By 1874 there were 147,000 buildings in the city.[14]

As if to signal the coming of more settled times, after several changes of location during the war the Union League opened its permanent home at Broad and Sansom on May 11, 1865. A few weeks later Gen. U. S. Grant was given a warm reception there.[15] The Masonic Temple at Broad and Filbert Streets, under construction from 1868 at a cost of more than a million dollars, was dedicated on September 26, 1873, with a parade of 11,000 Masons. The Philadelphia Freemasons had dedicated the first Masonic building in America on Lodge (Morris) Alley west of Second and north of Walnut in 1755; the new temple was their sixth in the city, in addition to transitory meeting places. The architect, James H. Windrim, himself a Mason, was commissioned to build "in popular Norman style."[16] The Philadelphia historian Thompson West-cott called the temple "the finest Masonic structure in the world" and boasted it was unlike anything else in Philadelphia, which in its fancifulness it surely was, with Corinthian, Renaissance, Gothic, Norman, Egyptian, Ionic, and Oriental Halls as well as a Doric Grand Foyer.[17]

Far less flamboyant, but already stylistically old-fashioned, was Addison Hutton's modified Parthenon, the Ridgway Library at Broad and Christian Streets. It was controversial from its inception. The concept of South Broad Street as an avenue of fine mansions, as North Broad Street became above Girard Avenue, spurred Henry J. Williams, the brother-in-law and executor of the estate of Dr. James Rush, to insist that Rush on his deathbed specify that the Library Company of Philadelphia must build there. Acceptance of the location became the price of what was left after construction costs of Dr. Rush's million-dollar bequest. Rush might well have so specified, for he was highly eccentric. He was the son of Benjamin Rush and himself a physician, but throughout his life a student of various types of esoterica (author of a *Philosophy of the Human Voice*) rather than a practicing physician. His bequest to the Library Company was in memory of his wife, Phoebe Ann Ridgway Rush, a famous hostess despite her husband's reclusive tendencies and the heiress whose fortune he inherited. The Library Company of Philadelphia maintained that a building so far distant from its members would not serve its purposes, but in 1877 the company decided to take the building anyway and opened it a few years later. It became a depository for the older books infrequently used.[18]

The Library Company had already made tentative plans to move from its old and elegant but now outmoded building at Fifth and Library Streets, opposite Independence Square, to a more suitable westerly (but not far southerly) site. Its directors had raised a building fund with which it assembled, property by property, an additional site at the northwest corner of Locust and Juniper Streets. Frank Furness, emerging as the most talented and exciting Philadelphia architect of his time, designed for this site in his characteristic eclectic style a fireproof structure (for its day, but with wooden walls and wooden shelves). The building included in its facade a niche for the Benjamin Franklin statue that had adorned the old structure, while reproducing inside much of the fine interior of the old quarters. In 1879–1880 the most frequently circulating part of the collection moved here, and the South Philadelphia building established by the Rush bequest became the "Ridgway Branch."[19] The Ridgway Branch proved an unfortunate place in unforeseen additional ways, impossible to heat adequately and with a forever leaking skylight atop its center block. Not until 1966 did the Library Company at last move its collections again to a new building on the south side of Locust Street between Juniper and Thirteenth. Since 1966 the Ridgway Library has been used for community activities.[20]

Ten blocks from Market Street was too far south—but such was the course

BROAD STREET.

WHEN William Penn laid out his city he divided it, east and west and north and south, by broad avenues, which he intended should be its principal thoroughfares. High or Market street, as it is now called, which runs east and west, as the city grew was occupied by merchants, who regarded not the dictates of fashion, and fashionable people in disdain forsook its pavement and selected Chestnut street for their promenade. Broad street, which runs north and south, and which is the longest street in the world, for a less accountable reason was also neglected by fashion, and until within a comparatively few years past the chief buildings on it were factories and warehouses of various kinds. A few fine residences having been erected upon the upper portion of

Synagogue of Congregation Rodeph Shalom, designed by Frank Furness (1839–1912), built 1870, demolished 1925, as seen in Earl Shinn, A Century After: Picturesque Glimpses of Philadelphia and Pennsylvania *(Philadelphia: Allen, Lane & Scott and J. W. Lauderbach, 1875).*

of the city's growth that a leap west across the Schuylkill all the way to the 3400 block of Walnut Street was a wise move for the University of Pennsylvania. The university purchased part of Andrew Hamilton's eighteenth-century country estate, the Woodlands, at $8000 an acre and in 1871 laid the cornerstone for the main building, College Hall. The architect was T. W.

University of Pennsylvania, College Hall, in A Century After *(1875). In 1872 the university sold its property at Ninth and Chestnut to the federal government and moved to this site in West Philadelphia where, with Drexel University (founded 1893), it is now the focus of the University City neighborhood.*

Richards, about to be promoted from instructor in drawing to professor of drawing and architecture; the architectural style was Collegiate Gothic and the building was ready for use in the academic year 1872–1873. The scale of the university was still such that the Department of Liberal Arts could occupy the west wing, the Department of Science the east wing, with library, chapel, and assembly rooms in the central pavilion.[21]

The city was still governed from Independence Square, with City Hall at Fifth and Chestnut Streets housing the central offices of the police and fire departments as well as the other principal municipal offices, while some other city offices and courts occupied Congress Hall at Sixth and Chestnut. Office and court space had become altogether inadequate for the government of a modern big city. On December 31, 1868, the city Councils appointed commissioners to plan new public buildings on Independence Square, with the existing buildings on the square except Independence Hall to be demolished. The proposed U-shaped new City Hall would have enveloped and dwarfed Independence Hall.[22]

An outcry followed, not only because of the sentiment surrounding the other historic buildings of Independence Square, but also because there was considerable support for moving the city offices westward with the flow of business and the tide of population. In response the state legislature on March 30, 1870, ordered a special election in October of that year at which Philadelphia's qualified voters could choose between Washington Square and Penn Square for the new city hall; either way, Independence Square would be preserved.[23] The result was a vote of 51,623 for Penn Square and 32,825 for Washington Square.

Construction of the new building was then placed in the hands of another commission. The cornerstone was laid on July 4, 1874. This mammoth pile, "The Temple of Philadelphia's Folly," as Alexander K. McClure called it, was not completed until almost the turn of the century, at a cost of $25 million instead of the $10 million originally estimated.[24] But however extravagant in cost and in the excesses of its late Victorian rendition of the French Renaissance style, John McArthur, Jr.'s City Hall capitalized on the decision favoring Penn Square. The structure used a potentiality always latent in Thomas Holme's plan for Philadelphia, to make the wide axes of Market and Broad Streets an étoile worthy of L'Enfant's Washington.

Independence Hall meanwhile needed attention and labor, within and without, if it were to be displayed suitably as a national shrine during the coming celebration of a century of national existence. Lt.-Col. Frank M. Etting, a member of one of Philadelphia's and Baltimore's most prominent colonial Jewish families, had volunteered for the Civil War and remained in the army afterward. In 1870 he returned to civilian life to dedicate himself to his conception of recovering the original furniture used in the Hall of the Declaration and restoring the chamber to an approximation of its condition in the revolutionary era. In 1871 the city Councils accepted the proposal to make Independence Square and its buildings a memorial forever to the establishment of the nation. With the Councils' authorization, the mayor appointed a committee to restore Independence Hall, including in its membership Colonel Etting and former Mayor Morton McMichael, civic leader and publisher of the *North American*.[25]

The Declaration chamber had become an oversized Victorian parlor, filled with furniture rejected by former city Councils and with masses of pictures covering every available space. One window was barricaded by a block of marble intended as Philadelphia's contribution to the still unfinished Washington National Monument.[26] Horace Binney's memories of the room as it had been in the early part of the nineteenth century led the restoration committee to place pillars in the Independence Chamber, to rebuild the president's dais, and to remove the clutter of portraits. Layer after layer of disfiguring paint was peeled from both interior and exterior of the building. The hunt for original furniture was pursued in private homes and especially at the state Capitol. The West Room was made into a national museum, for preservation of objects associated with the principal events of United States history. Much of the financing was through private funds raised by the restoration committee.[27]

Fairmount Park was a place of recreation for all. Until 1867 the chief engineer of the waterworks and the commissioner of city property jointly had custody of the park. Following the rapid growth of the park just before the Civil War, and once the end of the war restored public attention to local affairs, a Fairmount Park Commission was established on March 26, 1867, for the administration and development of the park. Morton McMichael, then mayor of the city and ex-officio a member of the commission, became first president of the Fairmount Park Commission. Other members included Eli Kirk Price and General Meade, who was vice-president.

The ordinance creating the commission also extended Fairmount Park deep into West Philadelphia by adding to the park a tract from the west bank of the Schuylkill opposite the original waterworks west and north roughly to the Pennsylvania Railroad tracks, Belmont Avenue, and Montgomery Avenue. Within this area were the West Philadelphia Water Works, opposite Lemon Hill, and the old country seats of Solitude, Sweetbriar, and Lansdowne. The ordinance declared that this land should be "laid out and maintained forever as an open public place or park, for the health and enjoyment of the people of the said city, and the preservation of the purity of the water supply." The latter clause, in addition to hearkening back to the genesis of the park, inspired the commissioners to recommend that ensuring the purity of the water supply made it desirable to extend the park boundaries still farther, roughly to the Falls of Schuylkill in the western section of the park and, with a road between Laurel Hill Cemetery and the Schuylkill, in the eastern section north to the Wissahickon, to include both banks of that stream. On April 4, 1868, the city Councils responded generously by directing the commissioners to appropriate ground all the way to City Avenue west of the Schuylkill, and on the east side, to the north bank of the Wissahickon and up the Wissahickon to Paul's Mill Road, about where Lincoln Drive now begins. While the commissioners were acquiring the new properties and planning roads and landscaping for them, an aged brother and sister, Jesse and Rebecca George, offered in return for annuities of $4000 each during their lifetimes (a small price; they died in 1869 and 1873, respectively) their ancestral tract just beyond the new western boundaries of the park: George's Hill, eighty-three acres with a superb view of the city. Thus when the new "grand road" of the west park, Lansdowne Drive, was opened on June 21, 1869, it ran from Girard Avenue to George's Hill, where General Meade ceremonially raised the flag.[28]

Fairmount Park now encompassed nearly 3000 acres. The walking or driving distance from the Callowhill Street entrance to the upper park was thirteen miles. In 1872 the park was used by some 750,000 pedestrians, nearly 400,000 vehicles, and 26,500 equestrians.[29]

II

The United States in 1865 was on the path toward preeminence as an industrial giant. Returning soldiers, capital released from wartime investment, the rapidly increasing use of the corporate form of business organization and financing, manufacturing plants needing to be readjusted to peacetime activity, an influx of immigrants, new techniques in communication and transportation, fabulous new machinery, American inventiveness, and American enthusiasm—all contributed to industrialization. All these assets were clearly discernible in Philadelphia at the end of the Civil War. The city's wealth and prominence in manufacturing, commerce, banking, and transportation sustained its mood of optimism and made possible the ambitious undertaking and fulfillment of the Centennial Exposition.

In the post–Civil War industrial age Philadelphia industry continued to benefit from the city's geographic situation, including the same amplitude of space that eased the pressures of population growth. Philadelphia remained close to productive farm, truck, and dairy areas, and it also still had near at hand the primary desiderata of the industrialism of the day, coal and iron. Since the railroads of the mid-century had begun bringing the mineral products of the earth to the city, the road to industrial wealth was even easier. Just before the beginning of the war another useful mineral product, petroleum, was discovered in western Pennsylvania. Although most of its diverse applications were still in the future, recognition soon came that petroleum could serve as a substitute for the ever-scarcer whale oil in lighting equipment. Railroads were the principal carriers of the black gold to its markets; the Pennsylvania Railroad had a large share of the early traffic, and Philadelphia, as a storage and refining center, benefited from the first surge of the petroleum boom.[30]

Philadelphia's business and industrial development was actively promoted by a Board of Trade that, founded in 1833, grew during the postwar period to be the largest such businessmen's organization in the country and a principal source of the movement that established a National Board of Trade in 1869. Much of the board's impetus came from John Welsh, its president from 1866 and throughout the period, a partner in an established mercantile firm, S. & W. Welsh, and one of the energetic original Fairmount Park commissioners. Welsh was soon to be the principal financial officer of the Centennial as president of the Centennial Board of Finance, and also served from 1877 to 1879 as United States minister to London. The treasurer of the board was Frederick Fraley, president of the Schuylkill Navigation Company and first president of the National Board of Trade. In large part the Centennial Exposition was a promotional project of the Board of Trade, and the board was most responsible for mobilizing the financial means to support the exposition.[31]

Not the least of the Board of Trade's services to the city was to provide annual statistical surveys that indicated the directions of Philadelphia's industrial development. These reports portray Philadelphia's industrialism in the postwar boom, and at the height of the city's prominence among the industrial centers of the world, as healthily diversified. Yet the promise for the future was less, for the city maintained the organizational patterns of the first industrialization; Philadelphia industry continued for the most part to be organized in a multitude of relatively small enterprises. Few individual firms employed large numbers of workers. The giant Baldwin Locomotive Works at Broad and Spring Garden Streets, with nearly 3000 employees before the Panic of 1873, was an exception to the usual Philadelphia scale of organization.[32]

Despite the city's proximity to coal and iron, Philadelphia had few producers of primary iron and steel products. The Midvale Steel Company in North Philadelphia, founded in 1867 by a group of investors headed by the banker Edward W. Clark, and the Roberts family's Pencoyd Iron Works on the Schuylkill opposite Manayunk were alone as major firms in this category. Henry Disston & Sons in Tacony—Disston saws—might be considered another primary producer. Otherwise the city's iron industry consisted of the manufacturers of such products as machinery, foundry products, locomotives, ships, stoves, cutlery, and tools.

Locomotive for the Boston and Maine Railroad, Baldwin Locomotive Works, Broad and Spring Garden Streets, 1870. From its founding in 1832 to 1870, the Baldwin works produced over 2600 locomotives for use throughout the world. The Baldwin factory site was closed in 1928.

LIBRARY COMPANY OF PHILADELPHIA

Lacking in primary industries that would have employed large numbers of unskilled workers, Philadelphia industry was a world of skilled and semi-skilled laborers. The textile and garment industries were continuing to grow around the large pool of skilled workers already in the city. These industries still employed traditional household labor while also developing factories. Such a work force, employed mostly by relatively small firms, does much to account for Philadelphia's persisting social conservatism and for the relatively low rate of foreign immigration into the city.[33]

Philadelphia had been the first great industrial city in the United States and remained the leading urban manufacturing center in the immediate post–Civil War era. In commerce she lacked the means to rival the port of New York. Although the completion of the Pennsylvania Railroad link to the Middle West in 1854 had given Philadelphia the ability to compete with New York in the scale of her domestic commerce for the first time since the building of the Erie Canal, the leadership that New York had won in the interval and the natural advantages of New York as a seaport ensured that as a transportation center Philadelphia would remain in its shadow. As the expansion of the United States across the continent created new transportation hubs and thus urban centers all the way to the Pacific coast, Philadelphia's very proximity to her old rival New York, when set against the vast scale of American distances, still further threatened her status even as a regional urban center. For commerce, in short, Philadelphia's geographic location was no longer nearly so advantageous as for manufacturing.

But the full implications of these circumstances had not yet revealed themselves; optimistic post–Civil War Philadelphia was still the second city of the United States, one of the largest cities of the world, and indeed still trying to retain greatness even in maritime commerce. In the summer of 1870 there was revived a project often discussed and occasionally attempted in the past—a direct, scheduled steamship connection from Philadelphia to Liverpool.[34] The American Steamship Company entered into a contract in 1871 with William Cramp & Sons to build four first-class iron propeller ships. At the beginning of 1874 these ships, the *Pennsylvania, Ohio, Indiana,* and *Illinois,* had been completed and were accepted. The American Steamship Company added four British-built steamers and was able to establish a semiweekly schedule to Liverpool. Furthermore in 1874 the Red Star Line opened regular service between Philadelphia and Antwerp, with four vessels at the outset and other ships added by 1877.[35]

When the Philadelphia and Reading Railroad decided in 1869 to transport virtually all its own coal from Port Richmond to ports of sale, it began acquiring a fleet of seagoing iron tugs. Fourteen were built by the end of 1874. These vessels delivered 450,000–500,000 tons of coal annually to ports along the Atlantic coast, mostly to Boston and way points, though sometimes as far as Portland, Maine. Port Richmond sent out 5,784,657 tons of coal in 1877 and was claimed as the "greatest point of water shipment of coal in the world."[36]

By now navigation to Philadelphia was assisted by the completed Delaware breakwater and a harbor of refuge at the entrance to the bay. The bay and river channels were cleared of all but relatively harmless shoals. The tide, rising six feet, enabled fairly large vessels to cross the bar.[37] In the Centennial year clearance was granted to 1457 vessels of 922,290 tons.[38] Imports reached a value of $20,298,763, while exports amounted to $50,552,300. The coastwise trade alone had a value of about $100 million yearly. Agricultural products still accounted for over half the total export value.[39]

Alexander Kerr, Bro., & Co., Salt Dealer, North Delaware Avenue (photograph c. 1875).

FREE LIBRARY OF PHILADELPHIA

Philadelphia's shipbuilding industry was a source of further sustenance for maritime commerce. The city's ancient wooden shipbuilding industry had enjoyed a final flurry of activity just before the Civil War, stimulated by the gold-rush trade to California and the diversion of European vessels from American commerce caused by the Crimean War; but wooden shipbuilding in Philadelphia never recovered from the combination of the devastating effects of the Civil War on the American merchant marine and the simultaneous rise of iron construction. Perhaps the final blow to the industry came when the Reading Railroad abandoned wooden vessels as coal carriers to build its fleet of iron steam colliers.[40] With wood construction nearly dead, from 1866 to 1870 no Philadelphia shipyards had much work; the government had ceased its war orders, iron was expensive, and Philadelphia shipyard wages were relatively high.

But improvement came for the iron shipbuilders after 1870, as iron fell in price, reaching its lowest level in United States history in 1878 at $16.50 a ton, and as the American merchant marine recovered enough to create a demand —reinforced by South American orders—for new iron ships. Obviously Philadelphia enjoyed a superior location for iron shipbuilding. It had good rail connections with the whole of the interior of Pennsylvania and thus with what was still the center of American iron production; the Delaware had a suitable depth of water; the city possessed a sufficient pool of workmen skilled in the use of iron.[41] In 1866, 243 vessels were built and in 1872, 303. By 1874 the trend was toward larger ships; the tonnage of the 120 vessels built that year exceeded that of the much larger number built in 1872.[42]

William Cramp & Sons and Charles Cramp successfully completed the transition from wooden to iron building and remained the leading Philadelphia shipyards. In 1872 William Cramp & Sons became a corporation, and by purchase shortly afterward it acquired the iron and engine-building works of I. P. Morris & Company. New capital was invested. With the reputation acquired in the Civil War and through building the vessels for the American Steamship Company, the firm soon had a steady stream of orders. The Russian government in 1876 engaged Cramp to do important repair work and then to build three cruisers. The firm's output included river steamboats as well as ocean-going vessels.[43]

The old Navy Yard at the foot of Federal Street had proved too small during the Civil War, but with the removal of the pressures of war the government was slow to transfer its Philadelphia shipbuilding to the League Island site donated by the city. Congress did not pass the necessary legislation to complete the acceptance of Philadelphia's offer until 1867. Moving the Navy Yard began in 1868; the government sold the old site for a million dollars.[44]

I V

Though a Philadelphia banking firm was directly associated with precipitating the Panic of 1873, the city's financial institutions in general weathered the depression with their reputation for sound, if increasingly conservative and cautious, practices intact. Long since secondary to New York in finance as well as in commerce, Philadelphia remained enough a center of banking and finance that the capital underlying its manufacturing and commercial enterprises was substantially home-based. There was reasonable pride in the fact that bankruptcy in the depression years showed the percentage of failures smaller than in any other large city of the United States.[45]

By 1875 Philadelphia had some forty banks, twenty-eight of them national, with a capital of $16,735,000.[46] Banks had doubled in number since 1859.[47] In addition there were four savings banks with aggregate deposits of about $12 million, over forty insurance companies of various types, and thirty-five private lending companies, to say nothing of the hundreds of building and loan associations.[48]

On September 18, 1873, the New York branch of the Philadelphia firm of Jay Cooke and Company failed. Its overextension of investment in Northern Pacific Railroad stock was symptomatic of a general American postwar overinvestment in new railroads, factories, and buildings, a credit inflation, and a currency inflation. Following upon a series of lesser banking failures earlier in the month, the closing of Jay Cooke burst the postwar inflationary bubble. Cooke's Philadelphia branch had to close its doors as well, and the Philadelphia investment banking house in which Jay Cooke had begun his career, E. W. Clarke & Co., also closed on September 18, though unlike Jay Cooke it later reopened. On September 20 another major Philadelphia firm, the Union

Banking Company, failed. The collapse of the Franklin Savings-Fund, declared bankrupt in federal district court on February 6, 1874, was a disaster of especially wide impact in the city because the fund had included many modest savings accounts.

But most of Philadelphia's banks survived and even extended their loans. The Farmers' and Mechanics' National Bank, the Philadelphia National Bank, the First National Bank, and the Bank of North America, among the largest of the city, continued to pay dividends. During the 1870s the Bank of North America "averaged nineteen per cent a year," while it maintained a proper surplus sum.[49] The Board of Trade report of 1874 somewhat prematurely congratulated its members on the "passing away of the financial pressure which had been so severely felt during the autumn months of 1873. Business is regaining its usual proportions and activity."[50] At least at the upper echelons of its business leadership Philadelphia did manage to retain its confidence during the depression of the 1870s; preparation for the Centennial probably cushioned the effects—especially psychologically. Still, many factories closed, many Philadelphians were out of work, hunger was apparent among the unemployed, and "a joyless winter followed" for thousands who did not have the reserve resources of the members of the Board of Trade.[51] The city Councils did nothing in particular for the relief of the unemployed; the prevailing theory among Philadelphia's business and political leadership, also enunciated by the Board of Trade, was that to the extent that hard times persisted, the remedy was a reconsideration of recent reductions in tariff duties, particularly to stem imports of foreign iron and steel.[52]

v

The composition of Philadelphia labor was not such as to foster militant class antagonisms. Rather, the city's mainly skilled and semiskilled workingmen remained dedicated to the preservation of the privileges of their trades and as many as possible of the remnants of independent artisanship. The skilled trades unions of Philadelphia took advantage of wartime and immediate postwar prosperity to rebuild and strengthen their local organizations and to stimulate a movement for national organization of the trades. The usual nineteenth-century pattern was for labor organizations to prosper when the whole economy prospered and to wane when the economy waned. Thus the 1860s were auspicious years for the Philadelphia trades unions; between 1860 and 1868 the wages of skilled workmen in the city rose by from 50 percent to more than 100 percent, and although the ten-hour day remained the general standard, some skilled workers won an eight-hour day.[53] The machinists, blacksmiths, and iron molders were especially successful in organizing in Philadelphia during the late years of the war. The Typographical Union and the Iron-Moulders Union were among old unions that took marked strides toward national organization. The National Union of Cigar Makers and the Plasterers' National Union were among new national organizations with notable strength in Philadelphia.

Probably the most influential labor journal of the time, *Fincher's Trades'*

Review, was published in Philadelphia for three years beginning June 6, 1863. At first a four-page weekly with less than 5000 circulation, by 1865 it printed over 11,000 copies and was an eight-page paper, national in appeal, ignoring advertising, and dependent on trades unions for support. Its editorial policy was that of the skilled workers with largely middle-class attitudes.[54]

Among the Philadelphia contributors to *Fincher's* was William H. Sylvis, who as early as 1859 had signed the call that led to the assembling in the city of the first convention of the Iron-Moulders International Union, and who was first treasurer and from 1863 president of that union. In February 1866 a meeting between Sylvis and William Harding of Brooklyn, president of the Coachmakers' International Union, produced a call for a national convention of workingmen to meet in Baltimore the following August. The Baltimore Labor Congress formed the National Labor Union. This organization stressed the injustices suffered by producers at the hands of nonproductive accumulators of capital, and advocated a government-regulated greenback currency and limitation of interest to 3 percent as a means of reducing excess capital accumulation by the nonproductive and assuring fair rewards to the producers of wealth. This was a prescription for encouraging modest property-holding by labor; reform was to be achieved without infringing liberty of contract, private enterprise, or private property. In September 1868 at a New York convention Sylvis was elected president of the National Labor Union. He was an able organizer and administrator; he established a committee of lobbyists to guard labor interests in Washington, and he pushed for the organization of a reform political party. Once currency and interest were properly regulated in the producers' interests, he believed, there would be no more necessity for a union movement.[55]

The National Labor Union met in Philadelphia in the summer of 1869. Shortly before the convention assembled, however, Sylvis died. Without his leadership nothing substantial was accomplished at the Philadelphia convention. The gathering was nevertheless noteworthy in that black delegates attended for the first time. Women fared less well; Susan B. Anthony, representing the Workingwomen's Protective Association, was rejected as a delegate because her organization was deemed not a labor organization and because she had tried to get jobs for women in printing offices at wages lower than those of striking men.[56]

However complacently the Philadelphia Board of Trade viewed the Panic of 1873, the panic and the ensuing depression were a watershed for labor. The advantages gained by unionization during the prosperous 1860s suffered predictable setbacks. The National Labor Union was already dying. During 1870–1871 trades unions defected, preferring concentration on immediate economic and status issues and disliking the emphasis on political action. Despite Sylvis, the Philadelphia unions were among those concerned with immediate issues. In the depression, however, many of the national trades unions themselves collapsed or clung to the mere appearance of existence. At the same time job insecurity made secrecy seem to many labor leaders an essential of union organization, the only safeguard against blacklists and the lockout. Under these conditions also socialism emerged to rival the greenback philosophy for the allegiance of American workingmen.[57]

Secrecy and socialism were to be principal themes of the labor movement in the 1870s, but neither was particularly congenial to the Philadelphia labor movement as it had evolved historically. Nevertheless Uriah Smith Stephens, a member of the Garment Cutters' Union, in Philadelphia on December 26, 1869, organized the first assembly of a labor union constituted as a secret society, the Knights of Labor. After some conflict, Assembly One of the Knights was opened to men of all callings with the same privileges as the garment cutters, except that they could not "participate in trade matters." With the combination of secrecy and this compromise of traditional trades unionism, the society early attracted considerable public attention, much of it unfavorable; but the society stated that its intent was to bring about cordial public feeling toward labor and its place in the economic scheme, to encourage favorable legislation, and to set up mutual benefits and aids. By May 1878 six additional assemblies were organized, all in Philadelphia. An early forerunner of the district assembly appeared in the establishment of a committee on the "good of the order." By Christmas 1873 the organization had sufficiently expanded—its secrecy now proving an asset in the face of the depression— that a coordinating district assembly was necessary, with thirty-one assemblies attached.[58]

Philadelphia also developed a surprising, though for the general life of the city highly peripheral, prominence in the history of socialism. By the beginning of the 1870s European radical emigrés were in the process of forming in New York and Chicago eight sections, with 293 members, of the Marxist First International, the International Workingmen's Association. When American intellectuals began to adopt an interest in Marxism, two native American sections of the International were formed in New York after 1870, Section 9 and Section 12. Section 12 was dominated by the Claflin sisters, Virginia Woodhull and Tennessee Claflin, who were all too well known in ways that injured the respectability of the movement, as traveling medicine-show clairvoyants and as proprietors of *Woodhull and Claflin's Weekly*, which advocated female freedom including free love. The European, mostly German, emigré socialists, for the most part thoroughly conservative in matters of private morality, persuaded the General Council of the International in London to read Section 12 out of membership. But Section 12 refused to accept extinction, and meeting in Philadelphia on July 9, 1872, it announced its independence of the International and called for political action in America through the Equal Rights party, which had nominated Mrs. Woodhull for the presidency of the United States. A few days later the remnant of the American wing of the International, the Marxists, also met in Philadelphia, declaring complete harmony with the General Council.

Following this meeting in the city the International Workingmen's Association enjoyed a modest recruitment of membership in Philadelphia, mainly among German workingmen. Meanwhile the headquarters of the International was itself transferred from London to New York, and in 1874 the First International met in convention in Philadelphia. At this depression-year assembly the International made a crucial decision, to reject the overtures of nonsocialist American labor organizations for cooperation, and to insist on purity of socialist doctrine and on political action only through a true workingmen's party, that is, a socialist party.

This rigidity pointed toward the next event in the loose historical association between Philadelphia and Marxism. The International Workingmen's Association was among the organizations meeting in Philadelphia during the Centennial year; but finding themselves making no progress in the United States and only tenuously linked to Europe, the delegates present—ten Americans and one German—chose to dissolve the First International. The American delegates hoped for better success by throwing in their lot with the Lassallean, rather than Marxist, Social Democratic Workingmen's party, organized in New York in 1874, which also met in Philadelphia in July 1876. A new Workingmen's Party of the United States came out of the merger of forces, but it also was to prove too rigidly Marxist for the American scene.

The Knights of Labor also met in Philadelphia in July of the Centennial year, "for the purpose of strengthening the order for a sound and permanent organisation, also the promoting of peace, harmony, and the welfare of its members." A constitution for a national body was drawn up, though the district assemblies were assured of almost complete autonomy in the national group. The delegates agreed that five cents per capita charged against the membership would be the only revenue collected. Not this national organizational meeting, however, but the accession of Terence V. Powderly to the presidency of the organization two years later was the key to transforming the Knights from a very slowly developing group into a national labor union of mass membership and major influence. Meanwhile, despite the comings and goings of labor leaders during Philadelphia's Centennial Exposition, unionization still floundered under the handicaps of the depression.[59]

V I

In Henry Adams's anonymously published novel of 1880, *Democracy*, a foreigner tells the heroine, Madeleine Lee, that all cities of the world are corrupt.[60] Post–Civil War Philadelphia might have been one of his object lessons. The city has long come to be regarded as "a classic study in machine politics on the municipal level."[61]

Postwar Philadelphia was machine-dominated in part because the Republican party alone dominated its politics. The Republican predominance in turn sprang largely from a postwar tendency to overlook local issues and concentrate political debate on the national scene. The epithets "Copperhead" and "rebel" remained effective weapons against the Democrats, both in national politics and in local contests that had little or nothing to do with the issues of the Civil War.

By the post–Civil War years, furthermore, the departure of the old Philadelphia upper class from civic and specifically political leadership was almost complete. The fall of Nicholas Biddle and his bank in the crash of 1841 had wrought a revolution in the social status of the city's leadership long ago, and the Civil War had destroyed most of the last vestiges of the old leadership. Sidney George Fisher and others of his class found the new political leaders vulgar and ignorant, the candidates of the current nominating conventions "wholly unfit for any public trust."[62] It is not necessary to absorb all of Fisher's prejudices to agree that the old Philadelphia political leadership, if often casual and lethargic, had demonstrated a sense of civic responsibility, a regard for tradition and the past that included a feeling of obligation to maintain a great city for the future, missing in the new politicians, ambitious for immediate advancement and for fulfillment of immediate interests, who had taken their places.

It was only a minimum of civic order and cohesion that the new machine politics provided. Taxes constantly increased, but the streets were "dirty, ill lighted and wretchedly paved."[63] Many Philadelphians constantly carried pistols; often the city seemed on the brink of returning to the riotous 1840s, with elections regularly the occasions for disorder, disturbances customarily piercing the quiet of the night—Charles Godfrey Leland said there were brawls nightly at Seventh and Chestnut—and a relatively quiet Fourth of July so unusual as to demand special comment in the press.[64]

The particular ills besetting Philadelphia's politics were many. First, although the city and county boundaries were now the same, one of the prices of the political parties' acceptance of the Consolidation Act had been the retention of numerous county offices that overlapped the jurisdiction of city offices. Thus there were too many elected officials and too many elections for the voters to keep track of, with resultant confusion and indifference that benefited only those who devoted full time to studying and controlling politics.

In addition the Registration Act of 1869 gave the Republicans as the dominant party control of every election board and kept the courts from interfering. Only those approved by the Republican organization were registered to vote. The minority members of the election boards, chosen in fact by the majority, were frequently selected for their stupidity or corruptibility.[65]

The Republicans were free on election days to flood the polls with repeaters and outsiders; many of them voted "on the thousands of fictitious names put upon the list of registered voters."[66] The *Inquirer* urged with little success: "To vote once today is a duty that every citizen owes to the Commonwealth. To prevent anybody voting more than once is equally a duty."[67]

The question of the franchise for the black man was constantly a potential source of trouble. Though Reconstruction was enfranchising black men in the South, Philadelphians were in no hurry to introduce the same reform in their own elections. The state legislature had ratified the Fifteenth Amendment to the United States Constitution in 1869 with considerable reluctance. In 1870 after the amendment had gone into effect, federal troops were sent into the city under the federal "Force Act" to protect the Negroes who chose to cast ballots, though few blacks as yet did so. At the next year's election there were no federal troops, and rioters trying to keep blacks from the polls killed three and wounded many more. One of the dead was Octavius V. Catto, principal of the Quaker-sponsored high school for blacks on Bainbridge Street above Ninth, the Institute for Colored Youth, a leader of the Pennsylvania State Equal Rights League in its fight to desegregate the streetcars, and at thirty-one the most magnetic and perhaps the most promising leader the Philadelphia black community had yet produced.[68]

Additional elements in Republican control of the city were the row officials such as the sheriff and coroner, who were paid no salary and depended on the fees of their offices and the cooperation of elected officials with their activities. The Republicans were also helped by the requirement that independent candidates for office provide at their own expense printed ballots for each of about 700 election districts, and twice as many ballots if they wanted votes from both Republicans and Democrats; the intimidation of voters by the police; the illegal placing of officeholders on election boards; and the false counting of votes and falsifying of election returns.[69]

For over a generation Philadelphia's volunteer fire companies had been a source of political power. But the fire companies, with their allied fighting gangs as the ultimate enforcers of their control over neighborhoods, were too unruly and unpredictable, too much inclined to adopt independent lines of action, to fit comfortably into Republican machine efforts to unify political control of the city; they tended instead to disrupt unity. Reformers had been trying to end the volunteer system at least since consolidation in 1854. The professional politicians were now ready for the change as well. By an ordinance of December 29, 1870, the city Councils eliminated the volunteer companies and created a paid fire department. Most of the volunteer companies became social clubs, but their parades and most of their political power disappeared.[70]

The Gas Ring became the hub of a much more centralized system of political power. In 1841 the city had bought out the private stockholders of the company supplying illuminating gas. Twelve trustees operated the gas system for the city. The purchase agreement stipulated that the trustees should pay no part of the profits of the works into the city treasury until all the gas company's loans were paid—but no provision was written into the agreement against the acceptance of further loans with the same priority claim against revenues. In consequence the trustees negotiated a seemingly endless succession of loans as a means of awarding favors and creating relationships of mutual dependence with various business interests. During the diversion of public attention to national politics in wartime the trustees used their financial power to become increasingly dominant in municipal administration, while in 1865 the Republicans took complete control of the board. Though the trustees were not paid, they saw to their own welfare when awarding about $2 million annually in contracts and when hiring, firing, and promoting among their thousand employees. Meeting secretly, they kept their records under lock and key and published an almost worthless, because confused and falsified, annual report. Popular dissatisfaction with the Gas Trust brought the city Councils to propose an investigation in 1866, but a machine-dominated judge blocked the inquiry. Nor did the legislature at Harrisburg offer much hope of reform.[71]

The leader of the Gas Trust, and—largely through his power there—the first citywide political boss of Philadelphia, was "King" James McManes. Born in County Tyrone, Ireland, McManes had come to Philadelphia as a young man in 1830 and had gone to work in a Southwark cotton mill. There he had saved enough to open a mill of his own, which through fire met the fate of many nineteenth-century buildings. Slowly regaining financial stability, he became an investor in real estate. He was a gentle and affectionate family man, never profane; he was also a tough and skillful organizer. As an early leader of the Seventeenth Ward (Frankford Road to Sixth Street, Girard Avenue to Oxford Street) People's Republican Club he was becoming an important political figure by 1858. Named a trustee of the Gas Works in 1865, he manipulated influential friendships in Washington and Harrisburg as well as locally to make himself within two years the strongest member of the board. McManes and the Gas Trust soon controlled enough public jobs to increase the number of those dependent on the "King" for their jobs from 1000 to over 5000. The control McManes exerted over other businesses, such as banks, contractors, and street railways, through his use of Gas Works funds made the tentacles of his power far-reaching.

On December 1, 1866, McManes took office as prothonotary in the district court, a position he filled for three years with scrupulous attention to punctuality and correctness. Although a fight with Simon Cameron in 1883 caused his defeat for the gas trusteeship, he was reelected the following year. In 1887, however, political reformism brought the dissolution of the Gas Trust itself.

The "King" left a considerable fortune when he died, but he had lived simply and austerely. He seldom spoke in public, and certainly was rarely given any kind of newspaper publicity in the period of the Centennial.[72] Lord Bryce, the British commentator on American politics, wrote that McManes had "courage, resolution, foresight, the judicious preference of the substance of power to its display." Gov. Samuel Pennypacker described the "King" as "an absolute autocrat, who tolerated no difference of opinion in his ranks."[73]

Other leaders of the Republican machine included William H. Kemble, president of the People's Bank of Philadelphia and former state treasurer; William B. Mann, longtime city district attorney; and William S. Stokley, often a Council member, and mayor from 1872 to 1881. During the war the mayor's term of office had been extended to three years. Mayor Henry, reelected in 1862, decided in 1865 not to run again. Morton McMichael of the

North American then headed the Republican ticket against Democrat Daniel M. Fox, and the atmosphere of military victory gave McMichael a lead of nearly 6000 votes.

McMichael was a successful newspaperman and well-intentioned civic leader, but he was not an effective political organizer or a magnetic personality. With the waning of the war's enthusiasms and McManes's Republican machine still in process of formation during the late 1860s, the Democrats were able to exploit McMichael's weaknesses and colorlessness to stage a brief comeback. They elected Peter Lyle sheriff in 1867. On October 13, 1868, with Sheriff Lyle reputedly swearing in "a large posse of bartenders, brothel keepers and proprietors of rat and dog pits to guard the posse" and importing voters from as far away as Baltimore and Washington, the Democrats elected Daniel Fox mayor over Hector Tyndale by a margin of 2239.[74]

With McManes's machine growing in centralized power, however, the Republicans rallied as early as the elections for state and row offices in 1869 and 1870. "Sweet William" Stokley, who had made his way from the confectionary business to Select Council, planned to ride the Republican comeback into the mayor's office, and he succeeded in doing so largely by presenting himself as a law-and-order man who would further attack the city's regression into the riotousness and disorder that consolidation was supposed to have ended. In this role he became the principal sponsor of eliminating the tumultuous volunteer fire companies. "[A]mid the usual riotous scenes" of Election Day, Stokley won the mayoralty by a margin of some 9000 votes over James S. Biddle in 1871.

Stokley achieved another reorganization and strengthening of the police —again by relying not on the police professionalism of a later era but on tough policemen who could beat the city's thugs and gangs at their own game of violence if they had to. By the Centennial year the *Evening Bulletin* was rejoicing over a police system so effective that not a bank had been broken into nor a savings institution robbed since Stokley's election.[75]

For all that, "Sweet William" was very much one of the new men of the postwar era, by no means possessing the substance or the image of the gentlemanly, old-family style of leadership of much of Philadelphia's earlier political history. Many respectable citizens thought that "a man of different type" from Stokley ought to preside over the Centennial observances. Alexander K. McClure, a rival Republican leader, sourly described Stokley as believing the "land belonged to the saints and his party were the saints." Reformers of both parties persuaded McClure himself to run for mayor in 1874 on an independent Citizens Centennial Constitution ticket.

Now practicing law in Philadelphia, McClure was a veteran newspaperman who had been prominent in Republican party affairs as long ago as the national convention of 1860, consistently as an ally of Governor Curtin against the Simon Cameron faction. But as an independent McClure would face a formidable obstacle in the entrenched Republican machine. His previous career, moreover, had been that of an ambitious behind-the-scenes manipulator eager to advance his own influence by borrowing on Curtin's prestige. The publisher and wartime Union League pamphleteer Henry Charles Lea, a major figure among Philadelphia reformers, called McClure a "reckless political adventurer" and supported Stokley as the lesser evil. In the course of the campaign McClure's running mate Charles Gray, candidate for receiver of taxes, withdrew from the ticket and accused McClure of participating in the doings of a Harrisburg gambling den. Stokley won reelection by a resounding 10,985-vote majority. McClure later claimed that his defeat was accomplished by stuffed ballot boxes substituted for the valid ones. But he never again ran for office, going on instead to do battle with his rivals from the editorial desk of the *Philadelphia Times*.[76]

Even McClure agreed that Stokley was a "man of unusually strong mental and physical force, generally clear in judgment, and scrupulously faithful to all his personal obligations in political life, and always exhibited a measure of courage that commanded the respect of friend and foe."[77] Never accused of personal venality, Stokley was nevertheless refused membership in the Union League, and he failed to win full support from many leading businessmen, a fact that was probably harmful to the gathering of funds for the Centennial Exposition. During the Centennial he behaved circumspectly with one possible exception, at the dedication of the Municipal Building on the Centennial Grounds on August 29, 1876. For several days after the event the newspapers debated whether the banquet hosted by the mayor had degenerated into a "disgusting orgie" and a "hideous debauch."[78] The *Bulletin* alleged that it might actually have been a group of reporters from a rival newspaper who were guilty of unseemly displays of drunkenness; the account in the *Times*, said the *Bulletin*, "was noticeably brief." The *Sunday Dispatch* reported that the mayor's own conduct was above reproach and that "Good order, sobriety, and geniality prevailed about him." It accused the mayor's foes of egging on some young men to a disgraceful exhibition. Very possibly, Stokley might have used the dedication ceremony and banquet to kick off his campaign for another reelection and thus encouraged spirits to flow freely. Whatever the truth, this minor tempest in possible fulfillment of the fears of the respectable did not prevent Stokley's reelection in 1877.

It is true that an intraparty fight over a third term for him developed, with the chief contender against Stokley being the rising business magnate Peter A. B. Widener, then city treasurer. McManes, however, backed Stokley. Widener soon decided his race was futile and withdrew in favor of Joseph L. Gaven, former president of the Select Council, who won the bipartisan reformers' support. Stokley's immunity to these challenges was widely credited at the time to his success in keeping law and order.[79]

Despite the general postwar disarray of the Democrats in both the city and the state, one Philadelphia Democrat contrived not only to retain considerable local power but also to gain national prominence: Cong. Samuel J. Randall. Born in 1828 of a politically minded Philadelphia family, Randall had prospered in early life in mercantile business and went on to develop his own iron and coal company. As an "American Whig," he served in the Common Council from 1852 to 1856. Shifting to the Democrats as did many Philadelphia Whigs in the late 1850s, in 1862 he won a seat in Congress. His was the old Pennsylvania First Congressional District, extending through the Delaware River wards and made up largely of mechanics, factory and dock workers, and small tradesmen. The Republicans might have gerrymandered the district out of existence had not Randall remained a stubborn high protectionist and thus a valuable Democratic ally of a major Republican national policy in the postwar era. He was usually the sole Democratic congressman from Philadelphia. Though his protectionism involved him in chronic feuding with other Democratic leaders, he was in the mainstream of his party in opposition to Republican tendencies toward generous federal spending and centralized federal power. He became chairman of the Democratic State Committee, and in 1876 his party elected him speaker of the House.[80]

Reformers unhappy with the new men and new methods in politics had somewhat better success in pursuing reform through changes in the state government rather than through direct attack on the city machine. In 1871 reform-minded Republicans, seeking a vehicle for change other than the Democratic party with its taint of Copperheadism, founded the Citizens' Municipal Reform Association. By 1872 an inner circle of reformers, possessing old-fashioned credentials, with Henry Charles Lea perhaps the prime mover among them and including George W. Childs, Joshua B. Lippincott, John Welsh, Joseph Harrison, Anthony J. Drexel, and John J. Ridgway, established a Reform Club, meeting at 1520 Chestnut Street.[81] The reformers helped nourish a drive for a new state constitution.

A resulting constitutional convention met to organize at Harrisburg on November 19, 1872, and beginning on January 7, 1873, convened in Philadelphia, in the Sixth Presbyterian Church on Spruce Street east of Sixth. It adjourned on November 3.[82] Among changes of the sort for which the municipal reformers hoped, the draft constitution sought to assure more careful checking of ballots and to prevent bribery of voters. It guaranteed uniform registration procedures and election laws throughout the commonwealth, dooming the infamous Registration Act. It provided that city debts could not be contracted except as the city government authorized them through a specific expense appropriation; it mandated that every city set up a sinking fund to pay its funded debt; it provided that officials of the more populous counties must be paid in salaries, not fees, according to a scale that the legislature would set.[83]

On December 16, 1873, the city somewhat surprisingly produced a majority of more than two to one for ratification of the reform constitution. McClure claimed later that the mayor had fraudulent returns prepared against ratification, but that the returns from the rest of Pennsylvania so strongly favored the new constitution that Philadelphia could not overcome them, and Stokley decided the authentic vote might as well stand. According to McClure, getting the honest returns reinstated was more difficult than readying a great many dishonest ballots and having them accepted.[84]

A new elections law passed the legislature in time for the Stokley-McClure mayoralty race of 1874, but in Philadelphia the administration of the law was in the hands of officials appointed under the old Registration Act. In this first test, the new constitution made little difference.[85]

The state legislature set out to provide the required sinking fund for Philadelphia. "The same bill, however, authorized a further increase in the debt of Philadelphia, which was already more than $80,000,000."[86]

The legislature also considered the subject of salaries in place of fees. District Attorney Mann and the city solicitor, Charles H. T. Collis, drew up a bill establishing local salaries far exceeding those of the governor and of the justices of the state Supreme Court. In the last days of the session Gov. John F. Hartranft vetoed the measure on the ground that it was poorly drawn in giving a different salary scale for Philadelphia County than for Allegheny and Luzerne Counties. The fee system continued.

So at the outset the constitution of 1873 proved a "hollow triumph for reform. The new constitution did indeed provide for a government of law, but the law would necessarily continue to be made and administered by men."[87] The remedies sought by the constitution constrained and limited the actions of government; but if the power of the political machine in the industrial city was to be broken, more governmental freedom of action rather than less would be necessary, so that government might legally provide to the citizens services now offered extralegally by the machine.

VII

Residents of Philadelphia occasionally anguished over political scandals and spoilsmen, over dirty streets and high taxes, but on the whole their civic mood remained one of complacency, not to say of pride. Never did the local press voice any thought that another city should be the site of the Centennial Exposition. On the contrary Philadelphia was the appropriate site, said the *North American*, because it was "of all parts of the country least given to radicalism, and sure always to be found safe, prudent, moderate, and what is known in England as liberal conservative."[88]

In so safe, prudent, and moderate a community, the fact that the city boasted 575 churches, or religious societies with "distinct places of worship," did not imply strong religious fervor or that the churches exerted great influence on city doings. The Protestant Episcopal, Methodist Episcopal, Baptist, and Presbyterian denominations claimed 359 of the churches; the Roman Catholics had 43, the Jews 9 synagogues, the Friends 14 meeting-houses.[89] There is no clue in these figures to church membership, financial support, or community influence. Sometimes attendance was impressive, but many religious groups lacked zeal enough to maintain services in Philadelphia's summer heat.[90] It was an indication of the changing urban population that perhaps the best known Philadelphia clergyman of the period was James Frederic Wood, who in 1875 became the first Roman Catholic archbishop of Philadelphia. Despite the contribution of immigration to his archdiocese, however, Wood was not notably sympathetic to the newcomers, particularly

Wanamaker's Grand Depot Store, Thirteenth and Market Streets, *wood engraving by Vaningen-Snyder after A. Blanc (c. 1876). The John Wana-maker Department Store remodeled the Pennsylvania Railroad's freight depot in 1876 and occupied the building until 1902 when the present store was built.*

the Irish. He himself was a convert of English Protestant ancestry, who had received his early education in England.[91]

The most spectacular religious event of the times was the Dwight L. Moody–Ira D. Sankey revival of mid-winter 1875–1876. The most famous evangelists of the day could be expected to draw crowds so large that for the occasion the Pennsylvania Railroad freight depot at the southwest corner of Thirteenth and Market Streets was transformed into a 10,200-seat auditorium; the depot was made available by the city's fastest rising merchant prince, John Wanamaker, whose men's clothing store, established in 1861, had grown into a department store big enough that Wanamaker purchased the depot to make it the new site of his store. With tracks removed, the depot received a new wooden interior whose floors sloped so everyone could see the speakers' platform, itself seating nearly 1000. Biblical texts decorated the walls. As many as 300 ushers were to officiate, many of them drawn from the ranks of the clerks at Wanamaker's Sixth and Market store. A thousand gas burners lighted the main audience room.[92]

Moody and Sankey came fresh from a triumphant two-year revival tour of Great Britain. The portly New Englander Moody, a onetime shoe salesman with little formal education and faulty grammar, began to be "always sincere and unaffected, to the point of brusqueness." His equally portly companion sang with deep feeling in a strong baritone. The close coordination of speaker and singer was the novelty of the Moody-Sankey technique, a device highly effective in these peak years of their evangelism and a model frequently emulated by later revivalists.[93] William F. Fischer, a Philadelphia piano dealer best remembered today as the composer of the music for "I Love to Tell the Story," trained a local choir of 300 for the Philadelphia revival and later went with Moody to New York.[94]

Moody and Sankey relied on force of personality and physical presence and fervor; their theology was coming to seem limited and dated even by the standards of emotional evangelism. Many leading ministers of Philadelphia supported their crusade, but enough doubts were simmering that the newspapers could sometimes voice skepticism, the *Sunday Dispatch* writing of Moodymaniacs as "weak minded men crazed by the harangues of the theological charlatan, Dwight Moody."[95]

The opening day of the crusade was Sunday, November 21, 1875. The crowds arrived aboard special streetcars with banners reading "Moody and Sankey Meetings." The chief of police, Kennard H. Jones, and his assistant posted themselves at the entrance to the Wanamaker Depot. Eight hundred persons occupied the platform, including the chorus of hundreds and many clergymen. In spite of a driving rain and services that started at 8:00 A.M., 8000 were in the congregation.[96]

The meetings went on for eight weeks, with a total attendance of about a million. President Grant ornamented at least one Sunday-night meeting. Leading citizens such as Jay Cooke, A. J. Drexel, and George W. Childs were persuaded to help shepherd converts forward. John Wanamaker had to miss the opening because he was abroad, but after he returned to the city he never missed a weekday service. The Sunday-morning meetings continued to be scheduled for an early hour, to avoid interfering with regular church services. Following the Sunday-evening services there were usually special meetings for young men, often held at the Arch Street Methodist Church and led by Wanamaker. From these meetings there developed a group of lay religious leaders called "Yoke Fellows." Private gifts of $30,000 covered the expenses, and no money was collected at the meetings except to benefit the YMCA. Although the hymnbook *Gospel Songs* that Moody and Sankey sponsored sold well, the revivalists took no profit from the sales but had established a trust for charitable purposes. Equipment used at the meetings was auctioned off afterward, even Moody's towels bringing four or five dollars each.[97]

Some ministers of the city met in January 1876 to discuss how to maintain religious enthusiasm after the departure of the revivalists. John Wanamaker, who was present, supported multidenominational union meetings once or twice weekly. The *Times* later concluded that Moody and Sankey had in fact brought a lasting increased vitality to the city churches. The same paper's earlier skepticism about a permanent impact was doubtless closer to the truth.[98]

Certainly the Moody-Sankey emphasis on personal salvation had little effect on benevolent efforts to cope with the social ills of the industrial city. Many churches were already engaged in charitable activities among the city's poor; so, to a limited degree, were the machine politicians whose reward was support at the polling place. Social action based on any larger conception of a responsibility of the municipality or the whole community was barely beginning. Soup societies and fuel associations offered a measure of private charity for the poor and the unemployed. Many partly social associations were intended also to mobilize such mutual self-help as their members could muster, especially within ethnic groups, as with various Hibernian societies, the Swiss Benevolent Society, and the Societé Française de Bienfaisance.[99] Otherwise, efforts to combat social problems tended like the Moody revivals to be directed toward the redemption of the fallen individual. The municipal House of Refuge was enlarged in 1872 for "employment of the idle, instruction of the ignorant and reformation of the depraved." The House of Correction opened at Holmesburg in January 1874 for vagrants, drunkards, and persons who had committed minor offenses.[100] These institutions and the Philadelphia Almshouse, or "Blockley," had to bear a surge of new admissions in the hard times following the Panic of 1873. Some newspapers did think that there ought to be general organization in the field of charities—in order to prevent swindling of the public.[101]

The public of the 1860s and 1870s recognized that there might be a connection between lack of education and idleness, and reformers argued that idleness in turn might well lead to criminality. Exposure to education kept the young from running the streets. One should attend school, acquire the fundamentals of reading, writing, and arithmetic, and then go on to further academic or technical training or use experience to fill remaining gaps in schooling.[102] But concern over education was not strong enough to prevent a closing of the city's night schools when funds were short during hard times, or to build enough classrooms—students had to be turned away from the city's schools for lack of space in September 1876. In 1876 the city also considered easing its financial problems with a 10 percent salary cut for teachers. This threat was averted in part by a mass protest meeting of teachers. The *Press* supported the teachers by declaring that reduced salaries would bring botched work and would be a blow to teaching as a profession. But a letter to the editor of the *Ledger* asked why teachers should be privileged, when everyone else had suffered salary reductions; besides, working only ten months, five days a week, six or seven hours a day was already a privilege![103]

The specific educational issues of greatest concern throughout the period were compulsory schooling and public aid to church, mainly Roman Catholic, schools. Compulsory schooling was an idea gaining in favor but not yet adopted by the Pennsylvania legislature. Too many voters still thought, like the *Sunday Tribune*, that it would take away the liberty of the individual and bring excessive governmental centralization and too heavy taxes.[104] As for aid to church schools, the prevailing view remained that of the *Bulletin*, that "The only safe method, the only Republican method, is to let children of all sects meet upon common ground in the schools." All sects, but not all races: the question of equal educational opportunity for blacks did not greatly disturb Philadelphians of the time, and the segregated black public schools remained generally inferior to schools for whites.[105]

For all that, concern for education ran deep enough to bring about a new code for teacher qualification, new laws regulating the Board of Education and the schools, and the completion of twenty-one new school buildings at a cost of $272,866.65. The Board of Education consisted of controllers, one for each section or district in the city, appointed by the Courts of Common Pleas. In each section or district there were annually elected school directors. By the beginning of 1875 there were 182 public school buildings with 108,631 pupils attending, including night-school students. There were 77 male and 1801 female teachers. The typical teacher of the period tended to be "white, female, native stock under twenty-five years of age who came from comfortable circumstances and continued to live with her parents while employed. She taught for twelve years at an annual salary of less than $450 and terminated her employment due to the lure of matrimony." Salaries in Philadelphia were low in comparison with other large cities.[106]

In higher education, Philadelphia's principal claim to distinction remained its cluster of medical schools. Apart from the medical schools, there was some truth to the opinion of several newspapers that the Philadelphia area had too many colleges with inadequate professors on poor salaries.[107]

The city's physicians and scientists as well as its medical schools still upheld its position as a medical center. Joseph Leidy of the Medical Department of the university was a paleontologist of note, president of the Academy of Natural Sciences, and a director of the Zoological Gardens, in whose establishment he was a leader. D. Hayes Agnew, professor of the principles and practice of surgery at the university and principal subject of Thomas Eakins's painting of the Agnew Clinic, was a prominent publishing scholar in surgery and anatomy and a world-famous practicing surgeon. He ranged from the Orthopaedic Hospital to the Wills Ophthalmic Hospital. William Pepper, following his father of the same name as professor of medicine at the university, and grandson of George Pepper, the brewer and merchant who founded the family fortune, used both his medical and his social connections to pave the way to acquire land and funds for the building and endowment of the University Hospital in 1871–1874. He became director of the Medical Services Bureau of the Centennial Exposition. The most famous Philadelphia physician of the day remains famous in our time, thanks to Eakins's painting of the Gross Clinic; Samuel D. Gross of the Jefferson Medical College was a great teacher as well as a great surgeon, and a champion of more rigorous medical education. S. Weir Mitchell was just beginning to make his mark. He was appointed to the Orthopaedic Hospital (on Ninth Street south of Market, later at Seventeenth and Summer) in 1870. He was already contributing numerous articles to a variety of medical journals and establishing himself as an expert in the treatment of nervous diseases.[108]

Dr. Leidy's Academy of Natural Sciences moved in 1876 from Broad and

Sansom Streets to its present building on Race Street at Logan Square. Space was provided there for a reading room, a lecture room, a laboratory, workshops, and "apartments" for the use of artists copying natural objects. The academy had accumulated by now a library of 30,000 volumes and a huge collection of botanical, mineralogical, and paleontological specimens, as well as specimens of shells, reptiles, fish, animals, and birds—of the latter, the largest collection in the world.[109]

The exhibits of the Academy of Natural Sciences took science to the public; so too, still more popularly, did the Zoological Society and its new Zoological Gardens. Subscriptions of stockholders made possible the landscaping and building of the zoo, which opened in 1874. It is difficult to imagine a more engaging location for the purpose than the thirty-three acres south of Fairmount Park on the west bank of the Schuylkill. The entrance pavilions at Thirty-fourth Street and Girard Avenue were designed by architects Frank Furness and George W. Hewitt. Furness also designed the elephant house. Hewitt designed the antelope house, which minus its porches is still standing.[110] Admission cost twenty-five cents, with half price for children. During the Centennial year admissions totaled $155,464, a figure not equaled for seventy years.[111]

Lovers of animals had their match in plant lovers, who had founded the Horticultural Society as long ago as 1827—it was the oldest society of its kind in the United States—and had given an annual flower show from the beginning. In May 1876 this society opened Horticultural Hall on Broad Street north of Spruce, a huge building with a fanciful Florentine facade and a magnificent interior stairway. It not only housed exhibitions of plants, flowers, fruits, vegetables, and horticultural tools, but also offered space for lectures, concerts, and balls. Rebuilt in 1895 after a fire, it was razed in 1917, but the Shubert Theater built on its site incorporated the lower part of its stairway.[112]

VIII

In the eyes of most upper-class Philadelphians, medicine and science were acceptable and commendable forms of activity. Probably for most Americans, but certainly for Philadelphians, the arts, pursued as potentially remunerative careers, were utterly different. One local journalist wrote: "The truth of the matter is that the accomplished portion of our native population manifest a very slight regard for American art, and consequently not much encouragement is extended in that direction."[113] Another declared:

Art in all its forms is after all with most people but a means of recreation after the serious business of life is attended to. . . . Good music is good, and good pictures are good, and good statuary is good, and good books are good, but we can do without them all and yet get along very comfortably and very happily. . . . An artist who is also a good business man will always do good work, the best he is capable of doing, but, like every other business man, he will manufacture the kind of goods his customers want to buy. . . .[114]

Still, at the time of the Centennial the city wanted to excel in everything —so that Philadelphia journalists also claimed more for local art than could be substantiated. The *Press* wrote: "Philadelphia, the cradle of art in America, assumes with each passing year a more important position as an art centre."[115] The city had a creditable art school and gallery, in addition to several small art associations and a number of fairly good private collections. It also boasted one or two artists whose reputations were destined to be international but who were not yet fully appreciated. But it was not an art center in the sense in which it was a medical center.

The Pennsylvania Academy of the Fine Arts had been relatively quiescent for a number of years. In 1876, however, it moved from its old home on Chestnut Street near Eleventh to the new building at Broad and Cherry designed for it by Frank Furness. When Furness attained in the twentieth century a much more distinguished as well as less merely local reputation than he enjoyed in his lifetime, his Pennsylvania Academy was to be hailed as "a building of great boldness and much personal character."[116] Immediately, however, its detractors began to say the sort of thing that those not liking Furness's work have said ever since, that the building looked like a railroad station or a market house. The *Evening Telegraph* thought its eclecticism so extreme that "many features are incongruous to the point of absurdity."[117]

The lower story of the Pennsylvania Academy was set up for educational

The Pennsylvania Academy of the Fine Arts, southwest corner of Broad and Cherry Streets, designed by Frank Furness (1839–1912) and George W. Hewitt (1841–1916), built 1872–1876 (photograph c. 1877 by Frederick Gutekunst, 1832–1917).

PENNSYLVANIA ACADEMY OF THE FINE ARTS, ARCHIVES DEPARTMENT

purposes, with rooms for life models and for other classes. The Academy offered instruction at no cost to the student, providing he showed a drawing indicating suitable talent. There were lectures on "artistic anatomy," on perspective, and on architectural styles. The display galleries were on the second floor and contained an appropriate collection of American works, as well as some examples of European art.[118]

There were a Philadelphia Sketch Club, at 524 Walnut Street, with a gallery; a School of Design for Women, at Merrick and Filbert, near Fifteenth, intended to instruct women in drawing, sculpture, and painting, with practical applications in mind; and a Fairmount Park Art Association, of 1300 members, for the purpose of providing the park with art objects.[119] A Social Art Club of twenty-five members, founded to promote "industrial, decorative, and antiquarian art," and looking toward the eventual establishment of a museum comparable to the Metropolitan in New York, met monthly at the homes of members to hear papers read.[120] There were several impressive private art collections, including that of Fairman Rogers at 202 West Rittenhouse Square.[121] Rogers, who occupied the chair of civil engineering at the University of Pennsylvania, became still better known in the art world through Thomas Eakins's painting of his four-in-hand; Rogers was a collector of coaches as well as of paintings and the author of a major book on coaching.

Rogers was also one of the first Philadelphians to perceive the merits of Thomas Eakins. For most of his life Eakins's home was at 1729 Mount Vernon Street. Born in 1844, he graduated from Central High School in 1861 and studied anatomy at Jefferson Medical College and art at the Pennsylvania Academy. From 1866 to 1870 he was abroad, studying in Paris with Jean Léon Gérôme and painting for a time in Spain. His first works after his return to Philadelphia were portraits of family and friends, such as *Margaret in Skating Costume* (1871), and genre scenes, such as *Max Schmitt in a Single Scull* (1871).[122] His interest in sports and in the body engaged in athletic contests was already evident.

In 1875 Eakins completed *The Gross Clinic*, intending it for the Memorial Art Galleries of the Centennial Exposition, probably assured in his own mind that the painting would establish his reputation. This work, "the most important by an American artist in the nineteenth century," depicts Dr. Gross explaining an operation—the removal of a diseased thighbone—while assistants do the work.[123] Genteel Philadelphians did not like the painting because it shows blood and suggests usually unmentioned parts of the anatomy: "Dr. Gross may have carved his way to eminence, but Philadelphia could not be troubled by exhibitions of his personal force carried on in a charity clinic."[124] While the painting was on display at Hesseltine's Galleries at 1125 Chestnut Street, the *Evening Telegraph* wrote that Eakins had exhibited very little and that his works had not attracted much attention, though his technical merits were great. "No American artist can compare with him as a draughtsman."[125] *The Gross Clinic* proved unacceptable for the Centennial art exhibits in Memorial Hall; instead it found a place with the medical section of the Centennial

Max Schmitt in a Single Scull, *painted by Thomas Eakins (1844–1916)*,
1871. Schmitt was a member of the Pennsylvania Barge Club. In 1866 and 1867 he
won the races for single scull held by the "Schuylkill Navy" or barge clubs. The
bridges crossing the Schuylkill just south of the sculls are the Pennsylvania Railroad
Bridge (now Amtrak) and the Girard Avenue Bridge.

METROPOLITAN MUSEUM OF ART, ALFRED N. PUNNETT FUND, GIFT OF GEORGE D. PRATT

Exposition, "among the exhibits of trusses, artificial limbs, and ear cleaners."[126] It brought Eakins only $300.[127] Eakins did place in the Centennial art
exhibition *The Chess Players* (1876), his portrait of Benjamin Howard Rand
(1874), and the watercolors *Baseball* (1875) and *Whistling for Plover* (1874).[128]

The disappointing rejection and the slight recognition accorded him,
however, did not cause Eakins to move off to some other city or to return to
Europe. He stayed on in his native place and in 1876 began teaching at the
Academy of the Fine Arts, where he thoroughly redesigned the curriculum.

As for Philadelphia music, Elizabeth Duane Gillespie remarked in her
Book of Remembrances that there were some so-called "musical entertainments," but of "real music there was none."[129] Such musical entertainments
as there were reflected a strong Germanic influence. The city had a Germania
Orchestra, a Männerchor, an Abt Male Chorus, a Beethoven Society, and a
Philadelphia Philharmonic Society with William Wolsieffer as leader. There
were also the Orpheus Club and the Theodore Thomas Symphony, whose
director was a kind of musical missionary trying to develop a taste for symphonic music both in the city and, by means of his tours, throughout America.[130] The 1874–1875 musical season featured the Kellogg English Opera at the
Academy of Music; English Opera Bouffe at the Chestnut Street Theatre,
where one leading lady was described as "somewhat substantial for light

opera"; and German Opera Bouffe at the Arch Street.[131] During the winter too the black Jubilee Singers gave several concerts mainly of slave songs at the Academy. After the first Jubilee concert, which was not especially well attended, a reporter wrote: "It is the duty—as it will in this way be certainly a pleasure—for us to give them the aid they most certainly deserve." Two weeks later the Academy was crowded for another Jubilee concert, and the audience, overflowing to the stage, was so enthusiastic that it called for many encores.[132]

Naturally the approach of the Centennial prompted discussion of music as one of the arts to be exhibited. Plans for opening day of the Exposition included the use of a large chorus and orchestra, and the Main Building was designed to house a series of concerts. Commissioning opening-day hymns from John Greenleaf Whittier ("Centennial Hymn") and Sidney Lanier ("Meditation of Columbia") nicely symbolized the reunited nation, but the award of $5000 to Richard Wagner for a "Grand Centennial March" predictably caused some carping from those who would have insisted on using native talent.[133] A Centennial Music Association was organized during 1875 under Prof. Jean Louis and by early January 1876 had over 600 singers, with Simon Gratz as president.[134] The Women's Centennial Committee meanwhile organized a Centennial Musical Festival, a series of concerts both choral and orchestral held at the Edwin Forrest mansion at Broad and Master Streets. Theodore Thomas initially conducted this series, but by July 31, 1876, he had withdrawn over complaints that his musical tastes were too heavy and serious.[135] Nevertheless a Women's Centennial Chorus survived after the close of the Exposition, reorganized as the Thomas Choral Society with Thomas as director.[136]

The theater in post–Civil War Philadelphia had the benefit of a resident company at the Arch Street, presided over by Mrs. John Drew, whom the *Evening Telegraph* characterized in 1876 as the most versatile of American actresses. Usually the offerings at the Arch Street were standard English comedies.[137] During January 1875 the Walnut Street Theatre presented both Augustin Daly's company in his *Divorce* and Edwin Booth in various Shakespearean plays. Several other theaters were operating, while minstrels and burlesque performed at the Eleventh Street Opera House. Colonel Wood's Museum, at Ninth and Arch, had *As You Like It* in February 1875, while *Measure for Measure* probably had its American première at the Walnut in the same month. It was reviewed as not fit for presentation, but played to the fullest house of the season, with every foot of standing room taken.[138]

The Chestnut Street Theatre, used for both musical events and drama, had *Jane Eyre* with Charlotte Thompson in early March 1875; hailed as one of the three best of young American actresses, the leading lady also presented *Camille, East Lynne,* and *Ingomar*. At the same time *Uncle Tom's Cabin* was featured at the Eleventh Street Opera House. *The Gilded Age* played in April at the Walnut, while at the American Theater, Buffalo Bill Cody appeared in *Scouts of the Plains; or, Red Men as They Are,* with Kit Carson, Jr., in the cast. By May, Dion Boucicault was appearing in his most recent Irish drama, *The Shaughraun,* and also in *The Octoroon.*[139]

By opening day of the Centennial Exposition in May the city boasted another major theater, the Alhambra Palace of the Kiralfy Brothers on the east side of Broad above Spruce. It seated over 1500 persons and did an "immense business," for according to the *Press,* its gardens and concerts alone were worth the price of admission, but in addition it presented a gorgeous spectacle and fine ballet, based on Jules Verne's *The Tour of the World in Eighty Days.*[140]

Philadelphia's own Edwin Forrest had become partially paralyzed in 1865 and thereafter could no longer march onto the stage with lordly air. He took to spending much of his time in his mansion, brooding in solitude over the way the world treated him. His last public appearance was in some readings in New York. On December 12, 1872, he died alone at his Broad Street house. In his will he left most of his estate to found a home for aged players; the Forrest country place near Holmesburg, Spring Brook, opened in the autumn of 1876 as the Forrest Home for Actors.[141]

Actors especially suffered the Philadelphia skepticism about cultural activities as a proper occupation; but publishers, journalists, and even writers seemed to fit naturally into a city claiming Benjamin Franklin as one of its great men. To be sure, the publishing families of the 1860s and 1870s—the Leas, Careys, Petersons, and Lippincotts—were generally involved as well in activities other than publishing. There was, for example, Henry Charles Carey. Long since retired from business to devote his time to research, writing, and lecturing, Carey had become the leader of a group that can be thought of as an American school of political economy. He published *Unity of Law* in 1872. In that same year he was a delegate to the Pennsylvania constitutional convention. Charles Godfrey Leland described him as a "handsome, black-eyed, white-haired man, with a very piercing glance." Alert and sensitive in face, kindly in manner, he held every Sunday afternoon at home an informal reception called "Sunday Vespers," a Philadelphia institution. Distinguished visitors and the eminent men of the city mingled there discussing topics of the day. Carey's fine collection of paintings, along with the best Rhine wines, encouraged guests to linger.[142]

By the 1870s Charles Jacobs Peterson's *Peterson's Magazine* enjoyed a circulation of 150,000. Theophilus Beasley Peterson and the other brothers of Charles Jacobs Peterson ran a publishing house which began to market popular books at cheap prices. Cousin Henry Peterson did some publishing and editing and became owner of the *Saturday Evening Post.* He also wrote poems and novels. His *Pemberton* appeared in 1873, a story of the American Revolution, dramatized at the Chestnut Street Theatre in 1876 as *Helen: or One Hundred Years Ago.* George W. Childs, publisher of the *Ledger,* was married to a daughter of one of the Peterson brothers, Robert E.[143]

From 1865 to 1880 Henry Charles Lea was sole head of the family publishing firm founded by his grandfather Mathew Carey. As a publisher he began to specialize in medical books and periodicals, an emphasis continued in the twentieth century when the firm became Lea and Febiger. As a citizen Lea was active in nearly every political reform movement of the day.

Joshua Ballinger Lippincott had established his own firm at mid-century, at first emphasizing Bibles and religious works. Until the early twentieth century he and his family also printed and published *Lippincott's Magazine*, a literary periodical.[144]

Rarely has the city boasted such a galaxy of journalists as in this period: George W. Childs at the *Ledger*, Alexander K. McClure at the *Times*, John W. Forney at the *Press*, Morton McMichael at the *North American*, Gibson Peacock at the *Bulletin*. Over a dozen newspapers offered their tales of public and private doings. The *Ledger* had the largest circulation of the city papers, with the *Times* offering strong competition.[145] The papers displayed considerable conscious pride in the Centennial City, but also offered considerable criticism of its faults and omissions.

The kidnapping of Charles Brewster Ross, aged four years and seven months, on July 1, 1874, gave the papers ample material for sensational reporting; but if they had a field day with the case, it was by later standards a dignified one. Little Charley Ross was held for ransom. Several persons were obviously involved, and one, William H. Westervelt, was given a lengthy trial but, to the disappointment of the press, convicted of but one charge, that of conspiracy. Little Charley was never recovered, and even today one feels the sensation of horror that always accompanies the kidnapping of a child.[146]

Most Philadelphia literary figures were also concerned with other, more practical, and perhaps more routine occupations than writing. The dramatist George H. Boker served his country as minister to Turkey and Russia, being absent from the city from 1871 to 1878.[147] While carrying on his publishing and political activities Henry Charles Lea was already engaged in the research for *A History of the Inquisition of the Middle Ages* (1888). He had three books behind him, *Superstition and Force* (1866), *An Historical Sketch of Sacerdotal Celibacy* (1867), and *Studies in Church History* (1869). Numerous pamphlets urging reform came from his pen, such as *Facts for the People*, describing what was wrong with Philadelphia's municipal services, why the city debt should not be increased, and why a new loan should not be floated.[148]

Horace Howard Furness, son of the Unitarian minister William Henry Furness and brother of the architect Frank, never achieved fame in the law, in which he was trained, but in his own lifetime gained renown as a scholar. His variorum editions of *Romeo and Juliet*, *Macbeth*, and *Hamlet*, the first of a massive series still being produced, were highly acclaimed, especially of course by the Shakspere Society of Philadelphia. His wife, the former Helen Kate Rogers, herself wrote *The Concordance to Shakespeare's Poems*.[149]

When Philadelphians wished to join with others of like mind for the encouragement of literature, art, or reform, or if they wished purely social activity, they usually formed a club. The Penn Club was an outgrowth of the *Penn Monthly*, a literary magazine designed especially for Philadelphia tastes and writers. It gave—and still does—an annual award to a person of international or local distinction. The Shakspere Society had been founded in 1851 under the inspiration of Fanny Kemble's readings and was especially active in the 1860s and 1870s.[150]

The Saturday Club or Saturday Parties originated in 1867, founded, according to Alexander K. McClure, because the influx of newly rich, uncultured persons prompted a nucleus of intelligent business and professional men to band together to revive cultivated entertainment and conversation on the Saturday evenings traditional for such activity. Everyone attended the meetings in regulation evening dress, but there was no "conventional suppression," and "generous intercourse" prevailed among the guests. There was no clubhouse, but from November to April the group met weekly at the house of one of the members. The *Press* declared that the Saturday Club provided a useful means of welcoming distinguished visitors during the Centennial.[151]

I X

With the expansion of the row-house blocks of the industrial city, the great outdoors, or whatever remnants were still accessible, beckoned more invitingly than ever. In addition to the expanding Fairmount Park, there was the Philadelphia Rifle Association's Schuetzen Park, on Indian Queen Lane north of Ridge Avenue, a popular scene of outings, not only for the German-American club that owned it. The park had shooting galleries and targets, and also facilities for concerts and dancing.[152] There were several racetracks around the city, including Belmont Driving Park and Point Breeze Park.[153]

Skating and sleighing naturally had their devotees. Sleighing parties went out through Fairmount Park or to the Wissahickon for waffles. Skating was possible on the lake at the zoo and at a rink at Broad and Montgomery; both featured music. Occasionally the ice on the Schuylkill was satisfactory for skating. Roller skating too was beginning to be thought of as a good sport.[154] Croquet, "more than a game . . . was a social function."[155] A croquet club sponsored matches, and the casual player often took his exercise in Fairmount Park, sending a boy ahead to set up the arches.[156]

With two rivers at their doors and boat clubs abounding, Philadelphians were fond of water sports. In the Centennial year, from the end of August until mid-September an aquatic carnival in the Schuylkill claimed attention.

OVERLEAF: The Centennial—Balloon View of the Grounds, *engraved for* Harper's Weekly *from sketches by Theodore R. Davis (1840–1894), September 30, 1876. Some of the avenues and drives created for the exposition have been preserved in Fairmount Park, but the only survivor among the large exhibition buildings is Memorial Hall, the domed art gallery above center in Davis's compiled view. The vast Machinery Building (at the lower right, west of the main entrance) covered fourteen acres along Elm (Parkside) Avenue in what is still known as the Concourse area of the park.*
ATHENAEUM OF PHILADELPHIA

Swimming had its followers, both in the rivers and at the Natatorium, on Broad Street between Walnut and Locust, which reported that it trained 600 to 700 swimmers every season.[157]

Various baseball clubs flourished, amateur and professional. The Civil War had spread awareness of the sport and interest in it; the soldiers played it in camps and even in prisons. The first candidly professional team, the Cincinnati Red Stockings, toured the country so successfully in 1869—they drew 15,000 spectators for a game in Philadelphia—that the first professional league was organized for the 1871 season, the National Association of Professional Baseball Players. At the organizational meeting in New York, James N. Kerns, a representative of the Philadelphia entry, an already well-established club founded in 1860 and called the Athletics, was elected league president. Furthermore the Philadelphia Athletics went on to compile a season's record of twenty-two wins and seven losses that captured the first league championship. Unhappily for the city, this triumph failed to prove an omen of consistent success for subsequent Philadelphia professional teams. The Athletics' seventh-place finish in an eight-team league during the National League's first season—the Centennial year—was a more accurate harbinger of things to come in the next century.[158]

X

Alexander McClure, nose in the air, called the period after the war "The Reign of Shoddy." Wealth had come suddenly to many who possessed little culture but plunged into "extravagant display." According to McClure, Mr. Caldwell, then a jeweler near the Girard House, said that the demand for diamonds was so great that it was hard to fill the orders from purchasers often unknown to him.[159] Women loaded themselves with diamonds, but their "general demeanor indicated entire ignorance of the proper use of such decorations."[160] McClure thought that many women of the older families gave up the wearing of jewels because of the tastelessness of the display by the newly wealthy.[161]

In 1866 Sidney George Fisher attended a party because he wanted to see "the young people & the fashions that have grown up since I was in the gay world." Though the party took place in handsome rooms, he found the company lacked "distinguished beauties" or those who had "style, elegance, accomplishment, & manner. . . ." He concluded: "I thought the tone of the party, its general effect, was deficient in refinement, in dignity, in short it was rather vulgar. And why not? *Business people* are now in society, here as in New York."[162]

There remained, of course, the inner circle of Philadelphia's upper class. To that august group there were some additions in the 1860s and 1870s, or at least there were some who managed to get one foot into the charmed circle. This select core was cohesive and self-sufficient and felt secure, perhaps because it knew where it had been if not precisely where it was going. An invitation to the dancing Assemblies remained an indicator of having arrived.

In the year 1874–1875 there were four Assemblies at the Academy of Music; usually there were two.[163] But others besides the select few danced, if not always at the Academy. Eight balls and at least five dancing schools advertised in one newspaper for one day alone in 1875.[164]

One of the most impressive social functions of the time, including many who had arrived in and who aspired to enter the upper class, was the reception given by George W. Childs to the emperor and empress of Brazil on their visit to the city for the opening of the Centennial. Over 600 guests came to the Childs mansion.[165] Another glittering reception was given on December 4, 1871, for the visiting Grand Duke Alexis of Russia, son of Czar Alexander II. McClure called it the "greatest social event in the history of Philadelphia," though the *Inquirer* was satisfied with the term "most successful." McClure's description of the event emphasized that the grand duke had been sent on a cruise around the world to help him forget a love affair with the wrong woman. Governor Curtin, now minister to Russia, helped arrange the visit to Philadelphia. Here Alexis was kept busy with a breakfast at Belmont Mansion and visits to Girard College, the Baldwin Locomotive Works, Independence Hall, and the Navy Yard. The climax to the day was a grand ball at the Academy of Music, for which patron subscribers paid as much as $100, but admission to which was only $15. General Meade was chairman of the sponsoring committee. Society ladies mingled with overdressed bejeweled women crowding the Academy. The grand duke danced with Miss Margaret Meade and Miss Fanny Drexel, but McClure remembered from the many belles of the evening Mrs. Col. Thomas A. Scott and Miss Emily von Schaumberg for the "sweet simplicity of perfect elegance."[166]

XI

On New Year's Eve, December 31, 1875, a visitor to Philadelphia described what went on in the streets at midnight as the "most extraordinary noise ever heard." John Lewis, an Englishman working in New York and visiting a son in Philadelphia, stated in a letter to his brother in England that "every bell, whistle, or other instrument that would make a noise" was sounded to welcome the Centennial year. Despite misty weather and dirty, muddy streets, the Independence Hall area was a solid mass of celebrators. Lights made the hall glow. Shortly before midnight Mayor Stokley appeared and sent to the top of the flagpole a replica of the flag unfurled by George Washington on January 1, 1776, over the camps of the Continental Army at Cambridge. The crowd responded with shouts and firecrackers. There were illuminations on many of the streets, where masked marching groups in fancy costumes, with noisemakers and musical instruments—the Mummers or New Year's shooters —celebrated even more jubilantly than usual. The reflection of the illuminations could be plainly seen in the countryside eighteen miles away. Thus was ushered in the Centennial year.[167]

Though the idea of fairs was old, the modern concept of an exposition, with exhibitors from many countries displaying new inventions and industrial

developments, was relatively new. The credit for linking the celebration of
100 years of American nationhood with such an exposition is usually given
to Prof. John L. Campbell of Wabash College, Indiana. As early as December
1866 he wrote to Mayor McMichael suggesting that a centennial exposition
be held in Philadelphia.

The idea of an American world's fair was a bold one. The recent successful
international expositions, beginning with the London Crystal Palace Exposition in 1851, had required the financial backing of their governments on an
increasingly lavish scale. Such governmental support was unlikely to be forthcoming in the United States. The previous American world's fair, the Exhibition of the Industry of All Nations in New York in 1853–1854, had been a
commercial venture and a failure. Could American industry, invention, and
art now provide an appropriate centerpiece for an American fair? Would
other nations bother to exhibit? If they did, would they put American products to shame at the most embarrassing moment possible?

Doubters repeated all these misgivings, but Professor Campbell's idea
nevertheless gathered momentum. Besides the doubts, the notion of a Philadelphia fair also had to face competition from Boston, New York, and Washington once the idea caught on. It says much about the vitality of industrial
Philadelphia just after the Civil War that these claims of rival cities were
overborne with relative ease. The big question, whether Philadelphia could
mount the first successful world's fair in the United States, then remained to
be answered.[168]

The Franklin Institute was an early supporter of the Centennial Exposition movement and asked the city Councils for the use of Fairmount Park.
In January 1870 the Select Council resolved to hold an exposition in Philadelphia in 1876, and both Councils created committees to study the project and
to seek the support of Congress. The Pennsylvania legislature also sponsored
the plan and sent a committee of ten to accompany the Philadelphia delegation to Washington. Cong. William D. Kelley spoke for the city and the state
to Congress. Cong. Daniel J. Morrell of Johnstown, chairman of the House
Committee on Manufactures, introduced a bill to create a United States
Centennial Commission to conduct an exposition in Philadelphia, but providing expressly that the United States government should not be liable for any
expenses. The bill passed on March 3, 1871.[169]

The United States Centennial Commission was organized on March 5,
1872, with Cong. Joseph R. Hawley of Connecticut, a newspaper editor and
former governor of his state, as president. With finances still a major problem,
Congress on June 1, 1872, set up a Centennial Board of Finance, authorized
to sell not more than $10 million worth of stock in ten-dollar shares. Most of
the members of this board were chosen from among the mercantile and
industrial leaders of Philadelphia, so there could readily be a quorum for
meetings in the city. John Welsh became president of the board; in addition
to his fifteen years as president of the Board of Trade and sixteen years as a
Fairmount Park commissioner, he had been chairman of the executive com-

mittee for the Great Central Sanitary Fair of 1864, no world's fair but the closest approximation Philadelphia had experienced, and a success that had raised a million dollars.

Welsh had considerable talents as a fundraiser and was attuned to voluntarism rather than government support as a means of getting things done. He needed all his talents and energy; even with them, money came in slowly. The stockholders of the Centennial Board of Finance eventually mustered sizable amounts, $1,784,320 by Washington's birthday, 1873. The City of Philadelphia contributed at least $1.5 million, the Commonwealth of Pennsylvania $1 million. Not until February 11, 1876, did Congress appropriate $1.5 million. The Centennial Board assumed that this amount was an outright subsidy, but after the fair was over the federal government sued for its return as a loan. The United States Supreme Court eventually reversed a lower court's finding for the city and forced repayment from the Centennial Board stockholders, so that in the end the federal government paid for nothing except a few of its own displays.

In 1873 the Centennial Commission chose Alfred T. Goshorn, an Ohio lawyer and manufacturer of white lead, as director-general of the Centennial Exposition. He was given broad executive powers and proved another able, energetic selection. Meanwhile the Fairmount Park Commission set aside 450 acres of West Fairmount Park for the Exposition. On July 4, 1873, Secretary of the Navy George W. Robeson officially dedicated the grounds, of which 236 acres were actually fenced off for the fair.[170]

The women of Philadelphia had contributed much time and effort to the Central Sanitary Fair of 1864, and John Welsh was eager to enlist them again. On February 16, 1873, the local arm of the Centennial Board of Finance, the Citizens' Centennial Finance Committee, met with thirteen Philadelphia women for help in organizing a grass-roots campaign of support for the Centennial within the city. Among the women present was (Mrs.) Elizabeth Duane Gillespie, a descendant of Benjamin Franklin, who undertook to create a women's committee representing all the city's wards, to knock on doors and solicit funds. Eventually women from across the country were added to create the Women's Centennial Executive Committee, with Mrs. Gillespie as president. In the first few months of its existence the Women's Committee raised over $40,000 and obtained 82,000 signatures in two days for memorials to the city Councils and the Pennsylvania Assembly to make appropriations for suitable buildings in which foreign countries might exhibit, to help assure the international aspect of the Exposition. When it became apparent that the men planning the Exposition would not do much to display women's work, the women went on to collect another $30,000 for their own exhibit building, the first women's building at any world's fair.[171]

The men may have come perilously close to botching the international aspect. It was not until June 5, 1874, that Congress was prevailed upon to pass a resolution inviting foreign governments to participate. Then, luckily, John W. Forney of the *Press* consented to head a Philadelphia commission to visit

Great Britain and Europe to drum up interest, and to pay for the trip out of his own pocket. Once more voluntarism at least partially offset governmental indifference by producing an able individual to take charge. Forney was gracious, sophisticated, and thoroughly knowledgeable about both the United States and much of Europe. He sailed amid skeptical expectations that the Europeans would boycott the Exposition, and against the obstacle that American tariffs might make European industrial exhibits seem a dubious investment—too few European goods could climb the tariff walls—but not a single European country declined Forney's invitation.[172]

The Centennial Commission sponsored a competition for building designs. Winners of a first round of judging had to be ready with full details including cost and construction time by a runoff deadline of September 20, 1873. The awards for the four best designs for the principal buildings then went to Philadelphia architectural firms, but none of them proved to have made enough allowance for the pressures of hasty construction on the one hand and financial stringency on the other. As the whole enterprise seemed about to founder on incompleted buildings, design as well as construction had to be taken from architects' hands and given to engineers. Henry Pettit and Joseph M. Wilson became the principal designers and constructors of the Main Building, a temporary structure begun in 1874. The largest building in the world, it covered about twenty-one and a half acres and extended one-third of a mile along the Elm Avenue concourse. It consisted of an iron framework resting on 672 stone piers, with generous use of glass between the frames to give a light and airy effect despite grandiose size. Its central avenue was 120 feet wide and 1832 feet long, the "longest avenue of that width ever introduced into an Exhibition Building." Directly to the west was Machinery Hall, a structure of similar design reaching 1402 feet along Elm Avenue and covering about fourteen acres.[173]

Intended to be permanent were Memorial Hall and Horticultural Hall. The guiding genius of both was German-born Hermann J. Schwarzmann, engineer for the Fairmount Park Commission, who had never before designed a building and had no professional training in doing so. His Memorial Hall indeed still stands, its great iron-and-glass dome commanding attention throughout much of Fairmount Park and from the river drives on both banks of the Schuylkill. For years it contained the Pennsylvania Museum of the School of Industrial Art, the forerunner of the later collections of the Philadelphia Museum of Art. Now it serves mainly as a police station.[174]

ON THE FACING PAGE: *Exterior and Interior of Agricultural Hall, north of Belmont Avenue and the Reservoir, Centennial Exhibition, 1876. Agricultural Hall, designed by Philadelphia architect James H. Windrim (1840–1919), was a huge structure of Gothic design. The elaborate iron and wood framework enclosed exhibitions of agricultural products in spacious, well-lighted naves.*

FREE LIBRARY OF PHILADELPHIA

Schwarzmann's other principal structure, Horticultural Hall, was yet more astonishing if not more impressive. It was a building mainly of glass, his tribute to the Crystal Palace of London's first modern world's fair and to the similar Crystal Palace of New York in 1853: a "Saracenic" tracery of glass and of iron "gaily polychrome in reds, greens, and yellows." It continued to exhibit exotic plants until it was battered so badly by Hurricane Hazel in 1954 that it had to be razed.[175]

There were eventually more than 200 buildings within the Exposition grounds, surrounded by a fence about three miles long.[176] President Grant and members of Congress came to Philadelphia in December 1875 to observe the progress of construction. By then the Main Building and Machinery Hall were nearly finished, and despite much mud the visitors appeared to be impressed. Congress may have been stimulated to vote its appropriation, however grudgingly, and out-of-town journalists began to pay more attention to the coming event.[177]

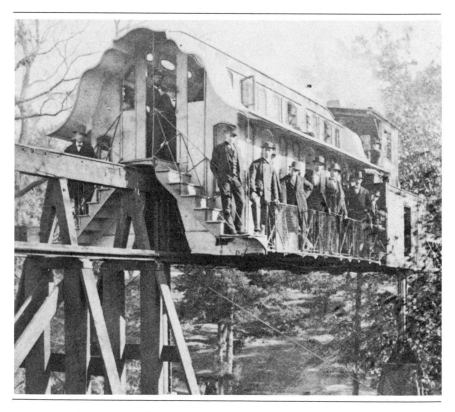

An elevated railroad and (on the facing page) the hand and torch of the Statue of Liberty were among the technological and artistic novelties to be seen at the Centennial Exhibition (photographs 1876).

The original plan had been to open in April 1876, to commemorate the anniversary of Lexington and Concord, but construction delays caused the date to be pushed back to May 10. On the first of May there was so much confusion on the grounds that it seemed impossible that the buildings could be ready in time. But ready they were. The chief of the Bureau of Installation put the matter in flowery language: "The great century plant which had been for so long a time tediously but steadily unfolding its intricate net-work of months, weeks, and days, had at last matured with a full bloom well worthy of the occasion."[178]

The bell at Independence Hall sounded to signal the opening, followed by all the bells of Philadelphia, while small boys, bringing out Christmas Eve tin horns, astonished visitors. Appropriate decorations were everywhere.[179] The day was fair and warm after an early rain, and from descriptions it seems as if everyone in the city must have been excitedly astir.

The *New York Herald* reported the opening day crowd as the "largest ever assembled on the North American continent." Official count set the number as 186,272, though about 110,000 entered on free passes rather than paying the fifty-cent admission charge. For modern exhibitions to equal this figure it would be necessary to have 800,000 people present.[180] The crowd that day concentrated between and around the Main Building and Memorial Hall, in front of each of which a platform had been erected. Many notables were on the platforms early. Eventually there arrived Emperor Dom Pedro of Brazil with Empress Theresa; somewhat later came President and Mrs. Grant. A rather tedious opening ceremony followed; it was difficult to hear, though certainly the chorus of 1000 voices must have been audible.

Finally President Grant and Emperor Dom Pedro grasped the valves that started the immense Corliss Engine in Machinery Hall, perhaps the greatest wonder of the Exposition. By means of cogs and underground shafts, this creation of a self-taught engineer, George H. Corliss, supplied the power to drive some 800 other machines at the fair. Its two cylinders, each forty-four inches in diameter with a ten-foot stroke, propelled a flywheel thirty feet in diameter and weighing fifty-six tons through thirty-six revolutions a minute, governing 1400 horsepower of energy. With the Corliss Engine beginning to hiss with steam and to turn its wheel, the fair was open. People cheered and threw their hats into the air, while guns roared from George's Hill, church bells pealed, and whistles were sounded.[181] The most amusing, perhaps the most apt, observation was that of Fukui Makota, the Japanese commissioner to the Exposition: "The first day crowds come like sheep, run here, run there, run everywhere. One man start, one thousand follow. Nobody can see anything, nobody can do anything. All rush, push, tear, shout, make plenty noise, say damn great many times, get very tired, and go home."[182]

But within two days the crowds fell off so drastically that few except the sponsors and the vendors had to say damn. On May 12, only 12,720 visited the fair. Opening day notwithstanding, the average daily attendance for May was only 36,000. In June it rose only to 39,000. A heat wave began in mid-June and sizzled unbroken through July, further discouraging visitors and threatening to deal the hopes of the promoters a fatal blow. "We swelter under a glassy sky from which the sun . . . beats down fierce and sullen. We walk streets . . . which are baked and which reflect back the heat as if it were thrown up to us from a fiery furnace."[183] For the four-week period ending July 22 the average weekly temperature was 81 ¾°F; for ten days the temperature reached about 100°F.[184]

Then the hot spell eased. The heat returned at the end of August, but attendance picked up from a 35,000 daily average in July to 42,000 in August. September turned cool, and the number of daily visitors to the fair soared to 94,000. September 28 was Pennsylvania Day, in commemoration of the 100th anniversary of the Pennsylvania Constitution of 1776; about a quarter of a million people were at the fair that day, hearing speeches, attending a reception, and watching fireworks. Pennsylvania Day was to prove the peak attendance day, but in October the daily average rose again to 102,000, and in November despite the chill and rains of autumn it reached 115,000. Philadelphia Day, November 9, brought out 176,000, but much of the astonishing rise in attendance represented visitors from more and more distant reaches of the Union. Planned amid skepticism and greeted at first with persisting popular doubts, the great American world's fair at last caught on as word of its wonders spread across the country through increasingly enthusiastic news reports and by simple word of mouth. In 1876 only the rich were accustomed to taking long vacation trips; but by autumn of the year the railroads' Centennial excursion fares, the justification that the Exposition was educational and not merely fun, and above all the lure of unprecedented excitement made the Philadelphia Centennial the country's first mass tourist mecca. The total of those admitted by the close of the Exposition on November 10 was 10,164,489, of whom 8,047,601 paid admission fees.[185]

Attendance at the fair having at last exceeded almost all expectations, could the city cope with the miracle of West Fairmount Park? Was it prepared to feed, house, transport, amuse, and protect the thousands of visitors?

Although the city Councils were at first reluctant, they had finally approved the erection of temporary hotels of wood near the Exposition grounds. These "huge caravanseries," like the Globe and the Transcontinental, were planned on a grand scale to house several thousand guests. The Centennial Lodging-House Agency compiled lists of available rooms, in hotels, boardinghouses, and private homes. Tickets for these rooms were then sold in cities promoting the Exposition or by special agents on the trains coming to Philadelphia. The tickets so distributed were eventually redeemed at the Lodging-House Agency by the hotel or boardinghouse keepers, or by private residents renting rooms. At times visitors complained about the expense of rooms, but the general verdict seems to have been that prices, perhaps not much more than $1.50 a night, were reasonable.[186]

Evidently the new hotels did very well in feeding their guests; there were few complaints about the general quality, quantity, and availability of food. Inside the Exposition grounds it was a different story. Prices were high enough that at least one reporter recommended that visitors go outside to eat and pay a new admission to come back to the grounds. Of course, one could take one's own lunch and get coffee or tea at the Public Comfort Building; there was plenty of ice water, while soda water and German lager beer stands enjoyed a brisk business, with beer at five cents a glass.[187] At any rate there is no indication that anyone went away hungry from Philadelphia, except perhaps President Grant, who it was reported could get no lunch on the grounds on opening day.[188]

A celebration at Fairmount Park on July 4, 1875, had demonstrated the deficiency of city transportation lines in providing access to the Exposition grounds. At that time over 130,000 persons had managed to get there by public transportation, but many more reportedly had to walk. All concerned bestirred themselves to improve matters, however, and by the time the Centennial opened it could claim among its distinctions to be the first world's fair providing satisfactory transportation for masses of visitors. All the European fairs had been deficient in this respect. The local streetcar lines increased their service, but the railroads outdid themselves. One of the showpieces of the Exposition was the Pennsylvania Railroad Depot across Elm Avenue from the main entrance; there were a circular turnabout and three platforms. The railroad ran special trains from Market Street and excursion trains from New York, Baltimore, and Pittsburgh. The Philadelphia and Reading Railroad also ran special trains to the Exposition from the heart of the city. All railroads lowered their rates to Philadelphia, though perhaps not as much as the Centennial promoters had hoped.[189]

To reach the Exposition grounds the visitor could also take a small steamboat from the east bank of the Schuylkill in Fairmount Park; the ride cost ten cents. And of course one could hire a carriage and ride to the Exposition in style; the cost was about three dollars. A narrow-gauge railway, the West-End, made the circuit of the Exposition grounds in thirty-five minutes, including stops. Nearly four million passengers rode in the open cars built for the West-End Passenger Railway Company, paying five cents for each ride. Rolling chairs were also available on the grounds, at sixty cents an hour.[190]

Crime at the Exposition was a less serious problem than many feared it would be. The total number of arrests made by the Centennial Guard was 675. A Scotland Yard inspector in charge of security at the British exhibits marveled that he saw scarcely a case of drunkenness; but in fact most of the arrests were either for that misdemeanor or for jumping the fence. The city's own Centennial Division force also reported that drunkenness and other minor offenses accounted for most of the arrests made during the Exposition. Stolen property to the value of $9412.60 was recovered and returned to the owners. In the admission money taken in at the Centennial, only $1001 was counterfeit.[191]

Philadelphia's health officers on the other hand felt conscious of straining their resources to the limit. Fortunately no epidemic erupted, but the heat wave added to the burden of visitors from all over the world. During the four hottest weeks ending July 22 there were, not surprisingly, 206 more deaths recorded than in the same period of 1875. The water supply on the Exposition grounds and various items of food eaten there naturally were cited as suspect whenever seemingly unusual illness appeared. Dr. William Pepper, director of the Medical Bureau of the Centennial, nevertheless stated that there were "no special conditions in the city, either at the Exhibition Grounds or elsewhere, whether in the form of imperfect drainage, impure drinking-water, or any other special local feature, which were calculated to induce sickness." He concluded that Philadelphia was the healthiest city in the world, save for London. With so many visitors yet few apparent health problems, he may not have been far wrong.[192]

Pepper's bureau established an efficient small hospital on the Centennial grounds, in Lansdowne Ravine on Lansdowne Avenue. Brisk efficiency was what made the Centennial the remarkable success that it came to be—efficiency in health care, in completing the buildings on schedule, in transportation to and from the fair, in the arrangements for overnight accommodations, and above all of course, in the constantly hissing machinery that kept the fair moving, provided its greatest source of wonder, and stilled the final doubts about America's and Philadelphia's capacity to host a great world's fair.

The Corliss Engine symbolized the Centennial Exposition on opening day and has loomed larger as the symbol of the fair with the passage of time. The first spectacularly successful American world's fair was a fair dominated by machinery. There was art too—two and a half miles of art exhibits on the walls according to John Sartain, chief of the Bureau of Art[193]—and there was the music of opening day and throughout, and there were foods and entertainment, but it was mainly the machinery that drew the crowds. This emphasis on mechanisms and invention was no doubt crucial to the success of an *American* world's fair furthermore because it meant that the focus of the fair was on the very areas of endeavor in which the United States was at least the equal of Europe and any other part of the globe.

Vying with the Corliss Engine for notoriety among the exhibits was a mechanism much smaller, yet also even more ingenious—Alexander Graham Bell's new telephone. "My God, it talks!" Emperor Dom Pedro is supposed to have said. Thomas Alva Edison exhibited the Quadruplex Telegraph, which transmitted several messages simultaneously. George Westinghouse exhibited the air brake, George Pullman the Pullman Palace Car. Three electric arc lights pushed back the darkness of night with a brilliant white glow. American machine tools, the vital machines needed to make other machines, impressed British observers as surpassing Britain's own—a possible portent of changing leadership in the industrial revolution. American machinery in general impressed the German commissioner, Prof. Franz Reuleaux, as surpassing the machinery of the burgeoning German industrial revolution in the key quality of efficiency; so much so that Reuleaux's subsequent book, *Letters from Philadelphia, (Briefe aus Philadelphia* Braunschweig (Brunswick): F. Vierling und Sohn, 1877) was a plea for Germans to emulate Americans in making efficiency and quality and not mass production alone the hallmarks of industry. Years later, in July 1941, while his armies were invading Russia, Adolf Hitler was to lecture his entourage on the Philadelphia fair as an event that had turned German production from the bad and the cheap to the qualitatively superior.[194]

For the first time the Philadelphia world's fair brought large numbers of foreign visitors to the United States for a single purpose, and they returned to their homes to make American efficiency and American machinery bywords for excellence. But the influence naturally did not run merely outward from the United States. Fifty nations exhibited at the Centennial, and their displays as well as the stream of foreign visitors in turn influenced America. Especially in industrial design, Americans took new ideas away from the fair, all the more because, in the manner of London's Victoria and Albert Museum but new to this country, industrial and artistic exhibits tended to stand side by side. A present-day art historian writes that "of the events of the second half of the nineteenth century none had more profound effects on American art and taste than the preparations made in Philadelphia to celebrate the completion of one hundred years of American independence."[195]

Yet it was not European but Oriental and particularly Japanese art that made the most lasting impression. An anonymous account in the *Atlantic Monthly* found the Japanese exhibit making everything else look "commonplace, almost vulgar. . . . The Japanese seem to possess the secret which the modern pre-Raphaelites have striven for without success, the union of detail and effect. . . . The commonest object of pottery or cotton-stuff for daily use has a merit of design or color which it does not owe to oddity alone. . . ."[196]

The Japanese had at first seemed figures of fun, when they puzzled Philadelphians by sending the materials for two prefabricated buildings—a species of efficiency the Americans themselves had scarcely begun to explore—and Japanese workmen to assemble them. It was at least equally puzzling that the workmen had no idea of how to use American building equipment—because they had never before seen a wheelbarrow, they carried it instead of pushing it—yet managed to put their buildings together. Of the finished Japanese structures, opinion soon changed from scoffing at them as oversized corncribs to accepting the praise of Richard Morris Hunt, as one of America's leading architects, of the "graceful lines of roofs and porches, the perfect tile work, and the rich ornamental carving, altogether offering a capital and most improving study to the careless and slipshod joiners of the Western world."[197] Opinion of the displays inside, especially the silks and porcelains, even more quickly reached a favorable verdict. The Centennial was perhaps the most important single source of the lasting American fascination with Oriental art.

For six months Philadelphia was host to a cosmopolitan stream of visitors from all over the American continent and from abroad. Among the inhabitants of the city, these visitors stimulated native curiosity and kindliness, and from all of them something could be learned. Philadelphians could again observe southerners as other than enemies, and become acquainted with fellow citizens of the United States from as far away as 3000 miles.

Over and above the economic benefits Philadelphia had acquired a sense of accomplishment, a conviction that its citizens could achieve results, that the city was no longer just a stop on the way to New York. "Strong local sympathy" from citizens, from Mayor Stokley, and from other municipal officials, wrote the director-general, was among the reasons for the success of the Exposition. For some glorious months Philadelphia might look upon itself as the "principal city in the United States."[198] Before the event the *Press* had hoped that "The Centennial is to ring the death knell of that non-enterprising, fearing-to-dare spirit which has so long ruled us."[199] The Centennial was altogether a lesson of self-respect for the city; it showed its present greatness and its potentialities.[200] It must have caused many Philadelphians pride to read the *Chicago Tribune* report of May 1, 1876, that staid old Philadelphia was gone, and that the city was "as cosmopolitan as Paris and as lively as Chicago."[201]

The Iron Age
1876-1905

by Nathaniel Burt and Wallace E. Davies

Anyone can be a shopkeeper, but a merchant is as much different as . . . a Rocky Mountain eagle from a mouse.

— JOHN WANAMAKER

Above all, the Quaker City lacks that discriminating enthusiasm for her own children . . . which enables more zealous towns to rend the skies with shrill paeans of applause. . . . If mistaking of geese for swans produces sad confusion . . . the mistaking of swans for geese may also be a serious error. The birds either languish or fly away to keener air.

— AGNES REPPLIER [1]

The period from the Civil War into the new century saw the transformation of Philadelphia into an industrial giant. Pennsylvania in general established itself as the Midlands or the Ruhr of America, the center of heavy industry, of iron and steel, coal and oil, America's foundry. Philadelphia became its Liverpool-Birmingham or perhaps Essen-Düsseldorf, chief port for the foundry, nerve center of transportation, producer of finished goods of an enormous variety but particularly of steam engines and steamships. The impact of this explosion of industry and technology almost obliterated Penn's green country town, the red-brick cultural capital, in a smog of steam and smoke, of endless gridirons of workers' housing, of railroads and factories, freight yards and warehouses. It was Philadelphia's Iron Age.

With the opening of the great Centennial Exposition of 1876 the city reemerged nationally. No longer the center of politics, religion, intellect, arts and letters, even of finance and commerce, Philadelphia presented itself as

---

OVERLEAF: *Aerial view of Philadelphia, photographed from a balloon by W. N. Jennings (1893). Lemon Hill Tower, the Fairmount reservoir, and the unfinished tower of City Hall are key reference points in this view of the city between the Schuylkill and Delaware Rivers looking to the southeast.*

Technology—Queen of the Engine. Let New York handle the finances and set the fashions, let Boston cling to its fading reputation as schoolmarm of the nation. Philadelphia was warming to business, albeit in a still slightly Quakerish subdued Philadelphia fashion. Domestic bliss and material comfort, those ultimate goals of middle-class Victorians, from the miles of row houses to the craggy new castles along the Main Line—this is what Philadelphia settled for. What it wanted, and what it got.

In the process Philadelphia's character crystallized, her society stabilized, her curiosity atrophied. Not the discovery of electricity or prison reform, but being a "city of homes," spawning associations and institutions and clubs, wallowing in contentment, conformity, and conversatism—these were now Philadelphia's chief interests. Politics became a necessary nuisance, to be left to self-paid professionals, despite constant abortive and bothersome reforms. Arts and letters were to be pleasantly inoffensive decorations of opulence. Science, medicine, engineering, the more practical professions, were enormously respected and dominated the mind of the city. Imagination and innovation were suspect. Safe and sound, prosperous and potbellied, this was the image Philadelphia liked to present, what Philadelphia now stood for.

This period was the culmination of that particular sort of Philadelphianism; yet in fact a new climax of the city's fortunes, a crest of a wave almost exactly corresponding to the climax of a century before. For almost in spite of itself this was perhaps Philadelphia's proudest period in just those areas in which it tried least hard. It was during this period that Philadelphia's greatest painter worked, that its only fictional classic was written, and that many other creative or performing talents emerged, some to stay, many more to leave and flourish elsewhere.

I

The basis, the root of all this was "business." The chief actors on the scene were businessmen—but businessmen with a difference. Unlike newer centers, Philadelphia did not totally glorify either business or businessmen. There were more important things. The holy professions of law and medicine, for instance, were much more respectable. Old money was much better than new money, blood counted as much as or more than accomplishment. Nonetheless, making money was certainly very important, and business unquestionably a good thing.

At the center and root of business, and most characteristic of this Iron Age, were those activities concerned with the basic trinity of iron and steel, railroads, and coal. This was the tripod on which the city's nineteenth-century industrial reputation and a large share of its prosperity rested. If there were to be any single symbol of Philadelphia during this period it would be a steam locomotive: an idol whose temple was, eventually, Broad Street Station; whose priests, wreathed in the incense of steam and soot, ranged from workers at the Baldwin Works or brakemen on the railroads to those almost sacred beings, the directors and presidents, particularly those of *The Railroad*, the Pennsylvania Railroad.

The Railroad was king. It was not only the most important single enterprise of the city, it also became and remained long afterward the single largest corporation in the country. Long after its great days the Pennsylvania Railroad held position as number one.[2] Its greatest days, however, were under the three presidents Thomas A. Scott (president 1874–1880), George B. Roberts (1880–1897), and Alexander J. Cassatt (1899–1906). (There was a brief interregnum, 1897–1899, of short-lived Frank Thomson, who died in office.) Under these men and their innumerable expert assistants, engineering, financial, and legal, the Railroad battled the nefarious manipulations of New York; battled the competition from the South represented by the Baltimore and Ohio; battled the octopus of Standard Oil; crept westward and southward and northward to Chicago, Washington, and New York; grew, consolidated, jockeyed, bargained, as deviously as any of its competitors, until by 1900 it was the keystone of the Keystone State. Philadelphia was its heart.

The Railroad's complicated history of engineering feats and improve-

Pennsylvania Railroad Depot (Broad Street Station), Broad at Filbert, designed by Wilson Bros. & Co. (1882, photograph taken in 1889). The elevated tracks, stretching west on Market Street, soon became known as Philadelphia's "Chinese Wall." The station was demolished in 1954 as part of the urban renewal project that became the Penn Center complex and John F. Kennedy Boulevard.

FREE LIBRARY OF PHILADELPHIA

ments, of mergers and consolidations, of rebates and politics and labor troubles is too specialized for a brief survey. Bit by bit it extended its rule over
the then-richest section of the country, that center belt delimited southward
by the Potomac and the Ohio Rivers, westward by the Mississippi. To the
north always breathed the fiery dragon of the New York Central and its allies
on Wall Street. Pennsylvania and New York fought over the way west and
over the control of Pennsylvania's coal and oil. Some of these battles the
Railroad lost; but its greatest victory, its final establishment on the island of
Manhattan itself, was signalled by the building of the Pennsylvania Station
on Seventh Avenue. This was essentially the triumph of Cassatt. The foundation for this success, the true high tide of Philadelphia's prosperity, was laid
by his predecessors.

Thomas A. Scott, one of eleven children of a western Pennsylvania tavern
keeper, got into transportation as a toll collector on turnpikes. He learned
railroading from J. Edgar Thomson, his predecessor as president, and turned
the Railroad from a state into a national affair. Scott was not Philadelphian,
though as president he moved to the city and died there.

George B. Roberts, however, was indigenous. Born in Pencoyd, one of
the most ancient and honorable Quaker homesteads of the so-called Welsh
Barony on what is now City Line, he was, also unlike Scott, an educated man
and a trained engineer. Whereas Scott's presidency was marked by labor
troubles, mostly in the west of the state, and abortive expansionist efforts
(Scott at one time controlled the Union Pacific before being ousted by Jay
Gould),[3] Roberts was a consolidator and centralizer. His monument was
Broad Street Station, opened in 1882 west of City Hall right at the hub of
Philadelphia, and connected to the former West Philadelphia terminal by a
blockwide massive stone viaduct nicknamed the Chinese Wall. The station
itself, a medieval castle of red brick, enlarged and made taller and fancier in
1892–1893 by Philadelphia's foremost architect of the period, Frank Furness,
was the fitting symbol of the Railroad's local power. The arched glass shed
into which trains arrived was the largest in the world. By 1894, 530 trains
carrying 60,000 people were arriving and departing each day. Fittingly, the
tracks dead-ended at Philadelphia's old Centre Square.[4]

Roberts was a small-boned, cautious, mustached man, deeply religious
(Episcopalian, no longer Quaker), quietly cultivated. Cassatt was large, handsome, sporting, expansive, fashionable. He too was from the barbarous West,
but not the son of a tavern keeper. His father had been the well-to-do mayor
of Allegheny City, suburb of Pittsburgh, but the family had moved to Philadelphia. Alexander had been educated in Germany and like Roberts was an
engineering graduate of Rensselaer Polytechnic Institute. There was a
shadow in mid-career. Like Roberts, Cassatt was a protégé of Scott, and by
1880 first vice-president. He may have expected to succeed Scott. When
Roberts became president instead, he resigned and spent seventeen years in
elegant exile on the Main Line raising horses, racing, coaching, and keeping
his hand busy in railroad affairs. As Roberts represented the centering of the

railroad in Philadelphia, so Cassatt represented its final expansion outward. As Broad Street Station illustrated Roberts's pulling inward, so the great Baths of Caracalla on Seventh Avenue in New York represented Cassatt's pushing outward. The tunnel under the Hudson River was in its day the most gigantic and daring engineering exploit of its kind. When the station in New York opened in 1910 it was dedicated to Cassatt. He, like Moses, never lived to see the promised land; but his monument stood for a generation as the Railroad's and Philadelphia's pride. Yet slowly and continuously thereafter, the Railroad's destiny was traveling on the downgrade.[5]

I I

The most immediate permanent impact of the Railroad upon Philadelphia was the creation of the Main Line. Suburbanization had begun long before, but it was George Roberts who really opened his native West to commuters. Stations along the main line of the railroad westward were rechristened, from the edge of the consolidated city to distant Paoli. "Old Maids Never Wed and Have Babies Period"—Overbrook, Merion, Narberth, Wynnewood, Ardmore, Haverford, Bryn Mawr, and, after others, Paoli at the end of the suburban circle—these names consciously reflected Roberts's own Welsh heritage. To some originally Welsh names like Merion and Haverford, new ones were added, obliterating rustic West Haverford, Elm, and Morgan's Corner. "Gothic" stations were built, and executives of the Railroad were expected to settle near them, which they did. Even rival Chestnut Hill owed its prosperity to the Railroad. Henry Houston, an officer of it, developed his great land holdings there as a model suburb. Unlike New York, where much of the earlier suburban movement was middle class, Philadelphia's suburbia was engineered from the top. The rich deserted city streets, even the sacred precincts around Rittenhouse Square, for a paradise of "country living" within comparatively few railroad minutes of City Hall. Gradually, anyone who could afford it followed suit.[6]

The other local railroad was the Reading; but its history was less fortunate than that of the Pennsylvania, and eventually after bankruptcies it became controlled by New Yorkers. Its reason for existence was coal. Coal of course was not mined in Philadelphia or its suburbs, but its mining and shipping was originally in the hands of Philadelphians, and much of the city's wealth was derived from it. By 1900 Philadelphia was exporting 447,000 tons of anthracite a year.[7]

The two most memorable characters associated with the Reading were its presidents Franklin B. Gowen and George T. Baer. Unlike the confident careers of Roberts and Cassatt, the careers of Gowen and Baer were attended by violence and unpleasant notoriety. Gowen, son of an Irish immigrant, was not an engineer. He got into railroads by means of the law. He made his reputation as the man who brought about the destruction of the Molly Maguires. After a famous trial in 1875 with Gowen as prosecutor, twenty reputed Mollys were convicted, ten were hanged. In 1870 Gowen had been made

The Anglecot, Evergreen and Prospect Avenues, designed by Wilson Eyre, Jr. (1858–1944), c. 1885, in S. F. Hotchkin's Ancient & Modern Germantown, Mount Airy and Chestnut Hill *(Philadelphia: P. W. Ziegler, 1889). The number of suburban houses conveniently located near the Pennsylvania Railroad's Main Line and the Reading lines to Germantown, Chestnut Hill, and Jenkintown grew rapidly in the last quarter of the nineteenth century. This building and its carriage house have recently been converted to multiple residences.*

PRIVATE COLLECTION

president of the Reading, whereupon he soon ruined the company by overinvesting in coal lands and being caught short in the depression of the 1870s. The company went bankrupt in 1880. Gowen resigned, and in 1889 shot himself.[8]

The Reading, though always busy carrying coal to Philadelphia, went into a long period of receiverships and eventually came under the influence of J. P. Morgan. Morgan returned the road to solvency and installed as president in 1901 George F. Baer, a lawyer and newspaperman from the city of Reading. Next year occurred the great and first successful strike of the United Mine Workers. Baer represented Morgan, and in the course of negotiations wrote to a gentleman in Wilkes-Barre saying: "The rights and interests of the laboring man will be protected and cared for . . . by the Christian men [to] whom God . . . has given control of the property interests of the country." This statement leaked to the press and probably did more for labor than the strike. Theodore Roosevelt stepped in with his big stick and forced a settlement in favor of the strikers.[9] Meanwhile the Reading Terminal of 1893 on Market Street was nearly as grand and impressive as Broad Street Station, but it was as much a symbol of Philadelphia defeat as Pennsylvania Station in New York was of Philadelphia victory, for control of the Reading rested in New York.[10]

Graver's Lane Station, Reading Railroad, Chestnut Hill, finished 1883 (photograph c. 1883), designed by Frank Furness (1839–1912). The station, now part of the Southeastern Pennsylvania Transportation Authority system, has been restored to its original profile.

CHESTNUT HILL HISTORICAL SOCIETY

The third of the city's great passenger terminals, that of the Baltimore and Ohio along the Schuylkill at Chestnut Street, built in 1886, was mainly distinguished as being one of the more characteristic works of Frank Furness. Like so many of his larger creations, it too has been destroyed. It also represented the threat of a rival, but in this case an unsuccessful one. The Baltimore and Ohio suffered a mortal blow when Roberts acquired the main line southward, the Philadelphia, Wilmington and Baltimore, snatching it from the B. & O. and others, and thus connecting Washington and New York with Pennsylvania Railroad through tracks.[11]

Philadelphia and its railroads were consumers and transporters of iron and steel, not producers; but the city was a center for the production of objects made from iron and steel. Of the manufacturers, two in particular were famous during the Iron Age: Baldwin's and Cramp's. Turning out three times as many locomotives as any other concern in the world (1500 a year by 1902), shipping them all over—South America, Russia, Palestine, Australia, Japan— the Baldwin Works was one of the wonders of the world and one of Philadelphia's industrial glories.[12] Equal in prestige and productivity was the William Cramp and Sons Ship and Engine Building Company. It made the Delaware into "the American Clyde," and from the days of the clipper ship through the First World War supplied the world not only with merchant ships but warships.

The genius of founder William (1807–1879), his sons, especially Charles (1828–1913) and the six sons of Charles, all of whom worked in and managed the works, helped the Cramp shipyards to survive the traumatic shift from sails and wood to steam and iron and emerge triumphant. By 1902 the works extended for fifty acres along the river in Kensington. Champion transatlantic passenger steamers like the record-breaking *St. Louis* and *St. Paul,* famous battleships like the U.S.S. *Maine,* famous yachts such as J. P. Morgan's *Corsair* —all were launched from the Cramp shipyards. In the late 1880s Cramp received a $13-million contract from the United States government, the largest up to then awarded to one company, for warships. Cramp like Baldwin had an international reputation, and supplied Russia, Turkey, and Japan with warships; Charles Cramp was decorated by the czar. The Railroad, Baldwin, and Cramp formed the cornerstone of Philadelphia's Iron Age.[13]

There were numberless other Philadelphia manufacturers in the field of iron and steel. Iron rolling mills made bar iron, ship plates, horseshoes, nails, and shoe machinery. The Kensington Iron and Steel Works was the largest such. Car wheels and ship propellers came from iron foundries that were said to produce one-third of the country's manufactured iron.[14] By the turn of the century William Sellers and Company, the leading foundry, was making and exporting machine tools, cranes, power hammers, locomotive turntables.[15] I. P. Morris, Towne & Co. in Port Richmond turned out boilers and engine works. Hoopes and Townsend made nuts, bolts, and rivets. Ice cream freezers, cast-iron building fronts, meters, pipes, elevators, sewing machines, and bath tubs (wooden tubs were banned by city ordinance in 1904) poured from smoke-belching factories along the industrial edges of the city, mostly along its two rivers.[16]

These iron and steel producers not only ringed the city itself, but intruded into the hinterland.

Of all the iron and steel works mostly owned or capitalized by Philadelphians, the most important was the Bethlehem Iron Company in the ancient Moravian center of Bethlehem, north of Philadelphia. This was the brainchild of that remarkable Philadelphian of birth, talents, and enterprise Joseph Wharton, who founded a Saucon Iron Company in 1857 which turned into the Bethlehem Iron Company in 1861 and finally in 1899 became the Bethlehem Steel Company. Wharton's fortune was actually made in nickel; for years he had an American monopoly in the production of refined nickel. More than any other single person he was the representative Man of Iron of this period of the city's life. He was a member of one of the oldest and most distinguished families of Quaker origin in the city, a man of learning, taste, and talents. He wrote poetry, collected art, sat on boards, interested himself in chemistry, geology, minerology, metallurgy, and became one of the richest men in the city—and one of the most individualistically philanthropic. His chief surviving beneficences are the Quaker Swarthmore College, one of America's early coeducational institutions, of which he was president of the Board of Managers for a quarter of a century, and the University of Pennsylvania's Wharton School of Finance and Commerce, first of its kind in the country and still one of the best.[17]

Two great depressions in the 1870s and 1890s marred this onward and upward expansion. Yet Philadelphia, though suffering, suffered less than other great industrial centers. One reason was that Philadelphia did *not* depend on the complex of iron, railroad, and coal for its sole support. It was the diffused diversity of the city's economy, its mixture of big plants and small, almost home industries, that kept the balance. This had been true of the eighteenth century with its multiple crafts and diversity of commerce. It remained true of the city in the nineteenth and even into the twentieth century.

During this period Philadelphia manufactured banjos, brooms, and buttons.[18] There were companies making wagons and carriages, wheelbarrows and watch cases (the Keystone Watch Company was the largest in the world),[19] cordage (Edwin H. Fitler and Company was especially important), glue, and electrical equipment. The Atwater Kent Manufacturing Company began making telephones and voltmeters as early as 1902; Morris E. Leeds from 1899 made precise electrical measuring instruments and became Leeds and Northrup in 1903. Factories turned out paper boxes and cigar boxes, parasols and umbrellas, "Fretz Foldwell Umbrellas" for example. Plumbing suppliers prospered; of Haines, Jones and Cadbury's excellent water closets nothing can be written, since "it would be useless to describe their working as their merits can only be appreciated after having seen them in actual use."[20]

A major industry of minor units was cigar making, carried on by small firms—490 of them in 1882—each employing only a few workers, many of them the recently immigrant Russian Jews of the 1890s. Bayuk cigars and the products of the Bobrow brothers eventually grew into major enterprises. In 1895 two Greek immigrants, Constantine and Stephen Stephano, started making cigarettes under the brand name Ramases. At first supplied only to the trade of hotels and restaurants, Ramases soon acquired a national reputation as a quality Turkish cigarette, mainly from their use by Philadelphia soldiers in the Spanish-American War.[21] Beers with German names such as Schmidt flourished up the Schuylkill;[22] ice creams like Bassett's and Breyers, and candies like Whitman's became nationally known.[23] The S. S. White Dental Company made false teeth and dental instruments, and pioneered with the first self-cleaning cuspidor.[24] Fels-Naptha soap soon became a household word, and manufacturer Joseph Fels one of the city's prominent philanthropists.[25] Above all it was during this period that the drug companies like Powers, Weightman & Rosengarten flourished,[26] an industry that today occupies much the same place in the city's economy that Cramp's or Baldwin's did a century ago.

However, it was not coal, iron, or railroads but textiles that continued to rank first among the city's enterprises, not only in the amount of capital invested but in number of establishments and employees. As of 1904, 19 percent of the city's 7100 manufacturers were textile plants, and they employed 35 percent of the city's 229,000 workers. Philadelphia produced more textiles than any other American city, and was also the world's largest and

most diversified textile center.[27] Yet none of the factories was famous in the
way that Baldwin's and Cramp's were, and no great families, like the Law-
rences in Massachusetts, were associated with the industry. Within the industry wool dominated; one-fifth of all domestic and imported wool in the
country was consumed by such Kensington plants as the Keystone Knitting
Mills.[28] Kensington in fact became a sort of textile enclave, inhabited by
English emigrant weavers who organized cricket teams that played with those
of gentlemen from the Main Line.[29] But there were mills all over the city. W.
H. Horstmann and Company manufactured silk hosiery.[30] Cotton was milled
in Manayunk.[31] John B. Stetson made big felt hats for westerners while J. H.
Fenton made tall silk hats for easterners.[32]

Carpets were Philadelphia's pride, and John Bromley and Sons, again in
Kensington, was the oldest carpet manufacturer in the city. The James Dobson Carpet Mills at the Falls of Schuylkill (once a famous beauty spot and
resort of budding eighteenth-century poets and painters) boasted 362 looms
and 1435 employees.[33] Fringes and upholstery coverings, lace curtains and
tapestries, eiderdown cloth and horse blankets all came from Philadelphia.[34]

Sugar and oil: these two seemingly rather uncharacteristic commodities
also founded Philadelphia fortunes. But the history of their establishment in
the city was attended by difficulties of various kinds. Like so many industries
of that time both these succumbed to national monopolies. Originally Philadelphia was second only to New York as a refiner of sugar. Of local refineries
the most important was that of Harrison, Frazier and Company, by 1887 one
of only three still in operation in Philadelphia as a result of low profit margin
and cutthroat competition.[35] The head of the company was Charles Custis
Harrison, who like Joseph Wharton represented old money refurbishing itself
with new money.[36] Harrison's grandfather John was the first manufacturing
chemist in the United States, and a very successful one. Harrison money sifted
into sugar in the next generation. But grandson Charles and his brothers,
along with the whole Philadelphia sugar business, were engulfed by a former
partner of the Harrisons, the New Yorker Theodore Havemeyer. In 1887
Havemeyer began to form the Sugar Trust that in 1891 was incorporated as
the American Sugar Refining Company. By 1892 Havemeyer had bought all
the Philadelphia refineries.

Like Wharton, Charles Harrison devoted his later years to education. He
became one of the more famous provosts (presidents) of the University of
Pennsylvania. He concentrated on raising money and expanding the plant,
the faculty, and the student body. His particular passion was for the University Museum and its archeological activities; everyone forgot about sugar, a
somewhat sore subject in Philadelphia by then, and thought of Harrison only
as one of the fathers of Philadelphia archeology.[37]

Oil refining in Philadelphia suffered similarly and succumbed earlier to,
of course, Standard Oil. The Atlantic Refining Company at Point Breeze had
been absorbed in 1874. Others, some owned by William L. Elkins the future
traction king, were taken over in 1880.[38] Oil was one of the Port of Philadel-

phia's important exports. Since Pennsylvania was then the oil state, it was only natural that this should be so. In 1891 the city was still exporting 35 percent of all the petroleum shipped from the United States, and the Pennsylvania Railroad tanked oil to the Point Breeze refineries from which it was shipped all over the world. (In 1901, when oil was used more for lighting than for fuel, nearly half the world's illuminating fluid was shipped from Atlantic's Point Breeze plant.)[39] But relations between John D. Rockefeller and the Railroad were not happy. Standard's ties were with New York, bypassing Philadelphia. The Railroad created an Empire Transportation Company in defiance of Rockefeller and in 1877 planned to build a large local refinery. Rockefeller cut off oil shipments to the city, and the Railroad had to give up.[40] In the end New York got 65 percent of all Standard's oil traffic and Philadelphia and Baltimore had to share the rest. However, Standard's Atlantic plant survived and flourished, and was the city's principal oil business.[41]

III

First seaport of the colonies during the eighteenth century, Philadelphia remained second only to New York in the late nineteenth. By the end of that century there were five miles of continuous wharves along the Delaware and four along the Schuylkill.[42] Imports, valued in 1901 at $67 million, included West Indian molasses, tropical fruit, wool from England, glassware from Germany, coffee from Rotterdam, iron from Scandinavia.[43] Exports were primarily coal, which Philadelphia practically monopolized even as late as 1900, and oil.[44] Grain was also exported, though always to a lesser extent than from New York and Baltimore.[45] There was a considerable amount of local tonnage—coastwise shipping, fishing craft, and excursion boats. Transatlantic steamers still left Philadelphia for Liverpool and Antwerp, under the control of the International Navigation Company, which bought the American Steamship Company and the Red Star Line.[46] Seafaring stores lined Front Street along the Delaware. Yet no city was less seafaring or seemed less like a great port than late-nineteenth-century Philadelphia. Perhaps its sheer physical extent back into the hinterland, as opposed to New York's insular water-surrounded concentration, and the fact that the city was in fact a long distance from the real ocean, diluted any salty atmosphere.[47]

Philadelphia in fact remained in area the largest city in the United States. By 1904 its 129 square miles supported some 300,000 families, many of them living in modestly comfortable small houses within walking distance of their work.[48] It was more a collection of almost separate villages—Kensington, Frankford, Manayunk—than the consolidated metropolis it was officially and politically supposed to be. Each neighborhood jealously guarded its special character, ethnic coloration, political integrity.[49] Each had its business district, the Italian street markets and Jewish shops in South Philadelphia, the local commercial areas on Girard or Ridge or Columbia Avenue to the north. As the population expanded the physical detachment of most of these various neighborhoods tended to decrease (though local pride and xenophobia prevails to this day), and the city became one gigantic fabric woven together by extended streets and above all by improved transportation.[50]

It was the network of street railways that more and more permitted workers to commute to jobs beyond walking distance from their homes and shoppers to patronize other than local stores. By 1880 Philadelphia led all American cities in the length of its horse-car lines—some 264 miles of track —and in 1885 these lines carried 117 million passengers. Gradually cable cars, in the 1880s and 1890s, and then electric trolleys, beginning in December 1892, took the place of horses; the last horse-car lines ran in 1897.[51]

Two men in particular played a leading role in this development and became, in the not always edifying process, two of the city's and the country's richest men. Peter Arrell Brown Widener began his career as a butcher boy in his brother's meat shop. William Lukens Elkins started as a clerk in a grocery store. Widener prospered in meat, Elkins in groceries. Widener also became involved in local Philadelphia politics. A fortunate contract to supply mutton to Union forces around Philadelphia during the Civil War gave him

The Independence, *ascending from a park or vacant lot in North Phila-delphia (1891). A "Model Philadelphia House," similar to the new row houses in this neighborhood, was exhibited at Chicago's Columbian Exposition in 1893.*

a nucleus of capital, to which his padded salary as city treasurer added. He began to invest in Philadelphia traction companies.

As Widener had prospered as owner of a chain of meat stores, so Elkins prospered as a grocer, building the city's first large refrigerator to store his fruit. When Pennsylvania oil was discovered, Elkins invested in storage plants and refineries, and by 1875 was a partner in Standard Oil. The first gasoline made was the product of one of these Elkins refineries. In the 1870s he also began to show interest in street railways and formed his association with Widener.

Together they bought up smaller companies, and by 1883 had effected a consolidation of all the lines in the city, first as the Philadelphia Traction Company, then as the Union Traction Company, and finally as the Philadelphia Rapid Transit Company. They expanded into other cities, helping Thomas Fortune Ryan and William C. Whitney in New York with capital and advice. They were conspicuously present in Chicago and involved in Pittsburgh and Baltimore. By the time Widener died he was probably the richest man in the city, Elkins perhaps the second.[52]

As a result of the amalgamation, electrification, and expansion toward the suburbs of street railways, and of course with the already extant suburban services of the Pennsylvania and Reading, it was possible for most Philadelphians to get to the center of the city easily for business and for shopping. Stores, hotels, business offices clustered about City Hall like filings to a magnet, and during this period most of the first skyscrapers, great hotels, and great department stores of the city were built. Lit by electricity (Chestnut Street was so illuminated as early as 1881)[53] and gas (the United Gas Improvement Company, the U.G.I., formed in 1882 with the backing of Widener, Elkins, and others, and the constant favor of City Hall, became the country's largest public utility),[54] and even linked by telephone (as early as 1878 the Bell Telephone Company opened its first exchange),[55] the concentration of business around City Hall became the focus for the city's transportation facilities. Broad Street Station, City Hall, John Wanamaker's department store all next to each other demonstrated Philadelphia's turn-of-the-century power—financial, political, and mercantile.

The latest Wanamaker's building, begun in 1902, was designed by Daniel H. Burnham of Chicago in the newfangled skyscraper style; as such it suggested the passing of the role of Second City to the westward, from Philadelphia to upstart Chicago. John Wanamaker himself remained one of the city's most conspicuous citizens. His combination of self-advertising publicity, religious conviction, political do-goodism, and making money tended to cause other Philadelphians both to admire and to snicker. Though he was sincere, there was a certain incompatibility among his various roles. He had been a secretary of the YMCA as a youth and had thought of a career as a clergyman. He became a merchant instead, and he always thought of merchandising as a sort of holy vocation. "Anyone can be a shopkeeper," he pronounced, "but a merchant is as much different as . . . a Rocky Mountain eagle from a mouse."[56] The famous bronze eagle in the center of the grand concourse of the store, for years a favorite meeting place for shoppers, proclaims this faith. His political career reached a climax when he first became postmaster general under Pres. Benjamin Harrison and then ran for nomination for the United States Senate as an antimachine Republican in 1897. He was defeated by the combined forces of evil represented by bosses Matthew S. Quay and Boies Penrose. Wanamaker died not a senator but a multimillionaire, his store unchallenged as the greatest of its kind in the city, and one of the greatest in the nation.[57] There were, however, other important department stores, most of them farther east on Market Street. Of these, Strawbridge & Clothier, founded and patronized by Quakers and other substantial Philadelphians, was the most respectable. Gimbel Brothers at Eighth and Market was one of the earliest important merchandising efforts of that family, whose early success began in Philadelphia in 1865, but who like so many other Philadelphians eventually flowered in New York.[58] Gimbels' across-the-street neighbor, Lit Brothers, occupying a whole block of by-now historic cast-iron– and pottery-fronted

Lit Brothers Department Store, Eighth and Market Streets, main section designed in 1893 by Collins and Autenrieth (photograph c. 1898). The Lits complex, now empty, which incorporated several older mercantile buildings on Market Street, extended to Seventh Street at the right. A corner of the Strawbridge & Clothier store appears at the left.

buildings, also prospered; today Lits is out of business, its cast-iron fronts threatened with demolition. The other great stores still remain in business.

The greatest and for years most fashionable hotel of the city, the Bellevue-Stratford, built in a mansarded style much like that of City Hall, opened in 1904.[59] Other skyscrapers, always kept just below the height of Calder's statue of William Penn on top of City Hall tower, pushed up roundabout. The John F. Betz Building of 1891, on the northeast corner of Broad and Chestnut, now replaced by the Philadelphia National Bank, was the first of them. The Land Title Building of 1898 and 1902 on the southwest corner, the Real Estate Trust Building of 1905 on the southeast corner, and many others followed.[60] As skyscrapers go, however, Philadelphia's lack the soar and flamboyance of those of New York and Chicago. Philadelphia moved into modern times with care, not to say trepidation. For a city with such a distinguished architectural tradition, its first modern business buildings were on the whole undistinguished.

United States Post Office and Federal Building, designed by Alfred B. Mullett (1834–1893), Ninth and Market (photograph c. 1895). The massive building opened in 1884 and was replaced in 1935.

FREE LIBRARY OF PHILADELPHIA

I V

Working in these mills, settling in these neighborhoods, riding these trolley cars, and as they made money, patronizing these stores, banks, and hotels—and almost all and always voting Republican—was a population rapidly changing from predominantly Protestant North European stock to one increasingly Roman Catholic and variegated in ethnic background. The city's industrial growth naturally stimulated a steady growth in population: 1880— 847,170; 1890—1,046,964; 1900—1,293,647.[61]

Nevertheless, Philadelphia still had a relatively small foreign-born population compared to other large American cities. Its 200,000 foreign-born in 1880 constituted only 24 percent of the total population, whereas in New York and Chicago they were 40 percent; in 1900 the percentage was even lower.[62] Although the makeup of this population was becoming more diversified, the "Old Immigration"—English, Irish, and Germans—was still predominant as the nineteenth century closed, a fact frequently commented on. One British writer, for example, noted that in Philadelphia one found "the purest Anglo-Saxon citizen body among all the large centers" in the nation.[63]

Many of the English who came to Philadelphia in these years continued to be absorbed as expert weavers into the textile industries of the northeastern sections of the city. Kensington was called "Little England."[64] German immigrants were readily assimilated into existing German settlements scattered throughout the city. Industrious and skilled, they often became independent businessmen, from watchmakers and gunsmiths to bakers and brewers. Their numbers were large enough to support at least three German-language newspapers.[65]

The largest foreign-born group in Philadelphia in this period remained the Irish, constituting half the city's foreign-born population in 1880 and one-third of it in 1900. Newcomers joined so many second- and third-generation Irish that in many ways Philadelphia was an Irish city, surpassed only by Boston and Providence. Philadelphia offered the Irish immigrants greater job opportunities than Boston, a lower death rate, and a higher standard of living with more housing, schools, and churches. Wherever the Irish settled they established churches until the Roman Catholic church became the largest religious group in the city. They favored large families. A French priest visiting Philadelphia in 1904 found 475,000 Catholics, an increase of more than a third in twenty years. As it was elsewhere in the United States, the Catholic church after the death of Archbishop Wood came to be Irish-dominated, a domination under which Polish and Italian Catholics became increasingly restive.[66]

Benefiting from a period of urban growth, the Irish were heavily involved in the construction industry as bricklayers, hod carriers, and bridge and railroad builders. Some rose to become powerful "contractor bosses" who effectively utilized Irish building skills, often through useful but corrupt political manipulation.[67] Politics also opened up opportunities for jobs as policemen, firemen, and watchmen. More of a stereotype was the Irish saloon-keeper, and of course the Irish cook and maid, whom Ethel Barrymore remembered so well in the home of her grandmother, Mrs. John Drew, on North Fifth Street.[68]

Gradually, as the century ended, the "Old Immigration" from Great Britain and northern Europe was supplanted by a "New Immigration" from

Russia, eastern Europe, and Italy. For many of these Philadelphia, unlike New York, was just a port of entry and a way station;[69] but some groups settled. Of these the Jews were the largest. In the late nineteenth century this community's upper class were German Jews who about 1880 began moving to the section around North Broad Street between Spring Garden Street and Columbia Avenue. By 1895 they had built on Broad Street not only two fine synagogues, Keneseth Israel and Rodeph Shalom, but their stylish Mercantile Club as well.[70]

In 1881 there were perhaps 5000 Jews in Philadelphia, including a small colony of eastern European Jews, largely from Poland and Lithuania, in "Jerusalem" in the Port Richmond industrial area. The Port Richmond Jews kept to themselves, were strictly Orthodox, with their own synagogue, and made their living for the most part as peddlers, rag pickers, and hucksters.[71] But the pogroms in Russia in 1881 began a tide of Jewish immigration that flowed into the next century. Early in 1882, 225 Russian Jews arrived aboard the Cramp steamer *Illinois* at the Christian Street wharf near Old Swedes' Church. It was the first such group to come directly to Philadelphia from abroad, and they were given a citywide welcome. Although some 2000 Jewish immigrants came to the city in 1882, these first arrivals were the largest single group for several years.[72] Since most of them were indigent, the United Hebrew Charities had to strain to meet their needs. In 1884 the Association of Jewish Immigrants was formed to give further assistance by locating relatives, finding jobs, and arranging temporary housing. In 1901 all the Jewish health and welfare agencies, hard pressed by the needs of the flood of immigrants, joined to form a united fundraising body, the Federation of Jewish Charities, with Jacob Gimbel as its first president.[73]

Most of the more than 40,000 Jewish immigrants who came through the Port of Philadelphia between 1881 and 1891 stayed in the city. While some went to "Jerusalem" in Port Richmond, others remained where they landed, and by 1894 the Jewish population of South Philadelphia had increased from about 300 to 30,000, most of them living in the river wards south of Spruce Street. Here they began to displace the long-settled black residents. The more well-to-do moved into the mansions of old Philadelphia families who had gone west to Rittenhouse Square. By 1905 there were about 100,000 Jews in the city, 70,000 of them Russian (compared to 286 in 1880); and of these, 55,000 lived in the southern wards, Philadelphia's "East Side."[74]

Unlike most immigrants of the period the Jews did not work in heavy industry, but in smaller businesses involving hand crafts—cigar factories, tailoring, and the garment trades; also in small neighborhood shops. South Street in particular became a sort of Jewish bazaar, with its housefront stores and Hebrew signs.[75] Adjustment for the newcomers into the already established Jewish community was not easy. The existing synagogues were Americanized, with a ritual quite different from that of the Russians. They had also adopted reforms repugnant to Orthodox traditions. New synagogues grew up around Fifth and Lombard, some of them in abandoned Christian churches and most of them Orthodox. By 1895 there were no fewer than forty-five of them in a half square mile south of Spruce Street.[76] Newspapers in "the Jargon—*Juedisch Deutsch*" were founded and served the immigrant groups more effectively than the Establishment-oriented English-language weekly *Jewish Exponent*, begun in 1887.[77]

Between 1870 and 1900 Philadelphia's Italian population increased sixtyfold, from about 300 to almost 18,000. By 1910 it had jumped dramatically to 77,000. Before 1909 few Italians entered the city through the port of Philadelphia, but rather came down from New York where thousands arrived yearly.[78] They were usually young unskilled laborers from southern Italy and Sicily who, unlike the Jews, came to America as temporary residents intending to earn enough money to improve their status at home.[79] Through New York employment firms, railroad agents, and *padroni* connected with contractors and politicians, the Italians found construction jobs in Philadelphia with the Pennsylvania and Reading Railroads and on the city's public works. They became street cleaners, trash collectors, stevedores, and laborers in the sugar, cement, and oil industries along the Delaware waterfront, and masons everywhere homes were built.[80]

For the most part the Italians settled in South Philadelphia, where many remain to this day. The earliest center was St. Mary Magdalene de Pazzi at

On South Street, photograph by Gilliame and Stratton Syndicate (c. 1895). Many Russian Jewish immigrants made hand-wrapped cigars. At the end of the century, South Street was the center of a thriving Jewish business community.

Seventh and what is now Montrose (until 1897 Marriott), founded in 1851 as the first Italian Catholic church in the United States.[81] Italians then moved westward toward the closer suburbs—Overbrook, Manayunk, Germantown. The Philadelphia political machine tended to organize them, displacing the system of *padroni*. As a result, instead of depending on the *padroni* for board and lodging[82] Italians, like other Philadelphians, rented or bought houses of their own. Many of them worked in these homes as tailors and finishers, or on the streets roundabout in the familiar roles of bootblacks, organ grinders, and fruit vendors. Their great market, then as now, extended along Ninth Street north and south of Christian.[83]

Other immigrant groups had less impact. A small Hungarian settlement worked in factories or became well known as makers of shoes and riding boots. Many incoming Poles merely passed through the city on their way to the coal and steel areas in the west of the state, giving Pennsylvania the largest Polish population in the country.[84] Those who did stay worked primarily in heavy industry—oil and sugar refineries, iron works like Pencoyd and Midvale.[85] The Christian Poles were predominantly Roman Catholic and as early as 1882 had established a parish of their own in the Northern Liberties, and in 1891 one in South Philadelphia.[86]

But of all the city's immigrant groups, the most consistent incoming flow was the result not of foreign but internal immigrations. Philadelphia's foreign-born population was small compared with other cities', but its black population was the largest of any northern urban center. Only the southward cities of Baltimore, Washington, and New Orleans had larger black populations.[87] By 1890 this population was close to 40,000, 4 percent of the city's total and a 24 percent increase over 1880. By 1900 the number had risen 60 percent to more than 62,000 and made up 5 percent of the total.[88] Between 1876 and 1896 some 15,000 blacks arrived to join the 25,000 already there.[89]

In 1896 W. E. B. DuBois was brought to Philadelphia by the University of Pennsylvania to study the city's blacks. His book *The Philadelphia Negro* was a pioneer in sociological and environmental research and is today a classic.[90]

DuBois found that most blacks lived in center city and had for many years. The heaviest concentration was in the Seventh Ward (Spruce to South, Seventh to the Schuylkill), where they were about 40 percent of the population and lived near the white families for whom they were domestic servants. This ward provided both high and low aspects of black life. The more prosperous Negroes, perhaps 3000, lived on Lombard Street west of Eighth and on Rodman and Addison Streets. They comprised an aristocracy of wealth and education that was not recognized by or even known to the whites. They tended to be alienated from their own people for whom they provided little or no leadership. They were largely Philadelphia-born, many of them descendants of freedmen of the past century.

The southeastern part of the Seventh Ward, on Lombard and South Streets, together with the Thirtieth Ward next to it, formed Philadelphia's first black ghetto, with the worst black slum in the city at Seventh and Lombard. Conditions had been exacerbated by the influx of Russian Jewish immigrants into the Fifth Ward, from which they steadily pushed the blacks west. In 1891, for example, the James Forten School on Sixth Street north of Lombard had equal numbers of black and Jewish students; in 1899 the number of blacks had dropped to 13 percent.[91]

During these years too Negroes were also to be found in Germantown and West Philadelphia, again living in the small streets near the wealthy homes where they worked. The almost fourfold increase of blacks in West Philadelphia between 1870 and 1900 was a harbinger of the future.[92]

The Philadelphia Negro of the late nineteenth century had few opportunities to better himself economically. Not only did the new industrialization require skills he did not possess, but he was forced to compete with white immigrants even for those jobs he could fill. Moreover there remained a strong racial prejudice in the city which expressed itself in a variety of ways. When the Republican National Convention was held in Philadelphia in 1900, black delegates were barred from hotels. Many whites refused to rent to blacks. There was prejudice in employment selection even of qualified blacks, and whites frequently refused to work with Negroes. Because blacks were not admitted to labor unions, a League of Colored Mechanics in 1897 tried to promote them in trades.[93]

The vast majority of black males were manual laborers, filling the ever-present need for cheap, unskilled labor—stevedores, street and sewer cleaners, trash collectors, livery men and bootblacks, porters and waiters. In 1890 only a little more than 1 percent of the black population was employed in the major industries of the city. Frederick W. Taylor, the champion of "scientific labor," was unusual when he hired 200 blacks to work with his white "gangs" at Midvale Steel in 1896.[94]

Negro women, who outnumbered the men, were virtually limited to domestic service and sewing; however, none of them was to be found in the sweatshops of the garment trade. Men also filled many domestic service jobs, and in 1880, 20 percent of adult Philadelphia blacks were domestics; this number increased to one-third by 1896, and they constituted one-fourth of all domestic servants. But as was happening in so many employment areas, in this traditional black occupation white immigrants were displacing them as coachmen, butlers, and nursemaids.[95]

A few blacks, however, were able to pull themselves out of this economic pit. By 1896 there were some 300 black-owned businesses in the city, mostly catering firms, restaurants, and barbershops. Christopher J. Perry founded the *Philadelphia Tribune*, a newspaper for blacks, in 1884. Walter P. Hall was one of the wealthiest blacks in 1892, making his money in the wholesale poultry business and using it lavishly through churches and welfare organizations. Two of the four black undertakers were women.[96]

Professionally, the black community had fifteen "reputable" physicians and three dentists in 1896, but only two out of their ten lawyers were successful. There were about forty teachers and more than sixty ministers. About 1

Franklin Court in 1912, after its improvement by the Octavia Hill Association, a housing reform group founded in 1896 by members of the Women's Civic Club. Standing with the family in front of the project are a representative from the association and a rent collector.

percent of the blacks were clerical, semiprofessional, or "responsible" workers. In 1896 there were sixty black policemen, working in or near black areas. It was Mayor Samuel G. King who in 1881 appointed the first Negro policeman, over great opposition. Although blacks had no equal chance for a job at Strawbridge & Clothier or Wanamaker's in 1888, a decade later the black postmaster and postal employees at Wanamaker's were highly successful in running the city's second-largest substation.[97]

To ease their existence, Philadelphia Negroes joined beneficial and mutual-aid societies and "secret" or fraternal organizations, paralleling similar groups in the white community. The Odd Fellows were perhaps the most influential of the fraternal societies: in October 1886, 2500 black Odd Fellows paraded in the city and then enjoyed a ball at the Academy of Music. The Freemasons too were active, celebrating the centennial of black Masonry in 1884. In May 1889 an exhibition illustrating black progress in industry and the arts was held in Horticultural Hall.[98]

The principal organizing and stabilizing body among the blacks remained the church. The church was the center of social life and amusements and a communication center. Each congregation formed its own circle, some being neighborhood-bound, some class-conscious or work-oriented. In 1885 there were twenty-five black churches and missions in the city, but with the migration of Negroes from the South their number more than doubled to fifty-five in 1897. The Methodists had the greatest number of communicants, followed by the Baptists, Presbyterians, and Episcopalians, and "springing up and dying a host of little noisy missions which represent the older and more demonstrative worship." In the 1890s the Catholic church, because of its "comparative lack of discrimination," made many converts among the blacks, enough in fact that in January 1892 Philadelphia was host to the third black Catholic congress of the United States.[99]

The new immigration, so predominantly Catholic and Jewish, brought to a close the "Protestant consensus" under which the nation had developed since its founding. In Philadelphia the most venerable of the Protestant denominations was the Society of Friends, but by 1880 less than 1 percent of the Quaker City's population was Quaker. Their numbers continued to decline in the last decades of the century until by 1900 there were only 16,000 Friends in the Orthodox and much larger Hicksite Yearly Meetings, and most of these lived outside the city. The plain dress and plain speech of the Quakers had all but disappeared by this time, and although many in the two branches of the Society still regarded each other with "holy abhorrence," a gradual easing of the separation was beginning to be felt. More important perhaps were the divisions within the two groups as they sought to reconcile their Disciplines to "worldly" challenges on all sides.[100]

One of Henry James's impressions of Philadelphia about 1906 was the persistent presence of Quaker "drab," but he also noted a "bestitching of the drab with pink and green and silver." More and more, wealthy Quakers were being caught up in the social world of the largely Episcopalian aristocracy of Old Philadelphians. Although most of this "Quaker-turned-Anglican gentry" retained nominal affiliation with the Society of Friends, other Quakers, as they had since colonial days, left their Discipline for the Episcopalian and Presbyterian churches.[101]

V

It might be expected that the sudden influx of immigrants would produce the same effect apparent in all other American big cities—overcrowding, exploitation, slums, labor troubles, political corruption, and party realignments. All these things did indeed appear in Philadelphia, but curiously mitigated in some areas and curiously distorted in others.

Perhaps the most important single factor in creating the differences remained architecture. That is, instead of being a city of jammed-together multifamily tenements packed with renters, Philadelphia was still a city of endlessly repeated small row houses, most of them one-family dwellings, many of them owner occupied. As of 1891 a Philadelphian who earned $25 a week was considered a potential homeowner. Few workers were actually paid that much money, but of course more than one person in a family was usually employed.

Baldwin Locomotive workers in 1882 earned $605 a year; the average iron and steel wage was $500. Textile workers earned an average of $350 or less in establishments using child labor. Women, 26 percent of the work force in 1900, earned less than men.[102] Income did not increase greatly by the turn of the century, and an eight-hour day was a rarity. Some employers, like Strawbridge & Clothier and John B. Stetson, provided amenities—lunchrooms, building and loan associations. John Wanamaker introduced profit sharing in 1887.[103] But it was generally believed that home ownership remained one of the principal reasons for the comparative lack of labor agitation in Philadelphia in this period. Widespread resistance to trade unionism by employers was certainly another. Even many Quakers, so conscious of the needs of the poor, saw organized labor as "an anarchic bomb."[104]

Nonetheless there were efforts, often sporadic and ineffective, to organize. Textile and garment workers joined socialist unions. In the 1890s the Knights of Labor attracted members among cigar makers, brewers, and trolley-car conductors; but the founding of the American Federation of Labor, organized by craft unions, brought to an end the influence of the Knights.[105]

For the most part Philadelphia was spared the violent labor troubles of this agitated period.[106] But the city did have its quota of strikes—by shoemakers, steamfitters, longshoremen, machinists. In 1895 at the height of the Christmas season the Amalgamated Association of Street Railway Employees paralyzed the newly consolidated Union Traction Company. There was some rioting and damage to trolley cars during the week of the strike. In the end there was a slight increase in wages and a limitation of the working day to twelve hours.[107]

It was not until 1903 that Philadelphia experienced its first major strike. That summer some 100,000 textile workers, always among the worst paid members of the city's labor force, shut down the industry with their demand for a fifty-five-hour week. The strike failed, but did bring to public notice one of the most deplorable aspects of the industry, child labor. Among the strikers, 10,000 of them were children, many only ten years old. Parades and protests raised the issue, but it still was many years before effective laws were passed and enforced against the exploitation of children.[108]

And the "city of homes" also included specimens of the worst kind. Whereas the labor force of North Philadelphia was early unionized and conscious of rights and problems, South Philadelphia remained a sort of urban backwater. Unionism failed to develop there, and it remained an area of squalid slums and unskilled workers. These slums were not tenements but narrow alleys and dark courtyards of tiny three-story houses known as Trinity—"Father, Son, and Holy Ghost"—houses, one room to a floor. Jammed together, the houses had little light or air, lacked sewerage and adequate water supply, smelt of humanity and decay. Sweatshops occupied the upper floors of the Jewish neighborhoods; in the overcrowded Italian sections chickens were often kept in bedrooms and goats in the cellar.[109]

For all this misery Philadelphia still had less of a concentrated slum problem than other big cities. On the other hand what there was was ignored by a complacent public.[110] Nonetheless special groups made special efforts, and by 1878 there were more than 800 active charitable organizations, many of them addressing these problems. A centralizing Society for Organizing Charity was founded in 1879,[111] and in the same period the settlement movement began in a rather haphazard fashion.[112] Religious groups spearheaded the movement, including Quakers in Kensington and Episcopalians in South Philadelphia.[113] One of the more effective such philanthropies was the housing program inspired by the London reforms of Octavia Hill. Theodore Starr, Hannah Fox, and Helen Parrish began in the 1880s to build or restore houses to rent cheaply, mostly to poor blacks. An Octavia Hill Association was founded in 1896 by members of the women's Civic Club, and not only provided houses but agitated for housing legislation, with eventual success.[114]

Some of the problems of Philadelphia's living conditions were basically political. Sewage disposal, water supply, road and street construction, paving, and upkeep were all lamentably inadequate, and attempts at improvement usually turned into excuses for corrupt contracts and padded payrolls. No respectable person would drink the city water, which came from the polluted Schuylkill, and everyone who could bought spring water from private companies.[115] The typhoid fever death rate was the highest of the major cities, three times that of New York after the turn of the century.[116] Joseph Wharton hoped to supply the city with good water from the aquifer under the vast pine-barren acreages he owned and set aside in South Jersey. Utilization of the upper Delaware and other sources was urged. Instead the city Councils had other ideas. Expensive new pumping stations and reservoirs, resulting in juicy plums for favorite contractors and perquisites for councilmen, were preferred, ineffective though they might be.[117] For example, cholera and typhoid epidemics in 1891 and 1899 caused agitation for an improved system of water filtration. The result was a $12-million dollar loan and a sand-filtered water system the contract for which was awarded to the brother of a Select Council member. According to the reformer Rudolph Blankenburg, "Such a piece of costly and useless hydraulic construction . . . could not be duplicated in the wide universe."[118]

V I

In most cities of the nation during this period city governments tended to be split between the two great parties. In the North the Republican party usually represented "decent government"—and money. The Democratic party represented "machine politics"—and the disadvantaged. The familiar pattern of Irish politicians in Boston battling the Brahmins, or the conflicts between gentlemen reformers like Theodore Roosevelt and Tammany in New York was paralleled in Philadelphia to be sure, but with one major and crucial difference. Philadelphia was in effect a one-party town. Both "decent citizens" and "grafters" were Republicans. Thus a Republican nomination was usually an election, and most battles had to be fought in the murky areas of the primaries, where bosses were most effective.

Resident Democrats did exist at the bottom and the top of the social pyramid. The river wards, overwhelmingly working class, inhabited by Irish and Germans, remained loyally Democratic.[119] The very best Old Philadelphia families—Cadwaladers, Biddles, Ingersolls—also remained quixotically Democratic, largely based on sympathy for the prewar South and its states' rights attitudes, and also from a taste for independence and scorning of middle-class taboos.[120] Democrats managed to elect Robert E. Pattison as reform city controller of Philadelphia in 1877; he was reelected as a result of his exposés of corruption printed in newspapers in 1880, and then went on to become governor of Pennsylvania in 1883 and again in 1891.[121]

Meanwhile decent citizens formed committees, temporarily elected honest officials, made laws. A typical example involved a new city charter. Drafted by three of the city's most prominent reformers and civic leaders, John C. Bullitt, E. Dunbar Lockwood, and the famous historian and publisher Henry C. Lea, and backed by one of the city's endless series of reform groups, the Committee of One Hundred, the charter's chief emphasis was on giving power to the mayor, streamlining the city departments by reducing them from twenty-five to nine, and then putting them under the direct supervision of the mayor. The charter was drawn up in 1882, but local boss James McManes saw to it that it was buried in committee in 1883. There it might have stayed, except that state boss Matthew S. Quay recognized that the charter could be a powerful weapon against Philadelphia boss McManes in the perennial struggle between state and city chieftains for control of Pennsylvania. With the help of Boies Penrose, a Philadelphian but then in Harrisburg as Quay's chief lieutenant, the charter bill passed the state legislature in 1885 and took effect in the city in 1887.[122] The end result was not that of a new order, as everyone hoped in 1887, but a victory of Quay over McManes.

It was through this fight that Quay's henchman David Martin took over in Philadelphia from the defeated McManes[122]—and that Boies Penrose, who began as a reformist champion of the charter, saw what was really happening and decided, since he couldn't lick 'em, to join 'em, becoming himself the most corrupt and devious of bosses. As a later henchman of Quay's, Isaac Durham, said, "We took that charter and went right on with our business."[124]

Nevertheless two good mayors were elected—the "reign of the Edwins" —Edwin H. Fitler, cordage manufacturer, serving from 1887 to 1891, and succeeding him Edwin S. Stuart, owner of Leary's bookstore, one of Philadelphia's landmarks.[125] But the Panic of 1893 (allegedly brought about by those Democrats) in the middle of Stuart's mayoralty helped the bosses back to power. It was "business as usual" again.[126]

Among the bosses, however, the election of 1895 proved crucial. New

Philadelphia boss Martin used the occasion to try to declare his independence from Quay. Quay backed Penrose for mayor. Martin backed a nonentity named Charles Warwick. Warwick won the primary (largely thanks to a publicized photograph of Penrose coming out of a brothel), and then defeated reform Democrat Pattison, but it was a Pyrrhic victory. Quay ousted Martin as his representative and replaced him with Iz Durham.[127] After Quay's death in 1904 Penrose, by then perennial United States senator, took his place and dominated the city's, the state's, and to some extent the nation's politics until he died in 1921.

Penrose was very much a Philadelphian, a member of one of the city's oldest, richest, and most distinguished colonial families. A brilliant graduate of Harvard in 1881, he began as a lawyer. His reforming ardor having been cooled by the politics surrounding the 1887 charter, he cynically allied himself with Quay, whom he succeeded, and to the end of his days followed Quay's example. A gargantuan eater, a cynical lecher, like Quay a master of intrigue, he played politics the way others played chess: not for personal profit, since he was a man of inherited wealth, but for the pleasure of winning.[128]

VII

Not only were physical aspects of the city's life dependent on and tarnished by the contented corruption of the city's government—streets and sewers, water supplies, police and fire departments—but even its intellectual life was touched at the roots. That is, free public education was a function of the city, and here too "business as usual" and reform alternated. At the turn of the century some 3500 teachers (200 of them men) were instructing 153,000 students in the city public schools.[129] The system of operation opened the doors to corruption since the schools came under the jurisdiction of the district school boards which were dominated by ward bosses. These boards appointed teachers and principals not on the basis of merit but of pull, often exacting pay for positions and promotions as well as "voluntary contributions" for political campaigns. Salaries were lower in Philadelphia than in any other large city in the country. Men were paid more than women, upper grades more than lower; married women as teachers were discriminated against. Schools were overcrowded, rundown, unsanitary. Funds were chronically inadequate and teachers themselves often had to help buy textbooks.[130]

Reforms, desperately needed, paralleled the reforms in city government, though eventually with more permanent success. The establishment of a central school board in 1883 and the appointment of the first woman member of the Philadelphia Board of Education in 1886, Anna Hallowell, were steps in the direction of honesty and sanity. Finally in 1905, after twenty years of effort, a Public School Reorganization Act was passed and the system was freed of the incubus of the wardheelers' corrupt control.[131]

Part of the battle for school reform involved compulsory school attendance. This of course attacked the ancient abuse of child labor, and was opposed not merely by employers but by many working-class parents who depended on their children for family support. Here it was not the Republicans but the Democrats who were most strongly against the various reform measures, and a series of bills in the legislature were defeated or vetoed by the reformer Governor Pattison. Nonetheless a child-labor bill was passed in 1893 and compulsory school attendance voted in 1895.[132]

The jewel of the system remained Central High School, devoted to the education of specially selected boys of superior intelligence. Many of the prominent figures of Philadelphia life then as now were graduates, notably the painter Thomas Eakins and the lawyer and art collector John G. Johnson.[133] Meanwhile private education grew and flourished, and there were almost as many parochial schools and private schools in the city as public ones. Catholics generally sent their children to parochial schools, the well-to-do to the various town or suburban private schools. Notre Dame Academy on Rittenhouse Square and Eden Hall in Torresdale were the fashionable Catholic girls' schools, Delancey School and Episcopal Academy the Protestant boys' schools in the city. Various suburban schools founded during this time, notably Chestnut Hill Academy for boys in 1895 and Springside School (Chestnut Hill, 1879) and Shipley School (Main Line, 1894) for girls were indications of the trend of the prosperous away from the city. Eventually older schools such as Penn Charter, Episcopal Academy, and the Agnes Irwin School also moved out of town.[134]

The most important such educational move, however, had been that of the University of Pennsylvania to West Philadelphia in 1872. It was after this move and during this post-Exposition period that the university was converted from a parochial academy for the more conservative Old Philadelphians, totally dominated by its famous schools of law and medicine, into a modern city university.

Somewhat paralleling the history of the Railroad, three important leaders transformed a rather patchwork institution into a great national one. Rather like Thompson of the railroad, Charles J. Stillé, professor of English and a literary dilettante of ancient Delaware Valley Swedish descent, as provost supervised the move west and began the process of growth and reorganization. He himself, however, felt that he was a failure. Battling with the entrenched and conservative Board of Trustees, which still held even disciplinary power over undergraduates, he resigned discouraged in 1880. He was succeeded by Dr. William Pepper, already a famous practitioner and teacher of medicine, and it was Provost Pepper who during his fourteen years of incumbency realized Stillé's plans.[135]

William Pepper was a member of a family of German origin whose ancestor Johan Heinrich Pfeffer had come to the country in 1769 and whose grandfather George had established the family fortune. William graduated from the university in 1862 and then two years later from the medical school, still the most prestigious in the country. He taught at the university, where he served in several capacities until his death, as well as serving on the staff of various local hospitals. He was the chief founder of the University Hospital in 1874, a project new to the country at that time—a teaching hospital associated with a university medical school, in which the faculty acted as the staff. Though continuing his active medical career, he accepted the position of provost of the university when Stillé resigned. As one of the city's most important doctors in an age when Philadelphia was considered the first medical city in the country, and as a Pepper, William had few of the problems with the trustees that plagued Stillé. The university burgeoned in every direction. Financially and educationally soundly established, the campus decorated by a new library, chemistry building, and gymnasium, the curriculum modernized, gifts pouring in (including a bequest of $60,000 from Uncle George Pepper), the university approached the twentieth century rebuilt and revitalized. Perhaps the emphasis seemed more on things than thoughts, on new buildings and departments rather than on purely academic distinctions—a process that was emphasized under the administration of Pepper's successor Charles Custis Harrison. But by the time Pepper resigned in 1894, worn out with his double career as college president and doctor, the university had been restored to its ancient prerevolutionary eminence as one of the country's prestigious universities.[136]

While this process of academic blossoming was taking place at the University of Pennsylvania, Temple University was founded by the efforts of one man, that extraordinary Yankee with the golden tongue Russell H. Conwell. Born poor in rural Massachusetts, he was a soldier in the Civil War. His war experiences had converted him from adolescent atheism to exuberant Christianity. In 1879 he was called to the Baptist ministry, and the following year came to take over a moribund Grace Baptist Church in North Philadelphia. In ten years, largely on the basis of his popularity as a preacher and lecturer, he had converted the church into the vast Baptist Temple, seating some 3000 persons. In the church basement he began a night school for workingmen which gradually emerged as a full-fledged university, bearing the name of Temple and chartered in 1888. To this institution Conwell donated the enormous earnings he made from over 6000 speaking engagements for his lecture "Acres of Diamonds." This set piece of uplift, which combined spirituality with money-making in the best vein of the Protestant Ethic, was one of the phenomenal successes of the turn of the century, and on its success was founded one of the city's most dynamic educational institutions, intended as a "workingman's university."[137]

The Drexel Institute, founded in 1891–1892 by financier Anthony J. Drexel, also was aimed specifically at the education of working-class youth of both sexes in the areas of technical expertise.[138] In the suburbs, Bryn Mawr College was founded in 1880 as a bequest of Friend Joseph W. Taylor. Intended as a college for women to match and balance the older Quaker college Haverford, for men, it rose above sectarianism particularly under its second president, M. Carey Thomas. From 1894 to 1922 Thomas set uncompromising intellectual standards and gave determined support to women's rights and the cause of world peace.[139]

Circulation Room of the Free Library of Philadelphia, 1221–1227 Chestnut Street (photograph c. 1900).

But of all the institutions of the Iron Age none has had a more far-reaching effect on the city's educational development than the Free Library. Though Philadelphia was the earliest of American cities to encourage libraries, they had always been private ones, supported by shareholders, and though open to all, they were not the equivalent of the modern public library. A bequest by George Pepper of some $250,000 led to the founding of the Free Library of Philadelphia in 1891, belatedly in comparison with other cities. Under the guidance of his nephew Provost William Pepper, this library soon established itself as a vital adjunct of the city's educational life. Branches, the creation of Andrew Carnegie's bounty, were built. The library attracted many other gifts, notably a million-dollar one from P. A. B. Widener, whose home at Broad and Girard for years housed a collection of incunabula and a branch library, as well as retaining all his gold fixtures in the bathrooms.[140]

VIII

Along with the founding of the Free Library, one of the most notable institutions to emerge after the Centennial was the museum of art in 1877. It was a direct outgrowth of the Exposition, a rather random and leftover collection gathered in Memorial Hall. At first conceived of as a museum of industrial art, bequests by the Wiltach and Bloomfield Moore families gave it a nucleus of paintings. These, surrounded by a vast assortment of bric-a-brac and casts, were the beginnings of the present great collection of the Philadelphia Museum of Art.[141]

Much more prestigious at this time, however, was the venerable Pennsylvania Academy of the Fine Arts. The period from 1876 till about 1910 was the high point of its national prestige. Not only was it famous as an art school, it also maintained an annual series of exhibits of American art second to none in the country. Every artist of importance showed there, and the Academy with its schools and exhibits made Philadelphia one of the more important artistic centers of the United States for half a century after the Civil War.[142]

This institutional flowering—novelties like the Art Museum and the Free Library, the revitalization of the University of Pennsylvania and the Pennsylvania Academy—was paralleled in Philadelphia by an artistic flowering. In painting, architecture, and literature especially it was one of the city's finest periods and produced some of Philadelphia's finest artists. Some of these talents stayed and worked in the city, some went away to flourish elsewhere. But whether they stayed or left, Philadelphia didn't seem to care.

One might think, given this intellectual and esthetic ferment, that an atmosphere like that of the Italian Renaissance or the Flowering of New England might have prevailed. Not at all. The evidence to the contrary is overwhelming. Agnes Repplier, essayist, grande dame of Philadelphia letters, summed up the situation as of 1898 with sardonic wit in her *Philadelphia, The Place and the People:*

Above all, the Quaker City lacks that discriminating enthusiasm for her own children . . . which enables more zealous towns to rend the skies with shrill paeans of applause. . . . Philadelphia is . . . "more than usual calm" when her sons and daughters win distinction in any field. She takes the matter quietly. . . . If mistaking of geese for swans produces sad confusion . . . the mistaking of swans for geese may also be a dangerous error. The birds either languish or fly away to keener air. Yet . . . the sharp discipline of quiet neglect is healthier for a worker than that loud local praise which wakes no echo from the wider world.[143]

The careers of three of the more important Philadelphia swans of this period offer illustrative contrasts. Six artists have been traditionally considered to be the most important American painters of this period after the Civil War: the nativists Thomas Eakins, Winslow Homer, and Albert Pinkham Ryder, and the expatriates Mary Cassatt, James McNeill Whistler, and John Singer Sargent. Of these, three were Philadelphians. Of them all, Eakins was the only one who stayed, studied, painted, lived, and died where he was born. He dominated the Academy, and hence art in the city, from 1876 until he was dismissed in 1886. He made of the Academy one of the leading teaching centers of the American art world. Neglected in Philadelphia, and indeed everywhere else, during most of his lifetime, his career may be one of the city's shames. On the other hand it must also be considered one of its greatest glories. In American history there has seldom been any important artist whose entire active career was so molded and colored by one specific locality. No better example can be found of the salutory, if painful, "discipline of quiet neglect."

Mary Cassatt represents equally clearly the flight to "keener air."[144] She was not as completely a Philadelphian as Eakins. She was born in Pittsburgh, but her family settled in Philadelphia when she was young and became totally identified, especially in the person of her brother Alexander, president of the Railroad. Mary studied at the Academy in the 1860s, but did not find herself as an artist until she moved permanently to France in 1873 and came under the influence of Edgar Degas. She and Berthe Morisot were the only two women prominently identified with the Impressionist movement. She was the only native of the United States to be so importantly identified. Her work, her artistic frame of reference, is entirely French. As an artist she was Parisian. As a person she remained American. Her technique may have been modeled after Degas, but her subject matter was basically Philadelphian: feminine Philadelphia, in total contrast to the overwhelming masculinity of Eakins. Though she lived in Paris, or outside it, most of her social life there was spent exclusively in a narrow circle of an imported family and of American friends. In a curious way she was as much circumscribed by the ambience of her native, or native-adopted, city as was Eakins. Of her portraits, it is those of her family and her Philadelphia friends or patrons that remain most typical.

The third of the six with Philadelphia connections was John Singer Sargent. Though born in Florence, a student in Paris, and a resident of England, who practiced his trade of portraiture in America largely in Boston and New York, he was nonetheless a Philadelphian by background. His mother, born Mary Newbold Singer, was completely Philadelphian. Her connection with the Newbolds gave her a claim to local social distinction. John's father Fitzwilliam, though of an established family of Gloucester, Massachusetts, moved to Philadelphia as a boy and was educated entirely in Pennsylvania. He graduated from the Medical School of the University of Pennsylvania in 1843 and set up successfully as a practitioner in Philadelphia. He was well on his way to professional success when the death of a first child drove him and his wife abroad in 1854. She was the artistic one; it was from her that John learned the rudiments of painting. It is an especially Philadelphian art that made him famous, fashionable portraiture, absolutely in the tradition of Gilbert Stuart and Thomas Sully. The splendors of Gainsborough and Lawrence became obsolete in Victorian England. In Philadelphia, the Philadelphia of Sargent's mother and father, the tradition flourished up to the Civil War. Sargent revived this tradition. He even identified himself with Philadelphia by citing the city (quite improperly) as his birthplace when he first exhibited in the Paris Salon.[145]

A painter neglected by his city, one who left for good, and one who never in fact lived there at all make an odd trio on which to base a claim for glory. There were, however, many other practitioners of painting in or from the city during the period from the Centennial to the new century, though none of them achieved the same national prominence, then or later. Cecilia Beaux was, much more than any other prominent painter of the time, a born Old Philadelphian. Along with Mary Cassatt she represents the emergence in America during this period of hundreds of talented women painters who exhibited at the Academy Annuals and had successful careers. Few of these seem to have survived as reputations. Of them all Cassatt and Beaux are the most highly thought of now. Like Cassatt she seemed to be at her best when painting members of her own family, but she had a very successful career as a professional portraitist. Eventually, like so many other Philadelphia painters, she moved to New York where the commissions were. But it is her Philadelphia works, full of life, light, vigor, and style, that are her best claim to present-day recognition.

When Eakins was forced to resign from the Academy, his tradition was carried on by his successor and former assistant, Thomas Anschutz. He was not a Philadelphian by birth and training, coming there via Kentucky and New York, but he certainly adopted the style of his master, if never able to achieve his force and grandeur. His fame as a teacher remains greater than his fame as an artist. Very different, but equally non-Philadelphian in origin, were the charming if mild semi-Impressionist Robert Vonnoh and the fashionable dazzler William Merritt Chase, both of whom also taught at the Academy, and helped make it, after its revitalization by Eakins, one of the most important art schools in this period.

More native to Philadelphia were the Afro-American Henry Osawa Tanner, pupil and friend of Eakins, who left to live in Paris as a painter of religious subjects, and Thomas Moran,[146] flamboyant landscapist.

Tanner at his best achieved something of the sober emotional quality of his teacher, especially in a few striking genre scenes of fellow blacks. He is now considered the best nineteenth-century painter of his race.

Moran, whose landscapes were first of the wilds of the Wissahickon, went on to make a reputation as a painter of the Far West, and along with Albert Bierstadt is now a favorite nineteenth-century landscapist of collectors of western Americana (a Moran was sold to a westerner in 1980 for over $600,-000). He was, however, very much a Philadelphian, though born in England and dying in California. His family were weavers, typical examples of the kind of English immigrants who went into the textile works of Kensington's "Little England." Not so typical was the precocious talent shown by the four Moran brothers, Thomas, Edward (a marine artist of Turneresque vitality), Peter (who specialized in animals), and John (one of Philadelphia's pioneer realistic photographers). Thomas, Edward, and John are all being "rediscovered." Peter has a rather unenviable distinction: it was his picture *The Return of the Herd* that was hung in place of Eakins's *The Gross Clinic* when that picture was removed from the artistic to the medical section of the Great Exposition of 1876.[147] Thomas Moran studied with his brother Edward and began to specialize in renderings of the American wilderness. He was a typical later member of the somewhat misnamed "Hudson River School"—celebrators of the majesty of God's American Country. He achieved instant fame and fortune by being the first artist to paint the Yellowstone. His colorful and faithful pictures of geysers and canyons were a decisive factor in the creation of the nation's first national park in 1872. Though Moran roamed the West and settled in a studio in East Hampton, Long Island, near Chase, his family kept their connections with Philadelphia. They and their children and their in-laws the Nimmos and Ferisses in several generations made up a family group, active in the arts and based on Philadelphia, exceeded in numbers only by the Peales.[148]

Far less prominent during their lifetimes yet far more essentially indige-nous were the members of a school of trompe l'oeil still life that flourished, successfully but obscurely, in or around the city at this time. This group of painters, who derived their tradition directly from the precise, humble school of still life, America's first, originated by James Peale, produced after the Civil War various artists who specialized in a somewhat more elaborate vein. Theirs was an art of visual trickery, objects hung against, or seemingly pasted or tacked to boards, simple objects piled on tables, all so lifelike that naïve patrons were filled with awe and delight at being fooled. These artists were ignored by true art lovers, but bought by simple folk and hung in bars. William Harnett, John F. Peto, J. D. Chalfant of Wilmington, and George Cope of West Chester were only brought to life again in mid-twentieth century.[149]

Expatriates like the Haseltines and Harrisons began in Philadelphia. Wil-liam, James, and Herbert Haseltine made Rome their center, Alexander and L. Birge Harrison were respected in France. And there were many other painters, also distinguished in their day, then forgotten, now being brought to life—and all Philadelphians: Charles Fussell and William Trost Richards, landscapists; William Sartain and his sister Emily, William Furness, brother of Frank and Horace Howard, all portraitists; Xanthus Smith, a marine artist, and his sister Mary who did chickens; and many, many others.

Much more famous during their lives were the Philadelphia illustrators. Two friends, Arthur B. Frost and Edwin A. Abbey,[150] studied together at the Academy, then went on to demonstrate again the split between nativist and expatriate that also divides Eakins and Sargent. Frost came to represent every-thing homespun and indigenous, the preferred illustrator of *Brer Rabbit*. Abbey settled in England and was beloved for his sensitive and archaistic designs for volumes of English classics—the poems of Herrick, Goldsmith's *She Stoops to Conquer*. The illustrator-lithographer Joseph Pennell[151] also settled in England and became a bosom friend of Whistler (his wife Elizabeth Robins Pennell wrote the authorized Whistler biography). Above all Howard Pyle, native of Wilmington, Delaware, but with many Philadelphia connec-tions, and his pupils, notably Newell Convers Wyeth and Maxfield Parrish,[152] became and remain among the most popular illustrators in the American tradition. Pyle and Wyeth were founders of the still-flourishing Brandywine School, south of Philadelphia.

None of the Philadelphia sculptors of the period achieved more than a local reputation. But Alexander Sterling Calder survives as much because of family as because of personal fame. He was the second in what is by now the most celebrated dynasty of sculptors in America. The first of the line, Alexander Milne Calder, emigrated from Scotland in 1868 and became a part of the "Scotch Mafia" that dominated the building of City Hall—architect John J. McArthur, mason and contractor William Struthers, and sculptor Calder. The kind of closed-corporation ethnic control of construction projects characteristic later on of the Irish and then of Italians seemed to have been during the nineteenth century in Philadelphia a prerogative of Scots. Calder designed the statuary and carving that crawls all over the bulk of Philadelphia's civic mammoth, crowned by his massive memorial to William Penn, the great statue that to this day dominates the city on the top of its tower, still by common consent if not actual law the highest thing in town. Alexander II, his son, was a more tasteful and imaginative artist, trained at the Academy and in Paris in the Beaux Arts tradition, whose chief memorial in Philadelphia is the graceful and conspicuous Swann Memorial Fountain in Logan Circle in the middle of that pseudo-Champs-Élysées, the Benjamin Franklin Parkway. Since the Art Museum at the far end of it is conspicuously decorated by huge abstracts by grandson Alexander III, it is now possible to take in with one sweeping glance all three generations of Calders—at City Hall, Logan Circle, Art Museum. Though Alexander I was born in Scotland, Alexander II lived much of his life away from the city, and Alexander III is definitely a product of Paris in the 1920s, the family roots are unquestionably Philadelphian.[153]

City Hall, on which the first Calder lavished his talents, is par excellence the monument to Philadelphia's Iron Age. Its construction, graft ridden and endlessly delayed, began in 1871 and was not complete until 1894.[154] From the beginning it was considered an insult to Philadelphia taste. Agnes Repplier lets herself go, as of 1898: "Its only claim to distinction should be the marvelous manner in which it combines bulk with sterling insignificance . . . squalid paltriness . . . decorations . . . mediocre or painfully grotesque."[155] For years people of discrimination continued to deplore it, and there was even talk of tearing it down. Sanity, or inertia (often equivalent) prevailed. Now it dominates the grandest of Philadelphia's vistas, Broad and Market Streets, the Benjamin Franklin Parkway, with craggy grandeur. It perfectly expresses the tastes of the industrial and political masters of the Iron Age, and stands to memorialize during the tricentenary the vast industrial might of the city's bicentenary, the age of Cramp and Baldwin, of Quay and Penrose.

Philadelphia's most imaginative architect of the period was Frank Furness.[156] Some of his greater monuments, notably the Broad Street and B.&O. stations, are gone. The lucky preservation of the "new" 1876 Academy of the Fine Arts building, where Eakins began his teaching, the "new" library at the University of Pennsylvania, one of the proudest additions of the Pepper regime, and the First Unitarian Church, where his father was minister, have managed to secure his reputation in modern times. But nearly everything else has vanished. His reputation rests largely on a laying-on of hands: he taught Louis Sullivan, Louis Sullivan taught Frank Lloyd Wright. But the Academy building, beautifully renovated for the 1976 Bicentennial under director Richard Boyle, gives a vivid picture of the riotously innovative fancy of this now

One of fourteen sections of the statue of William Penn awaiting assembly in the courtyard of City Hall, November 1892.

PHILADELPHIA DEPARTMENT OF RECORDS, ARCHIVES DIVISION

(and most recently) famous of Philadelphia's late-nineteenth-century architects. Even twenty years ago he and City Hall were both still in the architectural doghouse.

More respectable during a slightly later turn of the century were the works of the firm of Walter Cope and John Stewardson,[157] who introduced into the life of the universities of the area the refined and archeological "collegiate Gothic" that set the tone of campus building at the University of Pennsylvania, Bryn Mawr, and above all Princeton, for the next half century. Far more than City Hall or Furness, this nostalgic, sensitively historical, dream-world-and-old-world architecture expressed true anglophile "Philadelphia taste" of this time. Now as much despised as City Hall used to be, this style remains at its best an unreproduceable example of esthetically delightful nonfunctionalism and extravagance of craftsmanship that the world can no longer seem to afford. It is as characteristic of the more graceful aspects of life in Philadelphia's Iron Age—and its turning away from all aspects of iron— as the craggy magnificence of City Hall expresses its cruder, material aspects.

Pupils of Furness, pupils of Eakins and Anschutz, went on to dominate

William Penn, *sculpture by Alexander Milne Calder (1847–1923), cast in bronze by the Tacony Iron and Metal Works (1892). Born in Scotland, Calder had studied at the Pennsylvania Academy of the Fine Arts under Thomas Eakins. Hired in 1873 to design and execute the sculptural program for City Hall, his final piece in the project—the twenty-six-ton statue of William Penn holding the charter of Pennsylvania—was raised to the top of the tower in 1894 after a two-year display in the courtyard.*

ON THE FACING PAGE: *Sectional drawing of the clock tower of City Hall. The statue of* William Penn *is thirty-six feet, eight inches tall. The statue of the Indian below is twenty-four feet tall.*

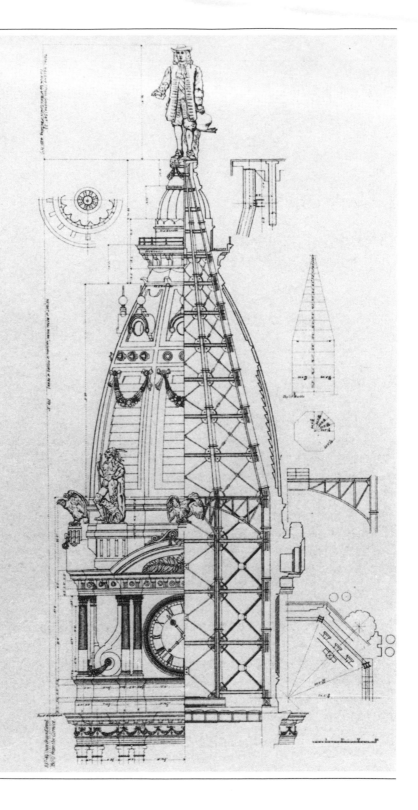

Philadelphia City Hall, Centre (Penn) Square, site preparation and construction 1870–1901, designed by John McArthur, Jr. (1823–1890), photograph 1899. The view, looking toward the southwest, includes corners of the United States Mint at the left and the Pennsylvania Railroad Station at the right.

FREE LIBRARY OF PHILADELPHIA

art and architecture in America, but in another time and in other places. Sullivan's imagination in the Midwest, the eventual triumphs of the painters of the Eight in New York—the talents of five of whom, Robert Henri, John Sloan, William Glackens, George Luks, and Everett Shinn were incubated in Philadelphia and in the Academy—had Philadelphia roots but bloomed elsewhere.[158]

I X

After the death of Whitman, Philadelphia produced or sheltered no iconoclastic Eakins of the word. Philadelphia literature of the time was characterized by accepted writers who were damned forever, it would seem, by one short two-syllable word—"genteel."

This period was probably Philadelphia's climax as a literary center, but its leading writers were unquestionably genteel. Overshadowed by booming New York and decaying Boston, Philadelphia still housed its most important resident writers and its best known and at the same time most indigenous group of talents. Whitman, Boker, Furness, Lea, Mitchell, Repplier, and Wister are names that have (often just) managed to survive. Most of them were friends or acquaintances, though their lives span three distinct generations. They were all in one way or another famous in their day, and famous in Philadelphia.

The high point of this Philadelphia flowering came in the 1880s. It was in 1881 that Walt Whitman, resident in Camden, New Jersey, across the Delaware since 1873, first became really nationally famous and successful—and first really became Philadelphian.[159] A new edition of *Leaves of Grass* was "banned in Boston." Censors there disapproved of it so his timid publishers Osgood and Company discontinued publication. In a blaze of notoriety the publication was transferred to Philadelphia, eventually under the imprint of D. McKay, and by 1882 the Philadelphia publishers sold out 3000 copies of the new edition in one day. From then on until his death in 1892 Whitman was a celebrity, and though his scandalous reputation in Boston horrified most Philadelphians, important individuals in Philadelphia knew him and even befriended him.

George Boker, very much a Philadelphian and his almost exact contemporary,[160] was not one of these friends. They knew of each other, but probably never met. Like Whitman, Boker was essentially a product of the 1850s, but his reputation was also made in the 1880s. In 1882 his poetic drama *Francesca da Rimini* was, like *Leaves of Grass*, an important success. First produced in 1855, it was revived by the famous tragedian Lawrence Barrett and remained a staple of his repertoire until his death in 1891.[161] It was then revived again in 1901–1902 by Otis Skinner (whose acting career had begun in Philadelphia in the late 1870s). Skinner had played the juvenile lead in Barrett's revival.[162] This resurrection of a thirty-year-old play, like the censorship of Whitman's thirty-year-old book of poetry, established Boker's reputation. His other poetic dramas, his nearly 400 sonnets, his ballads and once-famous Civil War poems still remain largely unknown. But as a total contrast and equal counterweight to Whitman—the conservative to Whitman's radical—he still looms as a powerful if still only dimly visible figure in American literary history.

A mutual friend of both Whitman and Boker was the Shakespearean scholar Horace Howard Furness,[163] brother of architect Frank. It was Furness with his sweetness of nature, wit, love of good conversation (despite the impediment of his ear trumpet), and hospitality at his country house Lindenshade who provided the center and cement of the Philadelphia literary group. Whitman referred to him as "friendly," not only personally but professionally —one of the few who were both.[164] Other Philadelphians of the group mixed admiration of the poetry with criticisms of the poet.

Dr. Silas Wier Mitchell[165] also knew everyone in the world of letters, not to mention medicine and society in general. He was the son of a physician with literary tastes, and his real profession was medicine. He was especially famous as a neurologist, and is usually considered one of the American pioneers in the treatment of nervous and psychological disturbances. After he was fifty he took up the career of writing with even more success and profit, and from 1885 when his first long novel *In War Time* appeared—another Philadelphia event of the 1880s—until his last book in 1913, *Westways,* he established himself as one of the country's most popular and esteemed writers of fiction. He was particularly famous for his series of historical novels about Philadelphia, carefully researched, vastly appealing to readers in that time of renewed interest in things colonial. *Hugh Wynne* of 1897 and *The Red City* of 1907, dealing with the eighteenth century in Philadelphia, particularly entranced the public. Nowadays his more psychological *Constance Trescott* and his novelistic essays *Characteristics* (1891) and *Dr. North and His Friends* (1900) seem more alive, particularly the latter two as pictures of the intellectual concerns of the Mitchell-Furness circle and its medical and scientific friendships with people like the world-famous naturalist Joseph Leidy. Mitchell also knew Whitman. Mitchell thought Whitman a monster of egoism and a "poetic tramp."[166] Whitman thought Mitchell blighted by worldliness. They disliked each other's poetry but liked each other personally.[167] Of all the Philadelphia group, the curse of "genteel" has fallen most heavily on Mitchell.

When Henry Charles Lea[168] found the strains of being simultaneously an active publisher, an earnest scholar, and a busy city reformer too much for him, his old friend Dr. Mitchell prescribed a regimen that he followed meticulously the rest of his life, enabling him to keep working into his eighties. He inherited the publishing firm that still bears his name, Lea and Febiger, from his forebears, the Leas (who were Quaker) and the Careys (the first of whom, Mathew, was Catholic). He devoted himself very early to the business, which had evolved from being the foremost general American trade book house of the earlier nineteenth century into a house specializing in medical publications.[169] His role in city affairs as a member of the Committee of One Hundred and an author of the city charter has already been mentioned. He also began to emerge as one of the country's most profound scientific historians.

From his first book in 1866, *Superstitions,* until his last in 1908, *The Inquisition in the Spanish Dependencies,* his works reflected his delvings in depth into the area where religion and law crossed and mingled, usually to their mutual detriment. Again a product of the 1880s, the three-volume *History of the Inquisition in the Middle Ages* first established his national reputation as the foremost expert in this area, and one of the few who, balancing perhaps his Quaker and Catholic inheritances, managed to remain objective in an area where objectivity would seem almost impossible. He insisted on letting the facts, as deduced from contemporary sources, speak for themselves. He became president of the American Historical Association in 1904 and remains the principal authority in his field.

Obviously neither Furness nor Lea has been or ever will be exactly popular. Mitchell's appeal was enormous, but does not seem enduring. The fourth charter member of this group was Agnes Repplier. Furness was her best male friend, Mitchell one of her oldest and best acquaintances.[170] Enormously popular too, and respected in her special field, the witty, reminiscent essay, her appeal would seem to be, and indeed should be, perennial. She belonged, however, to a culture and period of magazines, genteel as could be, like the *Atlantic Monthly* in Boston, *Scribner's, Harper's,* and the *Century* in New York, and *Lippincott's* in Philadelphia, that catered to people of literary tastes and general culture who liked to read about something besides current events. With the disappearance of this kind of magazine and reader, the Repplier sort of essay on lesser woman novelists of the eighteenth century, on tea, and on cats, for all their wit, erudition, and caustically keen observations on human nature, has disappeared too.

No one represented this aspect of American culture better than this plain, direct, commonsensical, appallingly well-read Philadelphia spinster. Fertilized by the enthusiasm of still-bookish Boston and tours of Europe, she yet remained, for all her criticisms, a permanent fixture in Philadelphia. She too took a somewhat dim view of her friend Furness's friend Whitman; but she admired him in spots as a poet, and was agreeably surprised when he spoke so well and so humanly at the Contemporary Club.[171] This organization was one of her favorites and a leading sponsor of thought in the city. Her other friend Henry James did not do as well. When he spoke to the club, no one could hear his mumbling, and the evening was saved only by Repplier's introductory remarks.[172] Eakins offered to paint her, but she refused. Made mortally ashamed of her homeliness by her sadistic mother, she could not bear to have her "character" revealed and recorded by the painter.[173]

Owen Wister[174] came in on the end of this group, as Boker and Whitman had at the beginning. He inherited the friendship of Furness and Mitchell. When, like Lea, the strains of his life were also too much for him—his frustrated desire to be a serious musical composer against his mother's supercilious intellectual condescension and his father's Philistine insistence that he be a lawyer—it was Dr. Mitchell who recommended the cure: a trip west. This again was in the fertile 1880s. He went to Wyoming in 1885 and the rest is literary history. In 1902, just after Mitchell had published *Circumstances* in 1901, Repplier *The Fireside Sphinx* (cats) in the same year, Lea *The Moriscos* and Furness his edition of *Twelfth Night*, Wister's *The Virginian; a Horseman of the Plains* hit the bestseller list. The book created one of America's most durable myths. Along with his friends the artist Frederic Remington, whom he met in Wyoming,[175] and the writer-politician Theodore Roosevelt, whom he met at Harvard, Wister in *The Virginian* converted the American cowboy into a romantic hero. Too genteel for modern tastes in its handling of the rather paper-doll romance with a priggish New England schoolmarm (though this was part of the thrill for readers of the period), the book's authenticity in sketching western character and conversation has seldom been equalled in vividness and accuracy. Like *Uncle Tom's Cabin* and *Gone with the Wind*, it is a classic without benefit of professor—along with the *Autobiography of Benjamin Franklin* the only such classic to come out of Philadelphia so far. (It is also, incidentally, the only novel to be personally edited by a president of the United States while in office. Roosevelt censored a passage as being too brutal, and the passage was altered.)[176]

This genteel literature was supported by those magazines of which *Lippincott's* was the Philadelphia representative. At this time the publishing company of that very Philadelphian name was at its height of success and reputation, taking the place of the earlier Carey and Lea, before it turned medical, as a general trade publisher. Less genteel perhaps but respectable enough and phenomenally popular were the magazines of the Curtis Publishing Company that rose during this period to dominate the field of the popular magazine for half a century, eventually from the Curtis Building on Independence Square. First of the fleet was the *Ladies' Home Journal* of 1883, with Mrs. Curtis, known professionally as Louisa Knapp, as editor. In 1889 a brash Dutch immigrant, Edward W. Bok, became editor, and by somewhat the same combination of piety and push that characterized John Wanamaker he made it the leading woman's magazine of the country.[177] A favorite of the time, Sarah Tyson Rorer, "Queen of Cookery," whose Philadelphia cookbook of 1886 became a standard and whose prolific writings were gospel to American housewives of the period, joined the staff of the *Journal* in 1897. The *Journal's* advice on clothes, food, house decoration, manners, and morals influenced the entire middle-class female populace of the United States.[178] The male population was soon equally influenced by the *Saturday Evening Post*, which Curtis bought in 1897 and which under the dynamic leadership of editor George Horace Lorimer from 1899 on became as powerful and influential as its older sister. The *Post's* success was based on its enticing fiction and its colorful advertising. The magazine, traced back to a semimythical foundation by Benjamin Franklin, was at the point of expiration when Curtis bought it. By 1903 its circulation had risen to 500,000, a triumphal progress that was finally halted by the advent of television after World War II.[179]

X

It was as a seedbed of actors and actresses that Philadelphia was most famous in the world of the theater at this time. The Chestnut Street, Walnut Street, and Arch Street Theatres supplied the city with drama during the nineteenth century, and kept actors and managers busy there until the gradual lure of Broadway took them up north. Joseph Jefferson, the greatest American comic actor of the nineteenth century, had been born in Philadelphia of a family associated with the Chestnut Street Theatre for three generations. But the association of the Drew-Barrymores with the Arch Street was longer lasting and even more famous. When Lionel (1878), Ethel (1879), and John (1887) Barrymore were born in Philadelphia, children of the rapscallion English charmer Maurice Barrymore and his equally charming wife, born Georgiana Drew, the Drews were on their way to becoming nearly as notable in America as the Kembles had been in England. Louisa Lane Drew was the center of the family, the grandmother in whose house the younger Barrymores grew up, the indefatigable manager of the Arch Street and unrivaled interpreter of Mrs. Malaprop in *The Rivals,* often playing in it opposite her old friend Jefferson. Born in England, she had come to America in 1827, and after a long stage career and her third marriage in 1850 to Irish comedian John Drew, she began her association with theater management. By 1861 she was sole manager of the Arch Street. She became a tremendous personage as Grand Old Lady of the American stage. In Philadelphia she managed to defy the conventions of the day which placed actresses only one step above harlots, and became a respected social figure. Her son John Drew, educated to be a perfect Philadelphia gentleman, with no intention of going on the stage, casually strolled into a part in his mother's theater in 1873. *Cool as a Cucumber* was the play, and so was John. His mother blasted him for not taking the stage seriously, and forced him to really work at being a comedian. In 1875 he was ready to go to New York, where from 1879 on, first as a member of the Daly company, he established himself as the essence of the swell—cool as a cucumber, nonchalantly charming, impeccably dressed—a role that he also played in real life, "adept in sports, a sartorial model, a punctilious gentleman." In other words a credit to his Philadelphia education. He went on to stardom on two continents, as well as to membership in the best clubs; he was third president, after Marylander Edwin Booth and Philadelphian Joseph Jefferson, of the prestigious Players Club in New York.[180]

His sister Georgiana, also carefully educated, went to New York as well. She and her husband left their children with Louisa while on tour. Her promising career was cut short by death, while Maurice, never a star, went on to become perpetual leading man to a series of notable actresses. Among them was the Polish Mme. Modjeska, for whom he wrote a Polish play called *Nadjezda.* The play was not overly successful, but was stolen by Sardou to make a vehicle for Bernhardt called *Tosca.* So there is a tenuous bond between Philadelphia, Puccini, and grand opera—one of two such bonds in fact, because *Madama Butterfly* was based on a short story by Philadelphian John Luther Long.[181]

As for the Barrymores, their careers were played out on the stages and sets of Broadway and Hollywood. Ethel, when she returned to Philadelphia on tour, liked to say in her wonderful throaty voice at her curtain calls, "It's good to be home!"[182]

Opera, not orchestral music, dominated the musical life of the city during this period. Nonetheless it was in 1900 that the Philadelphia Orchestra began its comparatively belated existence. It was a descendant of smaller orchestras, notably a Germania which had disbanded in 1895 and a Philadelphia Symphony Orchestra (1893–1900). More significant was the Thunder Orchestra, named not so much for its sound as for the conductor Henry G. Thunder, who played a leading role in the city's musical life at the end of the century.[183] In 1899 the German Fritz Scheel, who had conducted successful summer concerts at Woodside Park, was induced to stay on with promises that a true symphony orchestra would be formed for him. This came into being in 1900, made up mostly of players from the Germania and the Thunder, and played its first concert under Scheel in the Academy of Music on November 16, 1900. A splendid board was built, wealthy people like Alexander Cassatt and Peter Widener were involved, and gradually the orchestra established itself as a civic monument. But it was not until the later days of Stokowski and Ormandy that it built up a truly national reputation, though it played out of town as early as 1902.[184]

Meanwhile opera reached a peak of prosperity and popularity it was never to know again, and the riches of opera in Philadelphia seem astounding opposed to the comparative poverty of today. From 1885 on the Metropolitan began its visits to the Academy of Music, which during more than a decade between 1891 and 1903 occurred weekly during the season. Besides this a local company survived for eight seasons (1888–1896) at its own grand opera house on North Broad. This was the so-called National Opera Company of Gustav Hinrichs, who presented the American premières of *Cavalleria Rusticana* and *Pagliacci*, among others, and all told some 1800 nights of opera during its years of operation.

Light opera had its public too, and local composers and companies and orchestras (like that of Mark Hassler) had their day. None, however, seems to have left any permanent trace.[185] The amateur Savoy company began in 1901 to present annual performances of Gilbert and Sullivan, the first of many such American companies to do so.[186]

X

It was a period when more indigenous and less high-toned amusements also flourished. The paintings of Eakins present a world of masculine sport more smiling than his portraits—bird shooting in the river marshes, sailing on the Delaware, boxing matches in smoke-filled halls, above all rowing on the Schuylkill. This was the time when this very Philadelphian sport began to establish itself among all classes, but particularly at the University of Pennsylvania. The line of boathouses belonging to various rowing clubs still fringes the river, below the acropolis of the Art Museum, with Victorian charm. Some of the clubs were those of gentlemen, others were not.[187]

This reach of the Schuylkill was part of Fairmount Park, and the park was, particularly in this period after the Centennial and before the automobile, the city's playground. Excursion boats, visible in the background of Eakins's rowing pictures,[188] went up the Schuylkill; there were endless bosky nooks for pedestrian picnics, and miles of carriage drives, where four-in-hands like that of Fairman Rogers, patron of Eakins, could bowl along, and where ladies in Victorias could loll as they drove under their parasols, nodding to passing acquaintances.[189] In the winter there was iceskating, and in 1887 William Singerly, editor of the *Philadelphia Record*, provided funds for a public 2200-foot toboggan slide.[190] In summer there were sacred music concerts, and great crowds came out to watch the fireworks on the Fourth of July from the Girard Avenue Bridge.[191] In 1896 Fairmount Park trolleys began to wander through seven miles of parkland, and took passengers to Woodside Park, an amuse-

Boat clubs and excursion boats above the Fairmount dam on the Schuylkill River (c. 1875). The observatory was called Lemon Hill Tower.

ment center opened in 1897 on the western edge of Fairmount.[192] Even automobiles, as early as 1899, were gingerly permitted, though such "horseless pleasure vehicles" were not to frighten the real horses.[193] Another novelty, but not in the park, were the motion pictures. By 1895 at Keith's Bijou, Philadelphia saw its first projected movies.[194]

In 1898 Sigmund Lubin, an optician, began using his "Life Motion Picture Machines and Films" on the roof of the Dime Museum at Ninth and Arch. A year later he built this motion picture theater, one of the first in the United States, on the midway at the National Export Exposition on the west banks of the Schuylkill.

FREE LIBRARY OF PHILADELPHIA

Another famous amusement park, out to the northwest, was Willow Grove, created by Widener and the Union Traction Company as part of the effort to build up trolley traffic to that part of the suburbs. It had a ferris wheel and a scenic railway, but above all wonderful concerts, eventually by bands such as Sousa's and orchestras such as Walter Damrosch's.[195] Bicycles of course were ubiquitous, and the "wheelmen" by 1887 had organized, in typically Philadelphian fashion, into five clubs. The first meeting of the League of American Wheelmen gathered 400 strong in 1883 to inaugurate a new

Gentlemen's Driving Park in Fairmount. Next year a race between a wheel-man and a trotter was a draw. The horse won the first race, the bicycle the second. At the height of the bicycle craze in 1897 professional races were held on a board track at Willow Grove, and 1,314,000 cycles entered Fairmount Park during that year alone.[196]

By the mid-1890s Philadelphia was known as the "best baseball city in the world." Until the demise of the American Association in 1891 the city had two major-league clubs, the Athletics, in the American Association from its begin-ning in 1882, and the Phillies. The Phillies were newcomers, a National League team that had moved from Worcester, Massachusetts, in 1883. The Philadelphia Baseball Park at Broad and Huntington was considered the best place to play. In 1901 the Athletics reappeared as members of a new American League. Next year baseball excitement in the city ran high, culminating on September 29 in a great night parade down Broad Street to welcome home the A's, along with one of Philadelphia's great citizens, their manager Cor-nelius McGillicuddy—Connie Mack—with the league pennant. The Athlet-ics won the pennant again in 1905, but lost their first World Series (the second of the kind ever played) to the New York Giants. The Phillies also seemed on the verge of a championship in 1901, but most of their best players deserted to join the American League. The great Napoleon Lajoie, jumping from the Phillies to the A's, was enjoined by a Pennsylvania court against playing for the new league; thereupon Philadelphia lost him altogether when Connie Mack traded him to Cleveland, and to avoid the court's jurisdiction he simply did not play when his club visited Philadelphia. The Athletics went on to become one of the American League's dominant teams for the next genera-tion, but the Phillies, after their players' defection, lapsed into a half century of almost unbroken futility.[197]

More special during this period was Philadelphian interest in cricket. Not only was it played, but it was also watched. A meeting on the lawns between English millhands from Kensington, collegians from Haverford, and anglo-phile gentlemen resulted in an enthusiasm that brought teams from England and sent Philadelphians there to compete. Philadelphia was the only city in America (Staten Island near New York was another, though lesser center) where British and colonial teams could find a real challenge. Various cricket clubs—Germantown, Belmont, Philadelphia, and Merion—established them-selves as active promoters of this sport. In the great days of cricket a match like that between the Gentlemen of Philadelphia and the Gentlemen of England might bring out as many as 20,000 spectators.[198]

When lawn tennis ousted cricket at the turn of the century, it too became something of a Philadelphia specialty, and from the old cricket clubs emerged national champions like R. Norris Williams and William T. Tilden II.[199] This all took place under the seals, blazers, boaters, and caps of the clubs, the membership of which was duplicated by the roster of the social clubs in town. The best of these town clubs, like the Philadelphia and the Union League, had been founded a good while before, but the Rittenhouse (1888) quickly took its place as what contemporaries called a "junior ultra-swell" organization despite its original unfortunate name of the Social Art Club.[200] Many clubs of special interests were founded at the same time. There were the literary Contemporary Club of 1886, beloved by Agnes Repplier, or the Franklin Inn founded by S. Wier Mitchell in 1902, the Penn Club (1875), or the Browning Society (1894). There were art clubs such as the Sketch Club (1889) and the Art Club (1887). Journalists had their Pen and Pencil (1891) and whist players could join a Hamilton Club (1887). The Manufacturers Club (1887) appealed to businessmen, the Racquet Club (1889) to the well-born athlete. Besides these there were innumerable sporting clubs, fox hunts, ethnic clubs like the German singing societies, patriotic societies, and clubs for such special interests as the Geographical Society of 1897.[201]

Most of these clubs were for men, but part of the rising stir of women's rights expressed itself in the formation not only of women's colleges like Bryn Mawr but of women's clubs. Of these the Acorn (1889) was and remains the most elect, a feminine counterpart of the Philadelphia Club.[202] The New Century (1877), the first women's club founded in Philadelphia, was more active in causes. It was organized to provide women "a forum for the discussion of their interests," and under its founder and first president Sarah C. F. Hallowell the club outgrew its first quarters and built a new clubhouse at Twelfth and Sansom whose architect was the Philadelphia professional Minerva Parker Nichols. The club had a special interest in working women, holding evening classes for them in dressmaking and typesetting, and playing hostess to an Association of Working Women's Societies founded in 1891 which grew to a membership of 4000. Many of the women leaders of the city in the arts (like Emily Sartain, head of the School of Design for Women and an old friend of Eakins) or politics (like Lucretia Blankenburg, woman's suffrage leader and the wife of reform mayor Rudolph) belonged to it.[203] However, Sara Yorke Stevenson, archeologist, lecturer at the university in 1894, and member of the Philosophical Society, was president not of the New Century but of the Acorn Club for twenty-five years.[204]

XI

This proliferation of clubs, old and new, city and country, male and female, was one visible evidence of the cohesive group consciousness, the basically conformist atmosphere that pervaded the city. Philadelphians liked to express themselves not as individuals but in groups: members of something —clubs, teams, societies, families. All these gatherings had their special character and quality, and most of them were subtly graded as to social position and superiority or inferiority. The boat clubs along the Schuylkill had their pecking order; clubs with ethnic or religious flavor like the august Catholic Philopatrian Literary Society or the Jewish Mercantile Club or the black Pyramid Club lent the same kind of distinction to their members, within their special groups, as the Rittenhouse or the Acorn, for all their newness, did to members of "good society."[205] But in general above and beyond anything in Philadelphia was that same good society. Battered and shaken during the earlier half of the century by the rise of Jackson and the fall of Biddle, the crashing advent of industrialism, the disruptions of the Civil War, this society despite the two great depressions regrouped itself in the postwar period, refreshed itself financially at the fountains of industry, and began a slow but sure process of both solidification and absorption that made of the Philadelphia upper class one of the most varied yet cohesive such groups in the country. While New York was being swamped by floods of gold and its mores and manners corrupted by the extravagances of pushing parvenus, while Boston society was becoming increasingly rigid and beleaguered in a city taken over by the despised Irish, the Philadelphians managed to have their cake and eat it too. Socially nowhere were standards supposedly more excruciatingly high, distinctions more carefully made; and yet nowhere was absorption going on at a more steady pace. Since, unlike Boston and New York during the Revolution, or the South during the Civil War, the Philadelphia upper class was never dispossessed or fractured, it could claim a seamless, uninterrupted web of prosperous continuity from the earliest days of the city's founding. At the same time it was always various. Some of the best names like Pepper and Wister were German. Jewish names like Hays or Etting or Phillips or Rosengarten were socially integrated (and religiously absorbed). There were the French Bories and Swedish Stillés and Mortons, the West Indian Danish Markoes, the Catholic Irish Meades and Careys, and of course the bedrock of Welsh and Scots and Scots-Irish and English names.

Segregation and inclusion were both expressed by that multitude of clubs. Not everyone could obviously belong to any one club, and equally obviously some clubs were bound to be thought "better" than others. But on the other hand there were clubs for nearly everyone. Old Philadelphians did not parade down Broad Street in the Mummers Parade, but thousands of South Philadelphians did—and every single one of them belonged to a club. The parades became official in 1901. The Mummers had been strutting unofficially for many years, but had become so numerous and well organized that the city had to recognize them. In 1901 the prizes amounted to $1725. The Elkton Association took first prize in the fancy division; the White Caps took the comic prize.[206]

At another end of the social scale, the Philadelphia Assemblies, at which few Mummers danced, became established in this period as a social ultimate. Begun in 1748, the dances languished in the Jacksonian Era, as the remarks of diarist Sidney George Fisher about sporadic "revivals" make clear. But up to and after 1904 when the Assembly began to hold its dances in the opulent golden ballroom of the new Bellevue-Stratford, when Joseph Widener, son of Peter, was heartbroken because he and his daughter were not asked to it, when couples stayed together because they could not go to the Assembly if they were divorced, when newspapers devoted columns of lush description to the toilettes of those who did go (though reporters were not among those invited), nothing in Philadelphia had become as characteristic, as distinguished, above all as exclusive. But by no means all the names were eighteenth century or even early nineteenth. Eventually, Gowens of the Reading, Scotts and Cassatts of the Railroad, the Drexels and the Harrisons, all of mid-nineteenth-century vintage or later, twirled with longer established Peppers, Wisters, and Newbolds, as well as the inevitable Biddles and Cadwaladers. Girls of new fortune married boys of old fortune (admission was always through the male line), and then the better bred kin of these girls seeped in. It was a perfectly continuous process, but never one that changed the basic Old Philadelphian character of the occasion—which was that of a family party where nearly everyone was slightly related or connected to everyone else and they had all grown up together.[207]

The yachts and private trains and winter castles and summer "cottages" of the Philadelphia rich were just as expensive as those of New York. But they were usually in a quieter key, avoiding the curse of "parvenu ostentation," hidden away on the Main Line or Northeast Harbor in Maine rather than flaunting themselves as on Fifth Avenue or in Newport. Something like the Farmers Club, originally an organization of twelve landed gentlemen who dined each other in rotation at the full of the moon and talked crops, developed in this period into an extravaganza for which directors of the Railroad sent their private trains to bring dozens of New York guests back to the Main Line. Yet it was an extravaganza about which nobody except those involved knew, of which the public never heard.[208] For despite all this wallowing in the luxury of yachts and private trains, this was still a careful world. It paid strict attention to the laws of conformity and convention. Codes of dress and manners and mores, even of sexual morals. Great license was permitted both ladies and gentlemen, everyone had "affairs"; but woe to the person who got caught, who "scared the horses." "Proper" was never, never the proper word for this rich, easygoing, in some ways tolerant world, but "discreet" most certainly was. Cool as a cucumber to anyone they did not know, cordial as a May day to anyone they did, the people of this Philadelphia believed above all in appearances.

Never before or afterward was the position of this upper class more secure or its influence more pervasive. If the 10,000 ten-year-old strikers of the textile workers union or the inhabitants of the "Father, Son, and Holy Ghost" houses did not dance at the Assemblies, or if Messrs. Martin and Durham did not make the Philadelphia Club, there were hundreds of thousands of middle-class Philadelphians at the level of the Reppliers or the Eakinses who looked forward to a better life and saw friends and relations who had attained it. It was not a great empty gap that yawned between rich and poor. It was a vast, spongey, interwoven social medium of infinite gradations. Held together by shared Victorian conventions and the universal solvent of the Republican party, the city as a whole, heart in home, ignored politics, ate good food, and resorted to Fairmount Park, whether on foot, by bicycle, or in a coach-and-four. For all its enormous variety and vitality, the Philadelphia of the period clung to its row-house, morally cautious, materially comfortable homogeneousness. Visitors, whether they thought it drably monotonous or cosily consanguinous—or both, like Henry James—were always struck by this emphasis

The great arch of the Court of Honor on Broad Street at Sansom was electrically illuminated on October 27, 1898, for the Peace Jubilee celebrating the American victory in the short war with Spain. The Union League was prominently festooned and lighted for the occasion.

on uniformity. Nowhere were the rich richer or the poor poorer, but nowhere did they all more seem to be striving toward the same ends: a respectable family, nestled in a respectable house at least as decorously comfortable as the neighbors', whether the house had three or thirty rooms.

The dull finish, the conformity of Philadelphia, oppressive to eager spirits, consoling to staid ones, was somewhat deceptive. The gravy-covered stolidity of the city was pierced by Eakins's scalpel and lit by the architectural fancy of Furness. Cricket and coaching, opera and baseball, the Annuals of the Academy of the Fine Arts, the excitement over archeology at the university, the Mummers Parades and the Assemblies brightened the massive digestive processes of industry and the dreary spoliations of politics with grace notes of amusement, solace, and charm. Philadelphia certainly was never before or afterward so typically, almost obsessively Philadelphian as during the Iron Age. In its own cluttered, obscured, smoke-shrouded way, this was one of Philadelphia's greatest periods.

Progressivism
1905-1919

by Lloyd M. Abernethy

There is a prospect of political regeneration such as I had despaired of seeing.

— HENRY C. LEA

When wrongs so outrageous as the gas lease are thrust at [the Philadelphian], he may rouse for a while, but it is grudgingly in his heart of hearts; and when the party of reform makes mistakes, he jumps at these to cover his retreat into the ranks of acquiescence.

— OWEN WISTER [1]

In the early years of the twentieth century a wanderer about Philadelphia could still find many quiet picturesque streets and quaint eighteenth-century and early nineteenth-century neighborhoods. Orange Street, south of Washington Square, and Summer and Randolph Streets, near Franklin Square, offered a vista of old brick houses with dormer windows and tall chimneys. Along Pine and Spruce Streets stood rows of plain but beautiful old white-shuttered town houses. Beyond the Shackamaxon, brightly painted red and green dwellings made Fishtown a charming storybook village. Three green pumps in Central Place, a gathering place for generations of city dwellers, still served as a source of gossip and water for women of the neighborhood.[2] Similar vestiges of an earlier and simpler life could be discovered in many other parts of the city, but at the same time the Philadelphia landscape was beginning to assume the sights and sounds of a modern metropolis.

The noise of the internal-combustion engine grew from an isolated wheeze, rattle, and bang to a reverberating clatter in the crowded streets of center city within a matter of a few years. In 1905 there were fewer than 500 automobiles registered in the city; by 1918 the number of motor vehicles had grown to more than 100,000.[3] Philadelphians' growing dependence on motor trucks and cars for business and pleasure was acknowledged by writer Christopher Morley in 1919, when he found his view of Market Street "dimmed by the summer haze that is part atmospheric and part gasoline vapor."[4]

Market Street at Twelfth (1909). A few horse-drawn vehicles were still found among the electric trolleys and automobiles at one of the city's busiest intersections. The Reading Terminal with its landmark shed and still-popular market was built in 1891.

FREE LIBRARY OF PHILADELPHIA

Besides air and noise pollution, congestion, traffic safety, and the host of other problems that accompanied the automobile, the city faced the task of building additional and wider streets. Although extensive highway construction was to come for the most part later in the twentieth century, several important boulevards were completed by 1918. In 1914 a seven-mile stretch of the Northeast (Roosevelt) Boulevard was opened, immediately enhancing land values in the northeastern part of the city—greatly to the benefit of political insiders—and leading to rapid residential development there. The Parkway from Broad Street to Fairmount Hill—the subject of debate, delay, and political manipulation for almost a quarter of a century—finally became a reality in 1918. It eventually brought Fairmount Park to the center of the city and became the city's cultural avenue, but it also offered a fast route to Germantown, Overbrook, and Wynnefield, and promoted the movement of center-city families in that direction.[5]

Another modern innovation and an important development for Philadelphia transportation came in 1907 with the opening of the two-mile Market Street Subway, the city's first underground railway. Extending from Fifteenth Street to the Schuylkill River (the section east of Fifteenth to the Delaware River was completed in 1908), it connected with the Market Street Elevated which ran to Sixty-ninth Street in West Philadelphia. The new line made the area beyond Fiftieth Street easily accessible to center city for the first time and transformed it from a country-like environment to a thriving business and residential district within a decade.[6]

In 1908 the opening of the giant Torresdale filtration plant marked a great leap forward in the city's efforts to end the threat of typhoid fever by purifying the water supply. As late as 1906 the yearly toll of typhoid victims in Philadelphia had reached 1063. The Torresdale plant, with a daily capacity of 200 million gallons, was not only the largest in the Philadelphia system but the greatest of its type in the world. It helped cut the number stricken by the fever in half for 1908. By 1915 further expansion of the filtration system and other health measures enabled the city to reduce typhoid deaths to only 109 for the year.[7]

The years between 1900 and 1919 also witnessed a dramatic change in the Philadelphia skyline, as the construction of steel-and-concrete skyscrapers accelerated. The city had been slower than Chicago and New York to accept the advantages of tall buildings, largely because of the prevailing opinion that it had an almost unlimited area in which to expand. Increasing congestion as well as rising land values in center city at the turn of the century gradually forced a change in this attitude. Once begun, high-rise construction proceeded rapidly, and numerous ten- to twenty-story apartment, hotel, and office buildings arose in the downtown area before the 1920s.[8] South Broad Street, in particular, took on an almost canyon-like appearance with its hotel and office buildings. The westward trek of business went on, indicating the foresight of John Wanamaker's early move. Wanamaker's prosperity was confirmed when Pres. William Howard Taft gave the dedication speech for the present main store in 1911.[9]

I

More significant for modern Philadelphia history than the physical and technological changes were perhaps the changes occurring in the population. Between 1901 and 1915 the city experienced its greatest numerical increase for any similar period before or since. The number of inhabitants grew by almost a third—from 1,293,000 to 1,684,000. The proclivity of Philadelphians for large families accounted for part of the increase, but much of it resulted from the flood of immigrants to America before the World War. Between 1905 and 1914 over nine million aliens were admitted to the United States. Although Philadelphia still did not attract the new immigrants from southern and eastern Europe in the same numbers as other cities (it ranked fourth as an entering port behind New York, Boston, and Baltimore), it did feel their impact. The percentage of foreign-born in the city's population rose from 23 percent in 1900 to 25 percent (421,000) in 1910. The percentage of Italians, Russians, Poles, and others of the new immigration in the total foreign-born population increased from 16 to 33 percent, a trend that continued until the European war drastically cut immigration in 1915.[10]

Largely poor, these new Philadelphians usually settled in the shabbiest sections of the central and southern wards along the Delaware River. Joining those who had preceded them, they created ethnic ghettos that offered the security of familiar languages and customs and helped to perpetuate traditional social and religious institutions.[11] All the new arrivals shared the problem of finding housing—any housing—in an area that was already overcrowded. Increasing competition for living space led to more division of dwellings for multifamily use, the erection of back-alley shacks, and a general deterioration of sanitary conditions, particularly in the river wards.[12] Those who lived in them did not soon forget the "vermin-infested matchboxes, boiling in summer, freezing in winter."[13]

One of the largest ethnic communities in the city consisted of the Italians in South Philadelphia. The center of "Little Italy" was the market area in the vicinity of Ninth and Christian Streets, where dozens of shops offered enough cheese, fish, eels, artichokes, Ligurian mushrooms, and rich pastries to satisfy

Percy Street, near Ninth, South Philadelphia (c. 1918).

PHILADELPHIA HOUSING ASSOCIATION PHOTOGRAPH, TEMPLE UNIVERSITY, URBAN ARCHIVES

831 Montrose Street, South Philadelphia (c. 1910). Taken as an example of "poor light and poor ventilation" by the Philadelphia Housing Association.

TEMPLE UNIVERSITY, URBAN ARCHIVES

the most homesick Sicilian. Italian theaters and restaurants between Seventh and Eighth Streets recreated a Neapolitan atmosphere for local residents while providing a continental adventure for visitors.[14] In the early years of the twentieth century Italians from Sicily and southern Italy were drawn to Philadelphia, usually by reports that jobs could easily be found there and by the knowledge that "their people were there." Those already in the city often provided the stimulus for relatives and friends to leave the old country, and sometimes contributed passage money as well. And the newcomers did find jobs, particularly as general laborers in unskilled occupations: construction work, road grading, street cleaning, railway maintenance, and trash collection. It was largely Italian labor that built City Hall, the Reading Terminal, and the Broad and Market Street subways. Skilled Italian workers could also be found among the city's bakers, shoemakers, masons, plasterers, stonecut-

View of Fourth Street on Market Day (c. 1913). Photograph made for the Octavia Hill Association.

TEMPLE UNIVERSITY, URBAN ARCHIVES

ters, waiters, and garment workers. Unlike some immigrants, many of them wanted only to return home as the rich American uncle.[15]

Most of the Russian immigrants to Philadelphia, as well as large numbers of Poles and other eastern Europeans, were Jews. Forced from their homelands by "poverty and pogroms," they came to America as true immigrants. While others had thoughts of returning to Europe, and some did go back, the Jews tended to settle in Philadelphia and remain there.[16] Between 1905 and 1918 their numbers grew from 100,000 to 200,000. Concentrated in South Philadelphia at the turn of the century, the Jewish population soon spread north of Market Street and came to dominate the small-business life of the north-central part of the city. The corner of Marshall and Poplar Streets, where the German Jews who had preceded them once lived, became the hub of a bustling business district that resembled a European shopping bazaar complete with exotic shops and dozens of pushcart vendors. While many Jews were engaged in commerce as peddlers, shopkeepers, and merchants, even more could be found in the skilled occupations for which the city, given the nature of its industry, had exceptional demand. In particular they became preeminent in the "needle trades" (all forms of clothing manufacture), and contributed many shoemakers, carpenters, butchers, coppersmiths, and similar artisans to the city's labor force.[17]

Christian Poles, largely unskilled laborers, found themselves competing

Market Street and Delaware Avenue (c. 1919, photograph from the City Parks Association files). The elevated extension of the Market Street subway toward Frankford is visible at the left.

TEMPLE UNIVERSITY, URBAN ARCHIVES

unsuccessfully with the more numerous and already established Irish and Italian workers for general labor jobs. Consequently many Poles continued to move on to those Pennsylvania regions having more heavy industry than Philadelphia, and thus greater need for unskilled labor.[18]

At the same time that they were competing among themselves for jobs and territory, the new immigrants faced the common problem of overcoming the nativism of the Philadelphia population. They were more "different" than earlier immigrant groups and found acceptance more difficult in the city that was still called "the most American of American cities."[19] Native-born workers, fearful of the loss of jobs to the immigrants, bitterly resented them; industrial employers often paid lower wages to them than to other workers; Anglo-Saxon homeowners generally viewed them with suspicion if not with contempt. One did not have to look beyond the newspapers' classified ads for domestic help—which required that the candidate be "Protestant" as well as "white"—to realize that the roots of intolerance ran deep in the "City of Brotherly Love."[20]

The sharp decline of foreign immigration in 1915 was closely followed by an abrupt increase in black migration to northern cities. Between 1916 and 1918 thousands of blacks left the South to escape crop failures and lynching threats and to seek the better economic opportunities that war work and a labor shortage offered. Before 1916 the black proportion of Philadelphia's population had remained stable at about the 5 percent level. Negroes lived in scattered areas throughout two-thirds of the city, with the heaviest concentration in the south-central part, particularly between Spruce Street and Washington Avenue in the Fourth, Seventh, and Thirtieth Wards, where there was a concentration of domestics.[21]

As a group blacks were generally still poorly paid and relegated to the least desirable jobs, but individual achievements indicated that chances for economic advancement were improving. *The Philadelphia Colored Directory* of 1910 revealed that Negroes were engaged in almost any enterprise to be named, including all the professions. Among those listed were 169 clergymen, 143 musicians, 78 physicians, 16 dentists, and 13 lawyers. One member of the black community, tobacco dealer Richard A. Cooper, served on the city Councils. The first black member of the Pennsylvania state legislature, attorney Harry W. Bass, was elected from Philadelphia in 1910. John T. Gibson established a successful theater for black performers, the Standard, on South Street in the early 1900s. Publisher Christopher James Perry had built the *Philadelphia Tribune* into one of the most prosperous, respected, and influential black newspapers in the country.[22] The first black to win a Rhodes Scholarship was Central High and Harvard graduate Alain LeRoy Locke. After studying abroad, Locke became a teacher at Howard University in 1912 and later received a doctorate from Harvard in 1918. He was to have a long career not only as a philosophy professor at Howard but also as a prominent literary figure who published more than a dozen books on Negro life and culture before his death in 1954.[23]

The northward migration of blacks during the war had a significant impact on Philadelphia. By the early summer of 1917 more than 800 migrants were arriving in the city each week.[24] The *Philadelphia Christian Recorder* (the official organ of the African Methodist Episcopal church and the oldest Negro newspaper in America) published a special migration edition to instruct blacks on how to arrange their affairs in the South upon leaving, how they should comport themselves in the North, and how to find jobs at their destinations.[25] By 1920 the city's black population had grown to 134,000, more than double that of 1900 (63,000).

Although Philadelphia was to escape a repetition of its nineteenth-century racial riots and the disastrous twentieth-century racial wars that occurred in East St. Louis, Chicago, and Washington, D.C., the rapid expansion of the black population led inevitably to increased tension and conflict between the races. The competition for jobs and housing gave rise to bitterness on both sides. Housing, already overburdened because of the new immigrants, became a particularly acute problem for blacks. In one of many such instances, ten Negro families lived in one three-story house in the Thirtieth Ward with only a single bath and toilet for all the residents.[26] Whites, who expected blacks to remain in those parts of the city where they had traditionally lived, resented their movement into other areas. The resentment erupted into violence in July 1918 when a black woman moved into a house at 2936 Ellsworth Street, a white neighborhood. Angry white mobs gathered in the street, stoned the house, and attacked Negroes near the scene. Two days of sporadic rioting and fighting between the two races followed, resulting in the deaths of two whites and one black.[27] Peace was gradually restored, but the tensions and resentments lingered on.

As new immigrants and blacks moved into the central and eastern sections of the city, older residents moved to the west and northwest. Grown more affluent, many German, Scots-Irish, and Irish families sought the less congested areas of Germantown and Chestnut Hill. Others, especially the Irish, followed the new subway and elevated line into West Philadelphia. By 1912 it was estimated that one quarter of the city's population lived beyond the Schuylkill River.[28]

The suburbs continued to be the domain largely of the rich. As Christopher Morley observed, Philadelphia was a "large town at the confluence of the Biddle and Drexel families . . . surrounded by cricket teams, fox hunters, beagle packs, and the Pennsylvania railroad."[29] Gentlemen executives of inherited wealth or established families built homes and lived on the Main Line to the west of the city. Those who had risen from the ranks to great fortunes —Wanamaker, Stetson, Breyer, Elkins, Widener—constructed huge mansions along Old York Road in Montgomery County. A recent example of the latter was Lynnewood Hall in Elkins Park—a vast 110-room structure completed for traction magnate Peter A. B. Widener in 1908.[30] Yet an increasing number of middle-class families were also attracted to the suburbs; they led the way for the mass movement to little towns along the Reading and Pennsylvania Railroads that followed in the 1920s. By the First World War more than 500,000 people lived in the three Pennsylvania counties—Bucks, Montgomery, and Delaware—bordering Philadelphia.[31]

II

After the depression of the 1890s, the first two decades of the twentieth century brought prosperity to the nation and to Philadelphia. A brief business dip in 1907 and a potentially serious decline in 1914—abruptly halted by the European war—were the only exceptions to the expansion of the economy. Philadelphia banks, with accumulating surpluses, found themselves especially prosperous. Several new banks were established, but because of the general trend toward consolidation the number of national banks in the city actually declined. The largest banking merger thus far in Philadelphia history came in 1918 when the Philadelphia National—the city's biggest bank—purchased the Farmers' and Mechanics' National.[32] In 1914 Philadelphia became the home of the Third District Bank of the new Federal Reserve System.

As an industrial area Philadelphia ranked third in the number of its wage earners and the value of its manufactures in the early twentieth century. The census of 1910 revealed that the city had 251,900 industrial workers who produced goods valued at $746 million. The textile industry—including woolens, hosiery, clothing, and carpets—remained by far the largest and most productive enterprise. The food and food products industry (sugar refining, meat processing, bakery and confectionary goods, et al.) ranked second in value, followed by printing and publishing, metal products, and leather goods. The variety of its manufactured products was still among the city's chief economic distinctions, and prompted the Chamber of Commerce to claim the title of "Workshop of the World" for Philadelphia.[33]

Although the city continued to be the nation's leading hat and carpet manufacturer, and some industries (notably ready-made clothing) showed rapid growth after the turn of the century, there was an ominous decline in the rate of industrial growth. Philadelphia found itself lagging behind national growth averages, largely because many mass-production industries moved to more central locations for national distribution or to areas with a cheaper labor force. The cotton goods industry, for example, suffered a steady decline after 1900 as new factories appeared in the South. Between 1909 and 1919 Pennsylvania state production decreased 31 percent, with Philadelphia bearing the brunt of the loss.[34] New industries appeared of course, but they were not able to offset the decline in the growth rate. The Autocar Company began manufacturing short-wheelbase trucks in 1908. The first company to manufacture rayon in the United States, the American Viscose Company, was organized in Philadelphia in 1910 and built its first factory at Marcus Hook in 1911. The Sun Shipbuilding and Dry Dock Company, incorporated in 1916, launched its first ship in October 1917.[35]

Important changes in business organization and marketing techniques occurred as Philadelphia kept pace with national patterns. Local manufacturing, like banking, followed the trend toward consolidation. In one example, the hazards of competition brought a number of carpet manufacturers together to form the Hardwick and Magee Company in 1910. The continuing growth and success of the retail chain store idea led to the emergence of numerous chains in the Delaware Valley, such as the American Stores Company, organized in April 1917. Another phenomenon of the early twentieth century was the evolution of localized pushcart businesses or small shops into large commercial enterprises. Originally a hand-freezer operation, ice cream became big business with the reorganization of the Breyer Ice Cream Company in 1908; by 1914 it was selling over a million gallons each year, adding new luster to the city's reputation for high-quality ice cream. A similar development occurred in the baking industry, as illustrated by the movement from community bakeshops to big companies like the Freihofer Baking Company.[36] The growth of the handmaiden of commerce, advertising, into a big business itself was acknowledged by the founding of the Poor Richard Club in 1906. A professional-social organization for "men who buy, sell, or make advertising," it was to become a widely known Philadelphia institution.[37]

The first decades of the twentieth century witnessed a vast expansion of the opportunities for and variety of popular entertainment. Vaudeville, in its heyday, offered such stars as Lillian Russell, George M. Cohan, Mae West, McIntyre and Heath, and Philadelphia's own W. C. Fields, most of whom appeared at some time on the stages of the two main vaudeville houses in the city, Nixon's Grand at Broad Street and Montgomery Avenue or B. F. Keith's at Chestnut and Eleventh Streets. Vaudeville's chief competition, the movies, became increasingly elaborate and prosperous. At the East Market Street Theater or one of a dozen other new and large motion picture houses the moviegoer might see Mary Pickford's latest film or one of Mack Sennett's two-reel comedies. Connoisseurs of the can-can choruses and daring dancers with the seven veils could find burlesque at the Casino or Trocadero. Those seeking more family-type entertainment packed shoebox lunches and took the northwest trolleys out to the Willow Grove Amusement Park.[38] Still another diversion became accessible to the average man when Philadelphia's first public golf links opened at Cobbs Creek in May 1916.

Baseball fans had more to cheer about than at any other time in the city's history—the years from 1910 to 1915 brought a succession of championships to one or the other of the two local teams. The Athletics, who had won their first American League pennants in 1902 and 1905, took the title again in 1910, 1911, 1913, and 1914 behind such stars as "Home Run" Baker, "Chief" Bender, Eddie Plank, and Eddie Collins. They won the World Series in 1910, 1911, and 1913. The Phillies, with a roster including future Hall of Fame pitchers Grover Cleveland Alexander and Eppa Rixey, and the home-run hitter Clifford "Gavvy" Cravath, emerged briefly from obscurity to win the National League championship in 1915.

The opening of Shibe Park in April 1909 gave the Athletics the most modern baseball stadium in America. Accommodating 30,000 spectators, it was the first of the great concrete-and-steel arenas that were indispensable in the transformation of a boys' game into a big business. The more penurious Phillies—one of the National League's less well-financed teams—remained content with old-fashioned wooden fences and seats at the Baker Bowl, which had a capacity of 18,800.[39] Even the increasingly shabby Baker Bowl, however, helped give Philadelphia leadership in the accessibility of its ballparks to public transportation. Shibe Park, at the northeast corner of Twenty-first Street and Lehigh Avenue, and the Baker Bowl, on the southwest corner of Broad and Lehigh, were both close to the convergence of the Pennsylvania and Reading Railroad lines and their North Philadelphia stations, as well as to trolley lines.

I V

Commentators on Philadelphia in the early years of the twentieth century seemed to be less impressed with the changes taking place than with the lack of changes. To most of them the city remained conservative, contented, and dull; they elaborated again and again on Lincoln Steffens's "corrupt and contented" theme. After his visit in 1906 novelist Henry James described Philadelphia as "the American city of the large type, that didn't bristle . . . settled and confirmed and content."[40] Ten years later the same characteristics impressed a writer for *Harper's Magazine*. "The one thing unforgiveable in Philadelphia is to be new, to be different from what has been," he explained. "The Philadelphian likes to know what to expect, novelty disturbs his contentment, ruffles him."[41]

Local observers voiced many of the same criticisms heard from outsiders. Essayist Agnes Repplier called her hometown "a droll city. . . . And tepid. Oh, so tepid."[42] Owen Wister wrote in 1907: "Well-to-do, at ease, with no wish but to be left undisturbed, the Philadelphian shrinks from revolt."[43] Baldwin Locomotive executive George Burnham, Jr., blamed the "natural conservatism of our people" for the failure of reform movements in the city.[44] Philadelphia's millionaires were considered to be more conservative and cautious than those of New York and other cities. "At their root [of Philadelphia fortunes] lie toil, thrift, and caution, and in these three things are their permanency. Seasoned millions are the best rebuke to speculation and hazard. It pays to be conservative."[45]

The rather commonplace view that Philadelphia had become complacent and unexciting had a more substantial basis than the standard jokes about the dullness of the city to which Philadelphians have grown accustomed. Apparently Franklin's town had lost much of the enterprising spirit and innovative characteristics of its earlier years. Even one of the city's biggest boosters inadvertently provided evidence for this conclusion. In 1926 journalist George Morgan published a collection of fragments of Philadelphia history entitled *The City of Firsts*. The book included a list of hundreds of achievements in which the city had been a pioneer. Of all the "firsts," only three (the first automatic restaurant, 1902; the invention of fused bifocal eyeglasses, 1906; and the first newspaper advertising campaign for church attendance, 1913) were credited to the first quarter of the twentieth century.[46] Compared to the number and significance of the achievements of former years they were hardly a testament to unusual enterprise or imagination.

Philadelphia's diminishing role in the cultural leadership of the nation offered further confirmation of a loss of vitality. The source of many of America's most illustrious writers, artists, and actors in the nineteenth century, the city could claim few such in the early twentieth century. The generation of writers that had dominated Philadelphia letters *fin de siècle* came to an end in the years before the war. Henry C. Lea died in 1909, Horace Howard Furness in 1912, S. Weir Mitchell in 1914. Owen Wister, who won literary fame with *The Virginian* in 1902, wrote little of significance after his second successful novel, *Lady Baltimore*, appeared in 1906. Only Agnes Repplier continued to uphold the city's literary tradition with her bookish, witty, and often personal essays on history, war, Catholicism, and numerous other subjects.[47] Other Philadelphia-born writers of prominence left the city to find success elsewhere. Richard Harding Davis—novelist, playwright, reporter, world traveler, and the most famous war correspondent of his day—spent most of his creative years in New York. James Gibbons Huneker, an internationally famous essayist and music critic, also made his reputation writing for New York newspapers.[48]

Many Philadelphia-trained artists similarly left the city to find careers elsewhere. The rebellious painters known as "The Eight" or the "Ashcan School," the five of them trained at the Pennsylvania Academy of the Fine Arts having already departed Philadelphia before this period, sponsored the famous International Exhibition of Modern Art (the Armory Show) in New York in 1913. There they introduced European postimpressionist, cubist, and abstractionist artists to the United States. The Philadelphia art establishment refused to embrace the modern movement represented by the show, thus causing a further decline in the city's artistic reputation.[49] One artist who fled from Philadelphia, George Biddle, later explained the reasons for the mass exodus of his colleagues from the city: "Philadelphia has its own brand of integrity. It believes in itself; although there is nothing much any longer worth believing in. It respects its own standards, although these standards are inconceivably shallow and antedate in great measure the birth of our nation."[50]

The professional theater in Philadelphia also declined partly because of the more cosmopolitan allure of New York. Compared to its golden years in the middle of the nineteenth century when the productions of numerous local companies occupied the stages of the Chestnut Street, the Walnut Street, the Arch Street, and other theaters, the legitimate theater had virtually disappeared by 1915 save for New York road companies and try-out productions. Some of the void in the theatrical bill of fare was filled by the emergence of Little Theater groups. The first such group, called "Plays and Players," was organized by Mrs. Otis Skinner in 1911. It was followed by dozens of others to become an important characteristic of theater life in the city.[51]

Aside from the Barrymores—Ethel, Lionel, and John—who were becoming established performers in the prewar years, few new talents emerged from Philadelphia. Of the ten locally born actors and actresses listed in the *World Almanac* in 1916, the youngest (besides Ethel Barrymore, who was thirty-six) was forty-two and the average age was sixty.[52]

Local opera productions suffered a fate similar to that of the theater, despite the efforts of impresario Oscar Hammerstein. Determined to provide Philadelphia with a new resident opera company, Hammerstein opened the Metropolitan Opera House at Broad and Poplar Streets in 1908. The building was well equipped and elaborately appointed, including a giant stage and seating for more than 4000. With many of the world's leading singers in starring roles, Hammerstein presented four operas each week over a twenty-week season. Despite many outstanding performances, however, the venture did not win sufficient support from the public for financial success and Hammerstein was forced to cease production after the 1910 season. Apparently the new house was located too far from center city for operagoers; they preferred the competing touring company of the New York Metropolitan Opera which performed at the more accessible Academy of Music.[53]

Philadelphia usually reacted to departures from its cultural standards by ignoring or refusing to support them, but occasionally its citizens actively and openly demonstrated their conservative approach to the arts. In February 1909 Catholic and Protestant clergymen became excited about the reported "indecency" of the Oscar Wilde–Richard Strauss opera *Salomé* and led a week-long protest against Hammerstein's scheduled production of it. Although the great soprano Mary Garden in the title role attracted many opera-lovers, the size of the record-breaking audience was probably due to the publicity given by the protest. Afterward, members of the audience admitted that they had found nothing indecent in the opera and wondered what all the "fuss" had been about.[54] Edmond Rostand's play about Christ, *La Samaritaine*, created an even greater stir in February 1911 and fared less well. Long before opening night for Sarah Bernhardt and Company at the Broad Street Theater, Philadelphia ministers had charged that the play was sacrilegious. When Republican politicians joined in the outcry and 175 members of what one newspaper called "the exclusive social set" signed a petition to ban the play, Mayor John E. Reyburn succumbed to the pressure and issued an order prohibiting the production.[55]

The generally floundering condition of the arts in Philadelphia during the first two decades of the twentieth century had one bright exception—the beginning of the rise to international fame of the Philadelphia Orchestra. The orchestra was never considered more than "adequate" or "respectable" under the batons of its first two conductors, Fritz Scheel and Carl Pohlig. The building of its reputation began when a young Pole, Leopold Stokowski, arrived to take command in 1912. A glamorous figure personally, Stokowski combined a Spartan discipline with a highly individualistic style and a flair for innovation to create a virtuoso orchestra and launch the modern musical position of the city. It is probable that tradition-directed Philadelphians failed to appreciate much of the unconventional music of modern composers favored by Stokowski, but the city was so enraptured by his style and personality that it accepted his programming willingly, at least in the early years. Perhaps his most flamboyant performance came in 1916, when he put more than 1000 musicians and singers on the stage in the American première of Gustav Mahler's Eighth Symphony.[56]

V

Along with its notoriety for conservatism and dullness, Philadelphia carried a reputation for political corruption into the twentieth century as well. Articles on "election frauds," "political bandits," the "Republican Tammany," and the "sad story of Philadelphia" appeared with embarrassing frequency in national periodicals.[57] In his famous investigation of municipal

Leopold Stokowski and the Philadelphia Orchestra (c. 1918). Stokowski (1882–1977) resigned in 1938 after leading the orchestra for twenty-six years.

corruption for *McClure's Magazine* in 1903, Lincoln Steffens found that "Other American cities, no matter how bad their own condition may be, all point to Philadelphia as worse—'the worst-governed city in the country.' "[58]

Whether Philadelphia deserved the ignominious trophy for "worst" or not, there is little doubt that graft, fraud, and mismanagement abounded throughout city government. The Republican "Organization," led by State Insurance Commissioner Israel Durham, had developed the manipulation of public jobs and contracts for self-serving purposes to a level envied by other urban machines. The 10,000 offices at the disposal of the organization were distributed only to loyal supporters who were expected to confirm their allegiance by returning part of their salaries to the machine.[59] Each employee was assessed according to a fixed schedule, which ranged from 3 to 12 percent of his annual salary depending on his income bracket. In 1903, for example, 94 percent of all city employees paid more than $349,000 into the funds of the Republican organization.[60]

Further profits and friends for the Durham machine came through the letting of contracts for maintenance and construction and the distribution of public franchises. A member of the Common Council estimated that $5 million was wasted in the city each year because of graft in the contracts for filtration, street paving, garbage removal, sewage disposal, and public lighting.[61] Municipal franchise awards went to favored "grabbers" with scant regard for revenue losses to the city.[62]

With the view that nothing should be left to chance, the organization made outright manipulation of elections a common practice. Ballot boxes were stuffed by ambitious ward leaders, votes were purchased for as little as twenty-five cents or a drink of whiskey, and voting lists were padded with phantom voters.[63] In one instance the Republican City Committee attempted to purchase poll tax receipts for a list of 30,000 names of which more than 27,000 later proved to be fraudulent.[64] In the electoral process, as in most other aspects of city government, corruption was more the rule than the exception.

Other than the beneficiaries of the organization's favors, most Philadelphians acquiesced in its rule largely because of a long-established loyalty to the Republican party and a mood of resignation about the inevitability of political corruption in modern urban life. The city's Democratic party, saddled with the national party's reputation for tariff revisionism and "Bryanism," and a local leadership rumored to be in the employ of the Republican organization, seldom offered a serious challenge to the machine. Consequently, significant opposition depended on the independent movements organized by good-government advocates from time to time and their success in attracting large numbers of Republican voters.[65]

In the early years of the twentieth century the nationwide trend toward municipal reform brought renewed hope to Philadelphia reformers. Encouraged by the progressive achievements of cities like Toledo, San Francisco, New York, and Cleveland, the leaders of the Municipal League launched a new attack on local corruption in the fall of 1904. At several mass meetings of business and professional men, presided over by publisher John C. Winston and physician John B. Roberts, a new organization—the Committee of Seventy—was created to war against election abuses and municipal mismanagement.[66] The *North American*, which had become the city's most zealous reform newspaper under the editorship of Tioga County native Edwin Van Valkenburg, optimistically called it "the most logical and inherently the most powerful [reform movement] that has yet been opposed to the confederation of evil that rules the city."[67]

In its first challenge to the organization, the Committee of Seventy entered a slate of candidates under the City party label in the election for magistrates and councilmen in February 1905. Despite endorsements from religious leaders and many distinguished citizens, as well as daily exposés of municipal corruption by the *North American*, the antimachine candidates were defeated. Yet the publicity given to the corruption abounding in City Hall by the reform campaign seemed to shake the complacency of Philadelphians for the first time in many years. In the wake of the election, religious and civic organizations held dozens of mass meetings to protest the "evils" in city government.[68] Laying sectarian differences aside temporarily, clergymen united to hold a series of prayer meetings for Mayor John Weaver, urging him to join the campaign for civic virtue. "There is a considerable turmoil made by the clergy," historian-reformer Henry C. Lea wrote to a friend, "who . . . are banging away at Mayor Weaver. . . . Next to the Russian Czar he is the most unfortunate ruler in Christendom."[69] Other observers reinforced the view that the first three months of 1905 had given rise to a significant escalation of concern for public affairs.[70] It is likely, though, that the reforming sentiment which had proved fickle so often in the past would have gradually faded away if Iz Durham and the organization had not ignored the charged atmosphere and selected this time to attempt one of their most notorious steals.

In the early spring of 1905 Durham was in failing health and anticipated retiring from active politics in the near future. Before stepping aside, however, he wanted to make provision for his own future needs and also reward faithful supporters of the organization. To do so, he and his friend Thomas Dolan devised a scheme to cancel the existing short-term lease of the municipal gasworks and give a new seventy-five-year lease to the United Gas Improvement Company headed by Dolan. Under the new terms, U.G.I. would pay the city $25 million over a period of three years in lieu of the annual rentals ($655,000 in 1904) which had been customary in the past. The bulk payments would provide a handsome kitty with which to award municipal contracts to firms associated with Durham and his friends. At the same time U.G.I. would be paying only a fraction of the value of the old lease. Since he had the city Councils in his pocket, Durham had little reason to doubt the success of his plan.[71]

On April 20 the Select Council set the stage for the new lease by passing a resolution citing the urgent needs of the city for large sums to carry out important public works recently undertaken and authorizing the Finance

Committee to "confer with the United Gas Improvement Company with the purpose of ascertaining whether the yearly payments the city now received under the gas lease can be anticipated."[72] Despite a protest from the Committee of Seventy that other syndicates should be allowed to bid against U.G.I. to get better terms for the city, the Finance Committee moved swiftly and introduced a bill implementing Durham's plan on April 27.[73]

As the nature of the gas steal became evident, a surprising wave of indignation spread throughout the city. The *North American,* the *Press,* and the *Public Ledger* devoted the bulk of their front pages to criticisms of the proposal, deploring the enormous loss of revenue to the city and the exorbitant profits (estimated at $884,572,000) for U.G.I. that would result from the new lease.[74] Hundreds of letters from angry Philadelphians protesting the "grab" poured in upon city councilmen. On the evening of May 3 nearly 5000 citizens gathered at the Academy of Music in a massive demonstration against the plan. There they heard a host of prominent Philadelphians, including editor Charles Emory Smith of the *Press,* John H. Converse of the Baldwin Locomotive Works, ex-minister to Italy William Potter, and merchant-reformer Rudolph Blankenburg, attack the gas crime and urge Mayor Weaver to join the fight against it.[75]

Impressed by the public outcry, Weaver responded the next day by issuing a statement that announced his opposition to the new lease and also expressed his dissent from the Council's argument that the city urgently needed large sums of additional money for current projects. The same day, the beleaguered Select Council acknowledged the public protest and Weaver's stand by directing the Finance Committee to advertise for additional bids on the lease of the gasworks, although it tempered its concession with the requirement that new bids had to be submitted within eleven days.[76]

When the bidding deadline arrived on May 15, the Finance Committee found a second bid had been submitted by the banking firm of E. B. Smith and Company in collaboration with attorney-banker George Norris and the *North American.* The Smith plan would pay the municipality an annual rent of $1,250,000, plus one-third of the profits for the first ten years and two-thirds thereafter, or in lieu of a share of the profits the city could have the option of reducing the price of gas to consumers. Furthermore, if the city needed and desired large sums immediately, the syndicate would advance $25 million, reimbursing itself from the annual payments. Despite the obvious advantages to the city of the new bid, the Councils rejected it in favor of the U.G.I. plan in an open session on May 18, much to the displeasure of the overflowing gallery.[77]

Mayor Weaver immediately announced that he would veto the gas bill although it was acknowledged that the Councils very likely would override his veto. A new wave of public protest, however, prevented the expected confrontation between the mayor and the Councils from taking place. Angry crowds gathered at numerous rallying points, paraded through the streets, and appeared menacingly before the houses of councilmen, compelling several to flee out their back doors.[78] Their will weakened by the ferocity of public indignation, many councilmen, as Henry C. Lea observed, "ran for cover"— they abandoned the U.G.I. to support the mayor.[79] By the end of the month even Durham was ready to concede that it would be inexpedient to jam such an unpopular measure through the Councils at that time. On June 1, the city Councils officially withdrew the U.G.I. ordinance from further consideration.

The defeat of the organization on the gas issue convinced many Philadelphia reformers that the day of deliverance from municipal corruption was near. "There is a prospect of political regeneration such as I had despaired of seeing," wrote Henry C. Lea.[80] While this prospect rose and fell dramatically over the next decade, the struggle between reformers and the machine largely describes Philadelphia politics until the World War. It was also the time during which Republicans continually faced the dilemma of choosing between loyalty to their party and the appeal of organized independent movements opposed to the Republican organization.

In the aftermath of the gas war, the prevailing view among reform leaders, including Winston, Van Valkenburg, and attorney William C. Bullitt, as to the most effective way to continue the fight for permanent political changes was to unite sympathizers from all groups into one independent organization, namely, the City party.[81] Mayor Weaver, who had not only come to enjoy his sudden fame as a reformer but also realized that his future within the organization was bleak after defying Durham, gave a boost to the independent movement when he committed himself to the City party in early summer and asked municipal employees to do likewise.[82] Further support came from the Democratic City Committee when it endorsed the City party ticket in the fall campaign for Philadelphia County offices.[83]

Meanwhile the insurgents had extended their attack to include the state Republican machine led by Sen. Boies Penrose, a close ally of Durham's. Independent Republicans throughout the state were particularly incensed by Penrose's choice of a candidate for state treasurer in 1905. State legislator J. Lee Plummer, known as "Penrose's Messenger Boy" for his services to the machine, presented a sharp contrast to the highly regarded and popular Democratic candidate, William H. Berry, the former mayor of Chester.[84]

On September 11, 1905, independent leaders from forty of Pennsylvania's sixty-seven counties met with local reformers in Philadelphia and organized the Lincoln party to fight "the criminal and corrupt combination masquerading as Republicans" led by Penrose. They adopted a platform demanding election reforms, the direct primary for nominating candidates, personal registration of voters, and the repeal of the Philadelphia Ripper Bill.[85] (The latter measure, enacted by the legislature at Durham's instigation during the height of the gas war, transferred the power to appoint the director of public works and the director of public safety from the mayor to city Councils where, presumably, the choices could more easily be dictated by the organization.) Although almost wholly Republican, the Lincoln convention agreed with the *North American* that no real Republican would prefer "a Republican thief for a cashier to an honest Democrat" and nominated Berry for state treasurer.[86]

Despite the opposition's appeals for party loyalty and warnings that victory for the insurgents would mean "the disorganization of Republicanism" and "the destruction of American institutions," the Lincoln-City party campaign gained momentum as Election Day approached.[87] None of the organization's stratagems could overcome the main strengths of the independent coalition: the lingering resentment toward the machine from the gas war; the support of the Weaver administration; enthusiastic promotion by most of the city's newspapers; and the dedication of hundreds of volunteer workers. The result on election night was, as one G.O.P. leader observed, "the worst defeat sustained by the Organization in its entire history."[88] Not only did the local reform ticket win in Philadelphia, but Berry captured the treasurership by 87,000 votes, thanks principally to the 94,000 Lincoln party votes cast for him in the city. It was a remarkable exhibition of independence on the part of Republican voters, and even those not wholly caught up in the enthusiasm of the reformers wondered if the era of submission to machine politics was coming to an end.[89]

The most enduring consequences of the reform upheaval of 1905 came a few months after the election as a result of the special session of the state legislature in early 1906. Although Philadelphia reformers had sought a special session since mid-1905, Penrose had opposed it before the election when he thought that the Republican ticket would "be elected by a substantial majority."[90] Once the returns had proved him wrong, he quickly reversed his position and attempted to woo the insurgents back to the party with the promise, as made to William C. Bullitt of the City party, to "have a special session of the legislature called, and your legislation passed."[91]

The thirty-day session, ending in mid-February 1906, produced a long list of political reforms, many of them sought for years by Philadelphia progressives. The most important measure provided for the personal registration of voters, which put an end to the old and usually fraudulent preparation of voting lists by boss-controlled assessors. Other significant achievements included a uniform system of primary elections for all candidates for city and county offices; a stricter civil service code to prohibit political activity by city employees; a corrupt practices act requiring candidates to file reports of campaign receipts and expenditures; and the repeal of the Ripper Bill of 1905.[92] Of course the enactment of the new laws did not guarantee that they would be administered as intended. The primary bill did not end boss-controlled nominations, and the civil service code and corrupt practices act were poorly enforced or virtually ignored by local officials. But despite later failures of implementation, the fact that the reformers had gotten such measures through the legislature was a remarkable and unprecedented achievement itself.

V I

Interest in reform on the part of Philadelphians noticeably and characteristically waned following the special session. Content with what had been

achieved, they apparently agreed with the numerous local and national observers who concluded that political rights had been secured by adequate
legislation in a return to government by the people.[93] Frustrated insurgent
leaders struggled vainly to maintain a sense of urgency about civic affairs and
also deal with the numerous debilitating problems within the reform inner
circles.[94] Of these, the most serious was the growing estrangement of Mayor
Weaver and his ultimate defection back to the organization.

Weaver's disillusionment with the independents began when he lost his
bid for the Lincoln party nomination for governor in the May 1906 convention to Lewis Emery, Jr., former state senator from McKean County. In
September the mayor's coolness turned to open hostility after his personal
friend Frederick Shoyer was passed over for the City party nomination for
district attorney in favor of attorney Clarence Gibboney, head of the vice-
hunting Law and Order Society. All subsequent efforts for reconciliation
failed; on November 2 Weaver publicly declared his support for the organization's ticket and intention to return to the Republican party. Both Emery and
Gibboney lost the election as many independent Republicans were lured back
to party regularity by gubernatorial candidate Edwin S. Stuart, the highly
esteemed former mayor of Philadelphia.[95]

During the next three years Philadelphia reformers had little to cheer
about. In 1907 they ran the distinguished former minister to Italy William
Potter for mayor, but saw him easily defeated by the organization's confident
campaign for Cong. John E. Reyburn. Thereafter desertions back to the
Republican party accelerated, particularly as the presidential election of 1908
approached and tugged at traditional loyalties.[96] Even so famous a Philadelphian as novelist Owen Wister could not attract a winning vote in his bid for
a councilman's seat on the reform ticket in the municipal election of 1908. In
the fall campaign Clarence Gibboney stumped energetically for sheriff but
could not withstand the overwhelming vote for William Howard Taft which
swept all local Republican candidates into office. The next year perennial
candidate Gibboney almost won the G.O.P. nomination for district attorney
because of public resentment toward the organization arising from a poorly
handled transit strike. But after losing the primary by only 400 votes, he ran
in the general election as the reform-Democratic candidate and finished second to incumbent Samuel Rotan by the substantially bigger margin of 45,000
votes.[97]

Temporarily thwarted politically by defections and the erosion of popular
support, reform leaders turned their attention to a less partisan approach to
the city's governmental problems. In 1908 they established a Bureau of Municipal Research, modeled after that of New York City, "to promote efficient and
scientific management of municipal business." Governed by a board of trustees headed by physician George Woodward, and financed by the voluntary
contributions of more than a hundred businessmen, the bureau sought to
improve the technical aspects of city administration rather than the political.[98]
Through investigations conducted by a staff of specialists it accumulated

masses of data on many specific problems, published numerous booklets on its findings, and made detailed recommendations to the city government. The bureau's most successful early investigation found that, based on purchases made and tested by its staff, most goods sold in the city were of inaccurate weight or measure. Concluding that an official system of regulation and inspection to enforce existing laws was needed, the bureau's recommendations led to the creation of a Bureau of Weights and Measures in 1913.[99] The Bureau of Municipal Research proved to become a lasting and important fixture in the city; its emphasis on technical efficiency placed it thoroughly in accord with the spirit of the Progressive Era.

Meanwhile a new set of political bosses had emerged with Reyburn's victory. Iz Durham finally made good his desire to retire and left the management of the organization to state Sen. James P. McNichol, a genial Irish Catholic who headed a large construction firm that had counted the city as its biggest customer since 1893.[100] "Sunny Jim," however, never really controlled more than the northern half of the city. In South Philadelphia the three Vare brothers—George, Edwin, and William, who had also built a huge contracting company on municipal business—had already united the leaders of the populous wards below South Street into an organization of their own. While each faction viewed the other with suspicion, both defended the organization against outside opposition, and they usually limited their rivalry to municipal contracts and other spoils. In the absence of a single local com-

Boies Penrose (1860–1921), 1919.
HISTORICAL SOCIETY OF PENNSYLVANIA

mander-in-chief, Senator Penrose assumed more direction over Philadelphia politics.[101]

After Weaver's brief fling with reform, the Reyburn administration marked a return to the moral bankruptcy and immunity to the public interest of the past. The new personal registration law did place some restraints on the wholesale padding of voting lists, but other reforms had little effect. Civil service regulations were virtually ignored by the mayor-appointed commission. Political assessment of officeholders continued in increased amounts; between 1907 and 1911 over $2 million went from the salaries of public employees to the Republican party treasury.[102] Graft siphoned off much of the expenditure meant to improve the city's plant and services, resulting in the accumulation of large amounts of "deferred maintenance."[103]

The inadequacies of the old approach, where political and private interests claimed priority, to the problems and needs of a growing modern metropolis became increasingly clear during the Reyburn era. Port modernization and development can be singled out as one obvious area of neglect. Despite having a long waterfrontage on two rivers, a huge industrial complex, and ready access by rail to vast interior sources of agricultural and mineral raw materials, Philadelphia had only a few more than twenty wharves in 1907. Three-quarters of the wharves could not accommodate ships drawing more than thirteen feet of water; some were so shallow that fireboats could not approach alongside. Moreover, practically all of those piers termed adequate belonged to private companies, principally railroads. Only one covered wharf was available for public use by ships of sizable draft. Such poor facilities had helped cause the city's rank among world ports in the amount of inbound tonnage handled to skid from thirty-eighth in 1900 to fifty-first in 1907.[104] Even the usually complacent Mayor Reyburn admitted that "Philadelphia's neglect of her harbor improvement has been more marked than that of any other American municipality."[105] A Department of Wharves, Docks, and Ferries was created in 1907 to initiate port improvement, but little was accomplished until the next administration.

Philadelphia's public education program lagged behind other competitive cities as well. After completing a survey of a dozen major American municipalities, Superintendent of Schools Martin G. Brumbaugh concluded that "not one of them presents such conditions as are present in our city."[106] Chicago, for example, had a population one-third larger than Philadelphia's, but the valuation of its school property in 1908 was two and one-half times greater ($39 million as against $16 million). Its school budget for the same year amounted to $8,209,000 compared to $5,803,000 for Philadelphia. Brumbaugh reported that the Quaker City's schools were so crowded and facilities so inadequate that one-third of the students were on half-time and over 1700 children on a waiting list. His yearly pleas for increased funding produced appropriations "not sufficient to do more than a very small portion of what was needed."[107] A similar report by the director of public health and charities cited the negligent and "deplorable conditions" that existed in the hospitals and public institutions for children and the feeble-minded. Moreover he revealed that the annual appropriation for the city hospital was the lowest of any leading American metropolis. "One repeats year after year urgent recommendations that remain unfulfilled," concluded his report.[108]

The city government's paucity of planning and development and its indifferent attitude toward public programs can be seen as the natural result of rule by a self-serving machine operating through *quid pro quo* arrangements with private interests. In a larger sense these deficiencies also reflected the conservative nature of what Sam Bass Warner, Jr., has called "the private city."[109] The long tradition of reverence for private enterprise on the part of Philadelphians had fostered an abiding resistance to the expansion of government programs and management even into those areas of essentially a public-service nature. When the gas issue arose again in 1907 at the expiration of the U.G.I. lease, the city had the option of operating the gasworks itself. Instead, despite the bad publicity given U.G.I. in the gas war and the arguments of reformers that municipal operation would mean lower gas prices, the city stuck by the private-enterprise principle and renewed the U.G.I. lease for twenty years under terms similar to the old lease. It should be added that the organization, fearful of inviting another uprising, made no efforts to include the most controversial provisions of the 1905 plan, the bulk payments and the seventy-five-year term.[110]

Another victory for private monopoly in 1907, which also testified to the absence of a watchdog of the public interest in City Hall, was the fifty-year contract given to the Philadelphia Rapid Transit Company (PRT). The holding company put together in 1901 by traction magnates Peter A. B. Widener and William L. Elkins to control all the transit lines in the city had soon become swamped by the difficulties arising out of the clash between its profit-making goals and the transit needs of a growing metropolis. Demands for improved and expanded service from an unhappy public; a precarious financial position owing to rising costs, internal stock manipulation, and a shortage of new investment capital; and failure to fulfill the terms of its subway franchise had brought the PRT to the brink of collapse by the end of 1906. Under similar circumstances other cities had put the transit system under municipal control, but this alternative was never seriously considered at the time in Philadelphia. Largely through the efforts of the Retail Merchants Association, a plan to help the PRT in its quest for capital by solidifying its long-term control of city transit was approved by the company and ratified by City Hall in July 1907.[111]

The new contract gave the PRT not only a monopoly of all existing transit operations but of all new construction as well, if done within the time limits set by the city. Critics of the contract contended that under this latest municipal crime Philadelphia surrendered its regulatory powers over the transit system and agreed essentially to subsidize the company by assuming the costs of maintaining streets and removing snow (formerly done by PRT) in excess of the $500,000 per year paid by the PRT. (Formerly the PRT had been responsible for the full cost of these services.) Nevertheless the contract evoked little protest from the public, largely because of confusion over the legal technicalities and the hope that it would lead to an improvement over the "rotten service" of the past.[112] A recent researcher has found that while the contract helped resolve some immediate problems for the PRT and also marked the beginning of the gradual assumption of more responsibility for local transit by the city, it did not provide the machinery to enforce service reforms.[113] Over the next few years the decisions of the PRT's management did little to alleviate the distress of the public and, even worse, they led to one of the most violent labor upheavals in Philadelphia history.

VII

In contrast to its distinction as the birthplace of American labor unionism in the 1820s, Philadelphia in the early years of the twentieth century had become known as "the graveyard of unionism."[114] Organizing workers had become extremely difficult in the face of industry's open-shop attitude and the close alliance of business with the Republican machine. The entrenched traditions of homework and piecework in some industries, particularly clothing, by isolating and scattering workers, added to the unions' frustrations in organizing and supervising them. Furthermore the divisions within labor itself between the skilled and the unskilled, native-born and foreign-born workers, and competing ethnic mutual-aid societies within the immigrant population, militated against a strong union movement in the city.[115]

Of the approximately 500,000 workers in Philadelphia in 1905 only 10 percent were union members. Most of the members belonged to various craft unions which, except for textile and railroad workers, were affiliated with the Central Labor Union—the local clearinghouse for the American Federation of Labor. Between 1905 and 1919 there was a steady growth in union membership among highly skilled workers in textiles and the printing trades, but most others, particularly those in the clothing and steel industries, had to await the 1930s for effective unionism.[116]

The most militant confrontation between labor and management, and the one that had the most serious consequences for the city, grew out of the efforts of the PRT to block the spread of unionism among its carmen. The same year that the PRT received its new contract also saw the establishment of a local in Philadelphia by the Amalgamated Association of Street and Electric Railroad Employees. In May 1909 after the transit company refused to recognize the union or meet any of its demands, including a wage increase to twenty-five cents per hour, the local went on strike. Despite the paralyzing effects of the shutdown of all mass transit, the public generally supported the strikers. Few sympathized with the PRT, not only because the hoped-for improvements in service had never materialized, but also because it had recently dropped the popular six-for-a-quarter "strip tickets." Nevertheless the company refused to make any concessions until Jim McNichol persuaded it to accept an agreement so that the strike would not hurt the organization's candidates in the upcoming municipal primary. The day before the election, and five days after the strike began, the PRT agreed to raise wages to twenty-two cents per hour, to permit carmen to purchase uniforms at the supplier of their choice, and to reinstate workers discharged during the strike; but the company did not recognize the union.[117]

In fact after the strike the transit company seemed more determined than ever to kill off the local. Before the end of 1909 the PRT established a company union—the Keystone Carmen—and brought pressure on workers to join by favoring Keystone members in promotions and assignments to preferred trolley routes. Fighting for its life, the AASERE local sought to preserve its hold on the carmen by asking for a new agreement in January 1910, charging that the company had not lived up to most of the terms of the 1909 settlement. In no mood to dicker, the PRT belligerently fired 173 union men on February 19. Immediately the carmen launched another strike, which was to become one of the bloodiest and most destructive in the city's history.[118]

The company's defiant efforts to operate the transit system by importing 175 strikebreakers from New York precipitated a violent reaction from the strikers. Along Market Street and Lehigh Avenue and at many other points throughout the city angry carmen attacked streetcars and other company property, leaving dozens of persons injured and almost 300 cars destroyed or seriously damaged. When the police proved helpless against the mobs of strikers and their sympathizers, Mayor Reyburn deputized more than 3000 special police, including park guards and other city employees, in an effort to contain the violence. They arrested hundreds of strikers during the first three days, including C. O. Pratt, the national union organizer and leader of the strike, who was charged with rioting and conspiracy. The disorders were finally brought under control when several hundred state police requested by the mayor arrived on February 23.[119]

Although the union requested that the dispute be submitted to arbitration, the PRT's board of directors, firmly backed by the mayor, refused. "I am not a believer in arbitration, even among nations," Reyburn said. "I believe that if you and I have a dispute, that we alone can settle that satisfactorily."[120] Newspapers and civic organizations also appealed for arbitration in vain. When a nonsectarian ministerial association added a similar plea, the mayor told the clergymen to "attend to their own affairs."[121] Clearly in sympathy with the company, he prohibited all public meetings by the strikers and even banned John Galsworthy's play *Strife* from the stage of the Adelphi Theatre because its theme coincidentally supported the use of arbitration as a peace measure.[122]

The unyielding stand of the company, its backing by the city government, and the potentially bleak consequences for the local union movement generally should the strike fail brought the Central Labor Union to the assistance of the carmen. At a meeting on February 27, CLU members voted to initiate a general strike if no settlement were reached by March 5. When the deadline passed with no movement from the company, the CLU asked all Philadelphia workers to strike. Within a week an estimated 146,000 workers had joined the sympathetic walkout, crippling many of the city's industries.[123]

Public distaste for the "socialistic" general strike soon became apparent, however, as a flood of protests assailed the CLU's "unfair" tactics. Shaken by the massive criticism, the will of the sympathetic strikers weakened further as they saw much of the business of the struck plants going to nonunion shops in Philadelphia and factories in other cities. When the Pennsylvania Federation of Labor decided not to support the Philadelphia union in a contemplated statewide strike, the CLU called off the general strike on March 27.[124]

As the strike of the carmen continued, the PRT restored some service with policemen riding on the cars to protect strikebreaking motormen, although accidents and fatalities continued to occur. In all twenty-nine deaths were attributed to the strike: about half of them came in the battles between strikers and "scabs" and policemen; the rest resulted from the dangerous operation of the cars by inexperienced strikebreakers.[125] Despite the resumption of service with police protection, it soon became apparent that the company could not soon break the strike, nor could it long continue to sustain the huge financial losses incurred from the walkout.

In mid-April, sixty-six days after the strike began, the PRT finally reached an agreement with the union. The weary strikers went back to work with a pay increase to twenty-three cents an hour, to be raised a half cent every six months until it reached twenty-five cents; a guarantee that all strikers would be rehired and the cases of the 173 discharged men arbitrated; and the freedom to join the AASERE local if they chose.[126]

The costs of the strike brought the already financially troubled PRT to the verge of bankruptcy again. In exchange for capital guarantees, the company directors surrendered control of the transit system to E. T. Stotesbury, head of Drexel and Company. Stotesbury then brought in Thomas E. Mitten, former president of the Chicago Street Railroad Company, to reorganize and operate the Philadelphia system.[127] Mitten's plan included a provision for the recognition of and a contract with the Amalgamated Association if two-thirds of the workers so voted. In two secret ballots in November 1911 and July 1913, however, disagreement among the carmen prevented union endorsement by a slight margin. Thereafter the union movement in the transit system received a further setback when Mitten established a Co-operative Association of management and employees to settle disputes and provide welfare benefits. Strongly influenced by management, the association was actually a type of company union that became widespread after the Great War.[128] Beyond the labor issue, Mitten's management of the transit company did produce some expanded capacity and better service, and improved the PRT's financial condition to the point where it could begin paying dividends in 1916.[129]

VIII

Meanwhile political reformers resumed the offensive in 1910 when both Republicans and Democrats nominated machine-tainted candidates for governor. Insurgents from both parties gathered in Philadelphia in July to create yet another independent organization, the Keystone party, and nominate William Berry for governor. Berry almost duplicated his 1905 victory, carrying upstate Pennsylvania by 11,000 votes, but lost to Republican John K. Tener because of a 45,000-vote G.O.P. margin in Philadelphia. The Keystoners prevailed in the Kensington, West Philadelphia, and northwestern sections of the city but lost heavily in the Vare wards of South Philadelphia.[130] Despite Berry's loss, reformers were buoyed by their strong showing of 1910 and believed that it brooked well for their prospects in the upcoming mayoralty campaign in 1911.

The independents' chances for electing a mayor rose sharply when a new rift occurred in the organization. Because of the decisive results in their wards in 1910, the Vares insisted that William—the youngest of the brothers—should be nominated for mayor.[131] Jim McNichol, fearful of the consequences for his contracting business and political organization should the Vares control City Hall, urged Penrose to help block their ambitions. Although Penrose appreciated the value of the Vares to the organization, he foresaw a potential challenge to his own party leadership if they dominated Philadelphia. Also, having just barely withstood a strong independent attack, he believed that it would be folly to provoke the reformers further with a candidate so closely associated with bossism as "Bill the Baby."[132] Instead, Penrose and McNichol eventually settled on George H. Earle, an able lawyer and respected financier who had not been active in organization politics. Angered by their rejection, the Vares determined to make a fight for the nomination in the September primary anyway.

Encouraged by the dissension within the organization, Philadelphia Keystoners pressed for the nomination of the "old war horse of reform" himself, Rudolph Blankenburg. A German-born Quaker and founder of R. Blankenburg and Company, merchants and manufacturers of dry goods, Blankenburg had participated in municipal reform movements since 1880. Elected county commissioner on the Lincoln ticket in 1905, the gray-bearded, cultured gentleman had not only zealously performed his duties but had also donated his entire salary to the pension funds of the police, firemen, and teachers. Affectionately known as the "Old Dutch Cleanser," his long civic career had been eminently complemented by that of his wife Lucretia, a respected champion of numerous causes including the women's suffrage movement.[133] Blankenburg's candidacy was warmly received by independents throughout the city. The Democratic City Committee, hopeful that a fusion ticket could best the organization, endorsed Blankenburg for the Democratic nomination for mayor as well.[134]

The Republican primary contest was close and filled with vituperation. Earle's supporters claimed that the chief issue was "civic decency v. contractor bossism," while the Vare forces presented their candidate as "the little fellow vs. the big boss and his rich friends."[135] Probably the most decisive turn in the campaign came when an investigating committee of the state legislature, headed by Sen. Sterling Catlin, appeared on the scene. The announced

Mayor Rudolph Blankenburg (1843–1918), 1914.

PHILADELPHIA DEPARTMENT OF RECORDS, DIVISION OF ARCHIVES

purpose of the Catlin Commission was a probe into suspected corruption in the Reyburn administration, but few doubted that it was actually one of Penrose's devices not only to embarrass Reyburn but to strike at his candidate for mayor, William Vare.[136] In two weeks of public hearings before the primary the commission uncovered numerous cases of fraud and misappropriation of municipal funds. The most damaging blow to the Vare campaign was the revelation that brother Edwin had contracted with the city to provide landfill for League Island Park at more than twice the going rate.[137] (The Vares' rate of sixty-two cents per cubic yard was reduced to thirty cents in a later contract with them.)[138] Fully publicized by the Earle campaigners, the findings of the Catlin Commission undoubtedly cost Vare votes if not the nomination.

The primary results indicated that the only hope of the reformers lay in attracting massive Republican backing. Earle outpolled Vare by 105,000 to 82,000; Blankenburg's combined Keystone-Democratic vote of 45,000 was less than half that of Earle.[139] In the five-week canvass before the general election the Keystoners devoted most of their oratory toward proving that Blankenburg was a good Republican as well as an incorruptible reformer. The candidate himself repeatedly stressed that he not only fought for honest and efficient government but to save the Republican party from a machine that had "enslaved freemen and made a mockery of free government."[140] Apparently he was convincing; numerous distinguished Republican stalwarts—including banker E. T. Stotesbury, treasurer of the national G.O.P. finance committee —declared for him.[141]

In contrast to Blankenburg's effective campaign, Earle's often proved inept. Because his main place of residence was in the suburbs rather than the city, doubts about his eligibility for the mayor's office plagued him throughout the campaign.[142] His speeches probably hurt his chances more than they helped. Interrupted by hecklers at a rally in South Philadelphia, he caused an uproar by angrily saying that the district was like "the slums of Moscow."[143] Probably his chief handicap was the breech in the organization left over from the bitter primary fight. Although the Vares had pledged their support for the ticket after Earle's nomination, their lack of enthusiasm for his candidacy— apparent throughout the campaign—was confirmed by the returns. Where their wards had given majorities of 16,000 votes to Mayor Reyburn in 1907 and 18,000 to Governor Tener in 1910, they furnished Earle only a 6800-vote margin, insufficient as it turned out to overcome Blankenburg's pluralities in North and West Philadelphia.[144]

The final results gave Blankenburg 134,700 votes to Earle's 130,200, a slender margin of 4500. The most common explanations for the outcome held that Blankenburg won less because he was a reformer than because he "had proved himself to be a better Republican than Earle in a city that was first and foremost Republican," and because of the "split in the 'gang.' "[145] Even though these interpretations were probably accurate, the reformers—after years of frustration—had finally won control of the city administration in their own right and with it, they believed, a mandate for reform.

In his inaugural address on December 4, 1911, Blankenburg promised that his would be a nonpartisan administration and reiterated his campaign pledge to put city operations on a sound business basis with experts rather than politicians at the heads of municipal departments.[146] The fact that he kept his word and surrounded himself with able and dedicated professionals distinguished his administration from preceding ones as much as anything else.

Probably the ablest member of the new cabinet was Morris Llewellyn Cooke, an industrial engineer and student of scientific management who later became the first director of the Rural Electrification Administration under Franklin D. Roosevelt.[147] As director of public works, Cooke made his department a model of efficiency and incorruptibility. He replaced inept political appointees from previous administrations with technical experts. He modernized office routine and initiated on-the-job training, paid vacations, and other benefits for municipal workers. Most significant, he ended, at least for the time being, the notorious contractor-boss system for letting municipal contracts that had been a foundation of the Republican organization. To prevent fat profits to political contractors who used inferior materials and paid off city inspectors, Cooke prepared contracts containing exact quality specifications, awarded them to the lowest bidder, and followed through with rigorous inspections to ensure proper work.[148]

To head the Department of Public Safety, Blankenburg appointed George D. Porter, a young insurance broker and one of the original founders of the City party in 1905. Porter eliminated political assessment of the police and instituted many changes in the operations of the fire and police bureaus, including the introduction of the three-platoon system for police in 1912 and the establishment of training schools for police and fire recruits. He also worked successfully for the creation of a Night Police Court to prevent overnight detention of innocent suspects.[149]

George W. Norris, a highly successful lawyer and banker, became director of wharves, docks, and ferries. With Cooke, he successfully negotiated an agreement in 1913 with several railroads to abolish grade crossings and relocate considerable trackage in South Philadelphia, which not only improved rail traffic in that area but also expanded its industrial and residential possibilities. He also initiated large-scale improvements in the city's port facilities, including the construction of the Southwark and Moyamensing piers. Although the money to complete all the proposed facilities for "the Port of Pennsylvania," as Norris called it, was not forthcoming from city and state budgets, the number of municipal docks quadrupled by the end of Blankenburg's administration.[150]

As head of the newly created Transit Department, railroad executive A. Merrit Taylor worked diligently to expand the city's rapid-transit system. Philadelphia's meager 14.7 miles of high-speed trackage in 1912 compared very unfavorably with other major cities: Boston had twice as much; Chicago, ten times more; and New York, twenty times as much. Taylor developed plans for increasing trackage to 59.3 miles with three new elevated lines and two new subways, including the Frankford Elevated and the Broad Street Subway.[151] Although a start was made toward the building of the new lines, delays by the city Councils in approving plans and passing necessary ordinances prevented their completion until the 1920s. A significant alteration in past policy came when the city decided to build the lines itself, permitting the PRT to rent and operate them on a profit-sharing basis.[152]

Blankenburg's four years in office saw numerous efforts to modernize and improve the efficiency of city services. Expenditures for public education, aided by a new state law giving the school board independent taxing power, rose from $7,230,000 in 1911 to $12,207,000 in 1915. A loan measure in 1914 authorized the expenditure of $1 million for the reconstruction of Philadelphia General Hospital.[153] Cost-cutting economies gave Philadelphians much more for their tax dollars. The municipal garbage contract, which cost $516,000 in 1911, was reduced to $278,000 in 1912 and $229,000 in 1913. The water department saved approximately $970,000 between 1912 and 1916. The director of supplies shaved the city's expenditure for coal by $88,000 per year and cut the cost of lumber by 41 percent. Altogether it was estimated that the Blankenburg administration saved the city $5 million during its four years.[154] The mayor also wanted to save Philadelphians some of the more than $6 million they spent on prostitution each year (after learning from his Vice Commission that Philadelphia had more bawdy houses than New York City), but there is no evidence that he succeeded.[155]

Blankenburg's projects of essentially an administrative nature had a high ratio of success; not so for most of those requiring legislative action by the unreformed Councils. A new housing code was crippled by the councilmen's refusal to vote adequate funds for its administration. The mayor's efforts to obtain additional revenue through tax reform and new levies, as well as his attempt to raise the city's debt limit, met continual opposition from the Common Council's Finance Committee. During the economic recession of 1914–1915, when thousands of Philadelphia workers were unemployed, the city Councils failed to vote funds for Blankenburg's modest public works program.[156] The mayor did persuade the legislative body to pass a bill reducing the price of gas to consumers in January 1913, but then felt obliged to veto it when no provision was included for additional taxes to offset the $1.8 million yearly loss in revenue resulting from cheaper gas.[157]

Besides the problems posed by the recalcitrant Councils, Blankenburg experienced increasing difficulties in satisfying the friends of reform. His failure to keep his campaign pledge to lower gas prices not only disappointed consumers but also disillusioned some of his staunchest supporters. Even the *North American* accused him of "shuffling evasion and final repudiation" of his gas promise.[158] Ironically, in keeping another campaign pledge to respect the civil service system and prohibit political activity by municipal workers he alienated other backers. Job-hungry Keystoners, disgruntled by his refusal to make room for them by firing lesser employees inherited from previous administrations, charged him with disloyalty to the party that had elected him.[159]

Further dissension within reform ranks and diffusion of support for Blankenburg's administration arose out of the three-way contest for president in 1912. When Theodore Roosevelt joined the race against President Taft and Woodrow Wilson as the Progressive party's candidate, Van Valkenburg and other Philadelphia reformers helped organize the Washington party (the Progressive party title had been preempted by the Republican organization) to campaign for Roosevelt in Pennsylvania. After Roosevelt carried the state, the Washington party leadership sought to maintain their organization as a permanent state reform party, asking Blankenburg to help by providing patronage for party workers. While the mayor had actively championed Roosevelt and lauded the goals of the new party, he refused to alter his nonpartisan approach to city government.[160] Thereafter criticisms of Blankenburg by former admirers noticeably increased; with the vengefulness of a jilted lover, Van Valkenburg aimed numerous barbed editorials in the mayor's direction, denouncing his "lack of political common sense" and general "feebleness and incompetence."[161]

Blankenburg's ambitions for an honest and efficient municipal government devoid of political manipulation were characteristic of the goals and political naïveté of many of his contemporary good-government reformers.

By counting on the good judgment of the citizens to maintain the reformers in power instead of building his own loyal organization through patronage and other means at his disposal, Blankenburg could not long compete with a machine whose promise of tangible rewards assured it of an active cadre of workers and the allegiance of large blocs of voters. Yet Blankenburg set a standard for responsible city management during his four years in City Hall that has rarely been equalled in Philadelphia.

The prospects for continuing or building upon Blankenburg's "Great Experiment" seemed remote long before a vote was cast for his successor in the mayoralty election of 1915. That the 1911 outcome had been due more to dissension in the organization than to the rise of a large reform bloc appeared clearer in the county elections of 1913, when the reunited McNichol-Vare combination elected all Republican candidates over the fusion ticket of the Washington party and the Democrats.[162] A further confirmation of the weakness of antimachine forces came in 1914 when, in the first popular vote for United States senator in Pennsylvania history, Philadelphia voters rejected Washington party candidate Gifford Pinchot and contributed a substantial margin to the reelection of the "big boss" himself, Boies Penrose.[163] Blankenburg, feeling his seventy-two years after a strenuous tenure in City Hall, added to insurgent woes by deciding not to seek a second term.

George D. Porter, the innovative director of public safety in Blankenburg's cabinet, received the retiring mayor's endorsement and the Washington party nomination to head the ticket. Shortly after the primary Porter and his backers adopted a new party label—the Franklin party—to avoid identification with the losing image of the statewide Washington party and to emphasize their focus on strictly local issues. Pledging to preserve Blankenburg's achievements, the Franklinites also vowed to work for the shift to a one-house city Council and a program to encourage industrial development in the city.[164]

To their dismay the Franklinites found that neither Blankenburg's achievements nor even old Ben's name offered much help in their futile campaign. Unlike 1911 the organization was united and its opponents were not. Several reform factions, including the remnants of the Keystone party, refused to support Porter. The Democrats opted to nominate one of their own, Gordon Bromley, instead of uniting on the Franklin candidate. Furthermore the publicity given Porter's membership in a secret fraternal and anti-Catholic organization, the Stone Man's League, probably cost him votes among Catholics and liberals.[165] The clergy, possibly influenced by Billy Sunday's eleven-week revival campaign in the city earlier in the year to turn from public issues back to saving souls and other pastoral cares, took a much less active role in the canvass of 1915 than in those of 1905 and 1911.[166]

The organization's campaign for Thomas B. Smith, an active party man and president of a bail-bonding company, harped on two issues of particular sensitiveness to Philadelphia voters. It was repeatedly emphasized that if Porter were elected he would renew Blankenburg's efforts to raise taxes. Smith's campaigners also claimed effectively, if inappropriately in a municipal election, that the tariff would be endangered if the regular Republicans did not win. "Tariff talk," George Norris concluded, "carried more weight than honest municipal government."[167] The rejection of the Franklin candidate was general; Smith carried forty-two of the forty-eight wards and won handily with 168,000 votes to Porter's 91,000. Democrat Bromley, a very unrespectable third, polled only 4500 votes.[168]

In the months following the election the frustration of defeat and the shifting interests of reform leaders themselves hastened the disintegration of the insurgent movement. Concern about municipal corruption increasingly gave way to worries about the war in Europe and the possibility of American involvement. That militant voice of reform, the *North American*, called a truce in its war on the machine and became almost totally immersed in championing the Allied cause and attacking the neutralist policies of President Wilson in the manner of its hero, Theodore Roosevelt.[169] Insurgency lost its appeal to most local Republicans, however, primarily because of fear of the tariff and business policies of the Democratic administration in Washington and the threat that Wilson might continue in office. The approach of the presidential election of 1916 and the need for Republican solidarity to reclaim the White House beckoned independents back to the G.O.P. What had been a constant dilemma for Philadelphians between loyalty to the Republican party and distaste for the corrupt local organization—which for a time had seen the latter prevail and produce an insurgent reform movement—was now finally resolved in favor of party loyalty by the even more undesirable alternative of another Democratic victory.

On January 23, 1916, eighty-two Philadelphia reformers—including George D. Porter, John C. Winston, the other Franklin party leaders, and many other battle-worn insurgents (but not Blankenburg, for some unexplained reason)—issued a statement disbanding the Franklin party and declaring their intention to return to the Republican fold:

The issues now before this country present to the Republican party the gravest responsibilities it has faced since the Civil War, and the great need of the hour is for unity of purpose and action in the Republican ranks.

For many years the political conditions in Philadelphia have prevented a host of loyal Republicans from acting with their party in local affairs, and, to some extent in national affairs, and the party has thus been deprived of an important element of strength. The issues involved in the approaching presidential election call for cooperation and party unity.[170]

On this note, the last of the independent reform parties that had arisen in the Quaker City during the prewar years to combat the organization departed from the scene. Six months later, after Theodore Roosevelt had refused a second Bull Moose nomination for president, Van Valkenburg's progressives disbanded the Washington party.

IX

Philadelphia's initial reaction to the war in Europe, like that of President Wilson, was to remain neutral in thought and action. After the German invasion of Belgium, however, the city's sentiments rapidly grew more sympathetic to the Allies. Public meetings protested the reported atrocities against the Belgian people, and hundreds of thousands of dollars were raised for Belgian relief.[171] Still, there were few hysterical cries for war. Even the sinking of the *Lusitania* in May 1915, whose death toll included twenty-seven Philadelphians (Paul Crompton's entire family of eight went down with the ship), found the local press calling for calmness and deliberation.[172] Three days after the sinking, President Wilson made a scheduled address at old Convention Hall in honor of 4000 newly naturalized citizens. More than 20,000 heard him make the famous statement that "There is such a thing as a man being too proud to fight. There is such a thing as a nation being so right that it does not need to convince others by force that it is right."[173] The rousing ovation given his remarks seemed to indicate that Philadelphians agreed with his views.

As the war progressed and events brought increasing American support for the Allies, protests came from Philadelphia's German-Americans, Socialists, and Quakers. The local branch of the German-American Alliance campaigned for a better understanding of the Fatherland's position and vigorously opposed sending munitions to England and France. Socialists urged strict neutrality and later opposed the draft. The Quakers found wide support for their antiwar stand until the United States officially became involved in April 1917. Despite the decision of the Yearly Meeting of Friends to oppose any participation in the war, many individual Quakers supported the war effort, and some went off to fight and more to serve in the noncombatant ambulance corps.[174]

When all-out mobilization came, the variety of industry in the "Workshop of the World" enabled Philadelphia to make substantial contributions to the procurement program. Ship construction, on the decline before the war, rapidly escalated to meet the needs of the Atlantic supply line. Organized as the Delaware River District under the Emergency Fleet Corporation, the Philadelphia area built 328 ships, which amounted to 20 percent of the tonnage constructed by the United States under the wartime program. All the major yards—including the oldest, Cramp's—participated in the emergency fleet construction, but the center of activity was a new yard at Hog Island. Considered one of the greatest achievements of the mobilization program, the new yard arose out of 947 acres of swampland at the end of 1917 in a matter of months. When finished, its fifty shipways employing 30,000 workers made it the largest shipyard in the world. The first keel was laid on February 19, 1918, and the first ship launched on August 5, 1918. By the end of the war a new ship came down its ways every four working days. A total of 122 cargo and transport vessels went to sea from Hog Island under the emergency program.[175]

Philadelphia's largest single manufacturer before the war, the Baldwin Locomotive Works, also became a valuable component of the industrial mobilization. In addition to more than 5000 locomotives of various types, Baldwin also manufactured artillery shells and railroad gun mounts. The Ford Motor Company made all the steel helmets used by American troops in its ten-story plant at Broad and Lehigh. Seventy-five percent of all the leather used in military boots, saddles, and shoes came from Philadelphia tanners. David Lupton's Sons made trench mortars; Fayette R. Plumb, Inc., manufactured trench tools and bolo knives; Jacob Reed's Sons made uniforms. Few Quaker City manufacturers went uninvolved in the production for war.[176]

Philadelphia women became almost as caught up in war service as the men. They took over jobs of men called to the armed forces; they worked for the Red Cross; they organized Liberty Bond Drives, and busied themselves in dozens of other ways. Knitting socks, ear bands, sweaters, gloves for the doughboys became a major operation. The city's S. B. and B. W. Fleisher wool manufactory provided most of the yarn. The first woman to enlist in the United States Navy was Philadelphian Loretta Walsh. Eventually more than 2000 women from the city served in various branches of the services. Others joined the Women's Land Army to work on farms and to cultivate vacant lots. Their "liberty gardens" contributed significantly both to morale and to food resources.[177]

Female welder, Naval Aircraft Factory, League Island, Philadelphia Navy Yard (1918).

HISTORICAL SOCIETY OF PENNSYLVANIA

The city suffered serious shortages in both food and fuel as the war wore on. Schools and many business establishments closed their doors during the winter of 1917–1918 because of insufficient coal supplies. There were numerous instances of mobs' raiding coal cars on railroad sidings to obtain fuel for their homes. Philadelphians were urged by public officials to conserve fuel and food supplies by observing "Heatless Mondays" and "Wheatless Mondays and Wednesdays."[178]

Despite the shortages and inconveniences the city's patriotic fervor and support for the war effort remained high. The three major "Liberty Loan" campaigns were all oversubscribed. (Schoolchildren could win a captured German helmet by getting family subscriptions.) The "Liberty Sing Movement," a popular phenomenon throughout the metropolis, brought thousands of people together in public to sing patriotic songs. The chief coordinator of most of the civilian activities was the Home Defense Committee, formed by representatives from business and civic organizations even before the United States entered the war. Hundreds of volunteers contributed thousands of hours to the various projects under its auspices.[179]

Unfortunately, some patriotic fervor became misdirected and disordered. Like much of the rest of America the "City of Brotherly Love" experienced a rash of anti-German hysteria and intolerance. Constant rumors abounded about German spies and enemy plots, very few of which had any basis in fact.[180] Perhaps the most far-fetched "plot" had enemy aliens planning to buy up all condensed milk in order to starve American babies. Many instances of anti-German intolerance were so extreme as to be humorous. Sauerkraut was renamed "Liberty cabbage"; German measles became "Liberty measles" for the duration. Even Black Forest Christmas legends and customs were considered unpatriotic. "It is seldom that one hears, at this time, the name of Kris Kringle," observed a *Bulletin* editorial in December 1917; "the name of Santa Claus has also been put under a war ban by many."[181]

Other acts of intolerance by misguided patriots were vicious and destructive. Statues of Goethe, Schiller, and Bismarck in the city were painted yellow or defaced in other ways. Some patriotic groups campaigned for the suppression of the German press and language. Mayor Thomas B. Smith suspended all city advertising in German-language newspapers. The offices of the Philadelphia *Tageblatt* were raided by federal agents and five of its staff indicted for treason. Although they were later acquitted of the treason charges, they were found guilty of violating the Espionage Act.[182] The climax to the wartime intolerance came in May 1918. Against the pleas of many educators, including the United States commissioner of education, the Philadelphia School Board voted to end the teaching of the German language in the public schools.[183]

While some citizens of Philadelphia were busy fighting an imagined German threat at home, thousands of its sons marched off to fight the real enemy abroad. Of the total of 60,000 men called to arms from the city, almost 7000 served in the Twenty-eighth Division. Known as the "Iron Division" of the

Pennsylvania National Guard, it was federalized in August 1917. Drafting troops first began in July 1917, and it eventually accounted for 53,000 servicemen from the city.[184] One Philadelphian who managed to avoid induction into the service became the most notorious "draft dodger" of the war. Grover C. Bergdoll, the son of a wealthy family of brewers as well as a playboy aviator and automobile racer, refused to be conscripted into the army, demanding that he be assigned as an aviator instructor. His disappearance and then his eventual discovery and arrest in 1920 made him the center of a *cause célèbre* into the next decade.[185]

Philadelphians served in all branches of the armed forces, although the largest proportion of the draftees went to the army's Seventy-ninth Division. Both the Twenty-eighth and the Seventy-ninth participated in heavy fighting. The "Iron Division" was almost constantly at the front in the Marne and Argonne campaigns from July to October 1918; the Seventy-ninth Division fought in the Meuse-Argonne offensive in late September and in the battle of La Grande Montagne, part of the same offensive, in early November 1918. Casualties from the city amounted to 1399 dead.[186]

In the last month of the war the horrors of wholesale death moved from the remote battlefields of Europe to the streets and homes of Philadelphia. The worldwide influenza epidemic of 1918 struck particularly hard at the city. Schools, theaters, movies, and saloons were closed for nearly four weeks during October in an attempt to hold back the spread of the infectious germs. Few measures seemed to have any effect; at its peak the flu claimed more than 700 lives each day. Corpses accumulated faster than they could be buried. Mass interment took place on city land at Second and Luzerne. The city government eventually guaranteed to pay funeral expenses up to seventy-five dollars to ensure prompt burial.[187] Before the epidemic had run its course in early November it had claimed many more Philadelphia lives than the guns of World War I.

x

The spirit of self-sacrifice and unity of purpose called forth by the war effort did not carry over into Philadelphia politics. The contest between the Penrose-McNichol forces and the Vare machine for domination of the city took on a "trench warfare" character of its own. With Thomas B. Smith's elevation to the mayor's office in 1916 the Vares had gotten the upper hand. Assisted by the flow of jobs and favors in their direction from City Hall, they won control of the Republican City Committee and thirty-nine of the forty-eight wards by mid-1917.[188] The prospect of a fratricidal upcoming primary election, however, brought the two factions together temporarily at a "harmony conference" in August 1917. They agreed upon a "fifty-fifty ticket" whereby the offices up for election were divided between them and each side named candidates for its half.[189] Subsequent events, however, soon cut short the brief interlude of harmony and showed just how vicious Philadelphia politics could be.

A bitter primary contest for Select Council had developed in the Fifth

Ward between James A. Carey, an ally of Penrose and McNichol, and a Vare man, Isaac Deutsch. The "Bloody Fifth" was an immigrant ward, as well as home of Independence Hall, with a long history of violence and "strong-arm" politics. While visiting a polling place on primary day, Carey was attacked and severely beaten by several members of a hired gang imported from New York City by the Deutsch camp. When policeman George Eppley tried to defend Carey, he was shot and killed by one of the gang.[190] The gunman was later convicted of second-degree murder; Deutsch and six policemen working for him were found guilty of conspiracy. Mayor Smith, who had said earlier that "clubs would be trumps" in the Fifth Ward contest, was believed to have misused his office to help Deutsch, including the assigning of policemen to work for the Vare candidate. He was indicted on charges of impeding a free and fair election and committing a misdemeanor in office. Although he was eventually acquitted after a nine-day trial in January 1919, he could not escape the cloud of suspicion that hovered over the last two years of his administration.[191]

Shocked by the murder of Eppley, thousands of Philadelphians gathered

Edwin H. Vare (1862–1922), 1914.

at the Academy of Music on September 27, 1917, in one of the largest protest demonstrations in the city's history. Many reform leaders of the past, including Blankenburg and Van Valkenburg, participated in the meeting and appealed for citizen action against the sort of politics that had spawned the violence.[192] The result was a decision to oppose the machine candidates in the November election with a reform slate under the title of Town Meeting party. Penrose, appalled by the violent turn in local politics with its possible harmful consequences for his state organization, and seeing an opportunity to untrack the Vare machine, joined with the reformers to campaign against the Vare candidates. However, the South Philadelphia combine proved to be better organized than its opponents; the Vares turned out a large vote in their wards and elected their entire slate.[193] Penrose received yet another blow when Jim McNichol, who had been seriously ill throughout the campaign, died a week after the election.

As events were to prove, the joint campaign of 1917 marked the beginning of a close association between Penrose and the good-government forces. Frozen out of the immigrant wards by the Vares, he cultivated the support of citizens' groups, the respectable businessmen-reformers, and others who wanted to see a general "housecleaning" in the city. It would be easy to dismiss his alliance with the reformers as just an opportunistic strategy to combat the Vares, but there is probably some truth to the view that he had a sincere desire to make Philadelphia a better governed city.[194] As a native son who took considerable pride in his city, and as a United States senator who was concerned with promoting the image of the city as he worked for its economic and political interests at the national level, he had likely reasons for wishing to eliminate the most embarrassing and sordid features from local government. The most significant consequence of the collaboration between Penrose and the reformers, however, was the new charter for Philadelphia enacted by the state legislature in June 1919.

In the aftermath of the violent primary of 1917 much attention had been focused on the need for legislation to prevent the involvement of the police in politics. While knowledgeable reformers were concerned about this problem, they were also aware that other fundamental changes were needed to modernize and improve municipal government. The experience of the Blankenburg administration had demonstrated just how obstructive and unwieldy the two-house, 146-member city Councils could be. The city legislature also provided unequal representation; the central-city and riverfront wards were overrepresented and the big residential wards in Germantown and West Philadelphia were underrepresented. As one writer observed, "A third of the population of the city elects a majority of both chambers, and that third is the happy hunting ground of the politicians."[195] It had been recognized for some years that Philadelphia should follow the successful examples of many other cities and move to a smaller one-house and more representative legislative body. Another step talked about locally for years, which had also been proven out in other cities, was the assumption by the municipality of the operation of basic services, such as garbage and trash collection, street cleaning, and street paving and repairing, instead of contracting them out to private companies usually tied to the political machine.[196] Since most of these and other changes contemplated involved the structure or function of Philadelphia government over which the state legislature had authority, action by that body in the form of charter amendment or revision became necessary.

The charter revision movement, which had been gathering support since 1915, was officially launched at a dinner attended by over 900 patrons in December 1918. A committee of 137, headed by venerable reformer John C. Winston, was chosen to draft the new charter. Using the Bullitt Charter of 1885 as the basis for making changes, and drawing upon data and staff services supplied by the Bureau of Municipal Research, the committee completed its work in the spring of 1919.[197] An intensive promotional campaign and the strong endorsement of newly elected Gov. William C. Sproul accompanied the introduction of the charter bill into the legislature. Longtime reformer state Sen. George Woodward directed it through the Assembly, but "the greatest single factor in securing the passage of the bill" was Boies Penrose.[198] Under the weight of his considerable influence the resistance of the Vare legislators was worn down and the final legislation passed with 90 percent of the original recommendations intact.[199]

The new charter's most important provision gave the city a trimmer and more representative one-house city Council of twenty-one members. The old council members were officially unpaid; the new ones were to receive an annual salary of $5000. They were to be elected for four-year terms from the eight state senatorial districts, each district to have one councilman plus one additional for each unit of 20,000 assessed voters. No councilman was to hold another political office simultaneously. Another significant change granted Philadelphia the authority to do its own street cleaning, paving, and repairing, as well as garbage and refuse collecting. Intended to provide more efficient and economical service in these areas, it was also a direct attempt to eliminate the political manipulation of public service contracts by the organization. New stricter civil service regulations placed the 15,000 municipal workers on a classified list and limited to two the number of eligible persons who could be certified for any one job. Political activity or political contributions on the part of policemen and firemen became a crime punishable by fine and imprisonment. All of the city's offices were to be accountable to the controller, whose department was in essence independent of the mayor's control. The mayor was required to submit a budget to the city Council annually, and that body was to hold public hearings on the budget. Unfortunately a capital budget to fund long-range planning was not called for. A Department of Welfare was to coordinate various social welfare activities.[200]

With the enactment of the new "epoch-making" charter the second decade of the twentieth century ended on a positive note for Philadelphia.[201] The instrument's modernizing changes offered the possibilities of eliminating some of the worst features of municipal government as practiced in the past.

The Wading Pool, Rittenhouse Square (1915).
HISTORICAL SOCIETY OF PENNSYLVANIA

The key question of course was how much use the citizens of Philadelphia would make of these possibilities. Could public interest be sustained long enough to produce enduring reforms, or would Owen Wister's observation of 1907 continue to be true? "When wrongs so outrageous as the gas lease are thrust at him [the Philadelphian], he may rouse for a while, but it is grudgingly in his heart of hearts; and when the party of reform makes mistakes, he jumps at these to cover his retreat into the ranks of acquiescence."[202] Would loyalties to the Grand Old Party and the defense of the tariff continue to beguile Philadelphians and hamper efforts to combat the local Republican machine? Would the city's bias in favor of private enterprise, which was shared by most good-government reformers as well as their opponents, continue to inhibit the development of public programs needed in an expanding metropolis? Would the general resistance to innovation and change, seen in many aspects of Philadelphia life between 1905 and 1919, continue to be a basic characteristic of the Quaker City? The ways in which Philadelphia answered these questions would largely determine whether it advanced into the twentieth century as a leading American city or continued its decline in prestige and influence from earlier years.

The City Embraces "Normalcy" 1919-1929

by Arthur P. Dudden

The average division leader can always be found at a certain place—the corner cigar store, the drug store. . . . He goes there every night. When the voter wants him, he knows where to find him.

— WILLIAM S. VARE

Law enforcement on an absolutely even basis has not had the support of the people of Philadelphia and does not have it now.

— SMEDLEY D. BUTLER [1]

Philadelphians greeted the war's end on November 11, 1918, with joy and relief. But long after the initial jubilant celebrations subsided, the city's affection and concern for the soldiers who fought the war remained. When the troopship *Haverford* docked at Washington Avenue on January 30, 1920, Christopher Morley followed a host of other Philadelphians walking southward to meet it. He found Jefferson Square "packed with people" and an "immense" crowd at the eastern end of Washington Avenue. Making a strategic detour by way of Gloria Dei Church, Morley reached the slip of the South Street–Gloucester ferry just as "whistles down the river began to blow a deep, vibrant chorus." Boarding the ferry, he continued to report the scene, now from a mid-river vantage point:

> . . . the first thing we saw was the reception boat . . . And then we came right abreast of the big liner. . . . Her upper decks . . . brown with men, all facing away from us, however, to acknowledge the roar of cheering from the piers.
>
> A ship is always a noble sight . . . and in the clear yellow light of the winter morning . . . [the *Haverford*] seemed to have a new and very lovely beauty. Her masts were dressed with flags, from the bright ripple of the Stars and Stripes at the fore to the deep scarlet of her own Red Ensign over the taffrail. Half a dozen tugs churned and kicked beside her as she swung slowly to the dock. Over the water came a continuous roar of cheering as the waiting thousands tried to say what was in their hearts. . . . They [America's soldiers] were home again and we were glad.[2]

Yet the sense of well-being that followed the end of the war and the moderating of the 1918 influenza epidemic was short-lived. Somber reality in the guise of strikes—a building-trades strike halting construction in the city and a tugboat and coal handlers' walkout at the Port Richmond and Greenwich piers—worsened an economy already unsettled by the older steel, rail, and coal strikes. These and the Red Scare, the alarm fed by troubles in Seattle, Boston, Pittsburgh, and nearby Camden, made gloomy headlines in the daily papers.[3] The old and comfortable, because familiar, ways of life were further jostled by two amendments to the federal Constitution: the Eighteenth, superseding temporary wartime restrictions against alcoholic beverages to make Prohibition permanent, went into effect on January 16, 1920; and the Nineteenth, giving women the right to vote, was declared ratified on August 26, 1920, and was first applied in the presidential election of that year.[4] Locally, Philadelphia, endowed by the Pennsylvania Assembly with the new charter of 1919, had chosen and was now prepared to welcome a new mayor and a new city Council.

I

"To make intelligent use [of the new charter] is now the fine old town's splendid opportunity," concluded F. P. Gruenberg in an article in the August 9 issue of *Survey*. John C. Winston, chairman of the Charter Commission, echoed the thought: "If this same public sentiment can now be organized for the purpose of electing councilmen who are free from allegiance to contractors and who will serve the public interest then we shall get the full benefit of the new charter."[5]

One of the compromises the reformers had been constrained to accept allowed the politicians to continue the "fiction" of an independent county government and to fix the elections to the "row offices"—the register of wills, city treasurer, and coroner—so that they were not chosen with the mayor and Council but in different years, making elimination of machine control doubly difficult. More important was the failure of a supplementary bill to place all county employees, as well as municipal ones, under civil service. Similarly although political activity and personal contributions to political campaigns were prohibited for police and firemen, nonuniformed workers were not restrained in the same way. Another problem that surfaced later arose from the provision that a mayor could not succeed himself, making him a lame duck during the last year or two of office.[6]

The fall primaries prior to the 1919 mayoralty election provided the first test of Philadelphia's charter and of the city's devotion to reform. After weeks of haggling the Penrose men who had formed the Republican Alliance as their vehicle for challenging the Vare brothers agreed with the independents to support Cong. J. Hampton Moore as their candidate for mayor. Moore had been around the city for a long time, as a *Ledger* reporter, as chief clerk to City Treasurer Richard Gardner Oellers, as private secretary to Mayor Samuel Ashbridge, then as city treasurer himself, and finally for the past fourteen years as congressman from the Third District. Campaigning on the issue of "contractor rule," Moore won a narrow victory over the organization's choice, Judge John M. Patterson, proving thereby, in the words of a writer in the October 1 *Outlook*, that 51 percent of Philadelphia's voters "refuse to be called 'corrupt and contented.' "[7]

In the ensuing campaign Moore was supported by all the Philadelphia newspapers. When the votes were counted, the independents found that they and their allies had elected not only Moore, who not unpredictably received about 90 percent of all votes cast, but also Robert Lamberton as sheriff. They also filled with their candidates eleven of the twenty-one Council seats. The *Ledger*'s lead editorial for January 5 called Moore's assumption of the mayor's office an "incoming attended with the Brightest Hopes for Philadelphia."[8]

One final comic note attended the demise of the last Councils to sit under the regulations of the 1854 charter: a taxpayers' suit instituted January 4 to prevent the members of the Councils from taking home their desks "as mementoes of their services to the city." This constituted a "looting of municipal property," said Bartley J. Doyle, the initiator of the suit.[9]

Moore's cabinet contained a mixture of reformers and experienced City Hall officials. James T. Cortelyou, a former chief of the district attorney's detective bureau, was named director of public safety; the perennial reformer and chairman of the Charter Commission, John C. Winston, became director of public works; George F. Sproule, director of wharves, docks, and ferries, a position he continued to hold later under Mayor W. Freeland Kendrick; A. Lincoln Acker, well known to the reform movement since 1905, purchasing agent; Ernest L. Austin, subsequently director-in-chief of the Sesqui-Centennial, director of public welfare; and David J. Smyth, an old Durham man, city solicitor. It was an imposing set of activists who "proposed to complete the sewage disposal system, lay new sewers, improve housing conditions in congested sections, repave and clean streets, bridge the Delaware, operate the Frankford L, extend the pier system, deepen the channel [in the Delaware], and beautify the city." They would accomplish a great deal, in spite of setbacks in some areas.[10]

Mayor Moore was the first of Philadelphia's mayors to have to enforce the Eighteenth Amendment. His director of public safety had to handle the new problems created by Prohibition and meet the ever-increasing challenge of automobile traffic, including a new kind of criminal, the motorized bandit, all without additional policemen. Every patrolman transferred from his beat to enforce the law against the sale of liquor, beer, and wine added to the burdens of officers reserved for regular duties. Together the tasks of upholding the Prohibition law and of controlling crime by automobile threatened to overwhelm the police department. Moore, publicly proud of his men in blue, complained of the Council's refusal to hire more of them so that a check might be kept on "those who would rather get money by robbery than work," and in 1920 managed to secure a pay boost for the policemen, firemen, and park guards. His administration saw the establishment of a Civic Safety Fund to reward acts of heroism by the same group of public servants. Several abuses were corrected: special-privilege police cards were abolished, many of which had fallen into the hands of gamblers and felons; and lawyers' runners were no longer allowed to loiter inside police stations waiting for culprits to be brought in under arrest and in need of legal aid. Indeed, as much as possible was done to free the police force from machine control.[11]

An attempt was made, however, to stop one of the more charming forms of special privilege. It was customary for some families to get license plates with a long series of sequential numbers recognized and saluted by the semaphore policemen on Broad Street and the police guards on the River Drives, who regularly received five-dollar gold pieces at Christmas.

Street cleaning by contract was ended, and by January 1922 municipal street cleaning citywide was substituted, not without problems for both the city and the householders. Handling the trash, except in the newer parts of the city where "team alleys" allowed containers to be placed at the rear of lots, created problems for residents; persuading householders to comply with the new regulations, spotily enforced by politically oriented magistrates, spelled trouble for the city.[12] The water supply, regularly the subject of complaint from 1914 on, was improved; the old plant was "strengthened" and additional facilities provided, putting the city's water supply in better shape than it had been for a long time.[13] Construction on the Delaware River Bridge began on January 6, 1922, and the Frankford "El," 80 percent finished by 1920 but without any agreement on who—the PRT or the city—was to operate it, was completed and running by November 1922. The city had built and equipped the facility at the cost of $14 million; the PRT would operate it free of charge for the first two months, then pay a rent of 1 percent of the total cost during the first year of operation, adding 1 percent more each year until 1927, when the rent would be fixed at 5 percent of the cost.[14]

It is possible that this was the best arrangement that the city could make, since it not only had to satisfy its own needs but meet the requirements of the Public Service Commission and of the PRT as well. Nonetheless, William S. Twining considered the operating condition of his Department of Transportation unsatisfactory, largely because of the "casual arrangements" between the city and the PRT. He was particularly disturbed by the lack of any long-term planning and recommended that before construction of other proposed subways or high-speed lines were begun, an "unbiased study" be made similar to the one done for New York City by the Russell Sage Foundation. The projects already suggested without genuine planning included subways for Broad Street and for the Parkway, the latter with a connection by way of Filbert Street to the Delaware River Bridge at Franklin Square; a midtown loop under parts of Arch, Eighth, Walnut—or Chestnut—and Broad Streets; and an "El" to Darby, all designed to serve the "long-haul" passengers from Delaware, Montgomery, and Camden Counties.[15] In spite of Twining's caveats, on July 12, 1923, the Council's Transit Committee adopted a $100-

million three-year program as its first step in high-speed construction.[16] This transit program was one of the most ambitious proposals for the development of the city on record. Had it been completed it would have linked effectively the outer areas of the city and the expanding suburbs with the "downtown" and have done much to ensure the continued vitality of the center.[17]

Problems of patronage which the provisions of the new charter failed to eliminate caused Moore to lose the support of both the Republican Alliance and the independent reformers by the middle of his term of office. The independents and Moore fell out over his repeated call for charter changes to give the mayor more power over the hiring and firing of city employees. The Republican Alliance separated themselves from him when he cold-shouldered their advice on patronage. In creating a civil service list with government employment in the hands of three commissioners elected by Council, the charter's framers had hoped to reduce the importance of the ward leader in the hiring of municipal workers.[18] The Republican organization, however, was experienced in the art of manipulating regulations in this and other areas of city government to make them serve its own ends, and thereby had a clear advantage over the integrity-burdened independents, a fact of political life that became clear even before Moore was succeeded as mayor by W. Freeland Kendrick.

After his defeat in the charter campaign and Moore's election to the mayor's office, William S. Vare noted that "for a time the future of the Vares in politics appeared extremely dismal, and there were many who were so unkind as to believe that we would be relegated to the background." Far from it, as events showed when the Vare candidate, Harry C. Ransley, defeated Charles Delaney, the Moore administration's man, in the Republican primary contest for Moore's old seat as representative for the Third Congressional District. This victory was followed in the off-year municipal elections of 1921 by a clean sweep by the Vare slate in both the primary and the November elections.[19]

The September 1923 primary once again forcefully reminded Philadelphians of the survival power of the professional politician and of the uses of loyal ward leaders and committeemen. The Vare organization's candidate was W. Freeland Kendrick, considered their "best-vote-getter," and at the time the city's receiver of taxes. He had successfully introduced efficient procedures to his office and an effective "follow-up" system that brought in about 95 percent of the annual assessments.[20] His opponent was Powell Evans, nominee of the Independent Republican Committee. Evans was a manufacturer and engineer, president of the Merchant and Evans Company, but no match for Kendrick on the political field. Out of a total of 280,604 votes, Kendrick received 208,163, decisively defeating Evans and going on to win the general election on November 6 by a plurality of 249,331 over his Democratic opponent, A. Raymond Raff, an antiorganization Democrat, president of A. Raymond Raff Co., builders, and a respected Philadelphian. In spite of his solid commercial standing and his opposition to the "regular" or Vare-controlled

Democrats, Raff failed to win any support from the independent Republicans, underscoring the Philadelphia habit of preferring even an organization man of indifferent qualifications to any Democrat however worthy. Early in the campaign the *Record* had ridiculed this "unreasoning belief . . . that all governmental virtue reposes in the Republican party," so that "the election of a Democrat to any important city office . . . would be reactionary, ruinous and in effect equivalent to a municipal disaster."[21]

Once elected, Kendrick and three of his department heads faced huge tasks. Henry E. Ehlers and his Department of Transportation had to take on the construction of the Broad Street Subway. George H. Biles, head of the Bureau of Public Works and construction chief of the Sesqui-Centennial International Exposition, had to ready grounds and buildings for that affair. Brig.-Gen. Smedley Darlington Butler, director of public safety, was supposed to force compliance with the Volstead Act on a reluctant city. All three began energetically. For Ehlers things moved along with no more than ordinary obstructions to overcome. Biles and Butler were not so fortunate.

I I

Proposals for an international exposition to be held in Philadelphia in 1926 in commemoration of the nation's 150th anniversary had been put forward as early as 1916 by John Wanamaker. In January 1922 the city Council agreed to spend $5 million to promote a fair, and two months later a site combining the advantages of space in Fairmount Park and the access to it provided by the Parkway was settled upon. Neither the proposal for an international fair nor the park-Parkway site was agreeable to everyone. Edward T. Stotesbury, Samuel M. Vauclain, and some 400 civic leaders opted for a local celebration in the park, a kind of "Old Home Week"; William S. Vare and his political allies advocated an international fair, but in South Philadelphia at a site near League Island. When the Council voted to build a municipal stadium on city-owned property at Broad and Pattison Streets, the dispute over where to stage the celebration was settled in Vare's favor. A stadium design by Simon and Simon, architects, was accepted and a contract for the stadium superstructure awarded to the Turner Construction Company. A professional director, Col. David C. Collier of San Diego, was hired and the "glorified side show," as Councilman W. W. Roper called it, was underway. Pres. Calvin Coolidge gave his official approval for an international exposition on February 14, 1925, and by the following April piles were being driven for the stadium's foundations as the first of the exposition buildings to move from the architect's drawing boards began to take shape.[22]

Before any construction could begin, however, some mammoth engineering problems had to be resolved and the marshy land on which the exposition buildings would sit drained and filled. To do this, earth from the excavation for the northern end of the Broad Street Subway was hauled south to provide the needed firmer foundation. Streets were surveyed, graded, and paved, sewers and water and electrical lines installed, and mosquitos controlled.

Albert M. Greenfield, banker and real estate dealer, successfully raised $3 million through the sale of participatory certificates to provide some much-needed money. This, incidentally, turned out to be the largest sum other than the Council's appropriations made available to the directors of the Sesqui-Centennial, either then or later. The Commonwealth of Pennsylvania, for example, contributed nothing at all, other than the state building at the fair site; the Congress of the United States, only $1 million.[23]

The building program was cut to meet the reduced budget, and other plans revised, causing Colonel Collier to resign on October 29, 1925. At this juncture Mayor Kendrick took charge. In view of the chaotic state of affairs and the few short months left in which to plan the revised program, announced by Kendrick on November 22, 1925, to construct the buildings and arrange the exhibits, a strong argument was made by E. L. Austin, at that time the Exposition's controller, and others for the postponement of the fair until 1927. Kendrick opposed postponement on the grounds that the Sesqui-Centennial was designed to commemorate the nation's 150th birthday which fell in 1926, and that the exposition could not therefore be delayed until 1927, if it were to do so in proper fashion. Tremendous efforts were called for to complete the Forum of the Founders, the state buildings, foreign pavilions, a "Gladway," a "High Street" in a colonial village, numerous small structures for restaurants, a bank, a radio broadcasting station, and a gigantic Liberty Bell, eighty feet tall, placed at the entrance to the Exposition. In spite of all the frantic activity, only a few exhibits were actually in place by opening day, May 31, 1926, and not until July 5 were as many as 90 percent of the exhibits on display.[24]

The Exposition, unready though it was, was formally declared open on May 31 by Mayor Kendrick. Secretary of State Frank B. Kellogg and Secretary of Commerce Herbert Hoover, members of the National Sesqui-Centennial Exhibition Commission, addressed those present. A concert by the 108th Field Artillery Band, aerial exhibitions, and fireworks entertained the public; a luncheon, dinner, and inaugural ball were offered to special guests. In spite of this brave front, the Sesqui's unfinished state was all too evident. The first group to see and complain were the Shriners, whose national convention was being held in Philadelphia concurrently with the Sesqui's opening. Some roads still unpaved, unfinished exhibits and exhibition buildings—Gov. Alfred E. Smith did not even break ground for the New York State building until June 14, and the Argentine pavilion was not finished until October 30 —and, worst of all, rain greeted the Shriners. "All seemed confusion." Returning home the Shriners spread the word that the Sesqui-Centennial was not worth traveling to see.[25] The word-of-mouth reports that had saved the Centennial Exposition helped make a fiasco of the Sesqui.

Rain and poor attendance notwithstanding, scheduled programs went on as planned. Crown Prince Gustavus Adolphus dedicated the Swedish Blockhouse on June 2; on Flag Day, June 14, troops from the original thirteen states paraded; a musical pageant, *America*, was presented on June 24—in the rain, of course; President Coolidge delivered the Fourth of July address; there was a governors' day, July 23; and on September 23 Gene Tunney met Jack Dempsey in a heavyweight title bout at the new stadium. It rained on the 120,757 gathered to see the match won by Tunney. One Philadelphia Quaker, who considered the fight a "disgraceful affair," thought the rain just retribution for the city's staging of a pugilistic contest; for the sports-minded the Tunney-Dempsey fight is probably still the best remembered event of the summer.[26]

The Liberty Bell, entrance to the Sesqui-Centennial Exposition, was still not finished when Philadelphia, "the Workshop of the World," staged a mammoth industrial parade with a hundred bands and 135 floats on June 4, 1926.

FREE LIBRARY OF PHILADELPHIA

Old High Street, sponsored by the Colonial Dames, and the Japanese pavilion were two of the more successful exhibits. The electric lighting too was much admired. The Liberty Bell when lighted was visible the length of Broad Street, southward from City Hall. Floodlights with amber caps illuminated the Forum of the Founders, and the lighting effects about the canals and lagoons of the amusement area were spectacular.[27] Unfortunately none of this was enough to counteract the effects of the weather. Rain fell 107 of the 184 days the Exposition was open, contributing to the poor attendance; three

and a half million fewer people came to the Sesqui than had viewed the
Centennial. Poor attendance, initially ascribed to the fair's unfinished state on
opening day, was given still another interpretation by critics in Chicago and
New York when plans were being discussed in each of those cities in the 1930s
for the staging of similar spectacles of their own. Both cities cited Philadelphia's dismal showing as proof that the day of successful international expositions was over.

Official tour of President and Mrs. Coolidge, through "High Street,"
Sesqui-Centennial Exposition (July 6, 1926).

FREE LIBRARY OF PHILADELPHIA

When the Exposition officially closed in November, the unpaid bills in
Mayor Kendrick's hands showed that it had run up a $5-million deficit. E. L.
Austin, the Sesqui's last director-in-chief, blamed the citizens of Philadelphia
and the mayor for the Sesqui's troubles. He scolded Philadelphians for their
habit of "destructive criticism" and their refusal to "subordinate personal
preference to the good of the city as a whole." Kendrick became the scapegoat
for insisting that the Exposition be opened on time, chiefly, it was thought,
because as Imperial Potentate of the Order of the Mystic Shrine, he wanted
opening day to coincide with the Shriners' visit to the city.

Unexpectedly high construction costs raised the question of the use of
political influence for financial gain and led Councilman Morris Apt to ask
for an examination of stadium costs. Kendrick countered by challenging the

"whisperers" who were speculating about possible graft, but when 400 of those to whom money was due for work done at the Sesqui-Centennial were found to be represented by one man, George C. Klauder, law partner of Harry A. Mackey, then city treasurer and leader of the Forty-sixth Ward, the "whisperers'" suspicions appeared to be well founded. Controller WillB Hadley refused to approve subsequent payment vouchers and on January 10, 1927, subpoenaed the mayor, calling for the Sesqui-Centennial accounts.[28] Legal action was not pressed, but the Sesqui's bankruptcy was inevitable, and on April 27, 1927, the United States District Court appointed Francis Shunk Brown, a prominent Republican attorney, and E. L. Austin joint receivers. The Council voted extraordinary appropriations to rescue the Sesqui from its insolvency, and eventually all creditors were paid in full and the good name of the city preserved.

In spite of its bad press and its financial troubles, the Sesqui was not without value to the city. Albert M. Greenfield, who had worked hard to solve some of the Exposition's problems, thought that "the development of the extreme southern end of the city," now possible because of the work done by the city on streets, sewer, water, and electrical lines there, would provide an "increased financial return to the city treasury," and improve the "health and environment of the many thousands who [now] make their home in South Philadelphia. . . ." Greenfield was echoing an opinion expressed in a report by the Department of Public Works in 1913 on the opportunities for commercial, industrial, and residential development of South Philadelphia, if proper attention were paid to the provision of playgrounds and parks and the integration of League Island Park into the city's park system.[29]

Further expansion was slower in coming to this area than Greenfield may have expected. Not until a need for new housing near the Navy Yard with the yard's increased activity preceding the entry of the United States into World War II, and the completion of the Broad Street Subway to Snyder Avenue, was there much growth. No division of the South Philadelphia wards, usually one sign of increased population, was made after the Forty-eighth Ward was separated from the old Thirty-sixth in 1914. Moreover, according to Bernard J. Newman of the Philadelphia Housing Association, this South Philadelphia area actually lost population between 1920 and 1930.[30] In time, however, the land reclaimed for the Sesqui-Centennial provided Philadelphia not only with housing sites but also with space for a major sports complex where the Spectrum and Veterans' Stadium keep company with each other and with the rarely used stadium where the young ex-marine Gene Tunney won the heavyweight title from Jack Dempsey in a drenching rain.

I I I

Perhaps Philadelphia had been unready for a celebration. The city appeared to lack that civic unity an international exposition like the Sesqui-Centennial needed if it were to succeed. Reasons for this pervasive unease were not hard to find. There had been several bank failures between 1919 and

"Gene Tunney Takes Jack Dempsey's Title in Sesqui Battle" (September 24, 1926). A crowd of 120,757 fight fans watched the match in the new stadium.

PHILADELPHIA BULLETIN

1924, a building and loan scandal with the closing of seventeen associations, plus the closing of three stock brokers' businesses in 1922; postwar unemployment continued high as some manufacturers, especially those in the textile trades, moved south in search of cheaper labor; and the question of the immigration of yet more foreign workers to Philadelphia and the United States called for resolution, as did a related issue, the "Americanization" of those already here.[31] Some Philadelphians felt put upon by the newly imposed Prohibition laws, while others were deeply worried by a growing lawlessness, and by the graft and the police connections with illegal activities evident in the city.

The habit of placing personal preference above the requirements of the law, cited by Boies Penrose as a Philadelphia trait, and the obduracy of some ethnic groups, in whose eyes Prohibition cut across old traditions senselessly, was making the enforcement of the Volstead Act hard to obtain.[32] A *Ledger* headline on January 1, 1920, declared: "1920 Trips in on Barley Corn's Arm: Old John mourned as dead, shakes a spry leg at New Year's festivities." On New Year's Day itself the Mummers clubs almost unanimously chose to comment on the coming of Prohibition as a permanent condition rather than a wartime aberration.[33] Neither headline nor Mummers' comments augered well for a positive reception of the new law in Philadelphia, and indeed the next several years saw what appeared to be no more than desultory attempts at enforcement. The Council's refusal to provide money for a larger police force, the tardy revocation of the state licenses for taverns and grog shops, illicit distilling, brewing, rumrunning, and bootleggers' sales hamstrung those trying to enforce the law. There were some raids on cafés, liquor dealers, and alcohol manufacturers, and officials charged in a "liquor conspiracy" were arrested; but by the fall of 1923 Philadelphia's flouting of the liquor laws was beginning to provide lively reading for a national audience.[34]

While campaigning for election as mayor, Kendrick had promised to run an administration on "sound business principles" and to give special attention to the obvious need for law enforcement. He declared that he would appoint a director of public safety not "subject to local political pressures." His man was Brig.-Gen. Smedley Darlington Butler of the United States Marine Corps. Honest, tough, and with a distinguished military record, Butler agreed to take a year's leave from the marines if he could have a free hand to administer the police department and enforce the law as he deemed it necessary to do. When the mayor promised "no interference from any source whatsoever," Butler took the job.[35] Once in office he lost no time in starting his campaign to turn Philadelphia into a law-abiding city.

Three "forty-eight-hour vice drives" and a dramatic shake-up of the police force during his first month startled the city.[36] Although applauded by the "drys," Butler's "pounce policy" soon met with opposition: magistrates balked at issuing search warrants for private homes even when the owners were believed to be using them as outlets for the sale of illegal spirits. If any were brought to trial and convicted, the magistrates usually suspended their sentences or substituted warnings. If fines were imposed they were invariably light. "Judge Harry S. McDevitt was the only judge who stood squarely and unflinchingly by me," Butler said later. Café owners reopened their businesses as soon as the raiding policemen left. Raided five times in Butler's first drive, the bartender at the Venice Café on North Twelfth Street told a reporter, "Sure, we got beer." Generally it was found that although a stranger might not find bars open to him as freely as before, the "regulars" had no trouble in getting whatever they wanted.

Councilmen, fellow members of the Kendrick administration, and others with political clout raised their voices both publicly and privately in protest of Butler's operations. Several tried giving the director of public safety lists of places "to be left running as usual." "The hell they are," said Butler, and when some real estate men, applauding his raids on the "little" places, asked that "our place" where the investment was large be spared, Butler queried, "Since when, in God's name, has a one-hundred-thousand dollar crime been less than a ten-thousand dollar one?"

Opposition to Butler's program reached a boiling point by the summer of 1924, when even the mayor called Butler's activity "intolerable."[37] Support from the Federation of Churches and the Pennsylvania Law Enforcement Association, along with the generally enthusiastic response to his work indicated by a mass meeting at the Academy of Music, carried Butler over the mounting dissension. Kendrick and his director of public safety were reconciled, and the mayor, expressing renewed confidence in Butler, asked the president and the secretary of the navy to extend his leave for an additional three years. Coolidge, making it plain that he did not think the federal government should police America's cities, granted Butler one year's additional leave.[38]

Meanwhile Butler continued to apply the law to the important nightspots like the Ritz Carlton grill as well as to the corner saloons. He kept up his raids, and pushed along his reorganization of the police districts in order to change the cozy old arrangement that had equated the district boundaries with those of the city's wards. Here the reality confronting Butler included not only magistrates' courts where the decisions given were dictated by politics not by law, but ward leaders who exercised the right to pick the police captains for their wards, making the police accountable to the politicians and not to the director of public safety. Finally, since only the Civil Service Commission could dismiss a policeman and since the commission too was a political creature, the director was rarely able to fire or discipline an officer. Even proven extortion or assault were not considered "reasons for dismissal" by the commission.[39]

By September 1925 Butler had grown disheartened. Earlier in his term of office he had told a reporter: "Sherman was right about war but he was never head of the police of Philadelphia."[40] Now, speaking to a reporter from the *Evening Bulletin,* he expanded his comment to include Philadelphians generally, saying:

Either I am unpopular, or the enforcement of the liquor laws is unpopular in this city. Law enforcement on an absolutely even basis has not had the support of the people of Philadelphia and does not have it now. When the people of Philadelphia or any other city stop playing the game of "Enforce the law against others but not against me," they will begin to win the fight against lawlessness.[41]

Philadelphia remained "ostentatiously wet." Groups like the Molly Pitcher Club and an organization for "Prohibition Enlightenment" worked actively for repeal of the Eighteenth Amendment; many breweries were reported to be operating and making "high-powered beer"; conversion of industrial alcohol, much of it poisonous, into bootleg whiskey was common, producing, according to a city coroner's report, ten to twelve deaths daily. Arrests were made, but bringing the arrested to trial and persuading the courts to convict them remained another matter. According to Mayor Kendrick's report for 1925, there had been 1413 speakeasy owners arrested in 1923; 905 were tried and 595 convicted. In 1925, on the contrary, 10,381 were arrested, only about 10 percent were brought to trial, and only about 4 percent of those apprehended met with even a minimal fine, often "considered a routine business expense."[42]

Although Philadelphians remained at best lukewarm supporters of Butler's efforts to secure obedience to the Prohibition laws, they were pleased with the general reduction of crime in the city and the increased safety of the streets that his regime produced. They were pleased, and they said so. Possibly this persuaded Kendrick to ask for still another extension of Butler's leave

from the Marine Corps. Accompanied by Sen. George Wharton Pepper, he
called on President Coolidge on October 30, 1925. The president listened to
Kendrick, but refused the request.[43] Keeping subsequent events in view, the
cynic cannot but wonder whether Kendrick's appeal was not purely pro
forma.

In any event, when Coolidge refused further leave for Butler, Kendrick
promptly appointed George W. Elliott, who from the beginning had been a
trusted and trustworthy assistant to Butler, to succeed him as director of
public safety, presumably at Butler's request. Then Butler, apparently suffering from an overactive Quaker conscience and feeling that he was breaking
his promise to Kendrick and the city by leaving with his job uncompleted,
resigned from the Marine Corps so that he could continue on at his Philadelphia post. This was too much for Kendrick, who fired his old director of
public safety when the latter refused to resign. The *Record* summed it up thus:
"He [Butler] was honest; that was taken for granted or he would not have
been appointed. But he was 100 percent honest. We think we are doing the
Mayor no injustice in expressing the belief that this was a little more than he
had counted on."[44]

When Butler left the city in January 1926 to take command of the marines
at the San Diego Naval Base, his resignation from the corps having wisely
been ignored, Philadelphia was left to face the consequences of the abortive
war against the liquor interests, and to struggle against other kinds of crime
and corruption among government departments. The unsavory mixture
evolved into a scandal that finally exploded in August 1928 in a spectacular
grand jury investigation ordered by Judge Edwin O. Lewis because of spreading gangland warfare and other crimes.[45]

I V

The crimes that produced this particular investigation were not those
normally listed as routine by a metropolitan police department. Philadelphia
had plenty of that variety, too. Payroll bandits and employees falsely declaring
that they had been victimized by hold-up men; bank robbers who sometimes
killed bank messengers, guards, and policemen in the process; ingenious
swindlers; auto thieves operating as a ring were headlined and doubtless were
looked upon by readers of the Philadelphia press as seasoning for the day's
hard news.[46] Lotteries in West Philadelphia and in the Forty-seventh Ward
of North Philadelphia, and gambling syndicates with Broad and Locust
Streets as one center for "the sportsmen" and David Lane's Twentieth Ward
another, operated freely with occasional arrests and modest fines, if punishment was imposed at all. Dope made the news less frequently—two cases of
smuggling narcotics into the Eastern State Penitentiary, another involving
the seizure of $100,000 worth of opium at Twelfth and Wallace. Vine Street,
Noble Street, and the lower part of Charles Hall's Seventh Ward were havens
for prostitutes. If the houses were closed by police raids, they reopened
promptly. One story is told of a madam put on two year's probation every

time that she was arrested, who had accumulated eighty-four years' probation by the mid-1920s while continuing to operate her establishment "at full blast."[47]

All these unlawful activities unsettled Philadelphians, but it was the mounting number of gangland murders, as bootleggers, numbers barons, and others tried to expand or protect their turf, that finally led Judge Lewis to charge the August grand jury with the duty of looking into crime in the city, especially into connections between the police, the bootleggers, and the gambling rings.[48] Much of the warfare that so disturbed the judge had erupted in South Philadelphia: Joseph Zangli and Vincent Cocozza had been shot at Eighth and Christian; John (Race Track Johnny) Paone was gunned down in front of his East Passyunk Avenue cigar store; and the DiSilvestro brothers' homes in South Philadelphia had been bombed.[49] Not all those involved were Italians, nor were all the killings south of South Street. The Club Cadix at Twenty-fourth and Chestnut was the scene of a gang-related murder; Hughey McLoon was killed at Tenth and Cuthbert; his killer, Daniel O'-Leary, was himself gunned down less than a week later; and "Big Arthur" Callen met his end at Forty-second and Parkside.[50] Meanwhile the suspicion grew that these troubles were somehow related to a police department over-protective of organized crime.

Harry C. Davis, the new director of public safety, a member of the City Committee, and Vare's "detail man" and friend, had scrapped Butler's redistricting of the police force and reinstituted the old system of districts organized along ward lines, almost guaranteeing that the "war on crime" decreed by the new mayor, Harry A. Mackey, would be ineffectual.[51] Matters would probably have gone on as usual with a certain amount of sound and motion but little useful action had not Boss Vare suffered a severe stroke on August 1, 1928. Two weeks later Judge Lewis issued his charge to the grand jury.

The rip tide running through the Republican organization as the result of Vare's incapacity, with the attendant scramble for power that ensued, affected the procedures of the grand jury and the actions of the mayor; District Attorney John Monaghan, a former common pleas judge; and the director of public safety. On September 3 Mackey ordered the police to "clean up" the city within twenty-four hours; in October, Director Davis transferred 4500 policemen in a shake-up of the force; and Monaghan reported a widespread system of graft tied to the Police Bureau and instituted a watch over the "clearing house numbers game" that led to the exodus of the principals who for the past twenty years had thought themselves safe from the law.[52] A "society bootlegger" was indicted, fined $20,000, and jailed; the Venice Café was padlocked; and Matthew Patterson, leader of the Nineteenth Ward and member of the state legislature, was found guilty of bribery and extortion, fined, and jailed. Max (Boo Boo) Hoff, "King of the Bootleggers," had been questioned but because of "insufficient evidence" was not held (this, in spite of the testimony of Edward S. Goldberg, who admitted selling machine guns and bulletproof vests to him). A question was also raised about the use Hoff could possibly have had, as a private person, for 175 telephones.[53]

Through it all the police were generally uncooperative. Michael Slavin, a lieutenant of detectives, went so far as to defy the grand jury. Criticism of Davis increased, and although Vare, now recovering, declared him both competent and honest, Davis resigned on November 23 under pressure from the mayor and was replaced by Maj. Lemuel B. Schofield, the state's assistant attorney-general.[54]

Between August and December eighty-nine members of the police force, from an assistant superintendent down to a group of patrolmen, were suspended; eighteen were dismissed; sixty-three were arrested. An additional eighty-five men were dismissed the following March on the recommendation of the special grand jury. The Union Bank and Trust Company was severely criticized for the $10 million in "bootlegger deposits" it held under fourteen fictious names, leading to the resignation of the president of the bank, Joseph S. McCulloch, and its takeover by the Corn Exchange National Bank and Trust Company.[55] An article in the December 1, 1928, issue of *Collier's*, citing the number of open bars in the city (1185), the number of speakeasies (13,000), and the amount of "protection" paid weekly by each owner ($25 weekly for bars, whatever the traffic would bear for speakeasies), the number of bawdy houses (300), and the amounts they paid ($160 to $200 each week), estimated that Philadelphia's annual bill for liquor and other amusements was $40 million, with $20 million of that sum going for "protection." The grand jury's disclosures had provided a reply to a question being asked by some Philadelphia newsmen: "How rich is a rich policeman?" A reasonable rejoinder could be any officer with a bank account "swollen into six-figure" size.[56]

The city shuddered for a while, then went about its ordinary business. The historian, murmuring "*plus ça change . . .*," notes that precisely ten years later in 1938 a similar grand jury investigation exposed with similar vigor the unholy alliance then existing between the city government, the police, and organized crime.

V

The year 1928 was a bad one for the Republican organization. The grand jury's disclosures, Vare's stroke, and the defection of large numbers of hitherto stalwart Republicans to Al Smith in the November presidential election raised questions about the continuing domination of the city's voters by the Vare team.

"Boss" William Scott Vare was the surviving member of a dynasty of three brothers whose base of power lay among the ethnically defined slum wards of center city and the crowded row-house neighborhoods, the shipyards, docks, and factories, hogpens, and dumps of the vast reaches below South Street. Vare was the last of a string of municipal barons who had ruled the Quaker City for almost a century: William B. Mann, James McManes, David Martin, Israel Durham, Boies Penrose, and Edwin H. Vare, his brother. Bill Vare believed impartially in God and the Republican party; his politics were fundamental and pragmatic. Never before were all the Republican leaders of the city's wards so firmly united behind the will of one man. "He

was not at the head of his organization because of any unusual intellectual or
social acumen," wrote J. T. Salter. He was "in no sense a cultured or highly
civilized person . . . [in fact] he was ignorant and uninformed about many of
the implications of the social process of which he was a part. But he was an
ultraspecialist in ward and city politics."[57]

Central to Vare's dominant position was his understanding of ward leadership, how to make it work effectively for him, and how to manage the ward
leader and his committeemen. Through the 1920s Philadelphia had forty-eight
wards incorporating some 1200 precincts that were represented by about 3000
committeemen. Each of these was typical of his area and, if representing one
of the first twenty or "organization" wards, probably holding down a public
job. Vare demanded that a committeeman

stay close to those that need him. He must always be on the job to help them. The
average division leader can always be found at a certain place—the corner cigar store,
the drug store. . . . He goes there every night. When the voter wants him, he knows
where to find him.[58]

William Scott Vare (1867–1934), August 9, 1928.

PHILADELPHIA BULLETIN

The ward leader controlled his ward by favors he himself did for voters, by jobs given "vote producing committeemen," and by the force of his personality. Some were also members of the G.O.P. City Committee where their continued tenure was dependent on their ability to see that the organization candidates won election to whatever offices they were standing for.[59]

The money Vare needed to support his role as head of Philadelphia's G.O.P. came from contracts won by the Vare Construction Co., $15 to $20 million between 1924 and 1928 alone. These lucrative contracts frequently came from the utilities, from Bell Telephone, the Pennsylvania and B. & O. Railroads, and serve to illustrate an observation of J. P. Morgan that the heads of many of the great corporations "preferred to deal with a boss" and in so doing helped to perpetuate the boss's power. For if the contracts came the boss's way because of his political muscle, they in turn produced money, more contracts, and more political power in what often seemed to be an unbreakable cycle.[60]

False voter registration, "help" given voters in marking their ballots or by issuing "floating ballots" (that is, premarked ones), false counting, ballot-box stuffing, and purchase of votes were all used with more or less regularity whenever an election was held in Philadelphia. The 1925 primary, for example, produced, first, an organization "sweep." Then a series of petitions asking that the ballot boxes be opened in a number of the divisions of the First, Tenth, Thirteenth, Fourteenth, and Fifteenth Wards were presented to the Board of Registration Commissioners. In the Fifth Division of the Thirteenth Ward it was charged that 40 percent of the vote had been cast by a "phantom phalanx" from jails, hospitals, vacant houses, graveyards. The commissioners asked the district attorney to investigate the "fraudulent lists" on October 23, but despite the furor the organization won the November election as usual. The following month, however, four registrars and the election officials of the Fifth Division of the Fourteenth Ward were sent to jail for voting "phantoms" in the primary; and two registry boards and Magistrate Evan T. Pennock were held "in bail." Eight other registrars were fired as the trials of those presented before Courts of Common Pleas proceeded. Shameless and secure, the G.O.P. used the same illegal means to win in 1926. Probes of the Third, Thirty-sixth, Thirty-ninth, and Forty-fifth Wards followed.[61]

This scandalous situation would seem to have offered a ready-made platform for Philadelphia's Democrats. And so it would have, had they been a real rather than a shadow party, existing only on sufferance and the organization's handouts. Led by John O'Donnell, a South Philadelphian and friend of Vare's, and occupying a party headquarters with the rent paid by the Vare machine, the Democrats were loyal to their Republican boss and remained unwilling to do anything likely to discourage the patronage he provided. Even in those appointive offices where the law required bipartisanship, the officeholders were lackeys of the G.O.P. and not inclined to forget it.[62]

Boies Penrose had died on New Year's Eve, 1921. Thereafter Vare controlled the Democrats and the G.O.P. in Philadelphia, but statewide his

machine came into conflict with the Republican party as represented by the
Mellons of Pittsburgh and Joseph R. Grundy of Bristol. To win the leadership
of the Pennsylvania G.O.P. outright was at the bottom of Vare's decision to
run for the United States Senate in 1926. In the September primary he was
opposed by the incumbent, George Wharton Pepper, appointed in 1922 by
Gov. William G. Sproul to fill out Boies Penrose's term; and by Gifford
Pinchot, governor of the state. Vare, believing that Prohibition was increasingly unpopular, chose to run as a "wet," Pinchot as a "dry," while Pepper
tried to straddle the issue. Both Pepper and Vare spent lavishly, Pinchot only
a modest sum. Pepper, supported by the Mellons, Grundy, and the press,
carried sixty-two of Pennsylvania's sixty-seven counties, Vare only one in
addition to Philadelphia. Yet gathering a majority of 228,000 votes in the city,
all that he needed to win the primary, Vare went on to victory in November.
The Democratic candidate, William B. Wilson, a former secretary of labor,
ran well on the issue of Vare and Vareism, but once again the 230,000-margin
Philadelphia gave Vare could not be overcome.[63]

Albert M. Greenfield, who had raised much of the money for Vare's
campaign and who had given $125,000 to it himself, expressed pleasure that
he had helped Vare to achieve his "life's ambition." Other Philadelphians
were less complaisant. Questions were raised about the reasons the city's
contractors were willing to spend large sums to aid Vare; whether the high
costs of the Sesqui-Centennial might be part of the story; and how men like
Sheriff Thomas Cunningham, with an annual salary of about $8000, could
afford to contribute $50,000 to the newly elected senator's campaign.[64]

Unwilling to concede defeat, Wilson petitioned the Senate to declare
Vare's election fraudulent—which it probably was. Governor Pinchot sent
his own "certificate of doubt" to the Senate, bolstering Wilson's contentions
by charging that Vare's victory was "partly bought and partly stolen." A
three-year investigation followed, headed by Sen. Key Pittman of Nevada,
Thomas Walsh of Montana, both Democrats, and George W. Norris of
Nebraska, a Republican. On December 6, 1929, the Senate voted fifty-eight
to twenty-two to deny Vare the seat. Although conceding that he had defeated Wilson, it was agreed that Vare had forfeited his right to a place in the
Senate because of excessive spending to win the nomination (Pepper had
spent more to lose it). Such was the assigned reason. In Salter's view, Vare's
real crime was that "he was a ward politician without social background."[65]

City politics in 1927 centered on the election of a new mayor. When the
organization picked Harry A. Mackey, Vare's recent campaign manager, a
lawyer and leader of the Forty-sixth Ward, as its candidate, J. Hampton
Moore announced his intention of running as an independent. Moore ran
strongly in the September primary, but he could not defeat the Vare-sup-
ported Mackey. Undismayed, Moore and his adherents launched the City
party, but they were ineffectually organized and on Election Day joined by
too few Democrats to elect even so popular a man as Moore. Mackey and the
entire organization ticket swept in, Mackey by a margin of two to one over

Moore. The ring wards, residential areas on the fringes of the city, gave Moore his largest share of the vote; Mackey won in the safe first twenty, and in those precincts where blacks accounted for more than 80 percent of the voters. It was a smashing victory for Vare, then probably at the height of his political power, in spite of the Senate investigation.[66]

It was the presidential election of 1928 and Alfred E. Smith, the Democratic candidate, the "happy warrior" from New York, that combined to open cracks in Philadelphia's G.O.P. and inaugurated what amounted to a revolution in the city's politics. Philadelphia's affection for Smith was spontaneous and heartfelt. His Irish descent, Catholic religion, and "sidewalk personality," his opposition to Prohibition and to limiting immigration appealed to the ethnically oriented voters. In addition he was, like the Vares, a veteran of the city streets and precinct-level politics, a plus in Philadelphia and other urban centers. When he invaded Philadelphia on October 27, 1928, riding from the Delaware River Bridge to the Bellevue-Stratford in a motorcade, Smith enjoyed an ovation from the throngs gathered along the route. This enthusiastic welcome was repeated later at a mass meeting at the Arena. Herbert Hoover and Charles Curtis won in Philadelphia of course, and Republican Sen. David Reed was reelected handily, but Smith amassed 40 percent of the vote and carried eight wards, five in Vare's own South Philadelphia, where Flora Vare, Ed Vare's widow, lost what had been a "family seat" in the Pennsylvania Senate since 1894. (The victor was Lawrence E. McCrossin, a journalist and a political novice.) Smith's showing had undoubtedly been helped by the caution against illegal activity at the polls issued to the organization's division chiefs, lest unfavorable reports reaching Washington further prejudice the Senate committee investigating Vare's election.[67]

Had Vare not suffered a severe stroke in August, Smith's impact on Philadelphia might have been less, but out of the city and ill, Vare was unable to exert the control needed to dilute Smith's appeal. The same circumstances were responsible for several attempts by the more ambitious of the ward leaders to seize the old leader's power. The first to try for the crown was Harry A. Mackey; the opportunity he used, the grand jury investigation. Joined by District Attorney John Monaghan and George Holmes, a county commissioner (both old Vare men), by Thomas E. Mitten, president of the PRT, and by Albert M. Greenfield, a former Vare supporter who now was detaching himself from the troubled senator, they seized on Smith's good showing as well as the emerging scandals to reach out for control of the party.[68] The investigation supplied them with material for a kind of political blackmail, useful to whip into line vulnerable ward leaders and committeemen. These men they then kept faithful with patronage jobs. Men like Charles Hall, Harry Trainer, William Campbell, and Samuel Salus, seeing a threat to their own interests, combined behind Vare in opposition to Mackey and the uncertain future a clear-cut victory by his alliance would leave them. Mackey's power peaked in January 1929 when his man, Judge Charles L. Brown, was elected president judge of the municipal courts over Judge Leopold C. Glass, a Vare loyalist. Both the Council and the Civil Service Commission also continued in the Vare camp, however, and Mackey's triumph was destined for a short life.[69]

The row-office elections in the fall set the stage for a showdown. Mackey and Greenfield, supported by the anti-Vare Republican League, of which Thomas Raeburn White was head, nominated John F. Dugan, then director of public welfare, for register of wills, and Thomas F. Armstrong, president of the Manufacturers' Club and a former purchasing agent for the city, for city treasurer. The old pillars of the Vare organization, joined now by Hampy Moore, persuaded Vare to oppose Dugan for register of wills by continuing Billy Campbell in that post, and to nominate WillB Hadley, able, honest, and without damaging political connections, for treasurer. They also prevailed upon Vare to support the voting-machine referendum advocated by the Republican League. With these last two maneuvers they took away much of the League's thunder. The Vare ticket carried thirty-eight of the city's forty-eight wards in the primary and was triumphant in November. Vare, the phoenix, with the help of his superb organization, had risen again. The fact that no one of his would-be successors, who in time would include both Hall and Trainer, was powerful enough to defeat both the boss and their rivals in pursuit of his power kept Philadelphia in Vare's control for a while longer.[70]

Not until Philadelphia voters began to show their independence of the G.O.P. would his sway be broken. The 1928 election foreshadowed a change, when ethnic and religious considerations temporarily took large numbers of Irish and others into the Democratic camp. Vare's own support of John Hemphill, the Democratic candidate for governor in 1930, after his nominee Francis Shunk Brown lost to Gifford Pinchot in the primary, showed Philadelphians that it was possible to cast a vote for a Democrat. Vare's move was motivated by his anger at Pinchot who was, Vare believed, responsible for his disgrace in the Senate. The investigation following Wilson's and Pinchot's charges Vare considered "the most merciless . . . ever conducted by any committee of the United States Senate." Vare, never a forgiving man, was thus quite willing to cross party lines to upset someone who was perceived as the enemy, and Hemphill, a West Chester attorney whose view of Prohibition was akin to Vare's own, was an easy candidate to back.

Ward leaders and Philadelphia businessmen, particularly those with utility interests, followed suit. Among the G.O.P. defectors were W. W. Atterbury, president of the Pennsylvania Railroad; John Hampton Barnes, the railroad's counsel; Samuel M. Vauclain, president of the Baldwin Locomotive Works; Effingham B. Morris, chairman of the board of the Girard Trust; and Cyrus H. K. Curtis, whose Philadelphia newspapers the *Ledgers* and the *Inquirer* came out for Hemphill. Pinchot ran disastrously in Philadelphia, with Hemphill gathering 76 percent of the vote. This time a large margin in Philadelphia was not enough to determine the outcome of the election, and in the end Pinchot not Hemphill went to Harrisburg. In spite of Al Smith in 1928 and the lead Vare supplied in 1930, it took FDR's New Deal to swing

Philadelphia away from the G.O.P., and it was those peoples of the city who were invisible to men like Henry James who broke the back of the organization.

V I

In the fifty years from 1870 to 1920 Philadelphia's population doubled. Immigrants from Russia, Poland, and Italy supplied the greater number of the alien newcomers, and blacks from the South, those who were native to the United States. In spite of this influx Philadelphia's immigrants represented a relatively small portion of the total population, only about 25 percent, where Boston's were almost a third and New York's as much as 40 percent.[71] Henry James commented that a visitor to Philadelphia did not feel the impact of the "grosser aliens," leading him to wonder whether there may not be "some virtue in the air for reducing their presence, or their effect, to naught."[72]

Most of the eastern Europeans arriving after 1900 were Jews from Russia, Poland, Lithuania, and Rumania, believers in strict orthodoxy whose religious practices were at variance with the established German Jews who had been in Philadelphia for a generation or two. Many of the older stock had successfully integrated themselves into the economic life of the city. Howard A. Loeb was the president of the Trademans Bank and his brother-in-law Frank Bachman a partner in the stock-brokerage house of Parrish and Company. Jerome H. Louchheim, a contractor whose Keystone State Construction Company was building the Broad Street Subway, figured influentially—as could be expected—in Republican politics. A. S. W. Rosenbach gained an international reputation as a dealer in and collector of rare books and manuscripts, and his competitor Charles Sessler also conducted a well-patronized modern bookstore. Jules E. Mastbaum, a realtor, founded the largest moving-picture theater chain in the city, and his friend Morris Wolf Philadelphia's first major Jewish law firm. J. David Stern added the *Record* to his newspaper holdings and made it, a lone Democratic voice, a factor in the incipient attack on the Republican machine. Solid evidence of Jewish mercantile enterprise were three large department stores on Market Street East: Snellenburg's at Twelfth Street, Gimbels at Ninth, and Lits at Eighth.

For several decades prosperous Jewish families had been moving away from their old communities to apartments in the Rittenhouse Square area and to a band several streets wide on either side of Broad Street between Girard and Diamond. A movement farther north had already begun with some families seeking tree-shaded lawns and the advantages of suburban living in Oak Lane and Cheltenham Township, closer to their Philmont Country Club.[73]

At the same time numbers of eastern European Jews were climbing up the economic and political ladder, foremost among them Lithuanian-born Albert M. Greenfield. In South Philadelphia, the center of Jewish orthodoxy, Rabbi B. L. Levinthal held sway. As they prospered these immigrants too moved away from their first place of residence to nicer homes in West Philadelphia and Strawberry Mansion, at the same time abandoning orthodoxy for the less stringent demands of Conservative Judaism. A spread of settlement from Parkside by the end of the 1920s included Wynnefield, where the Conservative synagogue Har Zion rapidly grew in size and influence.[74] To be sure, a good many Jews of the prewar waves of immigration—the war and the restrictive Johnson Act of 1924 brought an end to the eastern European flow as it did to those from Italy and Greece—remained in the older areas of settlement, but the census figures for 1930 showed that South Philadelphia had 41 percent fewer Jews living there than in 1920. In 1919 the Federation of Jewish Charities, the community's central fundraising organization for health and welfare agencies which had been dominated by members of the older German-Jewish families, expanded its scope by taking in under its aegis a host of agencies founded by and for the new immigrants. These included Mount Sinai Hospital (now the Daroff branch of the Einstein Medical Center) and the Associated Talmud Torahs, traditional Hebrew schools. So began the slow melding of the Jewish community.

The cultural and economic background the immigrant brought with him and the economic opportunities of the area to which he came determined where he would settle. For example, 70 percent of the Jews who came to Pennsylvania settled in Philadelphia, but 71 percent of the Poles went elsewhere, although many of them had landed at the city's Washington Avenue docks. This variation directly reflected Philadelphia's economy which "stresses skill, diversity, precision and quality" but had little need for many unskilled workers. The immigrant Poles were generally without special skills and could best find employment in Philadelphia only in the leather industry, in some of the steel mills, or as longshoremen, jobs where muscle was of more importance than previous training. Here they were in competition with the blacks, whose presence in the city reduced the need for immigrant blue-collar laborers. Those Poles who did stay settled chiefly in Southwark, near St. Stanislaus Church at 242 Fitzwater, and worked on the docks. Another group turned a segment of Hunting Park Avenue near St. Ladislaus Church into a "Little Warsaw" and worked at Midvale.[75]

If the foreign-born contributed but a relatively small part of the city's total numbers, the blacks, although only about 7.4 percent of the whole in 1920, added a preponderantly large part for a northern city.[76] Many Negro families still lived along the corridor of Lombard Street in the neighborhood of Mother Bethel A.M.E. Church and on other streets in the Fourth, Seventh, and Thirtieth Wards. A strong if small black community had developed in the Northern Liberties close by Zoar Church, around the Berean school and Presbyterian church, opposite Girard College, on Diamond Street near Twenty-ninth, and in West Philadelphia. After World War I blacks began to take over houses left vacant by Jews "moving up the ladder," and North Philadelphia started to assume its present ethnic orientation.[77] The new arrivals usually held jobs as street and sewer cleaners, trash collectors, and servants, or worked on the railroads in maintenance jobs. Although the opportunities were severely limited, by 1930 Philadelphia was home to nearly 220,000 blacks.[78]

Among the more secure older families, the professions, particularly law, medicine, teaching, and the church, offered both men and women the best chance for advancement. Two hospitals—Mercy, founded in 1907 by Dr. Henry M. Minton, a graduate of Jefferson, and Douglass, then at Sixteenth and Lombard, founded in 1895 by Dr. Nathan F. Mossell, a graduate of the University of Pennsylvania Medical School—supplied the best health-care services generally available to the community. A newspaper, the *Tribune*, a bank, the Citizens and Southern, beneficial societies, organizations like the Armstrong Association, and the many black churches tried to help the new-comers withstand the frustration and loneliness of life in an inhospitable city. The churches, however, were not always seen as the stabilizing force they had been in the nineteenth century. Writers like Carter Woodson accused the clergy and the educated Negroes of shirking their responsibilities as the black community like its white counterpart divided along social and economic lines.[79]

Political exploitation of the black community, most of whom were "Lincoln Republicans," was easy for the Vare machine. There was only one black ward leader in 1925, Edward W. Henry, and most of the jobs he had in his pocket were the traditional ones, plus a handful of appointments to the police force, or to positions as marshals' or sheriffs' deputies. When the organization failed to deliver its expected aid, the black voters could and on occasion did make their displeasure felt. For example, when Amos Scott, a black tavern keeper of 1140 Pine Street, failed to receive a promised magistrate's office, G. Edward Dickerson, a Negro attorney with offices at 628 South Sixteenth Street, made sure that the Thirtieth Ward blacks heard the story. The result at the next election was "evident."[80] In the main, however, residents of the largely black Twelfth, Fourteenth, Twentieth, and Thirtieth Wards remained subject to the organization's whims until the New Deal's humanitarian response to the misery caused by the Depression drastically altered their party affiliation.

For Philadelphia's 55,972 Italian adults the 1920s were a time of change and adaptation. Although Italians had lived in South Philadelphia in sufficient numbers to make possible the establishing of their own church, St. Mary Magdalene de Pazzi, by 1851, it was not until the Pennsylvania Railroad began to invite Sicilian laborers to come to Pennsylvania to work on the railroad that immigrants from that country became a major presence in the city.[81] The earlier nineteenth-century immigrants were northern Italians, skilled craftsmen, musicians, and others with specific contributions to make to Philadelphia's culture and economy. The later comers were generally laborers, employed by the railroads, or in construction work on public buildings like City Hall, or in building subways. By the 1920s marked differences, both cultural and economic, increasingly divided the middle-class minority from the blue-collar majority.[82]

The separation between them was most evident in their attitudes toward education. For the laborer and his wife, both often illiterate, economic need determined that a son's attendance at school should end at fourteen when he could obtain working papers. Italian boys aged fourteen to sixteen, working as messenger boys, office boys, in the clothing industry, were the largest number of white youths employed in Philadelphia. It was the others, the sons of the middle-class families, who were able to finish high school and even go on to college. Middle-class parents—skilled artisans, specialty manufacturers, merchants—saw education as a way to preserve their Old World status as well as a means of advancement in the New World. Given these aspirations, Philadelphia's public schools with their emphasis on vocational training as the most appropriate kind of education for the children of immigrants, regardless of their inclination and ability, and the emphasis on a standardized variety of Americanization, irritated many Italians.[83]

Equally hard for the Philadelphia Italians to accept was the determination of the Irish hierarchy of Philadelphia's Catholic church, under the leadership of Dennis Joseph Cardinal Dougherty, to bring the "individualistic" and often anticlerical Italians into the fold of an Americanized church and his own program of "obedience and orthodoxy." Ten Italian parishes had been created before 1920 and five more were added in the 1920s. The Italian priests assigned to serve these were "carefully screened," and great efforts were put forth to bring the religious practices of the Italians into harmony with the cardinal's ideas of sound doctrine. An able administrator, Dougherty had a limited "ability to convey a sense of warmth, charity and human sympathy to the immigrants." In time, and not without some open rebellion, the Italians "made an accommodation" with Dougherty's church, but they did so "in their own fashion and with traditional reservations."[84]

Most Italians, unlike many of their Jewish neighbors, elected to remain in South Philadelphia in spite of improvement in their financial position. Many had invested in South Philadelphia real estate and found that ownership of property offered a useful way up the economic ladder. Their holdings were often small and not infrequently placed the owners in the category of slum-lords, operators of licensed tenements. Charles C. A. Baldi, banker, under-taker, politician, was one of the first and most successful of the Italian real estate tycoons, owning a hotel, a factory, a warehouse, an office building, and numerous houses. His activity and that of his lesser comrades in this business shows that Philadelphia slum properties were often in the hands of a member of an ethnic minority who might himself have lived in a tenement that he owned.[85]

Like the Italians the Irish had first settled in South Philadelphia, in South-wark and Moyamensing. After the Civil War they began to scatter through the city into Port Richmond, along the South Street–Bainbridge Street corri-dor to the Schuylkill, to Germantown, Chestnut Hill, and the northeastern sections of the city.[86] Both Italians and Irish subscribed to the Roman Catholic theology, but if the Italians found the American church uncongenial, the Irish, whose fellow nationals formed Philadelphia's archdiocesan hierarchy, were on familiar ground. Their children went, as they were expected to do, to the parochial schools; families, not just the feminine part thereof, went to mass; contributions were made to the parish for the building of churches, schools, and other useful projects, not for colorful festivals with the pagan undertones the parishioners of the Italian churches enjoyed. Again, unlike the Italians who gave total allegiance to the G.O.P., the Irish, perhaps more given to faction, supported both parties with little real power in either until the 1928 presidential election united them behind the twin issues of religion and ethnicity. Then the builder-developer or contractor-boss with the right political connections, a breed that first came to prominence in Philadelphia in the 1850s, found in the Democratic party a suitable vehicle for political and financial advancement, a means used with increasing effectiveness ever since.[87]

Immigration into the city after World War I continued even after Congress enacted a new quota law in 1924. The number of aliens settling here was small, however, when compared with the crowds that had helped to swell Philadelphia's population in the 1880s and 1890s. Migration replaced immigration as Philadelphia families of foreign parentage found in the prosperity of the 1920s a good time to take advantage of the city's transportation system to put some distance between home and work, to leave the old neighborhood for newer and pleasanter places, to buy a house with the aid of the ubiquitous building and loan society. For the most recent immigrants, foreign-born or black, opportunities were limited. If unskilled they competed with each other for scarce laborers' jobs, and for housing they accepted the old tenements, alleys, and courts whose amenities consisted of a pump and a privy in the yard. The separation, along economic, social, and cultural lines, between those who had achieved middle-class status and those who had not deepened. This was particularly noticeable among the Jews, distancing the well-established German Jews from the newly arrived adherents of eastern orthodoxy; among the middle-class artisans and professionals from northern Italy and their fellow nationals who remained blue-collar workers; and among the well-to-do blacks whose professional interests and upper-class outlook kept them aloof from the uneducated and untrained newcomers from the rural South. The city as a whole seemed both ignorant of and rather indifferent to the troubles of these the least fortunate among its people—unless they made headlines as bootleggers, gangsters, IWWs, or suspected Communists.

Another kind of Philadelphian, not a numerical minority but with only minor options to choose among when job hunting, and with hampering legal restrictions, were the women of the city. With the ratification of the Nineteenth Amendment on August 26, 1920, better times seemed in view, and on September 26 Philadelphia women celebrated this their first step into a fuller citizenship. Before year's end they had voted for a president of the United States and elected three women to the state legislature. Women's names were placed in the jury wheel, there were two women on the school board—Anna Lane Lingelbach and Laura H. Carnell—and a woman on the Art Jury, Mrs. H. S. Prentiss Nichols. Violet E. Fahnestock, the city's first woman magistrate, was sworn in on January 2, 1925, and heard her first case a week later, January 8. Before the end of the decade amenities available for women were enlarged as the Women's City Club settled into its spacious new quarters at 1622 Locust Street, and Warburton House, Philadelphia's hotel for women, opened. Nonetheless the greater number of working women were employed in factories or as servants. Others were clerks, saleswomen, bookkeepers, stenographers, or teachers. There were women doctors, the greater number trained by the Women's Medical College of Philadelphia, and lawyers, notable among these Sadie Turner Mossell Alexander, a graduate of the University of Pennsylvania Law School, member of both the Philadelphia and Pennsylvania bars, and assistant city solicitor during 1928–1930. Women held graduate degrees in the liberal arts and sciences, but if they wanted a bachelor of arts degree as an undergraduate they could not expect the University of Pennsylvania to admit them to its program.[88]

VII

Men and women, Old Philadelphians and newcomers, contributed to the cultural as well as to the economic life of the city, some as board members, some as fundraisers, some as audience, and some as performers. South Philadelphia and Kensington sent in the Mummers, the blacks offered jazz greats, including singer Bessie Smith and stride pianist Lucky Roberts, and the Italians stood behind the local opera companies. In sports there were Jack Kelly, Olympic champion in the single sculls at Antwerp in 1920, William T. Tilden II, with multiple tennis championships won at Forest Hills and Wimbledon, and Dorothy Campbell Hurd, who won the women's amateur golf championship at Merion in 1924.[89] The Philadelphia Athletics added a touch of professionalism to the gentlemanly sports in which other Philadelphians chose to excel with their World Series victory in 1929. This event was given the proper Philadelphia accolade when Connie Mack, the team's owner and manager, was handed the Philadelphia Award for 1929.[90]

In literature as well as in sports, old and new Philadelphians made reputations for themselves and a limited local coterie. Agnes Repplier was counted the best of America's essayists. A. Edward Newton's *Amenities of Book Collecting* in 1918 and his subsequent popular essays on the joys of books made the check-suited, red-tied manufacturer of electrical equipment an international figure. Contributing to the creation of Philadelphia genre works were Francis Biddle with *The Llanfair Pattern*, Struthers Burt in *Along These Streets*, and William C. Bullitt with *It's Not Done*.[91] Both Biddle's and Bullitt's books, on the theme of love of a lower-class girl by an upper-class man, titillated Philadelphians who thought they could recognize the characters. Owen Wister's *The Virginian* turned up as a silent film in 1920, and in 1929 was remade with Gary Cooper, Walter Huston, and a soundtrack. Joseph Hergesheimer supplied a pair of bestsellers, *Three Black Pennys* and *Java Head*, to the roster of writings by Philadelphians. George Kelly, Jack's brother, brought home a Pulitzer Prize in 1925 with his play *Craig's Wife*. At about the same time Arthur Huff Fauset and some other men and women, students or recent graduates from Penn, began to publish *Black Opals* (1927–1928), Philadelphia's first black literary magazine since 1909. (Up to this time the blacks, more than any other of Philadelphia's minorities, expressed in writing, in the theater, and in music their sense of self and of their own community.)[92] Fauset was a writer—his "Symphonesque" had won the O'Henry Memorial Award in 1926 —who turned publisher. Edward W. Bok, an editor, who began to write after he retired from the *Ladies Home Journal,* produced *The Americanization of Edward Bok* in 1921 and *A Man from Maine,* a biography of his father-in-law Cyrus H. K. Curtis, publisher of the *Ladies Home Journal* and the *Saturday Evening Post.*

Both Bok and Curtis exemplified the old Philadelphia habit of offering opportunity for the newcomer to establish himself in the city, to prosper, and to become a force in the community at large. Bok's "civic endeavors" live on in the Philadelphia Award, established in 1921, and appropriately enough given first to Leopold Stokowski, another newcomer under whose direction the Philadelphia Orchestra achieved a national reputation for excellence. Stokowski's interest in the science of sound brought the orchestra a chance to join with RCA in making the the first electrical recordings for Victor by their "orthophonic process," and in 1929 to make the first commercially sponsored radio broadcast by an orchestra. Backed by the Philadelphia radio manufacturer Philco, this program was carried by fifty NBC stations across the United States and by shortwave to Europe, South America, and Asia. For the production, Stokowski served as announcer, continuity writer, and conductor. The city recreation centers were opened specially on that Sunday afternoon so that persons without radios could hear the city's orchestra, and prizes were offered in the schools for the best essay on this new beginning for Philadelphia and for symphony orchestras elsewhere.[93]

Opera, which had been a staple of Philadelphia's musical life since 1830, tended to upstage the orchestra, which did not celebrate its twenty-fifth anniversary until 1925. During the 1920s the city had three professional opera companies, the Philadelphia Civic Opera Company, the Philadelphia Grand Opera Company, and the Pennsylvania Grand Opera Company, as well as a quasi-amateur group, the Philadelphia Operatic Society, all offering regular programs. Added to this were the appearances of New York's Metropolitan Opera Company.[94]

Philadelphia had 164 movie houses and about sixty theaters. Of these latter, eight were downtown, surely enough to serve up whatever variety of entertainment the city's diverse population could wish for. But if there was something for everybody, there was also bound to be something that displeased somebody. The *Ledger* on January 4, 1920, published a "New Year's Greeting" by C. H. Boute, the burden of which was the growing number of protests against plays; it cited the objections of the Jewish community to the *Merchant of Venice,* and of the League of Scottish Veterans to *Macbeth.* The protests were both vigorous and numerous enough to cause Mayor Kendrick to appoint Thomas M. Love, a theater manager, to head an "unofficial board" of theater censors in 1924. The following year, 1925, the police censored *Earl*

Carroll's Vanities, not surprisingly objected to by conservative groups upset by the changing values and liberated manners of the Jazz Age. More surprising was the Garrick Theater's withdrawal of *Revelry,* a play critical of the Harding administration, evidently an example of the persistence of the blind loyalty to a person or a cause by some even after that person or program has been discredited.[95]

The city's conservative stance surfaced in the world of art as well. Repeating a familiar lament, the acerbic Joseph Pennell remarked: "No artist of international reputation . . . born in Philadelphia has ever been able to live here, or, if he leaves . . . and returns, the bourgeois by whom the place is entirely overrun drive him out again."[96] Thomas Eakins and Frank Furness had managed to remain, although not always to universal applause; so for much of their careers did Howard Pyle, Cecilia Beaux, and the Calders. Nonetheless there was a sad truth in Pennell's diatribe. Yet Pennell's opinion might be balanced by Nathaniel Burt's comment that although Philadelphia has at times seemed to cherish the little talents while denying the big ones recognition, nevertheless in the "Philadelphia circles where arts are genuinely appreciated art is more quietly at home than in any other American milieu as part of the pleasures of life, not merely a form of chic or conspicuous consumption."[97]

Several associations, generally informal but one organized, illustrate Burt's assertion. The Philadelphia Art Week Association held its first exhibit in 1923, using store windows along Chestnut and Walnut Streets, galleries, the Art Alliance, and the Pennsylvania Academy of the Fine Arts to show off the work of contemporary Philadelphia artists. The other groups, weekly or biweekly gatherings of musicians, painters, architects, and amateurs, met to enjoy each other's company "in a cheerful belief that something was happening," hardly the mark of an uncaring city.[98] Caroline Sinkler and Emily Balch were hostesses at two of the city's more famous such assemblages. *The* salon was run on alternate Saturdays after the orchestra concert by the R. Sturgis Ingersolls on Rittenhouse Square and the Maurice Speisers of Tasker Street. (Speiser was a lawyer who represented artists, musicians, and writers, including James Joyce and Ernest Hemingway.) It included Adolph Borie, the Carroll Tysons, the Francis Biddles, the Edwin Dannenbaums, and Stokowski, and it fostered Edgar Varese and Franklin Watkins.

None of this, however, could ensure an immediate and positive response to the paintings by Cézanne, Matisse, Picasso, and Modigliani when Albert Barnes, persuaded by Arthur Carles and Henry McCarter, showed his collection of these and other moderns at the Academy in 1923. Barnes, best described as an eccentric millionaire who had made his money through his invention of Argyrol, a much-used antiseptic, was outraged by the adverse reaction of both critics and public and removed his paintings from the sight of Philadelphia's philistines. Housing his collection in a neo-Renaissance building in Merion designed for him by Paul Cret, he took pleasure in denying access to his paintings to most Philadelphians, and verbally thumbing his nose at them.[99]

The Benjamin Franklin Parkway (1925) designed in 1917 by Jacques Gréber (1882–1962). Looking down the Parkway, past Logan Circle and the Free Library (opened 1927), the two wings of the Philadelphia Museum of Art can be seen at the end. The museum was partially opened to the public in 1928. A corner of the Pennsylvania Railroad's Broad Street station appears in the foreground, and the new (1925) building for the Insurance Company of North America nears completion on Sixteenth Street.

At the same time that Barnes was severing diplomatic relations with Philadelphia, the city was engaged in building a new art museum to replace Memorial Hall, considered too small, and inconveniently located in Fairmount Park. Designed by Horace Trumbauer's firm, the neoclassical revival building elegantly crowns a vista down the Benjamin Franklin Parkway from City Hall. It was almost universally criticized in Philadelphia when built— either for not being modern in design or for being the wrong color (yellow rather than white), or, although complementing the design of the old waterworks nestling at the base of Fairmount, because it was thought by some to diminish them by its size and superior elevation. The museum had a new

director, a New Englander from New York University, Fiske Kimball, a
flamboyant, sometimes rude, impresario as well as a first-rate museum man
who had the job of turning a minor collection into one worthy of a major city
with a long tradition of concern for the arts. When the museum opened
officially on March 26, 1928, it was almost empty. Sixteen rooms had been filled
with seventy paintings borrowed from the collection of Flemish and early
Italian masterworks assembled by John G. Johnson, a successful Philadelphia
attorney, and with additional borrowings from other private collections of
modern artists including Renoir, Van Gogh, Braque, and Picasso. In the next
years Kimball managed to gather materials for the medieval wing, for additions to the period rooms, representative of the best architectural interiors of
eighteenth-century England and France, and to display the museum's holdings in them. Depression economics slowed the completion of the building's
interior spaces and made the acquisition of funds needed for the purchase of
additional works of art hard to come by. Here Kimball had some monumental
disappointments, the loss of the Widener collection to the National Gallery
being one, and some astonishing successes. When he retired in 1955 he left a
museum whose collections could no longer be ignored.[100]

VIII

In 1927, the year that Fiske Kimball was struggling to get an unfinished
museum ready to open, the city was boasting that it was "The World's
Greatest Workshop," producing more "articles necessary for Twentieth Century living, comfort and convenience than any other American municipality."
Statistics give a certain support to this assertion: Philadelphia was the third-
largest city in the United States, the country's third-richest city, and third too
in the overall value of its products, with a billion dollars invested in 266
distinct lines of manufacturing, and a work force of 670,865, almost evenly
divided among persons in professional, industrial, and service categories.[101]
Philadelphia's port, with 300 wharves and 159 piers, three trunk lines, and a
belt line connecting these with the piers, was the largest freshwater port on
the Atlantic and handled more tonnage than any other but New York. Coal,
oil, grain, lumber, and sugar were the principal items of trade.[102] Cramp's,
among Philadelphia's older firms, had two large ships on the ways when, just
before the yard launched the second of these, it was announced that no more
ships would be built, signaling an end to a company and a craft that had played
an important part in Philadelphia's economic life for generations.[103] Cramp's
projected closing was not the only cloud on the economic horizon, and the
more thoughtful of the city's businessmen determined to try to counteract
what some saw as a trend. An article in the Review of Reviews for December
1929, "Philadelphia Outgrows Its Past," described the program of the city's
Business Progress Association, founded the year before, which had raised $1.4
million to study "Philadelphia's industry and commerce, assess her geographical, cultural and social structure, invite new industries to settle here, and
generally keep the city from leaning on its past."[104]

Electricity had become an important part of the daily life of most Philadelphians. After World War I all new houses were expected to be lighted by electricity and were wired as a matter of course. The wiring of older homes kept electricians busy as the demand for better lighting and the new appliances—irons, toasters, cleaners, and radios—grew. One of the most important of the city's new companies, the A. Atwater Kent Company, was making Philadelphia a center of radio manufacturing. Two other inventions destined to change significantly the domestic habits of her householders, the electric refrigerator and the electrically operated oil burner, also came on the market in the 1920s but caught on rather slowly, possibly because of their cost. To serve all of its customers, particularly the PRT, for the "El," trolley lines, and the new subways, and the railroads, then electrifying their suburban lines, as well as businesses and homeowners, the Philadelphia Electric Company built new generating stations, expanded old ones, and developed a new hydroelectric plant at Conowingo, Maryland.[105]

While these improvements were going forward, rumors of a merger between the Philadelphia Electric Company and the United Gas Improvement Company were continuous. The U.G.I., a holding company with interests in gas and electric companies and in street railways, offered Philadelphia Electric connections with suburban companies that were previously lacking, and the merger of the two utilities was generally supported by both the press and the public. The rumors became fact in 1927, and shortly thereafter the PE's customers were made happy by a reduction in the rates charged for electrical current.[106] The response to the U.G.I.'s proposals to the city, made in advance of the expiration of their twenty-year lease of Philadelphia's gasworks, had been less enthusiastic. Suggesting a flexible gas rate and an annual payment of $4,448,000 to the city, the company, dealing with a friendly Council, expected no opposition. The city solicitor thought the arrangement "both unbusinesslike and of extremely doubtful legality," but the Council gave it unanimous approval and the mayor signed the new lease, to take effect in 1927.[107]

Automobiles were beginning to change the appearance of Philadelphia's streets and the regulations governing their use. In 1920 Christopher Morley could write a newspaper column celebrating Ridge Avenue, where a farmers' market still flourished, as the "stronghold of the horse." The same year the *Ledger* was carrying advertisements of agencies like the Firestone Ship by Truck Bureau, urging Philadelphia businessmen to ship by truck. Big cities were learning to cope with a new kind of traffic. Both New York and Philadelphia banned parking along major streets in 1922, and Philadelphia designated some 200 city streets as one-way thoroughfares shortly thereafter. In 1924 the city tried to control traffic on Broad Street by installing a master light in City Hall Tower. It did not work out as hoped, and the less spectacular "wooden policemen" at street level were substituted.[108] The PRT, with an eye to holding on to its present customers and possibly attracting new ones, installed parking lots at either end of the Frankford–Sixty-ninth Street

Parking Lot, Thirteenth and Arch Streets (c. 1926). This photograph, from the records of the City Parks Association (founded 1888), is labeled "a typical eyesore of its kind." A bus terminal now occupies the site.

TEMPLE UNIVERSITY, URBAN ARCHIVES

"El."[109] The city's own bridge-building program added to the problem, notably the construction of the Delaware River Bridge, a joint project with Pennsylvania and New Jersey, begun in 1922 and formally opened in 1926. Statistics reporting the tolls paid between that year and 1930 are eloquent testimony to the growing domination of transportation by automobile and truck. Even before the bridge was finished the PRT, sensing a new source of profit, applied for an exclusive franchise to operate bus lines over the bridge. This offer was rejected, but when the company agreed to accept a nonexclusive franchise and raised its yearly fee to the city, the Bridge Commission and the Public Service Commission approved the operation of trolley cars on the bridge.[110]

The PRT was accustomed to finding both the Council and the Public Service Commission willing to consider its proposals favorably, whether for the leasing of the Frankford "El," for new bus lines through the city, or for the purchase of the Yellow Cab Company.[111] When the management of the PRT asked for a monopoly of the bus and trolley lines running on any of the city streets, however, they went too far. Three hundred Philadelphia businessmen traveled to Harrisburg to protest the proposal and the Public Service Commission turned it down. The United Businessmen's Association was equally successful in opposing the new lease for the Frankford "El," refuting management's claims that they were operating that line at a loss.[112]

The Delaware River (Benjamin Franklin) Bridge, designed 1919–1926 by Paul Cret (1876–1945), photograph 1929. The nearly two-mile expanse was then the longest suspension bridge in the world. Municipal Piers Three and Five North, in the middle foreground of the photograph at Filbert and Arch Streets, are scheduled to be developed as condominium residences with marina facilities and restaurants in 1984. Piers Four and Five South, at the lower right, and the Camden Ferry, at the foot of Market Street, have been demolished. Penn's Landing (begun 1967), a mile-long development of quays, esplanades, and a boat basin, has replaced them.

PHILADELPHIA DEPARTMENT OF RECORDS, ARCHIVES DIVISION

During the next several years the relations between the city and the PRT grew increasingly acrimonious and ended when Controller Hadley demanded an audit of all PRT records.[113] The result was an exposé of the Mitten Management, which a few years before had been praised as an "Adventure in Industrial Democracy" for providing PRT workers with a share in the company, with wages indexed to the cost of living, with insurance, sick benefits, and pensions.[114] A less attractive side of Mitten Management now appeared as the relations between that management and the PRT were made clear. Evidence was brought before Judge Harry S. McDevitt that the management had ignored the city's right to representation on its board of directors, had failed to supply annual reports or an audit of its accounts, and had rigged the fees charged the PRT annually, raising them from $158,000 to $2.4 million. The city had not received its share of profits, and PRT funds had been manipulated and mismanaged by improper use of stockholders' proxies. Thomas Mitten drowned at about the time that Hadley started a suit to secure the money owed to the city, and eventually almost all of his estate was transferred to the PRT to replace that company's misappropriated funds.[115]

I X

Mitten's career was illustrative of the economic and administrative climate of Philadelphia about 1928. Money appeared to be readily available for the alert, with few questions asked. Profits were handsome and apparently endless. George W. Norris, president of the Third District Federal Reserve Bank in Philadelphia, compared the wild speculation he saw everywhere to the Mississippi and South Sea Bubbles, but those caught by the fever claimed that the world had entered a "New Era," with such an abundance of capital that equities could not fail to hold up.[116] With bigness looked upon as the key to success, bank mergers were frequent. Among the most important were those joining the Fidelity and Philadelphia Trusts; the Provident and Commonwealth Consolidated; the Philadelphia National, Girard National, and Franklin Fourth Street National; and the Bank of North America and Trust Company with the Pennsylvania Company, making this the largest trust company in the city. Banks merged to expand their services or to acquire enough capital to finance the needs of Philadelphia's utility and industrial companies, and sometimes to save a weaker institution from collapse.[117]

Norris was not the only banker alarmed by what the newspapers called the "Orgy of Speculation," a fever that infected all classes from stenographers and waiters to professional men and business executives. The Philadelphia National Bank in the spring of 1929 began to reduce loans to brokers and to individuals borrowing to buy stocks. In October securities prices began to come down. A "technical readjustment," the sophisticated called the decline, but by the end of the month a "selling stampede" was in full swing. Although the shock of the stock market crash was enormous to the banks, only one Philadelphia bank, the United Strength Bank and Trust Company, was forced to close that year, and for many of the city's banks 1930 turned out to be a profitable twelve months. The next year, 1931, was not so profitable, as the winds of economic depression strengthened nationwide.[118]

Depression and War
1929-1946

by Margaret B. Tinkcom

[Philadelphia's] voice is the voice of a city of contrasts—a city of wealth and poverty, of turmoil and tranquillity, of stern laws often mitigated by mild enforcement; a city proud of its world-molding past and sometimes slow to heed the promptings of modern thought.

— Federal Writers' Project guide to Philadelphia

Brother Alexander, I been thinking that my people has got to get two things. They got to get theyselves homes where the roof don't leak, and they got to get hospitals. God has given me a concern for my people. Now you take that sweepstakes money and build some homes.

— PEARL MASON, winner of the Grand National
Steeplechase Sweepstakes [1]

Philadelphia Faces the New Year Confident of Brighter Future" proclaimed the headline over the principal essay on the *Inquirer*'s financial page, January 3, 1930. The optimism of the writer was not altogether without solid support: there had been an 82 percent gain in real estate valuation in the city since 1920; both the Philadelphia Electric Company and the United Gas Improvement Company had announced plans for expansion, and U.G.I. had declared an increase in its annual dividend rate; the proposal to develop an air, marine, and rail terminal at Hog Island was "virtually assured"; Mayor Harry A. Mackey was expected to ask for an engineering study for a parkway between Race and Vine Streets from Broad Street to the Delaware River Bridge; while an *Inquirer* editorial suggested the demolition of City Hall, except for the tower, and the building of a new municipal office building on Reyburn Plaza just to the northwest, in order to relieve traffic congestion on both Broad and Market Streets.[2] Philadelphians had responded to the Christmas season splendidly, sending out a record seventy carloads of mail, and filling the stores to purchase a variety of gifts, possibly even including such frivolities as J. E. Caldwell's "diamond necklace suitable for almost every occasion."[3]

On New Year's Day 1930 the Mummers paraded, with the Funston, Ferko, and League Island clubs the prize winners, and if one may trust news reports, crime and the woes of Prohibition weighed more heavily on the city than did the uncertain future of jobs, banks, real estate investments, and the stock market. There were signs, however, that the coming year would bring difficulties: the United Strength Bank and Trust Company at Fourth and Market Streets had closed on Christmas Eve because of "frozen assets"; both local and New York bond and stock markets were clearly under pressure; and an *Inquirer* editorial writer noted, a bit too casually, that semiskilled and unskilled laborers might have to expect "a certain amount of unemployment."[4]

I

In 1930 Philadelphia, with a population of 1,950,961, up 7 percent since the 1920 census, was the third-largest city in the United States. The overwhelming majority of her citizens, 1,359,833, were native-born whites; 219,599 were blacks; and 368,624 were foreign-born.[5] Although the census figures show that the city was still growing, they also indicate that metropolitan Philadelphia, the city plus its surrounding suburbs, was growing at an even faster rate, with an increase of 42.1 percent during the same decade.[6] Nevertheless real property in the city, assessed at $1.80 per $100 of valuation, was listed at $3,451,528,364, cash receipts from taxes were reported to be $105,540,334, and the Council, fixing the city's budget for 1930 at $88,973,300, was thought to have provided for a comfortable surplus.[7]

Philadelphia's downtown in 1930 did not reflect on its surface the troubled financial picture worrying the directors of insurance companies, banks, brokerage houses, and building and loan associations. A number of important buildings had just been erected, were in progress, or were on the architects' drawing boards. The Aldine Trust Building (Twentieth and Chestnut), the Lewis Tower (Fifteenth and Locust), the Fire Association office (Fourth and Walnut), and three apartment houses—the Drake (Fifteenth and Spruce), the Rittenhouse Plaza (Nineteenth and Walnut), and the Chateau Crillon (Nineteenth and Locust)—had been completed in 1929. The Pennsylvania Railroad's Suburban Station Building (Sixteenth and Pennsylvania Avenue), the Sun Oil Company's office (1616 Walnut Street), the Market Street National Bank (Market at Juniper), a twenty-story addition to the Penn Mutual Life Insurance Company's building (Sixth and Walnut), and the Architects' Building (Seventeenth and Sansom) were opened in 1930. Work was in progress on the Pennsylvania Railroad's Thirtieth Street Station, on an addition to the Strawbridge & Clothier store at Eighth and Market, and on the Lincoln-Liberty Building (now the Philadelphia National Bank) at Broad and Chestnut, where Wanamaker's intended to establish a store catering to the "Philadelphia gentleman." Workmen were also completing a thirty-story addition to the Girard Trust (Broad Street at South Penn Square); the PSFS Building (Twelfth and Market), a technological and architectural landmark; the Medical Tower (Seventeenth and Latimer); and the Reading company's Terminal Commerce Building (401 North Broad Street), standing on stilts over the

Reading tracks; and at the time the only air-right property in existence with a public freight station beneath it as well as having the city's first underground parking garage. The Convention Hall, at Thirty-fourth Street and Civic Center Boulevard, and the Benjamin Franklin Institute on the Parkway were going up. Four new federal buildings were in planning stages: a new Federal

Philadelphia Saving Fund Society Building, built 1930–1932 (photograph c. 1932), designed by George Howe (1886–1955) and William E. Lescaze (1896–1969).

PHILADELPHIA SAVING FUND SOCIETY

Reserve Bank at Tenth and Chestnut; a courthouse at Ninth and Chestnut; the Customs House at Second and Chestnut; and the central post office, at Thirtieth and Market Streets. Not until the 1950s was Philadelphia to enjoy a similar architectural explosion. All these buildings except the post office, Thirtieth Street Station, the Federal Reserve Bank, and the Convention Hall were skyscrapers, the twentieth century's mark of a city's coming of age. It is probable that Henry James, who had found Philadelphia comfortably scaled for humans when he visited the city in 1903, would have been saddened by her somewhat belated succumbing to the "New York, the Chicago note" of the "perpetual perpendicular."[8]

The Philadelphia Planning Commission, established by ordinance on April 13, 1929, was preparing to submit to the Council a Fifty Year Plan for the city's immediate development with the coordinated expansion of a variety of municipal projects, including a proposal for a "memorial court of honor providing an ornate approach" to Independence Square, to be created in the block between Chestnut and Market, Fifth and Sixth Streets.[9] The City Beautiful concept for which Paul Cret received the Philadelphia Award in 1930 was to be furthered by the Schuylkill River Development Project, a proposal calling for two new bridges, University Bridge and one to connect

Convention Hall, Thirty-fourth and Civic Center Boulevard, opened 1931 (photograph c. 1932), designed by Philip H. Johnson (1868–1933). The 1936 Democratic National Convention which nominated Franklin Roosevelt for his second term was held in Convention Hall, as were the 1940 Republican convention which nominated Wendell Willkie and the 1948 conventions of both parties.

Pennsylvania Boulevard with Thirtieth Street Station; the extension of the "west embankment drive" both north and south from Market Street; and a new station for the Baltimore and Ohio Railroad with the realignment of its tracks so that the city could bring the East River Drive south from Fairmount Plaza to Walnut Street. Of vital importance to the success of the whole were plans to upgrade the system of sewage disposal in the area to relieve the Schuylkill of "its present offensive dumpage."[10] The Philadelphia Board of Trade proposed that consideration be given to improving the approaches to the Delaware River Bridge and the building of a crosstown, high-speed, elevated traffic boulevard to connect the city's two riverfronts. Meanwhile the mayor's office, with the intention of presenting Philadelphia in the role of international city, had issued a pamphlet in both English and Spanish entitled "Philadelphia, Historic in the Past, Inviting in the Present, Superb in the Future."[11] The foreword to this publication outlined a ten-year program for the city's beautification, and the text was interspersed with pictures of Philadelphia's parks, fountains, Parkway, old residential streets, and new apartment houses, and perspective drawings of its proposed airport.

There were solid accomplishments as well as "showy" proposals to which the Mackey administration could point as that mayor's term of office closed. Following the passage of a zoning enabling act, the draft of a zoning ordinance and zoning maps of the city were prepared. Major improvements in mass transportation had been carried through as Philadelphia chose to add to and improve existing rail, subway, and trolley lines rather than join Los Angeles and Detroit in highway building. The fact that 80 percent of the traffic into Philadelphia was carried by public transport doubtless influenced the city's decision. In any event both the Pennsylvania and the Reading Railroads were in the midst of an electrification program for their suburban lines. The Pennsylvania's was 70 percent complete, and the Reading expected to finish its by 1933. The Broad Street Subway had been extended to South Street. The tube to take the Frankford–Market Street El under the Schuylkill was being completed, and plans to continue the el underground west to Forty-second or Forty-sixth Streets were under discussion. The underground pedestrian concourse around City Hall was well along. The excavation for the Locust Street Subway had begun.[12]

As usual there was a negative side to municipal development. Those owning property in developing areas and the contractors specializing in municipal jobs could be expected to act as behind-the-scenes proponents of all purported improvements. Council aid, and in accordance with Philadelphia custom, Council profit had to be arranged, possibly by Charles Hall, leader of the Seventh Ward, whose ties with W. W. Atterbury, president of the Pennsylvania Railroad, and with Jerome H. Louchheim, whose Keystone State Corporation regularly won municipal contracts, were well known. At any rate Hall was accused by William S. Vare of promoting the "City Beautiful" to ease access to the Thirtieth Street Station, while "Mackey the Menace and Greenfield the Octopus" were charged with using political machinery to achieve power and financial gain. Although these were the agonized cries of the outsiders, there was doubtless more than a little truth behind the rhetoric.

By the time many of the development proposals and the formal report of the Regional Planning Federation were ready for publication, Philadelphia had a conservative mayor, and the region and the nation were of necessity more concerned with surviving an unprecedented depression than they were with planning future expenditures to safeguard the physical environment. Although much that was then proposed or partially executed died on the drawing boards, silent victims of the Depression, the plans and the unfinished public works of the Mackey era were ready at hand when a new Planning Commission and a reform government took charge of the city twenty years later.[13]

I I

Philadelphia's Christmas cheer and New Year's euphoria were short-lived. As 1930 moved on from month to month the critical weakness of the nation's economy made itself felt in Philadelphia's boardrooms. The lack of liquid assets and the attendant problems facing the city's banks, indicated by the closing of the United Strength Bank and Trust Company, were prophetic of trouble to come. During the next three years fifty Philadelphia banks that had overextended their resources, granting credit on insufficient security or on property with unrealistically inflated valuations, closed their doors. Of the fifty, only two were big banks: Albert M. Greenfield's Bankers Trust Company, with over 100,000 depositors and $35 million in deposits; and the Franklin Trust Company, with deposits of some $37 million.[14]

In July of 1930 Greenfield, head of the largest real estate firm in Pennsylvania as well as a banker, had taken over the Bank of Philadelphia and Trust Company, with $15 million on deposit and a large share of its funds in builders' construction and mortgage loans, and at the time in a shaky state. Before doing so, Greenfield had received the assurance of C. Stevenson Newhall, president of the Pennsylvania Company for Insurance on Lives and Granting Annuities, and Joseph Wayne, president of the Philadelphia National Bank, the two principal commercial bankers in the city, that the banking community would support the Bankers Trust should need arise and "good and sufficient collateral" be available. Newhall and Wayne did extend $7 million in loans to the Bankers Trust in November, but at a conference on December 21, to which Greenfield was not invited, the heads of Philadelphia's principal banks agreed to allow the Bankers Trust to close. The next day, December 22, 1930, the Great Depression became a reality for thousands of Philadelphians, moving from newspaper headlines about others' problems into their own kitchens. Some contemporary accounts imply that had Greenfield been a Proper Philadelphian rather than a Jew the rescue operations would not have been halted so quickly, citing in contrast the more extensive efforts made in behalf of the Integrity Trust Company, which survived until 1940 when its liquidation was announced by the Federal Deposit Insurance Corporation and the state Banking Department.[15]

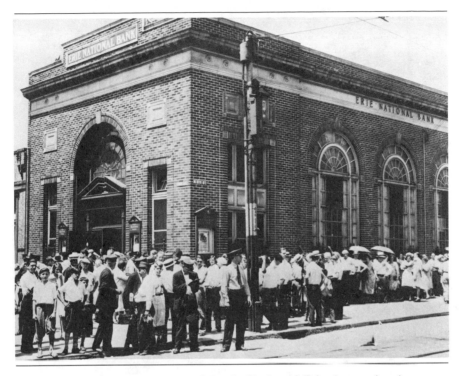

Run on the Erie National Bank, Sixth and Erie Avenue (1931).

HISTORICAL SOCIETY OF PENNSYLVANIA

Greenfield, who had kept his own funds in the Bankers Trust throughout, now had to start afresh. This he did so energetically and so effectively that half a dozen years later he had virtual control over the $15-million Bankers' Securities Corporation, an investment banking house, and over the recently reorganized City Stores, an umbrella corporation operating Lits, Bonwit Teller of Philadelphia, other department stores, and the Benjamin Franklin Hotel, and doing a $35-million business annually. Greenfield had also completed his switch of party allegiance. By 1932 he was working with John B. Kelly, Matthew McCloskey, and others to build up a real Democratic party in Philadelphia.[16]

In 1930 and at least through the succeeding decade, men listed in the *Social Register* and for the most part living on the Main Line dominated the boardrooms of Philadelphia's major banks and other institutions of equal prestige, such as the Insurance Company of North America and the Pennsylvania Railroad. In consequence a relatively small and interrelated group of socially prominent families exerted "more active control" over finance and industry in Philadelphia than did those of any other town.[17] An interesting exception to this Blue Book domination of Philadelphia's financial world was the Citizens and Southern Bank and Trust Company, with 11,000 depositors and

John B. Kelly (1889–1960) and Matthew B. McCloskey (1893–1973), photograph 1936.
HISTORICAL SOCIETY OF PENNSYLVANIA

about $2.5 million in deposits. Founded in 1921 by Richard Robert Wright with the help of a national Negro Teachers Association, it survived the turmoil of these years and was one of the first of the city's banks allowed to reopen at the end of the moratorium on all banking operations ordered by President Roosevelt immediately upon his inauguration in 1933.[18]

After the worst was over and the solvent banks were again in operation with individual deposits guaranteed by the Federal Deposit Insurance Corporation, Philadelphia was left with sixteen national banks and thirty-eight others, that is, state banks and trust companies, along with four mutual savings banks, to supply the capital for running the city and its industries.[19] As head of the Third District of the Federal Reserve system, Philadelphia also enjoyed the prestige of a Federal Reserve Bank whose new building at Tenth and Chestnut Streets was just being completed.

Philadelphia's building and loan associations, in most cases with smaller resources than the city's banks, had been similarly decimated. The large number of Philadelphians owning their own homes—more than in Boston and New York combined—reflected both the low cost of houses in the city (a two-story, six-room-and-bath house cost about $7000 in 1930), and the popularity of the building and loan association, a Philadelphia invention. A million and a quarter Philadelphians owned shares in 3400 building and loan associations in 1930. If times were good and work plentiful, everyone prospered; but with jobs hard to come by and many homes carrying 80 percent mortgages, both lenders and borrowers were in trouble. Citywide, mortgages on 19,000 properties were foreclosed in 1932. In just one block of North Van Pelt Street, thirty-six out of sixty houses were repossessed for debt between 1928 and 1938, twenty-three of them between 1932 and 1934. The real estate market was glutted, with an inevitably disastrous effect on the smaller and weaker associations, and by 1934, 1600 of the 3400 had been wiped out.[20]

The progressive collapse of a large number of the city's financial institutions (though not many of the major ones), with the loss to investors of some $5 billion, created havoc in Philadelphia's business community and in the lives of the citizens whose money and jobs, whose very ability to survive, were threatened by the growing chaos. More than 10 percent of the city's wage earners were unemployed even before the stock market crashed in the fall of 1929, reflecting the decline of local industries. By April 1930 the count of persons out of work stood at 15 percent, and by the end of the year it was clear that extraordinary measures had to be taken at once to cope with what had become a major emergency.[21]

III

In November 1930 the Committee on Unemployment Relief, headed by Horatio Gates Lloyd, was organized by concerned citizens and a drive to raise $5 million to aid Philadelphia's jobless and their families begun. The committee collected and distributed $3,840,000, most of which was used to purchase food and to provide make-work jobs for the heads of 14,000 destitute families, each man working three days a week and earning four dollars a day. The committee also supervised a shelter for homeless men in the eight-story loft of the Baldwin Locomotive Works at Eighteenth and Hamilton Streets. Between November 28, 1930, when it opened, and July 1, 1931, when lack of funds closed it down, the shelter cared for some 12,000 men. Half a dozen years later, in 1937, George W. Wilkins, superintendent of this shelter, was given the Philadelphia Award for his work there. All in all some 40,000 families received the committee's aid, and even the professional social workers, who generally opposed private charity as being more beneficial to the egos of the givers than responsive to the real needs of the recipients, commended Lloyd and his committee, noting that slim resources had been well handled and all without political entanglement.[22]

This original *ad hoc* group was replaced in June 1931 by the Bureau of Unemployment Relief, working by ordinance of the city Council within the city's Department of Public Welfare. The bureau, again with Lloyd at its head, and with $3 million of municipal funds, gathered a staff of interviewers and clerical assistants from among the unemployed, opened a headquarters at

112 North Broad Street, and set up five regional offices—in Germantown, Kensington, and North, South, and West Philadelphia. An applicant, his need verified, usually received aid—food, shoes, fuel—in two or three days, but by December 1931 the city's funds were exhausted and the bureau's official existence ended.[23] In the meantime a Community Chest Campaign, combining efforts of the Welfare Federation and the Federation of Jewish Charities, had raised $10 million. Even the notoriously tight-fisted Edward T. Stotesbury gave $100,000, and so did the always-generous Cyrus H. K. Curtis. Of this sum, $5 million was assigned to Lloyd, working as a dollar-a-year deputy to Clinton Rogers Woodruff, director of the city's Department of Welfare. Although the state added $2 million to the fund, by June all this too had been distributed. The Lloyd committee was disbanded and organized relief in Philadelphia stopped. From November 1930 to June 1932, $14 million had been gathered to help 80,000 families and 30,000 homeless men.[24] Philadelphians had contributed magnificently, but the problems the city faced were too big for private charity to handle, even with city and state aid.

With money for relief exhausted, unemployed workers and their families depended for survival principally on the help that relatives and neighbors could give, on community soup kitchens and breadlines set up by churches or other social organizations, and on fruit and vegetables scavenged at the docks and market stalls. The Unemployed Citizens League, sponsored by the hosiery and carpet workers unions, was organized in May 1932 to stop evictions wherever possible and prevent the cutting off of gas and electricity from the homes of the jobless. The league also managed to feed between 800 and 1000 families weekly thanks to donations from local merchants.[25] For most of the jobless credit had long since been exhausted. A survey of 400 families by the Community Council found that two-thirds owed for gas, electricity, or both; three-fourths were in debt to the milkman, grocer, and coal dealer. The surveyors added that the contributions to relief made by some landlords in the form of uncollected rents were "substantial."[26]

Unofficial aid came from other sources as well. Leopold Stokowski assembled a group of unemployed professional musicians for a concert in Reyburn Plaza and later directed the same ensemble in a benefit performance at Convention Hall to assist their fellows who were in need.[27] The American Institute of Architects' Philadelphia chapter proposed to map the city's landmarks and file the data on Philadelphia's eighteenth- and nineteenth-century buildings with the Free Library and the Library of Congress. Fifty-seven draftsmen, working with a committee headed by Sydney E. Martin and earning a weekly wage of fifteen dollars, began the task in February 1931. By October they had produced a notable archive of measured drawings and photographs, later documented by a map drawn by William M. Campbell and an essay on Philadelphia's architecture and architects by Horace Wells Sellers. When the Historic American Buildings Survey began operation in December 1933 under the United States Department of the Interior as part of the National Recovery Act, architects with experience in Philadelphia's earlier program were at hand to assist in organizing the new project.[28]

In addition to these programs, all of somewhat limited scope, a little extra help for the jobless living in the old townships of Philadelphia County—Germantown, Roxborough, Bristol, Oxford, Lower Dublin, Moreland, and Byberry—came from the local Poor Boards, relics of a system in force since the eighteenth century, and still assessing and collecting a poor tax in each of these districts.[29] Goodwill there was in all of this, but means were woefully inadequate to the situation, and soon Philadelphia hospitals began to report "definite cases of starvation" among their patients. By January 1932 the Community Council was speaking of the "slow starvation" facing those out of work and noted the "progressive disruption of family life" that seemed the inevitable result of prolonged joblessness.[30]

In the face of all the evidence to the contrary, J. Hampton Moore, mayor for the second time upon succeeding Harry A. Mackey in January 1932, decried all talk of a depression, claiming that people in trouble were so because they were thriftless and lazy. "I toured the lower section of South Philadelphia," Moore said, "I went into the small streets, and saw little of poverty. . . . I have counted automobiles and watched them pass a given point. Rich and poor, white and colored, alien and native born, all riding by. . . . There is no starvation in Philadelphia."[31]

He then proceeded to make matters worse by firing 3500 city workers, thus saving Philadelphia $12 million in salaries. Moore also instituted pay cuts; required police and firemen to take two weeks' vacation without pay; and by drastically reducing the number of contracts awarded during the first quarter of his first year, saved another $4.5 million. All work on the subways was ordered suspended upon the completion of the contracts then in force. This allowed the Ridge Avenue extension of the Broad Street Subway to be finished, as well as the el tunnel under the Schuylkill, but disallowed any funds for installing signal systems in both the Locust Street and Broad Street Subways.[32] Moore's procedures kept the city from defaulting on its bonded indebtedness and subsequently enabled it to borrow money at 5 percent when New York could not find any at 6 percent.[33] These tactics appealed to the business interests but hardly endeared Moore to the jobless for whom the welfare of their families was of more immediate concern than the health of the city's Sinking Fund.

Ironically enough, as the mayor was taking what he considered to be appropriate steps to meet the city's critical financial situation, a University of Pennsylvania study, "Municipal Planning to Prevent Unemployment," was published and among other points urged the value of public works projects in depression years, when they could absorb 10 percent of the unemployed and when the city's dollars could be expected to accomplish more, since materials and wages would then cost less. It is debatable whether in the long run all of Moore's economies were wise. For example, his refusal to seek a federal loan to continue work on the municipal airport at Hog Island not only deprived Philadelphians of jobs, but delayed for years the city's direct communication by air with other parts of the country.[34]

In spite of the evident need and in spite of some outspoken disapproval of his actions, Mayor Moore continued to find it impossible to consider any increase in city jobs or to accept federal funds for this purpose. In 1934, for example, Philadelphia might have had $1.5 million to pay the wages of men working on public projects if the city had agreed to use funds received from the Delaware River Joint Commission for the purchase of the necessary materials and supplies. Moore's insistence on adding this sum to the Sinking Fund for the redemption of city bonds caused David Stern, owner of the *Record*, to advise him to "take off the dunce cap," and even the conservative *Inquirer* thought the mayor's decision "too complacent."[35] Although Moore's position seemed astonishingly wrongheaded to many, in the comfortable climate of the Manufacturers' Club and the Union League it was applauded roundly.

Fortunately for Philadelphia's and Pennsylvania's jobless, both Gifford Pinchot, then serving his second term as governor, and his Democratic successor, George H. Earle III, were deeply concerned about the effects of the Depression on the state. Not long after Mayor Moore had precipitated the "Battle of Reyburn Plaza" by sending the police to meet representatives of the Unemployed Councils when they marched to City Hall on August 25, 1932, in a vain attempt to awaken the mayor to their plight,[36] Pinchot appointed the Philadelphia County Relief Board and designated Philip C. Staples chairman, with H. Gates Lloyd, experienced in Philadelphia's problems, and two highly regarded professionals, Karl de Schweinitz and Dorothy Kahn, among its members. From its inception until November 1934 the board issued orders for food and milk, and provided coal, gas, clothing, and medicine for those needing aid. Thereafter help was given in cash "sufficient to maintain minimum living standards."[37]

By the summer of 1936, however, the state's relief funds on which Philadelphia depended had run out. The situation of those without work again appeared to be desperate, while in Harrisburg a conservative Republican Senate feuded with Governor Earle and the necessary legislation to increase appropriations for relief languished. A demonstration in May persuaded the Assembly to transfer $3,630,000 from the Motor Fund to carry relief payments through the balance of that month. A second "hunger march" in July was more effective and resulted in an appropriation of $45 million to be used for relief payments statewide. This sum lasted through January 1937, when a new legislature, fortunately with more humanitarian views, took over.[38]

For five years, from 1932 to 1937, Philadelphia's city government had contributed nothing to direct relief, leaving it to the state to fund unemployment relief, outdoor poor relief, aid for dependent children, old-age assistance, and pensions for the blind, a considerable outlay when the Philadelphia County Board of Assistance had 60,000 cases covering 157,700 persons on its rolls, as it did by October 1937. The worst year for Philadelphia had been 1933, however, when 11.5 percent of whites were out of work, 16.2 percent of blacks, and 19.1 percent of foreign-born whites, who fared worst of all. Women, probably because they could be hired for less money, found work more easily than did men. (More than half of the women working in the sweatshops of the garment trade earned less than $6.58 a week.)[39]

In spite of these appalling statistics Philadelphia, because of the diversity of its manufacturing, including chemicals, steel, leather goods, and textiles, weathered the Depression rather better than did the one-industry cities like Detroit or Pittsburgh. Even so, neither private charity nor public welfare nor jobs created by public works projects could accomplish the mammoth task of restoring financial independence to out-of-work Philadelphians. Only a world war with its monstrous need for men and weapons did that.

Moore's successor, elected in November 1935, was S. Davis Wilson, nominally a Republican who had made the New Deal a campaign issue, declaring that it must be "utterly repudiated." Once in office, however, Wilson quickly showed that he had no qualms about setting up programs that could be financed with Works Progress Administration money. Thereafter Fairmount Park roads, bridle paths, and park areas, the Zoo and League Island Park benefited from the attention it was now possible to give them. City streets and the runways for the airport at Hog Island Road and Tinicum Avenue— renamed the S. Davis Wilson Airport—were graded. Improvements were made in more than 900 public buildings, money was secured for public housing, the city's water plant was overhauled, and construction projects at the Frankford and Schuylkill Arsenals, the Navy Yard, and the Naval Home were undertaken. Under the wing of the WPA's Division of Community Service, educational and recreational projects were started, nursery schools and tot playlots set up. The number of guides at the Museum of Art was increased and twenty-seven period rooms were installed there. The Federal Writers' Project produced *Philadelphia: A Guide to the Nation's Birthplace*, still considered a standard work of reference forty years later. At the peak in June 1936, 40,000 Philadelphians were working at WPA-financed jobs,[40] although not always within a friendly climate. At one venerable library, for example, the clerks sorting a hitherto unexplored and very dusty collection of manuscripts were firmly admonished, "WPA workers must not sneeze." Work, and probably sneezes, continued.

IV

The sad state into which many of Philadelphia's older houses had fallen accounted indirectly for a large share of jobs financed with federal funds. Before he had been in office a month Wilson commented that twenty-five miles of blighted areas in the city needed rehabilitation. A survey of Philadelphia housing undertaken in 1934 at the direction of the United States Department of Commerce, but carried out by the state's Emergency Relief Board as a make-work project, had reported on 433,796 dwellings of which 83 percent were row houses, about the same percentage occupied by a single family, and more than half of these owner-occupied. The survey showed that although hot and cold water were generally available (in 98 percent of the homes), eight in every thousand homes had no water at all, the occupants depending either on a hydrant in the yard or on wells or on their neighbors for their supply. Coal was the fuel used for heating, but again about 3000 homes had no way at all to heat their rooms. There was a 10 percent vacancy rate, and about 7000 houses were considered unfit for occupancy. Not surprisingly, houses available to blacks were generally older and in poorer condition than those for whites.[41]

When a WPA survey was made for the Philadelphia Housing Authority in 1939, conditions had improved somewhat. There were now more houses in the city (515,527), and more families to live in them. There were fewer vacant dwellings, only 3.5 percent, and a slightly smaller percentage of all needed major repairs to make them habitable. Nevertheless 17.5 percent were classed as substandard, and conditions for nonwhite tenants had not improved by much.[42]

Until the era of the New Deal even public interest agencies like the Philadelphia Housing Association had opposed government subsidies for low-cost housing, defined as dwellings priced from $3900 to $6200, believing that better results could be obtained by showing businessmen the possibilities of building for the largest market and selling their product through building and loan associations.[43] The Depression upset this theory by virtually eliminating the entrepreneur, the would-be purchaser, and the building and loan associations from the scene. Subsequently three nongovernmental housing projects, each of which made an important statement about a different segment of the Philadelphia community, were built, and each received the national recognition it merited.

The most orthodox of these, and the only one likely to appeal to the business world, was the salvage program devised by a real estate dealer, Arthur W. Binns. In 1939 Binns, believing in the profitability of using private capital "with a sense of service," undertook to rehabilitate 500 houses in the Thirty-fourth and Forty-fourth Wards of West Philadelphia at a cost of $1500 each. Rents were fixed at about twenty dollars a month, plus an award for tenants' good housekeeping of a once-yearly rent refund. Binns claimed about 10 percent profit after taxes, the result, he said, of good, on-the-spot management.[44] Binns was of course operating in a comparatively stable area of Philadelphia, in a rising market and an economy beginning to respond to impending war.

The second project, still seen as an architectural and social landmark, was the Carl Mackley Apartments at Castor and Juniata Park. Commissioned by the American Federation of Hosiery Workers, one of the largest and most progressively led of all Philadelphia's locals, and named for a young worker killed in 1930 in a strike-related incident, the apartments were designed by Oskar Stonorov, a European-trained architect, and financed by a loan from the Public Works Administration. Construction began in January 1934 and the first tenants, all hosiery workers, moved in a year later. The way the three-story buildings of the Carl Mackley Apartments were arranged in the open space on which they sat, with their gardens, lawns, play areas, and

Carl Mackley Houses, M and East Bristol Streets, Juniata Park, built in 1933 (photograph for the Philadelphia Record, *1940), designed by Oskar Stonorov (1905–1970) and Alfred Kastner (1900–1975). The accompanying article states that the model worker residences with underground garages and rooftop nursery schools rented for $22.50 to $45 a month. They are now privately owned, middle-income apartments.*

HISTORICAL SOCIETY OF PENNSYLVANIA

underground access to garages, and the invitation given to sculptors and painters to enliven the buildings with works of art, were new and highly sophisticated architectural ideas. The organization of life within the complex, around the credit union, the co-op market, and the tenants' committees, had roots in the labor-related utopian communities of the nineteenth century, old ideas being used to help twentieth-century workers counter the effects of the Depression.[45]

The third project, also an apartment complex, was a gift to Philadelphia's black community by Benjamin and Pearl Mason. The Masons had been on relief for five years when they won $150,000 in the Grand National Steeplechase Sweepstakes in 1940. Shortly thereafter the most heartwarming proposal of all was under way. Having paid the debts they owed, the Masons invested some $80,000 of their winnings in building the Frances Plaza Apartments at Nineteenth and Lombard Streets. Twenty-eight tenements were bought around that corner with the aid of Raymond Pace Alexander, a well-known black attorney. Frank V. Nickels, architect, designed a three-story, cream-colored brick apartment house, with court, play space, and gymnasium so arranged that about 40 percent of the land remained open, carrying out Mrs. Mason's wishes as she had expressed them to Alexander:

Brother Alexander, I been thinking that my people has got to get two things. They got to get theyselves homes where the roof don't leak, and they got to get hospitals. God has given me a concern for my people. Now you take that sweepstakes money and build some homes. The rain water been pouring through the roof all my life. I never had a inside toilet. My kids have to play in the alley and get theyselves cool in summer under a fireplug. I want green grass and flowers, too. I never did have no flowers. They's got to be a fountain where the kids can fuss around and play and not be getting hit by no automobiles.

The apartments were completed, using black contractors, and with loans from the Federal Housing Administration, the Reconstruction Finance Corporation, and the Citizens and Southern Bank.[46] Through this undertaking the Masons not only benefited some of their fellowmen for whom decent housing had seemed unattainable, but upset the almost ineradicable notion that all those on relief were out to take all they could gather in without making any return. They also probably shook up the sober souls who would have found it unsettling to discover that the use of welfare money for so frivolous an object as a sweepstakes ticket could produce such generous fruit.

The Frances Plaza Apartments are now called Rittenhouse Village and the play space is a parking area. The surrounding district, once characterized by shabby houses, sometimes empty, by garages, service stations, yards for scrap iron, rags, and paper storage, is now a semifashionable residential neighborhood, its physical improvement almost certainly begun with the construction of the Frances Plaza Apartments.

In October 1935, in spite of Republican misgivings, federal money for low-cost housing in the amount of $1.8 million was made available through the PWA working with the United States Housing Authority for the purchase of twenty-four acres of land at Adams and Rising Sun Avenues. Three months later, in January 1936, ground was broken for the Hill Creek Housing Project, the first such in the city.[47] The Hill Creek Homes were initially under the care of the United States Housing Authority, but after the state enabling act established the Philadelphia Housing Authority in the fall of 1937, the Hill Creek project was turned over to the new agency to manage. Four years later it was possible for the Philadelphia Housing Authority, using 90 percent federal funds, to build the James Weldon Johnson Homes at Twenty-fifth and Ridge on the site of the old Glenwood Cemetery, and between 1939 and 1940 to add two other projects, the Tasker Homes, on vacant ground at Thirtieth and Tasker, and the Richard Allen Homes, on a slum-clearance site at Ninth and Poplar. These three provided the city with 2859 new dwellings varying in size from three to six rooms each and renting from fourteen to twenty-six dollars a month. The greater number of the dwellings in these projects represented additional housing for the city and were the more welcome for that. Only the Richard Allen Homes had required the relocation of any families —900 families had occupied the 450 buildings demolished there.[48]

The Housing Authority offered the families that came to live in these projects new, sanitary dwellings that met the standards of the building code then in force. They also attracted attention nationally through efforts to show renters that a new house did not require a major expenditure for new furniture. To this end the authority furnished and decorated a model house, using reconditioned furniture from the Salvation Army shops. The idea proved popular. Tenants asked for and got a home-furnishing workshop where they could work on their own furniture, and one of the city schools set up a new program to provide practical experience for its students in this kind of work. Later the school board expanded the program, adding visiting homemaking consultants to the staffs of all the public schools near housing projects. These consultants worked with parents to help them improve nutrition, to learn how to keep cleaner, safer homes, and to see that both landlord and tenant assumed responsibility for repairs within their appropriate spheres.[49] Alas, the glow was not permanent; Tasker and Allen have become high-crime areas.

Unfortunately, after Mayor Wilson's resignation on August 11, 1939, and his death eight days later, a change in administration brought a conservative philosophy back to the city government, and when the United States Housing Authority allotted $19 million to Philadelphia for additional houses in 1940, oilman Joseph N. Pew, Jr., and Pennsylvania Manufacturers Association leader Joseph R. Grundy, Philadelphia's powerful Republican bosses, advised the city Council to refuse the offer. The Council obeyed, over labor's protest, and gave Philadelphia the distinction of being the only city to prefer the status quo to the possible pain of again grasping Washington's helping hand.[50]

A year later, when it was clear that the United States would soon become involved in World War II, the Philadelphia Housing Authority, working with the federal Defense Housing coordinator, turned to the task of finding shelter for the hundreds of newcomers to the city, men and women here to work at defense jobs. The Passyunk Homes, at Penrose Avenue and Magazine Lane, with 1000 houses for Navy Yard personnel, were begun in April 1941. In September work started on the Abbotsford Homes, at Henry Avenue and Abbotsford Road, which with Bartram's Village, at Elmwood and Fifty-fourth Streets, and Oxford Village, at Oxford and Comly Streets, added 1400 more. At the end of the war the Housing Authority found itself in charge of four low-cost housing developments, the Johnson, Tasker, Allen, and Hill Creek Homes; and of eight war-housing projects, the four just mentioned and four others built to provide temporary homes only for persons engaged in war-related occupations: the Ship Yard Homes (Twentieth and Packer), the League Island Homes (Thirty-sixth and Morris), Tacony Homes (Lewis and Tacony), and Oxford Village II (Comly and Langdon). After 1946 these last four were used as a part of a temporary housing program for veterans.[51]

V

The Depression was of incalculable importance for Philadelphia's workers. It brought Roosevelt's New Deal program and the enactment in 1937 of Pennsylvania's "Little New Deal" encouraging the formation of labor unions.

Government encouragement to unionization and the inception of the Congress of Industrial Organizations, the CIO, in 1936, sparked a burst of union activity in Philadelphia.

Labor's dissatisfaction with its condition had produced a rash of strikes during Mayor Mackey's term of office as Philadelphia's open shops began to yield to union pressure. In this context the Amalgamated Clothing Workers of America, with the object of unionizing Philadelphia's clothing industry, and the American Federation of Full-Fashioned Hosiery Workers made notable gains. As the result of a strike by the hosiery union the management of many of the Philadelphia mills agreed to the organization of their mills, while the union, accepting wage cuts, helped to keep union mills solvent and make them more profitable than nonunion plants. In consequence Philadelphia remained for the time being Pennsylvania's biggest production center for hosiery, in spite of the "yellow dog" tactics of the Reading and southern mills. But it was only for the time being; eventually the hosiery unions were to drive the hosiery factories out of Philadelphia, once the hosiery center of the country, to the nonunion South.[52]

After the organization of the CIO, union benefits were sought by workers in many additional trades, and by January 1937 union activity and worker unrest had reached such a peak that the *Inquirer* reported the current situation in a column headed "Along the City's Strike Front Yesterday." Listed in the column were a walkout by 700 men at Crown Cork and Seal Company, striking in protest of the dismissal of 100 of their fellows; the failure of the

Strike violence at the Apex Hosiery Mill, Fifth and Luzerne Streets (1937).

HISTORICAL SOCIETY OF PENNSYLVANIA

mayor's labor representative and the Exide workers who had staged Philadelphia's first sitdown strike to come to an agreement; the continuation of another sitdown strike, this one by 450 workers at the Brownhill and Kramer Knitting Company who were demanding union recognition and the check-off system; and a smaller strike at the Marshall Field Company plant. On a more cheerful note the reporter indicated that the striking seamen were moving toward settlement, but added that 8000 garment workers from 150 local plants were likely to walk out in pursuit of a thirty-five-hour week, a 20 percent wage rise, union recognition, and "establishment of union conditions in the shops."[53]

Other strikes made headlines subsequently, among them one by the Workers' Alliance, an organization of jobless WPA workers; several by the city ash and garbage collectors; another by employees at the J. G. Brill Company; and an oddity reported on the *Inquirer*'s financial pages, the action against the numbers "bankers" by 200 "pick-up men," the "minor racketeering gentry." Truckers struck in support of both the bakery drivers, at odds with the A & P, and the drivers having trouble with the Supplee, Wills, Jones milk company. Strikes were called for a variety of reasons: because of dissatisfaction with wages, hours, working conditions; and as the result of jurisdictional conflicts between the conservative, craft-oriented American Federation of Labor (AFL) and the more democratic, industrially oriented CIO. Some of the strikes were long, bitter, and violent, and by August 1937 the city's labor problems were acute. Mayor Wilson created his own labor board, and later claimed that he himself had taken a hand in settling some 200 disputes, spending as much as twenty-four hours at a time trying to bring opposing forces together. Wilson believed, with some justification, that he should receive credit for having saved the city from a kind of anarchy.[54]

With expert leadership from their own well-established textile unions, headed by David Dubinsky and Sidney Hillman, Philadelphians meanwhile turned a town with old craft unions but thousands of unorganized industrial workers into a city where a high proportion of all wage earners were also union members. It must have seemed an appropriate star for the top of labor's Philadelphia tree when the delegates from forty-one nations, members of the International Labor Organization, met in April 1944 at Temple University to plan programs and policies for the postwar world. Here they drafted what is sometimes called a "code of rights for the common man," or the "Philadelphia charter," a "classic" statement of the social aims of a hoped-for Allied victory.[55]

V I

The Great Depression left two marks on Philadelphia: it made the city truly a union town; and politically turned it from a Republican stronghold into one that could be counted on to give the Democratic candidate an ample majority in presidential elections, while for the time being maintaining its Republican complexion in local affairs.

The cracks in the monolithic G.O.P., evident in 1931 as a consequence of William S. Vare's slipping control, were widened by Mayor Moore's insensitivity to human need and made disastrously visible by his lack of action in behalf of those without work or hope. At the same time the small wind stirring among the Democrats began blowing more strongly in response to the bread-and-butter issues handed to their party by Moore.

Some years earlier Vare is reported to have tried to dissuade Charles Hall from continuing his efforts to develop the banks of the Schuylkill through the Vine–South Street section of the city by saying: "Charlie, the day of the contractor combine in politics was buried with my brother Ed." Perhaps it may have been buried for the G.O.P., but it was a combination of new men in the construction business, Matthew McCloskey and John B. Kelly, joined by the real estate entrepreneur and banker Albert M. Greenfield, and aided by the forum David Stern's *Record* provided, that built a real Democratic party in Philadelphia in 1932 and 1933.

In an interview with Greg Walter in 1969 McCloskey recalled his visit to New York in 1932 to see James Farley and discuss with him the state of the Philadelphia Democrats, then led by a man dependent for his position on the Vare organization, and with the Republicans even paying the rent on his

Albert M. Greenfield (1887–1967) and Mayor S. Davis Wilson (1881–1939), photograph 1937.

office. Coming back to the city, McCloskey with Kelly organized the Independent Democratic Committee, with Kelly as chairman and McCloskey as treasurer. The new committee worked hard for the election of Franklin Delano Roosevelt, and although the Republican ward leaders and committeemen managed to carry Philadelphia for Herbert Hoover, they discovered when the votes were tallied that Roosevelt had received an astonishing 45 percent of all votes cast, and that Hoover had won by the uncomfortably small margin of 70,000 votes.[56]

The following year the Democrats registered 179,000 new adherents. As one disgruntled committeeman put it, the people "are suffering from the depression and going toward the Democratic party like an ocean." In the row-office elections that November John O'Donnell, Vare's tame Democrat, and the members of his city committee pledged as individuals and as a group "to refrain from entering into any deals, agreements or understandings" with the Philadelphia G.O.P. Plans for coordinating the ensuing campaign were made in David Stern's office, and the *Record*'s coverage contributed not a little to Democratic success. All of Vare's major candidates were defeated. The Democrats, with the support of Governor Pinchot and the independent Town Meeting party, or Fusion ticket, won two important city offices, electing S. Davis Wilson controller and WillB Hadley city treasurer, as well as filling some lesser posts. Among those running, albeit unsuccessfully, was Joseph S. Clark, Proper Philadelphian, and a member of the Warriors' Club, young Democrats with reform of their party in mind. Clark's campaign for a seat on the city Council was managed by another Warrior, Richardson Dilworth, and marked the emergence within the Democratic party of a number of socially prominent Philadelphians, among them Francis Biddle, Walter Phillips, R. Sturgis Ingersoll, William C. Bullitt, and John F. Lewis, Jr. The following year Clark managed Dilworth's losing campaign for a seat in the state Senate. Although losing that race, the Philadelphia Democrats contributed significantly to the election of George H. Earle III as governor of Pennsylvania.[57]

Shaken by these events, a group of Republicans, including Henry J. Trainer, a member of the Council, Judge Charles L. Brown, and Jerome H. Louchheim, organized a successful revolt against Vare. Their action could hardly be considered a movement toward reform, but simply a recognition of an impending vacuum that allowed a shift in power from the old Vare gang to a party dominated for years to come by Joseph R. Grundy and Joseph N. Pew.[58] Hereafter, Democratic success in elections to city offices slowed down. In 1935 the G.O.P. made a clean sweep, electing a "solid" Council and a mayor, S. Davis Wilson, who had changed his party allegiance to become at least nominally a Republican. John B. Kelly was Wilson's opponent, and Wilson's victory, if indeed he did actually win—Kelly thought he had been counted out by manipulation of some of the voting machines, and the question remains unsettled to this day—was by a margin of 50,000 votes.[59]

In his campaign Kelly had pledged to apply for federal money for local work relief programs, to remove unnecessary city employees, and to leave no more abandoned subways and airports. Wilson was backed by Pew, the fanatically anti-Roosevelt head of Sun Oil; by contractor Louchheim; and by the city workers both uniformed and nonuniformed whose welfare he had cultivated as controller, always finding money to maintain payrolls and avoid increasing taxes. Wilson took the Republican candidate's obligatory stance of opposition to the New Deal, but once installed in City Hall in January 1936, he quickly accepted $1.9 million in WPA funds, and joined with Greenfield and Stern in a determined effort to bring the Democratic National Convention to Philadelphia. Always a promoter of his own interests and of Philadelphia's, Wilson was a partisan politician only if it suited his larger purposes.[60]

The Democratic convention did come to Philadelphia, the first major political gathering in town since 1900 when McKinley and Theodore Roosevelt were nominated on the Republican ticket. Businessmen and politicians now collected $200,000 to take the palm away from San Francisco or Chicago, and McCloskey arranged a successful $100-a-plate dinner, a fundraising device he later claimed to have invented, to aid the cause. Some of the newly acquired federal money was used to improve Convention Hall where the assembled delegates would meet, and the city suspended its famous Blue Laws against Sunday drinking to make the delegates welcome. So successfully was this done that in the opinion of one visitor the city needed only a change in local politics to be perfect. In fact the only visible hostility in this Republican city was the Union League's giant electric sign: "Landon and Knox, 1936. Love of Country Leads." For the Democrats, happy days were here again indeed, and on June 26, 1936, FDR was nominated by acclamation after a "wild" sixty-two-minute demonstration.[61]

This time Roosevelt carried all but seven of the city's fifty wards, winning by 209,876 votes. Democrats were elected in all of Philadelphia's congressional districts, and the Philadelphians helped their party gain control of both houses of the Pennsylvania legislature for the first time since 1845. Registered Democrats now numbered 364,259, up from 101,729 in 1928, and were only 86,000 fewer in number than those claiming Republican allegiance. Money for needed jobs, available through the WPA, and a consequent shift among ethnic and racial minorities from the G.O.P. to FDR's banner help to explain these changes. Hitherto labor had exerted little political muscle. J. Hampton Moore, for example, who had a history of antilabor votes, was nonetheless elected mayor twice, both times carrying the heavily industrial wards where the influence of the committeeman and ward leader had continued to be greater than that of the union leader. The new state of affairs was therefore shocking to the Republican ward leaders, and not only because this time their voters "couldn't be bought." As one man who had failed to deliver his district put it: "I lost by three votes. First time in twenty years. My friends double crossed me. They taken my money and voted the other way." Some of those friends perhaps were acting on the principle that determined the choice of one black woman who, given five dollars to vote for the Republican candidate and two dollars by the Democrats to vote for their man, cast her ballot for FDR because the Democrats were "poor, too." It also came as a surprise to the G.O.P. party workers that their constituents "knew where the second [Democratic] lever was, and *pulled* that *one.*" From that time on until after World War II Philadelphia, Janus-like, showed two faces in politics: turning in resounding victories for FDR in 1940 and 1944, but for the most part continuing to elect a Republican-dominated city government and usually supporting the Republican candidates for state office, although sometimes by slim margins.[62]

VII

Five mayors headed the city government between 1930 and 1946. Officially all were Republican when elected, and S. Davis Wilson, controversial, overly fond of intoxicating liquors, but colorful, may have been the ablest of the lot. Wilson owed a great deal to the intelligence of his city solicitor, Joseph Sharfsin, who was a kind of gaunt dark presence behind the mayor's chair. It was Sharfsin who made the administration's contacts with bankers and lawyers and individuals weighty in the community. Wilson's successor, Robert Lamberton, was another organization man who died nineteen months after taking office without leaving much to mark his presence. The last, Bernard (Barney) Samuel, was a political hack, easy to make fun of but hard to truly dislike, who held office from Lamberton's death until a new broom swept the Democrats into power in 1951.

During these administrations the city experienced continued monetary difficulties, the usual number of scandals, grand jury investigations and prosecutions, some of which led to convictions, and frustrations when state law interfered with proposed reform of the city government. The gasworks, the Philadelphia Rapid Transit Company, the water supply and sewage system, the courts, especially the magistrates' courts, police protection of racketeers and gamblers, and the illegal management of city elections made headlines regularly. Some of this stir led to improvements in city government, some appeared to produce more sound and fury than change.[63] Appropriately many of the issues came to a head shortly after Wilson, the muckraking deputy to the controller in the Mackey administration, was himself inaugurated as mayor in January 1936. Wilson's first months in office were tumultuous— whole departments suspended or their resignations requested, agency heads fired, suits begun. The first of these actions brought Wilson into conflict with the Civil Service Commission, then a haven for politicians moved more by considerations of friendship than by examination scores, and had little permanent effect. An attempt to improve the Civil Service Board was declared unconstitutional, and it was not until 1940 that a new commission was installed, after a grand jury had indicted the old one on grounds of fraudulent practices in the administration of the exams for police posts.[64]

The U.G.I., the public utility holding company operating the Philadelphia gasworks, was another of Wilson's targets. Claiming mismanagement and favoritism, the mayor asked that the company be compelled to repay the city $12,741,457, due, in his opinion, in accordance with the terms of their lease signed February 8, 1926, by Mayor Kendrick, and now up for renewal, renegotiation, or cancellation. In 1936 the committee of the city Council in whose hands the matter rested decided to terminate the old lease on December 31, 1937. Five bids for the operation of the gasworks were subsequently received, but the Council changed its mind and on December 17 voted sixteen to five to renew the lease with the U.G.I. on the old terms. Since this would not require the company to reduce its charges to consumers in accordance with Wilson's campaign pledge, the mayor vetoed the bill, and when it was repassed by the Council, refused to sign it.[65]

At that point the gasworks became entangled with the city's bleak financial position. The preceding month the Mayor's Advisory Finance Committee had reported that the city's debts exceeded the legal limit by $35 million and recommended a flat-rate income tax, a sales tax, and a tax on unincorporated businesses as sources of new revenue. Previously the Council had enacted a variety of small taxes—an amusement tax, a parking lot tax, a mutual insurance company tax, and a documentary stamp tax, some of which were later voided by the state Supreme Court and none of which produced revenue sufficient to eliminate the deficit. In January 1938 the Council, in a further attempt to rectify the situation, passed a 2-percent sales tax which the mayor promptly vetoed only to have the bill passed over his veto to become law on March 1, 1938. In spite of this flurry of activity year's end brought the Council face to face with a deficit now grown to $41 million, and the assignment of the gasworks rentals for a term of years in return for a loan in that amount was proposed. The state Supreme Court ruled that the Council had the right to balance the city's budget in this way, and although 60 percent of Philadelphians opposed the proposition the necessary agreements were made to borrow the money at 3½ percent for twelve and a half years from the Reconstruction Finance Corporation, securing the loan by agreeing to hand over for that period of time the annual rent of $4.2 million the city received from the U.G.I. under the lease agreements. Philadelphia's budget was balanced, but with the loss of considerable future revenue.[66]

And the city needed still more money. The subways and the fire, water, and streets departments lacked up-to-date equipment. Money to service the $400-million bonded debt, to light the city's streets, and to keep a sufficient number of policemen on patrol at any one time had to be found. The Council now proposed that a 1½ percent tax be levied on all wages and salaries and on the net profits of businesses and professions earned in Philadelphia. It was thought that this tax, to go into effect on January 1, 1940, would bring in $18 million annually, and with this rosy prospect before it the Council passed the 1940 budget on schedule, the first time a budgetary deadline had been met in four years. Predictably the labor unions attacked the legality of the new tax, the first such to be collected in the United States. Federal workers also disputed the propriety of their wages' being taxed by Philadelphia, but the courts, including the Supreme Court of the United States, upheld the city's position. At last Philadelphia had found a way to keep reasonably solvent, and by 1942 the city controller, Robert C. White, could even report a surplus, the first in fifteen years.[67]

Another long-standing problem reached crisis proportions during Wilson's term of office, namely, the dispute of the city with the PRT and its underlying companies regarding their conflicting financial interests. In November 1935 the Council had given Mayor-elect Wilson authority to explore ways for Philadelphia to condemn the entire transit system. Suits and countersuits between underliers, the company, and the city made headlines for the next four years. Finally Judge George A. Welsh of the U.S. District Court, the city Council, the PRT stockholders, and the Public Utility Commission were able to agree on a plan considered fair to all. On January 1, 1940, the PRT, the Philadelphia Rapid Transit Company, ceased to exist, and the PTC, the Philadelphia Transportation Company, came into being. The underliers agreed to accept $84 million in city bonds for their interests (a bonanza for the underliers of a shaky system); the city would collect half of the company's net annual income in excess of the amount needed to pay holders of common stock an agreed-upon sum, and would have the right to buy, on July 1 of any year, all of the company's property including bonds, common stock, and outstanding mortgages, having previously given six months' notice of its intentions. Further, the city's consent must be obtained for any increase in capital stock, funded indebtedness, or change in fares, and the PTC board of directors must include the mayor and four members elected by the city Council. In this case, unlike the U.G.I. affair, the city's position vis-à-vis an important independent agency with potential for advancing or hindering Philadelphia's growth was somewhat improved when the matters under adjudication were resolved—temporarily.[68]

The magistrates' courts, reviewed in 1926 by the Philadelphia Bar Association and criticized then because of the magistrates' lack of legal training, dishonesty, casually kept records, and political subservience, had not improved during the intervening decade. Magistrates were more politicians than judges and "not permitted to forget that they could never have been judges if they had not first been successful politicians." If a party member involved in the numbers racket, for example, were arrested and his committeeman or ward leader was notified, the latter spoke to the magistrate, who "understood." Acquittal followed. The opportunities for profit were sizable. One magistrate, pleading guilty to malfeasance in office, admitted to having banked more than $87,000 collected from defendants in just one year. A probe of this disgraceful system, demanded in 1935 by the Criminal Justice Association, led to a grand jury investigation and ultimately to the indictment of all magistrates in office except one, William H. Belcher. When Chief Magistrate John J. O'Malley was duly acquitted, the cases against the others fizzled. Enough public ire had been aroused, however, to assure the introduction and passage by the Assembly in 1937 of the Magistrates Court Act. Promptly tested in the courts, the act was upheld on August 6, 1937, by the Court of Common Pleas, but stripped of much of its force the following January by action of the state Supreme Court.[69]

In 1938 another grand jury investigated the ties between the police and other city officials and the Philadelphia gambling establishment. Thirty-nine gambling houses were said to exist "with official knowledge," and five police officers, including Inspectors James E. Clegg and Earl P. La Reau, forty-seven policemen from Eleventh and Winter Streets, and Superintendent of Police Edward Hubbs, were indicted, as were 142 operators of gaming establishments, among them Nathan Schaeffer, reputed "overlord" of the rackets.[70] Mayor Wilson was also charged on September 9, 1938, with failure to suppress gambling, especially rife in Wards Seven and Twenty; with firing city employees without regard to civil service regulations; and with interference with the attendance of witnesses before legislative committees. Two months later, on November 19, 1938, Harry S. McDevitt, president judge of the Courts of Common Pleas, quashed the charges against Wilson, and contemporary opinion generally held that they had been brought only because the G.O.P. hoped to get something on the mayor for his failure to support the regular Republican slate in the spring primaries.[71] The charges against Police Superintendent Hubbs were dismissed in April 1939 by Judge Lamberton, elected mayor later that same year, and none of the other changes recommended by any of the grand juries before which these problems had come was implemented.

Complaints about election fraud, including the presence on the rolls of phantom voters, the manhandling of opposition-party poll watchers at election time, the giving of illegal assistance to voters or of money to vote the right way, were frequently heard. A bill to provide for the permanent registration of voters, enacted in March 1937, was designed to correct the first of these abuses, but a federal grand jury called in November 1940 to investigate election fraud discovered the names of 50,000 ineligible voters still on the lists. The Registration Commission, a body of five appointed by the governor for a term of four years, was charged forthwith with failure to perform its duties properly. Thomas D. Starr, the chairman, resigned in July, and on August 1 the governor appointed a new commission, retaining only one member of the old board, Mrs. Sara McNeil. A Democratic governor had appointed the old board, a Republican one the second; but since in both cases the appointments were politically inspired, improvement was not notable.[72]

For those Philadelphians who were not in thrall to bossism the future of the city seemed uncertain. The organization, whether in Harrisburg or among the ward leaders in Philadelphia, appeared to be all but immovable and generally uninterested in the public weal. Meanwhile Philadelphia senses were offended by open garbage wagons, unpalatable water, smelly sewers, and rivers so polluted that their water took the paint off the hulls of the warships at the Navy Yard and on the hot, humid days of summer filled the air over center city with what the eighteenth century would have called "noxious vapors."

Philadelphia's drinking water and system of sewage disposal had long been objects of public complaint and professional concern. To get around the difficulty of low legal bonded debt limits and state legislative hostility the Council introduced an ordinance creating the Philadelphia Authority (chartered by the state in September 1938) in order to fund programs, financed by authority bonds, to curb the pollution of the city's rivers; to improve the city's water supply by upgrading pumping stations, filter plants, and water mains; and to provide high-pressure fire service to West Philadelphia. Philadelphians supported the Council's action and voted in favor of an $18-million water loan, approved by the courts as self-liquidating.[73] A larger expenditure, involving the sale of $42 million of sewer bonds to be backed by real estate taxes, did not fare so well, being declared unconstitutional by the state Supreme Court.[74]

Changing mayors—until Samuel's time no mayor could succeed himself, so that a new one came on the scene every four years—did relatively little to halt corruption. Furthermore, Philadelphia still had separate sets of officials, chosen in different election years, for the city and the county governments, with the patronage belonging to the county row officers sufficient to limit any reforms a mayor and his cabinet might put in motion. Proposals to merge the two governments were presented to the Assembly periodically from 1935 to 1945, always unsuccessfully. Again and again the Pennsylvania Assembly and the state Supreme Court became stumbling blocks in the way of those who wished to find a better means of managing their civic affairs.[75]

For any long-term reform the city needed a new charter. In 1922 the Pennsylvania constitution was amended to give cities the right to frame and adopt their own charters, but only in accordance with whatever "restrictions, limitations and regulations" the Assembly might impose. In 1929 and 1931 bills to permit Philadelphia to establish a council–city manager form of government were defeated in Harrisburg. A Charter Commission appointed by Governor Earle in 1937 produced a report that formed the basis for the Woodward-Shapiro Bill introduced in the Assembly the following year. The principal proposals of both were the establishment of a council–city manager government, the placement of both city and county offices under civil service, and the creation of a Department of Finance, a Budget Bureau, and a City Planning Commission. The four leading Philadelphia newspapers supported the bill and, according to polls, so did 76 percent of the Philadelphia voters. The bill passed the state Senate, thirty-eight to eight, but the special subcommittee of the House Committee on Cities of the First Class, responding to pressure from Republican leaders, took no action and the bill died when the Assembly adjourned on May 30.[76]

The organization of two legal-aid agencies designed to help the indigent, although independent of the attempt to reform Philadelphia's government, arose from a similar concern for the creation of a better and more responsive system of law. The old Legal Aid Society had resumed operations in November 1933 under the presidency of John Hampton Barnes, when the city eliminated its Bureau of Legal Aid. Two years later the society reported that it had assisted 12,000 clients involved in civil suits. Similarly the Voluntary Defenders Association, chartered in April 1934, undertook criminal cases when those under indictment lacked funds to hire a competent attorney. Francis Fisher Kane, the founder of the latter agency, received the Philadelphia Award in 1936 largely because of his work with this organization.[77]

Contrary to common belief, the Depression had not produced an increase in reported crimes in Philadelphia. Statistics on arrests in the city and a report in the *Journal of Criminal Law* for November 1936 both indicated that crimes against persons had actually diminished, and the author of the *Journal* article, A. C. Wagner, also pointed out that there was little evidence that "economic stress increases crimes against property." Some credit for the city's relatively safe streets was given to the juvenile courts, commended in an article in the *Survey* in April 1935 for cooperating with the Council of Social Agencies to provide supervision for discharged offenders and for boys picked up by the police but not held for trial, through referral to social clubs. This program continued one begun in 1932 by the Crime Prevention Association working with the police Crime Prevention Bureau, set up in the same year by Kern Dodge, the director of public safety.

In addition a variety of technological aids in the early 1930s improved police performance. These included radio connections between squad cars and police headquarters; a new city morgue with laboratories for testing for poisons and performing autopsies, and with better x-ray and photographic equipment; a medical research library; and adequate space for ballistics tests. The Bar Association, too, unhappy at the *Saturday Evening Post*'s exposure of ties between some of its members and the local crime ring, did its part to clean up this link between law and the underworld. Herbert and Samuel Salus and six other attorneys were charged and disbarred for their complicity with known criminals. Eight other lawyers were disciplined for the same offense.[78]

The collapse of Mayor Wilson, his resignation on August 11 and death eight days later on August 19, 1939, slowed the impetus toward reform. His successors, Lamberton and Samuel, were party stalwarts, not inclined to do anything to upset the usual flow of power and patronage. The outbreak of the war in Europe in September 1939 turned the attention of Philadelphians elsewhere for a large part of the next decade.

VIII

Philadelphians had five major newspapers to choose among when the 1930s began: the *Public Ledger*s, morning and evening; the *Inquirer*, like the *Ledger*s following the Republican line; the *Evening Bulletin*, nominally independent but very conservative; and the *Record*, which after its purchase by David Stern in 1928 offered a Democratic challenge to the political status quo. The city's neighborhoods and its demographically and religiously diverse population gathered news of special interest to themselves from periodicals like the *Philadelphia Tribune* (reporting on matters of concern to the black community), the *Jewish Exponent*, the *Catholic Standard and Times*, *L'Opinione* (later *Il Opinione Progresso*), *Patryota* (a Polish journal), *Nord Amerika* (a German one), *Pravda*, the *Germantown Courier*, the *Kensingtonian*, the *South Philadelphian*, the *Union Labor Review*, and many others.

Official corruption and an inept city government did not provide the only news to fill their pages. Racket-associated crimes as lurid as any found in mystery novels titillated Philadelphia readers. Until the repeal of the Prohibition Amendment on December 21, 1933, the suppliers of illegal liquor with their internecine wars, trigger-happy enforcers, and all-important payoffs contributed hugely to local crime news. Thereafter the elite among the purveyors of liquor on what might be called a retail level continued their businesses, now operating their clubs or nightspots openly as did Jack Lynch on the Walton Roof at Broad and Locust or going into the restaurant and catering business as did Jimmy Duffy. The Lanzetti brothers, dealers in dope, prostitutes, numbers, and bootleg liquor, continued to be the racket kings of South Philadelphia, maintaining their dominance by whatever means were necessary. Mickey Duffy until his murder in 1931 was boss of Philadelphia's numbers game, except in Lanzetti territory. After about twenty-five other killings attributed to the struggle for control of that business, an uneasy peace was reached between Pius Lanzetti and John ("Big Nose") Avena. These two shared the spoils until August 1936 when Avena was disposed of on orders from his partner Pius. The latter met a like fate a few months afterward, being gunned down on New Year's Eve 1936. Willie Lanzetti prudently left town.

Teo Lanzetti, one of the six notorious Lanzetti brothers—Ignatius, Lucien, Willie, Pius, Teo, and Leo—three of whom (Leo, Pius, and Willie) had met violent deaths by July 3, 1939, when this picture appeared in the Evening Bulletin.

PHILADELPHIA BULLETIN

He came back in 1939, but gangland's memories are long, and he too was murdered on July 1, 1939.[79]

Willie's demise was but one of several sensational crimes to make headlines in 1939. A coroner's inquest in February of that year turned up evidence of an arsenic insurance ring suspected of having been responsible for as many as fifty-five deaths over a period of years. By December nineteen convictions or confessions had been obtained and the heads of the ring, Herman and Paul Petrillo, were tried, found guilty, and sentenced to death. The principal prosecution witness, John Jerry Cacopardo, was framed for one of the murders and served fifteen years in prison before being exonerated and released to write a book, *Show Me a Miracle,* and study for the ministry, ending his days as the Rev. John Jerry Cacopardo.[80]

Willie Sutton, "Slick Willie," kept another kind of crime, bank robbery, in the news throughout the 1930s. Caught, tried, and sentenced to twenty-five to fifty years in prison after his 1934 holdup of the Corn Exchange Bank at Sixtieth and Ludlow Streets, Sutton added to his notoriety as a bank robber by engineering a series of clever escapes or attempted escapes from the Philadelphia prisons. These kept his picture in the papers and earned him a certain awed, if reluctant, admiration.[81]

The case that attracted the most attention nationally, however, because of its relevance to the bona fides of the Fourth Estate, swirled around Moses Annenberg, since 1936 owner of the *Inquirer.* Formerly an enforcer for Chicago's Hearst-controlled newsstands, Annenberg made sure that his employer's wares were well displayed and that those of rival publishers were banished from sight. He was also owner of the General News Bureau, a wire service to bookmakers, and of racing and gambling papers in New York, as well as assorted mystery and sex pulp magazines. Like Al Capone, in the end Annenberg was indicted not for his principal crime—running an illegal racing wire service—but for tax evasion. He pleaded guilty, was convicted, paid $10 million to the United States in back taxes and interest, and was sentenced to three years in prison. Paroled in June 1942, he died a few months later.[82]

Not long after Annenberg went to prison, leaving his son Walter to take over as publisher of the *Inquirer,* it became apparent that a constriction of the Philadelphia journalists' world was taking place. Depression economics affected newspapers as well as the news they printed. Both the *Public Ledger* and the *Evening Ledger* had disappeared from the newsstands by 1942. The *Record* died because of longtime labor supporter Stern's indignation at a bitterly fought strike a few years later ("How could they do it to *me?*"). Some of the neighborhood papers and those that appealed to a special group of readers also found profitable publication impossible to continue.[83]

IX

Defining society in *Social Register* terms, a reader of the "society" sections of the city's papers would have noticed that during the 1930s and 1940s debutantes' parties were becoming less extravagant. Instead of individual balls where each young woman held center stage at her very own fete, group debuts, imposed first by the Depression, later by the war, became the usual thing, the two principal ones being the Emergency Aid–sponsored June Ball and the Junior League's Christmas Presentation Ball. Other extravaganzas like the Benedicts Ball disappeared altogether.[84] The Manufacturers' and Jewish Mercantile Clubs vanished. The Assembly and the Philadelphia, Rittenhouse, and Acorn Clubs remained to show the enduring validity of Henry James's remark that Philadelphia was less a place than a "state of consanguinity."[85]

Two writers, Philip Barry and Christopher Morley, described the Philadelphia society of the 1930s: Barry in the play *Philadelphia Story*, and Morley in a novel, *Kitty Foyle*. Both were published in 1939 and both subsequently appeared on film. *Philadelphia Story*, an entertaining, well-made movie with a superior cast—most notably a Bryn Mawr graduate named Katharine Hepburn—has become something of a classic; Morley's book, which looked more deeply into Philadelphia's worlds, now appears dated and is probably more often read by students of the city's bygone mores than by those hunting entertainment and a good book.

Philadelphia gentlefolk did not limit their appearances in the columns of the city's newspapers to the society pages, however. Their control of many of Philadelphia's financial institutions, their interest in the reviving Democratic party, and their activity in charitable matters during the worst of the Depression has been noted. They dominated the board of the Philadelphia Orchestra, were the principal subscribers to its concerts, and supplied its necessary operating funds. Since both board and audience were musically conservative, they were in frequent conflict with Leopold Stokowski, the musical director of an orchestra called "incomparable" and Philadelphia's "chief contribution to civilization" by the *New York Herald Tribune*'s music critic Lawrence Gilman.[86] That the Philadelphia audiences usually preferred to listen to Bach and Beethoven rather than struggle to understand the new did not prevent Stokowski from trying to pull them forward into the world of contemporary musicmakers. In the spring of 1930, for example, Stokowski conducted a memorable performance of Igor Stravinsky's *Le Sacre du Printemps*, rechoreographed by Leonide Massine with Martha Graham as principal dancer. The following year he offered Alban Berg's opera *Wozzeck*. This brought the cognoscenti flocking to Philadelphia, but although a resounding success with the critics, it was a financial failure because of local indifference. Disagreements like these eventually led to Stokowski's resignation and the hiring in 1937 of Eugene Ormandy, less flamboyant and more receptive to local tastes.[87]

Among the orchestra's more successful innovations were remarkably well-received children's concerts and, beginning in 1933, the youth concerts. Tickets for the latter were offered to young people thirteen to twenty-five years old, and the concerts were "sold out" within hours of the opening of the box office. Regular symphonic programs were played, enlivened by "surprises," one such, a specially commissioned "Youth Song" by Jan Sibelius.[88] Stokow-

Eugene Ormandy (1899–1985) became conductor and music director of the Philadelphia Orchestra in 1936.

FREE LIBRARY OF PHILADELPHIA

ski also inaugurated the orchestra's transcontinental tours in 1936. The first of these, underwritten by RCA for $250,000, took the orchestra to more than twenty cities from Boston to San Francisco.[89] Stokowski had led his orchestra into radio broadcasting in 1929. In 1937 he took them to Hollywood, first for the making of a film, *The Big Broadcast of 1937*, and later to do the more notable *Fantasia*. With RCA, for whom the orchestra was then recording exclusively, Stokowski experimented with the concept of longplaying records ($33\frac{1}{3}$ rpm), and with the Bell Laboratories made the first-ever stereophonic recording of a symphony orchestra from the stage of the Academy of Music in 1932. The longplaying records did not yet catch on, but Stokowski's hiring of harpist Edna Phillips in 1930, the first woman member of a major symphony orchestra, did, and since then the orchestra has never been a wholly male ensemble.[90]

Miss Phillips was not the only woman to turn the orchestra in a new direction. That same year, 1930, (Mrs.) Clara Barnes Abbott, director of the city's newly created Bureau of Music, with the help of Dr. Herbert J. Tily, president of Strawbridge & Clothier, proposed that the orchestra present a summer series of concerts in Fairmount Park. Walter H. Thomas, city architect, built the necessary shell at Robin Hood Dell, and the first concert was played on July 8, 1930. About 12,000 persons attended, and Philadelphia's long tradition of concerts out of doors was once again in operation.[91] Mrs. Abbott's Bureau of Music was, incidentally, another Philadelphia "first." Planned to expand the opportunities for musical education citywide, a sixty-five-piece symphony orchestra was organized, as were classes in sight singing, a Municipal Jubilee Choir, and programs to train playground instructors. Music therapy in hospitals was attempted, and street concerts by way of the "melody wagon" carried radio broadcasts of the Philadelphia Orchestra to the neighborhoods.[92] This lively enterprise, like so many others, was a Depression victim, abolished as a useless frill by Mayor Moore.

Opera as produced by the Met during its Philadelphia season was high priced and, if magnificently sung, was often indifferently staged and acted. To attract an audience put off by the ticket prices and the language barrier of standard operatic productions, a new (1937) Philadelphia Opera Company began to present opera in English, with young singers, a well-trained orchestra, good sets and costumes, and tickets priced no higher than $2.50. The company did well on its shoestring budget of about $100,000 and in 1943 was able to take its show on tour. "Street-car opera," as *Newsweek* called it, had proved its worth.[93]

Although she did not appear in opera at this time, the singular ability of another Philadelphia musician, Marian Anderson, was celebrated by the world at large and recognized by her hometown with the Philadelphia Award in 1940.[94]

Not so well known outside of musical circles, the Free Library's Fleisher collection of about 11,000 orchestral scores must be counted as one of the city's major musical resources. These scores were made available without charge for use by recognized musical organizations. Additions were made in 1934 by WPA musicians who copied the works of about 350 contemporary American composers to fill in a great gap in the original collection. Still later, collecting trips to South America in the 1940s made Philadelphia's Fleisher collection the largest body of orchestral music in the world. With such resources for study and performance at hand it is no wonder that the city's music schools attracted students from all over.[95]

Not all of the music enjoyed by Philadelphians was of a serious nature. Billy Krechmer's jam sessions made Ranstead Street a mecca for visiting musicians. The popularity of Ted Weems, Joe Venuti, and Charlie Kerr was above question, and the stage shows at the Earle Theater at Eleventh and Market brought Harry James, Gene Krupa, Lionel Hampton, Benny Goodman, Frank Sinatra, and others to town. Louis Armstrong was well known to the audiences at the Lincoln Theater, at Broad and Lombard Streets. There were also top-flight shows of black performers for the delight of black audiences at the Golden Dawn, later the Bijou, just across the street.[96]

As a try-out town and one with an established association with the Theatre Guild, Philadelphia could expect a reasonable variety of plays and musicals to appear annually. Eleven houses—the Forest, the Walnut (dark much of the time), the Locust, the Erlanger, the Shubert (which flirted with burlesque to keep going), Keith's, the Lyric, the Adelphia, the Chestnut Street Opera House, the Broad Street, and the Garrick—the last five demolished or scheduled for destruction by 1940—presented plays by Noël Coward, George Kelly, Philip Barry, Clifford Odets, Maxwell Anderson, Robert Sherwood, Shaw, Shakespeare, and Aristophanes. These performances brought to town the Lunts, Tallulah Bankhead, Katherine Cornell, John Gielgud, and the perennial Walter Hampton, among other well-liked actors. *On Your Toes* with Ray Bolger, Gershwin's *Porgy and Bess,* the ILGWU's *Pins and Needles,* Gilbert and Sullivan operettas with the D'Oyly Carte company, the Piccolini (an Italian marionette theater), and the Ballet Russe de Monte Carlo contributed music, color, and a certain lightness of heart—sometimes combined with social comment—to the dramatic fare. By the end of the decade a somber mood infused many of the productions (Odets's *Waiting for Lefty,* Sherwood's *There Shall be No Night,* Hemmingway's *The Fifth Column*) and reflected the social disruption of the Depression and the coming storm of World War II.

When the Philadelphia Museum of Art was opened at the head of the Parkway, its architectural style was derided and its unfinished state and stored collections sharply criticized.[97] Nonetheless the museum and its director, Fiske Kimball, managed to stage attention-getting shows, beginning in 1930 with a memorial exhibition of paintings by Thomas Eakins.[98] An exhibit of "Surrealism, Dadaism, and Fantasia," called by the *Inquirer* "the goofiest art show that this town has ever seen," opened in February of 1937. It was followed by a "lively" Daumier exhibition, a show of WPA art, a loan exhibit of international sculpture effectively presented out of doors on the museum's grounds, the first major show in America of William Blake's work in 1939, and finally, in 1941, the first full-dress showing of the John G. Johnson collection.[99]

New ideas in the arrangement of exhibits as well as dynamic special shows marked the museum's program for the 1930s. Plans to hang paintings in period rooms surrounded by appropriate furniture and art objects were announced. A medieval wing was put on display in 1931; a gallery of modern art to "foster interest in contemporary art, particularly American art," followed in 1933; and in 1937 ten new galleries of French art were opened in style by the French ambassador, M. Georges Bonnet.[100] In view of Depression-induced financial restrictions, the museum's record overall was impressive.

Philadelphia and Philadelphians graced the sports pages of the newspapers with pleasant regularity in 1930. Behind the pitching of Robert Moses "Lefty" Grove and the defense of their "million-dollar infield," Connie Mack's Athletics won the American League pennant and the World Series for the second consecutive year. (Some connoisseurs consider this A's team the greatest baseball club of all time.) The Phillies, playing in the old Baker Bowl at Fifteenth and Huntingdon, were dismal as a team, but in newcomer Chuck

Klein fielded possibly the most exciting ballplayer in either league. Klein batted .386 and scored 158 runs that season, a National League record that still stands. Bill Tilden was once again singles champion at Wimbledon, and the Penn A.C. eight-oared crew, rowing on the Meuse River at Liège, Belgium, on August 17, 1930, won the world championship with a record time over a 2000-meter course that still stands. During the rowing seasons 1929 to 1931 this crew, now in the Helms Hall of Fame, won thirty-one consecutive races; in 1950 it was voted the greatest crew of the first half of this century by the Associated Press.[101]

After 1930–1931, however, the city's teams lost much of their luster. Shortage of funds compelled the Phillies to sell Klein to the Chicago Cubs at the end of the 1933 season; and the A's, although American League champions in 1931, also began to feel the pinch of the Depression. Within the next few years Connie Mack sold off most of his star players and the A's joined the Phillies at the bottom of their respective leagues for the balance of the decade.[102] In 1938 the Phillies left the Baker Bowl to share Shibe Park with the A's, where the following year floodlights were installed and Philadelphians enjoyed their first night ballgame on May 15, 1939.[103] Philadelphia was truly a baseball town in those days, giving the fans a choice not only between two major-league teams but also among some twenty-two city teams that were organized into three minor leagues: the Philadelphia Baseball League, the Quaker City Baseball League, and the City Baseball League. The Philadelphia Stars of the Negro National League, playing at Forty-fourth and Parkside, pleased a host of loyal followers.[104]

Professional football did not yet amount to much. The Eagles, a "shoestring operation" with two former Temple University players, Swede Hansen and Bull Lipski, as their mainstay, were founded in 1933 and were playing in the Baker Bowl by 1938. They endured lopsided losing seasons until 1943, but with "Greasy" Neale as coach, beginning in 1941 they improved gradually until by 1944 and 1945 they held second place in their division.[105]

Interestingly enough, Philadelphia women made the city's best showing in the world of sports after the early 1930s. In golf two women, Glenna Collett Vare and Helen Sigel Wilson, won national and state championships; and in field hockey Philadelphia frequently supplied more than half of the All-American team and particularly one of the sport's greatest players, Anne Townsend.[106]

X

With the advent of war in Europe in September 1939 the tempo of Philadelphia living changed. Here as elsewhere in the United States a steady reorientation of business and industry began to turn a sluggish, Depression-dominated economy into a booming, war-centered one.

Two major propaganda groups emerged almost at once and began to compete for attention and popular support. One, the Committee to Defend America by Aiding the Allies, was determined to secure as much help for beleaguered Britain as possible. The other, the Philadelphia America First Committee, was isolationist and dedicated to the view that the United States must remain neutral. Both found adherents: the Committee to Defend America among the anglophiles of the Philadelphia establishment; among labor, happy with a growing number of jobs and expanding paychecks; and among the academic community, alarmed by the Nazi threat to freedom of inquiry and expression. The America First Committee discovered its supporters among the ultraconservatives and some others who because of their national origins were inclined toward a more favorable opinion of the Axis powers than Philadelphians generally held. The divergent views of these committees indicated the split in Philadelphia's emotional climate and reflected as well the growing tensions in the nation.

Possibly with the hope of rekindling the old Republican flame and reestablishing Philadelphia as a safe G.O.P. town, the city was chosen as the site of the Republican National Convention in 1940. The convention began with an open-air rally at Independence Hall, enjoyed a Mummers' parade and an address by elder statesman Hoover, and ended with the nomination of Wendell Willkie on the sixth ballot. The balconies' chant, "We want Willkie!" may have contributed to his success. Willkie campaigned resolutely through Philadelphia; Roosevelt, seeking an unprecedented third term, came twice to tour defense projects and to speak at Convention Hall, always producing his magical effect and causing one G.O.P. ward leader to remark: "This man Roosevelt could win against the Lord in my division." The Democrats were helped not a little by Willkie's local campaign manager Robert T. McCracken, who made the injudicious comment that "only paupers will vote for Roosevelt" and therewith gave his opponents opportunity for some effective street theater. The Democrats sent out, to the delight of many, shabbily dressed men wearing "stove-pipe" hats and sporting huge buttons with the legend, "I am a pauper for Roosevelt." On Election Day the city gave Roosevelt 532,149 votes to Willkie's 354,878.[107]

The sense of urgency and unease abroad in the city was increased in 1939 by the decision of the Pennsylvania National Guard to double its regular drills, and by the enactment the following year of a federal law to draft young men into the armed forces, the first peacetime draft in the country's history. Almost 246,000 Philadelphians were registered for the draft, and in November 1940 the first of the city's draftees left for Fort Meade and their introduction to military life. Shortly thereafter, in February 1941, the Twenty-eighth Division of the National Guard and other units including the First City Troop were inducted into federal service.[108] Meanwhile Philadelphia prepared to take up once again her old role of supplier of materials of war to the nation.

The Chamber of Commerce established a committee on defense; took an inventory of facilities available for production of war-related goods; started a program, underwritten by the federal government, to train workers for defense industries using the city's vocational high schools; and discussed plans to improve transportation to the airport and to build a truck route around the city. New jobs, particularly in the metal trades, in textiles, and in construction, brought prosperity to workers as old companies increased their payrolls and about 200 new ones set up shop in the city.[109] In November 1940 the chamber's Business Research Bureau could report that the production of durable goods was up 33 percent, that exports through Philadelphia's port were up 29 percent, car loadings up 20 percent, payrolls up 12 percent, and retail sales up 6 percent over those of 1939. About $1 billion in defense contracts had been placed with Philadelphia firms. Philadelphia, whose peacetime slogan had been the "Workshop of the World," was well on her way to becoming for the second time in three decades the "Arsenal of America," producing everything from paper containers to battleships.[110]

Increased activity at the Navy Yard, the Schuylkill and Frankford Arsenals, the Quartermaster and Signal Corps Depots, and other federal agencies based in Philadelphia in 1940 and 1941 added to the profits of the PTC, to the sales of new automobiles, and to the demand for housing as military personnel and workers in industrial plants and in the newly opened offices of the War Production Board and the Office of Emergency Management descended on Philadelphia.[111] The Tasker Homes at Thirty-first and Morris, a WPA housing project, were taken over to provide shelter for navy personnel, and more than 8000 two-story dwellings were built in the area between 1940 and 1941.[112]

Thirty-one-ton M-3 tank, made at the Baldwin Locomotive Works, en route to Henry Disston & Sons, Inc., plant in Tacony to dedicate a new armor factory. This photograph, taken from the east side of Broad Street above Locust, was published in the Philadelphia Ledger *on June 16, 1941.*

FREE LIBRARY OF PHILADELPHIA

After the United States entered the war in December of the latter year, federal restrictions limited construction to those projects relating to national defense and city-issued building permits were severely cut back. Eventually rent controls, freezing Philadelphia rents at their March 1, 1942, rate, provided some aid for the harassed worker.[113] Problems remained, however. Maintenance costs formerly assumed by landlords now usually became the tenant's responsibility, and a prospective tenant was often expected to make under-the-table arrangements with the owner if he wished to occupy an available house or apartment.

X I

It was Defense Week in Philadelphia, December 1–6, 1941, and the newspapers mingled stories of parades and mock air-raid drills with advertisements of Christmas wares and notes of sporting events, coming-out parties, and other seasonal items. During the week, the front pages of the *Inquirer* headlined reports from Washington of the continuing negotiations with Tokyo; of the Japanese determination not to abandon their southward expansion; of the United States's demands for an explanation of Japanese troop movements into Indo-China (they claimed to be defending that land from the Chinese); and on December 6, of the personal note sent by President Roosevelt to Emperor Hirohito in a final effort to avert war. Nonetheless Congress was hopeful of peace, and many Philadelphians seem to have shared this optimistic view. Christmas spending was not notably less than usual. Toys and Christmas-tree ornaments might be made of plastic instead of metal or foil, housewives might have been advised to use economy in holiday wrapping, but Santa Claus reigned unchallenged, and the money put into Philadelphia's collective pocket by defense work flowed merrily into shopkeepers' cash registers. On Sunday, December 7, the *Inquirer*'s travel editor reported a record season in prospect for resorts in both North and South America as winter vacationers made ready to enjoy their holidays away from home.[114]

Almost before the newspapers had been read and laid aside, a short, incredible report of the bombing of the United States fleet at Pearl Harbor crackled from radios tuned in for the broadcast of the New York Philharmonic concert and other Sunday diversions and brought an abrupt stop to the city's normal way of life. After weeks of play at war and of defense against war, Philadelphia was shocked into reality. Mayor Bernard Samuel and his cabinet met to plan for the protection of the city's docks, bridges, highways, and water supply. Sailors on leave were sought out by the Shore Patrol and the police and hurried back to their stations. Philadelphians, reacting to the need for the reassurance that the companionship of their fellows brings, or relying on the old notion that more news is always to be found "downtown," congregated around City Hall. Here both city officials and "the man in the street" responded to reporters' questions confidently, sure that America would ultimately win the war into which she had been thrust so unceremoniously.[115]

The next day, December 8, the United States Customs House was jammed with men trying to enlist in the armed forces. In the week following, women and those too old or too young for the army overwhelmed the Civil Defense Volunteers office seeking posts as air-raid wardens, auxiliary firemen and police, or airplane spotters, these last to work under the direction of the Civil Air Patrol. The Red Cross organized special classes in first aid and home nursing; the public schools started training programs for the new air-raid wardens; and the city Council passed an ordinance to enforce blackouts. Mayor Samuel took charge of these operations as defense coordinator for Philadelphia, aided by five field directors, Leon J. Obermayer, George W. Elliott, Philip Staples, Raymond Rosen, and Mrs. John Frederick Lewis, Jr. Ordinary citizens familiarized themselves with the regulations relating to air-raid drills and set about providing their households with the recommended firefighting and blackout equipment.[116]

Memories of the Battle of Britain were fresh, and few believed that the Atlantic Ocean was a sure defense against Hitler's Luftwaffe. At first fear lent urgency to the implementation of the city's plans for 1000 air-raid shelters, and to the blackout tests and air-raid drills held intermittently from February 1942 to October 1943, by which time the danger was seen to be nonexistent.[117] Public apprehension aroused by the potential threat to the city from the 91,000 Philadelphians registered in 1940 under the Alien Registration Act led many to applaud FBI raids on German and Italian social clubs, homes, and offices.[118] These raids continued through 1942, but in retrospect it is difficult to regard them as more than grandstand plays and equally difficult not to be ashamed of the public panic that condoned them. The raids inevitably alarmed other Philadelphians of non-English stock, and it was possibly in the hope of heading off a recurrence of the World War I trials that the German-American League of Culture staged a rally on December 12, 1941, at which representatives of eleven nationalities pledged aid to the United States. The America First Committee too declared its intention to support the government unreservedly.[119]

Later, bond and Red Cross drives, with stars from the entertainment world as extra attractions; parades, rallies, and army war shows at Reyburn Plaza; and "I am an American Day" ceremonies at Independence Hall offered relief for pent-up emotions. A Philadelphia United Service Organization (USO) was formed. Hospitality centers for servicemen and a Stage Door Canteen, this under the direction of the American Theater Wing and housed in the basement of the Academy of Music, provided an outlet for the energies of volunteers as well as fun for servicemen and women on leave in Philadelphia or temporarily stationed in the city.[120] All was not parades and the half-pleasurable excitement of volunteer activity, however. The realities of rationing, most important of meat, gasoline, and fuel; of the draft, which made workaday Philadelphia often seem like a women's town; the loneliness; the arrival of one of those terrible, polite telegrams from the War Department reporting the loss of son or husband; the long hours of exhausting work,

whether in the heat and clatter of a mill or in the tense clamor of a government
office, gradually took hold of all Philadelphians, shook them out of their old
habits, and made them in one way or another an extension of the war machine.

As in all other American wars a small, quietly firm group of Philadelphians
who believed that any fighting was wrong, however just the cause appeared
to be, refused to take part in any military activity. A few went to prison; others
participated in one of the possible alternative services, in medical research or
as workers in understaffed hospitals at home, in the forestry service, or in
other similar activities. Quaker-owned businesses also had to find a peaceable
solution to the problem of survival in a war-dominated world. J. E. Rhoads
& Sons, manufacturers of industrial leathers, for example, asked to be excused
from defense contracts. This was a legitimate solution, although one fraught
with problems as both workers and materials became increasingly scarce.[121]

Philadelphia's contribution to the war was a significant one: in money,
bond quotas were met or exceeded regularly; in men and women sent to the
armed forces, there were 183,850 Philadelphians in the service when the war
ended in August 1945; in science and medicine, there was the development
of the proto-computer ENIAC at the University of Pennsylvania under the

*Dr. J. Presper Eckert, Jr., and the Electronic Numerical Integrator and
Computer (ENIAC), Moore School of Electrical Engineering, University of Pennsylvania, February 1946. The "world's fastest calculating machine" was developed
for the Army Ordnance Department.*

direction of J. Presper Eckert and John W. Mauchly, and of the seventy-five-millimeter recoilless rifle at the Frankford Arsenal, the manufacture of the radar bombsight at the Philco plant, and of plexiglass for gun turrets and bomber noses by Rohm and Haas, and the thousands of books supplied to the Medical Corps by W. B. Saunders, official publishers for the National Research Council. Before the war ended production of ordnance and other military supplies was the raison d'être for about 3500 Philadelphia businesses. The Baldwin Group made guns, tanks, shell forgings, armor plate, propellers, and diesel engines as well as the locomotives for which they were famous; the E. G. Budd Company, aircraft parts and ammunition components. Instead of trolleys, the J. G. Brill Company manufactured gun carriages; Henry Disston Sons, Inc., substituted light armor plate for saws. Other firms supplied blood for dried plasma, ski equipment for mountain troops, mosquito netting for the tropics, and parachute silk for the air forces.[122]

And since Philadelphia in spite of her inland position has always been a maritime city, shipbuilding—at the United States Navy Yard, at New York Ship, at old Cramp's, at Sun Ship and about a dozen other companies with yards along the Delaware River, whose channel had been deepened—played a major role in Philadelphia's wartime economy. In fact the accomplishment of the shipbuilders of the Delaware was truly magnificent. The Navy Yard not only built warships but fitted out almost 500 vessels launched elsewhere, and repaired and serviced many ships for America's allies. Operating under the yard's aegis, the Naval Air Materiel Center produced flying boats and served as an experimental station where new ideas could be tested and developed. New York Ship, based in Camden, worked exclusively for the navy. Sun Ship, with headquarters in Philadelphia and yards in Chester, constructed 250 ships for the United States Maritime Commission between December 1941 and September 1945, and emerged from the war as the world's largest builder of tankers. Cramp's, during the nineteenth and early twentieth centuries Philadelphia's most important yard, was closed and in financial difficulties in 1939. Formally reopened two years later with the laying of the keel of the cruiser *Wilkes-Barre*, the yard was modernized and subsequently built submarines, floating workshops, cruisers, and a variety of smaller vessels until the end of the war again emptied its ways.[123]

With factories and mills operating at capacity, problems of manpower soon became acute. As early as August 1940 a writer in *Business Week* noted the scarcity of workers needed to man the Philadelphia shipyards and suggested that men be "imported" to fill the need.[124] The suggestion was hardly necessary, for as in World War I a flood tide of migrants, many from the rural South, flowed into the city. Since these men rarely came with the required skills, training programs were begun in the city's vocational schools, in factories, and at government installations like the Frankford Arsenal. The Free Library, through posters and book lists displayed wherever workers were found, developed a new clientele and soon was circulating more technical books, particularly elementary ones, than fiction. Industries such as the Bendix Aviation Company set up plant libraries, and bookstores whose stock in trade was composed solely of technical books proliferated.[125] To help to fill the need for men with more sophisticated engineering skills the University of Pennsylvania compressed its engineering course, normally a four-year program, into two and a half years. Nevertheless the supply of qualified workers failed to keep up with the demand and by the summer of 1944, with the military forces at a peak of activity in Asia and Europe, the War Manpower Commission put Philadelphia's labor market in the critical class, ordered a forty-eight-hour week for workers in certain industries, and froze almost half a million men and women in their jobs. The Selective Service System at about the same time threatened with immediate draft all men between thirty and thirty-eight years of age who left work in a defense plant for a post elsewhere. In spite of these measures the Quartermaster Corps was so shorthanded at one point that German prisoners were put to work in its depot.[126]

Under the circumstances a certain amount of labor unrest was inevitable. By 1945 a long war seemed on its way to a conclusion, while fatigue and boredom combined with an uncertain job future disturbed the worker's world. Labor restlessness throughout the United States and the threat it had posed to the continuous flow of war-related products had been a matter of concern since the spring of 1941; in 1943 it led Congress to pass the Smith-Connally Act and to sanction the National War Labor Board's powers, originally derived from executive order, banning jurisdictional strikes, picketing, and violence in defense industries, and making mandatory mediation of all disputed issues by the board, of which Dr. George W. Taylor, professor of economics at the University of Pennsylvania, was chairman. Another Philadelphian, William L. Batt, on leave from SKF to head the Office of Production Management (later the War Production Board), was outspoken about the problems labor disputes could create when rival unions engaged in argument, as the CIO's Industrial Union of Marine and Shipbuilding Workers and the AFL's Metal Trades Council had done in 1941 at Cramp's shipyard, each attempting to secure company recognition as the workers' legal bargaining agent.[127]

During the first year of the war, 1942, no major strikes disturbed Philadelphia, although laundry workers, street cleaners, city mechanics, and the PTC's union members took "holidays" or struck briefly. More serious trouble came in the fall of 1943 with a one-day walkout at Cramp's, a prelude to a full-blown strike there the following January. Sun Ship and SKF also had labor problems ending in strikes; and in December 1944 the army had to be called in to unload the ships in Philadelphia's port when the longshoremen walked out.[128] On one occasion only, however, was the city seriously threatened by a major labor dispute: when PTC workers, protesting the upgrading of blacks to positions of motormen and conductors, struck in August of 1944 with potentially disastrous consequences for all offices and industries by almost immobilizing their work forces and bringing the city to a stop.

Trouble began when the transportation company's management refused to obey an order from the Fair Employment Practices Commission directing it to hire blacks to work on buses and streetcars as motormen and conductors. The company expressed readiness to comply with the order but claimed that its contract with the union, an independent one so-called, made doing so impossible. A contest that was going on simultaneously among the old company union, the AFL, and the CIO for the right to represent the workers further complicated the situation. In March 1944 the CIO was chosen as bargaining agent and declared that it would place no obstacles in the way of hiring and upgrading blacks. In July the PTC agreed, after the War Manpower Commission threatened to cut off its labor supply, to hire blacks for all kinds of jobs. On August 1, as training of black streetcar operators was to start, all trolleys, subways, and buses stopped running.

The strike, led by the "independent" union officials, was curiously unopposed by the company. When workers refused to return to their jobs in spite of CIO urging and a War Labor Board order, President Roosevelt sent a detachment of troops under Maj.-Gen. Philip Hayes to take charge. The

To ensure continued operation of Philadelphia Transportation Company vehicles, President Roosevelt ordered troops to the city in response to a union strike in August 1944 against the hiring of blacks as conductors and motormen.

PHILADELPHIA BULLETIN

soldiers arrived in Philadelphia on August 5 and General Hayes gave the workers until 12:01 A.M. on August 6 to return to their posts. Otherwise, he said, the army would run the system, and striking workers' draft deferments would end, while they would be barred from any other defense work and denied unemployment compensation. On August 6 the PTC was again in operation with soldiers riding on all vehicles as a safeguard against possible violence. A federal grand jury investigation was ordered by Attorney-General Francis Biddle, and four strike leaders were arrested and charged with violating the Smith-Connally Act. Ten days later the situation had so far returned to normal that the troops were able to leave the city and the PTC again assumed control of its transportation system.[129]

The strike was over but it had interfered with production of war materials and, it was said, "disgraced the United States in the eyes of the world."[130] It showed, moreover, that neither the Fair Employment Practices Commission, the CIO, nor the federal government could eliminate racial prejudice by fiat. It showed as well a black community willing and able to maintain self-discipline in the face of great provocation, and it showed the fear of white blue-collar workers who saw in the large number of blacks attracted to Philadelphia by war-created jobs a threat to their future, and in this instance to their old, favored positions. It was a classic case, and one that could have erupted into riots of the sort that tore the city apart in the 1840s.

The war and its prosecution to a successful end were the central concerns of most Philadelphians in 1944. Should Roosevelt, already holding office for a third term, be given a fourth to finish the task? The tone of the debate was bitter, and both Thomas E. Dewey, the Republican candidate, and FDR came to Philadelphia to speak. Once again on Election Day, November 7, the Philadelphia Democrats had the satisfaction of carrying the city, giving the president 496,367 votes to Dewey's 346,380. They sent six of their party to the House of Representatives and saw Francis X. Myers defeat Republican incumbent James J. Davis to win a seat in the United States Senate.[131]

Three months after his inauguration for a fourth term Roosevelt died, on April 12, 1945, at the Little White House in Warm Springs, Georgia. The city heard the news about six o'clock as many workers were homeward bound. Mayor Samuel ordered a thirty-day period of mourning for Philadelphia, with flags at half staff. City and county offices closed on April 14, the day of the funeral services in Washington. Many theaters, business houses, and non-war-related industrial plants also closed. Memorial services were held in most churches, including about 150 belonging to black congregations in the metropolitan area, calling their members together "in abject and bitter mourning," and the historic old bells of Christ Church and the bell in the tower of Independence Hall tolled in tribute. That night thousands of Philadelphians jammed Thirtieth Street Station and lined the bridges over the railroad tracks from Gray's Ferry to Holmesburg to see the funeral train as it made its way north from Washington to Hyde Park, New York. Judge Harry E. Kalodner spoke for many when he said that, losing Roosevelt, "Humanity has lost its greatest champion." A taxi driver put it more simply: "The country doesn't realize how badly they are going to miss that guy."[132]

XII

Peace, heralded by as many harbingers as any spring, finally came on August 14, 1945. The surrender of Germany in May, cutbacks in defense contracts, continuing military success in the Pacific, and the news of the use of a new and frighteningly devastating weapon, the atomic bomb, at Hiroshima and Nagasaki were clear indications of the approaching end of the war. The city waited anxiously from August 10 until, four days later, President Truman announced the Japanese surrender and the end of the fighting. The *Inquirer*'s banner headline on August 15 was one word, "PEACE"—in six-inch capitals. Under a story captioned "Philadelphia Roars a Salute to Victory" a reporter tried to capture in print the wild, joyous, noisy celebration that rocked City Hall and filled the center of town with cars and people from late afternoon of August 14 to the early morning of the next day. Relief, thankfulness, good cheer, and the need to let off steam possessed Philadelphia. Street merchants selling confetti and horns appeared magically; students at the University of Pennsylvania predictably staged a spectacular rowbottom; churches and synagogues were filled. All this was in marked contrast to the mild celebration of V-E Day, May 8, the highlight of which had been a service at Independence Hall and a tap on the Liberty Bell by Mayor Samuel. Now Gov. Edward Martin declared a two-day holiday for Pennsylvania, and with shops, restaurants, courts, and offices closed, Philadelphia rested from its "peace jag."[133]

Peace brought as an agreeable aside the collapse of the black market. Dealers began to unload hoarded items—gas rationing stamps, counterfeit or stolen; poultry and meat, particularly hams, bacon, and pork. Signs appeared in butcher shops saying "We have meat! Come in and take your pick." Scarce canned goods, once kept out of sight and reserved for favored customers, moved from beneath counters to open shelves. Motorists freed of hated restrictions went on a gas-buying spree and for a time threatened Philadelphia with a gasoline famine.[134]

The end of the fighting brought difficulties as well as joy. Economic dislocations were bound to be severe. Twelve warships were under construction in the Philadelphia area when the war ended. The navy immediately ordered building stopped, and thousands of workers were suddenly jobless. Long before this Philadelphia had shown an awareness of the problems that were bound to occur as war-oriented factories were returned to civilian activity. Early in 1942 a group of the city's industrialists, bankers, labor leaders, welfare workers, and others began to discuss ways to finance reconversion programs, keep factories in operation, and maintain payrolls and workers' purchasing power after the war was over. They also worried about the quality of urban life in Philadelphia, about the appearance of the city, about slum clearance, the rehabilitation of the water and sewage systems, about the city government and the public services it should provide, about taxes, about labor, postwar unemployment, and industrial peace. This concern was warranted. Values of Philadelphia's real estate as assessed for tax purposes had fallen from a 1932 high of $3,454,008,026 to not quite $2.5 billion in 1941. Similarly, assessments on personal property had declined from $1,041,811,121 to $732,968,980.[135]

Many of these matters had been aired before. In February 1942 *Business Week* published an article, "Philadelphia's Ills: Diagnosis by a Real Estate Specialist." The author, Richard J. Seltzer of the Urban Land Institute, looked at the city's center and found it a slum area dying from the "creeping paralysis" of blight. To stop further decay he recommended that the city be surveyed and "decadent" parts condemned and cleared, then rebuilt with private capital, on the theory that the community would be better served if persons with a cash stake in the results were in charge rather than do-gooders. Seltzer also made a number of suggestions for the improvement of the town's traffic problems: among them that a three-level highway be constructed at Sansom Street with three-deck parking areas along it to keep the shopping district free of cars; that merchandise be loaded and unloaded between 5:30 P.M. and 8:30 A.M. only; that no horse-drawn vehicle be allowed on center-city streets; and that owners of high-rise buildings be required to make provision for the traffic their buildings created.[136]

Seltzer's concern for the future of Philadelphia's center was shared by many. The preceding year, 1941, after a national conference of city planning met in Philadelphia, a Joint Committee on City Planning, composed of members of the Philadelphia Housing Authority, the City Policy Committee, the Junior Chamber of Commerce, and the Lawyers' Council on Civic Affairs, was formed and a proposal made to Mayor Lamberton recommending the creation of a planning commission for the city. An ordinance establishing such an agency was introduced in the Council in April 1942, but it was not until December, and after considerable prodding by the Action Committee on City Planning, a group composed of members of fifty civic organizations, that the Council was persuaded to act. Subsequently Edward Hopkinson, Jr., was appointed to be chairman of the new commission and Robert W. Mitchell of Washington, a highly regarded professional planner, hired as its first director.[137] Planning appeared to be good politics, and the following autumn both Acting Mayor Samuel and his Democratic opponent, William C. Bullitt, endorsed the concept as part of their campaigns.[138]

The importance of planning in the broadest terms for a peacetime economy surfaced in the summer of 1944 when two naval contracts, held by the Brewster Aeronautical Corporation and the E. G. Budd Manufacturing Company, were cancelled.[139] A Committee for Economic Development was promptly organized and by April 1945 could report that Philadelphia firms expected to spend $98 million for postwar construction and new equipment. Simultaneously efforts were being made to keep in the city those federal agencies that had moved there because of lack of housing and office space in Washington.[140] The City Planning Commission proposed a $200-million postwar program for the city; the PTC announced a five-year improvement schedule which would include the acquisition of new buses and streamlined trolley cars; the West Philadelphia Chamber of Commerce wanted the Market Street El put underground to Sixty-third Street and reminded the authorities that the tunnel to carry the el under the Schuylkill had been completed in the 1930s when plans to make it a subway to Forty-sixth Street were drawn up. Editorials in the *Inquirer* urged the clean-up of the polluted Delaware and Schuylkill Rivers and the creation of a Redevelopment Authority to oversee the rehabilitation of rundown neighborhoods. Several airlines and the Chamber of Commerce urged the mayor and Council to expand Philadelphia's Southwest Airport by building a two-level terminal with thirty-two gates, subterminals for international flights, and cargo facilities. The *Inquirer*, in an editorial on August 15, 1945, exhorted the Council not to "muff" this chance because of sectional bickering. The Council, however, unable to decide whether to support the Southwest or the Northeast Airport, appropriated $15 million to be divided between the two, with the not-unexpected result that nothing much happened at either.[141]

Most imaginatively and perhaps most appropriately of all, the city proposed in November 1945 that Philadelphia become the permanent home of the United Nations. Ten square miles on Belmont Plateau were offered the U.N.'s site-seeking committee, but although the committee was impressed, New York won the day.[142]

One more significant proposal was offered in August 1945. At a regional meeting of the Negro Business League, Dr. J. S. Benn, executive secretary of Philadelphia's Negro Chamber of Commerce, spoke of the need for cooperation between the black and white business communities and suggested plans for a joint conference of businessmen of both races to explore ways of increasing "the effectiveness of Negro enterprise along the Eastern seaboard." The local chapter of the NAACP, thinking along similar lines, appointed Walter C. Beckett, a black civic leader, chairman of a special committee to help Philadelphia's returning black veterans and to see that they received the same kind of consideration that was accorded whites.[143] That such actions needed to be taken, such conferences called, is evidence of the frustrating experiences of Philadelphia's blacks. They had hoped for better things from Penn's city.

All Philadelphians were ready for a change. Those who had been in the armed services were anxious to get on with the business of living, to continue their education, return to their jobs or professions, settle down, and get reacquainted with their families. Civilians who had spent the war at home hoped to shake off the restrictions of rationing, to buy a new car, order a telephone, move into a new house. The demand for more education, now possible under the G.I. Bill, crowded Philadelphia's schools and colleges. A building boom began to fill the fields and meadows of East Germantown, West Oak Lane, and the Northeast with rows of small houses and garden apartments.[144] As these were built and sold or rented it became apparent that a major demographic shift was in progress. Italians moved from South Philadelphia to East Mount Airy. Blacks came in ever-increasing numbers into Nicetown and Germantown. Jewish families deserted North Philadelphia for Oxford Circle and the northeast generally. Many middle-class professional families left the city altogether, going to the suburbs or even farther into the country. Even the city's two major universities, Penn and Temple, flirted with the notion of moving to suburban campuses.

Philadelphia was a city on the move. The mindless adherence to the standpat politics of the Republican machine was loosening. The city had given FDR its support since 1936; now the welfare programs of the New Deal were eroding the committeeman's hold on his constituents. Bankers and businessmen interested themselves in plans for the city's future and appeared to be abandoning their indifference to everything but their own concerns as narrowly defined. Men and women unhappily surveyed a shabby city and an inept municipal government and thought about the possibility of changing an increasingly unsatisfactory situation. By 1946 Philadelphia was rather like the sea, hiding a deceptive undertow beneath an unruffled surface.

Rally and Relapse
1946-1968

by Joseph S. Clark, Jr., and Dennis J. Clark

Early planners considered the business of the city to be economic growth and, therefore, concentrated their efforts on Center City and allowed the strictly residential areas to grow haphazardly. When a new interest in planning began in the early 1940s, it also focused on Center City problems.
— Richard Saul Wurman, architect,
and John Andrew Gallery, urban planner

The reformers have had to cast around for a new general to lead their troops. And, tardily, they realize he needs more troops to lead.
— Lorin Peterson, commenting on Philadelphia in the 1960s [1]

As the fantastically garbed Mummers strutted up Broad Street to the jingling music of their traditional tunes in the New Year's Parade of 1946, the city of Philadelphia was poised to enter one of the most exciting periods it would experience in the twentieth century. The Mummers' troupes, composed of working men from tightly knit neighborhoods throughout the city, symbolized one of the great strengths of Philadelphia, its local community cohesion and the solid reliability of its residents. It was this local neighborhood vitality that had enabled the ordinary people to withstand the abuses of the industrial revolution, the struggles and privations of the age of immigration, and the neglect of a city government whose corruption had become a national byword. In the face of their postwar problems and amid bitter winter weather, the throngs of Philadelphians along Broad Street could still celebrate in a great democratic demonstration of enjoyment as if to testify that despite prejudice and failure, despite generations of urban misfortune, they still had the hope and capacity for something better.

The city itself before 1950 still physically reflected the forms and achievements of the Victorian age. Downtown the rectangular blocks were crammed with office and retail buildings whose fronts were heavy with artifice, statuary, and crennellation. On City Hall a miscellany of many figures sat high above dingy gray porticos. The Witherspoon Building on narrow Juniper Street had brown ranks of Protestant saints and heroes standing rigidly along its elaborate cornices. All through the old financial district that occupied the most historic streets of the city near the Delaware, banking and brokerage houses and insurance firms were encased in tomb-like Victorian dignity behind massive doors and huge carved stone fronts. Shopping streets, fashionable Rittenhouse Square, railroad terminals, and government buildings all conveyed the same image of Philadelphia's public character: heavy, old-fashioned immobility. A view across the city's skyline from the gloomy upper reaches of City Hall tower provided a perspective on the institutions that made the city great. Looming among the row-house neighborhoods in all directions were the dark-windowed factories and mills that had roared with productive energy for over a century. Set among them were the steeples and domes of the churches that bound the city's people together in committed congregations. Ranged around the mills and churches were thousands of row-house streets, broad and narrow, in which lived the city's working families, skilled and unskilled, attentive to labor, accustomed to the sacrifices and small rewards of the unlovely industrial metropolis.[2]

Philadelphia and its suburbs from 1946 through 1970 formed a microcosm of the problems affecting cities wherever population shifts, changing technology, and social transformations were altering the shape and conditions of urban life. If, as Aristotle said, "Men come together in cities to live. They remain to live the good life," then Philadelphians were confronted continually with new difficulties in trying to achieve the good life in the turbulence of the modern city. An examination of the politics and government of the city in the post–World War II era reveals how altruism must grapple constantly with the forces of decay and irresponsibility to maintain a humane urban environment.

I

The period after World War II was one of vast change in American life, change that followed swiftly after the great dislocations of the war years. Shortages of all kinds occurred because of lags in production of civilian goods. Major strikes of railroad workers, miners, and plant workers, feverish anti-Communist crusades, and the hasty resettling of veterans in sprawling new suburbs all frustrated the postwar yearning for normalcy.[3] In Philadelphia all of these influences affected the conditions of family and community life. The story of the changes in the city's public life provides perhaps the most dramatic evidence of sweeping change in the postwar era.

In 1946 the politics of Philadelphia was still largely controlled by the Republican party organization, in close alliance with the business community. The Republican organization, and particularly Sheriff Austin Meehan, dominated Mayor Bernard Samuel and the city Council. The national and state elections of 1946 were a disaster for the Democrats, who had shown some signs of taking over the city just before World War II.

Yet there were many Philadelphians who, in common with that staunch Republican Elihu Root, speaking in 1908, felt: "I have a strong desire that the City of Philadelphia, whose history and good name are so dear to every

Independence Hall and Chestnut Street (c. 1948). The nineteenth-century buildings on Chestnut Street were demolished by the Commonwealth of Pennsylvania in 1953 to make way for Independence Mall. The Philadelphia Bourse, Fifth Street between Market and Chestnut, in the left middle ground of the photograph, reopened in 1981 after adaptation of its galleries and atrium for use by restaurants and specialty shops.

INDEPENDENCE NATIONAL HISTORICAL PARK COLLECTION

American, shall be relieved from the stain which a corrupt and criminal combination masquerading under the name of Republicans have put upon her."[4] Unfortunately the Democratic party had offered little alternative, even though it made occasional noises about reform to capture the so-called independent vote in local elections.

Stirrings of genuine reform surfaced in 1947. Richardson Dilworth, lawyer and returning war hero, was selected by a desperate Democratic City Committee to run for mayor. He summoned such friends as Abraham L. Freedman and Walter M. Phillips, young and energetic attorneys; Joseph S. Clark, son of a socially prominent family who had been interested in politics before World War II; and John Patterson, an activist local businessman. He persuaded them to organize an independent group of politically discontented younger people. All five of these leaders had become active in Americans for Democratic Action, organized at the end of World War II to perpetuate the ideals of Franklin D. Roosevelt. The Philadelphia branch of the A.D.A. under the leadership of three intrepid women, Ada Lewis, Emily Ehle, and Molly Yard Garrett, was destined to play an active role in the municipal reform movement for the next twenty years.

Dilworth took to the street corners in a gaily decorated sound truck to declaim the vices of the incumbent Republican administration and the political machine that shored it up. He was defeated by the incumbent mayor, Bernard Samuel, by 93,000 votes in the election of 1947, but a new political force had arisen in Philadelphia with the slogan "Sweep the rascals out!" In some of his appearances Dilworth carried the symbol of a broom prepared to sweep the city clean.

It was during Dilworth's 1947 election campaign that the exposure of municipal corruption was raised to a new level. Philadelphians had long since become inured to the intermittent charges of public stealing that the newspapers carried. Dilworth expanded such charges until they were so extensive and specific that they were irrefutable. Standing at a campaign street rally in Mayor Bernard Samuel's own Thirty-ninth Ward, he named names and amounts of bribes and peculations. His charges included 128 officials, ward leaders, and magistrates. The city Council was compelled by business and press opinion to create a Committee of Fifteen, five councilmen and ten representatives of civic groups, to investigate the charges. On March 1, 1948, the committee after months of effective research revealed a huge catalog of scandalously haphazard and crooked city practices. The city Council, in transports of fear and loathing, was forced to provide a larger budget for the Committee of Fifteen. The battle was on full scale after that.

In the following months $40 million in city spending was found to be unaccounted for. One employee of the Department of Supplies and Purchases was arrested on forty-nine counts of embezzlement, forgery, and other crimes. In May 1948 William B. Foss, an official in charge of part of the tax collection office, committed suicide when faced with the prospect of testifying before the committee. A grand jury was appointed to continue the investigation, and in the following four years one revelation after another rocked the city and amazed observers in the nation whose interest was focused on Philadelphia. A Water Department employee, a plumbing inspector, and the head of the police vice squad all killed themselves in the light of exposures. The fire marshal went to prison. The president judge of the Court of Common Pleas was shown to have tampered with cases in collusion with the chief of city detectives. These scandals were of staggering proportions, overwhelming in their flagrancy, in the amounts involved, and in the damages to orderly government. The public howled for reform as the newspapers relentlessly headlined the findings of such civic groups as the Committee of Seventy, the Bureau of Municipal Research, and the Pennsylvania Economy League, all of which aided the Committee of Fifteen. The press was particularly effective, and four years of outrage preceding 1950 set the stage for the momentous overthrow of the nation's most entrenched and incredibly corrupt political machine.[5]

In 1948 the Democratic City Committee was reorganized under the inspiring leadership of handsome, white-haired James A. Finnegan, a former army colonel, who was able for the time being to control the Democratic ward leaders who were no better and no worse than their Republican opposite numbers. Once again the Democrats carried the city in a presidential election, Harry S. Truman taking Philadelphia by 8000 votes. More significant for the local party, five Democratic congressmen from the city were elected, and Democratic strength in the Pennsylvania legislature was much increased.[6]

Dilworth again took the lead in challenging the incumbent city machine in the campaign of 1949. One fine spring night he used a sound truck to call forth a public rally near Sheriff Meehan's home in the northeast section of the city to denounce the sheriff and other Republican leaders. His stock in trade was to challenge his opponents to public debate on corruption in Philadelphia. A friend of Meehan's in the crowd stated that he was authorized to accept the challenge on behalf of the sheriff. July 12 was agreed on as the date, the Academy of Music as the place.

When newspapermen brought the news to the sheriff he was both furious and nonplussed. A man of little formal education, he knew he would be no match for Dilworth the skilled trial lawyer. But he was a man of considerable courage and a sincere conviction that he and his friends were being libeled by Dilworth. So he did not repudiate the unauthorized agreement.

Press and radio built up the debate as a political spectacular. The audience of some 3000 consisted, by agreement, of an equal number of partisans of each contestant. But it seems likely that all who owned a radio in the city, perhaps half a million people, were listening. Enormous publicity was given in the newspapers.

Dilworth won the debate hands down. At the end of his speech he announced that he would run for city treasurer and Joseph Clark would run for controller in the coming September 13 primary election. Finnegan strongly supported the self-appointed ticket, and it won both the primary and the general elections handily, the latter by a majority of some 112,000 votes. The forces of reform attained their first vantage points of power.[7]

Clark and Dilworth were anomalies in modern Philadelphia politics. They came from similar backgrounds, well-to-do families, Clark from Philadelphia, Dilworth from Pittsburgh. They were regarded as representatives of the old patrician tradition. They had known each other in their youth; Clark wrote, "We learned the American way of life together on the beaches of Southampton, Long Island before World War I." In the 1930s both had run unsuccessfully for public office as Democrats. When they came back to Philadelphia and urban life in 1946 after their military service, both still had ambition for public service. They were friends and in a sense rivals. But although the strains of postwar politics sometimes stretched their friendship, it never broke. Clark, the less spectacular of the two, wrote admiringly of Dilworth as "D'Artagnan in long pants and a double breasted suit." Together they led the reform movement in Philadelphia and Pennsylvania for twenty years.

For the two years following the 1949 election Dilworth and Clark busied themselves with politics, unearthing Republican scandals in City Hall and discovering, as they had expected, that the tools for municipal government were hopelessly obsolete and inadequate. So they joined in a bipartisan fight for a new city charter.

Philadelphia's business leadership also had come to realize that a new charter was essential for responsible municipal government. Robert T. McCracken, a leading old-line Republican lawyer, looked into the Allegheny Conference which under the Mellon interests and Mayor David L. Lawrence had improved city government in Pittsburgh, and on his return east organized the more imaginative businessmen of the city into the Greater Philadelphia Movement. Robert K. Sawyer, an attractive, energetic, and able engineer, was hired as its executive director. As president of the city Council, Frederick R. Garman, a respected Republican, helped the G.P.M. get the necessary state legislation to create a Philadelphia Home Rule City Charter Commission with power to reorganize the city government, their proposals to be submitted to the voters. The Democrats in the state legislature as well as the leadership of the AFL and the CIO, always Democratic by self-interest, also put their weight behind the reform movement.

The new city charter was drafted and ready for voter action by the end of 1950. It was largely the work of three able lawyers, Abraham L. Freedman, a Democrat and later a federal judge, and William Schnader and Robert T. McCracken, Republicans and heads of two prestigious Philadelphia firms. After much discussion, the reformers decided to place the charter on the ballot in the April 1951 primary; this was taking a calculated risk, for if either or both of the two political organizations decided to oppose the charter it would have little chance of approval.[8]

Finnegan, the Democratic city chairman, placed a somewhat reluctant Democratic organization squarely behind the charter. Despite the pressure of the Republican leaders in the Greater Philadelphia Movement, the Republicans held back and in the end took no position. An aggressive "Citizens' Charter Committee," co-chaired by John Morgan Davis, a Democrat, and Judge Nochem Winnet, a Republican, waged an active campaign. The vote was light, but the charter was approved by the substantial majority of 119,790.

The importance of the new charter in the reform of Philadelphia's government was great indeed.[9] It was described by competent observers as "a shining new weapon in the arsenal of good government." It created a strong-mayor form of government and a relatively weak city Council of seventeen members, ten elected by districts and seven at large. Two of the citywide councilmen were required to be members of the minority, or opposition party, one to propose and the other to second a minority position, thus assuring a minority-party vote.

Another important feature of the charter was its strong merit system. Civil service had been a scandal in Philadelphia for many years, with positions in the government being too often awarded solely as a reward for political activity. Henceforth city positions were to be filled by the mayor's administrators from lists submitted by the Civil Service Commission. Non–civil service appointments could be made by the mayor and needed no confirmation by the city Council. Only the city solicitor, who was to be the lawyer for the Council as well as for the mayor, needed councilmanic approval. The city solicitor was wisely made a member of the mayor's Cabinet.

The charter also created a large number of boards and commissions—the City Planning Commission, the Board of Managers of the Philadelphia General Hospital, and the Commission on Human Relations—to consist of citizens usually serving without pay. The mayor was thereby given power either to create a vibrant group of able and creative thinkers and administrators or to follow the old tradition and fill the commissions with political hacks or personal friends.

Administration generally was streamlined and decentralized. While the mayor was chief executive officer, a managing director was created and placed in charge of ten line service departments such as police, fire, welfare, recreation, and health. A director of finance would have charge of the executive budget, the Department of Collections, and the Department of Purchases and Supplies. These two officials plus the mayor constituted the administrative board that ran the city.

Also in the mayor's Cabinet was to be an amorphous office called city representative and director of commerce. This individual was given the impossible task—as it later turned out—of being the chief of public relations, director of the airport, and secretary of commerce, charged with supervision of the port and implementation of the city's efforts to attract industry.[10]

At the same time that the city charter was approved by the electorate, Clark was nominated for mayor and Dilworth for district attorney in the Democratic primary, and a relatively strong slate of Democratic politicians, headed by Finnegan, was nominated for the Council. The Republicans were in a dilemma. To nominate an old regular was, after the debacle of 1949, to invite disaster. McCracken and a number of other conservatives prevailed upon Meehan and the other organization stalwarts to slate a nonorganization candidate, the Rev. Daniel E. Poling, a nationally known Baptist minister and a man of impeccable integrity.

Unfortunately for their cause Dr. Poling was a resident of Philadelphia in name only. His real home was in New York City, and he had not bothered to come back to vote for the city charter in the primary. In the end the effort to drape the mantle of his respectability around the Republican organization failed. Clark was elected by a majority of 124,000 votes, Dilworth by slightly less. All Democratic candidates for district councilman and the five Democrats running at large were elected. The result was a city Council of fifteen Democrats and two Republicans. The reformers seemed secure in the saddle, and for the first time in generations the city of Philadelphia had a Democratic mayor and administration.[11]

*Mayor Joseph S. Clark, Jr., with city officials and Democratic party leaders
(January 10, 1952).* Standing: *George T. Guarnieri, Maurice Osser, William
Lennox, Michael Byrne, the Rev. Marshall Shepard, Joseph Scanlon, Lennox L.
Moak, and Thomas McHenry.* Sitting: *Richardson Dilworth, Mayor Clark,
Abraham E. Freedman, and James A. Finnegan.*

PHILADELPHIA BULLETIN

It became the Democrats' task to staff their municipal administration.
Finnegan was elected president of city Council and was to work closely with
Mayor Clark.[12] He also remained chairman of the Democratic City Committee until he left Philadelphia for Harrisburg early in 1955 to become secretary
of the commonwealth and political adviser to Gov. George M. Leader.

A new type of administrator was brought to City Hall, the professional
as opposed to the political appointee. The reform government, moreover,
attracted younger men to serve, men like Robert K. Sawyer as managing
director, and Lennox Moak as director of finance, with his assistant Robert
McConnell. Despite some grumblings in the Council, non-Philadelphians
were brought into positions requiring technical skill. For example, Robert
Crawford, recommended by the National Recreation Association, came from
Oakland, California, as deputy to Fredric R. Mann, recreation commissioner.

The next four years saw a drastic change in the spirit as well as the
administration of the city government. The provisions of the city charter
were rigorously complied with. The Civil Service Commission was revolutionized under the chairmanship of Sidney B. Dexter and his fellow commission members, Shippen Lewis, a political independent, and the Rev. Luther
Cunningham, a black minister active in the reform movement. Appointments
to the police and fire departments were made on a strict merit basis, not always
to the wishes of the Council and the Democratic ward leaders.

The police and fire commissioners on the other hand were appointed with
some concern for political considerations. Thomas Gibbons, police commis-

sioner, was a lifelong friend of Jim Finnegan's, but highly capable, and Fire Commissioner Frank McNamee, although sponsored by both the Democratic organization and the Variety Club, was effective. It is noteworthy that for five years the Philadelphia Fire Department won the National Fire Prevention Award.

Dilworth reorganized the district attorney's office, eliminating political control and establishing for the first time in many years a set of reliable criminal case records. Aided by his young and able first deputy, red-headed Michael von Moschzisker, son of a very conservative former chief justice of the Supreme Court of Pennsylvania, he appointed a capable staff of young lawyers and investigators who devoted full time to their jobs. They cut the period prior to trial in nonbail cases from ninety to thirty days, and the delay in reaching trial in bail cases from nearly two years to seven months. Dilworth worked closely with Police Commissioner Gibbons to break up long-standing alliances between ward politicians and the police. Criminal justice was put on as honest and compassionate a basis as the prosecuting attorney was able to do.

These were years of great activity. A logjam of critical problems had built up during the years of Republican control. World War II had left severe dislocations in its wake, among which were a terrible housing shortage and complex difficulties of industrial conversion back to civilian production. Not all problems were solved at once, but strong foundations of a municipal government of ability and integrity were laid to address the problem.

II

The city was changing in ways that put the morale of its citizens on a roller-coaster. Led by the outstanding pitching of Robin Roberts and Curt Simmons and the batting of other young "Whiz Kids" like Richie Ashburn and Del Ennis, the Phillies baseball team won the National League pennant in 1950—its first pennant since 1915 and its second in history; but then the Phillies lost the World Series to the New York Yankees in an embarrassing four-game sweep. In 1952 the Athletics made their first serious run for the American League pennant in two decades, only to falter when their twenty-four-game-winning pitcher, Bobby Shantz, suffered a broken pitching wrist in early September. The A's sank to fourth place and then to seventh and eighth in 1953 and 1954. Their latest collapse resulted in Connie Mack's family's—the old leader himself had finally retired from managing after the 1950 season—inability to continue to afford the operation of a major-league team, and the A's opened the 1955 season under new ownership in Kansas City; they moved again, to Oakland, in 1968.

College football in Philadelphia, popularized by great Penn teams that filled Franklin Field and briefly by the Temple team that played in the first Sugar Bowl in 1936, declined precipitously in quality and appeal during the 1950s.

The football professionals also rode the roller-coaster. Coach Earl

"Greasy" Neale's steady upbuilding of the Eagles achieved fruition soon after the war, when led by fullback Steve Van Buren the Eagles won the Eastern Conference championship of the National Football League in 1947 and then the league championship in 1948 and 1949. After they fell to a .500 record in 1950, however, Neale retired, and the team floundered in mediocrity until Coach Buck Shaw and quarterback Norm Van Brocklin raised it to respectability in 1959 and another league championship in 1960. But Shaw as coach and Van Brocklin as a player were both at the end of their careers, and their retirement after 1960 was followed by another decade of mediocrity. Speeding the descent also was the retirement after 1962 of almost the last sixty-minute (that is, both offensive and defensive) player, center and linebacker Chuck Bednarik, who had come out of Penn in time to play on the Eagles' 1949 championship team and remained to seal the victory over Coach Vince Lombardi's Green Bay Packers in the 1960 championship game by forcing a Packer fumble in the final seconds.

The Philadelphia 76ers of the National Basketball Association played more consistently, but perennially lost out in championship playoffs to the Boston Celtics—except for the 1966–1967 season when center Wilt Chamberlain led the team to a regular-season record of sixty-eight wins and only thirteen losses, the season and playoff championships, and eventual recognition as the greatest NBA team of all time. The 76ers' roller-coaster days came later, when the departure of Chamberlain to Los Angeles and the aging of their other stars brought them crashing to a nine-wins, seventy-three-losses season in 1972–1973, before they began to rise again in the later 1970s.

Professional baseball and football both benefited from wide public exposure through the new medium of television. In 1952 the Federal Communications Commission approved four television channels for Philadelphia, a communications event destined to have profound effects on politics and education as well as almost all areas of entertainment in addition to sports. The first TV spectaculars, however, were the antics of Red-baiter Sen. Joe McCarthy.

Throughout the physical city there was a feeling of movement. In the same year that the four television channels arrived, the decrepit ferry service to Camden at last ended, and a new bridge to South Jersey farther down the river was authorized. The old Broad Street Station across from City Hall was closed on April 27, 1952, and the Philadelphia Orchestra serenaded passengers on the last train. Attendance at Army-Navy games on the Saturday following Thanksgiving grew to over 100,000, and many fans could see the Schuylkill Expressway under construction as they drove through traffic jams to the game. In 1955, when Matthew McCloskey closed a $35-million deal with the Pennsylvania Railroad for a complex of buildings to replace the Broad Street Station and its tracks, plans for the downtown centerpiece of the city's renovation drew a chorus of approval and disapproval from citizens, who were excited but uncertain about the city's future.

This sense of movement contrasted with tensions in the city's life that betrayed growing social friction. A curfew was adopted in 1955 to bar youths under seventeen from the streets late at night as a result of juvenile delinquency incidents. In the same year twenty-six teachers were dismissed by the Philadelphia School District for refusing to answer questions about Communist affiliations on the basis of their rights under the Fifth Amendment. In 1953 Prof. Barrows Dunham had been dismissed from his position at Temple University on similar grounds and Jefferson Medical School was placed on the American Association of University Professors' censure list for like summary firings. In the city's neighborhoods a steady rash of small-scale racial conflicts occurred as blacks moved into previously all-white areas. Thus while improvement highlighted the city's skyline, the social fabric of Philadelphia was continuing to be subjected to stress and disruption.

The economic underpinnings of the city were changing in fundamental ways. In August 1954 Congress approved the deepening of the Delaware River ship channel to a depth of forty feet by the United States Army Corps of Engineers to facilitate passage of ore boats to a new steel plant outside the city in Morrisville, Bucks County. The location was symbolic of the enormous shift of business and industry to the suburbs. In another symbolic move the Board of City Trusts sold the Girardville Coal Mines, part of the wide hinterland of resources once, but no longer, controlled from Philadelphia. In 1958 the Pennsylvania Railroad was forced to merge with the New York Central Railroad, a step that failed to halt the slide into bankruptcy of the once-mighty Pennsylvania rail empire.

In 1955 Joseph Clark, whose ambition was to go to the United States Senate and to which he was ultimately elected, announced that he would not run for a second term as mayor. His obvious successor was Richardson Dilworth, who was triumphantly elected in the fall of 1955 over Thacher Longstreth, the attractive, argyle-socked, but inexperienced Republican nominee.

Dilworth was mayor of Philadelphia from January 1956 until February 1962, when under the terms of the city charter he resigned to run for governor of Pennsylvania. He continued in large measure the policies of his predecessor. Many of his principal assistants had been aides to Clark and continued a high level of competence. The Police Department under three splendid commissioners, Thomas Gibbons, Albert Brown, and Howard Leary, was probably the best in the country. Dilworth's six years in City Hall were a story of ongoing administrative successes accompanied by a series of turbulent political crises.

Cong. William J. Green, who had succeeded Finnegan as the "boss" of the Democratic party, had sufficient votes in the Council to place amendments to the city charter on the ballot, amendments that could seriously cripple the merit system. Under the circumstances Dilworth thought it wise to compromise with Green.[13] He agreed to support charter amendments that would remove from the merit system employees of Philadelphia County offices that had not been merged into the city government. These included the traditional offices of sheriff and recorder of deeds which were held by elective officials not responsible to the mayor. The patronage that would thus be released to the organization was avidly coveted by the ward leaders and the city chairman. The reform element in the city was highly critical of Dilworth for this action. The amendments would also have eliminated the charter requirement that an elected municipal officeholder must resign if he sought other elective office during his term.

Although the amendments were declared illegal by Common Pleas Court on a technicality and then roundly defeated in the primary election of 1956, by midsummer, less than a year after his election, Dilworth's political honeymoon seemed over. He was under attack from all sides, from the reformers for having deserted them, from the organization for not having put the amendments across with the voters.

Then came one of those unpredictable happenings in the life of a politician. Returning with his wife from a European vacation in the summer of 1956, Dilworth was aboard the transatlantic liner *Andrea Doria* when she sank after being rammed in a fog by another liner, the *Stockholm*. The Dilworths behaved with conspicuous courage and were greeted as heroes on their return to Philadelphia. The adventure at sea almost completely eliminated the unfavorable reaction from the so-called Charter Ripping.

After the fiasco of 1956 Congressman Green was wise enough not to tinker again with the city charter, but he did not abandon his efforts to utilize the Democratic City Hall government for patronage and political favors to contributors.[14] Over Dilworth's opposition, Green was successful in securing the renomination and election of Victor H. Blanc as district attorney and of Alexander Hemphill as city controller. He was also successful in thwarting Dilworth's bid for governor in 1958, the candidacy going to Mayor Lawrence of Pittsburgh. Despite this organizational opposition, Dilworth was reelected mayor in 1959 over Harold E. Stassen, lawyer, perennial presidential candidate, and former president of the University of Pennsylvania, by more than 205,000 votes, the greatest majority ever received by an elective candidate for a Philadelphia municipal office.

Yet Dilworth's second term continued to have its share of political fireworks. An effort to solve the problem of inadequate parking facilities in South Philadelphia by issuing parking licenses for which car owners would have to pay resulted in a tumultuous public meeting in 1961 at which the Dilworths were pelted with rocks, fruit, and vegetables. The mayor escaped injury, but the proposed parking tax died a swift death. Dilworth also had difficulty because of some offhand remarks about South Philadelphia which came out in the press as anti-Italian slurs. Conscious of the *faux pas*, Dilworth was perhaps only too ready to make an Italian-American career policeman from South Philadelphia a district police commissioner, and advanced Frank Rizzo to that post, a decision with long-term unforeseen results.

Dilworth resigned his mayoralty in February 1962 to run for governor. Republicans believed that a series of minor scandals that had created a tempest in a teapot would be damaging to his campaign. Although Dilworth lost the election to William W. Scranton, the comedy of errors that the grand jury investigations revealed proved to have little impact on the result.

Much of the public thought of the reform years in terms of Clark and Dilworth, but the politically active spectrum of the city included a wide array of personalities many of whom were remarkable and not easily categorized. In the Democratic party, for instance, Cong. William J. Green was an astute and energetic leader who represented effectively the interests of the city's blue-collar population. James P. Clark, a trucking magnate and chief promoter of the Liberty Bell racetrack, was a key financial backer of the party. John B. Kelly, Olympic oarsman and a major building supplier—"Brick Work by Kelly"—had long been a power in the city, and contractor Matthew H. McCloskey was chief financial adviser to the Democratic National Committee. Real estate entrepreneur Albert M. Greenfield remained involved in many important economic and political issues, so much so that for a time he became known as "Mr. Philadelphia." Harry A. Batten, an advertising executive, was one of the most imaginative figures of the period in his persistent advocacy of sweeping plans for downtown renovation, which included the establishment of the Food Distribution Center in South Philadelphia. G. Holmes Perkins, of the School of Fine Arts of the University of Pennsylvania, and Dr. Stephen B. Sweeney, of the Fels Institute of Local and State Government, were valuable advisers concerning municipal change and public administration. All of these talented people and many more were engaged in the reform movement.[15]

I I I

With the departure of Dilworth, James H. J. Tate, who had been president of the city Council since 1955, succeeded as acting mayor under the provisions of the city charter. Jim Tate, unlike Clark and Dilworth, whose programs he committed himself to support, started in politics as a committeeman and moved up the ladder rung by rung, acquiring administrative experience to supplement his political background as a staunch organization Democrat. A graduate of Temple University and a student for several years at its law school, he had the drive to lead the organization forces. It was said of him that he never missed an important man's or a neighbor's funeral. Amazingly enough, he was Philadelphia's first Irish-Catholic mayor.

In 1963 he ran for election in his own right. By this time the independent element in the Democratic party, which had supported Clark and Dilworth, particularly the A.D.A., was disillusioned with Tate; he was too much an organization man. The independents ran Walter M. Phillips for mayor in the spring primary, but were unable to summon any effective political support for him. Tate defeated Phillips easily and went on to win in the fall from James T. McDermott, the Republican candidate, by a margin of 68,268 votes, somewhat less than half of what had become the expected Democratic majority.

In retrospect Phillips's defeat marked the end of "independent" good-government influence in City Hall. The reform movement of the 1940s and 1950s really died when Dilworth resigned as mayor, although Mayor Tate pursued many of the public plans and projects that had been set in motion.

A working politician, never at ease with the big-business leaders of the city, Tate was much more a mayor of the row-house constituency than of the downtown business and liberal echelons. He made an earnest effort to continue the policies of his predecessors, but he fell out with the business community and with a number of other leaders who since 1951 had had their way in Philadelphia's life. Nevertheless he was a strong mayor as the charter required; some said he was a "big-city boss" in the old tradition. A number of Clark appointments and more of the Dilworth appointments stayed with him, but his top management was new, if uninspired. The complexion of a number of politically sensitive bodies consisting of mayoral appointees, such as the Zoning Board of Adjustment, changed for the worse. Middle management, largely under civil service, continued to be competent.

Paul D'Ortona, the South Philadelphia leader who had moved from a magistrate's office into the city Council in 1951, succeeded Tate as chairman of that body. He and Tate were often at odds. There was constant turmoil in City Hall among the mayor, the Council, and the Democratic City Committee with respect to administration, finance, and the implementation of policy.

The rising protest movement of the 1960s, focused on civil rights for blacks and other minorities, roared into the city's streets fueled by both resentment and idealism. One target of protests was historic Girard College, which a United States Supreme Court opinion in 1957 had declared to be publicly aided to a sufficient degree to require nondiscriminatory entrance policies admitting blacks. After that decision a separate governing board independent of the Board of City Trusts was formed for Girard. Blacks saw this as evasion of the court decree. Picketing on a large scale followed. By 1965, 1000 police had to be detailed to handle the pickets and crowds. The Rev. Martin Luther King, Jr., addressed a rally at the college urging nonviolent pressure for open admissions.[16]

The federal government had launched a "war on poverty," and a young black lawyer, Charles Bowser, was appointed by Mayor Tate to head the Anti-Poverty Action Committee. Disputes over local community participation became a regular feature of the program.

In the spring of 1965, Arlen Specter, an able and politically ambitious Democratic lawyer, accepted the Republican nomination for district attorney, feeling he had nowhere to go in the Democratic party. Charging that incumbent James C. Crumlish had failed to push the war on crime and to follow up evidence of the use of political influence in city affairs by the Democratic City Committee, he defeated Crumlish in November by 37,212 votes. Once elected, Specter went on the offensive against the Democratic organization.

The Democratic City Committee already had troubles enough in its quarrelling with the mayor. As all mayors must, Tate had contested the committee's patronage and financial demands from the first, but it was not until the death of Tate's good friend Congressman Green, on December 21, 1963, and the succession of Francis X. Smith, that the breach became an open one. Tate and Smith, for years political allies, became involved in an old-fashioned donnybrook in 1967 when Smith supported for mayor Alexander Hemphill, who had begun as a reformer but as city controller had broken with Dilworth and since then conducted a running feud with the mayor's office. Tate flexed his muscles and by doing so proved able to defeat Hemphill readily in the spring primary. Smith persisted in refusing to support Tate in the autumn general election, whereupon Tate's victory rendered inevitable Smith's resignation and retirement from politics. Tate was able to prevail on the city committee to elect as its new chairman Cong. William J. Green, Jr., the handsome son of the former Democratic leader.

Tate's Republican opponent in the fall election of 1967 was Arlen Specter, a strong candidate. It was widely believed in early summer that Specter would win. Tate, however, had several powerful groups working for him. Philadelphia's large Roman Catholic population was grateful for his influence in obtaining state aid for textbooks and bus transportation for parochial schools. The Italian-American community appreciated his intention to reappoint Frank L. Rizzo as police commissioner. (Rizzo had first been appointed by Tate when Howard Leary, Dilworth's last police commissioner, went to New York to serve under Mayor John V. Lindsay.) Rizzo's relations with Specter were cool. Indeed in a time of violent racial confrontations in many cities and of threatened riots in Philadelphia, Tate's support of Rizzo as a tough law-and-order cop held an appeal far beyond any one ethnic group or economic class, even if civil libertarians regarded the commissioner with suspicion. Of crucial importance was the compliance of the Tate administration at the negotiating table with city government employee unions. Agreements were signed for pension and fringe benefits that would escalate inordinately in the following years with disastrous financial results for the city. These decisions in the mid-1960s were a watershed for the erosion of municipal fiscal integrity. For all this, Tate was reelected by the very narrow margin of 11,000 votes.[17]

Tate's second elective term was a continuing succession of scandals and political quarrels. The familiar charges of zoning concessions, extortion, and conflict of interest brought a series of resignations in high places. Some of the most publicized troubles surrounded the building in South Philadelphia of the Spectrum for indoor sports. The principal contractor was Matthew H. McCloskey & Company, a firm deeply involved in Democratic politics. Not only did costs skyrocket, but early in 1968, soon after the Philadelphia 76ers, the National Basketball Association defending champions, and the new Philadelphia Flyers National Hockey League entry began to play there, part of the roof blew away. Similarly the cost of the contract for a new sports stadium in South Philadelphia to house the Phillies and the Eagles soared to unimagined heights as early as the submission of the first bids, requiring the voters to approve new loans. Completion was delayed for more than a year.

By the time the 1969 municipal election came around both the Tate administration and the Democratic City Committee were in disarray beyond the valiant efforts of young Chairman Green to rescue them. The Republicans won the election. Thomas Gola, a sports hero with an accounting degree, a star of La Salle College's 1954 national championship basketball team and later of professional basketball, was elected controller. Arlen Specter handily won another term as district attorney. The Republicans also gained two new seats in the city Council, leaving that body with twelve Democrats and five Republicans.

Tate blamed city Chairman Green and his preoccupation with his congressional duties for the loss of the election. Green had won his seat in Congress at the age of twenty-six to succeed his father. But he was a different character from his father. Idealistic and intelligent, he had the future of the Democratic party as a liberal reform group very much at heart. He in turn placed the blame for the Democratic defeat squarely on the mayor's doorstep, claiming that the party had come into the control of a small group headed by the mayor who lacked the vision and imagination to bring the Democratic organization back to the position it had occupied some fifteen or twenty years earlier when Jim Finnegan was chairman. Green proposed a reform plan for the organization, pressed it to a vote, and, since Tate was opposed to it, was badly beaten. Thereupon Green resigned as city chairman.

Joseph Scanlon, a ward leader from the northeast and an intimate of Tate's, was elected in Green's place as the mayor's candidate in December 1969, but Scanlon died in the fall of 1970. He was succeeded by Peter J. Camiel, a wise party war-horse with none of the aura of reform about him.

The effect of national trends on the city in the 1960s was powerful. The youthful protest movement and agitation for civil rights advances primed the city for large-scale antiwar protests as the decade ended. In 1969 some 15,000 rallied all over the city opposing the Vietnam War. In May of 1970 more rallies protested the killing of students at Kent State University in Ohio. Students took over the new Philadelphia Community College in a sit-in and, joined by most of the faculty, demanded changes in college administration. Racial outbreaks added to the turmoil. Mayor Tate had constant problems with juvenile and racial clashes. Race riots broke out at the city's Holmesburg Prison. Commissioner Frank Rizzo's police raided coffeehouses full of young "hippie" couples in center city, and the resulting publicity irritated thousands throughout the city. The temper of Philadelphia had changed greatly from the staid days before 1950.[18]

As the decade of the 1970s opened, troubles descended on the Tate administration from all sides. Philadelphia was in a desperate financial plight. Its operating expenses outran its revenues, as in almost all other big cities in the country. The budget for municipal services increased from $100,720,633 in 1947 to $535,361,000 in 1970. The need for increased revenue was apparent as early as 1939, and under the Samuel administration the city wage tax was first imposed to supplement the inadequate real estate tax. The postwar prosperity of both municipal and national economies made increases in taxation unnecessary during the Clark and Dilworth years, but from 1961 onward increases in both real estate and wage taxes had become almost annual.

Special taxes were added from time to time to meet specific needs, especially those of the schools.

Federal and state grants helped in such areas as urban redevelopment, highways, public housing, and health and welfare activities. Such grants tended to escalate from the Truman administration onward, though political shifts in Washington and Harrisburg made them alternately easier or harder to come by. On the state level the worsening fiscal condition of the commonwealth during the 1950s and 1960s virtually dried up state aid to Philadelphia. The legislators, always suspicious of the state's largest city, became increasingly less willing to help resolve Philadelphia's crying needs.[19]

Clark, Dilworth, and Tate all made unending pilgrimages to Washington and Harrisburg in search of funds. Much of their lobbying was done through two municipal government organizations, the League of Cities, tending to represent smaller municipalities, and the United States Conference of Mayors, largely confined to major cities. Clark was vice-president of the League of Cities, which held its convention in Philadelphia in 1954, and he would have become president two years later had he not been elected to the United States Senate. Dilworth and Tate—both well thought of among their peers—served as presidents of both organizations during their terms in City Hall.

Federal and state grants and lobbying notwithstanding, in the summer of 1970 the financial condition of the city was so precarious that Tate refused to spend $400,000 that had been appropriated by the Council to combat warfare among street gangs, a species of violence that was producing an alarming number of deaths. At the same time the Police Department was seriously undermanned, with some 700 vacancies.

Among the other difficulties facing the Tate administration were confusion at the airport with respect to improvements; the long delay in beginning a subway extension to the northeast and its ultimate deferral; another delay in the construction of the Delaware Expressway from north to south through the city to carry New York–Washington traffic, and the problem of putting this expressway underground in the vicinity of Society Hill; and a related controversy over, and eventual abandonment of, a plan to construct a crosstown expressway between the Delaware and the Schuylkill just south of center city.

IV

Of critical importance to the Democratic party and so to the city government during these administrations was the leadership of organized labor, the AFL and the CIO. Until they merged in 1955 the two labor groups functioned in loose cooperation in their political contacts with City Hall. Unlike the business leaders, their membership and leadership for the most part lived in the city and could vote. They also had access through various devices never questioned legally to large sums of money and much political manpower that they placed at the service of the Democratic party. Labor leaders served under Clark, Dilworth, and Tate on many of the boards and commissions where conflict of interest was not apparent. Tate, however, broke with the position of Clark and Dilworth when in 1969 he appointed a labor leader to the three-man Civil Service Commission.

Labor gave lip-service to good government, but its primary political interest was economic. Its leaders wanted a sympathetic city administration when disputes arose with management that on occasion resulted in strikes where inevitably the police were involved. Labor also urged higher wages and better working conditions for city employees.

Despite the strong support given them by organized labor, Clark and Dilworth managed to steer a sufficiently neutral course in their official conduct during labor disputes to hold the support of the business community as well. But Tate's loss of business establishment support was in no small measure due to his open advocacy of the labor cause in industrial disputes. Moreover his acquiescence in the demands of municipal employees for large wage increases and fringe benefits was a major reason for the fiscal difficulties in which the city found itself toward the end of his administration.

The labor movement operated politically through the Council on Political Education (COPE), a coalition of all the important unions having Philadelphia locals except the Teamsters, who were expelled from the national movement in 1957 and went their own generally Democratic way. For most of the 1947–1970 period COPE's leadership was in the hands of Ed Toohey from the building trades and Joe Kelley of the Electrical Workers. Both were shrewd politicians. Frequently quarreling not only with the Democratic City Committee but with each other over the selection of candidates, they nevertheless exerted important influence over policy, turned in their dollars to the party treasury, and supplied effective manpower on Election Day. Their relationship with the Clark-Dilworth independents and the A.D.A. was also excellent until 1967, when they broke with the liberals' support of Arlen Specter for mayor. The alliance has never been reformed.

By far the most serious labor disturbances during the period were the almost biannual rows between the Transport Workers Union and the management of the Philadelphia Transportation Company. The pattern repeated itself every time a union contract was about to expire. The union would demand a wage increase, allegedly to match higher wages in other cities, and management would refuse on the ground that there was no money to pay for it. At the last minute, or after a short strike, the dispute would be settled with a significant increase in wages. The PTC would then apply to the Pennsylvania Public Utility Commission for a fare increase. The city would offer token opposition, contending that the company was more prosperous than it would admit.

There were seven transit strikes between 1946 and 1967, and in almost every other year strikes were averted at the last moment as a result of City Hall mediation. In 1953, for example, a two-year contract between the T.W.U. and PTC was to expire in the middle of December. The union had insisted on a termination date at the height of the Christmas shopping season, to exert the maximum pressure on the company. Control of the PTC had been acquired that year by a holding company whose principal office was in New York, but Albert M. Greenfield, who had been instrumental in selling control of the company, was still on the board of directors and was placed in charge of management negotiations in Philadelphia. The ordinary process of collective bargaining having failed, negotiations were moved to Mayor Clark's office. As the contract expiration date approached, labor's *deus* (or *diabolus*, to his opponents) *ex machina*, Michael J. Quill, president of the national union, appeared from New York with his shillelagh and an Irish brogue entirely worthy of County Kerry's best. Quill and Greenfield were old but friendly antagonists who had squared off against each other in many a previous negotiating session.

After much palaver brought the parties within measurable distance of an agreement, Clark went back and forth from one room in the mayor's suite of offices to another, from the headquarters of Quill and the local union's bargaining committee—all somewhat suspicious of each other—to the place where Greenfield and the company labor experts gathered around a table. The mayor would cajole each group to yield further in the public interest. Two days before contract expiration, Greenfield told Clark he had gone as far as his instructions would permit. Quill, equally adamant, named a final figure still above what Greenfield was authorized to accept.

A strike seemed unavoidable. As Clark shuttled from one room to another he passed the desk of his executive secretary, on which, as a precaution for such a crisis, a bottle of whiskey was sitting. Appropriating it, Clark returned to persuade Greenfield, with the aid of the whiskey, to call New York and get authority to raise the ante, provided Quill would meet him halfway. Greenfield agreed, but only if Quill would agree first. With the bottle and ice at hand, Clark sent for Quill. After a couple of drinks and an Irish song or two, Quill agreed to a new figure. Greenfield called New York and obtained a new offer that Quill then sold to his labor colleagues, with the aid of what was left of the whiskey. Greenfield, Quill, and Clark celebrated labor peace with a final drink, each of the three convinced he had made a good settlement for his client.

But the end was not yet. At a union meeting, rank and file refused to ratify the agreement and a strike began. Clark called Quill and insisted that the union members be polled by secret ballot conducted by the American Arbitration Association. Quill agreed, and came back to Philadelphia to urge acceptance of the company's offer at a second union meeting. It took four days to work out the procedures for the ballot, but the members then approved the agreement and the strike was called off. The men received a sixteen-cents-an-hour increase over two years and a number of fringe benefits. The Public Utility Commission granted an increase in fares early in 1954. Patronage declined, the PTC's financial condition deteriorated again, but the trolleys and buses ran without substantial further interruption until 1961—not, however, without further tense negotiations at City Hall, further wage concessions, further fare increases, and further reduced ridership.

It was hoped that public ownership of the system in conjunction with operation of suburban bus lines and commuter railroads might break this vicious circle. The Southeastern Pennsylvania Transportation Authority (SEPTA), a quasi-public nonprofit company, was formed to operate the Philadelphia area transit system in 1968, purchasing the PTC for a little under $48 million. Philadelphia County had its representatives on a directing board, as did the suburban counties of Montgomery, Bucks, and Delaware. Their interests conflicted.

A labor area of vexatious difficulty was that of the port, and its problems were symbolic of the city's changing fortunes. Always turbulent, the long-shoremen of the port had for generations led a hazardous and exploited existence. Fr. Denis Comey, a Jesuit priest, had long campaigned for better working conditions for them. With the institution of more regular hiring and work assignment practices in the 1950s, some improvement resulted. But the growing use of large cargo container units for shipping reduced longshore work. Other cities were quicker to adopt container shipping technology. Philadelphia lagged. As a result the fading of the longshoremen from the docks signified the waning of a portion of the port's business as competition from other areas reduced Philadelphia's share of cargo handling.[20]

V

By the end of this period Philadelphia was the fourth-largest city in the United States, losing third place to Los Angeles in the census of 1960. Phila-delphia's population in 1970 was 1,927,863, a slight drop from the 2,002,512 count of 1960, which in turn was less than in 1950.

One of the overriding developments of this period was the astonishing growth of the suburban counties around Philadelphia. While the city's popu-lation declined by 6 percent from 1950 to 1970, the adjacent counties of its metropolitan hinterland were increasing by almost 30 percent. This enormous suburban growth took place largely at the expense of old working-class neigh-borhoods. People, industries, retail facilities, and many other sorts of interests diffused throughout the region. Repeated attempts were made to bind the suburban energies to the city, but the traditionally Republican suburbs were extremely wary of close ties. Commuters from the suburbs resented the city's wage tax; they had fled the increasingly black and crime-afflicted old neigh-borhoods. Richardson Dilworth's proclamation that the city and suburban school districts should be merged appalled suburbanites who had left the city precisely because of inadequate schools.

The Pennsylvania–New Jersey–Delaware Planning Association sought to chart regional functions in transportation and other areas, but had no statu-tory power. The Delaware River Port Authority, the Southeastern Pennsyl-vania Transportation Authority, and the Delaware Valley Regional Planning Commission all sought more regional coordination, but the scattering of local and state governments and deeply interwoven patterns of public authority simply defied any major structural changes. America was not France, and any plan for highly concentrated control of regional affairs was doomed because of ingrained antiurban hostility. Only in the area of sharing water resources was there a decent record of collaboration.[21]

The city's concentrations of people created an ever-present problem of land use. Philadelphia's tradition of low-rise row-house residences and a limit on high-rise apartments generated pressures to encroach on available parkland and open space for housing. Public opinion seemed resolved, however, to protect the city's remaining open space. Philadelphia's city planners, with the help of Robert Crawford and the Recreation Department, managed to set aside significant amounts of real estate as green retreats from the asphalt jungle of the city's core. These might be only tot lots, bocce courts, playgrounds, or open squares, but they were an achievement in the face of an almost inflexible development pattern determined by land costs and population density.

World War II had left the city with a critical housing shortage. In 1950 over 70,000 dwellings lacked a bath or were dilapidated, and overcrowding affected a huge proportion of the inner-city housing supply. Central to the problem was the age and character of the residential stock. About 50 percent of the city's housing had been built in the nineteenth century. Age of structure was the most significant variable related to deterioration. Overcrowding, neglect, illegal subdivision, and the financial, legal, and tenancy complications that blocked reinvestment to maintain good housing quality all conspired to erode residential neighborhoods. The attraction of new suburban housing, more stylish and spacious than the old row-house stock, also was a major factor in diminishing the desirability of the old housing stock. Added to this was the cultural difference between the growing black population and the whites of the city, leading to steady movement of whites out of neighborhoods that blacks entered in large numbers.

In North Philadelphia the Irish and Ukrainian residents moved out slowly as blacks expanded. Similar patterns developed in West Philadelphia. Thus blacks came to occupy the housing areas that were oldest and hardest to maintain and that provided the occupying families with the worst shelter for the most disadvantageous payment of rents and mortgages. The racism and prejudice that were a historic part of the American mentality were woven through the housing market, and all the problems of supply and finance were complicated by a seemingly inescapable segregation process that distorted the housing market. Throughout the city and its suburbs, whenever blacks sought to move freely in the housing market there was community tension and frequently vandalism, intimidation, street riots, and evacuation of whole neighborhoods by whites. The city's Commission on Human Relations worked diligently to relieve these situations, but the small staff was inadequate to the broad scope of the problem.[22]

The ever-growing needs of the congested black neighborhoods continued to challenge the efforts of various agencies to provide low-rent housing for low-income families. Between 1937, when the Philadelphia Housing Authority was organized, and 1970 that agency built, rehabilitated, or acquired and leased on a subsidy basis some 21,000 low-rent housing units. Housing some 106,475 persons, these units were far from adequate, but they were more than a beginning, particularly when one realizes that no low-rent housing at all was constructed in the decade prior to 1952.

The cost of this public housing was underwritten by the federal government. The Philadelphia Housing Authority built the units through private contractors, and administered the projects on completion and occupancy. Initially, high-rise elevator apartments were built with a few surrounding row houses to provide a self-contained community, like the Harrison Plaza and the Raymond Rosen and Schuylkill Falls developments. But these projects tended to create new low-income ghettos, perpetuating the evils public housing was supposed to eliminate. The last elevator project was built in 1967. Other housing in scattered areas was being rehabilitated and then rented to families at a percentage of their certified income, a plan more socially desirable and more generally acceptable.[23]

Larger than the Philadelphia Housing Authority and more active in this period was the Philadelphia Redevelopment Authority, created by federal statute in 1945. Although federally subsidized like the Housing Authority, the operations of the Redevelopment Authority were quite different. Government funds, covering approximately three-fourths of the ultimate cost of a project, were used to acquire land and either to demolish buildings being put to undesirable uses—slum dwellings or "skid row" commercial properties— or in some cases to rehabilitate existing properties, as in the Washington Square East–Society Hill area. The land was sold to private developers at a price less than the acquisition cost, the authority assuming the difference.

From its first project in 1950 through 1968 the Redevelopment Authority financed more than sixty separate projects involving 3368 acres. Although the tracts were widely scattered, major activity was centered in center city. Some of the money went into slum rehabilitation, partly in the black belt, but more of it to such diverse projects as University City and redevelopment around Temple University, the Food Distribution Center, Washington Square West, and Market Street East. The Redevelopment Authority was a major force in remaking the face of the city.

A third housing agency, the Philadelphia Housing Development Corporation, was created in 1965 to assist its larger associate authorities in further relieving the ongoing housing shortage. A quasi-public corporation with both city and "public" directors, the PHDC used both a $2-million city fund and federal bonds to acquire rental and sales housing units on a subsidy basis for low-income families. Unfortunately cuts in its budget because of the city's financial difficulties soon curtailed the corporation's effectiveness. Furthermore by the late 1960s all the housing programs were suffering from rising construction costs, rising interest rates on mortgages, and the shrinkage of federal housing money as the Vietnam War absorbed federal spending.

For all the accomplishments of the various housing agencies, moreover,

Renewal on of Spruce Street near Second (1965). The Philadelphia Redevelopment Authority, established in 1945, exercised its right of eminent domain to acquire blighted properties to sell or lease for private or public redevelopment. The Washington Square East (Society Hill) project was the authority's earliest major effort.
PHILADELPHIA BULLETIN

deterioration proceeded faster than rehabilitation. The continuing flow of poor black and, later in the period, Puerto Rican families into the city aggravated housing and related social problems that Philadelphia, like many another city, could not solve. The large majority of applicants for low-rent housing were black, but eligible whites were generally unwilling to live in predominantly black developments. White middle- and working-class residents were also violently opposed to public housing projects in their neighborhoods, thus confining them to black areas. Attempts by the Clark administration to disperse sites to outlying white areas in the 1950s led to a furor in the city Council and mob scenes in City Hall as neighborhood groups protested. Too often new housing projects in black areas displaced the poorest people in favor of those somewhat less poor; while federal housing law required that the displaced be relocated, usually their new housing was at least as bad as that from which they had been removed.

The chief defect of the housing improvement policy of the city in the 1950s and 1960s was probably the overreliance on public housing and large-scale

urban-renewal clearances. These were both necessary, but they did not address the problems of the enormous extent of the row-house supply that was
the main residential resource of the city. This aging row-house residential
fabric held the city together socially and in terms of community life. It was
declining at a rate that led people to abandon it, yet public housing or
clearance to replace the worst areas did not capitalize on the old neighborhood
stability characteristic of the city, nor did it induce widespread conservation
and reinvestment in older housing by working people themselves. In Society
Hill, Queen Village, and Fairmount the results of such reinvestment for
upper- and middle-class families could be seen, and a delightful center-city
ambience was created. The same thing never happened for blue-collar families, and the result was that dozens of neighborhoods continued to decline.
This condition altered the social character of the city more than all of the
ambitious rebuilding projects of the post–World War II decades.[24]

V I

Concern for human needs, or social compassion, is part of a civilized
society and Philadelphia had a great tradition of social concern, yet nowhere
in a great urban community was this ideal harder to achieve than in public
health and public welfare. When lack of funds required the setting of priorities, these areas were the first to be neglected. Relief from state and federal
governments was inadequate and badly managed, and an administrative complexity of overlapping agencies resulted. Despite such obstacles Philadelphia
achieved substantial progress in public health and welfare from 1946 to 1970.

In 1946 there were few public health services in the city. The commonwealth maintained a mental hospital at Byberry in the northeast. The Board
of City Trusts, a quasi-public agency, operated the Wills Eye Hospital. By
far the largest facility was Philadelphia General Hospital in West Philadelphia, an 1800-bed charitable institution that since 1920 was the successor to the
old Almshouse founded in colonial times and to "Old Blockley." Administration of the PGH was mediocre at best.

During Dilworth's administration the reformers finally succeeded in giving the medical schools control of the PGH's services. A committee appointed
by the Tate administration and chaired by Dr. James F. Dixon, the commissioner of health, considered a plan to rebuild the PGH complex at a possible
cost of $110 million. Eventually, however, the squeeze of public indifference,
municipal impecuniousness, and low priorities for welfare when cost rises
caught up with the PGH, the flurry of reform activity proved short-lived, and
instead of being rebuilt the hospital was closed altogether in the late 1970s.

In the summer of 1949, before his election as controller, Joseph Clark had
asked a committee of public health experts to make a survey and prepare a
plan for a public health program for the city. The plan became a plank in his
platform when Clark ran for mayor. In addition to reform of the PGH the
plan called for creating ten district public health centers to be fed by a group
of neighborhood centers all of which would operate a decentralized public

health program. Instead of enlarging the PGH or building new municipal general hospitals the plan called for contracts with existing private hospitals for indigent patient care.

The construction of the health centers progressed slowly as funds became available. By 1970 seven district health centers had been built and were in operation, and two older centers were renovated and placed in service. The district health centers were not hospitals. They offered medical and surgical services on an outpatient basis, however, and they improved the health services available to the people of Philadelphia.

Thus Philadelphia progressed in the public health field from 1946 to 1970. But the legitimate demands of the people for services, spurred on by federal programs and appropriations, were never fully met. At the end of the period health services were available to citizens thanks to federal Medicare and Medicaid to an extent hardly dreamed of twenty-five years earlier, yet the demands of a compassionate and civilized society were far from being met in areas of poverty.

Much the same was true of Philadelphia's welfare activities. For many years before 1947 the administration of such activities in the city was a hodge-podge of conflicting and overlapping public and private agencies attempting to breast a vast sea of misery. Unlike many other cities Philadelphia saw much of the welfare or relief for the indigent handled by the state, not the city, under the auspices of the state Department of Public Assistance and the Philadelphia County Relief Board, a state-affiliated agency. The city charter of 1951 attempted to bring a measure of order out of chaos and to strengthen the city's hand by creating a city Department of Public Welfare. As with other city departments under the Clark administration, it was led first by men of professional competence whose employees were under a strict merit system. Randolph E. Wise, commissioner of welfare, and his assistants Manuel E. Kauffman, Edward Hendrick, and Johannes Hoeber were the principal architects of the new organization.[25] The department operated its activities under three divisions: Child Care and Custody, Problems of the Aged, and Penal Affairs.

Child-care activities were comprehensive, including the placement and support of children in foster homes or institutions, adoption proceedings for the children of unmarried parents, and protective services for the neglected or abused child. The department generally provided for these services through contracts with voluntary agencies that were reimbursed by the department. Before the adoption of the charter many of these services had been provided either by the county commissioners or by the Juvenile Division of the Municipal Court, both of which had a record of mediocrity and political interference. Administration by the Welfare Department substantially improved their caliber.

Services to the aging primarily involved supervision of Riverview, until the mid-1950s known as the County Home. Riverview was basically a custodial-care facility moving toward nursing home care with medical support for elderly men and women who were still able and willing to take care of themselves, but who had been living alone and were without relatives or friends. At one time a dreary institution where callousness toward the then-called "inmates" was all too frequent, Riverview later enjoyed renovated physical facilities and a somewhat improved quality of supervision.

The charter gave the Department of Public Welfare responsibility for general supervision over all city penal reformatory and correctional institutions, as well as the county prisons at Moyamensing and Holmesburg. These and the House of Correction for less serious cases were brought under a single superintendent and one board of trustees in 1955. In 1963 a new Detention Center for untried adults was opened on State Road in Holmesburg, and the old county prison at Moyamensing, one of the city's architectural monuments, built in 1835, was closed. About this time a series of decisions of the United States Supreme Court concerning defendants' rights in the field of criminal justice resulted in an enormous increase in the case load of prisoners awaiting trial. In 1963 the ratio in prison had been 66 percent sentenced and 34 percent untried; in 1969, 26 percent were sentenced and 74 percent untried or unsentenced.

Much of the activity of the Welfare Department dealt with black and elderly citizens. The relationship of employees of the department with clients was made difficult because of a chronic shortage of caseworkers. The case load on the welfare rolls administered by the public assistance program of the state increased steadily from 64,760 in 1946 to 183,000 in 1969. Despite general prosperity there continued to be hunger among the poor in Philadelphia. School board officials confirmed the fact in appraising the condition of youngsters going into the public school system. To help meet the need the federal government initially sent surplus food into Philadelphia, to be distributed by the city Welfare Department. Some 75,000 families obtained some of their subsistence from these generally unattractive commodities in the early 1960s. In 1966 the federal food stamp program was instituted, making it possible for the poor to purchase more than surplus foods. By 1970 at least 15,000 families were receiving food stamps; none was any longer getting surplus food. The problem of food for the poor was part of the tangle of bureaucracy and persistent dependency that reflected the complex toll exacted from the poor by urban conditions.

Private agencies, most of them joining in the annual private United Fund appeal (later the United Way), and whose activities were planned with the private Health and Welfare Council, still carried a large part of Philadelphia's total welfare load. Because of the constantly increasing demands of an ever-rising population of indigents, the United Fund tried each year to raise more and more money to support its constituent agencies. The Philadelphia establishment always dominated the United Fund, and generally ran it well. However, there were increasing complaints from the black population that the fund spent too much money on middle-class agencies and neglected the needs of the ghetto.

VII

Philadelphia, like other large American cities, showed a shocking increase in crime of all sorts between 1946 and 1968. Many streets in the city became unsafe, particularly at night. At the same time there had been evidence, but not strong enough to stand up in court, of organized crime operating in Philadelphia under affiliates of nationwide syndicates. The police and court systems had become terribly complex and overburdened in trying to confront crime conditions, and an experienced lawyer, later a judge, Lois Forer, termed juvenile courts "the delinquent juvenile courts."

Authorities and civic groups continually strove to maintain order with justice and to rehabilitate the offenders. The Voluntary Defender, financed in part with city funds, and the Legal Aid Society both had admirable accomplishments, but their financial and manpower resources were inadequate to assure equal justice under law to those who could not afford a lawyer and to those in need of civil legal aid. The funds for Community Legal Services, part of the Federal Anti-Poverty Program, were cut drastically in the fall of 1970.

The police themselves came in for justifiable criticism in the later years of the period. The earlier police commissioners, Gibbons, Brown, and Leary, were humane and effective. Frank Rizzo was a more controversial commissioner. His determination, supported by Mayor Tate, to eliminate the Police Review Board as a check on possible police brutality was widely criticized by the black community and others. Despite efforts to eliminate the feeling, the police were widely regarded as enemies in the most blighted areas of the black community. The proportion of blacks on the police force, after rising in the 1950s and 1960s, began to decline, and blacks sued the city to compel broader black recruitment. Yet the percentage of unsolved crimes was lower than in most other large cities. Police education, centered on the Police Academy, improved in the 1960s. Still, recruiting of capable young men has always been difficult except in times of economic depression. "Who wants to be a cop when you can make more money as a bartender?" was a common sentiment. No matter how zealous the police were in their efforts to prevent crime, to arrest violators, and to bring alleged offenders to justice, their work was no more effective than the prosecution by the district attorney and the trial and sentencing of those indicted by the courts.

The district attorney's office, brought to a peak of efficiency under Richardson Dilworth, fell into the doldrums under his two successors. Prosecutions were routine, delays mounted, court calendars became clogged. The administration of criminal justice again became infected with the virus of political favoritism. Many a decision was made in the headquarters of the Democratic City Committee rather than in the district attorney's office. The county detectives, eyes and ears of criminal prosecution, tended to respond to political pressure in preparing cases for trial. The election of Arlen Specter as district attorney in 1965 changed this. Specter successfully resisted any effort of the Republican leadership to run his office on a political basis.

Nevertheless the prosecutor's hands were often tied in his efforts to reduce crime. Among the obstacles that confronted him were nineteenth-century court machinery; mounting case loads; too few judges; too few and poorly paid assistant district attorneys; inadequate detention facilities; the slow pace at which justices disposed of cases and released the innocent; failure of rehabilitation of prisoners in jails, with the resulting alarming rate of repeat offenses; and finally the chronic complaint of all district attorneys and police, inadequate sentencing by the judges.

At the lower levels of justice, particularly in the magistrates' courts, political favoritism rather than justice continued to be the rule. Elected by the people, magistrates were usually politicians at the ward level. Fortunately state constitutional amendments in 1968 provided that henceforth magistrates seeking new ten-year terms would have to be lawyers, and this requirement brought improvement.

Like other major cities Philadelphia suffered riots. Philadelphia shared amply in the discontents that caused so many "long hot summers" in American cities during the 1960s, and the credit that Police Commissioner Rizzo received, rightly or wrongly, for keeping the lid on rioting in Philadelphia was a major factor in his eventual ascent to the mayor's office.

Philadelphia's longest, hottest summer came in 1964, when the simmering ghetto of north-central Philadelphia exploded along Columbia Avenue west of Broad Street in late August. The precipitating incident was trivial; an intoxicated couple refused to let police unblock traffic by moving their stalled car. Bad feeling toward the police and the other resentments of the crowd that swiftly gathered—as many as 2000 people inhabited single blocks in the area—created a crescendo of scuffling with the police and then a first night, to be followed by several others, of breaking storefronts and looting. The police barricaded the area and slowly battled their way back into control. Two people died, 339 were injured, and an estimated $3 million of property was destroyed.[26]

Fighting between blacks and police broke out in two additional widely publicized disturbances, in the Girard College area on May 1, 1967, and at the Board of Education building on the Benjamin Franklin Parkway in 1969; the latter was a climax to frequent racial incidents in many schools. Rivaling the summer of 1964 for the tensions they produced throughout the city were the problems of crime, violence, and race that polarized Philadelphia in the first week of September 1970. On Saturday, August 31, a Fairmount Park guard was killed and another injured in an unprovoked attempt by seven persons to blow up a guardhouse. Five suspects were arrested and identified as black militants. The following day two other policemen were wounded by different gunmen not apparently involved in the earlier crime. On Monday three headquarters locations of the militant Black Panthers were raided by police. In ensuing gun battles three policemen were injured. Fourteen persons, presumably Black Panthers, were arrested in these raids. No connection, however, had been established between the targets of the raids and the earlier

murder and assaults against law enforcement personnel. The fourteen individuals arrested were searched for weapons but none was found. Nevertheless Judge Leo Weinrott, summoned from bed in the middle of the night, held
the fourteen in $100,000 bail. Meanwhile during Monday and again on Tues-
day other policemen were wounded in violent outbreaks that also appeared
to be without direct connection to earlier events.

The Black Panthers were sponsoring a People's New Revolutionary Convention to meet in Philadelphia over the weekend of September 5. About ten
days earlier Mayor Tate had declared a limited state of emergency in the
Tasker and Fairmount sections, which had agitated most of the black population. Feelings were now exacerbated by the shootings and arrests and the
imminence of the Black Panther convention.

Police Commissioner Frank Rizzo was the sparkplug of the raids and the
arrests.[27] Some of his comments, to say the least, tended to arouse rather than
to allay emotionalism. Following one of the shootings of a policemen, that of
Tom Gibbons, Jr., son of the former police commissioner, Rizzo said: "We
need 2,000 more policemen to stop them. The only thing we can do now is
to buy tanks and start mounting machine guns. . . . it is sedition. This is no
longer a crime, but revolution. It must be stopped even if we have to change
some of the laws to do it." Philadelphia was split down the middle. As one
reporter wrote: "The atmosphere of crisis, apprehension and anticipation"
spread over the city. Those concerned for their personal safety and for the
maintenance of order rallied to Rizzo's support. The black community as a
whole made heroes of the Black Panthers.

Voices of reason fortunately prevailed. Calling for order and restraint on
both sides were civic leaders such as Gustave Amsterdam of Bankers Security;
Richard Bond, a retailing executive; R. Stewart Rauch, president of the
prestigious Philadelphia Saving Fund Society; Thacher Longstreth, president
of the Chamber of Commerce; and Charles Bowser, a black leader, speaking
through the Urban Coalition and the Greater Philadelphia Movement. Temple University, with the approval of Gov. Raymond Shafer, opened its facilities for the convention of the Panthers and other black militant groups. The
event went off peaceably. The police were not obviously present at Temple
during the proceedings, though a number of plainclothes men monitored the
meeting. Fears of violence turned out to be unwarranted. The visiting militants departed. A still-nervous city returned to calm. The controversy between the police and civil libertarians continued, but it was no longer front
and center stage.

The increase in the number of juvenile delinquents between 1946 and 1970
was appalling. Gang warfare among blacks in the slums became worse in
Philadelphia than in other cities. There were forty-one gang killings in 1969.
Of all arrests for major crimes in 1968, 46.9 percent were of juveniles eighteen
years of age or under. Drug traffic played a role in this deadly conflict.

The initially splendid Youth Study Center on the Parkway for a time did
an excellent job in diagnosing the ills of youthful offenders and recommend-

ing punishment and rehabilitation procedures for judges sitting in the Juvenile Division of the County Court. But the facilities of the center became badly overtaxed. Some judges, notably J. Sydney Hoffman, later on the Superior Court, took a compassionate interest in the scores of cases marched before them every day. The reform schools and prisons to which the youth were sent had little success in preventing recidivism. The number of juvenile offenders who became hardened criminals was frightening. When drug use spread as a source of delinquency and crime among juveniles, a problem not only in Philadelphia but elsewhere in the nation, the treatment for narcotics addiction remained primitive.

By the 1970s crime was found to be ranked as the number one problem in a survey of public opinion by the City Planning Commission.

VIII

It was commonly assumed that Philadelphia's mingling of races and ethnic groups had in the past worked pretty well, but this assumption was questionable.[28] The surrender of political power by white Protestant to Catholic Irish and Italian and to Jewish hands, first in the Democratic party but more recently in the Republican as well, increased at the close of the 1950s. Dilworth and Stassen were the last two Protestants to oppose each other for mayor. Changes in the ethnic composition and the leadership of banks, law firms, and major institutions moved slowly as Jews and Catholics reached higher echelons, but blacks were even more slowly advanced. Blacks nevertheless appeared on the city Council, on the Civil Service Commission, in important positions in city government, and on the bench from the early days of the Clark administration.

A large percentage of municipal employees were black, and many private businesses, nudged by the Fair Employment Practices Ordinance passed under Clark and given teeth by the Human Relations Commission, opened their ranks to blacks of both sexes. No one could say that racial discrimination in employment had disappeared in Philadelphia. What could be said was that some employment opportunities had opened to the educated black, but that the unskilled remained at a terrible disadvantage. The black middle class increased greatly as a result. The "Philadelphia Plan" sponsored by the federal Nixon administration to some extent opened employment opportunities in the formerly white building trades unions. Serious discrimination decreased in public accommodations and in recreational facilities.

Leadership in areas of human relations was always a serious problem in Philadelphia, even during the era of reform. But Dilworth's departure from City Hall in 1962 brought with it a realization that succession for blacks had not often been provided for. In the 1950s and early 1960s a high level of black leadership was provided by the black Protestant clergy, such men as Luther Cunningham, Marshall Shepard, and William Gray. They devoted themselves to the spiritual leadership of their followers while at the same time engaging in the rough and tumble of municipal politics. Their potential successors, men like the Rev. Leon Sullivan, Judge Leon Higginbotham,

Principal Marcus A. Foster of Simon Gratz High School, the Rev. Henry Nichols of the school board, and Fr. Paul Washington, continued this tradition, but they faced the inevitable competition and pluralist buffeting of a city in which there was a whole constellation of contending ethnic and special interest groups.

Cecil Moore, a tempestuous lawyer and for some years chairman of the local branch of the NAACP, was often in the news. An expert agitator, he led his followers for several years through controversies like that surrounding Girard College. His younger successors were unable to summon more than fragmented support as the problems of blacks became increasingly complex and linked to grave urban ills.

Throughout the period, nevertheless, men and women of goodwill labored untiringly to bridge the racial gap. Much of their work was done through the Fellowship Commission, a coalition of civic groups seeking to create a unified solution to the many indignities that minority groups suffered. Founded in October 1941 by Marjorie Penney, a social worker, and Maurice B. Fagan, a former teacher with an intense interest in improving human relations, the commission was in the forefront of efforts that sought and obtained effective legislation to open public accommodations, employment opportunities, housing, and educational opportunities to all citizens. It had excellent establishment support. Charles J. Simpson, member of the Union League and president of the Philadelphia Gas Works, was long its president and principal fundraiser, Maurice Fagan its executive. Polarization set in about the time Dilworth resigned as mayor, and thenceforth the commission and many other like-minded civic groups had to struggle against grave difficulties to maintain communications between both sides of the racial barrier.

In addition to the rise of greater group consciousness on the part of blacks, other ethnic groups experienced a renewal of identity and solidarity due to various stimuli. Urban renewal had threatened or displaced some old ethnic neighborhoods. Religious changes, especially among Roman Catholics after Vatican Council II, challenged accepted rituals and folk religious attachments. Changing youth behavior made ethnic groups conscious of the indifference of some young people to old values. A great increase in popularity of folk music, ease of travel back to "the old country," and a broader acceptance in society of cultural differences all influenced the ethnic revival. Also, Italians, Poles, Ukrainians, and Irish responded to the new black assertiveness with assertion of their own identity. More and more interest in history and social science showed the extensive role such groups had played in building the industrial city, and hence there was a revival of pride, ethnic festivals, and ethnic cultural events. Race relations may have been inflamed, but young blacks were also experiencing a surge of positive ethnic appreciation of their own background. The Library Company's remarkable 1969 exhibition of black history helped. All of these developments gave the city that had been largely ruled by the image of a "Protestant establishment" in 1946 a whole new pluralist orientation by 1970.[29]

I X

The political reform movement of the 1940s and 1950s in Philadelphia bypassed public education. In 1947 there were three parallel systems of primary and secondary education. The public school system was operated by a Board of Education of fifteen members selected by the Board of Judges of the Courts of Common Pleas. The second system, of comparable size, was the parochial school system conducted by the Roman Catholic Archdiocese of Philadelphia. The third was a spectrum of private schools, some of them related to Protestant denominations, some of the oldest conducted by the Society of Friends.

The members of the Philadelphia Board of Education served without pay, and few of them knew anything about education or the public school system when they took office. Leon Obermayer, a respected lawyer and chairman of the board from 1955 to 1961, was at that time the only member whose childen had gone to the public schools, but he nonetheless adopted a laissez-faire policy. For all practical purposes during the period 1947–1961 the Board of Education and the school system with it were run by Add B. Anderson, business manager. His philosophy was to keep education as inexpensive as possible in order to prevent increases in school taxation. At the time the board was financed entirely by a tax on real estate fixed by the state legislature; the city Council and the mayor had nothing whatever to do with the system of public education.

Teachers in the public school system were badly paid. As late as 1960 the starting scale for an accredited teacher was $4000 a year; $7600 a year was the maximum that could be paid to a teacher with a Ph.D. The results were a mediocre teaching staff, high vacancy rates, teacher unrest, and many temporary uncertified teachers. The pay was better in the surrounding suburban counties. Among the pupils, the drop-out rate was extraordinarily high, averaging about 33 percent per annum in the high schools. Student achievement was significantly below the national average.

While schools were generally coeducational, those that sent the highest proportion of their graduates on to college were not: Central High and Girls High were selective, highly academic schools. There was also a system of vocational and technical schools for children not interested in an academic program, but little effective on-the-job training was provided.

In 1954 the Supreme Court of the United States in *Brown v. Board of Education of Topeka* decreed an end to *de jure* segregation in all public school systems. Philadelphia moved lethargically to carry the opinion of the court into effect. One dramatic test involved Girard College in North Philadelphia, endowed by Stephen Girard in the nineteenth century for poor, white, orphan boys. (Girard College was not a part of the public school system, but it was administered by the Board of City Trusts.) Despite the 1954 Supreme Court decision the board refused to open the school to black students, alleging that Girard's will superseded as well as antedated both the *Brown* case and the Fourteenth Amendment to the Constitution.

Two young blacks represented by Raymond Pace Alexander, a distinguished black lawyer and member of the city Council, applied for admission to the school. Alexander's request was turned down, although Joseph Clark and James Finnegan as mayor and president of the city Council and ex-officio members of the Board of City Trusts attempted to persuade the board to admit the youngsters and seek a later decision in the courts. Lengthy litigation ensued, with a final ruling by the Supreme Court of Pennsylvania, affirmed by the Supreme Court of the United States, that the will was superseded by the *Brown* decision. After 1968 black youngsters did gain admission to Girard College, but not before the litigation and dispute greatly agitated public opinion.

The public schools had experienced increasing racial problems as the black population expanded around the center of the city. In the 1950s, for example, Simon Gratz High School, in Nicetown or lower Germantown, was equally divided between white and black students. Ten years later because of changing neighborhood housing patterns the school was almost 100 percent black. Marcus Foster, the black principal at Simon Gratz, exerted outstanding leadership in this situation and in 1969 received the Philadelphia Award for his efforts in improving the quality of education at the school.

As the white population of Philadelphia declined and the black population grew, the change was reflected in the enrollment in the public schools. In 1961 there were approximately 125,000 white and the same number of black students enrolled. In 1970, out of a total enrollment of 291,000 pupils, nonwhite enrollment was 174,660. By 1970 Puerto Ricans formed 2.8 percent of the pupil population. Spanish-speaking students presented a special problem both because of the language difficulty and because of antagonism between them and non–Puerto Rican students. The school district was simply not prepared to deal with the special needs of a large number of students whose primary language was not English.

By the early 1960s public interest in the schools began to quicken. The Greater Philadelphia Movement became involved, and a Citizens Committee on Public Education was revitalized. As a result of this awakening a Philadelphia Educational Home Rule Charter was passed by the legislature in 1965 in the form of an amendment to the 1951 city charter. Taxing power for the schools was given to the city Council. The nine members of the Board of Education were to be appointed by the mayor from a list submitted by a citizens' educational nominating panel. Members of the board were to serve for six-year staggered terms and were to be registered voters living in the city. Richardson Dilworth was appointed chairman of the board, and the young, capable educator Mark Shedd was brought in as superintendent of schools.

With Dilworth's accession as chairman of the board, reform came to the Philadelphia school system. In addition to a continuing teacher recruitment problem and a demoralizing drop-out rate, the problems that the new board faced in 1965 were many and crucial: overcrowded schools, many of them firetraps; a tremendous backlog of essential school maintenance to accommodate the children of the baby boom of the 1950s; a need for widespread use of busing to which there was great public objection; an increasingly strong teachers' union with seniority principles that made it difficult to obtain qualified, experienced teachers for black or Puerto Rican schools; a totally inadequate school budget and financial chaos approaching bankruptcy; serious racial unrest; an obsolete curriculum; and a public educational system designed for children with middle-class mores and quite unsuited to the majority of black and Spanish-speaking and low-income white children.

Faced with this Augean stable, Dilworth, Shedd, and a majority of the board took Herculean measures. By drastically increasing teachers' salaries they reduced the vacancy rate from 20 percent to less than 1 percent, in the process eliminating practically all of the temporary uncertified teachers. The salary scale was increased from $4000 a year for a beginning certified teacher to $7300. Expenditures for school construction were increased from an annual average of $16 million to $90 million by 1968. New methods of meeting community resentments and community problems were devised through a series of conferences throughout the city with parents and others interested in the educational system. The curriculum was drastically revised. Magnet schools were created to give special priority to different subjects at particular schools. Through a variety of devices, successful appeals were made to potential drop-out students with the result that the drop-out rate was reduced from 33 percent a year to 17 percent.

All of this, of course, cost money. The school budget for 1960 was $102,-867,682; for 1969 it was $270,563,963. In order to raise the large sums necessary to meet capital and operating budget demands, Dilworth and Shedd were constantly before the city Council, the legislature and governor in Harrisburg, the Congress and the Department of Health, Education and Welfare in Washington, attempting to get more money for the Philadelphia schools. To some extent they were successful. As costs increased, however, there was a recurring fiscal deficit that caused grave concern. The situation was aggravated by demands of the Federation of Teachers in 1970 for increases in salaries and other benefits totaling $28 million, resulting in a strike in September and October that closed the schools. The public school system of Philadelphia faced a critical financial condition with no adequate help in sight from any of the supporting governmental bodies.[30]

A running feud between Dilworth and Mayor Tate that erupted shortly after Dilworth's appointment, along with dissensions within the Board of Education defying Dilworth's powers of conciliation, complicated all the other problems. By 1970 the highly touted school reforms were widely questioned, and black parents especially perceived increasing deficiencies in policy and practice in the schools. The financial problem mounted yearly, and the teachers union and the Board of Education seemed in a deadlock within a declining system.[31]

The history of the parochial school system during the period 1946–1968 closely paralleled that of the public schools. Both systems were beset by overcrowding, inadequate revenues, serious teacher problems, and an old-fashioned curriculum having little relevance to modern life. Orthodox Catholic religious instruction contradicting more unfettered trends in youth behavior raised additional major difficulties for the parochial schools. On the other hand bureaucratic problems confronting the public school system did not always exist in the parochial schools. The latter had a much milder race problem. Most blacks in Philadelphia and those who moved into the area after World War II were Baptists, or Methodists. No more than 10 percent of the children in Catholic schools were black, despite efforts over the years to convert blacks to the Catholic faith.

From the late 1950s until about 1965 there was an enormous increase in the number of pupils in the parochial schools and a corresponding building program.[32] Starting about 1965 school construction tapered off, in part because of financial problems, and enrollment expansion slowed. The parochial school system was operated under the Archdiocese of Philadelphia headed by John Cardinal O'Hara and later John Cardinal Krol. It was immediately under the care of the superintendent of archdiocesan schools, who for nine years was Monsignor Edward K. Hughes, until he was succeeded in 1970 by his assistant Monsignor Francis B. Schulte. Historically the teaching in the parochial schools was done by members of religious orders. As enrollment increased, however, it was necessary to bring in lay teachers. In 1960, 10 percent of the instructional force was lay teachers; by 1969 the proportion had risen to 40 percent. Since lay teachers in the Catholic schools were not paid as well as teachers in the public schools, there was concern that the caliber of instruction in the parochial schools would suffer, and the demands for higher salaries became more insistent.

In 1967 the lay teachers won collective bargaining rights and a salary agreement after a long and hotly contested dispute with the archdiocese. A further salary dispute in 1970, settled by a considerable increase, required a rise in tuition putting the parochial schools out of the reach of some low-income families. Even with the tuition increase the wage negotiations and the growing number of lay teachers accelerated the growth of the schools' financial problems and the schools had to continue to operate at a loss. Financial aid from the federal and state governments after Congress passed the National Defense Education Act, and more particularly the Elementary and Secondary Education Act in 1965, gave some relief but, as usual, not enough.

Bridging the gap for the poor student between high school and college was the Philadelphia Community College. It was established pursuant to state legislation in 1964 and opened for classes the following fall, with Dr. Allen T. Bonnell as president, in quarters in the former Snellenburg department store on Market Street between Eleventh and Twelfth. In 1969 full-time enrollment was 4200, with another 2000 students attending part time; another 1500 or more could have been enrolled if facilities and funds had permitted. The curriculum was in effect a thirteenth and fourteenth grade for high school graduates. Some students went on to complete their baccalaureate elsewhere, but most went directly into the labor market. Human service careers, business administration, health occupations, and paraprofessional engineering courses were the principal subjects taught.[33]

Institutions of higher education experienced extraordinary growth after World War II because of the population boom and the G.I. Bill giving veterans tuition-free education privileges. Among the institutions making Philadelphia a center for higher education, Temple University, which had enjoyed a remarkable growth since 1947, became part of the Commonwealth System of Higher Education in 1965. The consequent increase in state support stimulated the university's further growth, especially in its graduate and professional schools. The Jefferson Medical College and its associated institutions became the Thomas Jefferson University on July 1, 1969, including in addition to the Medical College a College of Allied Health Sciences, a College of Graduate Studies, and the Thomas Jefferson University Hospital. The institution that the financier Anthony J. Drexel founded in 1891 as the Drexel Institute of Art, Science, and Industry, to emphasize engineering and business studies, known since 1936 as the Drexel Institute of Technology, became Drexel University on February 27, 1970. Its graduate degrees include the Ph.D. in engineering science and in library and information science. The Women's Medical College of Pennsylvania, after its Board of Corporators voted in 1969 to admit male students to its only remaining all-female department, its M.D. program, changed its name on July 1, 1970, to the Medical College of Pennsylvania.

The University of Pennsylvania was a quiescent place in 1947. Its president, Thomas S. Gates, though a distinguished New York and Philadelphia banker, did not much more than keep the institution afloat; he was not an educator and did not pretend to be. His successor from 1949, Harold Stassen, former governor of Minnesota, more interested in his political than his educational career, did, however, travel all over the country raising for the university an estimated $34 million, which provided a start for a rebuilding and renaissance program.

Gaylord P. Harnwell, a professor of physics in the university, succeeded Stassen in 1953 and served until his retirement in the fall of 1970. Major credit for the revival of the University of Pennsylvania must go to President Harnwell. In the twenty years from 1950 to 1970 the university's faculty doubled, and it became a younger, more cosmopolitan, more sophisticated, more liberal faculty. There was an extraordinary increase in faculty salaries, necessary to obtain individuals of distinction. As late as 1953 the average annual salary of a professor at Penn was $8000; by 1969 it was $19,838, with fringe benefits bringing it to a total of $22,175.

The student body did not greatly increase in the period. In the fall of 1969 there were 19,021 students, about 13,500 of them full time. An effort was made to enroll more black students, but not nearly so successfully as at Temple. Of the 250 black applicants who were offered admission to Penn in 1969, only about half matriculated. As a result of student unrest a Student Committee on Undergraduate Education was created, and students sat as members of the Committee on Instruction of the College and on the Graduate and Undergraduate Curriculum Committees.

Many new programs were instituted, relating to the needs of modern society. The graduate schools of the university achieved national distinction in such fields as archeology, law, and business administration. It was a mark of the caliber of the university's graduate work that research grants and contracts rose from $8.5 million in 1956–1957 to $45 million in 1968–1969.

Penn's renaissance, of course, cost large sums of money, which was forthcoming to an extraordinary extent. In 1947 annual support for the university from alumni, friends, foundations, and corporations (not including contract grants for specific research projects) was less than $2 million. By 1969 the comparable figure had increased more than tenfold. The university successfully completed its development drive, which went over the top in 1969 with a total of $102,318,599. Nineteen new endowed professorships were established. Scholarship and fellowship endowment was increased by more than $10 million.

At the end of World War II the university campus was physically rundown, and its renewal was planned with the aid of its city planning and fine arts departments. All branches benefited. The Gates Memorial Pavilion and I. S. Ravdin Institute added enormously to the capacity of the University Hospital; new athletic facilities were provided; the Van Pelt and Dietrich Libraries, which functioned together, became a significant regional educational resource; a student housing program in 1968 was financed by the Pennsylvania Higher Education Facilities Authority. The surface trolley cars that used to bisect the campus along Woodland Avenue were relocated underground. Streets were closed, and landscaping and walkways created. In addition to the university's own fund drives, money for campus development included a vast array of city, state, and federal agencies, especially the Philadelphia Redevelopment Authority and the General State Authority.

Much of the building and improvement for the university during the 1960s resulted from a redevelopment plan known as University City, a joint project of the University of Pennsylvania and Drexel University. On the basis of plans submitted by both these institutions, the Philadelphia Redevelopment Authority obtained from the federal government approximately 90 percent of the cost of tearing down unsafe and unsound structures in the area between the Schuylkill River and Forty-fourth Street, bounded on the north by Market Street and on the south by Spruce Street, together with a smaller area reaching north of Market toward Powelton Village.[34]

Across the Schuylkill River in north-central Philadelphia, Temple University also experienced an enormous expansion after World War II, and with the aid of federal and state funds transformed what was formerly one of the worst slum areas of Philadelphia into a great university center. Much of the credit must go to the three presidents of Temple during the period: Robert H. Johnson, formerly an executive of *Time* magazine and director of the Pennsylvania State Welfare Program during the Earle administration of the 1930s; Millard Gladfelter, long associated with Temple, during whose term the university entered the Commonwealth System of Higher Education; and Paul R. Anderson, who came to Temple initially as vice-president for academic affairs from the presidency of Chatham College in Pittsburgh.

In its undergraduate schools Temple was a commuters' university, two-thirds of its students living at home. Like Penn, Temple encountered bitter opposition to its steady accession of land while displacing poor blacks. Conscious thereafter of the problems created by its growth in the midst of a ghetto neighborhood, Temple formed a steering committee of university officials, community representatives, and delegates from federal, state, and city agencies to explore ways in which the university, in partnership with the community, might help revitalize the whole community surrounding the campus with the assistance of government. The university later made special efforts to recruit able young people from low-income families. Scholarship aid increased significantly. In 1969 about one-third of all Temple students received some form of assistance through various programs administered by the university.

Total enrollment that year was 44,779, including summer school. The university had twenty-four separate colleges and schools and a faculty that had doubled in the preceding ten years. The main campus changed from a crowding together of row houses and a few academic buildings into a coherent arrangement of such new buildings as the Samuel Paley Library, the 481-seat Tomlinson Theater, and humanities and social science towers centering on a Bell Tower Plaza. In addition to its main campus, Temple took over the former Pennsylvania School of Horticulture in Ambler. The university's Tyler School of Art was located in Cheltenham Township, and a Health Sciences Center including the medical school and Temple University Hospital expanded around Broad and Ontario Streets north of the Broad Street and Montgomery Avenue complex.

Because Temple is a state-related university, twelve of its thirty-three trustees were appointed by the governor. Presiding over the Board of Trustees from 1939 to 1969 was Judge Charles Klein of the Orphan's Court of Philadelphia, who shared with the university presidents a major role in the extraordinary growth of a trolley-line college into a great university. Probably the most surprising aspect of Temple's academic and physical expansion was its swiftness. From an institution with an undistinguished profile to one with remarkable scholarly and teaching resources in little more than a decade was a quantum leap.[35]

X

Philadelphia's universities and colleges contributed much to the cultural climate of the city. During the years 1946–1968 there was solid achievement in a wide variety of disciplines that make for a civilized community. On February 28, 1955, at the request of the Clark administration, the Philadelphia Museum of Art held a festival to honor six Philadelphians who had made their mark in seven disciplines of the humanities: Eugene Ormandy, conductor; George Howe, architect; Grace Kelly, actress; Alexander Calder, sculptor; Franklin Watkins, painter; Marian Anderson, singer; and Edna Phillips, harpist. They were each recognized for the honor they had brought to their native city. The mayor presented the awards, and more than 30,000 Philadelphians turned out for the occasion.

One area of considerable change was in the religious life of the city. All of the major religious groups experienced an increase in social activism among portions of their clergy and laity. Much of the black leadership in the city came from the ministry of Baptist and Methodist churches. The Rev. David Gracie and others led Episcopalians in marches for civil rights goals and stormy protests against the war in Vietnam. Picketing Quakers protesting the war were arrested by the police, and they sued for infringement of their rights of free speech and won in the higher courts. Jews continued their remarkable expansion of educational and service institutions and were deeply engaged with support for the State of Israel. Catholics emerged from the forty-year episcopate of Dennis Cardinal Dougherty and were confronted with an onrush of ecumenical and internal church change following Vatican Council II in the 1960s. While traditional religious allegiances weakened during the period, new suburban churches, new religious orientations, and ecumenical cooperation on a wide variety of social projects grew with notable rapidity.

The Philadelphia Museum of Art, supported by the city, continued to open more areas of its sprawling building and acquire more treasures during the period through the gifts of the still-opulent Philadelphia establishment and of those who sought entry into the establishment through the art donation route. The Museum of Art reached a peak popularity with a Van Gogh exhibit in 1970 that drew 400,000 visitors. The Pennsylvania Academy of the Fine Arts, the oldest art school in the country, with its fine collection of masterpieces by American painters and sculptors, opened a second building in 1964, the Peale House on Chestnut Street, for student activities as well as gallery space. The Philadelphia College of Art, founded in 1876, came out from under the Philadelphia Museum's umbrella as a separate entity and inaugurated in the 1960s a redevelopment program not only to improve the school's facilities but to revitalize the area immediately around its main building, the former Asylum for the Deaf and Dumb designed by John Haviland at Broad and Pine Streets. On the Parkway, the Moore Institute of Art, the oldest professional art college for women in America, attained full college status in 1962 and expanded its facilities. Despite a constant drain of talent to New York, a vigorous artistic community remained in Philadelphia, both in creative work and in the many exhibitions in public and private galleries.

The cultural life of the city was also ornamented by institutions whose reputations were international. The Curtis Institute of Music sent forth talent to concert halls all over the world. The Rosenbach Museum held literary treasures of unequalled value. The Library Company of Philadelphia continued to increase its extraordinarily rich collections of original research materials, as did the archives of its neighbor the Historical Society of Pennsylvania. To these scholarly institutions were added the growing renown of the Pennsylvania Ballet, the Singing City Choir, and the Philadelphia Drama Guild, all of which performed at the restored Walnut Street Theatre. Private

Leviathan, *sculpture at Penn Center by Seymour Lipton, photograph by A. K. Strobl (1967). The Philadelphia Art Commission, chartered as an official city agency in 1919, sponsored an ordinance that requires an expenditure of 1 percent of net construction costs for art in all major development projects in which city money is involved.*

PHILADELPHIA CITY PLANNING COMMISSION

philanthropies like the William Penn Foundation, created by the Haas family, the Philadelphia Foundation, and the Samuel S. Fels Fund all aided the arts in the city.

Post–World War II architecture in Philadelphia remains a controversial subject.[36] The wide variety of design, from the airport to Penn Center to Independence Mall and the Society Hill Towers, the high-rise and low-rise public housing, the two television and radio station buildings (WFIL and WCAU) on City Line Avenue, supplied the subject of much cultural debate. Practicing in the city and contributing to the cityscape were men like Vincent Kling and Louis I. Kahn. The former's Municipal Services Building at Broad Street and John F. Kennedy Boulevard, built in 1964, achieved a difficult harmony with a surrounding profusion of architectural styles; the latter's Alfred Newton Richards Medical Research and Biology Building of the University of Pennsylvania, also completed in 1964, was cited in 1961 by the Museum of Modern Art as "Probably the most consequential building constructed in the United States since the war," a work of solid geometrical

Alfred Newton Richards Medical Building, University of Pennsylvania, built 1957–1960, designed by Louis I. Kahn (1901–1974), photograph 1976 by Will Brown.

integrity. Late in the 1960s Romaldo Giurgola arrived in the city and Robert Venturi began his practice, and both belatedly received the recognition or commissions in Philadelphia that had been bestowed on them elsewhere.

Restored during the period and designated a National Historical Landmark in 1963 was Napoleon Le Brun's Academy of Music. Instituted by Stuart F. Louchheim, the Academy Ball, now the city's premier social event, pro-

vided most of the funds for rehabilitation. The Academy remained the home
of the Philadelphia Orchestra, perhaps justly considered by Philadelphians to
be the finest in the world. Throughout the period the orchestra's great tradition, bequeathed by Leopold Stokowski, was maintained by its conductor
Eugene Ormandy.

Most of the city's cultural institutions, though founded many years ago,
emerged from their past into a vigorous and effective existence. Two of the
most venerable of them erected new buildings: the American Philosophical
Society built its library across from Philosophical Hall on Fifth Street in 1959,
and in 1966 the Library Company of Philadelphia moved from its neo-Greek
Revival temple on South Broad Street to a modern multistory home on
Locust Street next to the Historical Society of Pennsylvania.

The Free Library of Philadelphia, under the inspiring leadership of Emerson Greenaway, revolutionized library service in the city. In the 1950s and
1960s the book stock of the Free Library doubled, to more than two and a half
million volumes. In 1951, ninety-two cents per capita was spent on library
service in Philadelphia; by the end of the 1960s the figure was over five dollars.
Seventeen new library buildings were constructed after World War II—alas,
building was more politically acceptable than staffing—another sixteen were
rehabilitated, and two others were located in more modern quarters. Traveling bookmobile routes were established. Approximately 30 percent of the
city's population became regular library users. Serving the readers in 1951 were
only fifteen staff members with library school degrees; by 1969 there were 307.
But many more were needed, and by 1970 when Keith Doms assumed its
direction the further progress of the Free Library, like that of so many
institutions, was imperiled by rapidly worsening financial stringencies.

XI

Philadelphia in 1946 had four daily newspapers—the *Evening Bulletin,* the
Inquirer, the *Daily News,* and the *Record.*

The *Record,* owned and operated by J. David Stern, was a partisan Democratic daily throughout the 1930s and early 1940s. Always entertaining, it made
no serious effort to separate news from editorial policy. Competition from the
other three dailies was keen, sometimes bitter. Advertising was not sufficient
to make the paper profitable and newsprint in the late 1940s was in short
supply. In a desperate effort to stay alive, Stern printed the *Record* on brown
paper for several weeks. Its staff compounded Stern's problems by joining the
Newspaper Guild and striking successfully for higher wages and shorter
hours than those of the other papers. Finally, on February 1, 1947, Stern gave
up. The *Bulletin* paid him a reputed million dollars for the *Record* and closed
it down.

For most of the period, then, Philadelphia had three daily newspapers, the
Inquirer in the morning, with its satellite the *Daily News,* and the *Bulletin* in
the afternoon. They were quite different in content and philosophy. The
Inquirer, aggressively Republican, handled the news in more colorful fashion

than its staid and respectable competitor the *Bulletin*. The *Daily News* was a tabloid making little effort to convey national or international news except that made available by the wire services. Its concentration was on matters of local human interest, with a high emphasis on sex, violence, and the bizarre.

The *Inquirer* was a one-man show. Walter H. Annenberg, who had inherited it from his father Moe, dominated its policy. He partly built and partly inherited a communications empire: a radio and television station, WFIL; a prosperous magazine for teens, *Seventeen;* a racing sheet, the *Morning Telegraph;* and a number of other ventures including *TV Guide.* They were all owned by Triangle Publications, which was owned by Annenberg. He established the Annenberg School of Communications at the University of Pennsylvania and donated Annenberg Hall to house the same activities at Temple.[37]

Notwithstanding its Republicanism, the *Inquirer* supported Dilworth and Clark in their initial efforts to win and hold city office. It opposed them in their efforts to achieve state and federal office, but never strongly so. There were times when the level of reporting in the *Inquirer* left much to be desired. In 1967 Harry Karafin, a prominent reporter whose by-line appeared almost daily, was indicted and subsequently convicted of extortion and blackmail using information he had uncovered as a reporter. It was difficult for Annenberg to find capable men of high integrity willing to work for him. He used his paper to wage his personal vendettas (the name of President Harnwell of the University of Pennsylvania was banned from the *Inquirer* after a minor altercation). Yet the *Inquirer* was a power not only in Philadelphia but throughout the eastern half of the state.

In October 1969 Walter Annenberg and John S. Knight jointly announced the sale of the *Inquirer* and the *Daily News* to Knight Publications, publishers of a chain of newspapers including the *Detroit Free Press* and the *Miami Herald.* When Knight took over in January 1970 there were major changes for the better in both personnel and policy.

The *Evening Bulletin*—"Nearly Everybody Reads the *Bulletin*"—which began to print a Sunday edition in 1947, was owned since 1895 by the McLean family. "Major" Robert W. McLean—the title came from World War I and stuck—was for many years its publisher. Long president of the Associated Press, he built the *Bulletin* into one of the better American newspapers by impartially printing the news gathered by a highly competent staff of reporters and refraining from taking controversial editorial positions. In 1960 the Major retired from the active direction of the newspaper to be succeeded by Robert Taylor, Mrs. McLean's nephew.

Brief mention should be made of *Philadelphia Magazine*, a bright, slick-paper monthly, full of advertising. Its publisher, D. Herbert Lipson, and its editor, Alan Halpern, built the magazine from an inconspicuous beginning as the voice of the Philadelphia Chamber of Commerce to a successful and widely read publication: an up-to-date muckraking sheet in the tradition of Lincoln Steffens.

Radio as a medium of communication was in full swing in 1947, and it remained an important source of capsule news, political comment, and entertainment, especially music. At the end of the 1960s there were forty-one AM and FM radio stations operating in the Philadelphia city market and a good many more in the suburbs. All of the major national networks owned stations, as did the *Bulletin* and the *Inquirer*. Special mention should be made of station WFLN, owned by Lawrence M. C. Smith, veteran supporter of liberal causes. From a shaky financial beginning in 1947 on an FM channel, it became a profitable venture, the "Good Music Station," offering programs of classical music and the news with relatively few commercials on both AM and FM channels.

Commercial television was in its infancy in 1947, but it grew in spectacular fashion. Local political television did not become feasible until after the 1951 mayoralty campaign. After that it was extensively used. Clark, Dilworth, and Tate all appeared on television to explain their programs to the people. Shows like "Tell It to the Mayor" and "Report to the People" were powerful tools for the mayor. Other local features included the televising of school board meetings. Philadelphia came to have seven television stations, including outlets of the three major networks and WHYY, the public television station which went into operation in 1961.

From the point of view of news and commentary television and radio probably had a greater impact on public opinion than the newspapers. In terms of politics television had an important effect in "selling" candidates, especially the young and personable. For other media of entertainment television became a fierce competitor, especially for the movies; many of the large movie theaters built in the 1920s heyday of the film industry, some of them monuments to the architectural tastes of their era, closed.

XII

Air in a big city, unlike talk, is a scarce resource that must be managed. Air pollution and the need to control it were recognized as a problem early in the Clark administration. The city charter created an Air Pollution Control Board, and a model air pollution ordinance was passed in 1954. It was thought that the principal city polluters were the Philadelphia Electric Company, which generated electricity at its several plants by burning soft coal; the five oil refineries along the Delaware south of the Schuylkill; open-dump burning of city refuse; and a few tanneries in the near northeast, most of which subsequently closed or left town. There was also considerable pollution across the Delaware from New Jersey when the wind blew from the east. Philadelphia, of course, returned the compliment when the wind blew the other way.

Under the gentle prodding of Morris Duane, chairman of the Air Pollution Control Board, the Philadelphia Electric Company and the oil refineries, notably the Atlantic Refining Company, installed expensive equipment in the 1950s to curb their pollutants. But much of this equipment soon became obsolete, more serious pollutant factors have since been uncovered, and the problem remains.

Toward the end of the Clark administration the city constructed a series of regional incinerators that eliminated much of the city's open-dump burning. Unfortunately the incinerators did not have perfect combustion and were inefficiently operated. Despite an excellent new air pollution control ordinance passed in 1969, Philadelphia remained one of the principal offenders in polluting its air. In September 1970 the Commonwealth of Pennsylvania announced that it was suing the city for violating state air pollution standards.

If in the matter of air the outcome of the race between civilization and disaster was in doubt, with respect to water civilization was perhaps running slightly ahead. Philadelphia obtained most of its water supply from the Delaware River, a tidal estuary from Trenton to the sea. A small part of the supply came from the Schuylkill River. Efforts to control pollution in the Delaware and its tributaries met with little success before 1952. Conditions indeed were worsening as raw sewage continued to be dumped in the Delaware and its tributaries by many upstream municipalities. Philadelphia's sewage treatment plants in the late 1940s and early 1950s were utterly inadequate. In 1955, however, Mayor Clark decided that the political situation was ripe for a four-state effort to control the uses and abuses of the Delaware River.

At that time Democrats held the governorships of Pennsylvania, New York, and New Jersey. Robert Wagner was the Democratic mayor of New York City. Only Caleb Boggs, liberal governor of Delaware, was a Republican. The four governors and the two mayors called into being the Delaware River Basin Commission and successfully solicited public and industrial support for an interstate compact to control the all-purpose use of water in the Delaware Basin.

The interstate compact creating a commission with power to regulate the flow of water in the Delaware required the approval of the United States Congress to become effective. Clark, moving from the mayor's office to the federal Senate, enlisted the support of Secretary of the Interior Stewart Udall, and together they secured the backing of the twenty-three separate federal agencies that had a legitimate part in the program. The interstate compact sailed through Congress almost without opposition in 1961. Thus an effective mechanism for purifying the waters of the Delaware River was provided. For the first time in many years shad survived the not-inconsiderable remaining pollution and swam to the upper Delaware to spawn, and the oyster beds in Delaware Bay were again considered safe from infection.[38]

In the Schuylkill River the same problems of pollution were made worse by the presence of acid drainage from the anthracite mines. The Delaware River Basin Commission undertook effective work to clean up the Schuylkill too. Swimming again came to be considered safe in many of the upper reaches of the Schuylkill as well as the Delaware—though it would be a rash man who would plunge into the waters near their confluence.

One of the major complaints against Philadelphia's city government in the 1940s was the inadequacy of trash and garbage collection. In the higher income areas the streets were kept clean and trash and garbage were regularly collected (to be disposed of by open-dump burning in South Philadelphia).

In less prosperous areas the situation was far different. Streets filthy with trash and open garbage cans smelling to heaven were the rule. Cleaning the streets was a rare event. Some of this neglect resulted from inadequate equipment and lack of city funds, but political operation of the streets and sanitation departments also played a major role. With the end of financial stringency for the time being and the coming to office of a reform administration, the situation quickly improved in the 1950s. Generally speaking the city continued to hold its own against the trash problem even into the 1970s.

The narrowness of the city's victories in the race with man's destructive tendencies, and the frequency of defeats, was a key factor that helped spur the exodus of Philadelphians to the suburbs. Industry fled along with people. Among the additional reasons for the exodus were a necessarily constantly increasing city tax rate; inadequate sites for industrial and commercial development in an era that required large amounts of space for automobile parking; an architectural tendency toward horizontal rather than vertical construction of commercial and industrial establishments. There was also the feeling by much of business and industry that the social composition of the city and the characteristics of the labor market, strongly unionized as it was, did not provide a climate in which business, and with it profits, could expand and flourish.[39]

Perhaps more disturbing was the "brain drain." Competent young people tended to leave the city to seek their fortunes elsewhere. There was a discernible belief among many of them that Philadelphia was a city without much imagination or intellectual stimulus. A similar situation arose from the transfer of ownership of many of Philadelphia's leading establishments to other places. The Atlantic Refining Company, for example, merged with Richfield Oil and its headquarters moved to Los Angeles. Philco was sold to the Ford Motor Company, transferring the decision-making to Detroit. Even banking leadership, which was supported by a solid core of inherited wealth, tended to gravitate to New York, in part because bank mergers that could have created financial institutions large enough to service the big Philadelphia industries were disallowed by the courts. Absentee ownership thus became a threat to leadership of the city in the philanthropic, business, and industrial world.

Beset though it was by so many problems and discouragements, there was steady planning for the development and improvement of the physical city. Under Mayor Samuel, Edward Hopkinson, Jr., a staunch and conservative Republican, had placed his considerable weight (over 225 pounds of it) behind a rejuvenated City Planning Commission, of which he became chairman. The commission, directed in turn by three brilliant urban planners, Robert Mitchell, Robert Leonard, and finally for many years Edmund Bacon, went to work planning public improvements ready to move from the drawing boards into construction as soon as municipal finances could be rehabilitated. In 1947 these men put on a Philadelphia Exhibition in Gimbels department store illustrating the plans and hopes for the new Philadelphia. The exhibition caught the imagination of the public, and a remarkable proportion of those plans and hopes eventually came to be realized.[40]

Edmund N. Bacon, executive director of the Philadelphia City Planning Commission from 1949 to 1970 (September 28, 1966). Society Hill Towers (1964), designed by I. M. Pei & Associates, are reproduced in the model of the Webb and Knapp 1960 proposal, at the left, and the building of the United States Customs Service, Second and Chestnut Streets, appears at the right.

PHILADELPHIA BULLETIN

XIII

A view of Philadelphia from the top of City Hall tower would reveal some of the changes that took place under the excitement of the post–World War II reform era and of the beginnings of comprehensive city planning.

The center city area extended from the Schuylkill on the west to the Delaware on the east, up to Spring Garden Street in the north and no farther south than South Street. It was the modern version of Penn's original city plan. Around this center city were brackets of immigrant and black areas, a vast district bounded on the southeast by an industrial wilderness of oil refineries, automobile graveyards, incinerators, and dumps. Only the Navy Yard, historic Fort Mifflin, the airport, Eastwick, and one or two new industrial plants relieved the squalor and smoke at the confluence of the Schuylkill and the Delaware. The old settled city arc covered much of West Philadelphia, ranged across the Schuylkill around Spring Garden Street, and ran north toward Germantown. Crossing Broad Street it included much of the area between the two rivers far north into Kensington. All of the city is not visible from City Hall tower, but with a powerful pair of binoculars one could see most of it on a clear day, because except for Roxborough, Manayunk,

Philadelphia Planning Commission model of Center City. The model was designed by Edmund Bacon for the Better Philadelphia Exhibition held at Gimbels department store in 1947.

TEMPLE UNIVERSITY, URBAN ARCHIVES

Chestnut Hill, and Mount Airy, it is generally flat.

Down by the Delaware River, to the south, below the Delaware's confluence with the Schuylkill, was the Philadelphia International Airport. The rudimentary S. Davis Wilson Airport existed at the end of World War II. It was obvious, however, that it had to be drastically improved and enlarged. This was done; the new airport was dedicated by Mayor Clark, who flew to the dedication in an army helicopter in 1954. At the time many thought it was a white elephant. Air traffic was light because of competition from Washington, New York, and Baltimore's new airport. Even though President Truman had it certified for international travel at Mayor Clark's request, naming the airport "International" was generally considered a joke.

It soon became apparent that the problem was not too little traffic but too much, and that the design of the airport was almost immediately inadequate to the demands of the air age. One building after another was added to provide for additional traffic, which through the 1950s and 1960s continued to increase at the rate of 25 percent a year. By 1970 traffic was up 800 percent since the opening of the terminal; from 1962 onward the city was unable to keep up with air traffic demands. By the end of the period the city had embarked on a $250-million expansion loan program, to be repaid out of airport revenues, but progress dragged. The failure to provide high-speed rail connections to center city and the congested highways made matters worse; nevertheless it takes less time to get from the airport to center city than in all but a few of the nation's major cities.

Across the road from the airport the Tinicum Wildlife Refuge was expanded, a unique development for a major metropolis. During the Clark administration, at the behest of Allston Jenkins, the city set aside this area as a wildlife sanctuary, a resting place for migratory wildlife including duck, heron, Canada geese, and snipe. The area was low-lying marshland, flooding and ebbing with tidewater from the Delaware.

Near the University of Pennsylvania was the Civic Center—the Civic Center Auditorium, the Grand Exhibition Hall, and the Commercial Museum. At the end of World War II Philadelphia was obsolete as a center for large conventions and trade shows. The Democratic and Republican National Conventions came in 1948, but the experience was not satisfactory. Part of the capital program of the City Planning Commission over the years was directed at remedying this deficiency through the modernization of existing facilities and the building of new ones. The completion of the Grand Exhibition Hall in 1967 largely finished the job as originally envisioned, and Philadelphia had far better facilities for a national gathering than ever before. But as with the airport and so much else, the original post–World War II plans failed to anticipate the acceleration of new demands; the Civic Center Auditorium, formerly called Convention Hall, remained inadequate particularly because of the limitations its design imposed on the television coverage of major conventions, while both inadequate hotel space and insufficient transportation between center city and the Civic Center also discouraged the largest national meetings from coming to the city.

North of Market Street, still in West Philadelphia, is Powelton Village, an area where partially successful projects for the integration of black and white families developed. Not far to the east, opposite the Thirtieth Street Station, the modern Bulletin Building, completed in 1955, one of the last structures designed by George Howe, was seen as a model of what a newspaper building should be. But north and south of Market Street in West Philadelphia were block after block of rundown slums, a tinderbox of political and social unrest and violence.

Running from South Philadelphia to Valley Forge was the Schuylkill Expressway, built in the early 1950s to serve the traffic needs of that horde of suburban Philadelphians coming into and through center city each day from the Main Line and as a truck route to and from the west. Many of them headed north over the Roosevelt Boulevard Extension, others east to New Jersey and south to the airport. With the opening of the Walt Whitman Bridge in 1959, traffic to Jersey shore points and to the New Jersey Turnpike only compounded commuter snarls at the southern end of the expressway. The route of the Schuylkill Expressway and its construction were subjects of great controversy during the years of the Clark administration.

John B. Kelly, well-known civic leader and sometime chairman of the

Democratic City Committee, was at this time a leading member of the Fairmount Park Commission. Stressing principles of conservation and recreation, he fought hard to persuade the state and the city to route the Schuylkill Expressway to the west of Fairmount Park. The state, however, was adamant, and the city under the Clark administration went along with the state. The state pinched pennies on both design and construction of the highway. By the time the route opened it was already obsolete. Congestion added to bad engineering and their consequences gave the expressway its jocular but apt nickname, the "Sure-Kill Crawlway." Yet it is an essential artery that has been widened several times. And it has not, as the worst scenario predicted, ruined the river aesthetics.

The Schuylkill Expressway, Art Museum curve near Spring Garden Street Bridge (c. 1956).

PHILADELPHIA OFFICE OF THE CITY REPRESENTATIVE

Another area that changed markedly after World War II was along City Line Avenue, which divides West Philadelphia from Montgomery County. The impact of lower taxes in the suburban county could be seen clearly. Most of the new development was on the Montgomery County side, although there were several high-rise apartment houses, a 500-room hotel, and one well-designed radio and television station, WFIL, built on the Philadelphia side of City Line.

East of the Schuylkill in northwest Philadelphia there was much less physical change. There was redevelopment in the lower end of Germantown, where $10.6 million was made available through the Redevelopment Authority for public housing for the ever-increasing number of black families who moved west and north. In the Roxborough area were some acres of still undeveloped land, much of it in woodland.

In the days immediately after World War II northeast Philadelphia north of Cottman Avenue contained huge areas of undeveloped acreage. The northeast was ripe for profitable development as population expanded and grew more affluent. Almost all the recently undeveloped land of the northeast was soon built up, most of it with row and apartment housing by two builders, A. P. Orleans and Hyman Korman and his sons. Most of the housing is not attractive, inviting a slum of the future. An effort was made during the Clark administration to prevent the exploitation of the area through a new zoning category that would have controlled the building of row houses and provided green areas. Unfortunately the zoning board granted variances in a number of key tracts to permit duplex housing and heavy density. In many tracts, moreover, the city Council itself downgraded higher zoning classifications. The pressure for new cheap housing in the northeast from white Jewish and Irish Philadelphians anxious to move away from the growing black population around center city resulted in disappointment to the hopes of the city planners. The exploitation of the northeast in the period 1946–1968 is one of the great tragedies of modern Philadelphia. Furthermore because the area became almost entirely white, a democratic solution to the citywide problems in housing and education was made more difficult.

The city did achieve the setting aside of substantial areas of the northeast for industrial parks. To be sure, this success accelerated the movement of workers seeking homes and the creation of housing density; but juxtaposing the job and the worker helped solve the traffic problem that had hitherto been a serious deterrent to the development of the northeast. There had never been high-speed facilities between center city and the northeast above the terminal of the Frankford Elevated at Bridge Street. Roosevelt Boulevard, despite improvements, was not an adequate highway to the northeast, but all kinds of facilities clustered along it. At the outer reaches of the northeast, near the Bucks County line, was the Liberty Bell Racetrack, licensed by the Commonwealth and opened on June 7, 1963.

The Delaware Expressway, under construction in 1968, carried the promise of swift traffic flow toward the center of town. This expressway ran through a heavily industrialized area that had seen few changes since World War II. The Frankford Arsenal was shut down by the federal government in 1977 because the army's needs for small arms were adequately filled elsewhere. There were a number of industrial parks where modern industry located, but also a good many abandoned factory sites. A few big estates along the river near Torresdale became new locations for cheaper housing. In Frankford and Kensington the abandonment of many multistoried factories no longer economical to operate brought more urban blight. The working-class families that lived there for generations, largely a white population, continued to live there amid the declining mills and aging facilities.

Farther west, on Broad Street, the Temple University campus, a product of the federal urban redevelopment program and of state and federal aid to higher education, was long surrounded by slums. Redevelopment accomplished some limited improvements in the area by 1968, and the Progress Plaza Shopping Center, operated by black businessmen on the block bounded by Broad, Oxford, Jefferson, and Thirteenth Streets, was a boon to the area. This project was conceived by the Rev. Dr. Leon H. Sullivan, black minister and civic leader, and was financed by the Redevelopment Authority for the sponsor, a nonprofit corporation formed by Dr. Sullivan's Zion Baptist Church.

In center-city Philadelphia many changes took place in the years after 1946. Looking out the Benjamin Franklin Parkway to the Art Museum on Fairmount above the Schuylkill River, a complex of post–World War II high-rise and high-rent apartments and office buildings could be seen. The broad tree-lined Parkway remained one of the most beautiful entrances to any city in the world, bringing residents of Germantown and Chestnut Hill and

Excavation at Penn Center, from Seventeenth Street, looking east (c. 1955). Three Penn Center is under construction and Suburban Station (Penn Center Station) at Sixteenth Street rises at the left.

the northwestern suburbs into town from the East and West River Drives of Fairmount Park and the Expressway.

On Market Street west of City Hall extraordinary changes took place. The Chinese Wall—the elevated tracks of the Pennsylvania Railroad from West Philadelphia into Broad and Market Streets—and the Broad Street Station came down in 1953. Thereafter all the major trains of the Pennsylvania, and later the Penn Central Railroad and Amtrak, operated through North Philadelphia and Thirtieth Street Stations; suburban trains came into center city on the old Pennsylvania lines, but their tracks ran underground east of Twentieth Street.

Directly west of City Hall the Penn Center development was largely built in the early 1950s on the site of the Chinese Wall. Here a series of modern, architecturally imaginative office buildings arose, housing some of the more important firms doing business in the city. Planning provided open walkways both above and below ground in much of this area. On the north side of Market Street commercial redevelopment made over the face of the city all the way to Thirtieth Street Station across the Schuylkill. Little Filbert Street west of Broad was widened to create Pennsylvania (later John F. Kennedy) Boulevard. Along both sides of the boulevard modern apartment houses, hotels, and office buildings transformed the area after 1946 from a commercial skid row to a place of architectural cleanliness and economic utility. Immediately north of Penn Center the Municipal Services Building on Reyburn Plaza, a Hospitality Center to welcome visitors to the city, a new Bell Telephone building, and a group of other modern structures were built.

A walk around the rim of William Penn's hat on City Hall tower viewing the part of center city to the east presented a prospect of plans in the making for the redevelopment of Market Street East. The area around Independence Hall in all directions had been redeveloped. The Commonwealth of Pennsylvania transformed the blocks directly north of Independence Hall to Race Street into a blockwide mall of grass and trees. On Fifth and Sixth Streets on both sides of the mall rose new and modern buildings, including a new United States Mint on the northeast corner of Fifth and Arch, a new federal courthouse, and the Rohm and Haas Building. Slightly to the north, on the Vine Street expressway to the Benjamin Franklin Bridge and just east of Philadelphia's Chinatown, a new Police Administration Building, a circular modern structure, was completed during the Dilworth administration.

To the east and south of Independence Hall the Society Hill redevelopment resulted in the demolition of most of the slum-like commercial structures that cluttered the area before 1946, including the "skid row" of the old Dock Street markets. Historic buildings such as Carpenters' Hall, the First and Second Banks of the United States, and the Merchants' Exchange were preserved and renovated by the federal government's Independence National Historical Park. Old houses were rehabilitated to restore Society Hill as a residential area, with high-rise apartments and newer houses—notably I. M. Pei's Society Hill Towers and Town Houses—interspersed among them.

Some of the business and professional leaders of the city moved to Society Hill, Mayor Dilworth among them; but not all of the housing of the area was in the highest cost category, and many a young lawyer, newspaper executive, or businessman also returned to the central city by moving to Society Hill. Furthermore a similar residential rebirth extended west from Society Hill along Locust, Spruce, Pine, and Lombard Streets to the Schuylkill River.

Beyond Society Hill to the east the Port of Philadelphia remained in 1968 the center of the largest freshwater port complex in the world. The wharves and docks had fallen into great disrepair during the years just before World War II. In 1965 the city, the state, and the Greater Philadelphia Chamber of Commerce formed the Philadelphia Port Corporation to work out a sensible plan for the rehabilitation of the port facilities and to handle the containerized packaging that was revolutionizing methods of handling cargo. The Packer Avenue Marine Terminal with complete modern facilities was opened in 1967. The Tioga Terminal followed in the 1970s. Both had facilities for container cargoes, but the port's modernization had not yet caught up with rival cities', and the ancient handicap of Philadelphia's considerable distance from the sea remained.

Mass transit into a large and congested urban center became an increasingly difficult problem in the years following World War II. Philadelphia drew workers from a wide region, including New Jersey across the Delaware. At least one partial solution to the transit problem came with the opening in 1969 of the high-speed line from Lindenwold, New Jersey, across the Benjamin Franklin Bridge to the former Locust Street Subway with a terminal at Sixteenth and Locust Streets. The Lindenwold line was a project of the Port Authority Transportation Company (PATCO), which developed the line and two new bridges across the Delaware at Chester and Pennsauken, begun in 1969 and opened in the 1970s, as part of a single financing package involving expenditures of over $300 million.

In Philadelphia itself construction began to extend the Broad Street Subway from Snyder Avenue south to the new sports complex of Veterans Stadium and the Spectrum at Pattison Avenue, a project completed in 1973.

Railroad traffic and passenger service into Philadelphia declined in the postwar years. The Baltimore and Ohio Railroad eliminated all passenger trains through the city. The advertised benefits of the merger between the Pennsylvania and New York Central Railroads suffered a severe setback when the Penn Central, the combined company, petitioned for reorganization in bankruptcy in 1970. In 1964 the Southeastern Pennsylvania Transportation Authority was created, leasing from the Pennsylvania and Reading Railroads most of their suburban lines. Initially SEPTA acquired new electric airconditioned aluminum coaches, reduced commuter fares, and began to operate the transportation system in a way that made a perceptible impact on highway traffic congestion. In 1968 SEPTA also took over the Philadelphia Transportation Company which operated the city's trolley lines, buses, subways, and elevated trains. Unfortunately by the 1970s the familiar economic squeeze of rising costs, including expensive union contracts, and limited and declining government subsidies began to wipe away the improvements in Philadelphia's mass transit systems, though Philadelphia was still considerably ahead of most American cities in the potential of its mass transit.

The face of Philadelphia had a very different appearance in 1968 from that of 1946. A combination of private and public investment had rendered the city in many areas more beautiful, more functional, and more modern than it was before World War II. In many other ways Philadelphia became a different city. In 1946 it was still corrupt and contented. In 1947 it began to find a new life, and for the next fifteen years experienced a time of great achievement. Late in the 1960s, however, came relapse, and as 1968 closed creative forces no longer appeared to control the city's destiny.

Bertram Zumeta, an economist who for some years served the Federal Reserve Bank in Philadelphia, has written that two paramount national influences were at work in shaping the life of Philadelphia after 1946. One was war. World War II left a legacy of problems and dislocation. Then the Korean War in the 1950s again taxed industry and the economy. The Vietnam War started a cycle of inflation that profoundly influenced municipal finance and standards, institutions, and the lifestyle of citizens. A second factor was the drop in rates of natural population increase beginning in the 1960s.[41] These national forces caused huge disruptions of plans and expectations. Schools were built, then population declined. Institutions modernized and then encountered a whole new set of priorities and operating conditions. Urban officials and civic leaders were unable to foresee the impact and consequences of suburbanization, dominance of the automobile, widespread racial change, alteration of industrial technology, and momentous changes in family composition and behavior.[42]

The period of political, civic, and physical reconstruction from 1946 to 1970 was profoundly important for Philadelphia even if the reform was gradually eroded and the physical changes were unevenly accomplished. The reform tested the determination of leadership and the idealism of the city's talented and wonderfully diverse population. The political renewal proved that from the very depths of municipal corruption a new spirit could be summoned. It demonstrated the capacity of a polyglot and ethnically varied urban citizenry for mobilization in behalf of improved standards of public responsibility and a new vision of urban life. It was testimony that even amid the contradictions and complexity of an industrial metropolis democracy could manifest itself vibrantly. The chief shortcomings of the entire effort were that standards were still not raised sufficiently to actually transform long-term social and political habits, and the changes made were not appropriately directed toward the root causes of social disability in the urban environment.

The Bicentennial City
1968-1982

by Stephanie G. Wolf

> . . . *much of that spirit is alive and well today . . . in ways and manners which may not have been invented by the Bicentennial experience, but which gained confidence through it. The city looks better, it feels better to walk its streets.*
>
> — *Philadelphia Inquirer* [1]

To invoke the spirit of the 1970s is to conjure up a kaleidoscope of media-generated images: the "Watergate era," the "me genera-tion," the "energy-crisis," loss of confidence, failure of credibility, alternative lifestyles, radical-chic, backlash, stagflation, unemployment. Hovering over the opening of the decade loomed the Vietnam War; over its closing, the Moral Majority. It began with a belief that established government controlled national policy, but that popular protest could significantly alter the directions of social and political life. It ended with a rejection of political participation and a perception that the establishment was irrelevant or impotent in the face of gigantic and insoluble problems. "Doing one's own thing" (another 1970s slogan) and caring only about those issues that had a direct effect on one's own life seemed preferable to dealing with worries and problems over which one had no control. Social goals of importance to the proper ordering of a society as a whole were impossible: if there was not enough money or concern to go around, why should it be expended on inadequate schools for other people's children, for example, while the houses in one's own neighborhood were deteriorating? And who had the right to set the priorities for the use of limited resources and make the final judgment on social needs? The liberal establishment had assumed that right since the early 1930s. Its members, well educated and often well heeled, articulated the goals, planned the methods of achieving them, implemented the plans, and evaluated the results. They represented an ideology and philosophy about the good of a community in which the individual was an abstract concept, part of an American melting pot in which ethnic, racial, class, or regional background had little significance. Richard Nixon had argued in the 1960s that there was a "silent majority" in the country that did not necessarily agree with the choice of social goals made by the liberal establishment. It was a group that when it was heard, Nixon and others thought, would speak in chorus for conservatism.

During the 1970s, perhaps with the aid of mechanisms developed by the broadcast media—talk shows on radio; debates, exposés, and interviews with private citizens on local television—the voices of the previously inarticulate began to be heard. What they had to say in part confirmed the notion of the "silent majority"—but in part did not. They did not identify first and foremost with a homogenized concept of an American but with their ethnic, racial, economic, and religious roots. But it was not a wide vision of any ideology they favored—either conservative or liberal—but improvement, or at least in the narrower expectations of the 1970s, maintenance of what they had already attained. They were violently antagonistic to the advancement of others at what they perceived to be their own expense. In the 1980s this realization would come to be associated with single-issue politics and pressure brought by small groups through new and creative uses of the political system. For the 1970s it remained largely a question of keeping what they had out of the clutches of an establishment in whose goals they were no longer willing to acquiesce, and of gaining control of their own lives and those of their children.

Philadelphia at night (1978). The view is toward the west, with Market Street at the left.

Other trends, functional rather than conceptual, were making vast changes in the face of America and on its power structure. These were largely demographic, and involved the movement of population and economic vitality from their traditional base in the Northeast to the South and West. Regional factionalism resulting from the changing balance played as large a part in the distrust of the old establishment as the ideological shifts already mentioned. Of course neither of these trends, material or philosophic, sprang up full-blown in the 1970s. Historical periodization is at its best arbitrary and at its worst deceptive; what appears as the product of one decade has its most significant roots and developments in earlier times. It is a basic fact that American populations have been moving westward since the first settlers arrived on these shores. The significance of a trend surfaces at the point at which it plays a primary role in the way people live and behave, and for this century it may be fair to characterize the 1970s as the decade when the great cities of the Northeast not only lost their power over national events but also over small but vocal factions and over government within their own boundaries. Philadelphia is almost a model of the working out of these changing national patterns; it is the *dramatis personae* and the particular events that make the history of Philadelphia unique.

I

If it were possible to take a huge group photograph of all the people who lived in Philadelphia and its surrounding area in 1982, and to contrast it with a similar photograph taken twenty, fifty, or a hundred years ago, one could get an immediate visual image of the primary changes that have taken place and on which all of the other changes rest. Since such a photograph is impossible even with the most modern sophisticated techniques, it is necessary to take the more tedious path of description in words and figures and letting the picture emerge as a mental image.

The overall figures for Philadelphia's population are well known, as are the general trends that they represent.[2] From a center, not insignificant in its time, of about 13,000 inhabitants in the mid-1740s, Philadelphia's population had surpassed all other cities in the revolutionary colonies by 1776 and stood at about 33,000. Despite a growth rate that remained about the same, it dropped to second place behind New York City by the end of the eighteenth century, a position that had psychological as well as physical implications. The first half of the nineteenth century with its emerging industrialization created enormous immigration into Philadelphia from both the surrounding countryside and abroad, and saw the fastest growth the city would ever undergo: by 1850 there were over 400,000 residents, eight persons crowding into the picture where only one had stood before. By 1880 the population had doubled again to 850,000, although the landscape in the photograph was also enlarged by a consolidation of the city with its surrounding county, establishing the geographic boundaries of present-day Philadelphia.[3] The city's population had topped one million by 1900, and despite a setback parallel to national trends during the 1930s depression, there were over two million people resident by 1950.

It was at this point that a twentieth-century historical phenomenon caught up with the cities of the Northeast in general, Philadelphia in particular. The trend began slowly at first and was not noticed by city planners, whose grandiose ideas were based on the economic and physical expansion of the past plotted upward on the graphs of the future. Certainly the baby boom of the late 1940s and 1950s helped to blind the planners to the plight that was about to overtake northeastern cities. Budgets and building programs were geared to rising expectations of populations, incomes, and tax base. But the very roads and transportation systems the planners were working to improve would place many of the people and much of the wealth on which the cities had to depend beyond their own inflexible political boundaries, out in the suburbs where land was cheaper, taxes lower, and free parking plentiful. During the 1950s Philadelphia lost 5 percent of its population and during the 1960s another 3 percent. While still the fourth-largest city in the United States, an enormous loss of more than 13 percent was registered in the decade between 1970 and 1980, dropping the total from just under two million to less than 1.7 million inhabitants. The thirty years since the highpoint of 1950 had seen nearly 400,000 people leave town, almost the same number that had con- stituted the entire population of the city at the time of its greatest growth back in 1850.

Moreover as an imaginary photograph of Philadelphia would show, this change in population was not merely one of numbers, but one of composition as well. Philadelphia, often called the most northern of the southern cities, had always had a substantial number of black citizens compared to the rest of the North. While the black population of other northern cities never made up more than 2 percent of their numbers before 1920, it remained consistently over 5 percent in Philadelphia through the early twentieth century, standing at about 11 percent in 1930. There was little change in the next decade, but during and following World War II, as a result of the demand for labor of any kind, the percentages rose sharply—by 5 percent in the decades of the 1940s and the 1950s, by 10 percent in the 1960s. Fewer opportunities during the 1970s slowed the rate at which the black population of the city grew in relation to whites, 5 percent for the decade according to the 1980 census figures. This meant that about 37 out of every 100 people in Philadelphia were black in 1980. At least another four were Asiatic or Spanish-speaking, four times the number that would have been present merely ten years before.

The visual image is less successful in illustrating the differences existing among the white faces smiling or frowning into that figurative camera. Ethnic and religious diversity had always characterized Philadelphia's population, but self-conscious political participation by different ethnic and religious groups became increasingly important during the 1970s. As one author has pointed out, in the bicentennial year Philadelphia's government was led by an Italian mayor, an Irish police commissioner, a Jewish president of the city

Council, and a Polish leader of the Democratic party.[4]

The loss of population in Philadelphia did not take place evenly through-out the city between 1970 and 1980. In the very center of Philadelphia the numbers have remained approximately the same although the composition has changed considerably. Those sections in most serious distress from deteriorat-ing housing, insufficient services, and poor economic conditions are the oldest areas clustering immediately around center city. North Philadelphia, Ken-sington, West Philadelphia, and South Philadelphia lost from 15 percent to 30 percent of their population during the 1970s. There was a more moderate decline, ranging from 4 percent to 14 percent in other areas, with the excep-tion of the far northeast which actually registered a gain of 6 percent (along with gains in a small portion of the southeast—the Eastwick development—and in a small part of center city—between Walnut and Spruce Streets, Broad Street and the Schuylkill). In many ways the far northeast is a part of Philadel-phia's political picture only by historical accident. Its actual development much more closely resembles the suburbs, and it still contains large amounts of open land on which construction has continued to take place.

Every photograph is limited by the arbitrary frame imposed by the pho-tographer: what is left out may distort the scene that would have emerged if a wide-angle lens had only been used. Nowhere is this more true than in trying to visualize Philadelphia in 1982 without looking beyond the political boundaries laid down almost 130 years ago. The huge urban centers of late twentieth-century America have been transformed by the post–World War II growth of their suburbs, turning the whole northeast corner of the country into a vast megalopolis of almost continuous urbanization. To study cities in their proper perspective population experts and sociologists examine the data for an entire region—the Standard Metropolitan Statistical Area (SMSA). This procedure enables them not only to look at cities themselves but to compare and contrast their changes with their surrounding counties, which originally grew as adjuncts of cities but have begun in recent years more and more to assume the real economic, political, and numerical power of their regions while the city's function has become more symbolic, less actual.

Philadelphia's SMSA includes, in addition to the city itself, the four Penn-sylvania counties of Bucks, Chester, Delaware, and Montgomery, and the three New Jersey counties of Burlington, Camden, and Gloucester. The SMSA remained in 1980, as it had been in 1970 and 1960, the fourth-largest such area in the United States. Like the projectors and planners for the city, however, those for the suburban counties for a time made the mistake of assuming that the temporary population boom of the 1950s was a permanent explosion. They could not, of course, predict worldwide events like the energy crisis and cultural changes in lifestyle, which in more recent years have had such drastic economic and demographic repercussions on the northeast-ern region as a whole.

At the start of 1970 the suburban counties could still look back on a decade of tremendous growth; the population of the SMSA, excluding the city itself, had increased by a whopping 23 percent to a total of over 2.25 million, greater than that of Philadelphia and much of it at the expense of the urban center. While the city had lost only 54,000 people in the preceding decade thanks to a high nonwhite birth rate, over 200,000 mostly white residents had "fled" to the neighboring suburbs to avoid urban problems, explicitly defined as more people, less money, and growing crime. As early as New Year's Day of 1970 the suburban section of the *Bulletin* carried a story that residents of the nearer suburbs were worried that the coming decade of the 1970s would see Philadelphia's problems following them out of the city, and these problems were defined as air pollution, abandoned houses, overcrowded schools, racial tensions, and inadequate transportation, health, and social services.[5]

Many of the expressed reasons for preferring life in the suburbs seem to be an elaborate code for racial attitudes, and it is hard to escape the conclusion that racism played a heavy role in the movement out of Philadelphia. People who have left the city will discuss the "black problem" in oral interviews, although for the record they will usually substitute some euphemism or mention issues in which the race question is implicit although unstated, such as "the quality of the schools." The horrified reaction by suburbanites to Richardson Dilworth's earlier suggestion that city and outlying schools be merged was partly an expression of these attitudes. The white nature of the migration is evident in the figures which show that as late as 1978 black people made up only 7.4 percent of the population in the SMSA, excluding Philadelphia but including the heavily black cities of Chester and Camden.

Worries about the other city ills that might evolve in the suburbs from simple overdevelopment seemed to surface but rarely as yet in the early 1970s. Enthusiastic population projections for Montgomery and Bucks Counties saw increases of 25 percent and 34 percent respectively during the 1970s. The actuality proved far different and must make one wary about predicting future trends: Montgomery County's growth was an almost imperceptible 2.5 percent while Bucks County increased a healthy 15 percent, but nothing like the earlier expectations. The suburban area as a whole slowed from its rapid pace in the 1960s to a mere 5 percent gain in population during the decade from 1970 to 1980, and in fact registered a very small decline (less than 1 percent) in the final year for which statistics are available (1979–1980). This slowdown of course is part of the larger national trend of population movement that signifies an end to the hegemony of the Northeast and the heyday of its cities and suburbs. When Philadelphia's losses are taken into account the total SMSA picture was 3 percent smaller in 1980 than it had been in 1970, standing at about 3.75 million inhabitants. The two major satellite urban areas of Camden and the city of Chester reproduced on a smaller scale all the difficulties experienced by Philadelphia, while the more rural and more affluent areas developed their own brands of rising crime rates, juvenile delinquency, drug abuse, school strikes, and economic dislocation, often without institutional facilities capable of coping. The rise of the national environmental movement of the 1970s caused many suburban communities to reevaluate their attitudes toward unchecked growth and development.

On the other hand growth of the suburbs has slowed down and stabilized in those counties closest to Philadelphia, while continued high growth has taken place in the more distant counties like Bucks and Chester. These areas are less affected by deteriorating conditions in the city, and perhaps less worried about being absorbed by its institutions. Active antagonism to the old center seemed less an attitude in the 1970s than did indifference. Local newspapers, museums, colleges, concerts, and parks may lack the "panache" of big-city "culture," but their presence during the 1970s contributed to a sense of community in which the urban niceties could be had close to home and parking. The one area in which regional identification with Philadelphia still seems to run high is in relation to its professional athletic teams: the hockey Flyers, the baseball Phillies, and the football Eagles all receive enthusiastic support and create huge traffic jams on the roads and bridges leading into the city when they play at home. Only the basketball 76ers have failed to capture the suburban imagination, and basketball in Philadelphia, as across the nation, has acquired the reputation of being a "black" sport.

II

The most readily observed difference in Philadelphia during the 1970s that was in part both caused and affected by the population changes just discussed is a fundamental change in its economic structure. In this realm too, long-term trends and national influences must be remembered as the context in which local developments have taken place.

The Frank L. Rizzo administration of 1972–1980 was particularly sensitive to the necessity for economic revitalization in Philadelphia, and its leaders believed that the only way in which this could be accomplished was by continued communication and closer cooperation between the city and private business. There was a constant stream of information about city resources and opportunities made available in forms particularly useful to potential business investors. There was even an attempt made in the mid-1970s to update printed economic statistics on a twice-yearly basis through the office of the city economist. Then in 1979 the Philadelphia City Planning Commission issued a paper on *Issues for the 1980's,* setting priorities for the future decade based on assessments of the ways in which the 1970s had differed from earlier expectations and predictions.[6] The situation as it had developed appeared bleak.

The structural changes in the national economy since 1951 that resulted in a smaller share of private-sector employment for manufacturing enterprises hit Philadelphia particularly hard; from the early nineteenth century industry had been the backbone of Philadelphia's economy. Worse still, the drop in Philadelphia was even steeper than that in the nation at large: while the proportion of America's work force involved in manufacturing between 1951 and 1977 fell from 43 percent to 29 percent, the city started higher and contracted further, from 46 percent down to 24 percent in the same period of time. Philadelphia's problem was twofold: it involved the physical problems endemic to most old cities—deterioration of buildings, outmoded building designs, inadequate truck access, lack of worker amenities, and lack of expansion space; but it also rested on a lack of available capital for investment in expanding and upgrading these facilities, or for constructing new ones. Despite the development of fifteen industrial parks within the city and particularly in its outlying regions, occupancy rates were low. By 1980 over 100,000 jobs in manufacturing had been lost, 44 percent of the 215,000 opportunities that had existed in 1970. Suburban communities that had been wary of industrial development in the 1960s, perhaps through fear of attracting the "wrong kind of people," had changed their policies by 1980. They realized the advantage it was to their tax bases to have successful industries located within their borders, providing jobs for their residents and customers for their shopping malls. Industrial development also eliminated the need for their residents to pay high commuting costs in time and fuel, or the city wage tax which had risen to over 4 percent. While the most aggressive pursuit of industry by Philadelphia's suburbs could not reverse the trends in which manufacturing jobs were declining across the nation and those that survived were leaving the Northeast, the loss of this kind of employment was held to only 6.5 percent in the Philadelphia suburbs during the 1970s.[7]

Of course, mental snapshots of people running machines, large or small, in a variety of settings, do not begin to cover the job choices available in the modern world in the complex urban environment. As old as civilization itself is the necessity to build structures in which people live and work, so the construction industry has always provided employment, as has the field of transportation, another basic necessity for interdependent society. Essential jobs in the technological twentieth century are also found in the distribution of communication and utility services. Trade—wholesale and retail—provides another cornerstone of urban development, and in association with modernization, finance, government, and service industries have all grown enormously to provide for increasing populations and the complexities of their lives and dealings. All of these areas provide job opportunities, although the work they offer is more and more likely to be dependent on specific skills and technical training. But a city like Philadelphia, where the proportion of people who acquire an education above the minimum legal requirement is only half the national average and less than half the average of its own suburbs, is at a great disadvantage in making use of these options. Consequently there are many thousands of unemployed persons looking for work, up from 5 percent in 1970 to around 8 percent in 1982.

Where job opportunities have risen sharply in Philadelphia's suburbs during the decade of the 1970s in every field but industry, only the service area has shown a steady, if modest, rise in the city itself throughout the same period. However, some of the gloomiest forebodings about the city made by authors who assessed the situation at the time of the 1976 Bicentennial have not come to pass. Although the total number of jobs is smaller in 1980 than it was in 1970, the effects of the recession of 1974–1975 which were more drastic in Philadelphia than in the country as a whole have begun to recede. Since

1977 the decline in numbers of jobs in most fields has flattened out. With their own peculiar use of the double negative, city financial experts forecast that "negative employment growth rates in employment levels will stabilize by mid-decade."[8]

A comeback in the construction industry has contributed not only to the actual improvement, but to a psychological feeling that the pulse of the city is quickening. Nothing gives onlookers a sense of continued life within a community quite like the sight of new metal skeletons rising against the sky, the inconvenience of perilous walkways around construction sites, and traffic jams caused by slow-moving pieces of huge construction equipment blocking the narrow streets. When all of this is accompanied by flying dust and dirt and the incessant noise of jackhammers, it is clear that things must be improving! Much of the money involved in expanding construction, which doubled in 1978 over 1977 and had doubled again by 1980, went into three private office buildings in center city, the Franklintown development just north of center city and the renovation of the Bellevue-Stratford Hotel, four major hospital projects, the center-city commuter tunnel, and a variety of public improvements. Government, medical, and educational institutions accounted for about 60 percent of this revitalization; residential and commercial activity provided another 18 percent or more each; and as might be expected in view of the grim manufacturing picture, only 3 percent of the $635.5 million invested in Philadelphia construction projects represented new industrial building.

Retail business in Philadelphia suffered the most during the 1970s, sales rising only 1.2 percent from 1974 to 1980 within the city, while they increased 90 percent for the SMSA, excluding Philadelphia, during the same years. In terms of billions of dollars, area residents spent about $4 billion in the city and over three times that much—$13.7 billion—in the huge regional malls that have come to blanket the suburban area. Movement in this direction began in the late 1950s when the large department stores began to open suburban branches near newly built developments. By the 1960s the merchants and developers were no longer waiting to see where housing would be located, but were leading the way, trusting in their special mix of department stores, supermarkets, family restaurants, movie theaters, and specialty shops focused on the growing market of the baby-boom generation to attract customers from a wide area and in fact encourage the building of housing nearby. Lack of any but the most rudimentary community public spaces and activities in many of the outlying suburbs turned the suburban mall into a kind of village green where it never rained, and where people could windowshop, watch the passing parade, and admire the greenery and fountains while resting on the benches which were usually provided. In competing with each other malls also began to offer entertainments; Santa Claus and his toy village, circus acts, traveling zoos, all aimed at potential customers of every generation.[9]

In many ways the city cannot compete. It is impossible to provide the easy access and parking that help to make the suburban malls so popular, nor can

Children's Hospital of Philadelphia, Thirty-fourth Street and Civic Center Boulevard, opened 1974, designed by Harbeson, Hough, Livingston, and Larson and William J. Amenta. The building is the fourth for the hospital, which was founded in 1855.

CHILDREN'S HOSPITAL OF PHILADELPHIA

the population of Philadelphia, with its significantly lower income ranges, spend anything like the money available to suburban residents. The last decade, however, has seen a variety of efforts to promote retail business in Philadelphia, both as part of center-city revitalization by the establishment and by local merchants in one or another of the many residential neighborhoods that form almost self-contained units within the sprawling borders of the city. Two projects in particular, undertaken during the 1970s, emphasized the pitfalls and possibilities of large-scale, aggressive attempts to attract shoppers back to center city.

Chestnut Street had a long and distinguished reputation as one of the best shopping areas in the city—branches of exclusive New York stores and specialty shops in an area surrounded by offices employing suburban commuters with money to spend. As part of the overall Bicentennial planning it was decided that this carriage-trade street would make an excellent downtown mall: the roadway would be narrowed, allowing only special nonpolluting buses carrying shoppers and tourists from Ninth to Eighteenth Streets, providing easy access to the most important of Philadelphia's historic sites at one end and high-class shopping at the other. New wide brick sidewalks, trees, artistically designed lighting, and places to rest would provide the aesthetic and practical amenities for strollers. Nevertheless many of the merchants were opposed from the beginning: their businesses would suffer severe losses during the building phase, the traffic and parking problems would discourage special shopping trips by suburbanites, there was not enough nearby residential business to draw on, and office workers really shopped only from noon to 2:00 P.M., not enough time from which to make a healthy profit. Yet the city more or less forced the issue and the mall was constructed. Even before it became operational in the late 1970s many of the better establishments had fled, to be replaced by fast-food restaurants, pinball arcades, and cheap shops catering more to the blacks in easy subway or bus access than the whites in the Society Hill and Rittenhouse Square districts. A cutback in municipal services left piles of litter, and by 1980 the failure of the project was visible in dreary, deserted night scenes which encouraged crime and discouraged business. As a partial remedy for the blight it had helped cause, the city again allowed automobile traffic at night.

On the other hand the Gallery I complex, completed in 1976–1977 with a combination of city, federal, and private investment, has been a commercial success of huge proportions, with average annual sales of $230 per square foot, making it one of the most financially productive shopping malls in the country. The first major retail facility to be constructed in the center of Philadelphia since a new Strawbridge & Clothier department store was built in 1931, the Gallery was carefully planned as part of the Market Street East development, envisioned many years earlier by city planner Edmund Bacon, which included improved transportation facilities and upgrading of offices and other buildings in the area. The complex itself was developed by the Rouse Company, which had successful national experience in such ventures. At a cost of $100 million the urban mall followed the traditional pattern of its suburban predecessors—a covered space, anchored by two major department stores—the existing Strawbridge & Clothier building and a new Gimbels—and including 125 other smaller specialty shops and restaurants. The usual open spaces, greenery, and strolling areas acquired individuality and architectural interest from a multilevel design suited to he urban nature of the location.

Gallery I, Market Street at Ninth, developed by the Rouse Company, 1976.
PHILADELPHIA CITY PLANNING COMMISSION

Crowds of customers and observers lent an atmosphere of excitement and busy activity, and the businesses catered to the kinds of Philadelphia consumers who could logically be expected to shop there. Further extension of Market Street East development in the 1980s calls for the addition of a Gallery II, undertaken by the same company, and including another department store and three new office towers. This was all tied to Philadelphia's largest construction project, the underground linkage of the old Reading and Pennsylvania Railroads with a new station at Eleventh and Market Streets.

Major undertakings on the retail scene do not adequately describe the trend of Philadelphia business during the 1970s. While small ventures may not have great influence on the huge dollar figures that make up the statistical charts of general economic developments, their proliferation is characteristic of life on a more individualized, less mass-produced scale, which has emerged as a feature of the decade. Thinking "small" is part of the general breakdown

of the conception of America as a large, monolithic culture and is reflected
in the business life of Philadelphia. As of 1980 there were only twenty-two
employers in the city who provided jobs for 2000 or more workers, and of
these only sixteen were strictly in the private sector, four of them in the retail
market.[10] Instead of the growth of the giants, the 1970s saw the increase of
small stores, sometimes franchised by large corporations, but often individual
enterprises, their owners banding together in neighborhood associations to
ensure the maintenance or improvement of the environment in which they
operated.

The most elementary of the small entrepreneurs were street vendors who,
following the generations-old tradition of chestnut and pretzel sellers on
Philadelphia street corners, offered a colorful profusion of merchandise from
fresh fruit and hot dogs to hats, bags, and costume jewelry. They annoyed
established merchants by blocking the sidewalks and perhaps by furnishing
cut-rate competition without the worries of overhead. Media focus, and therefore public awareness and government response to the street vendors, peaked
in the mid-1970s. Articles in all of the newspapers and in *Philadelphia Magazine* both stimulated letters from the public and reported attempts to pass
ordinances restricting their activities, with related court actions on both sides.
Racial and class overtones surrounded the issue of the street vendors—as they
did almost every aspect of civic life in Philadelphia during the 1970s.

Small shopping areas associated with specific neighborhoods within the
city also sought to keep the local shoppers at home and to attract outsiders
as well. Those located in areas where the residents had higher income levels
or where tourists could naturally be expected to congregate were the most
successful. A strong businessmen's association, a vigorous community organization, and an excellent neighborhood newspaper in the prestigious Chestnut
Hill section, for example, swinging into action well before the 1970s, countered the threat of nearby suburban malls with the use of several strategies.
They forced through the acquisition of land for several conveniently located,
jointly owned parking lots free to those who patronized the shops; the retailers engaged in a beautification project of tree planting, building repair, and
shop-window display; and a land-use committee maintained strict control
over the type and quality of the stores moving into the community. Aided no
doubt by the fact that many of the most important Philadelphia politicians on
the local, state, and national scene lived in the immediate vicinity, Chestnut
Hill received public financial support for repairing its main street with hand-
set Belgian paving blocks. This allowed the area to maintain the old-fashioned
ambience of its original cobblestones—disintegrated finally beyond repair—
as well as to improve the quality of its roadway at a time when many sections
of the city suffered from axle-breaking potholes and other deteriorating street
problems for which funds were not forthcoming. Association events—the
Santa Claus parade, window decoration competitions, open-air sales of season's end merchandise—assumed the nature of community celebrations. The
businessmen's association aimed at a specific carriage-trade market, indicated

Maplewood Mall, Germantown, opened 1974. This neighborhood project of shops and offices was accomplished by the combined efforts of the Rizzo administration, the Redevelopment Authority, the City Planning Commission, and the Germantown Businessmen's Association.

PHILADELPHIA CITY PLANNING COMMISSION

New Market, Head House Square (Second Street), 1980. The shopping and restaurant complex combining eighteenth-century structures with contemporary architecture and graphics opened in 1975.

NEWMARKET

by the tone and placement of its ads for "the extraordinary shops of Chestnut Hill" on the local classical music radio station.

Other shopping areas such as Society Hill or the South Street Renaissance in the tourist-oriented section of center city began later and had different problems to face in identifying their markets, but have also created individualized areas of strong local character. Long-established shopping districts with distinctive personalities, including the Italian Market on South Ninth Street, the Reading Terminal Market, jewelers' row on Sansom Street, and antiques row on Pine Street, continued to prove that sheer urban size could provide an opportunity not available in the suburban malls.

III

This focus on the plans and operations of the private-business sector has an old-fashioned ring to it, for if, as one author has expressed it, the eighteenth century was characterized by "nationalist optimism and confidence in science [and the nineteenth century by] faith in commerce and industry,"[11] the twentieth century must be thought of as the time when public belief rested in the ability of governmental systems to direct and implement society's progress. In looking at the history of the period from 1968 to 1982, however, it becomes clear that this reliance on government to produce progress, and in fact faith in "progress" itself as a concept, are exactly what has disappeared. The older, progressive attitude generally assumed a continual increase of government funding for constantly improving services that would make urban living ever more civilized and humane. As a corollary this attitude also accepted government decisions and control as the most efficient, objective way to accomplish desired ends. A certain amount of dishonesty and venality was expected, although they could be counted on to stir indignation and a cry for reform. The reform itself when it came, as it did to Philadelphia in the 1950s, was intended to "clean up the mess" so that the city government and the institutions it controlled would work better.

High hopes for better transportation facilities and services were entertained, for example, when the old, private Philadelphia Transportation Company was taken over by the publicly controlled Southeastern Pennsylvania Transportation Authority (SEPTA) in 1968. Sale negotiations and attendent court battles over price had lasted for five years, and when the PTC, the largest transit company in the United States still in private hands, finally wound up its affairs on December 31, 1969, the *Bulletin* provided its obituary. In an article that expressed the feeling of the time and its reliance on government to protect the interests of the citizens at large, the *Bulletin* stated: "For years critics said [the PTC's] facilities were less than ideal because its first loyalty was to its shareholders, who wanted a profit, rather than to the public, which wanted convenient, comfortable transportation." When the city government in 1979 looked back on a decade of public control, however, it admitted that "the quality of the service on the system is . . . unacceptably low. This is manifested by buses which break down during their runs, subway stations which are dark, dank and dirty, transit cars which are noisy, uncomfortable and covered by graffiti . . . and commuter trains which are habitually behind schedule." The task facing Philadelphia in the 1980s "is to improve the quality of service on its transportation network to a level which satisfies the expectation of its citizens."[12]

Little by little in most areas of municipal management the 1970s witnessed an erosion of the long-held basic belief in the ability of public-sector technocrats, intellectuals, and politicians to cope with the massive problems of the twentieth-century city. The national failure of government credibility is often considered a legacy of the Watergate scandals, but American faith in public solutions to social problems had survived scandals before. Exposés of corruption, local or national, form the backbone of media reporting in every decade, whether the administration is billed as independently reform or politically dependent. The Vietnam War may have played a more immediate role in creating the new frame of mind: it had a measurable end, and that end was failure. Both sides, those who wanted to win and those who wanted to get out, could agree on that. Once there was a general recognition that failure was possible, that government money and government planning might be incapable of a successful solution to problems, there were plenty of problems that could be measured by the same yardstick and judged with the same result.

In Philadelphia there· was an abundance of difficulties, far beyond the power of City Hall to control, based on world economics and changing social patterns. The numbers were all bad: public assistance recipients increased from around 200,000 in 1970 to almost 340,000 in 1980, even more dramatic as a factor of the city's population—from 10 percent to 20 percent of the total; the illegitimate birth rate climbed from 21 percent of all births in 1970 to 36 percent in 1976; in 1979–1980 alone murders rose by 13 percent in Philadelphia and robberies by 8 percent, compared to national increases of 7 percent and 8 percent respectively. Even if Philadelphia's citizens did not expect the city government to solve these problems, at the beginning of the 1970s they expected it at least to make things better. Here too the established political solutions were tried and found wanting. As other urban Americans seemed to be doing, Philadelphians lowered their expectations and turned inward to seek their own answers. People took karate lessons and bought guns; private organizations formed to counsel women who had been raped and provide legal services for poor and minority citizens. Emphasis early in the decade on increased police protection in the subways was turned by 1980 to an acceptance of the Guardian Angels, a branch of a New York group of youths with no official status but a private commitment to the public cause of improving the personal safety of subway riders. Some called them vigilantes, some saw grave dangers to the political and social process in their barely regulated assumption of civic power, but the general response—including that of City Hall—seemed to be to give them a chance.

Both in physical and human geography, lines of cleavage had long existed among the citizens of Philadelphia. The myth of the melting pot and the ideal of equal opportunity had obscured these differences during the years when establishment ideologies and policies controlled city life. The differences began to surface as Americans rediscovered their ethnic roots and as shifting economic patterns within neighborhoods brought widely disparate groups into close contact. The most visible, if not the most statistically significant of these changes was "gentrification," and as with any historical development the seeds were planted well before the time in which the name was coined, or its impact felt. Foresighted upper-middle-class Philadelphians, tired of the long commute from the suburbs and eager to be closer to the cultural excitement of the city, had begun to renovate individual houses in the Society Hill area of center city in the mid-1950s. As the federal government continued its massive job of restoring the national monuments in the area, real estate values rose and the movement gathered momentum. City Hall recognized the economic potential of this revitalization, and public agencies worked with private groups to change a slum into solid tax-paying homes. The private Old Philadelphia Development Corporation sold many of the houses that were restored, but the city's Redevelopment Authority also provided property, while the City Planning Commission and the Philadelphia Historical Commission worked on overall planning and provided the historical information needed for proper restoration. By 1976, according to the Historic American Buildings Survey, a program of the National Park Service, almost 800 individual houses had been restored, 200 new houses had been built to harmonize aesthetically with other buildings in the area, and three thirty-story high-rise apartment buildings—Society Hill Towers, designed by I.M. Pei—had risen to "serve not only as focal points in Society Hill in relation to its primary historic sites and open spaces but also in relation to the rest of downtown Philadelphia and its traffic flow."[13]

When the trickle of returning "gentry" into center city became a flood, Society Hill served as a model not only for other cities but for other neighborhoods in Philadelphia as well. Those who could not afford the soaring real estate values of the already successful area (often younger people with traditional backgrounds but more bohemian lifestyles) began "gentrifying" Queen Village south of South Street, the Fairmount section near the Art Museum, and the streets around Rittenhouse Square which maintained their long-settled affluent population of apartment dwellers.

Old-style reformers and planners assumed that the economic and social goals achieved in center city met with the approval of all the city's citizens. The newly refurbished areas, however, had not for the most part been previously uninhabited. The people who had lived in them had sometimes been there for decades and had established close-knit relationships. They formed enclaves, small and large, of working-class ethnics—Irish, Polish, German, Italian, Russian, Lithuanian, Greek, and a host of others—inhabiting an intricate mosaic of neighborhoods which had always seemed secure because largely ignored, except at election time. They were extremely resentful of being forced out by "improvements" like expressways and institutional expansions, or by real estate values they could no longer afford. They were as suspicious of newcomers as any rural village inhabitants, and were far from willing to consider the abstract good of Philadelphia as a fair exchange for their long-established communities.[14] Intellectuals disenchanted with the failure of establishment goals and programs, and sensitive to what they saw essentially as a class struggle between the power structure and working people, lent support to "the articulation of the values of neighborhood, community or parish as essential to the arguments against certain forms of 'outside' intervention."[15] In truth the problem did not belong to white ethnic groups alone; black neighborhoods were dislocated by the same factors of gentrification and institutional expansion of the city's hospitals and universities.

The disaffected Philadelphia residents, both black and white, were also confronted by a threat to their communities that was far more frightening. It was unfortunate to be forced to take a profit on one's property, if one really wanted to remain where one was. For working-class people, however, destruction of the value of one's home, often representing a family's whole capital investment, was disastrous. This was the prospect that faced many Philadelphia neighborhoods as large numbers of immigrants—blacks from the South, Puerto Ricans, and other Spanish-speaking newcomers, Asian refugees—arrived in the 1950s and 1960s. Most of the immigrants were of economic and cultural milieux as foreign to Philadelphia blacks as they were to the white ethnic communities, and black residents fought their intrusion with the same sentiments and for the same reasons that white inhabitants complained, sold out, and left.

Dispassionate analysis might show that the conflict was really one in which lower-middle-class neighborhoods, black and white, were being squeezed from both above and below, but the lines of the battle—and a real battle it became during the 1970s—were drawn on the basis of race. A simplistic viewpoint among white Philadelphians failed to distinguish the varieties of black communities, forcing blacks to define themselves by race foremost and ignoring or suppressing cultural differences among blacks. Once this was simply seen as a black/white issue, strange combinations of unlikely allies and even stranger combinations of incompatible goals controlled the political life of Philadelphia throughout the 1970s. Among other things the white liberal establishment was left without a power base.

Many militant groups operated outside the formal political process entirely. Domination of Philadelphia by the Democratic party had become almost total, and within the party the machine excluded much of the old liberal/black coalition on which its strength was formerly based, as well as the smaller interest groups that had begun to characterize Philadelphia political life.[16] As in the rest of the country, participation in the political process as measured by registration and voting statistics declined continuously, although other avenues for political expression and action multiplied. Using the local media, which are always hungry for controversial local news to spice up front pages and broadcast time, special interest groups for civic causes, labor and business organizations, and social issues can engage in confrontational activities and make provocative statements to rally the public and effect municipal action. Most of these groups, most of their ideologies, are not powerful enough to create policy, but they do have the strength, in the face of a government without a strong set of positive goals and objectives of its own, to stop things from happening—government by veto, it might be called. This is particularly true when money is as extremely tight as it had become in the 1970s, when easy federal and state assistance was no longer forthcoming and when City Hall had to order and choose among its priorities rather than create a shopping list as it could in more expansive economic conditions.

Black exercise of political voting power, vocal and determined during the 1960s, achieved a limited success. It was reflected in city hiring policies and in moneys (often acquired from special project funds of the federal government) for setting up new authorities to deal with special problems like housing and neighborhood medical facilities. There was even an attempt to make the outside Police Review Board an effective agent against police abuse of citizens, widely admitted to be racially motivated. In 1958 Mayor Dilworth had created the board to "consider citizens' complaints against the police when the charge involved brutality, false arrest, discrimination based upon race, religion, or national origin, or other wrongful conduct of police personnel toward citizens."[17] Throughout the following decade the board limped along, underfunded and underpublicized, facing constant opposition from the Fraternal Order of Police. After years of litigation, a final decision upholding the board was issued by the Supreme Court during Mayor Tate's administration, but by then the political climate of Philadelphia as well as of the country at large had changed considerably, and the mayor decided not to reactivate the board. While citizens' suits against the Police Department succeeded in the earlier 1970s, these were reversed by the Supreme Court, and the attempts by various civic organizations during the decade to force reform of the department from within met with little success until the advent of Mayor William J. Green's administration in 1980. For the most part citizen complaints against the police, when plotted on the map of Philadelphia, overlay almost exactly the map of racial distribution in the city.

I V

The disruptive and occasionally violent nature of black protest during the activist years of the 1960s produced an equally strong white response. Fear of crime—usually defined as black—united many ethnic groups, often across traditional class and party lines. In this context Frank L. Rizzo was elected mayor in 1971 and again in 1975. As police commissioner during the tumultuous years of the 1960s Rizzo had received much of the credit for "keeping the lid on," so that Philadelphia avoided the worst of the violence that had broken out in other cities like Los Angeles and Washington. Rizzo was also antipathetic to young radicals, white as well as black, homosexuals, and other nonconformists, as were white traditionalists including both bankers and labor leaders.

In a total reversal of the ideals that had directed city policy since the early 1950s, government was regarded by Rizzo and his supporters primarily as an institution for providing citizens with protection and only secondarily as an instrument for the delivery of social services. While close attention was paid to the maintenance of the police and fire departments during the 1970s, limited funds and escalating municipal union demands caused personnel to be sharply reduced in other areas of city administration—up to 50 percent in some cases —in the Departments of Welfare and Recreation, the Fairmount Park Commission, the City Planning Commission, the Committee on Human Relations, the Free Library, and the Streets Department. Street cleaning stopped on a regular basis in 1975, as did much road repair. Instead of maintaining the roads, the city tried to shift the responsibility by erecting signs advising residents "This is a STATE HIGHWAY. For repairs call 255-1415."[18] The state, however, had enough troubles of its own, and the result was an almost shocking deterioration of Philadelphia's street system. On the other hand the Rizzo administration was generally good to cultural institutions; for the first time the Library Company, the Historical Society, and other such groups received a city grant.

Visible decay in the material environment during the decade did nothing to improve the "quality of life" in Philadelphia, and contributed to an atmosphere in which the human environment exhibited less of civility, more shrill rhetoric and physical self-expression. Rizzo's frequent outspoken comments, voicing sentiments previously unthinkable among responsible government officials, couched in imagery of physical intimidation, set a tone for many of the actions and reactions that dominated Philadelphia life in the 1970s. While the mayor's methods and style offended and repelled many liberals and intellectuals, they had great appeal to others as a kind of populism of the urban North.

The events of the Philadelphia controversy over the radical black cult known as MOVE, which played out its tragic dénouement in the 1970s, formed merely one, though probably the best publicized, of the many acts in this drama. MOVE had begun in 1972 as the Community Action Movement, an antiurban, back-to-nature group which espoused the goal of African lifestyle and expressed hostility toward modern technology and research. All of its members, even those few who were white, adopted the surname "Africa." They were obtrusive not only in their vocal objections to all established authority but also in their manner of living "in harmony with nature." Many of their neighbors, both black and white, saw MOVE's rejection of normal standards of living as promoting rats, filth, disease, child neglect, and neighborhood deterioration. Verbal abuse, physical intimidation, and rumors of a weapons arsenal at the MOVE headquarters on Thirty-third Street in the Powelton section of West Philadelphia increased the atmosphere of tension and anxiety. From an escalation of jailings of MOVE members, hunger strikes, weapons collections, neighborhood protests, eviction notices, and police surveillance, to the storming and destruction of the MOVE headquarters and the death of a police officer in 1978, the crisis was covered by a press that took sides pro and con along with the public and the city administration. The almost anticlimactic final act, including both the trials of MOVE members for murder and the investigation of the police involved, illustrated the climate of the end of the 1970s, much as the birth of MOVE had been indicative of the decade's beginning.

For many who lived in Philadelphia during the 1970s, their mental image of the decade will always be fixed by television scenes of angry people waving picket signs, shouting epithets at each other, and even engaging in physical combat. A strong state law prohibiting strikes by public employees, which had been passed in 1947, was liberalized in 1970 and set the stage for many of the disturbances that followed. With increasing regularity throughout the decade municipal employees, particularly teachers and transportation workers, sought to improve their benefits in the face of rising inflation, from municipal budgets teetering on the edge of bankruptcy. City services were frequently paralyzed. Huge protest rallies around City Hall held by supporters of these special-interest groups created that new 1970s phenomenon, "grid lock" traffic on center-city streets. Shouting matches became fist fights on the floor of the city Council, and civility declined another notch. Ordinary citizens also engaged in fights and rock-and bottle-throwing melees about equally directed at the police and at each other, often with racial overtones. Those occasions that were serious enough to be designated "riots" usually began at some small personal level and lacked the ideological content of the protests and demonstrations of the 1960s.

Mayor Frank L. Rizzo, parade on Chestnut Street below Sixth (1976). A corner of the Rohm and Haas Building, completed in 1964, appears at the right.

PHILADELPHIA DEPARTMENT OF RECORDS, ARCHIVES DIVISION

Frank Rizzo, as mayor of Philadelphia, a troubled city in a troubled time, did not inspire neutral or objective response. His strong, partisan feelings and his expressions of them provoked unreasoned loyalty on one side, violent opposition on the other. The loyalty triumphed over scandals, increased taxes, lie-detector tests, and national derision, and elected him to a second term. The opposition used lawsuits, the press, and intraparty warfare in its attempt to loosen his control. In the spring and summer of 1976 a petition to recall the mayor was circulated under provisions of the Home Rule Charter. While more than the required 145,448 signatures (25 percent of the votes cast in the previous mayorality election) were collected, technical political maneuvering through the courts prevented the vote from taking place. When Rizzo decided to run a third time in 1979 it was necessary to change the Home Rule Charter, which limited the mayor to two consecutive terms. The battle was fought ostensibly on ideological grounds, "charter reform" against "no change," but the hidden agenda was whether or not Rizzo would be reelected, for there were few who doubted that this would be the result of a change in the rule. The change in the charter was in fact defeated by a majority of two to one. In the ensuing 1979 election campaign William J. Green, Jr., became the Democratic nominee and therefore inevitably mayor of Philadelphia. The election left unanswered, however, the question of whether the voters had responded to the stated or hidden agenda. Were they rejecting Frank Rizzo and signaling the end of a political phenomenon of the 1970s? Or were they making a statement that belief in government tradition was still strong, and the machinery was not to be tampered with for the sake of a single election or a single individual?

V

The 1970s was not merely the decade of race awareness, Rizzo, and gentrification. It was also, in Philadelphia, as in the nation at large, the decade of the 200th birthday of the United States. The life and death of Philadelphia's Bicentennial celebration illustrate in a neatly self-contained form the way in which municipal paralysis could develop in a city where sharp factions indulged in government by veto.[19]

Mindful of the problems encountered by the great Centennial Exhibition of 1876 because planning began only four years before the event, and noting that the National Park Service had been restoring the Independence National Historic Park since 1951, a group of citizens had formed the Bicentennial Celebration Committee as early as 1964. In December of 1965 Mayor Tate appointed a committee of nineteen "representative citizens" to study and evaluate their plans. The group included some of the best known names in Philadelphia, leaders of business and industry and publishers of the major newspapers, all men at the height of their careers and known for participation in civic affairs. Ethnicity and race were represented by the president of the Italian American Cultural Society and by a black judge of the United States District Court. The committee was to make the decision on how the 200th birthday of the country was to be celebrated, but in so doing it was expected to "invite expressions from the community as to the kind of observance it would be most appropriate for Philadelphia to undertake and provide a forum for interested citizens and organizations to present their views."[20]

A year and a half later the group was reorganized as the 1976 Bicentennial Corporation. While some of the original members were still involved, there also were more City Hall people included: the executive director of the City Planning Commission, the president of the city Council, the mayor, the city finance director, the city representative and director of commerce, along with representatives of the Old Philadelphia Development Corporation and the Philadelphia Industrial Development Corporation, and the international representative of the United Steel Workers of America. Although the chairman announced boldly that Philadelphia would absolutely have a celebration in 1976 to mark the 200th anniversary of the nation's independence, it was clear that no agreement could be reached on the form of the celebration. Some clung to the traditional major exposition and world's fair located on a single site, but others favored instead a series of celebrations and conventions. By August 1967, $135,000 of the city's money had already been spent with no particular results.

In true 1960s fashion a "counter group" of prominent Young Philadelphians, as they were called, proposed that the fair grounds be built over the Thirtieth Street Station at a cost of $1.2 billion, the permanent structure to pay for itself eventually in taxes. Membership in this group was both larger and more diverse than the city-backed corporation, and it tended to reflect the rising ambitious establishment of the future: its lawyers and businessmen were still forging their careers; its government people were middle echelon, and more of them were involved in the delivery of human services; its news people included the broadcast media; and there were members of the arts and design communities, of the universities, and even a psychiatrist. The Young Philadelphians suggested use of the theme "The Permanent Revolution," while other, more local or narrowly defined, groups entered the controversy, presenting plans to involve the whole city and turn it into a vast renewal project. All the ideas were expensive, based on the expectation that the Congress would agree that the national birthday should be celebrated in Philadelphia where it had all started, and that therefore most of the needed development money would be federal. If their backers had reread the history of the Centennial perhaps they would have known better. Boston too had competed in Washington for the right to the Bicentennial, but prudently withdrew in mid-1969 when it became obvious that the idea (as well as the money) would be sunk in the morass of national politics. Philadelphia continued to chase the elusive pot of national gold until 1972 when the Nixon administration decided against a single-site celebration and adopted a scattered-site plan. Philadelphia's eventual share of the federal funds was a modest $50 million.

The problem was of course ideological as well as functional. The late 1960s were a bad time nationally and locally to plan expensive panegyrics to the

American dream. Leaders of the "new" black community threatened to disrupt the plans if they were not given jobs in the organization: black membership on the board of the Bicentennial Corporation rose to six, including three blacks and one Puerto Rican who were regarded as activists, but the corporation had hired no black staff members. Nor was this the only dispute that arose to indicate minority disaffection with establishment goals. The corporation was called "lily white" and a "bigot organization" by the citywide Black Community Council, while other black activists questioned the propriety of holding a national birthday before tackling such problems as education and housing. A city Council member of Polish background accused the corporation of excluding Polish-American activists. Since another member of the Polish community was in fact a member of the corporation, this complaint accented the complex divisions between local community leaders and accepted members of the political structure.

In the ensuing years plan after plan was expensively plotted and discarded, the idea of Thirtieth Street Station or Fairmount Park returning every now and then like a symphonic refrain. State, county, and municipal governments dragged their feet about contributing funds until they were sure that the federal government was going to come through. Businessmen worried that they would get stuck with the bill, and community action leaders continued to object to spending money on window dressing while the city rotted away underneath. By the time the newly elected mayor, Frank Rizzo, reorganized the planning and implementation unit in its final form as Philadelphia '76, $3 million had already been spent and, as an editorial in the *Daily News* put it, "The price of baloney comes high. . . . Philadelphians are weary of Bicen [*sic*] talk (and bills) and no specifics. . . . This, remember, is a city that doesn't have enough money to keep its kids in school. If the Bicen planners expect to survive, we suggest that they come up with something more than high-sounding phrases."[21]

Much of the facelifting, however, while billed as part of the Bicentennial, was actually done with funds slated for general improvements to Philadelphia without reference to the celebration. They became part of the plan because their completion coincided with the dates of the celebration. They included the final five-year, $30-million stage of the restoration of Independence National Historic Park by the federal government, including Franklin Court, the Liberty Bell pavilion, the Visitor's Center, the restored First and Second Banks of the United States, and the Old City Tavern; the Art Museum with $8 million in new improvements; and the Penn's Landing area from Market

---

OVERLEAF: *Aerial view of Penn's Landing and Route I-95 (Skyphotos, 1981). Society Hill Towers rise at the left near Dock Street which covers Dock Creek where, traditionally, William Penn disembarked at the Blue Anchor Tavern (Front Street at Dock Creek) in October 1682.*

PHILADELPHIA CITY PLANNING COMMISSION

to South Streets along the Delaware River, where $12 million in public improvements provided a walkway along the river, a boat basin to serve as a home for historic ships, and a landscaped "world sculpture garden."

Municipal projects expressly undertaken for the Bicentennial reflected the ideology of the 1970s both in their conception and in their eventual failure to attract popular support. All were oriented toward the "people" approach to the American experience, in sharp contrast to the 1876 Centennial with its stress on technology and nationalism, its explicit faith in progress. The Living History Center, a huge modern building on Independence Mall, was designed to serve as a museum of contemporary Philadelphia and as the centerpiece of the city's Bicentennial effort. An impressive, highly professional film costing over $2 million was produced to tell the Philadelphia story, and was shown in the central space of the center on a giant 100-foot screen at regular intervals daily, but a lack of other exhibits or attractions left the Living History Center without any public appeal. It closed soon after the Bicentennial and the building became an enormous white elephant, feeding on the city budget until it was sold to the educational television station, Channel 12, and its sister radio outlet, WUHY. The "Design for Fun" exhibit at the Civic Center was never intended for permanence despite its $2-million price tag, but it accurately reflected a 1970s approach to life, with its focus on the average American's pursuit of leisure. The other two municipal endeavors were indicative of the deep split that weakened Philadelphia from top to bottom. One was a Black History Museum (later the Afro-American Historical and Cultural Center) and the other was a Mummers' Museum, honoring one of the oldest, best known attractions in Philadelphia—the New Year's Day Mummers Parade—but seen by many citizens as a bastion of white exclusiveness, partly because participants were almost exclusively white and also because of the heated controversy that had arisen in 1964 over the use of blackface in the parade.

In the end the planners created what they called a "scaled-down" celebration. The director of Philadelphia '76, political survivor William L. Rafsky, wanted to "give the city the appearance of being exciting—of being a city of fun." Critics expressed reaction to the plans in a much less flattering way: "what Dilworth envisioned as a monument to the twentieth century renaissance, Frank Rizzo has reduced to a giant ward picnic."[22] Ward picnic or not, Philadelphia '76 presented the city as a performance. The emphasis was on entertainment, with many different parts of the city serving as a backdrop. The summer before the celebration actually took place a kind of dress rehearsal for "the big bash" was held along the Benjamin Franklin Parkway. It was for this Philadelphia Festival '75 that the colorful banners of the nations of the world were first raised along the Parkway. There were an Art Caravan, ethnic foods, a children's amusement park, the sounds of music from "Bach to bluegrass," open-air dancing and theater. Much of the activity was sponsored by the cultural institutions that border the Parkway, but Bicentennial '76 cooperated with the Greater Philadelphia Cultural Alliance and firmly established the idea of entertainment as the key to success.

Liberty Bell Pavilion, Independence Mall. The bell was moved from the hall to the mall on January 1, 1976.

INDEPENDENCE NATIONAL HISTORICAL PARK COLLECTION

The events of the Bicentennial Year began at midnight on New Year's Eve with a formal ceremony in which the Liberty Bell was moved out of Independence Hall to its new home on the Mall. January 1 saw a balloon ascension from the square, as well as the traditional Mummers' Parade which featured a Bicentennial theme. Throughout the rest of the year, every week, almost every day had its special event, and the patriotic motif was visually extended to the smallest details; even many fire hydrants were painted red, white, and blue. The celebration itself drew mixed reviews. The usual charges of corruption, favoritism, and ineptitude were leveled at Bicentennial '76. There were fears about the inadequacy of facilities—hotel space, public toilets, parking, and transportation—for the twenty million expected tourists. When fewer than half that number actually visited the city, there were complaints, often from the same sources, that money had been wasted on overpreparation. Some of the entertainments, such as the play *1776* presented every night in a huge tent on Independence Mall, were poorly attended and lost money or closed early. Others, like big-band concerts on the Art Museum steps, were highly successful and were extended. Despite a tragic conclusion to the summer in the outbreak of "Legionnaires' Disease" among visiting American Legion conventioneers, the *Inquirer*, looking back a year later, judged the Bicentennial a success. It noted, "much of that spirit is alive and well today ... in ways and manners which may not have been invented by the Bicentennial experience, but which gained confidence through it. The city looks better, it feels better to walk its streets."[23]

One permanent legacy of the Bicentennial does indeed seem to be an improved image and atmosphere in the city. The cultural institutions and private businesses of Philadelphia have continued to stress public entertainment and activity. Since the Bicentennial the list of public events taking place around the city has grown longer and longer and reflects the diversity of Philadelphia's neighborhoods and its people. There have been Polish fairs, Lithuanian days, German dances, and a street fair and parade put on by the South Street Renaissance. In Society Hill the old Second Street market shelters a flea market on weekend days during the summer, while classical music groups (many of the players students from one of the music academies in Philadelphia) entertain on the sidewalk just beyond, as do mimes and musicians. Other concerts take place regularly at Penn's Landing. The restaurant renaissance that began in the early 1970s as a response to gentrification has continued to boom, giving Philadelphia a new reputation as a good place to dine out. On Olde City Day each of the eateries of the Front and Chestnut Streets area sets up a table on the sidewalk and offers its wares to passersby. Super Sunday, an annual one-day festival on the Parkway, continues to attract huge crowds annually, and to publicize the cultural institutions that sponsor it.

The new image of Philadelphia had made an even greater impression beyond the local area. The august *New York Times* devoted a lead article in its Sunday Travel Section to the fun that could be had where once it was only pretzels, the Liberty Bell, and rolled-up sidewalks.[24] The steps of the Art Museum have become a strong visual image of Philadelphia for the whole country through a climactic scene in the internationally popular moving picture *Rocky*, as have City Hall, the Italian Market, and the distinctive quality of the red-brick row houses. Since nothing succeeds like success, winning (or almost-winning) sports teams have led to a new phrase—the "City of Champions": the Philadelphia Flyers, led by center Bobby Clarke and goalie Bernie Parent, won the National Hockey League's Stanley Cup—the first expansion team to do so—in 1974 and 1975; the Phillies, after winning the National League Eastern Division championships in 1976, 1977, and 1978, at last captured their third league pennant and their first World Series championship in 1980 on the strong left arm of pitcher Steve Carlton and the home-run power— and all-around skills—of perhaps the best baseball player of his era, Mike Schmidt.

No quantity of cultural bandaids can cure the very real problems that

Super Sunday at the Eakins Oval at the Art Museum end of the Benjamin Franklin Parkway (September 9, 1980).

PHILADELPHIA BULLETIN

Phillies Fans celebrate the 1980 World Series victory.

PHILADELPHIA PHILLIES

Philadelphia faces in 1980. These are endemic to the nation, to the Northeast, and to large urban complexes, and may be insoluble. Certainly they are beyond the power of a single municipality to solve by itself. Within that framework it remains to be seen if the trends of the 1970s toward suspicion and division will continue on the local scene or whether the 1980s will foster a new spirit of consensus and reform, as the difficult days ahead make Philadelphians conscious of the truth in the saying of Benjamin Franklin, famous resident of earlier times: "Surely, if we do not hang together, we shall all hang separately."

Epilogue

by Edwin Wolf 2nd

It was to be a city ecologically—William Penn knew not the word —perfect, free in a libertarian seventeenth-century sense and all-welcoming before the Statue of Liberty beckoned the oppressed. Philadelphia was at one time or another all and none of those things. Like the patterns of a kaleidoscope the civic fluxes and refluxes changed as movements of social, economic, and political forces pulsed over a period of 300 years.

There is no history of a city. There are many histories, each valid in its way, many localized in time or space, some sectarian by race, creed, or color, others biased as they present groups or concepts in a favorable or unfavorable light, a few more modern ones gaunt with charts and figures. Each has its contribution to make to a mainstream. The synthesis, the ultimate appraisal, cannot be the product of those fettered by time, place, and personalities. The Roman Empire had long come to an end before Edward Gibbon was able to anatomize and then recreate its latter years. Boswell did not publish his biography of Dr. Johnson until the subject of it was dead.

In 1876 the *North American* wrote: "Of all parts of the country least given to radicalism, and sure always to be found safe, prudent, moderate, and what is known in England as liberal conservative," that was Philadelphia. When the president of the United States, pained by the blow of an assassin's bullet, is reported to have said "All in all, I'd rather be in Philadelphia," one wonders if this is not a summation of Philadelphia history. He was mimicking the one-liner of the red-nosed comic W. C. Fields, who used Quaker-gray, quiet Philadelphia as a target for jests. On the other hand President Reagan, a onetime liberal and trade unionist, may subconsciously have yearned for that liberal conservatism.

From its origins as the keystone of William Penn's Holy Experiment the city has reflected his and then its own duality. The proprietor planned and hoped for all the good things that his eulogists have claimed for it: a fertile land, a "greene Country Towne," self-supporting in food and trade, peaceful, tolerant, prosperous, a haven for Quakers seeking an unimpeded right to dissidence and for members of any other sect that wanted to settle. But Penn also planned and hoped to profit financially from his huge real estate promotion. This was not to be. It may have been the dichotomy of trying to be at one time an idealist and a landlord that, triggered by the treachery of his agent, Philip Ford, drove Penn in his last years to mental instability. It was his own Quakers who created the political turmoil that was Philadelphia and Pennsylvania during his lifetime—and for many years thereafter. They—early on, David Lloyd *primus inter pares*—flourishing, tasting their rights and privileges and with one foot in the countinghouse, wanted more of everything.

Cresheim Bridge at Devil's Pool, Wissahickon Creek, Fairmount Park (photograph by Al Strobl, c. 1975).

PHILADELPHIA CITY PLANNING COMMISSION

I

The *rus versus urbem* syndrome, one of the major negative influences on Philadelphia, existed from the time restless pioneers moved north and west and, contrary to the treaties with the Indians, settled. The march on Philadelphia from Lancaster in 1764 by the Paxton Boys who had, as a kind of reflex action, massacred some peaceful Indians, was only one of the early expressions of hostility. There was a Whiskey Rebellion in western Pennsylvania against a federal tax, but there was no rebellion, as in Massachusetts, by farmers against mortgage holders. Nonetheless there was the same suspicion of the money man, the banker. In 1791–1792 Pennsylvania had only one United States senator, Robert Morris. A 1792 satirical broadside *Dialogue* had a Citizen and a Farmer look at that anomaly: "We have but one senator," stated the Citizen, "but he alone, unembarrassed by any companion, is equal to many. Fully informed on every subject of commerce, versed in every system of funding, banking, brokerage, and stockjobbing, the concerns of the city are safely lodged in his hands." That was just what the Farmer feared as he set forth what was to become the Jeffersonian doctrine of agrarianism. It was fear of the influence of money, the seductive charms of a metropolis, the corruption of luxury, and—always, it seems, repetitively—the banks that led the southern planters to force the move of the national capital to the isolation of a muddy District of Columbia. So too did the country folk move the capital of Pennsylvania first to Lancaster and then to Harrisburg. These were psychic shocks which, following hard on the heels of several yellow fever epidemics, shook the city's urban confidence.

No study of Philadelphia can explain itself without a backward look over the shoulder at the upcountry hostility against the stereotype of the city slicker. When Joseph Ritner was running for governor in 1838, he had a campaign portrait print made showing himself in shirtsleeves, hand on plow, and top hat lying by a stump. At the convention that wrote the state constitution of 1838 Thaddeus Stevens referred to Philadelphia as "a great and growing ulcer on the body politic."

In the century from 1820 to 1920 only four Philadelphians were elected governor, and of those only Edwin S. Stuart was a native of the city. From 1808 to 1883 no Philadelphian won the governorship. In the century from 1820 to 1920 only two Philadelphians served in the United States Senate, George M. Dallas in 1831 and Boies Penrose for the first time in 1897. A rise in Philadelphia's political power occurred when the state's Republican machine allied itself with the city's bosses, and first Matthew Quay and then Penrose held the reins. Over the years urban needs were often blocked until concessions were offered to rural legislators. Highways were built where there was little traffic as Philadelphia's transport was starved. A minority dominated a commonwealth which thereby belied its literal meaning: it was not government for the common weal.

More recently with the growth of suburbia in the counties surrounding the city there has been fear on the part of the suburbanites that blacks, who account for just under 40 percent of the population of the city proper, would begin to emigrate to houses with trees and lawns in Delaware and Montgomery Counties. There was fear that the problems of the city, notably crime, would be exported. In a study recently made of the cultural and recreational resources and organizations of Philadelphia, it was noted that one of the factors inhibiting greater use of facilities was suburban parents' almost unreasoned concern about crime on buses and on the streets. The suburbs, let it be said, without great success have tried to build a wall to keep out all baleful elements while at the same time enjoying the benefits of a mature urban culture. The Southeastern Pennsylvania Transportation Authority (SEPTA) which runs the area's buses, subways, and commuter railroads has been hamstrung for much of its existence by the uneasiness on the part of the counties served that they might do something to the city's advantage. Funds for education coming from the state are voted only after a political *quid pro quo* for the rural legislators. Speaking of the block grants to be transferred to the state by President Reagan's program and the chance for Philadelphia to get a fair share, an editorial in the Philadelphia *Inquirer* asked if history provided "much ground for expecting that anti-urban legislators in Harrisburg, for example, will go out of their way to help Philadelphia and Pittsburgh solve their special fiscal, educational and social problems."

I I

Although intrastate conflict was one factor that affected the social and political health of the city, economic change was even more important and far more deleterious. In good King George's glorious days, before he was thought to have been seduced into illiberalism by wicked ministers, Philadelphia enjoyed all the benefits of flourishing mercantilism. Its backcountry supplied the natural produce—wheat, lumber, and meat—that went in its ships to the West Indies, England, and the Continent. The warehouses in return received oranges, lemons, wine, and manufactured goods that the colonies did not grow or make. When the almost interminable European wars did not severely restrict trade, Philadelphia merchants made good money. Skilled artificers chased silver, carved furniture, built elegant mansions, brewed excellent beer, constructed sturdy ships, printed books, and created for themselves a comfortable way of life. Benjamin Franklin was the epitome of the successful craftsman who, having gained his competence, devoted the rest of his life to the acquisition and propagation of useful knowledge—and to political action. At a lower economic level were the unskilled laborers—sailors, longshoremen, hostlers at inns, domestic servants, and farmhands—some indentured servants, a number of black slaves and some black freemen, and most poor Irish, Scots-Irish, English, and German immigrants. They found it better to be poor in America than in Europe. When times were good they made a living; in bad times they suffered. There was much home industry, stocking making in Germantown and linen weaving throughout the city. Families lived above their stores, and during most times before the Revolution there were ample and varied goods for the inhabitants to buy.

There were of course ups and downs in the economy. A glut of imported goods at the close of the French and Indian War, the massive interruption to regular trade caused by the Revolution, the yellow fever epidemics of 1793, 1798, and 1799, problems with the warring European powers at the turn of the century, Jefferson's embargo and then the War of 1812—all impeded the normal course of sea-borne commerce. Some men, outstandingly Stephen Girard, did well in the China and East Indian trade. Contrary to the bias of New England historiography, Philadelphia ships were frequent visitors to Canton and Calcutta in considerable numbers. There was a period after the Peace of Aix-la-Chapelle in 1814 when locally owned vessels plied the seas to take on cargoes of lemons in Italy, opium in Turkey (the port of Smyrna was dominated by ships from the Delaware River), hides in South America, and tea and blue-and-white tableware in China. To many, with Nicholas Biddle's second Bank of the United States controlling credit and currency with an even hand, the golden future seemed to stretch far ahead, even though New York had surpassed the city as a shipping center.

Yet there were some who saw the future at home and on a developing American continent. The waterpower that had made profitable the clusters of mills along rushing streams and creeks in Frankford, Bridesburg, Kensington, Darby, Germantown, Chestnut Hill, and Cheltenham was being replaced by steam. Oliver Evans at his Mars Iron Works was making high-pressure steam engines, the beginning of Philadelphia's more than a century of fame as the builder of machines and tools of all kinds. To fuel the steampower plants and the foundries in the 1820s coal began to be brought down the city's two rivers by way of an ingenious series of canals.

Coal, iron, steel, machinery, and railroads combined to create an economic upsurge in Philadelphia that lasted roughly for a century from the mid-1830s. The Philadelphia and Columbia Railroad reaching out westward was the harbinger of the Pennsylvania Railroad system which, in competition with the New York Central to the north and the Baltimore and Ohio to the south, emerged as the largest and richest railroad system in the world. The "Pennsy" became an integral part of Philadelphia's life. Along the Main Line on its way to Pittsburgh and beyond, officers of the company and promoters built stations to serve the luxurious country houses that soon became the chief residences of the leaders of industry. To the north and northwest the competing Reading Railroad, which owed its success to its fingers of steel rails in the coal country, countered with suburban stations to Chestnut Hill and Ogontz.

John Fitch's steamboat which chugged up the Delaware in 1786, the waterworks established in Centre Square at the end of the eighteenth century and developed into the best water system in the nation in 1822 with its pumps at Fairmount, Oliver Evans's amphibious steam dredge of 1804, the successful 340-foot single-span Fairmount Bridge, and the ships that slipped down the ways from yards on the Delaware were examples of mechanical and engineering aptitude that culminated in Philadelphia's sobriquet "Arsenal of Democracy" at the time of World War I. In the mid-nineteenth century Joseph Harrison's locomotives helped bring Russia into the railroad age. In 1917 the Baldwin Locomotive Works manufactured first-generation tanks, huge artillery pieces and shells, and from Cramp's shipyard and the federal Navy Yard fighting ships and merchant ships flowed at a rate that astonished the world. In World War II, in a diminished degree but still impressively, Philadelphia turned out war matériel from the Frankford Arsenal and a host of factories. Gradually high labor costs and antiquated equipment squeezed most of the city's heavy industries out of existence. When the Navy Yard got the job of rehabilitating the U.S.S. *Saratoga* in 1981 there was vast rejoicing, but on the dark side the future of Sun Shipbuilding a little down the Delaware was uncertain.

The change in the city's economy over the years has been one of the disappearance of primacy in many fields, the out-migration of industries and the takeover of local businesses by national corporations with headquarters and loyalties elsewhere. Once upon a time Benjamin Franklin's *Pennsylvania Gazette* had the largest circulation in the British colonies. The publishing firm of Carey and Lea in the third and fourth decade of the nineteenth century was the nation's largest. *Godey's Lady's Book,* founded in 1830, set a new circulation record for a monthly periodical, and almost a century later the Curtis Publishing empire with its *Saturday Evening Post* and *Ladies Home Journal* dominated the magazine world. Today J. B. Lippincott and Company, the last survivor of Philadelphia's major general publishing houses, is part of New York's Harper & Row.

Employing many more people than found jobs in printing and publishing was the textile industry—woolen and worsted cloth, carpets, lace, and stockings. But almost all of Philadelphia's soft-goods industries, a considerable number of clothing manufactories excepted, gradually moved to the South in the twentieth century to take advantage of cheap nonunion labor. As a result of the National Recovery Act of the Depression union membership blossomed; Philadelphia became a union town. Strikes for ever-higher wages to keep abreast of or ahead of inflation have closed schools, halted buses and subway trains, forced hospitals to carry on with supervisory staff, and prevented the delivery of newspapers. The building trades unions and the one representing municipal workers have exerted impressive political muscle in recent years. There are some who see the high price of labor as the cause of the financial problems of the public schools, the near insolvency of the commuter railroads, the exodus of heavy and other labor-intensive industries, and the malaise of municipal finances.

Yet the economic problems cannot be attributed solely or perhaps even to a major extent to the demands of labor. While Arco still plays a major role in the city's life, when Atlantic Refining merged with Richfield Oil the headquarters of the company was moved to Los Angeles. All the newspapers became parts of national corporations controlled elsewhere: the successful Philadelphia *Inquirer* and *Daily News* of the Knight-Ridder chain, and the recently failed *Bulletin* of the Charter Corporation. N. W. Ayer, once the city's largest advertising agency, decamped to New York. Even so traditionally a Philadelphia banking and brokerage firm as Drexel is now one branch of New York's Drexel Burnham Lambert. In order to escape urban problems and municipal taxes a number of large companies have moved their main offices to or established themselves in the suburbs: Sun Oil Company and

Triangle Publications to Radnor, television Channel 10 and a host of other businesses just across the city line in Bala-Cynwyd, and scores of large and small light industries along the Pennsylvania Turnpike at Valley Forge and Fort Washington.

All is not gloom and doom. The service industries and light, computer-based businesses in and around the city are doing well. Arco Chemical is a major factor in the economy, as are the oil refineries down the river on both sides of the Delaware. The banks—but, as nationally, not the savings banks —and insurance companies in the main are doing well. And that field with the greatest promise, medicine and collateral medical sciences, with hospitals, medical schools, and pharmaceutical houses clustered in the area, flourishes. Philadelphia's history as a medical center began with the Almshouse which after a good many transformations became the now-defunct Philadelphia General Hospital. The other early facilities, outstandingly the Pennsylvania Hospital and the medical school of the University of Pennsylvania—the first in the country—continued to make their contributions to the medical health of the city and an international community of scientists. Thomas Jefferson University and its hospital rank with the best in the world. The University City Science Center, growing almost from month to month, draws upon the technical know-how of its academic sponsors to offer research facilities and personnel to a variety of enterprises. It has been a long time since the city's ego was, paradoxically, inflated by the international reputation of Dr. Benjamin Rush and traumatized by a series of late-eighteenth-century yellow fever epidemics. Of all trades and professions, it has been Philadelphia doctors who have gained the greatest acclaim throughout the world.

III

Most of the men who managed large businesses or made their reputations practicing law or medicine have been satisfied to exert their influence behind the scenes, and emphatically after the Civil War era the socially elect chose not to run for political office. There were, it is true, a few exceptions. But when Joseph S. Clark and Richardson Dilworth entered the political arena in the 1950s, the novelty of their appearance in municipal affairs was not only because they became victorious Democrats in a city for decades dominated by Republican machines, but because they were blue-bloods. The novelty passed. Democrats remained, but upper-class citizens turned their backs once more on vote-getting campaigns. Even the judiciary in the city, once considered respectable and honorable enough for any gentleman, has, the federal bench excepted, been looked upon askance by the city's best and brightest.

As the railroad web around the city made commuting easy, more and more of the gentry made their country houses permanent domiciles or built themselves new homes well outside the city limits. From nine to five, bankers, brokers, insurance, railroad, and utility executives tended to their affairs in the center of town, and perhaps after a drink or two at a club scampered home to the freshness, quiet, and privacy of the suburbs. They would indeed come

in, or stay in, for a concert, a play, the opening of a museum exhibition, or
a dinner at the house of a dwindling number of friends who still lived on
Delancey Street or Rittenhouse Square. Although the prestige of redeveloped
Society Hill has brought some of the self-exiled back, most of the economically powerful still live in Montgomery, Delaware, or Chester County. They
do not use the buses or subways. They do not see the empty houses, the piles
of rubbish, the vandalized factories, and the squalor of the ghetto. They have
insulated themselves from the groups of blacks listening to the sound of a
transistor radio in front of a corner taproom because they cannot find employment. At a corporate level they are enthusiastic supporters of the United Way,
although in many instances the corporate contribution masks the inadequacy
of their personal one.

On the other hand these aristocrats by birth or business have built from
colonial times to today a complex of cultural institutions of superior achievement. The historicity of Philadelphia has been reinforced by the development
of the Old City (some would denominate it the "Olde" City). Philadelphia
needs none of the tricks of the pseudo-antique. There are more eighteenth-
century buildings standing and now used in the city than even in Boston,
which was founded half a century earlier. It has more eighteenth-century
foundations flourishing: the Library Company of Philadelphia, now recognized as one of the nation's great scholarly research libraries; the American
Philosophical Society, with Nobel Prize winners gilding its membership as
did the virtuosi of Europe in Franklin's days; the Pennsylvania Hospital,
modernizing, expanding, and making itself felt as a major component of the
city's huge medical reservoir of assets; the University of Pennsylvania, which
has had its periods of distinction and lack of distinction, today reasserting
itself as a prestigious undergraduate and graduate school.

The dichotomy of the withdrawal from personal involvement with sordid
matters and the long-term Quaker underlay of—and present Quaker concern
with—the poor and the suffering has created "The Private City." In his
influential study with that title, Sam Bass Warner chose Philadelphia as an
example of American urban development:

Under the American tradition, the first purpose of the citizen is private search for
wealth; the goal of the city is to be a community of private money makers. Once the
scope of many city dwellers' search for wealth exceeded the bounds of their municipality, the American city ceased to be an effective community. Ever afterwards it lacked
the desire, the power, the wealth, and the talent necessary to create a humane environment for all its citizens.

There were few cities in the United States where more private charitable
enterprises were founded and supported. From the early Almshouse through
the era of do-goodism of the nineteenth century, when fallen women, destitute orphans, the worthy poor, and upper-class women dispensing food and
fuel with one hand and moral tracts in the other, expressed voluntary philanthropy, to the impersonality of federated giving, Philadelphia's charitable

institutions have been successfully and typically American. A United Way includes both Catholic and Jewish charities, although the two sectarian groups also separately support their own educational systems and other aspects of their denominational interests.

IV

In many old cities the area of abandonment has been the core, with gradual slum conditions, torn-down and derelict homes and factories creating a bombed-out appearance in ever-widening circles. In Philadelphia since the 1950s the redevelopment of center city, expanding year by year, has brought many of the well-to-do and the downright wealthy back to the core. The blessing—or blight, for poor blacks and Puerto Ricans—of gentrification has graced other sections just on the periphery of the first housing renaissance: the Fairmount district north of the Parkway, Queen Village near Old Swedes' Church, and clusters of warehouses converted into lofts north of Market Street. As the price of housing has risen in the newly fashionable sections, the poor, chiefly blacks, who had lived there moved farther away from the core, and the hard-hatted white workmen, as in Kensington and Fishtown, moved out of the city completely, or stayed in uncomfortable despair. Some districts have found a more comfortable compromise in integration: the middle-class neighborhoods of Wynnefield, which in the 1920s were the residence of the economically upward-mobile Russian Jews, and Mount Airy, between largely black Germantown and largely white Chestnut Hill.

The business part of town has been changing too. The transformation of the jumble of offices, stores, and warehouses due north of Independence Hall into a mall extending to Franklin Square and the Benjamin Franklin Bridge over the Delaware—the latter one of the very, very few benefits that came to the city from the unfortunate Sesqui-Centennial celebration of 1926—brought a new zone of handsome buildings into being: several banks, two television stations (the city's Public Broadcasting System station in one of the more expensive mistakes of the Bicentennial celebration of 1976), the United States Mint and modern facilities for federal agencies and the federal courts, and the headquarters of the Rohm and Haas Company. The renewal has speared west from Independence Mall up Market Street to include a new structure for Gimbels department store, an extension of Strawbridge & Clothier, and the first of the Rouse Company's Gallery, a complex of many stores. Underway are a new railroad station at Eleventh Street on the connecting link of the former Reading and former Pennsylvania lines, and Gallery II.

Where the old Broad Street Station of the Pennsy stood with the Chinese Wall enclosing its tracks inhibiting the development of Market Street west of City Hall, a new office building complex has arisen and a new boulevard has been cut through to Amtrak's main Philadelphia station at Thirtieth Street. Architecturally exciting the structures are not. But corporate and law offices have moved into them as the center of Philadelphia's business activity has shifted westward—and north toward the Parkway on the far side of which

SmithKline has built a new headquarters and the new Franklin Plaza Hotel has risen. In a strong attempt to increase its room capacity so that the city can once more become a convention center, new hotels are under construction. Philadelphia's reputation as a visitor's delight is being restored. It boasted in the 1840s the United States Hotel—the nation's finest—where Charles Dickens stayed, the Continental on whose balcony Lincoln stood and spoke on the way to his inauguration, and the Lafayette and La Pierre that graced South Broad Street. Now the Bellevue-Stratford, a hostelry of Edwardian elegance, has been rehabilitated and has recovered from its 1976 attack of Legionnaires' disease.

When the First Continental Congress came to town in 1774 and the delegates stayed at the many available inns and boardinghouses (usually run by widows) they were overwhelmed by the quantity and quality of the food and drink offered them. John Adams wrote home to his Abigail of the sinful plenitude. Through the streets sellers cried "Pepper Pot, smoking hot," and in 1814 the Russian artist Pavel Petrovich Svinin pictured theater-goers stopping to patronize an oyster barrow in front of the Chestnut Street Theatre. Little Italy a century later brought forth an effusion from Christopher Morley:

Christian street breathes the Italian genius for good food. After lunching in a well-known Italian restaurant on Catharine street, where the Epicure [newspaper man Jimmy Craven] instructed me in the mysteries of gnocchi, frittura mista, rognone, scallopini al marsala and that marvelously potent clear coffee which seems to the uninstructed to taste more like wine than coffee, and has a curious shimmer of green round the rim of the liquid, we strolled among the pavement stalls of the little market.

The colorful Italian Market on Ninth Street is still where epicures shop for the fresh and the unusual, and politicians make their pitch for the South Philadelphia vote. Once there were many markets: the main one which extended down Market Street; a row of sheds on Second Street south of Pine, the Head House of which still stands as an introduction to a revived avenue of restaurants and boutiques; an excellent one on Ridge Avenue; and what was once a huge farmers' market back of the Reading Terminal, a remnant of which still functions. Bassetts Ice Cream, sold there, is the best made, and Margerum's meat was served in all the finest homes.

It may be that the revival of Philadelphia's city center owes as much to food as to houses. For many years after the exodus to the suburbs began a good meal could be obtained only in private homes and private clubs, and Philadelphians were renowned for their dinner parties. Today gourmet food is served in dozens of restaurants, and even suburbanites stay in town for dinner of an evening. At the same time there has been a daytime increase in street vendors who formerly sold chiefly the city's specialty, soft pretzels with mustard, but now offer hot dogs, soda pop, and even eggrolls. Fast-food chains have of course multiplied, but at the same time so have restaurants serving Indian, Japanese, Thai, Chinese, and Lebanese foods.

V

It may be a sign of the times that the owner of a Middle Eastern restaurant is a member of city Council. Politics in Philadelphia has been one of the city's most interesting public phenomena, but like the restaurant business it has recently enjoyed a special new verve. As Mayor Joseph S. Clark gave way to Richardson Dilworth, and Dilworth to James H. J. Tate, great government became merely good government, but politics made its way again. The end of Tate's terms began a roller-coaster era. With bitterness, Tate's commissioner of police, Frank L. Rizzo, wrested the mayoralty from his former friends and patrons. Crime on the streets became the issue, and, physically large and popularly exuberant Rizzo captured the hearts and the votes of Philadelphians. He had presence; he had charm; South Philly and the policemen loved him. He built a political machine à la Vare by giving jobs to friends and relatives of friends, by agreeing with school teachers that liberal superintendants were a menace and that the teachers were underpaid, and by enthusiastically raising the salaries of municipal workers upon demand. There were a few stumbles on the way. The Bicentennial was a fiasco as money was spent on buildings as if there were no future accounting; but the building unions were the mayor's strong supporters. A call for federal troops on the Fourth of July 1976 to protect Independence Hall and the president from the Communists made out-of-town tourists wary. When Mayor Rizzo sought to change the city charter so that he could succeed himself for a third term, the electorate turned him down.

Rizzo's legacy to the city in the late 1970s was an educational system, once one of the best and most forward-looking in the nation, now running out of inspiration and money. On Wall Street Philadelphia's credit was low; that made borrowing for capital purposes overexpensive. When a new administration came into power in 1979 with William J. Green as mayor, the bravura of Rizzo was replaced by an eminently commonsensical approach to life, finances, and the running of a government, less dramatic and less colorful, to be sure. There was a certain sobering effect on the politicians after Philadelphia's chief advocates in the state Senate and House were convicted of illegalities, after some congressmen and three members of the city Council were found guilty in the Abscam caper and other investigations. The present councilmen, however, still disgust and amuse the citizens of Philadelphia as they indulge in fisticuffs and verbal attacks on one another (the councilwomen behave far better). Yet a greater sense of responsibility for the fiscal health of the city has penetrated the ornate council chamber.

For the first time since the heady Clark-Dilworth days the major municipal departments are headed by intelligent and competent men. Some of the excess fat in the form of no-show or only-a-few-hours-a-day political appointees has been trimmed. Contracts are being scrutinized. Mayor Green has faced up—or down—to the demands of labor unions and kept raises in salaries and fringe benefits to a minimum. No solution has yet been found to get the

Mayor William J. Green (1980).
PHILADELPHIA OFFICE OF THE CITY REPRESENTATIVE

overstaffed school system within the bounds of prudent management, nor to raise the quality of the teaching, increase the receptivity of the students, and control the violence in the schools. But—amazingly—an effort coordinated with the Chamber of Commerce has cleaned up the streets noticeably.

V I

All has not come up roses. While the municipal government is less volatile, less subject to personal whims and personal pressures, the economy of the city is. like that of all older urban areas, still troublesome. Manufacturing has moved south and west. Although it was in Philadelphia during World War II that the first computer, ENIAC, was constructed by J. Presper Eckert and John W. Mauchly, the local entrepreneurs were late in getting into the computer game. It is now realized that the future of the city's fortunes will depend on service and light industries, pharmaceuticals and medical science, and tourism.

Philadelphia has indeed suffered from an inferiority complex—unnecessarily and irrationally so. Its place in American history as "The Birthplace of the Nation" is so appealing that over four million tourists annually visit Independence Hall and the inappropriate shack the federal government built to house the Liberty Bell. Few people realize that the Bell was brought to Philadelphia to resound from the State House tower to celebrate the jubilee, the scriptural fifty years, of Penn's Charter of Liberties. It had nothing at all to do with the Declaration of Independence, may not even have been rung in the dangerously shaky clock tower in July 1776, and was made a symbol by a group of New England Abolitionists. But of history it is a part and the whole complex of Independence National Historical Park is so redolent with the eidola of the past that one might expect Thomas Jefferson to walk out the State House door muttering about the flies that pestered the delegates equally with the horses stabled at the inn across Chestnut Street. Certainly the presence of Nicholas Biddle can be felt at both the strong, simple Grecian Second Bank of the United States and the more sophisticated elegance of Girard College.

The architecture of the city is the history of American architecture. From the Palladian beauty of Capt. John McPherson's Mount Pleasant to Louis I. Kahn's Richards Medical Building, Philadelphia has provided examples of the most fashionable, the most modern, and the best. An ordinance requiring that for any project receiving city funds 1 percent of its cost be expended on artworks has resulted in a remarkable bloom of civic statuary and murals. If the city can capitalize on its extraordinary two-river frontage, a commercial-residential development on the Delaware and a park downtown on the Schuylkill, one of Philadelphia's most exciting potentials can be realized.

A historical asset that does, sometimes with flickering flames, seem to illuminate the local scene is the longtime resilience of its cultural institutions. As a center of art it is still a stewing pot. From it have come the great portraitists Charles Willson Peale and Thomas Sully, and more and more in the mainstream of critical appreciation, almost supreme, the adventurer Thomas Eakins, and locally esteemed Cecilia Beaux and Franklin Watkins. The Pennsylvania Academy of the Fine Arts, the nation's first teaching academy, is still as stimulating to its students and as shocking to its patrons as it was in the days of Eakins, now almost a century in the past. Modern Realism is "in" now.

All over the world symphony orchestras try to match the high standard set by the Philadelphia Orchestra, brought to its original excellence by the electric, shock-haired Leopold Stokowski, maintained at that level by Eugene Ormandy, and recently placed under the baton of the dashing Riccardo Muti. It was quite a feather in the cap of the Philadelphia Museum of Art to convince Nigeria to make Philadelphia an unanticipated stop for the country's traveling exhibit of its national art treasures in 1982, and then to raise the funds to make it possible. In a city now one-third black, the museum presented the creations of two millennia of African culture to huge appreciative audiences of many races and colors. Founded in 1876, the museum is one of the great encyclopedic collections in the United States. In 1981 the venerable Library Company of Philadelphia celebrated its Quarter of a Millennium by bringing to the city librarians and scholars from many lands

---

OVERLEAF: *Aerial view of center city Philadelphia, toward the east from the Schuylkill River to the Benjamin Franklin Bridge and the Delaware River (Skyphotos, 1980).*

PHILADELPHIA CITY PLANNING COMMISSION

who participated in a symposium on "The Intellectual World of 1731." The consensus is that Philadelphia has a tremendous amount to offer. And so it does.

As Philadelphia's 300th anniversary begins, the city is looking forward. Century IV, the celebration is called. It will not be an international exhibition such as the triumphantly successful Centennial of 1876 or the dismally inept Sesqui-Centennial of 1926. It will not be a pouring out of money for buildings and administrative staff with small return in terms of visitors and critical acclaim as was the Bicentennial of 1976. Instead, Century IV will be a series of community and international events honoring the people of the city—recognizing their unique achievements in the past and present, and most important, their plans and hopes for the future. Century IV will go into neighborhoods to promote pride and interest in an expression of who, what, and where—and where from. A major community history program will show how the city has changed in the hundred years since the Industrial Revolution; it will explore how these changes have affected the neighborhoods in which families work and play; and it will examine how the industrial city has been transformed into today's service-based city. A series of festivals called "Only in Philadelphia" will focus on the distinctive character, history, and ethnic mix of each city neighborhood. The idea is to encourage neighborhood-to-neighborhood visiting and thereby broaden Philadelphians' knowledge and appreciation of their city. A Pennsylvania Horticultural Society project called "The Greening of Philadelphia" is designed to bring William Penn's dream of a "greene Country Towne" to every corner of the city. There will be a Folk Festival and exhibits documenting the contributions made by women, minorities, and ethnic groups to the city's history.

Special projects, conceived with an eye toward nurturing the growth and development of existing businesses and institutions, will draw attention to the fields in which Philadelphia is outstanding. There will be an international law congress, a world insurance congress, an exhibition of notable woman fashion designers, an international culinary exposition, a Feasting Festival, an international conference of art publishers, a Festival of American Music, a symposium on "The Philadelphia Tradition in Art," a Black Music Association Convention. A series of concerts by the Philadelphia Orchestra will honor Stokowski's 100th birthday; and the première of the opera *William Penn*, composed over a twenty-four-year period by the Philadelphia composer Romeo Cascarino and with a libretto by Philadelphia poet Peggy Oppenlander, will be presented on October 24, William Penn's birthday. The Annenberg Center for the Performing Arts will present its first Award of Merit to Philadelphia's Grace Kelly, now Monaco's Princess Grace.

Philadelphia's past—and future—as a port city is being celebrated by the visit of the Tall Ships, the fleet of canvas-sailed training ships that will race from Venezuela to the Delaware Bay Lighthouse, then sail up the river to berth at Penn's Landing. Another visitor will be the last of the mammoth ocean liners, the *Queen Elizabeth II*, renamed for the occasion after William

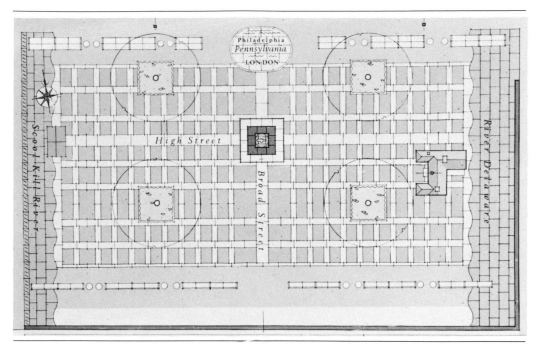

Architect's plan for Welcome Park. Architects are Venturi, Rauch and Scott Brown, for the Friends of Independence National Historical Park (1982). A new park is being built for the Tercentenary on the site of Penn's Slate Roof House, Second Street at Sansom. The paving of Welcome Park will illustrate Penn's 1682 plan for the city: the streets will be marble, the lots, gray brick. Four trees will represent the original city squares.

Penn's ship *Welcome,* and tracing the *Welcome*'s voyage across the Atlantic Ocean and up the Delaware River.

Century IV will be a hopeful celebration. By looking at the richness of the city's past and appreciating and exploring the vitality of the present, it will, it is hoped, set Philadelphia on course for a bright future. There is reason to be optimistic. The economic etiolation of the city may have come to an end. The municipal government seems to be inching its way past solvency to creative excellence. And Philadelphia, combining as it does the best of the urban experience and a setting scaled to human dimensions, is being discovered as a city that is eminently livable. Perhaps this "City of Firsts" in America —the first hospital, the first library, the first theater, the first museum, the first university, the first computer—may now be the first to point the way for a restoration and rebirth of the older industrial cities of America. Certainly, after Century IV Philadelphia will no longer be, as Mayor Green has called it, one of America's best kept secrets.

NOTES

THE FOUNDING, 1681–1701

1. *Some Account*, quoted in Hannah Benner Roach, "The Planting of Philadelphia, A Seventeenth-Century Real Estate Development," *Pennsylvania Magazine of History and Biography* (hereafter cited as *PMHB*) 92 (Jan. 1968): 8; William Penn to Gulielma Penn, Aug. 4, 1682, Etting Collection, Historical Society of Pennsylvania (hereafter cited as HSP).

2. "Instructions of William Penn to the Commissioners for settling the colony, 30 7th Mo. 1681," Mary Maples Dunn and Richard S. Dunn, eds., *The Papers of William Penn, 1680–1684* (Philadelphia: University of Pennsylvania Press, 1982), p. 121. There is no standard, comprehensive biography of William Penn. The best to date are Edward C. O. Beatty, *William Penn as a Social Philosopher* (New York: Columbia University Press, 1939), and Catherine O. Peare, *William Penn: A Biography* (Philadelphia: Lippincott, 1957). Penn's career in the 1670s, when most of his energy was devoted to the defense of Quakerism, is most fully documented in Mary Maples Dunn and Richard S. Dunn, eds., *The Papers of William Penn, 1644–1679* (Philadelphia: University of Pennsylvania Press, 1981); see especially the documents on New Jersey, pp. 381–421. Penn's negotiations for a royal charter for Pennsylvania are discussed in Joseph E. Illick, *William Penn the Politician: His Relations with the English Government* (Ithaca, N.Y.: Cornell University Press, 1965), chap. 1.

3. Penn's relationship with the First Purchasers is described in John E. Pomfret, "The First Purchasers of Pennsylvania, 1681–1700," *PMHB* 80 (April 1956): 137–63. See also Roach, "The Planting of Philadelphia," *PMHB* 92 (Jan. 1968): 3–47, and (April 1968): 143–94.

4. For further details on the settlement of the Delaware Valley before 1681, see C. A. Weslager, *The Delaware Indians: A History* (New Brunswick, N.J.: Rutgers University Press, 1972); id., *Dutch Explorers, Traders and Settlers in the Delaware Valley, 1609–1664* (Philadelphia: University of Pennsylvania Press, 1961); John E. Pomfret, *The Province of West New Jersey, 1609–1702* (Princeton, N.J.: Princeton University Press, 1956); and Carl Bridenbaugh, "The Old and New Societies of the Delaware Valley in the Seventeenth Century," *PMHB* 100 (April 1976): 143–72.

5. Edward Armstrong, ed., "The Record of the Court at Upland, in Pennsylvania, 1676 to 1681," *Memoirs of the Historical Society of Pennsylvania* 7 (1860): 35–203.

6. "Certaine Conditions or Concessions agreed upon by William Penn . . . & those who are the adventurers and purchasers, July 11, 1681," in Dunn and Dunn, eds., *The Papers of William Penn, 1680–1684*, p. 98.

7. For fuller details on Penn's initial plans for Philadelphia, see Sylvia Doughty Fries, *The Urban Idea in Colonial America* (Philadelphia: Temple University Press, 1977), pp. 79–107; Roach, "The Planting of Philadelphia"; Gary B. Nash, "City Planning and Political Tension in the Seventeenth Century: The Case of Philadelphia," *Proceedings of the American Philosophical Society* 112 (1968): 54–73. For general background, see Gary B. Nash, *Quakers and Politics: Pennsylvania, 1681–1726* (Princeton, N.J.: Princeton University Press, 1968), chaps. 1–2; Edwin B. Bronner, *William Penn's "Holy Experiment": The Founding of Pennsylvania, 1681–1701* (New York: Columbia University Press, 1962), chaps. 1–4. On commerce, see Marion V. Brewington, "Maritime Philadelphia, 1609–1837," *PMHB* 63 (Jan. 1939): 93–100.

8. See John F. Walzer, "Colonial Philadelphia and its Backcountry," *Winterthur Portfolio* 7 (1972): 161–75.

9. Bronner, *William Penn's "Holy Experiment,"* p. 64.

10. Penn's proposals of 1681 concerning his "large Towne or Citty" are printed in Dunn and Dunn, eds., *The Papers of William Penn, 1680–1684*, pp. 98–101, 118–21, and have been variously interpreted. See esp. Anthony N. B. Garvan, "Proprietary Philadelphia as Artifact," in Oscar Handlin and John Burchard, eds., *The Historian and the City* (Cambridge, Mass.: Harvard University Press, 1963), pp. 189–90.

11. Albert Cook Myers, ed., *Narratives of Early Pennsylvania, West New Jersey and Delaware, 1630–1717* (New York: Scribner's, 1912), p. 243.

12. This view is advanced by Garvan, "Proprietary Philadelphia as Artifact," pp. 190–91; and Fries, *The Urban Idea in Colonial America,* pp. 97–98.

13. Roach, "The Planting of Philadelphia," p. 36; and John W. Reps, *The Making of Urban America: A History of City Planning in the*

United States (Princeton, N.J.: Princeton University Press, 1965), pp. 15–19, 161–64; Margaret B. Tinkcom, "Urban Reflections in a Trans-Atlantic Mirror," *PMHB* 100 (July 1976): 287–313.

14. Everts B. Greene and Virginia D. Harrington, *American Population Before the Federal Census of 1790* (New York: Columbia University Press, 1932), p. 117; J. Thomas Scharf and Thompson Westcott, *History of Philadelphia* (3 vols.; Philadelphia: L. H. Everts, 1884), 1:145.

15. The 1693 tax list for Philadelphia is printed in *PMHB* 8 (1884): 85–94; the 1696 tax list is in Miscellaneous Papers of Philadelphia County, HSP, L/25–28. The 1689 quitrent roll is printed in *Pennsylvania Genealogical Magazine* 23 (1963): 68–94; the 1703 rent roll is printed in Commonwealth of Pennsylvania, *Internal Affairs Monthly Bulletin* 20, no. 4 (March 1954): 13–23, and no. 5 (April 1954): 27–29. For slightly higher estimates, see Gary B. Nash, *The Urban Crucible* (Cambridge, Mass.: Harvard University Press, 1979), pp. 4, 407–9; John K. Alexander, "The Philadelphia Numbers Game: An Analysis of Philadelphia's Eighteenth-Century Population," *PMHB* 98 (1974): 323–24.

16. Information on the caves can be found in *Minutes of the Common Council of the City of Philadelphia* (Philadelphia: Crissy and Markley, 1847), pp. 161, 163, 167, 201 (hereafter cited as *Common Council Minutes*); Roach, "The Planting of Philadelphia," p. 42; *PMHB* 33 (1909): 310; ibid., 90 (July 1966): 326. On housing in the new town, see Myers, *Narratives of Early Pennsylvania*, pp. 261, 269–72, 290–91, 317–18, 403–5. On streets, see *Common Council Minutes*, p. 381; and Staughton George et al., eds., *Charter to William Penn and Laws of the Province of Pennsylvania* (Harrisburg: Lane S. Hart, 1879), pp. 187–259. Hannah Benner Roach has identified brickmakers and bricklayers in "Philadelphia Business Directory, 1690," *Pennsylvania Genealogical Magazine* 23 (1963): 109–12. For fire laws, see George et al., eds., *Charter to William Penn*, pp. 259–60.

17. Roach, "The Planting of Philadelphia," p. 176.

18. Ruth L. Springer and Louise Wallman, "Two Swedish Pastors Describe Philadelphia, 1700 and 1702," *PMHB* 84 (April 1960): 207.

19. Nash, "City Planning and Political Tension," p. 67.

20. This discussion is based on an analysis of the 1689 and 1703 quitrent rolls (see note 15 above).

21. Roach, "Philadelphia Business Directory, 1690," p. 116. Our tabulation of the residential distribution of Philadelphia businessmen is drawn from Mrs. Roach's excellent article.

22. Myers, *Narratives of Early Pennsylvania*, p. 327.

23. For differing opinions on the justification for colonists' discontent, and to a lesser extent on the degree of discontent, see Nash, "City Planning and Political Tension," pp. 54–73; and Roach, "The Planting of Philadelphia," pp. 3–47, 143–94. The following discussion of division of land is based on these two articles.

24. Roach, "The Planting of Philadelphia," pp. 187–88.

25. James T. Lemon, "Urbanization and the Development of Eighteenth-Century Southeastern Pennsylvania and Adjacent Delaware," *William and Mary Quarterly*, 3d ser., 24 (Oct. 1967): 501–42; id., *The Best Poor Man's Country: A Geographical Study of Early Southeastern Pennsylvania* (Baltimore: Johns Hopkins Press, 1972), ch. 5.

26. U.S. Bureau of the Census, *Historical Statistics of the United States: Colonial Times to 1957* (Washington, D.C.: U.S. Government Printing Office, 1960), p. 757; Arthur L. Jensen, *The Maritime Commerce of Colonial Philadelphia* (Madison: University of Wisconsin Press, 1963), pp. 5, 290–92.

27. Gary B. Nash, "The Free Society of Traders and the Early Politics of Pennsylvania," *PMHB* 89 (April 1965): 147–73.

28. For documentary evidence concerning the rise and fall of the Free Society of Traders, see Samuel Hazard, ed., *Annals of Pennsylvania*, (Philadelphia: Hazard & Mitchell, 1850), pp. 541–50, 577–79; *The Articles, Settlement and Officers of the Free Society of Traders in Pennsylvania* (London, 1682), reprinted in *PMHB* 5 (1881): 37–50; Myers, *Narratives of Early Pennsylvania*, pp. 240–42, 380, 399, 404; Marion Balderston, ed., *James Claypoole's Letter Book: London and Philadelphia, 1681–1684* (San Marino, Calif.: Huntington Library, 1967), pp. 132–33, 239–42.

29. Frederick B. Tolles, *Meeting House and Counting House: The Quaker Merchants of Colonial Philadelphia, 1682–1783* (Chapel Hill: University of North Carolina Press, 1948), pp. 43–44.

30. George et al., eds., *Charter to William Penn*, pp. 133, 140, 239–40, 283–84. The 1693 meat inspection act was repassed in an act of 1700, which Arthur L. Jensen mistakenly supposes was the first inspection act in Pennsylvania ("The Inspection of Exports in Colonial Pennsylvania," *PMHB* 78 [July 1954]; 278).

31. Bronner, *William Penn's "Holy Experiment*," pp. 196–97.

32. Roach, "Philadelphia Business Directory, 1693," pp. 95–129.

33. Tolles, *Meeting House and Counting House*, pp. 29–32, 38–42.

34. This analysis is based on Mrs. Roach's "Philadelphia Business Directory, 1690."

35. Nehemiah Allen account book, 1698–1736, HSP.

36. Gregory Marlow and James West account book, 1676–1703, HSP.

37. Unfortunately there is no large body of Carpenter papers available, and knowledge of Samuel Carpenter's affairs must be pieced together from scattered letters and references. There is a genealogical work, Edward Carpenter, *Samuel Carpenter and His Descendants* (Philadelphia: Lippincott, 1912).

38. Roach, "The Planting of Philadelphia," p. 176.

39. Nash, *The Urban Crucible*, p. 73; Carpenter, *Samuel Carpenter*, pp. 21–23, 32.

40. Gary B. Nash, "The First and Second Generations of Philadelphia Merchants: A Comparison," conference paper, The World of William Penn, Philadelphia, March 20, 1981.

41. Myers, *Narratives of Early Pennsylvania*, pp. 380, 390–91, 399, 407, 416–17.
42. Stephanie Grauman Wolf, *Urban Village: Population, Community, and Family Structure in Germantown, Pennsylvania, 1683–1800* (Princeton, N.J.: Princeton University Press, 1976), pp. 29, 32, 41, 113, 129.
43. Gary B. Nash, "Urban Wealth and Poverty in Pre-Revolutionary America," *Journal of Interdisciplinary History* 6 (Spring 1976): 549.
44. For the 1693 and 1696 tax lists, see note 15 above. The 1700 list seems to have disappeared, but it is summarized in C. M. Andrews, *The Colonial Period of American History* (4 vols.; New Haven, Conn.: Yale University Press, 1934–1938), 3:293*n*. See also *Council Minutes*, pp. 462–521. For analysis of the 1693 tax list, and of late seventeenth-century inventories, see Nash, *Quakers and Politics*, pp. 278–86.
45. The charter is printed in *Votes and Proceedings of the House of Representatives of the Province of Pennsylvania*, in *Pennsylvania Archives*, 8th ser. (8 vols.; Harrisburg: State Library, 1931–1935), 1:393.
46. For fuller details on the establishment of the corporation and its English antecedents, see Judith M. Diamondstone, "The Philadelphia Corporation, 1701–1776" (Ph.D. dissertation, University of Pennsylvania, 1969); and id., "Philadelphia's Municipal Corporation, 1701–1776," *PMHB* 90 (April 1966): 183–201. For the request of 1684, see Roach, "The Planting of Philadelphia," p. 187. For the charter of 1691, see *PMHB* 18 (1894); 504–8. For an extended discussion of political factionalism in the city and province, see Nash, *Quakers and Politics*, pp. 202–7.
47. For fuller details of this interpretation, see Mary Maples Dunn, *William Penn: Politics and Conscience* (Princeton, N.J.: Princeton University Press, 1967); Nash, *Quakers and Politics;* Bronner, *William Penn's "Holy Experiment";* and Ethyn Williams Kirby,

George Keith (New York: D. Appleton-Century, 1942).
48. For the Pennsylvania legal-moral code, see George et al., eds., *Charter to William Penn*, pp. 101–3, 110, 112, 114–16, 128, 136–37, 145, 151, 154, 239.
49. See Penn's treatise on "Right Marriage" in Dunn and Dunn, eds., *The Papers of William Penn, 1644–1679*, pp. 231–37.
50. Nash, "Free Society of Traders," p. 162; Darold D. Wax, "Quaker Merchants and the Slave Trade in Colonial Pennsylvania," *PMHB* 86 (April 1962): 146–51; Thomas E. Drake, *Quakers and Slavery in America* (New Haven, Conn.: Yale University Press, 1950), chap. 1; Jean Soderlund, "Conscience, Interest, and Power: The Development of the Quaker Opposition to Slavery in the Delaware Valley, 1688–1780" (Ph.D. dissertation, Temple University, 1981).
51. *Common Council Minutes*, pp. 380–81.
52. Springer and Wallman, "Two Swedish Pastors Describe Philadelphia," p. 205.
53. Marion Dexter Learned, *The Life of Francis Daniel Pastorius* (Philadelphia: William J. Campbell, 1908), pp. 175–80; Etting Collection, Pemberton Papers, 1:76–77, 83, HSP.
54. Jon Butler, *Power, Authority, and the Origins of American Denominational Order: The English Churches in the Delaware Valley, 1680–1730* (Philadelphia: American Philosophical Society, 1978), pp. 32–38.
55. The anti-Keithians were led by Thomas Lloyd and his fellow officeholders. The Keithians were Lloyd's political opponents; some were wealthy supporters of the absent proprietor, others factors of English merchants, lesser merchants, and artisans. Like most seventeenth-century Quakers these people resented prescriptive authority, and they particularly objected to the way in which Lloyd and his circle had taken over management of the colony, the city, and the Friends' meeting structure. See Nash, *Quakers and Politics*, pp. 144–61.

VILLAGE INTO TOWN, 1701–1746

1. James Logan, *The Charge Delivered from the Bench to the Grand Jury . . .* (Philadelphia, 1723), p. 9, quoted in Thomas Wendel, "The Keith-Lloyd Alliance: Factional and Coalition Politics in Colonial Pennsylvania," *Pennsylvania Magazine of History and Biography* (hereafter cited as *PMHB*) 92 (July 1968): 294; Carl Van Doren, ed., *Benjamin Franklin's Autobiographical Writings* (New York: Viking, 1945), p. 55.
2. Ruth L. Springer and Louise Wallman, "Two Swedish Pastors Describe Philadelphia, 1700 and 1702," *PMHB* 84 (July 1960): 229; Carl Bridenbaugh, ed., *Gentleman's Progress: The Itinerarium of Dr. Alexander Hamilton, 1744* (Chapel Hill: University of North Carolina Press, 1948), pp. 193, 194.
3. For a description of early meeting houses, see Edwin B. Bronner, "The Center Square Meetinghouse," *Bulletin of the Friends Historical Association* 44 (Autumn 1955): 67–73; and id., "Quaker Landmarks in Early Philadelphia," *Transactions of the American Philosophical Society* 43, part 1 (1953): 210–16. This volume, edited by Luther P. Eisenhart,

was published separately as *Historic Philadelphia: From the Founding Until the Early Nineteenth Century: Papers Dealing with Its People and Buildings with an Illustrative Map* (hereafter cited as Eisenhart, ed., *Historic Philadelphia*).
4. Carl Bridenbaugh, *Cities in the Wilderness: The First Century of Urban Life in America, 1625–1742* (New York: Knopf, 1964), pp. 181, 204, 331–35; Arthur L. Jensen, *The Maritime Commerce of Colonial Philadelphia* (Madison: University of Wisconsin Press, 1963), passim.
5. For the 1693 tax list, see *PMHB* 8 (1884): 85–94; for 1709, see Peter J. Parker, "Rich and Poor in Philadelphia, 1709," *PMHB* 99 (Jan. 1975): 8.
6. Leonard W. Labaree et al., eds., *The Autobiography of Benjamin Franklin* (New Haven, Conn.: Yale University Press, 1964), p. 124.
7. On immigration, see Wayland F. Dunaway, *The Scotch-Irish of Colonial Pennsylvania* (Chapel Hill: University of North Carolina Press, 1944); Albert B. Faust, *The German*

Element in the United States (2 vols.; Boston: Houghton Mifflin, 1909); Bertha Hamilton, "The Colonization of Pennsylvania" (Ph.D. dissertation, University of Wisconsin, Madison, 1932); Richard Hofstadter, *America at 1750: A Social Portrait* (New York: Knopf, 1971); Guy S. Klett, *The Scotch-Irish in Pennsylvania* (Gettysburg, Penna.: Pennsylvania Historical Association, 1948); Israel D. Rupp, *Foreign Immigrants to Pennsylvania, 1717–1776* (Philadelphia: Leary, 1898); S. H. Sutherland, *Population Distribution in Colonial America* (New York: Columbia University Press, 1936).

8. James G. Lydon, "Philadelphia's Commercial Expansion, 1720–1739," *PMHB* 91 (Oct. 1967): 408.

9. This discussion is based on Lydon's excellent article, ibid., pp. 401–18.

10. Richard A. Lester, "Currency Issues to Overcome Depressions in Pennsylvania, 1723 and 1729," *Journal of Political Economy* 46 April (1938): 324–75; C. W. MacFarlane, *Pennsylvania Paper Currency* (Philadelphia: American Academy of Political and Social Science Publication no. 178, 1896).

11. Frederick B. Tolles, *James Logan and the Culture of Provincial America* (Boston: Little, Brown, 1957), p. 190. This book underlies the discussion of Logan.

12. Frederick B. Tolles, *Meeting House and Counting House: Quaker Merchants of Colonial Philadelphia* (Chapel Hill: University of North Carolina Press, 1948), p. 65.

13. Edwin B. Bronner, "Intercolonial Relations among Quakers before 1750," *Quaker History* 56 (Spring 1967): 3–17.

14. Frederick B. Tolles, *Quakers and the Atlantic Culture* (New York: Macmillan, 1960), chap. 1.

15. Thomas Woody, *Early Quaker Education in Pennsylvania* (New York: Teacher's College Press, Columbia University, 1920), esp. chap. 4; Howard H. Brinton, *Quaker Education in Theory and Practice* (Wallingford, Pa.: Pendle Hill pamphlet no. 9, 1949), pp. 27–29; Tolles, *Meeting House and Counting House*, pp. 148–49, 207–9.

16. Tolles, *Meeting House and Counting House*, esp. ch. 5.

17. Two copies of the manuscript "Book of Discipline" of 1704 are in the Quaker Collection, Haverford College Library.

18. Several manuscript copies of the 1719 "Discipline" are in the Quaker Collection, Haverford College Library. For commentary on the nature of the Friends' influence, see Brent E. Barksdale, *Pacifism and Democracy in Colonial Pennsylvania* (Stanford, Calif.: Stanford University Press, 1961); Daniel J. Boorstin, *The Americans: The Colonial Experience* (New York: Knopf, 1958); Dietmar Rothermund, *Layman's Progress: Religion and Political Experience in Colonial Pennsylvania* (Philadelphia: University of Pennsylvania Press, 1961), esp. pp. 14–15.

19. Thomas E. Drake, *Quakers and Slavery in America* (New Haven, Conn.: Yale University Press, 1950), p. 22.

20. Darold D. Wax, "Quaker Merchants and the Slave Trade in Colonial Pennsylvania," *PMHB* 86 (April 1962): 147–48.

21. See Wax's entire article, ibid., pp. 143–59.

22. Tolles, *James Logan*, pp. 154–55. See also Robert Proud, *The History of Pennsylvania . . .* (2 vols.; Philadelphia: Zachariah Poulson,

Jr., 1797), 1:468–77, 2:22–34, 55–57; Edwin B. Bronner, "The Quakers and Non-Violence in Pennsylvania," *Pennsylvania History* (hereafter cited as *PH*) 35 (Jan. 1968): 1–22; *Votes and Proceedings of the House of Representatives of the Province of Pennsylvania*, in *Pennsylvania Archives*, 8th ser. (8 vols.; Harrisburg: State Library, 1931–1935), 2:986–1002.

23. Allan Tully, *William Penn's Legacy: Politics and Social Structure in Provincial Pennsylvania* (Baltimore: Johns Hopkins University Press, 1977), p. 54.

24. Joseph Henry Dubbs, "The Founding of the German Churches of Pennsylvania," *PMHB* 17 (1893): 241–62; Rothermund, *Layman's Progress*.

25. Adolph B. Benson, ed., *Peter Kalm's Travels in North America* (2 vols.; New York: Wilson-Erickson, 1937), 2:22.

26. Labaree et al., eds., *Autobiography of Franklin*, p. 177.

27. Ibid., p. 179.

28. William L. Turner, "The Charity School, the Academy, and the College," in Eisenhart, ed., *Historic Philadelphia*, pp. 179–80.

29. John Tracy Ellis, *Catholics in Colonial America* (Baltimore: Helicon, 1965), esp. pp. 372–79.

30. Edwin Wolf 2nd and Maxwell Whiteman, *The History of the Jews of Philadelphia from Colonial Times to the Age of Jackson* (Philadelphia: Jewish Publication Society of America, 1957), pp. 18–35.

31. Robert C. Smith, "The Decorative Arts," in Louis B. Wright, George B. Tatum, John W. McCoubrey, and Robert C. Smith, *The Arts in America: The Colonial Period* (New York: Scribner's, 1966), p. 269 (illustration, p. 271).

32. Tolles, *James Logan*, pp. 194–95.

33. Bridenbaugh, *Cities in the Wilderness*, pp. 438, 439.

34. Ibid., p. 438; for quotation, Manuscript Minutes of Philadelphia Yearly Meeting, Sept. 17–21, 1743, Philadelphia Yearly Meeting.

35. *A History of the Schuylkill Fishing Company of the State in Schuylkill* (Philadelphia: Privately printed, 1889).

36. On the Library Company, see Edwin Wolf 2nd, *"At the Instance of Benjamin Franklin": A Brief History of the Library Company of Philadelphia, 1731–1976* (Philadelphia: Library Company of Philadelphia, 1976); on the American Philosophical Society, see Carl Bridenbaugh and Jessica Bridenbaugh, *Rebels and Gentlemen: Philadelphia in the Age of Franklin* (New York: Reynal & Hitchcock, 1942), pp. 190, 321–22, 334–53; American Philosophical Society, *Early Proceedings, Compiled by One of the Secretaries from the Manuscript Minutes of Its Meetings from 1744 to 1838* (Philadelphia, 1884).

37. Robert Earle Graham, "The Taverns of Colonial Philadelphia," in Eisenhart, ed., *Historic Philadelphia*, pp. 318–25.

38. Judith M. Diamondstone, "Philadelphia's Municipal Corporation, 1701–1776," *PMHB* 90 (April 1966): 190.

39. Bridenbaugh, *Cities in the Wilderness*, passim.

40. Norman S. Cohen, "The Philadelphia Election Riot of 1742," *PMHB* 92 (July 1968): 318.

41. Bridenbaugh, *Cities in the Wilderness*, pp. 201, 224, 359, 380, 381; W. E. B. DuBois, *The Philadelphia Negro: A Social Study*

(paperback ed.: New York: Schocken, 1967), pp. 11–15.

42. Hostadter, *America at 1750*, p. 34, citing Abbot E. Smith, *Colonists in Bondage* (Chapel Hill: University of North Carolina Press, 1947), p. 27; M. W. Jernegan, *Laboring and Dependent Classes in Colonial America* (Chicago: University of Chicago Press, 1931), p. 55.

43. Bridenbaugh, *Cities in the Wilderness*, pp. 235–36, 394–95.

44. Ibid., pp. 208, 213, 365–68.

45. Ibid., pp. 193, 349, 350; id., *Cities in Revolt: Urban Life in America, 1743–1776* (New York: Knopf, 1964), p. 81.

46. Bridenbaugh, *Cities in the Wilderness*, pp. 195, 193.

47. Ibid., pp. 192, 348.

48. *Minutes of the Common Council of the City of Philadelphia* (Philadelphia: Crissy and Markley, 1847), pp. 462, 482–85; Henry J. Biddle, "Colonial Mayors of Philadelphia," *PMHB* 19 (1895): 65–66; John F. Watson, *Annals of Philadelphia, and Pennsylvania, in the Olden Time* (3 vols.; Philadelphia: E. S. Stuart, 1898), 1:63, 64.

49. Norman S. Cohen, "William Allen, Chief Justice of Pennsylvania, 1704–1780" (Ph.D. dissertation, University of California, Berkeley, 1966).

50. Labaree et al., eds., *Autobiography of Franklin*, p. 43.

51. Charles S. R. Hildeburn, *A Century of Printing: The Issues of the Press in Pennsylvania, 1685–1784* (2 vols.; Philadelphia: Matlack and Harvey, 1885–1886), 1:50, 51, 58; Anna Janney DeArmond, *Andrew Bradford, Colonial Journalist* (Newark: University of Delaware Press, 1949), pp. 1–10.

52. Leonard W. Labaree et al., eds., *The Papers of Benjamin Franklin* (21 vols. to date; New Haven, Conn.: Yale University Press, 1959–), 1:112, 124.

53. Labaree et al., eds., *Autobiography of Franklin*, p. 171.

54. Bridenbaugh, ed., *Gentleman's Progress*, p. 193.

TOWN INTO CITY, 1746–1765

1. *Votes and Proceedings of the House of Representatives of the Province of Pennsylvania* (6 vols.; Philadelphia, 1752–1776), 4:538 (hereafter cited as *Votes of Assembly*); Carl Van Doren, *Benjamin Franklin* (New York: Viking, 1938), p. 303. Galerm was an Acadian exile; see below and Lawrence Henry Gipson, *The British Empire Before the American Revolution* (15 vols.; Caldwell, Idaho: Caxton Press; New York: Knopf, 1936–1970), vol. 6, *The Great War for the Empire: The Years of Defeat, 1754–1757*, p. 311.

2. J. Thomas Scharf and Thompson Westcott, *A History of Philadelphia, 1609–1884* (3 vols.; Philadelphia: L. H. Everts, 1884), 2:874; Carl Bridenbaugh, *Cities in Revolt: Urban Life in America, 1743–1776* (New York: Knopf, 1964), pp. 33–34; *Pennsylvania Gazette*, Oct. 3, 1751.

3. Ellis P. Oberholtzer, *Philadelphia: A History of the City and Its People* (4 vols.; Philadelphia; S. J. Clarke, 1912), 1:185, citing Franklin's *Autobiography*. See Leonard W. Labaree et al., eds., *The Autobiography of Benjamin Franklin* (New Haven, Conn.: Yale University Press, 1964), p. 204.

4. Harold E. Gillingham, "Philadelphia's First Fire Defenses," *PMHB* 56 (Oct. 1932): 372; Edward Allinson and Boies Penrose, *Philadelphia, 1681–1887: A History of Municipal Development*, Johns Hopkins University Studies in Historical and Political Science (Philadelphia: Allen, Lane and Scott, 1887), p. 37; Joseph Jackson, *Encyclopedia of Philadelphia* (4 vols.; Harrisburg: National Historical Association, 1931–1933), 4:1172.

5. Ruth L. Butler, *Doctor Franklin, Postmaster General* (Garden City, N.Y.: Doubleday, Doran, 1928), pp. 49, 50, 51; John F. Watson, *Annals of Philadelphia, and Pennsylvania, in the Olden Time* (3 vols.; Philadelphia: E. S. Stuart, 1877), 2:393.

6. Oberholtzer, *Philadelphia*, 1:212; *Pennsylvania Journal*, Jan. 14, April 10, 1755; Watson, *Annals*, 1:218–19.

7. Theodore Thayer, *Israel Pemberton: King of the Quakers* (Philadelphia: Historical Society of Pennsylvania, 1943), pp. 9 ff; Nicholas B. Wainwright, "An Indian Trade Failure," *PMHB* 72 (July 1948): 355n; Edwin Wolf 2nd and Maxwell Whiteman, *The History of the Jews of Philadelphia from Colonial Times to the Age of Jackson* (Philadelphia: Jewish Publication Society of America, 1957), p. 27; Carl Bridenbaugh and Jessica Bridenbaugh, *Rebels and Gentlemen: Philadelphia in the Age of Franklin* (New York: Reynal & Hitchcock, 1942), p. 7.

8. Cheesman A. Herrick, *White Servitude in Pennsylvania: Indentured and Redemption Labor in Colony and Commonwealth* (Philadelphia: J. J. McVey, 1926), pp. 172, 176, 178; Gipson, *British Empire*, 3:171–72; Ralph B. Strassburger and William J. Hinke, *Pennsylvania German Pioneers* (3 vols.; Norristown: Pennsylvania German Society, 1934), 1:xxx–xxxi; Bridenbaugh, *Cities in Revolt*, pp. 134–35.

9. Herrick, *White Servitude*, pp. 161–64; Gipson, *British Empire*, 3:167; Strassburger and Hinke, *Pennsylvania German Pioneers*, 1:771–74.

10. Darold D. Wax, "Quaker Merchants and the Slave Trade in Colonial Pennsylvania," *PMHB* 83 (April 1962): 145, 157, 158–59; Ruth M. Kistler, "William Allen, Provincial Man of Affairs," *Pennsylvania History* (hereafter cited as *PH*) 1 (April 1934): 170; Herman L. Collins and Wilfred Jordan, *Philadelphia: A Study of Progress* (4 vols.; Philadelphia: Lewis Historical Publishing Co., 1941), 1:61; Bridenbaugh, *Cities in Revolt*, p. 88.

11. Scharf and Westcott, *History of Philadelphia*, 1:253; Harry D. Berg, "Economic Consequences of the French and Indian War for Philadelphia Merchants," *PH* 13 (April 1946): 186; Winfred T. Root, *The Relations of Pennsylvania with the British Government, 1696–1765* (Philadelphia: University of Pennsylvania; New York: Appleton, 1912), pp. 82–83, 123; Thayer, *Israel Pemberton*, pp. 14, 17; Kistler, "William Allen," p. 171; Bridenbaugh and Bridenbaugh, *Rebels and*

Gentlemen, p. 6; Victor L. Johnson, "Fair Traders and Smugglers in Philadelphia, 1754–1760," *PMHB* 83 (April 1959): 127–29, 134, 139, 145–46; Nicholas B. Wainwright, "Governor William Denny in Pennsylvania," *PMHB* 81 (April 1957): 194, 195; Benjamin W. Labaree, *The Boston Tea Party* (New York: Oxford University Press, 1964), pp. 9, 11.

12. Gipson, *British Empire,* 3:6–7n, 184; Jackson, *Encyclopedia,* 4:1085; Bridenbaugh, *Cities in Revolt,* p. 72.

13. Bridenbaugh and Bridenbaugh, *Rebels and Gentlemen,* p. 10; Watson, *Annals,* 1:228, 238–39; Collins and Jordan, *Philadelphia,* 3:44; Board of Trade Papers, Proprietaries, 18 (1748–1754), vol. 73, Historical Society of Pennsylvania.

14. Bridenbaugh, *Cities in Revolt,* p. 94.

15. "Extracts from the Diary of Daniel Fisher," *PMHB* 17 (1893): 263–64; Oberholtzer, *Philadelphia,* 1:149n.

16. Jackson, *Encyclopedia,* 4:973; id., *Market Street: The Most Historic Highway in America* (Philadelphia, 1918), pp. 31, 92.

17. Watson, *Annals,* 1:393–94; Scharf and Westcott, *History of Philadelphia,* 2:855.

18. Bridenbaugh, *Cities in Revolt,* p. 113.

19. *Minutes of the Common Council of the City of Philadelphia* (Philadelphia: Crissy and Markley, 1847), pp. 486, 487, 519–20, 556 (hereafter cited as *Common Council Minutes*).

20. Ibid., pp. 561, 576.

21. Oscar Handlin and John Clive, eds., *Journey to Pennsylvania by Gottlieb Mittelberger* (Cambridge, Mass.: Harvard University Press, 1963), pp. 38–39.

22. Bridenbaugh, *Cities in Revolt,* p. 113; Oberholtzer, *Philadelphia,* 1:185; Allinson and Penrose, *Philadelphia . . . Municipal Development,* pp. 35–36; John R. Young, *Memorial History of the City of Philadelphia from Its First Settlement to the Year 1895* (2 vols.; New York: New York History Co., 1895–1898), 1:263; *Common Council Minutes,* pp. 512–13, 522; James T. Mitchell and Henry Flanders, eds., *The Statutes at Large of Pennsylvania from 1682 to 1801* ([Harrisburg:] W. S. Ray, State Printer, 1898), 5:111–28; *Votes of Assembly,* 4:176, 179, 183–84. The act was approved on Feb. 9, 1750/51.

23. Oberholtzer, *Philadelphia,* 1:145–46; Bridenbaugh, *Cities in Revolt,* pp. 102–3; Gillingham, "Philadelphia's First Fire Defenses," p. 358; Allinson and Penrose, *Philadelphia . . . Municipal Development,* pp. 42–43; Bridenbaugh and Bridenbaugh, *Rebels and Gentlemen,* p. 24.

24. Nicholas B. Wainwright, *A Philadelphia Story: The Philadelphia Contributionship for the Insurance of Houses from Loss by Fire* (Philadelphia: Privately printed, 1952), pp. 20–29; Gillingham, "Philadelphia's First Fire Defenses," p. 370.

25. John K. Alexander, "The Philadelphia Numbers Game: An Analysis of Philadelphia's Eighteenth-Century Population," *PMHB* 98 (July 1974): 314–24, esp. p. 317 for the Boston and New York statistics and p. 324 for Philadelphia. See also Gary B. Nash and Billy G. Smith, "The Population of Eighteenth-Century Philadelphia," *PMHB* 99 (July 1975): 362–68; Lord Adam Gordon, as quoted in Newton D. Mereness, ed., *Travels in the American Colonies* (New York: Macmillan, 1916), p. 410.

26. Leonard W. Labaree et al., eds., *The Papers of Benjamin Franklin* (21 vols. to date; New Haven, Conn.: Yale University Press, 1959–), 3:118–19.

27. Michael Kraus, *The Atlantic Civilization: Eighteenth-Century Origins* (Ithaca, N.Y.: Cornell University Press, 1949).

28. Brooke Hindle, *The Pursuit of Science in Revolutionary America, 1735–1789* (Chapel Hill: University of North Carolina Press, 1956), p. 90; *Dictionary of American Biography* (hereafter cited as *DAB*), s.v. "Ebenezer Kinnersley."

29. Hindle, *Pursuit of Science,* pp. 23–24, 25–26, 76; id., *David Rittenhouse* (Princeton, N.J.: Princeton University Press, 1966); Bridenbaugh and Bridenbaugh, *Rebels and Gentlemen,* pp. 270–71, 313–14; Watson, *Annals,* 1:548.

30. Esther Louise Larsen, "Peter Kalm, Preceptor," *PMHB* 74 (Oct. 1950): 501; Jackson, *Encyclopedia,* 1:124–27; Oberholtzer, *Philadelphia,* 1:210.

31. Whitfield J. Bell, Jr., "John Redman, Medical Preceptor, 1722–1808," *PMHB* 81 (April 1957): 158–67; id., *The Colonial Physician and Other Essays* (New York: Science History Publications, 1975).

32. *DAB,* s.v. "Thomas Bond"; Whitfield J. Bell, Jr., *John Morgan: Continental Doctor* (Philadelphia: University of Pennsylvania Press, 1965), pp. 25–26; Bridenbaugh and Bridenbaugh, *Rebels and Gentlemen,* pp. 270–75.

33. Harold Donaldson Eberlein and Cortlandt Van Dyke Hubbard, *Diary of Independence Hall* (Philadelphia: Lippincott, 1948), pp. 76–78; Young, *Memorial History,* 1:264; Oberholtzer, *Philadelphia,* 1:180–84; Agnes Repplier, *Philadelphia: The Place and Its People* (New York: Macmillan, 1898), pp. 118–22; William H. Williams, "The Industrious Poor and the Founding of the Pennsylvania Hospital," *PMHB* 97 (Oct. 1973): 431–43; id., *The Pennsylvania Hospital, 1751–1841* (Wayne, Penna.: Haverford House, 1976).

34. Labaree et al., eds., *Papers of Franklin,* 4:62.

35. Carl Van Doren, *Benjamin Franklin* (New York: Viking, 1952), p. 779.

36. Leonard W. Labaree et al., eds., *The Autobiography of Benjamin Franklin* (New Haven, Conn.: Yale University Press, 1964), p. 181.

37. Oberholtzer, *Philadelphia,* 1:179–80; Watson, *Annals,* 3:274–75; Whitfield J. Bell, Jr., "Some Aspects of the Social History of Pennsylvania, 1760–1790," *PMHB* 62 (July 1938): 291; Young, *Memorial History,* 1:264.

38. Bridenbaugh and Bridenbaugh, *Rebels and Gentlemen,* pp. 36, 48–50.

39. Ibid., pp. 254–55; Sydney V. James, *A People Among Peoples: Quaker Benevolence in Eighteenth Century America* (Cambridge, Mass.: Harvard University Press, 1963), p. 136; Richard I. Schelling, "Benjamin Franklin and the Bray Associates," *PMHB* 63 (July 1939): 284–86.

40. Bridenbaugh and Bridenbaugh, *Rebels and Gentlemen,* pp. 42–45; Frederick B. Tolles, *Meeting House and Counting House: The Quaker Merchants of Colonial Philadelphia, 1682–1763* (Chapel Hill: University of North Carolina Press, 1948), p. 151; Oberholtzer,

Philadelphia, 1:178–79; *Common Council Minutes*, p. 529; Nancy S. Hornick, "Anthony Benezet and the Africans' School," *PMHB* 99 (Oct. 1975): 399–421.
41. Bridenbaugh and Bridenbaugh, *Rebels and Gentlemen*, pp. 87–88; Carl Bridenbaugh, "Philosophy Put to Use: Voluntary Associations for Propagating the Enlightenment in Philadelphia," *PMHB* 101 (Jan. 1977): 70–80.
42. Bridenbaugh and Bridenbaugh, *Rebels and Gentlemen*, pp. 79–80.
43. Frank L. Mott, *A History of American Magazines, 1741–1850* (Cambridge, Mass.: Harvard University Press, 1957), pp. 25, 80–81; Robert E. Spiller et al., eds., *Literary History of the United States* (3 vols.; New York: Macmillan, 1953), 1:106–7.
44. Labaree et al., eds., *Papers of Franklin*, 3:263; Bridenbaugh, *Cities in Revolt*, p. 185.
45. William Sawitzky, *Catalogue Descriptive and Critical of the Paintings and Miniatures in the Historical Society of Pennsylvania* (Philadelphia: Historical Society of Pennsylvania, 1942), pp. 131–32, 134–35; Nicholas B. Wainwright, *One Hundred and Fifty Years of Collecting by the Historical Society of Pennsylvania, 1824–1974* (Philadelphia: Historical Society of Pennsylvania, 1974); Jackson, *Encyclopedia*, 1:157.
46. *Pennsylvania Gazette*, Dec. 2, 1746–March 3, 1746/7, March 24, 1746/7–April 9, 1747; Bridenbaugh and Bridenbaugh, *Rebels and Gentlemen*, p. 165.
47. Bridenbaugh and Bridenbaugh, *Rebels and Gentlemen*, p. 167; Jackson, *Encyclopedia*, 1:157.
48. Thomas C. Pollock, *The Philadelphia Theatre in the Eighteenth Century* (Philadelphia: University of Pennsylvania Press, 1933), pp. 6–7; *Common Council Minutes*, p. 523; Jackson, *Encyclopedia*, 1:20, 22; Scharf and Westcott, *History of Philadelphia*, 2:864.
49. Luther P. Eisenhart, ed., *Historic Philadelphia: From the Founding Until the Early Nineteenth Century: Papers Dealing with Its People and Buildings with an Illustrative Map* (Philadelphia: American Philosophical Society, 1953), p. 313; *Pennsylvania Gazette*, April 11, 1754; Pollock, *Philadelphia Theatre in the Eighteenth Century*, pp. 7–11, 13–17; William S. Dye, "Pennsylvania Versus the Theatre in the Eighteenth Century," *PMHB* 55 (July 1931): 352–57; Brooks McNamara, "David Douglass and the Beginnings of American Theater Architecture," *Winterthur Portfolio* 3 (1967): 117–18, 121; *Pennsylvania Statutes at Large*, 5:445–48; *Votes of Assembly*, 5:65; Jackson, *Encyclopedia*, 3:920, 4:-943, 1135; Scharf and Westcott, *History of Philadelphia*, 2:1075; Oberholtzer, *Philadelphia*, 1:166–67.
50. Scharf and Westcott, *History of Philadelphia*, 2:1324, 1420; Bridenbaugh and Bridenbaugh, *Rebels and Gentlemen*, p. 147; "Diary of Daniel Fisher," pp. 267, 272; Eisenhart, ed., *Historic Philadelphia*, p. 200; Adolph B. Benson, ed., *Peter Kalm's Travels in North America* (2 vols.; New York: Wilson-Erickson, 1937), 1:24; Gottlieb Mittelberger, *Journey to Pennsylvania in the Year 1750* . . . (Philadelphia: J. J. McVey, 1898), pp. 114–15.
51. Watson, *Annals*, 3:154; Bridenbaugh and Bridenbaugh, *Rebels and Gentlemen*, p. 150.
52. Tolles, *Meeting House and Counting House*, pp. 8–9, 135, 141–42; *Pennsylvania Gazette*, Jan. 20, March 16, 1746/7; Watson, *Annals*,

2:483; Thayer, *Israel Pemberton*, pp. 27, 29–30.
53. See Grant Miles Simon, "Houses and Early Life in Philadelphia," and Robert C. Smith, "Two Centuries of Philadelphia Architecture, 1700–1900," in Eisenhart, ed., *Historic Philadelphia*, pp. 280–88, 289–303.
54. Bridenbaugh and Bridenbaugh, *Rebels and Gentlemen*, pp. 89–90, 94–95; Frederick B. Tolles, *James Logan and the Culture of Provincial America* (Boston: Little, Brown, 1957), p. 193; Bridenbaugh, *Cities in Revolt*, pp. 95–96, 182.
55. Bridenbaugh and Bridenbaugh, *Rebels and Gentlemen*, pp. 1–12.
56. Eberlein and Hubbard, *Diary of Independence Hall*, pp. 63–64, 79–80, 94–95; *Pennsylvania Gazette*, March 24, 1757.
57. [Alexander Graydon,] *Memoirs of a Life, Chiefly Passed in Pennsylvania Within the Last Sixty Years* . . . (Harrisburg: John Wyeth, 1811), pp. 51–52; Thayer, *Israel Pemberton*, p. 29.
58. Watson, *Annals*, 1:277–78; Oberholtzer, *Philadelphia*, 1:210.
59. Young, *Memorial History*, 2:43. See also Robert F. Oaks, "Big Wheels in Philadelphia: Du Simitière's List of Carriage Owners," *PMHB* 95 (July 1971): 351–62.
60. Jackson, *Encyclopedia*, 1:173–77; Thomas W. Balch, *The Philadelphia Assemblies* (Philadelphia: Allen, Lane and Scott, 1916), pp. 17–50; Watson, *Annals*, 1:283–85; Oberholtzer, *Philadelphia*, 1:164–65.
61. Bridenbaugh and Bridenbaugh, *Rebels and Gentlemen*, p. 2.
62. Randolph S. Klein, *Portrait of an Early American Family: The Shippens of Pennsylvania* (Philadelphia: University of Pennsylvania Press, 1975); Bridenbaugh and Bridenbaugh, *Rebels and Gentlemen*, chap. 6; Tolles, *Meeting House and Counting House*, pp. 119–20.
63. Allinson and Penrose, *Philadelphia . . . Municipal Development*, pp. 19–20; Scharf and Westcott, *History of Philadelphia*, 2:862; Bridenbaugh and Bridenbaugh, *Rebels and Gentlemen*, pp. 205–7; Carl Bridenbaugh, *The Colonial Craftsman* (New York: New York University Press, 1950), pp. 78–79, 157–58.
64. Bridenbaugh and Bridenbaugh, *Rebels and Gentlemen*, pp. 206–7; Francis James Dallett, Jr., "John Leacock, Playwright," *PMHB* 77 (Oct. 1954): 458, 466.
65. Bridenbaugh, *Colonial Craftsman*, p. 111; Alfred Coxe Prime, *The Arts & Crafts in Philadelphia, Maryland and South Carolina, 1721–1785* (Topsfield, Mass.; Walpole Press, 1929), p. 108.
66. Carolyn W. Stretch, "Early Colonial Clockmakers," *PMHB* 56 (July 1932): 225–27; George H. Eckhardt, *Pennsylvania Clocks and Clockmakers* (New York: Devin-Adair, 1955), pp. 32, 64, 86; Watson, *Annals*, 1:574; Hindle, *Pursuit of Science*, p. 153.
67. Harold E. Gillingham, "Some Colonial Ships Built in Philadelphia," *PMHB* 56 (April 1932): 171–73, 180–81.
68. Bridenbaugh and Bridenbaugh, *Rebels and Gentlemen*, pp. 9–10, 13; Sam Bass Warner, Jr., *The Private City: Philadelphia in Three Periods of Its Growth* (Philadelphia: University of Pennsylvania Press, 1968), p. 19.
69. Watson, *Annals*, 3:236–37; Young, *Memorial History*, 1:258.

70. Benson, ed., *Peter Kalm's Travels*, 1:18, 33; Young, *Memorial History*, 1:266–67.
71. Watson, *Annals*, 1:450; Eisenhart, ed., *Historic Philadelphia*, p. 221.
72. Jackson, *Encyclopedia*, 4:1065; Scharf and Westcott, *History of Philadelphia*, 2:1419–20.
73. Oberholtzer, *Philadelphia*, 1:187–88, 233; Scharf and Westcott, *History of Philadelphia*, 2:1250; Eisenhart, ed., *Historic Philadelphia*, p. 212; Bridenbaugh and Bridenbaugh, *Rebels and Gentlemen*, p. 16.
74. Guy S. Klett, *Presbyterians in Colonial Pennsylvania* (Philadelphia: University of Pennsylvania Press, 1937).
75. Oberholtzer, *Philadelphia*, 1:197; Eisenhart, ed., *Historic Philadelphia*, p. 202; "Diary of Daniel Fisher," p. 274; Scharf and Westcott, *History of Philadelphia*, 2:1370.
76. Sister Blanche Marie, "The Catholic Church in Colonial Pennsylvania," *PH* 3 (Oct. 1936): 248–49, 252; Eisenhart, ed., *Historic Philadelphia*, pp. 200, 201; Jackson, *Encyclopedia*, 2:392–93.
77. Handlin and Clive, eds., *Journey . . . by . . . Mittelberger*, p. 113; Gipson, *British Empire*, 3:175–76; Theodore Thayer, *Pennsylvania Politics and the Growth of Democracy, 1740–1776* (Harrisburg: Pennsylvania Historical and Museum Commission, 1953), p. 59.
78. Mereness, ed., *Travels in North America*, p. 411.
79. Young, *Memorial History*, 1:258; Wainwright, *A Philadelphia Story: The Philadelphia Contributionship*, p. 6; "Diary of Daniel Fisher," p. 267; "Ezra Stiles' Diary," *PMHB* 16

(1892): 375; Watson, *Annals*, 1:493–94.
80. *Common Council Minutes*, p. 622; Jackson, *Encyclopedia*, 4:1170, 1206.
81. Handlin and Clive, eds., *Journey . . . of . . . Mitteiberger*, p. 48.
82. Labaree et al., eds., *Papers of Franklin*, 3:184; Scharf and Westcott, *History of Philadelphia*, 1:214–15.
83. Eberlein and Hubbard, *Diary of Independence Hall*, p. 73; Scharf and Westcott, *History of Philadelphia*, 1:215–16; Thayer, *Pennsylvania Politics*, p. 22.
84. Scharf and Westcott, *History of Philadelphia*, 1:215; Young, *Memorial History*, 1:261–62.
85. Labaree et al., eds., *Papers of Franklin*, 3:220–21, 221n, 274n; *Common Council Minutes*, pp. 492, 499; Scharf and Westcott, *History of Philadelphia*, 1:214.
86. *Pennsylvania Gazette*, Sept. 1, 1748; Labaree et al., eds., *Papers of Franklin*, 3:221, 274n, 283n.
87. Labaree et al., eds., *Autobiography of Franklin*, pp. 171, 172.
88. *Pennsylvania Gazette*, Sept. 1, 1748.
89. Labaree et al., eds., *Autobiography of Franklin*, p. 236.
90. E. Douglas Branch, "Henry Bouquet, Professional Soldier," *PMHB* 62 (Jan. 1938): 43; *Common Council Minutes*, pp. 601–2; Scharf and Westcott, *History of Philadelphia*, 1:252; Young, *Memorial History*, 1:283; Oberholtzer, *Philadelphia*, 1:200; Thayer, *Pennsylvania Politics*, p. 60.
91. Van Doren, *Benjamin Franklin*, p. 310.

THE REVOLUTIONARY CITY, 1765–1783

1. Allen to Benjamin Chew, in David A. Kimball and Miriam Quinn, "William Allen–Benjamin Chew Correspondence, 1763–1764," *Pennsylvania Magazine of History and Biography* (hereafter cited as *PMHB*) 90 (April 1966): 225; Bradford to James Madison, quoted in David Hawke, *In the Midst of a Revolution* (Philadelphia: University of Pennsylvania Press, 1961), p. 49, citing an undated letter probably written late February 1775, in Bradford Letterbook, 1775, Historical Society of Pennsylvania (hereafter cited as HSP).
2. Marc Egnal and Joseph A. Ernst, "An Economic Interpretation of the American Revolution," *William and Mary Quarterly*, 3d ser., 29 (Jan. 1972): 3–32.
3. Ibid.
4. James H. Hutson, "An Investigation of the Inarticulate: Philadelphia's White Oaks," *William and Mary Quarterly*, 3d ser. 34 (Jan. 1971): 18.
5. [Thomas Clifford] to Harper and Hartshorne, Philadelphia, Nov. 1, 1765, Thomas Clifford Letter Book, 1759–1766, Pemberton Papers, HSP.
6. [Thomas Clifford] to Hide and Hamilton, Philadelphia, Nov. 23, 1765, Thomas Clifford Letter Book, 1759–1766, Pemberton Papers, HSP.
7. J. Thomas Scharf and Thompson Westcott, *A History of Philadelphia, 1609–1884* (3 vols.; Philadelphia: L. H. Everts, 1884), 1:272–73.
8. Carl Bridenbaugh and Jessica Bridenbaugh, *Rebels and Gentlemen: Philadelphia in the Age of Franklin* (New York: Reynal & Hitchcock, 1942), p. 25.
9. *A Report of the Record Commissioners of the City of Boston, Containing the Selectmen's Minutes from 1764 through 1768*

(Boston, 1889), 20:273; Albert Bushnell Hart, ed., *The Commonwealth History of Massachusetts: Colony, Province and State* (5 vols.; New York: States History Co., 1927–1930), 2:496; Isaac Jones to the Boston Selectmen, Dec. 22, 1767, *Minutes of the Common Council of the City of Philadelphia* (Philadelphia: Crissy and Markley, 1847), Dec. 22, 1767, pp. 725–26 (hereafter cited as *Common Council Minutes*).
10. Theodore Thayer, *Pennsylvania Politics and the Growth of Democracy, 1740–1776* (Harrisburg: Pennsylvania Historical and Museum Commission, 1953), p. 144.
11. Arthur M. Schlesinger, Sr., "Politics, Propaganda, and the Philadelphia Press, 1767–1770," *PMHB* 60 (July 1936): 309, 321.
12. The letters are printed in William E. Leuchtenberg and Bernard Wishy, eds., *Empire and Nation* (Englewood Cliffs, N.J.: Prentice-Hall, 1962). See the introduction by Forrest McDonald, p. xiii.
13. A Petition to the Crown, March 5, 1771, Papers of the Continental Congress, 1774–1789, in microfilm (Washington, D.C.: National Archives Microfilm Publications, Microcopy No. 247, 1959), Roll 83, 1:87–89 (hereafter cited as PCC/NAMP).
14. John C. Miller, *Origins of the American Revolution* (Stanford, Calif.: Stanford University Press, 1959), pp. 338–41.
15. *Pennsylvania Packet*, Oct. 11, 1773.
16. Ibid., Oct. 18, 1773; Jan. 3, 1774.
17. Thayer, *Pennsylvania Politics*, p. 154.
18. John C. Miller, *Sam Adams: Pioneer in*

Propaganda (Stanford, Calif.: Stanford University Press, 1960), p. 288.
19. *Pennsylvania Packet*, Dec. 13, 1773.
20. Ibid., Dec. 27, 1773.
21. Miller, *Sam Adams*, pp. 289–90.
22. J. Paul Selsam, *The Pennsylvania Constitution of 1776* (Philadelphia: University of Pennsylvania Press, 1936), p. 50.
23. *Pennsylvania Journal*, June 22, 1774; Selsam, *Pennsylvania Constitution of 1776*, pp. 55–56.
24. Thomas Willing to William Maclay, William Plunkett, and Samuel Hunter, June 28, 1774, Society Miscellaneous Collection, Box 15B, HSP.
25. *Votes and Proceedings of the House of Representatives of the Province of Pennsylvania*, in *Pennsylvania Archives*, 8th ser. (8 vols.; Harrisburg: State Library, 1931–1935), 6:516–17 (hereafter cited as *Votes and Proceedings*).
26. Ibid., p. 520.
27. Carl Bridenbaugh, *Cities in Revolt: Urban Life in America, 1743–1776* (New York: Knopf, 1964), pp. 75, 217, 247.
28. Nicholas B. Wainwright, *Colonial Grandeur in Philadelphia: The House and Furniture of General John Cadwalader* (Philadelphia: Historical Society of Pennsylvania, 1964), pp. 1, 2, 39, 60; *PMHB* 56 (April 1932): 120.
29. Silas Deane to his wife, Sept. 1–3, 1774, in Edmund C. Burnett, ed., *Letters of the Members of the Continental Congress* (8 vols.; Washington, D.C.: U.S. Government Printing Office, 1921–1936), 1:4–5.
30. *PMHB* 56 (April 1932): 120.
31. *Pennsylvania Journal*, Nov. 2, 1774.
32. *Journals of the House of Representatives of the Commonwealth of Pennsylvania . . .* (Philadelphia, 1782), 1:32–33; Selsam, *Pennsylvania Constitution of 1776*, pp. 70–72.
33. *PMHB* 56 (April 1932): 124, 128; Douglas Southall Freeman, *George Washington: A Biography* (7 vols.; New York: Scribner's, 1948–1957), 3:419, 437, 459–61.
34. *Votes and Proceedings*, 7:647.
35. W. C. Ford et al., eds., *Journals of the Continental Congress, 1774–1789* (34 vols.; Washington, D.C.: U.S. Government Printing Office, 1904–1937), 4:342, 357–58 (hereafter cited as *JCC*).
36. *Votes and Proceedings*, 6:726–27; Peter Force, comp., *American Archives . . .* , 4th ser. (6 vols.; Washington, D.C.: M. St. Clair Clarke and Peter Force, 1837–1846), 6:-517–18.
37. Robert L. Brunhouse, *The Counter-Revolution in Pennsylvania, 1776–1790* (Harrisburg: Pennsylvania Historical and Museum Commission, 1971), p. 13.
38. Ellis P. Oberholtzer, *Philadelphia: A History of the City and Its People* (4 vols.; Philadelphia: S. J. Clarke, 1912), 1:251.
39. Carl Van Doren, *Benjamin Franklin* (New York: Viking Press, 1938), p. 551.
40. Oberholtzer, *Philadelphia*, 1:252.
41. Victor Rosewater, *The Liberty Bell: Its History and Significance* (New York: Appleton, 1926).
42. *Pennsylvania Archives*, 1st ser., 1664–1790 (12 vols.; Philadelphia: Joseph Severns, 1852–1856), 4:598–99 (hereafter cited as *Pa. Arch.*, without series number); Thayer, *Pennsylvania Politics*, pp. 55–56.
43. Scharf and Westcott, *History of Philadelphia*, 2:1017.
44. *Votes and Proceedings*, 6:593.
45. *Pa. Arch.*, 5:3–5.
46. Ibid., 4:598; Scharf and Westcott, *History of Philadelphia*, 2:1026–27.
47. "The Course of Delaware River from Philadelphia to Chester," a British military map, dated 1777, photostat at the Philadelphia Historical Commission; Brooke Hindle, *David Rittenhouse* (Princeton, N.J.: Princeton University Press, 1964), pp. 129–30.
48. *PMHB*, 85 (Jan. 1961): 36.
49. *Pa. Arch.*, 5:3–5.
50. John W. Jackson, *The Pennsylvania Navy, 1775–1781: The Defense of the Delaware* (New Brunswick, N.J.: Rutgers University Press, 1974), chap. 4.
51. Resolution of the Pennsylvania Council of Safety, Oct. 8, 1776, PCC/NAMP, microcopy 247, roll 83, 1:233.
52. *JCC*, 6:940.
53. Ibid., p. 977.
54. Ibid., p. 979.
55. Hindle, *David Rittenhouse*, p. 173.
56. *Colonial Records*, 9:38. This is the binder's title for *The Minutes of the Supreme Executive Council of Pennsylvania from Its Organization to the Termination of the Revolution*, the final six volumes of *Minutes of the Provincial Council of Pennsylvania from the Organization to the Termination of the Proprietary Government* (16 vols. and index; Philadelphia: Joseph Severns; Harrisburg: Theo Fenn, 1852–1860).
57. *JCC*, 6:1025–28.
58. Robert Morris to the Commissioners in France, Dec. 21, 1776, in Peter Force, comp., *American Archives . . .* , 5th ser. (3 vols.; Washington: M. St. Clair Clarke and Peter Force, 1848–1853), 3:1334.
59. Nicholas B. Wainwright, ed., "'A Diary of Trifling Occurrences': Philadelphia, 1776–1778," by Sarah Logan Fisher, *PMHB* 82 (Oct. 1958): 419.
60. *Colonial Records*, 11:204–5.
61. *JCC*, 7:268–69.
62. *Pennsylvania Gazette*, April 23, 1777.
63. Ira D. Gruber, *The Howe Brothers and the American Revolution* (New York: Atheneum, 1972), p. 234; Troyer S. Anderson, *The Command of the Howe Brothers during the American Revolution* (New York: Oxford University Press, 1936), p. 277; Bernhard Knollenberg, *Washington and the Revolution, A Reappraisal: Gates, Conway, and the Continental Congress* (New York: Macmillan, 1940), p. 24.
64. Wilbur H. Siebert, *The Loyalists of Pennsylvania* (Columbus: Ohio State University Press, 1920), pp. 23–24.
65. Arthur J. Mekeel, "The Quakers in the American Revolution" (Ph.D. dissertation, Harvard University, 1940), pp. 10–11.
66. Anne T. Gary, "The Political and Economic Relations of English and American Quakers, 1750–1785" (doctoral thesis, St. Hugh's College, Oxford, 1935, on microfilm at the American Philosophical Society), p. 365.
67. Mekeel, "Quakers in the American Revolution," p. 68, 77.
68. Gary, "Political and Economic Relations of English and American Quakers," p. 372.
69. Mekeel, "Quakers in the American Revolution," pp. 116–17.
70. Ibid., pp. 91, 124, 143.
71. Frederick B. Tolles, *Meeting House and Counting House: The Quaker Merchants of*

Colonial Philadelphia, 1682–1763 (Chapel Hill: University of North Carolina Press, 1948), pp. 236–39.
72. JCC, 8:694.
73. Colonial Records, 11:283–84.
74. Elizabeth Drinker's Diary, Sept. 2, 1777, HSP; John Pemberton, "Account of the Life of John Hunt," Pemberton Papers, 32:12, in a manuscript of eight pages, HSP.
75. Pa. Arch., 5:472, 473, 543, 551.
76. William Howe, The Narrative of Lieut. Gen. Sir William Howe . . . (London: H. Baldwin, 1780), pp. 18–19.
77. Christopher Ward, The War of the Revolution, edited by John Richard Alden (2 vols.; New York: Macmillan, 1952), 1:334, 335.
78. Charles Biddle, Autobiography of Charles Biddle, Vice-President of the Supreme Executive Council of Pennsylvania, 1745–1821, edited by James S. Biddle (Philadelphia: Collins Printing House, 1883), p. 101.
79. John F. Watson, Annals of Philadelphia, and Pennsylvania, in the Olden Time (3 vols.; Philadelphia, E. S. Stuart, 1887), 2:283; JCC, 8:735.
80. Wainwright, " 'A Diary of Trifling Occurrences,' " p. 448.
81. "The Diary of Robert Morton," PMHB 1 (1877): 7–8; Alfred Hoyt Bill, Valley Forge (New York: Harper, 1952), pp. 65–66.
82. Wainwright, " 'A Diary of Trifling Occurrences,' " p. 450.
83. Anne Bezanson, Prices and Inflation During the American Revolution: Pennsylvania, 1770–1790 (Philadelphia: University of Pennsylvania Press, 1951), pp. 17–18.
84. Knollenberg, Washington and the Revolution, p. 194n.
85. Clarence S. Brigham, History and Bibliography of American Newspapers, 1690–1820 (Worcester, Mass.: American Antiquarian Society, 1947), pp. 907–62; JCC, 8:754; Freeman, Washington, 4:499–500.
86. Howe, Narrative, p. 54.
87. Watson, Annals, 2:407.
88. For the battle of Germantown, see Ward, War of the Revolution, vol. 1, ch. 33. For the actions on the Delaware, see ibid., chap. 34; and Jackson, Pennsylvania Navy, chaps. 9–12.
89. Frank Moore, ed., Songs and Ballads of the American Revolution (New York: D. Appleton, 1856), pp. 209–11. For a historian's account, see Jackson, Pennsylvania Navy, pp. 288–89.
90. A Plan for the City and Environs of Philadelphia, with the Works and Encampments of His Majesty's Forces . . . , published Jan. 1, 1779, photostat from the original at HSP.
91. Howe, Narrative, pp. 54–55.
92. Van Doren, Franklin, p. 535.
93. JCC, 10:74.
94. Watson, Annals, 2:300–2.
95. Siebert, Loyalists of Pennsylvania, pp. 43–44.
96. Proclamation of Sir William Howe, broadside, HSP.
97. Howe, Narrative, pp. 42, 56.
98. Ibid., p. 153.
99. "The Examination of Joseph Galloway in the House of Commons," in Pennsylvania Journal, Nov. 17, 1779.
100. Whitfield J. Bell, Jr., John Morgan: Continental Doctor (Philadelphia: University of Pennsylvania Press, 1965), pp. 205, 210.
101. Willard O. Mishoff, "Business in Philadelphia

During the British Occupation, 1777–1778," PMHB 61 (April 1937): 171–72.
102. "Diary of James Allen," PMHB 9 (Oct. 1885): 429.
103. Wainwright, " 'A Diary of Trifling Occurrences,' " p. 454; Benjamin Rush to James Searle, Nov. 9, 1777, Conarroe Collection, HSP, 1:26; Phineas Pemberton to James Pemberton, Nov. 21, 1777, Pemberton Papers, HSP, 31:40; Watson, Annals, 2:285.
104. Bezanson, Prices and Inflation, p. 18; Proclamation by General Howe, Dec. 8, 1777, broadside, HSP.
105. Pa. Arch., 6:265.
106. Molly Pemberton to James Pemberton, Feb. 2, 1778, Pemberton Papers, HSP; 31:102; "Diary of James Allen," p. 432.
107. Robert Morris to John Brown, June 26, 1778, Dreer Collection, HSP.
108. James Thomas Flexner, The Traitor and the Spy: Benedict Arnold and John André (New York: Harcourt, Brace, 1953), p. 209.
109. Watson, Annals, 2:290–93.
110. Richard R. Murdoch, "Benedict Arnold and the Owners of the Charming Nancy," PMHB 84 (Jan. 1960): 27–28.
111. Pennsylvania Packet, July 18, 1778; Mishoff, "Business in Philadelphia," p. 179.
112. Pennsylvania Statutes at Large, 9:45–46.
113. Howe, Narrative, p. 33.
114. "The Examination of Joseph Galloway in the House of Commons," in Pennsylvania Journal, Nov. 17, 1779.
115. Siebert, Loyalists of Pennsylvania, pp. 57–58.
116. Ibid., pp. 52, 57–58.
117. Henry D. Biddle, Extracts from the Journal of Elizabeth Drinker (Philadelphia: Lippincott, 1889), p. 106.
118. JCC, 11:571.
119. Proclamation of General Benedict Arnold, June 19, 1778, in Pa. Arch., 6:606–7; Willard M. Wallace, Traitorous Hero: The Life and Fortunes of Benedict Arnold (New York: Harper, 1954), pp. 163–64.
120. Benedict Arnold to Henry Laurens, June 24, 1778, PCC/NAMP, microcopy 247, roll 179, item 162, pp. 114–15.
121. JCC, 13:337.
122. See both Flexner, The Traitor and the Spy, and Wallace, Traitorous Hero.
123. Henry Laurens to Rawlins Lowndes, July 18, 1778, in Burnett, ed., Letters of the Members of the Continental Congress, 3:332–33; JCC, 11:662.
124. Siebert, Loyalists of Pennsylvania, p. 55.
125. PMHB 8 (Oct. 1884): 430.
126. Pennsylvania Packet, May 27, 1778.
127. Ibid., July 9, 1778.
128. Ibid., July 25, 1778.
129. John F. Roche, Joseph Reed: A Moderate in the American Revolution (New York: Columbia University Press, 1957), pp. 145–47.
130. Mekeel, "Quakers in the American Revolution," pp. 142–43.
131. Edward Potts Cheyney, A History of the University of Pennsylvania, 1740–1940 (Philadelphia: University of Pennsylvania Press, 1957), p. 120.
132. Pennsylvania Statutes at Large, 9:175–76.
133. Brunhouse, Counter-Revolution, pp. 77–78.
134. Cheyney, History of the University of Pennsylvania, p. 122.
135. Hindle, David Rittenhouse, pp. 220–21.
136. Bezanson, Prices and Inflation, pp. 12–14, 88.
137. Brunhouse, Counter-Revolution, pp. 68–69.
138. C. Page Smith, "The Attack on Fort Wil-

son," *PMHB* 78 (April 1954): 177–85; John K. Alexander, "The Fort Wilson Incident of 1779: A Case Study of the Revolutionary Crowd," *William and Mary Quarterly*, 3d ser., 31 (Oct. 1974): 589–612.

139. *JCC*, 19:126, 180.
140. Robert Morris, circular letter of Jan. 8, 1782, Dreer Collection, HSP.
141. Brunhouse, *Counter-Revolution*, p. 123.
142. George A. Abbot, *A Short History of the Library Company of Philadelphia* (Philadelphia: Library Company of Philadelphia, 1913), p. 13; Scharf and Westcott, *History of Philadelphia*, 2:1178.
143. *Pennsylvania Packet*, March 2, 1779; Scharf and Westcott, *History of Philadelphia*, 2:-1192.
144. Whitfield J. Bell, Jr., "Some Aspects of the Social History of Pennsylvania, 1760–1790," *PMHB* 62 (July 1938): 303.
145. Bridenbaugh and Bridenbaugh, *Rebels and Gentlemen*, p. 253.
146. *Pennsylvania Packet*, Nov. 20, 1783.
147. Elias Boudinot to his wife, July 29, 1781, in Burnett, ed., *Letters of the Members of the Continental Congress*, 6:162n; *Pennsylvania Packet*, July 26, 28, 1781.
148. Col. F. Johnston to Anthony Wayne, Sept. 20, 1780, Anthony Wayne Papers, HSP, 10:75.
149. See Bell, *John Morgan*.
150. Scharf and Westcott, *History of Philadelphia*, 2:1477.
151. *Pennsylvania Packet*, Sept. 26, 1780.
152. *Pa. Arch.*, 7:134.
153. *Pennsylvania Packet*, Jan. 8, 1782.
154. Nicholas B. Wainwright, "Philadelphia's Eighteenth-Century Fire Insurance Companies," in Luther P. Eisenhart, ed., *Historic Philadelphia: From the Founding Until the Early Nineteenth Century: Papers Dealing with Its People and Buildings with an Illustrative Map* (Philadelphia: American Philosophical Society, 1953), pp. 250–51.
155. *Pennsylvania Statutes at Large*, 9:490, 511.

156. Wainwright, "Philadelphia's Eighteenth-Century Fire Insurance Companies," pp. 251–52.
157. Miller, *Sam Adams* (1936 ed.; Boston: Little, Brown), p. 353.
158. Scharf and Westcott, *History of Philadelphia*, 2:893.
159. Charles Henry Hart, "Mary White—Mrs. Robert Morris," *PMHB* 2 (1878): 162.
160. Col. Walter S. Stewart to Anthony Wayne, Nov. 29, 1778, Anthony Wayne Papers, HSP, 6:31.
161. Scharf and Westcott, *History of Philadelphia*, 2:901.
162. Col. F. Johnston to Anthony Wayne, July 25, 1780, Anthony Wayne Papers, HSP, 10:46.
163. *Pennsylvania Packet*, Feb. 8, 1780.
164. Ibid., Jan. 12, 1782.
165. Ibid., Nov. 28, Dec. 12, 1780.
166. Ibid., July 18, 1782.
167. Ibid., scattered issues for March and April 1783.
168. Ibid., April 12, 29, 1783.
169. Extracts from the Minutes of the Pennsylvania Executive Council, June 27, 1783, United States Army Photostats on the Mutiny of 1783, Society Miscellaneous Collection, HSP; Elias Boudinot to George Washington, June 21, 1783, in Burnett, ed., *Letters of the Members of the Continental Congress*, 7:193.
170. Edmund C. Burnett, *The Continental Congress* (New York: Macmillan, 1911), pp. 575–80; Willard M. Wallace, *Appeal to Arms: A Military History of the American Revolution* (New York: Harper, 1951), pp. 267–68; Harry M. Ward, *The Department of War, 1781–1789* (Pittsburgh: University of Pittsburgh Press, 1962), pp. 28–30; United States Army Photostats on the Mutiny of 1783, Society Miscellaneous Collection, HSP.
171. A Proclamation by Elias Boudinot [June 24, 1783], in Burnett, ed., *Letters of the Members of the Continental Congress*, 7:195–96.
172. Oliver Ellsworth to Jonathan Trumbull, June 4, 1783, in Burnett, ed., *Letters of the Members of the Continental Congress*, 7:180.

THE FEDERAL CITY, 1783–1800

1. *Freeman's Journal*, Dec. 13, 1786; Miranda, representative of Latin American independence movements, quoted in John S. Ezell, ed., *The New Democracy in America* (Norman: University of Oklahoma Press, 1963), p. 57; Luther P. Eisenhart, ed., *Historic Philadelphia: From the Founding Until the Early Nineteenth Century: Papers Dealing with Its People and Buildings with an Illustrative Map* (Philadelphia: American Philosophical Society, 1953), pp. 168–69, from William S. Baker, *Washington After the Revolution* (Philadelphia: Lippincott, 1898), p. 203.
2. Douglas Southall Freeman, *George Washington: A Biography* (7 vols.; New York: Scribner's, 1948–1957), 5:469–70.
3. Ibid., pp. 470–71.
4. Eric Foner, *Tom Paine and Revolutionary America* (New York: Oxford University Press, 1976), pp. 204–6 (p. 205 for shipbuilding).
5. David Hawke, *In the Midst of a Revolution* (Philadelphia: University of Pennsylvania Press, 1961); Robert Brunhouse, *The Counter-Revolution in Pennsylvania, 1776–1790* (Harrisburg: Pennsylvania Historical Commission, 1942), pp. 60–68.

6. Brunhouse, *Counter-Revolution*, pp. 176–90; Roland M. Baumann, "The Democratic-Republicans of Philadelphia: The Origins, 1776–1797" (Ph.D. dissertation, Pennsylvania State University, 1970), pp. 56–58.
7. Richard G. Miller, *Philadelphia—The Federalist City: A Study of Urban Politics, 1789–1801* (Port Washington, N.Y.: Kennikat Press, 1976), pp. 20–22.
8. William Bingham to Benjamin Rush, May 3, 1784, Gratz Collection, Historical Society of Pennsylvania (hereafter cited as HSP); William Bingham to Richard Price, Dec. 1, 1786, *Proceedings of the Massachusetts Historical Society*, 2d ser. 17 (1903–1904): 361; Jackson Turner Main, *Political Parties Before the Constitution* (Chapel Hill: University of North Carolina Press, 1973), pp. 174–211.
9. On incorporation and the similar issue of the Test Acts, see *Pennsylvania Packet*, Oct. 1, 1784; *Evening Herald*, Nov. 20, 1785; *Pennsylvania Journal*, Sept. 10, 1783; Brunhouse, *Counter-Revolution*, pp. 16–18, 40–41, 152–55, 184–85, 195, 220, 221, 247, 277–78.
10. Bray Hammond, *Banks and Politics in America: From the Revolution to the Civil War*

(Princeton, N.J.: Princeton University Press, 1957), pp. 42–56 (quotation from p. 54, citing Mathew Carey, ed., *Debates and Proceedings of the General Assembly of Pennsylvania on the Memorials Praying a Repeal or Suspension of the Law Annulling the Charter of the Bank* [Philadelphia: Carey, 1786], p. 21).

11. Lawrence Lewis, Jr., *A History of the Bank of North America* (Philadelphia: Lippincott, 1882); Cyril James, "The Bank of North America and the Financial History of Philadelphia," *Pennsylvania Magazine of History and Biography* (hereafter cited as *PMHB*) 64 (Jan. 1940): 56–87; Janet Wilson, "The Bank of North America and Pennsylvania Politics, 1781–1787," *PMHB* 66 (Jan. 1942): 3–28; Minutes of the Directors and the Minutes of the Stockholders of the Bank of North America, HSP.

12. Charles S. Olton, *Artisans for Independence: Philadelphia Mechanics and the American Revolution* (Syracuse, N.Y.: Syracuse University Press, 1975), pp. 99–102; Brunhouse, *Counter-Revolution*, pp. 195–97.

13. Edward Potts Cheyney, *History of the University of Pennsylvania, 1740–1940* (Philadelphia: University of Pennsylvania Press, 1940), pp. 129–47 (quotations from p. 146).

14. Ibid., pp. 144–45.

15. Ibid., pp. 149–53; Brunhouse, *Counter-Revolution*, p. 220.

16. Freeman, *Washington*, 6:87–88.

17. Ibid., pp. 102, 110 (quotation), 112.

18. Brunhouse, *Counter-Revolution*, pp. 200–2.

19. John Bach McMaster and Frederick D. Stone, eds., *Pennsylvania and the Federal Convention, 1787–1788* (Philadelphia: HSP, 1888); Jonathan Elliott, ed., *The Debates in the Several State Conventions on the Adoption of the Federal Constitution . . .* (5 vols.; Philadelphia: Lippincott, 1888), 2:415–542; Brunhouse, *Counter-Revolution*, pp. 202–9 (quotations from p. 209).

20. J. Thomas Scharf and Thompson Westcott, *History of Philadelphia, 1609–1884* (3 vols.; Philadelphia: L. H. Everts, 1884), 1:447–452 (quotation from p. 452).

21. *Statutes at Large of Pennsylvania, 1682–1801* (Harrisburg: Harrisburg Publishing Co., 1908), 13:197–205; Tench Coxe to William Irvine, March 13, 1789, Irvine Papers, HSP; Samuel Miles to Tench Coxe, Feb. 4, 1789, and Daniel Coxe to Tench Coxe, Feb. 12, 1789, Coxe Papers, HSP; *Pennsylvania Gazette*, Feb. 11, March 11, 18, 1789; Scharf and Westcott, *History of Philadelphia*, 1:455–56.

22. Cheyney, *History of the University of Pennsylvania*, pp. 162–69.

23. Freeman, *Washington*, 6:170–73.

24. Tench Coxe to James Madison, July 23, 1788, Madison Papers, Library of Congress; Coxe to Samuel Miles, July 29, 1790, Coxe Papers, HSP; Benjamin Rush to John Adams, Feb. 21, March 19, 1789, in Lyman Butterfield, ed., *Letters of Benjamin Rush* (2 vols.; Princeton, N.J.: Princeton University Press, 1951), 1:500–1, 506–9; Kenneth R. Bowling, "New Light on the Philadelphia Mutiny of 1783: Federal-State Confrontation at the Close of the War for Independence," *PMHB* 101 (Oct. 1977): 419–50; Lawrence D. Cress, "Whither Columbia? Congressional Residence and the Politics of the New Nation, 1776–1787," *William and Mary Quarterly*, 3d ser. 32 (Oct. 1975): 581–600.

25. Fisher Ames, quoted in Claude G. Bowers,

Jefferson and Hamilton: The Struggle for Democracy in America (Boston: Houghton Mifflin, 1925), p. 65, from Seth Ames, ed., *Works of Fisher Ames* (2 vols.; Boston: Little, Brown, 1854), 1:79–80; Bowers, *Jefferson and Hamilton*, pp. 65–66; Charles A. Beard, ed., *The Journal of William Maclay* (New York: Ungar, 1927), pp. 284–85; Irving Brant, *James Madison* (6 vols.; Indianapolis: Bobbs-Merrill, 1941–1961), 3.313–14.

26. *Federal Gazette*, May 28, June 16, 1789; ibid., March 25, July 12, 1790.

27. Thomas Fitzsimons to Miers Fisher, June 15, July 16, 1790, Miers Fisher Papers, HSP; Minutes of the Philadelphia City Council, July 12, 16, 23, Sept. 9, Nov. 22, 1790, HSP; *Federal Gazette*, Sept. 22, 1790; Robert Morris to Mary Morris, July 2, 1790, Robert Morris Papers, Huntington Library, San Marino, Calif.

28. Beard, ed., *Journal of Maclay*, pp. 230–31, 234; William Bradford to Elias Boudinot, Sept. 20, 1789, Wallace Papers, HSP; Richard Peters to Thomas Jefferson, June 20, 1790, in Julian Boyd, ed., *The Papers of Thomas Jefferson* (19 vols. to date; Princeton, N.J.: Princeton University Press, 1950–), 16:345; Samuel Miles to Tench Coxe, July 29, 1790, William Maclay to Coxe, April 30, 1790, and William Irvine to Coxe, Aug. 20, 1790, Coxe Papers, HSP; Jacob E. Cooke, "The Compromise of 1790," *William and Mary Quarterly*, 3d ser. 27 (Oct. 1970): 534–35; Kenneth R. Bowling, "Dinner at Jefferson's: A Note on Jacob E. Cooke's 'The Compromise of 1790,'" *William and Mary Quarterly*, 3d ser. 28 (Oct. 1971): 632.

29. Beard, ed., *Journal of Maclay*, pp. 185–88, 238–39.

30. Freeman, *Washington*, 6:278–79 (quotation from p. 279, from John C. Fitzpatrick, ed., *The Writings of George Washington* [39 vols.; Washington, D.C.: U.S. Government Printing Office, 1931–1944], 31:110); Harold Donaldson Eberlein, "190, High Street (Market Street below Sixth): The Home of Washington and Adams, 1790–1800," in Eisenhart, ed., *Historic Philadelphia*, pp. 161–67.

31. Henry Wansey, *An Excursion to the United States of North America* (Sailbury, England: J. Easton, 1798), pp. 184–86; Marquis de Chastelleux, *Travels in North America . . .* Introduction by Howard C. Rice, Jr. (Chapel Hill: University of North Carolina Press, 1963), pp. 253–63; Benjamin Rush to William Cullen, Dec. 22, 1784, in Butterfield, ed., *Letters of Rush*, 1:346–47; Ferdinand M. Bayard, *Travels of a Frenchman in Maryland and Virginia with a Description of Philadelphia and Baltimore . . .* translated and edited by Ben C. McCary (Ann Arbor, Mich.: Edward Bros., 1950), pp. 125–33; Duke de La Rochefoucault, *Travels through the United States of North America . . .* translated by H. Neuman (2 vols.; London: J. Phillips, 1799).

32. Anthony N. B. Garvan, "Proprietary Philadelphia as Artifact," in Oscar Handlin and John Burchard, eds., *The Historian and the City* (Cambridge, Mass.: Harvard University Press, 1963), pp. 197–98; Thomas R. Winpenny, "The Nefarious Philadelphia Plan and Urban America: A Reconsideration," *PMHB* 101 (Jan. 1977): 103–12; *Colonial Records of Pennsylvania* 12:688–89, 772 (*Colonial Records* is the binder's title for *The Minutes*

of the Supreme Executive Council of Pennsylvania from Its Organization to the Termination of the Revolution, the final six volumes of a series that begins with *Minutes of the Provincial Council of Pennsylvania* . . . [16 vols. and index; Philadelphia: Joseph Severns; and Harrisburg: Theo Fenn, 1852–1860]).

33. John K. Alexander, "The Philadelphia Numbers Game: An Analysis of Philadelphia's Eighteenth-Century Population," *PMHB* 98 (July 1974): 314–24; Gary B. Nash, "Slaves and Slaveholders in Colonial Philadelphia," *William and Mary Quarterly*, 3d ser. 30 (April 1973): 223–56; Gary B. Nash and Billy G. Smith, "The Population of Eighteenth-Century Philadelphia," *PMHB* 99 (July 1975): 362–67; David T. Gilchrist, ed., *The Growth of Seaport Cities, 1790–1825* (Charlottesville: University of Virginia Press, 1967), pp. 39–41; W. S. Rossiter, *A Century of Population Growth in The United States* (Washington, D.C.: U.S. Government Printing Office, 1909), pp. 11–25.

34. William E. Lingelbach, "Philosophical Hall: The Home of the American Philosophical Society," in Eisenhart, ed., *Historic Philadelphia*, pp. 45–51; Edward M. Riley, "The Independence Hall Group," in ibid., pp. 26–29.

35. Charles E. Peterson, "Library Hall: Home of the Library Company of Philadelphia, 1790–1880," in Eisenhart, ed., *Historic Philadelphia*, pp. 130–36, 144; Edward Teitelman and Richard W. Longstreth, *Architecture in Philadelphia: A Guide* (Cambridge, Mass.: MIT Press, 1974), p. 32.

36. Edward B. Krumbhaar, "The Pennsylvania Hospital," in Eisenhart, ed., *Historic Philadelphia*, pp. 237, 243–44.

37. Teitelman and Longstreth, *Architecture in Philadelphia*, p. 200, for the Woodlands; Alexander Mackie, "The Presbyterian Churches of Old Philadelphia," in Eisenhart, ed., *Historic Philadelphia*, pp. 217–18, for the Market Street Presbyterian Church.

38. James O. Wettereau, "The Oldest Bank Building in the United States," in Eisenhart, ed., *Historic Philadelphia*, pp. 70–73 (quotation from Blodget from p. 72).

39. Grant Miles Simon, "Houses and Early Life in Philadelphia," in Eisenhart, ed., *Historic Philadelphia*, p. 285 and pocket map; Bowers, *Jefferson and Hamilton*, p. 128 (quotation, from Wansey, *Excursion*, p. 136). For this and other buildings of the period, see also George B. Tatum, *Penn's Great Town: 250 Years of Philadelphia Architecture* (Philadelphia: University of Pennsylvania Press, 1961), pp. 39–52.

40. Earl E. Lewis, "Anne Willing Bingham," in Edward T. James et al., eds., *Notable American Women, 1607–1950: A Biographical Dictionary* (3 vols.; Cambridge, Mass.: Belknap Press of Harvard University Press, 1971), 1:146–47 (quotation from p. 146). See also Ethel Rasmusson, "Capitalism on the Delaware: A Study of Philadelphia's Upper Class, 1789–1800" (Ph.D. dissertation, Brown University, 1952).

41. Lewis, "Anne Willing Bingham"; Bowers, *Jefferson and Hamilton*, pp. 127–31.

42. Freeman, *Washington*, 7:360.

43. Eberlein, "190, High Street," pp. 169–70 (quotation from p. 170).

44. Ibid., pp. 168–69 (first quotation from pp. 168–69, second from p. 169).

45. Freeman, *Washington*, 6:295–96.

46. Fitzpatrick, ed., *Writings of Washington*, 31:177n.

47. J. H. Powell, *Bring Out Your Dead: The Great Plague of Yellow Fever in Philadelphia in 1793* (Philadelphia: University of Pennsylvania Press, 1949), pp. 1–12. The following account is based mainly on Powell's book. See also the most vivid contemporary account, Mathew Carey, *A Short Account of the Malignant Fever Lately Prevalent in Philadelphia* (Philadelphia: Carey, 1794; reprint, New York: Arno Press, 1970).

48. Powell, *Bring Out Your Dead*, pp. 12–32, 64–65; Freeman, *Washington*, 7:119–21; the quotations are from Laurence Farmer, "Moschetoes were uncommonly numerous," *American Heritage* 7, no. 3 (April 1956): 55; Freeman, *Washington*, 7:119n; Butterfield, ed., *Letters of Rush*, 2:645, see also Paul Leicester Ford, ed., *Writings of Thomas Jefferson* (10 vols.; New York: Putnam, 1892–1899), 6:403.

49. Powell, *Bring Out Your Dead*, pp. 36–51, 72–89 (quotation from p. 77).

50. Ibid., pp. 281–82.

51. Freeman, *Washington*, 7:131–35; Powell, *Bring Out Your Dead*, pp. 273–74.

52. Appendix VI-2 of Freeman's *Washington*, 6:393–413, is an excellent overview of "American Newspapers and Editorial Opinion, 1789–93" (see esp. pp. 396–401).

53. Ibid., pp. 402–7; the quotation is from *National Gazette*, May 10, 1792, p. 3.

54. Quoted in Powell, *Bring Out Your Dead*, p. xvi.

55. Charles Coleman Sellers, *Mr. Peale's Museum: Charles Willson Peale and the First Popular Museum of Science and Art* (New York: W. W. Norton, 1980); id., "Peale's Museum," in Eisenhart, ed., *Historic Philadelphia*, pp. 253–59.

56. Arthur Hobson Quinn, "The Theatre and Drama in Old Philadelphia," in Eisenhart, ed., *Historic Philadelphia*, pp. 314–15; Eberlein, "190, High Street," in ibid., p. 173; Brunhouse, *Counter-Revolution*, pp. 147, 169, 183–84, 219.

57. Quinn, "The Theatre and Drama," pp. 315–16.

58. Freeman, *Washington*, 7:258, 259.

59. *American State Papers, Foreign Relations* (6 vols.; Washington, D.C.: Gales and Seaton, 1832–1859), 1:576.

60. Freeman, *Washington*, 7:435, 428 (quotation from p. 428, citing Moncure Daniel Conway, ed., *The Writings of Thomas Paine* [4 vols.; New York: Putnam, 1894–1896], 3:252).

61. Quoted in Bowers, *Jefferson and Hamilton*, p. 357.

62. Quinn, "The Theatre and the Drama," p. 316; Scharf and Westcott, *History of Philadelphia*, 1:493.

63. Scharf and Westcott, *History of Philadelphia*, 1:490, 494; Michael A. Palmer, "The Quasi-War and the Creation of the American Navy, 1798–1801" (Ph.D. dissertation, Temple University, 1981), pp. 117–22, 490.

64. Martin S. Pernick, "Politics, Parties, and Pestilence: Epidemic Yellow Fever in Philadelphia and the Rise of the First Party System," *William and Mary Quarterly*, 3d ser. 29 (Oct. 1972): 559–87; Scharf and Westcott, *History of Philadelphia*, 1:490–91; Kenneth R. Rossman, *Thomas Mifflin and the Politics of the American Revolution* (Chapel Hill:

University of North Carolina Press, 1952), pp. 285–89; Bowers, *Jefferson and Hamilton*, pp. 380–81.

65. Scharf and Westcott, *History of Philadelphia*, 1:491.

66. Ibid., pp. 498–99.

67. Merrill Jensen, *The New Nation: A History of the United States During the Confederation, 1781–1789* (New York: Knopf, 1950), pp. 191, 195–218; Forrest McDonald, *We the People: The Economic Origins of the Constitution* (Chicago: University of Chicago Press, 1958), pp. 167–68; Samuel Woodhouse, "Log and Journal of the Ship 'United States' on a Voyage to China in 1784," *PMHB* 55, no. 3 (1931): 225–58; Eugene S. Ferguson, *Truxtun of the Constellation: The Life of Commodore Thomas Truxtun, U.S. Navy, 1755–1822* (Baltimore: Johns Hopkins Press, 1956), pp. 52–77.

68. Jensen, *New Nation*, p. 215.

69. James A. Henretta, *The Evolution of American Society, 1700–1815* (Lexington, Mass.: D. C. Heath, 1973), pp. 191–92; John Sitgreaves to Robert Smith, Dec., 22, 1792, John Sitgreaves Letterbook, Thomas Biddle Business Papers, HSP; Stephen Kington to Tench Coxe, April 29, 1793, Jefferson Papers, Library of Congress; Alice B. Keith, "Relaxations of British Restrictions on American Trade with the British West Indies, 1783–1802," *Journal of Modern History* 20 (March 1948): 11.

70. Thomas Smith to William Irvine, Aug. 15, 1791, Irvine Papers, HSP; Tench Coxe to Fisher Ames, June 7, 1791, and Coxe to A. Lee, June 10, 1791, Coxe Papers, HSP; Benjamin Rush, *The Autobiography of Benjamin Rush: His "Travels Through Life" Together with his "Commonplace Book" for 1789–1813* (Princeton, N.J.: Princeton University Press, 1948), pp. 204, 217; Thomas Jefferson to Edward Rutledge, Aug. 29, 1791, in Ford, ed., *Writings of Jefferson*, 5:376; *General Advertiser*, April 17, 1792; *National Gazette*, April 19, 1792.

71. Miller, *Federalist City*, pp. 37–51; Ronald P. Formisano, "Deferential Participant Politics: The Early Republic's Political Culture, 1789–1840," *American Political Science Review* 68 (June 1974): 473–87. Formisano argues that political parties were not formed during the 1790s. See also John B. Kirby, "Early American Politics—The Search for Ideology: An Historical Analysis and Critique of the Concept of 'Deference,'" *Journal of Politics* 32 (Nov. 1970): 808–38; Frank J. Sorauf, "Political Parties and Political Analysis," in William Nisbet Chambers and Walter Dean Burnham, eds., *The American Party Systems: Stages of Political Development* (New York: Oxford University Press, 1967), pp. 33–55.

72. *Federal Gazette*, Oct. 26, 1790; William Bingham to Lafayette, April 8, 1791; Bingham to W & J Willink, April 1, 1793, and Bingham to John Wilcocks, April 11, 1793,

William Bingham Letterbook, HSP; Thomas Hartley to Tench Coxe, March 26, 1793, Coxe Papers, HSP; Alexander DeConde, *Entangling Alliance: Politics and Diplomacy Under George Washington* (Durham, N.C.: Duke University Press, 1958), chaps. 3, 4; Jerald Combs, *The Jay Treaty: Political Battleground of the Founding Fathers* (Berkeley: University of California Press, 1970), chap. 7; Albert H. Bowman, *The Struggle for Neutrality: Franco-American Diplomacy During the Federalist Era* (Knoxville: University of Tennessee Press, 1974), chaps. 2, 3; Ralph L. Ketcham, "France and American Politics, 1763–1793," *Political Science Quarterly* 78 (June 1963): 198–223.

73. Minutes of the Democratic Society of Pennsylvania, HSP; Eugene Link, *Democratic-Republican Societies, 1790–1800* (New York: Columbia University Press, 1942), pp. 15, 71–72; Philip S. Foner, ed., *The Democratic-Republican Societies, 1790–1800* (Westport, Conn.: Greenwood Press, 1976), pp. 53–140; *Independent Gazetteer*, July 13, 1793.

74. *General Advertiser*, April 15, 1793; Harry M. Tinkcom, *The Republicans and Federalists in Pennsylvania, 1790–1801: A Study in National Stimulus and Local Response* (Harrisburg: Pennsylvania Historical and Museum Commission, 1950), pp. 82–83; Foner, ed., *Democratic-Republican Societies*, pp. 53–63.

75. John C. Miller, *Alexander Hamilton: Portrait in Paradox* (New York: Harper, 1959), pp. 399–400; James T. Callender, *A Short History of the Nature and Consequence of Excise Laws* (Philadelphia: Snowden & M'Corkle, 1795), pp. 11, 20, 56–69, 75–86; Tench Coxe to John Pintard, June 12, 1794, Coxe Papers, HSP; Samuel Hodgdon to Alexander Hamilton, May 9, 1794, in Harold Syrett, ed., *The Papers of Alexander Hamilton* (26 vols.; New York: Columbia University Press, 1961–1979), 16:397–98; *General Advertiser*, May 12, 1794.

76. Miller, *Federalist City*, pp. 82–90; Seymour Martin Lipset and Stein Rokkan, "Cleavage Structures, Party Systems, and Voter Alignments: An Introduction," in Stein Rokkan and Seymour Martin Lipset, eds., *Party Systems and Voter Alignments: Cross-National Perspectives* (New York: Free Press, 1967), pp. 5, 6, 53; Richard L. McCormick, "Ethno-Cultural Interpretations of American Voting Behavior," *Political Science Quarterly* 89 (June 1974): 351–77.

77. Miller, *Federalist City*, pp. 64–90.

78. Ibid., pp. 126–39.

79. Ibid., pp. 139–44; Richard A. Pride, *Origins of Democracy: A Cross-National Study of Mobilization, Party Systems, and Democratic Stability* (Beverly Hills, Calif.: Sage, 1970), pp. 692–94.

80. Freeman, *Washington*, 7:549–56.

81. Ibid., pp. 650–51; Scharf and Westcott, *History of Philadelphia*, 1:591–92.

82. Lewis, "Anne Willing Bingham," p. 147.

THE ATHENS OF AMERICA, 1800–1825

1. William T. Whiteley, *Gilbert Stuart* (Cambridge, Mass.: Harvard University Press, 1932), p. iii; Charles V. Hagner, *Early History of the Falls of Schuylkill . . .* (Philadelphia: Claxton, Remsen and Haffelfinger, 1869), p. 43.

2. For the general background for this chapter's portrait of Philadelphia, see:(1) On geography, James Truslow Adams and R. V. Coleman, *Atlas of American History* (New York: Scribner's, 1943); Charles O. Paullin, *Atlas of the Historical Geography of the United States*

(Washington and New York: Carnegie Institution of Washington and the American Geographical Society of New York, 1932). (2) On population, United States Census Office, 2nd census, 1800; 3rd census, 1810; 4th census, 1820; 5th census, 1830 (Washington, D.C.: Printed by order of the House of Representatives, 1801, etc.); W. S. Rossiter, *A Century of Population Growth, From the First to the Twelfth Census of the United States, 1790–1900* (Washington, D.C.: U.S. Government Printing Office, 1909). (3) On social and economic background, Daniel J. Boorstin, *The Americans: The National Experience* (New York: Random House, 1965); David T. Gilchrist, ed., *The Growth of the Seaport Cities, 1790–1825* (Charlottesville: University Press of Virginia, 1967); Oscar Handlin and John Burchard, eds., *The Historian and the City* (Cambridge, Mass.: Harvard University Press, 1963); John Bach McMaster, *A History of the People of the United States, From the Revolution to the Civil War* (8 vols.; New York: D. Appleton, 1883–1913); Russel Blaine Nye, *The Cultural Life of the New Nation, 1776–1830* (New York: Harper, 1960); Richard C. Wade, *The Urban Frontier: The Rise of the Western Cities, 1790–1830* (Cambridge, Mass.: Harvard University Press, 1959).

3. *The Port Folio* 5 (April 6, 1805): 97–99.
4. Rhoda M. Dorsey, "Baltimore Foreign Trade," in Gilchrist, ed., *Growth of the Seaport Cities*, pp. 54 ff; James Weston Livingood, *The Philadelphia-Baltimore Trade Rivalry, 1780–1860* (Harrisburg: Pennsylvania Historical and Museum Commission, 1947).
5. *Poulson's American Daily Advertiser*, July 3, 1804.
6. Albert J. Gares, "Stephen Girard's West Indian Trade, 1789–1812," *Pennsylvania Magazine of History and Biography*, (hereafter cited as *PMHB*) 72 (July 1948): 311–42.
7. Marion V. Brewington, "Maritime Philadelphia, 1609–1837," *PMHB* 63 (Jan. 1939): 93–117; Samuel W. Woodhouse, "The Voyage of the 'Empress of China,'" *PMHB* 63 (Jan. 1939): 24–36; id., "Log and Journal of the Ship 'United States' on a Voyage to China," *PMHB* 55, no. 3 (1931): 225–58; William Bell Clark, "Postscripts to the Voyage of the Merchant Ship 'United States,'" *PMHB* 76 (July 1952): 294–310.
8. Foster Rhea Dulles, *The Old China Trade* (Boston: Houghton Mifflin, 1930); Brewington, "Maritime Philadelphia, 1609–1837"; Marius Barbeau, *Pathfinders in the North Pacific* (Caldwell, Idaho: Caxton Press, 1958).
9. Van Braam's *Voyage* and Waln's *China* are in the Library Company of Philadelphia. On van Braam himself, see George R. Loehr, "A. E. van Braam Houckgeest: The First American at the Court of China," *Princeton University Library Chronicle* 15 (Summer 1954): 179–93; and Edward R. Barnsley, *History of China's Retreat* (Bristol, Penna.: Bristol Printing Co., 1933). There are watercolor views of Charles Blight's house and of the interior of Nathan Dunn's museum by D. J. Kennedy in the Historical Society of Pennsylvania (hereafter cited as HSP). For the beginning of South American trade, see Brewington, "Maritime Philadelphia, 1609–1837," p. 115.
10. J. Thomas Scharf and Thompson Westcott, *History of Philadelphia, 1609–1884* (3 vols.; Philadelphia: L. H. Everts, 1884), 1:523.

11. Brewington, "Maritime Philadelphia, 1609–1837," p. 111, for Wharton quotation; Scharf and Westcott, *History of Philadelphia*, 1:530.
12. *Appletons' Cyclopaedia of American Biography* (7 vols.; New York: Appleton, 1887–1900), s.v. "Isaac Hull," 3:309–11.
13. J. F. Loubat, *Medallic History of the United States of America, 1776–1876* (2 vols.: New York: Privately printed, 1878).
14. Scharf and Westcott, *History of Philadelphia*, 1:554–555.
15. Ibid., pp. 570–76.
16. Robert G. Albion, "New York and Its Rivals, 1815–1830," *Journal of Economic and Business History* 3 (Aug. 1931): 602–9; id., *The Rise of New York Port, 1815–1860* (Hamden, Conn.: Archon, 1961); Henry T. Reath, "Ebb Tide at Philadelphia, 1815–1830" (Ph.D. dissertation, Princeton University, 1942).
17. Woodhouse, "Log and Journal of the Ship 'United States,'" pp. 230, 238, 251.
18. *Appletons' Cyclopaedia of American Biography*, s.v. "William Wagner," 6:315.
19. Albion, "New York and Its Rivals," p. 611.
20. Brewington, "Maritime Philadelphia, 1609–1837."
21. Scharf and Westcott, *History of Philadelphia*, 2:901.
22. The descriptions of the roads leading out of the city by Townsend Ward, in *PMHB*, 1879–1882, although written much later, are helpful in visualizing the early city before its great growth.
23. *The Port Folio* 5 (April 6, 1805): 97–99.
24. Quoted by Ellis P. Oberholtzer, *Philadelphia: A History of the City and Its People* (4 vols.; Philadelphia: S. J. Clarke, 1912), 1:382.
25. Franklin D. Scott, ed., *Baron Klinkowström's America, 1818–1820* (Evanston, Ill.: Northwestern University Press, 1952), p. 17; Harry M. Tinkcom, ed., "Sir Augustus in Pennsylvania," *PMHB* 75 (July 1951): 369–99.
26. *The Port Folio* 5 (April 6, 1805): 98.
27. Thomas G. Morton and Frank Woodbury, *The History of the Pennsylvania Hospital, 1751–1895* (Philadelphia: Times Printing House, 1895), pp. 331–33; *The Port Folio* 2 (1816): 340.
28. Thomas G. Morton and John B. Garrett, *Addresses Delivered . . . on the Unveiling of West's Picture, Christ Healing the Sick* (Philadelphia: Pennsylvania Hospital, 1884).
29. Henri Marceau, *William Rush* (Philadelphia: Philadelphia Museum of Art, 1937).
30. *Journal of the House of Representatives*, February 2–8, 1808; see also the pamphlet *The Speeches of Messieurs Gardinier and Tallmadge on the Resolution for removing the seat of Government to Philadelphia. Delivered in the House of Representatives of the United States, on the third and eighth of February, 1808*, copy at Library Company of Philadelphia.
31. Thomas Moore, *Epistles, Odes and Other Poems* (Philadelphia: John Watts, 1806). Epistle VIII and its footnote (pp. 237–239) contain Moore's tribute to Dickins and his circle. See also his "Lines written on leaving Philadelphia" in *The Port Folio*, 5 (Aug. 31, 1805): 271; Burton Alva Konkle, *Joseph Hopkinson, 1770–1842: Jurist, Scholar, Inspirer of the Arts, Author of Hail Columbia* (Philadelphia: University of Pennsylvania Press, 1931), gives an attractive picture of an evening gathering, including Moore, at Hopkinson's house on Spruce Street.

32. H. B. Adams, *Jared Sparks*, quoted in Charles Coleman Sellers, *A Catalogue of Portraits and Other Works of Art in the Possession of the American Philosophical Society* (Philadelphia: American Philosophical Society, 1961), p. 95.

33. Albert H. Smyth, *The Philadelphia Magazines and Their Contributors, 1741–1850* (Philadelphia: R. M. Lindsay, 1892), p. 88.

34. Roy F. Nichols, *The Invention of the American Political Parties* (New York: Macmillan, 1967); William M. Meigs, "Pennsylvania Politics Early in This Century," *PMHB* 17 (1893): 462–90; Raymond Walters, Jr., "The Origins of the Jeffersonian Party in Pennsylvania," *PMHB* 66 (Oct. 1942): 440–58; Harry M. Tinkcom, *The Republicans and Federalists in Pennsylvania, 1790–1801: A Study in National Stimulus and Local Response* (Harrisburg: Pennsylvania Historical and Museum Commission, 1950).

35. Edward M. Riley, "The Independence Hall Group," in Luther P. Eisenhart, ed., *Historic Philadelphia: From the Founding Until the Early Nineteenth Century: Papers Dealing with Its People and Buildings with an Illustrative Map* (Philadelphia: American Philosophical Society, 1953), pp. 7–42.

36. Abraham Ritter, *Philadelphia and Her Merchants . . .* (Philadelphia: Privately printed, 1860), p. 46.

37. Edward P. Allinson and Boies Penrose, *Philadelphia, 1681–1887: A History of Municipal Development*, Johns Hopkins University Studies in Historical and Political Science (Philadelphia: Allen, Lane and Scott, 1887); Scharf and Westcott, *History of Philadelphia*, passim.

38. Allinson and Penrose, *Philadelphia . . . Municipal Development*, pp. 109–10.

39. Scharf and Westcott, *History of Philadelphia*, 1:551.

40. John F. Watson, *Annals of Philadelphia, and Pennsylvania, in the Olden Times* (3 vols.; Philadelphia: E. S. Stuart, 1905), 1:294.

41. Edward Potts Cheyney, *A History of the University of Pennsylvania, 1740–1940* (Philadelphia: University of Pennsylvania Press, 1940), p. 186.

42. Scharf and Westcott, *History of Philadelphia*, 3:1925.

43. Edwin Wolf 2nd and Maxwell Whiteman, *The History of the Jews of Philadelphia from Colonial Times to the Age of Jackson* (Philadelphia: Jewish Publication Society of America, 1957), p. 333; Scharf and Westcott, *History of Philadelphia*, 1:501, 514.

44. Louise Gilchrieese Walsh and Matthew John Walsh, *History and Organization of Education in Pennsylvania* (Indiana, Penna.: R. S. Grosse, 1930), p. 122.

45. Ibid., pp. 94 ff.

46. Ibid., pp. 101–3, 104.

47. Allinson and Penrose, *Philadelphia . . . Municipal Development*, p. 92.

48. Theo B. White et al., *Philadelphia Architecture in the Nineteenth Century* (Philadelphia: University of Pennsylvania Press, 1953), p. 22, plate 2; George B. Tatum, *Penn's Great Town: 250 Years of Philadelphia Architecture, Illustrated in Prints and Drawings* (Philadelphia: University of Pennsylvania Press, 1961), pp. 57, 167, plates 40, 41; Fritz Redlich, "The Philadelphia Waterworks in Relation to the Industrial Revolution in the United States," *PMHB* 69 (April 1945): 243.

49. There is dispute about where credit is owed for the ideas and innovations decisive for the success of the waterworks. Thomas Gilpin, "Fairmount Dam and Water Works, Philadelphia," *PMHB* 37 (Oct. 1913): 471–79, gives credit to Joseph S. Lewis for the shift from steam to hydraulic power, as does the long inscription on Lewis's tomb in Laurel Hill Cemetery. Lewis was president of the Watering Committee. Gilpin also gives the credit for the design and construction of the dam and waterwheels to the millwright Thomas Oakes. The author of Lewis Wernwag's biography in *Appletons' Cyclopaedia of American Biography*, 6:437 (who was probably Col. Josiah Granville Leach), says that the dam and waterworks "were erected in accordance with his [Wernwag's] plans." But see the Reports of the Watering Committee; also Scharf and Westcott, *History of Philadelphia*, 1:560, 605; Allinson and Penrose, *Philadelphia . . . Municipal Development;* and the biography of Graff by Horatio Gates Jones in *Appletons' Cyclopaedia of American Biography*, 2:700. For Graff's technical innovations, see *The Engineering Drawings of Benjamin Henry Latrobe*, edited by Darwin H. Stapleton, Maryland Historical Society Publication no. 53 (New Haven, Conn.: Yale University Press, 1980), pp. 196–98, for illustration of Graff's hydrant and stopcocks adopted by Latrobe for the New Orleans water system.

50. Scharf and Westcott, *History of Philadelphia*, 1:530; Allinson and Penrose, *Philadelphia . . . Municipal Development*.

51. *Hazard's Register* 1 (1828): 298–99.

52. Scharf and Westcott, *History of Philadelphia*, 3:2141; Charles E. Peterson, "Iron in Early American Roofs," *Smithsonian Journal of History* 3 (Winter 1968): 48–50.

53. *Report of the Patent-Office, February 22, 1805* (covering patents issued 1790–1804). "Number 148. Improvement in Bridges," Jan. 21, 1797.

54. Scharf and Westcott, *History of Philadelphia*, 3:2142; *United States Gazette*, no. 4185, Jan. 22, 1806, p. 3.

55. Scharf and Westcott, *History of Philadelphia*, 1:524; Peterson, "Iron in Early American Roofs," pp. 51–52.

56. [Col. Josiah Granville Leach,] "Lewis Wernwag," *Appletons' Cyclopaedia of American Biography*, 6:437.

57. Mill Creek in West Philadelphia, Falls Run, Cohocksink Creek, and Gunner's Run all provided valuable mill sites, but like the once-useful tributaries of Frankford Creek they have all disappeared.

58. Hagner, *Early History of the Falls of Schuylkill*, p. 32.

59. Scharf and Westcott, *History of Philadelphia*, 1:515. The role of waterpower in the growth of the city's manufacturing is not a well-understood phenomenon. The contributors to the chapter on manufacturing in Gilchrist, ed., *The Growth of Seaport Cities* (1967), assumed without discussion that Philadelphia, like Boston, New York, and Charleston, lacked waterpower. The simple observation of the countryside, old maps, and local histories like Scharf and Westcott or Hagner's history of Manayunk shows how erroneous this assumption is. Baltimore also had waterpower but did not exploit it as did Philadelphia. R. Malcolm Kerr, "Causes for the Growth of Philadelphia as an Industrial Center," *Bulletin*

of the *Geographical Society of Philadelphia* 13 (July 1915): 101, says there were fifteen creeks in the vicinity of the city developed for their waterpower.

60. Scharf and Westcott, *History of Philadelphia*, 1:522.

61. *Aurora*, Nov. 15, 1808.

62. Ibid., Nov. 22, 1808.

63. Sam Bass Warner, Jr., "Innovation and Industrialization of Philadelphia, 1800–1850," in Handlin and Burchard, eds., *The Historian and the City*, pp. 63–69; Ian M. G. Quimby, "The Cordwainers Protest," *Winterthur Portfolio: A Journal of American Material Culture* 3 (1967): 83–101.

64. Hagner, *Early History of the Falls of Schuylkill*, p. 43.

65. Henry Simpson, *The Lives of Eminent Philadelphians, Now Deceased, Collected from Original and Authentic Sources* (Philadelphia: William Brotherhead, 1859).

66. Greville Bathe and Dorothy Bathe, *Oliver Evans: A Chronicle of Early American Engineering* (Philadelphia: Historical Society of Pennsylvania, 1935); Eugene S. Ferguson, *Oliver Evans, Inventive Genius of the American Industrial Revolution* (Wilmington, Del.: Hagley Museum, 1980).

67. *United States Gazette*, Sept. 29, 1809.

68. John Stevens, Jr., "A Letter Relative to Steamboats," *American Medical and Philosophical Register* 2 (1812), gives Stevens's own account of his experiments with steamboats, in answer to an anonymous article (generally admitted to be the work of Robert R. Livingston), "An historical account of the application of steam to the propelling of boats," in the same volume; Henry William Dickinson, *Robert Fulton, Engineer and Artist: His Life and Works* (London: John Lane, 1913); George Dangerfield, *Chancellor Robert R. Livingston of New York, 1746–1813* (New York: Harcourt, Brace, 1960); James Thomas Flexner, *Inventors in Action: The Story of the Steamboat* (New York: Collier Books, 1962). See also Talbot Hamlin, *Benjamin Henry Latrobe* (New York: Oxford University Press, 1955), p. 370n, citing a letter of Oct. 1, 1798, from Roosevelt to Livingston, reprinted in J. H. B. Latrobe, *A Last Chapter in the History of the Steamboat*, Fund Publication 5 (Baltimore: Maryland Historical Society, 1871), for Roosevelt's claim to the invention of the paddlewheel.

69. Brooke Hindle, *David Rittenhouse* (Princeton, N.J.: Princeton University Press, 1964), pp. 94–96, 250–51.

70. [George Armroyd,] *A Connected View of the Whole Internal Navigation of the United States, Natural and Artificial, Present and Prospective* (Philadelphia: H. C. Carey & I. Lea, 1826); S. Alpach, *Schuylkill Navigator* (Philadelphia, 1827); Henry S. Tanner, *A Brief Description of the Canals and Railroads of Pennsylvania and New Jersey* (Philadelphia: Privately printed, 1834); Simpson, *Lives of Eminent Philadelphians*; J. Lee Hartman, "Pennsylvania's Grand Plan of Post-Revolutionary Internal Improvement," *PMHB* 65 (Oct. 1941): 439–57; Francis D. Klingender, *Art and the Industrial Revolution* (London: N. Carrington, 1947); [Pierre Stephen] Robert Payne, *The Canal Builders: The Story of Canal Engineers through the Ages* (New York: Macmillan, 1959).

71. Arthur H. Frazier, "Joseph Saxton's First Sojourn at Philadelphia, 1818–1831, and His Contributions to the Independence Hall Clock," *Smithsonian Journal of History* 3 (Spring 1968): 45–76.

72. *United States Gazette*, Nov. 3, 1800.

73. Don Taxay, *The U.S. Mint and Coinage: An Illustrated History from 1776 to the Present* (New York: Arco, 1966), p. 15.

74. Hindle, *David Rittenhouse*, pp. 334–35.

75. Taxay's *U.S. Mint and Coinage* gives the best and most recent review of the technical problems and the development of the mint.

76. Scharf and Westcott, *History of Philadelphia*, 3:2339–40.

77. Ibid., 2:1192.

78. The first two presidents of the academy, George Clymer and Joseph Hopkinson, were members of the APS.

79. Maurice E. Phillips, "The Academy of Natural Sciences of Philadelphia," in Eisenhart, ed., *Historic Philadelphia*, pp. 266–74.

80. Arthur M. Kennedy, "The Athenaeum: Some Account of Its History from 1814 to 1830," in Eisenhart, ed., *Historic Philadelphia*, pp. 260–65.

81. Henry Butler Allen, "The Franklin Institute of the State of Pennsylvania," in Eisenhart, ed., *Historic Philadelphia*, pp. 275–79.

82. *The Early History of Science and Learning in America, With Special Reference to the Work of the American Philosophical Society During the Eighteenth and Nineteenth Centuries*, special issue, *Proceedings of the American Philosophical Society* 86, no. 1 (Sept. 1942): 34.

83. Ibid., p. 48.

84. Ibid., pp. 63, 108.

85. Ibid., p. 126.

86. *Appletons' Cyclopaedia of American Biography*, s.v. "Alexander Wilson," 6:545; *Dictionary of American Biography*, s.v. "Alexander Wilson," 14:49.

87. E.g., *Early History of Science and Learning in America*, pp. 52–62, 91, 153–55, 157–61.

88. Ibid., p. 189.

89. Richard H. Shryock, "A Century of Medical Progress in Philadelphia, 1750–1850," *Pennsylvania History* 8 (Jan. 1941): 7–28; id., *Medicine and Society in America, 1660–1860* (New York: New York University Press, 1960).

90. Carl A. L. Binger, *Revolutionary Doctor: Benjamin Rush, 1746–1813* (New York: W. W. Norton, 1966).

91. Edward Louis Bauer, *Doctors Made in America* (Philadelphia: Lippincott, 1963), pp. 3–15; Edward Kremers and George Urdang, *History of Pharmacy: A Guide and a Survey* (2d ed.; Philadelphia: Lippincott, 1951), pp. 241–47; Joseph W. England, ed., *The First Century of the Philadelphia College of Pharmacy, 1821–1921* (Philadelphia: Philadelphia College of Pharmacy and Science, 1922).

92. Horace Binney, *The Leaders of the Old Bar of Philadelphia* (Philadelphia: H. E. Ashmead, 1859).

93. Charles Coleman Sellers, *Mr. Peale's Museum: Charles Willson Peale and the First Popular Museum of Natural Science and Art* (New York: W. W. Norton, 1980).

94. E. P. Richardson, "Joseph Allen Smith," *American Art Journal* 1 (Spring 1969): 5–19.

95. Helen W. Henderson, *The Pennsylvania Academy of the Fine Arts and Other Collections in Philadelphia . . .* (Boston: L. C.

Page, 1911); Charles Coleman Sellers, *Charles Willson Peale* (New York: Scribner's, 1969); id., "Rembrandt Peale, 'Investigator,' " *PMHB* 79 (July 1955): 331–42; Edward J. Hygren, "Art Instruction in Philadelphia, 1795–1845" (Winterthur thesis, 1969).

96. [Columbian Society of Artists,] *First Annual Exhibition of the Society of Artists of the United States, 1811* (Philadelphia: Tho. L. Plowman, 1811); *Second Annual Exhibition of the Society of Artists of the United States and the Pennsylvania Academy, 1812* (Philadelphia: Tho. L. Plowman, 1812); Anna Wells Rutledge, *Cumulative Record of Exhibition Catalogues, The Pennsylvania Academy of the Fine Arts, 1807–1870* . . . (Philadelphia: American Philosophical Society, 1955).

97. Martin P. Snyder, "William Birch—His Philadelphia Views," *PMHB* 73 (July 1949): 271–315; id., "William Birch—His Country Seats of the United States," *PMHB* 81 (April 1957): 225–54.

98. Richardson, "Joseph Allen Smith"; Harold E. Dickson, *Arts of the Young Republic* (Chapel Hill: University of North Carolina Press, 1968); George C. Grace and David H. Wallace, *The New-York Historical Society's Dictionary of Artists in America, 1564–1860* (New Haven, Conn.: Yale University Press, 1957); Nicholas B. Wainwright, *Philadelphia in the Romantic Age of Lithography* (Philadelphia: Historical Society of Pennsylvania, 1958).

99. Joseph Hopkinson, *Annual Discourse Delivered Before the Pennsylvania Academy of the Fine Arts on the 13th of November, 1810* (Philadelphia: Bradford and Inskeep, 1810); also printed in *The Port Folio* 4 (1810).

100. Hopkinson modestly omitted the first American edition of Shakespeare, of which he himself is supposed to have been the editor, published by Bioren and Madan in eight volumes: *William Shakespeare, The Plays and Poems . . . with notes by Samuel Johnson, L.L.D.* (Philadelphia, 1795–1796).

101. Alexander Wilson, *American Ornithology; or The Natural History of the Birds of the United States, Illustrated with Plates Engraved and Colored from Original Drawings Taken from Nature* (Philadelphia: Published by Bradford and Inskeep, Printed by Robert Carr, 1810), 2:vi.

102. Abraham Rees, D.D., F.R.S., F.L.S., S.Amer. Soc., *The Cyclopaedia; or Universal Dictionary of Arts, Sciences and Literature. Illustrated with numerous engravings by the most distinguished artists. First American Edition, Revised, Corrected, Enlarged, and adapted to this country, by several literary and scientific characters* (41 vols. and 6 vols. of plates; Philadelphia: Samuel P. Bradford & Murray, Fairman & Co., 1810–1822).

103. Mathew Carey's autobiography was published in the *New England Magazine* of 1833 and 1834. See also Earl L. Brasher, *Mathew Carey, Editor, Author, Publisher: A Study in American Literary Development* (New York: Columbia University Press, 1912); H. Glenn and Maude O. Brown, *A Directory of the Book Arts and Book Trade in Philadelphia to 1820* (New York: New York Public Library, 1950).

104. Scharf and Westcott, *History of Philadelphia*, 1:508–9; Smyth, *Philadelphia Magazines;* Ellis Paxson Oberholtzer, *The Literary History of Philadelphia* (Philadelphia: George W. Jacobs,

1906); Lewis Leary, "Joseph Dennie on Benjamin Franklin: A Note on Early American Literary Criticism," *PMHB* 71 (July 1948): 240–46.

105. Smyth, *Philadelphia Magazines*, pp. 145, 178–80.

106. Scharf and Westcott, *History of Philadelphia*, 3:1967.

107. James D. Reese, *Old Drury of Philadelphia* (Philadelphia, 1932); Arthur Hobson Quinn, "The Theatre and the Drama in Old Philadelphia," in Eisenhart, ed., *Historic Philadelphia*, pp. 313–17. The *Diary and History of the American Theater* (New York, 1832) gives vivid contemporary accounts of actors and actresses and of the kaleidoscopic fortunes of theatrical companies.

108. Robert A. Gerson, "Music in Philadelphia" (Ph.D. dissertation, University of Pennsylvania, 1940).

109. The best summaries of Philadelphia architecture in general are given in White et al., *Philadelphia Architecture in the Nineteenth Century*, and Tatum, *Penn's Great Town*. Joseph Jackson, *Early Philadelphia Architects and Engineers* (Philadelphia: Privately printed, 1923), though out of date in some details, is still useful also.

110. Tatum, *Penn's Great Town*, pp. 164, 165, plates 33, 35; William J. Murtagh, "The Philadelphia Row House," *Journal of the Society of Architectural Historians* 16 (March 1957): 8–13; George B. Tatum, "Thomas Carstairs," in *Two Centuries of Philadelphia Architectural Drawings* (Philadelphia: Philadelphia Museum of Art, 1964).

111. Joseph Jackson, *Development of American Architecture, 1783–1830* (Philadelphia: David McKay, 1926), pp. 99–107.

112. Talbot Hamlin, *Greek Revival Architecture in America* (New York: Oxford University Press, 1944), pp. 31, 63–66; White et al., *Philadelphia Architecture in the Nineteenth Century*, p. 22, plate 2.

113. Ritter, *Philadelphia and Her Merchants*, p. 199.

114. Hamlin, *Greek Revival Architecture*, pp. 66–68; Helen Mar Pierce Gallagher, *Robert Mills, Architect of the Washington Monument* (New York: Columbia University Press, 1935); Charles C. Watson, "Robert Mills, Architect" *Bulletin of the University of South Carolina*, no. 77 (Feb. 1919); Kenneth Ames, "Robert Mills and the Philadelphia Row House," *Journal of the Society of Architectural Historians* 27 (June 1968): 140–46.

115. Hamlin, *Greek Revival Architecture*, pp. 68–73; Norman B. Johnston, "John Haviland, Jailor to the World," *Journal of the Society of Architectural Historians* 23 (June 1964): 101–5.

116. Agnes A. Gilchrist, *William Strickland, Architect and Engineer, 1788–1854* (Philadelphia: University of Pennsylvania Press, 1950); Bray Hammond, "The Second Bank of the United States," in Eisenhart, ed., *Historic Philadelphia*, pp. 80–85.

117. Ritter, *Philadelphia and Her Merchants*, pp. 66–67, gives an account and an engraving of this plan. See also Joseph Jackson, *Market Street, Philadelphia* (Philadelphia, 1918), p. 5. Horace Mather Lippincott, *Early Philadelphia, Its People, Life and Progress* (Philadelphia: Lippincott, 1917), p. 182, says that when the yellow fever returned in 1820, the city asked the advice of the College of

Physicians. A committee composed of Doctors Howson, Griffiths, and Emlen recommended "the prosecution of the plan now in contemplation for removing the whole of the buildings from the east side of Front Street, inclusive, to the river, beginning at Vine and ending at South Street. . . ."

118. John H. Powell, *Bring Out Your Dead: The Great Plague of Yellow Fever in Philadelphia in 1793* (Philadelphia: University of Pennsylvania Press, 1949), gives a very moving account of their heroism in this terrible year.

119. W. E. B. DuBois, *The Philadelphia Negro: A Social Study* (paperback ed.; New York: Schocken, 1967); Edward Raymond Turner, *The Negro in Pennsylvania: Slavery, Servitude, Freedom, 1639–1861* (Washington, D.C.: American Historical Association, 1911); Philip St. Laurent, "James Forten," *Tuesday Magazine*, Nov. 1968, pp. 12 ff; Edwin Wolf 2nd, *Negro History, 1553–1903* (Philadelphia: Library Company of Philadelphia, 1969).

120. Nicholas B. Wainwright, *History of the Philadelphia National Bank: A Century and a Half of Philadelphia Banking, 1803–1953* (Philadelphia: Philadelphia National Bank, 1953); F. Cyril James, "The Bank of North America and the Financial History of Philadelphia," *PMHB* 64 (Jan. 1940): 56–87.

121. Herman E. Krooss, "Financial Institutions," in Gilchrist, ed., *Growth of the Seaport Cities*, pp. 104–38.

122. Ibid.

123. Raymond Walters, Jr., *Alexander James Dallas: Lawyer, Politician, Financier, 1759–1817* (Philadelphia: University of Pennsylvania Press, 1943).

124. Reminiscences of Charles N. Birch . . . from 1791 to 1841, HSP, pp. 194–95.

125. Quoted by William M. Gouge, *A Short History of Paper Money and Banking in the United States* (Philadelphia: T. W. Ustick, 1833), p. 110.

126. Ibid., p. 123.

127. Whiteley, *Stuart*, p. iii.

128. Dennis C. Kurjack, "St. Joseph's and St. Mary's Churches," in Eisenhart, ed., *Historic Philadelphia*, p. 262.

129. Whitfield J. Bell, Jr., "The Cabinet of the American Philosophical Society," in Walter Muir Whitehill, ed., *A Cabinet of Curiosities* (Charlottesville: University of Virginia, 1967), p. 166.

THE AGE OF NICHOLAS BIDDLE, 1825–1841

1. *United States Gazette*, Nov. 21, 1831; Nicholas B. Wainwright, ed., *A Philadelphia Perspective: The Diary of Sidney George Fisher Covering the Years 1834–1871* (Philadelphia: Historical Society of Pennsylvania, 1967), p. 154 (hereafter cited as *Fisher Diary*).

2. *Fisher Diary*, p. 155.

3. Ibid., p. 158.

4. Craig Biddle and James S. Biddle, *Autobiography of Charles Biddle: Vice President of the Supreme Executive Council of Pennsylvania* (Philadelphia: Privately printed, 1883).

5. Nicholas B. Wainwright, "Nicholas Biddle, 1786–1844" (senior thesis, Princeton University, 1936), p. 52.

6. Thomas Payne Govan, *Nicholas Biddle: Nationalist and Public Banker, 1786–1844* (Chicago: University of Chicago Press, 1959).

7. R. C. H. Catterall, *The Second Bank of the United States* (Chicago: University of Chicago Press, 1903), p. 51.

8. *American Daily Advertiser*, April 1, 1825.

9. *Niles' Weekly Register* 29 (1825–1826): 31.

10. *American Daily Advertiser*, May 28, 1825.

11. *National Gazette*, Jan. 1, 1827.

12. *American Daily Advertiser*, April 1, 1825.

13. *Niles' Weekly Register* 28 (1825): 162.

14. Ibid., 31 (1826–1827): 307.

15. Ibid., 33 (1827–1828), p. 132.

16. Sanford W. Higginbotham, "Philadelphia Commerce with Latin America, 1820–1830," *Pennsylvania History* (hereafter cited as *PH*) 9 (Oct. 1942): 252–66.

17. *Fisher Diary*, p. 14n.

18. Samuel Hazard, *The Register of Pennsylvania* 2 (1828): 177–78, 204–5, 217 (hereafter cited as *Hazard's Register*).

19. *National Gazette*, Feb. 6, 1827.

20. *American Daily Advertiser*, Jan. 1, April 12, 1825; *National Gazette*, Jan. 15, 1827.

21. *Fisher Diary*, p. 187.

22. Diary of Samuel Breck, March 26, 1828, April 22, 1834, HSP.

23. *National Gazette*, April 16, 1827.

24. Ibid., Feb. 16, Oct. 13, 1827.

25. *Hazard's Register* 1 (1828): 28.

26. Diary of Samuel Breck, June 11, 1834.

27. Ibid., May 5, 1834.

28. *Verses of Nicholas Biddle* (Philadelphia, 1889).

29. Diary of Samuel Breck, Feb. 15, 1828; *Fisher Diary*, p. 70.

30. *American Daily Advertiser*, Jan. 21, 1825.

31. *Niles' Weekly Register* 30 (1826): 153.

32. Ibid., 34 (1828): 288, 36 (1829): 85.

33. Ibid., 34 (1828): 264, 21 (1826–1827): 166.

34. Ibid., 28 (1825): 191.

35. *United States Gazette*, June 28, 1831; *Niles' Weekly Register* 21 (1826–1827): 100.

36. Philip S. Klein and Ari Hoogenbaum, *A History of Pennsylvania* (2d, enlarged ed.; University Park: Pennsylvania State University Press, 1980), p. 202.

37. Richard I. Shelling, "Philadelphia and the Agitation in 1825 for the Pennsylvania Canal," *Pennsylvania Magazine of History and Biography* (hereafter cited as *PMHB*) 62 (April 1938): 175–204; *American Daily Advertiser*, Jan. 28, March 23, April 26, 1825.

38. *United States Gazette*, June 23, 1831.

39. John C. Trautwine, Jr., "The Philadelphia and Columbia Railroad in 1834," *Publications of the City History Society of Philadelphia* 2 (1825): 139–78.

40. *The Schuylkill Navigation Company* (Philadelphia: Crissy and Markley, 1852), p. 10.

41. *The Story of the Old Company* (Lansford, Pa.: Lehigh Navigation Coal Company, 1941).

42. *Hazard's Register* 7 (1831): 24.

43. Frederick M. Binder, "Anthracite Enters the American Home," *PMHB* 82 (Jan. 1958): 82–91; Diary of Samuel Breck, Dec. 22, 1827; *Hazard's Register* 15 (1835): 352.

44. Marion V. Brewington, "Maritime Philadelphia, 1609–1837," *PMHB* 63 (Jan. 1939), 116–117; *United States Gazette*, Jan. 16, 1830.

45. Carroll W. Pursell, Jr., *Early Stationary Steam Engines in America: A Study in the Migration of Technology* (Washington, D.C.: Smithsonian Institution Press, 1969), pp. 40, 72, 87, 95–96, 132.
46. *United States Gazette*, Oct. 19, 20, 1829.
47. *Hazard's Register* 1 (1828): 67–68.
48. *Niles' Weekly Register* 33 (1827–1828): 404.
49. *United States Gazette*, Jan. 30, Feb. 7, 1832.
50. Ibid., Feb. 3, March 19, 1836, Jan. 2, 1837; *Hazard's Register* 16 (1835): 194.
51. Diary of Joseph Sill, March 18, 1836, HSP.
52. *United States Gazette*, Feb. 23, March 3, Aug. 19, 1837, Dec. 27, 1838.
53. *Niles' Weekly Register* 52 (1837): 304.
54. *United States Gazette*, July 18, 1837.
55. *Hazard's Register* 3 (1829): 214, 384.
56. *United States Gazette*, Aug. 24, 1838, Feb. 19, 1839; Diary of Samuel Breck, Aug. 16, 22, 1838.
57. *Hazard's Register* 8 (1831): 95, 9 (1832): 378; *United States Gazette*, March 22, 1831.
58. *United States Gazette*, June 7, 1832, Oct. 20, 1834, Aug. 17, Sept. 29, 1835.
59. Barbara Fisher, "Maritime History of the Reading," *PMHB* 86 (April 1962): 161–65; *United States Gazette*, July 19, 1838.
60. *United States Gazette*, Dec. 21, 24, 1830, June 2, 1832, April 24, 1834; *Hazard's Register* 6 (1830): 391, 16 (1835): 59.
61. *United States Gazette*, Oct. 29, 31, Nov. 4, 30, 1836, April 28, Oct. 2, Dec. 8, 1837, Feb. 7, 1839.
62. Ibid., Dec. 18, 1832.
63. Ibid., July 24, 1837; Sept. 27, 1838.
64. As quoted by Brewington, "Maritime Philadelphia, 1609–1837," p. 117; from John Bristed, *The Resources of the United States of America* (New York: James Eastburn & Co., 1819), p. 64.
65. *Niles' Weekly Register* 37 (1829–1830): 132.
66. *United States Gazette*, Nov. 6, 1829.
67. *Hazard's Register* 6 (1830): 396.
68. *Niles' Weekly Register* 28 (1825): 3.
69. Ibid., 34 (1828): 19.
70. Ibid., 33 (1827–1828): 211; Diary of Samuel Breck, July 29, 1825.
71. William A. Sullivan, "Philadelphia Labor During the Jackson Era," *PH* 15 (Oct. 1948): 305–20.
72. Malcolm C. Clark, "The Birth of an Enterprise: Baldwin Locomotives, 1831–1843," *PMHB* 90 (Oct. 1966): 426.
73. For sketches of Norris and Harrison, see the *Dictionary of American Biography (DAB)*.
74. Diary of Joseph Sill, Nov. 17, 1840.
75. *National Gazette*, Nov. 17, 1827, April 9, 1828; *United States Gazette*, March 30, 1835.
76. *United States Gazette*, Aug. 21, 1838, Aug. 22, 1839.
77. Ibid., March 29, 1832, Jan. 24, 1833, Nov. 22, 1837; *Hazard's Register* 15 (1834): 77–78.
78. *Niles' Weekly Register* 33 (1827–1828): 370.
79. *National Gazette*, June 14, 19, 1827.
80. William A. Sullivan, "A Decade of Labor Strife," *PH* 17 (Jan. 1950): 23–28.
81. Lewis H. Arky, "The Mechanics Union of Trade Associations and the Formation of the Philadelphia Workingmen's Movement," *PMHB* 86 (April 1952): 142–176; Arthur M. Schlesinger, Jr., *The Age of Jackson* (Boston: Little, Brown, 1945), pp. 201–4.
82. Leonard Bernstein, "The Working People of Philadelphia from Colonial Times to the General Strike of 1835," *PMHB* 74 (July 1950): 336–39; *United States Gazette*, June 4, 1835; *Niles' Weekly Register* 48 (1835): 235, 249.
83. *United States Gazette*, May 10, 1836.

84. William S. Hastings, "Philadelphia Microcosm," *PMHB* 91 (April 1967): 164–80.
85. *United States Gazette*, Aug. 30, 1828.
86. Ibid., May 27, 1828, Sept. 28, 1831.
87. Diary of Samuel Breck, March 4, 1828, Nov. 20, 1830.
88. Diary of Joseph Sill, Dec. 26, 1831.
89. *United States Gazette*, Nov. 21, 1831.
90. Diary of Samuel Breck, Oct. 23, 1838.
91. *United States Gazette*, April 13, 1831.
92. Ibid., Aug. 28, 1833; Diary of Samuel Breck, May 13, 1838.
93. Agnes Addison Gilchrist, *William Strickland, Architect and Engineer, 1788–1854* (Philadelphia: University of Pennsylvania Press, 1950), p. 85.
94. *United States Gazette*, June 6, 1827, June 6, 1835, April 27, 1836; Joseph Jackson, *Encyclopedia of Philadelphia* (4 vols.; Harrisburg: National Historical Association, 1931–1933), 1:98–99; *Hazard's Register* 3 (1829): 209.
95. *United States Gazette*, May 25, 1828.
96. Negley K. Teeters, "The Early Days of the Eastern State Penitentiary at Philadelphia," *PH* 16 (Oct. 1949): 261–302.
97. *United States Gazette*, Aug. 12, 1835.
98. Ibid., April 18, 1836, Oct. 17, 1839.
99. Ibid., Oct. 1, 1835.
100. Frederick Moore Binder, "Gas Light," *PH* 22 (Oct. 1955): 361–65; *United States Gazette*, Nov. 1, 1831, Nov. 10, 1832.
101. *United States Gazette*, April 11, 1837; Diary of Joseph Sill, Feb. 26, 1836.
102. *Hazard's Register* 11 (1833): 368; *United States Gazette*, Dec. 23, 1833, Aug. 1, 1834.
103. Diary of Samuel Breck, March 28, 1839; *United States Gazette*, March 28, 1839.
104. *National Gazette*, April 11, 1827; Nicholas B. Wainwright, *The Irvine Story* (Philadelphia: Historical Society of Pennsylvania, 1964), p. 23; *United States Gazette*, Feb. 2, March 12, 1836, Aug. 31, 1837.
105. Edward Biddle and Mantle Fielding, *The Life and Works of Thomas Sully* (Lancaster, Penna.: Wickersham Press, 1921); Diary of Samuel Breck, Sept. 21, 1838.
106. Oliver W. Larkin, *Art and Life in America* (rev. and enlarged ed.; New York: Holt, Rinehart and Winston, 1960), p. 127; Alexander Eliot, *Three Hundred Years of American Painting* (New York: Time Incorporated, 1957), pp. 50–51.
107. Virginia E. Lewis, *Russell Smith, Romantic Idealist* (Pittsburgh: University of Pittsburgh Press, 1956); *United States Gazette*, Oct. 5, 1836.
108. *United States Gazette*, June 12, 1830.
109. Ibid., July 25, 1834, Oct. 26, Nov. 7, Dec. 2, 1835, Feb. 9, 1836.
110. *Hazard's Register* 2 (1828): 375; *United States Gazette*, Oct. 20, 1831, April 14, June 4, 1834; *Niles' Weekly Register* 52 (1837): 304.
111. *United States Gazette*, June 12, 1830.
112. Ibid., March 8, 1830, April 23, 1832, May 30, 1836.
113. Ibid., Feb. 24, 1831. Persico was working in Philadelphia as early as 1831.
114. Ibid., Nov. 4, 1833.
115. Ibid., Oct. 9, 1835, Sept. 19, 1837, Sept. 4, 1838, June 4, 1839.
116. Ibid., June 19, 1835.
117. Ibid., April 23, 1832, Feb. 3, 1837; *Fisher Diary*, pp. 44, 76.
118. *United States Gazette*, Feb. 17, 1836. See Nicholas B. Wainwright, *Philadelphia in the Romantic Age of Lithography* (Phila-

delphia: Historical Society of Pennsylvania, 1958).

119. Jackson, *Encyclopedia of Philadelphia*, 4:998.
120. Ibid., p. 1055.
121. *United States Gazette*, Feb. 14, June 22, 1834, Sept. 21, 1835; *Hazard's Register* 16 (1835): 321.
122. *United States Gazette*, March 28, 1840; *Hazard's Register* 11 (1833): 232–36.
123. *United States Gazette*, Feb. 21, 24, 1832; Diary of Joseph Sill, Feb. 22, 1832.
124. Diary of Joseph Sill, Dec. 30, 1831; *United States Gazette*, Dec. 31, 1831, July 20, 1836, Sept. 18, 1839.
125. *United States Gazette*, July 7, 18, 1835.
126. Ibid., Aug. 16, 1834.
127. Ibid., Nov. 6, 1834, Dec. 30, 1837.
128. Ibid., June 7, 1828, June 13, 1835.
129. *Hazard's Register* 7 (1831): 105–11.
130. *American Daily Advertiser*, March 14, 1825; *Niles' Weekly Register* 28 (1825): 178.
131. *United States Gazette*, Feb. 17, 1837; *Hazard's Register* 7 (1831): 128.
132. *United States Gazette*, Nov. 1, Dec. 19, 1838, Feb. 9, 1839.
133. Ibid., Feb. 1, 1839.
134. Jackson, *Encyclopedia of Philadelphia*, 1:-179–80, 299–300.
135. Diary of Samuel Breck, Sept. 25, 1840.
136. Robert L. Bloom, "Robert Montgomery Bird, Editor," *PMHB* 76 (April 1952): 123; *DAB*, s.v. "Robert Montgomery Bird," 2:287.
137. Jackson, *Encyclopedia of Philadelphia*, 2:-342–44.
138. Ibid., 1:239–41.
139. *United States Gazette*, Sept. 15, 1836, Sept. 12, 1839; *Hazard's Register* 16 (1835): 175.
140. Jackson, *Encyclopedia of Philadelphia*, 2:374.
141. Wainwright, *The Irvine Story*, p. 23.
142. *Fisher Diary*, p. 105.
143. [Owen Wister,] *The Philadelphia Club, 1834–1934* (Philadelphia: Privately printed, 1934), p. 12.
144. Joseph J. McCadden, "Roberts Vaux and His Associates in the Pennsylvania Society for the Promotion of Public Schools," *PH* 3 (Jan. 1936): 1–17.
145. *Hazard's Register* 2 (1828): 28–29.
146. Ibid., 15 (1835): 278–81; Leroy B. De Puy, "The Triumph of the 'Pennsylvania System' at the State's Penitentiaries," *PH* 21 (April 1954): 128–44.
147. Negley K. Teeters, "The Early Days of the Philadelphia House of Refuge," *PH* 27 (April 1960): 165–87.
148. *Hazard's Register* 5 (1830): 176.
149. Frank Freidel, "A Plan for Modern Education in Early Philadelphia," *PH* 14 (April 1947): 175–84.
150. *Hazard's Register* 7 (1831): 172–73.
151. A Southerner [Joseph P. Wilson], *Sketches of the Higher Classes of Colored Society in Philadelphia* (Philadelphia: Merrihew & Thompson, 1841), pp. 19, 70, 74–75, 96; Elizabeth M. Geffen, "Philadelphia Protestantism Reacts to Social Reform, . . ." *PH* 30 (April 1963): 201.
152. *United States Gazette*, Aug. 25, 1835; *Hazard's Register* 16 (1835): 164–65.
153. Edward D. Snyder, "Whittier Returns to Philadelphia after a Hundred Years," *PMHB* 62 (April 1938): 140.
154. Ira V. Brown, "Miller McKim and Pennsylvania Abolitionism," *PH* 30 (Jan. 1963): 56–72.
155. Leonard L. Richards, "Gentlemen of Property and Standing": Anti-Abolition Mobs in Jack-

sonian America* (New York: Oxford University Press, 1970), pp. 7, 43, 66, 69.
156. Elizabeth M. Geffen, "William Henry Furness, Philadelphia Antislavery Preacher," *PMHB* 90 (April 1958): 267.
157. Richards, "Gentlemen of Property and Standing," p. 69.
158. Jackson, *Encyclopedia of Philadelphia*, 4:982; Diary of Samuel Breck, May 19, 1838.
159. Joseph J. L. Kirlin, *Catholicity in Philadelphia from the Earliest Missionaries to the Present Time* (Philadelphia: John Jos. McVey, 1909), pp. 263, 278, 290, 294.
160. Robert W. Doherty, "A Response to Orthodoxy: The Hicksite Movement in the Society of Friends," *PMHB* 90 (April 1966): 233–46; id., *The Hicksite Separation: A Sociological Analysis of Religious Schism in Early Nineteenth Century America* (New Brunswick, N.J.: Rutgers University Press, 1967).
161. [Wister,] *The Philadelphia Club*, p. 17.
162. Geffen, "William Henry Furness," pp. 259, 263.
163. Joseph J. McCadden, *Education in Pennsylvania, 1801–1835, and Its Debt to Roberts Vaux* (Philadelphia: University of Pennsylvania Press, 1937), pp. 4, 96, 104, 179, 221; Jackson, *Encyclopedia of Philadelphia*, 2:-402–4, 618.
164. *Fisher Diary*, p. 553.
165. Richard H. Shryock, "A Century of Medical Progress in Philadelphia, 1750–1850," *PH* 8 (Jan. 1941): 24.
166. George M. Gould, *The Jefferson Medical College of Philadelphia* (2 vols.; New York: Lewis Publishing, 1904), 1:53, 107.
167. Elisabeth D. Freund, *Crusader for Light, Julius R. Friedlander, Founder of the Overbrook School for the Blind, 1882* (Philadelphia: Dorrance, 1959).
168. William Campbell Posey and Samuel Horton Brown, *The Wills Hospital of Philadelphia* (Philadelphia: Lippincott, 1931), p. 57.
169. David Kaser, *Messrs. Carey & Lea of Philadelphia: A Study in the History of the Book Trade* (Philadelphia: University of Pennsylvania Press, 1957), pp. 51–52. See Charles E. Rosenberg, *The Cholera Years: The United States in 1832, 1849, and 1866* (Chicago: University of Chicago Press, 1962).
170. *United States Gazette*, June 11, 1840.
171. Kaser, *Messrs. Carey & Lea*, pp. 24–51, 58, 65.
172. Rollo G. Silver, *The American Printer* (Charlottesville: University Press of Virginia, 1967), p. vii.
173. The information on the Philadelphia press is based on Nicholas B. Wainwright, "The History of the *Philadelphia Inquirer*," supplement to the *Philadelphia Inquirer*, Sept. 16, 1962.
174. George H. Callcott, *History in the United States, 1800–1860: Its Practice and Purpose* (Baltimore: Johns Hopkins Press, 1970), p. vii.
175. Hampton L. Carson, *A History of the Historical Society of Pennsylvania* (2 vols.; Philadelphia: Historical Society of Pennsylvania, 1940), 1:54.
176. Edward M. Riley, "The Independence Hall Group," in Luther P. Eisenhart, ed., *Historic Philadelphia: From the Founding Until the Early Nineteenth Century: Papers Dealing with Its People and Buildings with an Illustrative Map* (Philadelphia: American Philosophical Society, 1953), p. 34.
177. Jackson, *Encyclopedia of Philadelphia*, 3:808, 882.

178. Bray Hammond, "Jackson, Biddle, and the Bank of the United States," *Journal of Economic History* 7 (May 1947): 2.
179. *Niles' Weekly Register* 35 (1828–1829): 75; Govan, *Nicholas Biddle*, pp. 100, 111; Wainwright, "Nicholas Biddle," p. 85.
180. Catterall, *The Second Bank of the United States*, p. 198.
181. *United States Gazette*, May 23, 1831.
182. Govan, *Nicholas Biddle*, p. 182.
183. Catterall, *The Second Bank of the United States*, p. 239.
184. Govan, *Nicholas Biddle*, p. 221.
185. *United States Gazette*, Nov. 3, 1832.
186. Govan, *Nicholas Biddle*, p. 214.
187. Catterall, *The Second Bank of the United States*, p. 291.
188. *United States Gazette*, Sept. 24, 1833.
189. Govan, *Nicholas Biddle*, pp. 244–45.
190. Ibid., p. 247; William Buckingham Smith, *Economic Aspects of the Second Bank of the United States* (Cambridge, Mass.: Harvard University Press, 1953), p. 169.
191. Govan, *Nicholas Biddle*, pp. 254, 260.
192. *United States Gazette*, March 21, 1834; *Hazard's Register* 13 (1834): 92.
193. *Niles' Weekly Register* 49 (1835–1836): 290.
194. Ibid., 50 (1836): 23.
195. Hammond, "Jackson, Biddle, and the Bank," p. 20.
196. Govan, *Nicholas Biddle*, p. 132.
197. Nicholas B. Wainwright, *History of the Philadelphia National Bank: A Century and a Half of Philadelphia Banking, 1803–1953* (Philadelphia: Philadelphia National Bank, 1953), p. 80; Diary of Samuel Breck, Dec. 16, 1839; Henry Simpson, *The Lives of Eminent Philadelphians, Now Deceased, Collected from Original and Authentic Sources* (Philadelphia: William Brotherhead, 1859), p. 62.

INDUSTRIAL DEVELOPMENT AND SOCIAL CRISIS, 1841–1865

1. *Report of the Sanitary Committee of the Board of Health of Philadelphia on the Subject of the Asiatic Cholera, Embracing Certain Sanitary Suggestions and Recommendations* (Philadelphia: Board of Health, 1848), p. 7; William H. Furness to Lucy Osgood, Jan. 14, 1846, Osgood manuscript correspondence in the possession of the author; William Chambers, *Things as They Are in America* (Philadelphia: Lippincott, Grambo, 1854), p. 317.
2. *United States Gazette*, Jan. 1, 1841; Samuel Hazard, ed., *United States Commercial and Statistical Register* (6 vols., Philadelphia: Samuel T. Hazard, 1841–1842), 5:5.
3. *United States Gazette*, Jan. 5, 1841.
4. J. Thomas Scharf and Thompson Westcott, *History of Philadelphia, 1689–1884* (3 vols.; Philadelphia: L. H. Everts, 1884), 1:687; Joseph Sill Diary, Jan. 8, 1841, Historical Society of Pennsylvania (hereafter cited as HSP), 2:341.
5. Job R. Tyson, *Letters on the Resources and Commerce of Philadelphia* . . . (Philadelphia: Sherman, 1852), p. 15; James Fenimore Cooper, ed., *Correspondence of James Fenimore-Cooper* (2 vols.; New Haven, Conn.: Yale University Press, 1922), 2:441.
6. Hazard, *Register*, 4:390–93; *The Seventh Census of the United States* (Washington, D.C., 1853), pp. 178–79; William J. Bromwell, *History of Immigration* (New York, Redfield 1856), pp. 109, 141, 161; Edwin T. Freedley, *Philadelphia and Its Manufacturers . . . in 1857* (Philadelphia: Edward Young, 1859), p. 57; *Population of the United States in 1860 . . . Eighth Census* (Washington, D.C.: U.S. Government Printing Office, 1864), p. xxxii; Ray A. Billington, *The Protestant Crusade, 1800–1860: A Study of the Origins of American Nativism* (New York: Macmillan, 1938); David Sulzberger, "Growth of Jewish Population in the United States," *Publications of the American Jewish Historical Society*, No. 6 (1897), p. 143; Maxwell Whiteman, "Isaac Leeser and the Jews of Philadelphia," *Publications of the American Jewish Historical Society* 48 (June 1959): 212.
7. W. E. B. DuBois, *The Philadelphia Negro: A Social Study* (New York: Schocken, 1967), pp. 32, 36, 303; Sam Bass Warner, Jr., *The Private City: Philadelphia in Three Periods of Its Growth* (Philadelphia: University of Pennsylvania Press, 1968), p. 55.
8. Scharf and Westcott, *History of Philadelphia*, 3:1762; Freedley, *Philadelphia and its Manufacturers*, p. 59; Tyson, *Letters on the Resources and Commerce of Philadelphia*, p. 34.
9. Thomas Baldwin and J. Thomas, *A New and Complete Gazeteer of the United States* . . . (Philadelphia: Lippincott, Grambo, 1854), p. 909.
10. George G. Foster, "Philadelphia in Slices," *Pennsylvania Magazine of History and Biography* (hereafter cited as *PMHB*) 93 (Jan. 1969): 59.
11. Baldwin and Thomas, *Gazeteer*, p. 912.
12. H. S. Tanner, *A New Picture of Philadelphia, or The Stranger's Guide to the City and Adjoining Districts* . . . (Philadelphia: H. Tanner, Jr., 1840), pp. 130–31, 135–36.
13. Baldwin and Thomas, *Gazeteer*, p. 908.
14. Nicholas B. Wainwright, ed., *A Philadelphia Perspective: The Diary of Sidney George Fisher Covering the Years 1834–1871* (Philadelphia: Historical Society of Pennsylvania, 1967), pp. 227, 237 (hereafter cited as *Fisher Diary*).
15. Tanner, *New Picture of Philadelphia*, p. 126; Scharf and Westcott, *History of Philadelphia*, 1:693, 690; Sill Diary, Nov. 17, 1847, 8:41.
16. Tanner, *New Picture of Philadelphia*, pp. 127, 133.
17. Baldwin and Thomas, *Gazeteer*, p. 918.
18. Alexander Mackay, *The Western World; or, Travels in the United States in 1846–47* . . . (2 vols.; Philadelphia: Lea and Blanchard, 1849), 1:93.
19. Baldwin and Thomas, *Gazeteer*, p. 911; George B. Tatum, *Penn's Great Town: 250 Years of Philadelphia Architecture* (Philadelphia: University of Pennsylvania Press, 1961), pp. 84, 181, 97; Charles E. Peterson, "Ante-Bellum Skyscraper," *Journal of the Society of Architectural Historians* (hereafter cited as *JSAH*) 9 (Oct. 1950): 27–28; R. A. Smith, *Philadelphia as It Is in 1852* (Philadelphia: Lindsay & Blakiston, 1852), pp. 109, 111; Theo B. White et al., *Philadelphia Architec-*

ture in the Nineteenth Century (Philadelphia: University of Pennsylvania Press, 1953), p. 17.

20. Foster, "Philadelphia in Slices," p. 50.

21. Baldwin and Thomas, *Gazeteer*, p. 911; Scharf and Westcott, *History of Philadelphia*, 1:711, 709.

22. *Public Ledger*, March 5, 1844; Jefferson Williamson, *The American Hotel: An Anecdotal History* (New York: Knopf, 1930), pp. 46, 61, 47; Scharf and Westcott, *History of Philadelphia*, 2:998; Tatum, *Penn's Great Town*, p. 98.

23. Francis and Theresa Pulszky, *White, Red, and Black* (2 vols.; New York: Redfield, 1853), 1:154; Chambers, *Things as They Are in America*, pp. 305–7, 312.

24. William J. Murtagh, "The Philadelphia Row House," *JSAH* 16 (Dec. 1957): 8–13; Kenneth Ames, "Robert Mills and the Philadelphia Row House," *JSAH* 27 (May 1968): 140–46; Isaac Parrish, "Report on the Sanitary Condition of Philadelphia," *Transactions of the American Medical Association* 2 (1849): 465.

25. Freedley, *Philadelphia and Its Manufactures*, pp. 250–51.

26. Scharf and Westcott, *History of Philadelphia*, 3:1851–52, 1848–49, 1:705.

27. Ibid., 1:675–76, 3:1854–56.

28. *United States Gazette*, Jan. 19, 1841.

29. John F. Watson, *Annals of Philadelphia, and Pennsylvania, in the Olden Time . . .* (3 vols.; Philadelphia: Privately printed, 1844), 1:221; *Public Ledger*, June 12, 1844; Tatum, *Penn's Great Town*, p. 87.

30. Baldwin and Thomas, *Gazeteer*, p. 919; Charles J. Cohen, *Rittenhouse Square* (Philadelphia: Privately printed, 1922), pp. 119–20; Scharf and Westcott, *History of Philadelphia*, 3:2200.

31. Smith, *Philadelphia as It Is in 1852*, pp. 407, 409, 411; Scharf and Westcott, *History of Philadelphia*, 3:2187; *Public Ledger*, July 16, Sept. 18 and 28, 1839; Michael Feldberg, "Urbanization as a Cause of Violence: Philadelphia as a Test Case," in Allen F. Davis and Mark H. Haller, eds., *The Peoples of Philadelphia: A History of Ethnic Groups and Lower-Class Life, 1790–1940* (Philadelphia: Temple University Press, 1973), pp. 58–61.

32. Archibald M. Maxwell, *A Run through the United States, During the Autumn of 1840* (2 vols.; London: Henry Colburn, 1841), 2:230–31; Mackay, *The Western World*, 1:97.

33. Charles R. Barker, "Post Office Buildings of Philadelphia," *City History Society of Philadelphia Publications* 2 (1930): 232–33, 254; *Twenty-first Annual Report of the Directors of the Philadelphia Board of Trade to the Members of That Association* (Philadelphia: Deacon & Peterson, 1854), pp. 18–19.

34. Watson, *Annals of Philadelphia*, vol. 3, edited by Willis P. Hazard (3 vols.; Philadelphia: Edwin S. Stuart, 1900), 3:130; Baldwin and Thomas, *Gazeteer*, p. 913; Scharf and Westcott, *History of Philadelphia*, 1:643, 676, 707; Charles R. Barker, "Philadelphia in the Late 'Forties,'" *City History Society of Philadelphia Publications* 2 (1931): 256–57.

35. Nelson M. Blake, *Water for the City: A History of the Urban Water Supply Problem in the United States* (Syracuse, N.Y.: Syracuse University Press, 1956), pp. 95–98; Baldwin

and Thomas, *Gazeteer*, p. 913; Scharf and Westcott, *History of Philadelphia*, 1:662–63; *Report of the Watering Committee for the Year 1853* (Philadelphia: Crissy & Markley, 1854), p. 34.

36. *Report of the Watering Committee for the Year 1848* (Philadelphia: Crissy & Markley, 1849), p. 6; *Report of the Watering Committee for the Year 1849* (Philadelphia: Crissy & Markley, 1850), pp. 8, 7.

37. Parrish, "Report on the Sanitary Condition," p. 478.

38. *Report of the Watering Committee for the Year 1849*, p. 45; Parrish, "Report on the Sanitary Condition," p. 479; *Report of the Watering Committee for the Year 1853*, pp. 7, 76.

39. Blake, *Water for the City*, pp. 258–59.

40. *Report . . . on the Subject of the Asiatic Cholera*, p. 7.

41. Charles E. Claghorn, *The Mocking Bird: The Life and Diary of Its Author, Sep. Winner* (Philadelphia: Magee Press, 1937), p. 14.

42. Richard H. Shryock, "A Century of Medical Progress in Philadelphia, 1750–1850," *Pennsylvania History* 8 (Jan. 1941): 10; James M. Newman, "Report on the Sanitary Police of Cities," *Transactions of the American Medical Association* 9 (1856): 434; Scharf and Westcott, *History of Philadelphia*, 1:690–91, 711; 3:1726; Parrish, "Report on the Sanitary Condition,'" p. 467; Committee on Epidemics, "Epidemics of Pennsylvania," *Transactions of the American Medical Association* 5 (1852): 308, 305; Baldwin and Thomas, *Gazeteer*, p. 919; Charles E. Rosenberg, *The Cholera Years: The United States in 1832, 1849, and 1866* (Chicago: University of Chicago Press, 1962), p. 4.

43. *Statistics of Cholera: With the Sanitary Measures Adopted by the Board of Health, Prior to, and During the Prevalence of the Epidemic in Philadelphia, in the Summer of 1849* (Philadelphia: King and Baird, 1849), p. 43.

44. Shryock, "A Century of Medical Progress," esp. pp. 13–15, 24, 25, 27–28; Henry B. Shafer, *The American Medical Profession, 1783 to 1850* (New York: Columbia University Press, 1936), pp. 11–12, 241–48; Richard H. Shryock, "Public Relations of the Medical Profession in Great Britain and the United States, 1600–1870," *Annals of Medical History* 2 (May 1930): 318; M. L. North, "A Glance at Medicine in Philadelphia," *Boston Medical and Surgical Journal* 26 (1842): 27; Harold J. Abrahams, *Extinct Medical Schools of Nineteenth-Century Philadelphia* (Philadelphia: University of Pennsylvania Press, 1966), pp. 49, 551; James F. Gayley, *A History of the Jefferson Medical College of Philadelphia* (Philadelphia: Joseph M. Wilson, 1858), p. 58.

45. William F. Norwood, *Medical Education in the United States Before the Civil War* (Philadelphia: University of Pennsylvania Press, 1944), p. 84, 88, 91, 93; Abrahams, *Extinct Medical Schools*, p. 562; Gayley, *Jefferson Medical College*, pp. 19–21; Samuel D. Gross, *Autobiography*, edited by Samuel W. Gross and A. Haller Gross (2 vols.; Philadelphia: George Barrie, 1887), 2:304.

46. Nathan S. Davis, *History of the American Medical Association from its Organization up to January, 1855* (Philadelphia: Lippincott, Grambo, 1855), p. 19; Abrahams, *Extinct*

Medical Schools, pp. 29–31, 35, 111, 112, 114, 162, 168.

47. Scharf and Westcott, *History of Philadelphia*, 2:1651; Davis, *History of the American Medical Association*, pp. 19–20, 31–32, 58.

48. Davis, *History of the American Medical Association*, pp. 43–44.

49. Ibid., pp. 49, 51–52; Scharf and Westcott, *History of Philadelphia*, 2:1632; Harry B. Weiss and Howard R. Kemble, *The Great American Water-Cure Craze: A History of Hydropathy in the United States* (Trenton, N.J.: Past Times Press, 1967), pp. 51–52.

50. Thomas L. Bradford, *History of the Homœopathic Medical College of Pennsylvania; The Hahnemann Medical College and Hospital of Philadelphia* (Philadelphia: Boericke & Tafel, 1898), pp. 1, 7–9.

51. *The American Illustrated Medical Dictionary* (22d ed.; Philadelphia: W. B. Saunders & Co., 1951), p. 686.

52. Bradford, *Homoeopathic Medical College*, pp. 405–6, 108, 111, 127–28, 139, 151.

53. Scharf and Westcott, *History of Philadelphia*, 1:698–99; Abrahams, *Extinct Medical Schools*, p. 232.

54. Weiss and Kemble, *The Great American Water-Cure Craze*, pp. 90–91.

55. Ibid., pp. 91–92, 189–90.

56. Gulielma F. Alsop, *History of the Women's Medical College, Philadelphia, Pennsylvania, 1850–1950* (Philadelphia: Lippincott, 1950), pp. 13, 4, 7, 9–12, 46, 53–54, 61, 72.

57. Abrahams, *Extinct Medical Schools*, pp. 111, 176–77, 179–81, 184, 194–98, 201, 550.

58. George B. Wood, *Addresses [1826–1856]* (n.p., n.d.), "Introductory Lecture, November 2, 1842," p. 22; *Wealth and Biography of the Wealthy Citizens of Philadelphia* (Philadelphia: G. B. Zieber, 1845), pp. 6, 19; *Spirit of the Times*, July 4, 1844.

59. Edward Kremers and George Urdang, *History of Pharmacy* (Philadelphia: Lippincott, 1940), pp. 144–45, 173–74, 175, 178, 189–91.

60. Scharf and Westcott, *History of Philadelphia*, 2:1682; Richard H. Shryock, *The Development of Modern Medicine: An Interpretation of the Social and Scientific Factors Involved* (New York: Knopf, 1947), p. 179.

61. North, "A Glance at Medicine in Philadelphia," p. 27.

62. Chester L. Jones, *The Economic History of the Anthracite-Tidewater Canals* (Philadelphia: John C. Winston, 1908), pp. 126, 136; *Niles' National Register* 61 (Jan. 8, 1842): 304; Freedley, *Philadelphia and Its Manufactures*, p. 115; Sill Diary, Jan. 10, 1842, 3:282.

63. Freedley, *Philadelphia and Its Manufactures*, p. 116; Barbara Fisher, "Maritime History of the Reading, 1833–1905," *PMHB* 86 (April 1962): 167–68; Jones, *Anthracite-Tidewater Canals*, pp. 134, 136–37, 138; Caroline E. MacGill et al., *History of Transportation in the United States before 1860* (Washington, D.C.: Carnegie Institution of Washington, 1917), p. 394.

64. Fisher, "Maritime History of the Reading," p. 168; Jones, *Anthracite-Tidewater Canals*, p. 141.

65. MacGill et al., *History of Transportation*, p. 394; Fisher, "Maritime History of the Reading," p. 171; *Twenty-first Annual Report . . . . of the Philadelphia Board of Trade* (Philadelphia, 1854), p. 23.

66. Robert G. Albion, *The Rise of New York Port* (New York: Scribner's, 1939), p. 135.

67. Louis Hartz, *Economic Policy and Democratic Thought: Pennsylvania, 1776–1860* (Cambridge, Mass.: Harvard University Press, 1948), p. 12.

68. Eliza Cope Harrison, ed., *Philadelphia Merchant: The Diary of Thomas P. Cope, 1800–1851* (South Bend, Ind.: Gateway Editions, 1978), pp. 479–80, 488–90, 492, 495, 496–97, 500, 502, 503; George H. Burgess and Miles C. Kennedy, *Centennial History of the Pennsylvania Railroad Company, 1846–1946* (Philadelphia: Pennsylvania Railroad Company, 1949), pp. 38–39, 92.

69. Charles C. Binney, *The Life of Horace Binney* (Philadelphia: Lippincott, 1903), pp. 245, 248–53; Harrison, ed., *Philadelphia Merchant*, pp. 516, 518–19, 523, 524–25; Burgess and Kennedy, *Centennial History of the Pennsylvania Railroad*, p. 43.

70. Burgess and Kennedy, *Centennial History of the Pennsylvania Railroad*, pp. 748, 755, 767, 31.

71. Advertisement in *O'Brien's Philadelphia Wholesale Business Directory and United States, South America and West India Circular . . . for the Year 1849*, noted in an unpublished manuscript of Francis James Dallett, "Philadelphia Oceanic Shipping in an 1849 Perspective," [p. 1,] in the possession of the author.

72. Francis Wyse, *America, Its Realities and Resources . . .* (3 vols.; London: T. C. Newby, 1846), 1:7.

73. George Rogers Taylor, *The Transportation Revolution, 1815–1860* (New York: Rinehart, 1951), pp. iv, 106.

74. Dallett, "Philadelphia Oceanic Shipping" [p. 1].

75. Ibid. [p. 2].

76. Ibid. [pp. 1–3].

77. Scharf and Westcott, *History of Philadelphia*, 3:2169–70, 1:693–95; Barker, "Philadelphia in the Late 'Forties,'" p. 250.

78. Taylor, *Transportation Revolution*, pp. 119, 121, 116–17; Scharf and Westcott, *History of Philadelphia*, 1:699.

79. Robert L. Thompson, *Wiring a Continent: History of the Telegraph Industry, 1832–1866* (Princeton, N.J.: Princeton University Press, 1947), pp. 219, 29–30, 41–42, 48, 168, 47, 222; A[lfred] M. Lee, *The Daily Newspaper in America* (New York: Macmillan, 1937), p. 66; *One Hundred Years in Philadelphia: The Evening Bulletin's Anniversary Book, 1847–1947* (Philadelphia: Evening Bulletin, 1947).

80. Scharf and Westcott, *History of Philadelphia*, 3:2133.

81. Baldwin and Thomas, *Gazeteer*, p. 917; Tyson, *Letters on the Resources and Commerce of Philadelphia*, p. 38; Freedley, *Philadelphia and Its Manufactures*, pp. 234, 301, 427–32; Victor S. Clark, *A History of Manufactures in the United States* (rev. ed.; 3 vols.; New York: McGraw Hill, 1929), 1:465.

82. Freedley, *Philadelphia and Its Manufactures*, pp. 252, 241; Rowland T. Berthoff, *British Immigrants in Industrial America, 1790–1950* (Cambridge, Mass.: Harvard University Press, 1953), pp. 39, 40.

83. Freedley, *Philadelphia and Its Manufactures*, pp. 432–33, 327, 434–35, 307, 450; Clark, *History of Manufactures*, 1:527; Baldwin and Thomas, *Gazeteer*, p. 917.

84. Freedley, *Philadelphia and Its Manufactures*, pp. 379–80, 383.

85. *Wealth and Biography of the Wealthy Citizens of Philadelphia*, pp. 1–23; E. Douglas Branch, *The Sentimental Years, 1836–1860* (New York: D. Appleton-Century, 1934), p. 45; Charles G. Leland, *Memoirs* (New York: D. Appleton, 1893), pp. 31–34. Edward Pessen in *Riches, Class, and Power Before the Civil War* (Lexington, Mass.: D. C. Heath, 1973) documents the great and growing maldistribution of wealth and its integral relationship to social status and power in the period 1825–1850.
86. Freedley, *Philadelphia and Its Manufactures*, p. 128; *Philadelphia City Directory*, 1857.
87. Mackay, *The Western World*, 1:130.
88. E. Digby Baltzell, *Philadelphia Gentlemen: The Making of a National Upper Class* (Glencoe, Ill.: Free Press, 1958), chap. 5. Stuart Blumin in "Mobility and Change in Ante-Bellum Philadelphia," in Stephan Thernstrom and Richard Sennett, eds., *Nineteenth Century Cities* (New Haven, Conn.: Yale University Press, 1969), finds that upward occupational mobility was fairly stable, while downward mobility seemed to have gradually increased between 1820 and 1860, but he notes that it may be invalid to infer economic mobility from occupational mobility.
89. *Fisher Diary*, p. 142.
90. Leland, *Memoirs*, p. 192.
91. Mackay, *The Western World*, 1:130.
92. Chambers, *Things as They Are in America*, pp. 317, 321.
93. Thomas W. Balch, *The Philadelphia Assemblies* (Philadelphia: Allen, Lane and Scott, 1916), p. 109.
94. *Fisher Diary*, pp. 221, 233. That Fisher exaggerated the breakdown of social exclusiveness is evident in the data presented by Pessen, *Riches, Class, and Power Before the Civil War*.
95. Balch, *Philadelphia Assemblies*, pp. 132–33, 121.
96. Job R. Tyson, *Sketch of the Wistar Party of Philadelphia* (Philadelphia: W. S. Young, 1846), pp. 12–13; (amended ed.; Philadelphia: Privately printed, 1898), p. 11.
97. Scharf and Westcott, *History of Philadelphia*, 1:819–20, 686; Cadwalader Collection, HSP.
98. William R. Wister, *Some Reminiscences of Cricket in Philadelphia Before 1861* (Philadelphia: Allen, 1904), p. 15.
99. Ibid., pp. 7–9, 12–13 (quotation), 22–30.
100. Foster Rhea Dulles, *America Learns to Play: A History of Popular Recreation, 1607–1940* (New York: D. Appleton-Century, 1940), pp. 64, 84, 146, 183.
101. *Fisher Diary*, pp. 189, 202, 228–30, 237, 564.
102. Anna R. Burr, *Weir Mitchell, His Life and Letters* (New York: Duffield, 1929), p. 27; *Godey's Lady's Book* 41 (Aug. 1850): 126, (July 1850): 62; *Public Ledger*, May 23, 1844; F. H. Shelton, "Springs and Spas of Old-Time Philadelphians," *PMHB* 47 (1923): 224, 227–30; Williamson, *The American Hotel*, pp. 235, 243–45.
103. Williamson, *The American Hotel*, p. 245; Sill Diary, July 20, 1854, 10:532.
104. Scharf and Westcott, *History of Philadelphia*, 1:712; Williamson, *The American Hotel*, pp. 245, 254–55.
105. Frank Luther Mott, *A History of American Magazines, 1741–1850* (2 vols.; Cambridge, Mass.: Harvard University Press, 1930–1938), 1:520, 521; John Sartain, *The Reminiscences of a Very Old Man, 1808–1897* (New York:

D. Appleton, 1899); Nicholas B. Wainwright, *Philadelphia in the Romantic Age of Lithography* (Philadelphia: Historical Society of Pennsylvania, 1958); Ruth E. Finley, *The Lady of Godey's: Sarah Josepha Hale* (Philadelphia: Lippincott, 1931), p. 243; *Godey's Lady's Book* 40 (Jan. 1850): 82.
106. Ellis P. Oberholtzer, *The Literary History of Philadelphia* (Philadelphia: George W. Jacobs, 1906), p. 231.
107. Mott, *History of American Magazines*, 1:506; Bertha M. Stearns, "Philadelphia Magazines for Ladies, 1830–1860," *PMHB* 69 (July 1945): 211.
108. Oberholtzer, *Literary History of Philadelphia*, p. 231; Mott, *History of American Magazines*, 1:509; Fred L. Pattee, *The Feminine Fifties* (New York: D. Appleton-Century, 1940).
109. Mott, *History of American Magazines*, 1:351–52, 2:301–11; Stearns, "Philadelphia Magazines for Ladies," pp. 212, 213.
110. Stearns, "Philadelphia Magazines for Ladies," p. 213; Smith, *Philadelphia as It Is in 1852*, p. 200.
111. Edgar W. Martin, *The Standard of Living in 1860* (Chicago: University of Chicago Press, 1942), p. 320.
112. Frank Luther Mott, *Golden Multitudes: The Story of Best Sellers in the United States* (New York: Macmillan, 1947), p. 307; Oberholtzer, *Literary History of Philadelphia*, p. 254; Roger Butterfield, "George Lippard and His Secret Brotherhood," *PMHB* 79 (July 1955): 287, 257, 293; Charles Durang, "History of the Philadelphia Stage Between the Years 1749 and 1855," clipped from the *Philadelphia Sunday Despatch*, 1854–1860, arranged in six volumes and illustrated by Thompson Westcott (1868), 5:246–47, in the Rare Book Collection of the University of Pennsylvania.
113. George Lippard, *The Quaker City* (Philadelphia: Leary, Stuart, 1876), pp. 3, 462.
114. Edith Abbott, "The Wages of Unskilled Labor in the United States, 1850–1900," *Journal of Political Economy* 13 (1905): 361; *Public Ledger*, March 12, June 12, May 21, 1844; Norman Ware, *The Industrial Worker, 1840–1860* (Boston: Houghton Mifflin, 1924), p. 33. On the working classes, the poor, and their living conditions, see also two works that appeared too late to be used in writing this book: Theodore Hershberg, ed., *Philadelphia: Work, Space, Family, and Group Experience in the Nineteenth Century: Essays Toward an Interdisciplinary History of the City* (New York: Oxford University Press, 1981); and Bruce Laurie, *Working People of Philadelphia, 1800–1850* (Philadelphia: Temple University Press, 1980).
115. *The Mysteries and Miseries of Philadelphia* . . . (Philadelphia, 1853), pp. 11, 15, 17, 18; Hazard, *Register*, 4:271.
116. *Public Ledger*, Feb. 25, 1841; Scharf and Westcott, *History of Philadelphia*, 3:2076; Joseph Jackson, *Literary Landmarks of Philadelphia* (Philadelphia: David McKay, 1939), pp. 9–10; Ira V. Brown, *Pennsylvania Reformers: From Penn to Pinchot* (University Park: Pennsylvania Historical Association, 1966), p. 43.
117. Rosine Association, *Reports and Realities From the Sketch-Book of a Manager of the Rosine Association* . . . (Philadelphia: Duross, 1855), pp. 25, 37.

118. Ibid., pp. 18, 27, 291, 34–35, 50–55, 36.
119. John R. Commons et al., *History of Labour in the United States* (2 vols.; New York: Macmillan, 1918–1921), 1:566.
120. *Public Ledger*, Feb. 2, 1844 et seq., Jan. 23, 1845; *Godey's Lady's Book* 34 (March 1847): 175.
121. *Public Ledger*, Aug. 2, 1842.
122. Ibid., Aug. 26, 1842.
123. Ibid., Aug. 27, 1842; Sill Diary, Aug. 26, 1842, 4:79–80.
124. *Public Ledger*, Aug. 19, 26, 29, Sept. 2, 1842, Jan. 10, 11, 12, 13, 14, 1843; March 22, April 17, 1844; April 18, 1846.
125. Ibid., Sept. 2, Aug. 19, 29, 1842; Jan. 10, 11, 12, 1843; Ware, *The Industrial Worker*, p. 63.
126. James W. Alexander, *The American Mechanic and Workingman* (rev. ed.; Philadelphia: Claxton, 1867), p. 197.
127. Butterfield, "George Lippard," pp. 291, 296–98; *The Quaker City*, Sept. 29, 1849.
128. Commons, *History of Labour*, 1:547–52, 543, 564; Ware, *The Industrial Worker*, p. 148.
129. Commons, *History of Labour*, 1:575, 596; Edgar B. Cale, *The Organization of Labor in Philadelphia, 1850–1870* (Philadelphia: University of Pennsylvania Press, 1940), pp. 12–18, 25, 110, 30.
130. Commons, *History of Labour*, 1:516; Joseph Dorfman, *The Economic Mind in American Civilization, 1606–1918* (3 vols.; New York: Viking, 1946–1949), 2:689–93.
131. Commons, *History of Labour*, 1:516.
132. Cale, *Organization of Labor in Philadelphia*, pp. 75, 94–95, 6; Roger Lane, *Violent Death in the City: Suicide, Accident, and Murder in Nineteenth Century Philadelphia* (Cambridge, Mass.: Harvard University Press, 1979), studies these types of violence as reactions to the social maladjustment caused by industrialization.
133. Edward Potts Cheyney, *History of the University of Pennsylvania, 1740–1940* (Philadelphia: University of Pennsylvania Press, 1940), p. 259.
134. Ibid., pp. 259–260, 217 ff, 340, 432, 232, 244–245.
135. James Mulhern, *A History of Secondary Education in Pennsylvania* (Philadelphia: Privately printed, 1933), pp. 478, 493–500; Scharf and Westcott, *History of Philadelphia*, 3:1931.
136. Scharf and Westcott, *History of Philadelphia*, 3:1947, 1950, 1953.
137. Ibid., p. 1936; *Public Ledger*, Jan. 16, 1845.
138. M. A. DeWolfe Howe, *Memoirs of the Life and Services of the Rt. Rev. Alonzo Potter . . .* (Philadelphia: Lippincott, 1871), pp. 162–65; Mulhern, *History of Secondary Education in Pennsylvania*, p. 472; Scharf and Westcott, *History of Philadelphia*, 2:1223.
139. Thomas Woody, *A History of Women's Education in the United States* (2 vols.; New York: Octagon, 1966), 1:524.
140. Ibid., p. 498; Scharf and Westcott, *History of Philadelphia*, 2:1698.
141. William B. Wood, *Personal Recollections of the Stage . . .* (Philadelphia: Henry Carey Baird, 1855), p. 436.
142. Arthur H. Wilson, *A History of the Philadelphia Theatre, 1835 to 1855* (Philadelphia: University of Pennsylvania Press, 1935), pp. 601–2, 583–84, 609–10, 638.
143. Sill Diary, Oct. 18, 1841, 3:181.
144. Dulles, *America Learns to Play*, p. 112.
145. Oberholtzer, *Literary History of Philadelphia*, pp. 241–44.
146. Sir Frederick Pollock, ed., *Macready's Reminiscences, and Selections from His Diaries and Letters* (2 vols.; London: MacMillan, 1875), 2:307–11.
147. Dulles, *America Learns to Play*, pp. 104–6; Wilson, *History of the Philadelphia Theatre*, pp. 36, 46.
148. Wilson, *History of the Philadelphia Theatre*, pp. 26, 35.
149. Ibid., pp. 5, 28, 109.
150. Dulles, *America Learns to Play*, p. 111.
151. Scharf and Westcott, *History of Philadelphia*, 2:1090–91.
152. Wilson, *History of the Philadelphia Theatre*, pp. 594, 604, 642; Sill Diary, May 4, 1848, 8:194.
153. Sill Diary, February-March 1842, 3:309 et passim; Jan. 25, 1843, 4:232; Jan. 28, 1843, 4:235–36; Jan. 1853, 10:209 et passim; Jan. 1854, 10:414 et passim; Carl Bode, *The American Lyceum: Town Meeting of the Mind* (New York: Oxford University Press, 1956), pp. 146–48; *Public Ledger*, Jan. 30, 1845; Elwyn B. Robinson, "The *Public Ledger*, An Independent Newspaper," *PMHB* 64 (Jan. 1940): 46; Lee, *Daily Newspaper in America*, p. 117.
154. Jackson, *Literary Landmarks*, p. 104; Butterfield, "George Lippard," pp. 293, 286; Scharf and Westcott, *History of Philadelphia*, 3:2012; Oberholtzer, *Literary History of Philadelphia*, p. 255.
155. Wilson, *History of the Philadelphia Theatre*, pp. 20–21, 30; Scharf and Westcott, *History of Philadelphia*, 2:980, 948–49, 979, 1:710–11, 713.
156. Neil Harris, *The Artist in American Society: The Formative Years, 1790–1860* (New York: George Braziller, 1966), pp. 275, 277; Sill Diary, Nov. 11, 1841, 3:205.
157. Sill Diary, Feb. 11, 1843, 4:25; Feb. 18, 1843, 4:255–56; Feb. 22, 1843; 4:258; March-May 1843, 4:268 et passim; Sept. 1843–Oct. 1844, 5:8 et passim; Nov. 23, 1844, 7:11; Dec. 1846–Sept. 1847, 7:240 et. passim; Oct. 1847–May 1849, 8:5 et passim; June 4, 1849, 10:11.
158. Ibid., Oct. 13, 1848, 8:316.
159. Harris, *The Artist in American Society*, pp. 272, 271; Sill Diary, June 4, 1849, 9:11, is the last recorded concern with attending meetings; George W. Dewey, "The Art-Union of Philadelphia," *Sartain's Union Magazine* 9 (Aug. 1851): 157.
160. Sartain, *Reminiscences of a Very Old Man*, pp 179–81.
161. Scharf and Westcott, *History of Philadelphia*, 1:711–12, 2:946–49.
162. Sill Diary, March 8, 1844, 5:198; Harris, *The Artist in American Society*, p. 111.
163. Harris, *The Artist in American Society*, pp. 109–10.
164. Edward J. Nygren, "Art Instruction in Philadelphia, 1795–1845" (M.A. thesis, University of Delaware, June 1969), pp. 6, 139, 147; Harris, *The Artist in American Society*, p. 273; Wainwright, *Philadelphia in the Golden Age of Lithography*, pp. 1–5.
165. Robert A. Gerson, *Music in Philadelphia* (Philadelphia: Theodore Presser, 1940), pp. 87, 89, 216–17; W. G. Armstrong, *Record of the Opera in Philadelphia* (Philadelphia: Porter & Coates, 1884), pp. 248–49.
166. Gerson, *Music in Philadelphia*, pp. 65, 66.

167. Watson, *Annals* (ed. Hazard), 3:125; Louis C. Madeira, *Annals of Music in Philadelphia and History of the Musical Fund Society from Its Organization in 1820 to the Year 1858* (Philadelphia: Lippincott, 1896), pp. 148–49.
168. Madeira, *Annals of Music*, pp. 155–57; Gerson, *Music in Philadelphia*, p. 67.
169. Madeira, *Annals of Music*, pp. 152–53.
170. *Godey's Lady's Book* 41 (Dec. 1850): 312.
171. Charles G. Rosenberg, *Jenny Lind in America* (New York: Stringer, 1851), p. 66.
172. Ibid., pp. 67–68.
173. Gerson, *Music in Philadelphia*, p. 68; Armstrong, *Record of the Opera in Philadelphia*, p. 78.
174. Gerson, *Music in Philadelphia*, p. 354.
175. Armstrong, *Record of the Opera in Philadelphia*, p. 43; Wilson, *History of the Philadelphia Theatre*, p. 23.
176. Gerson, *Music in Philadelphia*, pp. 72–73; Armstrong, *Record of the Opera in Philadelphia*, pp. 48–49.
177. Gerson, *Music in Philadelphia*, p. 76; Armstrong, *Record of the Opera in Philadelphia*, pp. 54–56, 72.
178. Gerson, *Music in Philadelphia*, pp. 90, 82–83; Claghorn, *The Mocking Bird*, pp. 19, 28–30; William A. Fisher, *One Hundred and Fifty Years of Music Publishing in the United States, 1783–1933* (Boston: Oliver Ditson, 1933), p. 89.
179. Scharf and Westcott, *History of Philadelphia*, 3:1912; Andrew H. Neilly, "The Violent Volunteers: A History of the Volunteer Fire Department of Philadelphia, 1736–1871" (Ph.D. dissertation, University of Pennsylvania, 1959), pp. 51–54, 69, 72–84; Bruce Laurie, "Fire Companies and Gangs in Southwark: The 1840s," in Davis and Haller, eds., *Peoples of Philadelphia*, pp. 71–88; Charles Lyell, *Travels in North America, in the Years 1841–42 . . .* (2 vols.; New York: Wiley & Putnam, 1845), 1:61.
180. Watson, *Annals* (ed. Hazard), 3:412; Neilly, "The Violent Volunteers," pp. 54, 70–72; Laurie, "Fire Companies and Gangs in Southwark," pp. 77–80; David R. Johnson, "Crime Patterns in Philadelphia, 1840–70," in Davis and Haller, eds., *Peoples of Philadelphia*, pp. 104–7.
181. Neilly, "The Violent Volunteers," pp. 54, 87, 90.
182. Scharf and Westcott, *History of Philadelphia*, 1:695–96, 700, 703–4.
183. Ibid., 3:1737.
184. Warner, *The Private City*, chap. 5.
185. Baltzell, *Philadelphia Gentlemen*, p. 12.
186. *Fisher Diary*, p. 126.
187. *Biographical Dictionary of the American Congress, 1774–1961* (Washington, D.C.: U.S. Government Printing Office, 1961), pp. 135, 1104–5.
188. Scharf and Westcott, *History of Philadelphia*, 2:1541–44; Baltzell, *Philadelphia Gentlemen*, pp. 132–39.
189. Charles M. Snyder, *The Jacksonian Heritage: Pennsylvania Politics, 1833–1848* (Harrisburg: Pennsylvania Historical and Museum Commission, 1958), p. 207.
190. Scharf and Westcott, *History of Philadelphia*, 2:1543.
191. Hazard, *Register*, 4:393; *Seventh Census*, p. 179. See John Hancock Lee, *The Origin and Progress of the American Party in Politics . . .* (Philadelphia: Elliott and Gihon, 1855),

for a contemporary, highly defensive account. Henry R. Mueller gives a scholarly appraisal in *The Whig Party in Pennsylvania* (New York: Columbia University Press, 1922), pp. 104–11, 118–20, 148–49, 155, 160–61, 163–64, 176. Michael Feldberg reviews the more recent scholarly interpretations of the phenomenon of nativism in *The Philadelphia Riots of 1844* (Westport, Conn.: Greenwood Press, 1975), chap. 3.
192. *Godey's Lady's Book* 34 (Jan. 1847): 8.
193. Malcolm R. Eiselen, *Rise of Pennsylvania Protectionism* (Philadelphia: Privately printed, 1932), p. 200.
194. Dorfman, *Economic Mind*, 2:799.
195. *Dictionary of American Biography*, s.v. "William D. Kelley," 10:299–300.
196. Henry C. Carey, *A Memoir of Stephen Colwell: Read before the American Philosophical Society, Friday, November 17, 1871* (Philadelphia: Baird, 1871), p. 7.
197. Stephen Colwell, *New Themes for the Protestant Clergy: Creeds Without Charity, Theology Without Humanity, and Protestantism Without Christianity* (2nd ed., rev.; Philadelphia: Lippincott, Grambo, 1853).
198. [S. Austin Allibone,] *A Review by a Layman, of a Work Entitled, "New Themes for the Protestant Clergy, etc."* (Philadelphia: Lippincott, Grambo, 1852), p. 65.
199. Carey, *Memoir of Stephen Colwell*, p. 7.
200. Dorfman, *Economic Mind*, 2:809–26.
201. Scharf and Westcott, *History of Philadelphia*, 1:678–79.
202. Ibid., pp. 679, 682; Sill Diary, Oct. 3, 1847, 8:4.
203. Clayton S. Ellsworth, "American Churches and the Mexican War," *American Historical Review* 45 (Jan. 1940): 301–26.
204. William H. Furness, *Doing Before Believing. A Discourse Delivered at the Anniversary of the Derby Academy in Hingham. May 19, 1847.* (New York: W. S. Dorr, 1847), p. 19; id., *The Son of Man Cometh. A Discourse Preached Before the Society of Cambridgeport Parish* (Boston: James Munroe, 1847), p. 19.
205. [William D. Willson,] *Sketches of the Higher Classes of Colored Society in Philadelphia* (Philadelphia: Merrihew & Thompson, 1841); Foster, "Philadelphia in Slices," pp. 60–64, 96–110; Edward Needles, *Ten Years' Progress: or A Comparison of the State and Condition of the Colored People in the City and County of Philadelphia from 1837 to 1847* (Philadelphia: Merrihew & Thompson, 1849), p. 8; Benjamin C. Bacon, *Statistics of the Colored People of Philadelphia* (Philadelphia: Ellwood, 1856), pp. 15–16; DuBois, *The Philadelphia Negro*, pp. 200, 222–24; Theodore Hershberg, "Free Blacks in Antebellum Philadelphia," in Davis and Haller, eds., *Peoples of Philadelphia*, pp. 111–34.
206. Hershberg, "Free Blacks," p. 114; DuBois, *The Philadelphia Negro*, p. 303.
207. Needles, *Ten Years' Progress*, p. 7; Hershberg, "Free Blacks," pp. 117–18; Bacon, *Statistics of the Colored People*, pp. 14–15; DuBois, *The Philadelphia Negro*, pp. 32, 34.
208. DuBois, *The Philadelphia Negro*, pp. 37, 238–39.
209. *Public Ledger*, Aug. 2, 1842, et seq.; Scharf and Westcott, *History of Philadelphia*, 1:660–61, 692–93; Elizabeth M. Geffen, "Violence in Philadelphia in the 1840's and 1850's," *Pennsylvania History* 36 (Oct. 1969): 387, 388.

210. Joseph Sturge, A Visit to the United States in 1841 . . . (London: Hamilton, Adams, 1842), p. 40.
211. [Willson,] Sketches of the Higher Classes of Colored Society, p. 64.
212. Herbert Aptheker, A Documentary History of the Negro People in the United States (New York: Citadel Press, 1969), p. 220; Gaffen, "Violence in Philadelphia," p. 388.
213. DuBois, The Philadelphia Negro, p. 88; Aptheker, Documentary History of the Negro People, pp. 359–60; Bacon, Statistics of the Colored People, pp. 4–11; Carter G. Woodson, The Education of the Negro Prior to 1861 (2nd ed.; Washington, D.C.: Association for the Study of Negro Life and History, 1919), pp. 146, 277.
214. William Still, The Underground Rail Road (Philadelphia: Porter & Coates, 1872); Larry Gara, The Liberty Line: The Legend of the Underground Railroad (Lexington: University of Kentucky Press, 1961), pp. 93–99, 104–5, 175–77, 99; Joseph A. Boromé, "The Vigilant Committee of Philadelphia," PMHB 92 (July 1968): 320–51; Minute Book of the Vigilant Committee of Philadelphia, May 31, 1839, to March 20, 1844, HSP; Leon F. Litwack, North of Slavery: The Negro in the Free States, 1790–1860 (Chicago: University of Chicago Press, 1961), p. 239; Benjamin Quarles, Black Abolitionists (New York: Oxford University Press, 1969), pp. 54–56.
215. Fourteenth Annual Report, Presented to the Pennsylvania Anti-Slavery Society, by its Executive Committee, October 7, 1851 (Philadelphia, 1851), pp. 11–13; Scharf and Westcott, History of Philadelphia, 1:701–2.
216. Fourteenth Annual Report . . . Pennsylvania Anti-Slavery Society, p. 11.
217. William H. Furness to Mary Jenks, April 14, 1851; Jenks manuscript correspondence in the possession of the author.
218. Proceedings of the Great Union Meeting, held in . . . the Chinese Museum, Philadelphia, on 21st of November, 1850 (Philadelphia: B. Mifﬂine, 1850).
219. Oberholtzer, Literary History of Philadelphia, pp. 310, 311.
220. "Black Letters; or Uncle Tom-Foolery in Literature," Graham's Magazine 42 (Feb. 1853): 209.
221. [Willson,] Sketches of the Higher Classes of Colored Society, pp. 85–86.
222. Elizabeth M. Geffen, "Philadelphia Protestantism Reacts to Social Reform Movements Before the Civil War," Pennsylvania History 30 (April 1963): 192–211; Henry J. Cadbury, "Negro Membership in the Society of Friends," Journal of Negro History 12 (1936): 167–69; Litwack, North of Slavery, p. 207; Quarles, Black Abolitionists, p. 72; Elizabeth M. Geffen, "William Henry Furness: Philadelphia Antislavery Preacher," PMHB 82 (July 1958): 259–92; Albert Barnes, Thanksgiving Sermon. The Virtues and Public Services of William Penn: A Discourse Delivered . . . November 27, 1845 (Philadelphia: William Sloanaker, 1845), p. 23.
223. L. C. Matlack, The Antislavery Struggle and Triumph in the Methodist Episcopal Church (New York: Phillips & Hunt, 1881), p. 117.
224. Albert Barnes, Our Position. A Sermon, Preached Before the General Association of the Presbyterian Church in the United States . . . May 20, 1852 (New York: Newman & Ivison, 1852); Timothy L. Smith, Revivalism and Social Reform in Mid-Nineteenth

Century America (New York: Abingdon Press, 1957), pp. 29–30; John B. Frantz, "Revivalism in the German Reformed Church in America to 1850 with Emphasis on the Eastern Synod" (Ph.D. dissertation, University of Pennsylvania, 1961), pp. 88 ﬀ; Henry S. Morais, The Jews of Philadelphia (Philadelphia: Levytype, 1894), pp. 89–91; Maxwell Whiteman, "Isaac Leeser and the Jews of Philadelphia," Publications of the American Jewish Historical Society 48 (June 1959): 207, 212, 215–18; Hugh J. Nolan, The Most Rev. Francis Patrick Kenrick, Third Bishop of Philadelphia, 1830–1851 (Washington, D.C.: Catholic University of America Press, 1948), pp. 270–72.
225. Frantz, "Revivalism in the German Reformed Church," p. 131; Albert Barnes, "Revivals of Religion in Cities and Large Towns," The American National Preacher 15 (Jan. 1841): 186; City Directory, 1841, pp. 339–40.
226. See Billington, The Protestant Crusade, 1800–1860, esp. pp. 168, 187; Scharf and Westcott, History of Philadelphia, 1:663.
227. Address of the Board of Managers of the American Protestant Association; with the Constitution and Organization of the Association (Philadelphia: American Protestant Association, 1843), pp. 5–12; Catalogue of the University of Pennsylvania, 1842–1843, p. 6; Cheyney, History of the University of Pennsylvania, p. 435.
228. Ruth M. Elson, Guardians of Tradition: American Schoolbooks of the Nineteenth Century (Lincoln: University of Nebraska Press, 1964), p. 53. In "The Shuttle and the Cross: Weavers and Artisans in the Kensington Riots of 1844," Journal of Social History 5 (Summer 1972): 411–46, David Montgomery presents the thesis that the confrontation between Protestants and Catholics produced by the political demands of evangelical Protestantism "fragmented the working class as a political force in ante-bellum Philadelphia" (p. 439).
229. A valuable review of the changing interpretations of the factors contributing to this outbreak of violence is provided by Feldberg, The Philadelphia Riots of 1844, pp. 41–50; see also The Truth Unveiled; or, A Calm and Impartial Exposition of the Origin and Immediate Cause of the Terrible Riots in Philadelphia, on May 6th, 7th and 8th, A.D. 1844 (Philadelphia: M. Fithian, 1844).
230. Alexander K. McClure, Old Time Notes of Pennsylvania (2 vols.; Philadelphia: John C. Winston, 1905), 1:203.
231. Scharf and Westcott, History of Philadelphia, 1:663–68; Billington, The Protestant Crusade, pp. 61, 78; Feldberg, The Philadelphia Riots of 1844, chap. 3, provides biographical data on many individuals among the nativists; Public Ledger, May 4, 1844, et seq.
232. Sill Diary, July 4, 1844; 5:333; Scharf and Westcott, History of Philadelphia, 1:668–73; Spirit of the Times, July 10, 1844; Billington, The Protestant Crusade, chap. 9.
233. Scharf and Westcott, History of Philadelphia, 1:673. The public controversy over the creation of this military force is described in Feldberg, The Philadelphia Riots of 1844, pp. 182–85.
234. Mueller, The Whig Party in Pennsylvania, pp. 109–11, 155, 160; Sill Diary, Oct. 16, 1846, 7:199; Scharf and Westcott, History of Philadelphia, 3:1738, 2015; biographical data on

Levin are provided in the *Dictionary of American Biography*, 11:200–1, and John A. Forman, "Lewis Charles Levin, Portrait of an American Demagogue," *American Jewish Archives* (Oct. 1960): 150–94; *Proceedings and Address of the Native American State Convention Held at Harrisburg, February 22, 1847* (Philadelphia, 1847), p. 2.

235. Eli K. Price, *The History of the Consolidation of Philadelphia* (Philadelphia: Lippincott, 1873), p. 55.

236. Ibid., p. 56.
237. Foster, "Philadelphia in Slices," p. 36.
238. William H. Furness to Lucy Osgood, Jan. 14, 1846, Osgood manuscript correspondence in the possession of the author.
239. Scharf and Westcott, *History of Philadelphia*, 1:666, 674; 3:1779; *Fisher Diary*, p. 226.
240. Price, *History of Consolidation*, pp. 51, 56.
241. Ibid., pp. 57, 22, 32–37, 47.
242. Ibid., pp. 90, 94.

THE BORDER CITY IN CIVIL WAR, 1854–1865

1. William Wells Brown, *The American Fugitive in Europe: Sketches of Places and People Abroad* (Boston: J. P. Jewett; New York: Sheldon, Lamport & Blakeman, 1855), p. 312; George W. Fahnestock Diary, June 30, 1863, Historical Society of Pennsylvania (hereafter cited as HSP).

2. Anthony Trollope, *North America*, edited by Donald Smedley and Bradford Allen Booth (New York: Knopf, 1951), pp. 290, 291. Population data cited for United States and foreign cities can be found in *Population of the United States in 1860 . . . Eighth Census* (Washington, D.C.: U.S. Government Printing Office, 1861), pp. ii–iii, 290–91; and Vladimir S. and Emma S. Woytinsky, *World Population and Production* (New York: Twentieth Century Fund, 1953), pp. 120–22. For the rate of Philadelphia population growth in the nineteenth century, see also W. E. B. DuBois, *The Philadelphia Negro: A Social Study* (paperback ed.; New York: Schocken, 1967), p. 46.

3. *The Seventh Census of the United States: 1850* (Washington, D.C.: Robert Armstrong, 1853), pp. 178–79; George H. Burgess and Miles Kennedy, *Centennial History of the Pennsylvania Railroad Company, 1846–1946* (Philadelphia: Pennsylvania Railroad Co., 1949), pp. 65–66, 74–79, 188–89.

4. For the background of consolidation, see Eli K. Price, *The History of the Consolidation of the City of Philadelphia* (Philadelphia: Lippincott, 1873). See also J. Thomas Scharf and Thompson Westcott, *History of Philadelphia, 1609–1884* (3 vols.; Philadelphia: L. H. Everts, 1884), 1:673–74, 691–92. For a statement on the motives for consolidation by the first postconsolidation mayor, Robert T. Conrad, see *Journal of the Select Council, 1855* (2 vols., Philadelphia: Crissy & Markley, 1856), vol. 2, Appendix, pp. 15–17. For a vivid description of the violence of the 1830s to the 1850s, including reference to the Moyamensing Killers, see Charles Godfrey Leland, *Memoirs* (New York: Appleton, 1893), pp. 216–18. There is a list of names and locations of Philadelphia street gangs in —notwithstanding the article's apparently unrelated subject matter—Stewart Culin, "Street Games of Boys in Brooklyn, N.Y.," *Journal of American Folklore* 4, no. 14 (July-Sept. 1891): 221–37.

5. The Consolidation Act can be found in *Laws of the General Assembly of the State of Pennsylvania, 1854* (Harrisburg: A. Boyd Hamilton, 1854), pp. 21–46 (see esp. pp. 24–25, 26–28), and in William Duane et al., eds., *A Digest of the Acts of Assembly Relating to the City of Philadelphia and of the Ordinances of the Said City & Districts in Force on the First Day of January, A.D. 1856 . . .* (Philadelphia: J. H. Jones, 1856), pp. 457–61. For complaints of Mayor Conrad about the return of the Councils to their preconsolidation habits, see *Journal of the Select Council, 1854* (Philadelphia: Crissy & Markley, 1855), pp. 132–35, 394–95.

6. *Laws of the General Assembly, 1854*, pp. 26–27; *Digest of the Acts of Assembly*, p. 33, and, for the act of May 3, 1850, pp. 454–58, esp. pp. 456–57.

7. *Journal of the Common Council, 1854–1855* (Philadelphia: Wm. H. Sichels, 1855), p. 387.

8. Scharf and Westcott, *History of Philadelphia*, 1:715; Ellis Paxson Oberholtzer, *Philadelphia: A History of the City and Its People* (4 vols.; Philadelphia: S. J. Clarke, 1912), 2:318. For census figures on foreign-born inhabitants, see Warren F. Hewitt, "The Know-Nothing Party in Pennsylvania," *Pennsylvania History* (hereafter cited as *PH*) 2 (Jan. 1935): 69–85; see also Ray A. Billington, *The Protestant Crusade, 1800–1860: A Study of the Origins of American Nativism* (paperback ed.; Chicago: Quadrangle, 1964), esp. chap. 12, pp. 289–321.

9. *Journal of the Select Council, 1854*, Appendix, pp. 85–87; ibid., *1855*, vol. 2, Appendix, pp. 8–9, 107–8 (and for Mayor Conrad's views on police, pp. 15–22); ibid., *1855–1856*, pp. 316–19; *Digest of the Acts of Assembly*, pp. 457–61; Scharf and Westcott, *History of Philadelphia*, 1:719–21; Oberholtzer, *Philadelphia*, 2:320.

10. Scharf and Westcott, *History of Philadelphia*, 1:719–21 (quotation from p. 721).

11. Sam Bass Warner, Jr., *The Private City: Philadelphia in Three Periods of Its Growth* (Philadelphia: University of Pennsylvania Press, 1968), pp. 91–98.

12. *Journal of the Select Council, 1856–1857*, Appendix, pp. 199–206; ibid., *1857–1858*, Appendix, pp. 135–67; Oberholtzer, *Philadelphia*, 2:319, 320–22; Scharf and Westcott, *History of Philadelphia*, 1:721–22.

13. *Journal of the Select Council, 1855–1856*, Appendix, p. 321; ibid., *1856*, Appendix, pp. 298–99; ibid., *1856–1857*, pp. 187, 195–98; ibid., *1857–1858*, Appendix, pp. 155–58; ibid., *1858*, Appendix, pp. 263–64; ibid., *1858–1859*, Appendix, pp. 216–27.

14. On Sutherland, see Warner, *The Private City*, pp. 86–91; on McMullen, see Oberholtzer, *Philadelphia*, 2:309.

15. Philadelphia Board of Health Annual Report, 1866, Philadelphia City Archives, pp. 8–12, 60; *Inquirer*, July 19, 1862. For investigation into health and sanitation conditions in mid-century Philadelphia I am indebted to John E. Daly, then of the Philadelphia City Archives, for his work when he was a member

of my graduate seminar at Temple University.

16. Warner, *The Private City*, pp. 50–61; id., "If All the World Were Philadelphia: A Scaffolding for Urban History, 1774–1930," *American Historical Review* 74 (Jan. 1968): 26–43; Norman J. Johnston, "The Caste and Class of Historic Philadelphia," *Journal of the American Institute of Planners* 32 (Nov. 1966): 334–49. For the Moyamensing slums, see DuBois, *The Philadelphia Negro*, p. 37. For the remark about "hangers-on," see Fahnestock Diary, March 26, 1863.

17. *McElroy's Philadelphia City Directory for 1863* (Philadelphia: E. C. & J. Biddle & Co., A. McElroy & Co., 1863), p. 522.

18. Leland, *Memoirs*, p. 9.

19. William Howard Russell, *My Diary North and South*, edited by Fletcher Pratt (New York: Harper, 1954), pp. 16–17.

20. Wm. Nelson West, ed., *Digest of the Laws and Ordinances Governing the City of Philadelphia in Force on the First Day of January, 1882* (Philadelphia: Thomas Nicholson, 1882), pp. 45–46 (for house numbers), 186 (for street names); *Journal of the Select Council, 1855*, vol. 2, Appendix, p. 119; ibid., *1856–1857*, Appendix, pp. 193–94; Oberholtzer, *Philadelphia*, 2:317–18; Trollope, *North America*, p. 291.

21. *Digest of the Acts of Assembly*, pp. 177–82; *Journal of the Select Council, 1855*, vol. 1, Appendix, p. 413; ibid, vol. 2, Appendix, pp. 202–4, 249; ibid., *1855–1856*, Appendix, pp. 1–3, 22–28, 48, 329–31, 344–46, 374; ibid., *1856*, Appendix, pp. 43–45, 132–33, 212–13, 235–39, 296–99; ibid., *1856–1857*, Appendix, pp. 278–79, 513; ibid., *1857*, Appendix, pp. 92–93; ibid., *1857–1858*, Appendix, pp. 37–42, 47; ibid., *1858*, Appendix, pp. 109–10, 136–38, 272, 308–9, 431; ibid., *1858–1859*, Appendix, pp. 75, 121, 509–11; ibid., *1859*, Appendix, pp. 91–92 (resolution offering a premium for the best plan for a paid fire department). For Conrad's report on fire department reorganization, see ibid., *1855–1856*, Appendix, pp. 319–21; for Vaux's reports, see ibid., *1856–1857*, Appendix, pp. 186–87; ibid., *1857–1858*, Appendix, pp. 134–35. On steam fire engines, see ibid., *1854*, Appendix, pp. 273–77; ibid., *1856*, Appendix, pp. 58, 278; ibid., *1856–1857*, Appendix, p. 301; ibid., *1858–1859*, Appendix, pp. 338–39. On fire detective police, see ibid., *1857–1858*, Appendix, pp. 143–46, 150–55; ibid., *1858–1859*, Appendix, p. 226.

22. Ibid., *1854*, Appendix, pp. 278–79; ibid., *1855*, vol. 2, Appendix, pp. 9–10, 215; ibid., *1856*, Appendix, pp. 89–90, 340–42; ibid., *1856–1857*, Appendix, pp. 481–85; ibid., *1857*, Appendix, pp. 24–27, 166–85; ibid., *1858*, Appendix, pp. 427–29; ibid., *1858–1859*, Appendix, pp. 479, 604–5; ibid., *1859*, Appendix, p. 49; ibid., *1859–1860*, Appendix, pp. 31–32, 44, 103–4 (with map insert showing Fairmount Park in 1860), 132, 154–56; Scharf and Westcott, *History of Philadelphia*, 1:675–76, 3:1851, 1854–55; George B. Tatum, "The Origins of Fairmount Park," *Antiques* 82 (Nov. 1962): 502–7.

23. Nicholas B. Wainwright, ed., *A Philadelphia Perspective: The Diary of Sidney George Fisher* (Philadelphia: Historical Society of Pennsylvania, 1967), pp. 432–33 (Aug. 15, 1862), 521–22 (Dec. 10, 1866) (hereafter cited as *Fisher Diary*); *Journal of the Select Council, 1857*, Appendix, pp. 68–70, 77–81; ibid., *1857–1858*, Appendix, pp. 360–61, 388–90, 417, 419–24, 439–89, 496–97; ibid., *1858*, Appendix, pp. 42, 55–56, 61, 68, 106–7, 134–36, 176–81, 224–27, 277–80, 283–86, 297–98, 331–32, 415–17, 439, 454–55; ibid., *1858–1859*, Appendix, pp. 48–53, 74, 77–79, 124–29, 139–41, 483–85, 492–94, 501–4, 595–96, 598–600, 624–26; ibid., *1859*, Appendix, pp. 15–16, 25, 59–60, 70–74, 78, 80–81, 87; ibid., *1859–1860*, Appendix, pp. 11–13, 29–30, 36–37, 160, 163; Philip S. Foner, "The Battle to End Discrimination Against Negroes on Philadelphia Streetcars: (Part I) Background and Beginning of the Battle," *PH* 40 (July 1973): 267, 274; Scharf and Westcott, *History of Philadelphia*, 1:717, 727, 729, 731, 789, 821; Frederic W. Speirs, *The Street Railway System of Philadelphia: Its History and Present Condition*, Johns Hopkins University Studies in Historical and Political Science, 15th ser., nos. 3–5 (Baltimore: Johns Hopkins University Press, 1897); Urban Traffic and Transportation Board, *History of Public Transportation in Philadelphia* (Philadelphia: Urban Traffic and Transportation Board, 1955). For Mayor Alexander Henry's views on horsecars and their problems, see *Journal of the Select Council, 1858–1859*, Appendix, pp. 235–37. For the removal of the Market Street market houses in connection with the extension of the street railways, see ibid., *1858*, Appendix, pp. 271–77; ibid., *1858–1859*, pp. 613, 626.

24. For the question of Negroes' riding streetcars, see *Report of the Committee Appointed for the Purpose of Securing to the Colored People in Philadelphia the Right to the Use of the Street Cars* (Philadelphia, 1867); William Still, *A Brief Narrative of the Struggle for the Rights of the Colored People of Philadelphia in the City Railway Cars* (Philadelphia: Merrihew, 1867); Foner, "The Battle to End Discrimination . . . on Philadelphia Streetcars: (Part I)," pp. 261–90, and "The Battle to End Discrimination Against Negroes on Philadelphia Streetcars: (Part II) The Victory," *PH* 40 (Oct. 1973): 355–79.

25. Austin E. Hutcheson, "Philadelphia and the Panic of 1857," *PH* 3 (April 1936): 182–94; Benjamin J. Klebaner, "The Home Relief Controversy in Philadelphia, 1782–1861," *Pennsylvania Magazine of History and Biography* (hereafter cited as *PMHB*) 78 (Oct. 1954): 421–23; Scharf and Westcott, *History of Philadelphia*, 1:726.

26. Masakiyo Yanagawa, *The First Japanese Mission to America (1860)* (New York: Stokes, 1938); Scharf and Westcott, *History of Philadelphia*, 1:734.

27. *Fisher Diary*, p. 268 (Feb. 25, 1857); John Harbeson, "Philadelphia's Victorian Architecture, 1860–1890," *PMHB* 67 (April 1943): 254–71; William Harbeson, "Mediaeval Philadelphia," *PMHB* 67 (April 1943): 227–53; Scharf and Westcott, *History of Philadelphia*, 1:724; Theo B. White, et. al., *Philadelphia Architecture in the Nineteenth Century* (Philadelphia: University of Pennsylvania Press, 1953), pp. 27–29. Phillips Brooks began his pastoral career at the Church of the Advent, York Avenue and Buttonwood Street, on July 10, 1859, and commenced his tenure at Holy Trinity on January 1, 1862 (Alexander V. G. Allen, *Life and Letters of Phillips Brooks* [3 vols.; New York: Dutton, 1901], 1:330, 386).

28. Leland, *Memoirs*, p. 136.
29. William Dusinberre, *Civil War Issues in Philadelphia* (Philadelphia: University of Pennsylvania Press, 1965), pp. 27–47, esp. pp. 41–43; A. K. McClure, *Old Time Notes of Pennsylvania* . . . (2 vols.; Philadelphia: J. C. Winston, 1905), 1:250–53; Scharf and Westcott, *History of Philadelphia*, 1:721–23, 727. For William B. Reed, see Foster M. Farley, "William B. Reed: President Buchanan's Minister to China, 1857–1858," *PH* 37 (July 1970): 269–80; Arnold Schankman, "William B. Reed and the Civil War," *PH* 39 (Oct. 1972): 455–68.
30. *Population of the United States in 1860*, pp. 431–32, and DuBois, *The Philadelphia Negro*, esp. p. 50, for population; Theodore Hershberg, "Free Blacks in Antebellum Philadelphia," in Allen F. Davis and Mark H. Haller, eds., *The Peoples of Philadelphia: A History of Ethnic Groups and Lower-Class Life, 1780–1940* (Philadelphia: Temple University Press, 1973), pp. 111–33, esp. pp. 117–18 for the decline of blacks practicing skilled trades; Dusinberre, *Civil War Issues in Philadelphia*, p. 21; Leon F. Litwack, *North of Slavery: The Negro in the Free States, 1790–1860* (Chicago: University of Chicago Press, 1961), pp. 84–86, 100–1, 150–51, 168–69, 191–93; Allen Weinberg and Dale Fields, comps., *Ward Genealogy of the City and County of Philadelphia* (Philadelphia: City of Philadelphia, Department of Records, n.d.).
31. Hershberg, "Free Blacks in Antebellum Philadelphia," pp. 118–20, 125–29.
32. Ira V. Brown, "Pennsylvania and the Rights of the Negro, 1865–1887," *PH* 28 (Jan. 1961): 46.
33. Hershberg, "Free Blacks in Antebellum Philadelphia," p. 125.
34. Foner, "The Battle to End Discrimination . . . on Philadelphia Streetcars: (Part I)," pp. 262, 266, quoting Brown, *The American Fugitive in Europe*, p. 312, and *Douglass' Monthly*, Feb. 1862.
35. DuBois, *The Philadelphia Negro*, p. 36; the census figure for Philadelphia blacks in 1840 was 19,833; in 1850, 19,761.
36. Ira V. Brown, "Miller McKim and Pennsylvania Abolitionism," *PH* 30 (July 1963): 53–72; Larry Gara, "William Still and the Underground Railroad," *PH* 28 (Jan. 1961): 33–37; William Still, Journal, Pennsylvania Society for Promoting the Abolition of Slavery MSS, HSP.
37. Larry Gara, *The Liberty Line: The Legend of the Underground Railroad* (Lexington: University of Kentucky Press, 1961), passim, esp. pp. 96–99, 104–6.
38. Fawn M. Brodie, *Thaddeus Stevens: Scourge of the South* (New York: W. W. Norton, 1959), pp. 115–18; Dusinberre, *Civil War Issues in Philadelphia*, pp. 57–60; Scharf and Westcott, *History of Philadelphia*, 1:701–2, 730.
39. Dusinberre, *Civil War Issues in Philadelphia*, pp. 51–52; Gara, *The Liberty Line*, p. 136.
40. *Biographical Directory of the American Congress, 1774–1849*, 81st Cong. 2d sess., House Doc. 607, s.v. "Thomas B. Florence," "Owen Jones," "James Landy," "John A. Marshall," "William Millward," "Edward Joy Morris," "Henry M. Phillips," "John P. Verree." Dusinberre, *Civil War Issues in Philadelphia*, pp. 40–45; Robert L. Bloom, "Kansas and Popular Sovereignty in Pennsylvania Newspa-

pers, 1856–1860," *PH* 14 (Jan. 1947): 77–93; id., "Morton McMichael's *North American*," *PMHB* 77 (April 1953): 164–80; Elwyn B. Robinson, "The *North American*: Advocate of Protection," *PMHB* 64 (July 1940): 345–55; id., "The *Pennsylvanian*: Organ of the Democracy," *PMHB* 62 (April 1938): 350–60; id., "The *Public Ledger*: An Independent Newspaper," *PMHB* 64 (Jan. 1940): 43–55.
41. Roy F. Nichols, *The Disruption of American Democracy* (New York: Macmillan, 1948), pp. 43–47, 55–57, 61–63, 86–87, 203–5; Elwyn B. Robinson, "The *Press*: President Lincoln's Philadelphia Organ," *PMHB* 65 (April 1941): 157–70.
42. Dusinberre, *Civil War Issues in Philadelphia*, pp. 65–79; Scharf and Westcott, *History of Philadelphia*, 1:727–29.
43. McClure, *Old Time Notes of Pennsylvania*, 1:340–59; Nichols, *Disruption of American Democracy*, pp. 204–5.
44. For an example of a comfortable, articulate Philadelphian's attitudes, see Letters of M. C. Meigs to Charles D. Meigs, M. C. Meigs Letter Book, 1859–1860, pp. 104, 100, Library of Congress; also see Dusinberre, *Civil War Issues in Philadelphia*, pp. 83–89; Scharf and Westcott, *History of Philadelphia*, 1:732.
45. Brown, "Miller McKim and Pennsylvania Abolitionism," pp. 68–69; Foner, "The Battle to End Discrimination . . . on Philadelphia Streetcars: (Part I)," p. 262; William Still, *The Underground Rail Road* (Philadelphia: Porter & Coates, 1872), pp. 81–84.
46. G. W. Curtis to Alexander Henry, Dec. 16, 1859, Box 1, Alexander Henry Papers, HSP; Isaac H. Clothier, "Philadelphia in Slavery Days," *Public Ledger*, Dec. 14, 1902; Dusinberre, *Civil War Issues in Philadelphia*, p. 90; Scharf and Westcott, *History of Philadelphia*, 1:733.
47. Fisher Diary, pp. 334 (Oct. 19, 1859), 339 (second quotation, Dec. 3, 1859), 343 (first and third quotations, Jan 2, 1860).
48. Alexander Henry to Wm. H. Allen et al., Dec. 11, 186[o], Box 1, Henry Papers, HSP; Dusinberre, *Civil War Issues in Philadelphia*, p. 90; McClure, *Old Time Notes of Pennsylvania*, 1:402; Scharf and Westcott, *History of Philadelphia*, 1:733.
49. Robert L. Bloom, "Newspaper Opinion in the State Election of 1860," *PH* 28 (Oct. 1961): 346–64; Dusinberre, *Civil War Issues in Philadelphia*, pp. 96–101; Scharf and Westcott, *History of Philadelphia*, 1:735.
50. Dusinberre, *Civil War Issues in Philadelphia*, pp. 96–101; Arthur M. Lee, "Henry C. Carey and the Republican Tariff," *PMHB* 81 (July 1957): 280–302; Reinhard H. Luthin, "Pennsylvania and Lincoln's Rise to the Presidency," *PMHB* 67 (Jan. 1943): 61–82; William H. Russell, "A. K. McClure and the People's Party in the Campaign of 1860," *PH* 28 (Oct. 1961): 335–45; Scharf and Westcott, *History of Philadelphia*, 1:735.
51. Dusinberre, *Civil War Issues in Philadelphia*, pp. 102–5; *Fisher Diary*, pp. 369–74 (Nov. 24–Dec. 16, 1860); Scharf and Westcott, *History of Philadelphia*, 1:738–40.
52. Dusinberre, *Civil War Issues in Philadelphia*, pp. 105–10.
53. Scharf and Westcott, *History of Philadelphia*, 1:740–53.
54. Ibid., pp. 746–47 (quotation from p. 747).
55. Dusinberre, *Civil War Issues in Philadelphia*, pp. 107–10; Elizabeth M. Geffen, *Philadel-

phia Unitarianism, 1796–1861 (Philadelphia: University of Pennsylvania Press, 1961), pp. 233–34.

56. Scharf and Westcott, *History of Philadelphia*, 1:749.

57. Roy P. Basler, ed., *The Collected Works of Abraham Lincoln* (9 vols. inc. index; New Brunswick, N.J.: Rutgers University Press, 1953, 1955), 4:240; Dusinberre, *Civil War Issues in Philadelphia*, p. 111; Joseph George, Jr., "Philadelphians Greet Their President-Elect, 1861," *PH* 29 (Oct. 1962): 381–90; Scharf and Westcott, *History of Philadelphia*, 1:750.

58. Geffen, *Philadelphia Unitarianism*, p. 234.

59. Dusinberre, *Civil War Issues in Philadelphia*, pp. 116–19; Scharf and Westcott, *History of Philadelphia*, 1:753.

60. Samuel P. Bates, *History of Pennsylvania Volunteers, 1861–1865* (5 vols.; Harrisburg; B. Singerly, State Printer, 1869–1871); Frank H. Taylor, *Philadelphia in the Civil War* (Philadelphia: The City, 1913), pp. 16–25, 40.

61. Scharf and Westcott, *History of Philadelphia*, 1:758–60; Taylor, *Philadelphia in the Civil War*, pp. 27–31.

62. Taylor, *Philadelphia in the Civil War*, pp. 33–39.

63. Bates, *History of Pennsylvania Volunteers*, 1:307–43, 539–906; Taylor, *Philadelphia in the Civil War*, pp. 5, 41–195.

64. Enrollment statistics are in Taylor, *Philadelphia in the Civil War*, passim.

65. Scharf and Westcott, *History of Philadelphia*, 1:779, 791, 797; Taylor, *Philadelphia in the Civil War*, pp. 196–99.

66. Erna Risch, *Quartermaster Support of the Army: A History of the Corps* (Washington, D.C.: Quartermaster Historian's Office, Office of the Quartermaster General, 1962), pp. 348, 350; Scharf and Westcott, *History of Philadelphia*, 1:780, 782; Taylor, *Philadelphia in the Civil War*, pp. 26–27; Russell F. Weigley, *Quartermaster General of the Union Army: A Biography of M. C. Meigs* (New York: Columbia University Press, 1959), pp. 251–53; *Inquirer*, July 15, 1862 (on Bridesburg).

67. *Statements Relating to a Navy Yard in the Delaware . . .* (Philadelphia, 1862); *Cramp's Shipyard, 1830–1910* (Philadelphia: William Cramp & Son, 1910); Scharf and Westcott, *History of Philadelphia*, 1:799; Taylor, *Philadelphia in the Civil War*, pp. 200–5; United States Navy Department, *Reports of the Secretary of the Navy and the Commission by Him Appointed on the New Iron Navy Yard at League Island* (Philadelphia: Collins, 1863).

68. James Moore, *History of the Cooper Shop Volunteer Refreshment Saloon* (Philadelphia: J. B. Rodgers, 1866); Scharf and Westcott, *History of Philadelphia*, 1:768, 770, 774; Taylor, *Philadelphia in the Civil War*, pp. 207–15.

69. Quoted in Taylor, *Philadelphia in the Civil War*, pp. 212–13.

70. Fahnestock Diary, Nov. 29, 1863; Taylor, *Philadelphia in the Civil War*, pp. 224–36; Nathaniel West, *A Sketch of the General Hospital of the U.S. Army at West Philadelphia* (Philadelphia: Ringwalt & Brown, 1862).

71. *Fisher Diary*, pp. 400 (quotation, Aug. 20, 1861), 402 (Aug. 29, 1861), 405 (Sept. 23, 1861); Scharf and Westcott, *History of Philadelphia*, 1:777, 781.

72. Dusinberre, *Civil War Issues in Philadelphia*, pp. 128–29.

73. For Fisher's relations with the peace Democrats in his circle, see especially his diary, Aug. 1, 1862, *Fisher Diary*, p. 431. An account of the Philadelphia peace Democrats, taking a relatively sympathetic view of them, is Nicholas B. Wainwright, "The Loyal Opposition in Civil War Philadelphia," *PMHB* 88, (July 1964); 294–315. For the historiography of the "Copperheads," see Richard O. Curry, "The Union as It Was: A Critique of Recent Interpretations of the Copperheads," *Civil War History* 13 (March 1967): 25–39.

74. *Biographical Directory of the American Congress*, p. 551; *Fisher Diary*, p. 395 (quotation, July 3, 1861); Francis B. Heitman, *Historical Register and Dictionary of the United States Army* (2 vols.; Washington, D.C.: U.S. Government Printing Office, 1903), 1:216.

75. *Congressional Globe*, 37th Cong., 2d sess., 32, pt. 2: 1169, 1644–45, 2503–5.

76. Dusinberre, *Civil War Issues in Philadelphia*, pp. 137–40; *Inquirer*, Aug. 25, 28, 29, 1862.

77. *Fisher Diary*, pp. 431 (quotation, Aug. 1, 1862), 433–37 (Aug. 26–Sept. 1, 1862); Irwin F. Greenberg, "Charles Ingersoll: The Aristocrat as Copperhead," *PMHB* 93 (April 1969): 198–201. The Charles Ingersoll case gained additional notoriety because some newspapers confused Ingersoll with his famous father, Charles Jared Ingersoll; an instance of such confusion is to be found in Frank Moore, ed., *The Rebellion Record . . .* (11 vols.; New York: Putnam, 1861–1863; Van Nostrand, 1864–1868), 5:69.

78. *Inquirer*, July 9, 1862, in an approving account of a mass meeting at Concert Hall.

79. Ellis Paxson Oberholtzer, *Jay Cooke: Financier of the Civil War* (2 vols.; Philadelphia: G. W. Jacobs, 1907).

80. Dusinberre, *Civil War Issues in Philadelphia*, pp. 151–52; George F. Lathrop, *History of the Union League of Philadelphia, from Its Origins and Foundation to the Year 1882* (Philadelphia: Lippincott, 1884), pp. 16, 21. The Democrats, it should be noted, won control of the state legislature in 1862.

81. [Anonymous], *Rifle Shots at Past and Passing Events . . . by an Inhabitant of the Comet of 1861* (Philadelphia: T. B. Peterson & Brothers, 1862), p. 110 (first quotation); *Constitution and By-Laws of the Central Democratic Club, Organized January, 1863* (Philadelphia, 1863); Ray H. Abrams, "The Copperhead Newspapers and the Negro," *Journal of Negro History* 20 (April 1935): 131–52; Dusinberre, *Civil War Issues in Philadelphia*, pp. 153–59; Wainwright, "The Loyal Opposition in Civil War Philadelphia," pp. 298–301; Schankman, "William B. Reed and the Civil War," p. 465 (second quotation).

82. Wainwright, "The Loyal Opposition in Civil War Philadelphia," p. 301.

83. Guy J. Gibson, "Lincoln's League: The Union League Movement During the Civil War" (Ph.D. dissertation, University of Illinois, 1957), pp. 49–51; Lathrop, *History of the Union League of Philadelphia*, pp. 26–34, 130–31; Union League of Philadelphia, *Chronicle of the Union League of Philadelphia, 1862–1902* (Philadelphia: Union League, 1902), pp. 34–50. On the rise of Philadelphia's new "business, industrial, and banking

elite" during the Civil War, see E. Digby Baltzell, *Philadelphia Gentlemen: The Making of a National Upper Class* (Glencoe, Ill.: Free Press, 1958), chap. 6. For a revealing insight into Charles Ingersoll's attitude toward the new business leaders, see his anonymously published *A Brief View of Constitutional Powers, Showing That the Union Consisted of Independent States United* (Philadelphia, 1864), pp. 27–31. A good example of Henry Charles Lea's wartime pamphleteering is his *The Record of the Democratic Party, 1860–1865* (1865).

84. Fahnestock Diary, June 4, 1863; Dusinberre, *Civil War Issues in Philadelphia*, pp. 159–60, 171; Taylor, *Philadelphia in the Civil War*, pp. 239–41.

85. Fahnestock Diary, June 15, 1863. William L. Calderhead, "Philadelphia in Crisis," *PH* 28 (April 1961): 142–55, concerns the city during Lee's invasion. Material on this topic can also be found in M[ichael] Jacobs, *Notes on the Rebel Invasion of Maryland and Pennsylvania and the Battle of Gettysburg, July 1st, 2nd and 3rd, 1863* (Philadelphia: Lippincott, 1864), and Winnifred K. MacKay, "Philadelphia During the Civil War, 1861–1865," *PMHB* 70 (Jan. 1946): 31–33.

86. Fahnestock Diary, June 16, 25, 26, 1863.

87. Fisher Diary, p. 455 (June 29, 1863). Similarly, A. K. McClure reported from Philadelphia that "Our people are paralysed for want of confidence & leadership . . ." (*The War of the Rebellion: A Compilation of the Official Records of the Union and Confederate Armies* [4 ser.; 70 vols. in 128 vols.; Washington, D.C.: U.S. Government Printing Office, 1880–1901], 1st ser., 27, pt. 3: 436 [hereafter cited as *O.R.*, with all citations referring to 1st ser.]).

88. *O.R.*, 27, pt. 3: 79–80.

89. Ibid., pp. 188, 408, 436; A. J. Pleasonton, *The Home Guard of the City of Philadelphia: Third Annual Report* (Philadelphia: King & Baird, 1864); Taylor, *Philadelphia in the Civil War*, pp. 40, 215–20, 242–51.

90. *O.R.*, 27, pt. 2: 211–19; ibid., pt. 3: 68–69, 243, 448.

91. Ibid., pt. 3: 365–66, 408; Correspondence, 1863, file in Box 2, Alexander Henry Papers; Scharf and Westcott, *History of Philadelphia*, 1:808; Taylor, *Philadelphia in the Civil War*, pp. 245–47.

92. *O.R.*, 27, pt. 2:211–19, 277–78; ibid., pt. 3: 68–69, 76–77, 79–80, 97, 111–13, 130–45, 162–67, 169, 187, 239–40, 264, 329–30, 342–44, 347–48, 363–65, 391–92, 408, 436, 480–81, 527; Edwin B. Coddington, *The Gettysburg Campaign: A Study in Command* (New York: Scribner's, 1967), pp. 134–41, 143–45; Taylor, *Philadelphia in the Civil War*, pp. 247, 249; Russell F. Weigley, "Emergency Troops in the Gettysburg Campaign," *PH* 25 (Jan. 1958): 45–50.

93. Fahnestock Diary, June 29–July 7, 1863;

Fisher Diary, pp. 454–56 (June 26–July 8, 1863).

94. Fahnestock Diary, June 30, 1863; Dusinberre, *Civil War Issues in Philadelphia*, pp. 160–65, 169–70; Foner, "The Battle to End Discrimination . . . on Philadelphia Streetcars: (Part I)," p. 270.

95. Scharf and Westcott, *History of Philadelphia*, 1:800, 809.

96. On the gubernatorial election of 1863 and wartime Pennsylvania politics generally, see Erwin S. Bradley, *The Triumph of Militant Republicanism* (Philadelphia: University of Pennsylvania Press, 1964), and Stanton L. Davis, "Pennsylvania Politics, 1860–1863" (Ph.D. dissertation, Western Reserve University, 1935). Neither contains as much material on Philadelphia as might be wished. On the judicial test of the draft law, see James G. Randall, *Constitutional Problems Under Lincoln* (rev. ed. Urbana: University of Illinois Press, 1951), pp. 247–48.

97. Charles J. Stillé, *Memorial of the Great Central Fair for the U.S. Sanitary Commission, Held at Philadelphia, June, 1864* (Philadelphia: United States Sanitary Commission, 1864); William Y. Thompson, "Sanitary Fairs of the Civil War," *Civil War History* 4 (March 1958): 51–68.

98. *Philadelphia Age*, June 6, 8, July 12, 13, Aug. 2, 31, 1864. In 1863 Lewis Cassidy had urged that the Democrats accept Governor Curtin's proposal of a Democratic-Union party fusion ticket in support of a War Democrat for governor (Davis, "Pennsylvania Politics, 1860–1863," p. 287).

99. Dusinberre, *Civil War Issues in Philadelphia*, p. 175; Scharf and Westcott, *History of Philadelphia*, 1:818.

100. Fahnestock Diary, Jan. 22, 1864.

101. Isaac Jones Wistar, *Autobiography of Isaac Jones Wistar, 1827–1905: Half a Century in War and Peace* (Philadelphia: Wistar Institute of Anatomy and Biology, 1937), pp. 4–5.

102. For an impression of Fairmount Park during the war, see *Fisher Diary*, (Nov. 21, 1861). pp. 408–9.

103. For private Philadelphia fortunes in wartime, see *The Rich Men of Philadelphia* [cover title only]: *Income Tax of the Residents of Philadelphia and Bucks County for the Year Ending April 30, 1865* (Philadelphia, 1865). Material on Philadelphia industry and the city's economy during the Civil War can be found in *Twenty-seventh Annual Report of the Philadelphia Board of Trade* (Philadelphia: Board of Trade, 1861); J. H. Perkins, *Thirty-second Annual Report of the Philadelphia Board of Trade* (Philadelphia: Board of Trade, 1865).

104. The following account is based on the detailed history by Philip S. Foner, "The Battle to End Discrimination . . . on Philadelphia Streetcars: (Part I)," pp. 261–90, and "(Part II)," pp. 355–79.

THE CENTENNIAL CITY, 1865–1876

1. *Evening Telegraph*, Aug. 14, 1876; George B. Tatum, *Penn's Great Town: 250 Years of Philadelphia Architecture Illustrated in Prints and Drawings* (Philadelphia: University of Pennsylvania Press, 1961), p. 102.

2. Nicholas B. Wainwright, ed., *A Philadelphia*

Perspective: *The Diary of Sidney George Fisher Covering the Years 1834–1871* (Philadelphia: Historical Society of Pennsylvania, 1967), p. 494 (hereafter cited as *Fisher Diary*); Samuel Whitaker Pennypacker, *Autobiography* (Philadelphia: John C. Winston, 1918),

p. 100; Ellis Paxson Oberholtzer, *Philadelphia: A History of the City and Its People* (4 vols.; Philadelphia: S. J. Clarke, 1912), 2:385.

3. *Fisher Diary*, p. 492.

4. Pennypacker, *Autobiography*, pp. 100–1; *Fisher Diary*, p. 494; Oberholtzer, *Philadelphia*, 2:385.

5. *Fisher Diary*, pp. 493–97. The *Evening Bulletin*, Oct. 28, 1875, explained that it was the Philadelphia custom that shutters be bowed and hung with black out of respect for someone dead in the immediate family or among other relatives; the observance might last as long as two years.

6. *Public Ledger*, July 2, 3, 6, 1865; Oberholtzer, *Philadelphia*, 2:387.

7. *Forty-third Annual Report of the Philadelphia Board of Trade* (Philadelphia: J. B. Chandler, 1876), Appendix B, p. 83. (Annual Reports of the Board of Trade were issued beginning in 1833; they are cited hereafter as *Board of Trade Report* and the year.) For a discussion, with illustrations, of the extension of the city westward, and of the houses built there, see Roger Miller and Joseph Siry, "The Emerging Suburb: West Philadelphia, 1850–1880," *Pennsylvania History* (hereafter cited as *PH*) 47 (April 1980): 99–145.

8. Oberholtzer, *Philadelphia*, 2:405; Dorothy Ditter Gondos, "The Cultural Climate of the Centennial City: Philadelphia, 1875–1876" (Ph.D. dissertation, University of Pennsylvania, 1947), p. 6.

9. John F. Sutherland, "Housing the Poor in the City of Homes: Philadelphia at the Turn of the Century," in Allen F. Davis and Mark H. Haller, eds., *The Peoples of Philadelphia: A History of Ethnic Groups and Lower-Class Life, 1790–1940* (Philadelphia: Temple University Press, 1973), pp. 175–202; Dennis Clark, *The Irish in Philadelphia: Ten Generations of Urban Experience* (Philadelphia: Temple University Press, 1973), pp. 40–60; Stewart A. Stehlin, ed. and trans., "Philadelphia on the Eve of the Nation's Centennial: A Visitor's Description in 1873–74," *PH* 44 (Jan. 1977): 25–36 (from Friedrich Ratzel, *Städte und Kulturbilder aus Nordamerika* [2 vols.; Leipzig: F. A. Brockhaus, 1876], 1: 201–5). In 1870 Philadelphia had 112,336 home dwellings, whereas New York had only 65,044 (ibid., p. 31).

10. *Board of Trade Report* (1874), Appendix 7, p. 155, reprinting the article "The City of Homes" from *Public Ledger*; Gondos, "Cultural Climate," pp. 12–13; Thompson Westcott, *The Official Guide Book to Philadelphia* (Philadelphia: Porter & Coates, 1875), pp. 76–83, for the car colors; Philip S. Foner, "The Battle to End Discrimination Against Negroes on Philadelphia Streetcars: (Part I) Background and Beginning of the Battle," *PH* 40 (July 1971): 261–92; and id., "(Part II) The Victory," *PH* 40 (Oct. 1971): 355–80.

11. Sutherland, "Housing the Poor," esp. p. 182; Clark, *The Irish in Philadelphia*, p. 50. Ratzel, a German geographer traveling in the United States in the 1870s, found the gridiron pattern lacked provision for enough wide streets and thought the right angles hindered traffic. He also deplored the lack of open parks along the Delaware and the growth there of ugly warehouses (Stehlin, "Philadelphia on the Eve," pp. 28–30).

12. Sutherland, "Housing the Poor," p. 183.

13. Caroline Golab, "The Immigrant and the City: Poles, Italians, and Jews in Philadelphia, 1870–1920," in Davis and Haller, eds., *Peoples of Philadelphia*, pp. 204–5; Sam Bass Warner, Jr., *The Private City: Philadelphia in Three Periods of Its Growth* (Philadelphia: University of Pennsylvania Press, 1968), p. 139; Clark, *The Irish in Philadelphia*, pp. 76–87.

14. *Board of Trade Report* (1875), p. 27.

15. Oberholtzer, *Philadelphia*, 2:386, 393.

16. Theo B. White et al., *Philadelphia Architecture in the Nineteenth Century* (Philadelphia: University of Pennsylvania Press, 1953), p. 29.

17. Ibid.; Westcott, *Guide*, p. 237.

18. Oberholtzer, *Philadelphia*, 2:407–9; *Fisher Diary*, pp. 551, 552; Westcott, *Guide*, p. 201.

19. Charles E. Peterson, "Library Hall: Home of the Library Company of Philadelphia, 1790–1880," in Luther P. Eisenhart, ed., *Historic Philadelphia: From the Founding Until the Early Nineteenth Century: Papers Dealing with Its Peoples and Buildings with an Illustrative Map* (Philadelphia: American Philosophical Society, 1953), p. 143.

20. Edwin Wolf 2nd, "At the Instance of Benjamin Franklin": A Brief History of the Library Company of Philadelphia, 1731–1976 (Philadelphia: Library Company of Philadelphia, 1976), pp. 44, 49–52.

21. Oberholtzer, *Philadelphia*, 2:406; Horace M. Lippincott, *The University of Pennsylvania, Franklin's College* (Philadelphia: Lippincott, 1919), p. 67; Edward Potts Cheyney, *History of the University of Pennsylvania, 1740–1940* (Philadelphia: University of Pennsylvania Press, 1940), pp. 262, 263.

22. Westcott, *Guide*, pp. 95–106; Edward M. Riley, "The Independence Hall Group," in Eisenhart, ed., *Historic Philadelphia*, pp. 7–42; Ordinances and Joint Resolutions of the City of Philadelphia (from January 1st to December 31st, 1868) (Philadelphia, 1869), pp. 571–73.

23. William E. Lingelbach, "Philosophical Hall: The Home of the American Philosophical Society," in Eisenhart, ed., *Historic Philadelphia*, p. 53, n.24.

24. Oberholtzer, *Philadelphia*, 2:403–4; Gondos, "Cultural Climate," p. 11.

25. Frank M. Etting, *An Historical Account of the Old State House of Pennsylvania* (Boston: James R. Osgood, 1876), pp. 166, 167, 189; Riley, "Independence Hall Group," p. 38. Etting's removal as chairman of the Committee on Restoration in July 1876 was attributed to his rudeness to the press and citizenry, but some members of the press evidently thought he did a good job (Stephen W. Stathis, "Returning the Declaration of Independence to Philadelphia: An Exercise in Centennial Politics," *Pennsylvania Magazine of History and Biography* [hereafter cited as *PMHB*] 102 [Jan. 1978]: 180).

26. Etting, *Historical Account of the Old State House*, p. 189.

27. Ibid., pp. 171, 172, 179, 182, 183; Riley, "Independence Hall Group," pp. 38, 39. Riley suggests (p. 38, n.24) that pillars were not part of the original room. For a discussion of a contribution to Independence Hall in the Centennial period, see Arthur H. Frazier, "Henry Seybert and the Centennial Clock and Bell at Independence Hall," *PMHB* 102 (Jan.

1978): 40–58. The return of the Declaration of Independence to Independence Hall for the Centennial is described in Stathis, "Returning the Declaration," pp. 167–183; the effort to keep the Declaration in Philadelphia after the Centennial failed (p. 182).

28. J. Thomas Scharf and Thompson Westcott, *History of Philadelphia, 1609–1884* (3 vols.; Philadelphia: L. H. Everts, 1884), 3:1855–60. John Maass, in *The Glorious Enterprise: The Centennial Exhibition of 1876 and H. J. Schwarzmann, Architect-in-Chief* (Watkins Glen, N.Y.: American Life Foundation, 1973), writes that appointment to the Fairmount Park Commission was "a mark of high social prestige in Philadelphia"; he adds that the tradition continues to the present (p. 18 and n.8).

29. *Board of Trade Report* (1874), Appendix 7, p. 157 (from reprint of *Public Ledger* article).

30. *Board of Trade Report* (1870), pp. 15–17, 19.

31. The Board of Trade reports are full of information on the city. By 1870 the reports contain a lengthy section with the names of the members categorized by occupation; e.g., *Thirty-eighth Annual Report* (1871), pp. 97–110; *Forty-third Annual Report* (1878), pp. 153–198. See *Board of Trade Reports, 1865–1877.* Specific references: Welsh elected president, March 1865, ibid. (1866), p. 11; Revision of Articles of Association, ibid. (1868), pp. 133 ff; on national organization, ibid. (1869), pp. 9–12; on currency, ibid. (1866), pp. 21, 22, and ibid. (1874), p. 19; on Department of Commerce, ibid., p. 18; on metric system, ibid. (1877), pp. 15 ff.

32. *Board of Trade Report* (1871), Appendix 5, p. 85.

33. See the various *Board of Trade Reports;* Scharf and Westcott, *History of Philadelphia,* 3:2226–2349.

34. *Board of Trade Report* (1866), p. 18; ibid. (1869), p. 15.

35. Commonwealth of Pennsylvania, *Annual Report of the Secretary of Internal Affairs,* part 3, Bureau of Industrial Statistics (Harrisburg: E. K. Myers, 1892), vol. 19, 1891, sect. C, pp. 48, 71; *Board of Trade Report* (1876), Appendix B, p. 87.

36. *Report of the Secretary of Internal Affairs,* 3:40–42 (quotation from p. 40).

37. *Board of Trade Report* (1876), Appendix B, p. 88.

38. Ibid. (1876), Appendix A, p. 90.

39. Ibid. (1877), Appendix A, p. 85; ibid. (1876), Appendix B, p. 88.

40. *Report of the Secretary of Internal Affairs,* 3:58.

41. Ibid., p. 67.

42. Ibid., p. 75.

43. Ibid., pp. 71, 72.

44. *Board of Trade Report* (1867), pp. 10, 13, 83; *Report of the Secretary of Internal Affairs,* 3:63. The Secretary's Report also stated that as of 1891 the Navy Yard had "never been put in a condition to construct or even make extensive repairs in modern vessels," though steps were being taken to remedy this situation.

45. Gondos, "Cultural Climate," p. 26.

46. *Board of Trade Report* (1876), Appendix B, p. 86.

47. Nicholas B. Wainwright, *History of the Philadelphia National Bank: A Century and a Half of Philadelphia Banking, 1803–1953* (Philadelphia: Philadelphia National Bank, 1953), p. 129.

48. *Board of Trade Report* (1876), Appendix B, pp. 86, 87.

49. Wainwright, *Philadelphia National Bank,* p. 130. On Jay Cooke, see Ellis Paxson Oberholtzer, *Jay Cooke, Financier of the Civil War* (2 vols.; Philadelphia: George W. Jacobs, 1907).

50. *Board of Trade Report* (1874), p. 21.

51. Oberholtzer, *Philadelphia,* 2:397.

52. *Board of Trade Report* (1874), pp. 117–19; *Journals of the Select Council, Journals of the Common Council* (Philadelphia, 1873–1874).

53. *Board of Trade Report* (1869), Appendix, p. 39.

54. John R. Commons et al., *History of Labour in the United States* (4 vols.; New York: Macmillan, 1918–1935), 2:15–16, 19, 45, 93–94.

55. Ibid., pp. 49–52, 55, 95, 96, 100, 130.

56. Ibid., pp. 132–34.

57. Ibid., esp. p. 196.

58. Ibid., pp. 197–99.

59. Ibid., pp. 208–11, 213, 214, 218, 270, 333, 334.

60. [Henry Adams,] *Democracy, A Novel* (paperback ed.; New York: New American Library, 1961), p. 48.

61. Frank B. Evans, *Pennsylvania Politics, 1872–1877: A Study in Political Leadership* (Harrisburg: Pennsylvania Historical and Museum Commission, 1966), p. 13.

62. *Fisher Diary,* p. 533 (Oct. 9, 1867).

63. Ibid., p. 33 (Oct. 9, 1867).

64. Oberholtzer, *Philadelphia,* 2:398; *Public Ledger,* July 6, 1866; Evans, *Pennsylvania Politics,* p. 13.

65. Evans, *Pennsylvania Politics,* pp. 13, 15, 75–76; A. K. McClure, *Old Time Notes of Pennsylvania* (2 vols.; Philadelphia: Winston, 1905), 2:237–38, 239, 284; Erwin Stanley Bradley, *The Triumph of Militant Republicanism: A Study of Pennsylvania and Presidential Politics, 1860–1872* (Philadelphia: University of Pennsylvania Press, 1964), p. 365.

66. McClure, *Old Time Notes,* 2:240. The *Times,* Oct. 5, 1875, stated that there had been an exposure of 15,000 fictitious names, "assessed on streets not yet paved and from houses of which foundations have not yet been dug."

67. *Inquirer,* Nov. 2, 1875.

68. Ira V. Brown, "Pennsylvania and the Rights of the Negro," *PH* 28 (Jan. 1961): 52–54; McClure, *Old Time Notes,* 2:282–88, 289.

69. Evans, *Pennsylvania Politics,* pp. 15, 16.

70. Oberholtzer, *Philadelphia,* 2:397, 398.

71. Howard Zink, *City Bosses in the United States: A Study of Twenty Municipal Bosses* (Durham: Duke University Press, 1930), pp. 194, 195; Evans, *Pennsylvania Politics,* pp. 14, 15, 27; Oberholtzer, *Philadelphia,* 2:400; James Bryce, *The American Commonwealth* (2 vols.; New York: Macmillan, 1927; first published 1888), 2:408. The *Evening Star,* Feb. 24, 1876, stated that the Gas Trust should be made to open its books.

72. Zink, *City Bosses,* pp. 196–202; Evans, *Pennsylvania Politics,* p. 15.

73. Bryce, *American Commonwealth,* 2:408, 409; Pennypacker, *Autobiography,* p. 176, quoted by Zink, *City Bosses,* p. 198.

74. Evans, *Pennsylvania Politics,* pp. 13–14; Oberholtzer, *Philadelphia,* 2:399, (quotation);

Public Ledger, Oct. 14, 1868. The *Ledger* wrote that it was a quiet election.

75. McClure, *Old Time Notes*, 2:365; Evans, *Pennsylvania Politics*, p. 14; Oberholtzer, *Philadelphia*, 2:399–400; *Evening Bulletin*, Aug. 12, 1876; *Times*, June 5, 1876; *Evening Star*, Nov. 15, 1876.

76. McClure, *Old Time Notes*, 2:365–68, 374 (p. 365 for quotation); Oberholtzer, *Philadelphia*, 2:401; Evans, *Pennsylvania Politics*, pp. 96–98 (p. 97 for quotation from Lea).

77. McClure, *Old Time Notes*, 2:364.

78. *Evening Telegraph*, Aug. 31, 1876; *Evening Bulletin*, Sept. 1, 2, 1876; *Times*, Aug. 31, 1876; *Sunday Dispatch*, Sept. 3, 1876; *Sunday Times*, Sept. 10, 1876. The short quoted phrases are from the *Evening Telegraph* and the *Times*.

79. *Evening Bulletin*, Sept. 2, 1876 (first quotation); *Sunday Dispatch*, Sept. 3, 1876 (second quotation); *Evening Star*, Nov. 17, 28, 1876; *Times*, Dec. 6, 1876; *Press*, Jan. 30, 1877; Hobart S. Perry, "Peter A. B. Widener," *Dictionary of American Biography (DAB)*, 20:185–86; Oberholtzer, *Philadelphia*, 2:416.

80. Evans, *Pennsylvania Politics*, pp. 21, 52, 53, 146–62, 289, 308, 309, 328; Albert V. House, Jr., "Samuel Jackson Randall," *DAB*, 15:-350–51.

81. Evans, *Pennsylvania Politics*, pp. 27, 79; Edward Sculley Bradley, *Henry Charles Lea: A Biography* (Philadelphia: University of Pennsylvania Press, 1931), pp. 177, 189.

82. Evans, *Pennsylvania Politics*, pp. 81–82; Oberholtzer, *Philadelphia*, 2:401.

83. Evans, *Pennsylvania Politics*, p. 84.

84. Ibid., pp. 92–93; McClure, *Old Time Notes*, 2:355–56.

85. Evans, *Pennsylvania Politics*, pp. 96–97, 98.

86. Ibid., p. 101.

87. Ibid., pp. 101–3 (quotation from p. 103).

88. *North American*, Feb. 14, 1876 (quotation); *Evening Bulletin*, Jan. 9, 1875; May 4, 1876; *Press*, March 17, Oct. 11, 1875; March 6, 1877; *Inquirer*, Sept. 29, 1875; *Manayunk Sentinel*, Feb. 19, 1875.

89. Lorin Blodget in *Board of Trade Report* (1876), Appendix B, p. 84.

90. *Public Ledger*, Nov. 4, 1876; *Evening Bulletin*, June 28, 1875.

91. *National Cyclopedia of American Biography*, s.v. "James Frederic Wood," 7:251; Richard J. Purcell, "James Frederick Wood," *DAB*, 20:462; *Press*, June 16, 1875. Though Wood's middle name is spelled with a "k" in *DAB*, printed documents issued under his name omit the "k."

92. Lefferts Loetscher, "Presbyterianism and Revivals in Philadelphia Since 1875," *PMHB* 69 (Jan. 1944): 57, 58; *Press*, Nov. 20, 1875. William R. Moody, *The Life of Dwight L. Moody* (New York: Fleming H. Revell, 1900), p. 267, says that 13,000 could be accommodated.

93. Loetscher, "Presbyterianism and Revivals," pp. 56, 59, 61.

94. James F. Findlay, Jr., *Dwight L. Moody, American Evangelist, 1837–1899* (Chicago: University of Chicago Press, 1969), p. 198; Loetscher, "Presbyterianism and Revivals," p. 62. See also Marion L. Bell, *Crusade in the City: Revivalism in Nineteenth-Century Philadelphia* (Lewisburg, Penna.: Bucknell University Press, 1977).

95. *Sunday Dispatch*, July 23, 1876.

96. Loetscher, "Presbyterianism and Revivals," p. 58.

97. Ibid., pp. 57, 58, 62, 64, 65; *Press*, Dec. 1, 1875, Feb. 5, 1876. The *Weekly Guide* 5, no. 8 (Jan. 22, 1876): 2, gave the total attendance as 900,000. There was quite a struggle over the chairs used by Moody and Sankey, Wanamaker, and Grant; see *Penn Monthly* 7 (March 1876): 172. On the hymnbooks, see J. C. Pollock, *Moody: A Biographical Portrait of the Pacesetter in Modern Mass Evangelism* (New York: Macmillan, 1973), p. 177.

98. *Times*, Dec. 4, 1875, Jan. 27, 1876; *Weekly Guide* 5, no. 8 (Jan. 22, 1876): 2; *Sunday Times*, Jan. 16, 1876; *Press*, Jan. 18, 1876; *Evening Bulletin*, Feb. 3, 1876; *Press*, Feb. 7, 1876.

99. Westcott, *Guide*, pp. 221–29, 234–36.

100. Ibid., pp. 109–18. The Radical Club, a women's organization, in January 1875 was investigating cruelty at the House of Refuge. It was a subject to which the newspapers did not tire easily; see *Press*, Jan. 21, 1875.

101. *Evening Star*, Dec. 30, 1876; *Press*, Jan. 31, 1876.

102. *Sunday Times*, Jan. 24, 1876; *Press*, Jan. 6, April 15, May 14, 1875, March 1, 1877; *Evening Bulletin*, Feb. 11, 1875; *Public Ledger*, June 26, 1875, Sept. 16, Nov. 3, 1876; *Evening Star*, Jan. 25, 1875, May 5, 1876; *Weekly Guide* 5, no. 40 (Sept. 2, 1876); *Times*, Oct. 27, 1875. See also John T. Custis, *The Public Schools of Philadelphia: Historical, Biographical, Statistical* (Philadelphia: Burk & McFetridge, 1897), p. 28.

103. *Evening Star*, April 19, 1875, Nov. 25, 1876; *Press*, Nov. 30, 1876; *Public Ledger*, Dec. 9, 1875, Supplement; *Inquirer*, June 15, 1875.

104. *Sunday Tribune*, Jan. 31, 1875; for opposing views, see *Press*, Jan. 6, 1875, and *Evening Bulletin*, Feb. 11, 1875.

105. *Evening Bulletin*, April 16, 1875 (quotation); *North American*, April 26, 1875; *Times*, June 21, Dec. 2, 1875. Evans, *Pennsylvania Politics*, pp. 195–96, states that an anti-Catholic campaign in Ohio greatly influenced Pennsylvania voters in the 1875 election year. On the neglected condition of the schools for blacks, see Harry C. Silcox, "Philadelphia Negro Educator: Jacob C. White, Jr.," *PMHB* 97 (Jan. 1973): 75–98.

106. Custis, *Public Schools*, pp. 28, 38; Westcott, *Guide*, pp. 119, 120; Blodget, in *Board of Trade Report* (1876), Appendix B, pp. 84–85. On the typical teacher and salaries, see Richard B. Fishbane, "The Shallow Boast of Cheapness: Public School Teaching as a Profession in Philadelphia, 1865–1890," *PMHB* 103 (Jan. 1979): 66–84 (quotation from p. 83).

107. Westcott, *Guide*, pp. 168–76; *Times*, July 14, 1875; *Press*, Feb. 9, May 26, 1875, March 20, 1877.

108. Westcott, *Guide*, pp. 177–79, 180–81; Ellis Paxson Oberholtzer, *The Literary History of Philadelphia* (Philadelphia: George W. Jacobs, 1906), p. 363; Henry C. Chapman, *Memoir of Joseph Leidy* (Philadelphia: Academy of Natural Sciences, 1891), p. 7; Oberholtzer, *Philadelphia*, 2:347, 348.

109. Westcott, *Guide*, pp. 183–84.

110. Westcott, *Guide*, pp. 188, 190; White et. al., *Philadelphia Architecture*, pp. 30–31.

111. *Evening Bulletin*, Dec. 11, 1946, p. 12.

112. Westcott, *Guide*, p. 190.
113. *Weekly Guide* 5, no. 18 (April 1, 1876).
114. *Evening Telegraph*, Aug. 14, 1876. These statements were written in response to Theodore Thomas's complaints that no one had built him a music hall.
115. *Press*, June 8, 1875.
116. Ibid., Jan. 8, 1875; White et al., *Philadelphia Architecture*, pp. 23, 29–30. The formal opening was on April 22, 1876 (*Press*, April 22, 1876).
117. *Evening Bulletin*, April 6, 1876; *Times*, April 22, 1876; *Evening Telegraph*, March 23, 1876.
118. Westcott, *Guide*, pp. 192–94; John Sartain, *The Reminiscences of a Very Old Man, 1808–1897* (New York: D. Appleton, 1899), p. 252.
119. Westcott, *Guide*, p. 197. The *Evening Telegraph*, Jan. 9, 1875, notes that the Sketch Club was at 10 Northwest Penn Square, in rooms just fitted up for its accommodation. A[nna] Margaretta Archambault. *A Book of Art, Architecture and Historic Interests in Pennsylvania* (Philadelphia: Winston, 1924), p. 61, states that the entrance building of the School of Design for Women was the former residence of the tragedian Edwin Forrest.
120. *Penn Monthly* 6 (June 1875): 402. Westcott, *Guide*, p. 250, gives the address of the club as 1525 Chestnut Street.
121. Westcott, *Guide*, pp. 195–96. See also *Press*, April 9, 1877, and Sylvan Schendler, *Eakins* (Boston: Little, Brown, 1967), p. 90.
122. Schendler, *Eakins*, pp. ix–x, 3–49 passim.
123. Ibid., pp. x, 54 (quotation from p. x).
124. Ibid., p. 55.
125. *Evening Telegraph*, April 28, 1876.
126. Schendler, *Eakins*, p. 60. Schendler (p. 292) suggests that John Sartain, chief of the Bureau of Art for the Centennial, did not like Eakins and must have had something to do with the failure to have *The Gross Clinic* properly displayed.
127. William Howe Downes, "Thomas Eakins," *DAB*, 5:591. The painting is now in the possession of the Thomas Jefferson University.
128. Schendler, *Eakins*, p. 60.
129. Elizabeth D. Gillespie, *Book of Remembrance* (Philadelphia: Lippincott, 1891), p. 366.
130. Nathaniel Burt, *The Perennial Philadelphians: The Anatomy of an American Aristocracy* (Boston: Little, Brown, 1963), pp. 466–67. The *Press*, Jan. 9, 1875, reports a concert by the Beethoven Society and Orpheus Club to be held the following January 22 at the Academy, both groups trained by Michael Cross. Ibid., March 1, 1875; notes a program by the Abt Male Singing Society. The Beethoven Society met in a hall at Eighteenth and Chestnut (ibid., June 22, 1875). For the Theodore Thomas Symphony and the Philadelphia Philharmonic Society, see ibid., Jan. 1, Nov. 13, 1875.
131. Ibid., Jan. 1, 1875. The Kellogg Opera Company was playing to large audiences in April 1875 (ibid., Jan. 5, April 16, 27, 1875). The quotation is from ibid., Jan. 5, 1875.
132. Ibid., Feb. 15, March 1, 1875.
133. *Weekly Guide* 5, no. 18 (April 1, 1876).
134. *Press*, Jan. 11, 1876.
135. Ibid., May 5, Sept. 26, 1876; *Inquirer*, May 18, 1876; *Evening Bulletin*, July 6, 1876; *Evening Telegraph*, July 31, 1876.
136. *Press*, Jan. 4, 1877. The *Evening Bulletin*, June 24, 1876, expressed the opinion that the chorus ought to become a permanent feature of Philadelphia musical life.
137. *Evening Telegraph*, Sept. 22, 1876; *Press*, Jan. 2, 4, 1875.
138. *Press*, Jan. 11, 25, 26, Feb. 4, 5, 12, 1875.
139. Ibid., March 1, 2, 8, 18, April 5, May 10, 25, June 21, 1875.
140. Westcott, *Guide*, "Changes, Additions and Corrections"; *Press*, May 29, 1876. Later, the Alhambra became the Broad Street Theater.
141. Walter Prichard Eaton, "Edwin Forrest," *DAB*, 6:529–31; *Evening Telegraph*, Sept. 22, 1876. The date for the scheduled opening was given as Oct. 2.
142. Broadus Mitchell, "Henry Charles Carey," *DAB*, 3:487, 489; Charles Godfrey Leland, *Memoirs* (New York: D. Appleton, 1893), p. 213; Joanna Wharton Lippincott, *Biographical Memoranda Concerning Joseph Wharton, 1826–1909* (Philadelphia: Lippincott, 1909), p. 74.
143. Frank Luther Mott, "Charles Jacob Peterson," *DAB*, 14:512, 513; Oberholtzer, *Literary History*, pp. 237–38; Frank Luther Mott, "Henry Peterson," *DAB*, 14:513, 514; Burt, *Perennial Philadelphians*, p. 417.
144. Gondos, "Cultural Climate," p. 234; John H. Frederick, "Joshua Ballinger Lippincott," *DAB*, 11:287, 288.
145. Gondos, "Cultural Climate," pp. 235–39.
146. Gondos, "Cultural Climate," p. 309. See also manuscript kept at the Library Company of Philadelphia, dated Jan. 26, 1875, from W. S. Stokley, mayor, concerning the search for the child; also a notice of reward, signed by Alan Pinkerton, Sept. 1, 1874, in Manuscript Division, HSP.
147. Gondos, "Cultural Climate," pp. 247ff. See also Bradley, *Henry Charles Lea;* Ernest Earnest, *S. Weir Mitchell, Novelist and Physician* (Philadelphia: University of Pennsylvania Press, 1950); Edward Sculley Bradley, *George Henry Boker, Poet and Patriot* (Philadelphia: University of Pennsylvania Press, 1927); Leland, *Memoirs;* Elizabeth R. Pennell, *Charles Godfrey Leland: A Biography* (2 vols.; Boston: Houghton Mifflin, 1906).
148. Gondos, "Cultural Climate," p. 267, citing Bradley, *Henry Charles Lea*, esp. p. 194.
149. Gondos, "Cultural Climate," pp. 256ff. Dates of editions of plays named are 1871, 1873, and 1877, respectively.
150. Ibid., pp. 223–24.
151. McClure, *Old Time Notes*, 2:249–50; Bradley, *Henry Charles Lea*, p. 136; Gondos, "Cultural Climate," p. 225. The holding of Wistar Parties had lapsed; the Saturday Parties were in the tradition of the Wistar Parties. McClure notes (p. 250) that among those present at any one meeting might be Gen. Robert Patterson, William D. Lewis, Gen. Simon Cameron, Gen. Thomas M. Cadwalader, and Morton McMichael.
152. Gondos, "Cultural Climate," p. 201.
153. Westcott, *Guide*, pp. 255–56.
154. Gondos, "Cultural Climate," pp. 202, 203.
155. Foster Rhea Dulles, *A History of Recreation: America Learns to Play* (New York: Appleton-Century-Crofts, 1966), p. 191. See also Eben Rexford, "The Van Heydens' Croquet Party," *Peterson's Magazine* 69 (April 1876): 253–55.
156. Gondos, "Cultural Climate," p. 203.
157. Ibid., pp. 199, 200.
158. *The Baseball Encyclopedia: The Complete and Official Record of Major League Baseball*

(New York: Macmillan and Information Concepts Incorporated, 1969), pp. 9–10, 176–77; David Quentin Voigt, *American Baseball: From Gentleman's Sport to Commissioner System* (Norman: University of Oklahoma Press, 1966), pp. 35–40.

159. McClure, *Old Time Notes*, 2:244, 246, 247.
160. Ibid., p. 247.
161. Ibid., p. 249.
162. *Fisher Diary*, pp. 508–9 (Feb. 1, 1866).
163. Gondos, "Cultural Climate," p. 170. See Thomas Willing Balch, *The Philadelphia Assemblies* (Philadelphia: Allen, Lane and Scott, 1916). *On Dangerous Ground: or Agatha's Friendship* (Philadelphia: Porter & Coates, 1876), a novel by a Philadelphian, Clara (Jessup) Bloomfield Moore, describes an Assembly of the time.
164. Gondos, "Cultural Climate," p. 171.
165. Ibid., pp. 172–73.
166. McClure, *Old Time Notes*, 2:247–48; *Public Ledger*, Nov. 30, Dec. 2, 4, 5, 1871; *Inquirer*, Dec. 4, 5, 1871.
167. William Randel, "John Lewis Reports the Centennial," *PMHB* 79 (July 1955): 367; Dee Brown, *The Year of the Century: 1876* (New York: Scribner's, 1966), pp. 7–9; *Times*, Jan. 1, 1876; *Press*, Jan. 3, 1876; *Inquirer*, Jan. 3, 1876; *Evening Telegraph*, Jan. 1, 1876.
168. Gondos, "Cultural Climate," pp. 2–4.
169. Ibid., p. 5.
170. Ibid., pp. 5, 6; *Report of the Director General, U.S. International Exhibition, 1876* (9 vols.; Washington, D.C.: U.S. Government Printing Office, 1880), 1:4, 5. (This first volume has the reports of various bureau chiefs that reported to the director general, and is hereafter cited as *U.S.I.E. Report of Director General*. A tenth volume, *Report of the Board on Behalf of U. S. Executive Departments at the International Exhibition held at Philadelphia, 1876,* ibid., 1:16, 17; ibid., Reports of Officers of Centennial Commission, U. S. International Exhibition, vol. 2, includes the Journal of the Final Session of the Centennial Commission, dated Philadelphia, Jan. 15, 1879, pp. 152–53; Regulations, etc., p. 5, National Archives, Record Group 43, E573; Westcott, *Guide*, p. 373; Dorsey Gardner, *Grounds and Buildings of the Centennial Exhibition* (Philadelphia: Lippincott, 1878), which also appears as vol. 9 of *U.S.I.E. Report of Director General*, p. 16. The Conference Committee Report, 1873, Subcommittee Report on Fourth of July Celebration and ceremony of transfer of control of exhibition lands to the Centennial Commission from the commissioners of Fairmount Park, along with other primary records, is in the Archives of the City and County of Philadelphia, Record Group 230.11.
171. *U.S.I.E. Report of Director General*, 1:25, 26.
172. Ibid., p. 6; *Times*, Jan. 5, 1876; *Inquirer*, March 1, 1876.
173. *U.S.I.E. Report of Director General*, 1:30–32. The original plans submitted in the summer of 1873 were exhibited in the large lecture rooms of the old buildings of the University of Pennsylvania at Ninth and Chestnut. Demolition of the university buildings was delayed for this purpose (ibid., p. 30*n*). See also Tatum, *Penn's Great Town*, pp. 103–7; Brown, *Year of the Century*, p. 115. White et al., *Philadelphia Architecture*, p. 31, states that the competition was for a combination permanent art gallery and temporary exhibit

building, a plan soon recognized as unworkable. On the site and cost, see *U.S.I.E. Report of Director General*, Report of the Chief of the Bureau of Installation (Henry Pettit), 1:111.
174. Maass, in *The Glorious Enterprise*, has recalled Schwarzmann to historical attention.
175. White et al., *Philadelphia Architecture*, p. 32, as well as Maass, *The Glorious Enterprise*, esp. p. 94.
176. *U.S.I.E. Report of Director General*, 1:32. The number of buildings varies according to the authority; Gardner gives 249 as the total; *Public Ledger*, May 8, 1876, gives 190.
177. *Press*, Dec. 18, 20, 1875, Jan. 25, 1876; *Inquirer*, Dec. 22, 1875; Brown, *Year of the Century*, p. 6.
178. *U.S.I.E. Report of Director General*, 1:22–23; Report of the Chief of the Bureau of Installation, ibid., p. 53.
179. Brown, *Year of the Century*, pp. 113–15; *Sunday Dispatch*, May 14, 1876; *Press*, May 11, 12, 1876; *Times*, May 10, 1876.
180. Brown, *Year of the Century*, p. 116.
181. Ibid., pp. 116, 117, 121–29; Howard Mumford Jones, *The Age of Energy: Varieties of American Experience, 1865–1915* (New York: Viking, 1971), pp. 139–43. Emperor Dom Pedro endeared himself to Philadelphians: he was intelligent and friendly, and visited the Centennial several times during the early months. On July 2, 1876, the *Sunday Dispatch* noted that his "shirt collars wilt just as do those of ordinary mortals."
182. Brown, *Year of the Century*, p. 131*n*, quoting *Harper's Weekly*, July 15, 1876, p. 579.
183. Gondos, "Cultural Climate," quoting *Inquirer*, July 21, 1876.
184. *U.S.I.E. Report of Director General*, 1:661, 664.
185. Gondos, "Cultural Climate," pp. 287–88; John Maass, "When the New World Dazzled the Old," *American Heritage* 27, pt. 4 (June 1976): 25–26; *U.S.I.E. Report of Director General*, Report of the Chief of the Bureau of Admissions, 1:439. For a description of the exposition during the hottest part of the summer, see William H. Crew, "Centennial Notes," *PMHB* 100 (July 1976): 406–13.
186. *U.S.I.E. Report of Director General*, 1:14, 15; ibid., Report of the Chief of the Bureau of Transportation, pp. 359–62. On prices, see Brown, *Year of the Century*, pp. 133–34; *Press*, May 17, 1876. On the wooden buildings, see ibid., June 29, 1875; *Evening Telegraph*, Feb. 25, 1875; *Inquirer*, July 2, 8, 1875. On hotels, see *Sunday Tribune*, Aug. 8, 1875; *Evening Bulletin*, Sept. 16, 1876.
187. Randel, "John Lewis Reports," pp. 369–72; Gondos, "Cultural Climate," pp. 282–83.
188. *Times*, Sept. 19, 1876; *Sunday Times*, May 14, 1876; Gondos, "Cultural Climate," pp. 181–82.
189. *U.S.I.E. Report of Director General*, Report of the Chief of the Bureau of Transportation, 1:342–46; Brown, *Year of the Century*, pp. 115, 133; Maass, "When the New World Dazzled the Old," p. 79; *North American*, Oct. 17, 1876.
190. *U.S.I.E. Report of Director General*, Report of the Chief of the Bureau of Transportation, 1:349, 355; ibid., Report of the Chief of the Bureau of Engineering, p. 239; Brown, *Year of the Century*, pp. 114, 132.

191. U.S.I.E. *Report of Director General,* Report of the Chief of the Bureau of Protection, 1:680–88, 693, 694, 696; also ibid., Report of the Chief of the Bureau of Admissions, p. 441.
192. Ibid., Report of the Chief of the Bureau of Medicine, 1:661, 664; *Sunday Dispatch,* July 16, 1876; Gondos, "Cultural Climate," p. 18, quoting *Press,* July 11, 1876.
193. U.S.I.E. *Report of Director General,* Report of the Chief of the Bureau of Art, 1:144, 145.
194. Maass, "When the New World Dazzled the Old," pp. 25–27, 76–79, is especially good on the impressions made on visitors, especially

foreign visitors; see p. 77 for Reuleaux and Hitler.
195. Tatum, *Penn's Great Town,* p. 102.
196. Jones, *Age of Energy,* p. 279, quoting *Atlantic Monthly* 38, no. 225 (July 1876): 89–90.
197. Maass, "When the New World Dazzled the Old," p. 27.
198. *Inquirer,* Aug. 30, 1876; U.S.I.E. *Report of Director General,* 1:5.
199. *Press,* Aug. 25, 1875.
200. *Evening Bulletin,* Nov. 16, 1876.
201. Brown, *Year of the Century,* p. 113, quoting *Chicago Tribune,* May 1, 1876.

THE IRON AGE, 1876–1905

1. Jos. H. Appel, *The Business Biography of John Wanamaker* (New York: Macmillan, 1930), p. 342; Agnes Repplier, *Philadelphia, The Place and the People* (New York: Macmillan, 1898), pp. 390–91.
2. *Fortune Surveys* (500 Largest U.S. Corporations), *1956 et seq.,* under "Transportation."
3. Patricia Davis, *End of the Line: Alexander J. Cassatt and the Pennsylvania Railroad* (New York: Neale Watson Academic Publications, 1978), pp. 61, 46, passim; Sylvester K. Stevens, *Pennsylvania: Birthplace of a Nation* (New York: Random House, 1964), p. 227; *Dictionary of American Biography* (hereafter cited as *DAB*), s.v. "Thomas A. Scott."
4. George H. Burgess and Miles C. Kennedy, *Centennial History of the Pennsylvania Railroad, 1846–1946* (Philadelphia: Pennsylvania Railroad Company, 1949), pp. 355, 433; Theo B. White et al., *Philadelphia Architecture in the Nineteenth Century* (Philadelphia: University of Pennsylvania Press, 1953), p. 32; George B. Tatum, *Penn's Great Town: 250 Years of Philadelphia Architecture Illustrated in Prints and Drawings* (Philadelphia: University of Pennsylvania Press, 1961), pp. 112, 196; Frank H. Taylor, ed., *The City of Philadelphia as It Appears in the Year 1894* (Philadelphia: George S. Harris & Sons, 1894), p. 97.
5. Davis, *End of the Line,* pp. 12, 19, 20, 83–84; *DAB,* s.v. "Alexander J. Cassatt."
6. Nathaniel Burt, *The Perennial Philadelphians: The Anatomy of an American Aristocracy* (Boston: Little, Brown, 1963), pp. 196 and *n,* 211; *Chestnut Hill; An Architectural Study* (Philadelphia: Chestnut Hill Historical Society, 1969), p. 27; E. Digby Baltzell, *Philadelphia Gentlemen: The Making of a National Upper Class* (Glencoe, Ill.: Free Press, 1958), p. 206; *Rand, McNally & Co.'s Handy Guide to Philadelphia* (Chicago and New York: Rand, McNally, 1900), p. 110; Richard J. Webster, *Philadelphia Preserved: Catalog of the Historic American Buildings Survey* (Philadelphia: Temple University Press, 1976), pp. 253–54.
7. Carol Ann Golab, "The Polish Communities of Philadelphia, 1870–1920: Immigrant Distribution and Adaptation in Urban America" (Ph.D. dissertation, University of Pennsylvania, 1971), pp. 82, 100, 390; Burgess and Kennedy, *Centennial History of the Pennsylvania Railroad,* p. 414; Moses King, *Philadelphia and Notable Philadelphians* (Philadelphia: Moses King, 1902), pt. 2:29; Edward Strahan, ed., *A Century After: Picturesque Glimpses of Philadelphia and Pennsylvania*

(Philadelphia: Allen, Lane & Scott and J. W. Lauderbach, 1876), pp. 176, 178; Taylor, ed., *City of Philadelphia, 1894,* pp. 97–98.
8. Burt, *Perennial Philadelphians,* pp. 205–6; Burgess and Kennedy, *Centennial History of the Pennsylvania Railroad,* p. 409; *DAB,* s.v. "Franklin B. Gowen."
9. Burt, *Perennial Philadelphians,* p. 208; *DAB,* s.v. "George F. Baer."
10. Taylor, ed., *City of Philadelphia, 1894,* pp. 97, 241; King, *Notable Philadelphians,* pt. 2:5; Richard Saul Wurman and John Andrew Gallery, *Man-Made Philadelphia: A Guide to Its Physical and Cultural Environment* (Cambridge, Mass.: MIT Press, 1972), p. 7; *Bulletin Almanac, 1971,* p. 417.
11. Burgess and Kennedy, *Centennial History of the Pennsylvania Railroad,* pp. 401, 404, 406–7; W. Wallace Weaver, "West Philadelphia: A Study of Natural Social Areas" (Ph.D. dissertation, University of Pennsylvania, 1930), p. 107; Ellis Paxson Oberholtzer, *Philadelphia: A History of the City and Its People* (4 vols.; Philadelphia: S. J. Clarke, 1912), 2:424; An Ex-Reporter, *Chestnut Street, Philadelphia* (Philadelphia, 1904), p. 47.
12. *DAB,* s.v. "Matthias Baldwin," "Matthew Baird." Golab, "Polish Communities of Philadelphia," p. 110; Sylvester K. Stevens, *Pennsylvania, Titan of Industry* (3 vols.; New York: Lewis Historical Publishing Co., 1948), 1:307; Lorin Blodget, *Census of Manufactures of Philadelphia* (Philadelphia: Dickson & Gilling, 1883), pp. 135, 198; Taylor, ed., *City of Philadelphia, 1894,* p. 182; King, *Notable Philadelphians,* pt. 2:40A; Paul de Rousiers, *American Life,* trans. from the French by A. J. Herbertson (Paris: Didot, 1892), p. 197; G. W. Steevens, *The Land of the Dollar* (Edinburgh and London: Wm. Blackwood & Sons, 1897), p. 121; Cyrus Adler, *I Have Considered the Days* (Philadelphia: Jewish Publication Society of America, 1941), p. 122; *City of Philadelphia: Leading Merchants and Manufacturers* (New York, Philadelphia, and Chicago: Historical Publishing Co., 1886), p. 72.
13. *DAB,* s.v. "William Cramp," "Charles Cramp"; Stevens, *Pennsylvania, Titan of Industry,* 1:333; David B. Tyler, *The American Clyde* (Newark: University of Delaware Press, 1958), pp. 33, 43, 72, 77, 83–84, 89–90, 112; Taylor, ed., *City of Philadelphia, 1894,* p. 111; King, *Notable Philadelphians,* pt. 1:10, pt. 2:41; J. Thomas Scharf and Thompson Westcott, *History of Philadelphia, 1609–1884* (3 vols.; Philadelphia: L. H. Everts, 1884), 3:2339; *Philadelphia and Popular Philadelphi-*

ans (Philadelphia: North American, 1891), p. 237 (hereafter cited as *Popular Philadelphians*); Steevens, *Land of the Dollar*, p. 121. Three other firms, all smaller than Cramp, also survived the earlier period: Neafie & Levy and Charles Hillman of Philadelphia, and John Roach of Chester (Taylor, ed., *City of Philadelphia, 1894*, p. 111; Stevens, *Pennsylvania: Birthplace of a Nation*, p. 222).

14. Golab, "Polish Communities of Philadelphia," pp. 112, 115; *City of Philadelphia* (1886), p. 72; Blodget, *Census of Manufactures*, pp. 134, 137, 138–39; Willard Glazier, *Peculiarities of American Cities* (Philadelphia: Hubbard Brothers, 1886), p. 387; King, *Notable Philadelphians*, pt. 2:42; Stevens, *Pennsylvania, Titan of Industry*, 3:717; *Popular Philadelphians*, p. 107.

15. Blodget, *Census of Manufacturers*, pp. 134, 140–45; King, *Notable Philadelphians*, pt. 2:43; *Popular Philadelphians*, pp. 121, 129.

16. Blodget, *Census of Manufacturers*, pp. 145–51; King, *Notable Philadelphians*, pt. 2:40C, 42; *Popular Philadelphians*, pp. 111, 113, 120, 124, 135, 176, 181; Stevens, *Pennsylvania, Titan of Industry*, 2:36; Taylor, ed., *City of Philadelphia, 1894*, p. 238; George Morgan, *The City of Firsts, Being a Complete History of the City of Philadelphia from its Founding in 1682, to the Present Time* (Philadelphia: Historical Publication Society, 1926), p. 432 (Aug. 8, 1904).

17. Baltzell, *Philadelphia Gentlemen*, pp. 121–22; Burt, *Perennial Philadelphians*, pp. 185–87; *DAB*, s.v. "Joseph Wharton."

18. *Popular Philadelphians*, p. 126; *Kensington: A City Within a City* (Philadelphia, Keighton Printing House, 1891), p. 99; *Annual Report of the Philadelphia Board of Trade* (Philadelphia, 1892), p. 8.

19. *Kensington*, pp. 8, 17, 21–23; King, *Notable Philadelphians*, pt. 2:48B; *Popular Philadelphians*, p. 118.

20. *Philadelphia and Its Environs* (Philadelphia: Lippincott, 1893), p. 156; Stevens, *Pennsylvania, Titan of Industry*, 2:237–38, 275, 368, 404; Golab, "Polish Communities of Philadelphia," p. 354; *Popular Philadelphians*, pp. 115, 116, 118, 144, 177; Baltzell, *Philadelphia Gentlemen*, p. 128; Taylor, ed., *City of Philadelphia, 1894*, p. 247; King, *Notable Philadelphians*, pt. 2:29; *Tales of the Trades* (Philadelphia: Merchants and Travelers Association, 1906; advertisement).

21. Blodget, *Census of Manufacturers*, p. 128; *Kensington*, pp. 53, 71; Stevens, *Pennsylvania, Titan of Industry*, 2:92, 119, 3:759.

22. Stevens, *Pennsylvania, Titan of Industry*, 1:331, 3:711; Taylor, ed., *City of Philadelphia, 1894*, p. 206; *Philadelphia and Its Environs* (1893), pp. 141, 185; *Popular Philadelphians*, pp. 232, 234; King, *Notable Philadelphians*, pt. 2:46; Stanley Baron, *Brewed in America: A History of Beer and Ale in the United States* (Boston: Little, Brown, 1962), pp. 268–69; *Philadelphia Business Directories* (1880–1904).

23. Stevens, *Pennsylvania, Titan of Industry*, 3:882; Taylor, ed., *City of Philadelphia, 1894*, p. 204; *Philadelphia Business Directories* (1880–1904).

24. The Special Correspondent of *The Times, A Visit to the United States* (London: G. E. Wright, 1887), p. 115; Taylor, ed., *City of Philadelphia, 1894*, p. 218; Blodget, *Census of Manufacturers*, p. 37; King, *Notable Phila-*

delphians, pt. 2:46; *Popular Philadelphians*, p. 116; Stevens, *Pennsylvania, Titan of Industry*, 3:871.

25. Arthur P. Dudden, *Joseph Fels and the Single-Tax Movement* (Philadelphia: Temple University Press, 1971), pp. 14, 24; Stevens, *Pennsylvania, Titan of Industry*, 2:270.

26. *Popular Philadelphians*, pp. 137, 163, 167; *Philadelphia and Its Environs* (Philadelphia: Lippincott, 1887), p. 76; Stevens, *Pennsylvania, Titan of Industry*, 1:334, 2:175, 176, 3:724.

27. Philip S. Klein and Ari Hoogenboom, *A History of Pennsylvania* (New York: McGraw-Hill, 1973), p. 304; Golab, "Polish Communities of Philadelphia," pp. 18, 110, 112–13; *Philadelphia and Its Environs* (1893), p. 11; Lorin Blodget, *The Textile Industries of Philadelphia* (Philadelphia, 1880), p. xii; Gustavus Myers, "The Most Corrupt City in the World," *The Living Age* 240 (Feb. 20, 1904): 451; *Tales of the Trades*, p. 33; Stevens, *Pennsylvania, Titan of Industry*, 1:325.

28. Golab, "Polish Communities of Philadelphia," p. 113; Blodget, *Census of Manufactures*, pp. 81, 177; *Philadelphia and Its Environs* (1893), p. 154.

29. Burt, *Perennial Philadelphians*, pp. 303–4; Golab, "Polish Communities of Philadelphia," pp. 19, 291, 345; *A Visit to the States*, p. 124; Rowland T. Berthoff, *British Immigrants in Industrial America, 1790–1950* (Cambridge, Mass.: Harvard University Press, 1953), pp. 40, 43; Elizabeth Robins Pennell, *Our Philadelphia* (Philadelphia: Lippincott, 1914), p. 19; Blodget, *Census of Manufactures*, p. 45; William B. Richter, *North of Society Hill* (North Quincy, Mass.: Christopher Publishing House, 1970), pp. 21, 22, 23; Taylor, ed., *City of Philadelphia, 1894*, p. 122; Harry W. Pfund, *A History of the German Society of Pennsylvania* (Philadelphia: German Society of Pennsylvania, 1944), p. 16.

30. Stevens, *Pennsylvania, Titan of Industry*, p. 324; *City of Philadelphia* (1886), p. 72; Taylor, ed., *City of Philadelphia, 1894*, p. 115; Blodget, *Census of Manufactures*, pp. 172–74.

31. Blodget, *Census of Manufactures*, pp. 78, 168; id., *Textile Industries*, p. xiii.

32. Golab, "Polish Communities of Philadelphia," p. 110; Stevens, *Pennsylvania, Titan of Industry*, 1:326, 2:88, 3:765, 766; Blodget, *Census of Manufactures*, p. 79; King, *Notable Philadelphians*, pt. 2:40A.

33. Blodget, *Census of Manufactures*, pp. 156, 157, 77, 182; id., *Textile Industries*, p. ix; Webster, *Philadelphia Preserved*, p. 317; *Philadelphia and Its Environs* (1893), pp. 154, 197–98; Taylor, ed. *City of Philadelphia, 1894*, p. 184; King, *Notable Philadelphians*, pt. 2:p. 44.

34. Klein and Hoogenboom, *History of Pennsylvania*, p. 285; *Tales of the Trades*, pp. 37, 43, 63, 77; Golab, "Polish Communities of Philadelphia," pp. 114, 138; Stevens, *Pennsylvania, Titan of Industry*, 1:324; King, *Notable Philadelphians*, pt. 2:45; *Kensington*, p. 51.

35. Alfred S. Eichner, *The Emergence of Oligopoly: Sugar Refining as a Case Study* (Baltimore: Johns Hopkins Press, 1969), pp. 42–44, 73, 169, 341; Stevens, *Pennsylvania, Titan of Industry*, 2:43, 44, 45, 3:511; *Popular Philadelphians*, p. 117; *Philadelphia:*

Pictorial and Biographical (Philadelphia and Chicago: S. J. Clarke, 1914), p. 151.
36. *DAB*, s.v. "John Harrison," Charles C. Harrison."
37. Ibid.
38. Allan Nevins, *Study in Power: John D. Rockefeller, Industrialist and Philanthropist* (2 vols.; New York: Scribner's, 1953), 1:228, 230, 269; *Popular Philadelphians*, p. 170; "100 Years of Progress: The Story of the Atlantic Refining Company," *Arco* 21 (Nov.-Dec. 1966): 15.
39. *Forty-fourth Annual Report of the Philadelphia Board of Trade* (Philadelphia, 1877), pp. 89, 121 (hereafter cited as *Board of Trade Report* and the year); *Board of Trade Report* (1878), pp. 109, 141; ibid. (1880), p. 129; Oberholtzer, *Philadelphia*, 2:389; Blodget, *Census of Manufactures*, p. 198; Taylor, ed., *City of Philadelphia, 1894*, p. 107; "100 Years of Progress," pp. 42, 47; King, *Notable Philadelphians*, pt. 2:40; Morgan, *City of Firsts*, pp. 417 (May 1, 1901), 418 (May 19, 1901).
40. Nevins, *Study in Power*, 1:232–36, 239–40, 241; Burgess and Kennedy, *Centennial History of the Pennsylvania Railroad*, pp. 362–63.
41. Nevins, *Study in Power*, 1:241–44, 248–49, 274; 2:5, 7; Burgess and Kennedy, *Centennial History of the Pennsylvania Railroad*, pp. 363–64; "100 Years of Progress," p. 31; *Popular Philadelphians*, p. 172.
42. Golab, "Polish Communities of Philadelphia," p. 147; *Popular Philadelphians*, p. 195; *Philadelphia and Its Environs* (1893), p. 11; King, *Notable Philadelphians*, pt. 2:59; *100 Years in Philadelphia, 1847–1947: The Evening Bulletin's Anniversary Book* (Philadelphia: Evening Bulletin, 1947), p. 11; Taylor, ed., *City of Philadelphia, 1894*, p. 107.
43. *Philadelphia and Its Environs* (1893), p. 11; King, *Notable Philadelphians*, pt. 2:29; *City Club of Philadelphia Bulletin* 1 (Dec. 16, 1909): 108; *Board of Trade Report* (1877), pp. 61, 67; ibid. (1878), p. 126; Golab, "Polish Communities of Philadelphia," p. 153.
44. Golab, "Polish Communities of Philadelphia," pp. 82, 100, 390; Burgess and Kennedy, *Centennial History of the Pennsylvania Railroad*, p. 414; King, *Notable Philadelphians*, pt. 2:29; Strahan, ed., *A Century After*, pp. 176, 178; *Philadelphia and Its Environs* (1893), p. 155; Taylor, ed., *City of Philadelphia, 1894*, pp. 97–98.
45. *Philadelphia and Its Environs* (1893), pp. 148–49, 155; Taylor, ed., *City of Philadelphia, 1894*, pp. 98, 99, 106, 107; King, *Notable Philadelphians*, pt. 2:5, 38; *Popular Philadelphians*, p. 99.
46. Pennell, *Our Philadelphia*, p. 278; *Popular Philadelphians*, p. 237; William A. Krauss, "In the Old Days, You Could Book a Berth," *Philadelphia Inquirer*, Jan. 20, 1980; Tyler, *The American Clyde*, p. 34; Burgess and Kennedy, *Centennial History of the Pennsylvania Railroad*, p. 271; John H. Morrison, *History of American Steam Navigation* (New York: Stephen Daye Press, 1958), pp. 482, 483; *Philadelphia and Its Environs* (1893), p. 149; Taylor, ed., *City of Philadelphia, 1894*, p. 112; *Handy Guide to Philadelphia*, p. 11.
47. Struthers Burt, *Philadelphia, Holy Experiment* (Garden City, N.Y.: Doubleday, 1945), p. 135.

48. *City of Philadelphia* (1886), p. 70; Robert Douglas Bowden, *Boies Penrose, Symbol of an Era* (New York: Greenberg, 1937), p. 85; Glazier, *Peculiarities of American Cities*, pp. 386, 387.
49. Oberholtzer, *Philadelphia*, 2:420; Taylor, ed., *City of Philadelphia, 1894*, p. 85; Clyde Kenneth Nelson, "The Social Ideas of Russell H. Conwell" (Ph.D. dissertation, University of Pennsylvania, 1968), p. 70; Sam Bass Warner, Jr., *The Private City: Philadelphia in Three Periods of Its Growth* (Philadelphia: University of Pennsylvania Press, 1968), pp. 184, 192; *Philadelphia and Its Environs* (1893), p. 7; *Travel & Leisure* 10 (Sept. 1980): 40.
50. Golab, "Polish Communities of Philadelphia," p. 288; Maxwell Whiteman, "Philadelphia's Jewish Neighborhoods," in Allen F. Davis and Mark H. Heller, eds., *The Peoples of Philadelphia: A History of Ethnic Groups and Lower-Class Life, 1790–1940* (Philadelphia: Temple University Press, 1973), pp. 238, 239; Charles S. Bernheimer, ed., *The Russian Jew in the United States* (Philadelphia: Winston, 1905), p. 52; Glazier, *Peculiarities of American Cities*, p. 378; Taylor, ed., *City of Philadelphia, 1894*, p. 85; *Handy Guide to Philadelphia*, p. 51; *Philadelphia and Its Environs* (1893), p. 8; Richter, *North of Society Hill*, p. 39; *Travel & Leisure* 10 (Sept. 1980): 40.
51. George Wilson, *Yesterday's Philadelphia* (Miami, Fla.: E. A. Seemann, 1975), p. 38; Adna Ferrin Weber, *The Growth of Cities in the Nineteenth Century* (New York: Macmillan, 1899), p. 469; Nicholas B. Wainwright, *History of the Philadelphia Electric Company, 1881–1961* (Philadelphia: Philadelphia Electric Co., 1961), p. 6; Frederic W. Speirs, *The Street Railway System of Philadelphia* (Baltimore: Johns Hopkins University, 1897), p. 32; Warner, *The Private City*, pp. 16, 169; Golab, "Polish Communities of Philadelphia," p. 286; A. K. McClure, *Old Time Notes of Pennsylvania* (2 vols.; Philadelphia: Winston, 1905), 1:599; Baltzell, *Philadelphia Gentlemen*, p. 124.
52. *DAB*, s.v. "William L. Elkins," "Peter A. B. Widener."
53. Wainwright, *Philadelphia Electric Company*, pp. 16, 17, 18, 19, 21; Federal Writers' Project, *Philadelphia: A Guide to the Nation's Birthplace* (Philadelphia: William Penn Association, 1937), p. 140 (hereafter cited as *WPA Guide*). On intracity transportation and the spatial arrangements of the city, there is much information in William W. Cutler III and Howard Gillette, eds., *The Divided Metropolis: Social and Spatial Dimensions of Philadelphia, 1800–1975* (Westport, Conn.: Greenwood Press, 1980).
54. Scharf and Westcott, *History of Philadelphia*, 3:1759; Wainwright, *Philadelphia Electric Company*, p. 12; Baltzell, *Philadelphia Gentlemen*, p. 125.
55. Wainwright, *Philadelphia Electric Company*, p. 8; Edwin Wolf 2nd, *Philadelphia: Portrait of an American City* (Harrisburg: Stackpole, 1975), p. 257; Joseph Jackson, *Encyclopedia of Philadelphia* (4 vols.; Harrisburg: National Historical Association, 1931–1938), 4:1131, 1132; Morgan, *City of Firsts*, p. 420 (Jan. 1, 1902).
56. Appel, *Business Biography of Wanamaker*, p. 342; *DAB*, s.v. "John Wanamaker."
57. *DAB*, s.v. "John Wanamaker"; Herbert

Adams Gibbons, *John Wanamaker* (2 vols.; New York: Harper, 1926).
58. *National Cyclopedia of American Biography*, s.v. "Isaac Gimbel," 23:133.
59. *WPA Guide*, p. 444.
60. King, *Notable Philadelphians*, pt. 1:8, pt. 2:37; William Harbeson, "Mediaeval Philadelphia," *Pennsylvania Magazine of History and Biography* (hereafter cited as *PMHB*) 67 (April 1943): 253; Webster, *Philadelphia Preserved*, pp. 115–16.
61. *Compendium of the Tenth Census of the United States* (Washington, D.C.: U.S. Government Printing Office, 1883), pt. 1:546; *World Almanac* (New York: New York World Telegram, 1941), p. 473; Golab, "Polish Communities of Philadelphia," p. 67.
62. Golab, "Polish Communities of Philadelphia," pp. 6, 12–15; William L. Quay, "Philadelphia Democrats, 1880–1910" (Ph.D. dissertation, Lehigh University, 1969), pp. 259–60.
63. Glazier, *Peculiarities of American Cities*, p. 397; Gladys L. Palmer, *Philadelphia Workers in a Changing Economy* (Philadelphia: University of Pennsylvania Press, 1956), p. 157; Steevens, *Land of the Dollar*, p. 115; *A Visit to the States*, p. 124.
64. Golab, "Polish Communities of Philadelphia," p. 19; *A Visit to the States*, p. 124; Berthoff, *British Immigrants in Industrial America*, pp. 40, 43; Pennell, *Our Philadelphia*, p. 19.
65. Golab, "Polish Communities of Philadelphia," pp. 19, 291, 345; *A Visit to the States*, p. 124; Blodget, *Census of Manufactures*, p. 45; Richter, *North of Society Hill*, pp. 21, 22, 23; Taylor, ed., *City of Philadelphia, 1894*, p. 122; Pfund, *History of the German Society of Pennsylvania*, p. 16.
66. Golab, "Polish Communities of Philadelphia," pp. 17, 19, 69, 226, 245, 248; Dennis J. Clark, "The Philadelphia Irish: Persistent Presence," in Davis and Haller, eds., *Peoples of Philadelphia*, p. 143. Scharf and Westcott, *History of Philadelphia*, 2:1393; Oscar Handlin, *This Was America* (Cambridge, Mass.: Harvard University Press, 1949), pp. 431, 433; Richard A. Varbero, "Philadelphia's South Italians in the 1920's," in Davis and Haller, eds., *Peoples of Philadelphia*, p. 264.
67. Dennis J. Clark, *The Irish in Philadelphia: Ten Generations of Urban Experience* (Philadelphia: Temple University Press, 1973), pp. 28–32; Clark, "The Philadelphia Irish," p. 143; Richter, *North of Society Hill*, p. 28.
68. John A. Saunders, *100 Years After Emancipation* (n.p., n.d.), p. 112; Ethel Barrymore, *Memories* (New York: Harper, 1955), p. 10; Tello J. D'Apéry, *Overbrook Farms* (Philadelphia, 1936), p. 81.
69. John F. Sutherland, "Housing the Poor in the City of Homes: Philadelphia at the Turn of the Century," in Davis and Haller, eds., *Peoples of Philadelphia*, p. 180; Golab, "Polish Communities of Philadelphia," pp. 49, 55.
70. Baltzell, *Philadelphia Gentlemen*, pp. 276, 280–87; Bernheimer, ed., *The Russian Jew in the United States*, p. 162.
71. Whiteman, "Philadelphia's Jewish Neighborhoods," pp. 233–37; Bernheimer, ed., *The Russian Jew in the United States*, p. 162; Golab, "Polish Communities of Philadelphia," p. 382.
72. Whiteman, "Philadelphia's Jewish Neighborhoods," p. 234; Bernheimer, ed., *The Russian Jew in the United States*, p. 77.

73. Baltzell, *Philadelphia Gentlemen*, p. 283.
74. Golab, "Polish Communities of Philadelphia," pp. 20, 157, 158, 271; Whiteman, "Philadelphia's Jewish Neighborhoods," pp. 238, 240, 246; Quay, "Philadelphia Democrats," pp. 304–6; Bernheimer, ed., *The Russian Jew in the United States*, pp. 51–52; Robert A. Woods and Albert J. Kennedy, *Handbook of Settlements* (New York: Russell Sage Foundation, 1911), p. 269; Sutherland, "Housing the Poor in the City of Homes," pp. 180–81; John F. Sutherland, "The Origins of Philadelphia's Octavia Hill Association: Social Reform in the 'Contented' City," *PMHB* 99 (Jan. 1975): 27; Emily W. Dinwiddie, *Housing Conditions in Philadelphia* (Philadelphia: Octavia Hill Association, 1904), p. 3; Pennell, *Our Philadelphia*, p. 460; Morgan, *City of Firsts*, pp. 424 (May 17, 1903), 425 (May 30, 1903); Baltzell, *Philadelphia Gentlemen*, p. 284.
75. Golab, "Polish Communities of Philadelphia," pp. 161, 162; Caroline Golab, "The Immigrant and the City: Poles, Italians, and Jews in Philadelphia, 1870–1920," in Davis and Haller, eds., *Peoples of Philadelphia*, pp. 213, 214; Richter, *North of Society Hill*, p. 41; Whiteman, "Philadelphia's Jewish Neighborhoods," pp. 238–39; Bernheimer, ed., *The Russian Jew in the United States*, p. 82.
76. Bernheimer, ed., *The Russian Jew in the United States*, pp. 161, 162, 163; Scharf and Westcott, *History of Philadelphia*, 2:1442; Baltzell, *Philadelphia Gentlemen*, pp. 284, 286; Whiteman, "Philadelphia's Jewish Neighborhoods," p. 240.
77. Henry Samuel Morais, *The Jews of Philadelphia* (Philadelphia: Levytype, 1894), pp. 197–99.
78. Joan Younger Dickinson, "Aspects of Italian Immigration to Philadelphia," *PMHB* 90 (Oct. 1966): 445, 446; Quay, "Philadelphia Democrats," p. 306; Golab, "The Immigrant and the City," pp. 205, 207; id., "Polish Communities of Philadelphia," pp. 158, 163.
79. Dickinson, "Aspects of Italian Immigration," pp. 454, 457; Golab, "Polish Communities of Philadelphia," pp. 163, 165.
80. Golab, "Polish Communities of Philadelphia," pp. 165–73; id., "The Immigrant and the City," pp. 210, 214–15; Dickinson, "Aspects of Italian Immigration," p. 455; Alexander DeConde, *Half Bitter, Half Sweet: An Excursion into Italian-American History* (New York: Scribner's, 1971), pp. 85–86.
81. Varbero, "Philadelphia's South Italians in the 1920's," pp. 264–65.
82. Golab, "Polish Communities of Philadelphia," pp. 171, 272; Dickinson, "Aspects of Italian Immigration," p. 463; *Chestnut Hill*, p. 35; Edwin Fenton, "Italians in the Labor Movement," *Pennsylvania History* 26 (April 1959): 135.
83. Dinwiddie, *Housing Conditions in Philadelphia*, p. 33; Golab, "Polish Communities of Philadelphia," pp. 163, 173, 174; id., "The Immigrant and the City," p. 215; Elizabeth Robins Pennell, *Charles Godfrey Leland: A Biography* (2 vols.; Boston: Houghton Mifflin, 1906), 2: 114; Webster, *Philadelphia Preserved*, p. 161.
84. Golab, "Polish Communities of Philadelphia," p. 19.
85. Woods and Kennedy, *Handbook of Settlements*, p. 266; Richter, *North of Society Hill*, p. 24.

86. Golab, "Polish Communities of Philadelphia," pp. 5, 64; id., "The Immigrant and the City," pp. 223, 225.
87. Id., "The Immigrant and the City," pp. 219–20; id., "Polish Communities of Philadelphia," pp. 109, 221, 224–26, 294, 297, 338–39, 402.
88. Id., "Polish Communities of Philadelphia," pp. 19, 222, 223, 250, 328, 385; id., "The Immigrant and the City," p. 220.
89. W. E. B. DuBois, *The Philadelphia Negro: A Social Study* (New York: Schocken, 1967), p. xxviii; Golab, "The Immigrant and the City," pp. 208, 209; Nelson, "The Social Ideas of Russell H. Conwell," p. 267. By 1910 the increase in Negro population had declined to 33 percent (DuBois, *Philadelphia Negro*, p. xxix).
90. DuBois, *Philadelphia Negro*, pp. ix, xv, xvi, xviii, xxv, xxx, xxxii, 58, 60–61, 316–18; Allen F. Davis, *Spearheads for Reform: The Social Settlements and the Progressive Movement, 1890–1914* (New York: Oxford University Press, 1967), p. 96; Burt, *Perennial Philadelphians*, p. 564. The focus of DuBois's study is on the Seventh Ward, but information used in this discussion relates to the city as a whole.
91. DuBois, *Philadelphia Negro*, pp. xxxiv, 58; Sutherland, "Housing the Poor in the City of Homes," pp. 180–81; id., "Origins of Philadelphia's Octavia Hill Association," p. 27; Dinwiddie, *Housing Conditions in Philadelphia*, p. 3; Bernheimer, ed., *The Russian Jew in the United States*, p. 205. Blacks in the Thirtieth Ward, just south of the Seventh, increased from 6 percent to 20 percent in the decade 1890–1900 (DuBois, *Philadelphia Negro*, p. xxxi).
92. Saunders, *100 Years After Emancipation*, p. 149; Weaver, "West Philadelphia," p. 141.
93. DuBois, *Philadelphia Negro*, pp. 45, 322–23, 327, 329–30, 333, 339, 348; *Sunday Bulletin*, Dec. 6, 1970; College Settlements Association, *Eighth Annual Report, 1896–1897* (Cambridge, Mass.: College Settlements Association, 1897), p. 26.
94. Golab, "The Immigrant and the City," pp. 208–9; DuBois, *Philadelphia Negro*, pp. 128, 129, 129–31, 131n, 133.
95. DuBois, *Philadelphia Negro*, pp. 54–55, 136, 139, 323; Dinwiddie, *Housing Conditions in Philadelphia*, p. 33.
96. DuBois, *Philadelphia Negro*, pp. xl, 118; Saunders, *100 Years After Emancipation*, pp. 136, 141, 146.
97. DuBois, *Philadelphia Negro*, pp. 111, 113, 114, 115, 131–33; Saunders, *100 Years After Emancipation*, p. 111; Quay, "Philadelphia Democrats," p. 35; *Sunday Bulletin*, Dec. 6, 1970.
98. DuBois, *Philadelphia Negro*, pp. 221–26; Morgan, *City of Firsts*, pp. 374 (May 24, 1883), 376 (Sept. 29, 1884), 384 (Oct. 7, 1886), 393 (May 13, 1889).
99. DuBois, *Philadelphia Negro*, pp. 200, 201, 203–4, 208–20; Morgan, *City of Firsts*, p. 399 (Jan. 5, 1892).
100. Philip S. Benjamin, "Gentlemen Reformers in the Quaker City," *Political Science Quarterly* 85 (Mar. 1970): 66; id., *The Philadelphia Quakers in the Industrial Age, 1865–1920* (Philadelphia: Temple University Press, 1976), pp. viii, 9, 14, 19, 155, 156, 173, 217–18 (tables); Taylor, ed., *City of Philadelphia, 1894*, p. 181; Alfred Lief, *Family Business:*

A Century in the Life and Times of Strawbridge & Clothier (New York: McGraw-Hill, 1968), p. 66; Frederica Ballard Westervelt, *A Victorian Childhood* (Chicago: Twentieth Century Press, 1938), p. 63; Logan Pearsall Smith, *Unforgotten Years* (Boston: Little, Brown, 1939), pp. 28, 31.
101. Henry James, "Philadelphia," *The American Scene* (New York: Scribner's, 1946), pp. 284–85; Benjamin, *Philadelphia Quakers*, p. 65; Baltzell, *Philadelphia Gentlemen*, pp. 247, 249, 265.
102. Sutherland, "Housing the Poor in the City of Homes," p. 178; Lorin Blodget, *The Social Conditions of the Industrial Classes of Philadelphia* (Philadelphia: Philadelphia Social Science Association, 1883), pp. 8, 9, 10, 11, 13, 14; *The Philadelphia Tradition of Work: Things To Do and Places To See* (Philadelphia: Philadelphia Area Cultural Consortium, 1979), p. 4; Blodget, *Textile Industries*, p. vi; id., *Census of Manufactures*, p. 79;
103. Josiah Strong, ed., *Social Progress: A Year Book and Encyclopedia of Economic, Industrial, Social and Religious Statistics* (New York: Baker and Taylor, 1904), p. 119; *WPA Guide*, p. 239; Stevens, *Pennsylvania, Titan of Industry*, 2:766; Morgan, *City of Firsts*, pp. 386 (Feb. 26, Apr. 8, 1887), 390 (May 7, 1888), 393 (May 17, 1889); King, *Notable Philadelphians*, pt. 1:6; Talcott Williams, "Philadelphia, A City of Homes," *St. Nicholas Magazine* 20 (March 1893): 331.
104. Sutherland, "Housing the Poor in the City of Homes," p. 178; *Popular Philadelphians*, p. 221; *Philadelphia Tradition of Work*, p. 5; Elden LaMar, *The Clothing Workers in Philadelphia: History of Their Struggles for Union and Security* (Philadelphia: Philadelphia Joint Board, Amalgamated Clothing Workers of America, 1940), p. 25; Edward C. Kirkland, *History of American Economic Life* (New York: F. S. Crofts, 1941), pp. 536–37; Hyman Kuritz, "The Labor Injunction in Pennsylvania, 1891–1931," *Pennsylvania History* 29 (July 1962): 311; *Board of Trade Report* (1900), pp. 13–15; ibid. (1903), pp. 17–20, 29–31; ibid. (1904), pp. 28–29; Benjamin, *Philadelphia Quakers*, p. 89.
105. Warner, *The Private City*, p. 180; Berthoff, *British Immigrants in Industrial America*, p. 95; Morgan, *City of Firsts*, pp. 370 (Feb. 6, 1882), 382 (Feb. 12, 1886); Louis Levine, *The Women's Garment Workers: A History of the International Ladies Garment Workers Union* (New York: B. W. Huebsch, 1924), pp. 65, 94, 96, 102–3; *WPA Guide*, pp. 154–57; Ira V. Brown, *Pennsylvania Reformers: From Penn to Pinchot*, Pennsylvania History Studies no. 9 (University Park: Pennsylvania State University, 1966), pp. 52, 53; Kirkland, *History of American Economic Life*, p. 535; Richard B. Morris, *Encyclopedia of American History* (New York: Harper & Brothers, 1953), p. 522; Norman J. Ware, *The Labor Movement in the United States, 1860–1895* (New York: D. Appleton, 1929), pp. 201, 224–25, 265, 348; *Philadelphia Tradition of Work*, p. 5.
106. Kirkland, *History of American Economic Life*, p. 590; Morgan, *City of Firsts*, p. 421 (Aug. 28, 1902); Mark Sullivan, *Our Times* (6 vols.; New York: Scribner's, 1926–1935), 2:423–26.
107. Morgan, *City of Firsts*, pp. 374 (July 19, 1883), 378 (Dec. 8, 1884), 379 (Feb. 25,

1885), 400 (Sept. 30, 1892), 404 (Dec. 17, 23, 25, 1895), 409 (June 1, 1898), 412 (Sept. 1, 1899), 414 (May 1, 3, 1900), 421 (Aug. 25, 1902), 422 (Dec. 1, 1902), 423 (Feb. 3, 1903), 430 (May 2, 1904); Ware, *Labor Movement in the United States*, p. 133; John A. Garraty, *The New Commonwealth, 1877–1890* (New York: Harper & Row, 1968), p. 153; John S. Ewing and Nancy Norton, *Broadlooms and Business* (Cambridge, Mass.: Harvard University Press, 1955), p. 90; Speirs, *The Street Railway System of Philadelphia*, pp. 104–12; Rudolph J. Walther, *Happenings in Ye Olde Philadelphia, 1680–1900* (Philadelphia: Walther Printing House, 1925), p. 118 (Dec. 17, 18, 1895).

108. Morgan, *City of Firsts*, pp. 425 (June 1, 1902), 426 (Aug. 17, 1903); *WPA Guide*, p. 155; C. K. McFarland, "Crusade for Child Laborers: 'Mother' Jones and the March of the Mill Children," *Pennsylvania History* 38 (July 1971): 284–90, 296; [Mary Harris Jones,] *Autobiography of Mother Jones* (Chicago: Charles H. Kern, 1925), pp. 71, 72, 83.

109. Morgan, *City of Firsts*, p. 414 (Apr. 30, 1900); Warner, *The Private City*, pp. 183–84; Fenton, "Italians in the Labor Movement," pp. 137, 139, 140; Dickinson, "Aspects of Italian Immigration," pp. 459, 461; Sutherland, "Housing the Poor in the City of Homes," pp. 175, 176, 181; "Certain Aspects of the Housing Problem in Philadelphia," *Annals of the American Academy of Political and Social Science* 20 (July 1902): 114–17; Klein and Hoogenboom, *History of Pennsylvania*, p. 310; Westervelt, *A Victorian Childhood*, p. 121; Golab, "Polish Communities of Philadelphia," p. 278; Dinwiddie, *Housing Conditions in Philadelphia*, pp. 1, 4, 21; Whiteman, "Philadelphia's Jewish Neighborhoods," pp. 241, 242.

110. Arthur Meier Schlesinger, *The Rise of the City, 1878–1898* (New York: Macmillan, 1933), p. 108; Steevens, *Land of the Dollar*, p. 116; Sutherland, "Origins of Philadelphia's Octavia Hill Association," pp. 20–22; Dinwiddie, *Housing Conditions in Philadelphia*, p. 1; "Certain Aspects of the Housing Problem," p. 111; Harlan B. Phillips, "A War on Philadelphia's Slums: Walter Vrooman and the Conference of Moral Workers," *PMHB* 76 (Jan. 1952): 47, 48.

111. Garraty, *The New Commonwealth*, p. 209; Leah Hannah Feder, *Unemployment Relief in Periods of Depression* (New York: Russell Sage Foundation, 1936), p. 59; *WPA Guide*, p. 305; Philadelphia Society for Organizing Charitable Relief and Repressing Mendicancy, *Manual for Visitors Among the Poor* (Philadelphia: Lippincott, 1879), pp. 3–4.

112. Anna F. Davies, "A Glance at the Philadelphia Settlements," *The Commons* 10 (May 1905): 299; Morgan, *City of Firsts*, pp. 362 (Dec. 8, 1878), 405 (March 12, 1896); Jackson, *Encyclopedia*, 4:1067; *The Columbia Encyclopedia in One Volume* (2d ed.; New York: Columbia University Press, 1950), p. 1744.

113. Benjamin, *Philadelphia Quakers*, pp. 183, 187; Davies, "A Glance at the Philadelphia Settlements," pp. 297, 298, 299; Woods and Kennedy, *Handbook of Settlements*, p. 267.

114. *History of a Street* (Philadelphia, 1901), pp. 21, 25, 38; College Settlements Association, *Fourth Annual Report*, 1892–1893 (Philadelphia: College Settlements Association, 1894),

p. 23; Allen F. Davis and John F. Sutherland, "Reform and Uplift Among Philadelphia Negroes: Diary of Helen Parrish, 1888," *PMHB* 94 (Oct. 1970): 496, 497–98; Sutherland, "Origins of Philadelphia's Octavia Hill Association," pp. 24, 26, 28, 30, 34, 37, 38; Benjamin, *Philadelphia Quakers*, p. 162; William H. Issel, "Modernization in Philadelphia School Reform," *PMHB* 94 (July 1970): 366; Edward T. James, ed., *Notable American Women, 1607–1950* (3 vols.; Cambridge, Mass: Harvard University Press, 1971), 2:599; Lucretia L. Blankenburg, *The Blankenburgs of Philadelphia* (Philadelphia: John C. Winston, 1929), p. 13.

115. John Russell Young, ed., *Memorial History of the City of Philadelphia from Its First Settlement to the Year 1895* (2 vols.; New York: New York History Co., 1895), 1:562; Warner, *The Private City*, p. 108; Myers, "The Most Corrupt City in the World," p. 458; *Board of Trade Report* (1894), p. 29; Garraty, *The New Commonwealth*, p. 194; Nelson, "The Social Ideas of Russell H. Conwell," pp. 239–40; Theophilus Baker, "Philadelphia, A Study in Political Psychology," *The Arena* 30 (July 1903): 1.

116. Sutherland, "Housing the Poor in the City of Homes," p. 188; Klein and Hoogenboom, *History of Pennsylvania*, pp. 311, 315; Schlesinger, *The Rise of the City*, p. 105; Warner, *The Private City*, p. 108; Davis and Sutherland, "Reform and Uplift Among Philadelphia Negroes," p. 490; Myers, "The Most Corrupt City in the World," p. 458; Milo Ray Maltbie, "A Tale of Two Cities: Water Supply in London and Philadelphia," *Municipal Affairs* 3 (June 1899): 208, 210; Baker, "Philadelphia, A Study in Political Psychology," p. 3.

117. Clinton R. Woodruff, "Philadelphia's Water: A Study of Municipal Procrastination," *The Forum* 28 (Nov. 1899): 307; Edward P. Allinson and Boies Penrose, *Philadelphia, 1681–1887: A History of Municipal Development* (Philadelphia: Allen, Lane & Scott, 1887), pp. 193, 195, 198; Joanna Wharton Lippincott, *Biographical Memoranda Concerning Joseph Wharton* (Philadelphia: Lippincott, 1919), pp. 52–56; Nelson Manfred Blake, *Water for the Cities: A History of the Urban Water Supply Problem in the United States* (Syracuse, N.Y.: Syracuse University Press, 1956), p. 275.

118. Morgan, *City of Firsts*, pp. 287, 411 (April 6, 1899), 412 (Sept. 21, 1899), 417 (March 14, 1901), 418 (May 28, 1901), 421 (Aug. 12, 1902), 425 (June 2, 1903), 433 (Nov. 19, 1904); Woodruff, "Philadelphia's Water," p. 314; *Board of Trade Report* (1900), pp. 44–46; ibid., (1903), p. 32; Myers, "The Most Corrupt City in the World," p. 459; Clinton R. Woodruff, "Philadelphia's Republican Tammany," *The Outlook* 99 (Sept. 21, 1901): 170; Blake, *Water for the Cities*, p. 263; H. D. Jones, "The New Philadelphia Filtration System," *Scientific American* 88 (March 14, 1903): 188; Maxwell Whiteman to Lois Given Bobb, Sept. 17, 1979.

119. Quay, "Philadelphia Democrats," pp. 21, 36, 200–7; William S. Vare, *My Forty Years in Politics* (Philadelphia: Roland Swain, 1933), p. 79; Warner, *The Private City*, p. 91; Edward Sculley Bradley, *Henry Charles Lea* (Philadelphia: University of Pennsylvania Press, 1931), p. 189.

120. Quay, "Philadelphia Democrats," pp. vii, 166, 195, 198, 209, 210, 228–33; Burt, *Perennial Philadelphians*, p. 541.
121. Benjamin, *Philadelphia Quakers*, p. 77; J. St. George Joyce, *Story of Philadelphia* ([Philadelphia: Privately printed,] 1919), p. 282; Young, *Memorial History*, 1:545; Bradley, *Henry Charles Lea*, p. 196; Quay, "Philadelphia Democrats," pp. 221–22; Stevens, *Pennsylvania: Birthplace of a Nation*, pp. 369–70; *DAB*, s.v. "Robert E. Pattison."
122. Joyce, *Story of Philadelphia*, pp. 283–84; Oberholtzer, *Philadelphia*, 2:426; Bradley, *Henry Charles Lea*, p. 198; Klein and Hoogenboom, *History of Pennsylvania*, p. 375; Allinson and Penrose, *Philadelphia . . . Municipal Development*, pp. 268, 269, 271, 272; James Bryce, *The American Commonwealth* (2 vols.; New York: Macmillan, 1889), 2:368, 369; Lincoln Steffens, *The Shame of the Cities* (New York: Hill and Wang, 1965), p. 142; id., *The Autobiography of Lincoln Steffens* (New York: Harcourt, Brace, 1931), p. 499; Walter Davenport, *Power and Glory: The Life of Boies Penrose* (New York: Putnam's, 1931), p. 44; Bowden, *Boies Penrose*, pp. 59–60.
123. Steffens, *Shame of the Cities*, pp. 136, 142, 144–45; Stevens, *Pennsylvania: Birthplace of a Nation*, pp. 258, 259; Clark, "The Philadelphia Irish," p. 145; Myers, "The Most Corrupt City in the World," p. 456; Woodruff, "Philadelphia's Republican Tammany," p. 170; Bowden, *Boies Penrose*, pp. 76–77; Bryce, *American Commonwealth*, 2:358; Wainwright, *Philadelphia Electric Company*, pp. 27–29; Morgan, *City of Firsts*, p. 285.
124. Bryce, *American Commonwealth*, 2:369; Steffens, *Shame of the Cities*; Blankenburg, *The Blankenburgs of Philadelphia* pp. 13–14; Steffens, *Autobiography*, pp. 408–9, 412; Klein and Hoogenboom, *History of Pennsylvania*, p. 136.
125. Steffens, *Shame of the Cities*, p. 137; Maxwell Whiteman, *Gentlemen in Crisis: The First Century of the Union League of Philadelphia, 1862–1962* (Philadelphia: The Union League, 1973), p. 116; Oberholtzer, *Philadelphia*, 2:427; Young, *Memorial History*, 2:421; Morgan, *City of Firsts*, p. 388 (Sept. 15–17, 1887).
126. Quay, "Philadelphia Democrats," pp. vi, 317–18; Klein and Hoogenboom, *History of Pennsylvania*, p. 332; Steevens, *Land of the Dollar*, p. 121.
127. Bowden, *Boies Penrose*, pp. 113, 115, 116; McClure, *Old Time Notes of Pennsylvania*, 2:592, 593, 600; Issel, "Modernization in Philadelphia School Reform," p. 367; Vare, *My Forty Years in Politics*, pp. 49, 53; Davenport, *Power and Glory*, pp. 109, 111; Burt, *Perennial Philadelphians*, p. 546; Blankenburg, *The Blankenburgs of Philadelphia*, p. 19; Joyce, *Story of Philadelphia*, p. 293; Quay, "Philadelphia Democrats," p. 95; Stevens, *Pennsylvania: Birthplace of a Nation*, pp. 259–60; Steffens, *Shame of the Cities*, p. 149.
128. Burt, *Perennial Philadelphians*, p. 546.
129. Issel, "Modernization in Philadelphia School Reform," pp. 359, 376, 378; King, *Notable Philadelphians*, pt. 2:29; J. M. Rice, "The Public School System of Philadelphia," *The Forum* 15 (March 1893): 38; Clinton R. Woodruff, "A Corrupt School System," *Educational Review* 26 (Dec. 1903): 433, 434,

436; Adele Marie Shaw, "The Public Schools of a Boss Ridden City," *World's Work* 7 (Feb. 1904): 4460, 4461, 4462; Steffens, *Shame of the Cities*, p. 155; "Political Bandits in Philadelphia," *The Outlook* 73 (April 11, 1903): 845–46; A Teacher, "Politics in Education," *The Outlook* 73 (Mar. 14, 1903): 648; Klein and Hoogenboom, *History of Pennsylvania*, p. 343.
130. Richard B. Fishbane, " 'The Shallow Boast of Cheapness': Public School Teaching as a Profession in Philadelphia, 1865–1890," *PMHB* 103 (Jan. 1979): 77; Shaw, "The Public Schools of a Boss Ridden City," pp. 4464, 4465; Klein and Hoogenboom, *History of Pennsylvania*, pp. 343–44; Morgan, *City of Firsts*, p. 417 (April 26, 1901), 424 (April 8, 1903).
131. William Issel, "The Politics of School Reform in Pennsylvania, 1880–1911," *PMHB* 102 (Jan. 1978): 71–72; *Notable American Women*, 2:122–23; Issel, "Modernization in Philadelphia School Reform," pp. 362–63; Rice, "The Public School System of Philadelphia," pp. 31, 32; Klein and Hoogenboom, *History of Pennsylvania*, p. 343.
132. Issel, "The Politics of School Reform in Pennsylvania," pp. 70–81 and passim; Warner, *The Private City*, p. 120; Shaw, "The Public Schools of a Boss Ridden City," p. 4465. See Anthony F. C. Wallace, *Rockdale: The Growth of an American Village in the Early Industrial Revolution* (New York: Knopf, 1978), for working-class resistance to child labor reform as a possible explanation for the Democratic party's attitude.
133. Shaw, "The Public Schools of a Boss Ridden City," p. 4466; William H. Cornog, *School of the Republic: A Half Century of the Central High School of Philadelphia, 1893–1943* (Philadelphia: Associated Alumni of Central High School, [1952]), pp. 53, 134, 163, 165, 168, 174, 178, 180; WPA *Guide*, p. 459; Oberholtzer, *Philadelphia*, 2:433.
134. *Handy Guide to Philadelphia*, p. 95; Baltzell, *Philadelphia Gentlemen*, pp. 297, 298, 299, 300–1.
135. *DAB*, s.v. "Charles Stillé," "William Pepper, Jr."; Martin Meyerson et al., *Gladly Learn and Gladly Teach: Franklin and His Heirs at the University of Pennsylvania, 1740–1976* (Philadelphia: University of Pennsylvania Press, 1978), pp. 104–5.
136. *DAB*, s.v. "William Pepper, Jr."; Meyerson et al., *Gladly Learn and Gladly Teach*, pp. 106–15.
137. *DAB*, s.v. "Russell H. Conwell"; Klein and Hoogenboom, *History of Pennsylvania*, p. 349; WPA *Guide*, pp. 162, 175, 464, 466; Nelson, "The Social Ideas of Russell H. Conwell," pp. 77, 79, 112, 115, 119, 120, 121, 162, 163, 164, 168, 169, 267; Taylor, ed., *City of Philadelphia, 1894*, p. 48; Webster, *Philadelphia Preserved*, p. 291.
138. Webster, *Philadelphia Preserved*, p. 201; *Chestnut Street*, p. 49; Taylor, ed., *City of Philadelphia, 1894*, p. 51; Saul Sack, "A History of Higher Education in Pennsylvania" (Ph.D. dissertation, University of Pennsylvania, 1959), pp. 736–37.
139. *DAB*, s.v. "Joseph W. Taylor," "M. Carey Thomas."
140. *DAB*, s.v. "George Seckel Pepper"; Taylor, ed., *City of Philadelphia, 1894*, pp. 66–67; *Handy Guide to Philadelphia*, p. 26; Donald W. Disbrow, "Herbert Welsh, Editor of City

and State, 1895–1914," *PMHB* 94 (Jan. 1970): 67; Jackson, *Encyclopedia*, 3:695–96; Morgan, *City of Firsts*, pp. 400 (Oct. 17, 1892), 423 (Jan. 6, 1903), 428 (Dec. 23, 1903).

141. Nathaniel Burt, *Palaces for the People* (Boston: Little, Brown, 1977), pp. 129, 139–42, 144n.

142. Ibid., pp. 130, 144.

143. Repplier, *Philadelphia: The Place and the People*, pp. 390, 391.

144. *Britannica Encyclopedia of American Art*, (Chicago: Encyclopedia Britannica, n.d.), s.v. "Mary Cassatt"; *DAB*, s.v. "Mary Cassatt"; Nancy Hale, *Mary Cassatt* (Garden City, N.Y.: Doubleday, 1975), p. 117 and passim.

145. *DAB*, s.v. "Fitzwilliam Sargent," "John Singer Sargent"; Charles H. Mount, *John Singer Sargent* (New York: W. W. Norton, 1955), pp. 1–40.

146. *DAB*, s.v. "Henry Osawa Tanner," "Thomas Moran"; Thurman Wilkins, *Thomas Moran* (Norman: University of Oklahoma Press, 1966); Thomas Moran, *Children of the Mountain*, Christie's sale catalogue, New York, May 22, 1980.

147. Sylvan Schendler, *Eakins* (Boston: Little, Brown, 1967), p. 60.

148. Wilkins, *Thomas Moran; The Moran Family*, Hecksher Miers exhibition catalogue (New York: Huntington, 1965).

149. Edgar P. Richardson, *Painting in America* (New York: Crowell, 1963), p. 323.

150. *DAB*, s.v. "Edwin A. Abbey"; *Britannica Encyclopedia of American Art*, s.v. "Arthur B. Frost," "Edwin A. Aubrey"; Richardson, *Painting in America*, pp. 326, 354.

151. *DAB*, s.v. "Joseph S. Pennell"; *The Reader's Encyclopedia of American Literature* (New York: Crowell, 1962), s.v. "Elizabeth Robins Pennell."

152. *DAB*, s.v. "Howard Pyle," "Newell Convers Wyeth"; Paul W. Skeeters, *Maxfield Parrish: The Early Years* (Los Angeles: Nash, 1933), pp. 347, 348, 349.

153. *Britannica Encyclopedia of American Art*, s.v. "Alexander S. Calder," "Alexander M. Calder," "Alexander Calder"; *DAB*, s.v. "Alexander S. Calder," "John McArthur."

154. *WPA Guide*, pp. 271, 379, 380.

155. Repplier, *Philadelphia: The Place and the People*, pp. 374, 375.

156. James F. O'Gorman, *The Architecture of Frank Furness* (Philadelphia: Philadelphia Museum of Art, 1973).

157. *DAB*, s.v. "Walter Cope," "John Stewardson."

158. *DAB*, s.v. "Robert Henri," "John French Sloan" (in Supplement 5).

159. *DAB*, s.v. "Walt Whitman"; *The Reader's Encyclopedia of American Literature*, s.v. "Walt Whitman."

160. *The Reader's Encyclopedia of American Literature*, s.v. "George Henry Boker"; *DAB*, s.v. "George Henry Boker," "Otis Skinner."

161. Bradley, *Henry Charles Lea*, pp. 143, 144, 149.

162. Ibid., pp. 147, 148.

163. Burt, *Perennial Philadelphians*, p. 382; *DAB*, s.v. "Horace Howard Furness"; *The Reader's Encyclopedia of American Literature*, s.v. "Horace Howard Furness."

164. Horace Traubel, *With Walt Whitman in Camden* (3 vols.; New York: Appleton, 1906–1914), 3:520.

165. *The Reader's Encyclopedia of American Literature*, s.v. "Silas Weir Mitchell"; *DAB*, s.v. "Silas Weir Mitchell."

166. J. P. Lovering, *S. Weir Mitchell* (New York: Twayne, 1971), p. 27.

167. Traubel, *With Walt Whitman*, 1:455, 2:271.

168. *DAB*, s.v. "Henry Charles Lea"; *Reader's Encyclopedia of American Literature*, s.v. "Henry Charles Lea."

169. *One Hundred Years of Publishing* (Philadelphia: Lea & Febiger, 1935).

170. George Stewart Stokes, *Agnes Repplier, Lady of Letters* (Philadelphia: University of Pennsylvania Press, 1949), pp. 108, 167.

171. Ibid., pp. 102, 105, 106.

172. Ibid., p. 102.

173. Ibid., p. 106.

174. *DAB*, s.v. "Owen Wister"; *Reader's Encyclopedia of American Literature*, s.v. "Owen Wister."

175. Owen Wister, *Owen Wister Out West*, edited by F. K. Wister (Chicago: University of Chicago Press, 1958), p. 164.

176. Owen Wister, *The Virginian*, preface by Struthers Burt (Los Angeles: Limited Editions Club, 1951), p. xiii.

177. Edward T. James, ed., et al., *Notable American Women, 1607–1950: A Biographical Dictionary* (3 vols., Cambridge, Mass: Belknap Press of Harvard University Press, 1971), 3:194; Frank Luther Mott, *A History of American Magazines* (5 vols.; New York: Appleton, Appleton-Century, and Appleton-Century-Crofts, 1930–1968), 3:194, 363, 4:536, 537, 539–40, 545, 546; Edward Bok, *The Americanization of Edward Bok* (Cambridge, Mass.: Harvard University Press, 1939), pp. 166, 170, 176, 179, 191, 233, 240, 244; James Playsted Wood, *The Curtis Magazines* (New York: Ronald Press, 1971), p. 10.

178. Emma Seifrit Weigley, "The Philadelphia Chef: Mastering the Art of Philadelphia Cookery," *PMHB* 96 (April 1972): 229, 231, 233, 238–40; *Notable American Women*, 3:194–95; Mott, *History of American Magazines*, 3:363.

179. See note 177 above; see also Wood, *The Curtis Magazines*, pp. 37, 38–39; Mott, *History of American Magazines*, 4:680–81, 682–84, 688, 689–90, 694, 703–6; *WPA Guide*, p. 195; Joseph Jackson, *Literary Landmarks of Philadelphia* (Philadelphia: David McKay, 1939), pp. 219–20.

180. *DAB*, s.v. "John Drew," "Edwin Booth," "Joseph Jefferson."

181. Burt, *Perennial Philadelphians*, p. 433n; Arthur H. Quinn, *Representative American Plays* (3d. ed.; New York: Century, 1917), p. 649.

182. Burt, *Perennial Philadelphians*, p. 446.

183. Herbert Kupferberg, *Those Fabulous Philadelphians: The Life and Times of a Great Orchestra* (New York: Scribner's, 1969), p. 10; Robert A. Gerson, *Music in Philadelphia* (Philadelphia: Theodore Presser, 1940), pp. 149, 168; Frances Anne Wister, *Twenty-five Years of the Philadelphia Orchestra, 1900–1925* (Philadelphia: Women's Committee for the Philadelphia Orchestra, 1925), pp. 11–12; Burt, *Perennial Philadelphians*, pp. 466–69.

184. Gerson, *Music in Philadelphia*, pp. 164, 168, 169, 171, 174; Wister, *Twenty-five Years of the Philadelphia Orchestra*, pp. 16, 17, 19, 20, 25; Kupferberg, *Those Fabulous Philadelphians*, pp. 17, 18, 19, 22, 48.

185. Jackson, *Encyclopedia*, 4:950; Gerson, *Music*

in *Philadelphia*, pp. 120–21, 127–28, 129, 132, 153, 154, 183, 231, 232.

186. Burt, *Perennial Philadelphians*, pp. 489, 490.

187. University Barge Club, *Centennial* (Philadelphia: Privately printed, 1954).

188. Schendler, *Eakins*, plate 13.

189. Ibid., plate 30.

190. Morgan, *City of Firsts*, p. 385 (Feb. 2, 1887).

191. Ibid., pp. 376 (June 24, Sept. 21, 1884), 383 (July 5, 1886), 387 (July 4, 1887), 391 (July 4, 1888), 411 (April 6, 1899), 412 (July 4, 1899), and numerous other July 4 entries.

192. Ibid., p. 406 (Nov. 10, 1896); Webster, *Philadelphia Preserved*, p. 226; Wilson, *Yesterday's Philadelphia*, p. 54; *100 Years in Philadelphia*, p. 137; Jackson, *Encyclopedia*, 3:643, 4:1207.

193. Wainwright, *Philadelphia Electric Company*, p. 4; Morgan, *City of Firsts*, pp. 412 (Oct. 5, 1899), 416 (Sept. 27, 1900).

194. Stevens, *Pennsylvania: Birthplace of a Nation*, pp. 249, 250; M. J. McCosker, "Philadelphia and the Genesis of the Motion Picture," *PMHB* 65 (Oct. 1941): 415, 417–18, 419; Jackson, *Encyclopedia*, 2:584, 3:906, 907.

195. Wainwright, *Philadelphia Electric Company*, pp. 46–47; *Evening Bulletin*, May 4, 1972; Lief, *Family Business*, p. 105; *Handy Guide to Philadelphia*, p. 31; Gerson, *Music in Philadelphia*, pp. 124, 162, 195, 196; Wister, *Twenty-five Years of the Philadelphia Orchestra*, p. 16.

196. Jackson, *Encyclopedia*, 1:284, 2:774; Taylor, ed., *City of Philadelphia*, 1894, p. 169; Richard Brinsley Sheridan, *Club Men of Philadelphia* (Philadelphia: Avil, 1894); Lief, *Family Business*, p. 68; Morgan, *City of Firsts*, pp. 373 (May 1, 1883), 374 (Sept. 29, 1883), 376 (June 9, 20, 1884).

197. Taylor, ed., *City of Philadelphia*, 1894, pp. 127, 164, 165; Jackson, *Encyclopedia*, 1:253; *Philadelphia and Its Environs* (1887), p. 74; ibid., (1893), p. 128; Morgan, *City of Firsts*, p. 421 (Sept. 29, 1902); *Public Ledger*, Sept. 30, 1902; *The Baseball Encyclopedia: The Complete and Official Record of Major League Baseball*, Bicentennial ed. (New York: Macmillan, 1976), pp. 68, 257, 269, 2029. The Athletics' ballpark was Columbia Park, at Twenty-ninth Street and Columbia Avenue, until Shibe Park was built in 1909 (Wilson, *Yesterday's Philadelphia*, p. 67).

198. Taylor, ed., *City of Philadelphia*, 1894, p. 165; Burt, *Perennial Philadelphians*, pp. 303, 305, 306; Cornelius Weygandt, *Philadelphia Folks: Ways and Institutions in and about the Quaker City* (New York: Appleton-Century, 1938), p. 38; Baltzell, *Philadelphia Gentlemen*, p. 359; *Handy Guide to Philadelphia*, p. 103; King, *Notable Philadelphians*, pt. 2:35; White et al., *Philadelphia Architecture*, p. 34.

199. Burt, *Perennial Philadelphians*, p. 310.

200. Sheridan, *Club Men of Philadelphia*; Charles J. Cohen, *Rittenhouse Square Past and Present* (Philadelphia: Privately printed, 1922), pp. 221, 223; Taylor, ed., *City of Philadelphia*, 1894, p. 125; King, *Notable Philadelphians*, pt. 2:24A.

201. Taylor, ed., *City of Philadelphia*, 1894, pp. 126, 125, 127; *WPA Guide*, p. 201, 425; Stokes, *Agnes Repplier*, p. 101; Davis, "The City of Homes," p. 9; Pennell, *Our Philadelphia*, p. 352; *Annals of the New Century Club, 1877–1952* (Philadelphia: Privately printed, [1952]), pp. 25, 34; *The Franklin Inn Club History* (n.p., n.d.); Jackson, *Encyclopedia*, 3:689, 735; id., *Literary Landmarks of Philadelphia*, pp. 61, 231; Sheridan, *Club Men of Philadelphia*; King, *Notable Philadelphians*, pt. 2:24; *Bulletin Almanac 1975*, p. 317; Geographical Society of Philadelphia, *Meetings and Programs, 1977–1978* (Philadelphia: Geographical Society of Philadelphia, 1977); *Philadelphia and Its Environs* (1893), p. 122.

202. *WPA Guide*, p. 435; Sheridan, *Club Men of Philadelphia*; *Philadelphia Record*, May 10, 1894; Baltzell, *Philadelphia Gentlemen*, p. 354.

203. Sheridan, *Club Men of Philadelphia*; *WPA Guide*, p. 399; Blankenburg, *The Blankenburgs of Philadelphia*, pp. 114, 124; Taylor, ed., *City of Philadelphia*, 1894, pp. 129, 130; *Annals of the New Century Club*, pp. 9, 11, 13, 17, 18; New Century Club, *75th Anniversary, 1877–1952* (program), pp. 13, 21; Morgan, *City of Firsts*, p. 399 (Jan. 4, 1892); *Notable American Women*, 1:170–71, 2:91, 629–30, 3:235–36, 486; New Century Club of Philadelphia, *The One Hundredth Anniversary Charter Luncheon, 1877–1977* (program); Davis, "The City of Homes," p. 9; Jackson, *Literary Landmarks*, p. 274; id. *Encyclopedia*, 4:1074; Benjamin, *Philadelphia Quakers*, p. 185; Brown, *Pennsylvania Reformers*, p. 27.

204. *DAB*, s.v. "Sarah Yorke Stevenson"; David J. Pivar, "Theocratic Businessmen and Philadelphia Municipal Reform, 1870–1900," *Pennsylvania History* 30 (July 1966): 302; Meyerson et al., *Gladly Learn and Gladly Teach*, pp. 126–27.

205. Burt, *Perennial Philadelphians*, pp. 258, 571, 577.

206. *Public Ledger*, Jan. 2, 1901; Morgan, *City of Firsts*, p. 417 (Jan. 1, 1901); Jackson, *Encyclopedia*, 2:912–13; Clark, *The Irish in Philadelphia*, p. 127.

207. Burt, *Perennial Philadelphians*, pp. 277–84; Joseph Sims, *The Assemblies, 1748–1948* (Philadelphia: Privately published, 1947), pp. 30, 36–51.

208. Burt, *Perennial Philadelphians*, pp. 251–55.

PROGRESSIVISM, 1905–1919

1. Henry C. Lea to E. P. Cheyney, June 9, 1905, Henry C. Lea Papers, University of Pennsylvania; Owen Wister, "Keystone Crime: Pennsylvania's Graft-Cankered Capitol," *Everybody's Magazine* 17 (Oct. 1907): 447.

2. Christopher Morley, *Travels in Philadelphia* (Philadelphia: David McKay, 1920), pp. 13, 31, 32, 72, 85.

3. Registration numbers are estimates based on

information supplied by the Pennsylvania Bureau of Motor Vehicles, Harrisburg.

4. Morley, *Travels in Philadelphia*, p. 28.

5. *Public Ledger*, Oct. 27, 1918.

6. Joseph Jackson, *America's Most Historic Highway: Market Street, Philadelphia* (Philadelphia: John Wanamaker, 1926), pp. 342–43.

7. J. St. George Joyce, ed., *Story of Philadelphia* (Philadelphia: Harry B. Joseph, 1919), p. 298;

Fifth Annual Message of Rudolph Blanken-burg, Mayor of the City of Philadelphia (Philadelphia: City of Philadelphia, 1916), 2:532.

8. George Morgan, *The City of Firsts* (Philadelphia: Historical Publishing Society, 1926), p. 310; *Philadelphia Year Book, 1918–1919* (Philadelphia: Chamber of Commerce, 1918), pp. H1–2.

9. Frank H. Taylor, ed., *Poor Richard's Dictionary of Philadelphia* (Philadelphia: Lippincott, 1916), p. 148; *Evening Bulletin*, Dec. 24, 1917.

10. See the summary of population statistics in Gladys L. Palmer, *Philadelphia Workers in a Changing Economy* (Philadelphia: University of Pennsylvania Press, 1956), p. 157. Complete statistics are in *Abstract of the Thirteenth Census of the United States with Supplement for Pennsylvania* (Washington, D.C.: U.S. Government Printing Office, 1913).

11. "The Foreign Population in Our Cities," *City Club Bulletin* 1 (Oct. 28, 1909): 12–19.

12. See John F. Sutherland, "Housing the Poor in the City of Homes," in Allen F. Davis and Mark H. Haller, eds., *The Peoples of Philadelphia: A History of Ethnic Groups and Lower-Class Life, 1790–1940* (Philadelphia: Temple University Press, 1973), pp. 175–201.

13. Nathan Kushin, *Memoirs of a New American* (New York: Bloch Publishing Company, 1949), pp. 59–60.

14. Morley, *Travels in Philadelphia*, pp. 15–20.

15. See Richard N. Juliani, "The Origins and Development of the Italian Community in Philadelphia," in John E. Bodnar, ed., *The Ethnic Experience in Pennsylvania* (Lewisburg: Bucknell University Press, 1973), pp. 233–62; Caroline Golab, "The Immigrant and the City: Poles, Italians, and Jews in Philadelphia, 1870–1920," in Davis and Haller, eds., *Peoples of Philadelphia*, pp. 203–30.

16. Golab, "The Immigrant and the City," p. 220.

17. See Maxwell Whiteman, "Philadelphia's Jewish Neighborhoods," in Davis and Haller, eds., *Peoples of Philadelphia*, pp. 231–54; Golab, "The Immigrant and the City," pp. 213, 214, 220; *Sunday Bulletin*, Oct. 27, 1968.

18. Golab, "The Immigrant and the City," pp. 221, 226.

19. "The Immigration Problem as It Affects Philadelphia," *City Club Bulletin* 2 (Jan. 13, 1910): 5.

20. *Public Ledger*, May 19, 1910.

21. John T. Emlen, "The Movement for the Betterment of the Negro in Philadelphia," *Annals of the American Academy of Political and Social Science* 49 (Sept. 1913): 84–88; *Christian Recorder*, May 31, 1917.

22. See *The Philadelphia Colored Directory* (Philadelphia: Philadelphia Colored Directory Company, 1910).

23. *Inquirer*, Mar. 22, 1970.

24. John Ihlder (Chairman, Committee on Negro Migration to Philadelphia, Philadelphia Housing Association) to Porter Johnson, June 20, 1917, in Philadelphia Housing Association Papers, Urban Archives, Temple University.

25. *Christian Recorder*, May 31, 1917.

26. Louise V. Kennedy, *The Negro Peasant Turns Cityward* (New York: Columbia University Press, 1930), pp. 154–58.

27. *Public Ledger*, July 29–31, 1918. For an extended account of the riot, see Vincent P.

Franklin, "The Philadelphia Race Riot of 1918," *Pennsylvania Magazine of History and Biography* (hereafter cited as *PMHB*) 99 (July 1975): 336–50.

28. Frank H. Taylor and Wilfred H. Schoff, *The Port and City of Philadelphia* (Philadelphia: International Congress of Navigation, 1912), p. 67; Morgan, *City of Firsts*, p. 305.

29. Morley, *Travels in Philadelphia*, p. 12.

30. *Sunday Bulletin*, June 9, 1968.

31. Taylor and Schoff, *The Port and City of Philadelphia*, p. 67.

32. Nicholas B. Wainwright, *History of the Philadelphia National Bank: A Century and a Half of Philadelphia Banking, 1803–1953* (Philadelphia: Philadelphia National Bank, 1953), pp. 166, 191.

33. *Bulletin Year Book, 1925* (Philadelphia: Bulletin Company, 1925), p. 309; *Harper's Weekly* 56 (April 27, 1912): 8–13.

34. Sylvester K. Stevens, *Pennsylvania, Titan of Industry* (3 vols.; New York: Lewis Historical Publishing Co., 1948), 1:380–84.

35. Ibid., 2:51–53, 76, 3:776.

36. Ibid., 2:41, 128–30, 283–85, 315; Morgan, *City of Firsts*, p. 306.

37. Jack Lutz, *The Poor Richard Club* (Philadelphia: Poor Richard Club, 1953), pp. 3–4.

38. Morley, *Travels in Philadelphia*, p. 57.

39. The proximity between fans and players in intimate Baker Bowl partially accounted for the reputation of Phillies' fans as "the league's most abominable." See David Quentin Voigt, *American Baseball*, vol. 2, *From the Commissioners to Continental Expansion* (Norman: University of Oklahoma Press, 1970), 2:90. Also see Harold Seymour, *Baseball*, vol. 2, *The Golden Years* (New York: Oxford University Press, 1971).

40. Henry James, *The American Scene* (New York: Harper and Brothers, 1907), pp. 264, 267.

41. Harrison Rhodes, "Who Is a Philadelphian?" *Harper's Magazine* 133 (June 1916): 9.

42. Quoted in George Stewart Stokes, *Agnes Repplier, Lady of Letters* (Philadelphia: University of Pennsylvania Press, 1949), p. 2.

43. Wister, "Keystone Crime," p. 446.

44. George Burnham, Jr., to Henry C. Lea, June 16, 1899, Henry C. Lea Papers.

45. Isaac F. Marcosson, "The Millionaire Yield of Philadelphia," *Munsey's Magazine* 47 (July 1912): 505.

46. Morgan, *City of Firsts*, pp. 15–19.

47. See Stokes, *Agnes Repplier*.

48. Federal Writers Project, *Pennsylvania* (Harrisburg: Pennsylvania Historical Commission, 1937), p. 196.

49. Ibid., p. 251; Nathaniel Burt, *The Perennial Philadelphians: The Anatomy of an American Aristocracy* (Boston: Little, Brown, 1963), p. 332.

50. George Biddle, *An American Artist's Story* (Boston: Little, Brown, 1939), p. 211.

51. Federal Writers Project, *Pennsylvania*, p. 221; Burt, *Perennial Philadelphians*, p. 451.

52. *The World Almanac* (New York: Press Publishing Co., 1916), pp. 644–45.

53. Burt, *Perennial Philadelphians*, pp. 478–79; Federal Writers Project, *Pennsylvania*, pp. 235–36.

54. *Public Ledger*, Feb. 7, 12, 1909.

55. Ibid., Feb. 1, 1911.

56. Herbert Kupferberg, *Those Fabulous Philadelphians, The Life and Times of a Great Orchestra* (New York: Scribner's, 1969), pp.

20–51; Frances Anne Wister, *Twenty-five Years of the Philadelphia Orchestra, 1925* (Philadelphia: Women's Committee for the Philadelphia Orchestra, 1925).

57. For a listing of articles on Philadelphia politics at the turn of the century, see Morgan, *City of Firsts*, p. 513.

58. Lincoln Steffens, "Philadelphia: Corrupt and Contented," *McClure's Magazine* 21 (July 1903): 249.

59. Robert D. Bowden, *Boies Penrose, Symbol of an Era* (New York: Greenberg, 1937), pp. 92–93.

60. *The Political Assessment of Office Holders: A Report on the System as Practiced by the Republican Organization in the City of Philadelphia, 1883–1913* (Philadelphia: Department of Public Works, 1913), pp. 7, 11–12.

61. *Public Ledger*, Jan. 5, 1905.

62. *City and State*, June 20, 1901.

63. *Public Ledger*, Dec. 18, 1904.

64. *City and State*, Feb. 1, 15, 1900. See also Clinton R. Woodruff, "Philadelphia's Election Frauds," *The Arena* 24 (Oct. 1900): 397–404.

65. Clinton R. Woodruff, "The Municipal League of Philadelphia," *American Journal of Sociology* 11 (Nov. 1905): 336–43; George W. Pepper, *Philadelphia Lawyer: An Autobiography* (Philadelphia: Lippincott, 1944), pp. 80–81.

66. *Public Ledger*, Nov. 15, 1904; *North American*, Dec. 20, 1904.

67. *North American*, Dec. 21, 1904.

68. *Public Ledger*, Feb. 27, 28, 1905.

69. Henry C. Lea to E. P. Cheyney, Feb. 21, 1905, Henry C. Lea Papers.

70. *North American*, March 15, 1905.

71. George W. Norris, *Ended Episodes* (Philadelphia: John C. Winston, 1937), p. 71; Franklin S. Edmonds, "The Significance of the Recent Reform Movement in Philadelphia," *Annals of the American Academy of Political and Social Science* 27 (Jan. 1906): 185; *North American*, April 24, 28, 1905.

72. *Journal of the Select Council, 1905* (Philadelphia: City of Philadelphia, 1905), p. 57, and Appendix, p. 36.

73. *North American*, April 28, 1905.

74. See *North American, Public Ledger*, and the *Press* for the period April 29–May 1, 1905.

75. *North American*, May 4, 1905.

76. Ibid., May 5, 1905; *Public Ledger*, May 5, 1905.

77. *North American*, May 16, 18, 1905.

78. William S. Vare, *My Forty Years in Politics* (Philadelphia: Roland Swain, 1933), pp. 91–93.

79. Henry C. Lea to E. P. Cheyney, June 9, 1905, Henry C. Lea Papers.

80. Ibid.

81. Norris, *Ended Episodes*, p. 82.

82. Edmonds, "The Significance of the Recent Reform Movement," pp. 185–86.

83. *Inquirer*, Sept. 21, 1905.

84. Vare, *My Forty Years in Politics*, p. 98; *North American*, Sept. 13, 1905.

85. *Public Ledger*, Sept. 12, 1905.

86. *North American*, Sept. 13, 1905.

87. Quoted in *Inquirer*, Oct. 19, 1905.

88. Vare, *My Forty Years in Politics*, p. 97.

89. *Public Ledger*, Nov. 9, 1905.

90. Boies Penrose to Samuel W. Pennypacker, Aug. 24, 1905, in Samuel W. Pennypacker, *The Autobiography of a Pennsylvanian* (Philadelphia: John C. Winston, 1918), p. 393.

91. Quoted in Norris, *Ended Episodes*, p. 82.

92. Clinton R. Woodruff, "Some Permanent Results of the Philadelphia Upheaval of 1905–06," *American Journal of Sociology* 13 (Sept. 1907): 252–71.

93. See Wayne MacVeagh, "The Great Reforms Secured in Pennsylvania," *North American Review* 183 (Oct. 1906): 600; editorial, *The Independent* 60 (Feb. 22, 1906): 466; "The New Spirit of Pennsylvania," *Review of Reviews* 33 (April 1906): 395; "Pennsylvania's Excellent Legislation," *The Outlook* 82 (March 3, 1906): 485; *North American*, June 18, 1906.

94. *Public Ledger*, May 11, 1906; Norris, *Ended Episodes*, p. 84.

95. *Public Ledger*, June 1, Sept. 19, 20, Nov. 3, 8, 1906.

96. Edwin A. Van Valkenburg to Arthur I. Vorys, Sept. 1, 1907, Edwin A. Van Valkenburg Papers, Harvard University.

97. Vare, *My Forty Years in Politics*, pp. 108–10; *Public Ledger*, Nov. 3, 1909.

98. William B. Munro, *The Government of American Cities* (New York: Macmillan, 1919), pp. 376–77.

99. *The Weights and Measures Situation in Philadelphia* (Philadelphia: Bureau of Municipal Research, 1911).

100. Dennis Clark, *The Irish in Philadelphia: Ten Generations of Urban Experience* (Philadelphia: Temple University Press, 1973), pp. 141–42.

101. See Harold Zink, *City Bosses in the United States: A Study of Twenty Municipal Bosses* (Durham, N.C.: Duke University Press, 1930); Vare, *My Forty Years in Politics*, pp. 106–7.

102. *Political Assessment of Office Holders*, p. 7.

103. Norris, *Ended Episodes*, p. 91.

104. Ward W. Pierson, "Harbor Facilities of Philadelphia," *Annals of the American Academy of Political and Social Science* 29 (March 1907): 366–69; "The Docks and Harbors of Some of the Great Commercial Cities of the World," *City Club Bulletin* 1 (Dec. 16, 1909): 108.

105. *Second Annual Message of John E. Reyburn, Mayor of the City of Philadelphia* (Philadelphia: Dunlap, 1909), 1:xlix.

106. "The Budget of the Board of Public Education," *City Club Bulletin* 1 (Nov. 25, 1909): 76.

107. *Ninetieth Annual Report of the Board of Public Education* (Philadelphia: City of Philadelphia, 1909), p. 59.

108. *Fourth Annual Message of John Weaver, Mayor of Philadelphia* (Philadelphia: Dunlap, 1907), 3:6, 25–31.

109. See Sam Bass Warner, Jr., *The Private City: Philadelphia in Three Periods of Its Growth* (Philadelphia: University of Pennsylvania Press, 1968).

110. J. Lynn Barnard and Jessie C. Evans, *Citizenship in Philadelphia* (Philadelphia: John C. Winston, 1919), pp. 137–38; Vare, *My Forty Years in Politics*, p. 93.

111. Charles W. Cheape, *Moving the Masses: Urban Public Transit in New York, Boston, and Philadelphia, 1880–1912* (Cambridge, Mass.: Harvard University Press, 1980), pp. 181–207.

112. Delos F. Wilcox, *Municipal Franchises* (2 vols.; New York: Engineering News Publishing Co., 1911), 2:213; Edwin O. Lewis, "Philadelphia's Relation to the Rapid Transit Company," *Annals of the American Academy of Political and Social Science* 31 (May 1908): 606–9.

113. Cheape, *Moving the Masses*, pp. 203–7.
114. Charles E. Zaretz, *The Amalgamated Clothing Workers of America* (New York: Ancon, 1934), p. 123.
115. Edwin Fenton, "Italians in the Labor Movement," *Pennsylvania History* 26 (April 1959): 136, 143–44.
116. Gladys L. Palmer, "History of the Philadelphia District Textile Council," *American Federationist* 39 (Oct. 1932): 1133–35; Elden LaMar, *The Clothing Workers in Philadelphia* (Philadelphia: Amalgamated Clothing Workers of America, 1940), pp. 27–28.
117. Selig Perlman and Philip Taft, *History of Labor in the United States, 1896–1933*, vol. 4, *Labor Movements* (New York: Macmillan, 1935), 4:343–44; Thomas Roberts, "A History and Analysis of Labor-Management Relations in the Philadelphia Transit Industry" (Ph.D. dissertation, University of Pennsylvania, 1959), pp. 20–32; "Strikes in the Public Service," *The Outlook* 92 (June 12, 1909): 339–40.
118. Perlman and Taft, *History of Labor*, 4:344; *Public Ledger*, Feb. 20, 1910; "The General Strike in Philadelphia," *Current Literature* 48 (April 1910): 363.
119. *Public Ledger*, Feb. 21–24, 1910; Perlman and Taft, *History of Labor*, 4:344–45.
120. Quoted in "The General Strike in Philadelphia," p. 364.
121. *Public Ledger*, March 2, 1910.
122. Ibid., March 11, 1910; Roberts, "History and Analysis," p. 50.
123. Perlman and Taft, *History of Labor*, 4:345.
124. *Public Ledger*, March 24, 1910; Roberts, "History and Analysis," pp. 48–49.
125. Roberts, "History and Analysis," p. 59.
126. "The End of a Futile Strike," *The Outlook* 94 (April 30, 1910): 963.
127. Roberts, "History and Analysis," pp. 62–84.
128. Ibid., pp. 70–114; Perlman and Taft, *History of Labor*, 4:346–48.
129. Cheape, *Moving the Masses*, p. 206.
130. *Smull's Legislative Handbook, 1911* (Harrisburg: Pennsylvania General Assembly, 1911), p. 553; Vare, *My Forty Years in Politics*, pp. 112–13.
131. Vare, *My Forty Years in Politics*, pp. 114–15.
132. Ibid., p. 115; *Public Ledger*, June 13, 1911.
133. For the careers of both Blankenburgs, see Lucretia L. Blankenburg, *The Blankenburgs of Philadelphia* (Philadelphia: John C. Winston, 1928).
134. *North American*, Aug. 1, Sept. 14, 1911; *Public Ledger*, Aug. 1, Sept. 18, 19, 1911.
135. J. Hampton Moore, *Roosevelt and the Old Guard* (Philadelphia: Macrae-Smith, 1925), p. 246.
136. Vare, *My Forty Years in Politics*, p. 116; *Public Ledger*, Sept. 20, Nov. 1, 1911.
137. *Public Ledger*, Sept. 20, 22, 1911.
138. Blankenburg, *The Blankenburgs of Philadelphia*, p. 67.
139. *Public Ledger*, Oct. 2, 1911.
140. Rudolph Blankenburg to Henry F. Walton, Oct. 10, 1910, Rudolph Blankenburg Papers, Historical Society of Pennsylvania.
141. *North American*, Oct. 24, Nov. 3, 1911.
142. Blankenburg, *The Blankenburgs of Philadelphia*, p. 43; *Public Ledger*, Nov. 9, 1911.
143. *Public Ledger*, Oct. 27, 1911. George Norris later wrote: "I have always believed that if he [Earle] had refrained from making speeches he would surely have been elected" (Norris, *Ended Episodes*, p. 87).
144. *Public Ledger*, Oct. 28, Nov. 9, 1911.
145. Ibid., Nov. 11, 1911; Karl de Schweinitz, "Philadelphia No Longer Corrupt and Unashamed," *The Survey* 29 (Jan. 18, 1913): 506.
146. *Public Ledger*, Dec. 5, 1911. The most comprehensive study of Blankenburg's administration is Donald W. Disbrow, "The Progressive Movement in Philadelphia, 1910–1916" (Ph.D. dissertation, University of Rochester, 1957); a shorter version by the same author is "Reform in Philadelphia Under Mayor Blankenburg, 1912–1916," *Pennsylvania History* 27 (Oct. 1960): 379–96.
147. For Cooke's philosophy of city management, see his book, *Our Cities Awake* (New York: Doubleday, 1918).
148. A summary report of Cooke's work can be found in Blankenburg, *Fifth Annual Message*, 2:1–35. See also T. Henry Walnut, "Reform in Philadelphia," *New Republic* 5 (Nov. 27, 1915): 92–94; de Schweinitz, "Philadelphia No Longer Corrupt and Unashamed," pp. 505–6.
149. "Police Progress in Philadelphia During the Year 1912," *City Club Bulletin* 6 (April 23, 1913): 405–16.
150. Norris, *Ended Episodes*, pp. 89–117. See report of Department of Wharves, Docks, and Ferries in Blankenburg, *Fifth Annual Message*, 1:377–405.
151. *Report of Transit Commissioner* (Philadelphia: City of Philadelphia, 1913), 1:5–30, 124, 130.
152. Barnard and Evans, *Citizenship in Philadelphia*, pp. 232–37.
153. Blankenburg, *Fifth Annual Message*, 2:138–51, 433, 446; George Norris, "Philadelphia Strabismus," *The Outlook* 110 (Dec. 29, 1915): 1050–51.
154. Blankenburg, *Fifth Annual Message*, 2:3; Charles F. Jenkins, "The Blankenburg Administration in Philadelphia: A Symposium," *National Municipal Review* 5 (April 1916): 212.
155. "The Vice Problem in Philadelphia," *The Survey* 30 (May 24, 1913): 259.
156. Disbrow, "Reform in Philadelphia," pp. 386–88; Norris, "Philadelphia Strabismus," pp. 1051–52.
157. *Public Ledger*, Jan. 31, 1913.
158. *North American*, Feb. 24, 1913; Blankenburg, *The Blankenburgs of Philadelphia*, p. 78.
159. *North American*, April 7, 1912; Norris, "Philadelphia Strabismus," p. 1051.
160. Disbrow, "Reform in Philadelphia," pp. 388–89.
161. *North American*, March 21, 1913. See also Van Valkenburg's evaluation of Blankenburg's administration in Jenkins, "The Blankenburg Administration," pp. 219–22.
162. *North American*, Nov. 7, 1913.
163. Ibid., Nov. 6, 1914. For the 1914 campaign, see M. Nelson McGeary, "Gifford Pinchot's 1914 Campaign," *PMHB* 81 (July 1957): 303–18.
164. *Public Ledger*, Sept. 22, 26, 30, 1915; *Press*, Sept. 30, 1915.
165. Disbrow, "Reform in Philadelphia," pp. 392–93.
166. Lefferts A. Loetscher, "Presbyterianism and Revivals in Philadelphia," *PMHB* 68 (Jan. 1944): 87–89.
167. Norris, "Philadelphia Strabismus," p. 1052.
168. *North American*, Nov. 3, 1915.
169. Pepper, *Philadelphia Lawyer*, p. 93; Robert L. Bloom, "Edwin A. Van Valkenburg and the Philadelphia North American, 1899–1924," *Pennsylvania History* 21 (April 1954):

121; Edwin A. Van Valkenburg to Hiram Johnson, Feb. 12, 1917, Van Valkenburg Papers.
170. Quoted in *Public Ledger*, Jan. 24, 1916.
171. Joyce, ed., *Story of Philadelphia*, p. 315; *Public Ledger*, Dec. 3, 1914.
172. *Public Ledger*, May 11, 1915.
173. Quoted ibid.
174. "Both Sides of the Quaker Argument," *Literary Digest* 57 (May 11, 1918): 31; *Public Ledger*, Jan. 16, 1918.
175. Philadelphia War History Committee, *Philadelphia in the World War, 1914–1919* (New York: Wynkoop, Hallenbeck, Crawford, 1922), pp. 378–80; Joyce, ed., *Story of Philadelphia*, p. 321.
176. War History Committee, *Philadelphia in the World War*, pp. 421–46.
177. Ibid., pp. 613–18.
178. *Public Ledger*, Nov. 21, 1917; Jan. 3, 28, 1918.
179. Joyce, ed., *Story of Philadelphia*, p. 336; War History Committee, *Philadelphia in the World War*, pp. 644–46.
180. Mark Sullivan, *Our Times: The United States, 1900–1925* (6 vols.; New York: Scribner's, 1926–1935), 5:469–74; Joyce, ed., *Story of Philadelphia*, p. 326.
181. *Evening Bulletin*, Dec. 24, 1917.
182. Carl Wittke, *German-Americans and the World War* (Columbus: Ohio State Historical Society, 1936), pp. 178, 185; *Public Ledger*, Sept. 28, 1918.
183. War History Committee, *Philadelphia in the World War*, p. 37; *Public Ledger*, May 15, 1918.
184. War History Committee, *Philadelphia in the World War*, p. 128; *Sunday Bulletin*, Nov. 10, 1968.

185. Sullivan, *Our Times*, 5:353–59.
186. War History Committee, *Philadelphia in the World War*, pp. 94–125, 134–52.
187. *Press*, Oct. 14, 19, 30, 1917.
188. William A. McGarry, "Government by Murder," *The Independent* 92 (Oct. 27, 1917): 191; Vare, *My Forty Years in Politics*, p. 133.
189. McGarry, "Government by Murder," p. 191.
190. "Philadelphia's Deplorable Murder," *Literary Digest* 55 (Oct. 13, 1917): 48–52.
191. Ibid., p. 52; Joyce, ed., *Story of Philadelphia*, p. 318; *Inquirer*, Jan. 14, Feb. 1, 1919.
192. *Inquirer*, Sept. 28, 1917.
193. Vare, *My Forty Years in Politics*, p. 134; McGarry, "Government by Murder," p. 191.
194. Clinton R. Woodruff, "Progress in Philadelphia," *American Journal of Sociology* 26 (Nov. 1920): 328–29.
195. Neva R. Deardoff, "To Unshackle Philadelphia," *The Survey* 42 (April 5, 1919): 20.
196. Frederick P. Gruenberg, "Philadelphia Stirreth," *National Municipal Review* 8 (Aug. 1919): 19–21.
197. Deardoff, "To Unshackle Philadelphia," p. 20; Woodruff, "Progress in Philadelphia," p. 328.
198. Woodruff, "Progress in Philadelphia," p. 328; "How Philadelphia Got Its New Charter," *The Outlook* 122 (July 16, 1919): 421.
199. Woodruff, "Progress in Philadelphia," p. 327.
200. Gruenberg, "Philadelphia Stirreth," pp. 420–22; "A New Charter for Philadelphia," *The Outlook* 122 (July 1919): 420–21.
201. "Philadelphia's Epoch-Making Charter," *The American City* 21 (Sept. 1919): 202.
202. Wister, "Keystone Crime," p. 447.

THE CITY EMBRACES "NORMALCY," 1919–1929

1. Quoted in J. T. Salter, "Party Organization in Philadelphia: The Ward Committeeman," *American Political Science Review* 27 (Aug. 1933): 621; quoted in Fred D. Baldwin, "Smedley Darlington Butler and Prohibition Enforcement in Philadelphia, 1924–1925," *Pennsylvania Magazine of History and Biography* (hereafter cited as *PMHB*) 84 (July 1960): 365.
2. Reprinted in Christopher Morley, *Travels in Philadelphia* (Philadelphia: David McKay, 1920), pp. 39–45.
3. *Public Ledger*, Jan. 3, 4, 5, 1920; Nicholas B. Wainwright, *History of the Philadelphia Electric Company, 1881–1961* (Philadelphia: Philadelphia Electric Co., 1961), pp. 143–44.
4. The first woman in Philadelphia was "assessed" to vote on Aug. 25, 1920 (George Morgan, *The City of Firsts* [Philadelphia: Historical Publications Society, 1926], p. 462).
5. F. P. Gruenberg, "Philadelphia's City Charter," *Survey*, Aug. 9, 1919, p. 701; "New Charter for Philadelphia," *The Outlook*, July 16, 1919, pp. 420–21.
6. Robert Edward Drayer, "J. Hampton Moore: An Old Fashioned Republican" (Ph.D. dissertation, University of Pennsylvania, 1961), p. 158; Gruenberg, "Philadelphia's City Charter," p. 701; Morgan, *City of Firsts*, p. 295.
7. Morgan, *City of Firsts*, pp. 292–93, 462.
8. "Philadelphia's Political Revolt," *The Outlook*, Oct. 1, 1919, pp. 170–71; *Public Ledger*, Jan. 2, 4, 5, 6, 1920; Morgan, *City of Firsts*, pp. 292, 457–58, 461.

9. *Public Ledger*, Jan. 1, 4, 1920.
10. Morgan, *City of Firsts*, p. 293.
11. Drayer, "J. Hampton Moore," p. 375; accounts of bandits' activities appear in both *Bulletin Almanac* (Philadelphia: Bulletin, annual) and Morgan's "Chronology" in *City of Firsts*.
12. *Municipal Street Cleaning in Philadelphia* (Philadelphia: Bureau of Municipal Research, June 1924), pp. 100–5.
13. *The Water Supply Problem of Philadelphia* (Philadelphia: Bureau of Municipal Research, May 1922), p. 53.
14. Morgan, *City of Firsts*, p. 463; William S. Twining, "Annual Report of Department of City Transit of the City of Philadelphia," a report to the city Council on the Frankford El, March 30, 1920, typescript in Historical Society of Pennsylvania (hereafter cited as HSP); *The First Operating Sections of the Frankford Elevated Railway and Bustleton Surface Line: A Souvenir Booklet Giving a Brief Account of Their Construction, Equipment and Operating Agreement* (Philadelphia, Nov. 4, 1922); *Bulletin Almanac, 1924*, pp. 52–53.
15. William S. Twining, Director, "Annual Report of the Department of City Transit of the City of Philadelphia"; Drayer, "J. Hampton Moore," pp. 202, 246, 247.
16. *Bulletin Almanac, 1924*, p. 212.
17. Sam Bass Warner, Jr., on the contrary, thinks that money spent on subways and elevated lines was a "misallocation of resources needed

for social and welfare projects." See his *The Private City: Philadelphia in Three Periods of Its Growth* (Philadelphia: University of Pennsylvania Press, 1968), pp. 193–94.

18. Morgan, *City of Firsts*, p. 293.
19. William S. Vare, *My Forty Years in Politics* (Philadelphia: Roland Swain, 1933), p. 136; Morgan, *City of Firsts*, pp. 462, 463.
20. Morgan, *City of Firsts*, p. 293.
21. Ibid., p. 243; Drayer, "J. Hampton Moore," p. 164; *Record*, Sept. 28, 1923; *Bulletin Almanac, 1924*, p. 212.
22. G. Burnap, "Park Foresight in Exposition Planning," *Architectural Record* 52 (Aug. 1922): 160–64; Wainwright, *Philadelphia Electric Company*, pp. 188–89; *Bulletin Almanac, 1924*, p. 211; ibid., *1926*, pp. 97, 330, 331, 332; Morgan, *City of Firsts*, pp. 463–64, 470.
23. Morgan, *City of Firsts*, p. 470; *Bulletin Almanac, 1926*, p. 337; E. L. Austin and Odell Hauser, *The Sesqui-Centennial: A Record Based on Official Data and Department Reports* (Philadelphia: Current Publications, 1929).
24. Morgan, *City of Firsts*, p. 477; Wainwright, *Philadelphia Electric Company*, p. 190; *Bulletin Almanac, 1926*, pp. 337, 338; ibid., *1927*, pp. 106, 352.
25. *Bulletin Almanac, 1927*, p. 352.
26. Ibid., pp. 352, 353; Wainwright, *Philadelphia Electric Company*, p. 189; T. Chalkley Matlack, "The Diurnal Record of the Life of T. Chalkley Matlack as Told by Him in His Diaries from 1887 Onward," typescript, HSP, 2:267.
27. Wainwright, *Philadelphia Electric Company*, p. 190.
28. *Bulletin Almanac, 1927*, p. 354; ibid., *1928*, p. 377; T. Henry Walnut, "S. Davis Wilson, Mayor of Philadelphia," in J. T. Salter, ed., *The American Politician* (Chapel Hill: University of North Carolina Press, 1938), p. 289.
29. *Abolition of Grade Crossings and the Creation of Opportunities for Commercial and Industrial Development* (Philadelphia: Department of Public Works, 1913), pp. 14–16.
30. "Map of Land Use" (Philadelphia: Zoning Commission, 1921), and map showing the "Location of Dwellings Built, 1927–1931," both in the Free Library of Philadelphia, Map Department; Alan Weinberg and Dale Fields, *Ward Genealogy of the City and County of Philadelphia* (Philadelphia: Department of Records, n.d.); Warner, *The Private City*, p. 172, n.13, reports that 4248 more persons lived in the Forty-eighth Ward in 1930 than had been there in 1920, but that South Philadelphia as a whole had lost 17,694 during the same decade.
31. Morgan, *City of Firsts*, pp. 462, 463, 464, 467, 468, 474; *Bulletin Almanac, 1925*, p. 337; ibid., *1926*, pp. 330, 331; Warner, *The Private City*, pp. 202–3; J. T. Salter, *The People's Choice: Philadelphia's William S. Vare* (New York: Exposition Press, 1971), pp. 58–59.
32. Boies Penrose, quoted in John Lukacs, *Philadelphia: Patricians and Philistines, 1900–1950* (New York: Farrar, Straus and Giroux, 1981), p. 59.
33. *Public Ledger*, Jan. 1, 2, 1920.
34. Ibid., Jan. 3, 1920; Morgan, *City of Firsts*, pp. 462, 463, 464; *Bulletin Almanac, 1924*, pp. 211, 212; "How Wet Is Pennsylvania?" *Literary Digest* 79 (Nov. 10, 1923): 38–44;

Baldwin, "Prohibition Enforcement in Philadelphia," p. 352; O. H. P. Garrett, "Why They Cleaned up Philadelphia," *New Republic* 38 (Feb. 27, 1924): 11–14.

35. *Record*, quoted by Baldwin, "Prohibition Enforcement in Philadelphia," p. 354.
36. *Bulletin Almanac, 1925*, pp. 332, 333.
37. Ibid., p. 334; Morgan, *City of Firsts*, pp. 467, 468; Baldwin, "Prohibition Enforcement in Philadelphia," pp. 355–56; William G. Shepherd, "Why Criminals Are Not Afraid: General Butler's Battle of Philadelphia," *Collier's* 76 (Nov. 28, 1925): 18–19; "Philadelphia Reformed and Discontented," *Literary Digest* 83 (Oct. 11, 1924): 14–15.
38. *Bulletin Almanac, 1925*, pp. 334, 336, 337, 338; Morgan, *City of Firsts*, p. 468; Baldwin, "Prohibition Enforcement in Philadelphia," pp. 361–62.
39. J. T. Salter, "The Corrupt Lower Courts of Philadelphia," *American Mercury* 33 (Oct. 1934): 237; William G. Shepherd, "The Price of Liquor: Philadelphia's Amazing Defiance of the Prohibition Law," *Collier's* 82 (Dec. 1, 1928): 41; id., "Crime in the Home of Its Friends," *Collier's* 76 (Dec. 5, 1925): 18–19; id., "Crime Preserved in Alcohol," *Collier's* 76 (Dec. 12, 1925): 7–9; *Bulletin Almanac, 1925*, p. 336; ibid., *1926*, pp. 330, 331.
40. Quoted in Baldwin, "Prohibition Enforcement in Philadelphia," p. 356.
41. Ibid, 365.
42. *Bulletin Almanac, 1925*, p. 334; ibid., *1926*, pp. 332, 336–37, 338; Wainwright, *Philadelphia Electric Company*, p. 187; *Annual Report of the Molly Pitcher Club of Pennsylvania, October 1924* (Philadelphia: Privately printed, 1924); Morgan, *City of Firsts*, pp. 475, 480; Baldwin, "Prohibition Enforcement in Philadelphia," p. 359; *Report of W. Freeland Kendrick, Mayor of the City of Philadelphia, 1925* (Philadelphia: City of Philadelphia, 1926), p. 29.
43. *Bulletin Almanac, 1926*, p. 337; Baldwin, "Prohibition Enforcement in Philadelphia," pp. 361–62.
44. *Bulletin Almanac, 1926*, p. 337; *Record*, Dec. 24, 1925, quoted in Baldwin, "Prohibition Enforcement in Philadelphia," p. 368.
45. Drayer, "J. Hampton Moore," p. 280; Walnut, "S. Davis Wilson," p. 294.
46. *Bulletin Almanac, 1925*, p. 333; ibid., *1926*, pp. 330, 335; ibid., *1927*, pp. 353, 354; ibid., *1928*, pp. 378, 379; ibid., *1929*, p. 410; ibid., *1930*, pp. 452, 453.
47. Ibid., *1925*, p. 332; ibid., *1926*, p. 334; ibid., *1928*, p. 378; Drayer, "J. Hampton Moore," p. 215; Shepherd, "Why Criminals Are Not Afraid," p. 18; *Fortune* 13 (June 1936): 179.
48. *Bulletin Almanac, 1929*, p. 411.
49. Ibid., *1928*, pp. 377, 378, 379.
50. Ibid., *1927*, p. 377; ibid., *1929*, p. 410; ibid., *1930*, p. 453.
51. Salter, *The People's Choice*, p. 80; *Bulletin Almanac, 1929*, pp. 409, 410, 411.
52. *Bulletin Almanac, 1929*, pp. 410, 411.
53. Ibid., pp. 410, 411; ibid., *1930*, pp. 451, 452; Shepherd, "The Price of Liquor," p. 38.
54. Shepherd, "The Price of Liquor," p. 9; *Bulletin Almanac, 1929*, p. 411.
55. *Bulletin Almanac, 1929*, p. 411; ibid., *1930*, p. 451.
56. Shepherd, "The Price of Liquor," pp. 8–9, 38–41; Nicholas B. Wainwright, *History of the Philadelphia National Bank: A Century and a Half of Philadelphia Banking, 1803–*

1953 (Philadelphia: Philadelphia National Bank, 1953), p. 199.

57. Taken from the author's review of Salter *The People's Choice*, in *PMHB* 94 (July 1972): 413–14.

58. Quoted in Salter, "Party Organization in Philadelphia," pp. 618–27.

59. Ibid.

60. Salter, *The People's Choice*, pp. 66, 67–68; Morgan, *City of Firsts*, p. 277.

61. Morgan, *City of Firsts*, pp. 474, 475, 476, 477, 478, 480; *Bulletin Almanac, 1926*, pp. 336, 337, 338; ibid., *1927*, p. 354; Drayer, "J. Hampton Moore," p. 256; Warner, *The Private City*, pp. 217–18.

62. Irwin F. Greenberg, "Philadelphia Democrats Get a New Deal: The Election of 1933," *PMHB* 97 (April 1973): 210–11, 234–240.

63. Salter, *The People's Choice*, pp. 32, 42–43; John Lukacs, *Philadelphia: Patricians and Philistines, 1900–1950* (New York: Farrar, Strauss, and Giroux, 1980). pp. 221, 225; Vare, *My Forty Years in Politics*, pp. 153, 154–55.

64. Drayer, "J. Hampton Moore," p. 358.

65. Vare, *My Forty Years in Politics*, p. 169; Salter, *The People's Choice*, p. 79.

66. Drayer, "J. Hampton Moore," p. 255; Vare, *My Forty Years in Politics*, p. 182; Salter, *The People's Choice*, p. 79; *Bulletin Almanac, 1928*, pp. 66, 378, 379.

67. *Bulletin Almanac, 1929*, p. 411.

68. Salter, *The People's Choice*, p. 82; Joseph P. Tumulty to Albert M. Greenfield, Dec. 3, 1927, Albert M. Greenfield Papers, HSP.

69. Salter, *The People's Choice*, p. 80; *Bulletin Almanac, 1929*, p. 450.

70. *Bulletin Almanac, 1930*, p. 453; Drayer, "J. Hampton Moore," p. 285; Salter, *The People's Choice*, pp. 81, 88.

71. Much of the material in this section is from Allen F. Davis and Mark H. Haller, eds., *The Peoples of Philadelphia: A History of Ethnic Groups and Lower-Class Life, 1790–1940* (Philadelphia: Temple University Press, 1973). The essays used are: Dennis J. Clark, "The Philadelphia Irish: Persistent Presence," pp. 135–54 (hereafter referred to as Clark, "Philadelphia Irish"); John F. Sutherland, "Housing the Poor in the City of Homes," pp. 175–201 (hereafter referred to as Sutherland, "Housing the Poor"); Caroline Golab, "The Immigrant and the City: Poles, Italians, and Jews in Philadelphia, 1870–1920," pp. 203–30 (hereafter referred to as Golab, "The Immigrant"); Maxwell Whiteman, "Philadelphia's Jewish Neighborhoods," pp. 231–54 (hereafter referred to as Whiteman, "Jewish Neighborhoods"); and Richard A. Varbero, "Philadelphia's South Italians in the 1920s," pp. 255–75 (hereafter referred to as Varbero, "South Italians"). Here see Golab, "The Immigrant," pp. 203–5.

72. Henry James, "Philadelphia," in *American Scene* (London: Chapman & Hall, 1907), p. 271.

73. Whiteman, "Jewish Neighborhoods," pp. 248–50.

74. Varbero, "South Italians," pp. 260–61.

75. Golab, "The Immigrant," pp. 210–12; R. T. Moriarty, "Little Warsaw," *Bulletin*, Feb. 18, 1968; *Bulletin Almanac, 1929*, citing U.S. estimate of Philadelphia's population in 1928, notes that the city had 15 percent more skilled workers than New York, and 10 percent more than Chicago (p. 107).

76. Golab, "The Immigrant," p. 208.

77. Emma Jones Lapsansky, *Before the Model City: An Historical Exploration of North Philadelphia* (Philadelphia: Philadelphia Historical Commission, 1969), p. 18.

78. Golab, "The Immigrant," p. 208.

79. Lapsansky, *Before the Model City*, pp. 44–45.

80. Drayer, "J. Hampton Moore," p. 105.

81. Whiteman, "Jewish Neighborhoods," p. 242; Varbero, "South Italians," p. 265.

82. Varbero, "South Italians," pp. 255, 258.

83. Ibid., pp. 257, 259, 262.

84. Ibid., pp. 266, 267, 270–72.

85. Ibid., pp. 260–61; Sutherland, "Housing the Poor," pp. 189–96.

86. Clark, "Philadelphia Irish," pp. 136–38; Rem Rieder, "Schuylkill: A 'Little Irish Village' Tucked into Center City," *Bulletin*, Nov. 23, 1969.

87. Clark, "Philadelphia Irish," pp. 143–47.

88. Morgan, *City of Firsts*, pp. 462, 464, 465; *Bulletin Almanac, 1924*, p. 211; ibid., *1926*, p. 330; ibid., *1928*, p. 377.

89. "Weekend," *Inquirer*, Feb. 27, 1981; Nathaniel Burt, *The Perennial Philadelphians: The Anatomy of an American Aristocracy* (Boston: Little, Brown, 1963), pp. 300, 310; *Bulletin Almanac, 1925*, pp. 71, 74; ibid., *1926*, p. 206.

90. *Bulletin Almanac, 1930*, p. 410.

91. Lukacs, "Agnes Repplier," in *Philadelphia: Patricians and Philistines*, p. 95; id., "Owen Wister," in ibid., p. 241; Burt, *Perennial Philadelphians*, pp. 390–93.

92. Vincent Jubilee, "In the Shadow of Harlem," *Pennsylvania Gazette* 79 (May 1981): 37–39. (The January 20, 1920, issue of the *Ledger* carried an advertisement for the Dunbar Theater, Broad and Lombard, where *The Silent Witness*, "a drama of today" was to be presented "by a carefully selected company of colored artists.")

93. *Bulletin Almanac, 1926*, p. 337; Herbert Kupferberg, *Those Fabulous Philadelphians: The Life and Times of a Great Orchestra* (New York: Scribner's, 1969), pp. 73–74.

94. "Philadelphia's Amazing Operatic Situation," *Etude* 47 (Sept. 1929): 668.

95. The downtown theaters were the New Forrest, the Walnut, the Chestnut Street Opera House, the Garrick, the Erlanger, the Fox-Locust, the Broad, Keith's, the Lyric, the Aldelphia, the Broad Street, and the Shubert (Morgan, *City of Firsts*, pp. 233, 465; *Bulletin Almanac, 1926*, p. 331; ibid., *1928*, p. 378; ibid., *1930*, p. 247).

96. Quoted in Joseph Jackson, *Literary Landmarks of Philadelphia* (Philadelphia: David McKay, 1939), pp. 250–51.

97. Burt, *Perennial Philadelphians*, p. 500.

98. M. Montgomery, "Art Week, Philadelphia's Innovation," *International Studio* 75 (July 1922): 352–355; Lukacs, "Albert Coombs Barnes," in *Philadelphia: Patricians and Philistines*, p. 268.

99. Lukacs, "Albert Coombs Barnes," p. 269.

100. Morgan, *City of Firsts*, p. 475; George and Mary Roberts, *Triumph on Fairmount: Fiske Kimball and the Philadelphia Museum of Art* (Philadelphia: Lippincott, 1959), pp. 88–93.

101. *Bulletin Almanac, 1927*, p. 259; ibid., *1929*, p. 107; ibid., *1930*, p. 272.

102. Ibid., *1930*, p. 274; Morgan, *City of Firsts*, p. 327; *World's Work* 60 (Feb. 1931): 40.

103. *Bulletin Almanac, 1925*, p. 338; ibid., *1926*, p. 333; ibid., *1927*, p. 352; ibid., *1928*, p. 377.

104. *Review of Reviews* 80 (Dec. 1929): 59–64.

105. Wainwright, *Philadelphia Electric Company*, pp. 148, 149, 150–51, 163, 173–74, 193–94, 196, 198; *Bulletin Almanac, 1928*, p. 379; ibid., *1929*, p. 410.
106. Wainwright, *Philadelphia Electric Company*, pp. 206, 212, 214.
107. Morgan, *City of Firsts*, p. 480; *Bulletin Almanac, 1927*, pp. 350, 351.
108. Morley, *Travels in Philadelphia*, p. 143; *Public Ledger*, Jan. 4, 1920; Blake McKelvey, *The Emergence of Metropolitan America, 1915–1966* (New Brunswick, N.J.: Rutgers University Press, 1968), p. 43; *Bulletin Almanac, 1925*, p. 335; ibid., *1928*, p. 377; Morgan, *City of Firsts*, pp. 473, 479.
109. *Bulletin Almanac, 1926*, p. 337.
110. Ibid., *1927*, pp. 351, 352; ibid., *1928*, p. 377.
111. Ibid., *1925*, pp. 332, 335, 336; ibid., *1926*, pp. 334, 337, 338; Morgan, *City of Firsts*, p. 323.

112. *Bulletin Almanac, 1926*, pp. 331, 335; ibid., *1927*, pp. 353, 354; ibid., *1928*, p. 377.
113. Ibid., *1927*, p. 354; ibid., *1929*, pp. 410, 411; ibid., *1930*, pp. 95, 450, 452, 453; Walnut, "S. Davis Wilson," p. 289.
114. *The Outlook*, Mar. 30, 1927, pp. 395–96; Drayer, "J. Hampton Moore," pp. 190–95.
115. Nicholas B. Wainwright, *Philadelphia National Bank*, pp. 209–10; "Managing Philadelphia's Rapid Transit," *National Municipal Review* 21 (April 1932): 252–53; *Bulletin Almanac, 1930*, p. 95.
116. George W. Norris, *Ended Episodes* (Philadelphia: John C. Winston, 1937), p. 209.
117. Wainwright, *Philadelphia National Bank*, pp. 189, 190, 194–96, 203, 204–5.
118. Ibid., pp. 200, 201, 205; Norris, *Ended Episodes*, p. 209.

DEPRESSION AND WAR, 1929–1946

1. Federal Writers' Project, *Philadelphia: A Guide to the Nation's Birthplace* (Philadelphia: William Penn Associates, 1937), p. 3; R. E. S. Thompson, "Winner Gives All: Private Housing Project for Negroes," *Survey Graphic* 30 (May 1941): 274.
2. *Bulletin Almanac, 1930*, p. 259; *Inquirer*, Dec. 21, 23, 1929, Jan. 3, 1930; Ford, Bacon & Davis, Inc., Engineers, "Report with Supplements, Location of Airport, Philadelphia, Pa., District," prepared for a Joint Committee of the Chamber of Commerce and the Regional Planning Federation on Air Terminal Survey, Philadelphia (in author's collection); a clipping, not identified by date or publication, in "City Architects' Scrapbook," 1920–c. 1939 (in City Archives and hereafter cited as "Scrapbook") proposed that Hog Island become a free port.
3. *Inquirer*, Jan. 3, 1930.
4. Ibid., Dec. 21, 1929, Jan. 3, 1930.
5. *Bulletin Almanac, 1933* (Philadelphia: Bulletin, annual), p. 105.
6. *American City*, March 1931, p. 128; Robert Edward Drayer, "J. Hampton Moore: An Old Fashioned Republican" (Ph.D. dissertation, University of Pennsylvania, 1961), pp. 246–47.
7. *Bulletin Almanac, 1930*, pp. 88, 98, 99; ibid., *1933*, p. 82.
8. Ibid., *1930*, pp. 255, 260–70, 282: ibid., *1933*, pp. 260, 286, 302; ibid., *1936*, p. 260; Russell Davenport, "Philadelphia," *Fortune* 13 (June 1936): 67, 69; clipping from *Public Ledger*, n.d., in "Scrapbook"; Blake McKelvey, *The Emergence of Metropolitan America, 1915–1966* (New Brunswick, N.J.: Rutgers University Press, 1968), p. 115; B. J. Newman, "Housing Research in Philadelphia," *Architectural Record* 74 (Sept. 1933): 170–74; D. Russell Connor, *Fifty Years on Chestnut Street: Federal Reserve Bank of Philadelphia* (Philadelphia: Privately printed, 1946), pp. 15–17; Richard J. Webster, *Philadelphia Preserved* (Philadelphia: Temple University Press, 1976), pp. 141, 374, n.44; Harvey W. Corbett, "The Skyscraper and the Automobile Have Made the Modern City," *Studies in the Arts and Architecture* (Philadelphia: University of Pennsylvania Press, 1941), pp. 107–13; Henry James, "Philadelphia," in *American*

Scene* (London: Chapman & Hall, 1907), p. 265.
9. "Scrapbook," clipping, Nov. 13, 1930, no publication noted.
10. *Bulletin Almanac, 1930*, pp. 273–74, 280–81; ibid., *1933*, pp. 103, 317; ibid., *1936*, pp. 260, 293–96. The Regional Planning Federation's report (Dec. 1931) noted that about 75 percent of the region's domestic sewage was discharged untreated into the area's streams (*Regional Planning: The Region—Past, Present and Future, A Digest of the Policies, Principles, Procedure and Findings of the Regional Planning Federation of the Philadelphia Tri-State District* [Philadelphia: Regional Planning Federation, Dec. 1931], p. 27).
11. "A Proposed Plan for the Philadelphia Approaches to the Delaware River Bridge . . . May 1930" (in author's collection). There were two new bridges north of the Delaware River Bridge: the Tacony-Palmyra Bridge (opened Aug. 14, 1929) and the Burlington-Bristol Bridge (opened May 2, 1931). The Delaware River Joint Commission, evidence of continued interest in regional cooperation, was appointed on July 1, 1931 (*Bulletin Almanac, 1933*, pp. 104, 105). See also *Bulletin Almanac, 1930*, pp. 260–62; and brochure in Historical Society of Pennsylvania.
12. *Bulletin Almanac, 1930*, p. 262; ibid., *1933*, pp. 96, 316–19; ibid., *1936*, p. 260; *Sunday Ledger*, Jan. 15, 1933, clipping in "Scrapbook"; C. E. Myers, "Underground Pedestrian Concourse for Philadelphia," *American City* 41 (Nov. 1929): 146–47; McKelvey, *Emergence of Metropolitan America*, p. 106.
13. On municipal ties with contractors, see Drayer, "J. Hampton Moore," pp. 180–85, 292, 320. The owners of property on the east side of the Schuylkill were rumored to be in line to gain $5 million. There were 11,006 building permits issued in 1927, in 1933 just 4672, and not until the architectural explosion of the 1950s was the 1927 figure reached again (Webster, *Philadelphia Preserved*, p. 357, n.65). Clipping, 1933, no date or newspaper noted, in the possession of the author, stated that many permits were for work to be done on newly legalized breweries.
14. Davenport, "Philadelphia," pp. 190, 192.
15. Ibid., pp. 186–90; J. David Stern, *Memoirs*

of a Maverick Publisher (New York: Simon & Schuster, 1962), pp. 180–82; for the closing of the Integrity Trust, see *Bulletin Almanac, 1941*, p. 516.

16. Davenport, "Philadelphia," p. 192; Stern, *Memoirs*, p. 200. Note the story of Greenfield's visit to the *Record* office after FDR's nomination and his comment that he was "thinking over" switching his support from Hoover to Roosevelt.

17. E. Digby Baltzell, *Philadelphia Gentlemen: The Making of a National Upper Class* (New York: The Free Press, 1966), pp. 37, 39, 389; Davenport, "Philadelphia," p. 208; *Time*, Nov. 30, 1936, p. 57.

18. Some banks opened within three days, others at longer intervals, depending on the FDIC's assessment of their stability (W. Waldron, "Massa, tell 'em we're rising! Career of R. R. Wright, leading Negro Banker," reprint from *Progressive*, March 12, 1945, in *Readers Digest* 46 [April 1945]: 53–56).

19. *Bulletin Almanac, 1936*, p. 69. Some closed banks later were adapted for use as state liquor stores (see *Bulletin*, Dec. 19, 1933).

20. *Bulletin Almanac, 1930*, p. 282, citing report of Philadelphia Housing Association; record of Van Pelt Street foreclosures in City Archives; Drayer, "J. Hampton Moore," p. 323; Davenport, "Philadelphia," p. 186.

21. *Bulletin Almanac, 1930*, p. 43; J. F. Dewhurst and R. R. Nathan, "Social and Economic Character of Unemployment in Philadelphia, April, 1930," *U.S. Bureau of Labor Bulletin* 555 (1932): 1–64; Karl de Schweinitz, "Philadelphia Takes Heart," *Survey* 66 (May 15, 1931): 217–19; "Unemployment in Philadelphia, April 1929 to May 1935," *Monthly Labor Review* 41 (Aug. 1935): 352.

22. De Schweinitz, "Philadelphia Takes Heart," p. 218; *Bulletin Almanac, 1932*, p. 51; ibid., *1938*, p. 472; Drayer, "J. Hampton Moore," p. 304.

23. *Bulletin Almanac, 1932*, pp. 51, 52; de Schweinitz, "Philadelphia Takes Heart," pp. 217–19.

24. Drayer, "J. Hampton Moore," p. 305; *Bulletin Almanac, 1933*, p. 102.

25. Drayer, "J. Hampton Moore," pp. 305, 306; "Unemployed Citizens League of Philadelphia," *Monthly Labor Review* 36 (March 1933): 495; E. Clague, "When Relief Stops What Do They 'Eat?" *Survey* 68 (Nov. 15, 1932): 583–85.

26. Clague, "When Relief Stops What Do They Eat?" p. 584; *Bulletin Almanac, 1936*, pp. 346–48.

27. George Wilson, *Yesterday's Philadelphia* (Miami: E. A. Seamann, 1975), p. 108.

28. Charles E. Peterson, "HABS—In and Out of Philadelphia," in Webster, *Philadelphia Preserved*, pp. xxviii–xxxi; *Ledger*, May 5, 1932, clipping in "Scrapbook"; "City of Past Preserved for City of Future," clipping, no date, no newspaper, file in author's possession.

29. *Bulletin Almanac, 1936*, p. 67.

30. Drayer, "J. Hampton Moore," p. 302.

31. Mauritz A. Hallgren, "Mass Misery in Philadelphia," *Nation*, 134 (Mar. 9, 1932): 276.

32. Clippings from the *Inquirer*, April 5, 1932, the *Bulletin*, July 6, 1932, and the *Morning Ledger*, Aug. 31, 1932, all in "Scrapbook"; Drayer, "J. Hampton Moore," pp. 321–22.

33. Drayer, "J. Hampton Moore," p. 325; editorial, "Balancing the City Budget," *Inquirer*, July 22, 1933.

34. Drayer, "J. Hampton Moore," pp. 321, 326; University of Pennsylvania study published in *American Labor Legislative Review* 22 (June 1932): 89–92.

35. *Record*, Jan. 5, 1934; clipping from the *Inquirer*, Aug. 23, 1933, in "Scrapbook"; Drayer, "J. Hampton Moore," pp. 308, 310.

36. Drayer, "J. Hampton Moore," p. 312; *Record*, Aug. 27, 1932.

37. *Bulletin Almanac, 1934*, p. 62; ibid., *1935*, pp. 61–62; ibid., *1936*, p. 464.

38. Ibid., *1937*, p. 483.

39. Davenport, "Philadelphia," p. 182; C. G. Shenton, "Relief Problems of Local Governments," *National Municipal Review* 27 (Jan. 1938): 30; *U.S. Bureau of Labor Bulletin* 555 (1932): 1–64; *Bulletin Almanac, 1935*, pp. 62, 63; ibid., *1936*, p. 502; ibid., *1946*, p. 355.

40. *Bulletin Almanac, 1936*, pp. 436, 505; ibid., *1937*, p. 486; ibid., *1939*, p. 474; ibid., *1943*, pp. 377, 378; *School and Society* 42 (Oct. 5, 1935): 462; Davenport, "Philadelphia," p. 74; C. H. English, "Playground Goes to the Children: Tot Lot Playgrounds," *Recreation* 32 (May 1938): 59–62; "Almost as Good as New, Philadelphia's Christmas Toy Shower," *Recreation* 32 (Oct. 1938): 381–82.

41. "Housing Problems in Philadelphia," *Monthly Labor Review* 37 (Sept. 1933): 626–31; "Housing for Negroes," *Monthly Labor Review* 40 (Oct. 1936): 885–86; *Bulletin Almanac, 1938*, pp. 310, 311.

42. Real Estate Property Survey, 7 vols. in City Archives, summarized in *Bulletin Almanac, 1941*, p. 329.

43. Bernard J. Newman, "Low Cost Housing, What the Rest of the Country Can Learn from Philadelphia," *American City* 40 (April 1929): 102–4.

44. A. Paxton, "Slum Clearance by Private Enterprise: Philadelphia's Black Belt," *Nation's Business* 27 (Dec. 1939): 29–30; "Lone Slum Clearer Makes Money: Mr. Binns of Philadelphia Turns Run-down Properties into Profitable Investments," *Business Week*, Dec. 9, 1939, pp. 32–33.

45. *Architectural Record* 78 (Nov. 1935): 289–98; "Arts Collaborate for Workers Houses, Philadelphia: Carl Mackley Houses," *American Magazine of Art* 27 (June 1934): 341; Catherine Bauer, *Modern Housing* (Boston: Houghton Mifflin, 1934), pp. 254–55; Webster, *Philadelphia Preserved*, pp. 319–20, 332.

46. Thompson, "Winner Gives All," pp. 274–76; *Inquirer*, Jan 10, 1940, clipping in "Scrapbook."

47. Clipping, Jan. 31, 1936, in "Scrapbook"; *Bulletin Almanac, 1936*, p. 504; ibid., *1938*, p. 475; ibid., *1939*, p. 473; ibid., *1942*, p. 344.

48. *Bulletin Almanac, 1942*, p. 344.

49. "Consumer Education in Furnishing for a Public Housing Project," *Journal of Home Economics* 33 (Sept. 1941): 468–70; T. E. White and S. L. Banks, "Adventures in Housing," *Journal of Home Economics* 37 (Feb. 1945): 72–73.

50. Stern, *Memoirs*, pp. 84–85; *Bulletin Almanac, 1941*, p. 517.

51. *Bulletin Almanac, 1942*, p. 344; *Philadelphia Forges Ahead*, report of the mayor for 1950 (Philadelphia: City of Philadelphia, 1951).

52. Davenport, "Philadelphia," p. 182; B. Amidere, "Styles in Strikes, Amalgamated Cuts a New Pattern for Philadelphia," *Survey* 63 (Dec. 1, 1929): 261–64. See transcripts of

hearings of Mayor Mackey's fact-finding committee, and report, May 29, 1931, in City Archives; "American Federation of Full-Fashioned Hosiery Workers," *Fortune* 5 (Jan. 1932): 49–53.

53. *Inquirer*, Jan. 23, 25, 1937; *Bulletin Almanac, 1938*, p. 472.

54. *Bulletin Almanac, 1938*, pp. 473, 474; ibid., *1939*, p. 475; *Inquirer*, Jan. 30, Aug. 2, 3, 4, 1937; Dec. 2, 1941; T. Henry Walnut, "S. Davis Wilson, Mayor of Philadelphia," in J. T. Salter, ed., *The American Politician* (Chapel Hill: University of North Carolina Press, 1938), pp. 297, 301; Edward B. Shils, "Philadelphia Streamlines Personnel Plan," *National Municipal Review* 32 (July 1943): 367–72.

55. "ILO Philadelphia Charter May Become a Classic," *Christian Century* 61 (May 24, 1944): 637; "ILO Exporting the New Deal: Social Aims of Victory," *Business Week*, May 20, 1944, p. 120.

56. Drayer, "J. Hampton Moore," p. 292; Stern, *Memoirs*, pp. 186–203; Greg Walter, "Sure and It's Matt McCloskey," *Philadelphia Magazine* 60 (Feb. 1969): 62, 65; J. T. Salter, "Election Episodes," *National Municipal Review* 23 (Sept. 1934): 459–60; id., "Party Organization in Philadelphia . . ." *American Political Science Review* 27 (Aug. 1933): 619.

57. O'Donnell's son was seeking appointment as Philadelphia's postmaster; J. T. Salter, "Tom Gibson vs. Public Opinion," *National Municipal Review* 24 (July 1935): 385–90; "O'Donnell Severs Ties Binding City Democracy to Vare," *Inquirer*, Aug. 4, 1933; Steven G. Neal, "Reflections of a Crusty Reformer," *Inquirer, Today Magazine*, Jan 7, 1973, p. 10; "Joe Clark, One Last Angry Man," *Inquirer, Today Magazine*, Aug. 3, 1975; Drayer, "J. Hampton Moore," pp. 354–55; Stern, *Memoirs*, pp. 205–8, 229–30.

58. Drayer, "J. Hampton Moore," p. 359.

59. J. T. Salter, "Introduction," in id., ed., *The American Politician*, p. xii; Struthers Burt, *Philadelphia, Holy Experiment* (Garden City, N.Y.: Doubleday, Doran, 1945), p. 358; Joseph S. Clark, "Spoilsmen Strike Back at Reformers," *Bulletin*, Sept. 22, 1971.

60. Drayer, "J. Hampton Moore," pp. 368, 370; Davenport, "Philadelphia," p. 201; Walnut, "S. Davis Wilson," pp. 293, 295, 301; Salter, ed., *The American Politician*, p. xii.

61. Clippings, *The Kensingtonian*, Jan. 17, 1936, and *Bulletin*, Jan. 1936, both in "Scrapbook"; Thomas R. Gillett, "Spirit of '36. In Philadelphia Americans Were Told of Their Rendezvous with Destiny," *Greater Philadelphia Magazine* 58 (Jan. 1967): 15–16; "Philadelphia Paradox: Republican Stronghold Stages the Democratic National Convention," *Business Week*, June 20, 1936, pp. 17–18; *Bulletin Almanac, 1937*, p. 485.

62. *Bulletin Almanac, 1937*, p. 486; ibid., *1938*, pp. 162, 465; ibid., *1939*, p. 475; ibid., *1940*, p. 483; ibid., *1941*, pp. 80, 473; ibid., *1942*, pp. 450–51, 521; ibid., *1944*, p. 519; ibid., *1945*, pp. 463, 477; Salter, "Letters from Men of Action," *National Municipal Review* 26 (Sept. 1937): 417–24; id., "Party Organization in Philadelphia," pp. 620–21, 624; Davenport, "Philadelphia," p. 74; "You're Another," *Time*, Nov. 15, 1943, p. 21.

63. Davenport, "Philadelphia," p. 73; Burt, *Philadelphia, Holy Experiment*, p. 352; Drayer, "J. Hampton Moore," pp. 38, 52–53; M. W.

Childs and J. C. Turner, "Real Philadelphia Story," *Forum* 103 (June 1940): 289–94; A. Frazier, "Philadelphia, City of Brotherly Loot," *American Mercury* 47 (July 1939): 275–82.

64. *Bulletin Almanac, 1937*, pp. 484, 486, 487; ibid., *1938*, p. 473; ibid., *1941*, pp. 78, 516, 517; "Fun in Philadelphia," *Time*, Jan. 10, 1938, pp. 52–55.

65. "Fun in Philadelphia," p. 55; Davenport, "Philadelphia," p. 205; *Bulletin Almanac, 1937*, p. 484.

66. *Bulletin Almanac, 1938*, p. 474; ibid., *1939*, pp. 473, 475; ibid., *1940*, pp. 341, 481, 482; ibid., *1941*, p. 83; "Sales Tax Voted in Philadelphia," *National Municipal Review* 27 (Mar. 1938): 171; C. Faber, "Low Tax Levies Precipitate Philadelphia Crisis," *National Municipal Review* 28 (April 1939): 321; "Philadelphia Almost Went Broke," *Inquirer*, May 21, 1975.

67. *Bulletin Almanac, 1940*, p. 483; ibid., *1941*, pp. 82, 516; ibid., *1943*, pp. 515, 516; *Time*, Jan. 8, 1940, p. 17. In 1933 the City Planning Commission recommended the appointment of a supervisory board to approve the city's budget, noting that 40 percent of current income was needed to service debt (see *Inquirer*, March 21, 1933).

68. *Bulletin Almanac, 1930*, p. 95; ibid., *1935*, p. 504; ibid., *1936*, p. 504; ibid., *1937*, pp. 484, 485, 486, 487; ibid., *1938*, pp. 472, 473, 474, 475; ibid., *1939*, pp. 308, 473; ibid., *1940*, pp. 482, 483; ibid., *1941*, pp. 327, 516; "Managing Philadelphia Rapid Transit," *National Municipal Review* 21 (April 1932): 252–53; Stern, *Memoirs*, pp. 173–74.

69. E. Ervin, "How Magistrates' Courts Defile Justice," *National Municipal Review* 20 (Oct. 1931): 573–76; J. T. Salter, "The Corrupt Lower Courts of Philadelphia," *American Mercury* 33 (Oct. 1934): 236, 238; *Bulletin Almanac, 1936*, pp. 502, 504.

70. *Bulletin Almanac, 1939*, pp. 473, 474, 475; ibid., *1940*, pp. 481, 482; *Newsweek*, Sept. 19, 1938, pp. 11–12.

71. *Newsweek*, Sept. 19, 1938, p. 12; Walnut, "S. Davis Wilson," p. 300; Frazier, "Philadelphia, City of Brotherly Loot," pp. 275–82.

72. *Bulletin Almanac, 1941*, pp. 88, 518; ibid., *1942*, pp. 77, 520.

73. Drayer, "J. Hampton Moore," pp. 344–45; "Philadelphia Flayed," *Time*, Feb. 14, 1938, p. 47; "Study of the Frequency of Tastes and Odors in the Philadelphia Water Supply," *American City* 48 (Aug. 1933): 53–54; "Report on Water Pollution," Special Advisory Committee to the Water Department (1935) and "Log Book of Public Complaints" (1943–1946), both in City Archives; "Action on Philadelphia Debt Limits," *National Municipal Review* 28 (July 1939): 554; *Bulletin Almanac, 1939*, p. 58; ibid., *1941*, pp. 516–17.

74. *Bulletin Almanac, 1941*, p. 518; ibid., *1942*, p. 520.

75. C. O. Shenton, "Philadelphia City and County Government," *National Municipal Review* 24 (May 1935): 273; F. P. Gruenberg, "Frontier Is the State . . ." *National Municipal Review* 28 (Dec. 1939): 824–31; id., "Philadelphia's City-County Dilemma," *National Municipal Review* 29 (June 1940): 385–87; id., "Legislation Sought for City-County Consolidation," *National Municipal Review* 34 (July 1945): 355.

76. "Official Report, Dec. 1938, of Committee Created by Act of Assembly, April 13, 1937," in City Archives; "Solid Press Backs the Philadelphia Bill," *National Municipal Review* 28 (May 1939): 398–99; J. U. Hoeber, "Philadelphia Carries On," *National Municipal Review* 28 (Sept. 1939): 646–52; *Bulletin Almanac, 1939*, pp. 37, 474; ibid., *1940*, pp. 481, 482.

77. *Bulletin Almanac, 1936*, p. 64; obituary notice for Barnes, *Bulletin*, May 14, 1952, and *New York Times*, May 15, 1952.

78. A. C. Wagner, "Crime and Economic Change in Philadelphia, 1925–1934," *Journal of Criminal Law* 27 (Nov. 1936): 483–90 (Dodge was dismissed shortly thereafter for failing to keep his department within strict budgetary limits); Clipping, 1933, no paper given, in possession of the author; "Boys at the Turning Point, Experiment by Philadelphia Juvenile Court," *Survey* 71 (April 1935): 106; "This Is Your Philadelphia . . . Report from the Mayor to the Citizens, 1948" (in City Archives), p. 40; *Bulletin Almanac, 1933*, p. 90; ibid., *1936*, pp. 502–3; George Sessions Perry, "Philadelphia Shows the Way," *Saturday Evening Post*, Sept. 1, 1934, p. 22.

79. "Frank Brookhouser's Philadelphia," *Bulletin*, March 9, May 12, 1968; *Bulletin Almanac, 1937*, p. 486; ibid., *1938*, p. 472; ibid., *1940*, p. 482.

80. *Bulletin Almanac, 1940*, pp. 481, 483; ibid., *1941*, p. 516.

81. Wilson, *Yesterday's Philadelphia*, p. 109.

82. Stern, *Memoirs*, pp. 239–43; "Moe Annenberg Buys Philadelphia's GOP Bible," *Newsweek*, Aug. 8, 1936, p. 30; "Moe Annenberg and the Fourth Estate," *Nation*, Aug. 15, 1936, p. 172; Gaetano Fonzi, "Annenberg," *Philadelphia Magazine* 60 (April 1969): 76, 128–29, 134; *Bulletin Almanac, 1940*, p. 482; ibid., *1941*, pp. 516–17.

83. Drayer, "J. Hampton Moore," pp. 247–48; "Philadelphia Story," *Time*, Jan. 19, 1942, p. 58; "Last of an Empire: Philadelphia Public Ledger," *Time*, Jan. 13, 1941, p. 52; "Ledger's Demise," *Business Week*, Jan. 17, 1942, p. 49; "Quiet Queen: Philadelphia Bulletin . . ." *Time*, April 10, 1944, pp. 49–50; "Newsprint Scrapple," *Newsweek*, March 27, 1944, pp. 88–90; Davenport, "Philadelphia," p. 192; H. Tatlow, "Philadelphia Acquires a Good Newspaper," *American Mercury* 28 (Feb. 1933): 185–87; Stern, *Memoirs*, pp. 121–22, 167–71; Oswald Garrison Villard, "The Press Today, VI: The Philadelphia Cabbage Patch," *Nation*, June 11, 1930, pp. 671–73.

84. Mary-Virginia Geyelin, "Debs Still Dance Till Dawn," *Bulletin*, May 4, 1969.

85. James, *American Scene*, p. 268.

86. Herbert Kupferberg, *Those Fabulous Philadelphians: The Life and Times of a Great Orchestra* (New York: Scribner's, 1969), p. 64.

87. Kupferberg, *Those Fabulous Philadelphians*, pp. 62, 86–87; "Walking Out on Music," *Literary Digest*, Oct. 29, 1932, p. 16; *Bulletin Almanac, 1937*, p. 484.

88. "Symphonic Jitterbugs: Sixth Season of Philadelphia's Youth Concerts," *Time*, April 17, 1939, p. 54; Kupferberg, *Those Fabulous Philadelphians*, p. 93.

89. Kupferberg, *Those Fabulous Philadelphians*, pp. 100–1; "Orchestra on Tour," *Time*, April

27, 1936, pp. 58–61; T. P. McMahon and C. Hoffman, "Front-page Maestro: Stokowski, Salesman of Symphony to America," *Readers Digest* 28, (June 1936): 35–38.

90. Kupferberg, *Those Fabulous Philadelphians*, pp. 73–76; "The Earliest Stereo Tape Comes to Stanford," *Stanford Observer*, June 1980, quoting from Robert McGinn, "Stokowski and Bell Laboratories: Collaboration in Development of High Fidelity Sound, 1930–1940," paper presented at the annual meeting of the History of Science Society, Dec. 1979.

91. *Record*, July 9, 1930; annual report, Bureau of Music, Department of Public Welfare, 1930 (in Historical Society of Pennsylvania); "Frank Brookhouser's Philadelphia," *Bulletin*, June 22, 1969.

92. "Philadelphia's Municipal Music Bureau," *American City* 42 (April 1930): 142; *Bulletin Almanac, 1930*, pp. 76–77, 157.

93. "Tchaikovsky in English," *Newsweek*, Nov. 11, 1940, pp. 74–75; "Street-car Opera," *Newsweek*, Mar. 15, 1943, p. 70.

94. *Bulletin Almanac, 1942*, pp. 349, 519; Frank Brookhouser, *Our Philadelphia* (Garden City, N.Y.: Doubleday, 1957), pp. 53, 171–75.

95. A. Bronson, "World's Greatest Musical Library," *American Mercury* 62 (April 1946): 444–47.

96. "Black Cafe Society," *Inquirer*, Jan. 25, 1975.

97. Davenport, "Philadelphia," p. 176; *Inquirer*, Jan. 25, 1937.

98. Mrs. Eakins had just given the museum sixty of her husband's paintings (George and Mary Roberts, *Triumph on Fairmount: Fiske Kimball and the Philadelphia Museum of Art* [Philadelphia: Lippincott, 1959], p. 98).

99. *Inquirer*, Jan. 21, 1937; "Philadelphia Program," *Time*, Feb. 8, 1937, p. 34; "Art in Philadelphia," *Time*, Feb. 14, 1938, pp. 43–44; "Philadelphia Museum Presents a Many-sided Daumier in Lively Show," *Newsweek*, Nov. 1, 1937, p. 26; "700-Year Panorama of Art; Huge Johnson Collection Given First Full-dress Showing," *Newsweek*, Nov. 10, 1941, p. 78; "Nudes and Lovers Brim Philadelphia Museum in Biggest Sculpture Show," *Life*, Aug. 12, 1940, pp. 54–55.

100. The General Education Board of the Rockefeller Fund gave $250,000 toward the program to develop period rooms ("New Gallery of Modern Art Opened," *American Magazine of Art* 26 [Feb. 1933]: 98; *Bulletin Almanac, 1933*, p. 281; ibid., *1938*, p. 473).

101. *Inquirer*, Feb. 8, 1976, Mar. 13, 1980; Nathaniel Burt, *The Perennial Philadelphians: The Anatomy of an American Aristocracy* (Boston: Little, Brown, 1963), p. 310. Another Penn A. C. crew, the "sprint crew" of 1940, also added to the prestige of Philadelphia's rowers (*Inquirer*, Aug. 13, 1980).

102. See team records in *Bulletin Almanac, 1936–1945*.

103. Ibid., *1940*, p. 482.

104. Ibid., *1936*, p. 471; Eugene Benson, "When Baseball Was a Matter of Black and White," *Inquirer*, Today Magazine, Aug. 9, 1981.

105. "Brookhouser's Philadelphia," *Bulletin*, May 11, 1969; *Bulletin Almanac, 1945*, p. 475; ibid., *1946*, p. 469.

106. *Bulletin Almanac, 1936*, p. 489; ibid., *1941*, pp. 502, 506; Burt, *Perennial Philadelphians*, pp. 312–13.

107. "Republican Party Has a Homecoming," *Life*, June 24, 1940, pp. 62–73; J. T. Salter, "Letters from Men of Action: Republican

Division Leaders of Philadelphia on the Eve of the 1940 Election," *National Municipal Review* 30 (Aug. 1941): 471–77; *Bulletin Almanac, 1941,* pp. 473, 517.

108. *Bulletin Almanac, 1940,* p. 483; ibid., *1941,* p. 518; ibid., *1942,* p. 519.

109. Ibid., *1942,* pp. 46, 325; C. F. Bender, "Philadelphia Program of Vocational Education for Defense," *Industrial Arts and Vocational Education* 31 (March 1942): 83–87.

110. *Bulletin Almanac, 1936,* p. 502; ibid., *1941,* pp. 319, 324; ibid., *1942,* pp. 45–48; "Defense Work Aids Philadelphia Trade," *Inquirer,* Dec. 1, 1941; "Defense, a Philadelphia Story," *Business Week,* Jan. 18, 1941, pp. 22–30.

111. "Defense, a Philadelphia Story," *Business Week,* Jan. 18, 1941, pp. 22–30; *Pennsylvania at War, 1941–1945* (Harrisburg: Pennsylvania Historical and Museum Commission, 1946), pp. 25–28; *Bulletin Almanac, 1944,* pp. 384–85.

112. *Bulletin Almanac, 1942,* p. 471; "Housing Project Joins the Navy," *American City* 58, (Jan. 1943): 58; McKelvey, *Emergence of Metropolitan America,* p. 121.

113. *Bulletin Almanac, 1943,* p. 515.

114. *Inquirer,* Dec. 1, 2, 3, 1941, and Travel Section, Dec. 7, 1941.

115. Ibid., Dec. 8, 1941.

116. *Bulletin Almanac, 1942,* pp. 51, 520, 521; *Pennsylvania at War,* pp. 39–41.

117. *Bulletin Almanac, 1943,* pp. 515–16; ibid., *1944,* p. 519.

118. Ibid., *1941,* p. 517.

119. Ibid., *1943,* p. 516; ibid., *1944,* p. 518.

120. Ibid., *1943,* pp. 515, 516, 517; ibid., *1944,* p. 518; ibid., *1945,* pp. 476, 477; ibid., *1946,* pp. 489, 490; Connor, *Fifty Years on Chestnut Street,* p. 24; M. Wall, "Labor Gives Canteens for Servicemen to Philadelphia," *American Federationist* 50 (Sept. 1943): 18–19.

121. Julia Cass, "The Rhoads: 11 Generations in the Quaker City," *Inquirer, Bicentennial Journal,* May 17, 1976, p. 18.

122. *Inquirer,* Aug. 8, 1945, Feb. 15, 1976; *Pennsylvania at War,* pp. 48, 50, 52; *Bulletin Almanac, 1942,* pp. 45–48.

123. *Bulletin Almanac, 1940,* p. 482; ibid., *1942,* pp. 48–50, 520; ibid., *1946,* pp. 441, 490, 491; *Pennsylvania at War,* p. 26.

124. "Shipyards Need Men," *Business Week,* Aug. 3, 1940, p. 36.

125. S. T. Woal, "Training Machinist Apprentices for National Defense, Frankford Arsenal," *Industrial Arts and Vocational Education* 31 (June 1942): 232; "How an Industrial City Supplies Its Workers with Technical Books," *Publishers' Weekly,* Oct. 10, 1942, pp. 1542–1551; F. H. Price, "Libraries and the War Program: The Philadelphia Free Library," *Library Journal,* May 15, 1942, pp. 464–65.

126. *Bulletin Almanac, 1945,* p. 477; ibid., *1946,* p. 489.

127. Ibid., *1946,* p. 490; Batt received the Philadelphia Award in 1943 for his work on the War Production Board (ibid., *1944,* p. 518); *Inquirer,* Dec. 2, 4, 1941.

128. *Bulletin Almanac, 1944,* p. 519; ibid., *1945,* p. 476; ibid., *1946,* p. 489.

129. "FEPC Challenged: Philadelphia Transit

Union Defies Order to End Discrimination," *Business Week,* Jan. 15, 1944, p. 95; *Bulletin Almanac, 1945,* pp. 476, 477; ibid., *1946,* p. 489; "FEPC on Spot: End of Philadelphia Transit Strike Leaves Basic Issue Unsettled," *Business Week,* Aug. 12, 1944, pp. 103–4; D. G. Redmond, "Trouble in Philadelphia: Analysis of the Philadelphia Strike Shows That the Real Issue Has Not Been Settled," *Current History* 7 (Sept. 1944): 186–92; "Trouble in Philadelphia: Transportation Strike," *Time,* Aug. 14, 1944, pp. 22–23; "Race Trouble in Philadelphia Brings Test of Wartime Powers," *Newsweek,* Aug. 14, 1944, pp. 36–38; "Racism in Philadelphia," *New Republic,* Aug. 14, 1944, pp. 176; "Philadelphia Strike," *Nation,* Aug. 12, 1944, p. 172.

130. "Philadelphia Strike," *Nation,* Aug. 12, 1944, p. 172.

131. *Bulletin Almanac, 1945,* pp. 463–64, 477.

132. *Inquirer,* April 13, 14, 15, 1945.

133. Ibid., Aug. 9, 10, 11, 14, 1945 (all front-page stories), and Aug. 15, 1945.

134. Ibid., Aug. 15, 16, 1945.

135. "Philadelphia's Plan: Post-war Business Problems," *Business Week,* July 4, 1942, pp. 18–19; H. C. Morris, "Youth Builds Today for a Better Tomorrow," *National Municipal Review* 32 (July 1943): 357–59; L. Dam, "Civic Plan to Bridge Eighteen to Twentyone Gap: Youth Civic Council of Philadelphia," *National Municipal Review* 34 (Jan. 1945): 10–13; "Planning Commission Recommends Philadelphia Freeway," *American City* 61 (Dec. 1946): 15.

136. "Philadelphia's Ills: Diagnosis by Real Estate Specialist," *Business Week,* Feb. 7, 1942, pp. 34–36.

137. E. N. Bacon, "How City Planning Came to Philadelphia," *American City* 58 (Feb. 1943): 62; id., "Capital Programming and Public Policy," *Journal of American Institute of Planning* 22, no. 1 (April 1956): 35–38; *Bulletin Almanac, 1944,* p. 519; ibid., *1945,* p. 84.

138. "Mayoralty Candidates Endorse City Planning," *American City* 58 (Nov. 1943): 87.

139. *Bulletin Almanac, 1945,* p. 348; "Bombshell No. 2," *Business Week,* June 24, 1944, pp. 36–37.

140. "Business Wanted: Group Will Wage Campaign to Keep Federal Agencies," *Business Week,* Nov. 18, 1944, pp. 65–66.

141. *Bulletin Almanac, 1945,* p. 477; ibid., *1946,* pp. 489, 490; editorials in *Inquirer,* Aug. 9, 11, 1945.

142. "Brotherly Love: Philadelphia Wants the U.N.," *Time,* Dec. 2, 1946, p. 21; *Philadelphia: Cradle of Liberty,* pamphlet prepared for U.N. representatives by the city government.

143. *Inquirer,* Aug. 12, 1945; A. D. Carlson, "Philadelphia's Stitch in Time," *Survey Graphic* 33 (July 1944): 324–25; N. L. Bok, "In Time of Crisis," *Survey Graphic* 33 (Nov. 1944): 435.

144. Areas of greatest growth were in the northwest, in Roxborough and Germantown; in the northeast; and in the southwest, in the Cobbs Creek section and Wynnefield (Public Information Bulletin no. 5, Philadelphia City Planning Commission, June 1952).

RALLY AND RELAPSE, 1946–1968

1. Richard Saul Wurman and John Andrew Gallery, *Man-Made Philadelphia: A Guide to Its Physical and Cultural Environment* (Cambridge, Mass.: MIT Press, 1972), p. 81; Lorin Peterson, *The Day of the Mugwump* (New York: Random House, 1961), p. 157.

2. For an interesting portrait of Philadelphia in 1950, see John Lukacs, *Philadelphia: Patricians and Philistines, 1900–1950* (New York: Farrar, Straus & Giroux, 1981), pp. 278–310.

3. Eric Goldman, *The Crucial Decade—and After: America 1945–1960* (New York: Vintage, 1960), pp. 3–91.

4. Philip C. Jessup, *Elihu Root* (2 vols.; Dodd, Mead, 1938), 1:444.

5. The Committee of Seventy, *The Charter: A History* (Philadelphia: The Committee of Seventy, 1980), pp. 6–8.

6. James Reichley, *The Art of Government: Reform and Organization Politics in Philadelphia* (New York: Fund for the Republic, 1959), and Kirk R. Petshek, *The Challenge of Urban Reform: Policies and Programs in Philadelphia* (Philadelphia: Temple University Press, 1973), both depict the reform movement.

7. "The Philadelphia Story: Citizens Clean Up Graft," *Newsweek*, June 14, 1948, pp. 27–28.

8. James Crumlish, *A City Finds Itself* (Detroit: Wayne State University Press, 1959).

9. Nochem S. Winnet, "The Form of Government," *Shingle* (Philadelphia Bar Association) 14, no. 4 (April 1951).

10. The provisions of the city charter are explained more fully in the Committee of Seventy, *The Charter: A History*, pp. 11–70.

11. For a brief overview of these events, see Peterson, *The Day of the Mugwump*, pp. 150–57.

12. A daily record of major decisions by Mayor Clark is contained in the "Daily Log of Mayor Joseph S. Clark," William L. Rafsky Papers, Urban Archives, Paley Library, Temple University. The account of events in this chapter is based upon Mayor Clark's firsthand experience.

13. Leon Shull, director of the Americans for Democratic Action, contended that Dilworth misled him and other liberals in making a secret deal with Green which Shull took credit for exposing (Leon Shull, interview, May 4, 1976, Walter M. Phillips, Sr., Oral History Collection, Urban Archives, Paley Library, Temple University, pp. 23–25).

14. Even during the reform few experienced people viewed the city Council as a full-time job, and members retained all kinds of outside business and professional ties (ibid., p. 16).

15. The differing views of many such figures about the reform are contained in the Walter M. Phillips, Sr., Oral History Collection.

16. R. Stewart Rauch, head of the Philadelphia Saving Fund Society in the 1960s, recounted that in 1968 the business community was brow-beaten into assembling a fund of $1 million to assuage militant black leaders, and that $250,000 of this fund was never adequately accounted for after it was funneled to ghetto groups (R. Stewart Rauch, interview, Oct. 11, 1978, Walter M. Phillips, Sr., Oral History Collection, p. 4; see also Miriam Ershkowitz and Joseph Zikmund, eds., *Black Politics in Philadelphia* [New York: Basic Books, 1973], pp. 55–145).

17. Paul D'Ortona, president of the city Council, attributed the growing problems with municipal unions to the decision of the Pennsylvania legislature to permit compulsory arbitration of labor issues for uniformed city employees. Thus Philadelphia had to live with a Harrisburg decision of enormous importance for the future (Paul D'Ortona, interview, May 17, 1977, Walter M. Phillips, Sr., Oral History Collection, p. 3).

18. Peter Binzen, *The Cop Who Would Be King* (Boston: Little, Brown, 1979).

19. Reed M. Smith, *State Government in Transition, 1955–59* (Philadelphia: University of Pennsylvania Press, 1961). The relation of the reform movement in Philadelphia to Pennsylvania politics is treated in Paul B. Beers, *Pennsylvania Politics: Today and Yesterday* (University Park: Pennsylvania State University Press, 1980), pp. 193–207.

20. Collection of the Oral History of the Port of Philadelphia, Philadelphia Maritime Museum; "War on the Waterfront," *Philadelphia Magazine* 53, no. 10 (Oct. 1962): 18.

21. William W. Cutler III, "Persistent Dualism: Centralization and Decentralization in Philadelphia, 1854–1975," in William W. Cutler III and Howard Gillette, Jr., eds., *The Divided Metropolis: Social and Spatial Dimensions of Philadelphia, 1800–1975* (Westport, Conn.: Greenwood Press, 1980), pp. 249–84.

22. Dennis Clark, *The Ghetto Game* (New York: Sheed and Ward, 1962), pp. 118–19, 163.

23. William L. Rafsky, in Stanley Newman, ed., "The Politics of Utopia," a report of a conference, April 28–May 23, 1975, Political Science Department, Temple University, 1975.

24. Edmund S. Bacon, executive director of the City Planning Commission in the Clark and Dilworth administrations, ruefully confessed the great toll exacted from low-income people through relocation and disruption of family and social life by the downtown and university rebuilding programs in Newman, ed., "The Politics of Utopia." Conrad Weiler, *Philadelphia: Neighborhood Authority and Urban Crisis* (New York: Praeger, 1974), is very critical of the reform administrations' programs.

25. Randolph Wise, interview, Jan. 12, 1978, Walter M. Phillips, Sr., Oral History Collection, pp. 2–23. Wise notes that even at the height of reform good personnel was superimposed on mediocre personnel without much displacement.

26. Lawrence Reddick, in Newman, ed., "The Politics of Utopia," provides background on the conditions producing the riots.

27. Binzen, *The Cop Who Would Be King*, pp. 70–110.

28. Peter O. Muller, Kenneth C. Meyer, and Roman A. Cybriwsky, *Philadelphia: A Study of Conflicts and Social Cleavages* (New York: Ballinger, 1976), pp. 11–34.

29. E. Digby Baltzell, "The Protestant Establishment Re-Visited," *The American Scholar* 45 (Autumn 1976): 499–518.

30. Weiler, *Philadelphia: Neighborhood Authority and Urban Crisis*, p. 101. Weiler sees the great weakness of the school reform to have been the failure to build a political base outside the schools to support the changes. Actually many of the reforms credited to

Dilworth and Shedd were set in motion by
the unglamorous previous superintendent, C.
Taylor Whittier, and board member Elizabeth
Greenfield, including nondiscrimination actions, early childhood education, and concentration of full-time teachers in black schools.
The big change came in 1965–1966 when
federal funds under the Elementary and
Secondary Education Act became available
(interview of Dennis Clark with Ezra Staples,
former school official, June 4, 1981). For a
view of school problems from the neighborhood level, see Peter Binzen, *Whitetown,
U.S.A.* (New York: Random House, 1970).
31. Graham Finney, a planner who worked for
the school district in the 1960s, saw the key
problem of sustaining school reforms affected
by two lines of policy he termed "short-
sighted," the attempt to "do too much too
soon," and the failure of not "heeding ethnic
and labor forces that are crucial in the school
system" (Graham Finney, interview, Jan. 1,
1978, Walter M. Phillips, Sr., Oral History
Collection, p. 16). For ethnic competition
among school district personnel, see Murray
Friedman and Daniel Elazar, *Moving Up:
Ethnic Succession in America* (Philadelphia:
American Jewish Committee, 1976). The disruption in the schools in the 1960s is
chronicled by Henry Resnick, *Turning on the
System: War in the Philadelphia Public
Schools* (New York: Pantheon, 1970).
32. Thomas J. Donaghy, *Philadelphia's Finest: A
History of Catholic Education in the Archdiocese of Philadelphia, 1692–1970* (Philadelphia: American Catholic Historical Society,
1972).
33. "A Guide to the Establishment of the
Community College of Philadelphia," Philadelphia Commission on Higher Education,
Jan. 1964, and Allen Bonnell, "Master Plan
for the New Campus," 1968 (both in the
office of the President, Official Records of the
Community College of Philadelphia).
34. Martin Meyerson et al., *Gladly Learn and
Gladly Teach: Franklin and His Successors
at the University of Pennsylvania* (Philadelphia: University of Pennsylvania Press, 1978).
35. John Rhoads, "Temple University Campus
Planning Report," Temple University, May
1969; Herman Niebuhr, "A Program for
North Philadelphians," mimeo, Center for
Community Studies, Temple University, 1961.
36. Valerie Sue Halverson Pace, "Society Hill,
Philadelphia: Historic Preservation and Urban
Renewal in Washington Square East" (Ph.D.
dissertation, University of Minnesota, 1976).
A visual record of changes in the cityscape
is contained in Edwin Wolf 2nd, *Philadelphia: Portrait of an American City* (Harrisburg: Stackpole Books, 1975), pp. 320–36. See
also Nancy Love, "Paradise Lost," *Philadelphia Magazine* 59 no. 7 (July 1968): 72.
37. "Annenberg," *Philadelphia Magazine* 60, no.
4 (May 1969): 64.
38. Rena Corman, *Air Pollution Primer* (Philadelphia: American Lung Association, 1969).
39. A critique of the emphasis on downtown
development was presented by Paul Levy and
Dennis McGrath, "Selective Resurgence: Corporate Strategy for the Urban Northeast,"
Institute for Civic Values, Philadelphia, 1980.
See also Muller, Meyer, and Cybriwsky,
*Philadelphia: A Study of Conflicts and Social
Cleavages,* pp. 35–64. A broad view of
metropolitan problems by key figures in the

reform effort is presented in Stephen B.
Sweeney, *Metropolitan Analysis* (Philadelphia:
University of Pennsylvania Press, 1958).
40. Cyril Bahr Roseman, "Public-Private Co-oper-
ation and Negotiation in Downtown Redevelopment: A Study in the Decision Process in
Philadelphia" (Ph.D. dissertation, Princeton
University, 1963). Roseman believed the complexity of the planning process at times
resulted in haphazard output. Another view
is given by Cynthia Pushaw, "Urban Renewal
in Philadelphia, 1942–1980: The Program, the
Process, the Proposals" (Honors thesis, Bryn
Mawr College, April 21, 1980). Graham
Finney, who served on the City Planning
Commission, believed that recommendations
for the Community Renewal Program stressing the social dimensions of planning were
rarely accepted by the commission (Graham
Finney, interview, Jan. 11, 1978, Walter M.
Phillips, Sr., Oral History Collection, p. 4).
41. Bertram Zumeta, in Newman, ed., "The
Politics of Utopia."
42. Conrad Weiler found the base of political
authority in the city during and after the
reform to be "tenuous and unstable," and
prey to "manipulation of ethnic and ideological symbols," its direction "largely determined
by national events" (Weiler, *Philadelphia:
Neighborhood Authority and Urban Crisis,*
pp. 211–12). Another observer found the
effect of the reform years to be "superficial,"
with politics not much changed (J. R. Fink,
"Reform in Philadelphia: 1946–51" [Ph.D.
dissertation, Rutgers University, 1971], p.
231). Former city Council Pres. Paul D'Ortona, responding to the question of "Who
subverted reform in Philadelphia?" said, "The
people themselves. The voters of Philadelphia
broke it down." He criticized the lack of
voter participation (Paul D'Ortona, interview,
May 17, 1977, Walter M. Phillips, Sr., Oral
History Collection, p. 5). Decreasing voter
participation is detailed in Peter McGrath,
"Bicentennial Philadelphia: A Quaking City,"
in Dennis Clark, ed., *Philadelphia 1776–2076:
A Three Hundred Year View* (Port Washington, N.Y.: Kennikat Press, 1975), pp. 69–
100.

BIBLIOGRAPHICAL NOTE

Study of recent Philadelphia history must
be undertaken through archival research, since
there are not as yet many secondary sources
and books relating to the period following
World War II. The *Bulletin Almanac,* published until 1976 by the *Evening Bulletin,*
provides a brief summary of annual events.
The Archives of the City of Philadelphia has
available papers and records of the executive
branch of city government and of the city
Council and the courts. The library of the
City Planning Commission and the records
of the Philadelphia Redevelopment Authority
and the Philadelphia Housing Authority provide detailed information on major physical
changes in the city. The Urban Archives of
the Paley Library at Temple University contain an excellent collection of personal recollections and agency records pertaining to this
period. *Philadelphia Magazine* has numerous
articles after 1960 dealing with city affairs,
as do the metropolitan and local community
newspapers, and such ethnic papers as the
Philadelphia Tribune.

Studies of particular community networks and situations can be reviewed with great profit, including the research reports of the Bureau of Municipal Research, the Pennsylvania Economy League, and the Philadelphia Council for Community Advancement. The studies and reports of the Fels Institute for Local and State Government and the Community Leadership Seminar provide background on problems of city administration and civic organization. Demographic and economic data in the files of the Chamber of Commerce of Philadelphia and the files of a wide array of institutions is generally accessible.

Dr. Henry Klein in his doctoral dissertation at Temple University, "The Network of Community Organization Leadership" (1964), gives a helpful profile of the power elite of the city. Recollections of city changes are contained in unpublished memoirs of the Hon. James H. J. Tate, former mayor, and such energetic citizens as Frank Delaney, former director of the Germantown Commu-

nity Council, but these are privately circulated at this point.

The extraordinary photographic collections of the Urban Archives of the Paley Library at Temple University and at the Library Company of Philadelphia and the newsfilms of local television stations are a great visual treasury, as is the slide collection of the Philadelphia Cultural Consortium.

Federal and state archives contain a massive amount of material, for the period was one of swift expansion of programs of all kinds at those governmental levels. Although United States Bureau of the Census materials have been placed on computers, there is no guide to the vast compilations of data dealing with the city that is even minimally adequate. The Center for Philadelphia Studies of the School of Public and Urban Policy at the University of Pennsylvania was launched in the 1970s to provide a continuing vehicle for study of the city with modern methodology.

THE BICENTENNIAL CITY, 1968–1982

1. Editorial, *Inquirer*, July 4, 1977.
2. The statistics for this section were figured on data compiled from several sources. Some general information can be obtained from the *Encyclopedia Britannica* (Chicago: University of Chicago Press, 1968), which has tables for the years 1950–1968, taken from the reports of the United States Bureau of the Census. The *1980 Yearbook* of the *Britannica* is also useful. Other sources consulted include *Preliminary Reports, 1980 Census of Population and Housing* (Washington, D.C.: U.S. Department of Commerce, Bureau of the Census), for Pennsylvania and New Jersey; *Philadelphia Statistical Data '77* (Philadelphia: City of Philadelphia Department of Finance, Office of the City Economist); *Tract Group Profile* (Philadelphia: City Planning Commission, July and Nov. 1977); *Technical Information Paper: 1980 Census, Special Population Summary for Philadelphia Census Tracts* (rev. ed.); Philadelphia: City Planning Commission, June 1981). Printed statistics for earlier periods can be found in Dennis Clark, ed., *Philadelphia 1776–2076: A Three Hundred Year View* (Port Washington, N.Y.: Kennikat Press, 1975), and Peter O. Muller, Kenneth C. Meyer, and Roman A. Cybriwsky, *Metropolitan Philadelphia: A Study of Conflicts and Social Cleavages* (Cambridge, Mass.: Ballinger, 1976).
3. Several good maps illustrating population and its movement within the city can be found in the *Technical Information Paper, 1980 Census*.
4. Muller et al., *Metropolitan Philadelphia*, p. 12.
5. *Bulletin*, Jan. 1, 1970, suburban section.
6. *Philadelphia Statistical Data* states in its forward: "originally conceived to serve as a source of basic statistical information on the economy of Philadelphia, and was intended for use primarily by the business community. . . . Our experience has demonstrated that the demand of the business sector for localized data transcends traditional economic interest in employment, transportation, systems, taxation, and the like. . . . the treatment accorded subjects included . . . has

also been amended . . . better to meet the requirements of business research." See also *Issues for the 1980's* (Philadelphia: Philadelphia City Planning Commission, 1979), esp. pp. 7–8, which also deals with economic developments.
7. These and most of the statistics which follow are based on "Preliminary Financial Statement for the Fiscal Year Ending June 30, 1980," City of Philadelphia, May 1981, typescript in files of the City Planning Commission. This report includes much data for all of 1980.
8. Ibid., p. I-3
9. For a good description of suburban mall development see Muller et al., *Metropolitan Philadelphia*, p. 49ff.
10. "Preliminary Financial Statement," p. I-4, Table I-3, lists the largest nongovernment employers in Philadelphia in 1980, based on figures supplied by the Philadelphia Chamber of Commerce. The largest by far is the University of Pennsylvania, with 12,500 paid personnel. Bell of Pennsylvania with 8695 is next, and the others over 5000 include Temple University; SEPTA; Sears, Roebuck, & Co.; the Budd Co.; and Philadelphia Electric. The overall list has twenty-four employers, with the smallest at 1755 employees; six of these are in education or delivery of public services, four are retailers, eight in production of goods, and six in money and finance.
11. Clark, *Philadelphia, 1776–2076*, "Philadelphia 1876: Celebration and Illusion," p. 51.
12. *Bulletin*, Jan. 1, 1970, p. 20; *Issues for the 1980's*, p. 20.
13. Richard Webster, *Philadelphia Preserved: Catalog of the Historic American Buildings Survey* (Philadelphia: Temple University Press, 1976), p. 8. This is an important book that not only presents complete coverage of identified historic buildings in Philadelphia, some of which have long since disappeared, but also provides an excellent historical overview of the significant neighborhoods.
14. For the ethnic background of Philadelphia neighborhoods, see Caroline Golab, *Immigrant Destinations* (Philadelphia: Temple University

Press, 1977). and Muller et al., *Metropolitan Philadelphia*, esp. Part I.

15. Letter from Paul R. Levy to the Advisory Committee of the Institute for the Study of Civic Values (late fall, 1977), author's personal files.

16. A good discussion of the political process in contemporary Philadelphia is found in Peter A. McGrath, "Bicentennial Philadelphia: A Quaking City," *Philadelphia 1776–2076*, pp. 74–81.

17. Memorandum, Oct. 25, 1977, from J. T. Kirkman on the "History of External Efforts to Curb Police Abuse in Philadelphia," *Inquirer* Library File, "Phila– Govt– Police Dept Advisory Board, 1970– ."

18. These signs are still posted in various parts of the city, although a new streets policy was initiated by the Green administration.

19. Information on the Bicentennial is mostly drawn from news sources, including the *Inquirer*, the *Bulletin*, the *Daily News*, and *Philadelphia Magazine*.

20. *Inquirer*, Dec. 1, 1965.

21. *Daily News*, Editorial, "The Invisible Bicen [sic]," Aug. 25, 1972.

22. Don Haskins and Fred Hamilton, "New Bicen [sic] Deadline Is Set," *Daily News*, Oct. 25, 1972; Mike Mallowe, "How They Blew the Bicentennial," *Philadelphia Magazine* 66, no. 6 (June 1975): 116.

23. Editorial, *Inquirer*, July 4, 1977.

24. Steven V. Roberts, "A foot in Philadelphia on a Car-less Weekend," *New York Times*, sect. 10, "Travel," May 27, 1979.

INDEX

Page numbers in *italics* refer to illustrations.

AUTHORS AND
CONTRIBUTORS

Russell F. Weigley, who served as editor of this project, is professor of history, Temple University. He is the author of *Eisenhower's Lieutenants, History of the United States Army, The American Way of War,* and *Towards an American Army: Military Thought from Washington to Marshall.*

Nicholas B. Wainwright, who served as associate editor of the project, has been research librarian, director, and director emeritus of the Historical Society of Pennsylvania. His books include *A Philadelphia Story, The Philadelphia National Bank,* and *Philadelphia in the Romantic Age of Lithography.*

Edwin Wolf 2nd, who served as associate editor of the project, is librarian of the Library Company of Philadelphia. He is the author of *The Library of James Logan of Philadelphia,* and *Philadelphia: A Portrait of an American City,* and coauthor of *History of the Jews of Philadelphia* and *Rosenbach: A Biography.*

Lloyd M. Abernethy is associate professor of history, Beaver College, Glenside, Pennsylvania. He is a contributor to *Pennsylvania Magazine of History and Biography,* and *Pennsylvania History.*

Dorothy Gondos Beers was for many years professor of history at American University. She is a contributor to *Military Affairs* and the *American Historical Review.*

Edwin B. Bronner is professor of history, curator of the Quaker Collection, and librarian of Haverford College. His books include (ed.) *William Penn's "Holy Experiment,"* and (ed.) *William Penn, 17th Century Founding Father.*

Nathaniel Burt is the author of a number of novels and nonfiction books including *The Perennial Philadelphians, First Families,* and *Palaces for the People.*

Dennis J. Clark has published many articles and books on urban problems and urban history including *Cities in Crisis, The Ghetto Game,* and *The Irish in Philadelphia.* He is executive director of the Samuel S. Fels Fund in Philadelphia.

Joseph S. Clark has been Philadelphia's mayor, city controller, and United States senator from Pennsylvania. He is the author of *The Senate Establishment, Congress: The Sapless Branch,* and *Readings in Congressional Reform.*

Wallace E. Davies was associate professor of history at the University of Pennsylvania. He was the author of *Patriotism on Parade: The Story of Veterans' and Hereditary Organizations in America, 1783–1900.*

Arthur P. Dudden is professor of history and chairman of the History Department at Bryn Mawr College. His books include (ed.) *Understanding the American Republic, Joseph Fels and the Single–Tax Movement* and *The Assault of Laughter: American Humor in Politics.*

Mary Maples Dunn is professor of history and dean of the Undergraduate College of Bryn Mawr. She is the author of *William Penn: Politics and Conscience.*

Richard Slator Dunn is the director of the Philadelphia Center for Early American Studies. His books include *Puritans and Yankees: The Winthrop Dynasty of New England, 1630–1717, The Age of Religious Wars, 1559–1689,* and *Sugar and Slaves: The Rise of the Planter Class in the English West Indies, 1624–1713.*

Elizabeth M. Geffen is professor of history and chairman of the History Department at Lebanon Valley College. She is the author of *Philadelphia Unitarianism, 1796–1861.*

Richard G. Miller has been professor of history and urban studies at the University of Texas at Arlington. He is the author of *Philadelphia—The Federalist City: A Study of Urban Politics, 1780–1801.*

Edgar P. Richardson has been the director of both the Detroit Institute of Arts and H. F. du Pont Winterthur Museum. He is the author of *Painting in America, The Way of Western Art,* and *American Romantic Painting,* and coauthor of the forthcoming *Charles Willson Peale and His World.*

Theodore Thayer was professor of history at Rutgers University. His books include *Israel Pemberton: King of the Quakers, Pennsylvania Politics and the Growth of Democracy, 1740–1770, Nathanael Greene: Strategist of the American Revolution,* and *As We Were: The Story of Old Elizabethtown.* He was a contributor to the book *George Washington's Generals.*

Harry M. Tinkcom was professor of history at Temple University. He is the author of *John White Geary: Soldier-Statesman,* and *The Republicans and Federalists in Pennsylvania,* and coauthor of *Historic Germantown.*

Margaret B. Tinkcom was historian of the Philadelphia Historical Commission for many years. She is the coauthor of *Historic Germantown.*

Stephanie Grauman Wolf is associate professor of history at the University of Delaware and coordinator of the Winterthur Program in Early American Culture. She is the author of *Urban Village: Population, Community, and Family Structure in Germantown, Pennsylvania, 1683–1800.*

Susan Detweiler, who did the picture research for the volume, is the author of *George Washington's Chinaware* and *Chestnut Hill: An Architectural History.*

Lois Given Bobb, who served as managing editor of the project, has been editor of the *Pennsylvania Magazine of History and Biography* of the Historical Society of Pennsylvania.

Joseph E. Illick, who served as editorial consultant on the project, is professor of history at San Francisco State University and the author of *Colonial Pennsylvania: A History* and *William Penn, the Politician.*

Thomas Wendel, who served as editorial consultant on the project, is professor of history at San José State University. He is the author of *Benjamin Franklin and the Politics of Liberty,* and the editor of Thomas Paine's *Common Sense: The Call to Independence,* the first annotated edition of Thomas Paine's *Common Sense.*